THE TIMES Atlas of WORLD HISTORY

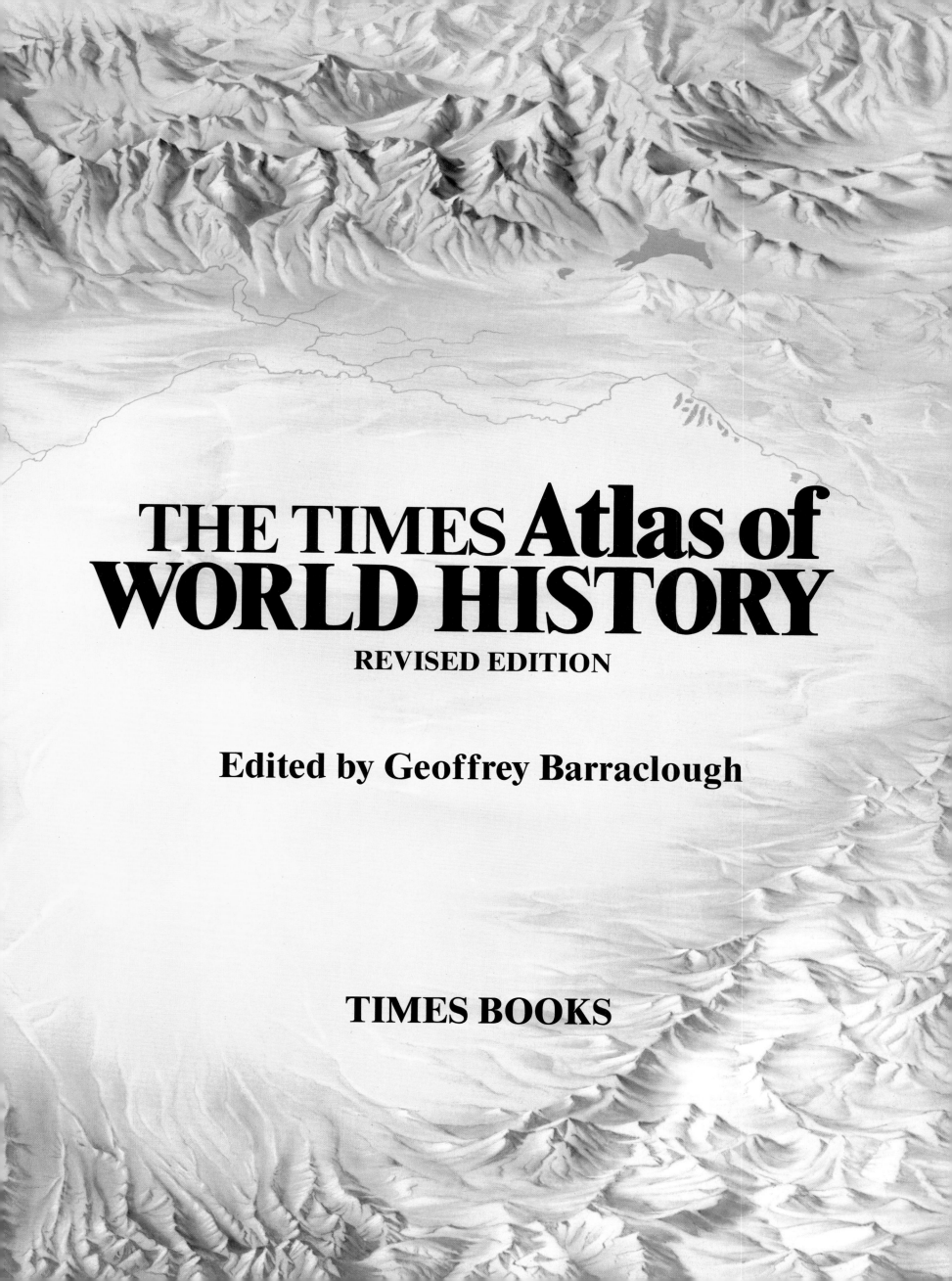

THE TIMES Atlas of WORLD HISTORY

REVISED EDITION

Edited by Geoffrey Barraclough

TIMES BOOKS

Revised edition
first published 1984 by
Times Books Limited
16 Golden Square, London W1

Reprinted 1985
Reprinted with revisions 1986
Reprinted 1988
First published in 1978
Reprinted with revisions 1979
Reprinted 1979, 1980, 1981, 1983
Copyright © Times Books Limited, London, 1978, 1979, 1980, 1981, 1983, 1984, 1985, 1986, 1988

Maps by
Duncan Mackay, Rex Nicholls, Hugh Penfold,
Malcolm Swanston, Alan Wormwell
of Product Support (Graphics) Ltd., Derby

Colour separations by
City Engraving, Hull

Editorial director:
Barry Winkleman
Place names consultant:
P.J.M. Geelan
Map design and layout by
Peter Sullivan

Revised edition:

Artwork and typesetting by
Swanston Graphics Limited, Derby
Colour separations by
Ensign Graphic Reproductions, Hull
Index set by
Stibo Sats, Denmark
Editorial:
Andrew Heritage, Ailsa Hudson
Printed and bound in Italy by
SAGDOS, Milan

**In addition to the contributors listed on pages 5 and 6
the publishers would also like to thank the following for their
generous advice and help:**
Professor C.D. Cowan, *Director*, and Professor Roland Oliver *of
the School of Oriental and African Studies, University of London;*
Professor M.C. Rickleffs, *Department of History, Monash
University, Australia;* Jonathan King *of the Museum of Mankind,
London;* Professor Donald Bullough, *University of St Andrews;*
Professor John Erickson, *Director of Defence Studies, University of
Edinburgh;* Correlli Barnett, *Fellow of Churchill College,
Cambridge;* Roger Vielvoye and Roy Lewis *formerly of The Times,
London;* Peter Wilsher *of The Sunday Times, London;* H.A.G.
Lewis, *formerly of the Directorate of Military Survey;* Robin
Bidwell, *Secretary of the Centre for Middle East Studies, University
of Cambridge;* W. Grenzebach, *Brandeis University,
Massachusetts;* George Maddocks; Andrew Wheatcroft
For revised edition:
J. Morland Craig; Professor Michael Crowder, *University of
Botswana;* Dr. Elizabeth Dunstan, *International African Institute;*
Dr. R.L. Sims, *School of Oriental and African Studies;* Dr. Michael
Leifer, *London School of Economics and Political Science;* Morton
Keller, *Spector Professor of History, Brandeis University,
Massachusetts;* Frans von der Dunk, *The Centre for the History of
European Expansion, Leiden University;* Dr. L.R. Wright,
Department of History, University of Hong Kong; Professor D.W.
Harding, *Department of Archaeology, University of Edinburgh;*
Dr. D.W. Phillipson, *Curator, Museum of Archaeology and
Anthropology, University of Cambridge*

Barraclough, Geoffrey
The Times atlas of world history. – Rev. ed.
1. Geography, Historical – Maps
I. Title
911   G1030

ISBN 0 7230 0261 4

Contributors

Editor:
Geoffrey Barraclough,
President, Historical Association, 1964-67,
formerly Stevenson Research Professor of
International History, University of London and
Chichele Professor of Modern History,
University of Oxford

R W Van Alstyne
Late Distinguished Professor of History
Callison College
University of the Pacific, California

Anthony Atmore
Research Fellow
School of Oriental and African Studies
University of London

John Barber
Fellow of King's College
University of Cambridge

W G Beasley
Emeritus Professor of the History of the Far East
School of Oriental and African Studies
University of London

Ralph Bennett
Emeritus Fellow of Magdalene College
University of Cambridge

A D H Bivar
Lecturer in Central Asian Archaeology
School of Oriental and African Studies
University of London

Hugh Borton
Formerly Professor of Japanese and Director
East Asian Institute
Columbia University, New York

A J Boyce
University Lecturer in Human Biology
University of Oxford

Warwick Bray
Reader in Latin American Archaeology
Institute of Archaeology
University of London

F R Bridge
Reader in International History
University of Leeds

Muriel E Chamberlain
Senior Lecturer in History
University College of Swansea
University of Wales

Irene Collins
Senior Fellow in History
University of Liverpool

James Cronin
Associate Professor of History
University of Wisconsin

Douglas Dakin
Emeritus Professor of History
University of London

Ralph Davis
Late Professor of Economic History
University of Leicester

Gordon East
Emeritus Professor of Geography
University of London

I E S Edwards
Formerly Keeper of Egyptian Antiquities
The British Museum, London

John Ferguson
President
Selly Oak Colleges,
Birmingham

David H Fischer
Warren Professor of History
Brandeis University, Massachusetts

John R Fisher
Director
Centre for Latin American Studies
University of Liverpool

W J Gardner
Formerly Reader in History
University of Canterbury, New Zealand

John Gillingham
Senior Lecturer in Medieval History
London School of Economics
University of London

D G E Hall
Late Emeritus Professor of South-East Asian
History
University of London

G A Harrison
Professor of Biological Anthropology
University of Oxford

Ragnhild Hatton
Emeritus Professor of International History
London School of Economics
University of London

M Havinden
Senior Lecturer in Social and Economic History
University of Exeter

W O Henderson
Formerly Reader in International Economic
History
University of Manchester

Colin J Heywood
Lecturer in the History of the Near and Middle
East
School of Oriental and African Studies
University of London

Sinclair Hood
Formerly Director
British School of Archaeology
Athens

Albert Hourani
Formerly Reader in the Modern History of the
Middle East
University of Oxford

Richard H Jones
Professor of History
Reed College, Oregon

Ulrich Kemper
University of the Ruhr
Bochum, Germany

Wolfgang Liebeschuetz
Professor of Classical and Archaeological Studies
University of Nottingham

John Lynch
Professor of Latin American History and
Director
Institute of Latin American Studies
University of London

James M McPherson
Professor of History
Princeton University, New Jersey

F R von der Mehden
Albert Thomas Professor of Political Science
Rice University, Texas

F S Northedge
Professor of International Relations
London School of Economics
University of London

D Wayne Orchiston
Senior Lecturer in Museum Studies
Victoria College,
Melbourne, Australia

Geoffrey Parker
Professor of Modern History
University of St Andrews, Scotland

W H Parker
Formerly Lecturer in the Geography of the USSR
University of Oxford

J H Parry
Late Professor of Oceanic History
Harvard University, Massachusetts

Thomas M Perry
Reader in Geography
University of Melbourne, Australia

E D Phillips
Late Professor of Greek Antiquities
Queen's University, Belfast

Sidney Pollard
Professor of Economic History
University of Bielefeld, Germany

T G E Powell
Late Professor of Prehistoric Archaeology
University of Liverpool

John Poynter
Deputy Vice-Chancellor
University of Melbourne, Australia

Benjamin Ravid
Associate Professor of Jewish History
Brandeis University, Massachusetts

Tapan Raychaudhuri
Reader in South Asian History
University of Oxford

A N Ryan
Reader in History
University of Liverpool

Göran Rystad
Professor of History
Lund University, Sweden

H W F Saggs
Professor of Semitic Languages
University College, Cardiff

S B Saul
Vice-Chancellor
University of York

Peter Sawyer
Formerly Professor of Medieval History
University of Leeds

D J Schove
Principal
St David's College, Kent

H H Scullard
Late Emeritus Professor of Ancient History
King's College
University of London

Andrew Sharf
Professor of History
Bar Ilan University, Israel

Andrew Sherratt
Assistant Keeper of Antiquities
Ashmolean Museum, Oxford

R B Smith
Reader in the History of South-East Asia
School of Oriental and African Studies
University of London

Frank C Spooner
Professor of Economic History
University of Durham

L S Stavrianos
Adjunct Professor of History
University of California, San Diego

Zara Steiner
Fellow of New Hall
University of Cambridge

W C Sturtevant
Curator of North American Ethnology
Smithsonian Institute, Washington DC

Alan Sykes
Lecturer in Modern History
University of St Andrews, Scotland

E A Thompson
Emeritus Professor of Classics
University of Nottingham

Hugh Tinker
Formerly Professor of Politics
University of Lancaster

Hugh R Trevor-Roper
Master of Peterhouse
University of Cambridge

Denis C Twitchett
Professor of East Asian Studies
Princeton University, New Jersey

Ernst Wangermann
Reader in Modern History
University of Leeds

D Cameron Watt
Stevenson Professor of International History
London School of Economics
University of London

Bodo Wiethoff
Professor of Chinese History
University of the Ruhr
Bochum, Germany

D S M Williams
Lecturer in the History of Asiatic Russia
School of Slavonic and East European Studies
University of London

David M Wilson
Director
The British Museum, London

For the revised edition:

Iris Barry
Formerly Research Student
Institute of Archaeology
University of London

David G Chandler
Head of Department of War Studies and
International Affairs
The Royal Military Academy, Sandhurst

R J W Evans
Lecturer in Modern History
University of Leeds

Michael Flinn
Late President
The Economic History Society

Carol Geldart
Formerly Adviser to the House of Commons
Foreign Affairs Committee

Norman Hammond
Professor of Archaeology
Rutgers University, New Jersey

John D Hargreaves
Professor of History
University of Aberdeen

Colin Jones
Lecturer in History
Department of History and Archaeology
University of Exeter

A R Michell
Lecturer in Economic History
Department of Economic and Social History
University of Hull

Christopher D Morris
Senior Lecturer in Archaeology
Durham University

A E Musson
Professor of Economic History
University of Manchester

B H Reid
Research Associate
Department of War Studies
King's College
University of London

Chris Scarre
Faculty of Archaeology and Anthropology
University of Cambridge

H M Scott
Lecturer in Modern History
Department of Modern History
University of St Andrews, Scotland

Peter Sluglett
Lecturer in Modern Middle Eastern History
Durham University

Jocelyn Statler
Adviser to the House of Commons Foreign
Affairs Committee

Norman Stone
Fellow of Trinity College
University of Cambridge

Malcolm Todd
Professor of Archaeology
University of Exeter

George D Winius
Lecturer in the History of Spain and Portugal
Centre for the History of European Expansion
University of Leiden

Contents

Contents *CONTINUED*

Contents *CONTINUED*

Contents *CONTINUED*

Introduction

Significant changes have occurred during the past quarter of a century in our conception of the scope and pattern of world history. The new *Times Atlas of World History* sets out to reflect these changes and thus to present a view of world history appropriate to the age in which we live.

Most historical atlases of an earlier generation were marked by their 'Eurocentricity', that is to say by their tendency to concentrate on the history of Europe (particularly of western Europe) and to refer to other regions or countries only when and where Europe impinged upon them. In the new *Times Atlas* we have broken away from this traditional western view because we believe such an approach is misleading and untenable. Our aim has been to present a view of history which is world-wide in conception and presentation and which does justice, without prejudice or favour, to the achievements of all peoples in all ages and in all quarters of the globe.

It is, of course, true that our knowledge of the past is unequal; but while we have tried to avoid the error of allotting less space to the history of the West than its achievements demand, no people has consciously been relegated to the margin of history and none singled out for specially favoured treatment. We have laid particular emphasis upon the great world civilisations and their links and interplay; but we have not neglected the peoples outside the historic centres of civilisation—for example, the nomads of central Asia—whose impact on history was more profound than is generally appreciated.

When we say that this is an atlas of world history, we mean that it is not simply a series of national histories loosely strung together. In other words, it is concerned less with particular events in the history of particular countries than with broad movements—for example, the spread of the great world religions— spanning whole continents. There are many excellent specialised atlases of national history. It is no part of our intention to compete with them; nor would it have been possible to do so, had we so wished, without dislocating the balance of the present work.

History is dynamic, not static; it is a process of change and movement in time; we have tried to avoid a series of static pictures of particular situations at particular moments in the past. In *The Times Atlas* a special effort has been made to emphasise change, expansion and contraction by the use of appropriate visual devices. In this way, we have endeavoured to convey a sense of history as a continuing process.

Any atlas seeking to present a conspectus of world history in approximately 130 plates must be selective. In singling out topics for inclusion we have adhered to the principle of selecting what was important *then* rather than what seems important *now*. Any other criterion, we believe, would put history through a distorting mirror.

If we have tried to ensure that the Atlas reflects the relative importance of different civilisations and the balance of world forces at any given moment in time, it is not merely out of piety towards the past but because we believe that, in the world as constituted today, the histories of India, China and Japan, and of other countries in Asia and Africa, are as relevant as the history of Europe. In the same way, and for the same reason, we have tried to hold a balance between eastern Europe and western Europe, and also to do justice to civilisations, such as the Ottoman Empire, which too often are treated as peripheral. It would be vain to hope that we have achieved a balance which all will find acceptable; but we believe that, granted the limits of space, this Atlas can fairly be described as comprehensive and ecumenical. Such, at least, has been our aim and endeavour.

Historical atlases have traditionally been concerned with political events and changes in political geography. Here again, the focus of interest has shifted during the past thirty or forty years. People today are more concerned with social history and with the cultural achievements of different civilisations than with political boundaries and military exploits. *The Times Atlas* pays considerable attention to such topics, and particularly to economic developments. Cultural and intellectual history does not, unfortunately, lend itself satisfactorily to cartographic documentation, and there are some subjects which ideally we should have wished to include and were forced reluctantly to omit. But we have sought in compensation to indicate the cultural connotations—and at the same time to make the presentation more vivid—by including, where space permits, visual records of the times or of historically significant tools, artefacts and other characteristic products of the peoples or civilisations with which the plates are concerned. Each plate also includes a commentary by a leading expert, providing the background to the maps and diagrams.

All atlases involve a number of specialised skills and disciplines, and none more so than an historical atlas. We have sought to make use of all available cartographic techniques, and in particular to emphasise different historical situations by employing a variety of different projections; thus the map of Islam, to take but one example, has been deliberately centred on Mecca, and the Mediterranean world has been viewed from there—as it might have been viewed by an Arab in the seventh century. In some instances we have used elaborate relief maps; in others we have deliberately simplified, sacrificing geographical detail to bring out the main historical facts. The results may not always be familiar, but we believe they may open new insights.

The original scheme for the atlas was drawn up by the present writer in 1973, and I was fortunate in being able to discuss it with L. S. Stavrianos and, before his death, with A. J. Toynbee. I am grateful to both not only for advice and criticism but also for encouragement. It is also no mere form of words to thank the contributors and other helpers (whose names are listed on pages 4, 5 and 6) for their unstinting efforts to present both familiar and unfamiliar material in an original and arresting way. Their collaboration is a guarantee of authenticity and of high scholarly standards. Finally, it is right to pay tribute to the pioneering work of our precursors, who have paved the way for us. A list of historical atlases is included in this volume. Though our purposes were often different from theirs, we have consulted them freely and they have been an indispensable source of guidance and information. Nevertheless *The Times Atlas of World History* is an entirely new venture. In particular, the plates in this volume are all original; not a few deal with topics which, to the best of our belief, have not been treated cartographically before, and all have been specially drawn to the specifications of contributors with the explicit aim of meeting the requirements and interests of present-day readers in all parts of the globe.

Geoffrey Barraclough
February 1978

The new edition of *The Times Atlas of World History* which is now offered to the public, has been prepared in response to the unparalleled success which it has enjoyed since its first appearance in 1978.

Since that time *The Times Atlas* has been translated into nine different languages, including Hebrew and Chinese; world-wide sales now exceed half a million copies; and at the same time the opportunity has been taken to incorporate a variety of corrections and improvements in successive impressions. After six years, however, it has become apparent that a totally revised edition is called for, and the present volume is the result.

It is our hope that the fundamental revisions carried out in all sections of this new edition will enhance the world-wide popularity of *The Times Atlas of World History* and ensure its continuing reputation as the most authoritative and comprehensive work of its kind. Every map has been re-examined in detail to ensure the highest standard of accuracy, and many thousands of revisions and corrections have been made. The Index of Place Names has been amplified and re-set, the Chronology has been updated, and the elaborate Glossary has been revised and updated. New projections have been introduced where appropriate, and maps redrawn; and we have taken pains to incorporate the results of the most recent research.

Particular attention has been paid to the plates dealing with the period after 1945. These have been updated and in some cases radically altered, to take account of developments since 1978 and to reflect more closely the situation in the mid-1980s. But this is in no sense an atlas of current affairs, and it makes no claim to keep up—if that were possible—with the changing panorama of contemporary international politics.

Geoffrey Barraclough
February 1984

A world chronology

The following twelve pages present a chronological synopsis of the major events in world history. The entries, necessarily abbreviated, are set out in columns under regional headings, which vary from period to period, reflecting changes in historical geography. A separate column lists important cultural events (in the broadest sense, including not only music, art and literature but also technological innovations and scientific discoveries) in all regions of the world.

Together with the Glossary and with the geographical Index (pages 297 to 360), the Chronology provides a key to the individual plates and maps, designed to help the reader to place the events there narrated in the broader context of world history. It also indicates the relative importance of different regions at different times, and the specific contributions of each to the development of civilisation and of civilised living.

The calendar of events starts with the beginnings of agriculture around the year 9000BC. For a time-scale of prehistory readers are referred to the time chart on page 36.

Asia excluding the Near East	Europe	Near East and North Africa	Other regions	Culture and technology
		c.9000-8000 Domestication of animals and crops (wheat and barley), the 'Neolithic Revolution', in the Near East; beginning of permanent settlements	c.9000 Hunters spread south through Americas	
		8350-7350 Jericho founded: first walled town in the world (10 acres)		
		c.7000 Early experiments with copper ores in Anatolia		
c.6000 Rice cultivation (Thailand)	c.6500 First farming in Greece and Aegean; spreads up Danube to Hungary (c.5500), Germany and Low Countries (c.4500) and along Mediterranean coast to France (c.5000). Farmers cross to Britain c.4000	6250-5400 Çatal Hüyük (Anatolia) flourishes: largest city of its day (32 acres)		c.6000 First known pottery and woollen textiles (Çatal Hüyük)
		c.5000 Colonisation of Mesopotamian alluvial plain by groups practising irrigation		
		c.5000 Agricultural settlements in Egypt		
		c.4000 Bronze casting begins in Near East; first use of plough		
c.3500 Earliest Chinese city at Liang-ch'eng chen (Lung-shan culture)				c.3500 Construction of Megalithic tombs and circles in Brittany, Iberian peninsula and British Isles (Stonehenge c.2000)
	3200-2000 Early Cycladic civilisation in Aegean			c.3500 Invention of wheel and plough (Mesopotamia) and sail (Egypt)
		c.3100 King Menes unites Egypt; dynastic period begins		c.3100 Pictographic writing invented in Sumer
c.3000 Use of bronze in Thailand	c.3000 Spread of copper-working	c.3000 Development of major cities in Sumer	c.3000 Arable farming techniques spread to central Africa	
			c.3000 First pottery in Americas (Ecuador and Colombia)	
c.2750 Growth of civilisations in the Indus valley		c.2685 The 'Old Kingdom' (pyramid age) of Egypt begins (to 2180 BC)		c.2590 Cheops builds great pyramid at Giza
		2371-2230 Sargon I of Agade founds first empire in world history	c.2500 Desiccation of Saharan region begins	c.2500 Domestication of horse (central Asia)
	c.2000 Indo-European speakers (early Greeks) invade and settle Peloponnese; beginnings of 'Minoan' civilisation in Crete	c.2000 Hittites invade Anatolia and found empire (1650)	c.2000 First metal-working in Peru	c.2000 Use of sail on seagoing vessels (Aegean)
		c.1800 Shamshi-Adad founds Assyrian state	c.2000 Settlement of Melanesia by immigrants from Indonesia begins	
		c.1750 Hammurabi founds Babylonian Empire		
c.1600 First urban civilisation in China, Shang Bronze Age culture	c.1600 Beginnings of Mycenaean civilisation in Greece	c.1567 Kamose and Amosis I expel Hyksos invaders and inaugurate Egyptian 'New Kingdom' (to 1090 BC)		
c.1550 Aryans destroy Indus valley civilisation and settle in N. India				c.1500 Ideographic script in use in China; 'Linear B' script in Crete and Greece; Hittite cuneiform in Anatolia
	c.1450 Destruction of Minoan Crete			c.1450 Development of Brahma worship; composition of Vedas (earliest Indian literature) begins
				c.1370 Akhenaten enforces monotheistic sun worship in Egypt
			c.1300 Settlers of Melanesia reach Fiji, later spreading to Western Polynesia	
	c.1200 Mycenaean civilisation in Greece collapses	c.1200 Collapse of Hittite Empire		c.1200 Beginning of Jewish religion (worship of Jahweh)
		c.1200 Jewish exodus from Egypt and settlement in Palestine		
		1166 Death of Ramesses III, last great pharaoh of Egypt		
			c.1150 Beginning of Olmec civilisation in Mexico	
c.1027 Shang dynasty in China overthrown by Chou; Aryans in India expand eastwards down Ganges valley	c.1000 Etruscans arrive in Italy	c.1100 Spread of Phoenicians in Mediterranean region (to 700 BC)		c.1100 Phoenicians develop alphabetic script (basis of all modern European scripts)
		c.1000 King David unites Israel and Judah		
		c.840 Rise of Urartu	c.900 Foundation of kingdom of Kush (Nubia)	
c.800 Aryans expand southwards in India		814 Traditional date for foundation of Phoenician colony at Carthage		800-400 Composition of Upanishads, Sanskrit religious treatises
				776 First Olympic Games held in Greece
771 Collapse of Chou feudal order in China	753 Traditional date for foundation of Rome			
	c.750 Greek city states begin to found settlements throughout Mediterranean			c.750 Amos, first great prophet in Israel
				c.750 Homer's *Iliad* and Hesiod's poetry first written down
	c.700 Scythians spread from central Asia to eastern Europe	721-705 Assyria at height of military power		
	c.700-450 Hallstatt culture in central and western Europe: mixed farming, iron tools			

Asia excluding the Near East

c.660 Jimmu, legendary first emperor of Japan

c.650 Introduction of iron technology in China

c.500 Sinhalese, an Aryan people, reach Ceylon

403-221 'Warring States' period in China

322 Chandragupta founds Mauryan Empire at Magadha, India

262 Asoka, Mauryan emperor (273-236), converted to Buddhism

221 Shih Huang-ti, of Ch'in dynasty, unites China (to 207)

202 Han dynasty reunites China; capital at Chang-an

185 Demetrius and Menander, kings of Bactria, conquer north-western India

Europe

c.650 Rise of 'Tyrants' in Corinth and other Greek cities

510 Foundation of Roman Republic

c.505 Cleisthenes establishes democracy in Athens

490 Battle of Marathon: Persian attack on Athens defeated

480 Battles of Salamis and Plataea (479): Persian invasion of Greece defeated

478 Foundation of Confederacy of Delos, later transformed into Athenian Empire

c.450 La Tène culture emerges in central and western Europe

431-404 Peloponnesian War between Sparta and Athens

356 Philip II, king of Macedon

338 Battle of Chaeronea gives Macedon control of Greece

290 Rome completes conquest of central Italy

241 First Punic War (264-241) with Carthage gives Rome control of Sicily

218 Second Punic War (218-201): Hannibal of Carthage invades Italy

206 Rome gains control of Spain

168 Rome defeats and partitions Macedonia

146 Rome sacks Corinth; Greece under Roman domination

Near East and North Africa

671 Assyrian conquest of Egypt; introduction of iron-working

612 Sack of Nineveh by Medes and Scythians; collapse of Assyrian power

586 Babylonian captivity of the Jews

c.550 Cyrus II (the Great) of Persia defeats Medes and founds Persian Empire

521 Persia under Darius I (the Great) rules from the Nile to the Indus

c.520 Darius I completes canal connecting Nile with Red Sea

494 Persians suppress Ionian revolt

334 Alexander the Great (of Macedon) invades Asia Minor; conquers Egypt (332), Persia (330) reaches India (329)

323 Death of Alexander: empire divided between Macedon, Egypt, Syria and Pergamum

304 Ptolemy I, Macedonian governor of Egypt, founds independent dynasty (to 30 BC)

247 Arsaces I founds kingdom of Parthia

149 Third Punic War (149-146): Rome destroys Carthage and founds province of Africa

Other regions

c.500 Iron-making techniques spread to sub-Saharan Africa

500-AD200 Period of Nok culture in northern Nigeria

Culture and technology

c.650 First coins: Lydia (Asia Minor) and Greece (c.600)

c.650 Rise of Greek lyric poetry (Sappho born c.612)

585 Thales of Miletus predicts an eclipse: beginnings of Greek rationalist philosophy

558 Zoroaster (Zarathustra) begins his prophetic work

550 Zoroastrianism becomes official religion of Persia

c.540 Deutero-Isaiah, Hebrew prophet, at work during exile in Babylon

c.530 Pythagoras, mathematician and mystic, active

528 Traditional date for death of Mahavira, founder of Jain sect

520 Death of Lao-tzu (born 605), traditional founder of Taoism

c.500 Achaemenid Persians transmit food plants (rice, peach, apricot, etc.) to western Asia

c.500 Caste system established in India

c.500 First hieroglyphic writing in Mexico (Monte Albán)

486 Death of Siddhartha Gautama, founder of Buddhism

479-338 Period of Greek classical culture. Poetry: Pindar (518-438); drama: Aeschylus (525-456), Sophocles (496-406), Euripides (480-406), Aristophanes (c.440-385); history: Herodotus (c.486-429), Thucydides (c.460-400); medicine: Hippocrates (c.470-406); philosophy: Socrates (469-399), Plato (c.427-347), Aristotle (384-322); sculpture: Phidias (c.490-417), Praxiteles (c.364); architecture: Parthenon (446-431)

479 Death of Confucius

350-200 Great period of Chinese thought: formation of Taoist, Legalist and Confucian schools; early scientific discoveries

312/11 Start of Seleucid era; first continuous historical dating-system

c.290 Foundation of Alexandrian library

277 Death of Ch'ü Yüan (born 343), earliest major Chinese poet

Asia excluding
the Near East

141 Wu-ti, Chinese emperor, expands Han power in eastern Asia

c.138 Chang Chien explores central Asia

130 Yüeh-chih tribe (Tocharians) establish kingdom in Transoxania

c.112 Opening of 'Silk Road' across Central Asia linking China to West

AD9 Wang Mang deposes Han dynasty in China

AD25 Restoration of Han dynasty; capital at Lo-yang

c.AD60 Rise of Kushan Empire

AD78-102 Kanishka, Kushan emperor, gains control of north India

AD91 Chinese defeat Hsiung-nu in Mongolia

184 'Yellow Turbans' rebellions disrupt Han China

220 End of Han dynasty: China splits into three states

245 Chinese envoys visit Funan (modern Cambodia), first major South-East Asian state

304 Hsiung-nu (Huns) invade China; China fragmented to 589

320 Chandragupta I founds Gupta Empire in northern India

c.350 Hunnish invasions of Persia and India

Europe

133-122 Failure of reform movement in Rome, led by Tiberius and Gaius Gracchus

89 All Italy receives Roman citizenship

49 Julius Caesar conquers Gaul

47-45 Civil war in Rome; Julius Caesar becomes sole ruler (45)

31 Battle of Actium: Octavian (later Emperor Augustus) establishes domination over Rome

27 Collapse of Roman Republic and beginning of Empire

AD43 Roman invasion of Britain

AD117 Roman Empire at its greatest extent

165 Smallpox epidemic ravages Roman empire

212 Roman citizenship conferred on all free inhabitants of Empire

238 Gothic incursions into Roman Empire begin

293 Emperor Diocletian reorganises Roman Empire

330 Capital of Roman Empire transferred to Constantinople

370 First appearance of Huns in Europe

378 Visigoths defeat and kill Roman emperor at Adrianople

406 Vandals invade and ravage Gaul and Spain (409)

410 Visigoths invade Italy, sack Rome and overrun Spain

Near East
and North Africa

64 Pompey the Great conquers Syria; end of Seleucid Empire

53 Battle of Carrhae: Parthia defeats Roman invasion

30 Death of Antony and Cleopatra: Egypt becomes Roman province

AD44 Mauretania (Morocco) annexed by Rome

AD70 Romans destroy the Jewish Temple in Jerusalem

AD116 Roman Emperor Trajan completes conquest of Mesopotamia

132 Jewish rebellion against Rome leads to 'diaspora' (dispersal of Jews)

224 Foundation of Sasanian dynasty in Persia

429 Vandal kingdom in North Africa

Other regions

100 Camel introduced into Saharan Africa

c.AD50 Expansion of kingdom of Axum (Ethiopia) begins

c.150 Berber and Mandingo tribes begin domination of the Sudan

c.250 Kingdom of Axum (Ethiopia) gains control of Red Sea trade

c.300 Rise of Hopewell Indian chiefdoms in North America and of Maya civilisation in Mesoamerica; large civilised states in Mexico (Teotihuacán, Monte Albán, El Tajín)

c.300 Settlement of eastern Polynesia

Culture
and technology

142 Completion of first stone bridge over river Tiber

79 Death of Ssu-ma Ch'ien, Chinese historian

46 Julius Caesar reforms calendar; Julian calendar in use until AD 1582 (England 1752, Russia 1917)

31-AD14 The Augustan Age at Rome: Virgil (70-19), Horace (65-27), Ovid (43-AD17), Livy (59-AD17)

5 Building of national shrine of Ise in Japan

c.AD30 Jesus of Nazareth, founder of Christianity, crucified in Jerusalem

AD46-57 Missionary journeys of St Paul

c.AD90-120 Great period of Silver Latin: Tacitus (c.55-120), Juvenal (c.55-c. 140), Martial (c.38-102)

AD105 First use of paper in China

c.125 Third Buddhist conference: widespread acceptance of the sculptural Buddha image

150 Earliest surviving Sanskrit inscription (India)

c.150 Buddhism reaches China

c.200 Completion of *Mishnah* (codification of Jewish Law)

c.200 Indian epic poems: *Mahabharata*, *Ramayana* and *Bhagavad Gita*

c.200-250 Development of Christian theology: Tertullian (c.160-220), Clement (c.150-c.215), Origen (185-254)

271 Magnetic compass in use (China)

274 Unconquered Sun proclaimed god of Roman Empire

276 Crucifixion of Mani (born 215), founder of Manichaean sect

285 Confucianism introduced into Japan

c.300 Foot-stirrup invented in Asia

313 Edict of Milan: Christianity granted toleration in Roman Empire

325 Axum destroys kingdom of Meröe (Kush)

350 Buddhist cave temples, painting, sculpture (to 800)

404 Latin version of Bible (Vulgate) completed

413 Kumaragupta; great literary era in India

426 Augustine of Hippo completes *City of God*

Asia excluding the Near East	Europe	Near East and North Africa	Other regions	Culture and technology
	449 Angles, Saxons and Jutes begin conquest of Britain			
	476 Deposition of last Roman emperor in West			
480 Gupta Empire overthrown	**486 Frankish kingdom founded by Clovis**			
	493 Ostrogoths take power in Italy			
				497 Franks converted to Christianity
				c.520 Rise of mathematics in India: Aryabhata and Varamihara invent decimal system
		531 Accession of Chosroes I (died 579): Sasanian Empire at its greatest extent		**529** Rule of St Benedict regulates Western monasticism
	533 Justinian restores Roman power in North Africa and Italy (552)			**534** Justinian promulgates Legal Code
				538 S. Sophia, Constantinople, consecrated
	c.542 Bubonic plague ravages Europe			**c.550** Buddhism introduced into Japan from Korea
				563 St Columba founds monastery of Iona: beginning of Irish mission to Anglo-Saxons
589 China reunified by Sui dynasty	**568** Lombard conquest of north Italy			
	590 Gregory the Great expands papal power		**c.600 Apogee of Maya civilisation**	**607** Chinese cultural influence in Japan begins
607 Unification of Tibet	**610** Accession of East Roman Emperor Heraclius; beginning of Hellenisation of (East) Roman Empire, henceforward known as Byzantine Empire	**611** Persian armies capture Antioch and Jerusalem and overrun Asia Minor (to 626)		
617 China in state of anarchy		**622** *Hegira* of Mohammed; beginning of Islamic calendar		**625 Mohammed begins his prophetic mission**
624 China united under T'ang dynasty		**632** Death of Mohammed: Arab expansion begins		
		636 Arabs overrun Syria		
		637 Arabs overrun Iraq		
c.640 Empire of Sri Harsha in northern India		**641** Arabs conquer Egypt and begin conquest of North Africa		
645 Fujiwara's 'Taika Reform' remodels Japan on Chinese lines				**c.645** Buddhism reaches Tibet (first temple 651)
658 Maximum extension of Chinese power in central Asia; protectorates in Afghanistan, Kashmir, Sogdiana and Oxus valley				
665 Tibetan expansion into Turkestan, Tsinghai				
676 Korea unified under Silla	**680** Bulgars invade Balkans			
	687 Battle of Tertry: Carolingians dominate Frankish state			**c.690** Arabic replaces Greek and Persian as language of Umayyad administration
				692 Completion of Dome of Rock in Jerusalem, first great monument of Islamic architecture
			c.700 Rise of empire of Ghana	**c.700** Buddhist temples built at Nara, Japan
	711 Muslim invasion of Spain			**700** Golden age of Chinese poetry: Li Po (701-62), Tu Fu (712-70), Po Chü-i (772-846)
712 Arabs conquer Sind and Samarkand		**718** Arab siege of Constantinople repulsed		**722** St Boniface's mission to Germany
				725 Bede (673-735) introduces dating by Christian era
	732 Battle of Poitiers halts Arab expansion in western Europe			**c.730** Printing in China
745 Beginnings of Uighur Empire in Mongolia		**750 Abbasid caliphate established**		
751 Battle of Talas River: sets boundary of China and Abbasid caliphate	**751** Lombards overrun Ravenna, last Byzantine foothold in northern Italy			**751** Paper-making spreads from China to Muslim world and Europe (1150)
755 An Lu-shan's rebellion in China				**760** Arabs adopt Indian numerals and develop algebra and trigonometry
	774 Charlemagne conquers northern Italy			**782** Alcuin of York (735-804) organises education in Carolingian Empire: 'Carolingian renaissance'
				788 Great mosque in Córdoba
794 Japanese capital moved to Kyoto from Nara	**793** Viking raids begin			
c.802 Jayaxarman II establishes Angkorean kingdom (Cambodia)	**800 Charlemagne crowned emperor in Rome;** beginning of new Western (later Holy Roman) Empire		**c.800** First settlers reach Easter Island and New Zealand (850) from Polynesia	**c.800** Temple at Borobudur (Java) constructed by Shailendra kings
836 Struggle for control of Indian Deccan		**809** Death of caliph Harun al-Rashid		
840 Collapse of Uighur Empire				
842 Tibetan Empire disintegrates	**843** Treaty of Verdun: partition of Carolingian Empire		**c.850** Collapse of Classic Maya culture in Mesoamerica	**853** First printed book in China

Asia excluding the Near East

907 Last T'ang emperor deposed

916 Khitan kingdom in Mongolia founded

918 State of Koryo founded in Korea

939 Vietnam independent of China

947 Khitans overrun northern China, establish Liao dynasty with capital at Peking

967 Fujiwara domination of Japan begins

979 Sung dynasty reunites China

1018 Mahmud of Ghazni sacks Kanauj and breaks power of Hindu states

1018 Rajendra Chola conquers Ceylon

1021 Cholas invade Bengal

1038 Tangut tribes form Hsi-hsia state in north-west China

1044 Establishment of first Burmese national state at Pagan

1126 Chin overrun northern China; Sung rule restricted to south

1170 Apogee of Srivijaya kingdom in Java under Shailendra dynasty

1175 Muizzuddin Muhammad of Ghazni, founds first Muslim empire in India

c.1180 Angkor Empire (Cambodia) at greatest extent

1185 Minamoto warlords supreme in Japan

Europe

862 Novgorod founded by Rurik the Viking

871 Alfred, king of Wessex, halts Danish advance in England

882 Capital of Russia moved to Kiev

911 Vikings granted duchy of Normandy

929 Abdurrahman III establishes caliphate at Córdoba

955 Otto I defeats Magyars at Lechfeld

959 Unification of England under Eadgar

960 Miesko I founds Polish state

962 Otto I of Germany crowned emperor in Rome

972 Beginning of Hungarian state under Duke Geisa

983 Great Slav rebellion against German eastward expansion

987 Accession of Capetians in France

1014 Battle of Clontarf breaks Viking domination of Ireland

1016 Cnut the Great rules England, Denmark and Norway (to 1035)

1018 Byzantines annex Bulgaria (to 1185)

1031 Collapse of caliphate of Córdoba

1054 Schism between Greek and Latin Christian churches begins

1066 Norman conquest of England

1071 Fall of Bari completes Norman conquest of Byzantine Italy

1073 Gregory VII elected Pope: beginning of conflict of Empire and papacy

1125 Renewal of German eastwards expansion

1154 Accession of Henry II: Angevin Empire in England and France

1198 Innocent III elected Pope

Near East and North Africa

936 Caliphs of Baghdad lose effective power

969 Fatimids conquer Egypt and found Cairo

1055 Seljuk Turks take Baghdad

1056 Almoravids conquer North Africa and southern Spain

1071 Battle of Manzikert: defeat of Byzantium by Seljuk Turks

1096 First Crusade: Franks invade Anatolia and Syria, and found crusader states

1135 Almohads dominant in north-western Africa and Muslim Spain

1171 Saladin defeats Fatimids and conquers Egypt

1188 Saladin destroys Frankish crusader kingdoms

Other regions

c.990 Expansion of Inca Empire (Peru)

c.1000 Vikings colonise Greenland and discover America (Vinland)

c.1000 First Iron Age settlement at Zimbabwe (Rhodesia)

1076 Almoravids destroy kingdom of Ghana

c.1100 Toltecs build their capital at Tula (Mexico)

c.1150 Beginnings of Yoruba city states (Nigeria)

c.1200 Rise of empire of Mali in west Africa

Culture and technology

863 Creation of Cyrillic alphabet in eastern Europe

865 Bulgars and Serbians accept Christianity

c.890 Japanese cultural renaissance: novels, landscape painting and poetry

910 Abbey of Cluny founded

935 Text of Koran finalised

c.1000 Great age of Chinese painting and ceramics

1020 Completion of *Tale of Genji* by Lady Murasaki

1020 Death of Firdausi, writer of Persian national epic, *The Shahnama*

1037 Death of Avicenna, Persian philosopher

c.1045 Moveable type printing invented in China

1094 Composition of old Javanese *Ramayana* by Yogisvara

c.1100 First universities in Europe: Salerno (medicine), Bologna (law). Paris (theology and philosophy)
c.1100 Omar Khayyam composes *Rubaiyyat*

1111 Death of al-Ghazali, Muslim theologian

c.1150 Hindu temple of Angkor Wat (Cambodia) built

1154 Chartres Cathedral begun; **Gothic architecture spreads through western Europe**
c.1160 development of European vernacular verse: Chanson de Roland (c.1100), El Cid (c.1150), Parzifal, Tristan (c.1200)

1193 Zen Buddhist order founded in Japan

1198 Death of Averroës, Arab scientist and philosopher

Asia excluding the Near East

1206 Mongols under Genghis Khan begin conquest of Asia

1206 Sultanate of Delhi founded

c.1220 Emergence of first Thai kingdom

1234 Mongols destroy Chin Empire

1264 Kublai Khan founds Yüan dynasty in China

1279 Mongols conquer southern China

1333 End of Minamoto shogunate: civil war in Japan

c.1341 'Black Death' starts in Asia

1349 First Chinese settlement at Singapore; beginning of Chinese expansion in South-East Asia

1350 Golden age of Majapahit Empire in Java

1368 Ming dynasty founded in China

1370 Hindu state of Vijayanagar dominant in southern India

1380 Timur (Tamerlane) begins conquests

1392 Korea becomes independent

1394 Thais invade Cambodia; Khmer capital moved to Phnom Penh

1398 Timur invades India and sacks Delhi

c.1400 Establishment of Malacca as a major commercial port of S.E. Asia

1405 Chinese voyages in Indian Ocean

1428 Chinese expelled from Vietnam

1471 Vietnamese southward expansion: Champa annexed

Europe

1204 Fourth Crusade: Franks conquer Byzantium and found Latin Empire

1212 Battle of Las Navas de Tolosa

1215 Magna Carta: King John makes concessions to English barons

1236 Mongols invade and conquer Russia (1239)

1241 Mongols invade Poland, Hungary, Bohemia
1242 Alexander Nevsky defeats Teutonic Order
1250 d. of Emperor Frederick II, collapse of Imperial power in Germany and Italy
1261 Greek empire restored in Constantinople

1291 Beginnings of Swiss Confederation

1309 Papacy moves from Rome to Avignon

1314 Battle of Bannockburn: Scotland defeats England

1325 Ivan I begins recovery of Moscow

1337 Hundred Years War between France and England begins

1348 Black Death from Asia ravages Europe

1360 Peace of Brétigny ends first phase of Hundred Years War

1361 Ottomans capture Adrianople

1378 Great Schism in West (to 1417)

1386 Union of Poland and Lithuania

1389 Battle of Kosovo: Ottomans gain control of Balkans

1397 Union of Kalmar (Scandinavia)

1410 Battle of Tannenberg: Poles defeat Teutonic Knights

1415 Battle of Agincourt: Henry V of England resumes attack on France

1428 Joan of Arc: beginning of French revival

1453 England loses Continental possessions (except Calais)

1453 Ottoman Turks capture Constantinople: end of Byzantine Empire

1475 Burgundy at height of power (Charles the Bold)

1478 Ivan III, first Russian tsar, subdues Novgorod and throws off Mongol yoke (1480)

Near East and North Africa

1228 Hafsid dynasty established at Tunis

1258 Mongols sack Baghdad; end of Abbasid caliphate

1299 Ottoman Turks begin expansion in Anatolia

1402 Battle of Ankara: Timur defeats Ottomans in Anatolia

Other regions

c.1200 Emergence of Hausa city states (Nigeria)

c.1200 Aztecs occupy valley of Mexico

c.1250 Mayapan becomes dominant Maya city of Yucatán

c.1300 Kanuri Empire moves capital from Kanem to Borno

c.1300 Emergence of empire of Benin (Nigeria)

1325 Rise of Aztecs in Mexico: Tenochtitlán founded

1415 Portuguese capture Ceuta: beginning of Portugal's African empire

1430 Construction of great stone enclosure at Zimbabwe (Rhodesia)

1434 Portuguese explore south of Cape Bojador

c.1450 Apogee of Songhay Empire; university at Timbuktu

c.1450 Monomatapa Empire founded

1470 Incas conquer Chimú kingdom

Culture and technology

c.1215 Islamic architecture spreads to India

1226 Death of St Francis of Assisi

1274 Death of St Thomas Aquinas: his *Summa Theologica* defines Christian dogma

1275 Marco Polo (1254-1324) arrives in China

1290 Spectacles invented (Italy)

c.1320 Cultural revival in Italy: Dante (1265-1321), Giotto (1276-1337), Petrarch (1304-71)

1339 Building of Kremlin (Moscow)

c.1350 Japanese cultural revival

1377 Death of Ibn Battuta (born 1309), Arab geographer and traveller

1387 Lithuania converted to Christianity

1392 Death of Hafiz, Persian lyric poet

1400 Death of Chaucer, first great poet in English

1406 Death of Ibn Khaldun, Muslim historian

1445 Johannes Gutenberg (1397-1468) prints first book in Europe

Asia

1498 Vasco da Gama: first European sea-voyage to India and back

1500 Shah Ismail founds Safavid dynasty in Persia

1511 Portuguese take Malacca

1516 Ottomans overrun Syria, Egypt and Arabia (1517)

1526 Battle of Panipat: Babur conquers kingdom of Delhi and founds Mughal dynasty

1550 Mongol Altan-khan invades northern China; Japanese 'pirate' raids in China

1557 Portuguese established at Macao (China)

1565 Akbar extends Mughal power to Deccan

1581 Yermak begins Russian conquest of Siberia

1584 Phra Narai creates independent Siam

1609 Beginning of Tokugawa shogunate in Japan

1619 Foundation of Batavia (Jakarta) by Dutch: start of Dutch colonial empire in East Indies

Europe

1492 Fall of Granada: end of Muslim rule in Spain; Jews expelled from Spain.

1494 Italian wars: beginning of Franco-Habsburg struggle for hegemony in Europe

1519 Charles V, ruler of Spain and Netherlands, elected emperor

1521 Martin Luther outlawed: **beginning of Protestant Reformation**

1521 Suleiman the Magnificent, Ottoman sultan, conquers Belgrade

1526 Battle of Mohács: Ottoman Turks overrun Hungary

1534 Henry VIII of England breaks with Rome

1541 John Calvin founds reformed church at Geneva

1545 Council of Trent: beginning of Counter-Reformation

1556 Ivan IV of Russia conquers Volga basin

1562 Wars of religion in France (to 1598)

1571 Battle of Lepanto: end of Turkish sea power in central Mediterranean

1572 Dutch Revolt against Spain

1588 Spanish Armada defeated by English

1598 Time of Troubles in Russia

1600 Foundation of English and Dutch (1602) East India Companies

1609 Dutch Republic becomes independent

1618 Outbreak of Thirty Years War

Africa

1492 Spaniards begin conquest of North African coast

1505 Portuguese establish trading posts in east Africa

1546 Destruction of Mali Empire by Songhay

1571 Portuguese create colony in Angola

1578 Battle of Al Kasr al Kebir: Moroccans destroy Portuguese power in north-western Africa

1591 Battle of Tondibi: Moroccans destroy Songhay kingdom

c.1600 Oyo Empire at height of power

1628 Portuguese destroy Mwenemutapa Empire

New World

1492 Columbus reaches America: discovery of New World

1493 First Spanish settlement in New World (Hispaniola)

1493 Treaty of Tordesillas divides New World between Portugal and Spain

1497 Cabot reaches Newfoundland

1498 Columbus discovers South America

c.1510 African slaves to America

1519 Cortés begins conquest of Aztec Empire

1520 Magellan crosses Pacific

1532 Pizarro begins conquest of Inca Empire for Spain

1545 Discovery of silver mines at Potosí (Peru) and Zacatecas (Mexico)

c.1560 Portuguese begin sugar cultivation in Brazil

1571 Spanish conquer Philippines

1607 First permanent English settlement in America (Jamestown, Virginia)

1608 French colonists found Quebec

1620 Puritans land in New England (*Mayflower*)

1625 Dutch settle New Amsterdam

Culture and technology

c.1500 Italian Renaissance: Leonardo da Vinci (1452-1519), Michelangelo (1475-1564), Raphael (1483-1520), Botticelli (1444-1510), Machiavelli (1469-1527), Ficino (1433-99)

1509 Watch invented by Peter Henle (Nuremburg)

c.1525 Introduction of potato from South America to Europe

1539 Death of Kabir Nanak, founder of Sikh religion

1543 Copernicus publishes *Of the Revolution of Celestial Bodies*

1559 Tobacco first introduced into Europe

1598 Shah Abbas I creates imperial capital at Isfahan

c.1603 Beginnings of Kabuki theatre, Japan

1607 Monteverdi's *La Favola d'Orfeo* establishes opera as art form

1609 Telescope invented (Holland)

c.1610 Scientific revolution in Europe begins: Kepler (1571-1610), Bacon (1561-1626), Galileo (1564-1642), Descartes (1596-1650)

1616 Death of Shakespeare (born 1564) and Cervantes (born 1547)

1620 First weekly newspapers in Europe (Amsterdam)

Asia

1638 Russians reach Pacific

1641 Dutch capture Malacca from Portuguese

1644 Manchus found new dynasty (Ch'ing) in China

1649 Russians reach Pacific and found Okhotsk

1674 Sivaji creates Hindu Maratha kingdom

1689 Treaty of Nerchinsk between Russia and China

1690 Foundation of Calcutta by English

1697 Chinese occupy Outer Mongolia

1707 Death of Aurangzeb: decline of Mughal power in India

1736 Safavid dynasty deposed by Nadir Shah

1747 Ahmad Khan Abdali founds kingdom of Afghanistan

1751 China overruns Tibet, Dzungaria and Tarim Basin (1756-9)

1751 French gain control of Deccan and Carnatic

1755 Alaungpaya founds Rangoon and reunites Burma (to 1824)

1757 Battle of Plassey: British defeat French

1761 Capture of Pondicherry: British destroy French power in India

Europe

1630 Gustavus Adolphus of Sweden intervenes in Thirty Years War

1642 English Civil War begins

1648 Peace of Westphalia ends Thirty Years War

1649 Execution of Charles I of England; republic declared

1652 First Anglo-Dutch War: beginning of Dutch decline

1654 Ukraine passes from Polish to Russian rule

1658 Peace of Roskilde: Swedish Empire at height

1667 Beginning of French expansion under Louis XIV

1683 Turkish siege of Vienna

1688 'Glorious Revolution'; constitutional monarchy in England

1689 'Grand Alliance' against Louis XIV

1699 Treaty of Carlowitz: Habsburgs recover Hungary from Turks

1700 Great Northern War (to 1720)

1703 Foundation of St Petersburg, capital of Russian Empire (1712)

1707 Union of England and Scotland

1709 Battle of Poltava: Peter the Great of Russia defeats Swedes

1713 Treaty of Utrecht ends War of Spanish Succession

1740 War of Austrian Succession: Prussia annexes Silesia

1756 Seven Years War begins

1772 First partition of Poland (2nd and 3rd partitions 1793, 1795)

1774 Treaty of Kuchuk Kainarji: beginning of Ottoman decline

Africa

1652 Foundation of Cape Colony by Dutch

1659 French found trading station on Senegal coast

1662 Battle of Ambuila: destruction of Kongo kingdom by Portuguese

c.1700 Rise of Asante power (Gold Coast)

c.1730 Revival of ancient empire of Borno (central Sudan)

New World

1645 Tasman circumnavigates Australia and discovers New Zealand

1664 New Amsterdam taken by British from Dutch (later renamed New York)

1684 La Salle explores Mississippi and claims Louisiana for France

1693 Gold discovered in Brazil

1728 Bering begins Russian reconnaissance of Alaska

1760 New France conquered by British: Quebec (1759) and Montreal (1760)

1768 Cook begins exploration of Pacific

1775 American Revolution begins

Culture and technology

c.1630 Apogee of Netherlands art: Hals (1580-1666), Rembrandt (1606-69), Vermeer (1632-75), Rubens (1577-1640)

1636 Foundation of Harvard College, first university in North America

c.1650 Beginnings of popular literary culture in Japan (puppet theatre, kabuki, the novel)

1653 Taj Mahal, Agra, India, completed

1656 St Peter's, Rome, completed (Bernini)

c.1660 Classical period of French culture: drama (Molière, 1622-1673, Racine, 1639-1699, Corneille, 1606-1684), painting (Poussin, 1594-1665, Claude, 1600-1682), music (Lully, 1632-1687, Couperin, 1668-1733)

1662 Royal Society founded in London and (1666) Académie Française in Paris

1687 Isaac Newton's *Principia*

1690 John Locke's *Essay concerning Human Understanding*

c.1700 Great age of German baroque music: Buxtehude (1637-1707), Handel (1685-1759), Bach (1685-1750)

1709 Abraham Darby discovers coke-smelting technique for producing pig-iron (England)

1730 Wesley brothers create Methodism

c.1735 Wahabite movement to purify Islam begins in Arabia

c.1760 European enlightenment: Voltaire (1694-1778), Diderot (1713-84), Hume (1711-76)

1762 J. J. Rousseau's *Social Contract*

c.1770 Advance of science and technology in Europe: J. Priestley (1733-1804), A. Lavoisier (1743-94), A. Volta (1745-1827). Harrison's chronometer (1762), Watt's steam engine (1769), Arkwright's water-powered spinning-frame (1769)

Asia

1796 British conquer Ceylon

1818 Britain defeats Marathas and becomes effective ruler of India

1819 British found Singapore as free trade port

1824 British begin conquest of Burma and Assam

1825-30 Java war: revolt of Indonesians against Dutch

1830 Russia begins conquest of Kazakhstan (to 1854)

1833 Death of Rammohan Roy (b.1772), father of modern Indian nationalism

1842 Opium War: Britain annexes Hong Kong

1843 British conquer Sind

1845-9 British conquest of Punjab and Kashmir

1850 T'ai-p'ing rebellion in China — (to 1864), with immense loss of life

1853 First railway and telegraph lines in India

1854 Perry forces Japan to open trade with US

Europe

1783 Russia annexes Crimea

1789 French Revolution begins; abolition of feudal system and proclamation of Rights of Man

1791 Russia gains Black Sea steppes from Turks

1792 French Republic proclaimed; beginning of revolutionary wars

1793 Attempts to reform Ottoman Empire by Selim III

1799 Napoleon becomes First Consul and (1804) Emperor of France

1805 Napoleon defeats Austria and (1806) Prussia

1805 Battle of Trafalgar: Britain defeats French and Spanish fleets

1807 Abolition of serfdom in Prussia

1812 Napoleon invades Russia

1815 Napoleon defeated at Waterloo, exiled to St Helena

1815 Congress of Vienna

1821 Greek war of independence

1830 Revolutionary movements in France, Germany, Poland and Italy; Belgium wins independence

1833 Formation of German customs union (Zollverein)

1845 Irish famine stimulates hostility to Britain and emigration to US

1846 Britain repeals Corn Laws and moves towards complete free trade

1848 Revolutionary movements in Europe; proclamation of Second Republic in France

1852 Fall of French republic; Louis Napoleon (Napoleon III, 1808-73) becomes French emperor

1854 Crimean War (to 1856)

Africa

1798 Napoleon attacks Egypt

1804 Fulanis conquer Hausa

1806 Cape Colony passes under British control

1807 Slave trade abolished within British Empire

1811 Mohammed Ali takes control in Egypt

1818 Shaka forms Zulu kingdom in SE Africa

1822 Liberia founded as colony for freed slaves

1830 French begin conquest of Algeria

1835 'Great Trek' of Boer colonists from Cape, leading to foundation of Republic of Natal (1839), Orange Free State (1848) and Transvaal (1849)

1853 Livingstone's explorations begin

Americas and Australasia

1776 American Declaration of Independence

1783 Treaty of Paris: Britain recognises American independence

1788 British colony of Australia founded

1789 George Washington becomes first President of United States of America

1803 Louisiana Purchase nearly doubles size of US

1808 Independence movements in Spanish and Portuguese America: 13 new states created by 1828

1819 US purchases Florida from Spain

1823 Monroe Doctrine

1840 Britain annexes New Zealand

1845 Texas annexed by US

1846 Mexican War begins: US conquers New Mexico and California (1848)

1846 Oregon treaty delimits US-Canadian boundary

1850 Australian colonies and (1856) New Zealand granted responsible government

Culture and technology

1776 Publication of *The Wealth of Nations* by Adam Smith (1723-90) and *Common Sense* by Tom Paine (1737-1809)

1781 Immanuel Kant's *Critique of Pure Reason*

c.1790 Great age of European orchestral music: Mozart (1756-91), Haydn (1732-1809), Beethoven (1770-1827)

1792 Cartwright invents steam-powered weaving loom

1793 Decimal system introduced (France)

1793 Eli Whitney's cotton 'gin' (US)

1796 Jenner discovers smallpox vaccine (UK)

1798 Malthus publishes *Essay on the Principle of Population*

1812 Cylinder printing press invented, adopted by *The Times* (London)

1817 Foundation of Hindu college, Calcutta, first major centre of Western influence in India

c.1820 Romanticism in European literature and art: Byron (1788-1824), Chateaubriand (1768-1848), Heine (1797-1856), Turner (1775-1851), Delacroix (1798-1863)

1821 Electric motor and generator invented by M. Faraday (Britain)

1822 First photographic image produced by J-N. Niepce (France)

1825 First passenger steam railway: Stockton and Darlington (England)

1828 Foundation of Brahmo-samaj, Hindu revivalist movement

1832 Death of Goethe (born 1749)

1833 First regulation of industrial working conditions (Britain)

1834 First mechanical reaper patented (US)

1836 Needle-gun invented (Prussia), making breech-loading possible

1837 Pitman's shorthand invented

1838 First electric telegraph (Britain)

1840 First postage stamp (Britain)

1848 Communist Manifesto issued by Marx (1818-83) and Engels (1820-95)

1849 Death of Chopin (b.1810); apogee of Romantic music with Berlioz (1803-69), Liszt (1811-86), Wagner (1813-83), Brahms (1833-97), Verdi (1813-1901)

1851 Great Exhibition in London

1853 Haussmann begins rebuilding of Paris

Asia

1857 Indian Mutiny

1858 Treaty of Tientsin: further Treaty Ports opened to foreign trade in China

1860 Treaty of Peking: China cedes Ussuri region to Russia

1863 France establishes protectorate over Cambodia, Cochin China (1865), Annam (1874), Tonkin (1885) and Laos (1893)

1868 End of Tokugawa Shogunate and Meiji Restoration in Japan

1877 Queen Victoria proclaimed Empress of India

1879 Second Afghan War gives Britain control of Afghanistan

1885 Foundation of Indian National Congress

1886 British annex Upper Burma

1887 French establish Indo-Chinese Union

1891 Construction of Trans-Siberian railway begun

1894-5 Sino-Japanese War: Japan occupies Formosa

1898 Abortive "Hundred Days" reform in China

1900 Boxer uprising in China

1904 Partition of Bengal: nationalist agitation in India

1904-5 Russo-Japanese War; Japanese success stimulates Asian nationalism

Europe

1859 Sardinian-French war against Austria; Piedmont acquires Lombardy (1860): **unification of Italy begins**

1861 Emancipation of Russian serfs

1864 Prussia defeats Denmark: annexes Schleswig-Holstein (1866)

1864 Russia suppresses Polish revolt

1866 Prussia defeats Austria

1867 Establishment of North German confederation and of dual monarchy in Austria-Hungary

1870 Franco-Prussian war

1871 Proclamation of German Empire, beginning of Third French Republic: suppression of Paris commune

1875 Growth of labour/socialist parties: Germany (1875), Belgium (1885), Holland (1877), Britain (1893), Russia (1898)

1878 Treaty of Berlin: Romania, Montenegro and Serbia become independent, Bulgaria autonomous

1879 Dual alliance between Germany and Austria-Hungary

1890 Dismissal of Bismarck; Wilhelm II begins new course

1894 Franco-Russian alliance

1898 Germany embarks on naval building programme; beginning of German 'world policy'

1904 Anglo-French entente

1905 Revolution in Russia, followed by Tsarist concessions

1905 Norway independent of Sweden

Africa

1860 French expansion in West Africa from Senegal

1869 Suez Canal opens

1875 Disraeli buys Suez Canal Company shares to ensure British control of sea route to India

1881 French occupy Tunisia

1882 Revolt in Egypt leading to British occupation

1884 Germany acquires SW Africa, Togoland, Cameroons

1885 King of Belgium acquires Congo

1886 Germany and Britain partition East Africa

1886 Gold discovered in Transvaal; foundation of Johannesburg

1889 British South Africa company formed by Cecil Rhodes, begins colonisation of Rhodesia (1890)

1896 Battle of Adowa: Italians defeated by Ethiopians

1898 Fashoda crisis between Britain and France

1899 Boer War begins

1900 Copper-mining begins in Katanga

Americas and Australasia

1861 Outbreak of American Civil War

1864 War of Paraguay against Argentina, Brazil and Uruguay (to 1870)

1865 End of American Civil War; slavery abolished in US

1867 Russia sells Alaska to US

1867 Dominion of Canada established

1869 Prince Rupert's Land, Manitoba (1870) and British Columbia (1871) join Canada

1876 Porfirio Díaz (1830-1915) gains control of Mexico (to 1911)

1879 War of the Pacific (Chile, Bolivia, Peru)

1885 Completion of Canadian Pacific railway

1898 Spanish-American war: US annexes Guam, Puerto Rico and Philippines

1901 Unification of Australia as Commonwealth

1903 Panama Canal Zone ceded to US

Culture and technology

1856 Bessemer process permits mass-production of steel

1859 Darwin publishes *The Origin of Species*

1859 First oil well drilled (Pennsylvania, US)

c.1860 Great age of European novel: Dickens (1812-70), Dumas (1802-70), Flaubert (1821-80), Turgenev (1818-83), Dostoyevsky (1821-81), Tolstoy (1828-1910)

1861 Pasteur evolves germ theory of disease

1861 Women first given vote (Australia)

1863 First underground railway (London)

1864 Foundation of Red Cross (Switzerland)

1867 Marx publishes *Das Kapital* (vol. 1)

1869 First trans-continental railroad completed (US)

1870 Declaration of Papal infallibility

1874 First electric tram (New York); telephone patented by Bell (US 1876) first electric streetlighting (London 1878)

1874 Emergence of Impressionist school of painting: Monet (1840-1926), Renoir (1841-1919), Degas (1834-1917)

1878 First oil tanker built (Russia)

1879 F. W. Woolworth opened first '5 and 10 cent store'

1882 First hydro-electric plant (Wisconsin, US)

1884 Maxim gun perfected

c.1885 Daimler and Benz pioneer the automobile (Germany)

1888 Dunlop invents pneumatic tyre

c.1890 Beginnings of modern literature in Japan on western models

c.1890 Europe - realistic drama: Ibsen (1828-1906), Strindberg (1849-1912), Chekhov (1860-1904), Shaw (1856-1950)

1895 Röntgen discovers X-rays (Germany); Marconi invents wireless telegraphy (Italy); first public showing of motion picture (France)

1896 Herzl publishes *The Jewish State* calling for Jewish National Home

1898 Pierre and Marie Curie observe radioactivity and isolate radium (France)

1899 Howard's *Garden Cities of Tomorrow* initiates modern city planning

1900 Planck evolves quantum theory (Germany)

1900 Freud's *Interpretation of Dreams*, beginning of psychoanalysis (Austria)

1903 First successful flight of petrol-powered aircraft (Wright Brothers, US)

1905 Einstein's theory of relativity (Germany)

AD1906

Asia

1906 Revolution in Persia

1910 Japan annexes Korea

1911 Chinese Revolution: Sun Yat-sen first President of new republic

1914 German concessions in China and Colonies in Pacific taken over by Japan, Australia and New Zealand

1917 'Balfour Declaration' promises Jews a National Home in Palestine

1919 Amritsar incident; upsurge of Indian nationalism

1919 May 4th movement in China; upsurge of Chinese nationalism

1920 Mustafa Kemal (Atatürk) leads resistance to partition of Turkey; Turkish Nationalist movement

1921 Reza Khan becomes leader and takes power in Persia, becomes Shah (1925) and introduces reform

1921-2 Washington Conference attempts to regulate situation in East Asia

1922 Greek army expelled from Turkey; last Ottoman sultan deposed; republic proclaimed (1923)

1926 Chiang Kai-shek (1886-1975) begins reunification of China

1931 Japanese occupy Manchuria

1932 Kingdom of Saudi Arabia formed by Ibn Saud

1934 'Long March' of Chinese Communists begins

1936 Japan signs anti-Comintern pact with Germany

1936 Arab revolt in Palestine against Jewish immigration

1937 Beginning of full-scale war between Japan and China

Europe

1907 Anglo-Russian entente

1908 Young Turk revolution: Ottoman sultan deposed

1908 Bulgaria becomes independent; Austria annexes Bosnia and Herzegovina

1912-13 Balkan wars

1914 Outbreak of First World War

1917 Revolution in Russia: Tsar abdicates (March), Bolsheviks take over (Nov); first socialist state established

1918 Germany and Austria-Hungary sue for armistice: end of First World War

1918 Civil war and foreign intervention in Russia

1919 Paris treaties redraw map of Europe

1919 World-wide influenza epidemic reaches Europe

1920 League of Nations established (headquarters Geneva)

1922 Mussolini takes power in Italy

1922 Irish Free State (Eire) created

1923 French occupy Ruhr; runaway inflation in Germany

1924 Death of Lenin

1925 Locarno treaties stabilise frontiers in West

1926 General Strike in Britain

1926 Salazar takes power in Portugal

1928 First Five-Year Plan and collectivisation of agriculture in Russia

1931 Spain becomes a Republic

1933 Hitler made Chancellor in Germany; beginning of Nazi revolution

1936 German reoccupation of Rhineland

1936 Spanish Civil War begins

1938 Germany occupies Austria

1938 Munich conference: dismemberment of Czechoslovakia

1939 German-Soviet non-aggression pact; Germany invades Poland; Britain and France declare war on Germany

1940 Germany overruns Norway, Denmark, Belgium, Netherlands, France; Italy invades Greece but is repulsed

1940 Battle of Britain

Africa

1908 Belgian state takes over Congo from King Leopold

1910 Formation of Union of South Africa

1911 Italy conquers Libya

1914 Britain proclaims protectorate over Egypt

1914-5 French and British conquer German colonies except German East Africa

1919 Nationalist revolt in Egypt

1921 Battle of Anual: Spanish army defeated by Moroccans

1926 Revolt of Abd-el Krim crushed in Morocco

1934 Italian suppression of Senussi resistance in Libya

1935 Italy invades Ethiopia

1936 Anglo-Egyptian alliance; British garrison in Suez Canal Zone

1940-1 Italians expelled from Somalia, Eritrea and Ethiopia

Americas and Australasia

1907 New Zealand acquires dominion status

1910 Mexican revolution begins

1914 Panama Canal opens

1917 US declares war on Central Powers

1918 President Wilson announces 'Fourteen Points'

1920 US refuses to ratify Paris treaties and withdraws into isolation

1921 US restricts immigration

1923 General Motors established: world's largest manufacturing company

1929 Wall Street Crash precipitates world Depression

1930 Military revolution in Brazil; Vargas becomes president

1932 Chaco War between Bolivia and Paraguay (to 1935)

1933 US President Franklin D. Roosevelt introduces New Deal

1935 Cárdenas president of Mexico: land redistribution and (1938) nationalisation of oil

1936 Pan-American congress; US proclaims good neighbour policy

1939 US proclaims neutrality in European War

Culture and technology

1907 Exhibition of Cubist paintings in Paris: Picasso (1881-1973), Braque (1882-1963)

1910 Development of abstract painting: Kandinsky (1866-1944), Mondrian (1872-1944)

1910 Development of plastics

1913 Henry Ford develops conveyor belt assembly for production of Model T automobile (Detroit, US)

1916 First birth control advice centre opened (New York)

1917 First use of massed tanks (Battle of Cambrai)

1919 Rutherford (1871-1937) splits atom (UK)

1919 Bauhaus school of design started by Gropius at Weimar (Germany)

1919 First crossing of Atlantic by air (Alcock and Brown)

1920 First general radio broadcasts (US and UK)

c.1920 Emergence of jazz in US: Louis Armstrong (1900-71), Duke Ellington (1899-1974), Count Basie (1904-1984)

1923 Development of tuberculosis vaccine (France)

1924 Thomas Mann (1875-1955) publishes *The Magic Mountain*; apotheosis of the novel with Proust (1871-1922), Joyce (1882-1941), Lawrence (1885-1930), Sinclair Lewis (1885-1951), Faulkner (1897-1962)

1925 Franz Kafka (1883-1924) publishes *The Trial*; Adolf Hitler publishes *Mein Kampf*

1927 Emergence of talking pictures. Rise of great film makers: D.W. Griffith (1874-1948), Chaplin (1889-1977), John Ford (1895-1973), Eisenstein (1896-1948), Clair (1898-1981), Hitchcock (1899-1980), Disney (1901-66)

1936 Keynes publishes *The General Theory of Employment, Interest and Money*

1936 First regular public television transmissions (UK)

1937 Jet engine first tested (UK)

1937 Invention of nylon (USA)

1939 Development of penicillin (UK)

1939 Development of DDT (Switzerland)

Asia

1941 Japan attacks US at Pearl Harbor

1942 Japan overruns SE Asia
1942 Battle of Midway; US halts Japanese expansion

1945 US drops atom bombs on Japan, forcing surrender

1946 Civil War in China (to 1949)

1946 Beginning of Vietnamese struggle against France (to 1954)

1947 India and Pakistan independent

1948 Establishment of state of Israel; first Arab-Israeli war

1949 Communist victory in China
1949 Indonesia independent

1950 Korean War begins

1954 Geneva conference: Laos, Cambodia and Vietnam become independent states

1955 Bandung Conference

1956 Second Arab-Israeli war

1957 Civil war in Vietnam

1960 Sino-Soviet dispute begins
1961 Increasing US involvement in Vietnam

1962 Sino-Indian war

1965 Indo-Pakistan war
1965 Military take-over in Indonesia

1966 Cultural Revolution in China

1967 Third Arab-Israeli war (Six-Day War)

1971 People's Republic of China joins UN
1971 Indo-Pakistan war leads to break-away of East Pakistan (Bangladesh)

1973 US forces withdraw from South Vietnam
1973 Fourth Arab-Israeli war

1975 Civil war in Lebanon: Syria invades (1976)

1975 Communists take over Vietnam, Laos and Cambodia

1976 Death of Mao-Tse Tung; political re-orientation and modernization under Deng Xiao-Ping

1977 President Sadat visits Jerusalem; Egypt/Israeli peace talks culminating in Camp David Peace Treaty (1978)
1977 Pakistan military coup by Zia ul-Haq; former president Bhutto executed in 1979

1979 Fall of Shah of Iran, establishment of Islamic Republic under Ayatollah Khomeini

1979 Afghanistan invaded by USSR
1979 Sino-Vietnamese War
1979 Vietnam invades Cambodia expelling Khmer Rouge government

1980 Military coup in Turkey, power assumed by General Evren
1980 Outbreak of Iran/Iraq War

1982 Israel invades Lebanon, expulsion of PLO from Beirut
1982 Israel withdraws from Sinai peninsula
1984 Britain and China agree on return of Hong Kong and New Territories to China in 1997. China initiates 'open door' policy to speed economic modernisation.
1984 Indira Gandhi assassinated following suppression of Sikh revolt at Amritsar
1985 Israel withdraws from all of Lebanon, other than 'buffer zone' in south

Europe

1941 Germany invades Russia; declares war on US

1943 German VI army surrenders at Stalingrad; Italian capitulation

1944 Anglo-American landing in Normandy; Russians advance in E. Europe

1945 Yalta Conference, **beginning of Cold War**
1945 Defeat of Germany and suicide of Hitler
1947 Intensification of Cold War; Truman Doctrine enunciated
1947 Greek Civil War (to 1949)
1947 Marshall Plan for economic reconstruction in Europe

1948 Communist take over in Czechoslovakia and Hungary; Berlin Airlift

1949 Formation of NATO alliance

1953 Death of Stalin

1955 Warsaw Pact signed

1956 Polish revolt, Gomulka in power; Hungarian revolt crushed by Russians

1957 Treaty of Rome: Formation of European Economic Community and (1959) of European Free Trade Association

1958 Fifth Republic in France: de Gaulle first President

1961 East Germans build Berlin Wall

1968 Liberalisation in Czechoslovakia halted by Russian invasion

1969 Outbreak of violence in N. Ireland

1970 Polish-German treaty; *de facto* recognition of existing frontiers

1973 Britain, Eire and Denmark join EEC

1974 End of dictatorship in Portugal
1974 Turkish invasion of Cyprus

1975 Death of Franco; end of dictatorship in Spain
1975 European Security Conference, Helsinki; recognition by W. Germany of post-war states of E. Germany and Poland

1977 Democratic election held in Spain, first in 40 years

1980 Death of Marshal Tito
1980 Creation of independent Polish trade union Solidarity; martial law (1981)
1981 Mitterand elected 1st Socialist President of France since World War II
1981 Widespread demonstrations against stationing of further nuclear missiles in Europe
1981 Greece joins EEC
1981 IRA hunger strikers die in Northern Ireland

1982 Death of USSR President Brezhnev, succession of Y. Andropov

1984 Death of Andropov, succession of K. Chernenko as USSR leader (d.1985)

1985 M. Gorbachev leader of USSR

Africa

1941 Germans conquer Cyrenaica and advance into Egypt (1942)

1942 Battle of el-Alamein; German defeat and retreat
1942 Anglo-American landings in Morocco and Algeria

1949 Apartheid programme inaugurated in S Africa

1952 Beginning of Mau Mau rebellion in Kenya
1952 Military revolt in Egypt; proclamation of republic (1953)

1954 Beginnings of nationalist revolt in Algeria

1956 Suez crisis: Anglo-French invasion of Canal Zone

1957 Beginning of **decolonisation in sub-Saharan Africa**: Gold Coast (Ghana) becomes independent

1960 'Africa's year'; many states become independent; outbreak of civil war in Belgian Congo

1961 South Africa becomes independent republic

1962 Algeria becomes independent

1965 Rhodesia declares itself independent of Britain
1967 Civil war in Nigeria (secession of Biafra) (to 1970)

1974 Emperor Haile Selasse deposed by Marxist junta

1975 Portugal grants independence to Mozambique and Angola

1976 Morocco and Mauritania partition Spanish Sahara
1976 Establishment of Transkei, first Bantustan in S Africa

1979 Tanzanian forces invade Uganda, and expel President Amin

1980 Black majority rule established in Zimbabwe (Rhodesia)

1981 President Sadat of Egypt assassinated

1984 Famine in the Sahel and Ethiopia; continuing war against secession
1985 Widespread civil unrest among blacks and coloureds in S. Africa

Americas and Australasia

1941 US begins 'lend-lease' to Britain

1941 US enters war against Germany and Japan

1944 Peron comes to power in Argentina

1945 United Nations established (headquarters New York)

1948 Organisation of American States established

1951 Australia, New Zealand and US sign Anzus Pact

1959 Cuban Revolution

1962 Cuba missile crisis

1963 President Kennedy assassinated

1964 US Civil Rights Bill inaugurates President Johnson's 'Great Society' programme

1966 Eruption of Black American discontent; growth of Black Power

1968 Assassination of Martin Luther King
1970 Allende elected president of Chile (killed 1973)

1971 US President Nixon and Secretary of State Kissinger initiate policy of detente with China and USSR
1971 USA abandons the Gold Standard and depreciates the dollar

1973 Major recession in US

1974 President Nixon resigns following Watergate affair

1979 Civil War in Nicaragua, President Somoza overthrown
1979 Military junta established, continuing civil war (El Salvador)

1980 Ronald Reagan President of USA

1982 Argentina occupies South Georgia and Falkland Is.; surrenders to UK Task Force June 15th

1983 Democracy restored in Argentina
1983 Coup in Grenada; US invades

1985 Democracy restored in Brazil and Uruguay

Culture and technology

1942 Fermi builds first nuclear reactor (US)

1945 Atom bomb first exploded (US)

1946 First electronic computer built (US)

1947 First supersonic flight (US)

1948 Transistor invented (US)

1951 First nuclear power stations (US and UK)

1952 Contraceptive pill developed (US)

1956 Beginning of rock and roll music (US): Elvis Presley (1935-77)

1957 First space satellite launched (USSR)

1961 First man in space: Gagarin (USSR)

1961 Structure of DNA molecule (genetic code) determined (UK)

1962 Second Vatican Council reforms Catholic liturgy and dogma

1964 Publication of *Thoughts of Chairman Mao*

1968 World-wide student protest movement

1969 First man lands on moon: Armstrong (US).

1976 1st supersonic transatlantic passenger service begins with Concorde

1978 Election of John Paul II, first Polish pope

1980s Computer revolution; spread of computers in offices and homes in the Western world

1981 First re-useable shuttle space flight (USA)

The geographical background to world history

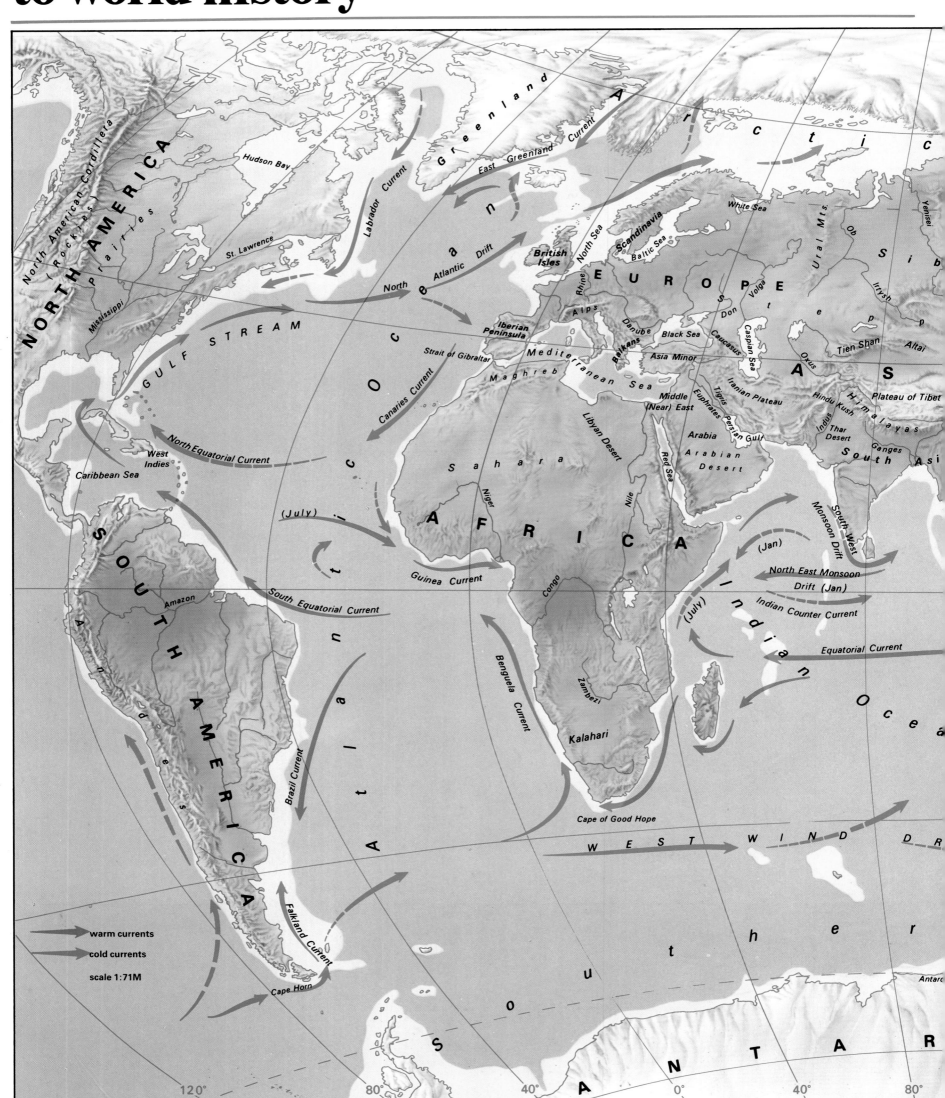

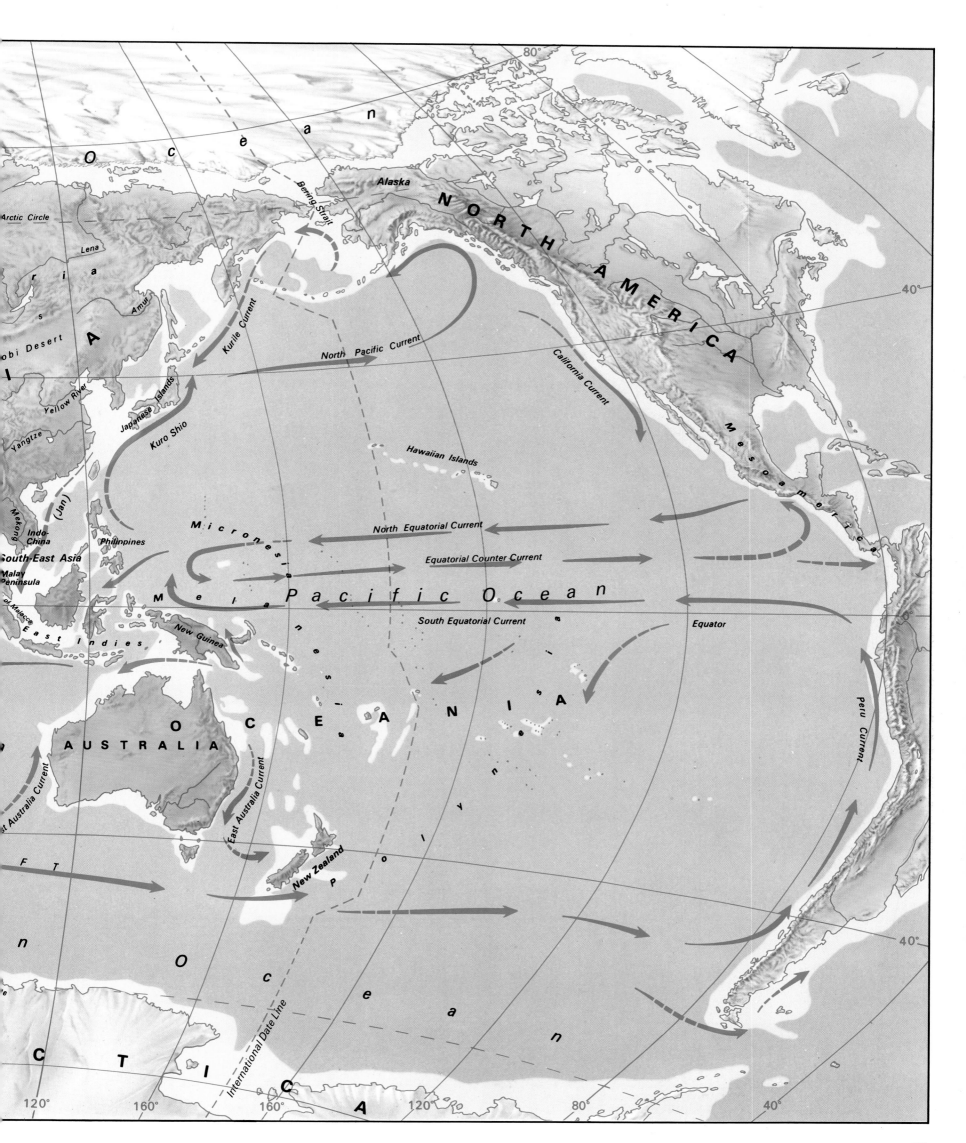

O c e a n

Arctic Circle

Lena

Gobi Desert

Yellow River

Yangtze

Mekong

(Jan)

Indo-China

South-East Asia

Malay Peninsula

of Malacca

East Indies

New Guinea

AUSTRALIA

East Australia Current

East Australia Current

New Zealand

F T

n

O

C

A

R

C

T

I

C

Bering Strait

Alaska

NORTH AMERICA

Kurile Current

North Pacific Current

California Current

Japanese Islands

Kuro Shio

Hawaiian Islands

M i c r o n e s i a

M e l a n e s i a

North Equatorial Current

Equatorial Counter Current

P a c i f i c   O c e a n

Philipines

South Equatorial Current

Equator

Mesoamerica

Peru Current

O C E A N I A

P o l y n e s i a

O   c   e   a   n

International Date Line

120°   160°   160°   120°   80°   40°

80°

40°

40°

1 The world

of early Man

Recorded history is only the tip of an iceberg reaching back through the millennia to the first appearance on earth of the species Man. Anthropologists, prehistorians and archaeologists have extended our vista of the past by tens and hundreds of thousands of years. We cannot understand human history without taking account of their findings. The transformation of Man (or, more accurately, of certain groups of men in certain areas) from a hunter and fisher to an agriculturist, and from a migratory to a sedentary life, is the most decisive revolution in the whole of human history. The climatic and ecological changes which made it possible have left their mark on the human record down to the present day. Agriculture not merely made possible a phenomenal growth of human population, which is thought to have increased some sixteen times between 8000 and 4000 BC; it also gave rise to the familiar landscape of village communities, which was still characteristic of Europe as late as the middle of the nineteenth century and even today prevails in most parts of the world. Nowhere are the continuities of history more visible. The enduring structures of human society, which transcend and outlive political change, carry us back through the centuries to the end of the Ice Age, to the changes which began when the shrinking ice-cap left a new world for Man to tame and conquer.

The origins of Man

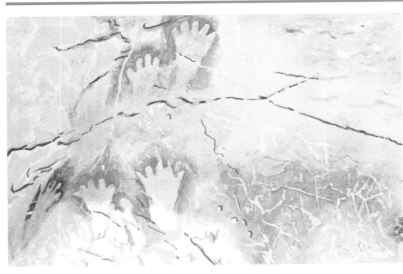

Cave painting *(above)* The evolution of man from animal to civilised life was made possible by the increased size of his brain and the development of his hand as a tool maker and tool user. These stencilled hand prints were made in a cave in France about 30,000 years ago.

2/Traces in western Europe *(below)* The oldest human relic found in Europe is the jawbone of Heidelberg man, discovered in 1907, and dated to approximately 400,000 years ago: roughly the same as Peking Man. *H. sapiens*, attested by the Swanscombe and Steinheim finds, goes back 250,000 years. The original Neanderthal skull was unearthed in a German gravel pit in 1856, while a Dordogne cave revealed an almost complete skeleton in 1911-13.

MAN and the great apes, particularly the African apes, it is now generally agreed, enjoyed a common ancestry some 15 to 20 million years ago. Fossil remains of various ape-like species, the *Dryopithecinae*, have been found dating from that period in east Africa, north India and in Europe. In body proportions and in the structure of their limbs for movement they were very different from either present-day apes or modern man, but from one of them descended, almost certainly, both the tree-living apes and the creatures who later left the forest for the open savannah grasslands and took to walking on two legs. No one knows precisely why these early hominids, whose lineage eventually gave rise to modern man, took to the ground, except that it may have been in search of some food supply – possibly plant seed and nuts – which was not being fully exploited by other animals.

Travelling upright on two feet (bipedalism) is not a particularly efficient form of movement, but it does free the hands and arms for other purposes. Primates in general had well-developed hands and were thus well equipped to grasp branches and to move freely in a varied and often precarious forest environment. Now these versatile forelimbs developed further, and could be used to make simple tools, carry food and building materials and thus establish a 'home', and hold infants closely to their mother's body and milk supply. With increasing refinement in these functions the brain's ability to record and interpret sensation and to control fine muscle movement evolved in parallel.

Increasing manual dexterity and the making of tools in turn favoured the development of communication systems, in particular spoken language, with all its distinctive and complex forms. The advantages offered by speech gave further impetus to brain evolution, while large snouts and powerful jaws, previously needed to seek out and masticate raw food, became largely redundant with the increase in manual dexterity, especially as all primates tend to rely far more on eyes than on their sense of smell.

Little is yet known about the very earliest hominids, fragments of whose jaws and teeth were first found in the Siwalik hills in India, and later duplicated in east Africa. These have been ascribed to the genus *Ramapithecus*, dating from about ten million years ago, but it is not established whether their owners even walked on two legs. This is, however, quite clear from the fossil remains of both pelvis and foot of the next evolutionary development, *Australopithecus*.

Australopithecine remains were first discovered in southern Africa, mainly in the Transvaal, where they occur in the debris of former limestone caves. Other sites have now been found in Tanzania, Kenya and southern Ethiopia. Some of these later finds, particularly those forms classified as *Homo habilis*, show rather advanced features by comparison with the southern African forms, and their precise status is currently in some dispute. There are certainly, however, at least two species of *Australopithecus*: *A. robustus* and *A. africanus*, dating from essentially the same period in south and east Africa. The first is larger and more rugged, and appears from its teeth to have lived wholly on vegetable matter. The smaller *A. africanus* probably added meat to his diet, and could well have been an active hunter. In east Africa, at least, simple stone tools have been found alongside the advanced Australopithecines, and in south Africa there is some evidence that horn, bone and animal teeth were already being used as weapons and tools. Although *Australopithecus* was certainly a terrestrial biped, in both species the braincase is still small and the jaws quite large. It has recently been possible to date some of these fossils, using mainly the potassium/argon method. One of the bones, the fragmentary Lothagam mandible, is about 5 million years old; but the Olduvai Gorge has Australopithecine remains dating from only 1.5 million years ago.

It was almost certainly from some part of the

A. africanus lineage that the first recognisably human creature, *Homo erectus*, finally evolved. Significantly advanced from *Australopithecus*, the undisputed specimens that have so far been discovered have all possessed smaller jaws, a larger brain capacity (averaging around 1000 cc) and a bone structure, apart from the skull, which is indistinguishable from that of modern man. The most numerous and best-known remains have been found in Asia (Java Man and Peking Man), but isolated examples have also been recognised in Africa and Europe. *Homo erectus* had a wider geographical range, a well-developed use of stone tools and also, at least at the Peking site, knowledge of fire. Some may in addition have practised ceremonial cannibalism: none of the Peking skulls discovered has its base intact.

H. erectus survived for an immense period,

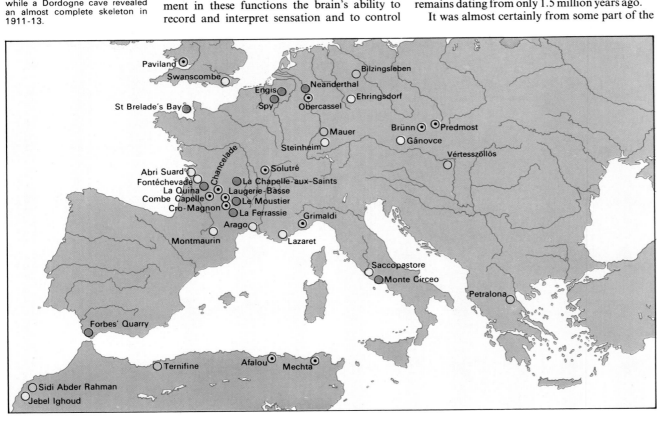

NORTH AMERICA

Midland
Minnesota
Natchez
Tepexpan

SOUTH AMERICA

Paviland
Swanscombe
Bilzingsleben
Engis
Neanderthal
Spy
Obercassel
Ehringsdorf
St Brelade's Bay
Mauer
Brünn
Predmost
Steinheim
Gánovce
Vértesszöllös
Abri Suard
Solutré
Fontéchevade
La Chapelle-aux-Saints
La Quina
Laugerie-Basse
Combe Capelle
Le Moustier
Cro-Magnon
La Ferrassie
Grimaldi
Arago
Montmaurin
Lazaret
Saccopastore
Monte Circeo
Petralona
Forbes' Quarry
Ternifine
Afalou
Mechta
Sidi Abder Rahman
Jebel Ighoud

at least one and a half million years, and possibly even longer. Eventually, natural selection brought about further development. Just when and how *Homo sapiens* became clearly differentiated from his *H. erectus* forebears remains a matter of debate, but even in quite early examples, such as those from Swanscombe and Steinheim (c. 250,000 BC), they were showing in their braincase characteristics of present-day Man. There is a considerable variety in the form of fossils dating from about a quarter of a million years ago; the skeletal remains become unquestionably those of 'modern' Man, with today's average cranial capacity of 1500 cc, at about 40,000 years ago. There are still important gaps in the record. One particular anomaly concerns the people known as 'classical' Neanderthals (as opposed to 'progressive' Neanderthals). These, apparently the first humans to live in a really cold climate, inhabited Europe in the late stages of the Pleistocene Ice Age (see page 36). In some respects they resemble *H. erectus* more than any *H. sapiens* predecessors. But their origins, the cause of their apparent extinction with the retreat of the glaciers, and their contribution, if any, to the ancestry of modern Man, remain a mystery.

Modern Man, once definitely established,

quickly spread over the whole world, including, for the first time, the Americas. For another 30,000 years, however, his technology, though highly advanced, was still based on unpolished stone tools, and his economy was that of hunting and gathering. Like all tool-making hominids, his culture is thus classifiable as Palaeolithic. It is in the next, Neolithic stage, with the advent of polished tools and settled agriculture, that man's society, rather than man himself, begins the process of rapid evolution.

3/The evolution of Man (right) The large, herbivorous man-apes, *A. robustus*, appear to have proved an evolutionary dead end. The main line of development led through *A. africanus* and *H. erectus* to the early forms of *H. sapiens*, known as 'progressive Neanderthal', and thence to Modern Man. The position of classical Neanderthal man is still a matter of considerable debate; it may represent another lineage from *H. erectus*. Whether he contributed further to the evolution of *H. sapiens* or suffered extinction is unknown.

1/Traces of Man's ancestors (below) This shows the main sites where early man's remains have been found. It is important to remember that the distribution probably relates as much to the intensity of fossil-seeking activity, and to the geological accidents of fossil-survival, as to the actual spread of the populations from which the fossils are derived.

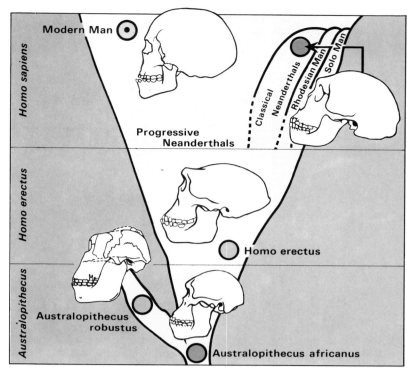

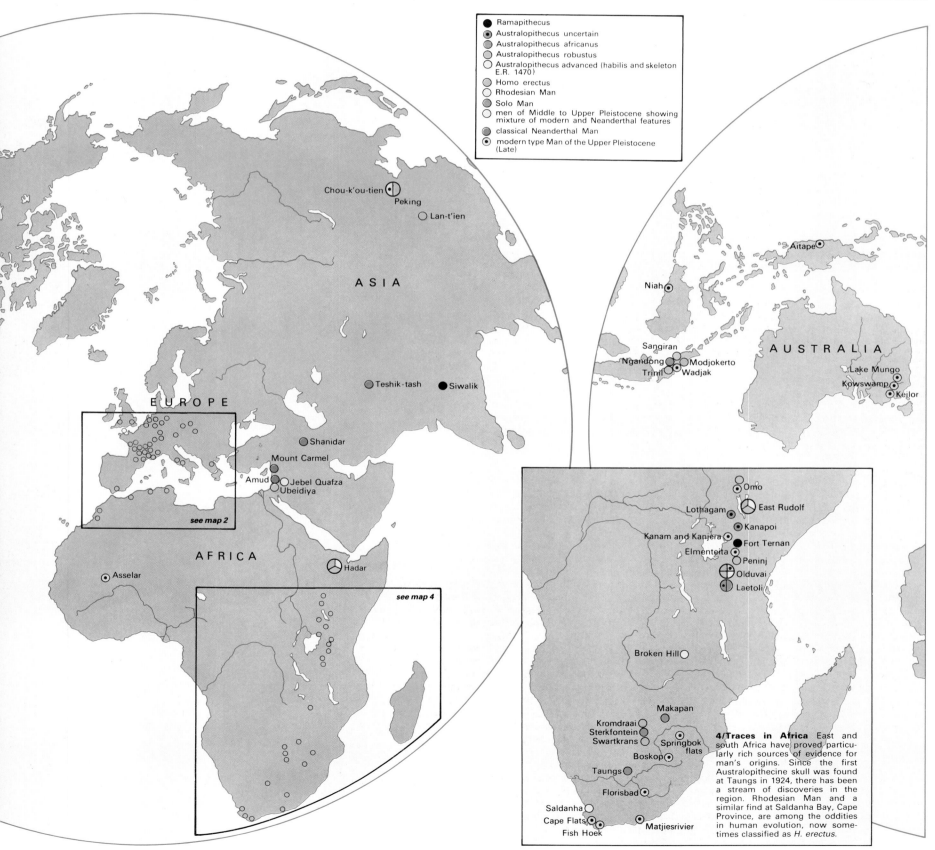

4/Traces in Africa East and south Africa have proved particularly rich sources of evidence for man's origins. Since the first Australopithecine skull was found at Taungs in 1924, there has been a stream of discoveries in the region. Rhodesian Man and a similar find at Saldanha Bay, Cape Province, are among the oddities in human evolution, now sometimes classified as *H. erectus*.

Hunters and gatherers: the economy of early Man

THE pathways of human evolution can now be traced back for over three million years. For more than 99 per cent of this time man lived as a hunter of wild game and as a gatherer of fruit, seeds and honey. This way of life was based on division of labour, on cunning, co-operation and intelligence, and was a social and technical achievement quite different from that of other hunting mammals. It was, until very recently, man's most persistent and successful adaptation. Only during the last few thousand years has the practice of agriculture, the domestication of plants and animals, replaced the earlier way of life; only in this brief period has man been able to make use of materials other than stone, wood or bone, or harness sources of energy other than those of the human body.

Knowledge and understanding of this way of life comes partly from the study of those people who still live by hunting and gathering today. They now form only a minute fraction of the world's population; many are relic groups living in marginal areas, their life-styles threatened with disruption or destruction by neighbouring agricultural and industrial populations. But in their activities and customs, and in the memories of their older members, they give a glimpse of the earlier pattern of life. Other evidence is provided by the remains and artefacts of early man, partly in the form of fossilised human remains (see page 32). Bones show that the earliest forms of man were upright, bipedal, with mobile hands capable of dexterity and precision. These unique physical characteristics, combined with emerging behavioural and cultural complexity, enabled man to develop to its full the hunting and gathering way of life and, in so doing, to spread from the original homelands of Africa across Asia and Europe and eventually into North and South America.

Evidence also comes from the dismembered bones of hunted animals, from the weapons and tools with which man wounded and killed his prey and prepared the meat, sinews, bones and hides, and later from the engravings, sculptures and paintings in his caves. Man extended his brain and hand by means of weapons and tools. Of these, mainly stone implements have survived from man's early period and provide its name – the Palaeolithic, the Old Stone Age. Not all rocks are suitable for tool-making, but those used included flint, obsidian, chert, quartzite and other glass-like substances capable of holding an edge. When the edge of a flint nodule is hit deliberately, a flake may be struck off. The form of the flake, or of its parent core, can be altered by shaping the outline to make a chopper, axehead, scraper or blade, and edges can be resharpened. Different cultural traditions and their development can be traced by distinguishing the various methods of manufacture.

The earliest implements, pebble tools such as those associated with *Australopithecus* in Africa, were crude and simple but adequate for cutting up meat and shredding plant food. Larger, more carefully worked choppers and other tools are found with *Homo erectus*, as in the Choukoutien cave near Peking, China. Associated remains show that some 400,000 years ago *Homo erectus* not only had fire to cook with, but was capable of applying group pursuit and intelligent co-ordinated action to the capture and slaughter of large animals – elephant, rhinoceros, horse, bison, water-buffalo, camel, wild boar, deer, sheep and antelope.

Elsewhere in the *Homo erectus* range, more versatile and sophisticated hand-axes are found in which the flaking process was continued all round the stone to produce a biface core with an irregular border; these were followed by hand-axes in which the flaking is more delicate, the edges straighter. This development is accompanied by increasing evidence of the use of the flakes themselves, and these flake cultures later

improved further when the technique was evolved of striking a flake from a carefully prepared 'tortoise-core'.

The industry associated with Neanderthal man consisted of a combination of hand-axes and flake tools – pointed scrapers, triangular knife blades, hammerstones and small hand-axes. The Neanderthal period, preceding and extending into the last European Ice Age (the Würm), provides the first clear evidence for the growth of ritual practices, for example ceremonial burials, but it is not until the forms of modern *Homo sapiens* appear, during the last Ice Age, that the hunting way of life reached its full richness and complexity. This later phase, the Upper Palaeolithic, is dominated by a new and more specialised range of flint tools – wooden or bone punches were used to pare blades from a flint; pressure-flaking, the pressing of pointed implements against the blades, was then used to detach further slivers. Burins, engraving tools bearing a variety of shaped working points, are also characteristic implements of the Upper Palaeolithic peoples. Other materials became widely used: bone, antler and ivory, for instance, were made into spearheads, harpoons and needles. There are signs that stone tools were hafted. From about 30,000 years ago dramatic new evidence of the hunters' life is provided by paintings, sculptures and engravings, at first of animals and later of the human, particularly the female body.

Some 10,000 years ago the ice sheets receded and the frozen plains, or tundra, where herds of game had previously wandered, became covered by large areas of forest. As the glaciers shifted northward other climatic zones were affected by the change. In a climate basically similar to today's, though slightly warmer, the Palaeolithic came to an end, and a transitional stage, the Mesolithic, developed, which saw the gradual beginnings of agriculture. The hunters survived, using much the same tools as before but with rather more application of bone and horn. The bow and arrow reached full development and the dog was domesticated as a trained hunting companion. Fishing became important as man familiarised himself with the use of fish-hooks, nets, harpoons, dugouts and paddles.

With the transition from the Mesolithic to the last of the Stone Ages – the Neolithic – hunting and gathering gave way before the advance of farming (see page 38). However, although in its overt form this mode of existence is now practised by only a handful of peoples, in a very real sense all human beings still carry the legacy of their Palaeolithic past. Intellect, interests, emotions and basic social life are all evolutionary products of the success of the hunting adaptation.

It was as a hunter that man first colonised all the continents except Antarctica. Beginning as a tropical animal, the elaboration of his culture and technology allowed him to spread through the temperate zone and, during the last glaciation, to tackle the game-rich steppe and tundra areas to the north – spreading from Africa through Eurasia and Australasia and ultimately to the New World.

Ten million years ago, before the Pleistocene ice age, man's ancestors could be found in a wide belt between Africa and India and up into central Europe. But remains of the earliest toolmakers (*Homo habilis*), around two million years ago, are found mainly in Africa; for as the world began to cool down, areas outside would have become less hospitable. Only when more sophisticated types of tools such as hand-axes and choppers were being made, did man (now *Homo erectus*) appear in large numbers in Eurasia – though as extensive glaciation had by then begun, Europe was occupied only in the warmer, interglacial, periods. Thus until the last glaciation, beginning around 110,000 years ago, man was confined to the south of the zone of

Tools of the early hunters *(below)*
Two million years ago chipped pebbles (a) were the first stone tools in Africa. More evolved choppers (b) then appeared in Asia, and pear-shaped hand-axes (c) in Africa and Europe, supplemented by simple flakes (d). Carefully-shaped flakes made into scrapers (e) became common as skin-clothing developed, as man spread northwards around 50,000 years ago. Finally, more advanced techniques of blade-making and pressure-flaking allowed handy small carving-tools (f) and projectile-points (g).

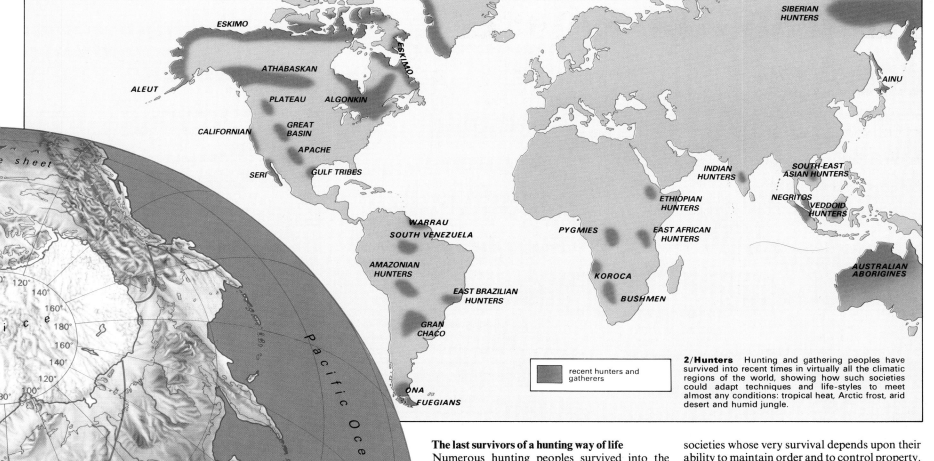

SIBERIAN
HUNTERS

ESKIMO

ATHABASKAN

ALEUT

PLATEAU   ALGONKIN

CALIFORNIAN   GREAT
BASIN

APACHE

SERI   GULF TRIBES

AINU

INDIAN
HUNTERS

SOUTH-EAST
ASIAN HUNTERS

NEGRITOS   VEDDOID
HUNTERS

WARRAU   ETHIOPIAN
SOUTH VENEZUELA   HUNTERS

PYGMIES   EAST AFRICAN
HUNTERS

AMAZONIAN
HUNTERS   KOROCA

EAST BRAZILIAN   BUSHMEN
HUNTERS

AUSTRALIAN
ABORIGINES

GRAN
CHACO

ONA
FUEGIANS

recent hunters and
gatherers

2/Hunters Hunting and gathering peoples have
survived into recent times in virtually all the climatic
regions of the world, showing how such societies
could adapt techniques and life-styles to meet
almost any conditions: tropical heat, Arctic frost, arid
desert and humid jungle.

The last survivors of a hunting way of life

Numerous hunting peoples survived into the
19th and early 20th centuries long enough to be
studied by ethnologists and anthropologists, both
physical and social, but today the hunting and
gathering way of life is only fully represented by
the pygmies, the bushmen, the eskimos and the
Australian aborigines, between them totalling
only a few hundreds of thousands out of a total
world population of nearly four thousand
million. Nevertheless, they provide a unique and
precious insight into man's earlier way of life.

Recent studies reveal the intimacy of the
relationship between hunting man and his
natural environment; the relative simplicity of
the material culture (only 94 different items exist
among the Kung bushmen); the lack of accumu-
lation of individual wealth; the mobility. The
units of society, the bands or hordes, are small:
groups of kinfolk and their friends who can live
and work well together. Recent work contradicts
the traditional view of hunting life as 'nasty,
brutish and short', as a constant struggle against
a harsh environment. In fact, bushmen's subsistence requirements are satisfied by only a
modest effort – perhaps two or three days work a
week by each adult; they do not have to struggle
over food resources; their attitudes towards
ownership are flexible and their living groups
open. Such features set hunters and gatherers
apart from more technologically developed

societies whose very survival depends upon their
ability to maintain order and to control property.

Evidence suggests that hunting and gathering
communities often have a high percentage of old
people, and that life expectancy is not necessarily
short; population control is not, as is often
thought, only or even mainly through high infant
or child mortality, but also through long intervals
between births, perhaps in part due to the long
periods of breastfeeding of the infant. Indeed
many hunting groups have proved highly adept
at population control – not merely in the crude
sense of restricting numbers, but in preserving
and developing desirable social characteristics,
while endeavouring to prevent (often by forced
celibacy) the passing on of any personal defects
that might prevent a member playing a full part
in his or her small community.

Such communities frequently show great
robustness and resilience in the face of normal
hazards. Illness, accident, climatic change or the
migration of food supplies can all be met from
within the resources of the group. It is usually
outside intruders, especially those introducing
modern methods and economic attitudes (not to
mention diseases) who shatter the delicate but
essential ecological balance between the hunters
and their environment. Unfortunately, given the
ubiquity of contemporary technology, it seems
unlikely that these life-styles will be left free to
survive for more than another generation or so.

coastline at the height of
the last glaciation (Ice
Age), 20,000 years ago

modern coastline and
rivers

Limits of human occupation in:

lower Palaeolithic
(to 100,000 years ago)

middle Palaeolithic
(100,000 to 40,000 years
ago)

upper Palaeolithic
(40,000 to 10,000 years
ago)

1/Hunters colonise the world (above) The earliest
tool-makers were restricted to the south of the Old
World. During the last glacial phase (70,000-10,000
years ago), when sea levels were low and ice-expansion
had restricted the forests, groups of hunters with
effective skin-clothing and heated dwellings managed
to penetrate northwards where they could exploit the
rich animal life of the enlarged steppe and tundra zones,
reaching Siberia and ultimately the New World. The
arrows indicate the main directions of population
expansion.

freezing winter temperatures.

The reason is not far to seek: without effective
clothing and shelter, survival in below-zero
conditions was impossible. It was the development (by Neanderthal man) of effective skin-
clothing and heated shelters which allowed the
dramatic increase in the area of human occupation and carried man to the north of the Arctic
Circle. By 35,000 years ago, men of fully modern
type had not only increased their density in the
area already occupied, but were pressing on
beyond into eastern Siberia.

The art of the hunters

One of the most striking achievements of the
Upper Palaeolithic and Mesolithic period was
its art – cave paintings, engravings and sculptures.
Animals predominate: human forms are rarely
rendered with the same naturalism as the
carefully observed wildlife. It seems likely that
these early creative imaginings were in part a
form of hunting magic, helping either to control
and capture the objects of the hunt or to increase
the amount of game. Perhaps they also provided
a way of illustrating myths and traditions, forming a 'backdrop' for sacred and ritual purposes,
or sometimes just enlivening and brightening
everyday life. Whatever the impetus, it developed
early in the history of *Homo sapiens* and spread
almost everywhere man himself was able to
pursue the food-providing herds. This picture
dates from the Mesolithic and shows a communal
hunt for red deer. Painted c.6000 BC, it adorns a
rock-face in the Cueva de los Caballos, near
Castellón in Spain. Such scenes, as opposed to
representations of individual animals are rare in
the 150 or so known sites of Palaeolithic art
in Europe.

Man and the Ice Age

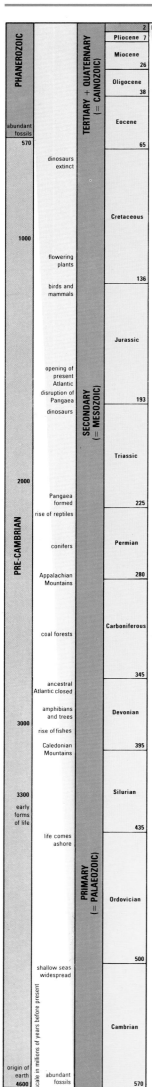

THE Pleistocene ice age, during which *Homo sapiens* made his first appearance on earth and ultimately spread out to occupy all the world's major landmasses, lasted roughly 2,000,000 years, ending about 10,000 years ago. It was a period of wide climatic variation, with all the continents experiencing frequent alterations and extremes of heat and cold, rain and drought, far sharper than anything recorded in recent centuries. Man's unique adaptability in the face of such violent environmental change was undoubtedly a crucial factor both in his survival and in his gradually developing dominance over other species.

In northern latitudes throughout the Pleistocene era, the main determinant of animal and vegetable existence was the advance and retreat of the glaciers. These frequently covered large parts of Europe, Asia and North America with impenetrable ice-sheets, locking up huge quantities of sea water and reducing average temperatures by 10°–12°C and ocean levels by over 450 feet – far below those of modern times. Only when they shrank back, allowing the northward spread of oak and spruce forests, and the subarctic vegetation on which the mammoths and reindeer browsed, was it possible for early humans to live much outside the equatorial regions; and even then it required the discovery of fire, and the ability to sew warm clothing, before they could survive a winter in the rich, but frozen, hunting grounds.

The main glacial advances have now all been accurately dated, and their associated meteorological, geographical, botanical and biological developments have been confidently established by a variety of techniques, from the study of

2/Geological periods and the emergence of Man
Using a complex variety of analytical techniques, it is now possible to reconstruct at least some aspects of the earth's climate as far back as the Pre-Cambrian era, more than 3000 million years ago. The chart sets out the broad patterns of change during the main geological periods down to the Cainozoic, which includes our own.

sedimentary lakes and the analysis of pollen zones to the use of radiocarbon and potassium-argon decay times. But it is the probably less-known pluvial epochs – the periods of favourable rain and vegetation conditions in tropical Africa – which played the first key climatic role in human history.

Certainly there were ape-like hominids in Africa, using weapons to kill their prey, even before the Ice Age began. As the expansion and contraction of the icecaps created a succession of more favourable conditions – making the rain forests drier in the cold epochs, and bringing more rainfall to the arid savannahs as the general temperature rose again – so a succession of progressively more advanced tool-using cultures emerged: the Aterian bow-and-arrow makers in the Maghreb and the Stillbay-Magosian settlements in south and east Africa, during the wet centuries c. 20,000 years ago, and the increasingly adept craftsmen of the Sangoan, Lupemban and Tshitolian groups who inhabited the sub-Saharan forests when the rain was light enough to keep the vegetation under control.

Among the very early anthropological discoveries, only Peking Man (c. 350,000 years ago) is known to have used fire, the vital attribute which enabled him to live north of the frost line in the north China caves of Chou-k'ou-tien; and there is no reliable evidence that Man actually knew how to make fire at will until the very end of the Pleistocene epoch. But once fire had been discovered, however accidentally, it was always possible to transport and sustain it, even over long distances and periods. By the time of the first advance of the Würm glaciers in central Europe, around 75,000 years ago, the Mousterian cave-dwellers of the Dordogne, with their cooking hearths, their bone needles, and their implements for scraping and shaping furs, could already survive the bitter conditions of a northern winter; and each time the ice retreated, the

peoples of Europe and Asia grew gradually more numerous and more advanced.

The water frozen into the Würm ice-sheets, and their equivalents in northern Europe and North America, the Weichsel and Wisconsin glacier-fields, reduced sea levels so far that land bridges appeared linking most major areas and many isolated islands into one single continental mainland. Helped by the three most southerly of those (see map 1) men were first able to reach Australia and Tasmania. The Bering Strait between eastern Asia and the glacier-free expanse of Alaska, which at most times has been traversible across the winter ice, now became a broad, dry land highway for the migration of peoples and animals of all kinds. The first groups to penetrate the Americas, sometime before 30,000 years ago, made little impact on their environment; and then the ice-sheets closed off the route South. An ice-free corridor opened up again about 12,000 years ago, letting the now more advanced big game hunters from Siberia through to the rich gamelands of the American plains.

Palaeolithic hunters, now making lethally

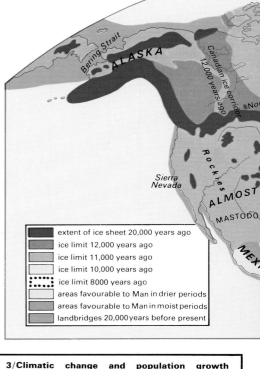

■	extent of ice sheet 20,000 years ago
■	ice limit 12,000 years ago
■	ice limit 11,000 years ago
□	ice limit 10,000 years ago
⋯	ice limit 8000 years ago
	areas favourable to Man in drier periods
	areas favourable to Man in moist periods
	landbridges 20,000 years before present

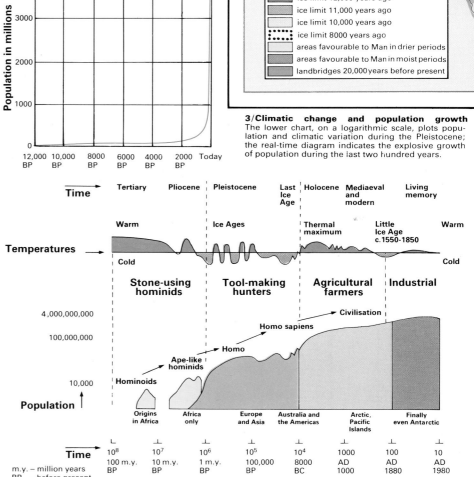

3/Climatic change and population growth
The lower chart, on a logarithmic scale, plots population and climatic variation during the Pleistocene; the real-time diagram indicates the explosive growth of population during the last two hundred years.

The Berezovka Mammoth This giant animal's entire carcass was preserved in frozen Siberian mud until its discovery earlier this century. Its death probably occurred in early autumn when it slipped while feeding on a high river-bank bluff. It fell, breaking many bones, and suffocated in the ooze, probably around 40,000 years ago.

tures called casteroides, camels, ground sloths, stag-moose, two types of musk-oxen, several varieties of large, often lion-sized cats, mastodons and three mammoths, woolly, Columbian and imperial. Within a thousand years of man's large-scale arrival most of them were gone – including all the horses, which had to be re-introduced from 16th-century Europe.

No one knows how far primitive man, with his limited numbers, was responsible for this wholesale destruction. No evidence has appeared, though, to suggest a climatic or topographical cause, and there are indications, both in cave paintings and in skeletal remains, that many of the now-extinct mammals were attacked by large groups of humans, and sometimes even stampeded in herds over high cliffs into swamps.

Whatever the explanation, there is little doubt that the greatly expanded populations of Late Palaeolithic Man, even though their hunting grounds now extended down to the far tip of South America, found their accustomed wild food-plants and wild game far sparser and more difficult to come by as the Pleistocene ice age came to its end, c.10,000 bp.

With the vanishing of major meat sources like the mastodon, which had weighed a ton or more, and sufficed on the frozen tundra to feed a whole tribe for weeks on end, men were now driven to devise new means of subsistence. It was now, as the world slowly started to warm up again, that all over the globe small groups of people first learned to domesticate animals and plants (see page 40) and embark on the Neolithic or agricultural revolution.

accurate use of flint-tipped spears and arrows, had long since begun to acclerate the extinction of once-numerous animal species. The mastodons and mammoths started to disappear from Africa and south-east Asia at least 40,000 years ago, and the process was well advanced in Australia and northern Eurasia by 13,000 bp (meaning before the present, or more precisely before 1950). But the rolling grasslands of the American west and south-west were a different matter. Roughly 11,000 years ago they were teeming with animal life – giant bison with a six-foot horn spread, towering, beaver-like crea-

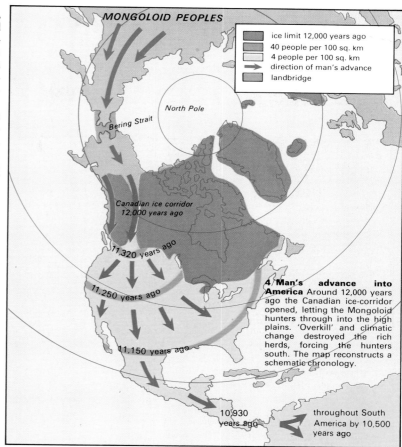

MONGOLOID PEOPLES

ice limit 12,000 years ago
40 people per 100 sq. km
4 people per 100 sq. km
direction of man's advance
landbridge

North Pole

Bering Strait

Canadian ice corridor 12,000 years ago

11,320 years ago
11,250 years ago
11,150 years ago
10,930 years ago

throughout South America by 10,500 years ago

4/Man's advance into America Around 12,000 years ago the Canadian ice-corridor opened, letting the Mongoloid hunters through into the high plains. 'Overkill' and climatic change destroyed the rich herds, forcing the hunters south. The map reconstructs a schematic chronology.

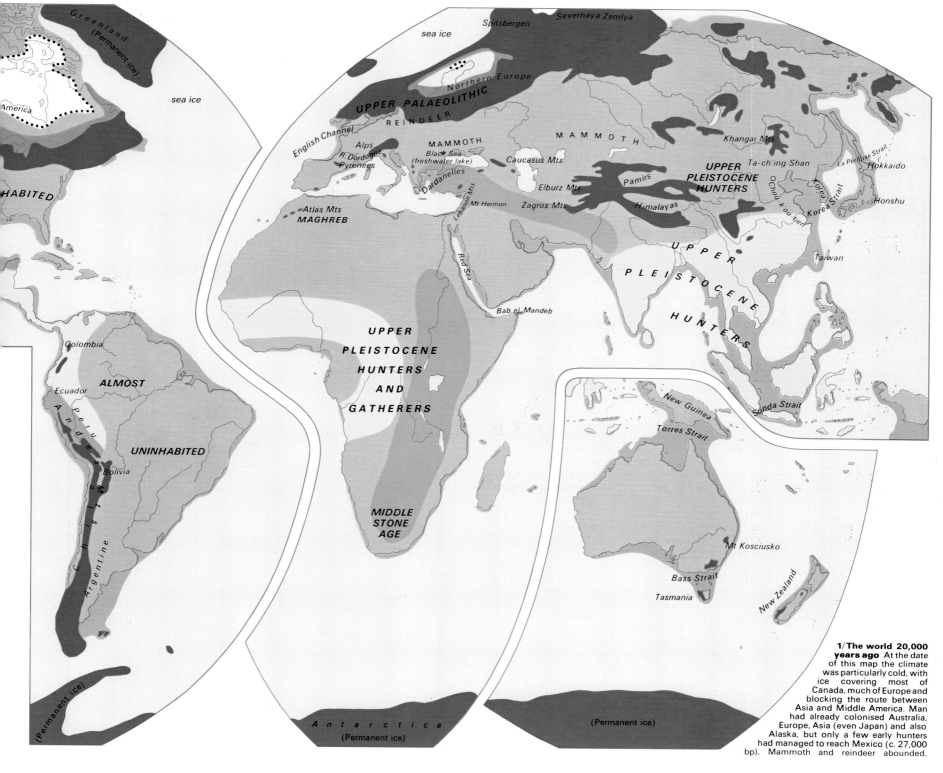

1/The world 20,000 years ago At the date of this map the climate was particularly cold, with ice covering most of Canada, much of Europe and blocking the route between Asia and Middle America. Man had already colonised Australia, Europe, Asia (even Japan) and also Alaska, but only a few early hunters had managed to reach Mexico (c. 27,000 bp). Mammoth and reindeer abounded.

From hunting to farming: the origins of agriculture

THE period of the last ten thousand years, during which present-day climatic conditions have existed, is only the last of a dozen or so warmer phases which punctuated the Ice Age. In one respect, however, it is unique: it has seen an unprecedented explosion in the numbers of the human species, and in their impact on the world as a whole.

In 8000 BC there were still only small bands of hunters and collectors, whose scale was little different from that of their predecessors up to half a million years before. Within two thousand years, however, some substantial villages had appeared; in another two thousand years, towns and cities; two thousand years later, city-states had grown to empires; two thousand years more and the technological foundations were laid for the achievements which in the next two thousand years were to include steam power, atomic energy, and man's first landing on the moon.

This decisive quickening of pace in certain areas can be attributed largely to the beginnings – independently in several parts of the world, but earliest and most importantly in the Near Eastern region of the Old World – of agriculture, which is the deliberate alteration of natural systems to promote the abundance of an exploited species or set of species.

Where this involves selective breeding and genetic change, the process is called domestication; and some species are now completely dependent on man's intervention for their survival. This is especially true of the cereals, the species which more than any other has sustained the tremendous growth of population since the last glacial. The yield from cultivated cereals made possible human communities of a larger size than ever before, and thus for the first time there arose settlements which can be described as villages or even towns. Because these yields came from a limited area of land, it was possible to support a growing population by converting more and more land to crops; and the productivity of this land could be increased by intensive techniques of cultivation, such as irrigation. Because such systems demand higher levels of organisation, more complex societies were often the result. How this self-sustaining process actually started, however, is still poorly understood. Certainly, by the end of the last glaciation, Man had a more complex technology and social organisation than before, and he was thus better equipped to respond to the challenge of environmental change than he had been at the beginning of previous interglacial periods. The altered distribution of rainfall and the changes in sea and lake levels after 8000 BC necessitated a greater use of the grasses which abounded in the mountain foothills; and the unconscious selection of certain forms which could be grown in lowland habitats revealed their potential as crops.

At least three major groups of cereals have independently taken part in this process, in different parts of the world becoming staple crops and causing fundamental changes in economy and society. In the Near East, and spreading out from there to Europe and India, wheat and barley formed the basis of village and city life among the most ancient civilisations. At the other end of Eurasia, in China, millet was

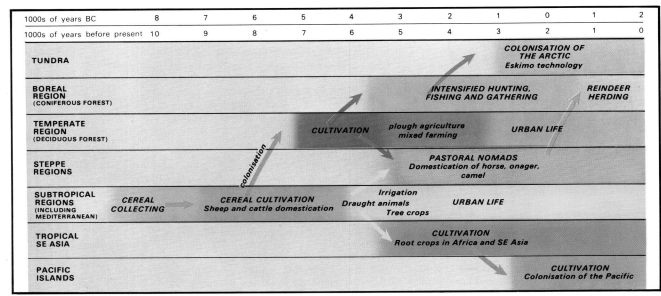

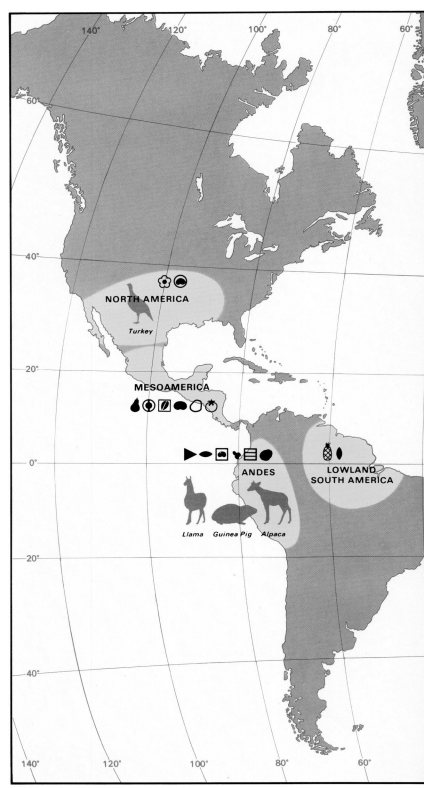

The cumulative consequences of the agricultural revolution *(above)* The pattern shown in map 2 developed in the ten thousand years of the post-glacial, following the initial impetus from the beginnings of cereal cultivation and the emergence of settled villages in the Near East. This diagram is based on the Old World, and shows the chain of consequences as it affected its different zones.

cultivated; and together with rice – which had been domesticated in South-East Asia – these crops supported the civilisation which has continued down to the present time. In Central America (Mesoamerica) and Peru, maize was developed from its tiny wild form to its present size, allowing the growth of the wealthy civilisations plundered centuries later by the Spanish *conquistadores* (see page 158). Thus the initial innovation of cereal cultivation had a cumulative effect, inducing not only fundamental changes in economy and social order, but also continuing pattern of change in subsequent millennia.

In the Old World, the cultivation of plants was complemented by new forms of animal exploitation: sheep, goats, cattle and pigs came to be herded near to the permanent settlements and fields, and became domesticated through isolation from their wild populations. Later it was discovered that some of these animals could be used for wool and milk as well as meat, and also to pull ploughs and carts, so raising agricultural productivity; and that other domesticable species such as horses and asses could be used to carry loads and human riders, improving communications and the possibilities of trade. With time, also, a wider range of plants came to be used – tree-crops such as figs, dates and olives were taken into cultivation, while as agriculture spread to the tropics, techniques of vegetative propagation were applied to roots and tubers.

In the New World, where few animals were domesticated, the lack of suitable draught animals prevented the development of the plough. Nevertheless several genera of plants were domesticated, many of which were widely adopted in Europe after the discovery of the Americas, and which are of worldwide importance today – maize, squashes and several sorts of beans from Mesoamerica, and potatoes, peppers and tomatoes from the tropical region further south. The use of cotton in the New World took the place of wool in the Old World. The parallel development of domestic plants and animals in different parts of the world has provided a valuable pool of diversity, allowing modern man a wide range of choice in selecting appropriate crops and stock for particular situations.

The spread of agriculture and domestication produced important effects even outside the core areas of cereal cultivation and urbanisation. In Africa a wide range of native species of plants was domesticated in the belt on the southern margin of the Sahara, supplementing the cereals

Early milling equipment *(above)* Found wherever grain crops were cultivated, the simple saddle-quern or flat grinding stone was a basic piece of early agricultural equipment, needed to convert the hard seeds to porridge or flour. It appears in Neolithic contexts both in the Old World and in the Americas.

and cattle introduced up the Nile. Thereafter, expanding populations in this zone tended to move southwards, pushing the native hunting groups into more marginal territories. The native species of domesticates were further supplemented in the first millennium by the arrival of crops including the banana, which was brought by a movement of colonisation starting in coastal South-East Asia and spreading both westwards across the Indian Ocean to Madagascar and eastwards to the as yet uninhabited islands of the Pacific.

In central Eurasia, animal-keeping was more important than cultivation, especially after the domestication of the horse, and some of the techniques of milking and riding spread northwards to the Siberian tribes whose economy was still based on reindeer. In the far north, the development of more advanced technologies allowed the colonisation of the Arctic by specialised Eskimo hunters and fishers. By the time of European expansion in the 16th century AD, the world had a roughly zonal arrangement of native economies, ranging from specialised hunter-fishers in the north, through herding groups, hunting and simple agricultural groups, complex plough- or irrigation-based urban economies, and tropical cultivators, to the marginal relict hunting and gathering populations of southern South America, South Africa and Australia – the last surviving examples of the way of life (see page 34) which man had followed for thousands of years.

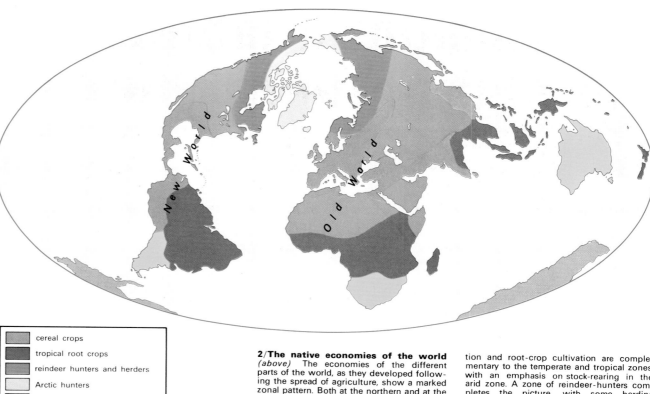

cereal crops

tropical root crops

reindeer hunters and herders

Arctic hunters

hunters and pastoralists

remnant hunting isolates

2/The native economies of the world *(above)* The economies of the different parts of the world, as they developed following the spread of agriculture, show a marked zonal pattern. Both at the northern and at the southern extremes, hunting economies survived — advanced Eskimo peoples in the Arctic, relict hunting groups in the often arid southern continental fringes. Cereal cultivation and root-crop cultivation are complementary to the temperate and tropical zones, with an emphasis on stock-rearing in the arid zone. A zone of reindeer-hunters completes the picture, with some herding techniques being used in the Old World where they have been learned from neighbouring pastoralists.

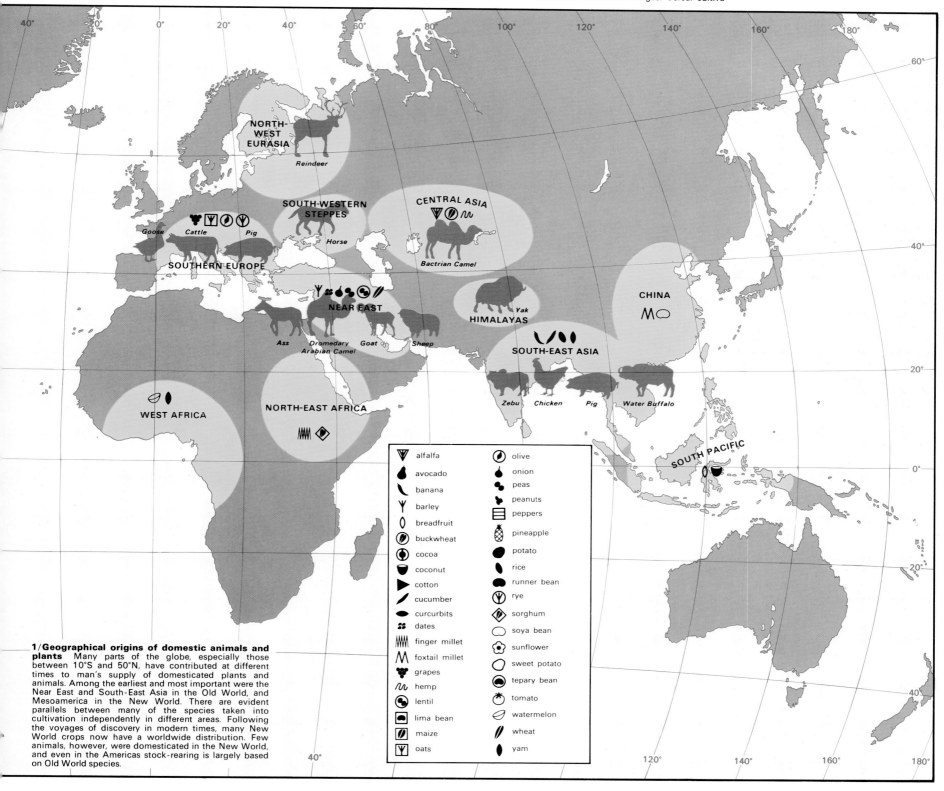

1/Geographical origins of domestic animals and plants Many parts of the globe, especially those between 10°S and 50°N, have contributed at different times to man's supply of domesticated plants and animals. Among the earliest and most important were the Near East and South-East Asia in the Old World, and Mesoamerica in the New World. There are evident parallels between many of the species taken into cultivation independently in different areas. Following the voyages of discovery in modern times, many New World crops now have a worldwide distribution. Few animals, however, were domesticated in the New World, and even in the Americas stock-rearing is largely based on Old World species.

alfalfa	olive
avocado	onion
banana	peas
barley	peanuts
breadfruit	peppers
buckwheat	pineapple
cocoa	potato
coconut	rice
cotton	runner bean
cucumber	rye
curcurbits	sorghum
dates	soya bean
finger millet	sunflower
foxtail millet	sweet potato
grapes	tepary bean
hemp	tomato
lentil	watermelon
lima bean	wheat
maize	yam
oats	

Before the first cities: the Near East 8000 to 3000 BC

THE beginnings of cereal cultivation in the lowland areas of the Near East during the 7th and 8th millennia BC produced, for the first time, communities which were large and permanent enough to develop brick and stone architecture for both private and public buildings, and a whole range of arts and crafts which went with them. The remains of these earliest mudbrick villages – now often forming prominent mounds as a result of rebuilding over hundreds of years – are a common feature of the lowland landscape, especially where abundant springs made the area a first choice for settlement. Most Near Eastern languages have a word to describe these ancient village mounds: *tell* in Arabic, *hüyük* in Turkish, for instance.

The earliest sites were not far from the mountain ranges which had been the original home of the wild ancestors of wheat and barley, and all lay either within the critical rainfall limit of 300 mm a year, necessary for rain-fed agriculture, or in a few cases in 'oasis' situations beyond this, where floodplain cultivation was possible. Two of the most famous, because largest and most developed, of these sites are Tell-es-Sultan at Jericho in the Jordan valley and Çatal Hüyük in the central plain of Turkey.

Jericho is the older of the two, and in the 8th millennium (when Europe was still only just recovering from the last ice age) it was defended by a rock-cut ditch and stone wall with a solid circular tower. Pottery had not been invented at this stage, and the lowest levels of the town are labelled 'pre-pottery Neolithic'. Stone bowls served as containers, and stone for tools came from as far afield as Turkey. Clay ovens were used for cooking. That some public buildings existed is shown by shrines, some of which contained plaster statues and even skulls, with the faces naturalistically modelled in plaster and cowrie-shells inset in the eyes.

The site of Çatal Hüyük is even more spectacular. Covering thirty-two acres (thirteen hectares), it was not defended by walls, although the tightly-packed agglomeration of houses could only be entered through the roof. Here, too, there is evidence of long-distance trade in desirable materials: volcanic glass for tools and weapons, for instance, or light blue apatite for ornaments. The fittings of the houses indicate a comparable sophistication. Frescoes showing hunting scenes covered some of the walls, while shrines were adorned with the plastered skulls of wild oxen set into the walls.

Although these two sites were larger than most of their contemporaries, it is uncertain whether they should be described as 'towns', and although they probably were regional centres of some kind they were largely agricultural. Nor is there any continuity between these early centres of population and the temple-centred administrative and manufacturing centres of later urban civilisation, with their literate élites and monumental architecture. These developments were made possible by more intensive agricultural techniques worked out in the intervening millennia.

Çatal Hüyük came to an end around 5000 BC, some 2000 years before the earliest writing was developed. Already, sophisticated kinds of pottery were being made, and woven textiles were in use. Flax was cultivated, as well as the full range of food crops. But the area under cultivation was small – restricted by rainfall and natural groundwater. One of the most important developments of the succeeding phase was the evolution of effective techniques of irrigation, which allowed settlement to spread beyond the zone of rain-fed 'dry-farming', and make use of the great rivers which flowed through otherwise semi-desert areas.

The earliest phases of this process are evidenced in the 5th millennium by the appearance of sites on the slopes where rivers entered the plains, where simple transverse trenches could divert the wandering streams into neighbouring fields. Such small-scale water-spreading by slight ditches or breaches of stream-banks were first used only as an insurance policy in areas already rain-fed; but during the 5th and 4th millennia this innovation allowed the colonisation of areas hitherto unoccupied because they were too dry. As a result, a large number of small sites appeared which had to be supplied with essential materials obtained from distant highland areas, whose products had to be exchanged with more mobile groups of herders and pastoralists, and whose competing needs for water had to be rationalised and organised. It was religion which provided the link between these functions, and the regional religious centres grew into administrative units based on the temple. It was from such sites, like Eridu in southern Mesopotamia, that urban, literate cultures came into being in the late 4th and 3rd millennia; and the classic pattern of Near Eastern civilisation was born.

One of the technological developments of this formative period was the beginning of copper metallurgy. While this was at first of very limited economic significance, metal came to play an increasingly important role as a raw material; and the experience of copperworking led to a knowledge of the properties of other materials. Among the rocks widely traded as ornaments among the Neolithic villages of the Near East, as far back as the 8th millennium, were certain attractive green stones, found only in the highland areas. One of these was malachite – a pure, high-yielding ore of copper. The technology of these early villages also involved the controlled use of heat, either in firing pottery, or even in merely baking bread in mudbrick ovens. This fertile combination of raw material and skill provided the milieu in which man's first experiments with metallurgy began. It was not until the 5th millennium, however, that effective techniques of smelting were developed, and it first became possible to cast objects like maceheads and axes. Weapons, status symbols and cult objects were the first products of this new technology; useful tools were a later application.

The output of the early copper industry was sustained by mining the rich surface ores of malachite at places like Timna, in southern Israel, where the shafts of ancient mines extend over a huge area. Production of finished objects was often under the patronage of the emerging temple centres, and the cult places were adorned by copper objects. The search for ways of moulding complex shapes led to the development of sophisticated casting processes, involving wax and clay moulds, and also led to an appreciation of the beneficial effects of certain impurities commonly found in the copper ores. Arsenical copper was the first deliberately produced alloy known to man, and produced to a consistent recipe for over a thousand years before the rarer but less dangerous metal tin became available through trade, and so allowed the production of bronze.

The purer copper ores such as malachite, important with simple techniques of smelting, did not last long after large-scale exploitation began. The early urban communities of the 3rd millennium had to develop ways of dealing with the more complex ores, often combined with sulphur and iron. It was thus as a waste-product to be removed that early smiths first encountered the metal which was later to supersede copper for tools and weapons.

1/Early centres of population *(right)* The wild ancestors of the cereals – wheat and barley – on which the first agricultural revolution was based, grew in remote upland areas of the Near East. The earliest villages appeared when these crops were first cultivated in the valleys, and from 8000 BC onwards such sites appeared in the regions surrounding the natural habitats of the wild cereals. Much of the adjacent lowland area, however, was too dry for cultivation. The development of irrigation techniques allowed settlements to extend to these areas by spreading water from the rivers draining from the mountains.

Terracotta figurine *(above)* Characteristic products of the earliest farming villages are small terracotta figurines of women, with emphasis on their sexual characteristics. This small cult statuette, only 6½ in (16.5 cm) high, came from Çatal Hüyük in south-central Turkey.

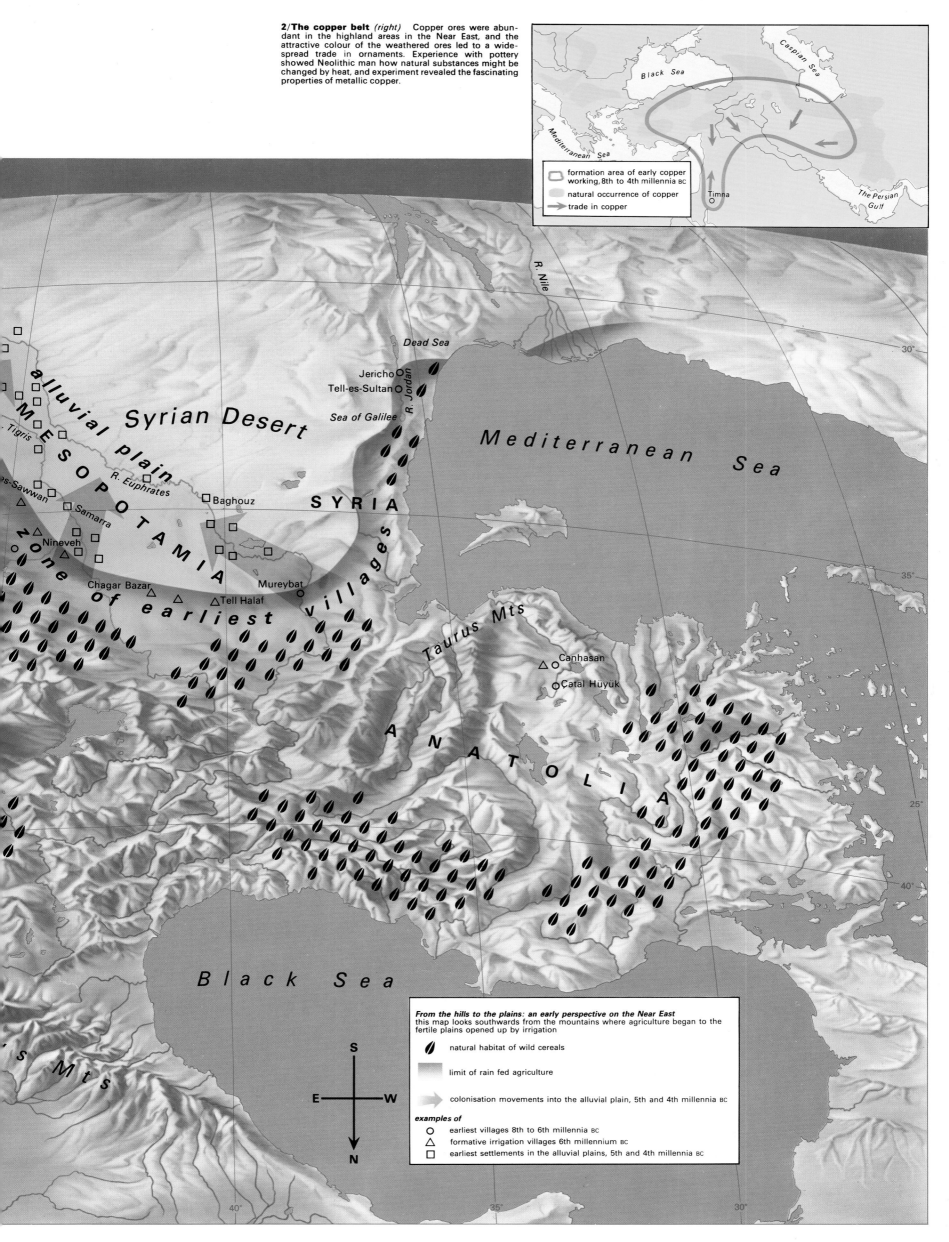

2/The copper belt *(right)* Copper ores were abundant in the highland areas in the Near East, and the attractive colour of the weathered ores led to a widespread trade in ornaments. Experience with pottery showed Neolithic man how natural substances might be changed by heat, and experiment revealed the fascinating properties of metallic copper.

Black Sea

Caspian Sea

Mediterranean Sea

The Persian Gulf

Timna

☐ formation area of early copper working, 8th to 4th millennia BC

natural occurrence of copper

→ trade in copper

R. Nile

Dead Sea

Jericho ○
Tell-es-Sultan ○

Sea of Galilee

R. Jordan

Syrian Desert

alluvial plain

MESOPOTAMIA

R. Tigris

R. Euphrates

es-Sawwan

Samarra

Nineveh

Chagar Bazar △

△ Tell Halaf

Baghouz ☐

Mureybat ○

z o n e   o f   e a r l i e s t   v i l l a g e s

S Y R I A

M e d i t e r r a n e a n   S e a

Taurus Mts

Canhasan △ ○

○ Çatal Hüyük

A N A T O L I A

B l a c k   S e a

Mts

From the hills to the plains: an early perspective on the Near East
this map looks southwards from the mountains where agriculture began to the fertile plains opened up by irrigation

natural habitat of wild cereals

limit of rain fed agriculture

→ colonisation movements into the alluvial plain, 5th and 4th millennia BC

examples of

○ earliest villages 8th to 6th millennia BC

△ formative irrigation villages 6th millennium BC

☐ earliest settlements in the alluvial plains, 5th and 4th millennia BC

S
E — W
N

41

Early Europe: the colonisation of a continent 6000 to 1500 BC

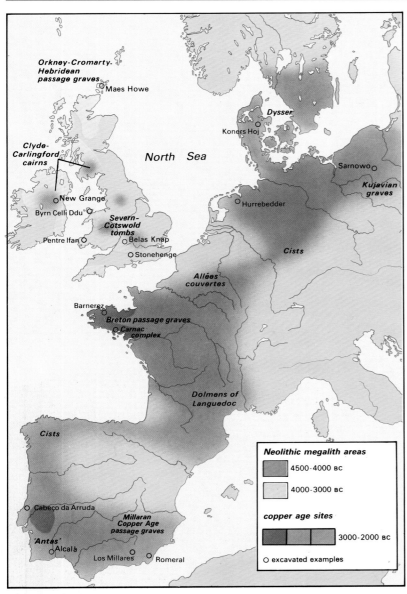

2/Megalithic monuments *(above)* The farmers of the loess-lands built their houses and cult-centres of wood. Further west, while houses continued to be mostly of wood, public monuments were constructed from large undressed boulders or slabs of stone. Such monuments, built to serve many generations, were mainly concerned with mortuary rituals and ancestor-worship. Three main areas began independently to build simple structures, but as the monuments grew more elaborate, ideas and techniques were exchanged. By the time copper had come into use many different kinds of monument were being built over much of western Europe, from simple cists to elaborate chambered tombs.

The cart *(above)* was introduced to Europe from the Caucasus via the steppe region in the 3rd millennium BC. This small model — in fact a drinking cup — came from a cemetery at Buda-kalasz, near Budapest, Hungary, and dates to around 3000 BC.

THE first experiments with the cultivation of cereals and the domestication of animals began in the Near East some ten thousand years ago, and the agricultural way of life was already fully established when farming villages appeared in adjacent parts of Europe two thousand years later. From here, farming spread rapidly across the more fertile parts of Europe at a rate of something like a mile a year, to reach the British Isles around 4000 BC.

The earliest mudbrick *tell* settlements (see page 40) in Europe, dating to about 6000 BC, are to be found on the western side of the Aegean, in the plain of Thessaly (e.g. Argissa) and Crete (e.g. Knossos). The earliest colonists must have come by sea from Anatolia, the routes being already well known through the obsidian trade. The material culture of the villagers was very similar to that of their contemporaries across the Aegean: the first colonists did not use pottery, but Anatolian techniques soon spread to the new areas, and both plain and sophisticated painted pottery were in use in Greece and Bulgaria by 5500 BC, when settlement had spread up the Vardar river valley to the north Balkans and the lower Danube area. The villages consisted of clusters of square mudbrick buildings each with an identical layout of hearths, cooking- and sleeping areas; though usually with one larger 'club-house' or village shrine. Their economy was based on keeping sheep and cultivating wheat and legumes. Such villages were situated in the plains, by areas of good soil with a plentiful water supply, and these sites often continued to be occupied for hundreds of years. Karanovo in Bulgaria is a good example: the mound of settlement debris is 12 metres (40 feet) high.

Villages of this Near Eastern character spread inland as far as Hungary (e.g. Hódmezóvásár-hely), but from here northwards a new pattern suddenly developed. The square mudbrick dwellings were replaced by wooden longhouses, and the villages, like Bylany in Czechoslovakia or Köln-Lindenthal in Germany, did not build up into *tells*. Settlement spread very rapidly across the whole of Europe, in a belt from north-east France to south-west Russia, on the expanses of soil produced by the weathering of loess – a highly fertile wind-blown dust laid down during the Ice Age beyond the margins of the glaciers. Over the whole of this area, the characteristic pottery is decorated with incised lines in spiral or meandering bands. This uniformity of culture reflects the rapid spread of settlement along the main river valleys (especially the Danube and the Rhine) which occurred around 5000 BC. In the eastern part of the area, villages continued to be grouped around a 'club-house'; but in the west, small strings of hamlets consisting of two or three longhouses were often found. Cattle seem to have been more important than sheep in the flat forested interior of Europe, but wheat continued to be the staple crop among the cereals. Where possible, settlements were placed next to small rivers or streams, and almost invariably on loess. Although small stone axes were used, the settlers did not clear wide areas of land away from the watercourses, where they practised an intensive horticulture.

This pattern continued, with developments and modifications, down to 4000 BC. Meanwhile, in the Balkans, population density had increased and there had been expansion into the foothills and lower slopes of the mountains. *Tell* settlements multiplied in the plains, and these prosperous communities traded and experimented with a wide range of raw materials for tools or for decorative purposes. Pottery came to be decorated in elaborate multi-coloured paints, using ochre, graphite and manganese. As in the Near East, abundant simple ores of copper in the mountains near to permanent settlements provided the opportunity of discovering the properties of metals, and the techniques of simple smelting and casting. Such early developments were confined to the Balkans and the Carpathian Basin (see map 3), and their products rarely spread beyond this region. Because of its relative isolation, this industry did not develop the sophistication of contemporary Near Eastern copper-working. Using only the simplest methods for casting unalloyed copper, it produced small ornaments and larger forms such as axes, though these were probably as much for prestige as for practical purposes. The technological significance of early copper-working was thus slight.

While the process of agricultural colonisation continued, small groups of hunters, fishers and collectors continued their older way of life in areas untouched by the new economy. Hunting populations were rather sparse in the areas first selected by agriculturalists, and the rapidity with which farming spread across the loess-lands may in part reflect the lack of local competition; but where the forests were more open they kept up their numbers. They survived especially in the morainic, lake-strewn landscapes created by the retreat of the ice sheets, on the Alpine foreland and on the northern edge of the North European Plain. The early stages of the post-glacial period – the time when the first experiments with agriculture were taking place in the Near East – had been a good time for the hunters of the European forests. As time wore on, however, life became more difficult for these hunters; the forest thickened as oak and beech moved northwards, the lakes filled in, and the coast-lands were drowned by rising sea levels. As the incoming farmers slashed and burned their way through the European forests, many of the aboriginal groups found themselves increasingly under stress, and eventually helped to swell the numbers of agriculturalists by adopting the new economy.

During the 4th and early 3rd millennia, important developments occurred which were to change the established pattern of life. New areas, previously peripheral, came into prominence; and their innovations in turn affected the older regions. The developing areas were the north European plain and the south Russian steppes (both colonised for the first time), and the Aegean – where fishing and maritime trade swung the emphasis from inland plains to the coasts and islands, and the domestication of vine and olive provided the agricultural economy which underlay Mycenaean civilisation. In south-east Europe many of the *tell* settlements came to an end, and in the Carpathian Basin appeared the large grave-mounds typical of the steppe area, suggesting the arrival of nomadic elements in the population. More definite evidence of eastward links is given by metallurgy, with the appearance of Caucasian types and techniques. Wheeled vehicles are evidenced for the first time, and this may be the point at which Indo-European languages first arrived in Europe.

Large areas of western Europe were now also settled by farmers for the first time, and the clearance of fields on the rocky Atlantic shores or in the boulder-strewn moraines of northern Europe provided an opportunity for making more durable monuments as tribal mortuary shrines for the scattered hamlets of the peasants. Vast unfaced blocks were piled one upon another to create the 'megalithic' monuments which were constructed by various groups of farmers beyond

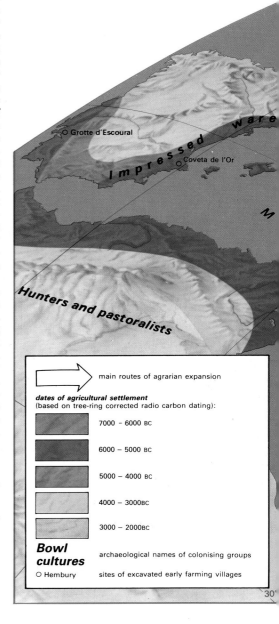

main routes of agrarian expansion

dates of agricultural settlement
(based on tree-ring corrected radio carbon dating):

7000 – 6000 BC

6000 – 5000 BC

5000 – 4000 BC

4000 – 3000 BC

3000 – 2000 BC

Bowl cultures   archaeological names of colonising groups

○ Hembury   sites of excavated early farming villages

3/Early metallurgy *(right)* Copper-working began in the Balkans in the 5th millennium, producing simple objects in one-piece moulds. A similar primitive industry also began in southern Iberia in the early 3rd millennium, shortly before Balkan smiths learned about alloying and two-piece moulds from the Caucasian school. The rich resources of central Europe and western Britain only came into large-scale use in the early second millennium, using local tin to make bronze.

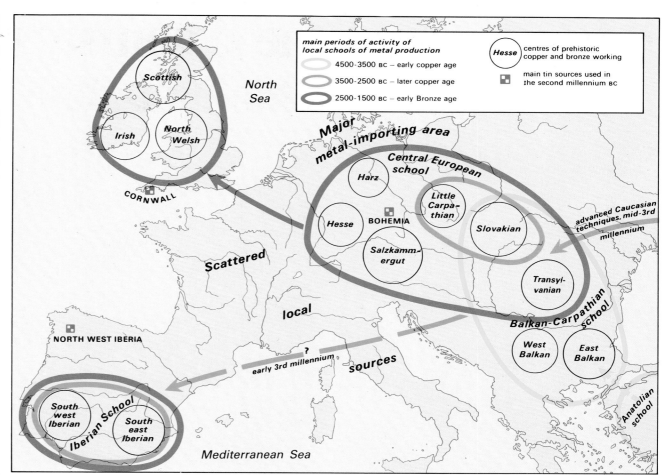

the loess-lands (see map 2). Some of the earliest occur in Brittany in the mid-4th millennium, but particularly elaborate forms were being made in Ireland and Spain up to a millennium later.

Such monuments were constructed with the aid of draught animals, now used both for carts and for the plough. The use of soils which were in general less productive than loess made the plough an essential aid in cultivating large areas of land. Widespread forest clearance became necessary, and mines for flint helped to provide the large quantities of stone needed for axes. The opening-up of northern and western Europe in this way produced a change in the cultural configuration of Europe in which the old 'Danubian' axis was less important: and with the continuing colonisation of sandy soils in northern Europe during the later 3rd and early 2nd millennia, the Balkans became something of a backwater between the rapidly-developing economy of north-central Europe and the nascent maritime civilisation of the Aegean (see page 66).

Note: All dates quoted above are based on the tree-ring correction of radiocarbon.

1/The colonisation of Europe *(below)* Early farmers spread from one side of Europe to the other by two main routes: the Vardar-Danube-Rhine corridor, and the Mediterranean littoral; the former was the more important. Archaeologists label the different groups involved by the characteristic kinds of pottery which each produced. For thousands of years the most 'developed' part of Europe was the south-east, which was the first to be settled.

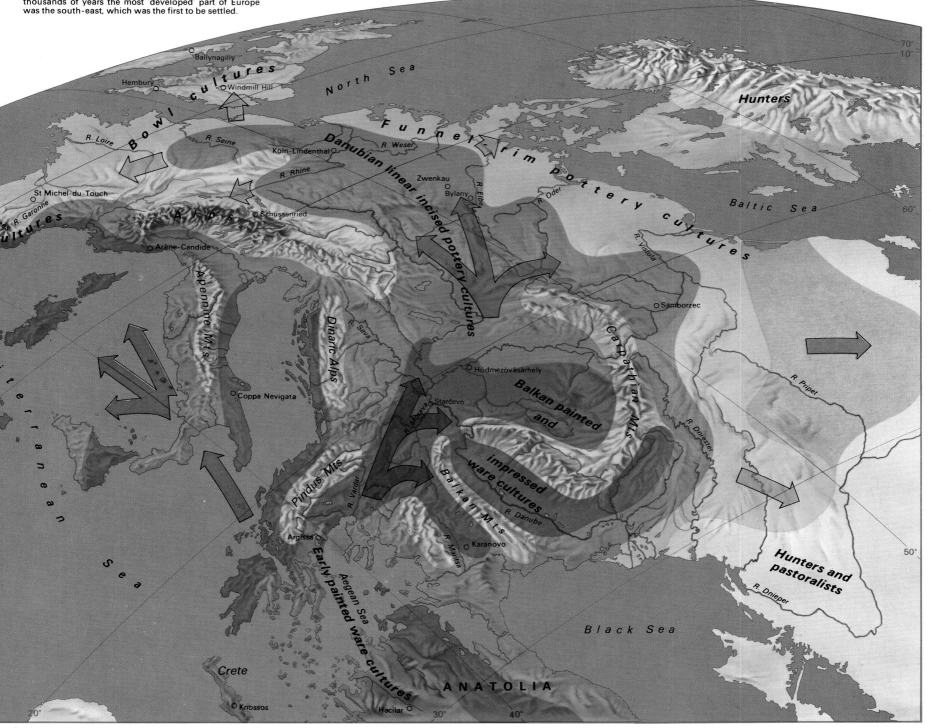

African peoples and cultures

to AD 1000

THE lands of Africa south of the Equator, though possibly the original setting for the emergence of *Homo* (page 32) were for thousands of years isolated from the technological and intellectual advances that were transforming the world elsewhere. North of the Equator, the transition from hunting and gathering to food-production occurred in the Late Stone Age. To the south, cut off by the huge marshes of the equatorial Nile and the almost impenetrable barrier of the tropical rain forest, settled agriculture mainly developed only with the coming of iron at the beginning of the Christian era.

Domesticated cattle and cereal-growing entered the continent from western Asia. The earliest sites, dating from the 6th and 5th millennia BC, show wheat and barley being cultivated on the edges of the Nile delta, and cattle-herding near the Hoggar massif in the Sahara, which was then undergoing a pronounced wet phase in which much of the present desert was habitable parkland. The discovery of bone harpoons throughout the area indicates the temperate aspect of the climate.

Desiccation of the Sahara set in during the 3rd millennium BC, causing some pastoralists to penetrate the Nile valley and its delta, and others to move south and east. Southward expansion of cereal-growing, however, required the domestication of suitable grains, such as millet and sorghum, which could be grown in the tropics. This probably took place only during the 2nd millennium BC, although there may have been some marginal cultivation of fruits and vegetables in the forest zone before this period. The increase of Negro populations in the Sudanic belt which now took place was mainly due to the development of the tropical crops.

Small numbers of early farmers penetrated the equatorial regions of Africa, particularly in eastern Africa, where a break in the forest enabled herdsmen and perhaps cereal growers to spread down the Rift Valley from Ethiopia into central Kenya and northern Tanzania during the 1st millennium BC. Elsewhere the jungle seems to have presented a fairly effective obstacle, although probably on the eve of the Iron Age an economy based mainly on fishing, with some supporting horticulture, spread from the northern to the southern margins of the forest.

In Egypt, copper-using began in the 4th millennium BC, and in the 3rd millennium was superseded by bronze. A few copper and bronze objects have been found along the north African coast, testifying to contacts with the early metal-using societies of southern Europe. Almost everywhere else in Africa, however, iron was the first metal to be produced in any quantity. The Near East was the source of the techniques of iron smelting and working. Occasional objects of native (unsmelted) iron have come from Egyptian royal tombs of the 2nd millennium BC, but it was only in the 1st millennium that it began to be produced in north Africa from the ore, and only in the 6th century BC that it came into common use in Egypt. At about the same period, iron-using spread among the Phoenician and Carthaginian colonies of the north African coast.

Iron-using came to sub-Saharan Africa by two routes. Firstly, there was a limited spread down the Nile Valley to Meroe, which seems to have been an important centre of iron production c.500 BC. The second route took iron-working from the Carthaginian cities to Nigeria, where it is attested by 450 BC at Taruga. The 1st millennium BC saw a decline in the fortunes of Egypt, which was conquered by a series of foreign powers. By contrast, the Kushite state of the south, with successive capitals at Napata (6th to 4th century BC) and Meroe (4th century BC to 4th century AD), experienced a period of prosperity. The cemeteries of small pyramids which mark the royal tombs of Kush illustrate the continuing importance of Egyptian influences. In the 4th century AD the kingdom of Meroe was overthrown by Axum, a trading state in northern Ethiopia. Axum derived its prosperity from the export of African ivory and maritime trade, and by the 4th century AD its fleet had become the dominant mercantile and military power in the Red Sea. The kingdom enjoyed close relations with Byzantium, and its rulers were converted to Christianity in the 4th century. In the 7th century Axum came into conflict with the rising power of Islam, and in AD 702 its fleet was destroyed by the Arabs, but the city of Axum survived as capital of a diminished kingdom until the end of the 9th century AD.

South of the Equator the earliest Iron Age sites date from around the beginning of the Christian era. The coming of iron marks a revolution far more dramatic than that in the north. It not only represented an important breakthrough in itself, but also it was in many regions associated with the earliest cereal agriculture, the earliest cattle-keeping and the earliest pottery. Since almost the whole of sub-Saharan Africa is now occupied by food-producers, speaking closely related Bantu languages, it is probable that Bantu was disseminated by these early agriculturalists.

It appears, then, that a Negro population, related in language and physical type to the Negroes of West Africa, established itself in late Stone Age times in the Congo basin, and expanded during the early Iron Age across the rest of southern Africa. Probably the process involved more intermixture than violence, with the better-watered and more densely settled sites of the food-producers superseding the hunters to provide linguistic and cultural foci for the region. By AD 1000 peoples of black Africa lived in settled agricultural societies, and some quite powerful political states were beginning to emerge.

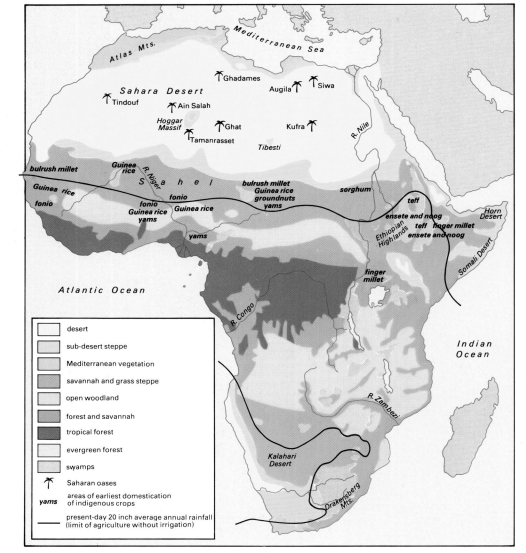

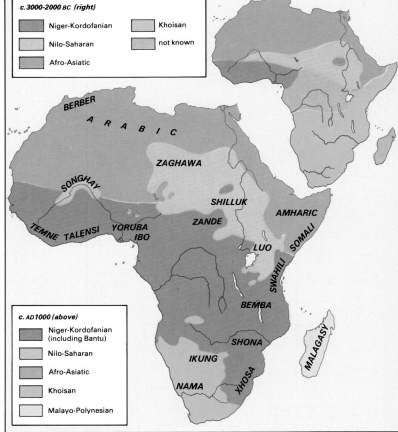

2/Rainfall and vegetation *(left)* The peopling of Africa was crucially determined by the continent's physical constraints. Over large areas the existence of desert and equatorial jungle made agriculture and communication virtually impossible. The areas of light forest and cultivable grassland retreated in the period 2000 BC to AD 1000, forcing major changes in the established methods of food production and food distribution.

3/African languages *(above)* The analysis of languages provides a possible clue to unravelling much of ancient African history, such as the spread of population across the Sudan, the problem of linking Bantu-speakers of the south with their origins north of the Congo, and the overlaying of Bantu upon earlier Khoisan cultures. This linguistic analysis is particularly important in regions which are totally without written records.

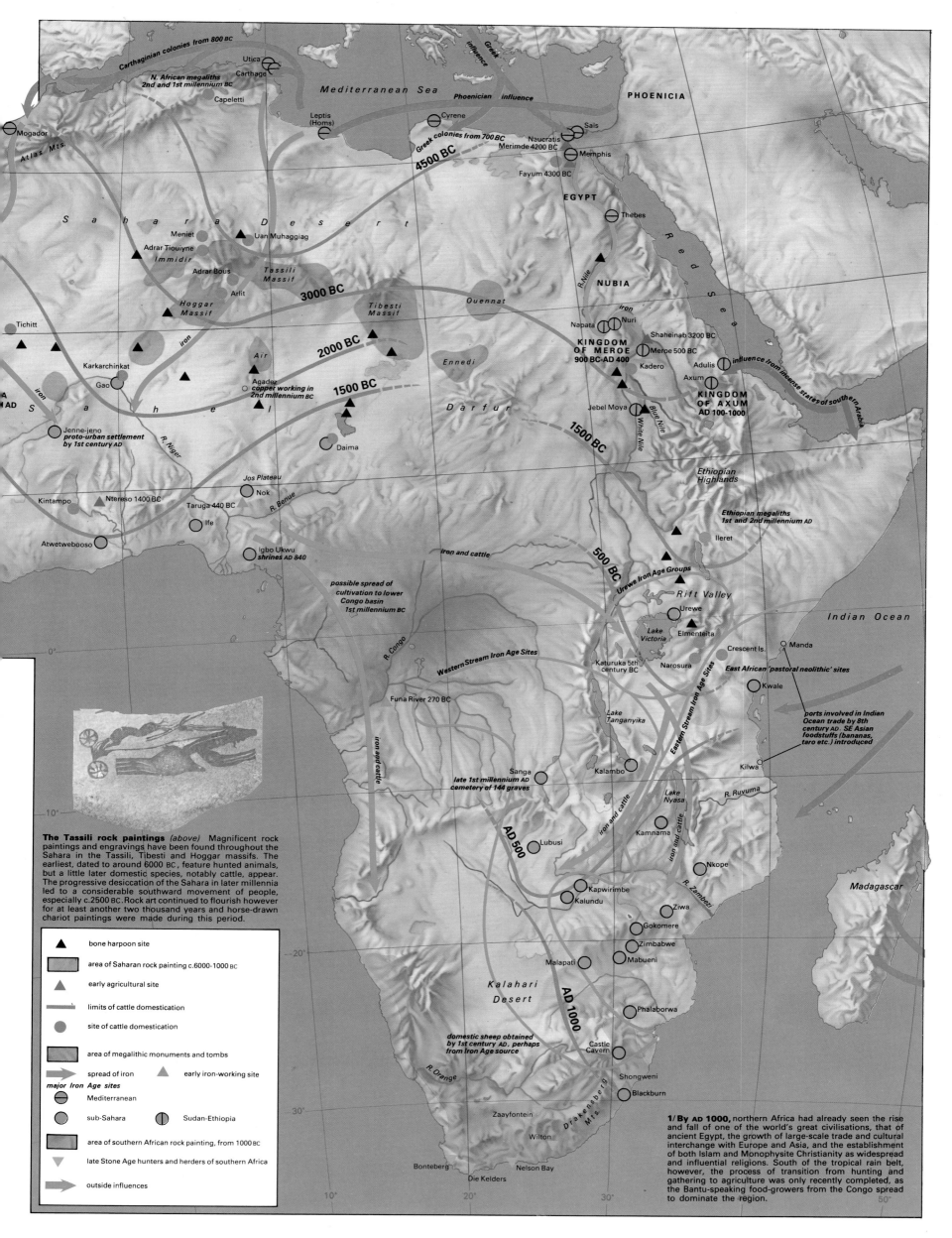

Carthaginian colonies from 800 BC

N. African megaliths
2nd and 1st millennium BC

Utica
Carthage
Capeletti

Mediterranean Sea

Phoenician influence

Greek influence

PHOENICIA

Mogador

Atlas Mts.

Leptis
(Homs)

Cyrene

Sais

Naucratis
Merimde 4200 BC

Memphis

Greek colonies from 700 BC

4500 BC

Fayum 4300 BC

EGYPT

Thebes

S a h a r a   D e s e r t

Meniet

Uan Muhaggiag

Adrar Tiouiyne

Immidir

Adrar Bous

Arlit

iron

*Tassili
Massif*

3000 BC

*Tibesti
Massif*

Ouennat

R. Nile

NUBIA

Napata   Nuri

Shaheinab 3200 BC

*Hoggar
Massif*

2000 BC

Air

Tichitt

Karkarchinkat

iron

Gao

Agadez
copper working in
2nd millennium BC

1500 BC

E n n e d i

D a r f u r

KINGDOM
OF MEROE
900 BC-AD 400

Meroe 500 BC

Kadero

Adulis

iron

influence from incense states of southern Arabia

Axum

KINGDOM
OF AXUM
AD 100-1000

Red Sea

iron

AD

S a h e l

Jenne-jeno
proto-urban settlement
by 1st century AD

R. Niger

Daima

1500 BC

Jebel Moya

White Nile

Blue Nile

*Ethiopian
Highlands*

Kintampo

Ntereso 1400 BC

Jos Plateau

Nok

Taruga 440 BC

Ife

Atwetwebooso

Igbo Ukwu
shrines AD 840

possible spread of
cultivation to lower
Congo basin
1st millennium BC

iron and cattle

500 BC

Ethiopian megaliths
1st and 2nd millennium AD

Ileret

Urewe Iron Age Groups

Rift Valley

Urewe

Elmenteita

Indian Ocean

R. Congo

Western Stream Iron Age Sites

*Lake
Victoria*

Katuruka 5th
century BC

Narosura

Crescent Is.

Manda

East African 'pastoral neolithic' sites

Kwale

0°

Funa River 270 BC

*Lake
Tanganyika*

ports involved in Indian
Ocean trade by 8th
century AD. SE Asian
foodstuffs (bananas,
taro etc.) introduced

Kilwa

iron and cattle

Sanga
late 1st millennium AD
cemetery of 144 graves

Kalambo

*Lake
Nyasa*

R. Ruvuma

-10°

Eastern Stream Iron Age Sites

Kamnama

iron and cattle

The Tassili rock paintings *(above)* Magnificent rock
paintings and engravings have been found throughout the
Sahara in the Tassili, Tibesti and Hoggar massifs. The
earliest, dated to around 6000 BC, feature hunted animals,
but a little later domestic species, notably cattle, appear.
The progressive desiccation of the Sahara in later millennia
led to a considerable southward movement of people,
especially c.2500 BC. Rock art continued to flourish however
for at least another two thousand years and horse-drawn
chariot paintings were made during this period.

AD 500

Lubusi

Nkope

Kapwirimbe

Ziwa

Kalundu

Gokomere

Zimbabwe

Malapati

Mabueni

Phalaborwa

R. Zambezi

▲ bone harpoon site

   area of Saharan rock painting c.6000-1000 BC

▲ early agricultural site

—— limits of cattle domestication

● site of cattle domestication

   area of megalithic monuments and tombs

➤ spread of iron

▲ early iron-working site

major Iron Age sites

◐ Mediterranean

◐ sub-Sahara   ◑ Sudan-Ethiopia

   area of southern African rock painting, from 1000 BC

▽ late Stone Age hunters and herders of southern Africa

➤ outside influences

*Kalahari
Desert*

AD 1000

domestic sheep obtained
by 1st century AD, perhaps
from Iron Age source

Castle
Cavern

Shongweni

Blackburn

Drakensberg Mts.

Zaayfontein

Wilton

Bonteberg

Die Kelders

Nelson Bay

Madagascar

-20°

-30°

1/By AD 1000, northern Africa had already seen the rise
and fall of one of the world's great civilisations, that of
ancient Egypt, the growth of large-scale trade and cultural
interchange with Europe and Asia, and the establishment
of both Islam and Monophysite Christianity as widespread
and influential religions. South of the tropical rain belt,
however, the process of transition from hunting and
gathering to agriculture was only recently completed, as
the Bantu-speaking food-growers from the Congo spread
to dominate the region.

R. Orange

10°   20°   30°   50°

The peoples and cultures of the Americas to AD 900

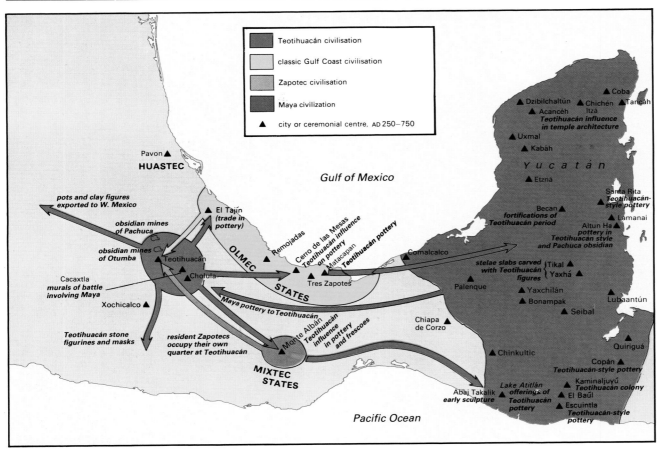

Map legend:
- Teotihuacán civilisation
- classic Gulf Coast civilisation
- Zapotec civilisation
- Maya civilization
- ▲ city or ceremonial centre, AD 250–750

2/The Classic Period in Meso-america, 400 to 900 *(above)*
During this period Teotihuacán was the dominant civilisation of Mesoamerica. Although the area under its direct control may have been limited to central Mexico and parts of Guatemala, the influence of Teotihuacán was felt all over Mesoamerica. Similarly, Maya cultural influence was not limited to the Yucatán peninsula alone.

3/North America 1000 BC to AD 1000 *(below)* The Adena culture of Ohio preceded the Hopewell, when chiefs obtained ornaments and exotic raw materials from all over North America. By AD 550 Hopewell influence had waned, and c.AD 700 saw the rise of the Mississippian culture in the southwest and southeast, where temple mounds and other features derived from Mexico were built.

M AN entered the New World from Siberia some time before 20,000 BC during a period of lowered sea level, when the Bering Straits were dry land. After spending thousands of years as semi-nomadic hunters and collectors of wild plant foods, certain groups of Indians in Mesoamerica and the Andean lands began to experiment with plant cultivation until by about 1500 BC maize-farming became the basis of life. Cultivation of tropical root crops may be equally ancient, but archaeological evidence is lacking. These farmers lived in permanent villages, some of which grew into large towns during the last thousand years BC. Craftsmen worked in luxury materials imported from long distances, and there is evidence for class distinctions between rich and poor, governors and governed. Rather than bands or tribes, these communities resembled present-day chiefdoms,

with control vested in a chief drawn from a single powerful lineage. Economic power derived from the chief's control over the distribution of land, foodstuffs and craft products, and his position was often reinforced by religious sanctions.

This stage of development was the takeoff point for civilisation and the growth of true states, with populations numbered in tens of thousands, with a hierarchy of social classes, an efficient civil service, professional priesthood, and specialists in all kinds of jobs from manufacturing to commerce, administration and government. Certain peoples (the Olmecs of the Mexican Gulf Coast plain, the Zapotecs of Monte Albán, and the inhabitants of Chavín in Peru) may have reached this stage c.1000-600 BC; by the early centuries AD most of Mesoamerica and the Central Andes was 'civilised'.

Around, and between, these nuclei of civilisa-

tion, other communities remained at the chiefdom level. Maize, beans and squashes were introduced from Mexico into north America, and the arrival of these crops initiated a period of rapid development. In Ohio and Illinois between 300 BC and AD 550, Hopewell chiefs built elaborate burial mounds and maintained trade contacts over an area stretching from Florida to the Rockies. Most American chiefdoms were agricultural, except along the north-west coast where unusually rich fishing grounds and an abundance of whales and seals supported large villages and a complex ceremonial life.

Towards the extremities of the hemisphere, where conditions were too harsh for farming, populations remained small and the old nomadic and tribal ways of life persisted. The conventional starting date for the Classic Period of Meso-american civilisation is AD 250, a time of intellectual and artistic climax. At about this date the Maya adopted hieroglyphic writing and began to erect stelae (stone slabs with carved historical or calendrical inscriptions). The Classic Maya were preoccupied with the passage of time. Their astronomers had calculated the exact length of the solar year, the lunar month and the revolution of the planet Venus, and were able to predict eclipses. These calculations demanded advanced mathematical skills, and the Mesoamericans independently invented the idea of place value and the concept of zero.

Classic Maya civilisation was not an isolated phenomenon. Important regional civilisations developed elsewhere in Mexico – along the Gulf Coast (El Tajín, etc.), in the Valley of Oaxaca (where Monte Albán became a great city), and at Teotihuacán in the Basin of Mexico. In its prime, around the year 600, Teotihuacán was a city of 125,000 people and covered 20 square kilometres, laid out according to a precise grid plan. The city's wealth came from agriculture, crafts and trade, in particular the export of obsidian (a natural volcanic glass used for knives and spear points) from the Otumba and Pachuca quarries. Diplomatic and commercial exchanges were kept up with the other civilisations of Mexico, and with the Maya by way of Teotihuacán colonies at Kaminaljuyú and perhaps Escuintla. All the regional civilisations of the Classic Period may be considered local variants of a pan-Mesoamerican culture pattern. Teotihuacán was destroyed and abandoned around 750; Monte Albán fell into disrepair during the 10th century, and Classic Maya civilisation collapsed, for reasons still not fully understood, between 800 and 900.

The Central Andes were the homeland of a second group of interrelated civilisations. Although not in direct contact with Mesoamerica, the level of development was very similar, the main technological difference being that the Andean peoples had developed how to work gold, silver and copper, and were using these metals for tools as well as jewellery. This region, with its vast distances and harsh topography, was always difficult to unify under the control of a single state, but the centuries between AD 600 and 1000 saw the rise and fall of a truly imperial power based on Huari (or Wari) in the Peruvian Andes. Many elements of Huari religion and art were first developed at Tiahuanaco in Bolivia, but were quickly adopted in Peru. From Huari, a modified version of the Tiahuanaco cult and its art style were carried by military force to many parts of the coast and highlands. For a short time, Huari became the capital of a political state which embraced most of Peru, but in about 800 the city was overthrown and abandoned forever. The fragile artificial unity soon broke down, and local states and local art styles reasserted themselves. It was not until the Inca conquest of the 15th and 16th centuries that Peru was once more unified under the control of a single power.

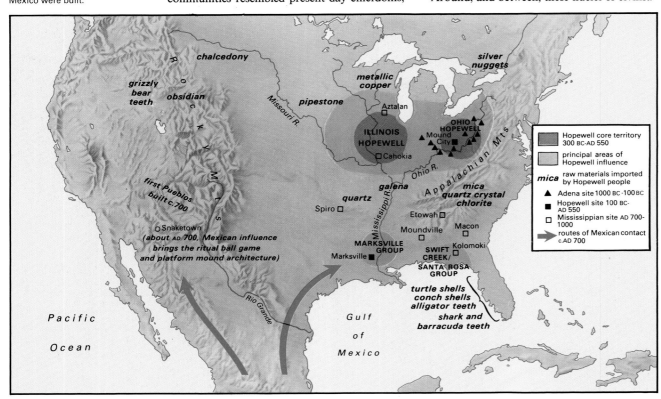

Map legend:
- Hopewell core territory 300 BC-AD 550
- principal areas of Hopewell influence
- *mica* raw materials imported by Hopewell people
- ▲ Adena site 1000 BC-100 BC
- ■ Hopewell site 100 BC-AD 550
- □ Mississippian site AD 700-1000
- → routes of Mexican contact c.AD 700

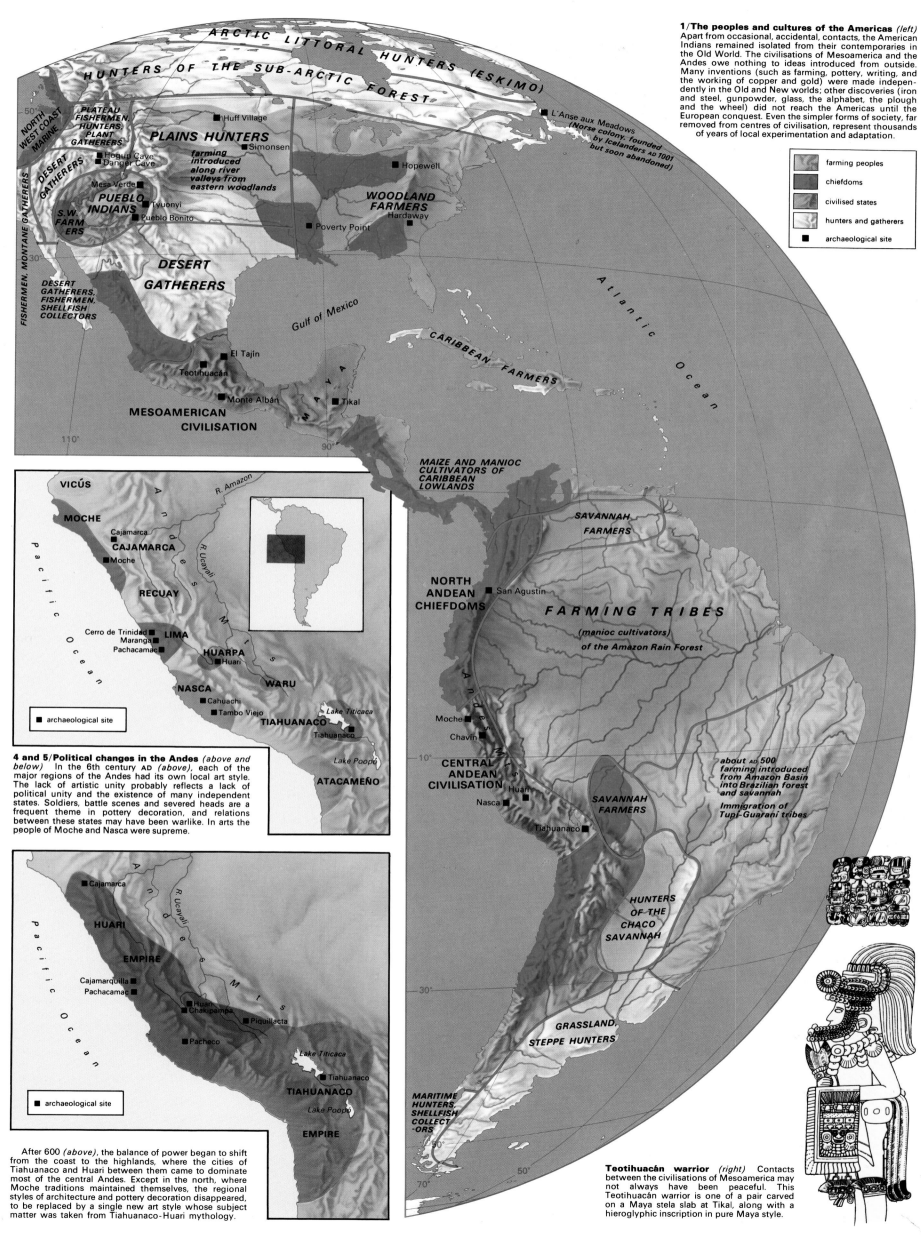

Apart from occasional, accidental, contacts, the American Indians remained isolated from their contemporaries in the Old World. The civilisations of Mesoamerica and the Andes owe nothing to ideas introduced from outside. Many inventions (such as farming, pottery, writing, and the working of copper and gold) were made independently in the Old and New worlds; other discoveries (iron and steel, gunpowder, glass, the alphabet, the plough and the wheel) did not reach the Americas until the European conquest. Even the simpler forms of society, far removed from centres of civilisation, represent thousands of years of local experimentation and adaptation.

▦	farming peoples
▦	chiefdoms
▦	civilised states
▦	hunters and gatherers
■	archaeological site

ARCTIC LITTORAL HUNTERS (ESKIMO)

HUNTERS OF THE SUB-ARCTIC FOREST

PLATEAU
FISHERMEN,
HUNTERS,
PLANT
GATHERERS

NORTH
WEST COAST
MARINE

DESERT
GATHERERS

PLAINS HUNTERS

■ Huff Village

farming
introduced
along river
valleys from
eastern woodlands

■ Simonsen

■ Hopewell

■ L'Anse aux Meadows
(Norse colony, founded
by Icelanders AD 1001
but soon abandoned)

■ Hogup Cave
■ Danger Cave

■ Mesa Verde

PUEBLO
INDIANS

■ Tyuonyi

S.W.
FARM-
ERS

■ Pueblo Bonito

WOODLAND
FARMERS

■ Hardaway

■ Poverty Point

FISHERMEN, MONTANE GATHERERS

DESERT
GATHERERS,
FISHERMEN,
SHELLFISH
COLLECTORS

DESERT
GATHERERS

Gulf of Mexico

CARIBBEAN FARMERS

Atlantic Ocean

■ El Tajín

■ Teotihuacán

M A Y A

■ Tikal

■ Monte Albán

MESOAMERICAN
CIVILISATION

MAIZE AND MANIOC
CULTIVATORS OF
CARIBBEAN
LOWLANDS

SAVANNAH
FARMERS

NORTH
ANDEAN
CHIEFDOMS

■ San Agustín

FARMING TRIBES

(manioc cultivators)

of the Amazon Rain Forest

■ Moche
■ Chavin

CENTRAL
ANDEAN
CIVILISATION

■ Huari
■ Nasca
■ Tiahuanaco

about AD 500
farming introduced
from Amazon Basin
into Brazilian forest
and savannah

Immigration of
Tupi-Guaraní tribes

SAVANNAH
FARMERS

HUNTERS
OF THE
CHACO
SAVANNAH

GRASSLAND,
STEPPE HUNTERS

MARITIME
HUNTERS,
SHELLFISH
COLLECT-
ORS

4 and 5/Political changes in the Andes (above and below) In the 6th century AD (above), each of the major regions of the Andes had its own local art style. The lack of artistic unity probably reflects a lack of political unity and the existence of many independent states. Soldiers, battle scenes and severed heads are a frequent theme in pottery decoration, and relations between these states may have been warlike. In arts the people of Moche and Nasca were supreme.

VICÚS

MOCHE

■ Cajamarca

CAJAMARCA

■ Moche

RECUAY

■ Cerro de Trinidad
■ Maranga
■ Pachacamac

LIMA

HUARPA

■ Huari

NASCA

■ Cahuachi
■ Tambo Viejo

WARU

Lake Titicaca

TIAHUANACO

■ Tiahuanaco

Lake Poopó

ATACAMEÑO

Pacific Ocean

R. Amazon

R. Ucayali

Andes

Mts

■ archaeological site

After 600 (above), the balance of power began to shift from the coast to the highlands, where the cities of Tiahuanaco and Huari between them came to dominate most of the central Andes. Except in the north, where Moche traditions maintained themselves, the regional styles of architecture and pottery decoration disappeared, to be replaced by a single new art style whose subject matter was taken from Tiahuanaco-Huari mythology.

■ Cajamarca

HUARI

EMPIRE

■ Cajamarquilla
■ Pachacamac

■ Huari
■ Chakipampa
■ Piquillacta

■ Pacheco

Lake Titicaca

■ Tiahuanaco

TIAHUANACO

Lake Poopó

EMPIRE

Pacific Ocean

Andes

Mts

R. Ucayali

■ archaeological site

Teotihuacán warrior (right) Contacts between the civilisations of Mesoamerica may not always have been peaceful. This Teotihuacán warrior is one of a pair carved on a Maya stela slab at Tikal, along with a hieroglyphic inscription in pure Maya style.

47

Australia and Oceania before the coming of the Europeans

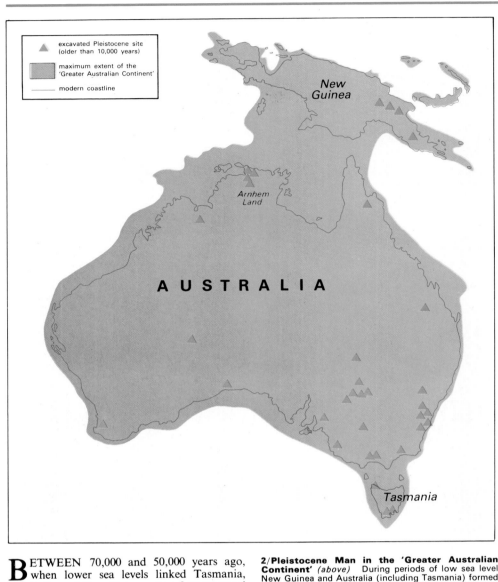

Legend:
- ▲ excavated Pleistocene site (older than 10,000 years)
- maximum extent of the 'Greater Australian Continent'
- modern coastline

New Guinea

Arnhem Land

AUSTRALIA

Tasmania

2/Pleistocene Man in the 'Greater Australian Continent' *(above)* During periods of low sea level New Guinea and Australia (including Tasmania) formed a single large landmass. Settlement was concentrated up the major river systems and along the coast, but Pleistocene coastal sites now lie submerged offshore. In this map, the comparative abundance of sites in south-eastern Australia is simply due to the greater attention devoted to this region by archaeologists.

BETWEEN 70,000 and 50,000 years ago, when lower sea levels linked Tasmania, Australia and New Guinea, man first ventured onto the Greater Australian Continent. His journey, from a south-east Asian homeland, was a pioneering one, as it involved at least one major water crossing. The original Australians were therefore among the world's earliest mariners. What a strange new world greeted these newcomers: enormous beyond comprehension, and ranging from tropical north to temperate south. Admittedly, some of the edible plants found in more northerly latitudes were related to those of Asia and were therefore familiar, but this was not so of the animals. In addition to the mammals which have survived, there was a bewildering assortment of giant forms: ten-foot tall kangaroos, various enormous ox-like beasts, a large native lion, and rangy emu-like birds. Despite this terrestrial abundance, it was the plentiful supply of fish and shellfish available along the coasts and in the rivers that drew most attention, and these are the areas in which Aboriginal settlements were concentrated. Regrettably, most of these sites are lost to us: between 70,000 and 10,000 years ago the sea was lower than the present level and they now lie offshore, on the continental shelf. Characteristic of these Pleistocene inhabitants are bone points, and the stone core implements and crude scrapers of the Australian Core Tool Tradition. While this tradition, which underwent remarkably little change in more than 40,000 years, is pan-Australian, there are a number of regional elements that have New Guinean and Asian links. One of these is the edge-ground axe, which has been dated to 22,000 years in Arnhem Land (much earlier than anywhere else in the world).

Around 6000 years ago the sea rose to its present level, and while Aboriginal settlements were still concentrated along the coasts, there was rapidly increasing exploitation of inland resources. It was also at about this time that the dingo was introduced, and that a range of small, finely-finished flake implements especially developed for hafting, and known as the Australian Small Tool Tradition, appeared across the continent, superimposed on the earlier lithic forms. Political, economic and religious development continued, and by the time of settlement Europeans found that there were some 300,000 Aborigines living in around 500 tribal territories. Although their way of life was still based on hunting and gathering (the Aborigines never became agriculturalists), they had developed some very intricate relationships with their environment. Morphologically, the Aborigines were found to exhibit considerable regional variation, though all belonged to the modern subspecies of man, *Homo sapiens sapiens*. However, archaeological research has shown that even greater heterogeneity occurred in Pleistocene times (that is, before 10,000 years ago) and that some individuals were remarkably like the earlier forms of man found in Java.

While it is likely that New Guinea was first settled at about the same time as Australia, the earliest known archaeological site, near Port Moresby, is only 26,000 years old. Other sites, in the highlands to the north-west, evidence the widespread distribution of man in New Guinea by 8,000 BC, and a crude flake tool-chopper stone industry with some additional elements also found in Australia and south-east Asia (e.g. the edge-ground axe and waisted blade). Major changes took place about 6000 years ago with the introduction of domesticated Asian plants and animals, though the hunting and gathering tradition of earlier times persisted.

Most of Island Melanesia (to the east, northeast and south-east of the New Guinea mainland) saw its first occupants during the first and second millennia BC, as maritime trading groups bearing domesticated plants and animals, and pottery belonging to the Lapita tradition, spread through the area. These Austronesian people and their distinctive pottery (which can be traced back to the Moluccas area of Indonesia) reached Fiji, the eastern boundary of present-day Melanesia, by 1300 BC, and soon after made their way into Polynesia via Tonga and Samoa. And it was in these two island groups, but particularly in the latter, that a typically Melanesian material culture gradually evolved into a Polynesian-like one, during more than a thousand years of

Early Australian-Asian links *(below)* Stone artefacts show that there were Pleistocene contacts between Asia and Australia-New Guinea: three artefact types found in both regions are shown here.

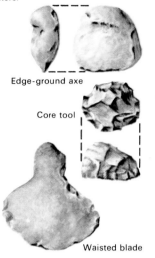

Edge-ground axe

Core tool

Waisted blade

120°   140°

Mariana Is.

Caroline Is.

MICRONE[SIA]

Moluccas

New Guinea

New Ireland

New Brit[ain]

AUSTRALIA

Tasmania

geographical isolation. Around AD 300, a time when Lapita pottery was disappearing throughout Island Melanesia and western Polynesia, prehistoric Samoans ventured eastward in their canoes and settled the distant Marquesas Islands. This ·is a key island group for Polynesian prehistory, for between AD 400 and 850 it served as a primary dispersal centre, radiating initial settlers, and their distinctive domesticated plants and animals, adzes, fishing gear, and ornaments, to the far corners of the 'Polynesian triangle' and to other nearby islands. The Hawaiian Islands were occupied around AD 400, the Society Islands and Easter Island by 800, and the Cook Islands and New Zealand by 850. All the other major island groups of Polynesia were first settled, mainly from Samoa-Tonga or Society Islands-Marquesas, between 1000 and 1300, and a multitude of largely independent cultures evolved on these little 'island universes', only to be shattered by the shock of European contact during the 17th, 18th and 19th centuries.

Because of its climatic range, comparative enormity, and unfamiliar plants and animals, New Zealand presented its initial Polynesian settlers with special adaptive problems. Most of the domesticated plants and animals characteristic of the ancestral Marquesan homeland were lost en route to New Zealand or else failed to withstand the more rigorous climatic conditions; the only principal survivors were the dog and native rat, and the taro, yam and sweet potato, and these last three were basically restricted to coastal North Island localities. Nevertheless, the New Zealand environment

offered these early settlers unexpected dietary compensation in the form of a whole suite of giant flightless birds, the best known of which are the moas. The original New Zealanders of the North Island and northern South Island thus became hunter-farmers, and a pattern of seasonal movement was developed to take advantage of these conditions. Settlements were predominantly coastal, and were restricted to several clearly defined regions. Meanwhile, superseded implements in the ancestral 'tool kit' were abandoned, and new forms were developed in response to the new environment. During the ensuing centuries the growing population expanded around the coasts of both islands, and South Island inland resources were intensively exploited. As hunting and man-made 'fires' continued there was a gradual change in the environment, culminating in the 13th and 14th centuries with widespread deafforestation, and virtual extinction of the avian megafauna.

It was probably at about this time that many of the implements derived from ancestral Polynesian types were abandoned, and that distinctly New Zealand artefacts began to emerge. So too did warfare, and with it the appearance of specially-developed fortified settlements termed *pa*. By the time of European contact, Cook and other explorers found New Zealand occupied by up to 250,000 Maoris. A hunting-farming lifestyle was still in evidence (except in the southern half of the South Island, beyond the limits of horticulture). European contact and settlement were accompanied by rapid breakdown of traditional Maori society and culture.

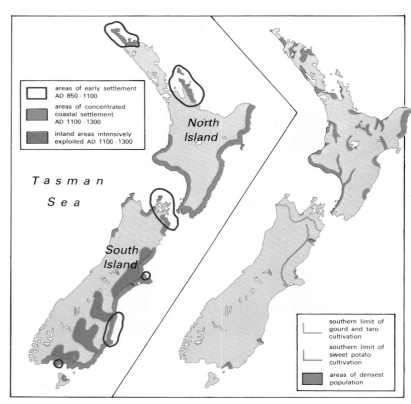

3/Early New Zealand settlement (above) New Zealand's early settlers were basically coastal hunters-gatherers, though South Island inland resources were seasonally exploited. Cultivated plants were only grown in sheltered North Island localities.

4/Maori settlement at European contact (above) By 1769 most Maoris were settled in the North Island, along the coast and rivers. Food obtained by hunting and gathering was in some areas supplemented by horticultural products.

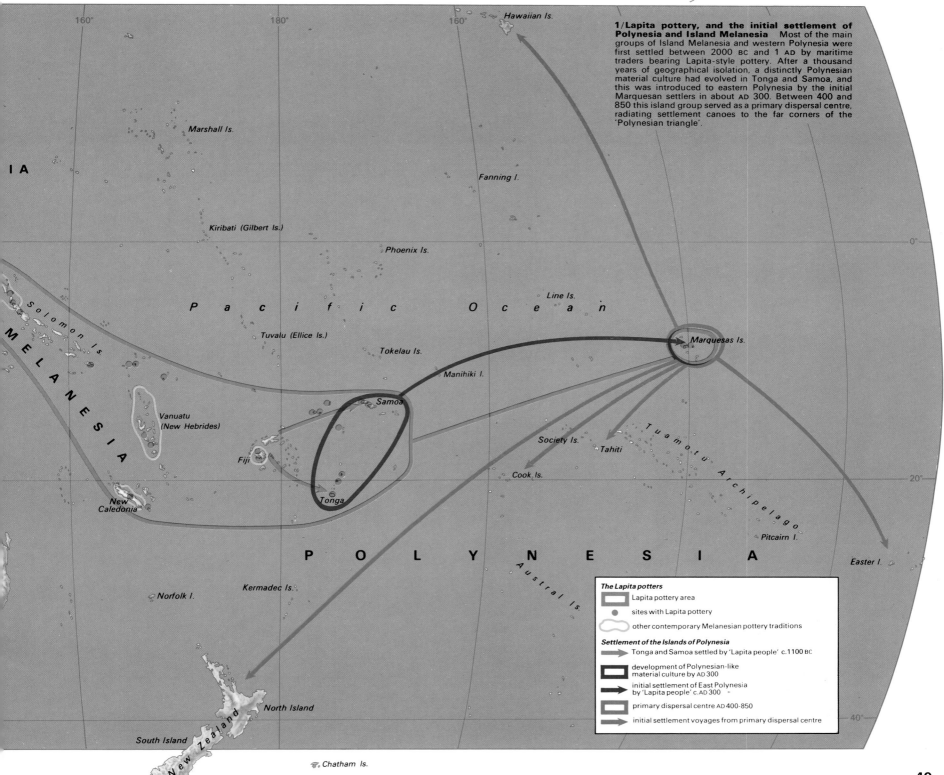

1/Lapita pottery, and the initial settlement of Polynesia and Island Melanesia Most of the main groups of Island Melanesia and western Polynesia were first settled between 2000 BC and 1 AD by maritime traders bearing Lapita-style pottery. After a thousand years of geographical isolation, a distinctly Polynesian material culture had evolved in Tonga and Samoa, and this was introduced to eastern Polynesia by the initial Marquesan settlers in about AD 300. Between 400 and 850 this island group served as a primary dispersal centre, radiating settlement canoes to the far corners of the 'Polynesian triangle'.

The Lapita potters
- Lapita pottery area
- sites with Lapita pottery
- other contemporary Melanesian pottery traditions

Settlement of the islands of Polynesia
- Tonga and Samoa settled by 'Lapita people' c.1100 BC
- development of Polynesian-like material culture by AD 300
- initial settlement of East Polynesia by 'Lapita people' c.AD 300
- primary dispersal centre AD 400-850
- initial settlement voyages from primary dispersal centre

2 The first

civilisations

About the middle of the fourth millennium before Christ, in a few areas where agriculture was particularly intensive, the dispersed villages of Neolithic Man gave way to more complex societies. These were the first civilisations, and their emergence marks the beginning of a new phase of world history. They arose, apparently independently, in four widely dispersed areas (the early civilisations of America were considerably later in date): the lower Tigris and Euphrates valleys, the valley of the Nile, the Indus valley around Harappa and Mohenjo-Daro, and the Yellow River around Anyang. The characteristic feature of them all was the city, which now became an increasingly dominant social form, gradually eating up the surrounding countryside, until today urban civilisation has become the criterion of social progress. But the city had other important connotations as well: a complex division of labour, literacy and a literate class (usually the priesthood), monumental public buildings, political and religious hierarchies, a kingship descended from the gods, and ultimately empire, or the claim to rule over the *oikumene*. Already there was visible the dichotomy between the civilised world and the barbarian world outside. The onslaught of nomadic peoples eager to enjoy the fruits of civilisation was a recurrent theme of world history, until the introduction of firearms in the fifteenth century AD decisively tilted the balance in favour of the civilised peoples.

The beginnings of civilisation in the Eurasian world 3500 to 1500 BC

THE first civilisations arose in the fertile alluvial basins of the major rivers which water the otherwise arid plains of southern Asia, draining from the mountain fringes where agriculture first began (see page 40). These more complex societies were the natural outcome of the increasing organisation needed to make use of these problematic, but potentially highly fertile, lowland environments.

To realise this potential, two things were necessary: a continuous flow of raw materials from neighbouring uplands to supply the stoneless, metalless and largely treeless plains, and a system of irrigation capable of spreading the copious floodwaters of the rivers over the thirsty lands nearby. As farming communities spread from the hilly flanks to the open plains and alluvial valleys, similar hierarchically organised societies sprang up–independently, but for similar reasons–in the basins of the Tigris-Euphrates, the Nile, the Yellow River and the Indus.

These societies had many features in common: the development of cities, writing, large public buildings, and the political apparatus of the state. They all stemmed from the need to organise local production and long-distance trade, and resulted from the emergence of regional centres where local produce was gathered and exchanged, trading expeditions organised, and irrigation systems planned. These functions were in the hands of either a priesthood or a secular ruler; in either case, the temple-centre with its literate élite was an important element, and large-scale public architecture a characteristic feature. Such centres supported craftsmen, and had an important role in defence. The centralised control required by these functions created a specialised legal system and a standing army; they created a permanent bureaucracy, and the first division of society into classes.

The great volume of raw materials needed to supply the rapidly-expanding populations of the plains led to very extensive trading activity in the hinterlands, and to interaction with the smaller nuclei in the minor river-valleys of the intervening areas, where similar processes of urbanisation were taking place on a smaller scale. It is hard to separate cause and effect in this growing network of major and minor trading centres and city-states, which sprang up in a great arc from the eastern Mediterranean to the Indus. Only Chinese civilisation developed in relative isolation, sheltered by the Himalayas and the jungles of south-eastern Asia. Its interaction was mainly with neighbouring peasant societies, some of which already had advanced skills, for instance in bronze-working. Urban societies did not, however, appear either in the tropical zone or in temperate Europe until much later, in the Iron Age.

In northern and western Europe, copper- and bronze-working were practised on a village basis, and the population was too small and scattered to necessitate elaborate organisation. Nevertheless, there is evidence of inter-regional links, facilitated by the major river systems, and also along the coasts, suggesting the importance of boats and fishing. But the wealth of the community was not communally stored, and there is nothing to compare with the fortified centres of the Near East.

More striking changes, involving the movement of people rather than goods, were taking place in the steppe regions (see page 60), where the horse and the cart began to make possible the mobile way of life of the nomadic pastoralist.

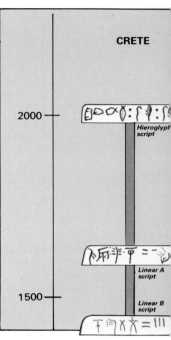

CRETE

2000 —

Hieroglyphic script

Linear A script

1500 —

Linear B script

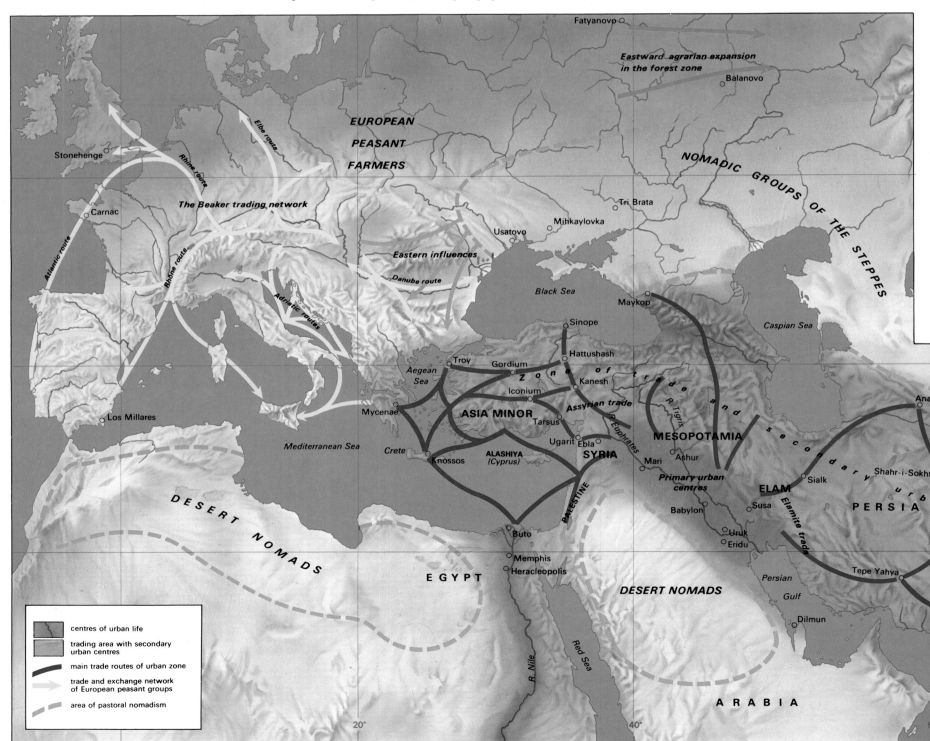

centres of urban life

trading area with secondary urban centres

main trade routes of urban zone

trade and exchange network of European peasant groups

area of pastoral nomadism

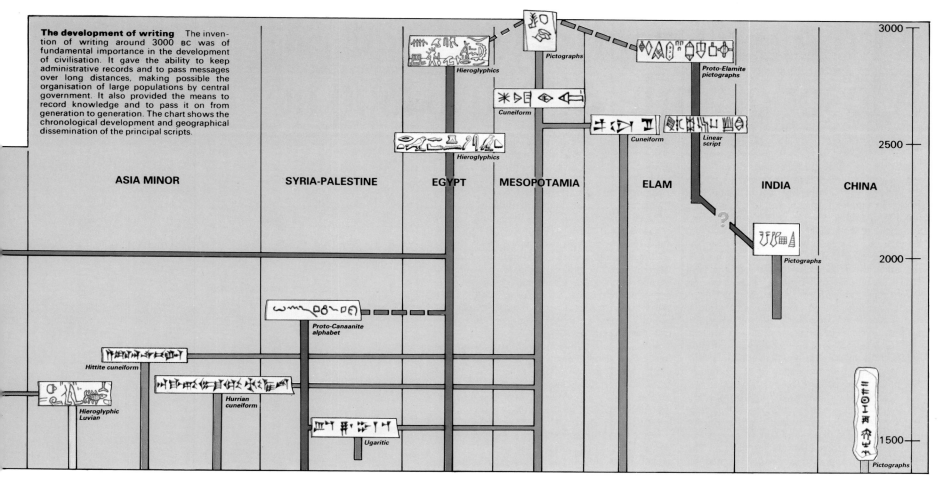

The development of writing The invention of writing around 3000 BC was of fundamental importance in the development of civilisation. It gave the ability to keep administrative records and to pass messages over long distances, making possible the organisation of large populations by central government. It also provided the means to record knowledge and to pass it on from generation to generation. The chart shows the chronological development and geographical dissemination of the principal scripts.

ASIA MINOR   SYRIA-PALESTINE   EGYPT   MESOPOTAMIA   ELAM   INDIA   CHINA

Hieroglyphics
Pictographs
Proto-Elamite pictographs
Cuneiform
Cuneiform
Linear script
Hieroglyphics
Pictographs
Proto-Canaanite alphabet
Hittite cuneiform
Hieroglyphic Luvian
Hurrian cuneiform
Ugaritic
Pictographs

3000
2500
2000
1500

A temple of the Late Prehistoric period, c. 3000 BC (above) at Eridu, modern Abu Shahrain, in southern Mesopotamia. The main structure, built of mud brick, stood on a stone-faced platform. This architectural combination developed, in mud brick, into the ziggurat or temple tower characteristic of later Mesopotamian cities.

At the same time, groups of peasant farmers continued to push eastward along the forest belt of central Russia, using hardy types of cereals. These groups penetrated as far as the region of modern Moscow and on to the southern Urals by 2000 BC. Movements along the forest/steppe margin opened up one of the earliest contact-routes between China and north-western Eurasia by the end of the second millennium BC.

The contrast between the early civilisations and their neighbours—mobile pastoralists to the north, and peasant groups in the temperate forests of Europe or the tropical jungles of Indo-China—lay in the centralisation of their economies. In these early urban societies, goods were collected and allocated in a system of administered redistribution. To keep track of these flows of products, some kind of permanent record was needed: the development of writing systems is a characteristic feature of such societies. The earliest written records were usually no more than lists of the contents of storehouses—though once a flexible system of writing had been invented, it was used to record myths, legends and poetry, as well as for administration.

In each region, the earliest script was pictographic, i.e. symbols were used for individual words and concepts. But such a system, requiring a new sign for each new word, soon became cumbersome, and eventually symbols were used for sounds rather than ideas. The original pictures thus lost their significance as representations, and took on more arbitrary forms and meanings. One of the most successful systems was that evolved in Mesopotamia, where the wedge was used to write on clay tablets (Latin *cuneus*—wedge: hence 'cuneiform'). This system was adopted by several groups for their own languages—initially Sumerian, then Akkadian, Babylonian and Assyrian, Eblaite (early Canaanite), Hittite and Hurrian; it thus included Semitic, non-Semitic and Indo-European languages.

It is possible that the earliest Mesopotamian pictographs spread, by way of Iran, to inspire those of the Indus—which never evolved beyond that stage. Chinese pictographs were probably an independent invention. Egyptian hieroglyphics ('priestly' pictographs) may similarly owe their initial inspiration to Mesopotamia, but developed their own strongly individual tradition. They may themselves have given the initial idea of writing to the palace-centres of Crete, which eventually developed their own 'Linear' scripts, Linear A and Linear B. Scribal inventiveness is best exemplified, however, in the creation of an alphabetic system on the basis of provincial Egyptian hieroglyphics, to write the Canaanite language. This system inspired an alphabetic cuneiform (Ugaritic) and became the ancestor of the alphabet which was taken over by the Greeks and passed on to the Romans to form the basis of the modern European script.

1/The spread of civilisation (below) As defined by urban life and writing, civilisation began in Mesopotamia and Egypt, and soon spread to Elam, the Indus Valley, and Crete and parts of Asia Minor. The spread of writing, largely from the two main stems, Mesopotamian cuneiform and Egyptian hieroglyphics (see chart above), is a good index of the spheres of influence of the two dominant centres, Mesopotamia and Egypt, and of the dissemination of civilisation from them. The beginnings of civilisation in Mesopotamia are exemplified at Warka (ancient Uruk), where several thousand pictographic clay tablets were found in levels of about 3000 BC associated with monumental architecture.

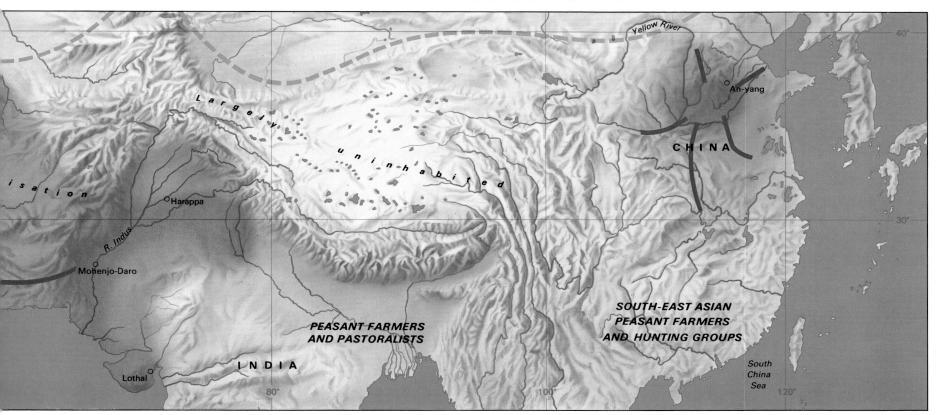

The early empires of Mesopotamia c. 3500 to 1600 BC

THE fertile plains and valleys drained by the Tigris and the Euphrates offered in antiquity the richest potential farming country between the Indus and the Nile. But it was a land held always in the most delicate and fragile balance, needing constant defence both against nature and against the hungry human predators from the desert to the west and the mountains to the north and east. Unlike the regular, benevolent rise and fall of the Nile, the flow of the twin rivers, rising in the Eastern Taurus range, was irregular and unpredictable, bringing near-drought conditions in one year and violent, destructive floods the next. To establish and maintain any kind of control, dykes, canals, and organisation of the most elaborate kind were required. In meeting this challenge, many of the most significant achievements of early civilisation gradually evolved.

The pressed-mud villages dating from the first beginnings of agriculture (see page 40), whose remains have been excavated in the Zagros mountains and the northern Tigris basin, began to give way to more elaborate settlements. The potter's wheel appeared (probably invented in the region), while from about 3000 BC architecture, sculpture and metal-working reached new levels of mastery. Most far-reaching of all,

writing was developed, first in the form of pictograms, later becoming cuneiform script (see page 52).

Underlying subsequent developments, during the late 4th to the mid-2nd millennium, was cultural cross-fertilisation between four major ethno-cultural groups: Sumerians, Semites, Indo-Europeans (Hittites) and Hurrians. In the Syrian area there were also significant contacts with Egypt. The underlying pattern of change involved expanding commercial contacts and the exploitation of economic resources, with initially short-lived attempts to consolidate the gains by military expansion from various centres, mainly in Mesopotamia itself.

In southern Mesopotamia it was the Sumerians, seen by some scholars as indigenous but generally taken to be immigrants via Persia from some more remote homeland (perhaps central Asia), who from 3000 BC onwards introduced writing and developed large compact social organisations which may properly be called cities. In material culture they perfected the irrigation techniques invented by their predecessors, and brought to a high standard the metal technology already developed in Anatolia and Persia.

Throughout history, Semitic-speaking peoples

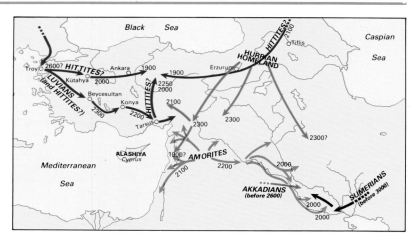

3/Ethnic movements *(above)* Long-standing controversy over the origins of, and the routes taken by, the Hittites is still unresolved: the map therefore indicates the three principal hypotheses. Very little is known for certain about the migrations of the Akkadians and Sumerians.

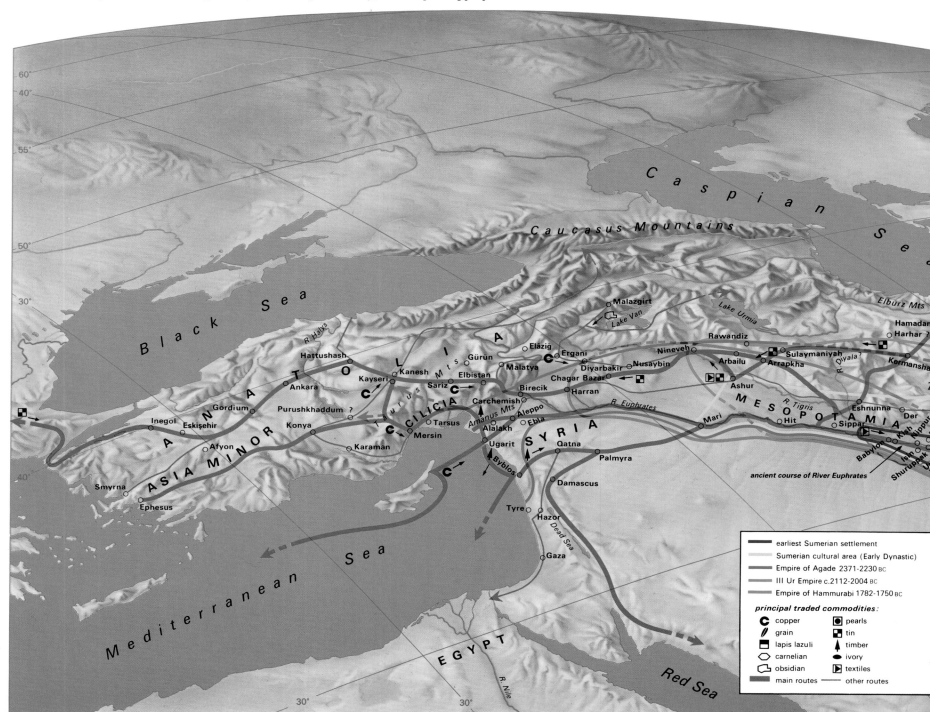

	earliest Sumerian settlement
	Sumerian cultural area (Early Dynastic)
	Empire of Agade 2371-2230 BC
	III Ur Empire c.2112-2004 BC
	Empire of Hammurabi 1782-1750 BC

principal traded commodities:

C	copper		pearls
	grain		tin
	lapis lazuli		timber
	carnelian		ivory
	obsidian		textiles
	main routes		other routes

Sandstone stele of Naram-Sin *(above)* One of the greatest rulers of the third millennium Agade Dynasty, which founded the first Mesopotamian Empire. It depicts his victory over the Lullubu, a people of the Zagros. The stele, two metres high, in antiquity taken by an Elamite conqueror to Susa in south-west Persia, is now in the Louvre Museum.

from the Syrian desert have filtered into Mesopotamia, but in this period there were two incursions of major significance: Akkadians in the first third of the 3rd millennium, and Amorites around the turn of the 3rd and 2nd millennia.

At least two waves of Indo-Europeans (represented later by Luvians and Hittites, the latter by far the more prominent politically) entered Asia Minor from the north before 2000 BC. The route of the Luvians in western and southern Asia Minor is generally agreed, but that of the Hittites is in dispute. The Hurrians were a people originally from the Caucasus, who began moving southwards and westwards in the 3rd millennium, becoming widespread in eastern Anatolia, Syria, and northern Mesopotamia from 1800 BC.

The political organisation of the Sumerians of the first half of the 3rd millennium (the Early Dynastic period) was based on city-states with a shifting hegemony among them. Their need of timber, metals and semi-precious stones, none of which southern Mesopotamia provides, led the Sumerians to begin exploitation of the Zagros and Amanus and to develop more distant trade routes into Persia and Asia Minor and by sea to Dilmun (Bahrein) and possibly beyond.

The first significant attempt at empire was under the dynasty of Agade, of Akkadian immigrant origin, whose rulers (most notably Sargon and his grandson Naram-Sin) reduced the importance of the old city-state system by moving towards centralised government. They undertook deliberate conquests from south-west Persia to Syria and (according to not improbable tradition) into central Asia Minor, in the interest of trade. Sea trade extended to the remote lands of Magan and Meluhha, possibly the Persian coast of the Gulf of Oman and the Indus Valley. Collapse, triggered by the invasion of hillmen (barbarous Gutians from the central Zagros) but ultimately due to internal stresses, was followed by a renaissance of the Sumerian city-state system in which Ur finally emerged as the dominant element, a highly bureaucratic empire more compact and stable than that of Agade.

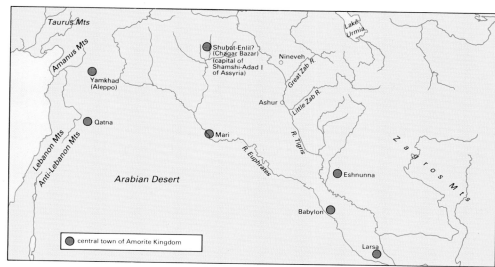

This empire in turn collapsed (c. 2000 BC) under the pressure of new Semitic invaders, the Amorites, probably from eastern Syria. The Amorites gradually settled, to establish dynasties from Syria to the Diyala area and south Mesopotamia on the basis of old kingdoms and city-states. (Map 2 marks the most prominent of these.) The two of greatest eventual significance were Assyria and Babylon. Assyria, which already had trading colonies in Anatolia, passed from a native dynasty to the Amorite Shamshi-Adad I, who extended it from the Zagros mountains to the middle Euphrates to make it the most powerful state in Mesopotamia. After the death of Shamshi-Adad and towards the end of the reign of Hammurabi (1792-1750 BC), Babylon emerged pre-eminent after a period of changing coalitions among Amorite city-states, to achieve a brief empire. The enduring importance of this was the development of the ideal (not always fulfilled) of a single south Mesopotamian kingdom with Babylon as its capital.

In Asia Minor, early trading contacts, possible military expeditions by the Agade dynasty,

2/Principal Amorite kingdoms *(above)* Babylon's eventual supremacy under Hammurabi was not foreseen by contemporaries, one of whom wrote, 'There is no king who is unquestionably powerful by himself'. Ten or fifteen kings, he reported, followed Hammurabi, but similar numbers supported Rim-Sin of Larsa, Ibalpiel of Eshnunna and Amutpiel of Qatna, while twenty backed Yarimlim of Yamkhad (Aleppo).

Assyrian merchant colonies, and indirect contacts via Syria and Cilicia, had already introduced some Mesopotamian cultural influence by the early 2nd millennium. By the 17th century BC the Hittites had crystallised into a kingdom in the Halys area, which expanded southwards from 1650 BC, eventually to control Syria north of Aleppo and west of the Euphrates. In a transitory further extension they broke past Aleppo and marched down the Euphrates to sack Babylon in 1595 BC. Further Hittite expansion towards Mesopotamia was held in check by the Hurrians, by that time consolidating to the east of the Euphrates bend. After the Hittite raid a dynasty of Cassites, a people from the Zagros, seized control of Babylonia. Rapidly assimilating to its culture, it ruled for over four centuries.

1/The early empires *(below)* Throughout this period, general areas of influence and control are clear, but the exact situation of many boundaries remains uncertain, and in some cases — such as Agade's frontier south of Susa or the northern extension of Assyria under Shamshi-Adad — completely unknown. Partly for this reason, partly because there were substantial overlaps between the empires of Shamshi-Adad and Hammurabi, the former is not shown here, though its geographical extent was at least as great.

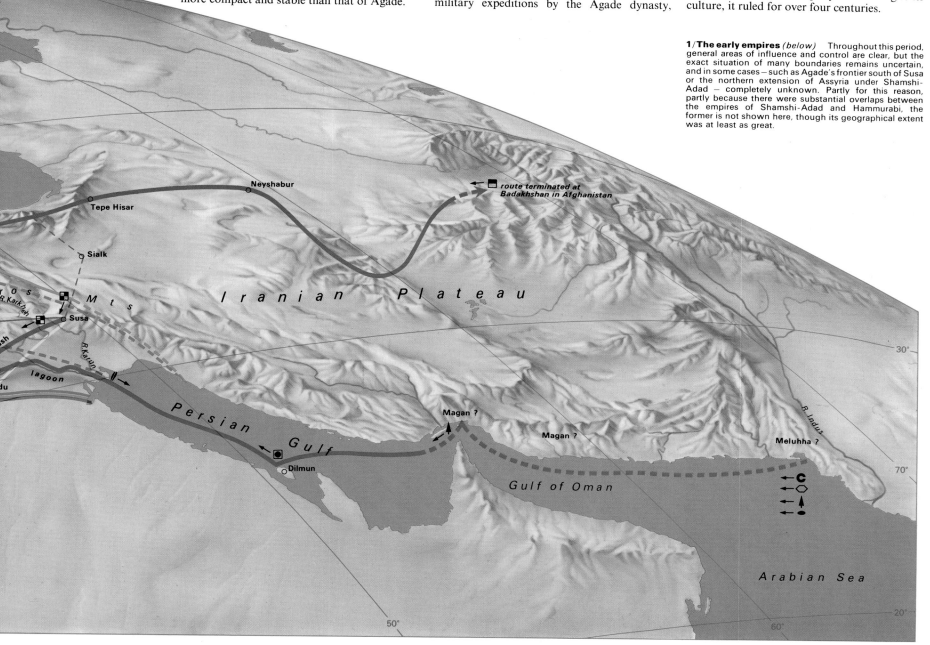

The Near East from the fall of Babylon to the fall of Assyria c.1300 to 612 BC

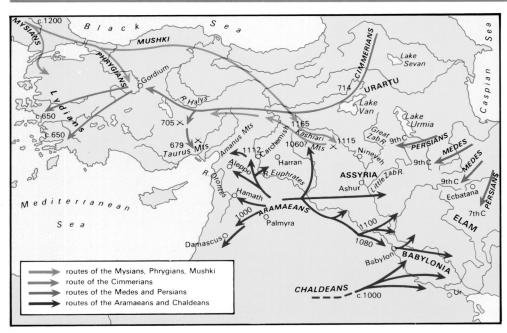

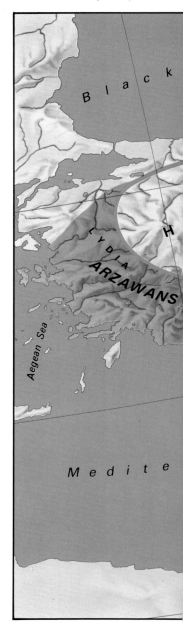

AFTER the collapse of the First Dynasty of Babylon, the centre of gravity of the Near East shifted towards Syria and north Mesopotamia, where Hittite and Hurrian zones of influence met. Syria was the junction for trade routes from the east, from Asia Minor and the Aegean, and from Egypt, and for this reason each of the major powers sought to control it.

The typical political unit in Syria at this time was the city-state. Such a state might be fully independent, and even (as Ugarit in the 15th century and Hamath and Damascus early in the first millennium) wield control beyond its own territory; but usually the city-states were vassals of some great power centred outside Syria. For the first three centuries three powers come into account. Egypt, the most distant, was interested in Syria both for its mercantile importance and because control there would safeguard Egypt from a recurrence of Asiatic invasion suffered earlier in the second millennium; the port of Byblos was of particular trading importance to Egypt. The second power was the Hittites, based in central Anatolia and gradually extending control towards the Aegean. The third was Mitanni, a predominantly Hurrian state centred on the Khabur and controlling much of north Mesopotamia, including Assyria; north of it lay the associated state of Hurri. At its maximum extent during the 15th century, when the Hittites were engaged in Asia Minor, Mitanni intermittently controlled all north Syria and Cilicia (Kizzuwadna). Subsequently the Hittites resumed their drive for Syria. Internal developments had weakened Egypt's hold on south Syria, so that under Shuppiluliumash (c. 1380-1346 BC), the Hittites were able to gain control of most of Syria by a system of vassal states, cutting Mitanni off from the Mediterranean.

Assyria, centred on the Tigris from Nineveh to Ashur, was a vassal of Mitanni as long as the latter was a major power, but Hittite pressure on Mitanni allowed Assyria's re-emergence. Assyria had adopted much of the military organisation of the Hurrians, notably the use of the war-chariot, and by the second half of the 12th century intermittently controlled former Mitannian territory up to the Euphrates.

In about 1200 BC the Hittite Empire collapsed. The immediate cause was belligerent movements of migrants from the Aegean region known from Egyptian inscriptions as 'Peoples of the Sea'. A technological consequence of these movements was the spread of the use of iron, for the production of which the Hittite area had hitherto been the main centre. Some relics of Hittite culture survived in neo-Hittite states in north Syria, notably Carchemish and Aleppo. The later kingdom of Lydia in western Asia Minor may indirectly represent another Hittite survival.

The vacuum left in central Anatolia by the Hittite collapse was filled not by the 'Peoples of the Sea' (although one group, the Danuna, probably settled in Cilicia) but by a new ethnic group migrating from Europe. The newcomers were the people known to the Greeks as Phrygians, with their eventual capital at Gordium. Another group, known to the Assyrians as Mushki, may (as shown here) have been a different wave of the same people, though other scholars think they came via east of the Black Sea and joined the Phrygians after an attempt to thrust southwards into Mesopotamia had been checked by Assyria in a battle in 1115 BC.

Further south another migration, in the 11th century, contributed to a significant change in the Near Eastern ethnic and political structure by the turn of the millennium. This was the migration of the Semitic Aramaeans, a people from the mountainous area east of Syria. This quickly produced a strong Aramaean element in the Syrian states, along the Euphrates, and in north Babylonia. In south Babylonia the Chaldeans, an associated group whose earlier history is not clear, settled at this time, particularly around Ur, known henceforth as 'of the Chaldees'.

Assyria, politically the successor of Mitanni, was subject to pressures from both the northern and southern migrations. But whereas in the north Assyria succeeded in deflecting the Mushki, to the south and west Aramaean pressure was so persistent that although Assyria once (c. 1100 BC) broke through to the Mediterranean its effective western boundary from soon after this time until the end of the 10th century was the Khabur.

In the first millennium the predominant characteristic of Assyria was its imperialism. What mainly motivated this were joint considerations of commercial interests and the quest for secure boundaries. The ultimate strength of Assyria lay in its fertile corn-plains in the rain-belt, but these had no natural defence against raids from the hillsmen to north and east. In addition, Assyria lacked metal ores and large timber. The Assyrian response to these factors was systematically to send armies through the petty states of the Zagros foothills to exact tribute in metals, timber and horses. This produced for Assyria border security, economic advantages and an efficient military organisation.

This policy, begun in the period between Mitannian decline and Aramaean pressure, was energetically resumed from the end of the 10th century. What made this possible is not wholly clear; a main factor was probably the international stability developing as many of the Aramaeans settled to form states in Syria. Ashurnasirpal II (883-859 BC) was able to force a

bridgehead through Carchemish to the Mediterranean; under his son Shalmaneser III (858-824 BC), this was extended both northwards to the Taurus (important for the trade routes to Europe and as a source of metals) and southwards to Damascus. The latter move brought Assyria directly into military conflict with the Aramaean states in Syria and their allies in Palestine, including Israel. With temporary setbacks, Assyria gradually extended control over these states, until the whole of Syria and Palestine, and for a short time in the 7th century north Egypt, were within the Assyrian Empire.

North of Assyria, the people around Lake Van, ethnically predominantly Hurrian, coalesced into a federation of states and then the kingdom of Urartu, which became notable for its metal technology and its engineering skill in irrigation works. Its developing trade, particularly in bronze objects, made it by the 8th century a serious rival of Assyria for control of northern Syria. The two states also clashed over control of the horse-rearing regions south of Lake Urmia.

Urartu was seriously weakened near the end of the 8th century by combined Assyrian pressure and invasion by Cimmerians, migrating hordes from east of the Black Sea. The Cimmerians subsequently clashed with Assyria in the Taurus, before their vanguard moved into western Anatolia, where they knocked out Phrygia in the early 7th century, and finally lost their momentum in an attack on Lydia a little later. The menace of the Cimmerians, and of the related Scythians who followed them, led to rapprochement between Assyria and Urartu.

Assyria's southern neighbour Babylonia, conquered by her in the late 13th century, was at most subsequent periods dominated politically by Assyria, even when formally independent. In turn, Assyria was strongly influenced by Babylonian culture; for example, many Assyrian royal inscriptions were written not in Assyrian but in Standard Babylonian.

To the east of Babylonia, and closely linked by economic interests, was Elam. Its political importance during this period was slight, except for a brief expansion into the Diyala area and eastern Assyria in the mid-12th century, probably seeking to gain control of the Zagros trade routes. From the late 8th century, the Chaldean tribes increasingly dominated Babylonia, requiring Assyrian military intervention there. Links of these tribesmen with Elam, and associated Elamite meddling in Babylonia, led Assyria to overrun and annex Elam in the 7th century.

Further north, east of the Zagros, Assyria had from the late 9th century been in contact with the Medes, Iranian migrants from north of the Caspian. During their two centuries as nominal vassals of Assyria, the Medes adopted features of Assyrian administrative practice and warfare which they later used against their tutors.

By the mid-7th century Assyria, attempting to control the whole Near East from Egypt to west Persia and northwards to the Taurus, was severely overstretched. Collapse had already begun when a Chaldean, Nabopolassar, seized the kingship of Babylonia in 625, and attacked Assyria. Nabopolassar was later joined by the Medes and Scythian hordes. The Assyrian capital, Nineveh, was sacked in 612 BC, the last organised Assyrian resistance ending in 605 BC at Carchemish.

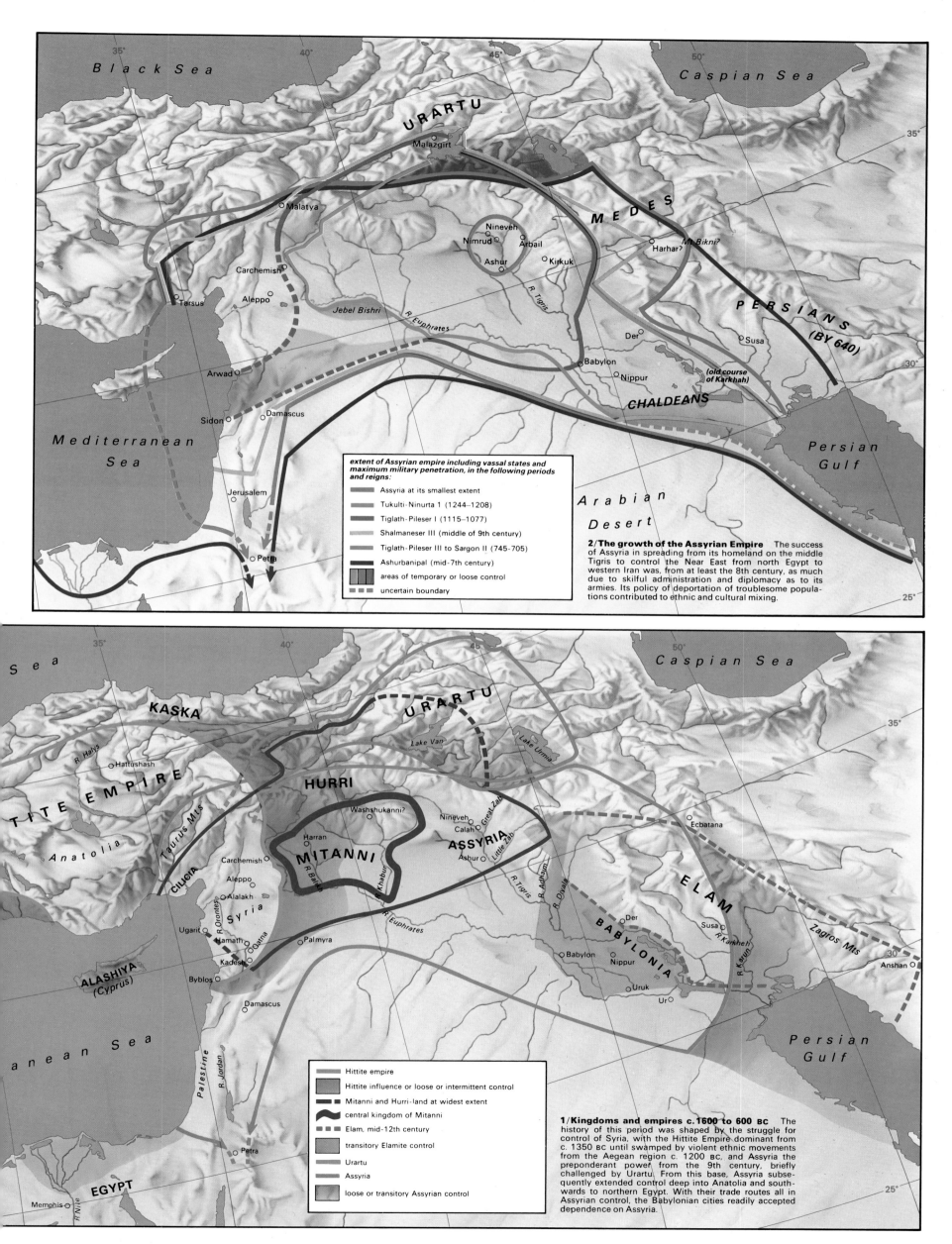

2/The growth of the Assyrian Empire

The success of Assyria in spreading from its homeland on the middle Tigris to control the Near East from north Egypt to western Iran was, from at least the 8th century, as much due to skilful administration and diplomacy as to its armies. Its policy of deportation of troublesome populations contributed to ethnic and cultural mixing.

extent of Assyrian empire including vassal states and maximum military penetration, in the following periods and reigns:

- Assyria at its smallest extent
- Tukulti-Ninurta 1 (1244–1208)
- Tiglath-Pileser I (1115–1077)
- Shalmaneser III (middle of 9th century)
- Tiglath-Pileser III to Sargon II (745-705)
- Ashurbanipal (mid-7th century)
- areas of temporary or loose control
- uncertain boundary

1/Kingdoms and empires c.1600 to 600 BC

The history of this period was shaped by the struggle for control of Syria, with the Hittite Empire dominant from c. 1350 BC until swamped by violent ethnic movements from the Aegean region c. 1200 BC, and Assyria the preponderant power from the 9th century, briefly challenged by Urartu. From this base, Assyria subsequently extended control deep into Anatolia and southwards to northern Egypt. With their trade routes all in Assyrian control, the Babylonian cities readily accepted dependence on Assyria.

- Hittite empire
- Hittite influence or loose or intermittent control
- Mitanni and Hurri-land at widest extent
- central kingdom of Mitanni
- Elam, mid-12th century
- transitory Elamite control
- Urartu
- Assyria
- loose or transitory Assyrian control

Ancient Egypt and her empires

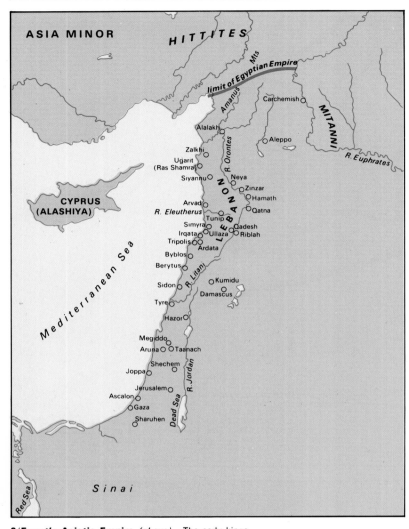

2/**Egypt's Asiatic Empire** *(above)* The early kings of the XVIIIth Dynasty embarked on a policy of expansion into western Asia. Having experienced the rewards of successful conquest they tried to add to what they had won. The dominion of Tuthmosis I (c. 1525-1512 BC) extended from the Euphrates to the Third Cataract in Nubia. His grandson, Tuthmosis III (c. 1504-1450 BC) fought seventeen campaigns in Palestine and Syria, taking Egypt's empire to its furthest northern limits in the region of Carchemish. After much of this empire had crumbled away in the next 130 years, the campaigns of Sethos I and Ramesses II recovered some of the lost territory, but Egyptian armies never again gained control beyond Qadesh on the Orontes.

FROM Early Palaeolithic times onwards, for very many thousands of years, the natural fauna and flora of the Lower Nile valley sustained semi-nomadic groups of hunters and food-gatherers, whose stone implements have been found in abundance in the terraces cut by the river, in the wadis adjoining the valley and on the surface of the high deserts flanking it. These primitive inhabitants were succeeded in Neolithic and pre-Dynastic times (c. 7000-3100 BC) by people who adopted a more settled mode of life, food-producers who brought arable land under cultivation and bred cattle. Their racial connections are obscure, but their artefacts are sufficiently distinctive to enable their different cultural groups to be easily distinguished and, in Upper (southern) Egypt at least, to allow their order of arrival in the Nile valley to be determined.

At first there was little intercourse between the peasant communities; each community worshipped its local deity or deities and each developed its own theological ideas. It was this insularity which was largely responsible for the multiplicity of deities and cults in historical times. When the communities were grouped into larger units (later called *nomes* by the Greeks), they retained much of their religious independence, and it was scarcely affected when, towards the end of the pre-Dynastic period, the *nomes* became two kingdoms with their respective capitals at Hieraconpolis, in Upper Egypt, and Buto. In c. 3100 BC Menes, the king of Upper Egypt, subdued Lower Egypt, united the 'Two Lands' under one crown and built a new capital, later called Memphis, near the junction of the two former kingdoms. It was at about this time that writing in the hieroglyphic script was invented and also that many of the conventions employed in Egyptian art for the next three thousand years were adopted. The Early Dynastic Period (c. 3100-2685 BC) was the most formative age of ancient Egypt, when proficiency advanced rapidly in stone-masonry, copper-smelting and working and technical skills of many kinds. Living conditions improved, and there can be little doubt that there was a considerable growth in the population. At the beginning of the Old Kingdom (IIIrd-VIth Dynasties, c. 2685-2180 BC) Imhotep was able to assemble the necessary skill and manpower to build for his king, Zoser, the famous Step Pyramid at Saqqara, the first monument in Egypt to be constructed entirely of hewn stone. Pyramids of step design were superseded at the beginning of the IVth Dynasty (c. 2613-2494 BC) by geometrically true pyramids, the most outstanding examples of which are the Great Pyramid of Cheops and the pyramid of his son, Chephren, at Giza. Throughout the remainder of the Old Kingdom kings and high officials continued to adorn their temples and tombs with sculptures in relief and in the round which were never surpassed in strength and quality, but politically it was a period of decline which culminated, at the end of the VIth Dynasty (c. 2180 BC), in the collapse of the central government. For the next 140 years (the First Intermediate Period, c. 2180-2040 BC), although kings existed in name, first at Memphis and then at Heracleopolis, the real rulers were the provincial governors, the nomarchs, who recruited private armies and levied taxes for their own use in their respective *nomes*. At times famine was general and struggles for supremacy developed between the nomes.

National unity was at length restored by the nomarchs of Thebes, who first gained control of the nomes south of their own and then advanced northwards. The final victory over the Heracleopolitan king was won by Mentuhotep II, whose namesake and ancestor, Mentuhotep I, had founded the Theban dynasty four generations previously. Apart from his military achievements, which also included the expulsion of Asiatic and Libyan settlers from the eastern and the western Delta, he re-established an effective central government, at Thebes, and laid the foundations of a new age of economic and cultural progress; it marked the beginning of the Middle Kingdom (XIth and XIIth Dynasties, c. 2060-1785 BC). Under the first king of the XIIth Dynasty, Ammenemes I, the capital was moved to Itj-towy, eighteen miles south of Memphis and near the entrance to the Faiyum. He and his six successors, three bearing his name and three named Sesostris, carried out important land reclamation and irrigation schemes, particularly in the Faiyum, probably in an effort to prevent a recurrence of the famines which had plagued the country since the end of the Old Kingdom. It was a time when the arts flourished, particularly sculpture and lapidary work; some of the best

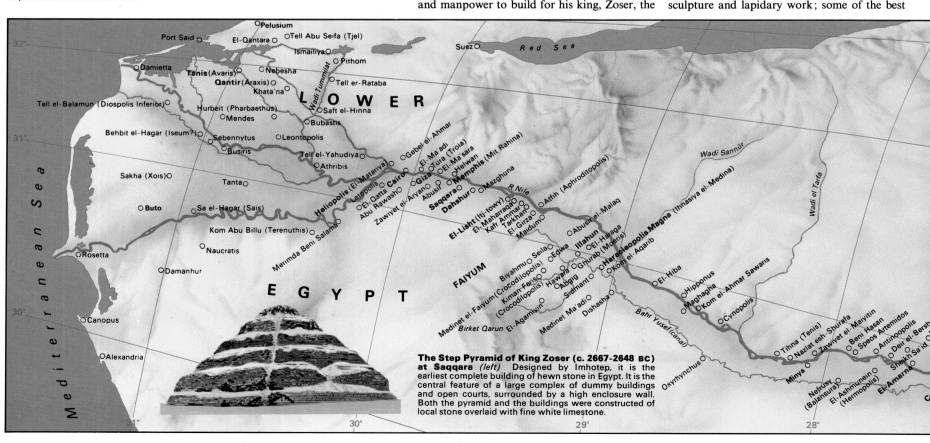

The Step Pyramid of King Zoser (c. 2667-2648 BC) at Saqqara *(left)* Designed by Imhotep, it is the earliest complete building of hewn stone in Egypt. It is the central feature of a large complex of dummy buildings and open courts, surrounded by a high enclosure wall. Both the pyramid and the buildings were constructed of local stone overlaid with fine white limestone.

surviving examples are the reliefs on the peripteral chapel of Sesostris I at Karnak and the jewellery found in tombs of princesses at the pyramids of Ammenemes II at Dahshur and of Sesostris II at Illahun.

In the unsettled period which followed the XIIth Dynasty (the Second Intermediate Period, c. 1785-1570 BC), a succession of, mainly ephemeral, kings failed to prevent a repetition of the infiltration of Asiatic immigrants into the northeastern Delta, this time, moreover, in large numbers. Known as the Hyksos, these intruders eventually subjected the Egyptian inhabitants of the Delta and the Nile valley as far as Cusae to their domination for more than a century. Farther south, the princes of Thebes ruled as vassals of the Hyksos kings until Kamose in c. 1567 BC succeeded in recovering nearly all the occupied territory. His brother, Amosis I, completed the conquest three years later by capturing Avaris, the Hyksos capital. The traditional representation of Hyksos rule as harsh and oppressive finds little contemporary support. There can be no doubt, however, that it provided Egypt with the incentive to safeguard her territory against further foreign domination by embarking on her conquest of neighbouring lands in western Asia. In its achievement she owed much to the horse-drawn chariot and the composite bow, both of which came to her knowledge through the Hyksos.

Amosis pursued the retreating enemy through Palestine into Syria in a campaign which lasted for at least three years. Never before had Egypt exercised government over foreign territory, except in Lower Nubia, between the First and the Second Cataracts, where the kings of the XIIth Dynasty had built a series of forts. In the XVIIIth Dynasty (c. 1570-1320 BC), however, the six warrior kings who followed Amosis I, each of whom was named either Amenophis or Tuthmosis, controlled an empire which ultimately stretched northwards to the Euphrates and southwards to about the Fourth Cataract. But its maintenance required frequent displays of strength and prompt action to counter threats of secession, neither of which suited the temperaments of the pleasure-loving Amenophis III or of his son, Amenophis IV, who adopted the name Akhenaten in about the fifth year of his reign. Inspired by religious fervour, Akhenaten proclaimed the god immanent in the sun's disk, Aten, to be the only god, suppressed the cults of Amun and all the other gods, confiscated their properties for the state, abandoned Thebes and built a new capital at El-Amarna. In art greater freedom was allowed in the subjects represented, and a new and distinctive style was introduced.

Akhenaten's heretical movement was already moribund when he died in c. 1362 BC. Three years

later the court returned to Thebes and his young successor immediately reinstated the ancient cults, signifying his own adherence to the cult of Amun by changing his name from Tutankhaten to Tutankhamun. As is evident from the Amarna letters (diplomatic correspondence, mostly written in Akkadian, between Egypt and the rulers of western Asia), much of the Asiatic empire had been lost by the time of Akhenaten's death, but Egypt still kept a foothold in Palestine; under Sethos I (c. 1318-1304 BC) and Ramesses II (c. 1304-1237 BC) her former possessions, as far as Qadesh on the Orontes, were regained. Some fierce but indecisive encounters with the Hittites, whose empire embraced the territory farther north, culminated in two peace treaties, the first with Sethos I and, some thirty years later, the second, a more permanent contract, with Ramesses II. Apart from being successful fighters, these two kings constructed some outstanding monuments, notably the temple of Abydus and the hypostyle hall at Karnak by Sethos I, and the rock-temples of Abu Simbel by Ramesses II.

There were still two warrior-kings to come, Merneptah (c. 1236-1223 BC) and Ramesses III (c. 1198-1166 BC). Their role, however, was not to expand the empire, but to defend the land of Egypt against a series of attacks, sometimes concerted, by Libyans (who had previously been defeated by Sethos I) and a mixed army of invaders from Asia Minor and the Aegean, collectively called 'peoples of the sea'. Having failed to achieve their aim by military means, the Libyans resorted to peaceful penetration, with the result that, some two centuries after the death of Ramesses III, the chief of one of their groups of settlers in the Nile valley was able to ascend the throne as the founder of a dynasty of nine Libyan kings (the XXIInd Dynasty, c. 935-730 BC).

For the next seven hundred years, until she became a province of the Roman Empire in 30 BC, Egypt was ruled in turn by Ethiopians of her former province of Nubia (the XXVth Dynasty, 751-656 BC), twice by Persians (525-404 BC and 341-333 BC) and, after the annexation by Alexander the Great in 333 BC, by Macedonians and Greeks. The two hundred years during which she was governed by native kings (the XXVIth Dynasty, c. 664-525 BC and the XXVIII-XXXth Dynasties, c. 404-341 BC) were periods when much attention was paid to the arts, but even under foreign rule the construction of monuments and other creative activities continued without either serious interruption or any fundamental change in character, and the same continuity can be observed in religion, government and society. No more telling tribute could have been paid to the essential worth of the Egyptian civilisation.

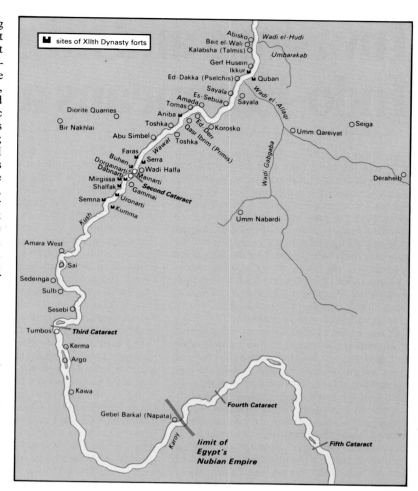

sites of XIIth Dynasty forts

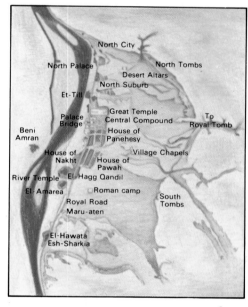

3/Egypt's Nubian conquests *(above)* Nubia, on Egypt's southern frontier, was an important supplier, above all of gold from the region of Wadi el-Allaqi and Wadi Gabgaba, and further south between Wadi Halfa and Kerma. In the XIIth Dynasty the whole territory from the First Cataract to Semna was annexed and brick forts were built at strategic points, the most northerly being near Aswan. The XVIIIth Dynasty kings pushed the boundary further south until, under Tuthmosis III, it reached Napata, near the Fourth Cataract.

4/El-Amarna *(right)* Only in one instance has it been possible to reproduce the ground-plan of an ancient Egyptian city and to reconstruct the design of some of its principal buildings. This is El-Amarna, built by Akhenaten as his new capital when he abandoned Thebes. It lies on the east bank of the Nile, approximately half way between Cairo and Luxor, in a natural amphitheatre formed by the cliffs of the high desert, about eight miles long and three miles wide at the centre.

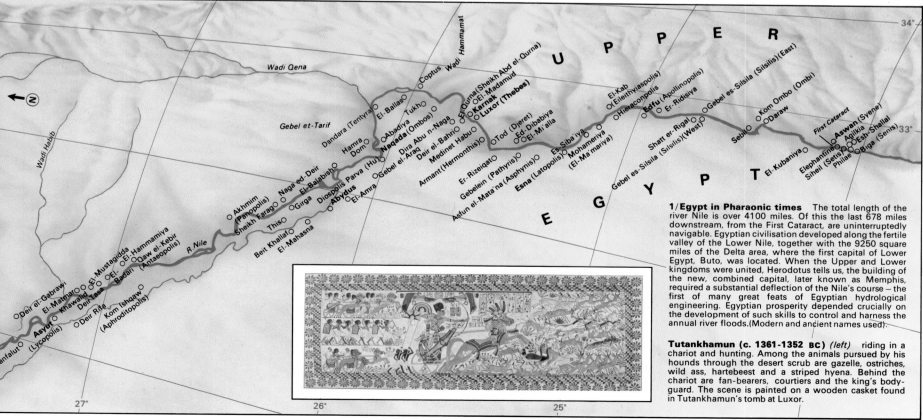

1/Egypt in Pharaonic times The total length of the river Nile is over 4100 miles. Of this the last 678 miles downstream, from the First Cataract, are uninterruptedly navigable. Egyptian civilisation developed along the fertile valley of the Lower Nile, together with the 9250 square miles of the Delta area, where the first capital of Lower Egypt, Buto, was located. When the Upper and Lower kingdoms were united, Herodotus tells us, the building of the new, combined capital, later known as Memphis, required a substantial deflection of the Nile's course — the first of many great feats of Egyptian hydrological engineering. Egyptian prosperity depended crucially on the development of such skills to control and harness the annual river floods. (Modern and ancient names used):-

Tutankhamun (c. 1361-1352 BC) *(left)* riding in a chariot and hunting. Among the animals pursued by his hounds through the desert scrub are gazelle, ostriches, wild ass, hartebeest and a striped hyena. Behind the chariot are fan-bearers, courtiers and the king's bodyguard. The scene is painted on a wooden casket found in Tutankhamun's tomb at Luxor.

Invasions and migrations: Indo-Europeans and Semites

ACROSS the north of Africa, through Arabia and the Near East, and far beyond into Asia north of the Himalayas, runs the arid belt which separates the temperate zone from the tropical forests of the Equator. Life in this area, away from the great river-valleys, depends on mobility, to take advantage of scattered seasonal pastures. As agricultural man domesticated the animals which were adapted to the steppe and semi-desert – the horse, the ass and the camel – so a new mode of life became possible: nomadic pastoralism. Ranging widely in quest of grazing lands, these peoples came into often violent contact with their settled neighbours.

It was in the third millennium BC, at a time when settled agricultural populations had already occupied Europe for two thousand years, and when urban civilisation was making its first appearance in the fertile river valleys of the Near East, that the first extensive colonisation of the steppe and semi-desert areas occurred. In different parts of the arid zone, the various animals without which these environments could not be used came to be domesticated. On the Eurasian steppeland north of the Black Sea, the Caucasus and the belt of the Taurus and Zagros Mountains, it was the horse which provided the key, as farmers and fishermen, formerly confined to the watercourses through the steppes, now had the means to exploit their scattered pastures. Wheeled vehicles, first invented on the fringes of the Caucasus where woodland and steppe meet, soon spread among these groups. This successful economy penetrated both westwards, into the zone of already established farming groups, and widely to the east, among the vast open corridors of steppeland leading to central Asia, and down, east of the Caspian Sea, to the edge of the Indian sub-continent.

This process is reflected most strikingly in the distribution of the closely-related languages of the Indo-European group, which embraces both Sanskrit and Persian at one end, and such European languages as Greek, Latin, French, German and English at the other. Words like *father* (Latin *pater*; Sanskrit *pitar*) for instance, show close similarities among the members of the group. The earliest-known written forms of Indo-European are the second-millennium texts from Greece, written in Mycenaean Linear B, and from Asiatic Turkey (Anatolia), written by peoples such as the Hittites and Luvians. There are also more scattered references in contemporary texts from Mesopotamia which refer to a tribe called the Mitanni, and which contain Indo-European personal names. Significantly, terms used in the training of horses turn out also to be Indo-European. It is clear that during the earlier second millennium BC there had been widespread penetration southwards from the steppe lands, bringing Indo-European languages from their still illiterate homeland into the fringes of the civilised world.

How this came about is not certain. Violent irruptions of nomadic groups have always gained the attention of historians, but it is probable that a gradual and continuous shedding of population from the steppe areas into the often disaster- and disease-ridden agricultural and urban communities surrounding them provided an ongoing process of dispersal.

A basic division can be seen between the western Indo-European group, whose members adopted the stable agricultural life of the European farmers, and the eastern Indo-European group, whose members ranged more widely over the steppe and semi-desert areas, and whose movements were often more complex and unpredictable. The southward extent of these movements may be seen from the movement of the 'Aryan' (Iranian Indo-European) peoples into northern India, following the collapse of the Dravidian-speaking cities of the Indus valley civilisation in the early second millennium BC –

a series of events recollected in the ancient Sanskrit hymns known as the Rig-Veda. Eastwards, the most far-flung members of the Indo-European group were those who reached Chinese Turkestan, where the language known as Tocharian was written down in the 8th century AD. Counter-currents also brought eastern Indo-Europeans westwards. During the first millennium BC, groups of peoples known successively as Cimmerians, Scythians and Sarmatians pressed on the eastern frontiers of Europe, and again penetrated over the Caucasus and into north-eastern Anatolia. Many elements of Iranian art were transmitted westwards in this way, as well as superior kinds of horse-gear.

The eastern and western branches of Indo-European are today separated from one another geographically by a wedge of languages from further east, disseminated during later episodes of expansion and migration across the steppes. Down to the birth of Christ, the steppes were dominated by Indo-European tribes; but in the following millennium various tribes from the region of the Altai Mountains in Mongolia also adopted a nomadic way of life, and began to move west. The first to reach Europe were the Huns, followed by their relations the Avars: then came various Turkish tribes, led by the Khazars. The tribes which penetrated into Europe were largely driven out or assimilated by Indo-Europeans of the Slav group, but when the Seljuk Turks finally took over the remains of the Byzantine Empire, the chain of related languages from Europe to India was severed.

In the zone of urban civilisations on the southern flanks of the mountain belt and the rivers running from it, a somewhat similar interaction between settled and semi-desert areas produced another set of wide-ranging linguistic relationships, reaching down into Arabia and across into northern Africa. The distribution of the Semitic languages reflects the nomadic character of life in these areas, based at first on the ass and onager, and later on the camel. Horses, obtained from the steppe area over the mountains and used to pull light, spoke-wheeled chariots, were the equipment of richer warriors from the cities rather than the desert nomads. The earliest urban communities, those of the Sumerians (third millennium BC; see page 54) were non-Semitic, but their neighbours and second-millennium successors, the Akkadians and Assyrians, represent the north-east Semitic branch. Their north-western neighbours on the Levantine coast and adjacent areas were the urbanised Canaanites, including the Aramaeans, Phoenicians and Hebrews; while to the south-west lay the major Semitic-speaking Egyptian civilisation, and south-east, the more nomadic Arabs – much later to carry their culture and the Islamic religion from the Atlantic to the Indian Ocean.

Even in the first millennium BC, however, Semitic languages and culture were carried well beyond the semi-arid area of the Near East by the process of maritime expansion throughout the Mediterranean. Back in the Bronze Age, in the later second millennium, the Levantine coast had been a noted trading area; but in the first millennium, following economic collapse during its early centuries, maritime trading networks and colonies were set up at increasing distances from the homeland. Chief among the traders and colonists were the Greeks and the Semitic Phoenicians. From their great Levantine ports of Tyre and Sidon, the Phoenicians sailed beyond the Greek colonial network in the Aegean and Adriatic, to found the north African cities of Carthage (814 BC) and Utica, and on to Cadiz in Spain. Some scholars have seen the Etruscans as part of a similar movement from Turkey. It was the sea-borne power of these Semitic west Mediterranean colonies that the Romans first encountered in the succession of Punic Wars.

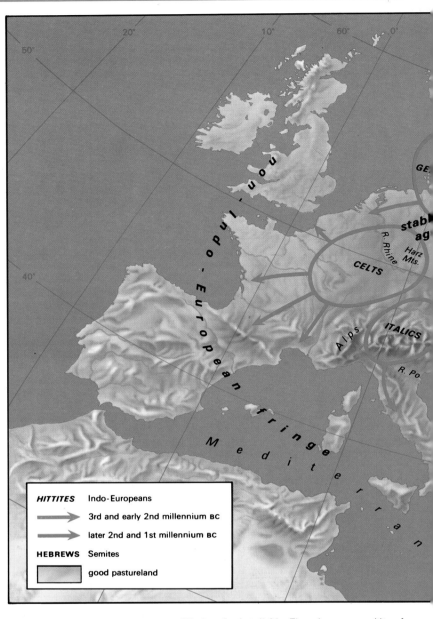

HITTITES — Indo-Europeans
→ 3rd and early 2nd millennium BC
→ later 2nd and 1st millennium BC
HEBREWS — Semites
good pastureland

Hittite chariot *(left)* The urban communities of the Near East obtained horses from the Steppes to the north, and with their own manufacturing skills produced the spoke-wheeled chariot, as seen in this Neo-Hittite relief.

2/Trading Empires *(below)* The first millennium BC saw a great expansion of maritime activity and the foundation of overseas colonies within the Mediterranean. Bypassing the main areas of Greek influence, the Phoenicians carried Semitic languages and culture to the other end of the Mediterranean world, and even sailed beyond to explore the Atlantic coasts.

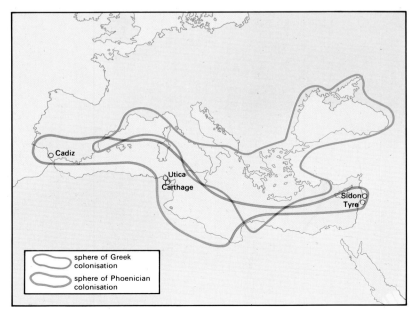

sphere of Greek colonisation
sphere of Phoenician colonisation

hunters of the Northern forests
(Finno-Ugrian)

Baltic Sea

BALTS

...MANS

...cultural
groups

SLAVS

ILLYRIANS

WEST INDO-
EUROPEAN

EAST INDO-
EUROPEAN

THRACIANS

zone of mobile pastoralists

SCYTHIAN

COMPLEX

pre-literate Indo-Europeans

R. Danube

Kuban Valley

zone of mobile pastoralists

L. Balkhash

Tien Shan

TOCHARIANS

R. Volga

R. Don

Caucasus Mountains

Aral
Sea

Syr Darya

Tibetan Plateau

GREEKS

Black Sea

IRANIAN
COMPLEX
(ARYANS)

Amu Darya

Pamirs

Hindu Kush

Himalayas

HITTITES

Caspian Sea

zone of mobile pastoralists

LUVIANS

Taurus Mountains

urban

MITANNI

ASSYRIANS

ARAMAEANS

PHOENICIANS

Syrian Desert

HEBREWS

civilisations

R. Tigris

R. Euphrates

Zagros Mountains

INDO-ARYANS

R. Indus

Indus
civilisation
(Dravidian)

...Sea

zone
of
semi-
mobile
pastoralists

EGYPTIANS

R. Nile

Red Sea

SOUTH SEMITES
(ARABS)

Arabian Sea

Arctic Circle

R. Ob

R. Yenisei

1/Indo-Europeans and Semites *(above)* The open
landscapes of the arid zone were the homelands of
nomadic peoples who spread their languages far and
wide. North of the Black Sea, peoples of the Indo-
European group domesticated the horse and colonised
the good grazing-grounds of the steppes. Semitic
peoples spread widely within the Near East, both as
nomads and as farmers and town-dwellers.

The beginnings of Chinese civilisation to 500 BC

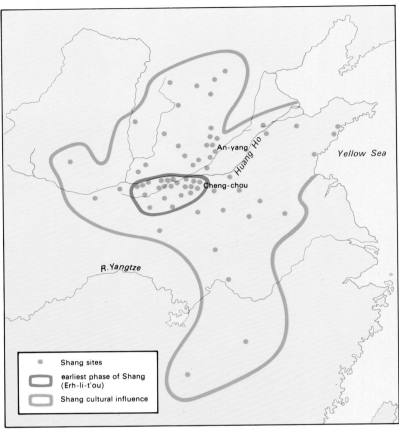

CHINA has been inhabited continuously by man since very early times. Remains of early hominids, similar to those from Java, have been found in Kwangsi, Yunnan and Shansi. About 500,000 BC Peking Man was living around Peking, in Shansi and possibly in Hupeh and Kwangtung. *Homo sapiens* first appears in Palaeolithic cultures in the Ordos region, Hopeh, and in the south-west, about 30,000 BC. Later Mesolithic cultures flourished along the northern frontier zone, in the south and south-west, and in Taiwan.

Neolithic agricultural communities, the immediate ancestors of Chinese civilisation, arose around 4000 BC in the loess-covered highlands of the north and north-west, where the well-drained soil of the river terraces was ideal for primitive agriculture. The Yang-shao, the first Neolithic culture, still subsisted largely by hunting and fishing. Agriculture was shifting, the settlements small and impermanent. Their pottery is strikingly similar to that from western Asia and the Ukraine. The second Neolithic culture, the Lung-shan, was more highly evolved. Its people lived in larger, more permanent villages. Relatively advanced, theirs was a sedentary culture with a high level of organisation and elaborate ritual. Their artifacts show great technical skill.

The use of bronze began around 1600 BC, and the beginning of the Bronze Age corresponded with the beginning of the first historical dynasty, the Shang. Traditionally there was a Hsia dynasty preceding Shang. This may refer to one of the later Neolithic cultures, but no site has yet been identified as from the Hsia.

The Shang (1523-1028 or 1751-1111 BC) was traditionally a powerful political regime controlling most of northern China. It was more probably a loose confederation of clan domains, many little more than village settlements. The Shang kings moved their capital six times, and two capitals, at Cheng-chou and An-yang, have been excavated. The capital, the king's 'Great Domain', contained the court, with many royal functionaries, supported by revenues from an extensive area. The Shang had trade relations with most of northern and central China, and with the steppes of north and west. Many smaller Shang sites have been found, most of them in areas which had been centres of Neolithic cultures. How far the Shang kings actually controlled these outer areas is uncertain.

In the 11th century BC the Shang were conquered by the Chou, a client people, possibly of different ethnic origin, living on the north-western border. They gradually extended their sovereignty over an area much larger than the Shang, including all of Hopeh, Honan, Shansi, Shantung, much of Shensi, Hupeh and Anhwei, and parts of the middle basin of the Yangtze. At first their capital was in the vicinity of Hsi-an (Sian), with a secondary capital near Lo-yang. Their state was divided into many separate domains. Many of these, especially around the capitals, were possessed by the king himself as a Royal Domain. Others were granted as fiefs to members of the royal clan, to the families that had helped the Chou to power, and to the clans of important subjects and office-holders. The Shang royal family was enfiefed in eastern Honan. This system of delegated authority was something like the later European feudal system.

Until the 8th century BC the Chou kings remained powerful, and constantly extended the area under their control. About 770 BC, however, internal disorders forced them to abandon their homeland in the Wei valley and move to their eastern capital at Lo-yang, where they soon became powerless figureheads. For the next two and a half centuries there was constant warfare between their former vassals. By the 5th century more than a hundred petty feudal states had been swallowed up by some twenty of the more powerful kingdoms. Real power was exercised by 'hegemon' states heading temporary alliances: from 667-632 Ch'i was predominant; after 632 Chin; during the 6th century Ch'u was the dominant power. But these alliances did not achieve political stability. Nevertheless, Chou culture and Chinese influence were consolidated and spread far beyond the political borders of early Chou times.

1/Prehistoric cultures *(below)* Most of the Palaeolithic and Mesolithic sites, as well as remains of earlier forms of man, have been found in the dry border regions of the north and north-west, and in the south, where these cultures spread into Vietnam and Laos. Neolithic cultures are concentrated in the northern region of easily worked loess soils.

2/Shang China *(above)* Most Shang sites are close to areas already occupied by Neolithic peoples. The very highly developed bronze culture of Shang was concentrated in the limited area along the Yellow River (Huang Ho). Shang culture was more widely diffused, but it is not known how far their political authority reached.

3/Western Chou China: 11th to 9th centuries BC *(below)* The early Chou dominions comprised a very large number of domains. Some remained under royal control, others were granted as fiefs to supporters and servants of the Chou, in a sort of feudal tenure. Much of the area shown on the map was still occupied by peoples of different ethnic origins who were gradually assimilated and conquered by the Chou and their vassals.

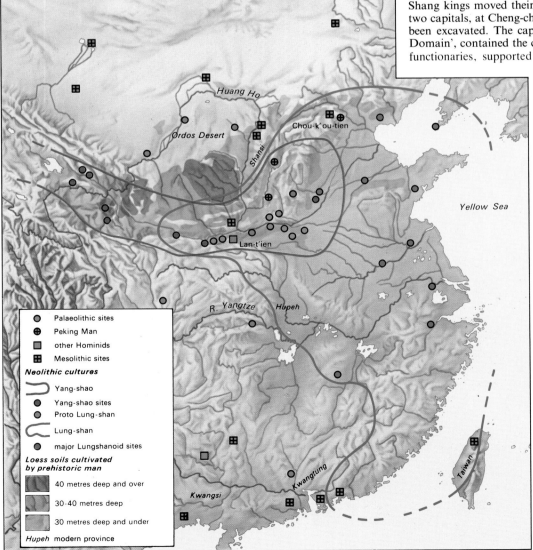

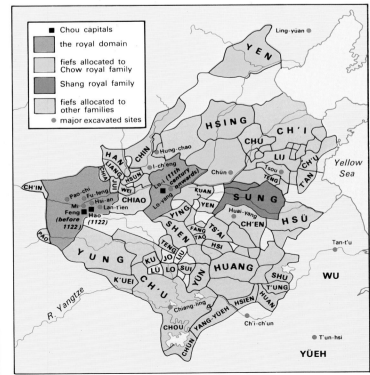

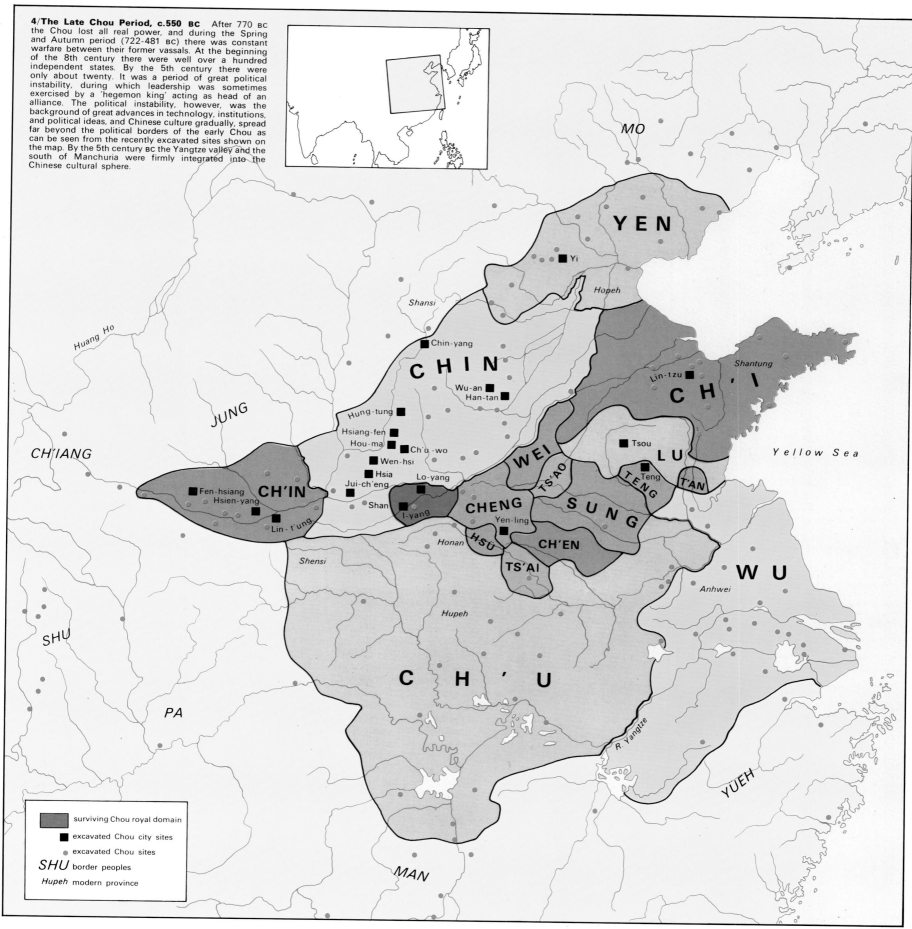

4/The Late Chou Period, c.550 BC

After 770 BC the Chou lost all real power, and during the Spring and Autumn period (722-481 BC) there was constant warfare between their former vassals. At the beginning of the 8th century there were well over a hundred independent states. By the 5th century there were only about twenty. It was a period of great political instability, during which leadership was sometimes exercised by a 'hegemon king' acting as head of an alliance. The political instability, however, was the background of great advances in technology, institutions, and political ideas, and Chinese culture gradually, spread far beyond the political borders of the early Chou as can be seen from the recently excavated sites shown on the map. By the 5th century BC the Yangtze valley and the south of Manchuria were firmly integrated into the Chinese cultural sphere.

surviving Chou royal domain

■ excavated Chou city sites

• excavated Chou sites

SHU border peoples

Hupeh modern province

The Shang and early Chou periods were differentiated from their predecessors not only by their political organisation and their bronze technology, but also by the use of writing, and their culture was already recognisably 'Chinese'. Their cities maintained a hierarchy of nobles, royal officers and court servants engaged in a constant round of warfare, hunting and elaborate religious ritual. They were supported by communities of craftsmen in bronze, wood, stone, ceramics and textiles, many of them slaves. The peasants working the various royal domains supplied them with revenues and grain.

Although the court and the nobility enjoyed a sophisticated Bronze Age culture, bronze remained rare and was used almost exclusively for ritual objects rather than practical tools. On the domains of the countryside farmers continued to use stone implements and to lead much the same life as in Neolithic times, living in permanent settlements and cultivating lands within a fixed territory with millet, barley and hemp, and

raising pigs, poultry and silkworms. There were only patches of cultivated lands, worked for a few years and then left fallow. The technology available could neither clear the dense woods on the mountains, nor drain and cultivate the heavy lands of the river valleys. Men still depended heavily on the wild lands surrounding every settlement, for game, wild fruits and herbs.

Towards the end of the period the old social order began to collapse. The more powerful states employed bureaucrats rather than the hereditary nobility of older times. Religious observances decayed. A new group of state servants (*shih*) emerged, as military officers and state officials. One of their number, Confucius, formalised many of the ideas current among them, and formulated them into a new ethos, which was to have currency far into the future. He was, however, only one of many thinkers who began to ponder the philosophical and practical problems facing man in this period of insecurity and rapid changes.

Shang ritual food vessel (14th-11th century BC) *(right)* The highly sophisticated bronze technology of the Shang period was devoted almost entirely to the production of ritual objects such as this. Ordinary tools continued to be made of stone rather than metal.

The beginnings of Indian civilisation

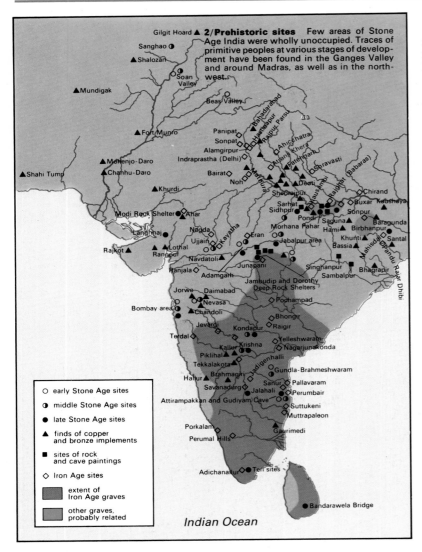

2/Prehistoric sites Few areas of Stone Age India were wholly unoccupied. Traces of primitive peoples at various stages of development have been found in the Ganges Valley, the Punjab foothills, the Soan and Beas valleys, Rajasthan, Malwa and as far south as Madras, as well as in the north-west.

○ early Stone Age sites
◑ middle Stone Age sites
● late Stone Age sites
▲ finds of copper and bronze implements
■ sites of rock and cave paintings
◇ Iron Age sites

■ extent of Iron Age graves

■ other graves, probably related

Indian Ocean

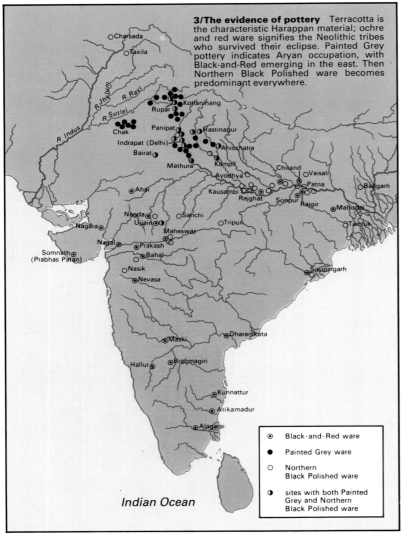

3/The evidence of pottery Terracotta is the characteristic Harappan material; ochre and red ware signifies the Neolithic tribes who survived their eclipse. Painted Grey pottery indicates Aryan occupation, with Black-and-Red emerging in the east. Then Northern Black Polished ware becomes predominant everywhere.

⊙ Black-and-Red ware
● Painted Grey ware
○ Northern Black Polished ware
◐ sites with both Painted Grey and Northern Black Polished ware

Indian Ocean

MEN have lived in India since the Second Interglacial Period, from 400,000 BC to 200,000 BC. The hand-axes, chopping tools and flakes of the Early Stone Age are found in the Punjab foothills, the Soan and Beas valleys, Rajasthan, Malwa and as far south as Madras. Middle Stone Age sites, with their more delicate flake-shaped tools, occur mainly in central and peninsular India, but also in the Soan valley and at Sanghao in north-west Pakistan. There are rock paintings, depicting a vigorous hunting culture, at several places in the Narmada valley and north-east India, and the microliths and mesoliths of the Late Stone Age are distributed, apart from Pakistan, almost throughout the sub-continent.

Five of the six large ethnic groups which make up the population of India today appear to have been already well-established by the 3rd millennium BC. The earliest, probably, were the Negritos, followed by the Proto-Australoids, the Mediterranean peoples, now mainly associated with Dravidian culture, the Mongoloids, of the north-east and northern fringes, and the western Brachycephals. Their settlements, gradually evolving and growing more elaborate, were widely scattered throughout Sind, Baluchistan and Rajasthan by the end of the 4th millennium BC, and a form of urban life was already beginning to develop, with copper and bronze appearing alongside the traditional stone blades and implements. Major sites have been discovered at Mundigak in south-east Afghanistan, Kulli near the Makran coast of south Baluchistan and Amri in south Sind.

These developments came to flower in the first of the great Indian civilisations. This spread out from its leading cities, Harappa and Mohenjo-Daro in the Indus valley, to cover nearly 500,000 square miles of territory and survived for the best part of 1000 years (c. 2550 to 1550 BC). The remains of typical Harappan towns, with their high citadels, solid buildings, uniform grids of streets and elaborate drainage systems, exist as far south as Cutch and Bhagatrav, at the mouth of the Narmada river, as well as at Rupar (Punjab) and Alamgirpur (Uttar Pradesh) in the east, and Judeirjo-Daro (Sind) and the Makran coast to the south-west. The Harappan script, mainly found on seals, is so far undeciphered, but it has been deduced from the vast granaries, the large houses, the proliferation of religious figurines (many of them anticipating Hindu deities) and the absence of royal palaces that this was essentially a society of priests, merchants and peasant farmers. Many typical Harappan goods have been found in Mesopotamia, and textual references there suggest that the traders of the country known as *Meluhha* were at this time in regular commercial contact with the Middle East via the land of *Dilmun* (probably Bahrein).

The Indus civilisation vanished without trace, until digging revealed the first of its lost treasures in 1925. Its disappearance is almost certainly linked with the rise of the sixth major Indian population group, the Nordics, normally known, from their Indo-European languages, as the Aryans. Though some still argue that these were of local origin, they were most probably invaders from Bactria and northern Iran who had broken away earlier from the main nomad hordes in south Russia (see page 60). Their archaeological remains include Iranian funeral furnishings and copper hoards of a 'Caucasian' type, and their likely part in the destruction of Harappa and Mohenjo-Daro is underlined by early Vedic references to hostile, dark-skinned *dasas* (the original untouchables) living in the broken ruins *(armaka)* left behind by the great god Indra, in his role as Purandara, the breaker of cities.

The Vedas, which form the earliest Indian literature, consist largely of hymns to the Aryan gods, but together with the two enormous early Indian epic poems, the *Ramayana* and the *Mahabharata*, the *Rig-veda*, in particular, gives some notion, however selective and stylised, of life in the period from about 1500 BC to 450 BC.

At first the newcomers appear to have been hunters and herdsmen, tending cattle, which were already acquiring sacred attributes, and breeding the horses which, though unknown to the Harappan painters and sculptors, now figure frequently on the Painted Grey pottery characteristic of early Aryan settlements. Gradually they adopted the techniques of settled farming from the peoples they had conquered and particularly after the advent of iron in about 800 BC, they proceeded with extensive clearance of the forests then covering northern India. At the same time they evolved a complex and pervasive set of cultural institutions, which in many ways have shaped the sub-continent to the present day. Their language, Sanskrit, formed the basis for a literature as developed as the Greek and Latin to which it is closely related. Their metaphysical subtlety, expressed in the *Upanishads*, held the seeds of many later systems of religious thought. Their emphasis on sacrifice, and the crucial importance which they were already attaching to the notion of caste set fundamental social patterns, and at the same time created objectives of social reform, which have continued to shape life in India for almost 3000 years.

In the first phase of their expansion, down to c. 1050 BC, the Rig-vedic Aryans, with their horses and light chariots extended their domain from Suvastu (the Swat valley in Pakistan) to *Sapta-Sindhava*, the land of the Seven Induses. From then on they began to move steadily eastward towards the Ganges. Painted Grey ware has been found in quantity at the site of Hastinapur, a city largely washed away by a great Ganges flood in about 900 BC. As land clearance then spread eastward along the valley, the river became a natural trade highway. Ships and voyages figure in the *Rig-veda*, though the Aryans probably did not venture far on the sea. Probably after 800 BC they began to penetrate increasingly further south, and though the *Ramayana*'s epic account of their conquest of Sri Lanka, generally believed to be Ceylon, has never been archaeologically substantiated, they undoubtedly moved into the Deccan, which from now on became an ever-more important route between north and south.

The physical geography of India at this time dictated a different form of development for the hilly, much-fragmented lands which make up the southern peninsula. Where the great northern plains lent themselves to large-scale agriculture and the growth of substantial kingdoms, the relatively tiny communities of the south evolved their own highly autonomous forms of religious, political and economic life. Distinctive megalithic cultures grew up around Madras, Kerala and Mysore, while the seafaring peoples of the southern tip continued to cultivate the close maritime ties with the Middle East which had been severed, as far as northern India was concerned, with the eclipse of the Harappans.

From 600 BC to 450 BC the pattern of kingdoms and republics begins to emerge more clearly (see page 82). Archaeological evidence, largely based on pottery styles, suggests that the heartland of the Aryan peoples had by now moved east from the western Punjab to Kurukshetra and the Doab, and the texts refer to land as far eastward as Magadha. Painted Grey ware and the Black-and-Red ceramics of the eastern regions were giving way to a single Black pottery, extending throughout the Indo-Gangetic region. A culturally unified northern India was ready for her first empire, that of Chandragupta Maurya who may have met and been inspired by his contemporary, Alexander the Great.

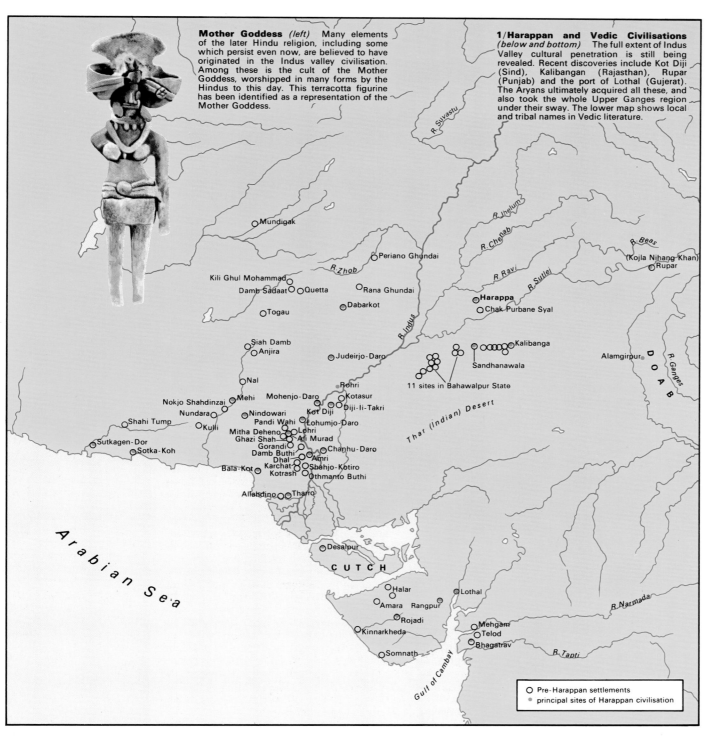

Mother Goddess *(left)* Many elements of the later Hindu religion, including some which persist even now, are believed to have originated in the Indus valley civilisation. Among these is the cult of the Mother Goddess, worshipped in many forms by the Hindus to this day. This terracotta figurine has been identified as a representation of the Mother Goddess.

1/Harappan and Vedic Civilisations *(below and bottom)* The full extent of Indus Valley cultural penetration is still being revealed. Recent discoveries include Kot Diji (Sind), Kalibangan (Rajasthan), Rupar (Punjab) and the port of Lothal (Gujerat). The Aryans ultimately acquired all these, and also took the whole Upper Ganges region under their sway. The lower map shows local and tribal names in Vedic literature.

○	Pre-Harappan settlements
●	principal sites of Harappan civilisation

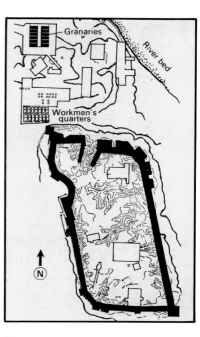

Harappa *(above)* and **Mohenjo-Daro** *(below)* are the first and most important discoveries of the Indus valley civilisation, the earliest developed urban culture on the Indian sub-continent. Excavations reveal an elaborate pattern of main roads at right-angles and houses opening onto narrow back alleys.

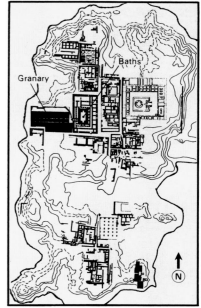

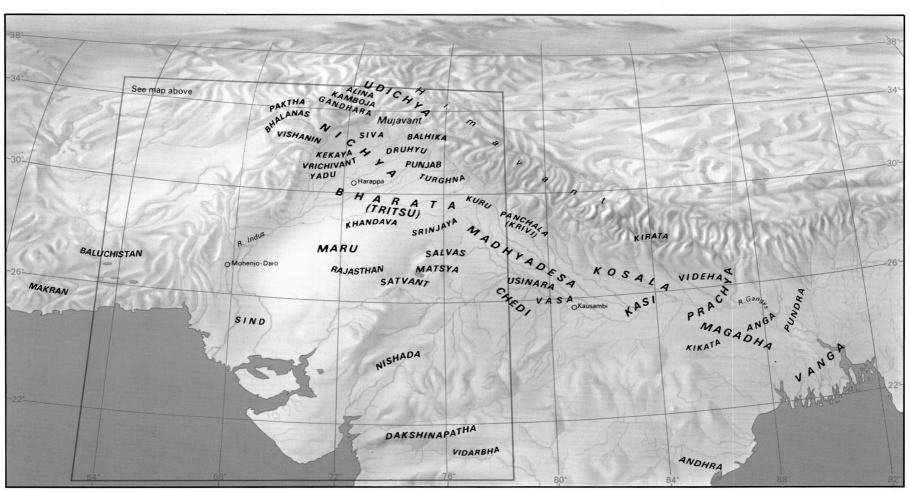

The early Mediterranean world c. 3000 to 1200 BC

THE island of Crete, mountainous but fertile, saw the rise of the first high civilisation on European soil. Until less than a century ago almost nothing was known about this civilisation. It has been named Minoan, after Minos, the legendary king of Knossos, which appears to have been from the first the chief city of the island. The Cretans learned to make tools and weapons of copper, and later of bronze, and evolved a system of writing. They were ruled by kings for whom they built spacious palaces; the goddesses whom they worshipped had sanctuaries on the tops of mountains and in caves.

The peoples inhabiting the mainland of Greece and the Aegean islands in early times were probably related to the Cretans in speech and race, sharing fashions of jewellery with them and using similar tools and weapons. But the development of civilisation there was arrested by massive invasions towards the end of the third millennium BC. The northern islands and most of the mainland were then overrun by relatively barbarous peoples from Anatolia. A century or so later, other invaders reached the Peloponnese from the north. These may have been the first Greeks; but the question of when the Greek language was introduced into Greece is much disputed, some believing that it originated in Greece itself in earlier times, others that it was brought by conquerors at the end of the Bronze Age, in about 1200 BC.

While the mainland languished after this period of invasions, the Minoan civilisation of Crete continued to develop, with exquisite pottery, superb gem-engraving, and decorative wall-paintings in palaces and houses.

This was evidently a period of flourishing trade. Egyptian stone vases, scarab seals and carved ivories found their way to Crete and were imitated there. Finely decorated pottery from Crete reached Egypt; some of it was recovered from the town of Kahun, built to house work-

4/Trade connections during the Neolithic and Bronze Ages *(below)* Much of the trade in the Aegean world was probably in raw materials. This has left few traces, apart from Spondylus shell, Melian obsidian, and large copper ingots of the distinctive ox-hide shape found throughout the eastern Mediterranean.

men and officials engaged in constructing a pyramid for one of the great pharaohs of the Twelfth Dynasty, Sesostris II (c. 1906-1888 BC). Much of the trade in these early times was no doubt in raw materials such as copper, and the tin required to mix with it to make bronze. Crete may have imported Egyptian linen, exchanging it for timber and for woollen cloth woven with colourful designs, as depicted in representations of the dress worn by Cretan men and women. The painted decoration on the ceilings of some Egyptian tombs from the time of the Twelfth Dynasty onwards seems to reflect the influence of imported Cretan textiles. Cretan fashions spread throughout the islands and eventually penetrated the mainland. Cretans had established a settlement at Kastri on Cythera some time before 2000 BC. In the 16th century BC Cretan settlers were established on Rhodes and at Miletus, and there were evidently Cretans living in Cycladic towns like Phylakopi (Melos) and Ayia Irini (Ceos). The islands and parts of the mainland may have paid tribute to Cretan kings, as later Greek legend hints in the story of Theseus and the exploits of Minos and his sons. Mycenae became a leading centre on the mainland, and royal tombs (shaft graves) of native rulers there dating from the 16th century BC have produced treasures of gold, silver and faience, many of them made in Crete.

It is ironical that the finest products of the flourishing period of the Cretan civilisation should come from these graves of comparatively barbarous chieftains living on the fringes of the Cretan world. Among the treasures of the Mycenae shaft graves are many exquisite drinking cups of precious metal, produced in Cretan workshops or by Cretan artists living at the court of the Mycenaean rulers. The men in these graves were buried with vast quantities of swords and daggers, the hilts of which were often adorned with gold or precious stones. The majority of these weapons were of Cretan types, and may have been imported from Crete. The most richly ornamented were the daggers, with blades inlaid with gold, silver and black niello. The more elaborate of the surviving inlays are in the form

of pictures, one showing men armed with bows and spears and great body shields (made of ox-hide) combating lions, which certainly lived on the Greek mainland and may have existed in Crete at the time. Another dagger is decorated with scenes of cats pursuing water fowl by silver streams stocked with fish and flanked by papyrus flowers. The ultimate source of inspiration for the scenes on this dagger was Egypt, where cats were trained, like gun dogs are now, to help in fowling in the marshes bordering the Nile. The richly mounted weapons and exquisite gold and silver vessels of the Mycenae shaft graves form a striking contrast to the barbaric splendour of most of the jewellery and of the gold masks placed over the faces of some of the dead, all clearly of local native workmanship.

About 1500 BC the flourishing settlements on the island of Thera were buried by a great eruption of the volcano there (as Pompeii was buried by Vesuvius in AD 79). Some fifty years after this, most of the important towns and cities of Crete were destroyed by fire. This havoc appears to have been the work of conquerors from the mainland, although the eruption of Thera has been falsely blamed for it. The conquerors may have been Greeks, if the system of writing afterwards found in use both in Crete and on the mainland has been correctly deciphered as Greek. This is still disputed.

Mainland fashions in pottery, architecture and burial customs now dominate Crete. In the 14th century BC a mixed civilisation, known as Mycenaean, and related to the Minoan as was the Roman to the Greek in later times, spread throughout the Aegean. Knossos appears to have been the only centre of government in Crete after the mainland conquest of c. 1450 BC, but eventually the palace there was destroyed, and the whole Aegean may have become a miniature empire ruled from Mycenae, although palaces at Tiryns, Pylos, and elsewhere suggest the existence of tributary kings. The story of the siege of Troy in Homer's *Iliad* may enshrine distant memories of these times.

Shortly before 1200 BC the palaces and walled citadels on the mainland were destroyed by fire.

'Ox-hide' copper ingots *(above)* This standard shape, fashioned as a convenient way of transporting raw metal, was flat, about an inch thick, and represented a load for one man carrying it on his shoulder.

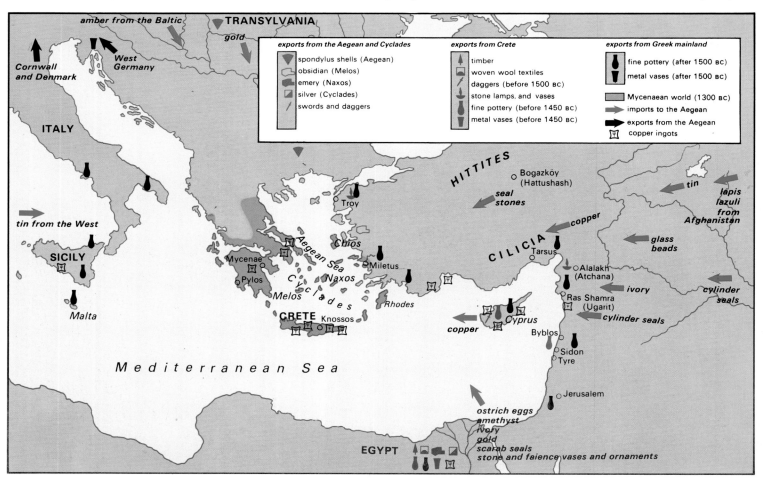

The destruction seems to have been due to invaders rather than to civil war or natural causes. Refugees from the mainland settled in Aegean islands like Naxos and Crete; some made their way as far afield as Cyprus and Tarsus in Cilicia. The invaders may have been Greeks, or a branch of them, the Dorians, traditionally the last to enter the Peloponnese from the north, or transitory migrants like the Sea Peoples.

About this time other Indo-Europeans, Armenians and Phrygians, poured into Anatolia from the Balkans, occupying Troy and destroying the Hittite empire with its capital at Bogazköy. Peoples expelled by them moved southwards, devastating Syria and settling there. Some, from coastal regions of Anatolia – the Sea Peoples of Egyptian records – took to their ships, occupied Enkomi in Cyprus and launched a grand assault on Egypt in alliance with the Libyans on her western borders, where they were defeated by the pharaoh Merneptah in 1232 BC. Some forty years later, Ramesses III overthrew another coalition of Sea Peoples, but some of them, notably the Philistines, afterwards settled on the coast of Palestine, which still bears their name.

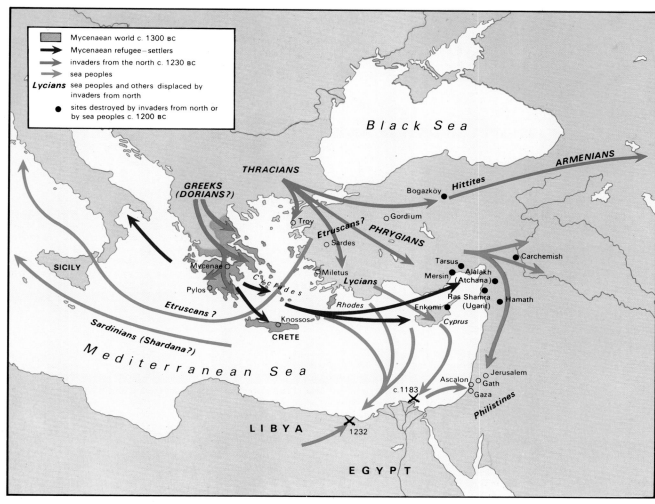

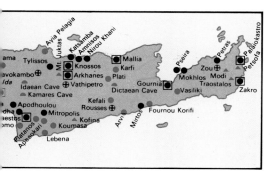

2/The island of Crete (above) Mountainous but fertile, and strategically placed in the centre of the eastern Mediterranean, Crete was the home of the first high civilisation in Europe. After a thousand or more years of undisturbed peace, it was conquered about 1450 BC by Mycenaean people from the Greek mainland, who had adopted many aspects of that civilisation.

3/Migrations in the eastern Mediterranean c. 1250 to 1150 BC (above) At the end of the Bronze Age barbarous peoples overwhelmed the Mycenaean and Hittite civilisations. Mycenaean refugees escaped overseas, while other groups, forced from homes in Anatolia and the Aegean, attacked Egypt and eventually settled in Syria, Palestine and the western Mediterranean.

1/The Aegean: main Bronze Age centres and movements of peoples c. 3000 to 1500 BC (below) Better supplied with water than today and relatively well wooded, with its genial climate and resources of olives, grapes and fish, the Aegean must always have acted like a magnet to peoples from less favoured regions. The pattern of invasions in the Bronze Age has been reproduced in historic times.

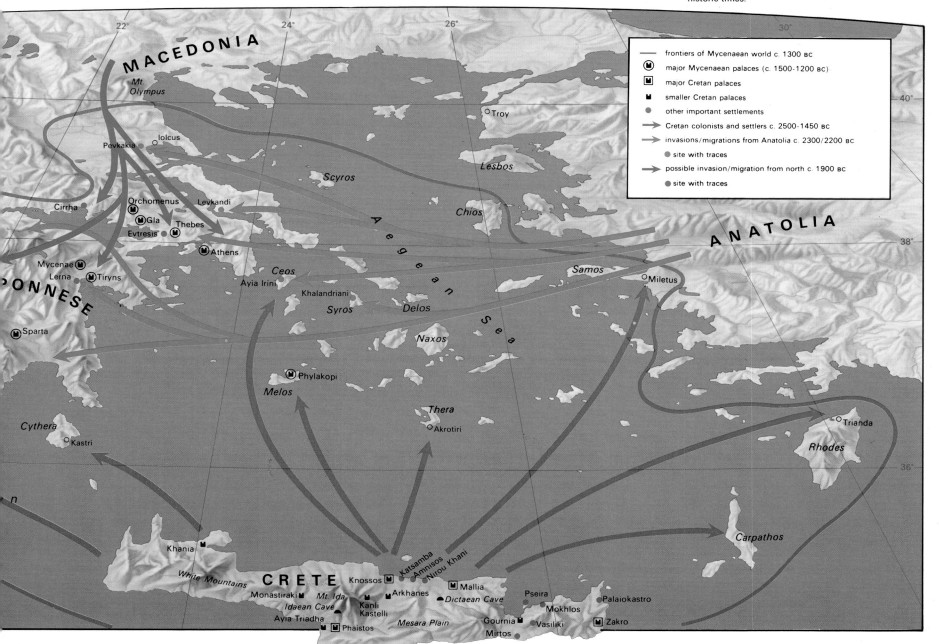

3 The classical

civilisations of Eurasia

The earliest civilisations had arisen at a few scattered points, like lighthouses in the night or oases in the vast uninhabited or sparsely inhabited Eurasian landmass. Between 1000 BC and AD 500 the pattern began to change. Although America, Australasia and Africa south of the Sahara still remained outside the mainstream of world history, and were to stay so for a further one thousand years, the civilisations of Europe and Asia now linked up in a continuous belt. By AD 100, when the classical era was at its height, a chain of empires extended from Rome, which encompassed the entire Mediterranean basin, via Parthia and the Kushan Empire to China, forming an unbroken zone of civilised life from the Atlantic to the Pacific.

This was a new and important fact in the history of the Eurasian world. The area of civilisation was still narrow and exposed to unrelenting barbarian pressures, and development in the different regions was still largely autonomous; but with the expansion of the major civilisations and the elimination of the geographical gaps between them, the way was open for inter-regional contacts and cultural exchanges which left a lasting imprint. In the west, the expansion of Hellenism created a single cultural area which extended over a period of time from the frontiers of India to Britain; in the east, the expansion of the Chinese and Indian civilisations resulted in something like a cultural symbiosis in Indo-China. These wider cultural areas provided a vehicle not only for trade but also for the transmission of ideas, technology and institutions, and above all for the diffusion of the great world religions. Beginning with Buddhism, and continuing later with Zoroastrianism, Judaism, Christianity and Islam, religion became a powerful unifying bond in the Eurasian world, with consequences that were political and cultural as well as religious.

The commercial and cultural bonds of Eurasia

FEW PEOPLE in the Near East, let alone in Europe, knew much about eastern Asia until the emergence of Achaemenid Persia in the 6th century BC (see page 78), and China itself remained almost unknown until shortly before the Christian era. But although there is little or no evidence of face-to-face meetings in the earlier centuries, it is clear that there were important influences and borrowings. Bronze was already giving way to iron in the west when it first appeared in China; and unparalleled technical excellence was soon achieved in the Shang and Chou kingdoms along the Huang Ho (Yellow River). Although the silk-moth was native to Assam and Bengal, it was in northern China that men first learned how to unravel a single, unbroken thread from its cocoon. Jade, the most prized material of the Chinese jewel-carvers, came from the western end of the arid and dangerous Tarim Basin. Wheat seeds originated in the west; water-buffalo and domesticated poultry in northern India; wet-rice cultivation was common throughout east and south-east Asia; cowrie shells, the first Chinese money, probably from the faraway Maldive Islands. All these, it seems, must have been first introduced by nomads and itinerant merchants from beyond China's traditionally self-contained borders.

Economic and cultural contact between the extremes of the ancient world reached its height in the 2nd century AD. Although Rome and Han China never established formal diplomatic relations, each was well aware of the other's existence. Goods flowed freely, particularly from east to west, and expensive and non-bulky goods like silk and spices could be transported by caravan or ship at a cost which was only a small proportion of their market value. In return, gold and silver, mostly in coins, moved in large quantities, both by land and by sea. Between the frontiers of these great classical civilisations, the Kushan Empire and the Parthian Empire of Persia both willingly fostered this trade, maintaining and garrisoning the roads, protecting the caravans and thriving on the tolls.

To the south, in the Indian Ocean, up to 120 substantial Greek ships a year plied between the Red Sea ports and India, exploiting the monsoon, while Arab ships traded from port to port along the north-west coast of India, the Persian Gulf, the incense-bearing shore of Arabia and the spice markets of Abyssinia and Somaliland. The Roman Empire exported glass, copper, tin, lead, red coral, textiles, pottery, and above all currency. The chief imports from the east were

Ferghana's 'Heavenly Horses' Ferghana was the homeland of the fabled 'heavenly horses' with which the Chinese were anxious to equip their cavalry as a counter to the agile ponies of the Hsiung-nu and other raiding mounted nomads north of the Great Wall. The fifth Han emperor Wu-ti sent emissaries and armies to subdue the nomad-infested areas of Sinkiang in order to control the source of these horses. China eventually received steady supplies of Ferghana stallions, and this painting from Tun-huang shows a Chinese official mounted on one of them.

Arabian incense, Chinese silk, and from India precious stones, muslin and spices, especially pepper. Other spices reached the Empire from the East Indies via Madagascar and East Africa. The main land route from the East entered the Empire via Nisibis and Zeugma. Caravans moving between the Empire and the Persian Gulf ports of Charax and Apologos were owned, organised and escorted across the desert by citizens of Palmyra. Until the city was destroyed in 273 Palmyra's role as a desert entrepôt earned it the wealth to finance spectacular public buildings. Further south, Petra performed the same function for the caravans travelling to and from the Red Sea ports of Leucecome and Aelana, and the Persian Gulf port of Gerrha. The most important entrepôt of all was Alexandria, a city of about 500,000 inhabitants which received the goods of the eastern trade from the Red Sea ports of Berenice, Myos Hormus and Clysma for shipment to all parts of the Roman Empire. It also exported its own manufactures: linen, processed Arabian drugs and Indian perfumes, papyrus, glassware and – vastly the greatest shipment of all – Egyptian grain, which helped to feed the population of Rome.

In the end the horse and the Bactrian camel were the means by which the central Asian steppes were opened up as a great commercial route. During Chinese efforts to control Sinkiang, the great general Pan Ch'ao, who held the northern and western oases against all comers, defeated a massive Kushan invasion from India in AD 90, led an army across the Pamir mountains to reach the Caspian, established contact with the Parthians and was only just persuaded, in AD 97, against sending an embassy to Rome.

By that time, however, regular caravans had linked the two mighty empires for almost 200 years. Few, if any, went straight through, but there were well-established change-over points where the Greek, Arab, Roman, Iranian and Indian traders of the west exchanged goods with the nomad merchants who undertook the middle stretches of the journey, handing over in turn to the Chinese at the further frontiers.

In the 2nd century AD these trade links were fully cemented when the Yüeh-chih and the Tocharians combined to create the vast Kushan Empire, extending from the northern half of India to include a great part of the central Asian landmass. Even under the Achaemenids, trade, roads and safe transportation had been matters of prime concern. Darius's Royal Road ran 1677 well-garrisoned miles from Ephesus to Susa; an even longer route linked Babylon with Ecbatana, and ultimately Ortospana (Kabul). The Seleucids maintained the tradition, with a major trading network across the Persian plateau, from Seleucia through Ecbatana and Merv to Bactra. When Bactria became independent (250-139 BC) it formed the junction for a web of caravan routes joining Siberia and China with India's great trading centre of Taxila and with Persia, the Red Sea, the Persian Gulf and the Mediterranean entrepôt cities such as Antioch and Alexandria. Great trading concerns centred in Bactria kept branches and agents in China. The Parthians under Tiridates (247-212 BC) deliberately transferred their capital to Hecatompylos on the caravan road from Seleucia to Bactra. Now the Kushans, with their 'thousand cities' of central Asia, completed the chain.

The chain did not hold for long. By the opening of the 3rd century AD all parts of the 2500-mile route from Syria to the Tarim were under pressure. The Chinese were driven completely from the Tarim Basin, cutting the major routes, and both Rome and China found themselves hard pressed by the barbarians to the north (see page 94). The demand for foreign products built up during the years of peace and security did not suddenly vanish, but increasingly it had to be met by the relatively unthreatened – and for

bulky cargoes very much more economical – sea route whose traffic had grown rapidly since the Greek pilot Hippalus discovered the monsoon, probably around 100 BC. Since then ships with a carrying capacity of up to 500 tons beat with the monsoon winds across to the Indian ports, Barbaricum at the mouth of the Indus, Barygaza further south and Muziris about 200 miles north of the southern tip of India. In winter the winds reversed and the Greek ships returned laden with the products of the east. The occasional Greek merchants may have gone further east than Muziris or Ceylon, but as a rule they did not, receiving Chinese wares from Indian merchants. The Chinese Empire now reached as far south as Haiphong; it is likely that Indians and Chinese met at Oc Eo in southern Cambodia. From there the Indians shipped the goods west, portaging them across the Malay Peninsula and the southern tip of India.

The development of the sea route greatly reduced the price of silk in the Roman world and significantly increased the use of eastern spices in Roman cookery. The volume of eastern trade no doubt fluctuated according to the internal conditions of the Roman and Chinese Empires and intervening lands. From time to time war between the Roman and Persian Empires interfered with the land route, while disorders among the Arabs might impede shipping along the coast of Arabia. From the 5th century AD the progressive takeover by barbarians of the Western provinces of the Roman Empire reduced – but did not end – the demand for eastern luxuries in those areas. The oriental provinces of the Empire remained prosperous until the end of the 6th century and the age of the Arab conquests.

trade routes from the Mediterranean used by Greeks, Phoenicians and Arabs with Roman permission

Persian trade

trade routes under Chinese control including nomad areas only intermittently under Chinese control

Kushan trade

Indian and other routes

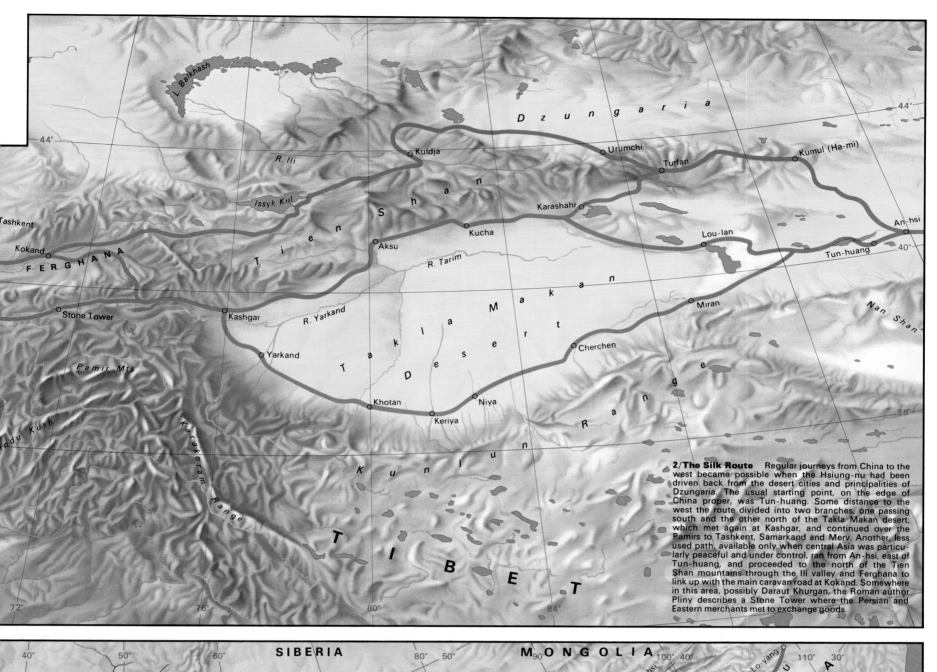

2/The Silk Route Regular journeys from China to the west became possible when the Hsiung-nu had been driven back from the desert cities and principalities of Dzungaria. The usual starting point, on the edge of China proper, was Tun-huang. Some distance to the west the route divided into two branches, one passing south and the other north of the Takla Makan desert, which met again at Kashgar, and continued over the Pamirs to Tashkent, Samarkand and Merv. Another, less used path, available only when central Asia was particularly peaceful and under control, ran from An-hsi, east of Tun-huang, and proceeded to the north of the Tien Shan mountains through the Ili valley and Ferghana to link up with the main caravan road at Kokand. Somewhere in this area, possibly Daraut Khurgan, the Roman author Pliny describes a Stone Tower where the Persian and Eastern merchants met to exchange goods.

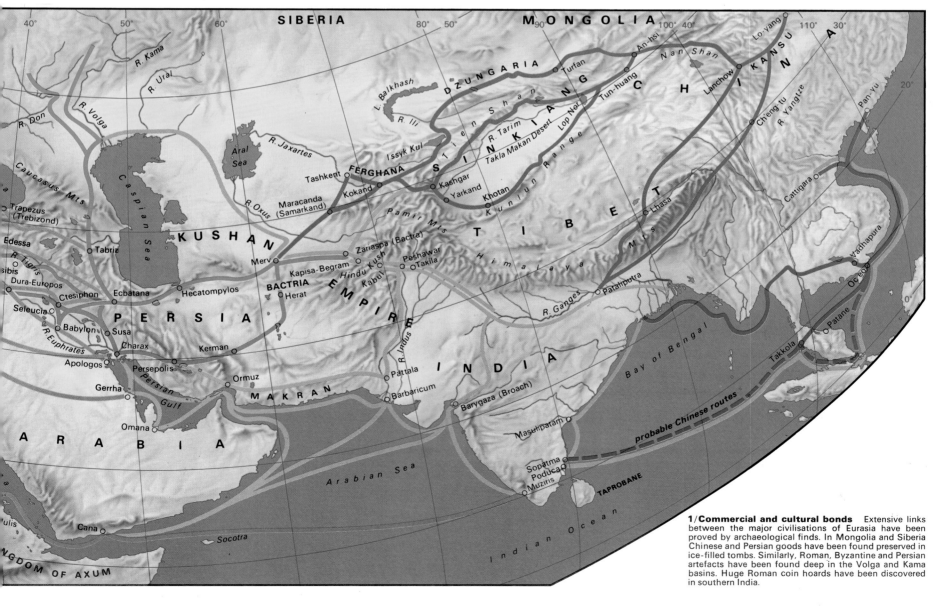

1/Commercial and cultural bonds Extensive links between the major civilisations of Eurasia have been proved by archaeological finds. In Mongolia and Siberia Chinese and Persian goods have been found preserved in ice-filled tombs. Similarly, Roman, Byzantine and Persian artefacts have been found deep in the Volga and Kama basins. Huge Roman coin hoards have been discovered in southern India.

The religious bonds of Eurasia
to AD 500

ALL the great world religions originated in Asia, and three of them – Judaism, Christianity and Islam – from a quite small area of western Asia. Equally noteworthy is the grouping of religious genius in different parts of the world in or close to the 6th century BC, an 'axial' age, as Karl Jaspers said. This was the period of Confucius and perhaps Lao-tzu in China and Zoroaster in Iran, of Gautama the Buddha in India, of the greatest of the Hebrew prophets, whom we call Deutero-Isaiah (*Isaiah* 40-59), and of Pythagoras in Greece. Possibly the emergence of civilisations which claimed to be universal called for the birth of universal religions; possibly the new religions were a response to tensions within the existing societies, and the need for a spiritual outlet and a religion which transcended a superstitious polytheism. There was a movement towards a belief in a single spiritual reality, at the same time as Greek thinkers were looking for a single principle to explain the material world. One aspect of this was the growth of monotheism.

The oldest of the world religions is Hinduism, although narrowly defined it is not a world religion at all. It is the religion of the people of India: 'Hindu' means 'belonging to the Indus'. It is comprehensive and enormously complex; it is a growth not a construction; it embraces vegetarianism and human sacrifice, asceticism and orgy, cults which express themselves in all the richness of external observance, and the devotion of internal meditation, the simplest beliefs of village folk and the abstruse ratiocinations of philosophers. Hinduism is not in any real sense a missionary religion. Buddhism, which began as a reformist movement within Hinduism, is one of the great missionary religions. Ironically, while its outreach has been so successful that it has spread over much of Asia, there are now virtually no Buddhists in India. Gautama, the Buddha (the title means 'Enlightened'), was an Indian prince who lived perhaps in the 6th and 5th centuries BC. He gave up his position in the Great Renunciation; six years later he received enlightenment under the Bo-tree. He attained Nirvana, obliteration of desire. The first great landmark in Buddhist history was the reign of the Indian emperor

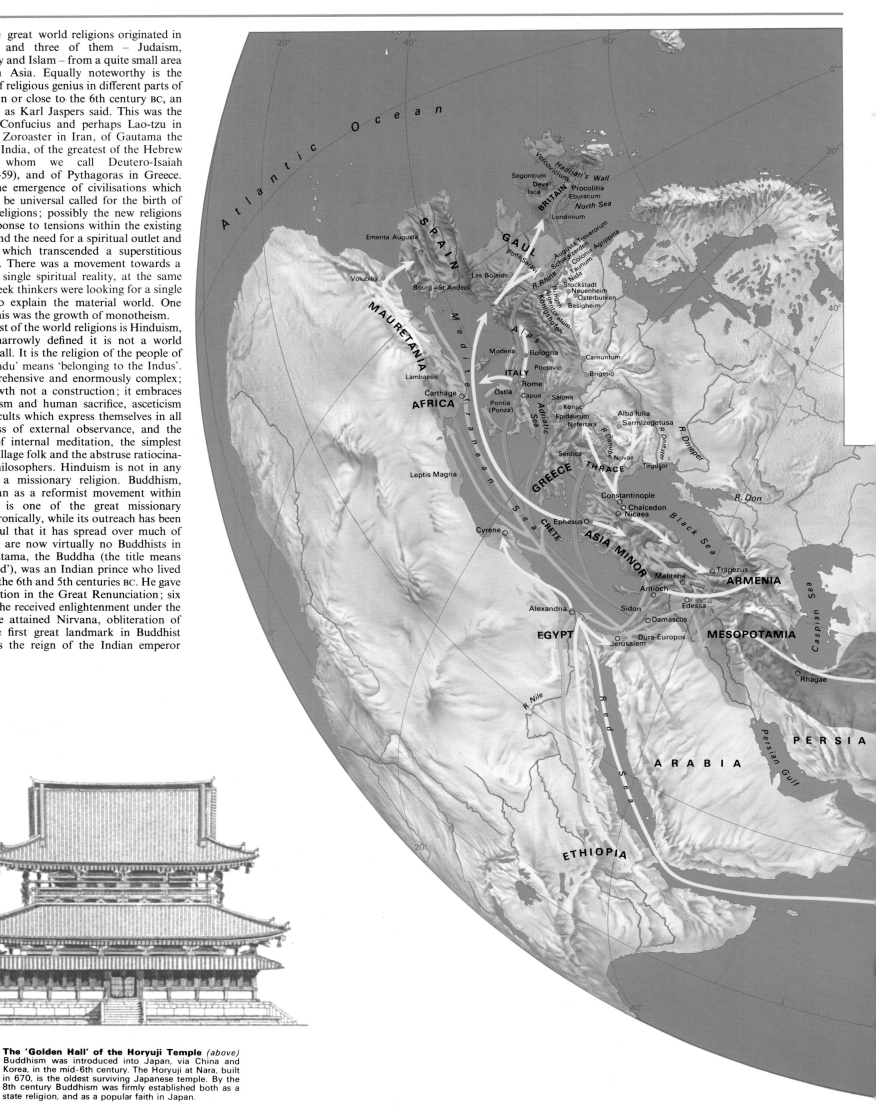

The 'Golden Hall' of the Horyuji Temple *(above)* Buddhism was introduced into Japan, via China and Korea, in the mid-6th century. The Horyuji at Nara, built in 670, is the oldest surviving Japanese temple. By the 8th century Buddhism was firmly established both as a state religion, and as a popular faith in Japan.

Asoka, 274-232 BC (see page 82). He was a convert, and after his conversion became a man of peace and high principle of a kind unusual in high places; his conversion stands in marked contrast to that of the Roman emperor Constantine to Christianity. Buddhism spread early to Ceylon and Burma, and reached China by the 1st or 2nd century AD, Korea in the 4th century, and Japan in the 6th century.

Buddhism is unusual among world religions in that it does not centre upon a god. Its message is one of deliverance from suffering through the annihilation of desire. This is the Doctrine which, with the Buddha and the Community, form the focal parts of Buddhism. There has been one great schism in Buddhism, which emerged five hundred years or so after the beginning: this is between the universalist Mahayana and the more conservative Theravada. The Theravada (also called Hinayana, but the name is insulting) is strong in Ceylon, Burma and Thailand; the Mahayana tended to have more appeal further east. Buddhism spread along the coast of southeastern Asia and also by the silk route through central Asia.

In China itself there were ancient traditions of ancestor-cult and the worship of spirits of nature. From about the 5th century BC two systems became dominant, at least among the upper classes. One was the ethical system of Kung Futzu or Confucius (551-479 BC). The other was the mystical religion of the Tao, associated with the shadowy figure of Lao-tzu. The Tao means 'the Way', the Way of the universe; man's call is to be in harmony with the Tao through the practice of quietude. These two, with Buddhism, constituted the 'three religions' of traditional China. In Japan, Buddhism challenged traditional Shinto and spirit-worship in the 6th century AD, and it was only towards the end of the Tokugawa era that Shintoism revived as the expression of Japanese national identity.

The Jews were a people, small in number, who by tradition moved from Mesopotamia to Palestine, and whose firm history began with their escape from oppression in Egypt under a leader named Moses. They attributed their escape to a divine being named Yahweh or the Lord, with whom they made a covenant that they would be his people and he would be their god, a covenant associated with the simple but profound moral demands of the Ten Commandments, the basis of the Torah or Law. They were an exclusive people, marked off by their foodlaws, circumcision, and other religious observances. The fact that Yahweh was a god who adopted them from outside had in it the seeds of universalism, and a succession of 'prophets' kept the challenge of ethical and religious righteousness before them. The Jews suffered continually from the political and military domination of others, and the consequent Dispersion carried them over much of the Mediterranean world and further east as well (see page 102). Later, as a result of Christian persecution, they spread still further.

Judaism gave birth to Christianity, which spread early over the Roman Empire and later still further afield (see pages 92 and 100). Islam too accepts the traditions of Judaism and Christianity, and sees Mohammed as standing in a line of prophets which includes Moses and Jesus. Islam was also to be a great missionary religion. In one direction it spread across North Africa, through Spain and into Europe; in another it reached India (see page 104).

One other world religion must be mentioned. This started in Persia, and is associated with the name of Zoroaster or Zarathustra, another shadowy figure. It sees life as a battleground between the forces of light and the forces of darkness, and is today represented by the comparatively small Indian sect of the Parsis. In the form of Mithraism it spread through the Roman

Empire, but was ousted by the growth of Christianity.

In addition, there are the tribal religions which never lasted as world religions. The Greek pantheon, adopted and adapted by the Romans, honoured a sky-god, Zeus (Jupiter), and other deities, each with a special function, who became identified with gods of conquered peoples. The Celts (whose priesthood, the Druids, was suppressed on a charge of human sacrifice), the Scandinavians (whose special gods Wotan, Thor and others provided English names for the days of the week), and Germanic peoples all had their own gods, as did Syrians and Nabataeans and the peoples of Asia Minor. The Egyptian goddess Isis was worshipped far to the west. In the end all these died out, although they have sometimes influenced the religions which superseded them, and their cult-practices sometimes survive today in other religions. It was the world religions which in the end provided the bonds that linked together areas of the world previously separate.

1/The diffusion of religions
(below) It is not surprising that there should be some association between the great world religions and the development of the great riverine civilisations of the Nile, Mesopotamia, the Indus and the rivers of China. But though the associations are there, and without these settled civilisations world religions might not have emerged, it was not the rivers alone which proved the nurse of religious genius.

Expansion generally followed the trade routes. Religions were exported through traders, soldiers, administrators, and by ordinary travellers, sometimes with a deliberate missionary purpose, naturally using the same routes. Buddhism spread along the coast of South-East Asia and also by the silk route through central Asia. The Roman and Chinese empires were points of attraction, and peaceable governments helped religious diffusion. Christian writers claim that the peace brought by Rome was providentially designed for the spread of Christianity.

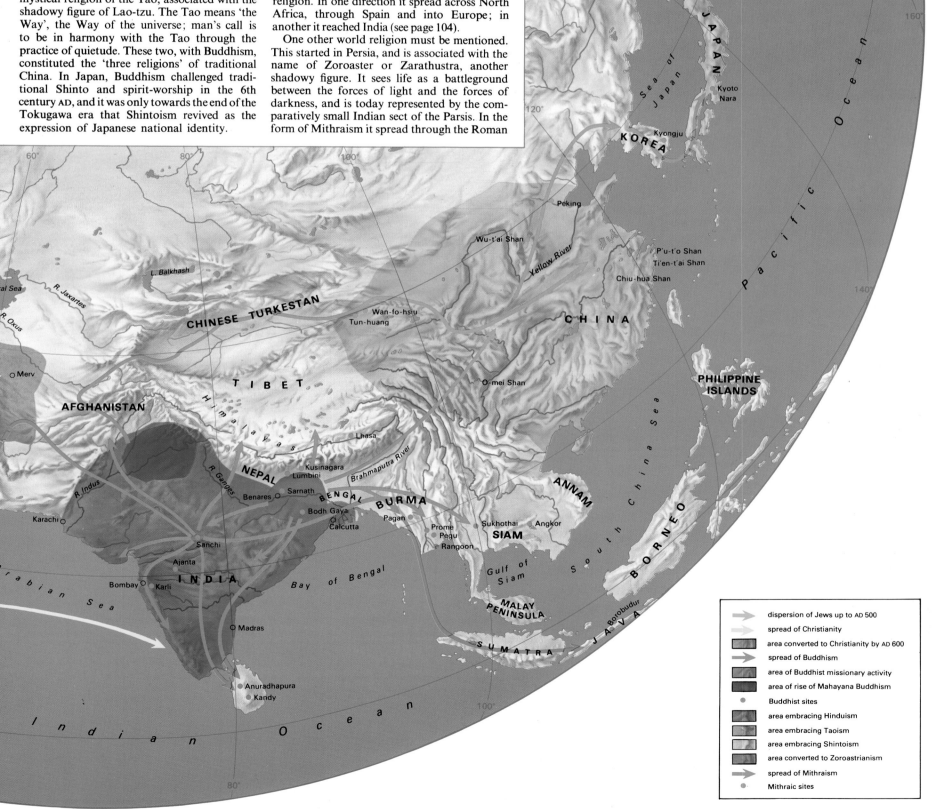

→	dispersion of Jews up to AD 500
→	spread of Christianity
▨	area converted to Christianity by AD 600
→	spread of Buddhism
▨	area of Buddhist missionary activity
▨	area of rise of Mahayana Buddhism
•	Buddhist sites
▨	area embracing Hinduism
▨	area embracing Taoism
▨	area embracing Shintoism
▨	area converted to Zoroastrianism
→	spread of Mithraism
•	Mithraic sites

73

The diffusion of Hellenic civilisation

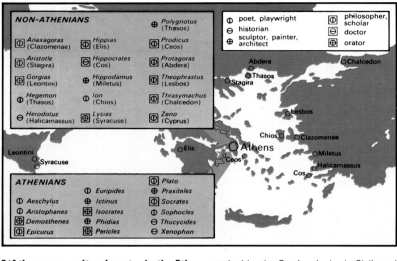
2/Athens as a cultural centre in the 5th and 4th centuries *(above)* From about 750 BC the Ionians in Asia Minor led the Greek world in culture; they were soon matched by the Greek colonies in Sicily and southern Italy. When they began to decline, Athens became, in the 5th century, the cultural centre of the Greek world.

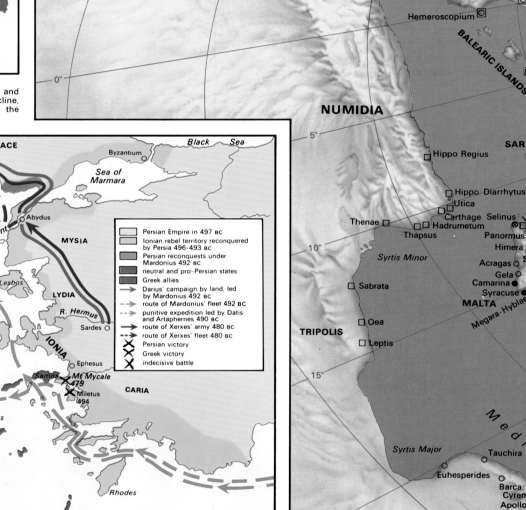

3/Greece and the Persian Wars 490 to 479 BC A Persian expedition against Athens in 490 was, incredibly, defeated at Marathon. Ten years later a massive Persian force was defeated by Athens, Sparta and other cities by sea at Salamis (480) and by land at Plataea (479). Argos and Boeotia were under Persian influence.

	Persian Empire in 497 BC
	Ionian rebel territory reconquered by Persia 496-493 BC
	Persian reconquests under Mardonius 492 BC
	neutral and pro-Persian states
	Greek allies
→	Darius' campaign by land, led by Mardonius 492 BC
→	route of Mardonius' fleet 492 BC
⇢	punitive expedition led by Datis and Artaphernes 490 BC
→	route of Xerxes' army 480 BC
⇢	route of Xerxes' fleet 480 BC
✕	Persian victory
✕	Greek victory
✕	indecisive battle

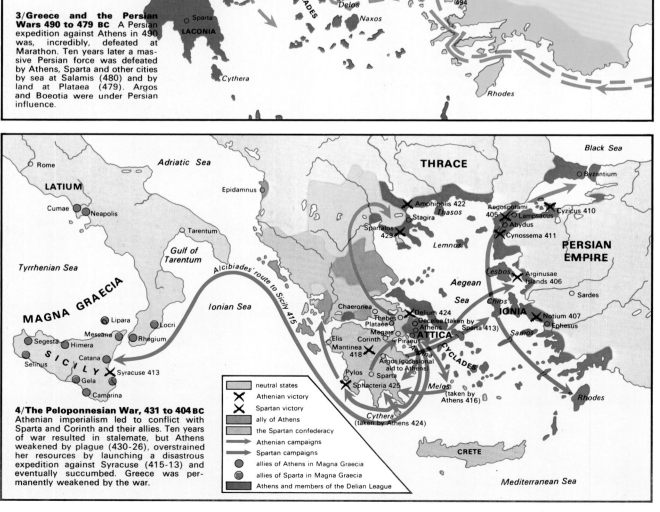

4/The Peloponnesian War, 431 to 404 BC Athenian imperialism led to conflict with Sparta and Corinth and their allies. Ten years of war resulted in stalemate, but Athens weakened by plague (430-26), overstrained her resources by launching a disastrous expedition against Syracuse (415-13) and eventually succumbed. Greece was permanently weakened by the war.

	neutral states
✕	Athenian victory
✕	Spartan victory
	ally of Athens
	the Spartan confederacy
→	Athenian campaigns
→	Spartan campaigns
●	allies of Athens in Magna Graecia
●	allies of Sparta in Magna Graecia
	Athens and members of the Delian League

THE key to Greek history is the *polis*, or city-state. The *polis* was a limited, independent, self-governing community which commanded the primary loyalty of its members. Its emergence was dictated by the facts of Greek geography. Greece, like Asia Minor, is a rough country, but all round the coast are comparatively small plains, separated from one another by mountain-barriers which might be impassable in winter and would be difficult to traverse at any time. These plains helped to form natural political units, often very small. Athens, for example, in her greatness with a total population of a quarter of a million or so, was far larger than any other *polis*; many would have numbered their people in four figures rather than five, let alone six. (Aristotle said that a *polis* of 100,000 citizens – free, adult males – would cease to be a *polis*.) In the settlements of Asia Minor they protected themselves with walls; in Greece proper it sufficed for a long time to withdraw to a fortified citadel (*acro-polis*) in an emergency. Around the main centre were farms, hamlets and villages stretching as far as the mountains. The *polis* was both a political community and a religious one, as religion was, under one aspect, the life of the community.

The eighth century saw a new enlightenment. The technological development of iron-working no doubt contributed to the cultural change. Another factor was the alphabet, developed from Phoenicia. Alpha, beta, gamma are not Greek words, but come from Semitic terms for ox, house and camel. Perhaps the bardic tradition of oral poetry had its climax in the poems which go with the name of Homer, and which were preserved in writing. This was also the age of the great vases decorated with systematic geometric patterns. It was the age of a dawning consciousness that these city-states were united by a common blood, a common language, a common culture and a common religion. Throughout Greek history there is a tension between the ideal of panhellenism and the divisiveness of the *polis*. Among the forces expressing unity the Olympic Games and the Delphic Oracle, both acknowledged and respected by the whole Greek-speaking world, now appear.

The eighth century also saw the beginning of two hundred years of colonial expansion, encouraged by land-hunger, political disaffection, or the desire for adventure or profit. These were not colonies in the modern sense; they were independent of the mother city, and although there was exploitation of natives it was on a much smaller scale than the land-grabbing of the nineteenth century. The main colonising cities were few in number: Eretria and Chalcis in Euboea, Corinth and Megara on the central neck of Greece, Miletus in Asia Minor, Rhodes. They founded settlements of lasting importance: Massilia (Marseilles), Neapolis (Naples, a colony of a colony, being founded from nearby Cumae), Syracuse, Byzantium (later Constantinople, and later still Istanbul).

These centuries saw new cultural forces especially in the eastern Aegean, at the meeting-point of influences coming up the coast from Egypt and Syria, overland from Mesopotamia and even India. One finds the development of legal structures; a new individualism, especially in poetry, of which Archilochus is the revolutionary forerunner and Sappho the supreme exponent; developments in vase-painting, at first with oriental motifs in bands, and then with black figures against red clay; the beginning of stone sculpture; the emergence of coinage developed in Lydia; and right at the end of the period the first steps to a scientific philosophy.

In general there was a well-marked pattern of political development. King was challenged by baron. The barons fell out among themselves and a discontented nobleman, perhaps with the backing of the power classes, might establish himself as dictator or 'tyrant'. Good dictators were followed by bad dictators, and revolution by counter-revolution. The fifth century BC saw the Greek world oscillating between oligarchs who wished the power to be confined to a relatively few, and democrats who stood for a wider and more radical extension of power. But democracy was only extended oligarchy: women, aliens and slaves had no political rights.

By the fifth century the situation had polarised into a confrontation between Sparta and Athens.

Sparta was an 'arrested civilisation'. It had retained its monarchy; power lay with a senate of two kings and twenty-eight elders, guided by five ephors or superintendents. Athens was a direct democracy, ruled by an assembly in which every citizen had the right to speak and vote, in which most of the offices were filled by lot from the whole citizen body, and in which a magistrate at the end of his year of office might find himself arraigned before a people's court.

At the beginning of the fifth century these two stood together to repel the forces of Persia. At the end they fought one another for the mastery of the Greek world in a bitter and bloody war which lasted twenty-seven years (431-404 BC); the story is told with incomparable power by the historian Thucydides. The war had arisen partly from fear and envy of Spartans and others, generated by the growth of the power of Athens, which had converted a free alliance of Greek maritime states into an Athenian empire.

Yet this century saw, especially in Athens ('the school of Greece' as her statesman Pericles called her) an unparalleled flowering of culture: the tragic drama of Aeschylus, Sophocles and Euripides; the comedy of Aristophanes; the historians Herodotus and Thucydides; the personality of Socrates; the marvellous 'red-figure' vases; the Parthenon; and the sculptures of Phidias and others. In the end it is for these achievements that Greece is of lasting importance. There is nothing else quite like it in human history – and Athens was no larger than Leicester or Miami.

The fourth century saw more jockeyings for power, with the shadow of Persia falling from the east. Plato and Aristotle produced their great metaphysical constructs, and tried to put the world back to the age of the city-state. Isocrates called vainly for the Greeks to unite. The unity which they would not find for themselves was forced upon them by the imperialistic power of Philip of Macedon. The battle of Chaeronea (338 BC) was the end of Greek liberty and the beginning, in some sense, of Greek unity.

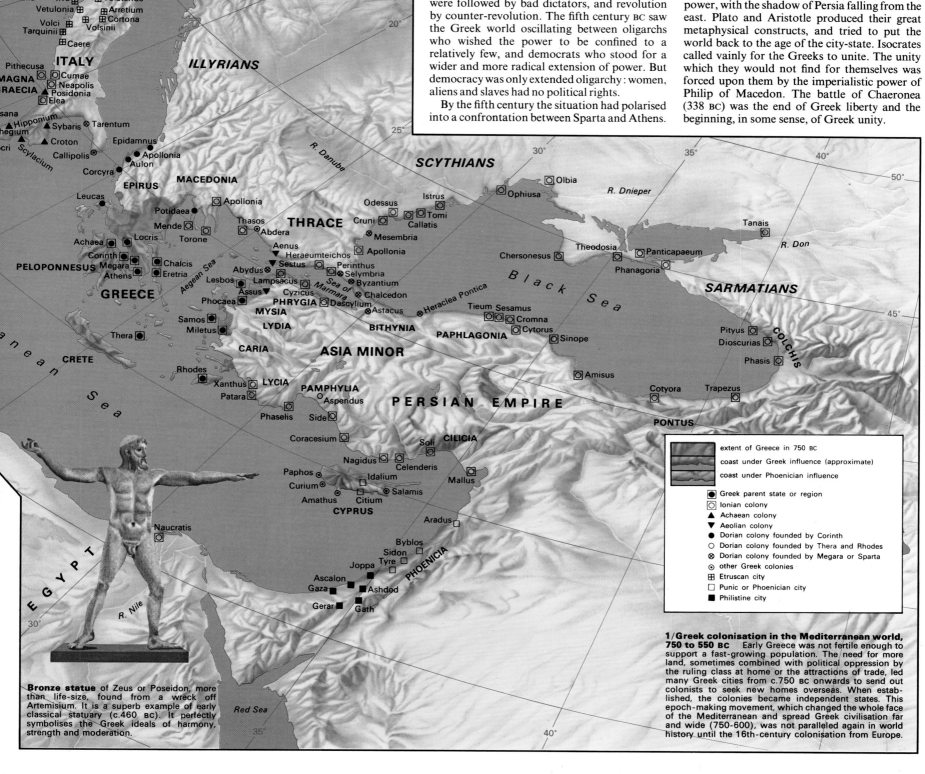

Bronze statue of Zeus or Poseidon, more than life-size, found from a wreck off Artemisium. It is a superb example of early classical statuary (c.460 BC). It perfectly symbolises the Greek ideals of harmony, strength and moderation.

	extent of Greece in 750 BC
	coast under Greek influence (approximate)
	coast under Phoenician influence
◉	Greek parent state or region
⊡	Ionian colony
▲	Achaean colony
▼	Aeolian colony
●	Dorian colony founded by Corinth
○	Dorian colony founded by Thera and Rhodes
⊗	Dorian colony founded by Megara or Sparta
⊙	other Greek colonies
⊞	Etruscan city
▢	Punic or Phoenician city
■	Philistine city

1/Greek colonisation in the Mediterranean world, 750 to 550 BC Early Greece was not fertile enough to support a fast-growing population. The need for more land, sometimes combined with political oppression by the ruling class at home or the attractions of trade, led many Greek cities from c.750 BC onwards to send out colonists to seek new homes overseas. When established, the colonies became independent states. This epoch-making movement, which changed the whole face of the Mediterranean and spread Greek civilisation far and wide (750-600), was not paralleled again in world history until the 16th-century colonisation from Europe.

The Hellenistic world 336 to 30 BC

ALEXANDER the Great transformed the Greek world by opening up for it the resources of the Middle East. In 334 BC he crossed the Hellespont from Europe to Asia, swept through Asia Minor, past Syria to Egypt, then east and south-east down the Tigris and Euphrates, pressing on into the heartlands of Iran and then through the Caspian Gates and the Hindu Kush to the neighbourhood of Bukhara and Tashkent. Here he retraced his steps, turned south into Kashmir and east again across the Indus as far as the Beas. He hoped to reach Ocean, the great mythical river which the Greeks believed to encircle the landmass of the world, but his troops would go no further. They turned back along the Indus to its mouth, and marched, with bitter sufferings, north-westward back to Persepolis and ultimately to Susa.

Alexander died in 323 BC, just before his thirty-third birthday. His mighty empire broke up between his warring generals; among them, three major powers gradually emerged. One, with its capital at Pella, was the old kingdom of Macedon, shorn of its Asiatic conquests but still dominating northern Greece, retaining a firm foothold in Greece proper and exercising substantial authority in Greek affairs, sometimes by diplomacy and sometimes by brute force. In wealthy Egypt, whose capital was now at Alexander's new foundation of Alexandria, an able soldier-historian named Ptolemy (Soter or Saviour) established a new dynasty and extended his interests into Palestine, where he confronted the third of the great kingdoms. Seleucus had been in authority in Babylonia; from there he extended his power over Syria and established a new capital at Antioch-on-the-Orontes, whence successive sovereigns named Seleucus, Antiochus or Demetrius ruled. These Seleucid kings, like Alexander earlier, founded many Greek cities within their realm. To this triumvirate of kingdoms must be added the breakaway Pergamum, which between 264 and 133 BC maintained an independence which came to overshadow much of Asia Minor, and further east the remarkable kingdom of the Bactrian Greeks who broke away from Seleucid control.

The new developments led to a diffusion of wealth and a great expansion of trade with east Africa, Arabia, India and central Asia, while to the east there was for the first time some commerce with China. To the west Pytheas of Marseilles sailed through the Straits of Gibraltar, circumnavigating Britain, laying the foundations for the Cornish tin trade, and probably reaching Norway and the river Elbe. Within the Mediterranean, silver flowed from Spain, copper from Cyprus, iron from the Black Sea coasts, corn from Egypt, North Africa and the Crimea, olive oil from Athens, dried fruit from Palestine, dried fish from Byzantium, linen, granite and papyrus from Egypt, woollen goods from Asia Minor, timber from Macedon, Asia Minor and the Lebanon, marble from Paros and Athens. Rhodes and Delos prospered as middlemen.

Alexander had flung back the horizons. The Greeks, with their new philosophies and religions, now found themselves members not only of a local community, the *polis*, but of *cosmopolis*, the whole civilised and increasingly Hellenised world. For a century, while Stoics and Epicureans alike proclaimed the brotherhood of man, and the more radical Cynics declared themselves citizens of the universe, the great post-Alexandrian powers maintained an often uneasy, but essentially stable equilibrium. Athens, seized by the Macedonians in the course of Chremonides' War (267 to 262 BC) remained an important cultural centre, but deliberately abdicated any further large-scale political ambitions. The main growth-points were now the newer capitals: Antioch, Pergamum, to some extent Pella, and above all Alexandria. Here the Museum, like the Library of Pergamum, formed an international

centre for higher learning and the arts. Here flourished the great 3rd century poets, Apollonius of Rhodes, Callimachus and Theocritus, and far-reaching advances in medicine, astronomy, mathematics, geography and science were made. It was the age of Eratosthenes and Archimedes.

Greece itself produced a variety of political experiments: different forms of confederation, particularly in the Achaean League, and the attempts by Agis IV and Cleomenes III in Sparta to establish an early form of communism before the regime was smashed by Antigonus Doson's Macedonians at Sellasia in 222 BC. To begin with, little of this disturbed the essential underlying balance, which lasted almost throughout the 3rd century. But with Rome's second war against Macedonia (200-197 BC) increasingly significant shifts began to develop, as rulers throughout the eastern Mediterranean were forced to adjust their policies to the rising might of Rome.

Roman imperialism was henceforth to be the crucial factor in the affairs of the Hellenistic kingdoms; but under the late Republic it grew only slowly. Direct annexation, except along the barbarian frontiers, was normally regarded as a policy of last resort, acceptable only when political aims could be achieved by no other means. Not until after 150 BC was there a single Roman governor or permanent army stationed east of the Adriatic. But other forms of intervention grew progressively more forceful.

Philip V of Macedon's provocative alliance with Hannibal in 215 had led to Roman military intervention in Greece which ended in 205 with the Peace of Phoenice, a treaty of mutual co-

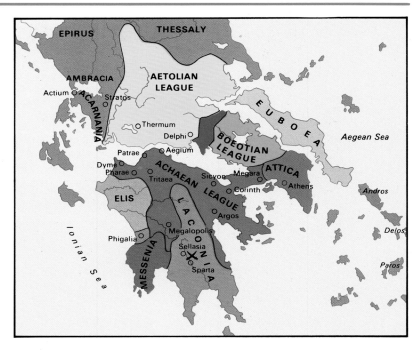

4/The Greek Leagues *(above)* Weakness in the 3rd century led to federalism. The Aetolians expanded their influence by force, while an Achaean League expanded by admitting non-Achaean members. Both Leagues were normally hostile to Macedon, but later Achaean hostility to Sparta led to reconciliation with Macedon whose king, Antigonus Doson, defeated Sparta at Sellasia (222 BC).

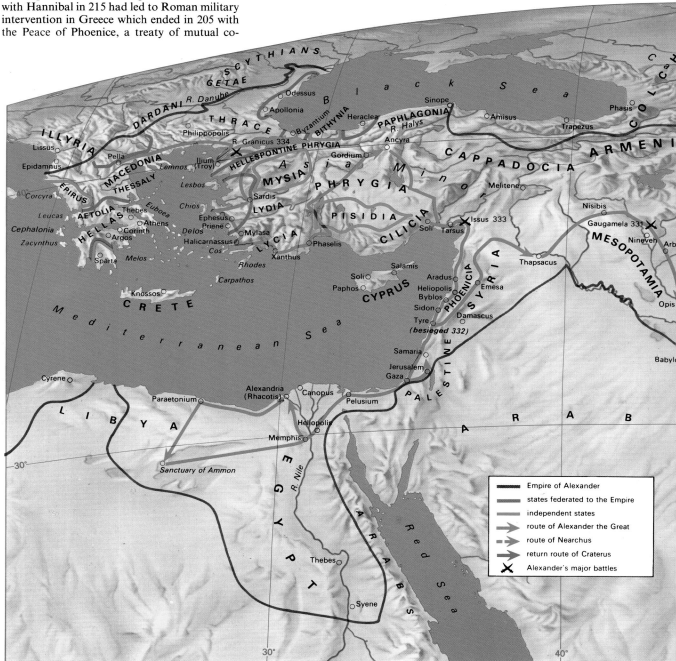

existence. But Philip's continued expansion, both into Greece, in the Aegean and along the Adriatic, brought retaliatory action, and a heavy defeat by the army of Flamininus at the Battle of Cynoscephalae. Shortly afterwards, in 190 BC, the greatest of the Seleucid monarchs, Antiochus III, after invading Greece was similarly humbled at the Battle of Magnesia, and stripped of his possessions in Asia Minor at the subsequent Peace of Apamea (188).

From then on, Rome had no serious rival in the Aegean and the Middle East. She could, and did, enhance the power of states like Pergamum and Rhodes and then, just as easily, break them. Even so, it took more than 150 years before the Hellenistic world fell fully under Roman control. Renewed Macedonian aggression, under Philip V's son Perseus, was decisively halted at Pydna (168) and the country divided into four independent territories; it only became a Roman province in 146, after further uprisings. The Seleucid Empire, weakened by internal conflicts and Parthian wars, was finally terminated by Pompey in 64 BC. Pergamum, unexpectedly bequeathed to Rome at the death of Attalus III (133), was only reluctantly accepted by the Senate; and Egypt, bestowed in an even more opulent gesture by Ptolemy Alexander I in 88 BC, was rejected outright. It was only after the defeat of Cleopatra VII, the last of the Ptolemies, at the naval battle of Actium in 31 BC, that Rome legally as well as effectively held the whole of Alexander's heritage in her hand. Long before that the framework of Greek civilisation had been irreparably broken; but its spiritual and intellectual legacy now permeated every aspect of Roman life.

1/The Empire of Alexander (below) The Macedonian conquests stretched to the limits of the known world and beyond, taking Hellenistic civilisation decisively beyond the Mediterranean and turning European minds and energies for the first time to the east; they probably also made it more vulnerable to the implacable Roman drive from the west.

2/The Hellenistic world in 240 BC (right) After two generations of war, the Ptolemies, the Seleucids and the Antigonid kings of Macedon had achieved a sustainable political and military balance. Athens had faded as a political force, but Pergamum, Rhodes, Delos, Pontus on the Black Sea were all independent rising powers, thanks not least to their commerce. Bactrian Greek rulers, breaking away from the Seleucid Empire (c. 240 BC) held Afghanistan (with parts of north-western India and Central Asia) for over a hundred years. The Parthians, whose era began in 247 BC, were beginning to build up their power, which was to stretch from the Euphrates to the Indus.

3/The Hellenistic world in 185 BC (right) With decisive victories over both the Macedonians (Cynoscephalae, 197 BC) and the Seleucids (Magnesia, 190 BC), Rome had established herself as the dominant force in the eastern Mediterranean.

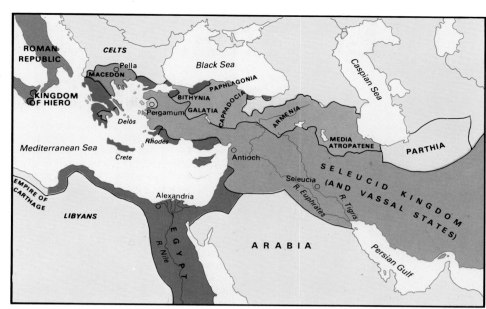

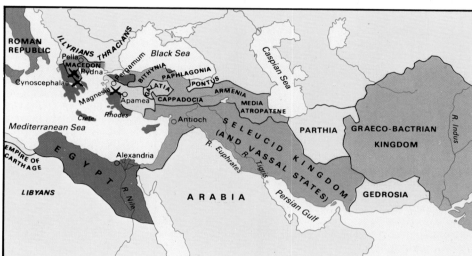

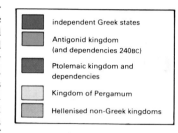

- independent Greek states
- Antigonid kingdom (and dependencies 240BC)
- Ptolemaic kingdom and dependencies
- Kingdom of Pergamum
- Hellenised non-Greek kingdoms

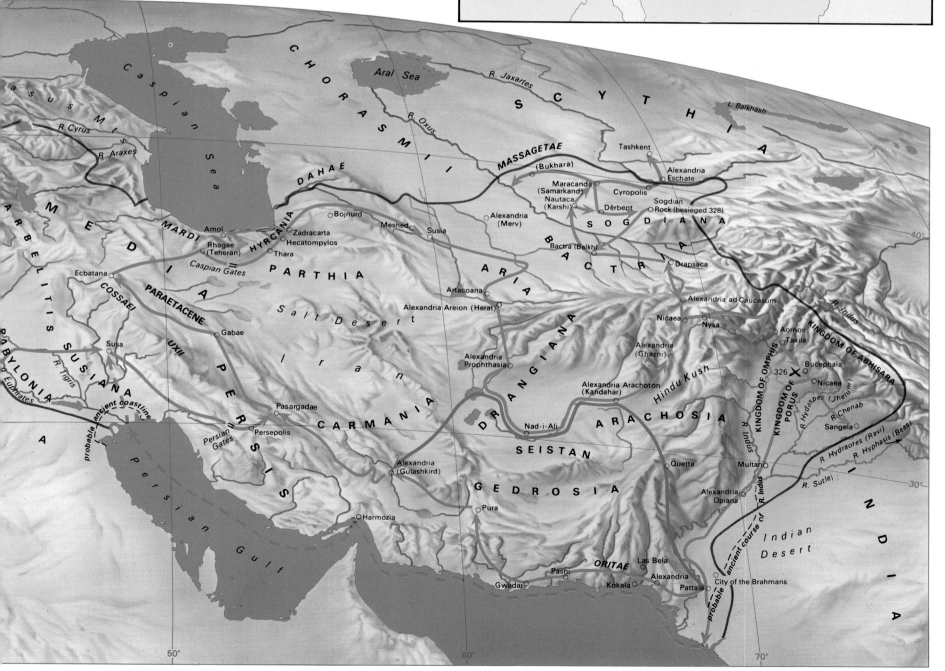

The Empires of Persia
550 BC to AD 637

2/The Persian Gulf *(above)* With the decline of the Seleucids in the 2nd century BC, the kingdoms of Characene and Elymais arose by the Persian Gulf. Here coastlines and rivers were continually changing. Lake Kataderbis disappeared after 300 BC, and Charax near the Tigris east bank was afterwards the main port.

AFTER the destruction of Assyria and the sack of its capital, Nineveh, in 612 BC, Babylon, one of the victors, retained the Mesopotamian lowlands, while the mountain country lying westward to the river Halys (modern Kizil Irmak) was incorporated in the kingdom of its allies the Medes. In 550 BC Cyrus, then Prince of Persia, rebelled, defeated the Median king, Astyages, and welded the Medes and the Persians together to make Iran the dominant power in Asia and the Near East. Its empire, enlarged by various successful military campaigns, soon incorporated Lycia, Lydia, the Ionian-Greek settlements of Asia Minor, Babylon and Afghanistan.

The Iranian peoples, newly arrived from central Asia, thus came to dominate the power centres of the Mesopotamian world. Their Iron Age technology, their ability to exploit the horse for communication and warfare, and above all their vigour and versatility, almost always gave them an edge over the forces of the more ritualised ancient civilisations. Soon after Cyrus's death, while one of his sons, Smerdis, held Iran, the other, Cambyses, defeated the last Egyptian pharaoh, Psamtik III, at Pelusium (525 BC). Later the brothers quarrelled, with fatal results, and a usurper seized the throne. But a cousin of theirs, Darius, led a group of confederates to restore the Achaemenid family line, reorganised the empire into twenty tribute-paying satrapies and established unified control, with a comprehensive code of laws, a stable currency and an efficient postal service. As organiser and financier Darius swiftly proved himself as great a genius as his uncle Cyrus had been in military affairs. His administration laid stress on regular, equitable taxes, accurate weights and measures and soundly cautious monetary policies. The Iranians' essentially ethnic religion, Zoroastrianism, sought no converts. So that tolerance, whether for Judaism or for the various Greek, Babylonian and Egyptian forms of polytheism, encouraged both communal harmony and loyalty to the king. Martial traditions, artistic sensibility and technical awareness, especially in engineering, all contributed to Iranian success, while an unshakeable national consciousness and an unusual respect for monarchic legitimacy helped the culture to survive the repeated invasions made inevitable by its position on the Asian landbridge.

This strength was soon put to the test. Darius's military enterprises were less uniformly successful than his administrative reforms. He was repulsed by the Scythians of the Ukraine in 513 BC, and his attempts to punish Athens and Eretria for their support of the rebellious Ionians led to a brusque defeat at Marathon in 490 BC. A massive invasion of Greece by his son Xerxes was similarly beaten off, both by sea at Salamis (480 BC) and by land at Plataea the following year. Persia itself remained impregnable to the Greeks for almost another century. Its weak-

nesses were revealed when Cyrus the Younger, the Iranian viceroy in the west, recruited a force of Greek mercenaries, the Ten Thousand, to revolt against his brother, the Emperor Artaxerxes II, in 401 BC. The knowledge gained attacking Babylonia paved the way for the later, devastating onslaughts of Alexander of Macedon, whose destruction of the Persian army at Gaugamela (331 BC) finally brought the Achaemenid rule to its end.

After the break-up of Alexander's own empire (see page 76) Iran became part of the Seleucid kingdom, as it remained, apart from the appearance of the local dynasty in the region of Persis, until 247 BC. In that year Ptolemy III of Egypt invaded Syria and claimed sovereignty as far east as Bactria. The nomad Parthians on the northern borders took advantage of the resulting upheaval to tear the whole territory of Parthia and Hyrcania away from Seleucid allegiance. Further east, Diodotus, satrap of Bactria, also declared independence, and founded the Graeco-Bactrian kingdom. Valiant efforts by the restored Seleucids, notably Antiochus III the Great, in 208 BC to suppress the Parthians and Graeco-Bactrians achieved little lasting effect, and finally, in 141 BC, Mithridates I of Parthia reversed the situation and entered Seleucia.

Ten years later, however, the situation on Iran's eastern frontiers drastically changed. The Yüeh-chi nomads, or Tocharians, driven back by Huns, clashed with the Scythians, beyond the river Jaxartes. The latter then destroyed the Graeco-Bactrian kingdom on their way southward to the Punjab. The Tocharians followed more slowly, by way of northern Afghanistan, sweeping away remaining Hellenic outposts. The brief period of Indo-Parthian dominance in Taxila, the great trading city of north India, was itself ended in AD 60 with the rise of the Tocharians' mighty Kushan Empire.

In the west, the Parthian borders soon marched with Rome on the Euphrates. Invasions by the elsewhere almost invincible legions were unsuccessful, for Parthia was the only major state consistently to withstand Roman power. In 53 BC the army of Crassus was destroyed at Carrhae by the relatively modest cavalry forces of a Parthian regional commander. Mark Antony, in 36 BC, led a formidable army from Armenia to Azerbaijan (Atropatene) but quickly got into difficulties and could barely extricate the survivors of his force. Augustus, seeking better relations, effectively accepted the Euphrates boundary line, and later emperors in the main limited their intervention to dynastic intrigues. It was only in AD 114 that Trajan, exploiting a moment of Parthian weakness, formally annexed Armenia as a Roman province. He then advanced down the Euphrates and Tigris to take Seleucia and reach the Persian Gulf. In AD 165, the general Avidius Cassius again sacked Seleucia and also Ctesiphon before being forced to retreat at an attack of smallpox. This feat was repeated by Septimius Severus in AD 198, but such incursions had little lasting effect. The real threat was internal, and came to a head in about 224 when Ardashir Papakan, Prince of Persia and founder of the Sasanian dynasty, defeated his Parthian overlord, Artabanus (Ardavan) V, at Hormizdagan, north of Isfahan.

The new king replaced Parthian feudalism with a highly centralised administration and reorganised the vassal kingdoms (Characene, Elymais, etc.) as provinces, each governed by a Sasanian prince. He crushed the Kushan state to the east. His son Shapur pushed the Asiatic frontiers back as far as Tashkent and Peshawar. Immediately on his accession in 244, Shapur repelled an invasion by the Roman Gordian III near Meshik on the Euphrates, grandiloquently renaming the place Peroz Shapur. In 253 he smashed a second Roman army at Barbalissus, higher up the Euphrates, and

finally, in 259, defeated and captured the Roman emperor Valerian at Edessa. Annexing Oman on the Arabian shores of the Gulf, he firmly established Sasanian Iran as the strongest power of late antiquity, with an elaborate and efficient bureaucracy, a powerful state religion, Zoroastrianism, and a strong tradition of craftsmanship, especially in the weaving of silk, now widely imported from China.

The peak of Sasanian power and prosperity was reached under Khosrau I Anohshirvan (531-79) when he invaded Syria, captured Antioch and deported its famous metal-workers to his own lands. But his son, Khosrau II Parviz (590-628), over-reached himself. Invading the Byzantine Empire, capturing Jerusalem, overrunning Anatolia and Egypt, and camping on the Bosphorus facing Constantinople, he was forced to retreat when the Byzantine emperor Heraclius outflanked him and sacked his favourite residence at Dastagerd.

Peace came too late for the two empires, for both quickly fell victim to the newly-emergent forces of Islam (see pages 104 and 112). The Arabs scored significant victories at Dhu Qar (c. 611), in the 'Battle of the Chains' and at Ullais, near the Euphrates (633), but the decisive action was at Al Qadisiya (637), when they smashed the Persians' metropolitan army and captured the capital, Ctesiphon. Yezdagird III, the last Sasanian king, fled to the Zagros, but further Arab victories at Jalula (637) and Nehavend (642) opened the road to the main Iranian plateau. Within a few years the Muslim armies reached the Oxus, and Iran became part of the Islamic world-empire.

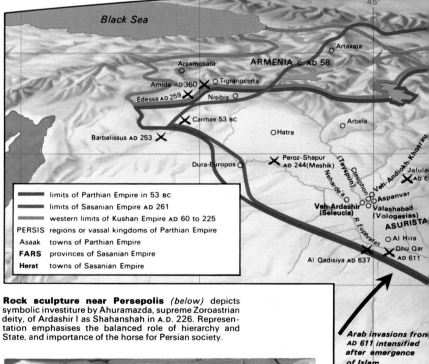

limits of Parthian Empire in 53 BC
limits of Sasanian Empire AD 261
western limits of Kushan Empire AD 60 to 225
PERSIS regions or vassal kingdoms of Parthian Empire
Asaak towns of Parthian Empire
FARS provinces of Sasanian Empire
Herat towns of Sasanian Empire

Rock sculpture near Persepolis *(below)* depicts symbolic investiture by Ahuramazda, supreme Zoroastrian deity, of Ardashir I as Shahanshah in A.D. 226. Representation emphasises the balanced role of hierarchy and State, and importance of the horse for Persian society.

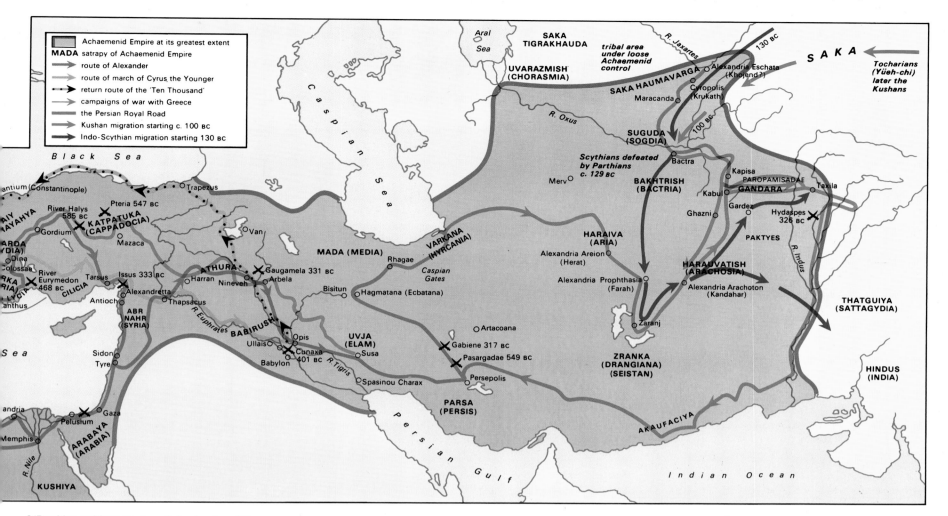

1/The Achaemenid Empire

Legend:
- Achaemenid Empire at its greatest extent
- **MADA** satrapy of Achaemenid Empire
- route of Alexander
- route of march of Cyrus the Younger
- return route of the 'Ten Thousand'
- campaigns of war with Greece
- the Persian Royal Road
- Kushan migration starting c. 100 BC
- Indo-Scythian migration starting 130 BC

Black Sea

Caspian Sea

Aral Sea

SAKA TIGRAKHAUDA

UVARAZMISH (CHORASMIA)

tribal area under loose Achaemenid control

SAKA HAUMAVARGA

130 BC

SAKA

Tocharians (Yüeh-chi) later the Kushans

Alexandria Eschata (Khojend?)

Cyropolis (Krukath?)

Maracanda

100 BC

R. Jaxartes

R. Oxus

SUGUDA (SOGDIA)

Scythians defeated by Parthians c. 129 BC

Bactra

BAKHTRISH (BACTRIA)

Merv

Kapisa

PAROPAMISADAE

GANDARA

Kabul

Taxila

Ghazni

Gardez

Hydaspes 326 BC

HARAIVA (ARIA)

Alexandria Areion (Herat)

PAKTYES

R. Indus

Alexandria Prophthasia (Farah)

HARAUVATISH (ARACHOSIA)

Alexandria Arachoton (Kandahar)

THATGUIYA (SATTAGYDIA)

antium (Constantinople)

Trapezus

Pteria 547 BC

River Halys 585 BC

KATPATUKA (CAPPADOCIA)

Gordium

Mazaca

Van

MADA (MEDIA)

Rhagae

VARKANA (HYRCANIA)

Caspian Gates

Bisitun

Hagmatana (Ecbatana)

Zaranj

ZRANKA (DRANGIANA) (SEISTAN)

HINDUS (INDIA)

ARDA (YDIA)

Dipa

Colossae

River Eurymedon 468 BC

Tarsus

Issus 333 BC

CILICIA

Alexandretta

Antioch

Thapsacus

ATHURA

Harran

Nineveh

Gaugamela 331 BC

Arbela

R. Euphrates

ABR NAHR (SYRIA)

BABIRUSH

Ullais

Opis

Cunaxa 401 BC

Babylon

R. Tigris

UVJA (ELAM)

Susa

Spasinou Charax

Artacoana

Gabiene 317 BC

Pasargadae 549 BC

Persepolis

PARSA (PERSIS)

Persian Gulf

AKAUFACIYA

Indian Ocean

Sidon

Tyre

andria

Pelusium

Gaza

ARABAYA (ARABIA)

Memphis

R. Nile

KUSHIYA

1/The Achaemenid Empire *(above)* The Medes and Persians were Indo-European peoples from central Asia. The centre of the Medes was founded at Ecbatana, and after the sack of Nineveh in 612 they became the chief power in the East. Their cousins the Persians moved southwards to Fars province (originally Parsa), and won the leadership under Cyrus the Great (550) who extended the rule of his line from the Aegean to the Indus. Under his successors the Empire flourished mightily until 330 BC, when Alexander the Great burnt its capital, Persepolis, to the ground.

3/Parthian and Sasanian Iran *(below)* From 247 BC when the nomad Parthians rose, under their chieftain Arsaces, and seized the Seleucid town of Nisa (Mihrdadkert), until AD 635, when the Arabs clinched their final victory. Iran, though often under attack, remained one of the richest and most powerful regions of the ancient world. The Parthians embraced the whole area from the Euphrates to northern India, but gave way, in AD 224, to the Sasanians, a Persian dynasty which only succumbed to the forces of Islam after fighting almost to the death with Byzantium.

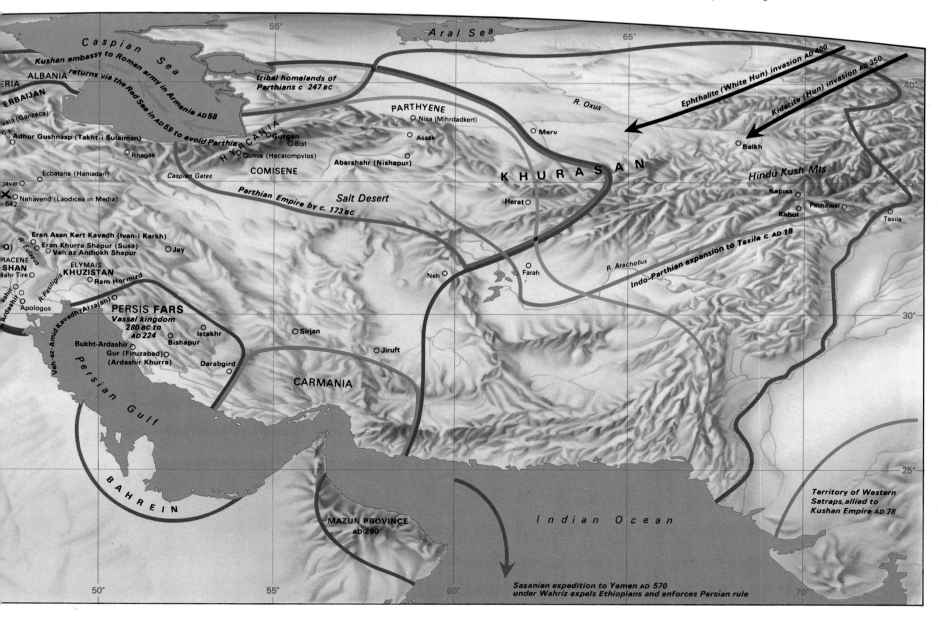

Caspian Sea

Aral Sea

Kushan embassy to Roman army in Armenia AD 58 returns via the Red Sea in AD 59 to avoid Parthia

ALBANIA

ERBAIJAN

ata (Ganzaca)

Adhur Gushnasp (Takht-i Sulaiman)

Rhagae

Ecbatana (Hamadan)

javar

Nehavend (Laodicea in Media) 642

Eran Asan Kert Kavadh (Ivan-i Karkh)

Eran Khurra Shapur (Susa)

Veh az Andiokh Shapur

Jay

ELYMAIS KHUZISTAN

Nahr Tire

Ram Hormizd

SHAN

Ardashir

Apologos

Veh az Amid Kavadh (Arrajan)

Bukht-Ardashir

Gur (Firuzabad) (Ardashir Khurra)

PERSIS FARS

Vassal kingdom 280 BC to AD 224

Istakhr

Bishapur

Darabgird

Persian Gulf

BAHREIN

MAZUN PROVINCE AD 260

tribal homelands of Parthians c 247 BC

PARTHYENE

Nisa (Mihrdadkert)

HYRCANIA

Gurgan

Asaak

Bist

Qumis (Hecatompylos)

COMISENE

Abarshahr (Nishapur)

Caspian Gates

Parthian Empire by c. 173 BC

Salt Desert

R. Oxus

Merv

KHURASAN

Ephthalite (White Hun) invasion AD 400

Kidarite (Hun) invasion AD 350

Balkh

Hindu Kush Mts

Kapisa

Kabul

Peshawar

Taxila

Herat

R. Arachotus

R. Euphrates

Parthian Empire c. 173 BC

Neh

Farah

Indo-Parthian expansion to Taxila c AD 18

Sirjan

Jiruft

CARMANIA

Indian Ocean

Territory of Western Satraps, allied to Kushan Empire AD 78

Sasanian expedition to Yemen AD 570 under Wahriz expels Ethiopians and enforces Persian rule

55° 65° 40°

35°

50° 55° 60° 70°

30°

25°

The unification of China
350 BC to AD 220

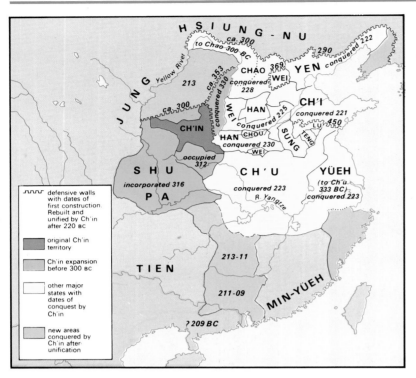

THROUGHOUT the Warring States period (403-221 BC) seven major states contended for supremacy. At first the main contenders were the old-established kingdoms of Ch'i, Ch'u, Han and Wei. Later (328-308 BC) the north-western border state of Ch'in established firm control over the north-west and west, and during the latter half of the 3rd century gradually destroyed its rivals to become master of all China in 221 BC. This was a period of constant warfare, waged on a massive scale by powerful and well-organised kingdoms which began to replace the old feudal social order with a centralised administration staffed by bureaucrats rather than hereditary nobles. They developed effective legal and fiscal systems to provide for their armies and public works.

Their emergence coincided with major economic and social changes. The introduction of iron tools from about 500 BC and the use of

1/The Warring States and the unification of China (left) Ch'in became a serious contender for supremacy over the other major states after her expansion and consolidation in the north-west and west from 328 to 308 BC. Later, the other states were eliminated until in 221 BC Ch'in controlled all China. Under Shih Huang-ti the Ch'in expanded its territories to the far south and north-east.

animal power for cultivation greatly increased agricultural productivity. The large-scale new states could undertake massive drainage and irrigation projects to bring much new land into cultivation. In these new lands a new social order arose, breaking away from the tight village community of the past. Population multiplied. Commerce and industry flourished as the states built roads and large cities emerged. It was a period of innovation in every field: in technology, science and government. There was a philosophical ferment, in which the main streams of Chinese thought, Confucianism, Taoism and Legalism, all took shape.

In the victorious state of Ch'in the old feudal aristocracy was abolished, and replaced by a rigid centralised bureaucracy. The population was organised in groups of families bearing mutual responsibility, and regimented to provide manpower for construction works and for the army. The new system was enforced through a savage penal code. When the first Ch'in emperor, Shih Huang-ti, unified China, these institutions were extended throughout the country. Although he ruthlessly eliminated all hostile factions, the burdens imposed on the people by his campaigns and vast construction works combined with surviving regional tensions to bring about the

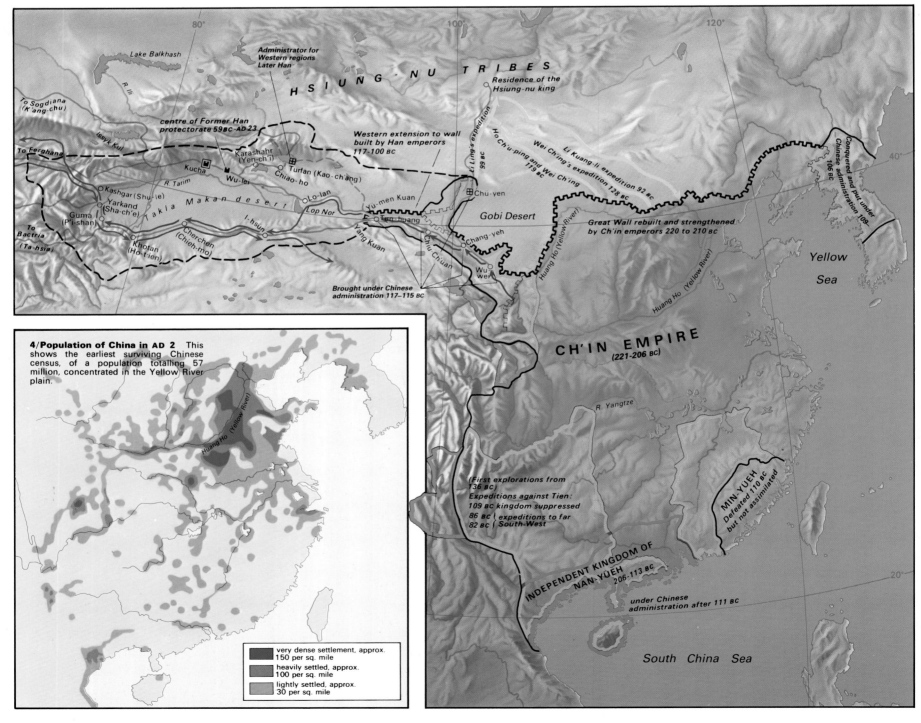

4/Population of China in AD 2 This shows the earliest surviving Chinese census, of a population totalling 57 million, concentrated in the Yellow River plain.

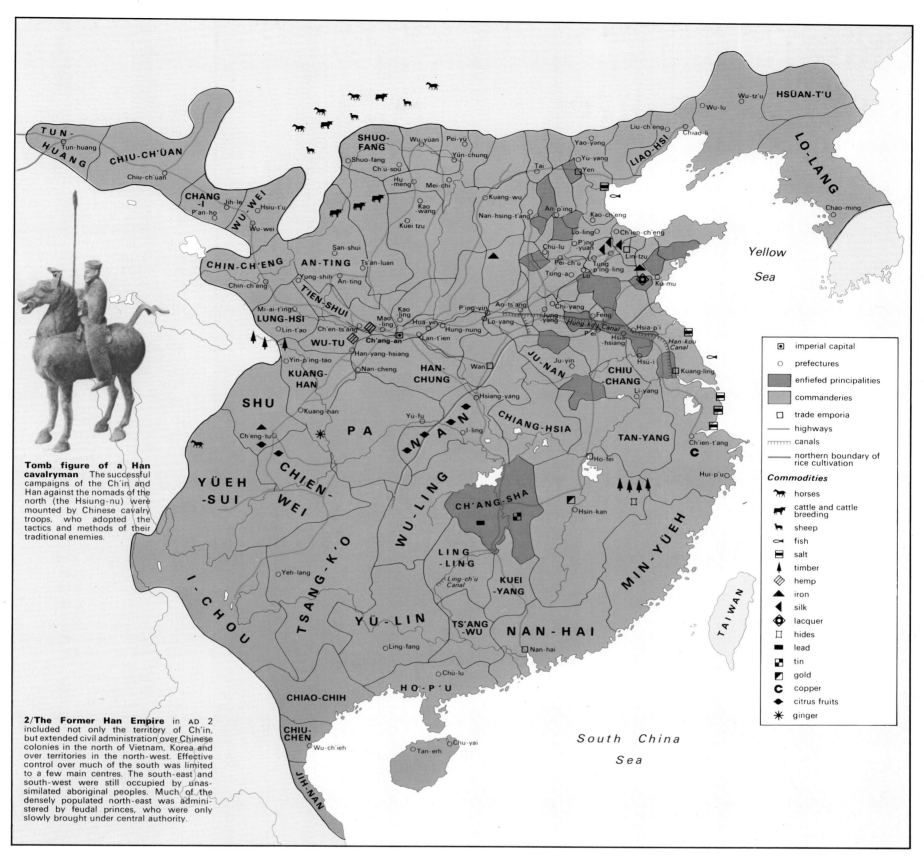

2/**The Former Han Empire** in AD 2 included not only the territory of Ch'in, but extended civil administration over Chinese colonies in the north of Vietnam, Korea and over territories in the north-west. Effective control over much of the south was limited to a few main centres. The south-east and south-west were still occupied by unassimilated aboriginal peoples. Much of the densely populated north-east was administered by feudal princes, who were only slowly brought under central authority.

Tomb figure of a Han cavalryman The successful campaigns of the Ch'in and Han against the nomads of the north (the Hsiung-nu) were mounted by Chinese cavalry troops, who adopted the tactics and methods of their traditional enemies.

⊡	imperial capital
○	prefectures
▨	enfiefed principalities
▨	commanderies
▫	trade emporia
	highways
	canals
	northern boundary of rice cultivation

Commodities

🐎	horses
🐂	cattle and cattle breeding
🐑	sheep
🐟	fish
▭	salt
▴	timber
◈	hemp
▲	iron
◀	silk
◈	lacquer
⬜	hides
■	lead
▣	tin
▨	gold
C	copper
◆	citrus fruits
✳	ginger

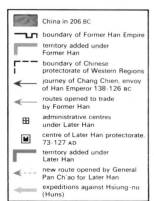

3/**The expansion of Han China** (*left*) Han expansion began under Wu-ti (140-86 BC). The Chinese took the offensive against the Hsiung-nu, extended the Great Wall far to the north-west to protect the route into central Asia. For a few decades after 59 BC the Chinese controlled the Tarim basin. Missions visited Parthia and Bactria, and extensive trade with the West began. Chinese power was again briefly extended to the west after AD 94. The Han eliminated the coastal Yüeh kingdoms, occupied north Vietnam and northern Korea.

▨	China in 206 BC
	boundary of Former Han Empire
	territory added under Former Han
	boundary of Chinese protectorate of Western Regions
←	journey of Chang Chien, envoy of Han Emperor 138-126 BC
	routes opened to trade by Former Han
⊞	administrative centres under Later Han
▣	centre of Later Han protectorate. 73-127 AD
	territory added under Later Han
◄--	new route opened by General Pan Ch'ao for Later Han
⇐	expeditions against Hsiung-nu (Huns)

collapse of his empire in 206 BC, shortly after his death.

After a period of civil war a new dynasty, the Han, regained control of all China. Founded by a man of humble origins, the Han were forced to reintroduce a system of feudal principalities allocated to their family and supporters, and these fiefs were not brought under strong central control until about 100 BC. Copying the general outlines of Ch'in government, but softening its harshness, the Han gradually evolved a strong central government and an effective system of local administration.

The Ch'in had taken strong defensive measures against the nomad Hsiung-nu in the north, and had expanded southwards into areas occupied by non-Chinese aboriginal peoples. The Han were at first preoccupied with internal affairs. Under Wu-ti (140-87 BC) China again took the offensive against the Hsiung-nu, rebuilt the Ch'in wall and extended it far to the north-west. They opened up the route to central Asia and after 59 BC Chinese military power was briefly extended over the oasis states of the Tarim Basin. The Chinese began a large export trade, largely in silk, to Parthia and to the Roman Empire. The Han also reaffirmed the Ch'in conquests in the Canton region, eliminated the Yüeh kingdoms of the

south-east coast at the end of the 2nd century, and occupied northern Vietnam. Chinese armies also drove deep into the south-west, establishing Han control over its native states. These southern conquests, however, led to little Chinese settlement. Away from a few main centres most of southern China remained in the hands of aboriginal peoples for centuries to come. Wu-ti's armies also occupied and placed under Chinese administration parts of southern Manchuria and northern Korea.

The Han Empire grew extremely prosperous. The rapid growth of the preceding centuries continued. During this period of stability, prosperity and growth China's population reached some 57,000,000 and many large cities grew up. The Han capital, Ch'ang-an, had a quarter of a million people, and was the centre of a brilliant culture. At the beginning of the Christian era the Han Empire rivalled that of Rome in size and in wealth.

Even the riches of the Han Empire, however, were severely taxed by Han Wu-ti's military adventures, and under a series of weak emperors during the latter half of the 1st century BC the authority of the throne was rivalled by the great court families. In AD 9 Wang Mang, an imperial relative by marriage, usurped the throne and

set up a brief dynasty (Hsin, AD 9-23) which embarked upon a drastic programme of reforms. His reign ended in widespread rebellion, and was followed by a restoration of the Han (Later Han, AD 25-220). Since Ch'ang-an had been sacked during the fighting, the capital was moved to Lo-yang and during the Later Han period the north-east of China steadily grew in importance relative to the north-west.

After some decades of consolidation, in the late 1st century the Chinese again began active hostilities against the Hsiung-nu, and in AD 94 again invaded the Tarim basin. But this revival proved short-lived. Trouble with the Chiang tribes of the north-west, the succession of several child-emperors and virulent factionalism at court had seriously weakened the Han state by about AD 160. A wave of agrarian distress culminated in the massive religious uprising of the Yellow Turbans which engulfed China from 184. Some degree of order was eventually restored by various regional warlords. Although the Han survived in name until 220, power in fact lay with these regional commanders. In 220 the last Han emperor abdicated in favour of one of them, and the empire was divided into three independent regional states. China was to remain politically fragmented until 589.

India: the first empires

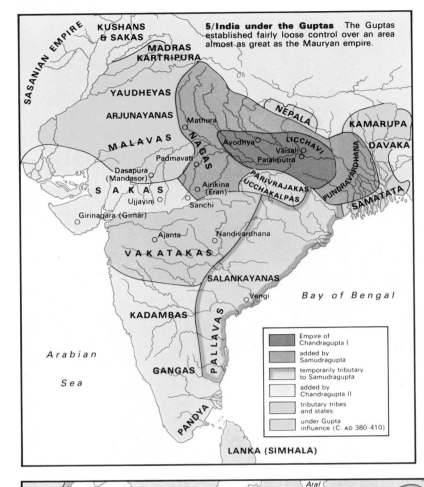

5/India under the Guptas The Guptas established fairly loose control over an area almost as great as the Mauryan empire.

Empire of Chandragupta I
added by Samudragupta
temporarily tributary to Samudragupta
added by Chandragupta II
tributary tribes and states
under Gupta influence (C. AD 380-410)

LANKA (SIMHALA)

B Y about 600 BC, northern India had at least sixteen well-articulated political units, some still essentially tribal republics, others already absolute monarchies, established in the rich Gangetic plain. In one of the smaller republics, Kapilavastu, Gautama Buddha, the founder of Asia's most pervasive religion, was born c. 566 BC, while on the Ganges itself his near-contemporary Mahavira (born c. 600 BC) was formulating the teachings of Jainism, the faith still followed by many of India's merchant community.

During the 5th century BC the number of *Mahajanapadas*, or great realms, was gradually reduced to four, and ultimately, after a century of mutual wars, these were all absorbed into the single kingdom of Magadha, with its splendid new capital of Pataliputra (Patna), strategically commanding the Ganges trade route. This was to be the nucleus of the first Indian Empire. When Alexander, having conquered Achaemenid Persia, was marching to the Indus in 327 BC, a young adventurer, Chandragupta Maurya, is said to have met him. Shortly after Alexander's invasion of India, Chandragupta seized the Magadhan throne. Then, exploiting the power vacuum left behind in the north-west after Alexander's departure, Chandragupta annexed all the land east of the Indus, swung south to occupy large parts of central India north of the Narmada river, and in 305 BC decisively defeated Alexander's successor, Seleucus Nicator, who then ceded the Greek province of Trans-Indus including a large part of Afghanistan.

The Mauryan Empire, extended by Chandragupta's son Bindusara, reached its zenith under his grandson, the Emperor Asoka, who with the conquest of Kalinga on the Bay of Bengal established his rule over the bulk of the subcontinent. Asoka's India was by this time a land of settled village agriculture, with an elaborate administrative and tax-collecting system, probably described in one of the world's earliest manuals of statecraft, the *Arthasastra*, attributed to Kautilya, Chandragupta's chief minister. Trade flourished and a special group of officials appears to have been made responsible for the building and maintenance of roads, including the Royal Highway (known to modern India as the Grand Trunk Road) from Pataliputra to the north-west. Probably neither Chandragupta nor his successors practised orthodox Hinduism, although this had now clearly established itself as the predominant religion of the Ganges plain, with the sacerdotal caste of Brahmans as the most powerful caste. After the bloody subjection of Kalinga, Asoka accepted conversion to Buddhism and abandoned the policy of conquest, *Digvijaya*, in favour of *Dhammavijaya*, the Victory of Righteousness. His ethical teachings are found inscribed on pillars and rock-faces all over India, and his emissaries visited the Hellenistic kingdoms, as well as Ceylon and the far south, to preach the new gospel of peace.

Mauryan rule, however, did not long survive Asoka's death in 232 BC. In the 2nd century BC, the north and north-west were extensively invaded, both by Greeks from the former Seleucid satrapies of Bactria and Parthia, and by new nomad groups on the move from central Asia. In particular the Kushan section of the Yüeh-chih horde (see page 78) who had settled in the Oxus valley after 165 BC, gradually extended their rule inland, reaching Benares in the first century AD. Large parts of Afghanistan and Khotan were included in their cosmopolitan empire, which became a melting-pot of cultures – Indian, Chinese, central Asian and Helleno-Roman. Meanwhile, various marauding families of Greek and Scythian origin established a number of kingdoms and dynasties in western and central India. Kushan emperors and Greek feudatories adopted Sanskrit names and followed Indian religions. Indian and Hellenistic influences mingled in Gandhara sculpture. Mahayana Buddhism, separating itself at this time from the fundamentalist teachings of the original Hinayana, developed a more eclectic outlook, much influenced by non-Indian faiths, with a pantheon of deities drawn from many lands. These are now the two great divisions of Buddhism, with Hinayana still dominant in Ceylon, Burma and South-East Asia, and Mahayana the leading sect in India, Tibet, China and Japan.

India's ancient trading links with the Middle East and Egypt were revitalised and greatly

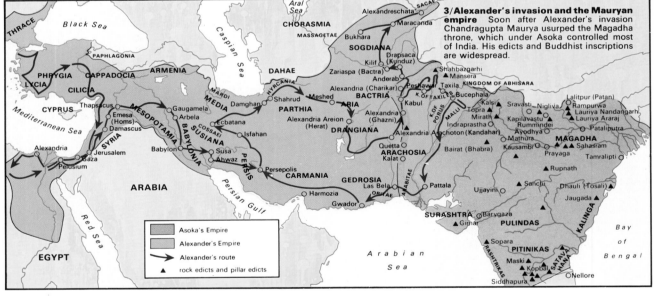

3/Alexander's invasion and the Mauryan empire Soon after Alexander's invasion Chandragupta Maurya usurped the Magadha throne, which under Asoka controlled most of India. His edicts and Buddhist inscriptions are widespread.

Asoka's Empire
Alexander's Empire
Alexander's route
rock edicts and pillar edicts

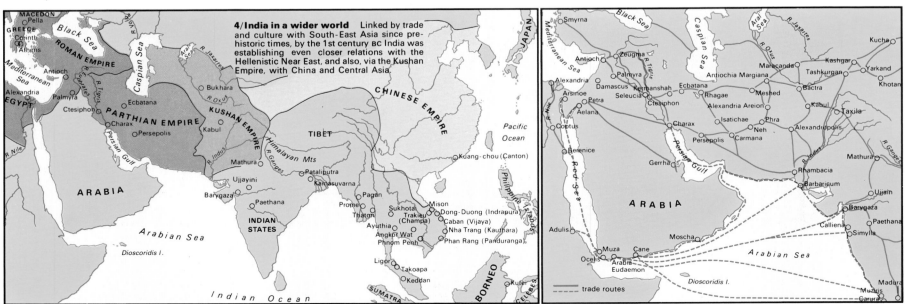

4/India in a wider world Linked by trade and culture with South-East Asia since prehistoric times, by the 1st century BC India was establishing even closer relations with the Hellenistic Near East, and also, via the Kushan Empire, with China and Central Asia.

trade routes

extended as the Hellenistic kingdoms gave way before the rising power of Rome. By the first century AD, Pliny was complaining that India's spices, jewels, muslins and exotic animals were costing the Romans 550 million *sesterces* a year in gold. Ports like Barbaricum, on the Indus delta, and the great entrepôt centre of Barygaza (Broach) shipped out turquoise, diamonds, spikenard, indigo, silk yarn and tortoise-shell, receiving in return an immensely varied flow of wine, pearls, copper, dates, gold and slaves, from Ethiopia, Arabia and the Mediter-ranean. Indian merchants, seeking spices for the Roman market, opened up buying agencies throughout South-East Asia, while much of the Chinese silk traffic (especially during the Roman wars with Parthia) found its way south to the trading city Taxila, in West Pakistan, before the caravans took it further west.

By the middle of the 2nd century AD the foreign kingdoms of the north were in deep decay, and new, indigenous groupings had begun to emerge. The Tamil-speaking peoples south of Madras had briefly occupied Ceylon and built important harbours on both sides of the southern tip, while the Satavahanas of the Deccan had become a formidable force, straddling the peninsula and driving significantly into the northern plain. Then in the 4th century, the native dynasty of the Guptas, based again on Magadha, imposed a new, almost imperial rule which extended, at its furthest stretch, from Sind and the Punjab to west and north Bengal.

Their suzerainty was acknowledged in regions even further to the east and the south. This was in many ways the classical age of north Indian civilisation, and it survived well beyond the political collapse of the empire, brought about by fresh invasions of Hunnish, or *huna*, nomads in the 5th century.

During this period the Puranas, recording the Hindu version of the Creation and early history of mankind, were composed in their final form, while Vedanta also began its decisive emergence as the dominant system of Hindu thought. But Buddhism, now carried far and wide by Indian merchants and travellers, proved permanently acceptable beyond the confines of the sub-continent. In 379 it became the state religion of China, and even in South-East Asia, where Hinduism initially enjoyed much success, it persisted and flourished long after its rival's decline in the 7th and 8th centuries.

In the mid-7th century, the warrior-king Sri Harsha, ruling from Kanauj, once more estab-lished a rough feudal unity over an extensive area from Gujerat to east Bengal, but his attempts to force the Deccan were blocked by a powerful southern dynasty, the Chalukyas. For many years Hsüan Tsang, the most famous of Chinese travellers to India, lived at Sri Harsha's court, leaving a vivid account of Indian life and politics, and at his death, Chinese troops intervened to place a suitable successor on his throne. Very soon, however, India once more relapsed into a tangle of warring states.

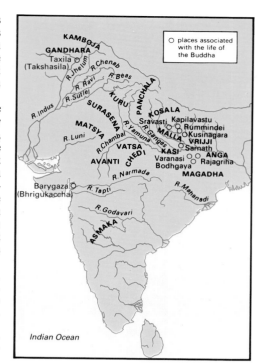

2/The Mahajanapadas (above) Each of the sixteen great realms of early India produced its quota of cities. Others, like Taxila and the port Barygaza were of great trading importance. By the 5th century they were reduced to four major rivals: the three kingdoms of Kasi, Kosala and Magadha, and the republic of the Vrijji, covering parts of modern Nepal and Bihar.

Lion capital (above) Asoka built the first of these at Sarnath where Buddha preached. The capital in its original form had a wheel of virtue atop the lions, symbolising the ascendancy of virtue over worldly pomp and power.

1/The ancient empires (below) The warring early kingdoms first gave way to a unified kingdom under Chandragupta Maurya, con-temporary of Alexander. The domain of the Scythian Kushans stretched from Khotan to Benares, but included nothing south of the Vindhyas. The 4th century AD Guptas and the 7th century Sri Harsha established the best-known of the later northern Indian empires.

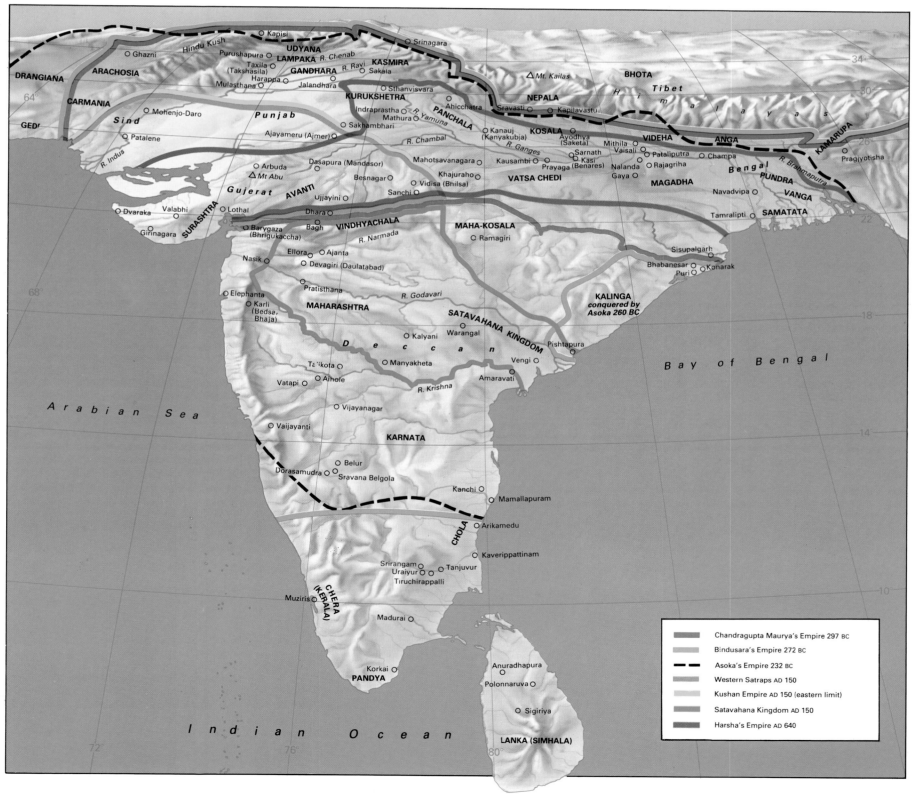

▬▬	Chandragupta Maurya's Empire 297 BC
▬▬	Bindusara's Empire 272 BC
▬ ▬	Asoka's Empire 232 BC
▬▬	Western Satraps AD 150
▬▬	Kushan Empire AD 150 (eastern limit)
▬▬	Satavahana Kingdom AD 150
▬▬	Harsha's Empire AD 640

The peoples of Northern Europe

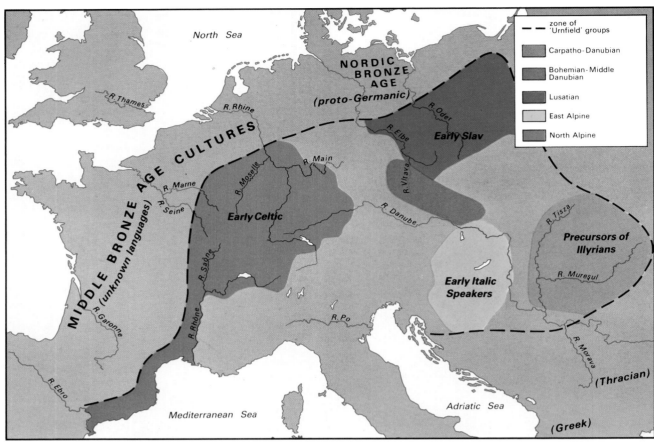

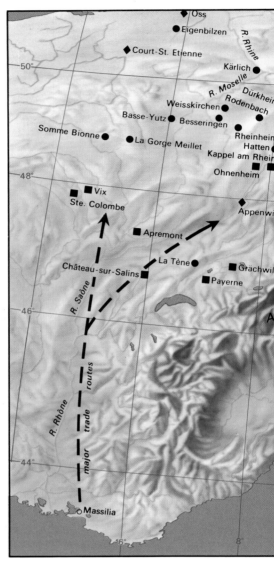

2/Middle Europe c. 800 BC *(above)* The broken line encloses the expanding groups of the Late Bronze Age 'Urnfield' complex, bordering on survivals of Middle Bronze Age cultures to the west and the proto-Germanic civilisation of the Nordic Bronze Age to the north. The North Alpine group were Celtic-speakers, and their descendants were to dominate much of Middle Europe: the Lusatian group were probably ancestors of the Slavs, and other groups of the Illyrians and Italians.

Maiden Castle *(left)* A great Celtic hill fort in Dorset, England, 400-100 BC. It was stormed by the Romans in AD 44.

3/The Expansion of the Celts *(below)* From their heartland on the Rhine and Upper Danube, Celtic groups spread to France and Czechoslovakia by the 6th century; by the 3rd century they had replaced the Scythians in the Middle Danube, and were raiding widely.

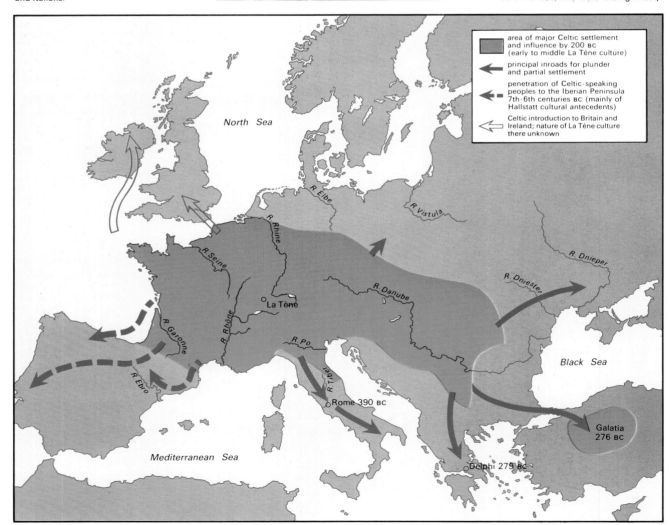

THE first millennium before Christ saw a great increase in the population of Europe north of the Alps. Many of the extensive areas of heavy land were opened up for the first time to agricultural settlement, and local expansion brought about movements of population into peripheral areas. As a result of these changes, a more centralised political system came into being, reflected in the hillforts which are found in most areas of Europe, dominating the landscape for miles around. Some of these grew to become towns and market-centres in the last two centuries before Christ. It was this growth which allowed the spread of Roman power by the conquest of one regional centre after another.

The rise in population was evident already in the Late Bronze Age, for instance in measures taken to economise in the use of bronze, even though new deep mines for copper had been opened. The adoption of ironworking when the technique became known around 800 BC was so rapid because the copper supplies no longer met the growing demand for metal. The main focus of these economic and technical developments lay in central Europe, in the territory of the various branches of the 'Urnfield' culture – a group of related tribes, with a common culture and burial practices, which dominated the Rhine/Danube axis. About 1000 BC, these tribes began to expand into adjacent areas along the main river thoroughfares. Their four main branches each gave rise to an important group of historic peoples: Celts in the west, Slavs in the north, Italic-speakers in the south, and Illyrians in the south-east. Outside this ring, to the north, lay a Nordic group of early Germans and Balts on the Baltic coast; while south-eastwards lay Dacians, Thracians and Greeks.

During the first millennium BC the Celtic areas greatly expanded at the expense of their neigh-

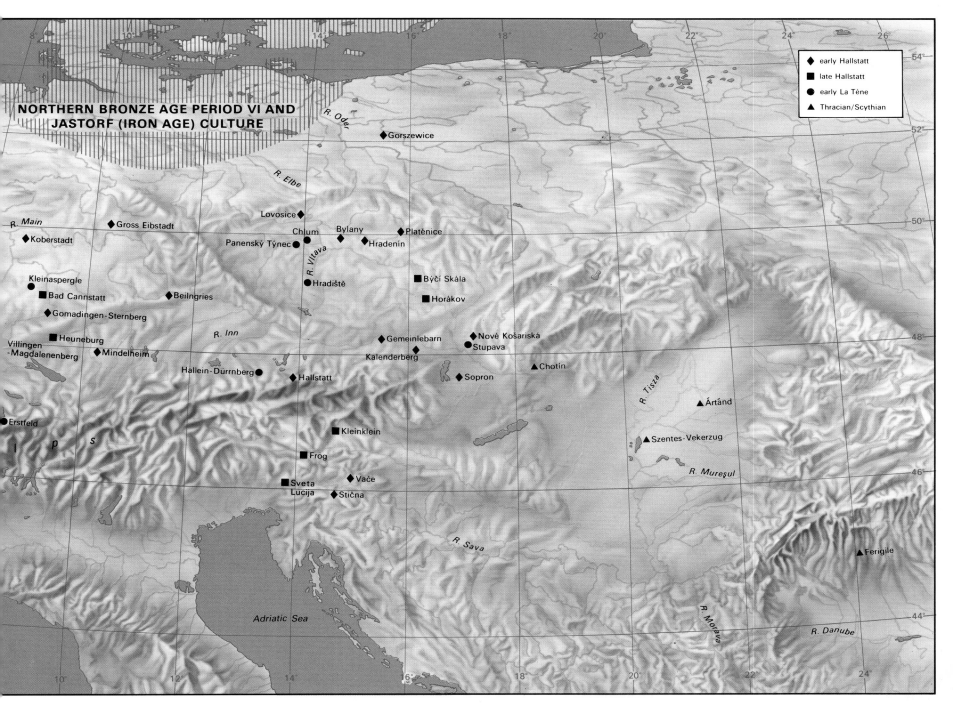

NORTHERN BRONZE AGE PERIOD VI AND JASTORF (IRON AGE) CULTURE

Legend:
- ◆ early Hallstatt
- ■ late Hallstatt
- ● early La Tène
- ▲ Thracian/Scythian

Map labels: Gorszewice, R. Oder, R. Elbe, Lovosice, R. Main, Gross Eibstadt, Koberstadt, Chlum, Bylany, Platěnice, Panenský Týnec, Hradenín, R. Vltava, Kleinaspergle, Bad Cannstatt, Beilngries, Hradiště, Býčí Skála, Gomadingen-Sternberg, Horákov, R. Inn, Heuneburg, Villingen-Magdalenenberg, Mindelheim, Gemeinlebarn, Nové Košariská, Stupava, Kalenderberg, Chotín, R. Tisza, Erstfeld, Alps, Hallein-Dürrnberg, Hallstatt, Sopron, Ártánd, Kleinklein, Szentes-Vekerzug, R. Mureşul, Frog, Sveta Lucija, Vače, Stična, R. Sava, Ferigile, R. Morava, Adriatic Sea, R. Danube

bours, just as in the first millennium AD the Germanic tribes overran large parts of western Europe (see page 98). In particular, large areas of present-day France came to be incorporated into the Celtic-speaking world. At the same time, important economic changes began to take place among the Celts as a result of growing contact with the Mediterranean world, for instance via the Greek colony of Massilia, founded in 600 BC. Some measure of the importance of commercial relations between the Greeks and their barbarian neighbours is given by the magnificent burial of a Celtic princess at Vix near Châtillon-sur-Seine, with a massive ornamented bronze punch-bowl of Italian workmanship, and other pieces of imported finery. These early Celtic aristocrats lived in hillforts such as the Heuneburg on the Upper Danube, partly designed by a Mediterranean architect, and members of their families were buried with a complete cart to carry their possessions to the grave – a practice followed all over the Celtic world, from Vix to Lovosice in Bohemia (see map 1).

The Celtic Iron Age is divided into two phases, named after the sites of Hallstatt in Austria and La Tène in Switzerland. The second, La Tène, phase (450 BC onwards) is characterised by an even wider extension of the area of Celtic raiding and settlement, now mainly to the east and south, though they also penetrated north as far as Britain, much of which they occupied, and by the emergence under aristocratic patronage of a characteristic decorative style known as 'Celtic Art'. This developed in the industrial and political heartland of the later Celtic world, in the Rhineland and Upper Marne. The most spectacular pieces of Celtic art are the bronze vessels and gold neck-rings with cast curvilinear decoration, which accompany

the burials of powerful chieftains in such cemeteries as Rheinheim, Basse-Yutz or Dürkheim.

The economic strength of the Celtic area was based upon growing industrialisation. Large numbers of iron ingots show the importance of the Rhineland in primary production, while the light, two-wheeled fighting chariots which were occasionally buried there with the warriors of this phase (e.g. at Somme-Bionne in France) are an indication of the skills of Celtic craftsmen. These advantages carried the Celts both eastwards, into territory which in the Hallstatt period had fallen largely under the control of the Scythians – semi-nomadic horsemen and herders whose homeland lay in the steppes of southern Russia; and at the same time southwards, to attack Rome in 390 BC and a century later to reach Delphi, and even as far as central Anatolia, where some settled, later to become the 'foolish Galatians' of St Paul's letters.

The Celts were the first of the peoples of temperate Europe to be incorporated within the Roman Empire as it spread beyond the confines of the Mediterranean. Already by the end of the second century BC, the Mediterranean part of Gaul was a Roman colony; and the intimate links northwards via the Rhône valley led Caesar into a series of campaigns which brought the western Celtic world under Roman control as far as the English Channel.

Thus the economically most advanced areas of the barbarian world were rapidly integrated within the framework of the Roman Empire. Yet beyond this frontier, and especially in Ireland, the Celtic world knew the mass-production of the Roman world, to flower again in the early Middle Ages, in such masterpieces of manuscript illustration as *The Book of Kells* and the *Lindisfarne Gospels*.

1/Middle Europe c. 700 to 400 BC
(above) The map shows important archaeological finds of the Iron Age Celts, and some of their Scythian neighbours to the east, including both graves with rich material, and the larger fortified centres. Note the density of finds between the Moselle and the Alps.

4/The Prelude to Germanic Expansion
(below) Place-names between the Aller and the Somme show remnants of a language neither Celtic nor German – the last traces of a prehistoric people squeezed between expanding Celtic and Germanic groups. Even this people, however, had already adopted many features of Celtic culture.

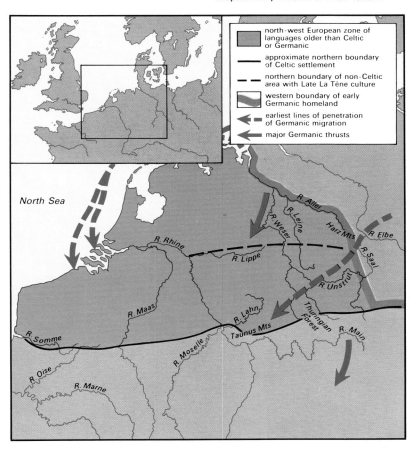

Legend:
- north-west European zone of languages older than Celtic or Germanic
- approximate northern boundary of Celtic settlement
- northern boundary of non-Celtic area with Late La Tène culture
- western boundary of early Germanic homeland
- earliest lines of penetration of Germanic migration
- major Germanic thrusts

Map labels: North Sea, R. Aller, R. Leine, R. Weser, Harz Mts, R. Elbe, R. Rhine, R. Lippe, R. Saal, R. Maas, R. Lahn, R. Unstrut, Thuringian Forest, R. Main, R. Somme, Taunus Mts, R. Moselle, R. Oise, R. Marne

The expansion of Roman power in Italy and the Mediterranean to 31 BC

ROME first grew from a cluster of villages into a city in the 6th century BC, influenced by its more civilised overlords, the Etruscans, whom in about 510 BC the Romans expelled, establishing a Republic which very slowly expanded its power. Thus while the Greeks were repelling the early 5th century Persian invasions and Athens was reaching its peak under Pericles, the Romans controlled only a small part of central Italy. But the Greeks had their own problems, and until after the days of Alexander they hardly noticed the advance of the 'barbarians' in the west. Equally the Carthaginians, with a trade monopoly and an overseas empire in the western Mediterranean, were not interested in central Italy, whose main concern was still agriculture. Rome could extend her power without much external interference. By 264 BC she led a single Italian confederacy, and little over a century later she dominated the whole Mediterranean. The contemporary Polybius felt able for the first time in Western history to write of a unified mankind.

The early Italian population was very mixed (map 2). The Bronze Age Apennine culture of the central highlands was outstripped early in the first millennium BC by an Iron Age Villanovan culture which flourished from the Po valley to Etruria and the site of Rome, and even reached Campania. In the 8th century BC a new culture emerged in Etruria, based probably on a fusion of the Villanovan population with an invading Etruscan aristocracy from Asia Minor. Other Iron Age groups included the Picentes, Veneti and Iapyges. From about 750 BC Greek settlers established colonies on the coast from Cumae southwards around the toe of Italy and Sicily.

The Etruscan empire, which at its height reached from the Po to Campania, was ultimately mastered by the Latins of central Italy. Among the Indo-European-speaking Latin towns Rome gradually gained the ascendency. Initial conflict soon developed into mutual support against the pressure of the surrounding tribes: Sabines, Aequi, Volsci and (in the 4th century BC) the Samnites. During these struggles Rome extended both her territory *(ager Romanus)* and her

alliances. By 500 BC she controlled some 350 square miles of territory; by 260 BC some 10,000 square miles. With conquest went an extension of Roman citizenship, either complete or with limited privileges. At the same time Rome built up a confederacy with special privileges for the Latins; in all, her allies controlled in 260 BC some 42,000 square miles, giving effective Roman dominance over some 52,000 square miles (map 1). By now her citizens numbered some 292,000 men, while the allies had perhaps 750,000; the total population numbered about 3 million.

With this manpower and territory Rome had become a potential world power. Her influence was strengthened by founding strategic colonies in Italy, linked by a network of roads. These colonies comprised either Roman citizens alone or Latins (originally joined by some Romans who surrendered their Roman citizenship): the former were part of the Roman state, the latter independent but privileged allies.

The emergence of this powerful confederacy was a potential challenge to Carthage, which then controlled the coast of north-west Africa, part of Spain, Sardinia and western Sicily. More by accident than by design they clashed in 264 BC. In the First Punic War (264-241), Rome, still essentially agricultural, had to become a naval power; by driving the Carthaginians first from Sicily and then (238) from Corsica and Sardinia, Rome gained two overseas provinces. The Second War (218-201), when Hannibal invaded Italy, saw the Carthaginians expelled from Spain, which then became two Roman

2/The peoples of Italy 500 BC (above) During the Bronze and early Iron Ages Italy contained many independent tribes. The Etruscans were the first to extend their power over a large part of the peninsula. But Etruria proper (Tuscany) was organised as independent city-states and although an Etruscan League was formed, its ties were more religious and cultural than political. It thus found concerted action difficult. Assailed by land and sea, the Etruscans were forced back into Etruria around 500 BC, and the way was left open for the more political Romans.

Lictor Fasces, thonged bundles of rods containing an axe, were carried by lictors, first before the early kings, and then in procession with the higher republican magistrates. They vividly symbolised Rome's powerful executive authority.

3/The Roman world 264 to 31 BC (below) Alexander the Great's empire split into three after his death: Macedon, Syria and Egypt. Their mutual struggles allowed Carthage to build an empire in the western Mediterranean. Rome and Carthage clashed in Sicily in 264 BC, and after three great wars Rome acquired five overseas provinces: Sicily, Corsica and Sardinia, Spain (two provinces) and Africa (roughly modern Tunisia). In the East, Rome's first annexation was Macedon (146 BC), followed by Asia (western Turkey), Cyrene, Crete, Bithynia, Pontus, Cilicia, Syria and Cyprus. But their administration overstrained the Roman constitution, which had not been designed for an overseas empire. The Republic finally collapsed in a series of civil wars, the last of which was won by Octavian (Augustus) over Antony and Cleopatra in 31 BC.

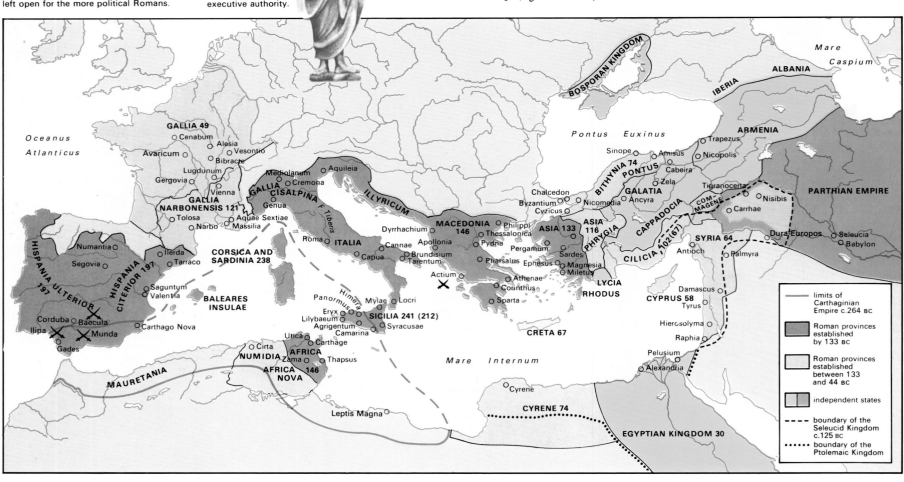

	limits of Carthaginian Empire c.264 BC
	Roman provinces established by 133 BC
	Roman provinces established between 133 and 44 BC
	independent states
---	boundary of the Seleucid Kingdom c.125 BC
····	boundary of the Ptolemaic Kingdom

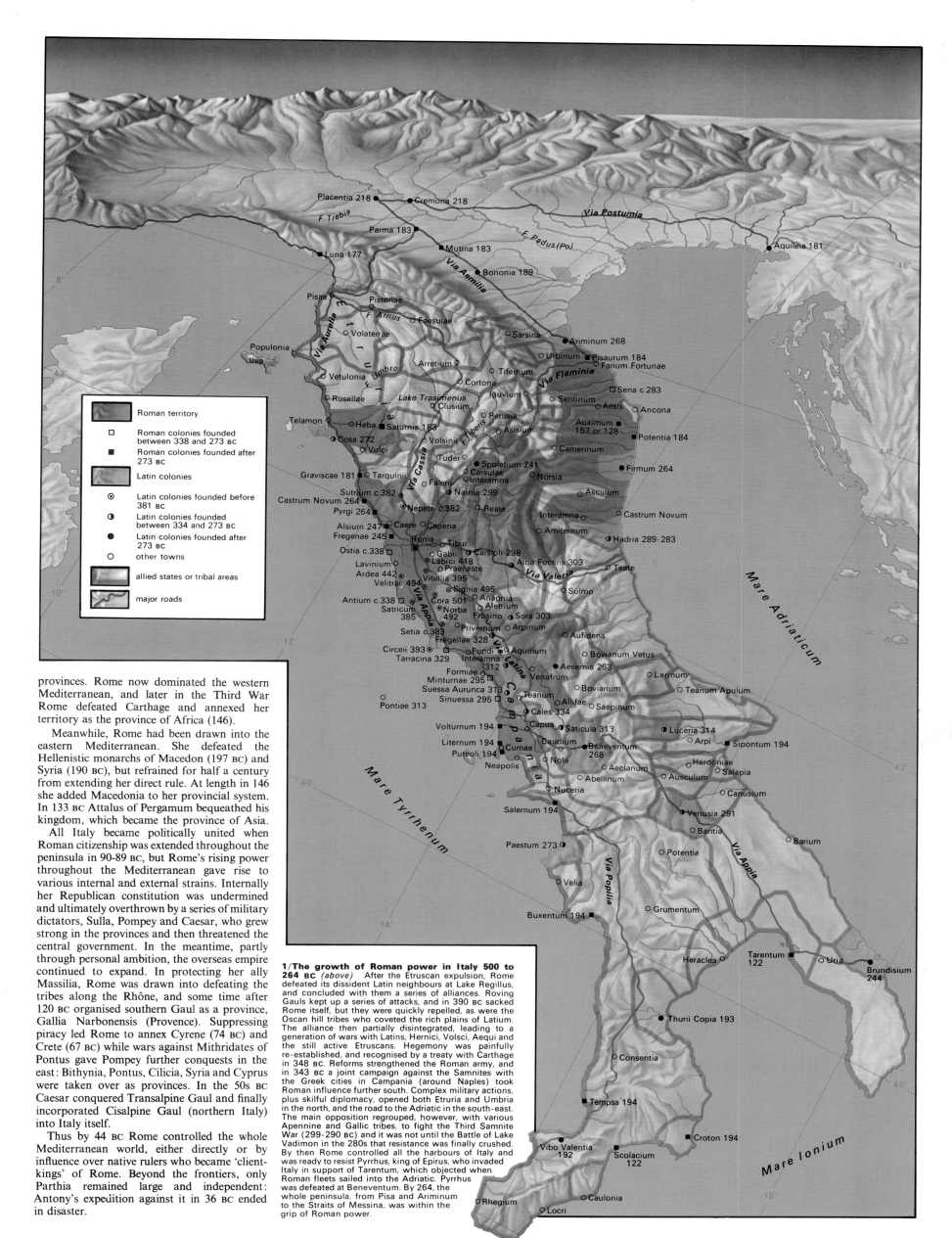

Roman territory

Roman colonies founded between 338 and 273 BC

Roman colonies founded after 273 BC

Latin colonies

Latin colonies founded before 381 BC

Latin colonies founded between 334 and 273 BC

Latin colonies founded after 273 BC

other towns

allied states or tribal areas

major roads

provinces. Rome now dominated the western Mediterranean, and later in the Third War Rome defeated Carthage and annexed her territory as the province of Africa (146).

Meanwhile, Rome had been drawn into the eastern Mediterranean. She defeated the Hellenistic monarchs of Macedon (197 BC) and Syria (190 BC), but refrained for half a century from extending her direct rule. At length in 146 she added Macedonia to her provincial system. In 133 BC Attalus of Pergamum bequeathed his kingdom, which became the province of Asia.

All Italy became politically united when Roman citizenship was extended throughout the peninsula in 90-89 BC, but Rome's rising power throughout the Mediterranean gave rise to various internal and external strains. Internally her Republican constitution was undermined and ultimately overthrown by a series of military dictators, Sulla, Pompey and Caesar, who grew strong in the provinces and then threatened the central government. In the meantime, partly through personal ambition, the overseas empire continued to expand. In protecting her ally Massilia, Rome was drawn into defeating the tribes along the Rhône, and some time after 120 BC organised southern Gaul as a province, Gallia Narbonensis (Provence). Suppressing piracy led Rome to annex Cyrene (74 BC) and Crete (67 BC) while wars against Mithridates of Pontus gave Pompey further conquests in the east: Bithynia, Pontus, Cilicia, Syria and Cyprus were taken over as provinces. In the 50s BC Caesar conquered Transalpine Gaul and finally incorporated Cisalpine Gaul (northern Italy) into Italy itself.

Thus by 44 BC Rome controlled the whole Mediterranean world, either directly or by influence over native rulers who became 'client-kings' of Rome. Beyond the frontiers, only Parthia remained large and independent: Antony's expedition against it in 36 BC ended in disaster.

1/The growth of Roman power in Italy 500 to 264 BC (above) After the Etruscan expulsion, Rome defeated its dissident Latin neighbours at Lake Regillus, and concluded with them a series of alliances. Roving Gauls kept up a series of attacks, and in 390 BC sacked Rome itself, but they were quickly repelled, as were the Oscan hill tribes who coveted the rich plains of Latium. The alliance then partially disintegrated, leading to a generation of wars with Latins, Hernici, Volsci, Aequi and the still active Etruscans. Hegemony was painfully re-established, and recognised by a treaty with Carthage in 348 BC. Reforms strengthened the Roman army, and in 343 BC a joint campaign against the Samnites with the Greek cities in Campania (around Naples) took Roman influence further south. Complex military actions, plus skilful diplomacy, opened both Etruria and Umbria in the north, and the road to the Adriatic in the south-east. The main opposition regrouped, however, with various Apennine and Gallic tribes, to fight the Third Samnite War (299-290 BC) and it was not until the Battle of Lake Vadimon in the 280s that resistance was finally crushed. By then Rome controlled all the harbours of Italy and was ready to resist Pyrrhus, king of Epirus, who invaded Italy in support of Tarentum, which objected when Roman fleets sailed into the Adriatic. Pyrrhus was defeated at Beneventum. By 264, the whole peninsula, from Pisa and Ariminum to the Straits of Messina, was within the grip of Roman power.

The Roman Empire from Augustus to Justinian 31 BC to AD 565

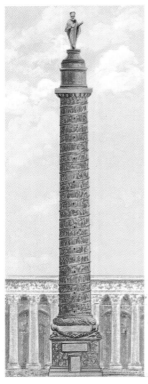

Trajan's column *(above)* Trajan, the first Roman emperor born outside Italy, came from Italica in Spain, near present-day Seville. His famous column, which still stands in Rome, is a unique work of art, sculptured in the form of a continuous spiral frieze, showing arms, armour, fortifications and battle scenes from the two great campaigns he fought during the Dacian Wars.

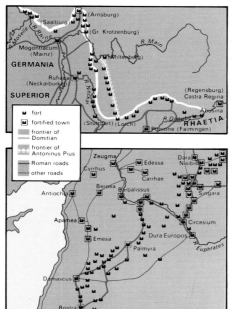

2/The frontiers in Germany *(left)* In 12 BC the Romans finally pushed across the Rhine from Gaul, to reach the Elbe in 9 BC. They failed to establish permanent occupation: in AD 9 a revolt led by Arminius (Herman) ended in the destruction of three legions in the Teutoburg Forest. In AD 74, Vespasian established Roman authority throughout the triangle known as the Agri Decumates, lying between the sources of the Rhine and the Danube and stretching to the Black Forest. Under his successor, Domitian, fortifications were erected as far as the Neckar Valley and the Taunus Mountains.

3/The Syrian 'limes' *(left)* Under Trajan and Hadrian, this once lightly-held frontier was equipped with a formidable screen of forts and military roads. It failed, however, to prevent the Sasanians sacking Antioch in AD 260, or to deter the Palmyran 'Empress' Zenobia, who won eastern Syria, Anatolia, Palestine and Egypt before her defeat by Aurelian in 272. The defences were later restored under Diocletian.

The Roman Peace *(left)* This marble slab from the Altar of Peace *(Ara Pacis)* which Augustus erected in Rome, symbolises the peace and prosperity which the Roman world enjoyed for two centuries after his death. The central figure is Mother Earth *(Terra Mater)* with fruit, flowers, corn, sheep, children and a bull representing agricultural plenty.

OCTAVIAN, by his defeat of Antony and Cleopatra at Actium in 31 BC, became undisputed master, not only of Egypt, which he took as his personal domain, but of the whole Roman world. In 27 BC he accepted the title of Augustus, under which, after his death, he was to become a Roman god. Without significant political rivals, and fully supported by the armies, he was able to introduce far-reaching reforms – in taxation, family and social life, the elimination of corruption at home and in provincial administration, the revival of many old Roman and Italian religious cults – which gave the now almost fully consolidated empire a new, intense surge of life. He established himself as First Citizen *(Princeps)*, reshaped the internal constitution, and extended the frontiers to a point where he hoped they would remain unchanged for ever.

While keeping undivided power in his own hands, he allowed the Senate, the old republican magistrates and the business classes (the Equestrian Order) to share with him the task of administering the Empire. Thus in theory 'the Republic was restored', and the government remained civilian and not military. At the cost of some loss of personal liberties, a stable government gave to the greater part of the civilised western world some two and a half centuries of peace and prosperity, with municipalities throughout the provinces enjoying a considerable degree of local independence, and with the predominantly Latin culture of the west complementing the Hellenism of the east. This more tranquil period was threatened by two brief civil wars (in AD 69 and 193), which emphasised the increasing importance of the army and the dominance of the Princeps. As external pressures on the northern and eastern frontiers increased, the civilian government collapsed in 235, and armies in different provinces tried to set up their own commanders as emperors (the so-called Thirty Tyrants) and economic life was shattered. However, a series of strong emperors in the years 268 to 284 managed to turn back the tide of Gothic and other invaders and to restore a semblance of orderly government.

In the early days of the Augustan Empire, the long frontiers had been guarded against the less civilised peoples beyond by a permanent army of some 300,000 men, stationed in camps and mostly deployed in units along the imperial boundaries, which at first consisted mainly of natural features such as seas, rivers and mountains. This was backed by an elaborate system of military roads, while naval vessels protected Rome's widespread commercial activity. Roman citizenship gradually spread more widely, and in 212 Caracalla granted it to all free inhabitants. When expansion ceased with Trajan (d. 117), permanent stone barriers were erected to protect the frontiers in northern England and Scotland, beyond the Rhine, along the Danube, in Syria and north Africa. By the mid-3rd century internal weakness threatened the whole system.

When Diocletian came to power in 284 it was obvious that one ruler could no longer hold the whole Empire together: hence his division of power between himself and a joint Augustus, with two subordinate Caesars, and his division of the empire into four prefectures and twelve dioceses. By now the principate was dead: the military had triumphed over the civilian. Further, a new basis had to be found for imperial authority: under the influence of eastern ideas the Princeps became Dominus (Lord), an absolute ruler, at the head of a vast bureaucracy. The centre of gravity was shifting eastwards: hence Constantine established a new capital and a Christian city at Byzantium, renamed Constantinople (330), while a new taxation system resulted in an economic revival. But further decline was merely postponed, not overcome. Although theoretically governed by joint rulers, the Empire gradually broke into an eastern and western half, and outlying provinces fell to barbarian invaders. Rome itself was sacked by the Visigoth Alaric (410) and the Vandal Gaeseric (455); and in 493 an Ostrogothic kingdom was established in Italy. The Western Empire had fallen to the invaders, while Justinian's attempt in the mid-sixth century to reunite the two halves led to no permanent union. Yet in the east the Byzantine Empire survived for another thousand years, until the capture of Constantinople by the Turks in 1453.

For two centuries after the breakdown of the Western Empire the Byzantine monarchy kept up Roman institutions and continued to use Latin in its courts. Although Greek then superseded Latin and the administration became less concentrated, it was the Eastern Empire that compiled the two great monuments of Roman law, the codes of Theodosius and of Justinian. Further, the east preserved and transmitted to the modern world much of the legacy of the ancient world. Even in the west many Roman traditions survived. The Latin tongue, although widely developing into the derivative 'Romance' languages, was still preserved in the Church and as the language of science; Roman law forms the basis of the law of most modern European states; the feats of Roman engineering genius are still visible in the Mediterranean world; the Roman Church lives on as a direct link with the past; and the German kings of the 'Holy Roman Empire' claimed that they were Roman rulers.

4/The Roman Empire from Diocletian to Justinian *(right)* Diocletian's major administrative reforms (see main text) put off the final splitting of the Empire which took place when Rome and the West were finally overrun by the barbarians in AD 476. The map shows the reforms (dioceses and prefectures) and the shrinkage that had occurred up to the death of Justinian. In the interim, German tribes had overrun Gaul, Spain, Britain, Italy, North Africa and Pannonia (see page 98). Justinian's partial reconquests from Vandal and Ostrogoth proved ephemeral: three years after his death the Lombards had taken Italy, Slavs soon poured into Pannonia and a century and more later the Arabs took North Africa and Spain.

1/The Roman Empire from Augustus to c.AD 280 *(below)* Augustus settled with Parthia, annexed Egypt, Galatia (25 BC) and Judaea (AD 6) and advanced over the Alps to the Danube and the Rhine, adding the provinces of Rhaetia, Noricum, Pannonia and Moesia. Settlement of colonies continued until Hadrian (d.138), after which *'colonia'* became a title for privileged *municipia*. Syria and Cappadocia were extended under the Flavians (69-96) and the German frontier advanced to the Black Forest (Agri Decumates). Trajan, whose reign marked the end of the Empire's significant territorial additions, fought wars for the annexation of Dacia (106), Armenia and Assyria (114), and Mesopotamia (115), to join Arabia Petraea, already taken in 106. His successor, Hadrian, decided to abandon these eastern acquisitions, apart from Arabia and Dacia, and to consolidate the frontiers of the Empire.

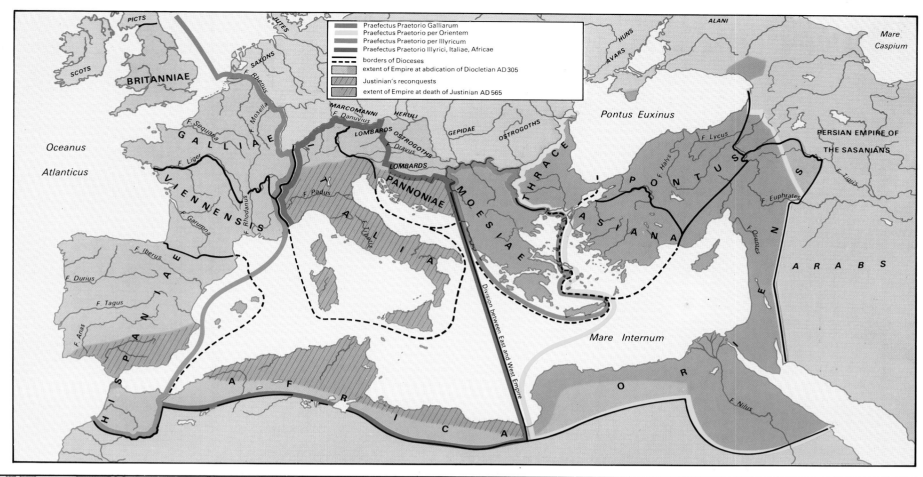

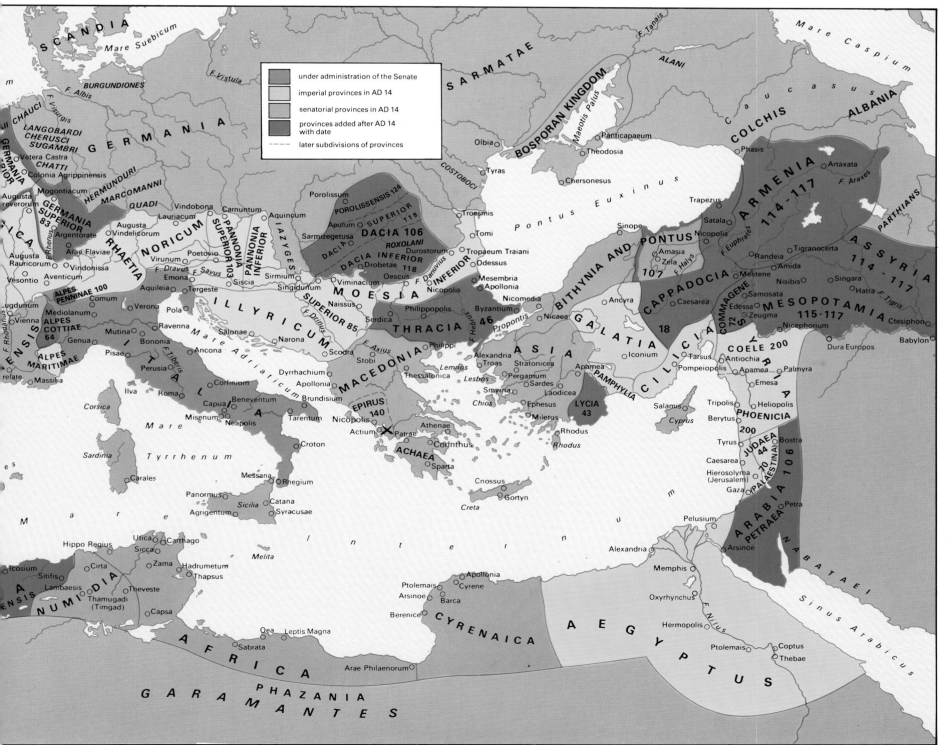

The economy of the Roman world c.AD 200

THE Roman Empire created a vast area, with a single currency and low customs barriers, in which commerce was hindered by neither pirates nor frontiers and was aided by an elaborate network of roads and protected harbours. While the basic needs of the great majority of the population were satisfied by local agriculture and craftsmanship, Graeco-Roman civilisation involved the long-distance movement of natural products and manufactured goods on a considerable scale. Many cities, especially those in Greece and Asia Minor, were regularly dependent on imported grain. Elsewhere, local crop failures produced a recurrent need for imports. Some parts of the Empire, notably Italy, Greece, Syria, Egypt and Africa (Tunisia) lacked local supplies of essential metals. All areas used Egyptian papyrus as a writing material. There was trade in expensive textiles from the wool and linen producing areas of the Empire. The luxuries of the eastern trade reached all provinces. Silk clothing was worn as a status symbol by the wealthiest; spices, especially pepper, seasoned the food of a wider segment of the population. The eastern trade caused a heavy drain of currency out of the Empire.

A great part of the long-distance movement of products or goods was a direct consequence of the existence of the Empire. Wealth was concentrated at Rome itself which, with a population of approximately 1,000,000, consumed most of the taxation in kind received from Sicily, Africa and Egypt as well as additional grain and a great deal of Spanish oil provided on a purely commercial basis. Stone for Roman building schemes and animals for the shows came from far afield. In addition, the armies stationed in frontier provinces created a large demand for both natural and manufactured products. As a result, these areas saw a considerable development in agriculture, mining and manufacture. Army supplies, like other goods, were if possible transported by river, notably the Rhine (Rhenus), Rhône (Rhodanus), Danube (Danuvius) and their tributaries. A number of large cities, such as Trèves (Augusta Treverorum), Lyons (Lugdunum), Aquileia and Antioch, combined the roles of a centre of administration and of distribution of supplies. In many parts of the Empire, city colonies with an attached territory were settled and farmed by the retired soldiers. Such settlements greatly contributed to the agricultural development of the Empire. Armies, colonies and the urbanisation of the wealthier of the provincials all created a new demand in the provinces of western Europe and the Balkans reflecting the Roman way of life – wine, olive oil, weapons, artistic metalware, fine pottery and glass. In the early 1st century AD Italy supplied wine, oil and metalware from Campania and pottery from Arezzo (Arretium) to Spain, Gaul, Britain

and the western Balkans. Then the pottery industry moved north through stages associated with La Graufesenque, Lezoux and the Rhineland. Glass-making grew up around Cologne (Colonia Agrippina) and metal industry in the hilly region south-west of it. Spain became a large-scale producer of wine, olive oil and other products, including a delicious fish paste *(garum)* which filled the amphorae that were shipped in very large quantities to Rome and also carried along the rivers of Gaul for destinations as far as Britain. Later, North Africa became a large-scale exporter of olive oil and fine pottery to the whole Mediterranean area. By the end of the 2nd century the export trade of Italy had dwindled and large areas of the Empire had become self-sufficient in the principal items of Roman living, but Britain and the northern Balkan provinces continued to import wine, olive oil, glassware and fine pottery from other parts of the Empire.

The distribution of cities reflects the degrees of development of different areas. Bithynia, Asia, Syria, Egypt, Africa (Tunisia), southern Spain, Greece, Italy and Provence were the most highly-developed regions. In the cities property was unequally divided, and the contributions of a small group of outstandingly wealthy men financed public building. The standing army, unoccupied in peacetime, was sometimes employed on the building of roads, bridges or fortifications. The spectacular nature of Roman remains tends to obscure the economic backwardness of the Roman Empire. It depended on a system of agriculture which required the land to lie fallow in alternate years and which could not work heavy clay soil. Development was limited by the slowness and expense of land transport, which depended on donkeys, mules and oxen rather than on horses. It was cheaper to ship grain across the Mediterranean than to cart it seventy miles.

The commercial classes were weak both in capital and in social esteem. The wealth of even the richest merchant fell below that of the local landowning notables, not to mention members of the imperial aristocracy. Much trading was carried on by humble men travelling with a small stock of goods. The shop, not the factory, was the standard unit of production; the economy was vulnerable. The political and military crisis after AD 230 permanently weakened the commercial classes in the western provinces. In order to pay its troops, the government gradually debased the silver currency. Debasement was accompanied by devaluation, which culminated in rapid inflation.

Around the year AD 300 Diocletian restored internal stability and inaugurated the Later Empire. Henceforth the government satisfied the needs of civil servants, soldiers and capital cities out of taxation in kind, the transport of which was itself a tax. A new currency based on gold was established, but rapid devaluation of the copper currency continued to the end of the 4th century. The scope of money and market economy, and thus of the private contractor and merchant, was greatly reduced. At the same time the western provinces saw a reversal of urbanisation in that both local aristocrats and craftsmen began to move into the countryside.

Throughout the imperial period slaves formed, by historical standards, a very high proportion of the population in many areas of the Empire. They provided dependent labour in domestic service, manufacture and agriculture. Positions of dependent management of, for instance, farms, workshops, ships or a bank were also normally held by slaves or freedmen. The evidence scarcely allows the establishment of quantitative trends in the employment of slaves, but it seems that a gradual decline in the social and legal status of the humbler free population worked to reduce the social and economic importance of slavery.

Seen in a global perspective, the Roman Empire represented a single economy which was self-sufficient in all essential commodities. Its cohesion was made possible by geographical factors such as the Mediterranean Sea and the river systems flowing into it. But the development of some areas rather than others and the direction and volume of the movement of goods was largely determined by the political organisation of the area. The break-up of the Empire in the west in the 5th century AD ended the massive government-directed transfer of resources to Rome, Italy and the frontier armies. The pattern of commercial exchanges lasted longer, even though their scale declined gradually. It was only in the 7th century, with the Arab conquests in the east and the establishment of the Carolingian monarchy in France, that new patterns began to form.

A 'silver' denarius of 44 BC *(above)* The standard coin of the early Empire was progressively debased until between AD 324 and 360 it depreciated from 4350 to 4,600,000 denarii to the new gold solidus.

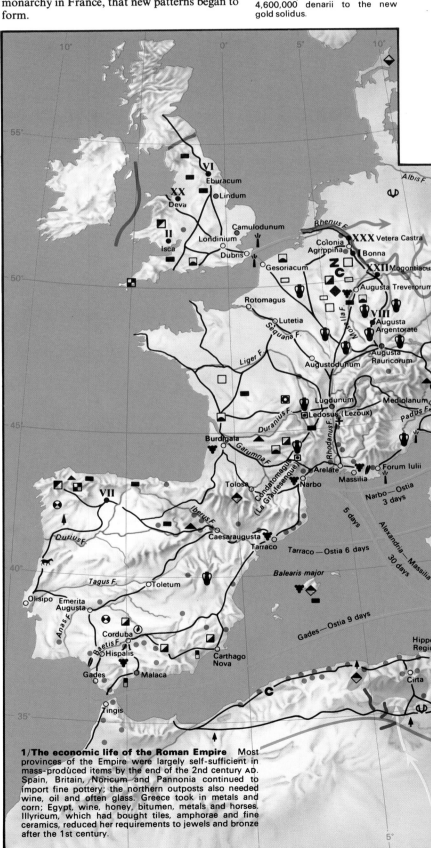

1/The economic life of the Roman Empire Most provinces of the Empire were largely self-sufficient in mass-produced items by the end of the 2nd century AD. Spain, Britain, Noricum and Pannonia continued to import fine pottery; the northern outposts also needed wine, oil and often glass. Greece took in metals and corn; Egypt, wine, honey, bitumen, metals and horses. Illyricum, which had bought tiles, amphorae and fine ceramics, reduced her requirements to jewels and bronze after the 1st century.

Amphorae *(left)* These two-handled, thin-necked pottery vessels, with pointed bases, could be either stood in a rack or stuck in the ground. They held several gallons of wine, olive oil, olives, fish sauce, salted fish, fruit, nuts, pepper, grain, flour, hair-remover or potter's clay. Their varied shapes, labels and origin-stamps give valuable information about trade.

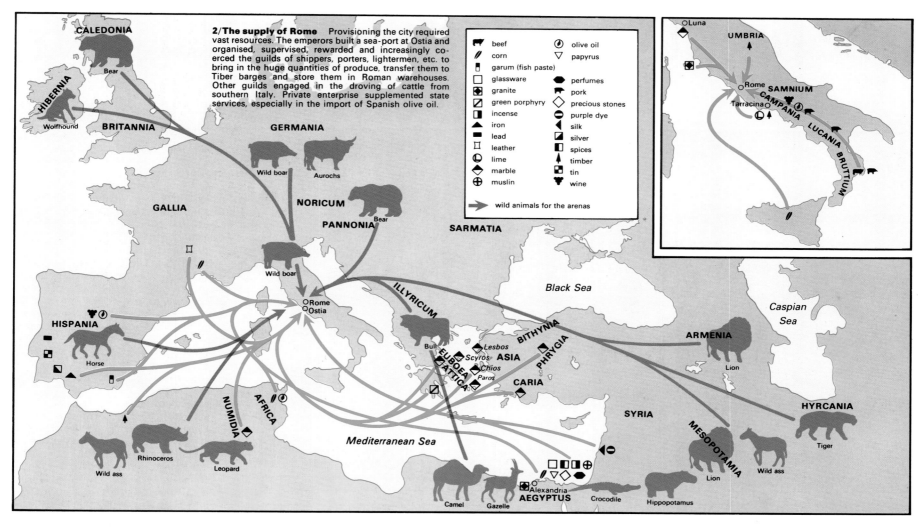

2/The supply of Rome Provisioning the city required vast resources. The emperors built a sea-port at Ostia and organised, supervised, rewarded and increasingly coerced the guilds of shippers, porters, lightermen, etc. to bring in the huge quantities of produce, transfer them to Tiber barges and store them in Roman warehouses. Other guilds engaged in the droving of cattle from southern Italy. Private enterprise supplemented state services, especially in the import of Spanish olive oil.

🐄	beef	olive oil
	corn	papyrus
	garum (fish paste)	
	glassware	perfumes
	granite	pork
	green porphyry	precious stones
	incense	purple dye
	iron	silk
	lead	silver
	leather	spices
	lime	timber
	marble	tin
	muslin	wine

→ wild animals for the arenas

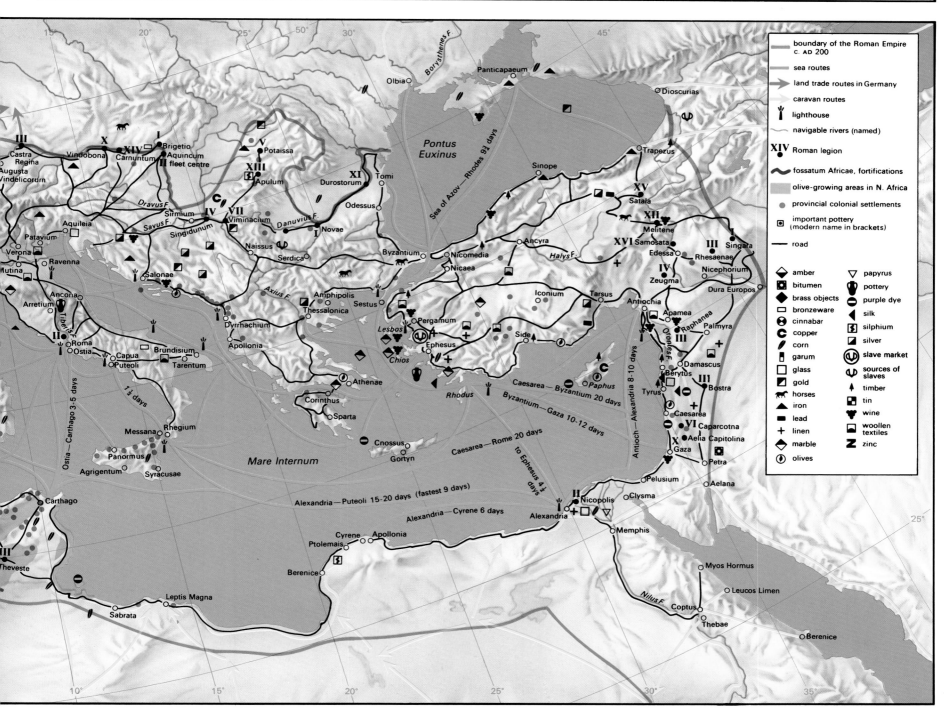

boundary of the Roman Empire c. AD 200
sea routes
land trade routes in Germany
caravan routes
lighthouse
navigable rivers (named)
XIV Roman legion
fossatum Africae, fortifications
olive-growing areas in N. Africa
provincial colonial settlements
important pottery (modern name in brackets)
road

amber		papyrus
bitumen		pottery
brass objects		purple dye
bronzeware		silk
cinnabar		silphium
copper		silver
corn		slave market
garum		sources of slaves
glass		timber
gold		tin
horses		wine
iron		woollen textiles
lead		zinc
linen		
marble		
olives		

91

The rise of Christianity
to AD 600

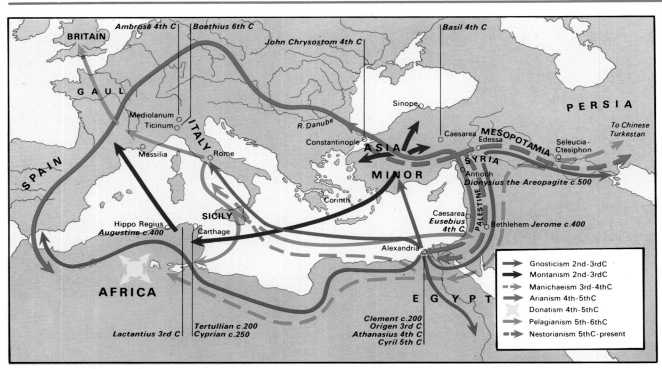

2/Writers and heresies (above)

As soon as Christianity became a subject of intellectual speculation in the second century AD, it was rent by doctrinal controversies, many of which represented a serious challenge to the Church's traditions and authority. The ideas of theologians like Donatus, Arius and Pelagius moved men and events almost as powerfully as the Christian revelation itself, and constantly threatened the unity of early Christendom.

The linking of pagan and Christian symbols In the pre-Constantinian inscription (below), the fish, an old religious symbol used because the Greek initial letters of 'Jesus Christ God's Son Saviour' spell IXθΥΣ, fish, represents Christ; so does the anchor, a firm point in a storm. But DM is a pagan formula, and the laurel is a Roman symbol of triumph. The symbol (above) is from a sarcophagus of about AD 350. Here the Roman laurel wreath is combined with the chi-rho, the first two letters of 'Christ' in Greek, linked to a vision of Constantine and resembling the 'sun-wheel'.

CHRISTIANITY, the last great world religion before Islam, originated in Palestine. Little is known of its founder, Jesus of Nazareth, before he began at the age of thirty to preach that 'the Kingdom of God is at hand'. It was a message for which many Jews were waiting. Their country, formally annexed by Rome in AD 6, was in turmoil; and there were many sects, some chiefly spiritual (like the Essenes), others more political (like those later called the Zealots), which hoped for the long-promised Messiah, or saviour, to liberate them. The crowds at first followed Jesus, seeing in him this Messiah; but the Jewish authorities were suspicious and his popular following soon dwindled. After three years of teaching and preaching he was seized, handed over to the Roman procurator, and crucified as a revolutionary.

The new faith proved tenacious, despite its founder's early death. His disciples, even their leader Simon Peter (the Rock), had initially abandoned Jesus, but their faith was restored by the Resurrection, when, they claimed, he appeared to them after death and charged them to proclaim the good news of God's reigning power. This revelation was at first presented in a purely Judaic context. Whether Jesus himself believed that God had sent him to convert the Gentiles remains unclear. It was left to Paul, a Jewish convert from Tarsus, to show the power and extent of Christianity's appeal as he preached in the Aegean islands, Asia Minor, Greece, Italy and perhaps as far as Spain. In all these areas there were Jewish communities (see page 102). The Christian preachers usually began with these, but the Jews in general were not won over; anti-Christian riots broke out, and the gap widened irretrievably when the Christians failed to support the Jewish uprising of AD 66.

Jesus's teaching appealed particularly – though not exclusively – to the poor and humble, who found in the kingdom of God a message of hope denied to them in the secular world. The number of converts steadily grew as economic conditions in the Empire deteriorated, though more among the urban masses than in the countryside, which largely retained its pagan beliefs. Outside the Empire, Antioch – 'the cradle of gentile Christianity' – spread its influence north and east. One disciple, Philip, is said to have converted an Ethiopian official, and there is a persistent tradition that Thomas reached India. At some point, date unknown, Edessa became a Christian stronghold. In the west, there were 1st-century churches in Puteoli, Rome, and possibly Spain;

by the mid 2nd century many existed in the Empire's eastern provinces and were starting to spread to the Rhine valley and North Africa.

By this time Christianity was significant enough to attract the attention of writers like Tacitus and Pliny the Younger. The former described how Nero used the Christians to divert hostility from himself. Conversions continued, despite repeated outbreaks of repression and persecution. The Christians' refusal to worship the emperors, serve as magistrates or carry arms made them officially suspect, but their beliefs appealed strongly to the oppressed and insecure, and as traditional Roman cults withered in the stormy 3rd century they became a force to be reckoned with.

Early in the 4th century the Emperor Constantine, whose family had worshipped the Unconquered Sun, decided to accept Christianity. His reasons were partly political, but it was a momentous decision. Recognised by the Edict of Milan (313), Christianity quickly established itself as the Empire's official religion, especially in the new capital, Constantinople. There was an abortive attempt to put the clock back by the Emperor Julian (361-63), but another tough militarist, Theodosius (379-95), further strengthened the Church's power. By now Christianity had also reached the barbarians beyond the imperial frontier. Soon after 340 Ulfilas converted the Goths near the mouth of the Danube. Many of the Germanic invaders after

376 were already Christian, though their preferred form of belief, Arianism, had been condemned as heretical at the Council of Nicaea (325).

Meanwhile, Christianity was becoming more organised. As time passed, those who had placed their faith in the second coming of Christ came to realise that this was not imminent. By the late 3rd and early 4th centuries, the sheer spread of churches demanded more complex structures to maintain discipline and safeguard doctrinal purity. The 'elders' of the early Christian communities had already been superseded by a hierarchy of bishops, and now a full-scale diocesan framework emerged.

Christianity was in any case never solely the simple faith of simple people. The great Alexandrian theologians, Pantaenus (active c.180-200), Clement (c. 150-215) and Origen (c. 185-254) had reconciled Christianity with Greek philosophy and made it intellectually respectable; but at the same time they opened the door to acute theological controversy. Already in the 2nd century, the mystical belief known as Gnosticism had developed at Alexandria. Other heresies and schisms which increasingly tended to split the Church were associated with Marcion (who regarded matter as evil), Novatian and Donatus (strict moralists), Arius (who subordinated the Son to the Father) and Pelagius (a moralist stressing free will). Another threat to Church unity was the withdrawal of monks and hermits by the thousand to a life of desert solitude. But Basil (c. 330-79) in the east and Benedict (c. 480-544) in the west curbed this trend by bringing the ascetics together in monastic communities, subject to strict ecclesiastical rules.

The Christian church modelled its structure on that of the Roman Empire. The dioceses mirrored the administrative divisions of Diocletian; bishops, based in the chief cities, met in synod in the provincial capitals, and those from the great metropolitan centres were accorded special dignity. Rome, the see of St Peter, was granted precedence in 'honour' but not in 'authority', and its bishops shared rank and power with those of Antioch and Alexandria, to which were later added Constantinople (381) and Jerusalem (451). Clear expressions of papal primacy are not found until the late 4th century. Meanwhile important decisions, particularly the definition of doctrine, were made by the assembled clergy. In the 2nd century local synods were called in Asia Minor to deal with the Montanist heresy, and in 325 the first ecumenical council, representing the whole Church, met at Nicaea. This was followed by the councils of Constantinople (381), Ephesus (431) and Chalcedon (451). Theoretically they were the voice of the Church; but in practice Christianity as the state religion was often subjected to imperial constraint. Some emperors – notably Justinian I (527-65) – ruled the Church with a heavy hand. This was the seed of conflict between Church and State, and underlay much of the later tension between Empire and Papacy (see page 122). However, when Rome succumbed to barbarian attack, it was the Church and its bishops, with their vast estates and pervasive influence, who emerged as guardians of the classical tradition, and guided Europe, as well as Christendom, into the new age.

3/The monastic movement (above) Almost from the beginning, a significant minority of Christians adopted a life of renunciation and withdrawal. By AD 700 monasteries had become centres of piety and learning in every Christian land, as well as great landowners.

1/The Early Christian churches (below) Starting with the journeys of St .Paul, Christian churches sprang up throughout the Roman world. By the time of Diocletian's persecutions (AD 304), they were thickly clustered around the Mediterranean, and scattered as far apart as Britain and the Nile.

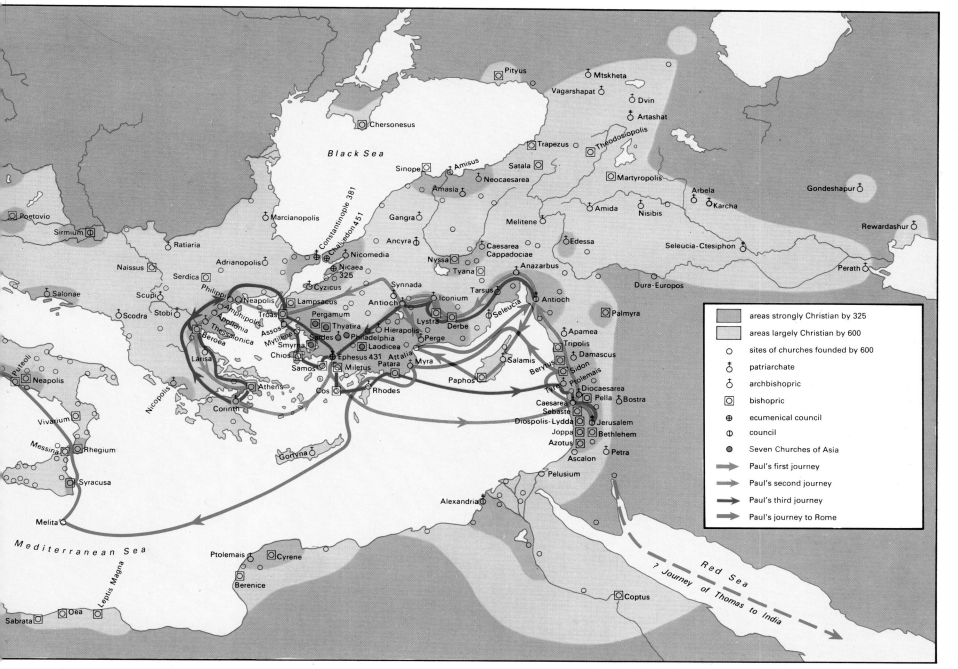

93

The crisis of the classical world

THE crisis of the classical world reached its height in the 5th century AD. It was prepared by earlier movements on the edge of China and affected all the great established civilisations of Eurasia, not merely the Greeks and the Romans. Its cause was the irruption of mounted nomad peoples from the north-west into the great crescent of ancient civilisations, which stretched from the Mediterranean to China. Its result was a setback to civilisation, which ushered in the so-called 'Dark Ages' not only in Europe but also in the whole of Eurasia. Only China coped successfully with the invaders; but even here their appearance saw a period of political fragmentation only ended by the Sui dynasty in AD 589.

The invading nomads whose incursions produced this crisis were no longer Indo-Europeans, though they had Indo-European peoples, mostly nomad, as subjects or allies. They were linked by common traditions and sometimes by actual kinship among their ruling groups; but they were not, unlike the Mongols seven centuries later (see page 128), under any form of central control, though their movements radiated from a common centre. Their physical type was not

uniform but was often Mongoloid Their languages were mostly of the Altaic groups of north-east Asia, now represented best by the varieties of Turkish. They all followed the pastoral mode of life with movable encampments of tents. In war they fought as mounted archers, using composite bows made of strips of bone, short, strong and convenient for riders. They also used sabres at close quarters and, when they came to possess taller horses and to use stirrups, the lance. This light and effective panoply was seldom adequately copied by civilised peoples, and accounts for the nomads' successes against them.

The centres of power among these Altaic nomads were not in arid steppe or desert, but in more favoured regions, such as the country along the Great Wall of China, and Mongolia north of the Gobi Desert. From here they struck both southward and westward. Their expansion began with the conquests of the people called Hsiung-nu in Chinese sources – a great nomad confederacy, the first to arise in eastern Asia, which grew up in continual rivalry with the Chinese empire of the Han. They were kept at bay only by a vast line of fixed fortifications. Finally the Han, using

cavalry modelled on that of the nomads, broke the power of the Hsiung-nu in the first century AD. But the Hsiung-nu did not vanish from history. Families of the ruling tribes appear to have established themselves in central Asia, where they gradually built up a new confederacy, now including Iranian nomads and some Mongoloid tribes from the Siberian forests. This revived confederacy was the origin of the Huns of later history. Mongolia, meanwhile, was ruled by other nomads, who were for the time less dangerous to the Chinese. But they finally broke into China at the beginning of the 4th century AD, after the short period of reunification under the Western Chin (265-317). Setting up an independent state in Shansi and Shensi, they took the two traditional capitals, Loyang in 311 and Ch'ang-an in 316. For the next 280 years northern China was dominated by invaders from the steppe, who established a bewildering succession of short-lived dynasties. Some of these were established by Hsiung-nu leaders, some by proto-Mongolian Hsien-pi, some by Turkic peoples, by the Avars, and by Tibetan tribes from the western borders, the Ti and Ch'iang.

These tribes had mostly had long contacts with

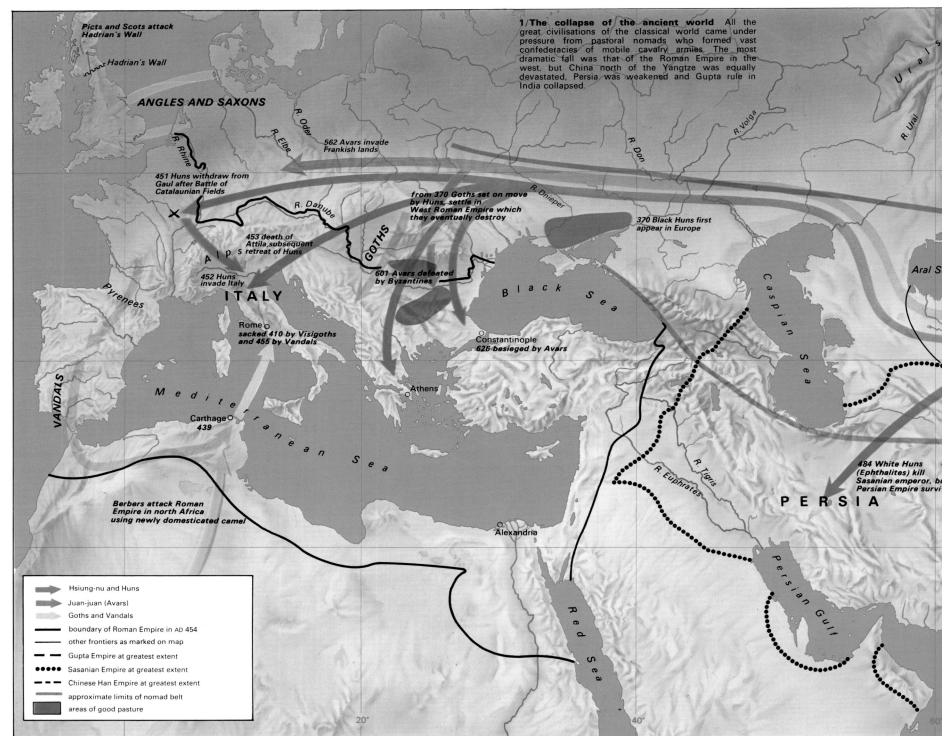

1/The collapse of the ancient world All the great civilisations of the classical world came under pressure from pastoral nomads who formed vast confederacies of mobile cavalry armies The most dramatic fall was that of the Roman Empire in the west, but China north of the Yangtze was equally devastated, Persia was weakened and Gupta rule in India collapsed.

Picts and Scots attack Hadrian's Wall

Hadrian's Wall

ANGLES AND SAXONS

R. Rhine

R. Oder

R. Elbe

562 Avars invade Frankish lands

451 Huns withdraw from Gaul after Battle of Catalaunian Fields

R. Danube

from 370 Goths set on move by Huns, settle in West Roman Empire which they eventually destroy

370 Black Huns first appear in Europe

R. Don

R. Volga

R. Dnieper

Urals

R. Ural

453 death of Attila, subsequent retreat of Huns

GOTHS

601 Avars defeated by Byzantines

Black Sea

Caspian Sea

Aral Se

452 Huns invade Italy

ITALY

Alps

Pyrenees

Rome sacked 410 by Visigoths and 455 by Vandals

Constantinople 626 besieged by Avars

Athens

VANDALS

Mediterranean Sea

Carthage 439

R. Tigris

R. Euphrates

484 White Huns (Ephthalites) kill Sasanian emperor, bu Persian Empire surviv

PERSIA

Alexandria

Berbers attack Roman Empire in north Africa using newly domesticated camel

Red Sea

Persian Gulf

→	Hsiung-nu and Huns
→	Juan-juan (Avars)
→	Goths and Vandals
—	boundary of Roman Empire in AD 454
—	other frontiers as marked on map
– –	Gupta Empire at greatest extent
••••	Sasanian Empire at greatest extent
– –	Chinese Han Empire at greatest extent
▨	approximate limits of nomad belt
▨	areas of good pasture

20°

40°

the Chinese; some, like the Hsiung-nu and Ch'iang, had been allowed to settle inside the Great Wall, and had served the Chinese as mercenary troops. When they established local states of their own in Chinese territory, however, they lacked the experience needed to administer a sedentary agricultural population, and were forced to adopt Chinese methods of government and to co-operate with the local Chinese elite families. The tension between the need to adapt tribal customs to Chinese conditions, and the desire to preserve their ethnic identity proved fatal to most of these regimes.

Eventually a powerful Turkic people, the Toba (Northern) Wei 386-534, succeeded in reunifying northern China. But they did so in the end by becoming completely sinicised. In the early 6th century this led to civil conflict, and their empire was again for a time split up. During these centuries, not only did the nomadic invaders adopt Chinese customs, literary culture and political institutions, but the Chinese upper class, particularly in north-western China (Kansu, Shensi, Shansi) collaborated widely with them, and themselves intermarried with the Turks and Hsien-pi. The result was the emergence of a distinctive Sino-nomad aristocracy, many of whom spoke both Chinese and Turkish, who lived a style of life much influenced by non-Chinese customs, and among whom women played a very powerful role. It was from this aristocratic group that emerged the ruling houses of the Sui (581-617) and T'ang (618-907) dynasties, which reunified the whole of China, and extended throughout the empire the institutions and style of government which had been developed in the northern successor kingdoms to the Toba Wei. They maintained a distinctive identity as a separate aristocratic group until the late T'ang.

The political chaos of the 4th century, when northern China was fragmented into many local states, led to immense physical destruction, and widespread depopulation. Vast numbers of Chinese fled to the south, where conditions were relatively stable. The flourishing internal and external trade of Han times fell away; the use of money even disappeared, and not only was trade carried on by barter, but the states' finances were collected entirely in commodities. It was only at the end of the 5th century that the Toba carried out a redistribution of land to bring more of their territory under cultivation, and began slowly to rehabilitate the economy.

The Black Huns of Europe, as they were called, moved into south Russia in the 4th century, and advanced in the 5th century into the fertile basin of the Danube, particularly the territories later known as Hungary. There they created an east European empire which threatened both the East and the West Roman Empires until the death of its leader Attila in AD 453. Their onslaught eventually destroyed the West Roman Empire, which fell under Germanic rule, but the East Roman or Byzantine Empire survived. Meanwhile, also in the 4th, 5th and 6th centuries AD the White Huns or Ephthalites overran much of the Sasanian Empire of Iran in constant wars, and went on to set up a dynasty in northern India. Byzantine sources and Indian coins represent them as people of a white race from central Asia, not Mongoloid, indicating that the name Hun (Khun in Iran, Huna in India) now denoted a political, rather than an ethnic, unity.

Both the Black Huns who invaded Europe, and the White Huns, have a record of devastation; the Hsiung-nu and their descendants and successors were thus the moving power in the crisis of established civilisations at the time. Not only did the effort to resist their incursions strain the resources of the states exposed to their attacks, but they also unsettled the tribes through whose territories they moved. Thus it was the Huns who set the Germanic peoples in motion (see page 98), and the withdrawal of garrisons to defend the Rhine frontier left the northern outposts in Roman Britain open to attack by the Picts. In eastern Asia, the successors of the Hsiung-nu were the Kök Türük – the Blue or Celestial Turks. They ruled during the 7th and 8th centuries over an empire which reached from Manchuria to the arid steppes west of the Syr Darya, and they appear to have driven other Turks westward, particularly the various tribes of the Ogur, who appear in Byzantine history. They also drove out the Juan-juan of Mongolia, once their rulers. The latter passed through northern Iran to reach the Russian steppes; here they amalgamated with other nomad Turkish or Hunnish tribes and reappeared in Hungary as the Avars, who threatened Constantinople and western Europe from the 5th to the end of the 8th century, when their empire was destroyed by Charlemagne. These movements among the nomad peoples of central Asia, whose causes are obscure and can only be surmised, mark the end of one period in world history, and set the stage for another.

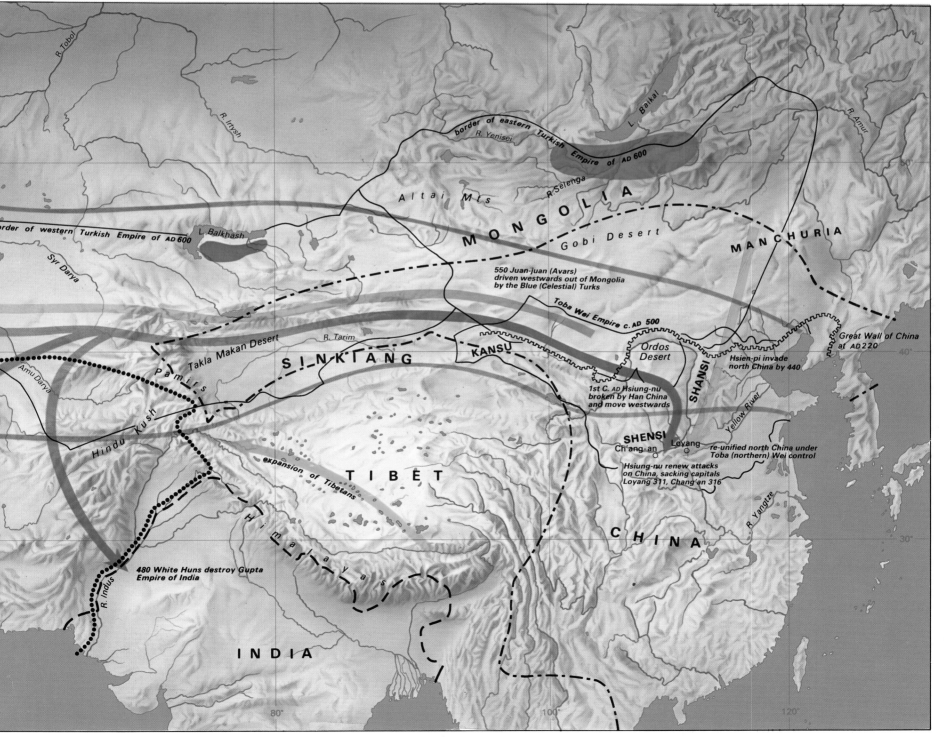

4 The world

of divided regions

The period around AD 500 was a time of upheaval throughout the Eurasian world, when nomads from the steppes of Asia descended upon all the existing centres of civilisation. Although the gains of the classical period were never entirely lost, there was a marked slackening of contacts between China and the West, and also between north Africa and Italy and between Byzantium and the lands of western Europe. Each region was thrown back upon its own resources to fend for itself.

In western Europe this period is traditionally known as 'the Middle Ages'. This description may be fitting in European history but makes little sense in the wider perspective of world history. Here, two outstanding events dominated the scene. The first was the rise and expansion of Islam, the second the emergence of the great Mongol Empire. After AD 632, when Mohammed died, Islam was incomparably the world's most dynamic civilisation, the true inheritor of the mantle of ancient Greece. At the same time, important developments were taking place in regions which hitherto had been isolated from the main stream. The appearance of the Maya, Aztec and Inca civilisations in America, the creation of the empires of Srivijaya and Majapahit in South-East Asia, and the rise of the empires of Ghana, Mali and Songhai in Africa, all attested to a new vitality and to the expansion of the area of civilised life.

Europe, by comparison, remained backward. Even here, however, it was a formative age, when primitive societies, such as the Anglo-Saxon heptarchy or the warbands of Frankish Gaul, were welded into feudal monarchies. But the process of consolidation was slow, interrupted by barbarian incursions and by economic setbacks. Not until the second half of the fifteenth century did Europe begin to draw level with the other world civilisations, and even then it was overshadowed by the expanding civilisation of the Ottoman Turks. If a relatively large space in this section is devoted to Europe, it is not so much because of its importance at the time, but rather because this period saw the beginnings of developments in European society which enabled it to advance to the centre of the stage in the following centuries.

Germanic and Slavonic invasions of Europe

3/The expansion of the Slavs (above) Following the Germanic migration westwards, the Slavs advanced into the vacated lands and also thrust south into Greece and the Balkans, accompanied by various non-Slav peoples such as Avars and Bulgars.

THE barbarian invasions of the 5th and 6th centuries and the settlement of Germanic and (later) Slav peoples on the soil of the Roman Empire are the traditional starting point of European history. Roman civilisation had been Mediterranean rather than European. With the Arab conquest of Palestine and North Africa (see page 104) and the descent of the Slavs into the Balkans, severing the links between Byzantium and the west, the Mediterranean framework of the Roman world was fractured, and the seat of power and influence shifted to the lands north of the Alps. Europe, cut off from the older civilisations of the Near East, began to go its own way under peoples who now moved from the periphery to the centre of the stage.

The Germanic peoples had moved before the Christian era, from Scandinavia to the shores of the Baltic around the mouth of the Vistula. Simultaneously the 'West Germans' were expanding into territory inhabited by the Celts east of the Rhine (see page 84). The 'East Germans' moved south c. AD 150 to the Carpathians and the lands north of the Black Sea. Pressure by both groups on the Roman frontiers began early; but it was the irruption of the Huns from Asia (see page 94) that threw the whole Germanic world into turmoil. First affected (c. 370) were the Ostrogoths in the Crimea and the Ukraine. Thrown back across the Dniester, they drove the Visigoths across the Danubian frontier of the Roman Empire into lower Moesia (Bulgaria), where they received permission to settle. Their defeat of the emperor Valens at the battle of Adrianople (378) destroyed Roman powers of resistance and opened the way for other barbarians fleeing westward. The Visigoths themselves first sought to settle in Greece (396-99), then moved on to Italy, when they astonished the civilised world by sacking Rome in 410, but quickly passed over into Aquitaine (418), where they founded the kingdom of Toulouse. They were followed in 406 by Alans, Vandals and Sueves from the Theiss valley and Silesia, who broke across the frozen Rhine frontier near Mainz and ravaged Gaul for three years, until in 409 they crossed the Pyrenees and entered Spain. Behind them came the Burgundians, who founded a kingdom around the city of Worms, but were settled in Savoy in 443 after Worms had been destroyed by the Huns in 437. In Spain the Sueves founded a kingdom in Galicia, which survived from 411 to 585, when it was absorbed into the Visigothic kingdom. The Vandals and Alans crossed from Spain to Africa in 429, and in 442 the imperial government recognised their king, Gaiseric, as an independent ruler. The Vandal kingdom survived until 533, when North Africa was reconquered by Justinian's general, Belisarius. Meanwhile, the defeat of the Huns at the climactic battle of the Catalaunian Fields near Troyes (451), the death of their leader Attila (453), and their retreat to the Russian plains, released the remaining Germanic tribes on the Danube, and the Ostrogoths moved south into Greece and subsequently into Italy, where they were in control by 493. North of the Alps, Franks and Alemans were infiltrating across the Rhine; while from about 440 Angles and Saxons were occupying the eastern and southern coastal areas of Britain, from which the Roman garrisons had withdrawn some thirty years earlier.

This great movement of peoples did not destroy the fabric of Roman civilisation. The Romans had long made a practice of settling barbarian 'confederate troops' within the empire. Salian Franks had been quartered in Belgium since c. 360. The Visigoths and others only sought settlement on a larger scale. Except for the Vandals, the Germanic leaders accepted a position within the Roman hierarchy of government. Their object was not to destroy but to share in the benefits of Roman civilisation. Their greatest leaders, notably Theoderic the Ostrogoth (493-526), saw it as their task to reconcile Romans and Germans. Nevertheless, except in the Frankish kingdom (see page 106), they did not succeed. The early Germanic kingdoms were inherently unstable. There were many reasons for this, not the least being hostility between the Arian ruling class and their Catholic subjects. But the main weakness was the fact that the warbands (averaging perhaps 80,000, of whom only some 20,000 were warriors), cut off from their homeland, were too small to exercise permanent control. The exceptions were the Franks and Anglo-Saxons, both able to draw on reinforcements from Germany. Otherwise, once Justinian embarked on reconquest in 533, their instability was soon apparent, although the Ostrogoths resisted fiercely from 536 to 554.

Justinian's reconquest was the turning point. Engaged simultaneously in war with Persia, the imperial government was over-extended and unable to restore effective control. The long Gothic wars irretrievably ruined Italy. In 568, only a few years after the capitulation of the last Gothic strongholds, the defenceless country was occupied – apart from the south, which remained Byzantine – by the Lombards, another Germanic people which had moved down from the Elbe to modern Hungary. The destruction of Gothic power, removing the main obstacle to Frankish expansion, also ensured the predominance of the Frankish kingdom in the west. East of the Adriatic the Slav peoples, who had expanded from their home in the region of the Pripet marshes as the Germanic tribes moved west, crossed the Danube c. 600, and descended into Greece. Just as the Germans had been propelled by the onslaught of the Huns, so it was the onslaught (beginning c. 560) of another Asiatic people, the Avars, which drove the Slavs (and the Lombards) into Roman territory. Apart from Salonica, protected by its walls, Macedonia was permanently occupied by the Slavs; Salona, the Roman capital of Dalmatia, fell to them c. 640. Only a few coastal cities of southern Greece and the Peloponnese remained Greek. In the eastern Balkans the Bulgars, an Asiatic people akin to the Huns, ruled over a largely Slav population and were recognised by the imperial government (681). The early history of the peoples of southeastern Europe is obscure; but by the end of the 8th century independent Croatian, Serbian and Bulgarian kingdoms were taking shape. Meanwhile the physiognomy of Europe had been permanently changed. The three centuries after the battle of Adrianople were a time of desperate confusion and material setbacks; but they were also a period when a new civilisation, 'Romano-Germanic' rather than Roman in character, was taking shape. Eventually it was to find its centre in the empire of Charlemagne (see page 106).

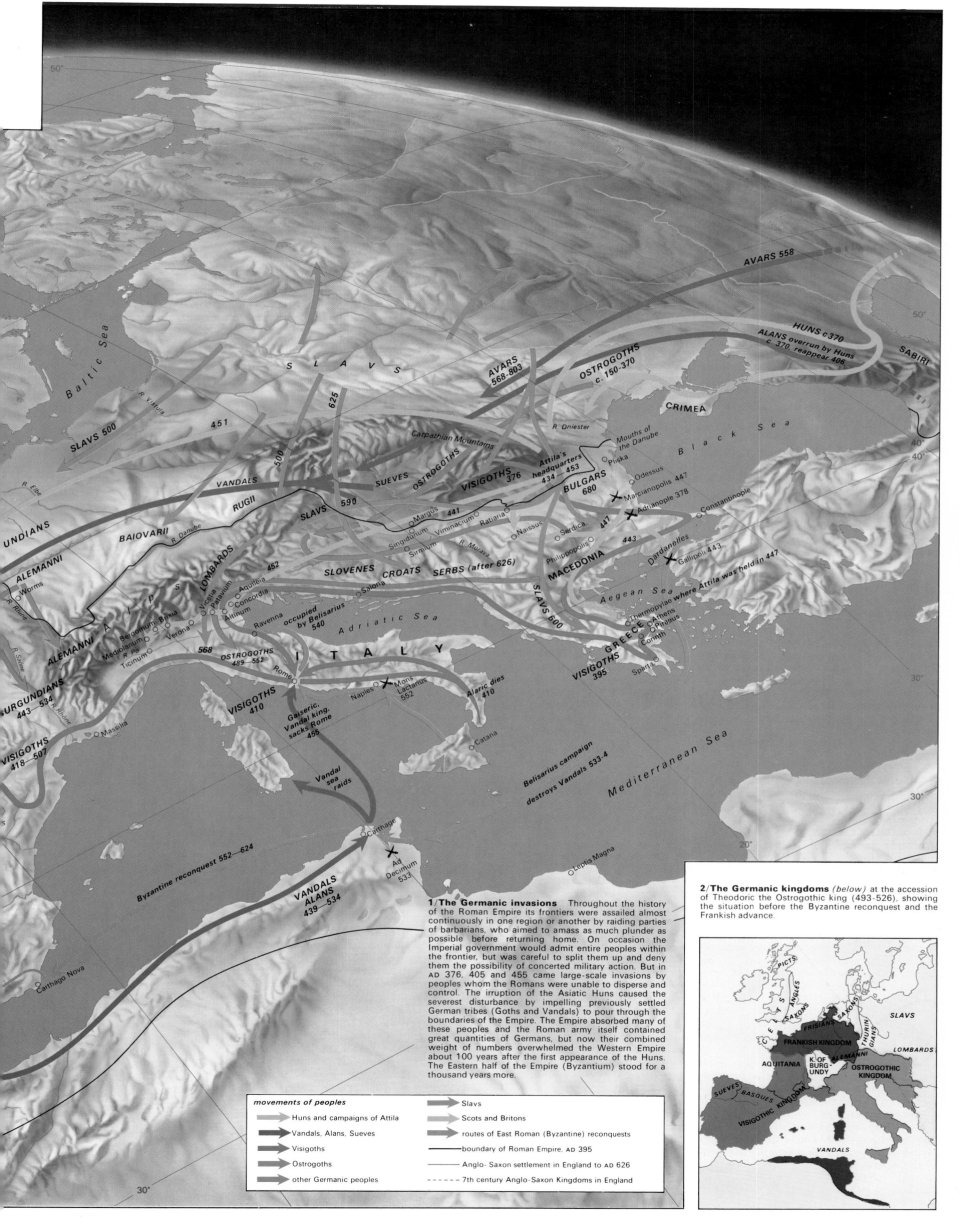

AVARS 558

HUNS c370

ALANS overrun by Huns
c. 370, reappear 406

SABIRI

OSTROGOTHS
c. 150-370

Baltic Sea

S L A V S

AVARS
568-803

CRIMEA

Black Sea

SLAVS 500

451

625

500

R. Vistula

VANDALS

RUGII

SLAVS

590

Carpathian Mountains

R. Dniester

Mouths
of the
Danube

Pliska

SUEVES

OSTROGOTHS

VISIGOTHS
376

Attila's
headquarters
434—453

BULGARS
680

Odessus

Marcianopolis 447

UNDIANS

BAIOVARII

R. Danube

LOMBARDS

SLOVENES

Margus

Singidunum

441

Viminacium

Ratiaria

R. Morava

CROATS

Naissus

Serdica

447

Philippopolis

443

MACEDONIA

Adrianople 378

Constantinople

Dardanelles

Gallipoli 443

ALEMANNI

Worms

R. Elbe

452

Aquileia

Concordia

Altinum

Ravenna

Salona

occupied
by Belisarius
540

Adriatic Sea

SLAVS
600

SLAVS 600

Aegean Sea

Thermopylae where Attila was held in 447

GREECE

Athens

Piraeus

Corinth

VISIGOTHS
395

Sparta

ALEMANNI

Bergomum

Brixia

Mediolanum

R. Po

Verona

Ticinum

568

OSTROGOTHS
489—552

Vicetia

Patavium

I T A L Y

Rome

BURGUNDIANS

R. Rhône

VISIGOTHS
410

Massilia

VISIGOTHS
418—507

Gaiseric, Vandal king,
sacks Rome
455

Naples

Mons
Lactarius
552

Alaric dies
410

Catana

Vandal
sea
raids

Belisarius campaign
destroys Vandals 533-4

Mediterranean Sea

Byzantine reconquest 552—624

Carthage

Carthago Nova

Ad
Decimum
533

VANDALS
ALANS
439—534

VANDALS
ALANS
439-534

Leptis Magna

1/The Germanic invasions Throughout the history of the Roman Empire its frontiers were assailed almost continuously in one region or another by raiding parties of barbarians, who aimed to amass as much plunder as possible before returning home. On occasion the Imperial government would admit entire peoples within the frontier, but was careful to split them up and deny them the possibility of concerted military action. But in AD 376, 405 and 455 came large-scale invasions by peoples whom the Romans were unable to disperse and control. The irruption of the Asiatic Huns caused the severest disturbance by impelling previously settled German tribes (Goths and Vandals) to pour through the boundaries of the Empire. The Empire absorbed many of these peoples and the Roman army itself contained great quantities of Germans, but now their combined weight of numbers overwhelmed the Western Empire about 100 years after the first appearance of the Huns. The Eastern half of the Empire (Byzantium) stood for a thousand years more.

2/The Germanic kingdoms (below) at the accession of Theodoric the Ostrogothic king (493-526), showing the situation before the Byzantine reconquest and the Frankish advance.

PICTS

CELTS

ANGLES

SAXONS

FRISIANS

SAXONS

THURIN-GIANS

SLAVS

FRANKISH KINGDOM

ALEMANNI

LOMBARDS

AQUITANIA

K. OF BURG-UNDY

OSTROGOTHIC KINGDOM

SUEVES

BASQUES

VISIGOTHIC KINGDOM

VANDALS

movements of peoples

Huns and campaigns of Attila

Vandals, Alans, Sueves

Visigoths

Ostrogoths

other Germanic peoples

Slavs

Scots and Britons

routes of East Roman (Byzantine) reconquests

boundary of Roman Empire, AD 395

Anglo-Saxon settlement in England to AD 626

7th century Anglo-Saxon Kingdoms in England

The expansion of Christianity 600 to 1500

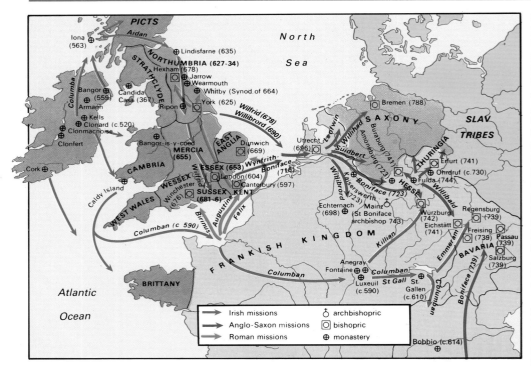

IN the first five centuries of its history Christianity was largely confined to the Roman Empire. Except for the missions of Ulfilas (c. 311-83) to the Goths and of St Patrick (c. 450) to Ireland, little effort was made to propagate the Gospel to the peoples outside. The decline of the Empire thus had decisive effects on the history of the Church. Already in the 5th century various attempts to shore up the tottering Empire by imposing religious orthodoxy, particularly the Council of Chalcedon (451), had alienated both the Monophysite churches of Egypt, Syria and Armenia, and the Nestorians in Upper Mesopotamia who, expelled from Edessa, took refuge in Persia. But the events which completely changed the position of the Church were the Germanic invasions of western Europe at the time of the pontificate of Pope Leo I (440-61), and the rapid advance of Islam after 635. The advance of Islam swamped three of the five patriarchates (Alexandria, Jerusalem and Antioch) and threatened a fourth (Constantinople). The western patriarchate (Rome) was similarly affected. North Africa and (later) Spain were lost; Illyria passed into the hands of heathen Slavs; while in the west most of the invaders, though Christian, were Arians and did not recognise papal authority. The Franks (though converted to Catholicism in 497) and the Anglo-Saxons were pagan.

By the time of Gregory I (590-604) Christianity was everywhere on the defensive. A century later the situation was worse. In place of a united Church in a united empire, disintegration and disruption were apparent on every side. Disputes between Rome and Constantinople over primacy compromised the Church's authority, and in the west the corrupt and secularised churches of Gaul and Spain were largely independent. Though Gregory himself sent a mission (596) to the heathen English, it accomplished little. At this crucial turning point salvation came from outside – not from the official Church, but from the Nestorians of Persia, the Copts of Egypt and the Celtic Christians of Ireland. These were the communities which initiated the expansion of Christianity at a time when, in its original Mediterranean homeland, it was under severe pressure.

In the long term the work of the Irish missionaries proved to be the most enduring, but to begin with the gains of the eastern churches were more impressive. Egypt was the home of cenobitic monasticism, and monasticism and asceticism gave the Egyptian, or Coptic, church a missionary fervour only equalled later by

Celtic Christianity. Already c. 340-50 Egyptian missionaries were active in Ethiopia; a century later Coptic missions, travelling upstream along the Nile valley, converted the Nubian kingdoms between Syene (Aswan) and Khartoum. The fact that Islam was not an intolerant or persecuting religion allowed these churches to flourish. It also permitted the rapid spread of Nestorian Christianity from its centre at Ctesiphon, the Persian capital on the Tigris. The expansion of the Nestorian church between the 7th and 11th centuries placed it, in size and influence, ahead of any other Christian church of the period. By the year 1000 its adherents probably numbered millions; it had some 25 metropolitan provinces and 200-250 bishoprics, stretching from eastern Syria across central Asia into China and south into Arabia. The Christian church in India (the so-called St Thomas church) was also almost certainly an offshoot of Nestorian Christianity.

The decline of eastern Christianity began with the mass conversions to Islam in the 11th century. The Coptic church in Egypt was particularly affected. Furthermore, the appearance of crusading armies in Asia Minor after 1097 bred a new intolerance on the Muslim side. In China, Christianity never made much headway except among the tributary peoples, such as the Uighurs. In central Asia the Mongols were tolerant and the Nestorian churches flourished until the 14th century; but with the accession of Timur (1362-1405) persecution began. A few Christian communities survived in remote places, as they did in India; but by the 15th century Christianity in Asia was a dying cause. It only revived, and then not very successfully, with the arrival of Catholic and Protestant missions in modern times. The exception was Siberia, where Russian missionaries were active from the 17th century.

In the west, the impetus for revival came from the Celtic church in Ireland, another monastic missionary church which directed its attention first to its Celtic neighbours in Scotland, Wales and Brittany, then to England, and later to the heathen tribes of continental Europe. The leading figures of the first generation were

Columba (d. 597) and Columban (d. 615). From Columba's Scottish foundation at Iona, Christianity was carried south to Northumbria (634), East Anglia (653) and Mercia (655), and from 664 the English church was united under the Roman obedience. Columban went further afield, to Burgundy and to the heathen Alemanni round Lake Constance. His missionary work was continued by the leading figures of the second generation, Willibrord (658-739) and Wynfrith (or Boniface) (675-754), the former among the Frisians around Utrecht, the latter in Hesse and Thuringia. Their target was the heathen Saxons, but the conversion of Saxony only followed later (804), at the point of the sword. Henceforward the expansion of Christianity in its western form was too often linked with political expansion. Nevertheless the missionary impulse remained strong. In 826 Anskar began the mission to Scandinavia, but here again resistance was fierce and Christianity was not finally accepted before the 11th century.

The Anglo-Saxon missions inaugurated the revival of Christianity in the west. Meanwhile Rome and Constantinople, slowly drawing apart into two separate obediences, Catholic and Orthodox, were vying for the allegiance of the Slav peoples of eastern Europe. The famous mission of Cyril and Methodius in 864 misfired owing to opposition from the Frankish church, but Serbia and Bulgaria were won over to orthodoxy. Constantinople also sent missions to the northern shores of the Black Sea. By 867 there was a Christian church at Kiev, and in 988 the Russian prince Vladimir was baptised. The conversion of Russia was a capital fact, opening up to Christianity an area larger than the rest of Europe combined. After 1169, when the capital was transferred from Kiev to Vladimir, Russian missionaries, moving north and east, carried Christianity to the heathen Karelians, Lapps, Permians, Votyaks and Mari. It was a major achievement, and once again ascetic monasticism provided the impetus.

Further west, Poland (966) and Hungary (1001) opted for Catholic Christianity, but sought to escape Frankish domination by placing their churches directly under the protection of Rome. The result was to enhance the Pope's authority. From the time of Leo IX (1048-54) a reformed Papacy actively asserted leadership, and the breach between Rome and Constantinople in 1054 hardened into a permanent schism. Papal authority was enhanced as a result of the Christian counter-offensive against Islam in Spain, still more by the Pope's sponsorship of the First Crusade (1095-99). The attempt to restore Christianity in Palestine was a costly failure, but the militant crusading spirit remained alive. The propagation of Christianity was underpinned by new monastic orders, the Cluniacs (particularly in Spain) and the Cistercians (in eastern Europe), but now the monks normally followed in the wake of the conquering armies. During the 13th century the friars (Franciscans and Dominicans) undertook peaceful missions to Asia and Africa, but their results were negligible. Heathen Prussia was conquered (1231-83) by the sword. In 1387 the prince of Lithuania, the last remaining heathen state in Europe, was converted to Catholicism, but only in order to succeed to the Polish throne. This was the last success of western Christianity until the Spanish *conquistadores,* imbued with the crusading spirit, carried the Catholic faith to America and opened a new chapter.

St Andrew and St Peter (above) This portrait, from the monastery of Bawit in the Libyan desert, exemplifies the ascetic spirit of eastern Christianity and helps to explain why, for a thousand years, it was so powerful a missionary force.

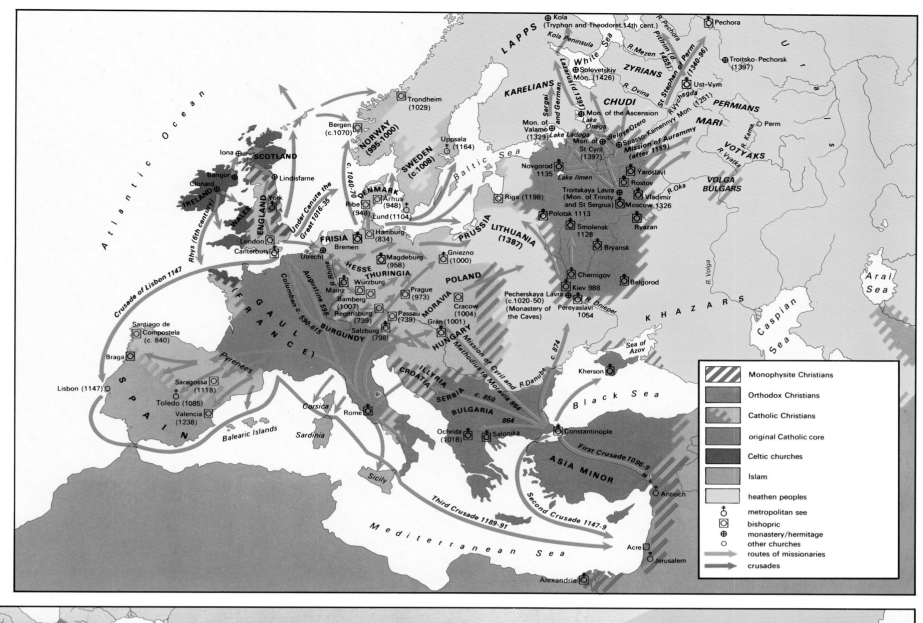

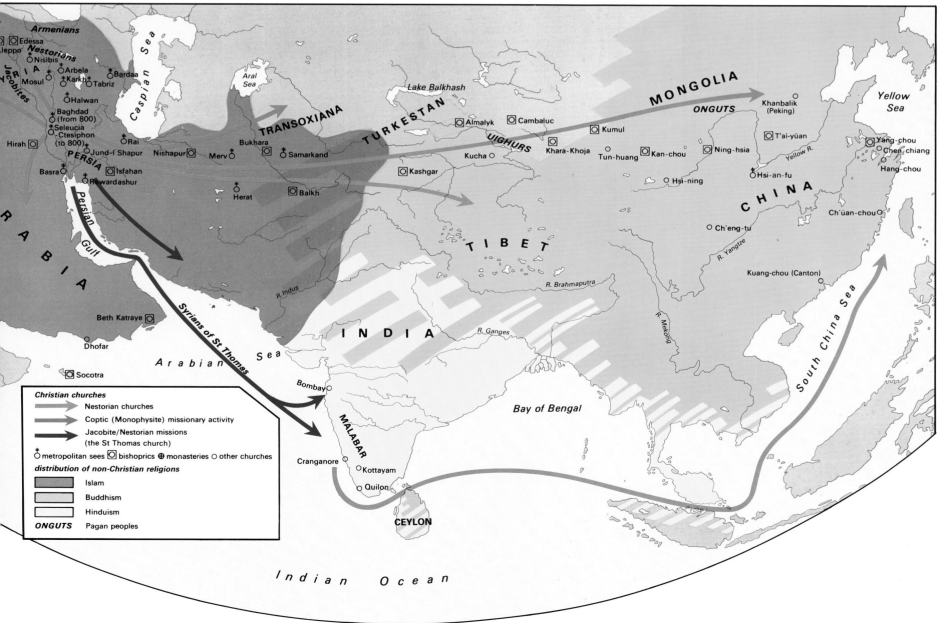

The Jewish diaspora
AD 70 to 1497

FOR over 2000 years the history of the Jews has been a story of external dispersion and internal cohesion. From the time of the destruction of the first Temple and the Babylonian exile (586 BC), the Jewish homeland was beset by powerful, predatory empires, of which the last was Rome. Conquered by the Roman general Pompey in 63 BC, Judaea became a Roman protectorate, and in AD 44 was finally placed under the direct rule of Roman procurators. The result was religious, political and nationalistic tension, which came to a head in AD 66 when a group of Jewish zealots revolted against Rome and gained control of Jerusalem. This uprising was crushed by Vespasian and Titus, who recaptured Jerusalem and destroyed the Temple in AD 70. Three years later the last zealot stronghold, the fortress Masada on the Dead Sea, also fell. Later, the apparent plan of the Emperor Hadrian to Romanise Jerusalem ended all prospects of rebuilding the Temple, and incited a second Jewish revolt in AD 132, which was finally suppressed three years later.

The political, military and religious reverses in Judaea in no way affected the status of Jews elsewhere in the Roman Empire, nor of the even larger number of Jews living in Babylonia. The movement of Jews from the main area of Jewish settlement (Palestine, Asia Minor, Babylonia, Egypt) into Europe had begun in the late Hellenistic period, and was stimulated by the incorporation of Judaea into the Roman Empire. By the middle of the first century BC, Jews already lived in the city of Rome, and later they spread out in the wake of the Roman legions. Exact figures are not known, but it has been estimated that they may have constituted as much as ten per cent of the population of the Roman Empire, playing a role in cultural and religious life, and enjoying legal privileges which facilitated their observance of Judaism.

The resilience of Judaism after the setback in AD 70 may be explained, at least in part, by the evolution of the Jewish religion following the destruction of the first Temple in 586 BC, when a system based on a Temple and sacrifices was complemented by one based on the synagogue and prayer. These new religious forms were developed after the Babylonian exile under the guidance of a new type of religious leadership, the *sofrim* (scribes or bookmen), who evolved into the Pharisees and finally the Rabbis. A second important factor was the codification of Jewish law, both civil and religious, carried out in Palestine around AD 200 by Rabbi Judah the Patriarch in a work called the *Mishnah*. This code became the basis of continuous study in the academies of learning in both Palestine and Babylonia, and the discussions were preserved in the *Talmud*, still today the basis for traditional Jewish behaviour and belief.

The adoption of Christianity as the official religion of the Roman Empire in the 4th century AD brought a change for the worse in the position of Jews. Restrictive legislation was enacted in the Empire and later in its successor states, particularly in Visigothic Spain, where Judaism was finally proscribed. However, the Muslim conquest of Spain in AD 711 brought a respite, which culminated in the 'golden age' of Spanish Jewry. At the same time, the break-up of the Roman Empire affected the economic activities of the Jews, which hitherto had been no different from those of other national groups. From about the 6th century this changed, and Jews became particularly identified with international and regional trade. Internal and external factors, including the widespread dispersal of Jews both in Islamic lands and throughout Christian Europe, Jewish group solidarity, facility of linguistic communication, and a uniform system of commercial law based on the *Talmud*, accounted for this change. The trend was encouraged by the increasing exclusion of

Jews from landowning, especially in northern Europe, the consolidation of the feudal system, and the constant threat of the confiscation of Jewish property and expulsion. Carolingian rulers, aware of the Jews' role in international trade, granted them special charters, assuring them of protection, commercial privileges, and the right to govern themselves according to their own law.

In the 10th and 11th centuries, Jewish settlements, apparently first consisting of merchants, were established in the Rhine valley. Later, they spread further east, and by the 13th and 14th centuries into Poland, where the Jews continued to speak their German dialect, which became known as Yiddish. But the pre-eminence of the Jews in commerce declined with the emergence of a native Christian merchant class and the exclusive policies adopted by the Christian merchant guilds. The Jews were forced more and more into the credit field (closed at least in theory to Christians by the Church's prohibition of usury), where they came to assume a predominant, though by no means exclusive role, especially in northern France, England, Germany and northern Italy. As such, they were invaluable, often as a source of small-scale loans to the urban poor in time of need and always as a source of credit and taxation to kings, princes and municipalities, who continued to grant them charters of protection, guaranteeing security of persons and property, the exercise of religious worship, and the right to communal self-government, thus making possible the development of Jewish law and institutions, the perpetuation of the Jewish religious tradition, and the evolution of intellectual and cultural life.

At the same time the Church adopted an increasingly hostile attitude (especially at the Third and Fourth Lateran Councils in 1179 and 1215), and as the inflammatory sermons of the wandering friars stirred the passions of the populace, the condition of the Jews deteriorated severely. They were subjected to arbitrary financial payments, severe restrictions of economic pursuits, the wearing of distinguishing badges (often yellow), confinement to special quarters known as ghettos *(ghetti)* – a term first applied to the Jewish quarter in Venice in 1516, though the institution existed earlier – and unsubstantiated charges of ritual murder, blood libel, desecration of the Host, and well poisoning (the last especially at the time of the Black Death in 1348). This combination of social, economic and religious animosity, coupled with the feeling that Jews were an alien body in a Catholic society, led to numerous expulsions. Though fairly often the Jews were recalled, because their departure caused a disruption of economic life, with the emergence of alternative sources of finance and the development of the western economies they became much less necessary. One by one the rulers of western Europe expelled them totally from their realms: England in 1290, France in 1394, Spain in 1492 (thereby initiating the Sephardic diaspora), Portugal in 1497 (though here large numbers, including many who had found refuge in Portugal at the time of the Spanish expulsion, were forcibly converted, though many escaped in the following decades).

Jews were also expelled from many German cities. Thus, after 1497, Jews no longer resided in western Europe or in large parts of central Europe. The centres of Jewish population and cultural life were located in northern Italy, a few cities in Germany, the Ottoman Empire, and especially in Poland and Lithuania. Not until the 17th and 18th centuries, under the impact of rationalism, mercantilism and the Enlightenment, were the Jews readmitted to England, France and the Netherlands; legal emancipation, though not always social acceptibility, had to wait until the late 18th and 19th centuries.

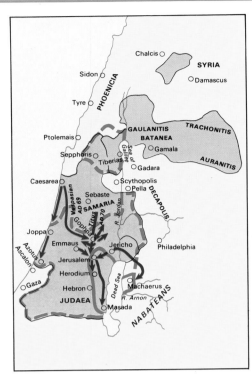

2/Judaea in the 1st centuries BC and AD *(left)* In 140 BC an independent Jewish state emerged under Simon the Hasmonean, a brother of Judah Maccabee. It became a Roman protectorate in 63 BC. Subsequently, the Edomite Herod I (37-4 BC), husband of the Hasmonean princess Miriam, divided it in his will between his three sons, Archelaus, Herod Antipas and Philip. Eventually it was reunited under his grandson, Agrippa I (AD 41-44), and after Agrippa's death governed by Roman procurators, whose rule led to the unsuccessful revolt by Jewish nationalists of AD 66-73. Their last stand was at the fortress of Masada.

	area of Roman procuratorial rule in Judaea
	Agrippa II's kingdom, AD 61
	area of major revolt at start of AD 66
	area of revolt at end of AD 69
→	Roman armies

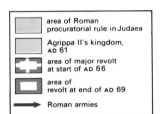

The seven-branched candlestick *(above)* from the Temple in Jerusalem was taken to Rome by Titus when the Romans destroyed the Temple in AD 70 during the suppression of the Jewish revolt.

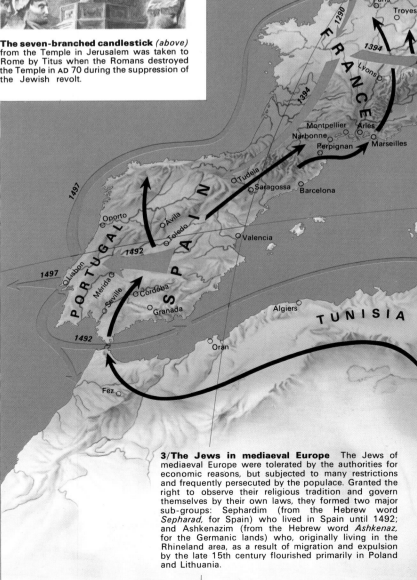

3/The Jews in mediaeval Europe The Jews of mediaeval Europe were tolerated by the authorities for economic reasons, but subjected to many restrictions and frequently persecuted by the populace. Granted the right to observe their religious tradition and govern themselves by their own laws, they formed two major sub-groups: Sephardim (from the Hebrew word *Sepharad*, for Spain) who lived in Spain until 1492; and Ashkenazim (from the Hebrew word *Ashkenaz*, for the Germanic lands) who, originally living in the Rhineland area, as a result of migration and expulsion by the late 15th century flourished primarily in Poland and Lithuania.

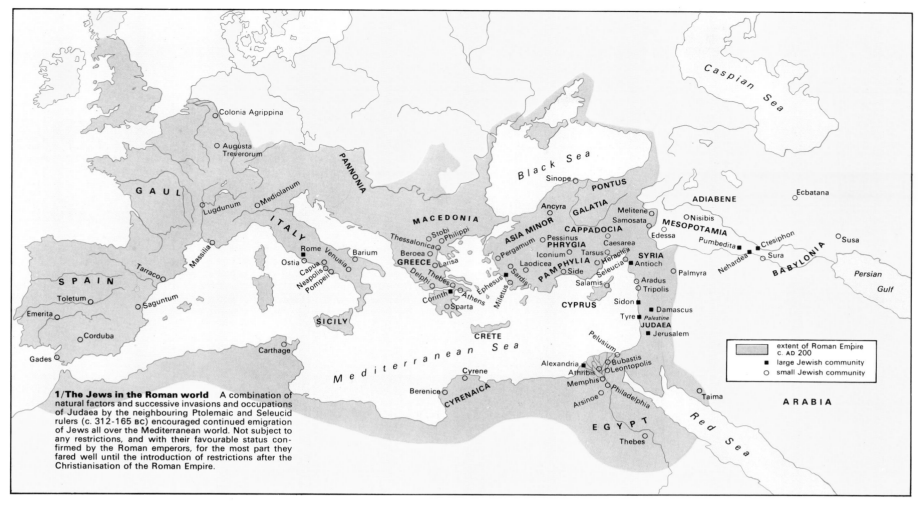

1/The Jews in the Roman world

A combination of natural factors and successive invasions and occupations of Judaea by the neighbouring Ptolemaic and Seleucid rulers (c. 312-165 BC) encouraged continued emigration of Jews all over the Mediterranean world. Not subject to any restrictions, and with their favourable status confirmed by the Roman emperors, for the most part they fared well until the introduction of restrictions after the Christianisation of the Roman Empire.

extent of Roman Empire c. AD 200
■ large Jewish community
○ small Jewish community

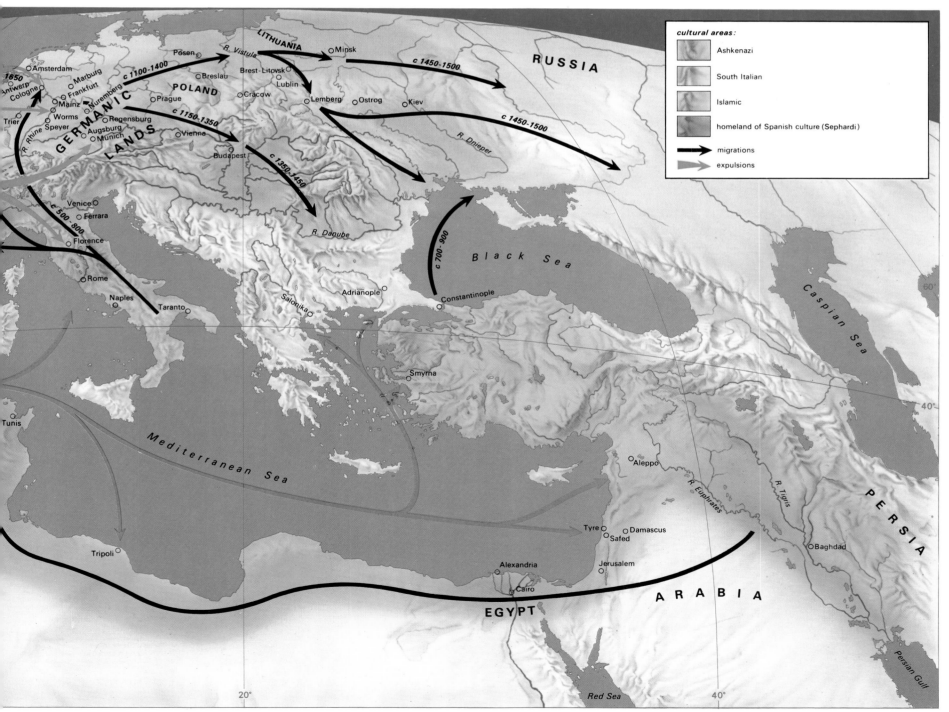

cultural areas:

Ashkenazi

South Italian

Islamic

homeland of Spanish culture (Sephardi)

→ migrations

→ expulsions

The spread of Islam from AD 632

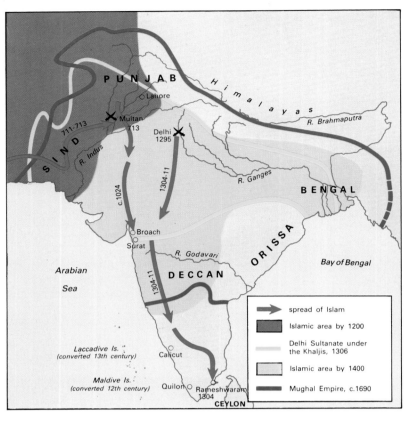

2 and 3/ India and Indonesia The spread of Islam in India *(above)* was partly the result of expansion by successive waves of Muslim conquerors, partly the consequence of conversion by missionaries and traders. Indonesia and the Malay peninsula *(below)* were converted to Islam by a gradual process of proselytisation, beginning in all probability with Muslim traders from Gujerat in India, who had acquired a permanent foothold at Perlak on the northern top of Sumatra

by 1290. From there they spread to Malaya (c.1400), where the new religion quickly took hold, and also to Java and the Moluccas (c.1430-90). By the end of the 16th century most of the islands in the archipelago had accepted Islam, notably Mindanao and the Sulu archipelago in the Philippines. This process continued despite successive waves of Spanish, Portuguese and Dutch colonisation and conquest.

THE rise and expansion of Islam was one of the most significant and far-reaching events in modern history, and its impact continues to reverberate in our own times. Islam means 'submission to the will of God'; God's message to mankind has been expressed through a series of prophets, culminating in Mohammed, the Apostle and Prophet of God. Muslims believe that God has spoken through Mohammed, and that the Koran, which means recitation, is the Word of God. Mohammed is the Seal of the Prophets, and no others will come after him, but he is not of course divine, for divinity belongs to God alone. Mohammed's message, to his fellow citizens in the western Arabian city of Mecca, was that they should cease to worship idols, and submit instead to the will of Allah.

Mohammed was born in Mecca about AD 570, and was orphaned in early childhood. At that time Mecca was the principal commercial centre in western Arabia, and was also an important pilgrimage centre, based on the cult of the Ka'ba, the Black Stone. He received his first revelations in 610. As his followers grew in number, Mohammed aroused the hostility of the merchant aristocracy of Mecca, who feared that acceptance of his message would pose a threat to the shrine. Hostility developed into persecution, and in 622 Mohammed and his followers withdrew to Medina, some 280 miles north-east of Mecca. This 'migration', *hijra* in Arabic, on 16 July 622, marks the beginning of the Islamic era and thus of the Muslim calendar.

In Medina, Mohammed organised the Muslims into a community, and consolidated his base with the assistance of his Medinan hosts. The Meccans made every effort to dislodge him, but after a series of defeats eventually accepted his message. Mohammed returned to Mecca in triumph in 630, and cast out the idols from the Ka'ba, transforming it into the focal point of the new religion of Islam. When Mohammed died in 632, his authority extended over the Hejaz and most of central and southern Arabia.

Over the next hundred years, the Arab armies brought the religion of Islam as far west as Spain, and as far east as northern India. This expansion owed much to the enthusiasm and religious conviction of the conquerors, but it was also

facilitated by the war-weariness of the empires of Persia and Byzantium. The first of Mohammed's successors, the caliph Abu Bakr (632-34) completed the conquest of Arabia and entered southern Palestine. His successor Omar (634-44) advanced to Damascus, and victory over the Byzantines at the Yarmuk river in 636 encouraged the Muslims to advance east into Mesopotamia and north-west into Asia Minor. By 643 Persia had been overrun, and the last Persian emperor, Yazdigird, was killed in 651 after his troops had put up a final stand at Merv. The conquest of Herat and Balkh (651) and the fall of Kabul (664) opened the way to India; Sind, in north-east India, fell to the Muslims in 712.

Simultaneously, Arab forces pushed west into Egypt, occupying Alexandria in 643, and advancing across North Africa into Cyrenaica. Further progress was held up by Berber resistance, but the advance was resumed after the construction of the fortress city of Kairouan in 670. After the subjection of the Maghreb, Arab forces crossed the Straits of Gibraltar in 711 and conquered Spain. There were further advances into southern France, but the Arab armies were defeated at Poitiers in 732, and in 759 they withdrew south of the Pyrenees. In the late 7th and early 8th centuries attacks were launched against Constantinople, but the Byzantines succeeded in preventing the Arabs from capturing the city and in fact retained control of much of Asia Minor until the 11th century.

Initially, Islam did not particularly encourage, far less insist upon, conversion. The Koran enjoins Muslims to respect the 'people of the book', that is, members of the other monotheistic religions with written scriptures, and the existence of substantial Christian (and until

The minaret *(left)* from which the *muezzin* chants the call to prayer, is attached to all mosques and is a distinctive feature of Islamic religious architecture. Originally square, the minaret later assumed the slender, lofty, circular form familiar in India and Constantinople. The minaret of the famous mosque of Ahmad ibn Tulun in Cairo, built in 879 and renovated in 1267, combines both forms.

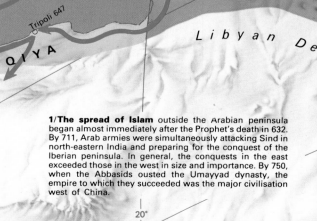

1/The spread of Islam outside the Arabian peninsula began almost immediately after the Prophet's death in 632. By 711, Arab armies were simultaneously attacking Sind in north-eastern India and preparing for the conquest of the Iberian peninsula. In general, the conquests in the east exceeded those in the west in size and importance. By 750, when the Abbasids ousted the Umayyad dynasty, the empire to which they succeeded was the major civilisation west of China.

comparatively recently, Jewish) communities throughout the Muslim world is ample evidence that this injunction was heeded. However, under the Abbasid dynasty (750-1258), large-scale conversion became common. This was partly because under the Abbasids, when the capital of the empire shifted from Syria to Mesopotamia, power passed from the conquering Arab minority to the non-Arab majority, and non-Arabs were no longer discriminated against as they had been under the Umayyads (661-750).

Although the Muslim world soon lost its original political unity — with the accession of the Abbasids and with the establishment of rival caliphates in Cairo and Córdoba in the mid 10th century it retained a considerable degree of cultural unity, largely through the Arabic language. In many ways, this unity overrode the sectarian divides which had already appeared in the first Islamic century, largely centring on the vexed question of the succession to the caliphate. With the seizure of temporal power by the Buyids in Baghdad in 936, the Abbasid caliphs were largely restricted to their religious functions. The Islamic world had fragmented into local dynastic entities, whose acknowledgement of Abbasid suzerainty was often only nominal.

Although the Islamic empire declined as a theocratic entity, Islam itself continued to expand as a religious force (see maps 2 and 3). This expansion was partly the result of conquest, and partly — particularly in South-East Asia and West Africa — the result of missionary activity by traders and preachers. The contemporary Islamic world (map 4) covers substantial parts of Asia and Africa, and the events of the 1970s and 1980s have shown that Islam has once more emerged as a decisive factor in world politics.

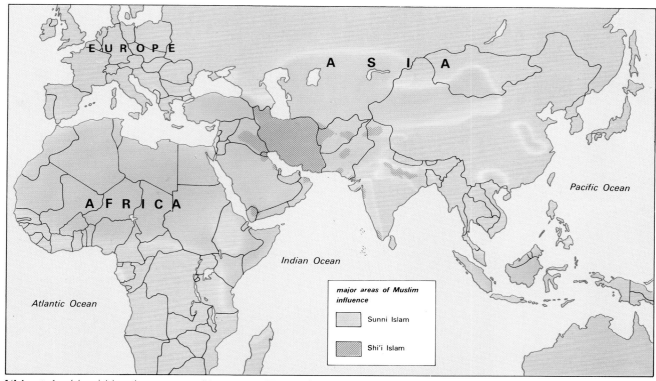

4/Islam today *(above)* Islam, the most recent of the great world religions, numbers some 400 million adherents, about one-seventh of the total population of the globe. Most Muslims are distributed in a broad band from Morocco to Indonesia, and from northern central Asia to Tanzania. The states with the largest Muslim population are Indonesia (148 million, 90% of total population), Bangladesh (88 million, 80%), Nigeria (81 million, 47%), Pakistan (80 million, 83%), India (70 million, 11%) and Egypt (41 million, 92%). The map shows the relative preponderance of Sunni (orthodox) Muslims, the Shi'i sect being largely confined to Iran, southern Iraq and Yemen.

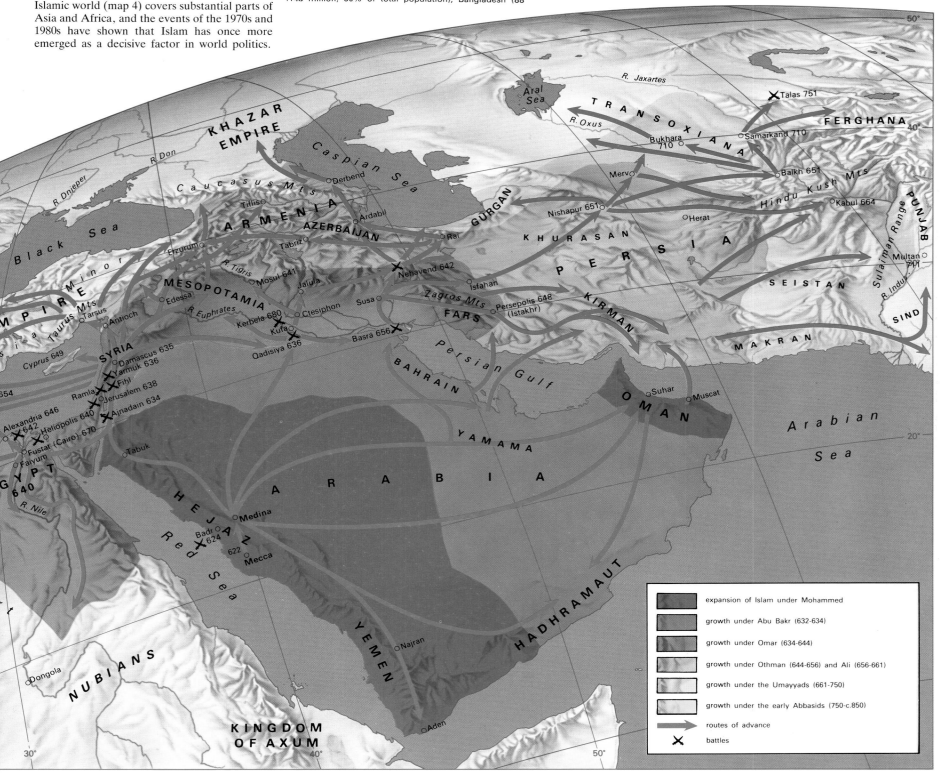

The rise of the Frankish Kingdom 482 to 814

THE conquests of Clovis, who died in 511, and his sons made the Franks the most powerful and important of all the barbarian successors of Rome, and created the basis for the Frankish hegemony that dominated western Europe for more than three centuries. The tomb of Clovis' father, Childeric, discovered in 1653, shows that he was buried with great, but not particularly barbarian, splendour in a Roman cemetery at Tournai, in the heart of the territory seized by the Franks in the 5th century. He was, however, not the only Frankish ruler, for the Franks who lived in the valleys of the Rhine, Mosel and Meuse had other chieftains or kings. Clovis not only destroyed the power of such rivals and so united the Franks under his rule, but also greatly extended his authority over neighbouring peoples to both east and west. His victories over the Thuringians and Alemans began that Frankish influence over the Germans east of the Rhine that was to be a major theme of Frankish, and of European, history; while his mastery of the greater part of Gaul was achieved by the defeat of Syagrius, 'king of the Romans', at Soissons in 486 and, some twenty years later, at Vouillé, near Poitiers, of Alaric II and his

Visigoths, who were thereafter confined to Spain and the coastal district of Septimania. Clovis' kingdom was enlarged by his sons and grandsons who not only extended Frankish overlordship in the east as far as the middle Danube, but also conquered the Burgundians and drove the Ostrogoths from Provence.

This expansion was achieved more by conquest than by colonisation; some Franks did settle in northern Gaul but most of them continued to live in the north-east in those areas where Germanic languages have persisted to this day (see map 2). Clovis ruled from Paris, but in Gaul itself there was little displacement of the native population, and the French language has developed from Latin with relatively few German words (e.g. *bleu*). The government largely remained in the hands of bishops and counts drawn from the Gallo-Roman aristocracy who, as a result of Clovis' conversion to Catholic Christianity, were ready to accept Frankish rule in preference to that of Burgundians and Visigoths, who had been converted earlier to the heretical Arian form of the religion.

However valuable Clovis and his successors found such Gallo-Roman support, their power

ultimately depended on the Frankish army, and one important motive for the conquests was the need to win booty, land and revenues with which the loyalty of the warriors could be rewarded and maintained. By the middle of the 6th century the first period of expansion was over and Frankish kings had to reward followers and endow the Church by granting away their own estates and revenues. In so doing, they diminished their resources, and in time their power passed to the families that had benefited most from royal favour. There were many of these, but by the middle of the 7th century two families had emerged as particularly important and were the principal agents of the kings, holding office as mayors of the royal palace. One family came from Austrasia, the eastern, traditionally Frankish lands, while the other family was associated with Neustria, the new lands north of the Loire. The conflict between these rivals was ended at Tertry in 687 when the victor was the Austrasian, Pepin of Herstal, near Aachen. He consequently gained a dominant position in the Frankish kingdom which he retained until his death in 714, and which was quickly re-established by his son Charles Martel, 'the Hammer' (d.741), who

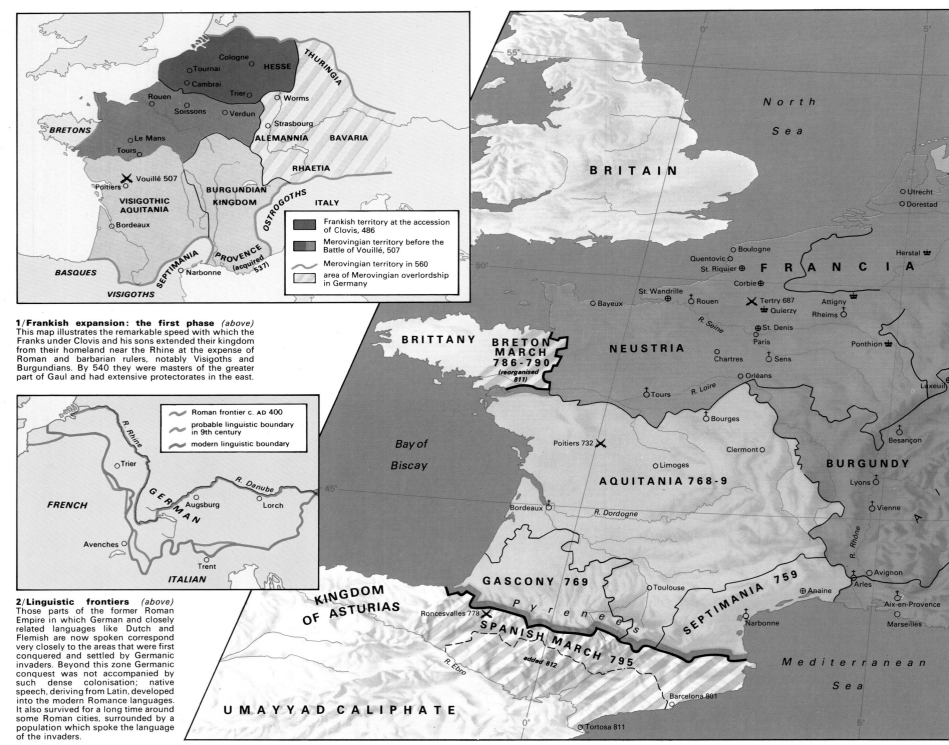

1/Frankish expansion: the first phase *(above)*
This map illustrates the remarkable speed with which the Franks under Clovis and his sons extended their kingdom from their homeland near the Rhine at the expense of Roman and barbarian rulers, notably Visigoths and Burgundians. By 540 they were masters of the greater part of Gaul and had extensive protectorates in the east.

2/Linguistic frontiers *(above)*
Those parts of the former Roman Empire in which German and closely related languages like Dutch and Flemish are now spoken correspond very closely to the areas that were first conquered and settled by Germanic invaders. Beyond this zone Germanic conquest was not accompanied by such dense colonisation; native speech, deriving from Latin, developed into the modern Romance languages. It also survived for a long time around some Roman cities, surrounded by a population which spoke the language of the invaders.

gave his name to the Carolingian family.

These men were prepared to rule while the Merovingians, so called because they traced their ancestry back to Clovis' grandfather, Meroveus, continued as kings, but in 751 the situation was transformed when, with the sanction and support of the pope, Charles Martel's son Pepin the Short (d.768) made himself king and so established the new Carolingian dynasty. The Church continued to be a pillar of the monarchy, and Alcuin of York was one of Charlemagne's main advisers. Meanwhile, the new dynasty assumed the traditional responsibilities of Frankish rulers, leading expeditions and defending their territory against such old enemies as the Frisians and the Saxons, as well as combating the new threat posed by the Muslim conquerors of Visigothic Spain. Charles Martel's most famous victory was, in fact, the battle of Poitiers in 732 against Muslim raiders, a victory that was remembered as being of the greatest moment, symbolising the role of the Franks, and of the Carolingians in particular, as defenders of Christendom. That role was first assumed by Clovis and later found its most dramatic expression on Christmas Day 800 at Rome in the imperial coronation of Pepin's son, Charlemagne (Charles the Great), who by conquering and converting the Saxons, by taking over the Lombard kingdom and so liberating the papacy from a persistent threat, and by creating a March, or buffer zone, between the Frankish lands and Muslim Spain, had created a truly imperial and Christian hegemony.

The hegemony was, however, personal. In 806 Charlemagne planned to divide his empire among three sons, a scheme that was frustrated by the death, in his lifetime, of all but one of them, thus making it possible for the survivor, Louis the Pious (814-40) to inherit the whole empire. In providing for such a division Charlemagne was following the Frankish custom of partitioning the royal demesne, a custom that had caused him to share his inheritance for three years with his brother Carloman (see map 4b). This practice can be traced back to the death of Clovis when his four sons partitioned their inheritance. The divisions, which could be very complicated, did not mean the dismemberment of the kingdom, which could still be regarded as a unit and was occasionally united, but they did create many opportunities for internal conflict which the later Merovingians appear to have preferred to external conquest.

Under the Carolingians Frankish expansion was resumed, but it was unlike that of the Merovingians for it led to the displacement of many bishops and counts of Gallo-Roman descent by Franks from Austrasia. The first generations of these Frankish agents of royal government were in general loyal to Pepin and Charlemagne, but their descendants tended to identify with the particular interests of their own localities at the expense of the kingdom, and during the 9th and 10th centuries, as they were able to free themselves from the restraints of royal authority, some established principalities over which the kings could, for a time, claim little more than a theoretical superiority. The Frankish hegemony was therefore disrupted by partition and fragmentation, but its framework and memory has remained, to this day, a powerful influence in European history.

4a/Francia in 587 *(above)* The treaty of 587 was one of many agreements dividing the Frankish kingdom between the descendants of Clovis. Childebert's portion was in effect ruled by his mother, the Visigoth Brunhild, who dominated Frankish politics until her execution in 613.

4b/Francia in 768 *(above)* The custom of partitioning the kingdom was continued by the Carolingians: on the death of Pepin the Short (768) his two sons divided their inheritance. The elder, Charlemagne, held most of the key area of Austrasia until Carloman died (771), when he inherited the whole.

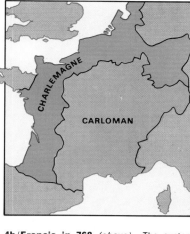

The Chapel at Aachen *(right)* Charlemagne's vast authority in western Europe was reflected by the construction of a large and complex palace in Aachen which was thought by some contemporaries to be a 'second Rome'. It included this chapel, modelled on the 6th-century church of San Vitale in Ravenna which commemorates Justinian, another great emperor who triumphed in Italy.

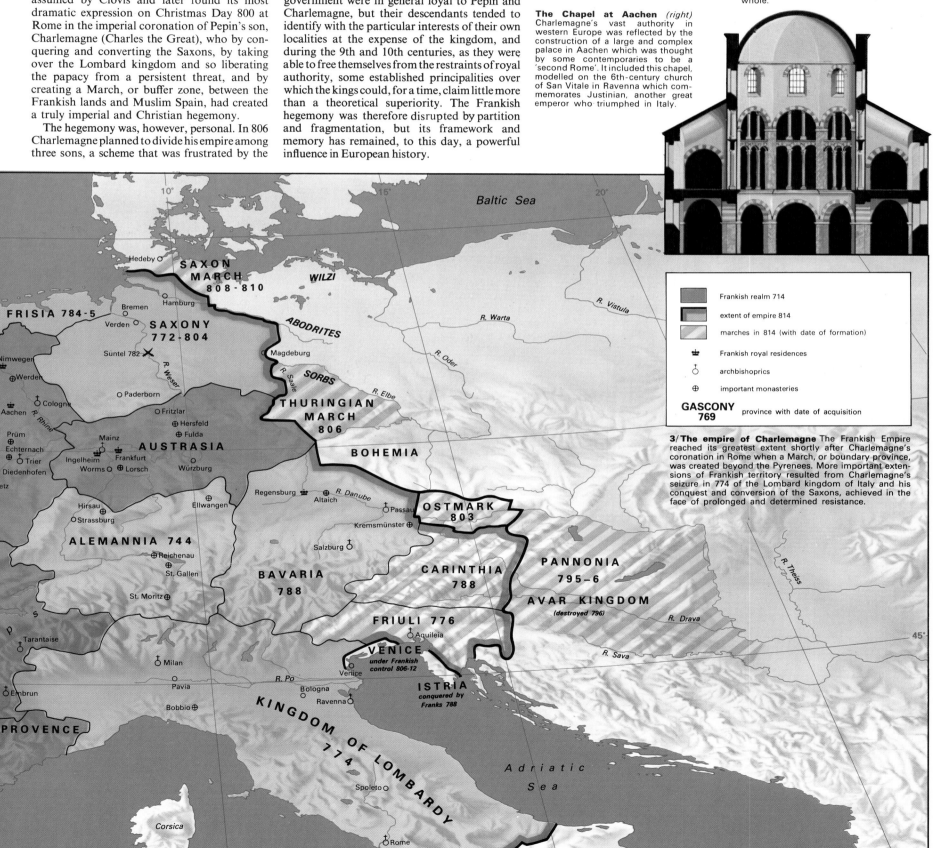

	Frankish realm 714
	extent of empire 814
	marches in 814 (with date of formation)
♛	Frankish royal residences
♙	archbishoprics
⊕	important monasteries

GASCONY 769 province with date of acquisition

3/The empire of Charlemagne The Frankish Empire reached its greatest extent shortly after Charlemagne's coronation in Rome when a March, or boundary province, was created beyond the Pyrenees. More important extensions of Frankish territory resulted from Charlemagne's seizure in 774 of the Lombard kingdom of Italy and his conquest and conversion of the Saxons, achieved in the face of prolonged and determined resistance.

The Eurasian world in 814

BY 814, the year of the death of the Frankish emperor, Charlemagne, Europe and Asia were recovering from the wave of barbarian invasion which, some four centuries earlier, had disrupted the civilisations of China, Rome and India and severed the trans-Eurasian ties of classical times (see page 94). It was, as events were to prove, a short-lived revival. During the century that followed all the civilisations of Eurasia suffered setbacks, some severe. But the gains at the expense of barbarism, particularly the expansion of the area of settled, civilised life, were more than temporary. By 814 a series of powerful empires stretched in unbroken sequence from the Atlantic to the Pacific, and under their shelter new states with a high level of civilisation took shape on their southern flank, among them the Srivijayan Empire of Sumatra and the Shailendra Empire of Java. In the far east the boundaries of T'ang China extended to the Tarim basin and the Pamirs. In the west the Franks had reunited the territories north of the Alps formerly a part of the Roman Empire. But the decisive factor was the astonishing expansion of Islam (see page 104) which carried the dominion of the Caliph to Bukhara and Samarkand by 710 and provided the essential link between Orient and Occident. After the Arab victory over China at the Talas river in 751 – one of the decisive battles of history – the two powers, with contiguous frontiers, dominated central Asia. Further north, at the western end of the Eurasian steppe, was the empire of the Khazars, the most civilised empire this region had seen since the collapse of Scythian power in the 3rd century BC. Converted to Judaism c. 740, the Khazars ruled a vast territory extending west as far as Sambat (the future Kiev) and south to Kherson, and their capital Itil, a populous and highly civilised city, was one of the great commercial centres of the period. Only India, after the collapse of Harsha's short-lived empire (606-47), failed to reconstitute some sort of unity, and the Arabs, who had conquered Sind in 711, remained in possession.

More stable conditions were accompanied by a revival of trans-Eurasian relations. China under the T'ang dynasty was unusually open to foreign contacts, and the unification of the vast areas under Arab rule led, particularly after the succession of the Abbasids in 750, to a great expansion of trade. Diplomatic relations also became closer. The caliph, Harun al-Rashid (786-809), who probably sent embassies to Charlemagne in 797 and 801, also despatched envoys to conclude a treaty of alliance with the T'ang emperor in 798. By 758 there was a large establishment of Muslim merchants in Kanfu (Canton) and a century later we hear of Chinese in Baghdad; and in far-away England Offa of Mercia (757-96), who had fairly close diplomatic relations with Charlemagne, issued a gold coin copied from the dinar struck by the Caliph al-Mansur in 774. All this suggests active commerce from one end of the Eurasian heartland to the other. Chinese porcelain, in particular, was prized throughout the Middle East and quantities have been found in 9th-century sites as far afield as Tarsus and Cairo. The art of paper-making, learned from Chinese prisoners taken at Talas in 751, spread rapidly across the Islamic world, reaching Spain by 900; already under Harun al-Rashid the first paper mills were operating in Baghdad.

Although T'ang civilisation had passed its peak after 755, the Chinese empire was still preeminent in 814. Measured by almost any standard of comparison, China and Islam, even India and the countries of Indo-China, far surpassed Europe in the level of civilisation. It is characteristic that, while Chia Tan in 801 was compiling a map of China drawn to a scale of 100 li to an inch (2.5 cm) – a map which measured roughly 9 by 10 metres and covered an area of 16,000 by 17,600 km – geographical knowledge in the West was so embedded in myth that Jerusalem was believed to be the centre of the world, and the Nile, Euphrates and Ganges were considered to have a common source in the Garden of Eden.

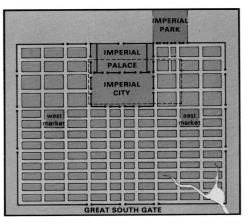

2/Ch'ang-an (left) Planned as a massive rectangle, 9.4 km from east to west and 8.4 km from north to south, with eleven great north-south avenues, the main avenue led from the imperial palace to the south gate. It was no less than 153 m wide, intersecting 14 east-west thoroughfares, and dividing the city into 106 separate wards. Ch'ang-an probably had a million inhabitants within the walls and another million in the suburbs outside. Already by 722 it contained 91 Buddhist and 16 Taoist places of worship, 4 Zoroastrian temples, and 2 Nestorian Christian churches.

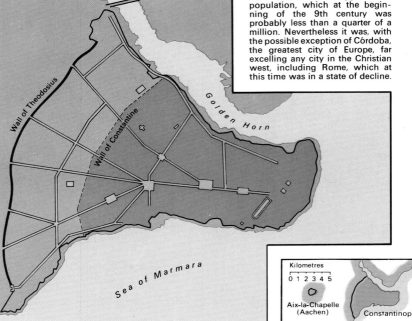

3/Constantinople (left) Constantinople never grew beyond the walls of Theodosius II (c. 447) and within the walls there was much vacant space. Historians have tended to exaggerate its population, which at the beginning of the 9th century was probably less than a quarter of a million. Nevertheless it was, with the possible exception of Cordoba, the greatest city of Europe, far excelling any city in the Christian west, including Rome, which at this time was in a state of decline.

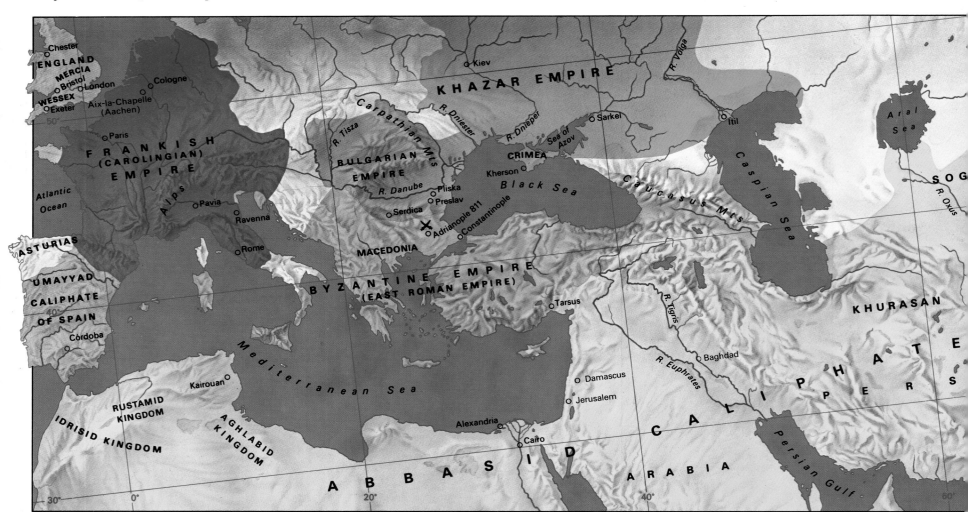

108

4/Baghdad *(right)* Founded in 762 by the caliph al-Mansur, who employed 100,000 men on the building. The circular city, with a diameter of 2638 metres, surrounded by a rampart with 360 towers, was almost immediately too small for the growing population. By the time of Harun al-Rashid it had expanded south to the suburb of *al-karh*, home of commerce and artisans, and east to the residential quarters near the Caliph's new palace, *Dar al-khilafa*. By 814 it was probably the world's largest city.

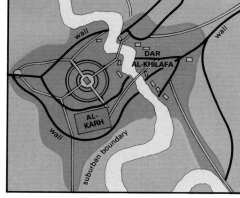

5/Córdoba *(right)* Córdoba, housing perhaps half a million Muslims, Christians and Jews, was already the leading city west of Constantinople by the end of the 8th century. Outside the original walled city, planned as a rectangle resting on the river front, with ramparts measuring about 4 km, was a series of suburbs. According to a contemporary Arab writer, Córdoba contained 471 mosques, 213,077 houses for workers and traders, 60,000 residences for officials and courtiers, and 80,455 shops. It was also the seat of a university of international repute.

6/Aix-la-Chapelle *(right)* Almost nothing is known of Charlemagne's residence before he built his palace and chapel there in the 790s. It was certainly in no sense a city, though the palace attracted a few Christian and Jewish traders, and some officials had built themselves houses by 828. The massive Romanesque church (48.6 m long and 35 m wide) is impressive, but Aix remained small, with a population probably of no more than two or three thousand, until it was destroyed by the Vikings in the second half of the 9th century. The modern city of Aachen descends from the new foundation of the 12th century.

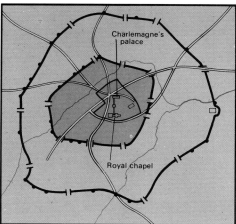

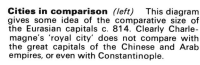

Cities in comparison *(left)* This diagram gives some idea of the comparative size of the Eurasian capitals c. 814. Clearly Charlemagne's 'royal city' does not compare with the great capitals of the Chinese and Arab empires, or even with Constantinople.

Architecturally, also, no contemporary European building approaches in majesty the magnificent temples erected during this period at Prambanan in Java.

The Carolingian Empire, though hardly as large as the area controlled by the Khazars, was impressive in size, but, like the Bulgarian Empire flanking the Byzantine Empire in the north, it was little more than the conquest of a barbarian warband, which fell apart, only thirty years after Charlemagne's death, when its warlike energies flagged. Such empires could be dangerous militarily, as was seen in 811 when the Bulgarians under Krum (802-14) inflicted a crushing defeat on the Roman emperor Nicephorus. But, unlike China and Rome and the Caliphate, they lacked the resources and organisation – particularly the financial and bureaucratic organisation – to give them stability. The East Roman Empire, hemmed in by Arabs and Bulgars, was weak and ineffective between 780 and 820. After 751, when the Lombards conquered Ravenna and drove out the emperor's viceroy (the Exarch), its authority in Italy was only nominal, and this made it possible for Charlemagne to usurp the imperial title in 800. But the sound administration inherited from the Heraclian and Isaurian emperors enabled Byzantium not only to survive but to mount a remarkable revival under Basil I (866-86) and Leo VI (886-912). In the West, by contrast, this was the period when feudalism, spreading from its home in northern France, became endemic. Charlemagne had attempted to hold the power of the aristocracy in check by making the counts into removable officials and sending out royal agents (*missi dominici*) to supervise their activities. But the system was too rudimentary to work; within a few years of Charlemagne's death the relationship of lord and vassal displaced that of ruler and subject as the bond of political society, and royal authority went into eclipse.

The contrast between the civilisations of Eurasia at this period is nowhere better illustrated than in their capital cities. Characteristically, the Frankish Empire, with its backward agricultural economy, had none. Rome, which Charlemagne never revisited between 800 and his death in 814, was in full decline, and there is no sign that he ever thought of reviving it. It is possible that he had a vision of creating a fixed capital at Aix-la-Chapelle, where he built himself a palace and a large and impressive chapel (see page 106) modelled upon San Vitale at

The temple of Shiva *(above)* The great 9th-century temple of Shiva at Prambanan in Java shows both the extension of Hindu influence and the remarkable artistic and architectural achievement of Indonesian civilisation at this period. Only the great mosques of Damascus, Kairouan and Córdoba compare in scale and magnificence.

Ravenna, the last capital of the Roman Empire in the west. But if so, little came of it. Carolingian writers described Aix grandiloquently as a 'royal city' *(urbs regalis)*, but it is unlikely to have had more than a couple of thousand inhabitants and did not compare in any way with Constantinople, the capital of the (East) Roman Empire, or with Córdoba, the capital of Umayyad Spain, still less with Ch'ang-an, capital of T'ang China. Even after the foundation of the Abbasid capital, Baghdad, in 762 Ch'ang-an remained the outstanding city of Eurasia, so impressive that the Yamato rulers of Japan used it as a model for their capitals at Nara (710) and Kyoto (794). In the West no city equalled Córdoba, though its period of greatest renown was the 10th century (912-61). But the most astonishing phenomenon was the stupendous growth of Baghdad, which had spilled out by the death of Harun al-Rashid from the original circular city, Madinat as-Salam ('the City of Peace'), and by 814 covered an area of approximately 10 by 9 km, the equivalent of modern Paris within the outer boulevards. The West had still a long way to go before it caught up.

1/Eurasia in 814 The expansion of Islam and the stabilising influence it exerted in central Asia did much to restore the contacts between the eastern and western halves of the Eurasian heartland which had been disrupted by barbarian invasions in the 4th and 5th centuries. But the west was still on the periphery and its participation in the recovery was limited.

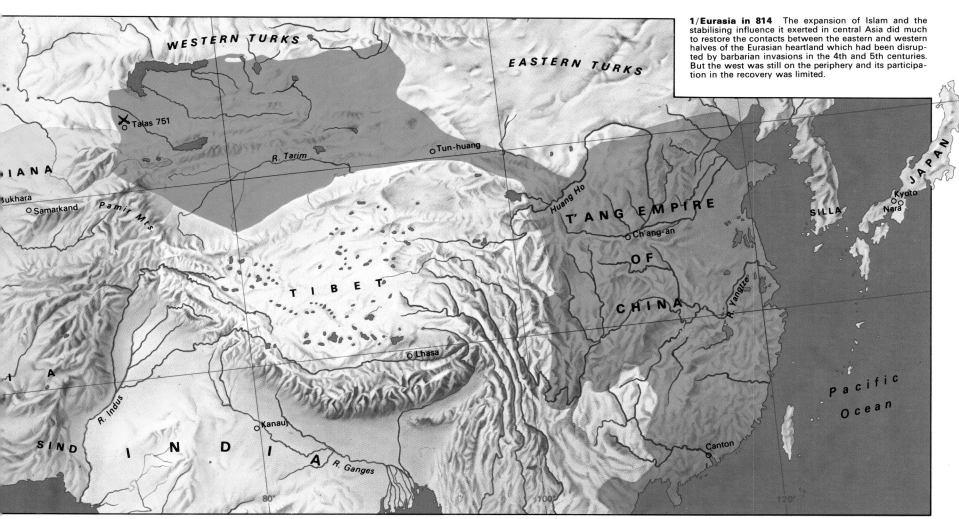

The 9th and 10th century invasions of Europe: Vikings, Magyars, Saracens

areas of Scandinavian settlement

Danelaw frontiers established by treaty 886

Norman frontier at end 11th century

2/Scandinavian colonies in Britain and France *(above)* The first Viking colonists were Norwegians; from their new homes they raided the coasts of Western Europe. The Danes, who had tended to raid the rich low-lands of England and Francia, astonished the English in 876 by sharing out some of the conquered land and beginning to farm it, leaving a permanent linguistic mark on eastern and northern England.

THE relatively effective rule of the Carolingians in western Europe (see page 106) and of the Mercians in England gave some assurance of security from internal attacks to both religious communities and merchants, and in the 8th century abbeys and markets were not fortified and Roman defences were not kept in repair. The accumulations of wealth in such places did, however, offer tempting bait to external raiders, men who accepted neither the religious sanctions that generally protected the holy places of the Christian west nor the authority of Christian kings, and in the 9th and 10th centuries western Europe suffered attacks from three separate groups of such strangers: Saracens, Magyars and Vikings.

The Saracen raids were an extension of Islamic conquest, and after the occupation of Sicily, completed by 827, Muslim pirates established bases on the coast of southern Italy, and later in southern Gaul, from which they were able to threaten large areas of southern Europe. Corsica and Sardinia were frequently attacked and many monasteries and towns in Italy (including Rome itself) and in Gaul were pillaged, while merchants and pilgrims were robbed or forced to pay large ransoms for their release from captivity. The main credit for driving the pirates from their Italian bases was due to the forces of the Byzantine Empire.

The Magyars posed a different kind of threat. They were horsemen who moved into the Hungarian plain in the last years of the 9th century and almost immediately began to plunder the neighbouring areas, first northern Italy, then Germany and on their longest raids deep into France. Their advantages of speed and surprise made opposition difficult, and in open country their horsemanship was markedly superior to that of their German or Italian opponents, but in mountainous country and at river crossings, especially when returning home laden with booty, they were more vulnerable and German rulers had some successes against them. The threat was finally ended by the victory of Otto I at Lechfeld near Augsburg in 955, after which the Magyar leaders were executed and the assimilation of the Magyars into western Christendom began.

The Vikings also had the advantage of surprise when they descended on the coasts and rivers of western Europe but, unlike the Magyars, they could be colonists as well as raiders. Once the Norwegians had discovered that there were islands in the North Atlantic with an environment very similar to that of their homeland, many were prepared to look for a better life overseas, particularly when Harald Fairhair tried to unify the country. The Danes also settled overseas, no doubt partly because there were better opportunities for plundering and extorting treasure in western Europe than in Scandinavia. The Norwegian and Danish leaders of expeditions appear to have been men who were forced to leave their homes, exiles who had been banished for offences, or members of unsuccessful branches of royal families who, having failed to make themselves kings, hoped to gain both wealth and reputation in the west.

The earliest Viking raids were towards the end of the eighth century – the best known though probably not the first, was on the Northumbrian monastery of Lindisfarne in 793. In the following century several Norwegian bases were established in Ireland, the most famous being Dublin, founded by 841, and from such places warrior chiefs led expeditions to plunder not only the monasteries and other centres in Ireland, but also in Britain and further afield. The Danish attacks began about a generation later than the Norwegian, with a raid on the market of Dorestad in 834, the first of a series of regular attacks on that place. By the middle of the century bands of Danes were making their way by boat and horse to attack churches and towns in many parts of Britain and the Frankish Empire. To facilitate these raids they established bases, some of which eventually became centres of permanent Scandinavian settlement, such as the Five Boroughs of the English Midlands. In such colonies the Vikings lost their advantages of mobility and surprise and were vulnerable to pressure that eventually led them to accept both the overlordship of French and English kings and conversion to Christianity.

At the same time as these western enterprises, Swedes were crossing the Baltic to visit markets, notably Bolgar on the middle Volga, in which Muslims were eager to acquire furs and slaves that the Swedes, and others, could gather in the forests of northern Russia. Swedish leaders who made themselves masters of such places as Kiev and Novgorod were soon slavicised, and maintained no more than dynastic links with Scandinavia. The rulers of Kiev came into contact with Byzantium but its influence was religious and cultural rather than economic, and the main markets for the produce of the Kiev region continued to be the Islamic east rather than the Byzantine south.

This sudden extension of Scandinavian activity overseas was in part caused by the growing demand for goods that could only be obtained from the north; walrus tusks were at that time the main source of ivory in Europe and furs from the arctic regions of Scandinavia and Russia were greatly prized. On the eve of the Viking period there was a growing commerce in coastal markets called *wics*. The greatest of these was the Wijk at Dorestad but there were many others, including Quentovic, near Boulogne, and Hamwic, later to develop into Southampton. Scandinavians were encouraged to search even further afield for fresh supplies of skins, furs and tusks and a contemporary account by a 9th-

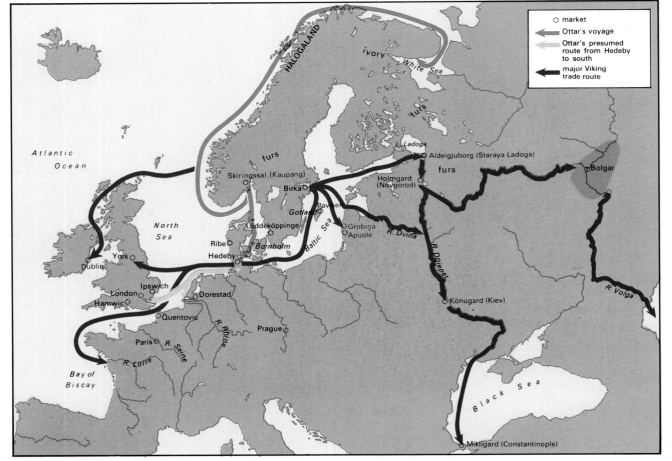

market

Ottar's voyage

Ottar's presumed route from Hedeby to south

major Viking trade route

3/Viking trade *(left)* Scandinavia and the lands east of the Baltic were important in the luxury trade of the Dark Ages as the only source of furs and ivory and a good source of slaves. In response to the demand for these goods, first in western Europe and later in the Muslim east, Scandinavians such as Ottar ventured far afield in search of new supplies.

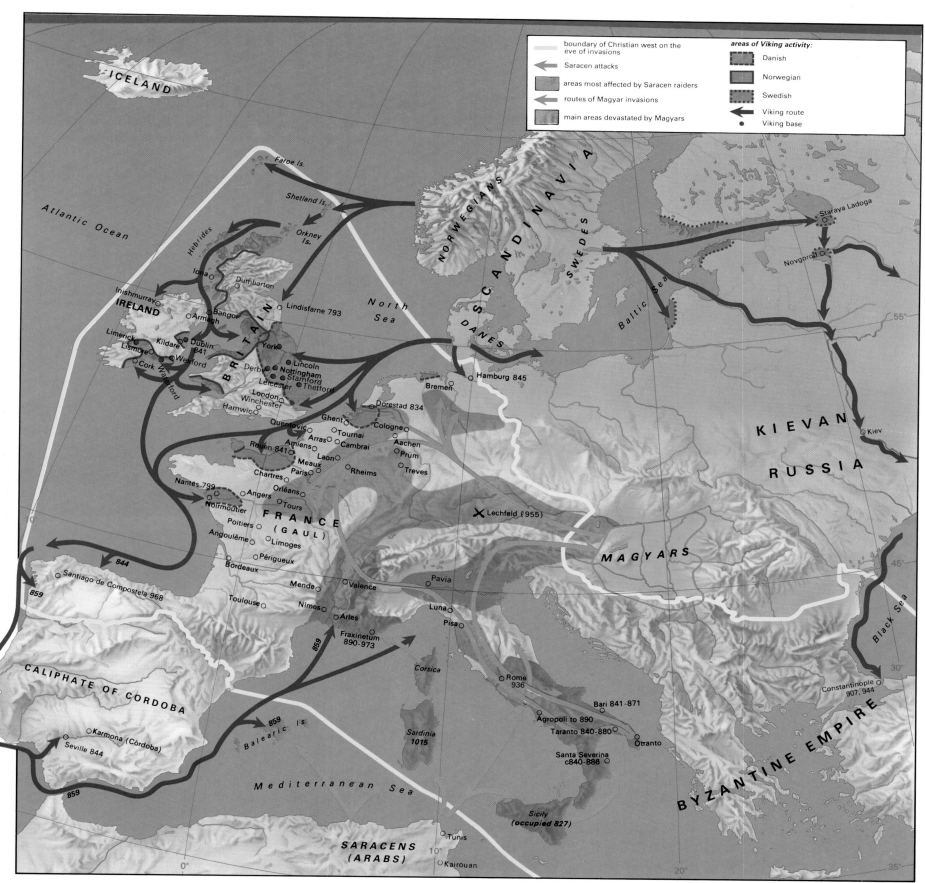

The invasions *(above)* labels on the map:

ICELAND

Atlantic Ocean

Faroe Is.
Shetland Is.
Orkney Is.
Hebrides
Iona
Dumbarton
Inishmurray
IRELAND
Bangor
Armagh
Limerick
Kildare
Dublin 841
Lismore
Wexford
Cork
Waterford
Lindisfarne 793
York
BRITAIN
Derby
Lincoln
Nottingham
Leicester
Stamford
Thetford
London
Winchester
Hamwic

North Sea

NORWEGIANS
SCANDINAVIA
SWEDES
DANES
Baltic Sea

Staraya Ladoga
Novgorod
55°

Quentovic
Ghent
Tournai
Arras
Cambrai
Amiens
Laon
Rouen 841
Meaux
Chartres
Paris
Rheims
Orléans
Angers
Tours
Nantes 799
Noirmoutier
Poitiers
FRANCE (GAUL)
Angoulême
Limoges
Périgueux
Bordeaux
Mende
Valence
Toulouse
Nimes
Arles
Fraxinetum 890-973

Bremen
Hamburg 845
Dorestad 834
Cologne
Aachen
Prum
Treves

KIEVAN RUSSIA
Kiev

Lechfeld (955)

MAGYARS

844
859
Santiago de Compostela 968

CALIPHATE OF CORDOBA
Karmona (Córdoba)
Seville 844
859

Balearic Is.
859

Corsica
Sardinia 1015

Pavia
Luna
Pisa
Rome 936
Bari 841-871
Agropoli to 890
Taranto 840-880
Otranto
Santa Severina c840-886

BYZANTINE EMPIRE
Constantinople 907, 944
Black Sea
45°
30°
35°

Mediterranean Sea

Tunis
Sicily (occupied 827)
Kairouan
SARACENS (ARABS)
0°
10°
20°

Legend:
- boundary of Christian west on the eve of invasions
- Saracen attacks
- areas most affected by Saracen raiders
- routes of Magyar invasions
- main areas devastated by Magyars
- areas of Viking activity: Danish / Norwegian / Swedish
- Viking route
- Viking base

century Norwegian, Ottar, tells of a voyage he made from his home in northern Norway into the White Sea in search of walrus.

Although the Vikings contributed to the consolidation of early Russia (see page 114), in England the kings of Wessex, particularly Edward the Elder (899-924) and Athelstan (924-99) fought back, and in Gaul the Frankish rulers virtually capitulated, leaving defence to the local magnates. The result was the fragmentation of public authority and a great upsurge of feudalism which, though it had originated earlier in the dark days of the 7th century, had been held in check by Charlemagne. Even in England the number of free cultivators declined, as freemen commended themselves to lords for protection. In Gaul peasant freemen virtually disappeared and society was polarized between nobles and serfs. In Germany also power devolved into the hands of dukes and margraves who guarded the frontiers. From the beginning of the 10th century the map of western Europe was a feudal map, an intricate interlacing of counties, communities, principalities and lordships, and it was not until the 12th century that consolidation again got under way.

1/The invasions *(above)* No part of the Christian West was immune from external attack in the 9th and 10th centuries. From their base in the Hungarian Plain the Magyars traversed vast distances, but as they moved fast the disruption they caused was short-lived. Saracens and Vikings established bases in the West and were consequently a more persistent threat; the Saracens were eventually expelled, but the Norwegian and Danish invaders were in time assimilated, as were the Swedes, who had gone east in search of wealth among the Slavs and Finns.

4/The Atlantic settlements *(below)* The settlement of Iceland by Norwegians began in about 870 and was completed in two generations. Later emigrants travelling in ships such as that illustrated below found limited opportunities there, but after the discovery of Greenland in the last years of the 10th century some went on to create new settlements which survived for some five centuries. The Vikings reached Newfoundland, but no permanent settlements have been found either here or further south. The location of Vinland of the sagas is disputed.

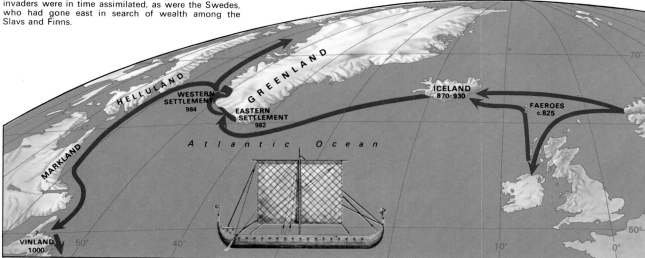

HELLULAND
WESTERN SETTLEMENT 984
GREENLAND
EASTERN SETTLEMENT 982
ICELAND 870-930
FAEROES c.825
70°
MARKLAND
Atlantic Ocean
VINLAND 1000
50°
40°
30°
10°
50°

The Byzantine Empire from Heraclius to the Fourth Crusade: 610 to 1204

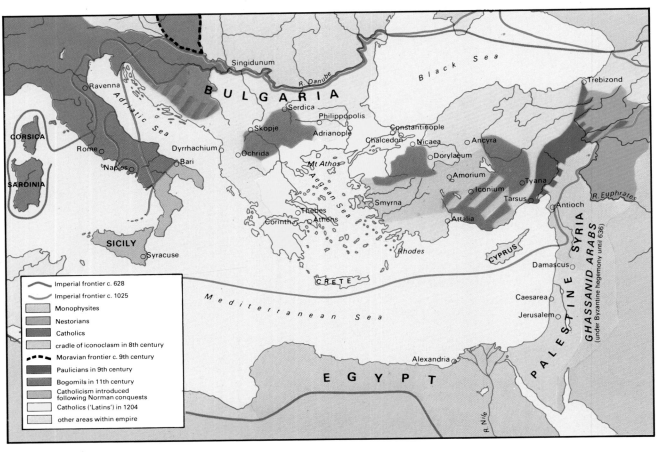

THE reign of Heraclius (610-41) marked in many ways the end of the East Roman Empire and the true beginnings of that distinctive, Greek-speaking, Christian, culturally heterogeneous form of civilisation known as Byzantine. Its first years saw the final titanic struggle with Persia, so long Rome's most formidable rival, culminating in Heraclius's crushing victory at Nineveh in 628. But before his death the Emperor saw his southern and eastern frontiers everywhere under attack, as the new forces of Islam (see page 104) burst out of Arabia, seized Palestine, Syria and the ruins of Persia, and embarked on their triumphant westward advance. For the next two centuries, increasingly isolated from the West, Byzantium was forced to mobilise its whole society for its struggle against Islam.

Constantinople withstood two long Arab sieges, from 674-8 and again in 717-8. But the struggle was not only with the Arabs. About 680, the Turkic Bulgars flooded into the land now known as Bulgaria. By the 8th century they too constituted a serious threat, with armed outposts less than sixty miles from Constantinople itself. Equally seriously, the Empire was wracked with internal religious dissension. Starting with Leo III, the emperor who forced the Arabs to abandon the second siege of Constantinople, successive emperors imposed a stringent ban on Christian images. Iconoclasm produced a large crop of martyrs and exiles, and lasted, with only one break, from 726 to 843.

Soon after it was reversed, Byzantium, under a fresh and vigorous Macedonian dynasty of emperors, embarked on a new era of aggressive expansion. Its dominions, which in 610 still stretched from Gibraltar to the Euphrates, had dramatically shrunk. In the west, the only remaining toeholds were in southern Italy, Sicily and along the Dalmatian coast; Greece, though reconquest had already begun, was still largely in the hands of barbarian Slavs; in the

2/The Conflict of Doctrines (above) Monophysite/Nestorian disputes over nature of Christ ended with Arab conquests. Paulicians and Bogomils (9th-10th centuries) preached varieties of Manicheism.

3/The 'themes' and Arab invasions (left) The *themes* were administrative districts and army units, peasants were granted farms in exchange for war service. They prevented Arab settlement, despite raids.

first four Themes:
- Opsician
- Anatolic
- Armeniac
- Theme of the Carabisiani

Arab invasion routes
- by land
- by sea
- ● invasion bases

final organisation of Themes

4/Byzantium and the Slavs (below) Basil II liquidated the first Bulgarian Empire, which had spread through northern Greece to Constantinople's doorstep. The introduction of Orthodox Christianity helped pacify Slav peoples, and took strong root despite the conflicts.

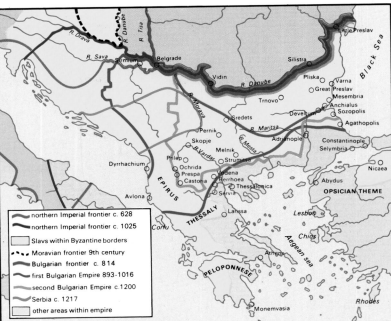

- northern Imperial frontier c. 628
- northern Imperial frontier c. 1025
- Slavs within Byzantine borders
- Moravian frontier 9th century
- Bulgarian frontier c. 814
- first Bulgarian Empire 893-1016
- second Bulgarian Empire c.1200
- Serbia c. 1217
- other areas within empire

Map 1 legend:
- Imperial frontier c. 628
- Imperial frontier c. 1025
- Monophysites
- Nestorians
- Catholics
- cradle of iconoclasm in 8th century
- Moravian frontier c. 9th century
- Paulicians in 9th century
- Bogomils in 11th century
- Catholicism introduced following Norman conquests
- Catholics ('Latins') in 1204
- other areas within empire

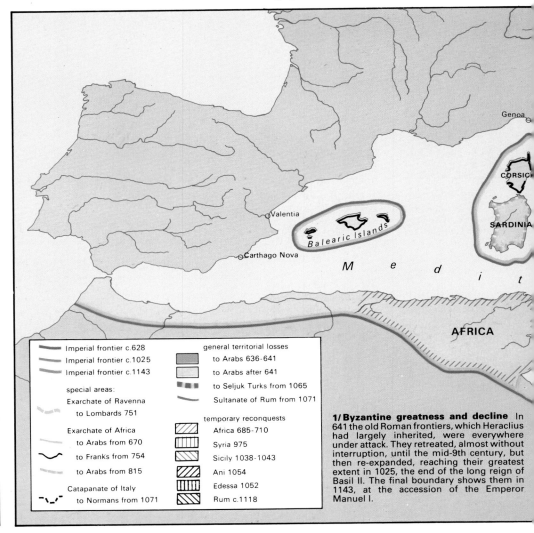

Map 1 legend:
- Imperial frontier c.628
- Imperial frontier c.1025
- Imperial frontier c.1143

special areas:
- Exarchate of Ravenna to Lombards 751
- Exarchate of Africa to Arabs from 670
- to Franks from 754
- to Arabs from 815
- Catapanate of Italy to Normans from 1071

general territorial losses
- to Arabs 636-641
- to Arabs after 641
- to Seljuk Turks from 1065
- Sultanate of Rum from 1071

temporary reconquests
- Africa 685-710
- Syria 975
- Sicily 1038-1043
- Ani 1054
- Edessa 1052
- Rum c.1118

1/Byzantine greatness and decline In 641 the old Roman frontiers, which Heraclius had largely inherited, were everywhere under attack. They retreated, almost without interruption, until the mid-9th century, but then re-expanded, reaching their greatest extent in 1025, the end of the long reign of Basil II. The final boundary shows them in 1143, at the accession of the Emperor Manuel I.

embattled and devastated wastes of Asia Minor the frontier ran roughly from Trebizond to Tarsus; and apart from Constantinople the great Roman cities of the past – Antioch, Alexandria, Beirut, Caesarea, Gaza – were all under Arab rule. But now all this was to change.

Between 863, when a strong force of Arabs was annihilated at Poson, on the Halys river in Anatolia, and the death of the great warrior-emperor Basil II (976-1025), a series of dramatic victories pushed back the frontiers, often close to where they had been in the heyday of Rome. In the south-east the Arabs had at one stage (976) been driven back to the very gates of Jerusalem; the Russian axe-men had been held and routed at Silistra, on the Danube; Bulgaria, after long, bitter campaigning, was now reduced to a group of Byzantine provinces; and Basil, after defeating Bulgars, Armenians, Georgians, Arabs and Normans, was preparing to retake Italy, and possibly Africa beyond.

But it was not to be. Byzantium, outwardly at the height of its prosperity and power, was seriously overextended. Basil, unmarried, was succeeded by women and weaker men. The new frontiers, exhaustingly won, proved indefensible, especially as the previously invincible Byzantine military machine now found itself starved of funds by a civilian administration which feared it. Within fifty years, in 1071, a much weakened Byzantine army was smashed by a force of Seljuk Turks at the battle of Manzikert (see page 134). In the same year, the last Italian possession fell to the Normans; and the period of greatness, when Constantinople ruled the wealthiest and best-governed realm in the Christian world, was at an end.

Paradoxically, the 11th and 12th centuries were artistically and theologically among the most fertile in Byzantine history when the social and institutional links which had previously held the multilingual Empire together gradually fell into decay. Indeed, despite the disasters of 1071-81, when the Turks established permanent occupation of the Anatolian plateau and the Normans consolidated their Sicilian gains, it proved possible, under the brilliant trio of Comnenian emperors, to sustain the illusion of Byzantium's universal dominion for another hundred years. But it remained an illusion. For all their genius, Alexius I, John II and Manuel I were unable to recover much of the vast territory that had been lost; and when they had gone, there was little spirit left to resist the final assault.

This came, not from the traditional enemy, the Muslim infidel, but from the Christian West. The real collapse, however, was from within. Byzantium's strength, apart from its religious cohesion, was two-fold – the themes with their independent freeholding peasantry, ready both to farm well and to defend its land, and an army and navy often manned by native Asian officers and troops. At least since 1000 these advantages had scarcely existed. In the 11th and 12th centuries, mercenaries (often themselves Seljuk, Muslim or Norman) formed the bulk of the armed forces, and the Empire, whose only hereditary office had been that of the Emperor himself, fell more and more into the ambitious hands of a few rich, dynastic families. These owed much of their new wealth and power to the Byzantine form of feudalism, the *pronoia* system, under which key state functions, including tax collection, were handed over to large local landowners – originally for their lifetime, but increasingly on a hereditary basis.

It was an already seriously weakened Byzantium which saw the arrival of the First Crusade in 1096, but hopes that Rome and Constantinople could co-exist peacefully were soon dashed. There had been tension, if not actual schism between the Roman and Orthodox churches since 1054 (see page 100). Both Seljuks and Normans resumed full-scale frontier aggression in the 1170s. By 1180 Serbia was virtually independent; Hungary absorbed Dalmatia; Bulgaria and Wallachia rose; independent feudal rulers detached whole provinces – Cyprus (1184), Philadelphia (1186), Eastern Morea (1189); and in 1204 the final blow fell when Constantinople itself was seized and ravaged by the swordsmen of the Fourth Crusade. The immediate beneficiary was the rising power of Venice, whose fleets had carried the Crusaders. But the attempt to set up a Latin Empire of Constantinople proved abortive. Now for the first time, the Greeks had become a majority within the truncated Empire, and in 1261, aided by Genoa, the rival of Venice, they drove out the westerners. But the Greek empire was only a shadow of the Byzantium of the past and, rent by civil war, was no match for the Turks when they advanced into Europe in the 14th century. It was a very different Byzantium which now entered the later Middle Ages.

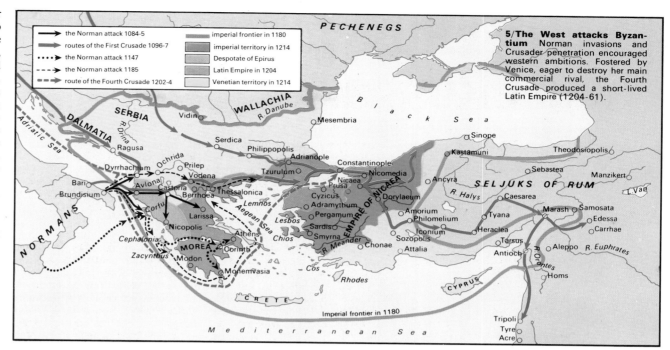

5/The West attacks Byzantium Norman invasions and Crusader penetration encouraged western ambitions. Fostered by Venice, eager to destroy her main commercial rival, the Fourth Crusade produced a short-lived Latin Empire (1204-61).

The City Walls (above) Constantinople is isolated from the land by a double line, and from the sea by a single line, of turreted walls. The inner landward bastion, 30 feet high and 16 feet thick, was breached only once, in 1453.

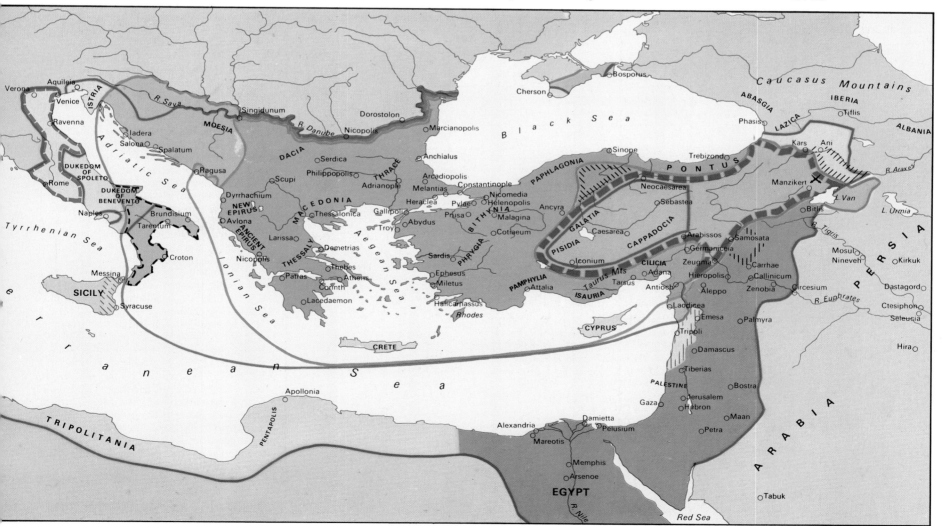

The first Russian state: Kievan Russia 882 to 1245

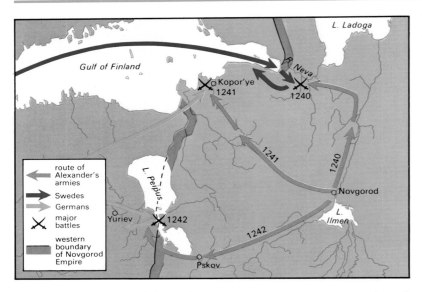

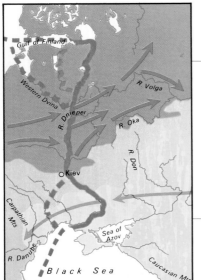

2/The campaigns of Alexander of Novgorod *(above)* An attempt by Swedes and Germans to drive Russia from the Baltic was frustrated. Alexander's decisive victory on the Neva earned him the title 'Nevsky' Two years later he defeated the Germans.

3/Vegetation belts and early migrations *(left)* The first Russian state was established by the Vikings with the Dnieper as its axis. It lay athwart the northern forest and the southern steppe. Kiev was a natural capital.

4/The Mongol onslaught on Russia *(below)* Until 1236 northern Russia was immune from the steppe nomads' raids, and its centres prospered, but in the winter of 1237-38 the Mongols struck north into the forest and subjugated its princes.

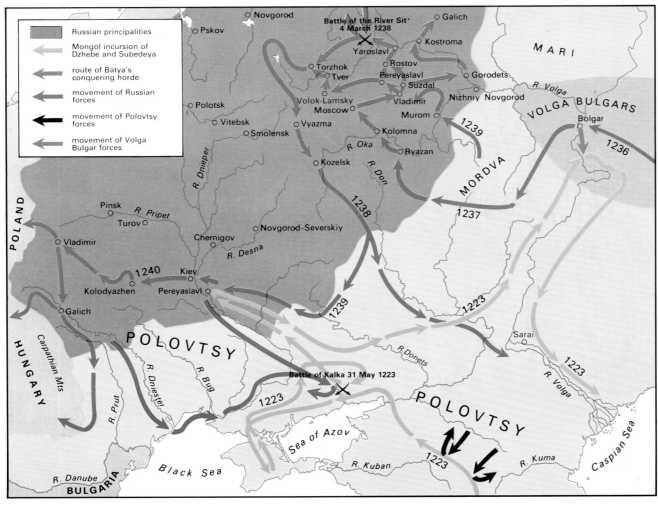

D URING the period 882 to 1242 Russia was subject to powerful external influences: as a political unit it was first hammered into shape by Vikings from the north; it then received Christianity from Byzantium in the south; and it was ultimately overthrown by the Mongol Tartars from the east.

The contrast between forest and steppe was of prime importance at this time. Before the arrival of the Vikings in the ninth century the East Slavs were pushing eastwards from Europe into the woodlands of central Russia, while hordes of nomadic horsemen moved westwards across the southern steppes from Asia. The rivers assumed significance with the coming of the Vikings, who established, dominated and exploited trade routes along the waterways; the first Russian state originated in their determination to control the lands adjoining them. Because the rivers of Russia have a general north to south and south to north direction, there was great potential for trade between northern Europe and the Baltic on the one hand, and southern Europe and the Black Sea on the other; both the main trade routes and the ensuing political unit ran north and south, across the east to west trending belts of forest and steppe which, however, proved too strong for a north-south alignment, based upon the rivers, to survive. The history of Kievan Russia, the first Russian state, is dominated by the constant struggle and ultimate failure of the Russians to hold on to their steppe territory, which became once more the undisputed realm of westward-migrating nomads. Instead, they resumed the historic eastward colonisation of the forest belt.

The principal waterway route established by the Vikings (known to the Slavs as *Varyagi* or Varangians) ran from the Gulf of Finland up the river Neva, through Lake Ladoga, the river Volkhov, and thence by portages to the Dnieper, and on across the Black Sea to Byzantium. This was the 'route from the Varyagi to the Greeks' referred to by the earliest writers. As the Vikings pushed their control southwards, Novgorod,

Smolensk and Kiev (in 882) became in turn their headquarters. Kiev grew rapidly as the new state's flourishing capital. Its links with Byzantium, its chief trading partner, were strong, and from Byzantium it received the Christian faith during the reign of Vladimir Svyatoslavich (980-1015).

At the time of the Viking incursions the Khazars and their vassals, the Magyars, held the steppes, but by the 10th century the formerly nomadic Khazars had largely become merchants and farmers. The Russians were able to hold the lands of the lower Pruth, the Dniester and Bug, and to maintain control of the Dnieper route to the Black Sea. Grand Prince Svyatoslav (962-72) determined to strengthen and expand this Russian grip by crushing the Khazars. But by destroying the relatively peaceful Khazars, Svyatoslav opened the way to the fierce Pechenegi who henceforth dominated the south Russian steppes until displaced by the equally warlike Polovtsy. Vladimir I (980-1015) had some defensive success against the Pechenegi, but Kiev was sacked by the Polovtsy in 1093.

Weakened by its perpetual conflict with the nomads, the Kievan state broke up into a number of independent and often warring principalities after 1054. While the southern lands emptied in the face of cruel Polovtsy raids, steady colonisation of the forest increased the populations of the northern and central principalities, giving them the strength to throw off Kievan suzerainty. Novgorod, which had built up a great fur-trading empire reaching to the Urals and beyond, and Vladimir-Suzdal, which contained the fast-growing commercial centre of Moscow (first mentioned in 1147), were the foremost of these forest principalities. On the eve of the Mongol attack of 1237, Vladimir-Suzdal was about to challenge the Volga Bulgars, whose stranglehold on the middle Volga region was an obstacle to further Russian expansion eastward. Nizhni Novgorod was built as a first move in this campaign.

The Mongol invasion was perhaps the most traumatic event in Russian history. The Mongols had made an exploratory raid into the steppes in 1221, defeating a combined Russian and Polovtsy force at the Kalka river in 1223. In 1237 they returned in strength and struck first at the middle and upper Volga regions, hitherto immune from nomadic attack. In the winter of 1237-38, when the protective rivers were frozen, they overcame the Volga Bulgars and set upon Vladimir-Suzdal, destroying its prosperous towns. Only the approach of spring saved Novgorod, as the invaders dared not be caught by the thaw among its surrounding marshes. In 1239 it was the turn of south-west Russia, which suffered annihilation. Kiev itself was sacked in 1240, along with hundreds of other settlements.

Novgorod, although it escaped the Mongol fury, had to stave off incessant attacks from Swedes and Germans in the Baltic region. Prince Alexander beat the Swedes decisively on the river Neva in 1240, and the Germans on the ice of Lake Peipus in 1242; yet even he had to recognise the Mongol overlordship.

The Mongol invasion had lasting economic, social and political effects. Those peasants who survived, oppressed by the tribute the Mongols exacted, lost all hope of rising above the barest subsistence. The destruction of the leading cities, where handicrafts had flourished, reduced life to a barbarous level. The Mongols themselves soon withdrew to the steppes, and although they restricted their direct intervention to punitive expeditions when necessary, and to the appointment of local, but immensely powerful, revenue collecting agents, their influence was all-pervasive. The elimination of the urban middle classes smoothed the path of an autocracy which imitated its Mongol overlords in ruthless terror and efficient extortion.

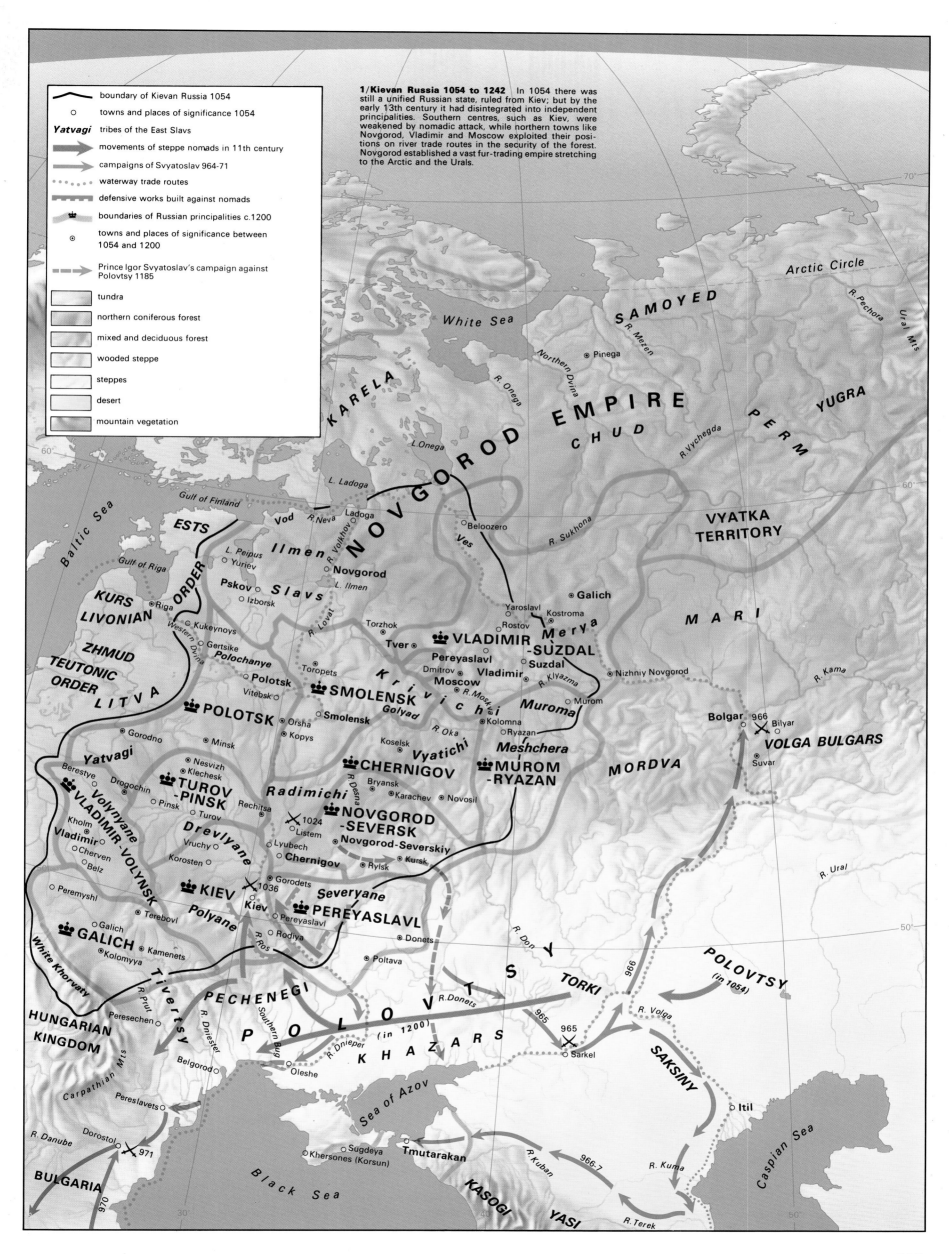

1/Kievan Russia 1054 to 1242
In 1054 there was still a unified Russian state, ruled from Kiev; but by the early 13th century it had disintegrated into independent principalities. Southern centres, such as Kiev, were weakened by nomadic attack, while northern towns like Novgorod, Vladimir and Moscow exploited their positions on river trade routes in the security of the forest. Novgorod established a vast fur-trading empire stretching to the Arctic and the Urals.

Legend:
- boundary of Kievan Russia 1054
- ○ towns and places of significance 1054
- *Yatvagi* tribes of the East Slavs
- movements of steppe nomads in 11th century
- campaigns of Svyatoslav 964-71
- waterway trade routes
- defensive works built against nomads
- boundaries of Russian principalities c.1200
- ⊙ towns and places of significance between 1054 and 1200
- Prince Igor Svyatoslav's campaign against Polovtsy 1185

- tundra
- northern coniferous forest
- mixed and deciduous forest
- wooded steppe
- steppes
- desert
- mountain vegetation

Arctic Circle

White Sea
SAMOYED
R. Mezen
R. Pechora
Ural Mts
KARELA
R. Onega
Pinega
Northern Dvina
NOVGOROD EMPIRE
CHUD
PERM
YUGRA
R. Vychegda
L.Onega
Beloozero
VYATKA TERRITORY
R. Sukhona
L. Ladoga
Gulf of Finland
Baltic Sea
Ladoga
R. Neva
Volkhov
Ves
Galich
MARI
Vod
Ilmen Slavs
Novgorod
L. Ilmen
Yaroslavl
Kostroma
R. Kama
ESTS
L. Peipus
Yuriev
Pskov
Izborsk
Rostov
Merya
ORDER
Torzhok
Tver
VLADIMIR-SUZDAL
Nizhniy Novgorod
KURS
LIVONIAN
Riga
Gulf of Riga
Kukeynoys
R. Lovat
R. Lovat
Pereyaslavl
Dmitrov
Vladimir
Suzdal
R. Klyazma
ZHMUD
Western Dvina
Gertsike
Toropets
Moscow
R. Moskva
Murom
TEUTONIC ORDER
Polochane
Polotsk
Krivichi
Golyad
R. Oka
Muroma
LITVA
Vitebsk
SMOLENSK
Meshchera
Bolgar
966 Bilyar
POLOTSK
Orsha
Smolensk
Kolomna
Ryazan
MUROM-RYAZAN
VOLGA BULGARS
Gorodno
Kopys
Suvar
Minsk
Koselsk
Vyatichi
Yatvagi
Nesvizh
Klechesk
CHERNIGOV
R. Desna
Bryansk
MORDVA
Berestye
Drogochin
TUROV-PINSK
Radimichi
Karachev
Novosil
Volynyane
VLADIMIR-VOLYNSK
Pinsk
Rechitsa
Turov
Drevlyane
1024 Listem
NOVGOROD-SEVERSK
Kholm
Vladimir
Vruchy
Lyubech
Novgorod-Severskiy
Cherven
Korosten
Chernigov
Rylsk
Kursk
Balz
Gorodets
1036
Severyane
KIEV
Peremyshl
Kiev
Pereyaslavl
PEREYASLAVL
Galich
Terebovl
Polyane
Rodiya
R. Ros
Donets
GALICH
Kamenets
R. Ros
Poltava
R. Don
POLOVTSY (in 1054)
Kolomyya
Tiverrty
Poltava
R. Ural
White Khorvaty
Peresechen
PECHENEGI
R. Prut
R. Donets
TORKI
966
HUNGARIAN KINGDOM
R. Dniester
POLOVTSY (in 1200)
R. Dnieper
Belgorod
Southern Bug
KHAZARS
965
SAKSINY
Carpathian Mts
965 Sarkel
Pereslavets
Oleshe
R. Volga
Dorostol
971
Sea of Azov
Itil
970
Sugdeya
Khersones (Korsun)
Tmutarakan
966-7
R. Kuban
R. Kuma
Caspian Sea
BULGARIA
Black Sea
KASOGI
YASI
R. Terek

115

The formation of states in northern and eastern Europe 900 to c.1050

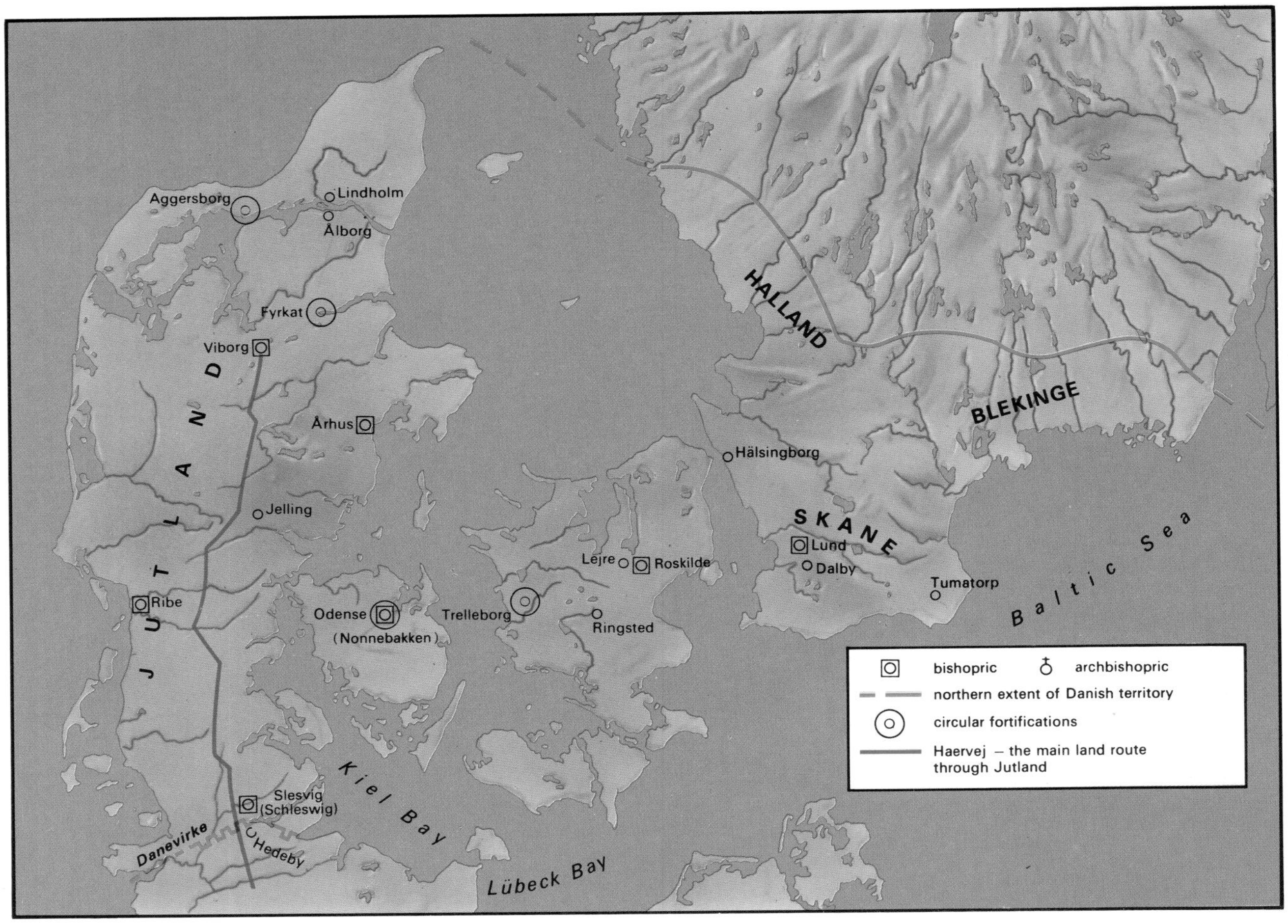

THE Carolingian Empire had established some sort of political order in those parts of western Europe (except Spain) which had formerly belonged to the Roman Empire. In northern and eastern Europe, it was different, and it was not until the period 900-1050 that the Scandinavian and Slav states emerged from pre-literate mists as organised, even aggressive, entities. Their emergence extended the area of civilisation, filled out the political map of Europe, and put pressure on other western European states which resulted among other things in the establishment of well-defined boundaries between kingdoms and principalities and of marches along the eastern frontiers of Germany.

As a result of the initial activity of the early Viking Age the Scandinavians were by 900 well established in the west. In England the Danelaw was only gradually reconquered and although the last Scandinavian king of York, Erik Bloodaxe, was expelled in 954, most of the incomers were apparently able to retain their land, giving permanent Scandinavian character to the customs and place-names of the region. The reconquest of the Danelaw by the kings of Wessex and an expanding population paved the way for the unification of England and for the political and religious reforms of Eadgar (959-75). But the wealth of England soon attracted the Scandinavians again, first as organised military expeditions seeking financial rewards (the Danegeld), then as conquerors, ruling England in tandem with Norway and Denmark under a Danish king, Cnut (Canute). But Cnut's northern empire was short-lived, and with the accession of Edward the Confessor to the English throne (1042), and still more after the Norman Conquest in 1066, England turned away from its role in northern Europe and aligned itself with the culture of France and the Mediterranean. It was an historic turning-point.

With the fall of York the position of the major ports of Ireland became important to the Scandinavians. These towns had been founded by them in the 9th century, and remained economically under their control, although often politically dominated by the Irish. The Irish, like the Welsh, were a society divided by many social and political factors. Sometimes united, often in disarray, they had neither the time nor the energy to develop economically. The history of much of this period is one of continuous warfare between the various Irish dynasties. Brian Bóruma, in the few years after 1000, was the first to unite Ireland (however shakily), but his power lasted only a short time; by 1014 he was dead and his achievement in ruins. The next man to attempt to unite Ireland was Diarmat, who became King of Leinster in the 1040s. Dublin's fortunes fluctuated politically, but rarely economically. The function of Dublin, the chief of the Scandinavian towns, as a market place is emphasised by the striking of the first Irish coins there in the 990s. From the late 10th century the economic power and international connections of Dublin – the chief market of the Scandinavians in the west – grew apace. The Isle of Man, the Western Isles of Scotland and the Atlantic islands also remained under Scandinavian control throughout this period. The mainland of Scotland, apart from Galloway and the far north, was gradually taken over by the Scots in the course of the 10th and 11th centuries and, by 1050, Scottish influence also extended into the northern counties of modern England. A firm boundary was drawn only in 1237.

Although Scandinavia had been economically stable for many centuries, it consisted at the beginning of the Viking Age of many provinces speaking a more or less common tongue. Now powerful states were founded out of the disarray. Denmark under three kings (Gorm, Harald and Sven) became in the course of the 10th century a powerful kingdom and, under Cnut the Great (1014-35), the centre of a great – but impossibly large – Anglo-Scandinavian empire.

After the battle of Hafrsfjord in the 890s Norway was first reorganised as a single kingdom under Harald Finehair. After his death in the 930s, however, Norway was largely under Danish control until the death of Cnut, when a Norwegian king again succeeded. The history of Sweden is more obscure: it was gradually united, however, under the kings of Uppland towards the end of the 10th century. By 930 Iceland was an independent state (without a king) and an attempt was made to settle Greenland from about 985. Through the medium of the newly-introduced Christianity (brought to Scandinavia by a handful of English and Saxon missionaries during the 10th and 11th centuries) Scandinavia emerged from heathen obscurity into the community of European Christendom.

Meanwhile, a similar process of consolidation was taking place in eastern Europe. The first organised state in this region, Moravia, was destroyed in 906 by the Magyar invaders. A new phase of political consolidation began in the 10th century, probably in response to German pressure under Henry I and Otto I. Although the lesser Slav peoples along the Elbe successfully resisted the Germans in the great Slav revolt of 983, they remained disunited and loosely organised, and it was further east, in Poland, that a major Slav state arose. Miesko I (960-92) united the tribes of northern Poland; his son Boleslav Chrobry (992-1025) extended control to Little Poland in the south. Meanwhile, the Magyars were settling the Hungarian plain, welded into a Hungarian kingdom by Duke Geisa (972-97) and his more famous son, King Stephen (997-1038). Bohemia, caught between Germany and Poland, had also emerged as a stable political unit by the time of Boleslav I (929-67), and even though the Přemyslid dukes were vassals of the German king they exercised more or less sovereign powers internally.

The creation of Bohemia, Poland and Hungary by the Přemyslid, Piast and Árpád dynasties respectively, was founded on agricultural

2/The rise of Denmark *(above)*

Denmark was the first Scandinavian kingdom to achieve full statehood in the Christian European tradition. Three kings were basically responsible: Harald Bluetooth (c.950-c.986), Sven Forkbeard (c.986-c.1014) and Cnut the Great (1014-35). Harald was instrumental in persuading the Danes to accept Christianity, while politically he countered a German threat and brought Norway under the political control of the Danish crown. Sven concentrated largely on warlike campaigns in England from which he drew large amounts of money – the Danegeld. His son, Cnut the Great, eventually came to the throne of England and ruled an empire which stretched, in theory at least, from North Cape to the Isles of Scilly. Cnut's North Sea empire collapsed at his death and Denmark was subject to the Norwegian king Magnus until 1046. Denmark then settled down within what were to become its boundaries for many centuries (including the modern Swedish provinces of Skåne, Blekinge and Halland) under Sven Estridsson. In the 10th and early 11th centuries the first towns were founded in Denmark, the first bishoprics established and a remarkable series of fortifications constructed by the central authority – including at least part of the Danevirke (the fortified southern frontier of Denmark) and the fortresses at Trelleborg, Odense, Fyrkat and Aggersborg.

The Jelling stone *(above)* is both a symbol and a fact of the unity of Denmark and its official conversion to Christianity in the 10th century. The inscription reads: 'King Harald had this monument made in memory of Gorm his father and in memory of Thyre his mother. That Harald who won for himself all Denmark and Norway, and made all the Danes Christian'. Harald died c.986.

Territories from maps 1 and 2
(right and above)

Bohemia Duchy conquered from Slavs by Otto II in 950 and made tributary to Emperor.
Brandenburg (Nordmark and Billungmark) 928 margravate under Empire; 982 reconquered by Slavs.
Brittany Independent Celtic-speaking duchy; 912-37 under Scandinavian control.
Danelaw Generic term for area of England under Scandinavian control in early 10th century.
Dublin Kingdom under Scandinavian control (although political power sometimes in Irish hands).
England Kingdom. North and east under Scandinavian control for much of first half of 9th century. Gradually united under kings of Wessex. 1016-42 under Danish rule.
Hungary Principality. After death of Kursan (904) united under one leader, Árpád. In 1001 Stephen (d.1038) became first king.
Iceland Republic.
Ireland Land of petty kings (*tuatha*). Five main kingdoms to which in this period was added a sixth, Brega. Northern dynasty of Ui Néill most important until Brian Bóruma produced semi-organised overlordship under Munster until 1000 (see also Dublin).
Man Norse kingdom; apparently independent, but in the early 10th century under Orkney control.
Moravia Empire; 906 fell to Hungarians; 1025 combined with Bohemia after a period in Polish hands.
Normandy Colonised by Scandinavian settlers; dukedom after 911.
Norway Kingdom. At first very disunited, for some time in late 10th and early 11th centuries under loose Danish control. Finally achieved independence and was united under Magnus the Good (1035).
Orkney Earldom under nominal control of Norway. For much of period also probably controlled western islands of Scotland (Sudreyjar), Shetland (Hjaltland), and also for a short period Man.
Scotland Kingdom centred in east. Edinburgh captured by Indulf (954-62), battle of Carham (1018) brought in Lothian. Strathclyde taken over after death of Owen the Bald (1015). Galloway not properly under Scottish rule; north and west controlled by Norse.
Strathclyde Kingdom incorporated in Scotland after 1015.
Sweden Political organisation obscure before c. 1000, when Olaf Skötkonung appears to have gained control.
Wales Land of petty kings (*gwlad*). Six main kingdoms struggled for power. After death of Hywel Dda (950) no consolidation until accession of Gruffydd ap Llewelyn of Gwynedd in 1039.
York Norse kingdom until 954.

Map labels: Aggersborg, Lindholm, Ålborg, Fyrkat, Viborg, Århus, Jelling, JUTLAND, Ribe, Odense (Nonnebakken), Trelleborg, Lejre, Roskilde, Ringsted, Hälsingborg, Lund, Dalby, Tumatorp, SKÅNE, BLEKINGE, HALLAND, Baltic Sea, Slesvig (Schleswig), Danevirke, Hedeby, Kiel Bay, Lübeck Bay

Legend: bishopric, archbishopric, northern extent of Danish territory, circular fortifications, Haervej – the main land route through Jutland

3/Poland under Boleslav Chrobry *(right)* After the unification of the tribes of Great (or northern) Poland under Miesko I, his son Boleslav Chrobry ('The Brave') attempted to create a great Slav empire, including Bohemia and Moravia. Most of the gains were temporary and involved long, debilitating wars on all frontiers; but Little Poland, centring on Cracow, was permanently acquired, and it was to Cracow that Casimir I (1037-58) transferred his residence when he began the restoration of the monarchy after the setbacks under Miesko II (1025-34). Poland was already Christian and a number of bishoprics had been founded. The towns of the Baltic coast came into their own as international trading stations in this period.

development, suppression of tribal differences and of the independence of the tribal aristocracies, and on the organising and civilising influence of the Christian church. At this stage, despite numerous wars (particularly after 1003) there was no racial confrontation between Germans and Slavs. Miesko I worked closely with the emperor Otto III, and the Bohemian nobility gladly became vassals of Germany when threatened by the Hungarians. Moreover, all three dynasties made use of Frankish institutions (counties, castellanies) to strengthen their position. Boleslav Chrobry had ambitions of founding a great Slav state from the Baltic to the Danube, including Bohemia and Moravia and certain Russian territories in the east; but the ensuing conflicts, involving wars with Slavs and Hungarians as well as Germans, overtaxed the monarchies and enabled the nobility to reassert itself. The result in all three countries was a setback to royal authority. Nevertheless a foundation had been laid, and none of them henceforth lost its identity, though it was not until the 14th century that a new stage of advance took place.

1/The emergence of states *(below)* The 10th century was marked by the emergence of stable political organisation in northern and eastern Europe. The marauders of the previous century (the Vikings in the north, the Magyars in the east) formed settled states; in England the successors of Alfred the Great reconquered the Danelaw; in Poland the Piasts not only extended their control over Little Poland (around Cracow) but also embarked on expansion at the expense of their Slav neighbours to the south, east and west. In eastern Germany, marches were established to defend the frontiers from incursions from the east.

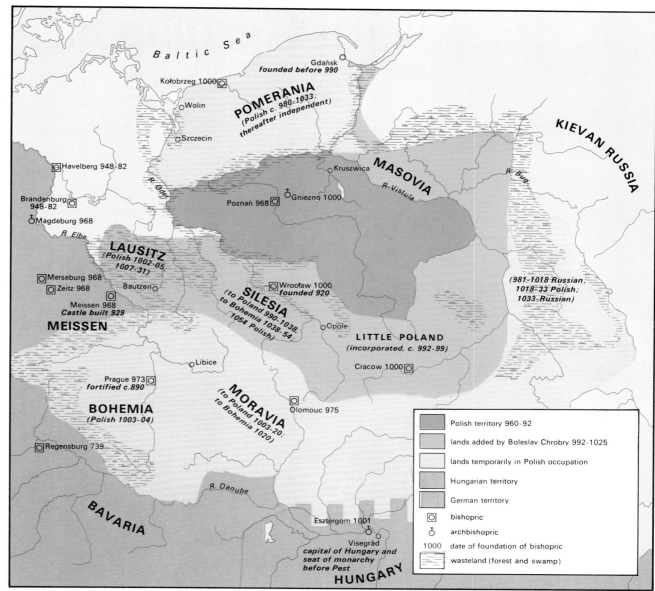

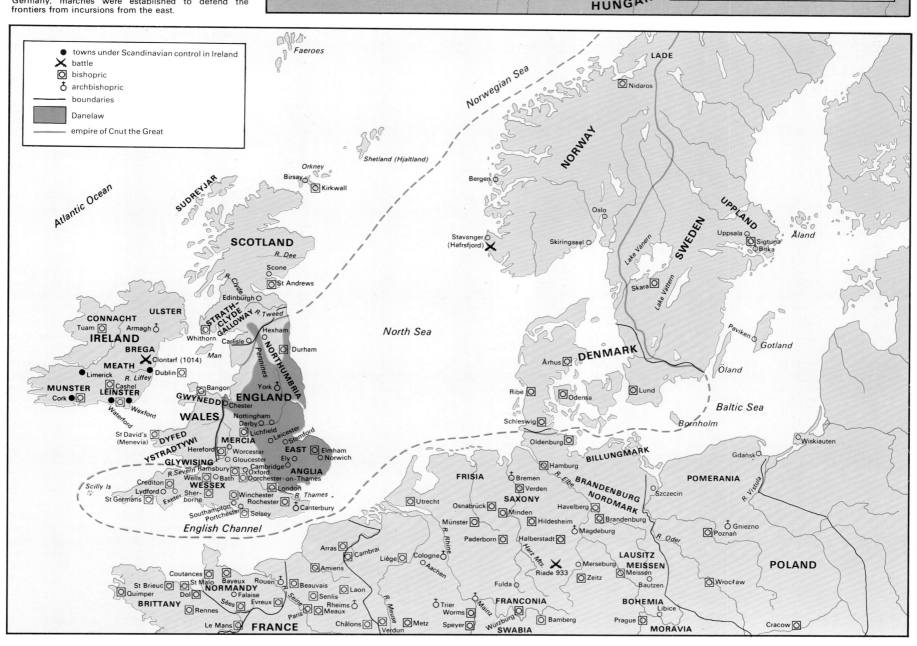

The mediaeval German Empire 962 to 1250

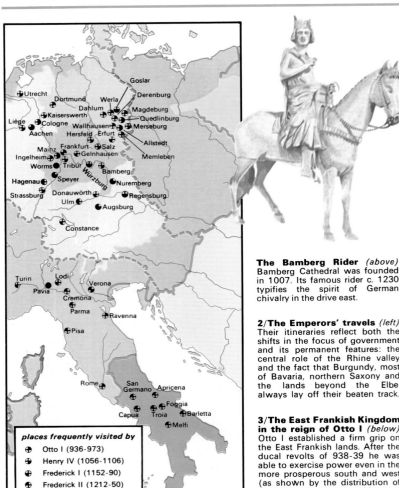

THE 9th century Viking, Magyar and Saracen invasions (see page 110) shook the foundations of the Carolingian Empire, already weakened by the Frankish custom of partible inheritance. After 887 the West Frankish (French) and East Frankish (German) lands went their own ways, and so did Italy. In 919 the East Frankish crown passed to Henry, Duke of the Saxons. This disputed election seemed to mark just another stage in the long-drawn out disintegration of the Carolingian world. Henry's power barely extended beyond the borders of Franconia and south-eastern Saxony. South of the Alps the imperial crown was now just a prize awarded to the most influential Italian magnate. West of the Rhine the forces of political fragmentation continued to operate for another 200 years (see page 124). But in the east the new Saxon dynasty emphatically reversed this process. By perseverance, skill and good fortune Henry I's son, Otto I, decisively extended his influence over the German duchies, defeated the Magyars at the Battle of the Lech (955), and conquered the kingdom of Italy. The imperial coronation at Rome (962) served to legitimise this vast acquisition. After the turbulence of the late 9th and early 10th centuries the Ottonian Empire emerged as the leading power west of the Adriatic, claiming equal status with Byzantium in the east.

Otto I's work could easily have proved ephemeral; but his survival by only one son, Otto II, allowed the Empire to remain intact. In 1033 it was extended even further by the acquisition of Burgundy. Owing to an extraordinary series of dynastic accidents, not until 1190 was an emperor (Frederick I) survived by more than one son. By this date a partition of the Empire was unthinkable. There had been times (in 1002, 1024 and 1037) when the Italian magnates who had

been emperor-makers in the early 10th century resisted the rulers thrust upon them from the north. But after 1037 they acquiesced in a custom which granted lordship over north Italy to the German king. Thus Germany, Burgundy and Italy remained together in the hands of one ruler, the emperor. Dynastic change, from Saxon to Salian (1024), and then to Hohenstaufen (1138), made little difference to the Empire's political structure. Nor, for all its high drama, did the Investiture Contest (1075-1122), when Henry IV tried to depose Pope Gregory VII, and in turn was excommunicated and forced to go in penance to Canossa, except that it cast doubt on the emperor's role as protector of the papacy.

The Empire's pre-eminence lasted until the death of Frederick II in 1250, although from the mid-12th century, with the recovery of the West Frankish territories and the rise of the Angevin Empire under Henry II of England, the balance was visibly changing. By 1200 Paris was the intellectual and artistic centre of Europe. Germany, with no capital city and no universities, lagged behind. German scholars, like Otto of Freising, studied philosophy and theology in Paris. Gothic architecture entered Germany from the West, advancing from Strassburg and Rhenish Franconia to Magdeburg and Naumburg. Although poetry, like sculpture and architecture, retained its specifically German characteristics, great poets like Wolfram of Eschenbach and Gottfried of Strassburg used French sources and subject matter.

Only gradually was the Empire's political structure undermined by the socio-economic developments of the 12th and 13th centuries: the growth of population and commerce, the clearing of waste and forest. From around 1140 internal colonisation was reinforced by the *Drang nach Osten*. But this concerned the eastern frontier princes far more than the German kings. The latter were always more interested in the West, especially the Rhineland, and in Italy. Only in these economically advanced regions were the profits of lordship sufficient to sustain an emperor and his following. Above all, there was the magnetic pull of urban wealth in Lombardy and Tuscany, the result of an unparalleled rate of economic growth. Frederick I (1152-1190) spent one third of his reign in Italy, whereas his predecessors in the previous 150 years had averaged only one-seventh. But the growing independence of the Italian towns made it more difficult for the king to collect royal dues. The Hohenstaufen were twice involved in hostilities with Leagues of Lombard Cities (founded 1167 and 1226) and were forced to compromise. Even so, inter-communal rivalries gave the emperors many opportunities. Chroniclers' estimates of Frederick I's income from Italy make it clear that it was this source that made him the equal of the Angevins. Then Henry VI's conquest of the prosperous kingdom of Sicily (1194) made him and his son Frederick II the richest rulers in Europe.

The machinery of government remained inadequate. Only in 13th century Sicily was there a centralised administrative system. In Germany and northern Italy the kings travelled continually, dispensing justice and supervising local government. In the 11th century they had begun to use *ministeriales* as local agents, but these men were no substitute for a salaried official class. To enforce their will, the kings had to be on the spot in person. The tremendous accession of landed wealth under Otto I had enabled the Ottonians to stay chiefly in their palaces, supplied by the produce of their estates. But the gradual alienation of royal domains forced Henry II and his successors to rely more heavily on church lands, particularly on episcopal towns and their developing markets. This meant an increasingly close relationship between king and church – and helps to explain the fierceness of the dispute over

The Bamberg Rider (above) Bamberg Cathedral was founded in 1007. Its famous rider c. 1230 typifies the spirit of German chivalry in the drive east.

2/The Emperors' travels (left) Their itineraries reflect both the shifts in the focus of government and its permanent features: the central role of the Rhine valley and the fact that Burgundy, most of Bavaria, northern Saxony and the lands beyond the Elbe always lay off their beaten track.

3/The East Frankish Kingdom in the reign of Otto I (below) Otto I established a firm grip on the East Frankish lands. After the ducal revolts of 938-39 he was able to exercise power even in the more prosperous south and west (as shown by the distribution of royal mints). Magyar raids were halted. The drive eastward against the Slavs was normally left to the margraves, while Otto himself ranged more widely.

places frequently visited by
- ☩ Otto I (936-973)
- ☩ Henry IV (1056-1106)
- ☩ Frederick I (1152-90)
- ☩ Frederick II (1212-50)
- --- boundary of E. Francia 950
- — boundary of Empire 1190

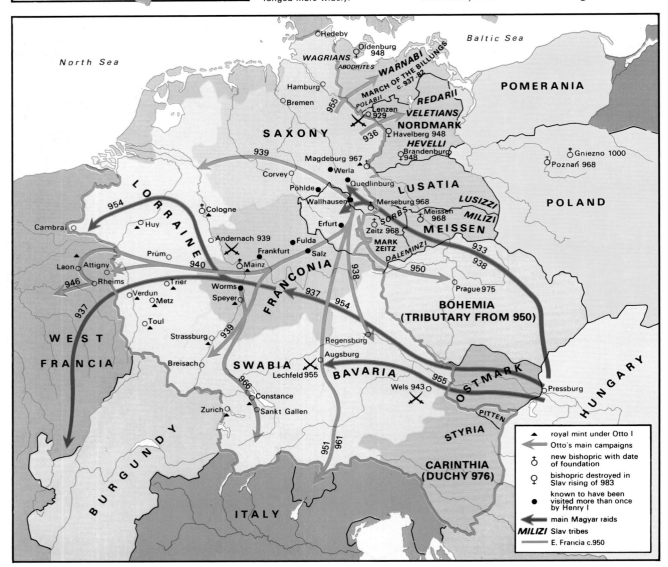

royal mint under Otto I
Otto's main campaigns
♂ new bishopric with date of foundation
♀ bishopric destroyed in Slav rising of 983
● known to have been visited more than once by Henry I
main Magyar raids
MILIZI Slav tribes
— E. Francia c.950

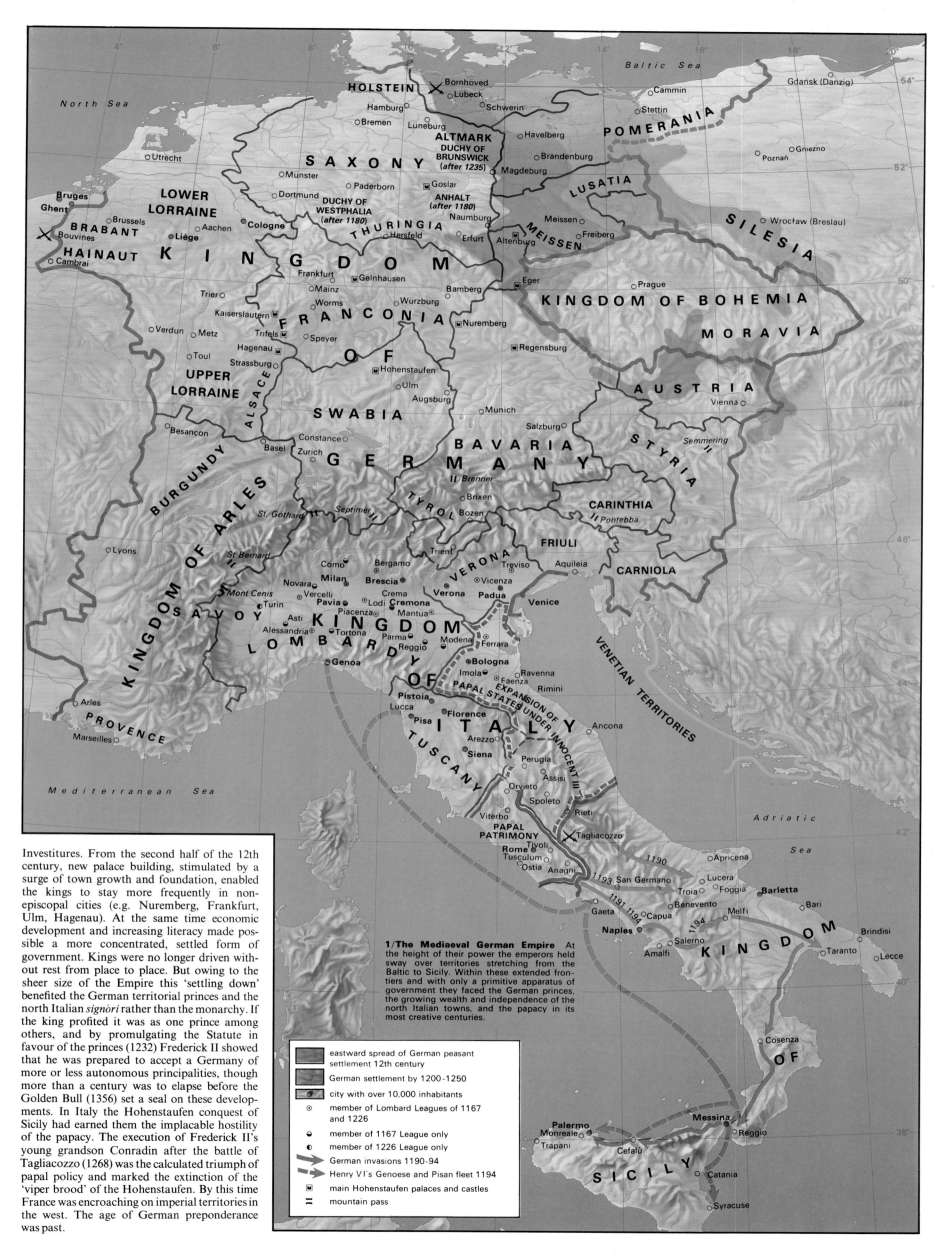

Investitures. From the second half of the 12th century, new palace building, stimulated by a surge of town growth and foundation, enabled the kings to stay more frequently in non-episcopal cities (e.g. Nuremberg, Frankfurt, Ulm, Hagenau). At the same time economic development and increasing literacy made possible a more concentrated, settled form of government. Kings were no longer driven without rest from place to place. But owing to the sheer size of the Empire this 'settling down' benefited the German territorial princes and the north Italian *signóri* rather than the monarchy. If the king profited it was as one prince among others, and by promulgating the Statute in favour of the princes (1232) Frederick II showed that he was prepared to accept a Germany of more or less autonomous principalities, though more than a century was to elapse before the Golden Bull (1356) set a seal on these developments. In Italy the Hohenstaufen conquest of Sicily had earned them the implacable hostility of the papacy. The execution of Frederick II's young grandson Conradin after the battle of Tagliacozzo (1268) was the calculated triumph of papal policy and marked the extinction of the 'viper brood' of the Hohenstaufen. By this time France was encroaching on imperial territories in the west. The age of German preponderance was past.

1/The Mediaeval German Empire At the height of their power the emperors held sway over territories stretching from the Baltic to Sicily. Within these extended frontiers and with only a primitive apparatus of government they faced the German princes, the growing wealth and independence of the north Italian towns, and the papacy in its most creative centuries.

- eastward spread of German peasant settlement 12th century
- German settlement by 1200-1250
- city with over 10,000 inhabitants
- member of Lombard Leagues of 1167 and 1226
- member of 1167 League only
- member of 1226 League only
- German invasions 1190-94
- Henry VI's Genoese and Pisan fleet 1194
- main Hohenstaufen palaces and castles
- mountain pass

The recovery of Europe c. 950 to 1150

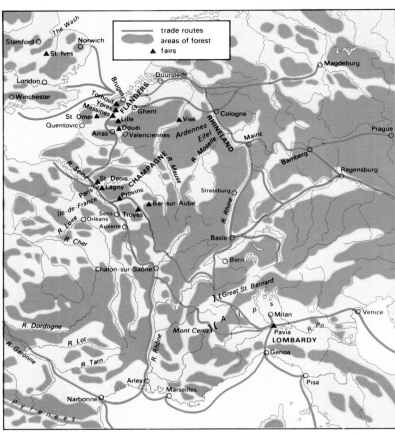

1/Western Europe, c. AD 1000 *(above)*
Before AD 1000 perhaps four-fifths of Europe north of the Alps and Pyrenees was covered by dense forest. The essential work of the next two hundred years was to clear the forest and make the land available for human settlement and agriculture. Even in the Rhineland the highlands bounding the river were still largely uninhabited (see map 3). Elsewhere, forests such as the Ardennes and the Eifel constituted an almost impene-trable barrier to communications. At this stage only the western Alpine passes were in regular use. Certain areas – Flanders, Lombardy, and the Rhine valley – were beginning by 1100 to become centres of commercial exchange. But it was only after 1150 that Italian merchants regularly attended the fairs of Champagne (Troyes, Provins, Bar-sur-Aube, Lagny), buying Flemish cloths in exchange for Oriental goods.

THE repulse of the Magyars by Otto I at the battle of the Lech in 955 (see page 110) is the conventional date for the beginning of the recovery of Europe from the preceding period of devastation and economic setback. After 950 – a little earlier, perhaps, in some regions, a little later in others – the economic graph of Europe was on an upward curve until around 1300-20 (see page 142). This economic recovery, and the sharp rise in population which accompanied it, was a capital fact in European history.

The preceding period had indubitably marked a time of recession. Villages were razed to the ground and cultivated land reverted to waste. Duurstede and Quentovic, leading Carolingian ports, were destroyed, never to be rebuilt; much of Normandy was depopulated when it was handed over to the Viking chief, Rollo, in 911. In the south the cities of Marseilles, Arles, Aix, Fréjus and Genoa, the targets of Saracen raiders, were abandoned. What is remarkable, once the invasions were halted, is the speed with which this situation was reversed. The population of Europe in 900 was probably at its lowest level since the fall of the Roman Empire. By 1000 it may have reached a total of 30 million; 150 years later it had probably increased by 40 per cent. Most of this increase was concentrated in western Europe, in France, Germany and England. The development of eastern and northern Europe and the *repoblación* of Spain only got under way after 1150.

The basic factor in this process of recovery was the opening up of new land. In a few regions (e.g. the Po valley of northern Italy, Flanders, the country around the Wash in England) marshes were drained and land re-claimed from the sea. But there is no doubt that the bulk of new land was won by sheer hard work from the vast, impenetrable forests which still covered most of Europe in the year 1000. This is a process which can only be followed step by step and locality by locality on large-scale maps. It took three main forms: steady encroachment by the peasants of the old villages on the woods which surrounded their fields; the migration of settlers, presumably driven by land-hunger, to the uninhabited uplands and mountains, where they carved out scattered fields and enclosures from the forest and scrub; planned development by lay lords and monasteries, wealthy promoters and speculators who founded villages and towns, at the foot of a castle or outside a monastery gate, with the aim of increasing their income. All three types of clearing are found juxtaposed in all countries, and their history is revealed by field patterns and by place-names (e.g. Newport, Neuville, Neustadt, Bourgneuf, Nieuwpoort). Occasion-ally the nomenclature is more fanciful. The small English market town of Baldock (Hertfordshire), founded by the Knights Templar in about 1148, was named optimistically after the great city of Baghdad.

No accurate estimate is possible of the amount of new land brought into cultivation in this way, but the effects of the great work of internal colonisation are indisputable. First and foremost an agricultural surplus became available for trade, and the result was to stimulate the foundation and growth of towns, markets and fairs. Historians formerly attributed the re-covery of Europe to the revival of long-distance trade at the time of the Crusades. We know today that the basis of recovery was local trade; the fairs (notably the fairs of Champagne) which became internationally renowned after 1150, still essentially served a local market in 1100. The gradual reassertion of European control over the northern shores of the Mediterranean after about 972 was a precondi-tion for the later efflorescence of the Italian cities; but in 1000 Pisa and Genoa were only beginning to emerge from the setbacks they had

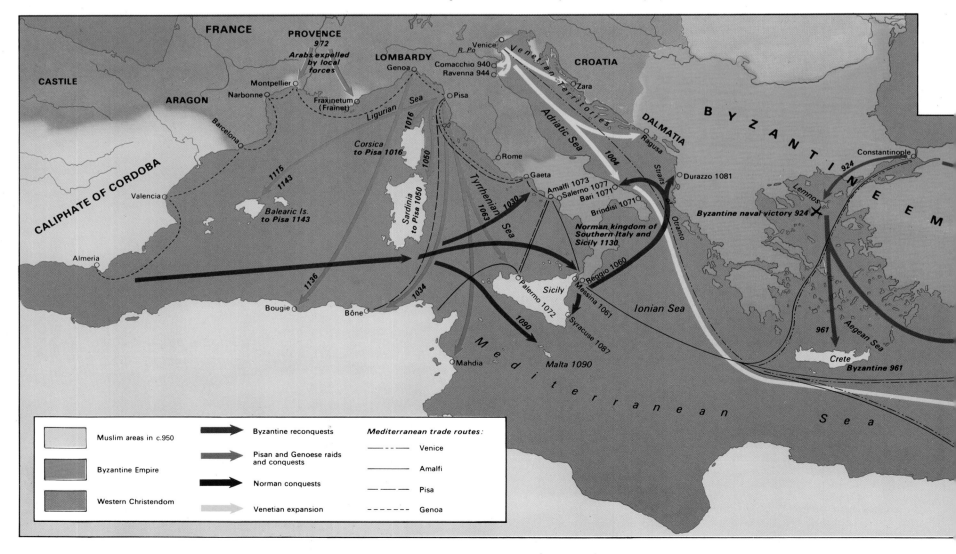

suffered at the hands of the Saracens, and Venice alone of the north Italian cities carried on a major overseas trade at the time. Significantly, the first two Crusades (1096-99, 1147-49) proceeded overland to Constantinople; not until the time of the third Crusade (1189-92) did the West possess a fleet capable of transporting an army the length of the Mediterranean, from Gibraltar to Palestine.

In Europe also, though a few Roman roads remained in partial use, communications were still primitive, and rivers (Rhine, Meuse, Po, Rhône) conveyed bulk transport. Only the western Alpine passes (Mont Cenis, Great St Bernard) were in regular use; the central passes (St Gotthard, Septimer, Splügen) and the Brenner in the east were not developed before the reign of the emperor Frederick I (1155-90) or later. The Mont Cenis and Great St Bernard provided a connection with the Rhineland, and thence with the cloth-towns of Flanders, and also with the Paris region. But the Capetians were still struggling (see page 124) to assert authority in the Ile-de-France, and until this had been achieved the Rhineland remained the focus of artistic and intellectual as well as of economic life. Cologne, in particular, was at the height of its prosperity, but the cathedral-building throughout the region – e.g. at Mainz and Worms – is a testimony to the new-found wealth which 'the great age of clearing' had made available.

5, 6, 7/Urban development (right and below) Throughout western Europe the 12th century was a time of town-foundation. Kings, nobles and ecclesiastics all competed in setting up new towns, hoping for enhanced land values as well as profits from markets and fairs. In England and Wales alone (right) more than a hundred new towns were founded between 1066 and 1190. By no means all these ventures were a success, and many other urban centres grew from existing villages, while ancient cities such as Cologne (see map 8) got a new lease of life. The counts of Flanders were particularly active in founding new towns; so were the dukes of Zähringen (see map 3). No less than nine towns in the north-west of modern Switzerland owe their existence to their initiative (far right). French kings, bishops and princes were equally enterprising. Louis VI (1108-37) and Louis VII (1137-80) planted *villeneuves* (in this case villages rather than towns) the length of the road from Paris to Orléans (below), seeking in this way to consolidate their hold over the region which was the core of their domain.

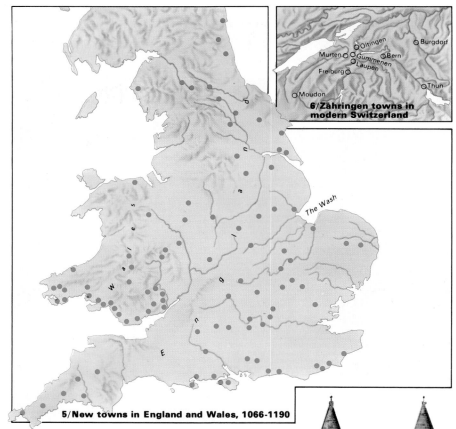

6/Zähringen towns in modern Switzerland

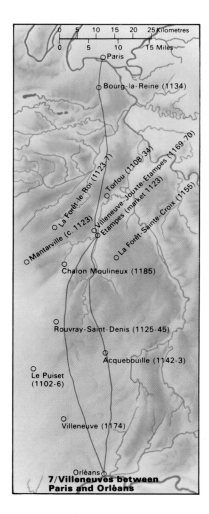

7/Villeneuves between Paris and Orléans

2/The reconquest of the Mediterranean (below left) In 950 the Mediterranean was almost entirely a 'Muslim lake'. Such trade as there was between western Europe and the Orient was in the hands of the cities of Byzantine Italy; Bari, Amalfi, Gaeta and Salerno. Amalfi, in particular, traded indiscriminately with Muslims (in Sicily and Egypt) and with Constantinople and Antioch. But its connections with northern Europe were at best indirect, and it was Venice, linked with the west by the Po valley, that first engaged in trade with Europe north of the Alps, once it had cleared the Adriatic of Dalmatian pirates and fought off the closure of the Straits of Otranto first by Muslims (who occupied Bari from 841 to 871) and then by Norman marauders. In the western Mediterranean trade was virtually at a standstill so long as the Saracens were in control of the Mediterranean islands, and from their base at Fraxinetum, of the Ligurian coast. Their dislodgement from Fraxinetum in 972 was therefore a capital fact. By this time Islamic unity was breaking up (see page 134), and this weakening enabled the fleets of Pisa and (later) of Genoa to wrest control of the Ligurian and Tyrrhenian seas from the Saracens. At this stage, however, these cities were freebooters and pirates rather than traders, but the loot from their raids on Saracen shipping provided capital for shipbuilding and eventually for commerce. The first Crusade (1096-99) opened up trading stations in the Levant; but it was only after the great Venetian naval victory off Ascalon in 1123 that the Italian cities came to dominate the Mediterranean from Spain to Syria.

5/New towns in England and Wales, 1066-1190

8/Cologne (below), the Roman Colonia Agrippina, was by the end of the 12th century the largest German city, commanding the trade of the river Rhine. In 900 less than half the area within the Roman walls was occupied, but a merchant quarter, with markets, was growing between the Roman city and the river. In the 10th century (presumably as protection against Viking raiders) this was enclosed by walls. In 1106 the walls were extended, but rapid growth required a new wall in 1180. This remained the city boundary until the 19th century.

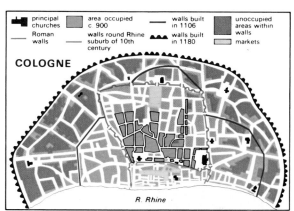

principal churches	walls built in 1106
Roman walls	walls built in 1180
area occupied c 900	unoccupied areas within walls
walls round Rhine suburb of 10th century	markets

COLOGNE

R. Rhine

The cathedral of Worms (above) The massive Romanesque cathedral illustrates the new wealth generated by the economic recovery of the 11th century.

3/The colonisation of the Black Forest (below) The Rhineland, a main artery of communications from Roman times, was settled at an early date; but the high, heavily wooded ranges which enclosed it on both sides (Hunsrück, Taunus, Spessart, Odenwald and Black Forest) had to wait until the 11th century before clearing and colonisation took place. In the Black Forest settlement of the mountainous areas only took place after c. 1075. The agents were the dukes of Zähringen and the monasteries under their control, particularly St Peter (1093) and St Georgen (1114). The Zähringer finally asserted control over the whole region by founding (c. 1120) the towns of Freiburg, Villingen and Offenburg, which dominated the few routes traversing the forest. The advance of clearing, evidenced by the new place name, from the old-settled areas to the high woodlands is a classic example of the progress of colonisation and settlement.

4/Clearance and settlement in north-eastern France (below) If in some areas (e.g. the Black Forest) colonisation and the clearing of woodland and waste was planned, in others it was the result of piecemeal encroachment by individual peasants on the less fertile uplands and woods. The forest of Othe, south-east of Sens, is an example of this process. Early settlement followed in the main the river valleys and existing roads; but in the 12th century scores of new settlements opened up the intervening afforested countryside. The result was an increase in the cultivated area assessed at one-third or more for Europe north of the Alps and Pyrenees and west of the Elbe: an accretion of territory and agricultural resources which gave a major impetus to the European economy.

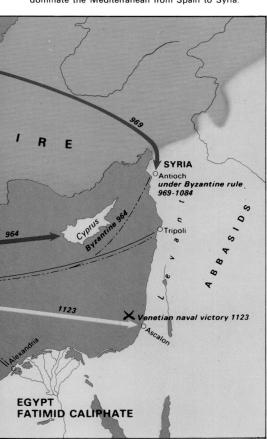

EGYPT
FATIMID CALIPHATE

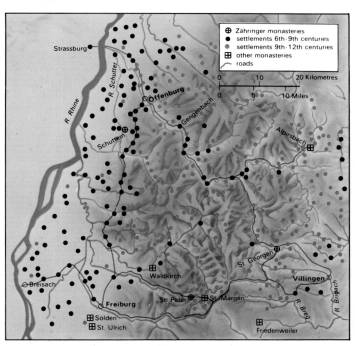

⊕	Zähringer monasteries
●	settlements 6th-9th centuries
●	settlements 9th-12th centuries
⊞	other monasteries
	roads

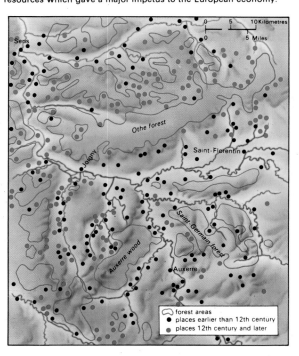

◯	forest areas
●	places earlier than 12th century
●	places 12th century and later

The conflict of Church and State in Europe 1056 to 1314

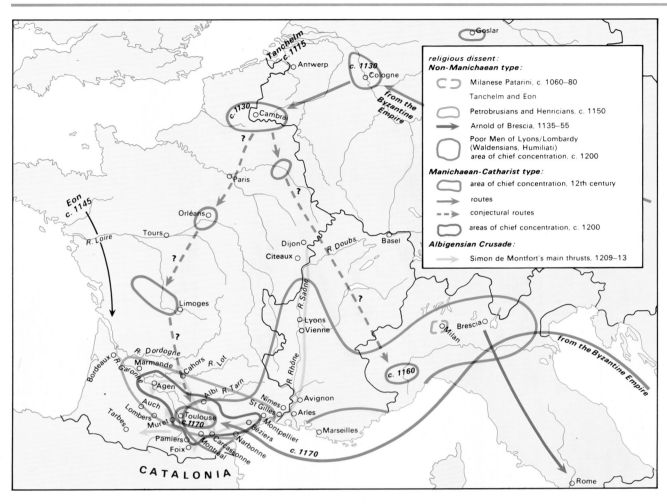

THE conflict of Church and State is a capital fact in European history. Elsewhere kings and priests tended to work in harmony, and the result was a 'monolithic' society. In Europe, particularly in western Europe, the co-existence of two powers helped to promote the emergence of 'pluralistic' societies, in which the individual had to balance the different claims made on his allegiance. Here were the distant origins of modern individualism.

From time immemorial, kings and emperors had claimed to rule by divine mandate. In imperial Rome, also, emperors assumed divine attributes and used the title 'supreme pontiff' *(pontifex maximus)*; and even after the adoption of Christianity as a state religion (see page 92), old habits died hard. Constantine (324-37),

Theodosius (379-95) and Justinian (527-65) all regarded themselves as rulers of Church and State, responsible to God for the spiritual and material welfare of their subjects. So did the kings of the Germanic successor-states of western Europe. Charlemagne (page 106) saw himself as 'king and priest', and acted as the head of both aspects of a single society, in which Christianity was important not only for its religious aspirations but also as the focus of daily life.

Popes challenged this outlook from at least the 5th century, but were seldom able to do much about it. In times of stress, like those which followed the Viking and Magyar invasions (see page 110), the secular arm was uppermost. The emperor Otto I and his successors (see page 118) used bishops as instruments of government and claimed to invest them with their spiritual as well as their secular functions. Once Europe began to recover, resistance to this usurpation grew and a movement to free the Church from secular control took shape. It began in scattered monastic centres in the west, notably at Cluny, and at Brogne and Gorze in Lorraine, spread quickly, and finally reached Rome when the emperor Henry III took in hand the reform of the papacy at the Synod of Sutri in 1046.

The connection thus forged between Church reformers and the papal see inaugurated the long struggle of Empire and Papacy, which eventually destroyed the former and fatally impaired the authority of the latter. The conflict came to a head under Gregory VII (1073-85), whose combative nature and insistence on ancient but exaggerated and hitherto largely ineffective papal claims resulted in a violent explosion. Gregory deposed the emperor Henry IV in 1076 and allied with the emperor's enemies – the Normans of southern Italy, the recalcitrant German nobility, and a chain of states around the periphery which feared German power. The result was a lasting setback to German monarchy. Although Gregory failed in his immediate objects, the launching of the First Crusade (see page 100) by Urban II (1088-99) showed how rapidly papal authority was advancing.

But by now both sides were exhausted, and the struggle begun in 1075 was settled in 1122 by the Concordat of Worms.

For the Church it was a pyrrhic victory. What had started as a movement to free the Church from secular control now seemed to be leading to the oppression of society by clergy and Pope. Gregory VII's legacy was a growing concern with temporal affairs, against which St Bernard warned Pope Eugenius III (1145-53). Papal centralisation caused an increasingly educated lay society to resent the clergy's privileges and stimulated popular religious movements, particularly in southern France and northern Italy, many of which ended in unorthodoxy and dissent. Nor did the Concordat of 1122 solve the question of Church and State, over which the kings of England and France as well as the German emperor frequently found themselves at loggerheads with the Pope. But now the conflict of Empire and Papacy had deteriorated from a conflict of principle to a struggle for control of Italy. The political involvement of the papacy became clear when Alexander III (1154-81) allied with the Lombard League of self-governing cities to resist Frederick I's attempts to restore German imperial authority in Italy. Once again, the issue was settled by a compromise (Peace of Constance, 1183), but the early death of Frederick's son, Henry VI (1190-97) and civil war in Germany (1197-1214) enabled Innocent III (1198-1216) to regain ascendancy for the Church.

Innocent III's pontificate marked a high point for the papacy. He established a papal state in central Italy to protect Rome; he nominated emperors; England bowed to his will, and France was his ally. He also had some success in dealing with anti-clericalism. The heretics of southern France were viciously suppressed in the Albigensian crusade (1208), but Innocent also encouraged the evangelism of the new orders of friars, the Franciscans and Dominicans, who were formally

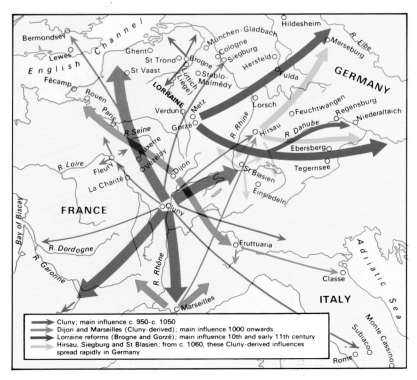

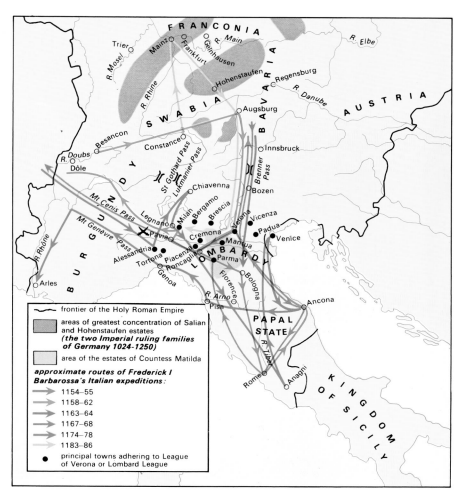

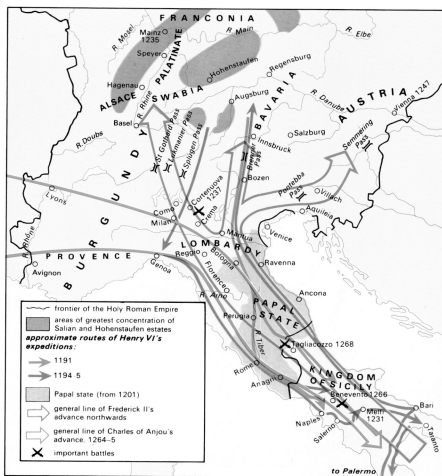

approved by his successor, Honorius III (1216-27), and sought to remove the sources of discontent by reforming clerical behaviour. But his successes were greater on paper than in practice. The papal state was never effectively controlled; the reforms of the Fourth Lateran Council (1215) were ineffective; and his choice of Frederick II (1214-50) as emperor was dictated by circumstances beyond his control.

After Innocent's death decline set in. It was accelerated by renewal of the struggle with the Empire. Like Alexander III before him, Innocent IV (1243-54) allied with the Italian cities to resist Frederick II's efforts to subject the whole of Italy to his rule (the Norman kingdom of Sicily

was his by inheritance) and to unite it with Germany by controlling the lines of communication between them. The bitterness of the struggle, in which the Pope openly expressed his intention of extirpating the Hohenstaufen dynasty, produced a strong reaction, and the papacy only succeeded when Clement IV (1265-8) called in Charles of Anjou, the brother of Louis IX of France, to evict the Germans from Italy.

Charles of Anjou's victories at Benevento (1266) and Tagliacozzo (1268) brought the Empire down in ruins, but the papacy had jumped from the frying pan into the fire. After Louis IX's death in 1270 disputes with the increasingly centralised French monarchy over

taxation of the clergy and royal sovereignty led to open conflict in 1296. Boniface VIII proclaimed papal authority undiminished, but was kidnapped by his French and Italian enemies in 1303, and in 1309 his successor, Clement V (1305-14), took up residence in Avignon, directly under French supervision. Although not always a tool of France, the 'papacy of Avignon' commanded little respect, and heresy and anticlericalism were again rife. The long conflict of Church and State had still produced no final victor, for France in its turn soon collapsed in face of English invasion (see page 142), but it had set the Church on the road which led, two centuries later, to the Protestant Reformation.

4 and 5/Conflicts of Empire and Papacy 1152-90 (above left) **and 1190-1268** (above right) The routes of the imperial expeditions illustrate the constant pressure from Germany which led Innocent III to found the papal state. By contrast, Frederick II's bases were in Apulia and Sicily. The broad arrow suggests the stages by which he tried, after about 1230, to beat a path back northwards by controlling Italian communications, and south Germany from Alsace to Austria. Charles of Anjou's invasion substituted a French for a German yoke upon Italy.

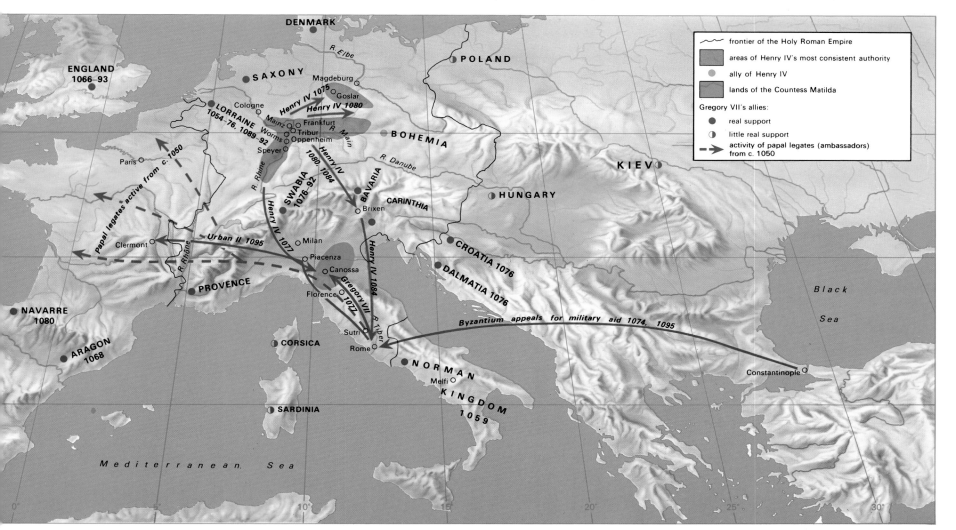

Feudal monarchy in Western Europe 1154 to 1314

2/Italy disunited *(above)* Papal-Imperial controversy and the wealth of the municipalities inhibited consolidation in Italy. After 1250, public power in independent city states was exercised by republican oligarchies or by despots who often succeeded as alternatives to the factional violence of civic politics.

3/Spain: the Reconquista *(below)* Displaced in Old Castile and León, where Christian freeholders settled, Muslims remained numerous in the Aragonese kingdoms. In Andalusia Christian military leaders, rewarded with great estates, dominated a mixed population.

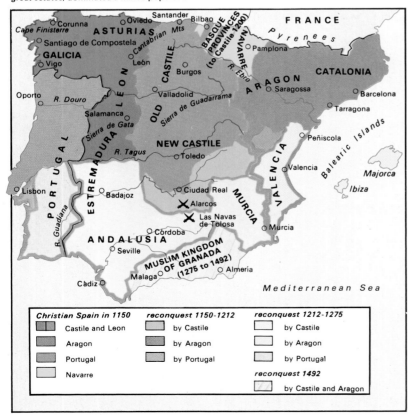

WESTERN Europe began its slow climb out of political dislocation and feudal anarchy during the 12th century. Viking and Magyar invasions (see page 110) had disrupted royal authority and strengthened the local feudatories, but kingship survived. Weak though the king might be in practice, his position was hallowed by religious sanctions, and in the 12th century kings used their position to assert their prerogatives at the head of the feudal hierarchy. They were helped by the reaction against papal attacks on the monarchy during the Investiture Contest (see page 122), when rulers turned to the arsenal of Roman law for weapons to defend their independence. In the hands of the emperor Frederick Barbarossa and later of the French Capetians, Roman law became a powerful instrument of royal authority. But the main weapons used by 12th and 13th century kings were feudal: the king's rights as 'liege lord', the duty of tenants-in-chief to render service, the theory that all land was held of the king, and all rights of justice were delegations of royal authority, and therefore reverted, or 'escheated', to the crown in case of abuse or treason. Step by step grave misdemeanours (felonies) were reserved to the king's courts as 'pleas of the crown'. By the beginning of the 13th century, at least in France and England, elective monarchy had been displaced by hereditary monarchy, and the electors, lay and ecclesiastical, shorn of their power. Much of this progress was piecemeal; but by the middle of the 13th century the great lawyers (Bracton in England, Beaumanoir in France) had created a systematic structure of royal government, which kings like Edward I of England (1272-1307) and Philip IV of France (1285-1314) proceeded to exploit.

Progress was most rapid in the Norman kingdoms of England and Sicily. Since both were acquired by conquest, the aristocracy was less firmly entrenched than elsewhere and the kings' hands correspondingly free. This enabled William the Conqueror (1066-87) to retain and build up the fiscal and jurisdictional prerogatives inherited from his Anglo-Saxon predecessors in England. In Sicily also the great Norman ruler, Roger II, who united Sicily, Apulia and Calabria in 1130, retained the institutions of his Byzantine and Muslim predecessors, particularly their efficient system of taxation. By the end of the 12th century Sicily, with its control of the Mediterranean sea-routes, was the richest, most advanced and tightly organised state in Europe. In France, on the other hand, where the anarchy of the 9th and 10th centuries was greatest, progress was slower. Louis VI (1108-37) spent his reign asserting authority over the petty barons of the Île de France, and it was scarcely before the reign of Philip Augustus (1180-1223) that expansion of the royal demesne began in earnest. The turning point was the conquest of Normandy in 1204, which effectively meant the destruction of the Angevin Empire, i.e. of the Anglo-Norman dominions across the English Channel. After 1214 English continental possessions were limited to Gascony, and a third of France was now under direct royal control. The defeat of the English also permitted the Capetians to turn elsewhere. Much of Languedoc was subdued in a campaign against the Albigensian heretics (1209-29) and royal authority now extended south of the Loire.

The other area in which monarchy made great strides was the Iberian peninsula. Here the kingdoms of Portugal (independent since 1139), Navarre, Castile and Aragon were creations of the progressive reconquest of the peninsula from the Arabs, whose decisive defeat at Las Navas de Tolosa (1212) led rapidly to the loss of Córdoba (1236), Valencia (1238), Murcia (1243), Seville (1248) and Cádiz (1262). A major role in the reconquest was taken by Castile, originally a tributary of the crown of León, with which it was permanently united in 1230. By the middle of the

13th century Castile controlled more than half the peninsula and was gradually welded into a monarchical state by Alfonso X (1252-84). In the eastern portion of the peninsula authority was wielded by the crown of Aragon after its union with the county of Catalonia (1137) and the conquest of Valencia (1238). Hemmed in on the west by Castile, Aragon turned its expansionist energies towards the Mediterranean. The Balearics were conquered between 1229 and 1235, and Sicily wrested from Charles of Anjou, the French prince called in by the papacy, in 1282. Though the tripartite structure of the kingdom left partial autonomy to the component states, the Aragonese empire was the creation of a powerful monarchy fortified by the commercial wealth of Catalonia and Valencia.

The exceptions to this process of feudal concentration were Germany and Italy. Here, despite the efforts of Frederick Barbarossa (1152-90), the monarchy never fully recovered from its setbacks during the Investiture Contest, and the long interregnum after the death of Frederick's son, Henry VI, in 1197, weakened it still further. Paradoxically, the feudal processes which strengthened monarchy in the west worked to its detriment in central Europe, where power passed to feudal princes or, in Italy, to city magistrates (*podestà*) or increasingly to tyrants (*signori*) who dominated the cities they ruled and the surrounding countryside.

In the west royal supremacy was well established before the end of the 13th century. Kings exercised powers of taxation and legislation (often in consultation with parliaments or 'estates of the realm') and controlled the administration of justice. They also used their authority to assert overlordship over neighbouring territories, where feudalism had resulted in an intricate network of overlapping rights and jurisdictions. Nowhere was the feudal map more complex than in France, where the English possessions at one time stretched from Normandy to the Mediterranean coast. The determination of the French kings to assert their overlordship over these lands and over Flanders gave rise to a series of major wars. Meanwhile the English kings were asserting similar claims in Scotland, Wales and Ireland. Henry II's attempt to conquer Ireland (1171) achieved only a precarious foothold, but Edward I subdued Wales, already harassed by marcher lords and the palatine earls of Chester, in 1284. His attempt to repeat the process in Scotland in 1296 resulted in fierce resistance under Wallace and Bruce, and the famous Scottish victory at Bannockburn in 1314.

Edward I's failure in Scotland was matched by Philip IV's failure in Flanders. Defeated by the Flemings at Courtrai (1302), the French king, who had seized Gascony in 1294, was compelled to restore it to the English in 1303. War expenditure and centralisation also produced severe internal strains. In Aragon the estates forced the monarchy to grant a General Privilege in 1283. In England Edward I was compelled in 1297 to confirm and extend the charters wrested from King John in 1215. In France the States-General met for the first time in 1302. Everywhere, in short, the new monarchies had overreached themselves; the result was a powerful aristocratic reaction. When, after the middle of the 15th century, recovery began (see page 150), the foundations were no longer feudal. Sovereignty had replaced suzerainty, and a new period in the history of western monarchy had begun.

1/The growth of the French and English monarchies *(right)* Early mediaeval rulers laid claim to supreme power but they depended primarily on personal and feudal allegiances over which not infrequently they had less command than their most powerful subjects. The institutional strength of monarchy, developing in the 12th century, expanded rapidly in the 13th century. By 1300 western kings were no longer primarily feudal overlords: they had become acknowledged executors of effective public authority.

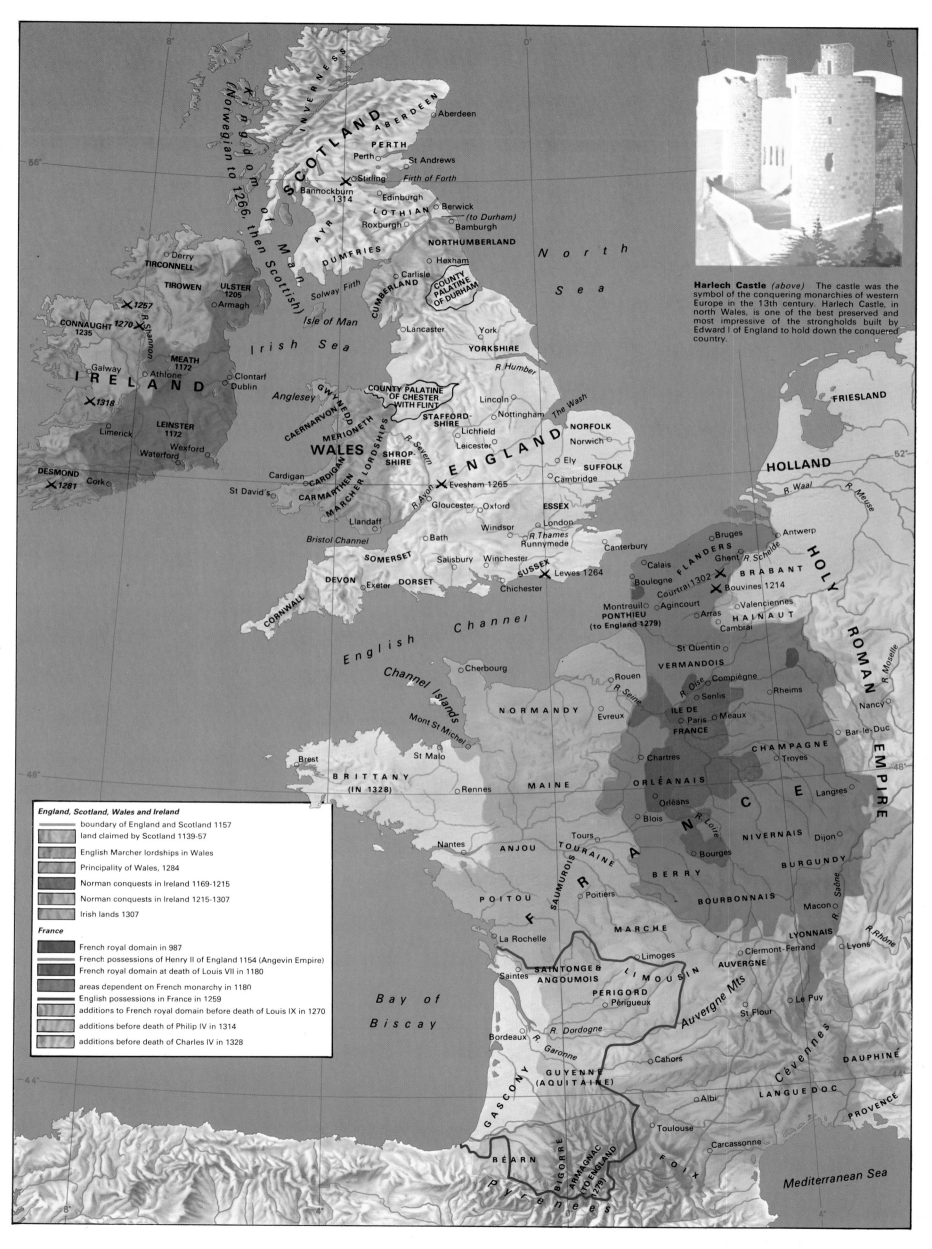

Harlech Castle *(above)* The castle was the symbol of the conquering monarchies of western Europe in the 13th century. Harlech Castle, in north Wales, is one of the best preserved and most impressive of the strongholds built by Edward I of England to hold down the conquered country.

England, Scotland, Wales and Ireland

	boundary of England and Scotland 1157
	land claimed by Scotland 1139-57
	English Marcher lordships in Wales
	Principality of Wales, 1284
	Norman conquests in Ireland 1169-1215
	Norman conquests in Ireland 1215-1307
	Irish lands 1307

France

	French royal domain in 987
	French possessions of Henry II of England 1154 (Angevin Empire)
	French royal domain at death of Louis VII in 1180
	areas dependent on French monarchy in 1180
	English possessions in France in 1259
	additions to French royal domain before death of Louis IX in 1270
	additions before death of Philip IV in 1314
	additions before death of Charles IV in 1328

Kingdom of Man (Norwegian to 1266, then Scottish)

SCOTLAND

INVERNESS

ABERDEEN
Aberdeen

PERTH
Perth
St Andrews

AYR
Stirling
Bannockburn 1314
Edinburgh
Firth of Forth
LOTHIAN
Berwick
Roxburgh
(to Durham)
Bamburgh
DUMFRIES
NORTHUMBERLAND

Derry
TIRCONNELL
TIROWEN
ULSTER 1205
Armagh

× 1257
CONNAUGHT 1235 × 1270 R. Shannon

MEATH 1172
Galway
Athlone
Clontarf
Dublin

IRELAND

× 1318

LEINSTER 1172
Limerick
Wexford
Waterford

DESMOND
× 1281
Cork

Solway Firth
Isle of Man
Carlisle
CUMBERLAND
COUNTY PALATINE OF DURHAM
Hexham

North Sea

Lancaster
York
YORKSHIRE

R. Humber
The Wash

Irish Sea

Anglesey
GWYNEDD
CAERNARVON
MERIONETH
CARDIGAN
CARMARTHEN
MARCHER LORDSHIPS
WALES
SHROP-SHIRE
Cardigan
St David's
Llandaff

COUNTY PALATINE OF CHESTER WITH FLINT
STAFFORD-SHIRE
Lichfield
Leicester
R. Severn

Lincoln
Nottingham

NORFOLK
Norwich

Ely
SUFFOLK
Cambridge

ENGLAND
R. Avon
Evesham 1265
Gloucester
Oxford
ESSEX
Windsor
London
R. Thames
Runnymede
Canterbury

Bristol Channel
SOMERSET
Bath
Salisbury
Winchester
SUSSEX
Lewes 1264
Chichester

DEVON
Exeter DORSET

CORNWALL

FRIESLAND

HOLLAND

R. Waal
R. Meuse

Bruges
Antwerp
Calais
FLANDERS
Ghent R. Schelde
Boulogne
Courtrai 1302
BRABANT
Bouvines 1214
Valenciennes
Montreuil
Agincourt
Arras
HAINAUT
PONTHIEU (to England 1279)
Cambrai

HOLY ROMAN

R. Moselle

English Channel

Cherbourg

Channel Islands

Mont St Michel

Brest
St Malo

BRITTANY (IN 1328)
Rennes

MAINE

NORMANDY
Evreux
Rouen
R. Seine

St Quentin
VERMANDOIS
R. Oise
Compiègne
Senlis
Rheims
ILE DE FRANCE
Paris
Meaux

Nancy
Bar-le-Duc

EMPIRE

Chartres
ORLÉANAIS
Orléans
Blois

CHAMPAGNE
Troyes
Langres

F R A N C E

NIVERNAIS
Dijon
BURGUNDY
R. Saône

Nantes
ANJOU
TOURAINE
SAUMUROIS
Tours
Poitiers
POITOU

BERRY
Bourges
BOURBONNAIS

LYONNAIS
Mâcon

La Rochelle
MARCHE
Limoges
LIMOUSIN
AUVERGNE
Clermont-Ferrand
Lyons
R. Rhône

Bay of Biscay

SAINTONGE & ANGOUMOIS
Saintes
PERIGORD
Périgueux
Auvergne Mts
St Flour
Le Puy

Bordeaux
R. Dordogne
R. Garonne
GUYENNE (AQUITAINE)
Cahors
Albi
LANGUEDOC
Cévennes
DAUPHINÉ

GASCONY
BÉARN
BIGORRE
ARMAGNAC (TO ENGLAND 1279)
Toulouse
FOIX
Carcassonne
PROVENCE
Pyrenees

Mediterranean Sea

Chinese civilisation from the T'ang to the Sung 618 to 1278

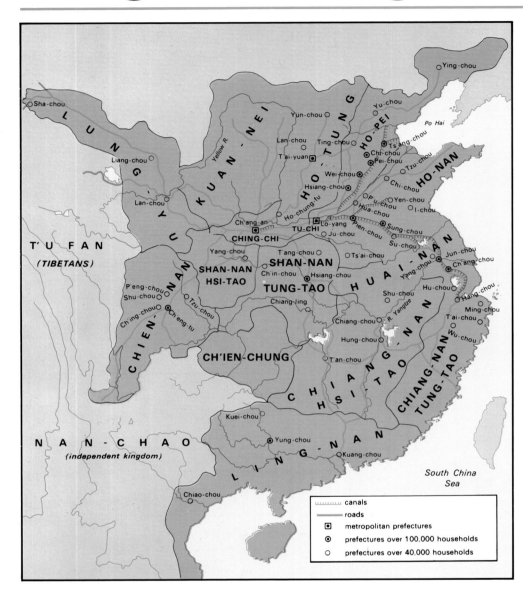

1/T'ang China *(above)* The whole of China proper, excepting the far south-west, was permanently organised under centralised administration. The empire was linked together by a network of post-roads, while transport of commodities between the rapidly developing regions of the Yangtze valley and the north was provided by an efficient system of canals and waterways. The road system centred on the capital, Ch'ang-an, which remained the political and strategic hub of the empire. However, the eastern plain and the area around the Lower Yangtze were the main economic centres.

A FTER centuries of disunion (see page 94), China was reunified in 589 by the Sui dynasty (581-617). Their empire was consolidated under the system of centrally codified institutions developed under the northern Wei and their successors, by the state patronage of a style of Buddhism acceptable in north and south alike, and by the construction of a canal system linking the Yangtze with the Yellow River (Huang Ho) and the Peking region. The Sui collapsed, partly from the burden imposed by these public works and the reconstruction of the Great Wall, partly because of repeated abortive attempts to conquer Koguryŏ (northern Korea).

After some years of widespread rebellions, the Sui were replaced by the T'ang, a dynasty of similar social origins which continued most of their policies. The T'ang state was a strong centralised empire, with a simple but effective administrative system designed to be uniform. At first the system worked well. But after some years of internal consolidation the T'ang began to expand abroad, and in the 8th century the growing complexity of the state and of society, and the costs of defence, produced many changes. By the 660s Chinese armies had intervened in India, central Asia and Afghanistan, the Chinese had occupied the Tarim Basin and Dzungaria, and briefly set up protectorates in Tukharistan, Sogdiana, Ferghana and eastern

Persia. At the same period Koguryŏ was finally conquered and for a few years the T'ang occupied northern Korea. The formidable northern Turks had been defeated in 630, and in the 660s the Chinese Empire reached its greatest extent prior to the Manchu conquests of the 18th century.

While Chinese military force was establishing this vast empire, Chinese culture, its written language and political institutions, were adopted in the states which were growing up around China's eastern periphery–in Silla (Korea), in Japan, in Po-hai (Manchuria) and Nan-chao (Yunnan). Thus began the Chinese ecumene in the Far East, which persisted long after T'ang military power had decayed.

In 755 An Lu-shan, a frontier general, began a rebellion which lasted seven years and almost destroyed the T'ang. As a result the Chinese withdrew from central Asia, and the Tibetans and Uighurs occupied their former territories. Islam had meanwhile reached Ferghana and later became the dominant cultural force in Turkestan. The deep cultural links between China and central Asia were broken, and China became more inward-looking.

The rebellion also set in motion major social and economic changes. The imperial authority was much reduced, and the uniform centralised policies of the 7th century were abandoned. Power passed to the provinces, and many provincial capitals grew into large and wealthy metropolises. There was a massive movement of population to the fertile Yangtze valley, where new methods of farming produced large surpluses of grain. Trade boomed, and a network of small market towns grew up everywhere.

At the end of the 9th century massive peasant uprisings reduced central authority to a cipher, and power passed to the provincial generals,

whose regimes became virtually independent. When in 907 the T'ang finally disappeared, China split into ten separate regional states, and was only reunified by the Sung in 960 to 979. In northern China there was constant warfare, and everywhere it was a period of insecurity and sweeping social change, in which the diversity of China was intensified. During this period of division China lost control of the north-eastern area to the Khitan (Liao) who had overwhelmed Po-hai to set up an empire in Manchuria and Inner Mongolia. In the north-west another powerful kingdom, the Hsi-hsia, was founded by the Tanguts in Ningsia and Kansu. These areas remained under alien domination until 1368.

The Sung state was organised on less uniform lines than the T'ang. The emperor enjoyed greater power, and military and financial experts were given greater influence. But there was constant and bitter factional strife between those who wished to rationalise government, and the conservatives, and this weakened the Sung state, which in spite of its power and resources faced grave external threats. The Sung was a far less cosmopolitan era than the T'ang, generally on the defensive and suspicious of the outside world. In 1126-27 this attitude was hardened when the Chin, who had replaced the Liao in the north-east, overran and conquered all of northern China, with terrible devastation. From 1127 to 1279 the Sung survived in control only of central and southern China, constantly on the defensive and forced to maintain huge armies and to pay vast subsidies to their aggressive neighbours.

Nevertheless, Chinese economic growth continued under the Sung. Between 750 and 1100 the population doubled; trade reached new levels, and a great concentration of industries arose around the early Sung capital, K'ai-feng. Even after the loss of the north, Sung China was immensely prosperous. Its southern territories were far more productive than the old northern heartland of China. Population continued to increase rapidly, trade and industry boomed, and the capital, Hang-chou, became indisputably the world's greatest city. It was also a

2/The Chinese world, 7th-8th centuries *(right)* During the 660s and 670s Chinese military power reached a peak, and briefly extended the power of the T'ang from Sogdiana to North Korea. The Chinese remained in control of the Tarim Basin and Dzungaria until 756; the Tarim and parts of north-west China fell to the Tibetans in 763-83 after Chinese garrisons were withdrawn. Chinese institutions and literary culture extended over parts of the Far East which were never controlled by China, but became parts of the Chinese ecumene.

A foreign merchant *(above)* T'ang China was an extremely cosmopolitan society. Many of the merchants, both in large-scale international trade and in local retail trade, were central Asians, like this tomb figure of a Sogdian merchant.

3/The fragmentation of China: the Five Dynasties and Ten Kingdoms 910-23 *(below)* After the widespread peasant rebellions of the 870s, culminating in the Huang Ch'ao uprising, the central power of the T'ang, already weakened since the mid-8th century, speedily collapsed, and a variety of independent local regimes developed on the basis of Late T'ang provincial regional divisions. These were finally reunified by the Sung only in 979.

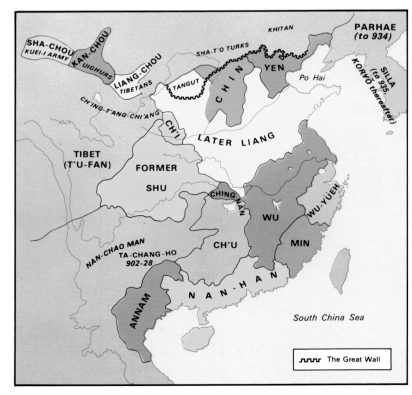

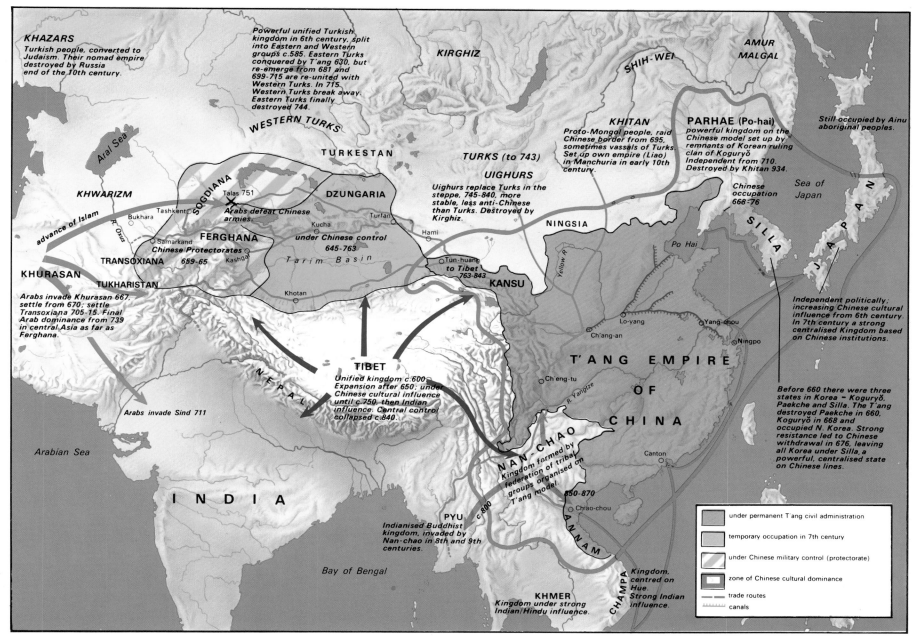

period of great cultural achievement. In the visual arts, in literature, philosophy, science and technology, new heights were reached. Education became more widespread, aided by the dissemination of printing, which had been invented during the T'ang and was now commonplace. The prosperous cities developed an urban middle class with their own life-style and culture, who became patrons of popular drama and of storytellers.

Society was transformed. State examinations for the recruiting of officials gradually replaced the old ruling aristocratic caste with a mandarinate – a meritocracy of career bureaucrats. Although merchants were excluded from official service, many became immensely rich and

held an important place in society, forming guilds and partnerships and setting up a complex commercial organisation with banks, credit systems and paper money. In the countryside the independent peasants of T'ang times, working lands allocated by the state, were replaced by many large estates farmed by tenant farmers and labourers. A free market in land emerged.

Since the old land routes to central Asia and the Middle East were no longer in Chinese hands, the Chinese slowly became a major sea power. Chinese shipping regularly traded with south-east Asia, Indonesia, India and the Persian Gulf. The southern Sung also had a powerful navy.

In the 13th century, after this period of rapid

change and growth, the pace of change slowed down markedly. This was partly the result of the immense destruction and social disruption caused by the Mongol conquest (see page 128), but in part because T'ang and Sung China had evolved an abiding social stability, developing conservative and conformist intellectual and political attitudes which militated against change. But in the 13th century China remained far more populous, productive and wealthy, her society far more orderly and stable, her science and technology far more advanced than that of contemporary Europe. During this whole period, China was the world's greatest power, and Chinese culture the world's greatest splendour.

5/Sung China (below) The Sung suffered considerable losses of territory compared with the T'ang: Vietnam was no longer Chinese territory; in the north, the Khitan state of Liao occupied the border areas on the north-east, and the Tangut state of Hsi-hsia the north-west. The centre of the Sung state was the great commercial city of K'ai-feng, centre of the canal system and of the eastern road network, which grew into the centre of a major complex of industries. The old strategic heartland of the north-west steadily declined in importance.

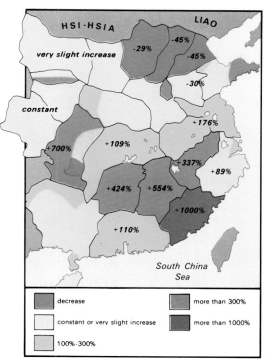

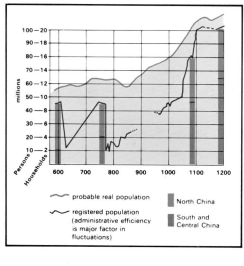

4/Population growth (above and left) The period from 750 to 1250 saw a very rapid growth of the Chinese population, which probably doubled. At the same time the distribution of the people completely changed. In the 7th century 73 per cent of the population lived in the north-east of China, and less than a quarter in south and central China. By the 13th century the situation was reversed and China's economic centre of gravity had shifted from the northern plain to the Yangtze valley.

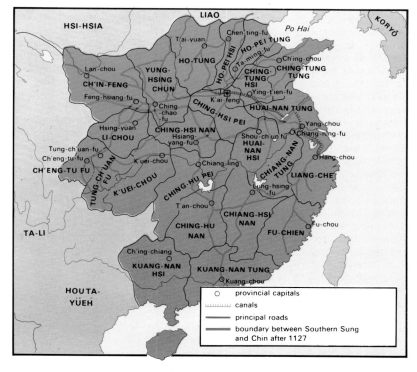

The Mongol Empire
1206 to 1405

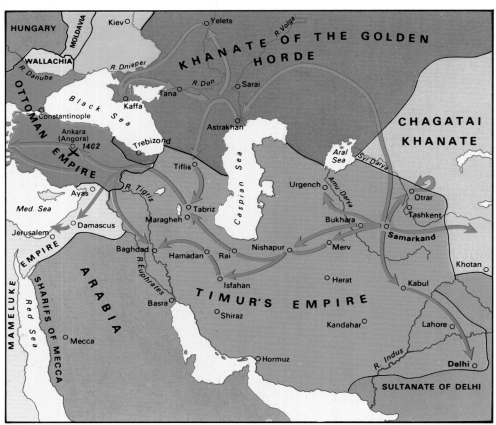

THE Mongols, a primitive nomadic people from the depths of Asia, made a tremendous impact on world history. Their conquests were of a scope and range never equalled, stretching from the eastern frontiers of Germany to Korea and from the Arctic Ocean to Turkey and the Persian Gulf. They even attempted seaborne invasions of Japan and Java. This was the last, and most violent, assault of nomadic barbarism that civilisation was called upon to endure, and its effects were considerable. The political organisation of Asia and a large part of Europe was altered; whole peoples were uprooted and dispersed, permanently changing the ethnic character of many regions; the strength and distribution of the principal religions of the world were decisively altered; European access to Asia and the Far East, interrupted for a thousand years, became possible again once the transcontinental routes were dominated by a single authority and travel made safe.

Ethnically the most striking result of the Mongol conquests was the wide dispersal of the Turkic peoples over western Asia. Since their barren land could not support a large population, the Mongols were not a numerous people, but from the outset Genghis Khan did not hesitate to augment his armies from Turkish tribes on whose fidelity he could rely, until Turks in the Mongol armies actually outnumbered the native Mongols. Thus the Turkish language advanced across Asia with the Mongol armies, the minority of Mongol speakers was absorbed by the Turkish mass and their language survived only in the original homeland. The Turks had already risen to prominence before the Mongol conquests, but the Mongols, by breaking up the old Seljuk sultanate of Rum, cleared the way for the greatest of the Turkish empires – the Ottoman.

In the course of their drive for empire the Mongols came into contact with three religions and their associated cultures – Buddhism, Islam and Christianity. Their attitude towards them was ambivalent. They professed an ancestral shamanism embodied in the *Yasa* or Law of Genghis Khan, but felt the powerful attraction of the new creeds which seemed invariably to be associated with higher cultures. Islam at first seemed unfavourably placed. Baghdad itself was captured and sacked and the caliph slain.

But the religion of the Prophet slowly established its ascendancy over the conquerors and a powerful revival began. This revival was closely bound up with the collapse of Asian Christianity, whose prospects had once looked so bright (see page 100). For a time Christianity was widely preached throughout the Asian continent, but the initial promise was never fulfilled. Buddhism, like Islam, emerged from the Mongol experience stronger than it entered it. It had little success west of the Altai mountains, but in eastern Asia the Mongol dynasty gave it a predominant place in Chinese society.

The early life of Genghis Khan is shrouded in a mist of legend. Primitive Mongol-speaking tribes had lived for centuries in the general area of present-day Mongolia, but it took an extra-ordinary leader to unite the Mongols and transform them into a world power. Temujin (later Genghis Khan) was born probably in 1167, the son of a tribal chief. After many years of struggle he succeeded, by 1206, in uniting all the Mongol tribes. After subduing other neighbouring tribes, in 1211 he invaded the independent Chin empire in northern China, piercing the Great Wall and opening a struggle that was to continue for twenty-three years, ending only in 1234, after Genghis' death, with the total destruction of the Chin empire. Peking fell in 1215, but Genghis was then drawn away to the west in campaigns against the Kara-Khitai and Khwarizm – the first Muslim state to experience the full fury of the Mongol onslaught. In spite of bitter resistance, the Mongols overwhelmed the Muslim states of central Asia and reached the Caucasus.

Genghis died in 1227, but his conquests were continued and extended by his successors. Before his death he made provision for the succession, dividing his empire among his four sons. Batu, a grandson of Genghis, directed the invasion of Europe. The northern Russian principalities were smashed in a lightning winter campaign in 1237-38, and the ancient city of Kiev was taken by storm and razed to the ground in 1240. The

same year a two-pronged assault was launched against Poland and Hungary. The Oder was passed at Raciborz and the Mongol army swept northwards down the river valley. Breslau was bypassed, and on 9 April 1241 a German/Polish army was annihilated at Legnica. A few days later the second Mongol army routed the Hungarians at Mohi. It is generally believed that only the death of the Great Khan Ogedei in December 1241 saved Europe. Disputes arose over the succession and Batu led the armies back to their old base on the lower Volga in the winter of 1242-43.

If Christian Europe was saved by the death of Ogedei in 1241, the death of the Great Khan Möngke in 1259 saved Muslim Asia. Möngke had resolved to extend the Mongol dominions in the east and west, against the Sung in China, and the Assassins and the Caliphate 'as far as the borders of Egypt'. Möngke himself was to take charge of the Chinese war, but the western campaign was entrusted to his younger brother, Hülegü. The Assassins were exterminated and Baghdad fell early in 1258. After the death

The Mongols, a primitive nomadic people... (see page 100).

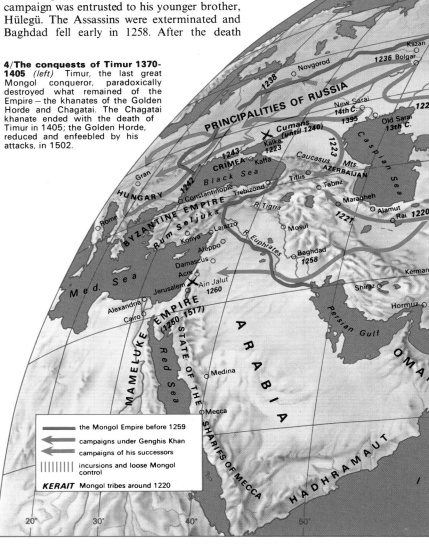

1/The Mongol Empire before 1259 (below) The greatest land empire in world history was conquered by the ruthless and brilliant cavalry armies of Genghis Khan and his successors. It stretched from Java and Korea in the east to Poland in the west, from the Arctic in the north to Turkey and Persia in the south. The armies became expert at siege warfare, learning from the Chinese, and their field intelligence and signals enabled them to mount bewildering flank attacks, encirclements and obstruction of escape routes. Byzantium and western Europe were saved by the death of Ogedei just as his advance guard reached the Adriatic, and Japan by the storms (or *kamikaze*, sacred wind) that destroyed Kublai Khan's navy.

4/The conquests of Timur 1370-1405 (left) Timur, the last great Mongol conqueror, paradoxically destroyed what remained of the Empire – the khanates of the Golden Horde and Chagatai. The Chagatai khanate ended with the death of Timur in 1405; the Golden Horde, reduced and enfeebled by his attacks, in 1502.

———	the Mongol Empire before 1259	
←	campaigns under Genghis Khan	
←	campaigns of his successors	
‖‖‖	incursions and loose Mongol control	
KERAIT	Mongol tribes around 1220	

2/The Mongol invasion of Europe 1237-42 (right) The Mongols conquered Russia in a winter campaign – their cavalry armies moving with great speed on frozen rivers, the only successful winter invasion of Russia in history. A meticulously planned and brilliantly executed campaign against Hungary followed, penetrating from at least three different directions.

of Möngke in 1259 armed conflict broke out between rival claimants, causing Hülegü to concentrate the bulk of his troops in Azerbaijan leaving only a skeleton force in Syria. This soon became known in Cairo, and the Mameluke sultan took the opportunity to march against the pagan enemies of the faith. At Ain Jalut near Nazareth on 3 September 1260 the superior Mameluke army inflicted a crushing defeat. This battle was a turning point in history. The Mongol advance in the West was never seriously renewed, and the spell of their invincibility shattered for ever.

The death of Möngke also ended the short-lived unity of the Mongol Empire. The direct authority of succeeding Great Khans was confined to the east, while the khanates of Chagatai, Persia (Il-Khan) and the Golden Horde went their several ways as independent states. In the settled kingdoms of Persia and China the Mongol dynasties came to an end in less than a century. In the khanates of the Golden Horde and Chagatai society was less urbanised and simpler and the population partly nomadic; in consequence Mongol rule lasted longer – in Russia for more than two hundred years. Their decline can in fact be dated from the time of Timur (Tamerlane), whose rise to power marks the final end of the Mongol age of conquests.

The appearance of the Mongols on the world stage was sudden and devastating. Old kingdoms and empires went down before them in monotonous succession. Their success was probably the result of superior strategy, an excellent and highly mobile cavalry, endurance, and a disciplined and co-ordinated manner of fighting. The Mongols even had an organisation that in some ways resembled a modern general staff. On the other hand the opposing armies, especially in Europe, were usually cumbersome and unco-ordinated. The invasion of Russia is a good example of Mongol methods. The strongest part of the country was conquered in a few months, and by means of a winter campaign, the Mongol cavalry moving with great speed on the frozen rivers – the only successful winter invasion of Russia in history. The Mongols did not make any startling innovations in the ancient traditions of the steppe nomads. They used the strategy and tactics of the earlier cavalry armies of the steppe peoples, but under a military genius these were brought to the highest pitch of efficiency and produced what was certainly the most formidable instrument of war in the world at that time.

Nevertheless the social and cultural legacy of the Mongol irruption is not easy to trace. Their rule was mostly comparatively brief. In fact the Mongols never succeeded in creating a distinctive, enduring civilisation. Rather their conquests can be seen as the end of an epoch. From the dawn of civilisation, city dwellers and the cultivators of the soil had been menaced by assault from the fierce riders of the steppes. But during the life of the Mongol Empire came the invention of gunpowder and firearms; no longer would battle be decided by endurance and stamina. During the succeeding centuries Russia and China, the two nations which had suffered most from nomad aggression, steadily moved in to contain once and for all the recalcitrant herdsmen of the steppes.

The Mongol 'soldier' (above)
The horsemanship of the Mongol cavalry was the most effective in military history.

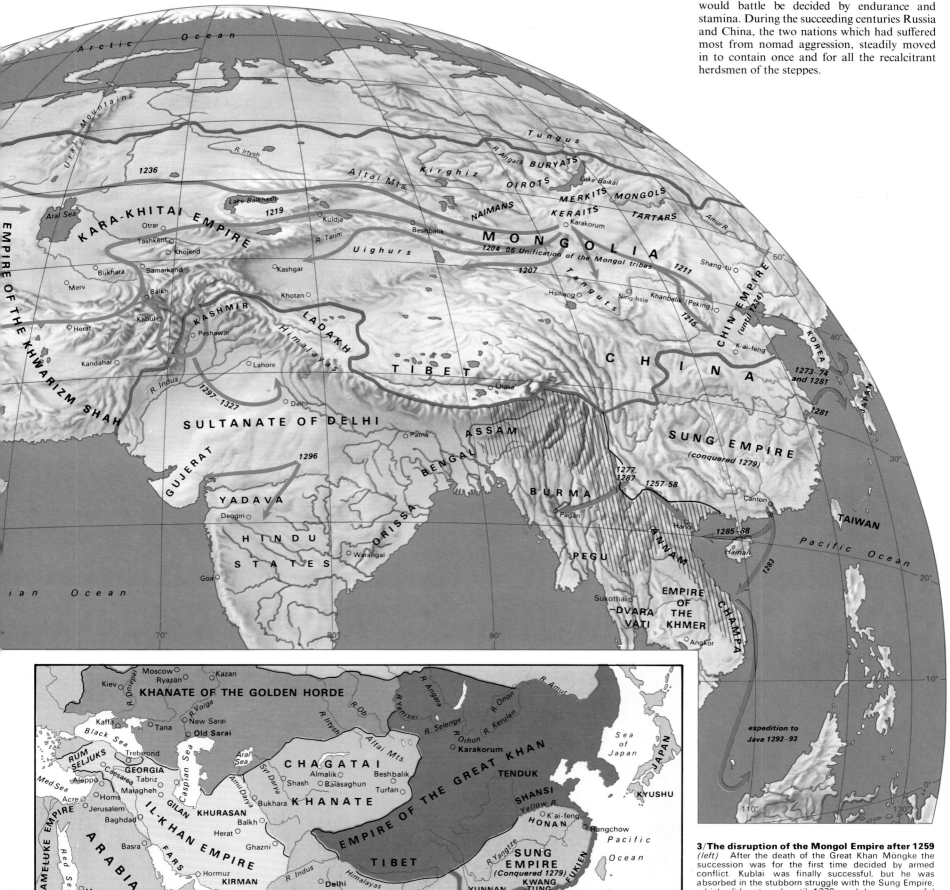

3/The disruption of the Mongol Empire after 1259 (left) After the death of the Great Khan Möngke the succession was for the first time decided by armed conflict. Kublai was finally successful, but he was absorbed in the stubborn struggle with the Sung Empire, which did not end until 1279, and by unsuccessful efforts to conquer Japan. A vast imperial realm comprising nearly all Asia and much of Europe could not be governed by one man.

129

India: the struggle for power and the Delhi Sultanate

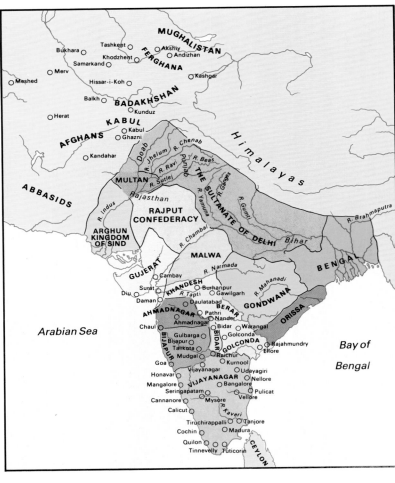

IN Harsha's time (see page 82) the city of Kanauj, in western Uttar Pradesh, gradually displaced the ancient dynastic capital of Pataliputra and soon came to dominate the Ganges plain. The tripartite struggle to control it (map 1) waged between the Gurjara-Pratiharas, the Palas and the Rashtrakutas, shaped north Indian history for most of the next 200 years. The Rashtrakuta kingdom, established around the year 753, constantly pressed on the lands to both north and south of its main power base in the north Deccan, and extended, at its peak, from south Gujerat, Malwa and Baghelkhand to Tanjore. The Pala Empire, maintaining strong Buddhist ties with Tibet and valuable commercial links with south-east Asia, included Bengal, Bihar, Orissa and the Andhra country. It flourished exceedingly after the election of a strong king, Gopala, ended a period of political chaos in the 8th century. The Pratiharas originated in Rajasthan and held power from 836 between the east Punjab and the north Bengal. The strengths of the three contenders proved to be almost exactly matched, and in the 10th century, after a last thrust by the Palas which reached as far as Benares, they all disintegrated into smaller warring states. The advancing Turks sacked Kanauj in 1018.

The invaders against whom the Pratiharas were keeping the door were almost certainly the Arabs, who in the 7th century penetrated Afghanistan and Baluchistan, and in the 8th century conquered Cutch, Saurashtra and Sind. When their further progress was checked by Indian resistance, the Sind Arabs broke away from the Abbasid Empire (827) and later split up into the twin kingdoms of Multan and Mansura. These became well-known trading communities under the Delhi Sultanate, although their political significance was very small.

Events in south India, as in the past, continued to be determined largely by geography. The high, mountain-ringed plateau lands to the west of the peninsula are linked to the fertile plains south of Madras by west-to-east flowing rivers,

notably the Krishna and the Godavari. During this period a succession of states and dynasties continually tried to control the waterways throughout their length, and out of the struggles two groups, the Tamil Cholas in the east and the Chalukyas in the west, emerged as major powers.

The Cholas were already an old people, first mentioned in the inscriptions of Asoka (page 82). Under Rajaraja (985-1014) and his son Rajendra, they now conquered most of the Tamil-nad, eastern Deccan, Ceylon and parts of the Malay Peninsula. Ceylon, involved in conflicts with assorted enemies (including the Rashtrakutas) finally expelled the Cholas in 1070, but this did not prevent the latter from successfully driving north, through Orissa and as far as the Ganges, to take part in the dismemberment of the Pala domains and threaten Bengal's independence.

The Rashtrakutas of the north were finally overthrown by the Chalukyas, who had built their kingdom on the ruins left behind by the Satavahanas (page 82) and their successors, the Vakatakas, whose fortunes had declined alongside those of their northern allies, the Guptas. In the 7th century they established control over Vengi, the land between the Krishna and the Godavari, adopted the Zoroastrians, later known as Parsees, who had been expelled by the Arabs, and spread far and wide from their homeland in north Mysore. Their power was broken, however, when the Cholas sacked their capital, Kalyani, in the early 11th century.

Civilisation flourished during this period of history despite the political disarray. Sankaracharya, a 9th century brahmin from Kerala, set out to cleanse the ancient Vedic philosophy from its accretion of obscurities. He became a famous interpreter of Vedanta, which proclaimed that the final object of existence was the union of the individual and the Absolute Soul, and also propagated the Monist philosophy of Advaita, holding that the world is an illusion. Earlier, in the 6th and 7th centuries, the Tamil saints, known as *alvars*, preached devotion to Vishnu in exquisite poetry, while their contemporaries, the *nainars*, similarly celebrated the cult of Shiva. The Tantric form of Buddhism, with its emphasis on magic, and the substitution of female for male deities, spread its mystically erotic influence from eastern India to Nepal and Tibet. The famous temples, at Tanjore and Gangaikonda-cholapuram in the Tamil-nad, Khajuraho in central India, with its richly sexual sculptures, and the more monumental style of Bhubaneswar, in Orissa, were all built in this period. Storytellers, royal biographers, regional historians, dramatists, and the mystic erotic poets like Jayadeva, with his *Gita Govinda* (Song of Krishna), preserved and developed Sanskrit literary traditions.

Early in the 11th century, new dynasties, including the Paramaras, Chandellas and Chedis from central India, and the Chalukyas from Gujerat, who now ruled in the north and north-west, came into conflict with the Yaminis of Ghazni. These former vassals of Bukhara had acquired an extensive empire in Iran and central Asia. Under their formidable leader, Mahmud of Ghazni, they repeatedly invaded as far as the Doab and the Gujerat coast, annexing parts of Baluchistan and the Punjab.

Mahmud's depredations revealed India's underlying political and military weakness. Systematic conquest by the Turkish peoples of central Asia began with the renewed annexation of the Punjab (1186) by Muizzuddin Muhammad, one of the Ghurid family who had lately overthrown their Ghaznavid suzerains. In 1191 he defeated the Rajput clans, commonly accepted descendants of earlier Hunnish invaders, and in 1206 his general, Qutbuddin Aibak, established the first Turko-Afghan dynasty in the strategically-placed city of Delhi, founded in 736.

The Delhi Sultanate remained the major

4/India on the eve of Babur's Invasion *(above)* In 1526, one of the Lodi sultans, who had assumed rule after Timur's sack of Delhi, held sway in the Punjab, and another controlled the Doab and Bihar. The Bahmani kingdom in the Deccan had broken up into five separate warring sultanates. Rajput dynasties controlled Rajasthan and also territories further to the north-west, including Delhi.

2/India in the 11th century *(below)* The conquests of Sultan Mahmud of Ghazni stretched deep into central Asia. The subcontinent is divided into two along the line of the river Narmada and the Vindhya mountains. To the south, the Chola Empire, including Ceylon, is shown at its fullest extent. But wars with the Rashtrakutas and others continually abraded the frontiers, both for the Cholas and for the Chalukyas in the west.

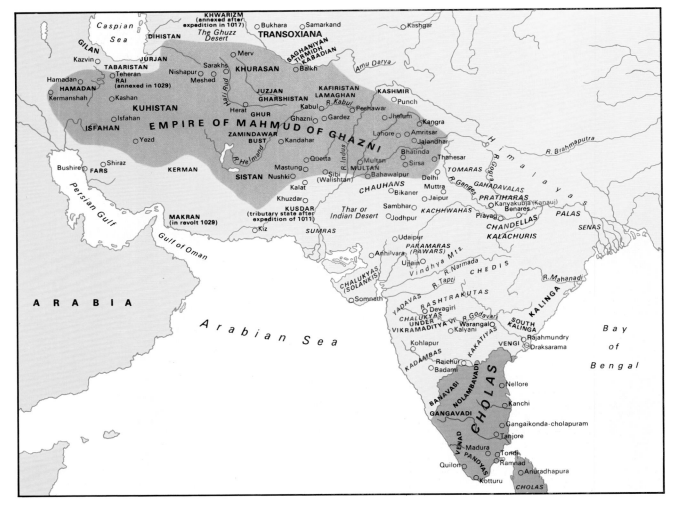

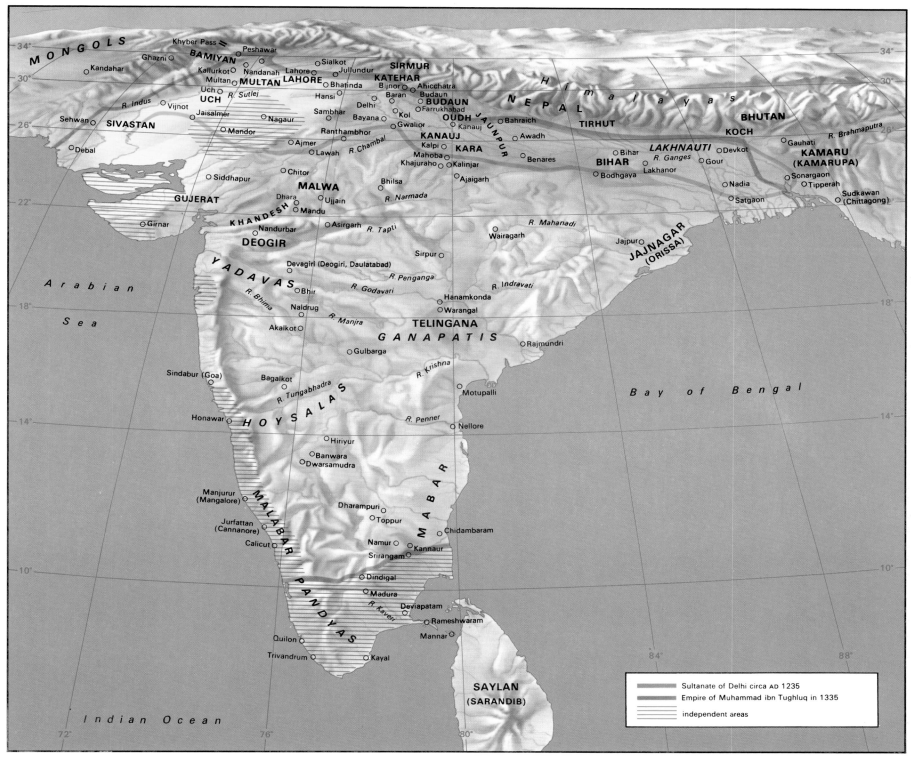

3/The Sultanate of Delhi (*above*) Turko-Afghan rule in India started in the 12th century and reached its height with the Sultanate under Muhammad ibn Tughluq. However, by 1398 Tughluq rule barely extended beyond Delhi.

1/Regional Kingdoms and the Struggle for Empire (*right*) The fluctuating territories held by the Gurjara-Pratiharas, the Rashtrakutas, the Palas, the Cholas and the Arabs in Sind, as they struggled both on their frontiers and for control of Kanauj from c. 750 to 1018.

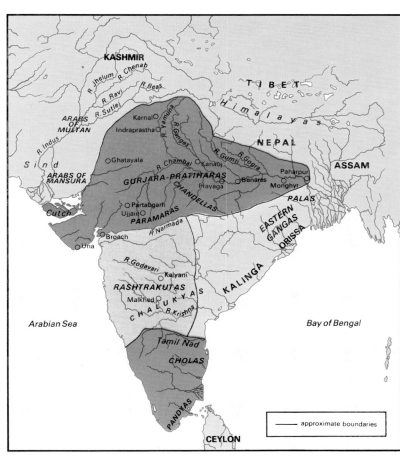

political factor in north India from the 13th to the 16th century, though it never controlled the whole area, and its power and territories fluctuated widely according to its current ruler's ability. By 1235, under Iltutmish, Qutbuddin's son, it stretched from Sind to Bengal (though hostilities continued in Rajputana). Iltutmish was then succeeded in turn by his daughter, Razziya (ultimately murdered) and by a former palace official, Balban. Expansion resumed when a new Turkish group, the Khaljis, succeeded. Under Alauddin Khalji they annexed Gujerat, Chitor, Ranthambhor, Ujjain, Dhar and Mandu, invaded southernmost India, and devised fiscal and administrative arrangements to support a powerful military machine. They also admitted Indian Muslims to high political office, thus easing much of the internal tension; Hindu kingdoms were reduced to vassalage.

Mongol harassment from the north started with Genghis Khan, who reached the Indus, and continued, with occasional forays to Delhi and beyond. But all were beaten back. Under Muhammad ibn Tughluq (1325-51) the Sultanate reached its maximum extent, with 23 provinces including all the southern kingdoms. But high taxes, an abortive attempt to move Delhi, with its entire population, south to a new capital at Devagiri in the Deccan (or to create a new capital, according to some authorities) and

the sheer size of the empire hastened its decline. Bengal broke away in 1341, the Deccan provinces in 1347 (to form the Bahmani kingdom), and Khandesh, Malwa, Jaunpur and Gujerat between 1382 and 1396. South of the Tungabhadra, the powerful new Vijayanagar empire was firmly established by 1374. After the invasion by Timur (Tamerlane) in 1398, Tughluq rule barely extended beyond Delhi.

During the centuries of Turko-Afghan rule, when a real *modus vivendi* between Muslim and Hindu gradually evolved, a stylistically unified architecture flourished, and a varied local literature grew up in the provincial kingdoms. Humbly-born saints, like Nanak (1469-1532) and Kabir (1440-1518) denied any contradiction between Muslim and Hindu ideas of God, and preached social egalitarianism. The cult of Bhakti, or devotion to a personal deity, revived through the efforts of preachers such as Madhva, who expounded dualism, and Chaitanya (1486-1533) led a revival of Vaishnavism in eastern and northern India. Magnificent temples were built by the Vijayanagar and Hoysala kings who now dominated the south. But the greater part of India was fragmented into a large number of local kingdoms, Hindu and Muslim, perpetually at war with each other. When Timur's descendant, Babur, invaded from Afghanistan in 1526, only the Rajputs were organised to resist.

The early civilisations of South-East Asia to AD 1511

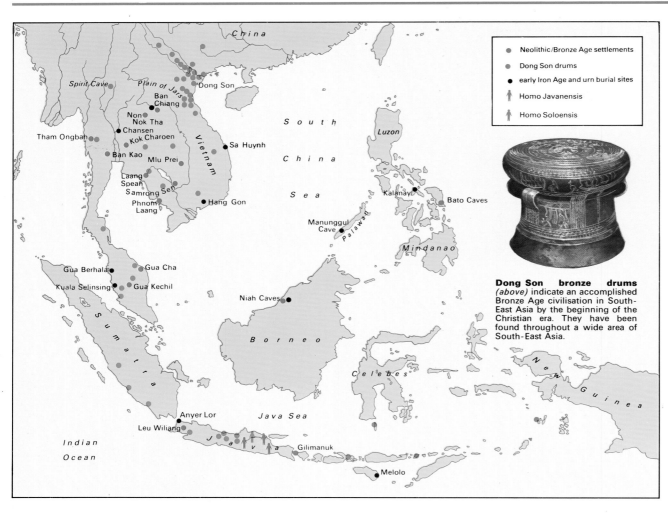

1/Prehistoric sites in South-East Asia (above) Neolithic and early Bronze Age sites indicate developed lowland cultures by the 2nd millennium BC. Later (late 1st millennium BC) we find more advanced cultures, characterised by 'Dong Son' bronze drums or by early Iron Age jar burials, all before the arrival of Indian and Chinese influences in the area.

Dong Son bronze drums (above) indicate an accomplished Bronze Age civilisation in South-East Asia by the beginning of the Christian era. They have been found throughout a wide area of South-East Asia.

SITUATED at one of the world's main crossroads, the countries of South-East Asia had their own history, with indigenous roots reaching back into early prehistory and beyond. 'Java Man', whose remains, belonging to the Middle Pleistocene, were found in the Solo Valley of central Java, may be related to the culture of 'Peking Man' in China. Java has also produced the earliest evidence of *Homo sapiens* in South-East Asia: remains of c.40,000 BC, from the Brantas Valley. A number of Palaeolithic and Mesolithic cultures have been identified in various parts of the region, notably the 'Bacsonian' and 'Hoabinhian' of Vietnam, Siam and Malaya. Early cave sites have been excavated in Sumatra, Borneo, Cambodia and Siam (Thailand), and in one (Spirit Cave, northern Siam) evidence was found suggesting rice cultivation as early as 6000 BC.

The Neolithic cultures of the region were formerly identified by axe types, including the rectangular adze which was undoubtedly of ancient origin. More recently, the excavation of burial and possibly habitation sites has provided information about specific Neolithic cultures and their highly localised pottery traditions. At sites in north-east Thailand (Ban Chiang, Non Nok Tha) there are indications of a gradual evolution towards bronze metallurgy. Attempts to date the earliest bronze, by Carbon-14 and thermo-luminescence methods, have yielded controversial results; some scholars claim a date earlier than 3000 BC, while others place it nearer to 1000 BC. A Neolithic and Early Bronze culture of around 1000 BC has also been explored in northern Vietnam. The first use of iron in the region seems to occur in central Siam, perhaps as early as 500 BC; it had spread to Borneo and Palawan by c.200 BC.

It is thus clear that South-East Asia had a number of flourishing cultures using bronze and iron before the advent of Indian and Chinese influences made itself felt in the 2nd or 3rd century AD. These influences left a permanent impact but they never obliterated the distinctive character of South-East Asian civilisation. Nevertheless, the next thousand years saw their assimilation to produce some distinctive South-East Asian societies. Chinese influence was predominant in Tonking (northern Vietnam), which had its own polity down to c.110 BC, but was subsequently annexed to China and ruled as a Chinese province down to c. AD 900. The remainder of the region gradually came under Hindu-Buddhist influences from India, beginning about the 2nd or 3rd century AD. Early trade routes appear to have linked India with southern Burma, central and southern Siam, lower Cambodia and southern Vietnam, where an ancient port city (3rd-6th century) was excavated at Oc Eo. By the 5th-6th century we find Buddhist images and votive tablets, and also the earliest Sanskrit inscriptions. In addition to the above areas, early Indianisation occurred in Java and southern Sumatra. Although Indian in culture, these areas had trade and political relations with China, which welcomed tribute missions from a growing number of states whose location it is not always easy to identify.

By the 7th century, small Hindu temples were being built in lower Cambodia, notably at Angkor Borei, and also in central Java; other early temples, probably Buddhist, have been excavated in southern Burma at Peikthano and Sri Ksetra. These three areas became the principal centres of temple-building and produced a number of major temple complexes: Borobudur and Prambanan (central Java, 8th-10th centuries); Angkor (9th-13th centuries); and Pagan (11th-13th centuries). All three combined Hindu and Buddhist elements, but Buddhism was especially strong at Pagan and Hinduism at Angkor. Another series of temples belonging to the Hindu-Buddhist kingdom of Champa is found along the coast of central Vietnam. A centre of Sanskrit culture, Palembang, in south-east Sumatra, emerged in the 7th century as the probable capital of the maritime empire of Srivijaya, which for centuries controlled international trade passing through the straits of Malacca and Sunda, and across the Isthmus of Kra.

The great temple states fell into decline by the later 13th century. In Java, the area of Prambanan was superseded in importance by eastern Java, where three states developed in succession: Kediri (12th century), Singhasari (13th century) and finally Majapahit (late 13th-early 16th centuries). On the mainland, Pagan was sacked by Mongol invaders and then by Shans (late 13th century), while Angkor fell to Thai attacks from 1369 onwards and was eventually abandoned. Sukhothai, the first of the lowland Thai cities, was itself in decline by the late 14th century. In place of the old temple cities new political centres emerged: in Burma, Ava (1364) on the upper Irrawaddy, Toungoo (1347) on the Sittang, and Pegu (1369), capital of a new Mon kingdom of the south; in Siam, Ayutthaya (1350) and Chiengmai (1296); in Cambodia, Phnom Penh and other capitals along the Mekong; in Laos, Luang Prabang (1353). All were Theravada Buddhist in the Sinhalese tradition, and had stupas, not temples. Meanwhile, in Vietnam the Chinese had failed to reconquer their former province despite invasions in 1075-77 and 1285-88; a new kingdom emerged calling itself Dai Viet, and gradually absorbed the kingdom of Champa, finally annexing its capital, Vijaya, in 1471. In the meantime, Srivijaya declined and at the end of the 14th century Malacca took its place. By that time the east Javanese empire of Majapahit was declining, and the west Javanese kingdom of Pajajaran was also to go down before Muslim pressure from the northern coast ports in the early 16th century.

Political change in the 14th and 15th centuries was accompanied by significant religious developments. Thus while Theravada Buddhism

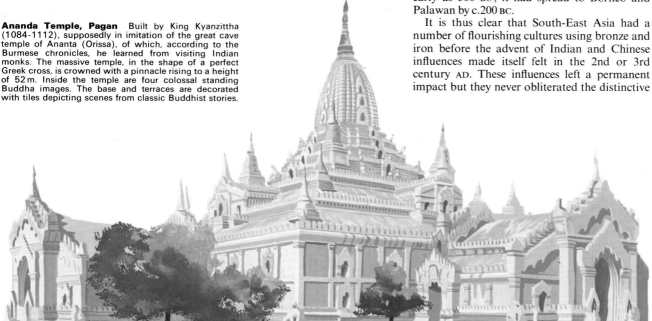

Ananda Temple, Pagan Built by King Kyanzittha (1084-1112), supposedly in imitation of the great cave temple of Ananta (Orissa), of which, according to the Burmese chronicles, he learned from visiting Indian monks. The massive temple, in the shape of a perfect Greek cross, is crowned with a pinnacle rising to a height of 52 m. Inside the temple are four colossal standing Buddha images. The base and terraces are decorated with tiles depicting scenes from classic Buddhist stories.

3/Cultural divisions of South-East Asia in 1500

(right) By 1500 the modern pattern of polities and cultures had begun to emerge, with the spread of Islam in the islands and Theravada Buddhism on the mainland, while Vietnam remained Confucian and Mahayana Buddhist. Malacca was the centre of a strong maritime, commercial empire which traded with the whole world, and was a main diffusion centre of Islam.

took firm root on the mainland, Islam, which had begun to influence northern Sumatra just before 1300, made its first big advances in the archipelago under the patronage of Malacca. The Malaccan empire in the peninsula and in Sumatra adopted Islam, and from it the faith was taken to the north Javanese trading ports and the Spice Islands, and also to north Borneo, and thence to Mindanao in the Philippines. Its advance in that direction was only halted by the Spanish seizure of Manila in 1571, and their introduction of Christianity. In Vietnam, this period saw the strengthening of Confucian scholarship, despite the repulse of a Chinese attempt at reconquest under the Ming. As before, Chinese cultural influence remained limited to Vietnam, but under the Ming the old system of tributary relationships was revived and strengthened, and a series of important voyages to the southern seas was made by the Muslim admiral, Cheng Ho (see page 146).

Thus by about 1500, South-East Asia had begun to take on its modern pattern of cultures and polities – on the eve of the arrival of the Europeans.

2/South-East Asia AD 500-1500

(below) Early Buddhist and Hindu images with isolated Sanskrit inscriptions (5th-6th centuries) were succeeded in some areas by temple complexes (8th-13th centuries) denoting major political centres, notably at Pagan and Angkor and in central Java. These were followed by Mon, Thai and Burmese kingdoms on the mainland and Malay sultanates in the maritime areas. Vietnam became Sinicised between the 1st and 9th centuries and subsequently developed as an independent kingdom absorbing the Cham kingdom to the south.

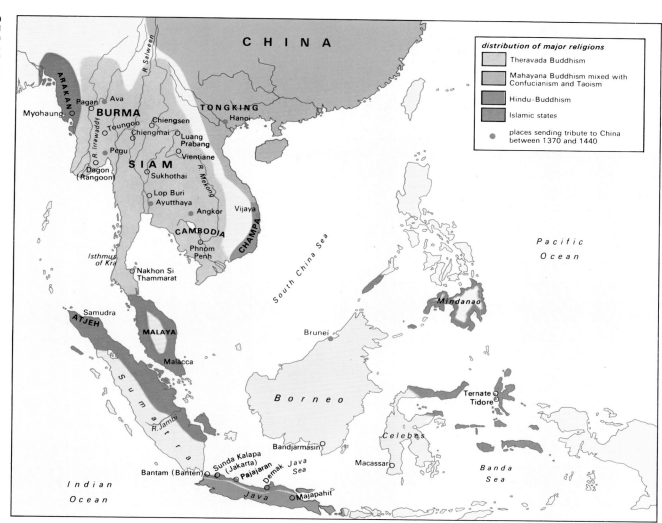

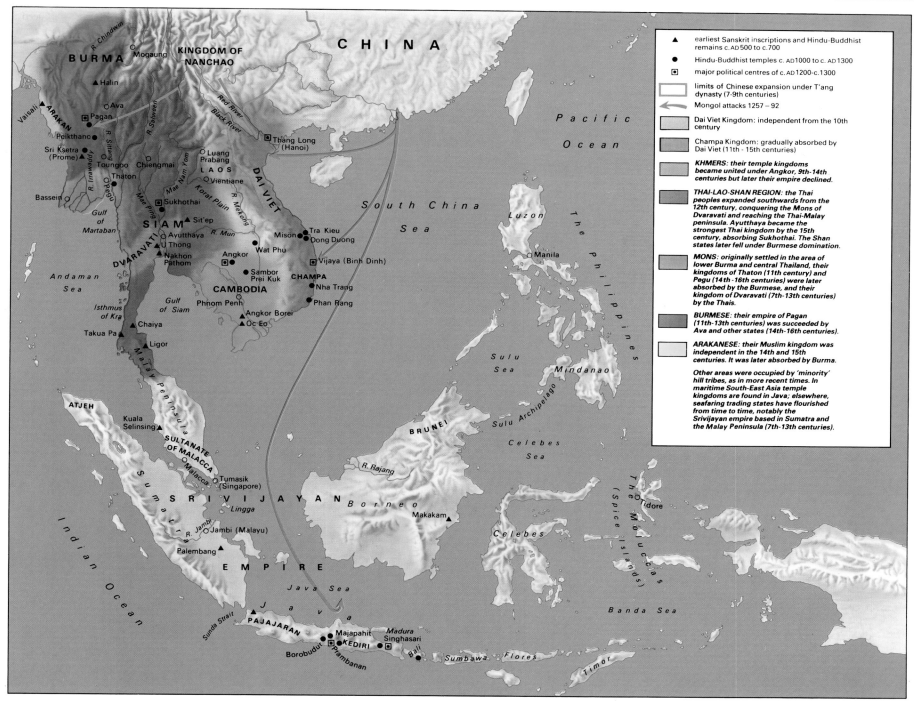

The Muslim world: the Middle East and North Africa 909 to 1517

BY the beginning of the 10th century, the efforts of the Abbasid caliphs to maintain the political unity of the Muslim world were faltering; provincial governors and army commanders were gaining local autonomy, and one military group, the Buyids, established itself in the capital, Baghdad, in 945, and ruled in the name of the Abbasids for more than a century. In some places, the bases of society were weakened; there were movements of social and political unrest, and differences concerning the succession to the caliphate and the nature of authority in Islam. These differences had emerged after Mohammed's death in 632, since the Prophet had left no guidelines for choosing his successor. The group that now forms the majority of Muslims, the Sunnis, claimed that authority passed to the caliphs, leaders whom the community designated, and who exercised supreme judicial and executive power. The Shi'is, however, believed that Mohammed's authority passed to his cousin and son-in-law Ali, and to his descendants; for the Shi'is the various imams are infallible because of their descent from Ali and from the Prophet's daughter Fatima. In political terms, the Umayyads and the Abbasids were Sunnis while many of the dynasties that challenged their authority in various parts of the Islamic world were Shi'is. In the 8th century one of these established a dynasty in Morocco, in the 9th century others created states in eastern Arabia and Yemen, and in the 10th century yet another, the Ismailis, set up a more important state, that of the Fatimids, first in Tunisia and then in Egypt and Syria. They took the title of caliph in opposition to the Abbasids; in opposition to them, so did the branch of the Umayyads who had established themselves in Spain after they had been defeated in the east by the Abbasids.

In most of the Middle East and North Africa, rainfall is scanty and irregular and vegetation sparse, and settled agriculture depends on strong government and good irrigation. In the 10th century there was some disturbance of the settled order, and a shift in the balance between sedentary cultivators and nomadic pastoralists, as Berbers expanded into Morocco, Arabs west along the North African coast, and Turks south and west from central Asia. But pastoral groups also provided the manpower and leadership which made possible a restoration of strong government. In Morocco, two successive movements of religious reform, those of the Almoravids and Almohads, gathered Berber groups around them and formed states; the former spread into Spain, the latter into Algeria and Tunisia. Another group, of Turkish origin, the Seljuks, established themselves in Baghdad. Their state was the first important example of a new type of Muslim state, based on a partnership between 'men of the sword', mainly of Turkish origin, and bureaucrats and men of the law, Persian or Arab in culture, and on an alliance with the interests of the merchant and landowning classes. In these states, officials and officers were paid by being given the right to collect and keep the tax on land in return for service; thus those who might be of alien or nomadic origin were given an interest in the prosperity of the countryside and the stability of society.

The Seljuks and their successors were called sultans, not caliphs, and ruled in the name of the Abbasid caliphs. They did not claim universal rule, but their limited kingdoms existed within a stable, international Islamic social order, which had by this time been brought into existence by gradual conversion (although Christian, Jewish and other communities still existed). This order was maintained by a common religion and law, the Arabic language and by widespread trade, the cities of Iraq, Baghdad and Basra playing an important part in this trade.

In course of time the geographical limits of this society had changed. Islam had expanded into northern India, and from the time of the Seljuks began to expand also into Anatolia. But the Normans ended Muslim rule in Sicily, and the southward expansion of the Christian states in northern Spain, checked for a time by the coming of the Almoravids and Almohads, continued after the battle of Las Navas de Tolosa (1212), until all that was left of Muslim Spain was the kingdom of Granada, and that ended in 1492. In Palestine and Syria, an attempt by Crusaders from western Europe to re-establish Christian rule led to the creation of a number of small states in the late 11th century, but a century later they were virtually destroyed by a new and strong government in Egypt and Syria, that of the Ayyubids created by Saladin.

In the 13th century the balance of Muslim society, at least in its eastern part, was again disturbed by a new conquering group, with Mongol leadership and largely Turkish manpower (see page 128); in 1258 they captured Baghdad ending the Abbasid caliphate. They were gradually converted to Islam and absorbed into Muslim society, but by this time it was in some ways a different society. The Muslim world was split into clearly defined regions. In the east, there ruled first the Ilkhanids, a branch of the conquering Mongol dynasty, and then another dynasty of similar origin, founded by Timur (Tamerlane); to the west, attempts by the Mongols to expand towards the Mediterranean were ended at the battle of Ain Jalut (1260) by a new ruling group in Egypt and Syria, the Mamelukes, an élite of soldiers from southern Russia and the Caucasus. Further to the west, North Africa fell under the control of two states: the Hafsids in Tunisia and the Marinids in Morocco.

These divisions were more than political. By now the decline of the irrigation works and a shift in trade routes had weakened the cities of Iraq; the main centres of Muslim society lay in Persia and in the Nile valley. Between these two there were deep differences of culture. The dominant Arabic culture of the west preserved its traditions of law, mysticism and literature but was no longer creative; in the east, the art of the miniature and architecture thrived, and the Persian language, revived in an Islamic form, was the medium of great poetry. In the east, too, Turkish pastoral elements continued to play an important part in the life of society and the creation of states. In Anatolia, Turkish frontier states expanded at the expense of the Byzantines, and in one of them there emerged a new dynasty, the Ottomans.

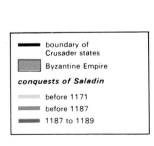

King Roger's Cape
The Norman king of Sicily, Roger II, was known for his fondness for Arabs and Islam. His marvellous coronation mantle, with Arabic inscriptions and the Hegira date 528 1133/4 was woven in Palermo.

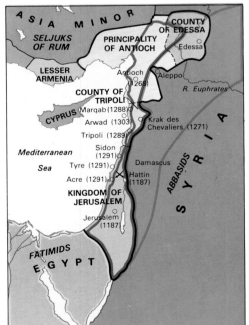

▬	boundary of Crusader states	
▓	Byzantine Empire	

conquests of Saladin

	before 1171
	before 1187
	1187 to 1189

3/The Muslim reconquest of Palestine *(left)* The Muslim reconquest began when Zengi, a Seljuk officer, built a strong Syrian state and occupied the Crusading county of Edessa in 1144. Saladin, an officer of this state, made himself master first of Egypt, deposing the Fatimids, and then of the interior of Syria. He attacked the Crusaders in 1187, and before his death in 1193 had captured Jerusalem and driven the Crusaders from all but a narrow coastal strip between Acre and Antioch.

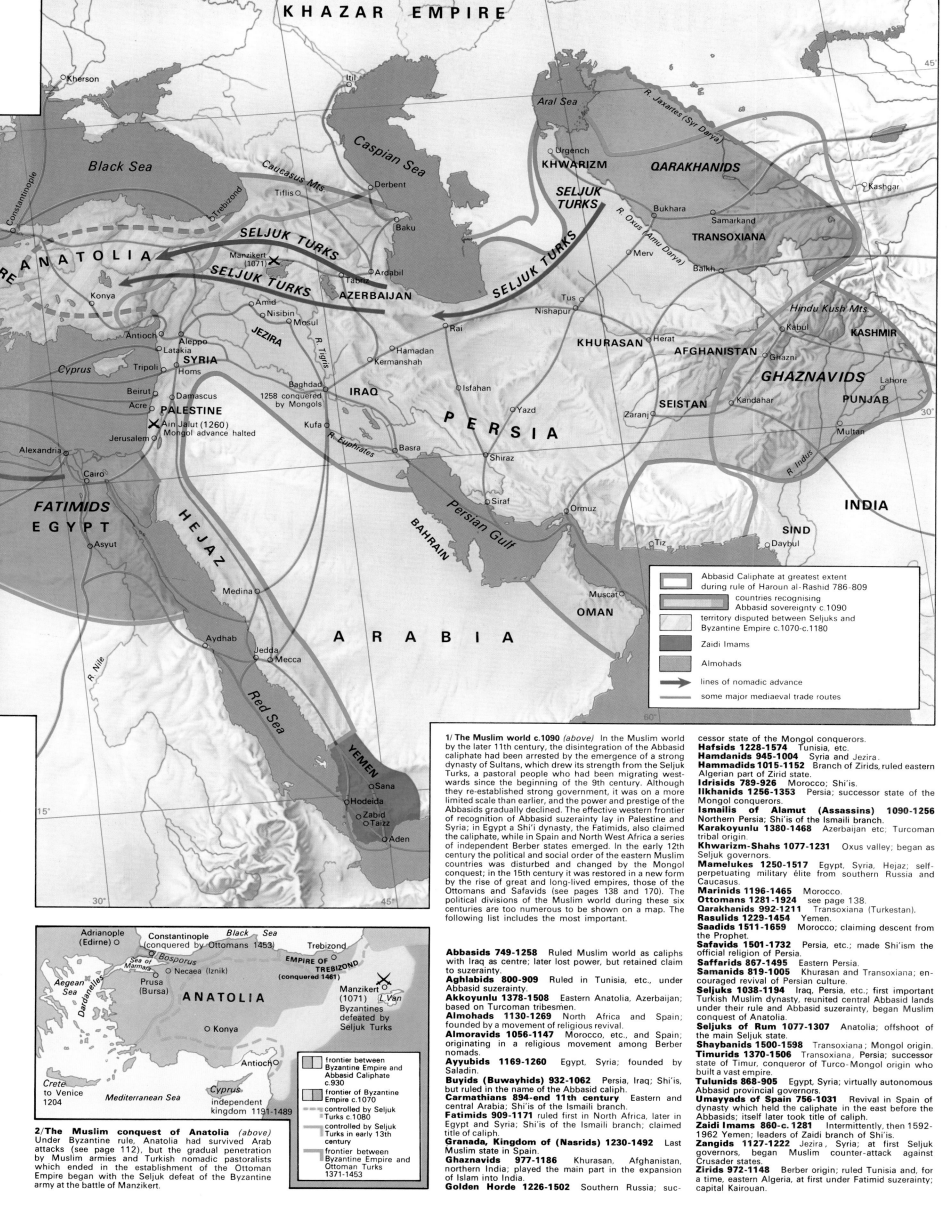

KHAZAR EMPIRE

Black Sea · Kherson · Itil · Caspian Sea · Aral Sea · R. Jaxartes (Syr Darya) · Urgench · KHWARIZM · QARAKHANIDS · Kashgar

Caucasus Mts. · Tiflis · Derbent · Baku · Ardabil · SELJUK TURKS · Bukhara · Samarkand · TRANSOXIANA · Balkh

Constantinople · Trebizond · SELJUK TURKS · Manzikert (1071) × · SELJUK TURKS · Tabriz · AZERBAIJAN · R. Oxus (Amu Darya) · Merv · Nishapur · Tus · Rai · Hindu Kush Mts.

ANATOLIA · Konya · Amid · Nisibin · Mosul · JEZIRA · KHURASAN · Herat · Kabul · KASHMIR · AFGHANISTAN · Ghazni

Antioch · Aleppo · Latakia · SYRIA · Homs · R. Tigris · Hamadan · Kermanshah · GHAZNAVIDS · Lahore · PUNJAB

Cyprus · Tripoli · Beirut · Damascus · Baghdad 1258 conquered by Mongols · IRAQ · Isfahan · Kandahar · SEISTAN · PERSIA · Yazd · Zaranj · R. Indus · Multan

Acre · PALESTINE · Ain Jalut (1260) × Mongol advance halted · Jerusalem · Kufa · R. Euphrates · Basra · Shiraz · Siraf · Ormuz · INDIA

Alexandria · Cairo · FATIMIDS EGYPT · HEJAZ · BAHRAIN · Persian Gulf · OMAN · Muscat · Tiz · SIND · Daybul

Asyut · Medina · ARABIA · Aydhab · R. Nile · Jedda · Mecca · Red Sea · YEMEN · Sana · Hodeida · Zabid · Taizz · Aden

Legend:
- Abbasid Caliphate at greatest extent during rule of Haroun al-Rashid 786-809
- countries recognising Abbasid sovereignty c.1090
- territory disputed between Seljuks and Byzantine Empire c.1070-c.1180
- Zaidi Imams
- Almohads
- → lines of nomadic advance
- some major mediaeval trade routes

1/ The Muslim world c.1090 *(above)* In the Muslim world by the later 11th century, the disintegration of the Abbasid caliphate had been arrested by the emergence of a strong dynasty of Sultans, which drew its strength from the Seljuk Turks, a pastoral people who had been migrating westwards since the beginning of the 9th century. Although they re-established strong government, it was on a more limited scale than earlier, and the power and prestige of the Abbasids gradually declined. The effective western frontier of recognition of Abbasid suzerainty lay in Palestine and Syria; in Egypt a Shi'i dynasty, the Fatimids, also claimed the caliphate, while in Spain and North West Africa a series of independent Berber states emerged. In the early 12th century the political and social order of the eastern Muslim countries was disturbed and changed by the Mongol conquest; in the 15th century it was restored in a new form by the rise of great and long-lived empires, those of the Ottomans and Safavids (see pages 138 and 170). The political divisions of the Muslim world during these six centuries are too numerous to be shown on a map. The following list includes the most important.

Abbasids 749-1258 Ruled Muslim world as caliphs with Iraq as centre; later lost power, but retained claim to suzerainty.

Aghlabids 800-909 Ruled in Tunisia, etc., under Abbasid suzerainty.

Akkoyunlu 1378-1508 Eastern Anatolia, Azerbaijan; based on Turcoman tribesmen.

Almohads 1130-1269 North Africa and Spain; founded by a movement of religious revival.

Almoravids 1056-1147 Morocco, etc., and Spain; originating in a religious movement among Berber nomads.

Ayyubids 1169-1260 Egypt, Syria; founded by Saladin.

Buyids (Buwayhids) 932-1062 Persia, Iraq; Shi'is, but ruled in the name of the Abbasid caliph.

Carmathians 894-end 11th century Eastern and central Arabia; Shi'is of the Ismaili branch.

Fatimids 909-1171 ruled first in North Africa, later in Egypt and Syria; Shi'is of the Ismaili branch; claimed title of caliph.

Granada, Kingdom of (Nasrids) 1230-1492 Last Muslim state in Spain.

Ghaznavids 977-1186 Khurasan, Afghanistan, northern India; played the main part in the expansion of Islam into India.

Golden Horde 1226-1502 Southern Russia; successor state of the Mongol conquerors.

Hafsids 1228-1574 Tunisia, etc.

Hamdanids 945-1004 Syria and Jezira.

Hammadids 1015-1152 Branch of Zirids, ruled eastern Algerian part of Zirid state.

Idrisids 789-926 Morocco; Shi'is.

Ilkhanids 1256-1353 Persia; successor state of the Mongol conquerors.

Ismailis of Alamut (Assassins) 1090-1256 Northern Persia; Shi'is of the Ismaili branch.

Karakoyunlu 1380-1468 Azerbaijan etc; Turcoman tribal origin.

Khwarizm-Shahs 1077-1231 Oxus valley; began as Seljuk governors.

Mamelukes 1250-1517 Egypt, Syria, Hejaz; self-perpetuating military élite from southern Russia and Caucasus.

Marinids 1196-1465 Morocco.

Ottomans 1281-1924 see page 138.

Qarakhanids 992-1211 Transoxiana (Turkestan).

Rasulids 1229-1454 Yemen.

Saadids 1511-1659 Morocco; claiming descent from the Prophet.

Safavids 1501-1732 Persia, etc.; made Shi'ism the official religion of Persia.

Saffarids 867-1495 Eastern Persia.

Samanids 819-1005 Khurasan and Transoxiana; encouraged revival of Persian culture.

Seljuks 1038-1194 Iraq, Persia, etc.; first important Turkish Muslim dynasty, reunited central Abbasid lands under their rule and Abbasid suzerainty, began Muslim conquest of Anatolia.

Seljuks of Rum 1077-1307 Anatolia; offshoot of the main Seljuk state.

Shaybanids 1500-1598 Transoxiana; Mongol origin.

Timurids 1370-1506 Transoxiana, Persia; successor state of Timur, conqueror of Turco-Mongol origin who built a vast empire.

Tulunids 868-905 Egypt, Syria; virtually autonomous Abbasid provincial governors.

Umayyads of Spain 756-1031 Revival in Spain of dynasty which held the caliphate in the east before the Abbasids; itself later took title of caliph.

Zaidi Imams 860-c.1281 Intermittently, then 1592-1962 Yemen; leaders of Zaidi branch of Shi'is.

Zangids 1127-1222 Jezira, Syria; at first Seljuk governors, began Muslim counter-attack against Crusader states.

Zirids 972-1148 Berber origin; ruled Tunisia and, for a time, eastern Algeria, at first under Fatimid suzerainty; capital Kairouan.

Inset map — The Muslim conquest of Anatolia:

Adrianople (Edirne) · Constantinople (conquered by Ottomans 1453) · Black Sea · Trebizond · EMPIRE OF TREBIZOND (conquered 1461) · Bosporus · Sea of Marmara · Necaea (Iznik) · Prusa (Bursa) · Manzikert (1071) × L. Van · Byzantines defeated by Seljuk Turks · Aegean Sea · Dardanelles · ANATOLIA · Konya · Crete to Venice 1204 · Mediterranean Sea · Antioch · Cyprus independent kingdom 1191-1489

Legend (inset):
- frontier between Byzantine Empire and Abbasid Caliphate c.930
- frontier of Byzantine Empire c.1070
- controlled by Seljuk Turks c.1080
- controlled by Seljuk Turks in early 13th century
- frontier between Byzantine Empire and Ottoman Turks 1371-1453

2/The Muslim conquest of Anatolia *(above)* Under Byzantine rule, Anatolia had survived Arab attacks (see page 112), but the gradual penetration by Muslim armies and Turkish nomadic pastoralists which ended in the establishment of the Ottoman Empire began with the Seljuk defeat of the Byzantine army at the battle of Manzikert.

135

The emergence of states in Africa 900 to 1500

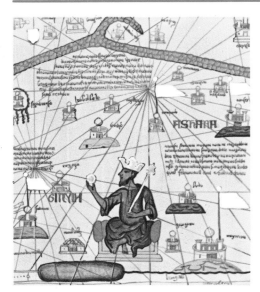

Africa's golden wealth *(above)* Western Europe abandoned the gold standard in the Dark Ages, but by the 13th century Italian city states and the Christian Spanish kingdoms were striking gold coins. Up to about 1350 at least two-thirds of the world's supply of gold came from West Africa. Mansa Musa, ruler of the great empire of Mali, epitomised the golden wealth of Africa.

THE period from the year 900 to 1500 saw the growth of states throughout much of the northern part of Africa, and coincidentally the forging of trade links. With few exceptions, we know much less about Africa south of the Equator, but even there the origins of states and of trading can be traced back to this time.

A series of foreign Muslim dynasties – the Fatimids, Ayyubids and Mamelukes – ruled Egypt, and these regimes stimulated commerce in the eastern Mediterranean, the Red Sea and the Arabian Sea. This flow of trade provided the economic basis for the revival, after the decline of Axum, of the political power of the Christian empire of Ethiopia, first under the Cushitic-speaking Zagwe dynasty in the 11th century, and then under the Amharic-speaking Solomonids in the 13th century. The Solomonids came into conflict with the Muslim coastal states of the Horn of Africa, notably Adal.

By AD 1000 the Maghreb (north-west Africa) had been Islamic land for over three centuries and was the site of the great Berber empires of the Almoravids and the Almohads (see page 134). During the period 1000 to 1500 Islam spread south: up the Nile into the Christian kingdoms of Nubia, along the northern and eastern coasts of the Horn (which faced southern Arabia), and across the Sahara into the states in what is called

the Sudanic belt (stretching from Senegal to the Nile, south of the great desert). Muslims crossed the Sahara as merchants and travellers with the caravans of camels which regularly made the hazardous journey from the trading depots on either edge of the desert, such as Sijilmassa, south of the Atlas mountains in Morocco, and Walata in Mali. This dangerous trade carried luxury goods (and in time firearms) and salt – a vital element in the diet in tropical countries – to the black African lands south of the Sahara. In exchange, gold, leather-work and slaves went northwards. By the middle of the period, the economies of Muslim Middle East and Christian Europe depended upon African gold.

This expanding trans-Saharan trade gave an impetus to the growth of states in the Sudanic belt. Two of the greatest of these were created by Mande-speaking peoples who had spread across the western part of west Africa. Ghana, which flourished from the 8th to the 11th centuries, was established by the Soninke group of the Mande in the area north of the Senegal and Niger rivers. Its successor, Mali, founded by the Malinke Mande, was a vast empire stretching from the Atlantic right across the great bend of the Niger. In 1324 the Mali king Mansa Musa went on pilgrimage to Mecca, and took so much gold with his retinue that en route the currency of Cairo was depressed. The empire of Mali was followed by that of Songhay, which was centred on the Niger cities of Gao and Timbuktu. East of Mali were the city states of Hausaland, some of which – Zaria, Kano, Katsina – became extremely prosperous, although they never united to form a single Hausa state. Further east lay the Kanuri empire. This had been founded by desert people in Kanem, to the east of Lake Chad, but by the 14th century had shifted its political centre to Borno, west of the lake. The Kanuri kings, known as *mais,* came from one of the longest surviving dynasties in history, being finally overthrown in the 19th century.

By the late Middle Ages, therefore, when western Europe was undergoing a decline as a result of the Black Death and the ravages of the Hundred Years War, the black kingdoms of the western and central Sudan were flourishing. A number of African kings – Mansa Musa and Sonni Ali, to name only two – were renowned throughout Islam and Christendom for their wealth, brilliance and the artistic achievements of their subjects. Their capitals were immense walled cities, to which thronged traders of many nationalities. Alongside the mosques of the Muslim townsmen grew up universities (at, for instance, Timbuktu and Jenne) which attracted

scholars and poets from far and wide. The rule of these African kings was acknowledged over many hundreds of miles, being enforced by a mixture of military force and diplomatic alliances with local leaders. Royal judges dispensed justice, and royal bureaucracies administered taxation and controlled trade, the life-blood of these empires.

To the south of these Sudanic states, Hausa and Malinke merchants (the latter known as Dyula) traded among the peoples on the edge of the tropical forests, especially in the gold-producing regions. By 1500 the foundations had been laid of many of the famous forest states such as Oyo, Benin and the Akan kingdoms, partly as a result of contacts with the northerners. Also by 1500 these kingdoms had been visited by the first European sailors, mainly Portuguese, who had explored the way around the great bend of west Africa into the Bight of Benin.

Down the east coast of Africa was a string of Muslim city states, such as Mogadishu and Kilwa Kisiwani on the mainland, and the island of Zanzibar, which were part of the Indian Ocean trading complex. Especially important to this system was the gold of the Zimbabwe region, which was shipped from the port of Sofala, south of the Zambezi. In addition to its original Indonesian colonists, Madagascar – a minor participant in the Indian Ocean trade – was being settled by mainland Africans. In 1498 Vasco da Gama sailed round Africa, and visited some of these east African ports en route for India. In a dramatic fashion, European interlopers were poaching upon a highly lucrative Indian Ocean Muslim trading preserve.

In the interior of the southern half of the continent, several African peoples were coalescing to form the nuclei of later kingdoms. These people were iron-working agriculturalists and pastoralists with material cultures known collectively as Later Iron Age; these developed into sophisticated civilisations. Many were Bantu-speakers. Centralised states, with rulers who were held to be divine, were emerging into the Kongo region south of the lower Zaire river, in Lubaland (Katanga or Shaba), Zimbabweland (Rhodesia) and the interlacustrine area between the great lakes of east Africa. By 1500 states were forming here as a result of the interaction between Bantu-speaking farmers and other Later Iron Age peoples, many of them pastoralists who had come down from the inland basin of the Nile (southern Sudan) and from the Horn of Africa, and who spoke Nilotic and other non-Bantu languages. But the great age of these Bantu African states was yet to come.

2/The trans-Saharan routes *(below)* Even with camels, which had been introduced into Africa in Roman times, the desert crossing was extremely hazardous. If the far-spread watering places dried up or if the fiercely independent desert people, the veiled Tuareg, attacked, whole caravans of hundreds of men and beasts perished; their skeletons were grisly reminders of the dangers. Yet for centuries the great trading system persisted.

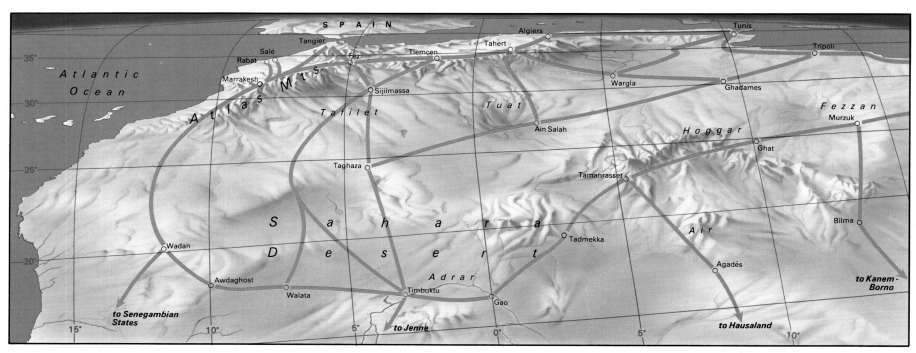

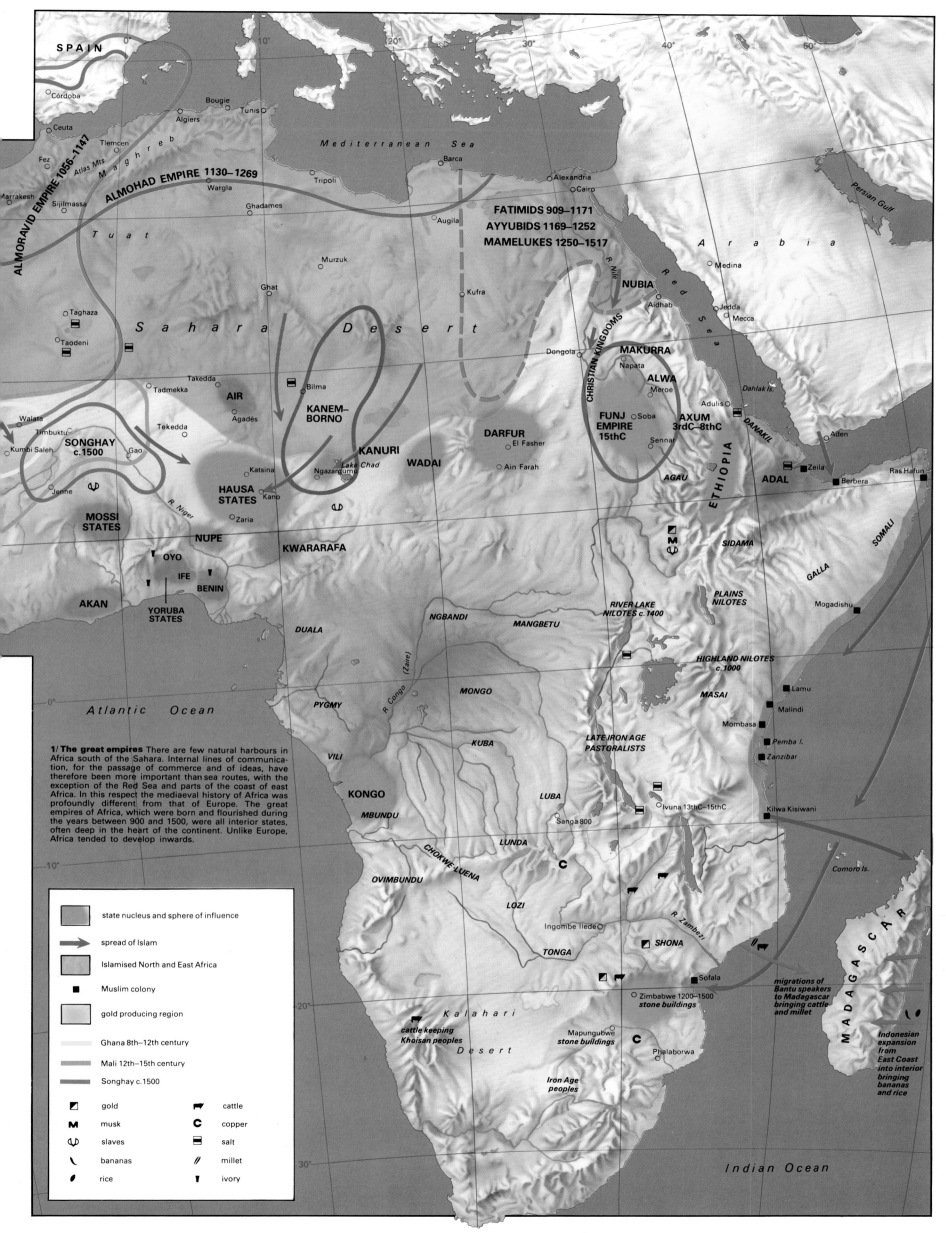

SPAIN

Córdoba
Ceuta
Fez
Marrakesh
Sijilmassa
ALMORAVID EMPIRE 1056-1147
Atlas Mts
Tlemcen
Maghreb
Bougie
Algiers
Tunis
ALMOHAD EMPIRE 1130-1269
Wargla
Tripoli
Ghadames
Mediterranean Sea
Barca
Alexandria
Cairo

Taghaza
Taodeni
Tuat
Sahara
Desert
Murzuk
Ghat
Augila
Kufra

FATIMIDS 909-1171
AYYUBIDS 1169-1252
MAMELUKES 1250-1517

R. Nile
NUBIA
Aidhab
Medina
Jedda
Mecca
Arabia
Red Sea
Persian Gulf

Takedda
Tadmekka
AIR
Agadès
Bilma
KANEM-BORNO
KANURI
Lake Chad
Ngazargumu
DARFUR
El Fasher
Ain Farah
WADAI
Dongola
MAKURRA
Napata
ALWA
Meroe
Soba
Sennar
FUNJ EMPIRE 15thC
CHRISTIAN KINGDOMS
Dahlak Is.
Adulis
AXUM 3rdC-8thC
DANAKIL
Aden
Zeila
ADAL
Berbera
Ras Hafun

Walata
Timbuktu
Kumbi Saleh
SONGHAY c.1500
Gao
Tekedda
Jenne
HAUSA STATES
Katsina
Kano
Zaria
MOSSI STATES
R. Niger

AGAU
ETHIOPIA
SIDAMA
GALLA
SOMALI
Mogadishu

NUPE
KWARARAFA
OYO
IFE
BENIN
AKAN
YORUBA STATES

PLAINS NILOTES
RIVER LAKE NILOTES c.1400
HIGHLAND NILOTES c.1000
MASAI
Lamu
Malindi
Mombasa
Pemba I.
Zanzibar

DUALA
NGBANDI
MANGBETU
PYGMY
R. Congo (Zaire)
MONGO
KUBA
VILI
LUBA
Sanga 800

Atlantic Ocean

1/ The great empires There are few natural harbours in
Africa south of the Sahara. Internal lines of communication, for the passage of commerce and of ideas, have
therefore been more important than sea routes, with the
exception of the Red Sea and parts of the coast of east
Africa. In this respect the mediaeval history of Africa was
profoundly different from that of Europe. The great
empires of Africa, which were born and flourished during
the years between 900 and 1500, were all interior states,
often deep in the heart of the continent. Unlike Europe,
Africa tended to develop inwards.

KONGO
MBUNDU
CHOKWE-LUENA
OVIMBUNDU
LUNDA
LOZI
TONGA
Ingombe Ilede
Ivuna 13thC-15thC
Kilwa Kisiwani
LATE IRON AGE PASTORALISTS
Comoro Is.

cattle keeping Khoisan peoples
Kalahari Desert
Iron Age peoples
Mapungubwe stone buildings
Phalaborwa
SHONA
Zimbabwe 1200-1500 stone buildings
Sofala
R. Zambezi

migrations of Bantu speakers
to Madagascar bringing cattle
and millet

MADAGASCAR

Indonesian
expansion
from
East Coast
into interior
bringing
bananas
and rice

Indian Ocean

state nucleus and sphere of influence
spread of Islam
Islamised North and East Africa
Muslim colony
gold producing region

Ghana 8th–12th century
Mali 12th–15th century
Songhay c.1500

gold   cattle
musk   copper
slaves   salt
bananas   millet
rice   ivory

137

The rise of the Ottoman Empire 1301 to 1520

ORIGINALLY a petty principality in Western Anatolia, the Ottoman state rose to become a world empire, which lasted, through many vicissitudes, from the late 13th century to 1924. Like that of the Habsburgs, its eventual rival, the Ottoman Empire was dynastic; its territories and character owed little to national or ethnic boundaries, and were determined by the military and administrative power of the dynasty at any particular time.

The rise of the Ottoman state, like the rise of Islam itself nearly seven centuries earlier, owed much to the weakness of the empires which surrounded it. The damage to the structure of the Byzantine Empire caused by the fourth crusade in 1204 facilitated the Ottomans' rapid advance into the Balkans in the course of the 14th century; the defeat of the Seljuks by the Mongols at the battle of Kösedag in 1243 gravely weakened that dynasty's power, and the gradual retreat of the Mongols from Anatolia into Iran created a vacuum in Anatolia which was filled by a number of small Turcoman states, each vying with the other for political supremacy in the area. The first recorded member of the Ottoman family, Ertoghrul, was the ruler of a small state around the town of Söğüt, then on the 'frontier' between the Seljuks and the Byzantines. In about 1281, Ertoghrul was succeeded by his son Osman, after whom the dynasty was named, and under whom the territory of the state first underwent significant expansion.

The Ottomans justified their conquests by describing themselves as *ghazis*, waging the Holy War against non-Muslims, and attempting to bring as much territory as possible into the Islamic fold, the Dar al-Islam. The non-Muslims living in these areas were then absorbed into the Empire as *dhimmis*, protected subjects. Under Osman I and his successors Orkhan (c.1324-60) and Murad (1360-89) the state gradually expanded; in 1326 Bursa was captured after a long siege, and became the Ottoman capital; the absorption of the emirate of Karasi in 1345 brought the Ottomans to the Dardanelles, and in 1354 they gained their first foothold in Europe with the capture of Gallipoli.

By 1361 Murad and his followers had taken Adrianople (Edirne), and transferred the capital there. Much of the first period of expansion in the Balkans seems to have been undertaken by quasi-independent Turkish warrior leaders rather than by forces directly controlled by the Ottomans, but with the accession of Bayezid I in 1389 and the decisive defeat of the Serbians and Bosnians at

Kosovo in the same year, Ottoman supremacy was definitively established. By 1393 the kingdom of Bulgaria had become part of the empire, and by the end of the century most of the independent emirates of Anatolia had also been absorbed into the Ottoman state, which now stretched from the Danube to the Euphrates. However, Bayezid's achievement was short-lived; his army was destroyed at Ankara in 1402 by Timur (Tamerlane), the last of the Mongol invaders to reach as far west as Anatolia. There followed an eleven year hiatus between 1402 and 1413, when the Balkan states and the Anatolian emirates took advantage of the opportunity provided by the Mongol victory to shake off Ottoman rule, although further Mongol advance ceased after Timur's death in 1405.

The reconstruction of the Ottoman state by Mehmed I (1413-21) and the revival of the conquests in the reign of his son Murad II (1421-51) again brought most of eastern and central Anatolia and the southern and eastern Balkans under direct or indirect Ottoman control. However, Ottoman rule in the Balkans was far less oppressive than the system it superseded, in which feudal dues and compulsory labour services weighed heavily upon the peasantry; in consequence, the Ottomans were often welcomed as deliverers. The rounding off of these conquests, and the emergence of the Ottoman state as a world power, was the work of Mehmed II al-Fatih, The Conqueror (1451-81), whose conquest of Constantinople in 1453 removed the last major barrier to expansion into northern Anatolia and enabled the Ottomans to dominate the Straits and the southern shore of the Black Sea. The disappearance of the Serbian kingdom, followed by the absorption of Herzegovina and much of Bosnia, left Hungary as the major European power facing the Ottomans. Mehmed's failure to take Belgrade in 1456 left the line of the middle Danube and lower Sava as the Ottoman boundary with Hungary for over sixty years. With the final re-absorption of Karaman in 1468 the last of the independent emirates disappeared, leaving the Turcoman confederation of the Akkoyunlu (White Sheep) as the Ottomans' major opponents in the area until their destruction by the Safavids of Iran in the early 16th century. Further north, Mehmed established a bridgehead in the Crimea by the capture of Caffa (Kefe) from the Genoese in 1475, subsequently bringing the Khanate of the Crimea, the most important of the successor states of the Golden Horde, under Ottoman control.

In Europe, the middle years of Mehmed's reign saw the ending of Byzantine and Frankish control over the Morea, and the gradual erosion of Venetian and Genoese power in the Aegean and the Black Sea. Mehmed's death in 1481 brought a temporary halt to these advances, and the struggle over the succession between Bayezid II (1481-1512) and Sultan Jem meant that the Ottomans were unable to undertake major campaigns against the west for many years. However, the securing of the land route from Constantinople to the Crimea was achieved in 1484 with the conquests of Akkerman and Kilia, and the Ottoman-Venetian war of 1499-1502 showed that the Ottomans had now become a major naval power.

The last years of Bayezid II's reign, and most of that of his successor Selim I (1512-20) were largely taken up with events in the east, in Iran, Egypt and the western fertile crescent. The rise of the Safavids in Iran had brought to power a state both militarily strong and ideologically hostile to the Ottomans as their eastern neighbour. Shi'ism, the form of Islam favoured by the Safavids, was also attractive to dissident forces and groupings within the Ottoman state, who rallied to support the new dynasty in Iran. A series of Shi'i-inspired risings among the Turcoman tribes of eastern Anatolia in the last years of Bayezid II's reign was a prelude to the war which broke out in the reigns of Selim and Shah Isma'il (1501-24), culminating in the defeat of the Safavids at the battle of Çaldiran in 1514. For a time, eastern Anatolia was secured for the Ottomans and the threat of religious separatism removed.

Selim's attempt to consolidate his conquests in this area led him to annex the emirate of Dhu'l-Qadr in 1515, thus bringing the Ottomans into direct contact with the Mameluke empire for the first time. Over the next two years Selim destroyed the Mamelukes politically and militarily, conquering Aleppo and Damascus in 1516, and taking Cairo in 1517. As well as bringing Syria and Egypt under Ottoman control, this campaign also added the Holy Places of Christendom and Islam to the empire, thus adding to the prestige and authority of Selim and his successors. At Selim's death in 1520 the Empire stretched from the Red Sea to the Crimea, and from Kurdistan to Bosnia, and had become a major participant and contender in the international power politics of the day. Furthermore, substantial Turkish Muslim migration to the Balkans had begun to make permanent changes in the demographic and ethnic structure of that area.

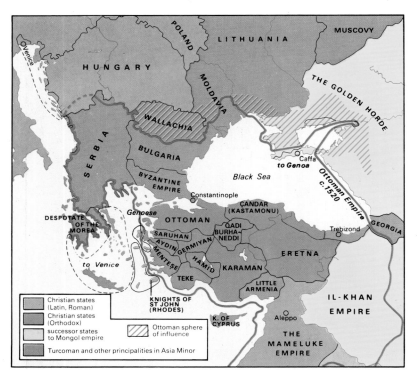

The siege of Rhodes 1522 *(right)* The élite of the Ottoman army is seen here storming the walls of the city, being defended by knights of St John. The élite was formed by the Janissaries, the famous infantry corps founded early in the Ottoman state's history, and the *sipahis*, the Muslim feudal cavalry. The Janissaries, seen here with firearms, were raised by the *Devshirme*, a compulsory levy of Christian boys begun late in the 14th century which soon became a fundamental institution of the Empire. They were regarded in Christian Europe as the most formidable component of the Ottoman army.

2/Before the Ottomans *(left)* Invasion and war between Latins, Byzantines and Muslims, and Mongols had destroyed the last shreds of the former Byzantine and Muslim empires in the Middle East. The Balkans and Anatolia, entirely fragmented by the early 14th century, were to become under the Ottomans the provinces of a single empire.

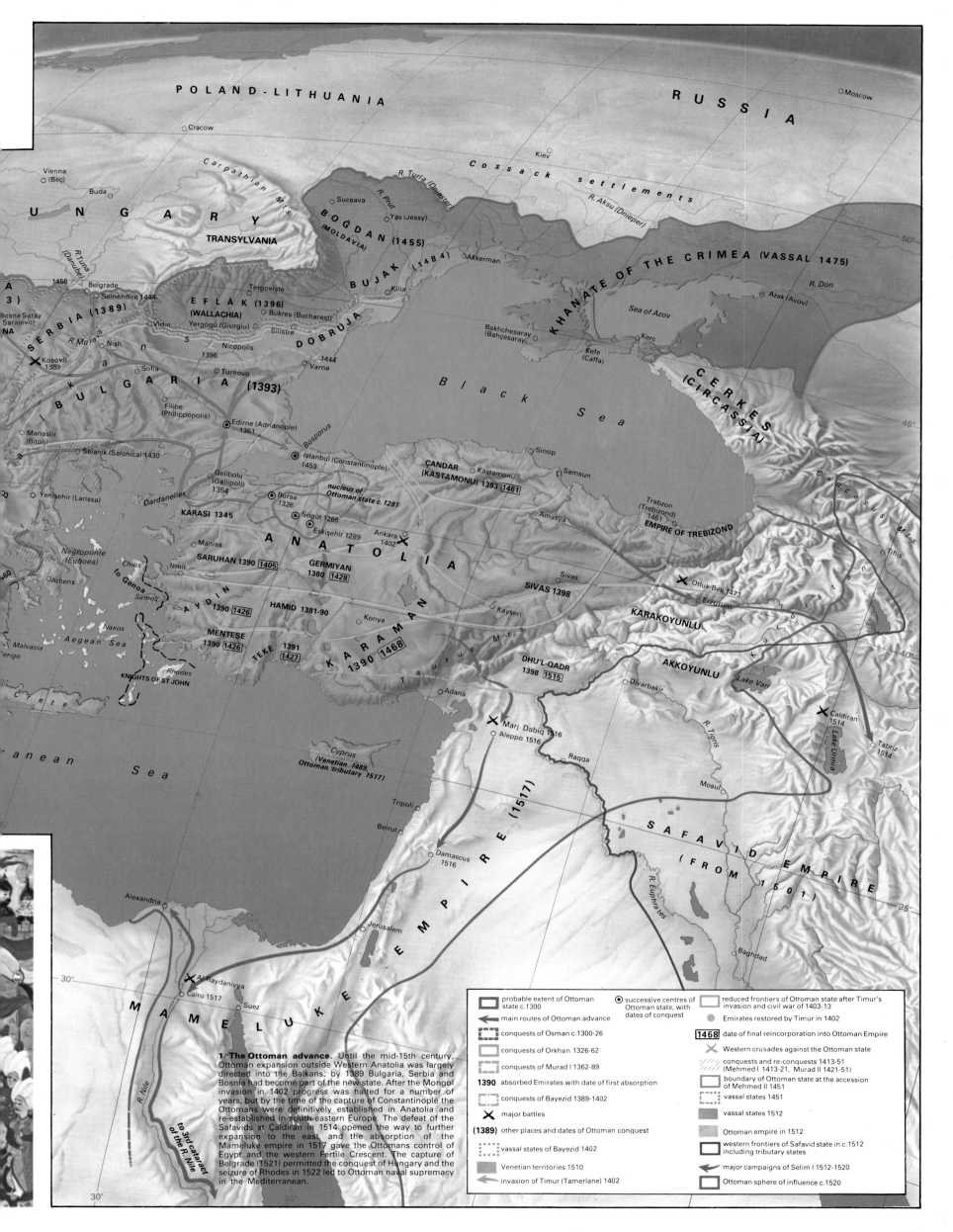

POLAND-LITHUANIA

RUSSIA

○ Moscow

○ Cracow

Vienna ○
(Beç)

Buda ○

Carpathian Mts.

Kiev ○

Cossack settlements

R. Turla (Dniester)

R. Prut

R. Aksu (Dnieper)

50°

H U N G A R Y

TRANSYLVANIA

BOĞDAN (MOLDAVIA) (1455)

Suceava ○

Yaş (Jessy) ○

KHANATE OF THE CRIMEA (VASSAL 1475)

Akkerman ○

R. Don

1456

Belgrade ○

Semendire 1444 ○

R. Tuna (Danube)

Bosna Saray Sarajevo) ○

SERBIA (1389)

NA

EFLÂK (WALLACHIA)

Tergovişte ○

Bükres (Bucharest) ○

Vidin ○

Yergöğü (Giurgiu) ○

Silistre ○

BUJAK (1484)

Kilia ○

DOBRUJA

Azak (Avov) ○

Sea of Azov

Bakhcesaray (Bançesaray) ○

Kerc ○

Kefe (Caffa) ○

ÇERKES (CIRCASSIA)

R. Morava ○ Nish ○

Nicopolis 1396

1444 Varna ○

Black Sea

Sofia ○

B U L G A R I A (1393)

Kosovo 1389 ✕

Turnovo ○

Sinop ○

Samsun ○

Trabzon (Trebizond) 1461

Caucasus Mts.

Manastir (Bitoli) ○

Filibe (Philippopolis) ○

Edirne (Adrianople) 1361

Bosporus

İstanbul (Constantinople) 1453

ÇANDAR (KASTAMONU) 1393 [1461]

Kastamonu ○

Amasya ○

EMPIRE OF TREBIZOND

Tiflis ○

Selanik (Salonica) 1430 ○

Gelibolu (Gallipoli) 1354

Bursa 1326

Söğüt 1265

nucleus of Ottoman state c.1281

Ankara 1402 ✕

Sivas ○

Yenişehir (Larissa) ○

Dardanelles

KARASI 1345

Eskişehir 1289

A N A T O L I A

SIVAS 1398

Otluk-Beli 1473 ✕

Erzurum ○

Negroponte (Euboea)

Manisa ○

SARUHAN 1390 [1405]

GERMIYAN 1380 [1428]

KARAKOYUNLU

Athens ○

Chios

to Genoa

Samos

İzmir ○

AYDIN 1390 [1426]

HAMID 1381-90

Konya ○

Kayseri ○

KARAMAN 1390 [1468]

Çaldiran 1514 ✕

AKKOYUNLU

Lake Van

Tabriz 1514

Malvasia ○

Naxos

Aegean Sea

MENTEŞE 1390 [1426]

TEKE 1391 [1427]

DHU'L-QADR 1398 [1515]

Divarbakir ○

Lake Urmia

Crete

Terigo

KNIGHTS OF ST JOHN

Rhodes

Taurus Mts.

Adana ○

R. Tigris

Mosul ○

Marj Dabiq 1516 ✕

Aleppo 1516

Raqqa ○

-ranean Sea

Cyprus (Venetian 1489, Ottoman tributary 1517)

S A F A V I D   E M P I R E   (F R O M   1 5 0 1)

O T T O M A N   E M P I R E   ('1517')

Tripoli ○

Beirut ○

Damascus 1516

R. Euphrates

Alexandria ○

Jerusalem ○

Baghdad ○

30°

M A M E L U K E   E M P I R E

Al-Raydaniyya ✕

Cairo 1517

Suez ○

to 3rd cataract of the R. Nile

R. Nile

1/The Ottoman advance. Until the mid-15th century, Ottoman expansion outside Western Anatolia was largely directed into the Balkans; by 1389 Bulgaria, Serbia and Bosnia had become part of the new state. After the Mongol invasion in 1402 progress was halted for a number of years, but by the time of the capture of Constantinople the Ottomans were definitively established in Anatolia and re-established in south-eastern Europe. The defeat of the Safavids at Çaldiran in 1514 opened the way to further expansion to the east, and the absorption of the Mameluke empire in 1517 gave the Ottomans control of Egypt and the western Fertile Crescent. The capture of Belgrade (1521) permitted the conquest of Hungary and the seizure of Rhodes in 1522 led to Ottoman naval supremacy in the Mediterranean.

☐ probable extent of Ottoman state c.1300	⊙ successive centres of Ottoman state, with dates of conquest
→ main routes of Ottoman advance	
⌐ ⌐ conquests of Osman c.1300-26	
☐ conquests of Orkhan 1326-62	
☐ conquests of Murad I 1362-89	
1390 absorbed Emirates with date of first absorption	
☐ conquests of Bayezid 1389-1402	
✕ major battles	
(1389) other places and dates of Ottoman conquest	
⌐ ⌐ vassal states of Bayezid 1402	
▨ Venetian territories 1510	
→ invasion of Timur (Tamerlane) 1402	

☐ reduced frontiers of Ottoman state after Timur's invasion and civil war of 1403-13	
● Emirates restored by Timur in 1402	
[1468] date of final reincorporation into Ottoman Empire	
✕ Western crusades against the Ottoman state	
▨ conquests and re-conquests 1413-51 (Mehmed I 1413-21, Murad II 1421-51)	
☐ boundary of Ottoman state at the accession of Mehmed II 1451	
⌐ ⌐ vassal states 1451	
▨ vassal states 1512	
▨ Ottoman empire in 1512	
☐ western frontiers of Safavid state in c.1512 including tributary states	
← major campaigns of Selim I 1512-1520	
☐ Ottoman sphere of influence c.1520	

139

Eastern Europe in the 14th century

2/German eastward colonisation *(above)* For two centuries after 1125 peasants, soldiers and merchants moved in a steady German-speaking stream into the rich, welcoming land between the rivers Elbe and Oder, swamping the local Slav tribes, developing the land and opening up the Baltic to new, profitable international trade. Monasteries, particularly the Cistercians, undertook large-scale land-drainage schemes, for which they called in peasants from Flanders.

3/The conquest of Prussia by the Teutonic Knights *(below)* In 1231 Hermann Balke crossed the river Vistula with a crusading army, swiftly founding new fortified cities such as Königsberg (1255). Systematic subjection of the pagan Prussian tribes gave way, after 1309, to seventy years of prosperity. In 1201, another military order, the Brethren of the Sword, had landed in Latvia and founded the bishopric of Riga, but in 1237 amalgamated with the Prussian Knights.

THE 14th century saw an important shift in the centre of gravity in Europe. The onset of economic depression, the prolonged and devastating wars between England and France (see page 142), and the political dislocation of Germany after the death of Frederick II in 1250 (see page 118), all resulted in a period of instability, weak government and unrest in western Europe. In eastern Europe the same period saw the rise and consolidation of powerful states with modern institutions. Under Charles the Great of Bohemia (1333-78), Casimir the Great of Poland (1339-70) and Louis the Great of Hungary (1342-82), the lands north of the Carpathians and east of the Elbe entered the mainstream of European history. Their cultural integration is symbolised by the foundation of the universities of Prague (1348), Cracow (1364), Vienna (1365) and Pécs (1367).

The early states established in eastern Europe had proved unstable. Like Kievan Russia (see page 114), they broke apart in the 12th century into warring principalities, and the Mongol invasions were a further setback, particularly in Hungary. After 1250 a new phase of concentration began. First in the field was Bohemia under Ottocar II (1253-78), who set out to build up a great territorial state including Austria and extending to the Adriatic. But Ottocar's ambitions provoked the opposition of the Bohemian nobility and of the German princes, and his defeat and death in 1278 left the way open for the Habsburgs to establish their power in Austria. Confusion and conflict in Germany, the bitter struggle between Ludwig IV of Bavaria (1314-47) and Pope John XXII (1316-34) over the imperial succession, the extinction of the Premyslid dynasty in Bohemia (1306) and the Arpad dynasty in Hungary (1301), all helped in the process. By the time of Rudolf IV (1356-65) the Habsburgs had consolidated their position, and Austria, along with Poland, Hungary and Bohemia, was a major territorial power. At the same time, in south-east Europe Stefan Dushan (1331-55) assumed the title of 'Tsar of the Serbs and Greeks' and put together a great Serbian empire which reached from the Mediterranean coast opposite Corfu to Salonica and controlled the whole of the Bulgarian hinterland.

The half-century between 1330 and 1380 saw a remarkable upsurge of government and civilisation in east and east-central Europe. In the case of Serbia, the foundations soon proved extremely fragile. After Dushan's death the Serbian empire was torn by separatism and faction, and succumbed to the Ottoman Turks

at the famous battle of Kosovo in 1389. The foundations on which the Polish, Bohemian and Hungarian rulers built were more solid. Bohemia's financial strength and early prominence owed much to the opening of the silver mines of Kutna Hora in the 13th century, and to Prague's strategic position on the trade routes from east to west. Poland profited from the opening of the Baltic sea-route by German merchants, and became a major exporter of timber and grain. Using their new-found economic power, the rulers of the period – Charles IV, Casimir III and Louis of Hungary – set about building centralised states on the western model. Their object was to curb the nobility, encourage new classes dependent upon themselves, codify the law, and set up royal tribunals to which all classes – particularly the nobility – would be subject. *The Statutes of Casimir the Great* (1347) and the *Majestas Carolina* are a monument to their efforts; Stefan Dushan also promulgated a code of laws, the *Dušanov Zakonik*, in 1349.

The decisive factor in the transformation of eastern Europe, however, was the influx of German and Flemish settlers, who cleared forest and waste land, drained swamps, founded villages, and created vast reserves of arable capable of sustaining a rapidly growing population. German eastern colonisation, checked by the great Slav revolt of 983 (see page 116), began again around 1125 as a result of population pressure, and quickly submerged the small west Slav peoples (Wagrians, Abodrites, Sorbs, Lusatians) inhabiting the country between the Elbe and the Oder. Military and predatory at first, it soon developed into a vast movement of peasants, often called in by Slav princes anxious to develop their territories, who granted the settlers the privilege of living under German law. A second thrust was by sea. The conquest of Wagria opened the Baltic to the Germans, and after the foundation of Lübeck (1143) a string of German cities (Wismar, Rostock, Stralsund, Greifswald, Cammin, Kolberg) sprang up along the Baltic coast. From these emerged the later Hanseatic League, established in 1358. The immediate consequence was a series of expeditions, beginning in 1186, intended to extend German sway as far as the Gulf of Finland. But although Livonia was formally subdued (1207), there was no appreciable German colonisation except in the cities (Riga, Dorpat, Reval) where German merchants played a prominent role in the Russian trade. German enclaves remained an important element in the Baltic states, right down to the 20th century, but the bulk of the peasantry retained their national characters.

Colonisation reached its peak in the half-century after 1220. By 1300 it was slowing down, except in the territories of the Teutonic Knights, who had been called in as auxiliaries in 1226 by the Polish dukes of Masovia against the heathen Prussians. That same year East Prussia was granted by the Emperor Frederick II to the Master of the Teutonic Order, who was also made an Imperial Prince. The conquest of Prussia, unlike German colonisation elsewhere beyond the Oder, was a ruthless military operation, followed by systematic settlement. Some 1400 villages and 93 towns were founded between 1280 and 1410. Under Winrich of Kniprode (1351-82), the greatest of the Grand Masters of the Order, the Teutonic Knights reached the zenith of their power. But their efforts to link up their territory in Prussia with Pomerania in the west and with Livonia in the north-east inevitably provoked hostile reactions. Poland, in particular, saw itself threatened, and further east, Lithuania, the largest territorial state of 14th century Europe, took shape in response to German pressure. Gedymin (1316-41) and Olgierd (1345-77) were the founders of modern Lithuania, and when Poland and Lithuania were united in 1386, under Wladislaw II, the first of the long-lasting

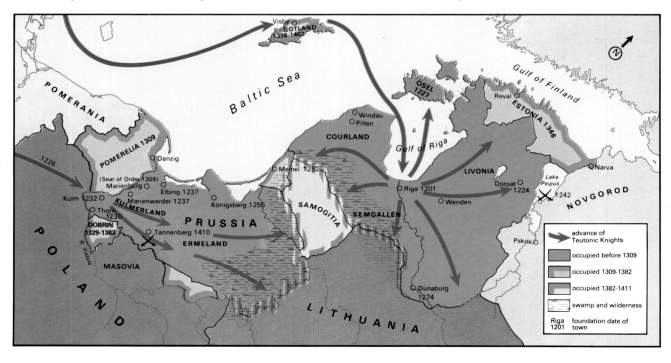

SWEDEN

HOLSTEIN
Lübeck
Hamburg MECKLENBURG
R. Elbe
BRANDENBURG 1373
LUSATIA 1368
MEISSEN
UPPER PALATINATE 1369
KINGDOM OF BOHEMIA
Prague
Kutna Hora
MORAVIA
Brünn
AUSTRIA 1282
Vienna
STYRIA 1282
CARINTHIA 1335
Graz
CARNIOLA 1335
Venice Trieste Fiume
SLAVONIA
CROATIA
Adriatic Sea

Baltic Sea

POMERANIA
POMERELIA
Danzig
Memel
Königsberg
SAMOGITIA
LIVONIA
TEUTONIC ORDER

Toruń (Thorn)
Poznań
Gniezno
POLAND
Breslau
SILESIA 1368
LITTLE POLAND
Cracow
Lublin
Sandomierz

Polotsk
Vitebsk
SMOLENSK
Smolensk
Vyazma
NOVGOROD
PRINCIPALITY OF MOSCOW
Vilna
Minsk
Novogrudok
LITHUANIA
Bryansk
Kursk
Chernigov
Kiev
VOLHYNIA
R. Pripet
PRINCIPALITY OF RYAZAN

RUTHENIA to Poland 1366
Lwów (Lvov)
Halicz
PODOLIA
R. Dniester
MOLDAVIA Hungarian suzerainty until 1365; independent until 1387, then under temporary Lithuanian control.
KHANATE OF THE GOLDEN HORDE
R. Dnieper
CRIMEA

Carpathian Mts.
Pest
KINGDOM OF HUNGARY
Pécs
Belgrade
Smederevo
WALLACHIA Hungarian suzerainty until 1369; then independent; from 1389 Ottoman tributary.
Black Sea

BOSNIA Hungarian rule 1328; independent from 1353
✗ Kosovo 1389
R. Danube
BULGARIA
BYZANTINE EMPIRE (to 1361)

SERBIAN EMPIRE under Stephen Dushan (1331-1355)
Skoplje
Durazzo
Salonica
CORFU EPIRUS
Aegean Sea
NEGROPONTE
PRINCIPALITY OF ACHAEA

Legend:

growth of Lithuania

- Lithuania to 1300
- Lithuania under Gedymin 1316-41
- Lithuania under Olgierd 1345-77
- Lithuania under Jagiello and Witold from 1377
- boundary of Poland-Lithuania after union of 1386
- Habsburg lands
- Bohemian lands
- Samogitia to Teutonic Order 1398-1411; to Lithuania 1422
- Polish territory under Casimir III
- Venetian territory
- swamp and wilderness

Jagiello dynasty, Prussia was outmatched. Defeated by the Poles at Tannenberg (1410), it entered a period of decline which culminated in the Peace of Toruń (1466) under which Pomerelia, Danzig and other parts of the former *Ordensland* passed under Polish rule.

The long conflict with Prussia also adversely affected Poland. To gain support in the wars, the Jagiellonian rulers were forced to make concessions to the gentry *(szlachta)*. Furthermore, the union between Poland (which was predominantly Catholic) and Lithuania (which was predominantly Orthodox) was far from untroubled. With the rise of Muscovy under Ivan III (1462-1505) and the inception of the policy of the 'reassembly of the Russian land' (see page 162), Poland came under pressure from the east, particularly as Casimir the Great, checked by the Prussian Knights on the Baltic, had expanded in the south-east and annexed the White Russian territories of Ruthenia and Galicia (1366).

Hungary, meanwhile, was exposed to Ottoman attacks (see page 138), and in Bohemia social and religious unrest beginning under Charles IV's son, Wenceslaus (1378-1419), undermined the power of the crown. After the condemnation and burning of Jan Hus, the Bohemian reformer, at the Council of Constance (1415), the long Hussite wars (see page 142) quickly took on nationalist, anti-German overtones and divided and ruined the country, preparing the way for the eventual rise of Austria (see page 150) to the leading position in eastern Europe.

Nevertheless the changes of the 14th century were of lasting importance. Just as the centre of political power in Germany had moved east from the Rhine to the Elbe and from the Elbe to the Oder, so the rise of Poland, Lithuania, Hungary and Bohemia marked the beginning of a new phase in which Moscow, Vienna, Sweden and Turkey struggled for succession to the Polish-Lithuanian inheritance.

1/Eastern Europe in 1386 *(above)* The crown of Poland descended traditionally in the female line. The marriage of Queen Jadwiga (1382-99) to Wladislaw II of Lithuania in 1386, brought the 'personal union' of these two already powerful kingdoms, and created a formidable new political force, threatening the Teutonic Knights.

Prague *(below)* Under Charles IV (1316-78), Prague became one of the great capitals and a symbol of the new eastern Europe. The St Veit cathedral and the famous royal residence, the Hradschin, were embellished and extended, the Charles University founded (1348) and lavish efforts made to attract merchants and trade.

PRAGA

The crisis of the 14th century in Western Europe

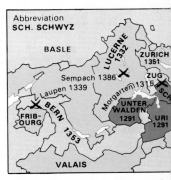

Abbreviation
SCH. SCHWYZ

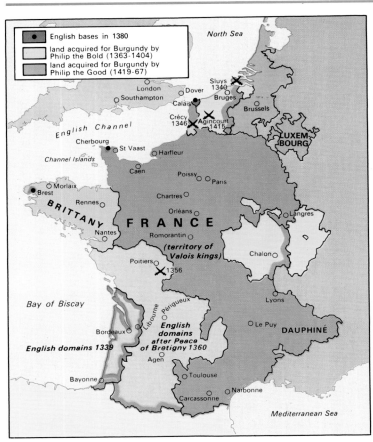

English bases in 1380

land acquired for Burgundy by Philip the Bold (1363-1404)

land acquired for Burgundy by Philip the Good (1419-67)

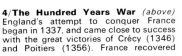

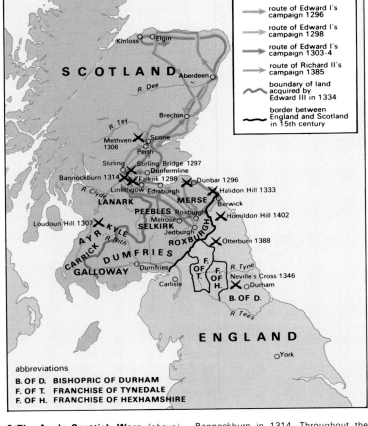

route of Edward I's campaign 1296
route of Edward I's campaign 1298
route of Edward I's campaign 1303-4
route of Richard II's campaign 1385
boundary of land acquired by Edward III in 1334
border between England and Scotland in 15th century

abbreviations

B. OF D. BISHOPRIC OF DURHAM
F. OF T. FRANCHISE OF TYNEDALE
F. OF H. FRANCHISE OF HEXHAMSHIRE

3/The Swiss Confederation (above) Characteristic of the disintegration of the 14th century was the success of the Swiss mountain cantons in throwing off Habsburg rule. The three cantons which formed the original Confederation in 1291 were joined by five others before the end of the 14th century, after the decisive defeat of Austria at the battle of Morgarten.

The Black Death (below) In 1347, plague of Asiatic origin spread from the south-east across the European continent, wiping out perhaps a third of the western population in about two years. Until the early 18th century scarcely a decade went by without a recurrent outbreak. Unlike famine, the pestilence affected every social rank and class, and the psychological impact was profound. The disease, spread by infected fleas carried by rats, was particularly virulent, and few who caught it ever recovered. This German print shows the holy men of the Church praying for plague victims.

4/The Hundred Years War (above) England's attempt to conquer France began in 1337, and came close to success with the great victories of Crécy (1346) and Poitiers (1356). France recovered after 1360 (Peace of Bretigny), but Henry V's invasion in 1415 again gave England control of northern France (see page 150). The last English garrisons except Calais were expelled in 1453.

2/The Anglo-Scottish Wars (above) The effort of Edward I of England (1272-1307) to subjugate Scotland culminated in Edward II's disastrous defeat at Bannockburn in 1314. Throughout the century and beyond, the Scots, often fighting in alliance with France, were a threat to English security.

THE monarchies of western Europe were confronted in the 14th century by an aristocracy eager to reassert position and privilege though not to dismember the state. Fragmentation was, nonetheless, a threat everywhere, conspicuously so in France after 1337, where the Hundred Years War exacerbated particularist dissension. French expansion to the east (Dauphiné, 1353) was checked by a royal fief, the Duchy of Burgundy, swollen by acquisition of the imperial county of Burgundy (1363) and Flanders (1384). Military successes in France under Edward III (1327-77) and Henry V (1413-22) eased English aristocratic restlessness, but in the long run the French wars only sharpened tensions of which Edward II (1307-27) and Richard II (1377-99) were victims. In England, war with the Scots was an ever-present threat and a frequent reality. In Germany, the Golden Bull of 1356 defined the pattern for a century of political strife: a king without real power and princes incapable of preserving peace in their separate domains. The Wittelsbachs, Habsburgs and Luxembourgs, who contested for the crown, were more concerned with strengthening their own patrimonies than with stabilising German monarchy. Papal intervention contributed to monarchical weakness. A complex network of leagues and confederations emerged to fill the political vacuum. Of these, the Swiss Confederation (after 1291) was the most successful and enduring.

By 1400 five Italian states were predominant: Florence, Venice, the Papal States, Naples and Milan, most powerful of the *signorie* under its Visconti lords, a threat to the security of the rest. Transfer of the papacy to Avignon (1305-77) and the Great Schism (1378-1417) which followed gravely diminished papal prestige, though Avignonese popes were no mere puppets of French kings. At the same time, failure to check corruption and incompetence in the Church inspired reformers, who advanced from complaints about abuses to assaults on hierarchical authority and even on orthodox doctrine. Religious and political objectives mingled in England and Bohemia among followers of John Wyclif and John Hus.

Spain, like Italy, was a theatre of operation for bands of mercenaries employed by every side in dynastic wars. Aristocratic reaction to Castilian royal authority triumphed in the Trastamara usurpation (1369). Regionalism surfaced after the death of Martin IV of Aragon in 1410, but the settlement of 1412 acknowledged the importance of monarchy to all component sections. Iberian boundaries in fact remained essentially unchanged despite intermittent warfare including a Trastamara threat to overwhelm Portugal, decisively terminated at Aljubarrota (1385). In Denmark, Norway and Sweden the crisis for monarchy loomed not as a prospect of domination by special interests but as a threat to the existence of more than a titular kingship. By 1400 what power remained to the three crowns had fallen to one ruler, Margaret of Norway (Union of Kalmar, 1397). The northern kingdoms, however, were not united and the overriding strength of the aristocracy was undiminished.

Though growth in population and productivity was steady until after the middle of the 13th century, both began to decline prior to the Great Famine of 1315-17. Textile manufacture in Flemish and Italian cities and maritime trade fell off sharply before 1330. Banking failures, beginning with the Buonsignori of Siena (1298), culminated in the collapse of the great Florentine banking houses in the 1340s. Mineral production slumped; in many regions reclamation and colonisation virtually ceased while land went out of cultivation and timber supplies were exhausted. Resources and wealth were redistributed as established commercial and industrial centres passed their peak and new rivals prospered. English producers gained a substantial share of a diminishing cloth industry. Portuguese and Castilian shipping burgeoned in 1400. Farmland was converted to pasturage for sheep in England and Castile and for cattle in the Netherlands and northern Germany. Monopolistic restrictions designed to secure established positions in a waning market adversely affected the volume of trade and enabled some large towns to prosper at the expense of neighbouring villages. At the same time, the putting-out system deprived townsmen of work in the cloth trades. Pestilence, beginning with the Black Death (1346-53), and popular insurrection exacerbated social and economic tensions. Erosion of the manorial system progressed unevenly, but throughout western Europe the servile tenant was transformed in a steadily increasing ratio into freeholder, leaseholder, sharecropper or wage-worker. In any of these capacities, or indeed if he remained a serf, he prospered from depopulation after mid-century. Meanwhile, urban labourers organised to bargain for economic improvement and political power, and revolts erupted in both cities and countryside. Most, apparently, were spontaneous; many were brutally repressed; and few accomplished enduring results. The Sicilian Vespers (1282) spreading from Palermo, drove the Angevins from Sicily. Hostility to the French also mingled with bitter antagonism toward burgher oligarchies and landlords in Flemish uprisings such as the Matins of Bruges (1302) and the ensuing battle of Courtrai. Non-violent takeovers of power by Jacques van Artevelde (Ghent, 1337), Cola di Rienzi (Rome, 1347), and Etienne Marcel (Paris, 1357) were bourgeois movements with popular support in which the leaders were ultimately victims of mob violence. Marcel attempted to collaborate in the best known of mediaeval peasant insurrections, the Jacquerie. Undercurrents of religious sentiment and anti-clericalism permeated much popular protest. In the Great Revolt of 1381 in England, it was radically reformist; in the popular frenzy against the Jews in Spain (1390-92), it combined outrage over social inequity with orthodox bigotry. Although these outbursts were assaults on privilege and exploitation – whether feudal and manorial vestiges, legal chicanery, clerical abuse, royal taxation or guild monopoly – demands in many instances were either visionary or unrelated to actual causes of complaint. Foreigners (French, Hansa merchants, Jews, Flemings) were often the victims.

the Great Schism 1378-1417

Avignon
Rome

THURGAU
Näfels 1388
GLARUS 1352
GRISONS

Shetlands
Orkneys
Hebrides
Bergen
NORWAY
SWEDEN
Oslo
Uppsala
Stockholm
Visby
North Sea
SCOTLAND
Edinburgh
Carlisle
Newcastle
York
Armagh
IRELAND
Wexford
Chester
Lincoln
WALES
ENGLAND
Norwich
Bristol
Bury St Edmunds
London
Winchester
Roosebeke 1382
FRIESLAND
Amsterdam
HOLLAND
Hamburg
Bremen
Lübeck
DENMARK
Copenhagen
Baltic Sea
Riga
Königsberg
Danzig
TEUTONIC ORDER
Novgorod
RUSSIAN STATES
PRINCIPALITY OF MOSCOW
Smolensk
R. Dnieper
LITHUANIA
Kiev
POLAND
Warsaw
POMERANIA
BRANDENBURG
SILESIA
SAXONY
Brunswick
Magdeburg
HOLY
Antwerp
Bruges
Ghent
Ypres
FLANDERS
Liège
Aachen
Cologne
R. Rhine
R. Elbe
R. Oder
Cracow
UKRAINE
R. Dniester
Agincourt
Crécy
Amiens
Rouen
Mello 1358
Paris
Meaux 1358
Chartres
Rheims
Troyes
MAINZ
Trier
FRANCONIA
Frankfurt
ROMAN
Prague
BOHEMIA
MORAVIA
Tabor
Regensburg
Strasbourg
LORRAINE
BRITTANY
BURGUNDY
Orléans
Poitiers
FRANCE
Augsburg
BAVARIA
Munich
Passau
Vienna
SWABIA
Basle
SWISS CONFED.
Constance
Lausanne
Geneva
AUSTRIA
Salzburg
Buda
Pest
HUNGARY
R. Danube
Belgrade
Bucharest
WALLACHIA
Bay of Biscay
R. Loire
Lyons
SAVOY
Alps
CARINTHIA
Trieste
Venice
EMPIRE
Bordeaux
R. Dordogne
ENGLISH GASCONY
AQUITAINE
Cahors
Massif Central
DAUPHINÉ
R. Rhône
Turin
Milan
Genoa
Ravenna
REPUBLIC OF VENICE
BOSNIA
SERBIAN PRINCES
BULGARIA
Black Sea
Avignon
PROVENCE
Marseilles
Toulouse
Montpellier
Narbonne
NAVARRE
Saragossa
ARAGON
Barcelona
Valencia
Pisa
Florence
Siena
PAPAL STATES
Rome
Ancona
Adriatic Sea
Ragusa
PRINCIPALITY OF ALBANIA
Salonica
Adrianople
Constantinople
OTTOMAN TURKS
Corsica
Sardinia
Balearic Islands
Mediterranean Sea
KINGDOM OF NAPLES
Naples
Amalfi
Palermo
Messina
KINGDOM OF SICILY
ACHAEA
DUCHY OF ATHENS
Athens
Rhodes
Crete

1/Famine, plague and popular unrest Inadequately financed and weakened by war and internal dissension, western European monarchy underwent severe strains throughout the 14th century. Recession, compounded by famine and pestilence, led to conflicts in all countries between the autocracy and the urban oligarchies on the one hand, and the peasants and urban proletariat on the other. The Western Church was also rent with schism.

Merchants and finance in Europe c.1500

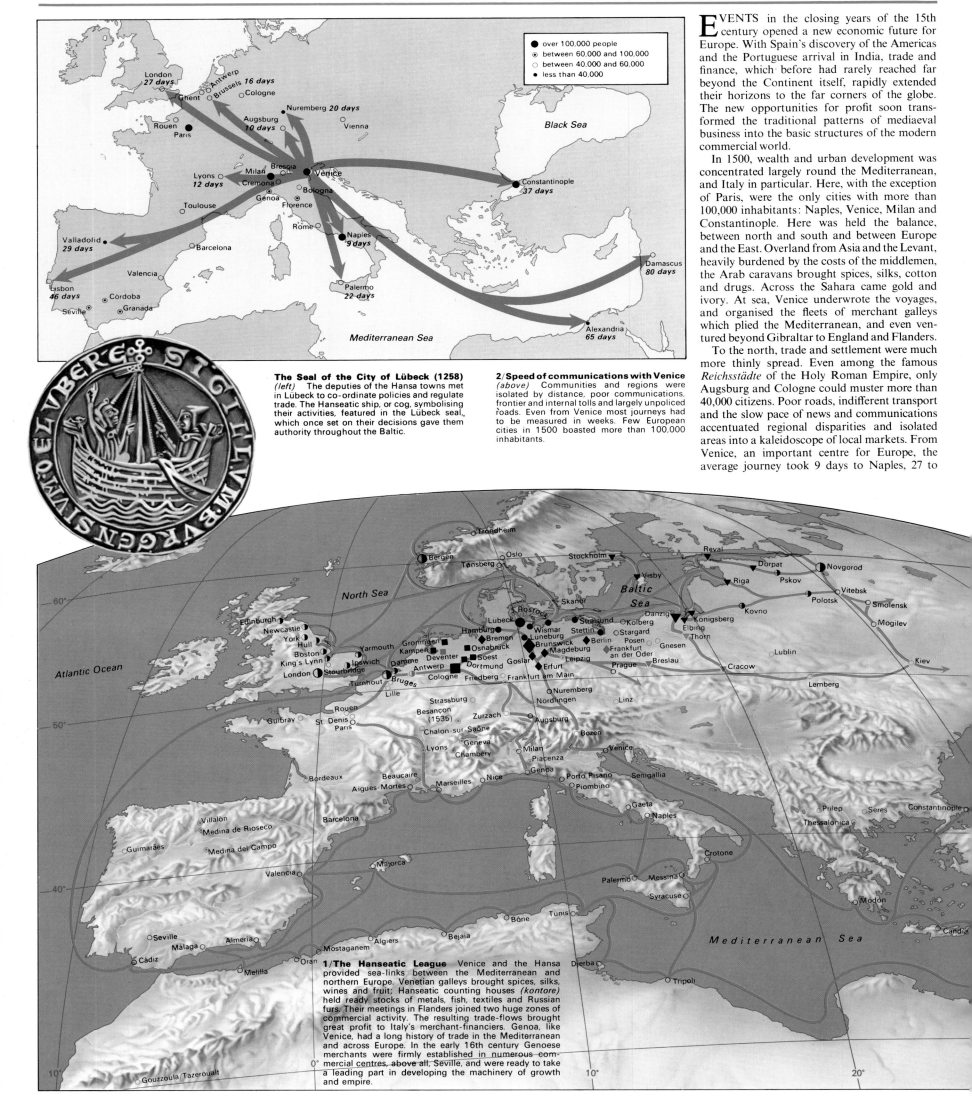

EVENTS in the closing years of the 15th century opened a new economic future for Europe. With Spain's discovery of the Americas and the Portuguese arrival in India, trade and finance, which before had rarely reached far beyond the Continent itself, rapidly extended their horizons to the far corners of the globe. The new opportunities for profit soon transformed the traditional patterns of mediaeval business into the basic structures of the modern commercial world.

In 1500, wealth and urban development was concentrated largely round the Mediterranean, and Italy in particular. Here, with the exception of Paris, were the only cities with more than 100,000 inhabitants: Naples, Venice, Milan and Constantinople. Here was held the balance, between north and south and between Europe and the East. Overland from Asia and the Levant, heavily burdened by the costs of the middlemen, the Arab caravans brought spices, silks, cotton and drugs. Across the Sahara came gold and ivory. At sea, Venice underwrote the voyages, and organised the fleets of merchant galleys which plied the Mediterranean, and even ventured beyond Gibraltar to England and Flanders.

To the north, trade and settlement were much more thinly spread. Even among the famous *Reichsstädte* of the Holy Roman Empire, only Augsburg and Cologne could muster more than 40,000 citizens. Poor roads, indifferent transport and the slow pace of news and communications accentuated regional disparities and isolated areas into a kaleidoscope of local markets. From Venice, an important centre for Europe, the average journey took 9 days to Naples, 27 to

The Seal of the City of Lübeck (1258) *(left)* The deputies of the Hansa towns met in Lübeck to co-ordinate policies and regulate trade. The Hanseatic ship, or cog, symbolising their activities, featured in the Lübeck seal, which once set on their decisions gave them authority throughout the Baltic.

2/Speed of communications with Venice *(above)* Communities and regions were isolated by distance, poor communications, frontier and internal tolls and largely unpoliced roads. Even from Venice most journeys had to be measured in weeks. Few European cities in 1500 boasted more than 100,000 inhabitants.

1/The Hanseatic League Venice and the Hansa provided sea-links between the Mediterranean and northern Europe. Venetian galleys brought spices, silks, wines and fruit; Hanseatic counting houses *(kontore)* held ready stocks of metals, fish, textiles and Russian furs. Their meetings in Flanders joined two huge zones of commercial activity. The resulting trade-flows brought great profit to Italy's merchant-financiers. Genoa, like Venice, had a long history of trade in the Mediterranean and across Europe. In the early 16th century Genoese merchants were firmly established in numerous commercial centres, above all, Seville, and were ready to take a leading part in developing the machinery of growth and empire.

London, 46 to Lisbon and 65 to Alexandria.

Despite the difficulties, however, Italian connections reached far and wide. The Medici of Florence, following the example of the Bardi and Peruzzi a century and a half earlier, controlled substantial banking agencies in the principal northern capitals. The north itself specialised in the products of sea, farm, mine and forest, many of them monopolised by the merchants of the Hanseatic League. The Hansa was an association of German cities which promoted trading monopolies and successfully sought exclusive privileges in Scandinavia, the Low Countries, Russia, Germany and England. Its activities were principally based on a network of towns in Germany and four great trading posts or *kontore*: the Tyskebrugge in Bergen (timber and fish); the Peterhof in Novgorod (furs); the Steelyard in London (wool and cloth); and the Assemblies in Bruges (cloth). Until its harbour silted up in the late 15th century, this last was the main *entrepôt* market, linking Mediterranean interests with those of the Baltic and the North Sea. Meanwhile, the substantial payment and credit requirements needed to facilitate the physical movement of goods were still mainly met by the great periodic fairs, which had emerged in the Middle Ages. After the brief prosperity of Geneva, the most famous of these in the 15th century was Lyons, strategically placed on the great trade route through the Rhône valley. There the merchants of Florence, Lucca, Genoa and Germany met, four times a year, under the freedom of the fairs from certain taxes and tolls, to settle accounts and clear bills of exchange from the principal markets of Europe.

But now the traditional mercantile structure was proving progressively less adequate. It could no longer cope fully with the opportunities presented by the Atlantic, the increasing flows of gold and silver, and the commercial exploits of the merchants of Portugal and Spain (see page 158). By the 1550s, these two great colonial powers had not only opened up the world, but also created huge demands for investment in new

methods and institutions. A more advanced technology had to be developed to conquer the oceans, discover the most profitable sea routes, and train seamen to cope with winds and currents different from those of the Adriatic and Aegean seas. New market structures emerged to cater for changing needs and demands. The intermittent fairs gradually gave place to more permanent markets and bourses, open each weekday throughout the year. With the eclipse of Bruges, the merchant community moved to Antwerp, on the Scheldt, with its access to the Rhine and the cloth towns of southern Flanders, and its versatile and convenient financial facilities, now a meeting point for Europe.

With growing, changing trade came a fresh generation of rich merchants and bankers, foremost among them the Fuggers of Augsburg. Although the Hansa and Bruges had progressively declined and the Iberian powers grown in strength, Venice managed after an initial set-back to come to terms with the Portuguese advance. But the balance of political as well as economic forces was shifting. When Charles V bribed his way to the imperial throne in 1519, not only the Holy Roman Empire but also Spain, the Low Countries, Germany, Austria and most of the New World now came under a single ruler, and it was largely the Fuggers who had furnished the money. Starting as peasant weavers and expanding into silver, copper and mercury mining, this German family grew immensely rich and powerful as moneylenders

to the Court and its aristocracy. As security, they normally demanded monopoly rights over various forms of mining trade and revenue collection. They controlled the Spanish customs, and gradually extended their influence throughout the Empire and its colonies overseas. Their operations stretched from Danzig to Lisbon, from Budapest to Rome and from Moscow to Chile. In 1552 their famous loan, made to Charles V at Villach, probably saved his military campaign from disintegration.

The private financing of great states, however, was a hazardous affair. Both the Fuggers, before their descendants turned from banking to landownership, and their thrusting Genoese competitors, were badly affected when the Spanish Court repudiated its debts, which happened on five separate occasions between 1557 and 1627. After the bankruptcy of 1575, the Fuggers increasingly withdrew from such business. The merchant bankers of Genoa, who took their place, had been forced to seek new commercial channels in the 1520s when their city chose the Emperor's side in France's Italian wars and they were barred from the Lyons fairs. Charles V compensated them for a while with the fairs of Besançon, which later moved to Piacenza, but such periodic meetings, as elsewhere, could no longer cater for the growing scale and volume of business. Nevertheless, their enterprise in the corridors of Spanish power helped to pave the way to modern finance, in the Atlantic markets of Amsterdam and London.

4/The Circle of World Trade *(above)* Columbus's voyages were extended across America to the West. Da Gama's ventures reached China and Japan. Macao, Nagasaki and Manila became trading centres holding out high promise for international trade. The Mediterranean still prospered, but the future lay with the Atlantic. Spain and Portugal closed the trading circle of the world.

The Fugger Correspondence Chest *(below left)* Fugger success and wealth grew from knowledge of Europe's markets. Letters poured in from all sides: from Danzig about copper, from Antwerp on the demand for silver, requests from Venice about spices, orders from the Emperor to pay his German armies.

3/The four major networks of trade *(below)* The mediaeval fairs proved inadequate as a means of channelling Spain's irregular landings of American bullion into European finance. Soon regular bourses opened in cities like Antwerp to handle the growing volume and complexity of business. The Fuggers, with their Europe-wide network of interests, bridged the gap.

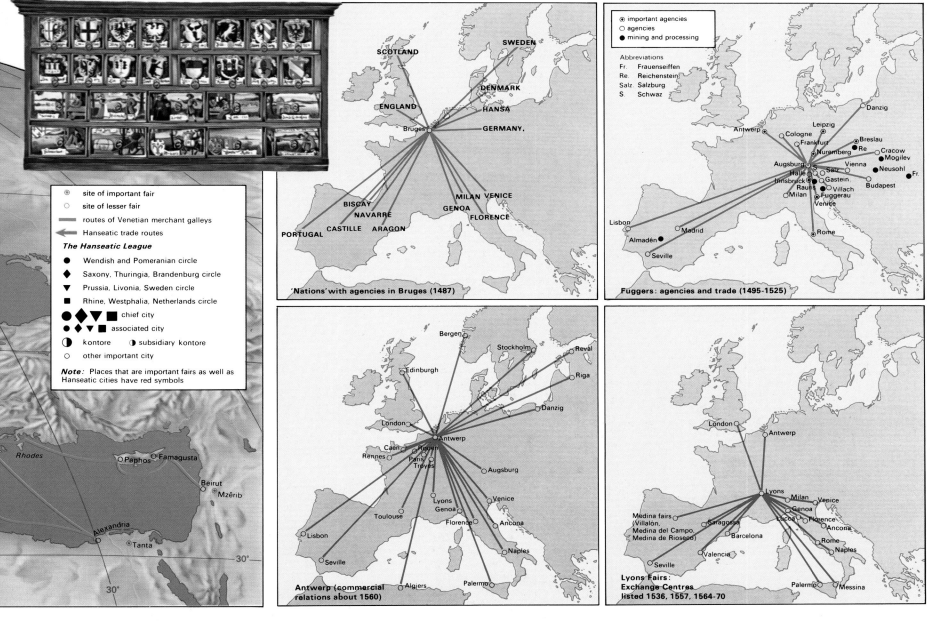

Eurasian trade routes from the Crusades to Bartolomeu Dias

AS long as the oceans of the world were thought to be unnavigable, they acted as barriers to the movement of men over the earth's surface, and the vast majority of the human race lived in ignorance of conditions in distant places. The great break through the barriers of ignorance and isolation came with the 15th-century voyages into the Atlantic and Indian Oceans, which brought European ships to the unknown shores of America, to hitherto unknown parts of Africa, and to Asia.

European interest in Asia, rekindled during the Crusades, developed considerably in the 13th century as the Mongols expanded their conquests and imposed order and relative security for travellers over an area extending from China to the Black Sea region. Suddenly Asia was open to European missionaries and merchants, the most famous traveller being the Venetian Marco Polo, whose *Description of the World* was based on a journey which lasted from 1271 to 1295 and included a period of service at the court of Kublai Khan. Colonies of Italian merchants, mostly Genoese, were established at Constantinople, Kaffa, Tana and Trebizond, the south-western termini of the 'silk roads' to Tabriz, Samarkand, and thence to China. Southwards from Tabriz ran the road to Baghdad and Ormuz.

Ormuz was one of the main entrepôts of the spice trade. Europe, like China, was dependent upon the spice-producing regions of Asia – south India, Ceylon, the Moluccas and the Malay archipelago – for cosmetic, culinary and other related products. As a result, Malacca became an international port shipping spices to China and to the Malabar cities of India, where they were purchased by Arab, Indian and Persian dealers for transit to Aden and Ormuz. From there they found their way to the Black Sea and the Mediterranean. But the roads opened by the rise of the Mongol Empire were closed by its decline in the mid-14th century. The chief victim was the traffic in Chinese silk, which wilted and dried up after the establishment of the proudly isolationist Ming dynasty in China. The steppe routes to Muscovy, Novgorod and the eastern outposts of the Hanseatic League, which dominated the Baltic trade, also fell out of use, and the spice trade was adversely affected. Plague, brigandage and hostility to Christians, as Islam spread in the disintegrating Mongol khanates, reduced to a trickle trade between Ormuz and the Black Sea. As a result, Europeans became heavily dependent upon Alexandria for spices, but the precariousness of the situation encouraged a search for alternative routes.

Dependence upon Alexandria also stimulated gold hunger in Europe, for there was little demand for European goods in the Levant and Egypt and payment for the most part had to be made in specie. The chief known source of gold was the Niger region of Africa. It was carried to the Mediterranean in trans-Saharan caravans to pay for European manufactures, particularly cloth. Some attempts were made by Italian merchants, such as the Genoese Malfante, to reach the African gold markets direct across the desert. But far more important and successful was the alliance of Italian finance and Portuguese seamanship to work down Africa's west coast in search of a reliable seaborne supply.

Many motives impelled Portugal to look beyond its own remote and impoverished shores: not only gold hunger, but shortages of grain, fish, and above all of slaves for its labour-starved sugar plantations in Madeira and elsewhere. Following the capture of Ceuta, one of the great North African gold ports, in 1415, Portuguese sea-captains pressed south, along the coast of Morocco, past the dreaded Cape Bojador (1434), finally reaching the Gold Coast where, from the 1480s, fortresses were built to protect Portugal's new-found wealth. By the end of

the 15th century some 700 kilograms of gold and around 10,000 slaves were arriving in Lisbon every year from west Africa. Meanwhile exploration continued. Angola was reached and 'annexed' in 1484, and in 1487 two further important expeditions of discovery were despatched. The first, under Bartolomeu Dias, was sent to explore the coast of Africa until a southern passage to the Indies was discovered. The second, under Dom Pero de Covilhã, was sent to Ethiopia to establish contact with 'Prester John', the legendary Christian ruler, and to discover how the trade of the Indian Ocean was organised. Both ventures were successful. Dias rounded the Cape of Good Hope in 1488 and saw the coast running north-east; Covilhã reached Sofala near the mouth of the Zambezi, only 1500 miles from the Cape, and saw the coast running south-west.

The Portuguese government – confused by the claim of Christopher Columbus to have found 'the Indies' by a westerly sea-voyage – hesitated

1/Eurasian trade routes *(right)* Land trade across central Asia enjoyed a renaissance under the Mongols, but dwindled away as various 14th-century crises affected routes, customers and sources of supply. The Chinese, under Admiral Cheng Ho, took ambitiously to the open sea in the early 15th century but soon retired, leaving what international exchange there was largely in the hands of coast-hugging Indian and Arab merchants. Alexandria and Venice almost monopolised the spice flow to Europe. It should be remembered that Marco Polo and Cheng Ho travelled along already established trade routes. (For routes within Europe see page 144.)

The Gagnières-Fonthill Vase *(left)* The existence of a direct link between China and the West in the Middle Ages may be proved by objects such as this vase. It probably arrived in Hungary with an Embassy of Nestorian Christians from China on their way to the Papal court at Avignon. It was given by Louis the Great of Hungary (1342-82) to Charles I of Durazzo.

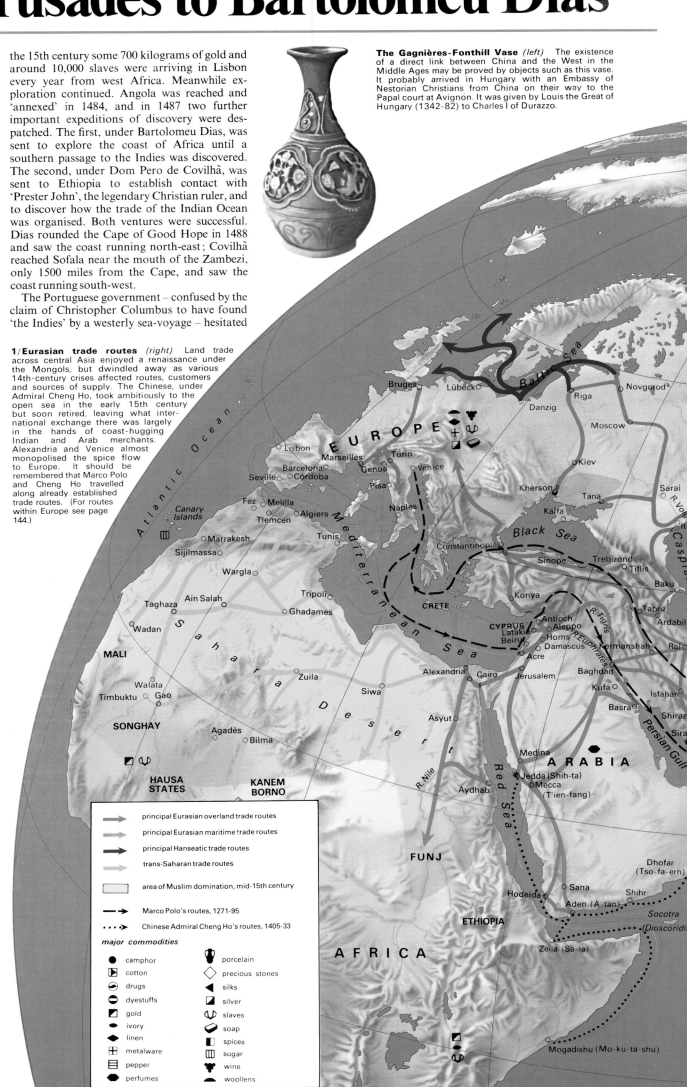

principal Eurasian overland trade routes
principal Eurasian maritime trade routes
principal Hanseatic trade routes
trans-Saharan trade routes
area of Muslim domination, mid-15th century
Marco Polo's routes, 1271-95
Chinese Admiral Cheng Ho's routes, 1405-33

major commodities

- camphor
- cotton
- drugs
- dyestuffs
- gold
- ivory
- linen
- metalware
- pepper
- perfumes
- porcelain
- precious stones
- silks
- silver
- slaves
- soap
- spices
- sugar
- wine
- woollens

to Kilwa, Malindi, Mombasa

at first, but in December 1496 concluded that Columbus could not possibly have found India and therefore decided to send an expedition there by the newly discovered route round Africa. A fleet of four ships, armed with twenty cannon, left Lisbon under Dom Vasco da Gama in July 1497. It was fortunate to meet little resistance. Earlier in the century, between 1405 and 1433, the Chinese admiral Cheng Ho had made seven voyages of discovery into the Indian Ocean, bringing back tribute and exotic products from as far afield as Java, Ceylon and east Africa. If the Chinese had persisted, the Portuguese would have found formidable rivals, for the Chinese

were better equipped and their fleet, comprising 62 ships and 28,000 men, was far larger. But their maritime enterprises ceased abruptly with Cheng Ho's death in 1434, and when the Portuguese arrived at Calicut on 17 May 1498 the sea route to India lay wide open. The 'Age of Vasco da Gama' in Asian history had begun.

2/The Portuguese in Africa *(right)* Under the patronage of Prince Henry the Navigator (1394-1460), Portuguese explorers steadily penetrated southwards in search of gold, spices and slaves. In 1488 one Portuguese expedition reached the Cape of Good Hope while another reconnoitered east Africa, preparing the way for Vasco de Gama's first direct seaborne journey to India in 1497.

coast revealed during life of Henry the Navigator, 1418-60

coast revealed under contract of Fernao Gomes, 1469-75

coast revealed by Diogo Cão

journey of Pero de Covilhã, 1487-90

route of Bartolomeu Dias, 1487-8

principal trans-Saharan caravan routes

The Americas on the eve of European conquest

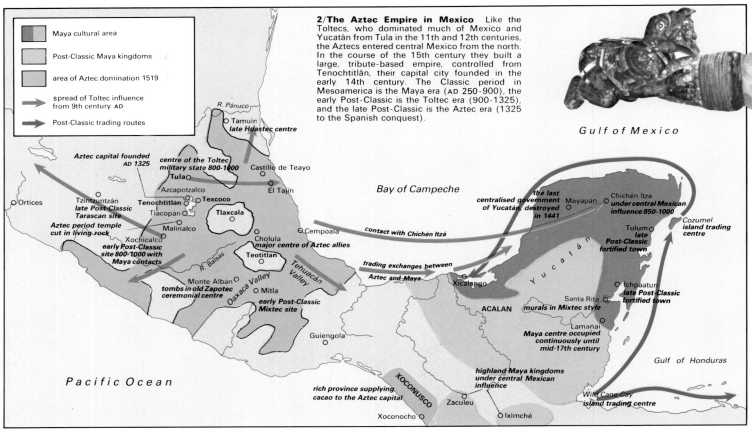

2/The Aztec Empire in Mexico Like the Toltecs, who dominated much of Mexico and Yucatán from Tula in the 11th and 12th centuries, the Aztecs entered central Mexico from the north. In the course of the 15th century they built a large, tribute-based empire, controlled from Tenochtitlán, their capital city founded in the early 14th century. The Classic period in Mesoamerica is the Maya era (AD 250-900), the early Post-Classic is the Toltec era (900-1325), and the late Post-Classic is the Aztec era (1325 to the Spanish conquest).

Aztec sacrificial knife (above) The Aztecs believed that the continuation of human society and of the present (fifth) creation required nourishing the sun and the earth with human blood and hearts. War was necessary to provide the sacrificial victims, whose hearts were removed with knives such as this one, about 32 cm long, made of chalcedony with an inlaid handle in the form of a warrior costumed as an eagle, *quauhtli*, which was also a name for the sun.

Inca silver (above) This Inca-made silver llama with gold and red stone inlay, about 21 cm high, illustrates both fine Inca metallurgy and the Andean domestication of the llama and alpaca. Guinea pigs were also domesticated here. In other regions of the Americas the only domesticated animals were the dog, brought from Asia by early immigrants, and turkeys domesticated in Mesoamerica and the south-west.

THE native inhabitants of the Americas had, despite their common Asiatic origin, achieved widely varying levels of development by the second millennium AD. In the Amazonian jungles, the Chaco and the sub-Arctic most were still nomadic Stone Age hunters, but in eastern North America and much of South America farming was well established. The Apaches and the Araucanians continued a gathering existence, but agriculture was being introduced to the plains hunters of North America from the east, while groups such as the Chibcha and the Caribs had formed settled societies with some degree of political organisation. All these cultures were overshadowed, however, by the more advanced civilisations of Mesoamerica and the central Andes, where two mighty empires, those of the Aztecs and the Incas, were at their most powerful by the late 15th century.

Like their Toltec predecessors, who controlled much of Mexico in the 11th and 12th centuries, the Aztecs came from the north, probably in the early 13th century, to a land being fought over by the semi-civilised tribes, known collectively as Chichimecs, which had destroyed the Toltec city of Tula. In this period of confused, continuous warfare they took refuge on a muddy island in Lake Texcoco, and founded there their town of Tenochtitlán as a place of safety rather than a centre of power. The surrounding swamps were drained, artificial islands were constructed to form gardens, and canals and causeways were built. By the end of the 14th century, following the transfer of religious and political authority from the tribal elders to a single ruler, Tenochtitlán had become the centre for a policy of aggression, first against overlords in Azcapotzalco, then against other neighbouring tribes. The Aztec strategy was brilliantly simple: they allied with their most powerful neighbours in the towns of Texcoco and Tlacopán against smaller groups, and then made war upon their former allies. This policy was particularly successful during the reign of Montezuma I, and by the second half of the 15th century the Aztecs, already in control of the greater part of Mexico, were beginning to enter Maya territory, where the inhabitants had reverted to a simpler way of life and the great cities of the Classic period had disappeared into the jungle.

The Aztecs allowed conquered tribes to retain their own gods and leaders, but failure to provide Tenochtitlán with an ever-growing volume of basic foods, textiles, pottery, metal goods and the other items required to support its nobles, priests and administrators (who numbered perhaps 100,000), would bring rapid retribution from the powerful imperial army. Increasingly war was waged without provocation, simply to ensure an adequate supply of captives for sacrifice to the principal Aztec god, Huitzilopochtli. It is estimated that at least 10,000 victims a year, rising to 50,000 on the eve of the Spanish conquest, had their still throbbing hearts pulled from their chests by Aztec priests.

Despite its material wealth, this civilisation had neither the wheel nor a written language, but its agriculture, although primitive in equipment, was intensive and produced a wide range of crops. Surviving pictorial tribute lists show that millions of peasants – total population was probably at least twelve millions – were expected to provide a surplus of some 20,000 tons of foodstuffs alone from their communal holdings for annual delivery by the empire's complex trading network to Tenochtitlán and its satellites. Facts such as this explain why it was that subject tribes like the Totonacs and the Tlaxcalans welcomed the Spanish *Conquistador*, Hernan Cortés, as a deliverer from Aztec oppression when he landed in Mexico in 1519.

The Incas were empire-builders, with an imperial ideal rather more comprehensive and coherent than that of the Aztecs. They imposed their culture, their socio-economic organisation, and to a degree their religion on conquered tribes as they pushed forward their frontiers from their base in the southern Andes in the 15th century. By the end of the century they had overcome the distinctive regional cultures which had emerged in Peru following the demise of the Huari empire in the 9th century, and had created an empire 200 miles wide and 2000 miles long, with a population of perhaps 10 millions. The origins of this mighty civilisation are shrouded in mystery. According to Inca legend the first emperor, Manco Capac, had been sent to Earth by his father, the sun (Inti), with instructions to found a city at the spot where a

golden rod he was carrying could be pushed deep into the ground. He wandered northwards from Lake Titicaca to the Valley of Cuzco, where he found soil rich enough for this purpose. This settlement seems to have occurred in the 12th century. For the next two hundred years the Incas were simply one of several small groups, vying for supremacy with their neighbours – the Chanca, the Colla, the Lupaca and others – in the southern Andes. Their expansion out of the Cuzco region began early in the 15th century in the reign of the eighth emperor, Viracocha, and was continued by his son Pachacuti, who completed the conquest of the Titicaca basin. Pachacuti's son, Topa, led the Inca armies northwards to subdue the powerful coastal Chimú civilisation, and then following his accession as emperor in 1471, pushed forward the frontiers of his empire into Chile and northern Argentina. Huayna Capac, emperor from 1493, concentrated his efforts in the north, where he founded Quito (in modern Ecuador) as a second capital. This decision, dictated by the need to decentralise an already over-large empire, proved fatal, for after Huayna Capac's death in 1525 it provoked a bitter civil war between the northern and southern halves of the empire, led respectively by his sons Atahuallpa and Huáscar.

As new territories were incorporated into the Inca Empire, large-scale movements of population occurred, with thousands of loyal colonists moving in to replace traditional inhabitants transferred to more secure areas. An impressive network of paved highways and bridges provided the means for rapid movement of troops through the hostile terrain. In Cuzco the divine emperor lived in great splendour, ruling through four members of his family, each responsible for one quarter of the empire. These nobles in their turn delegated authority to provincial rulers, in a highly-stratified political structure which descended through a complex hierarchy to officials responsible for every ten families at village level. Here the life of the common Indian was dominated by the need to provide tribute for local and central rulers, to work on a rota basis on road and bridge maintenance, and periodically to serve in the army. In exchange he was guaranteed freedom from famine –

Navajo sand painting (above) Maise (corn), beans and squash formed a triad of domesticated plants on which settled life depended over much of the Americas. Maise, especially, is a sacred plant, as is illustrated by this 'corn person' from a 20th-century painting.

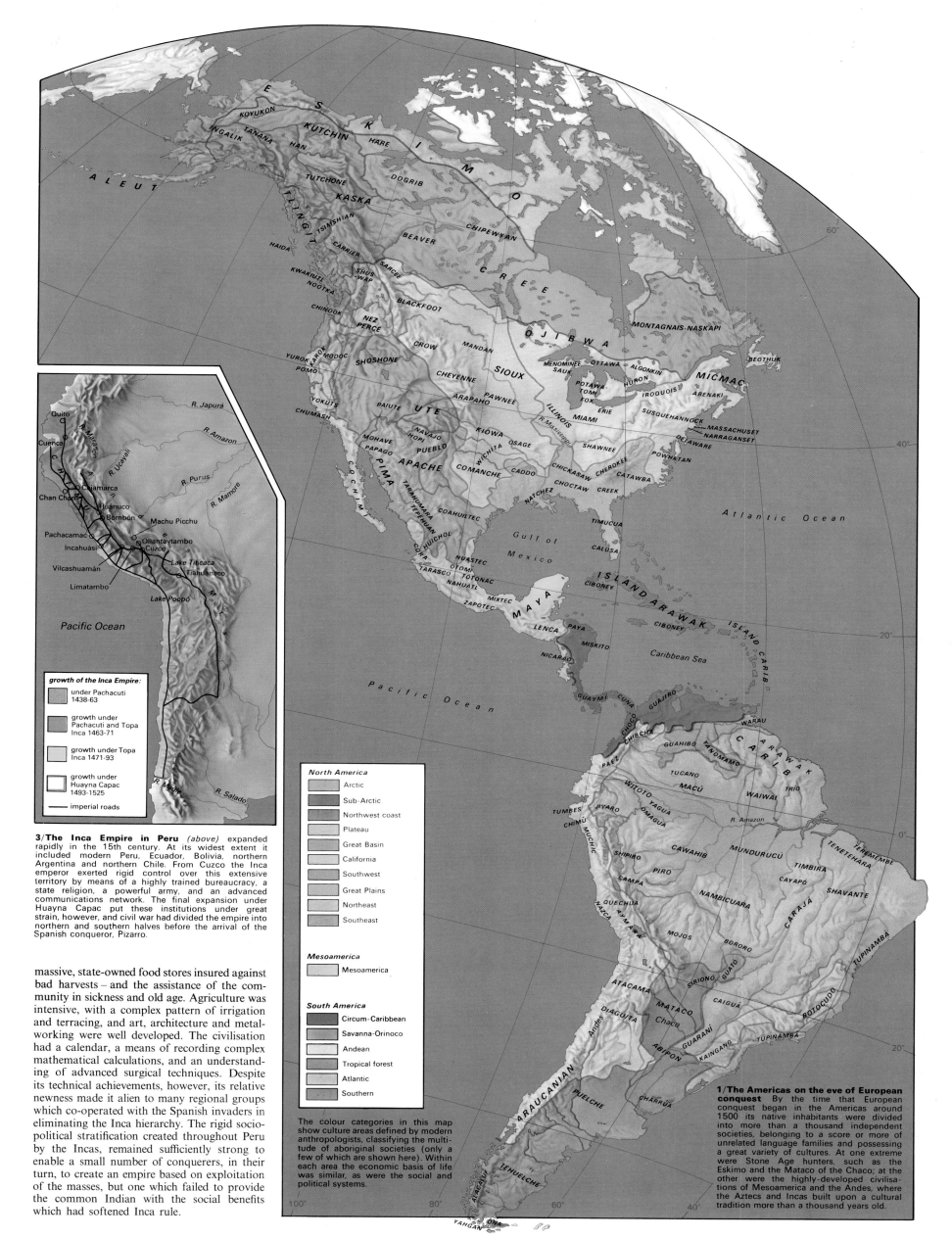

growth of the Inca Empire:

under Pachacuti 1438-63

growth under Pachacuti and Topa Inca 1463-71

growth under Topa Inca 1471-93

growth under Huayna Capac 1493-1525

— imperial roads

3/The Inca Empire in Peru *(above)* expanded rapidly in the 15th century. At its widest extent it included modern Peru, Ecuador, Bolivia, northern Argentina and northern Chile. From Cuzco the Inca emperor exerted rigid control over this extensive territory by means of a highly trained bureaucracy, a state religion, a powerful army, and an advanced communications network. The final expansion under Huayna Capac put these institutions under great strain, however, and civil war had divided the empire into northern and southern halves before the arrival of the Spanish conqueror, Pizarro.

massive, state-owned food stores insured against bad harvests – and the assistance of the community in sickness and old age. Agriculture was intensive, with a complex pattern of irrigation and terracing, and art, architecture and metal-working were well developed. The civilisation had a calendar, a means of recording complex mathematical calculations, and an understanding of advanced surgical techniques. Despite its technical achievements, however, its relative newness made it alien to many regional groups which co-operated with the Spanish invaders in eliminating the Inca hierarchy. The rigid socio-political stratification created throughout Peru by the Incas, remained sufficiently strong to enable a small number of conquerers, in their turn, to create an empire based on exploitation of the masses, but one which failed to provide the common Indian with the social benefits which had softened Inca rule.

North America

Arctic

Sub-Arctic

Northwest coast

Plateau

Great Basin

California

Southwest

Great Plains

Northeast

Southeast

Mesoamerica

Mesoamerica

South America

Circum-Caribbean

Savanna-Orinoco

Andean

Tropical forest

Atlantic

Southern

The colour categories in this map show culture areas defined by modern anthropologists, classifying the multitude of aboriginal societies (only a few of which are shown here). Within each area the economic basis of life was similar, as were the social and political systems.

1/The Americas on the eve of European conquest By the time that European conquest began in the Americas around 1500 its native inhabitants were divided into more than a thousand independent societies, belonging to a score or more of unrelated language families and possessing a great variety of cultures. At one extreme were Stone Age hunters, such as the Eskimo and the Mataco of the Chaco; at the other were the highly-developed civilisations of Mesoamerica and the Andes, where the Aztecs and Incas built upon a cultural tradition more than a thousand years old.

The new monarchies: Europe at the close of the 15th century

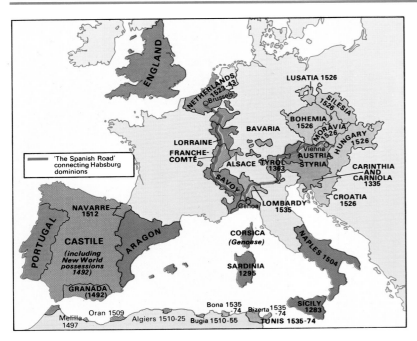

2/The Habsburg Empire in Europe *(above)* The emperor Charles V was heir to four separate inheritances, one from each of his grandparents. From Ferdinand of Aragon he acquired Sicily, Naples, Sardinia and Aragon, adding Milan and Tunis in 1535. The legacy of Isabella the Catholic provided Castile, Granada and the West Indies; Charles added Mexico (1519) and Peru (1533). Mary of Burgundy provided most of the Netherlands, Charles adding a number of provinces (see map 3). Maximilian of Habsburg's legacy gave him Austria, Tyrol, Carinthia, Alsace and the title of Holy Roman Emperor; he added Bohemia, Moravia, Silesia and parts of Hungary in 1526.

Key:
- Aragonese inheritance of Charles V
- acquisitions by Charles V, with date
- Castilian inheritance of Charles V
- Austrian inheritance of Charles V
- acquisitions by Charles V, with date
- Burgundian inheritance of Charles V
- acquisitions by Charles V, with date
- states favourable to Charles V

As a result of the economic and political setbacks of the 14th century (see page 142), by about 1400 there was no dominant state in Europe. Germany and Italy were already fragmented, and in neither was there any clear preponderance. In the east, the powerful states of the 14th century (see page 140) crumbled and new empires, such as those of Casimir IV of Poland (1447-92) or Matthias Corvinus of Hungary (1458-90), proved ephemeral. In the west, the Iberian peninsula was a prey to civil war, while France was torn apart by the feud between Burgundians and Armagnacs, a situation made far worse when Henry V of England (1413-22), the ally of Burgundy, invaded Normandy in 1415 and extended English control to the Loire.

This unstable balance was destroyed after 1450. The Muscovites and the Ottoman Turks rapidly subjugated large areas of the steppes and plains of eastern Europe (see map 1, and pages 138 and 162). In the west, Burgundy, the rising star of the 15th century, which seemed destined to become a major power between France and Germany, was partitioned after Charles the Bold was killed in battle in 1477 (see map 3), and the English were expelled from French soil (except from Calais) by 1453. In Spain, the warring kingdoms of Castile and Aragon were united in 1479, and in 1492 their combined forces completed the reconquest of the last Islamic strongholds in Spain. In England, failure in France and the loss of Normandy (1453) provoked civil war ('The Wars of the Roses'), but after 1485 a new dynasty, the Tudors, succeeded in restoring order and extended royal control in the turbulent outlying regions through the Council of the North and the Council of the March of Wales. In Germany, a series of dynastic alliances united the Habsburg lands with those of Luxemburg (1437) and Burgundy (1477). All these possessions, and later those of the Spanish royal family, came to the Emperor Charles V (1519-56), making him the greatest Christian ruler since Charlemagne. He systematically expanded each of these inheritances (see maps 2 and 3) and fear of Habsburg hegemony dominated Europe for two centuries.

The states which achieved these territorial successes were very different from the 'feudal monarchies' of the 12th and 13th centuries (see page 124). New conceptions of statecraft, exemplified for later generations by Machiavelli's famous treatise, *The Prince,* were in the air, and new institutions were created to enhance the king's authority. New courts, such as the English Star Chamber, were set up to impose law and order; new taxes were introduced, such as the French *taille* (1439), and new machinery to collect them; permanent ambassadors monitored the actions of neighbouring states. There was also a marked expansion of armies and navies. In France, regular royal regiments, the beginning of the standing army, were raised after 1445, and Louis XI (1461-83) could rely, in his struggles with foreign enemies and overmighty vassals, on the best train of artillery in Europe. The armed forces of the king of Spain numbered about 30,000 in the 1470s, but 150,000 some sixty years later.

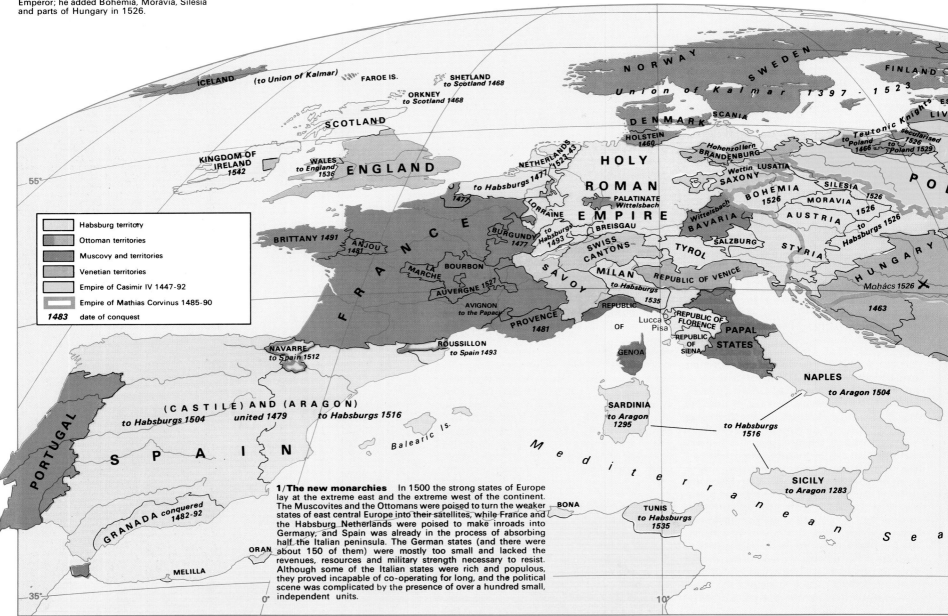

1/The new monarchies In 1500 the strong states of Europe lay at the extreme east and the extreme west of the continent. The Muscovites and the Ottomans were poised to turn the weaker states of east central Europe into their satellites, while France and the Habsburg Netherlands were poised to make inroads into Germany; and Spain was already in the process of absorbing half the Italian peninsula. The German states (and there were about 150 of them) were mostly too small and lacked the revenues, resources and military strength necessary to resist. Although some of the Italian states were rich and populous, they proved incapable of co-operating for long, and the political scene was complicated by the presence of over a hundred small, independent units.

Map legend:
- Habsburg territory
- Ottoman territories
- Muscovy and territories
- Venetian territories
- Empire of Casimir IV 1447-92
- Empire of Mathias Corvinus 1485-90
- *1483* date of conquest

The attitude of the new monarchs was expressed by Matthias Corvinus when he told a Silesian assembly in 1474 that he was 'lord and king' and that 'what he with his councillors held to be best, it was for them as dutiful subjects to perform'. The inhabitants of many countries, particularly the commercial classes, were prepared to tolerate this form of royal absolutism in return for security and the suppression of civil war. The economic recovery visible from c. 1450 also helped by providing more taxes. Civil war and economic setbacks had weakened the old nobility, and the church also was brought increasingly under royal control. In 'concordats' with Austria (1448), France (1516) and Spain (1526), the papacy was forced to concede far-reaching rights over the national churches, and in a number of Protestant countries the ruler openly assumed control of spiritual affairs. Henry VIII of England, for example, declared himself 'Supreme Head' of the church in England in 1534. Nevertheless the institutional armature of the 'new monarchies' was more fragile than it seemed, their apparent modernity often superficial. The new exalted sense of the prince's authority might point to the future, but rulers like Charles the Bold of Burgundy and Maximilian I of Austria, even Charles V himself (who abdicated in 1556 and spent his last years in monastic seclusion), clung to the ideals of the age of chivalry which was passing. The secular state, in which politics are divorced from religion and organised around an impersonal, centralised and unifying system of government, was still two centuries away (see page 184); the 'new monarchies' were at best its forerunner.

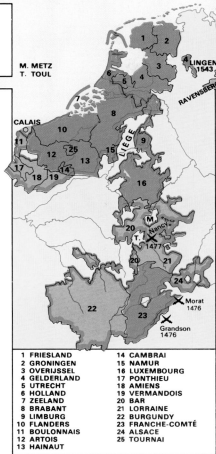

Legend (map 3):
- Charles the Bold's possessions, 1477
- Burgundian possessions lost at the death of Charles the Bold, 1477
- Emperor Charles V's Burgundian possessions, 1548
- provincial frontiers

M. METZ
T. TOUL
CALAIS
LINGEN 1543
RAVENSBERG
LIÈGE
Nancy 1477
Morat 1476
Grandson 1476

1 FRIESLAND	14 CAMBRAI
2 GRONINGEN	15 NAMUR
3 OVERIJSSEL	16 LUXEMBOURG
4 GELDERLAND	17 PONTHIEU
5 UTRECHT	18 AMIENS
6 HOLLAND	19 VERMANDOIS
7 ZEELAND	20 BAR
8 BRABANT	21 LORRAINE
9 LIMBURG	22 BURGUNDY
10 FLANDERS	23 FRANCHE-COMTÉ
11 BOULONNAIS	24 ALSACE
12 ARTOIS	25 TOURNAI
13 HAINAUT	

3/State-building in the Low Countries
(above) In the 15th century the dukes of Burgundy succeeded in building up a compact territory at the expense of France and the Empire. Including Flanders and Brabant, it was the richest land in Europe and effectively an independent state, very active in European politics. Duke Charles the Bold (1467-77) was defeated by the Swiss at Morat and Grandson (1476) and killed at the battle of Nancy (1477). His French fiefs (Burgundy and Picardy) were confiscated by Louis XI, but the rest of the Burgundian inheritance passed to Maximilian I of Austria, husband of Charles's heiress, and thence to their son, the emperor Charles V, who added further territories in the north-east.

Calais 1558
ST POL (1477)
ARTOIS
PICARDY
NORMANDY
VALOIS
RETHEL
Verdun 1552
CHAMPAGNE
Metz 1552
BAR
Toul 1552
BRITTANY
MAINE
ALENÇON 1525
PERCHE 1483
ANJOU
VENDÔME
ORLÉANAIS
NEMOURS 1503
BURGUNDY
TOURAINE
BLOIS
POITOU
BERRY
NEVERS
LA MARCHE
BOURBONNAIS
CHAROLAIS
Habsburg possession
ANGOUMOIS
PÉRIGORD
LIMOGES
AUVERGNE
FOREZ
GUYENNE
ALBERT
ROUERGUE
LANGUEDOC
DAUPHINÉ
ARMAGNAC
COMTAT VENAISSIN
Papal state
BIGORRE
ASTARAC
COMMINGES
FOIX
PROVENCE

4/The reunification of France 1440 to 1589
(above) The possessions of the French monarchy in the mid-15th century were surprisingly small. Until 1430, most of the land north of the Loire was in the hands of English and Burgundian forces, and even in the remaining area to the south the actual domain was less than half the total territory. The reconquest of Normandy, Gascony and the other areas held by the English in the 1440s doubled both the area obeying Charles VII and the royal domain. But the area under the crown's direct control was still relatively small until a series of confiscations brought in the lands of the dukes of Burgundy (1477), Anjou (1481), Brittany (1491) and Bourbon (1527). This left only a handful of semi-independent fiefs (of which many came to the crown when Henry of Navarre became King Henry IV in 1589).

Legend (map 4):
- frontier of France in 1492
- Royal domain, c.1475
- lands annexed from Burgundy, 1477
- lands of René of Anjou, annexed 1481
- lands of Duke of Brittany, annexed 1491
- lands brought to the crown by Louis XII, 1498
- lands brought to the crown by Francis I, 1515
- lands of Duke of Bourbon, annexed 1527
- lands brought to the crown by Henry IV, 1589
- other fiefs annexed, with date
- fiefs still independent at the end of the sixteenth century
- lands recognising English suzerainty, 1429

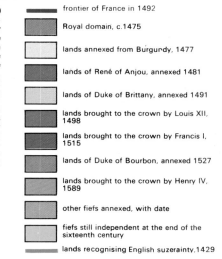

acquired by Ivan III 1462-1505
PSKOV
LITHUANIA
Moscow
MUSCOVY
1462
acquired by Vassily III 1505-33
TRANSYLVANIA 1541
MOLDAVIA 1504
1520's
1504
WALLACHIA
TARTARS
1459
Black Sea
OTTOMAN EMPIRE
1478
in 1451
ANATOLIA
1453
EUBOEA 1470
Lesbos 1462
Chios (Genoese)
MOREA 1460
conquered 1470s
1461
1488
1514-17
Rhodes 1522
CRETE
(Venetian)
CYPRUS
(Venetian)
20°
30°
40°

The Renaissance *(below)* The 'new monarchs' of Europe left lasting monuments to their wealth and power. Patronage on an unprecedented scale produced the rich cultural harvest known as the Renaissance. The movement began in two areas at the end of the 14th century: in the Netherlands, at the court of the Dukes of Burgundy and in the great commercial centres such as Bruges and Antwerp; and in the major city-states of Italy – Florence, Milan, Venice, Naples and Rome. From these centres new styles in art, architecture, literature and music soon spread over the whole continent, as far as Moscow. Italian architects had been employed by Ivan III since the 1470s. The purest Renaissance building in Moscow is the Cathedral of the Archangel Michael *(below)* designed by Alevisio Novi, in the Kremlin. The external decoration is distinctly Italianate, although the main structure was Russian in inspiration.

For most of the 16th century Italians continued to dominate architecture as Netherlanders dominated music, and both were prominent in art; but the Renaissance brought a flowering of vernacular literature in every country, from Spain to Sweden. Thanks to the spread of printing after 1455, the new cultural advances could be shared and improved upon by others.

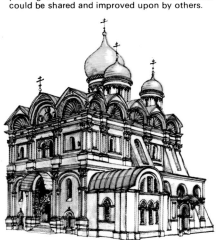

5 The world of

the emerging West

The Indian historian Panikkar described the period from 1498 to 1947, from Vasco da Gama's discovery of the sea route to India to the declaration of Indian independence, as the European age in history. Other historians have pointed out the element of exaggeration in this definition. If the Europeans had withdrawn from their settlements on the Asian coastlands in 1750, they would have left behind 'a few relics of historical curiosity', but nothing more substantial. Nevertheless, round about 1500 the balance, which hitherto had weighed heavily on the side of Asia, began to change, and by 1750 the change was momentous.

Before 1500 civilisation had been essentially land-centred, and contacts by sea were relatively unimportant. If the year 1500 marks a new period in world history, it is because henceforward direct sea contact was established between the different continents. This resulted not only in an extension of the stage of history to regions which hitherto had gone their way in isolation, but also in a challenge to the age-old land-centred balance between the Eurasian civilisations. Only Australia and the smaller islands of the Pacific remained immune; but even they fell into European clutches before the end of the eighteenth century.

Even so, the speed of European expansion should not be exaggerated. The sixteenth century saw a remarkable resurgence of Muslim power in the Ottoman Empire, Safavid Persia and Mughal India. China and Japan closed their doors to the western barbarians. As late as the days of Voltaire, Turkey and China were the exemplars of civilised living, to which Europe could only look with envy and respect. The advent of the Industrial Revolution put Europe ahead; but the fruits of that – some of them poisonous fruits – were only garnered in the nineteenth century. The period from 1500 to 1815 was a transitional period in world history, and European society, for all its thrusting novelty, was still essentially an agricultural society of lords and peasants, closer to its agrarian past than to its industrial future.

The world on the eve of European expansion c.1500

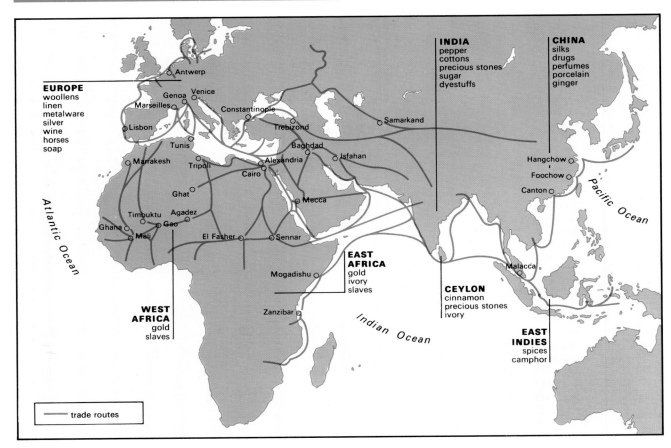

EUROPE
woollens
linen
metalware
silver
wine
horses
soap

INDIA
pepper
cottons
precious stones
sugar
dyestuffs

CHINA
silks
drugs
perfumes
porcelain
ginger

EAST AFRICA
gold
ivory
slaves

WEST AFRICA
gold
slaves

CEYLON
cinnamon
precious stones
ivory

EAST INDIES
spices
camphor

— trade routes

THE central feature of world history between 1500 and 1815 was the expansion of Europe and the spread of European civilisation throughout the globe. Down to 1500 the world had, on the whole, pressed in on Europe; after 1500 Europe pressed out into the world. By 1775 a new global balance was in existence.

In 1500 western Europe still stood on the periphery of the civilised world, overshadowed by the Ming Empire of China, the most powerful and advanced state of the period, and by the rising Ottoman and Safavid empires of the Middle East. Both in wealth and in population China, with over 100 million inhabitants (more than the whole of Europe), loomed far ahead, while the most expansive of the great world religions was Islam, still actively making converts in central and south-east Asia and among the peoples of sub-Saharan Africa.

The area occupied by the major civilisations, roughly equivalent to the area of plough cultivation, was nevertheless still relatively small in 1500. Over three-quarters of the world's surface was inhabited either by food gatherers and herdsmen – as in Australia and most of Siberia, north America and Africa – or by hand cultivators, especially in south-east Asia, Africa and central and south America. But the plough cultivators were far more productive, and it

2/Trade on the eve of Portuguese expansion *(left)* When Vasco da Gama set out for India, the world's richest trade routes ran from East to West. They made fortunes for the Muslim kingdoms of the Near East and for ports handling the western end.

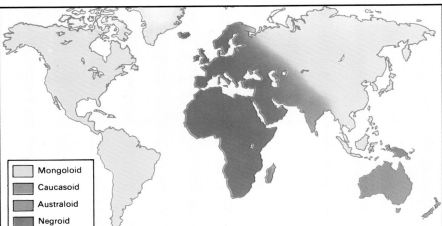

3/Distribution of races in 1500 *(left)* **and subsequent diffusion** *(below)* Before 1500 there existed, in effect, worldwide racial segregation. The Negroids were concentrated in sub-Saharan Africa and a few Pacific islands; the Mongoloids in central Asia, Siberia, Madagascar and the Americas; the Caucasoids in Europe, north Africa, the Middle East and India; and the Australoids in Australia and India. By 1775 this pattern had fundamentally altered as the result of six principal intercontinental migrations: from Europe to north, central and south America; from Great Britain and other northern European countries to Africa (and later Australia). There was also an enforced movement of African slaves to the Americas; a steadily growing trickle from Russia across the Urals into Siberia; and a substantial flow from India to east Africa, south Africa and the Caribbean, and from China into south-east Asia. By far the greatest change occurred in the Americas, where the native population declined by 90 per cent within a century, to be replaced by white Europeans, black Africans and a mixed race of *mestizos*.

☐ Mongoloid
☐ Caucasoid
☐ Australoid
☐ Negroid

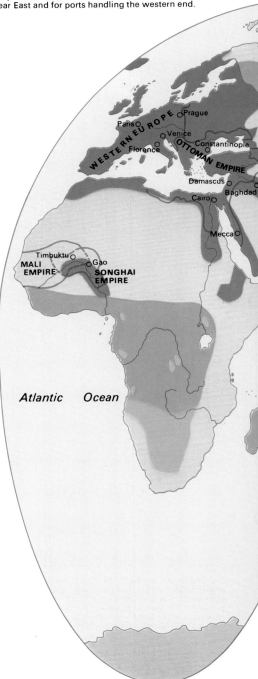

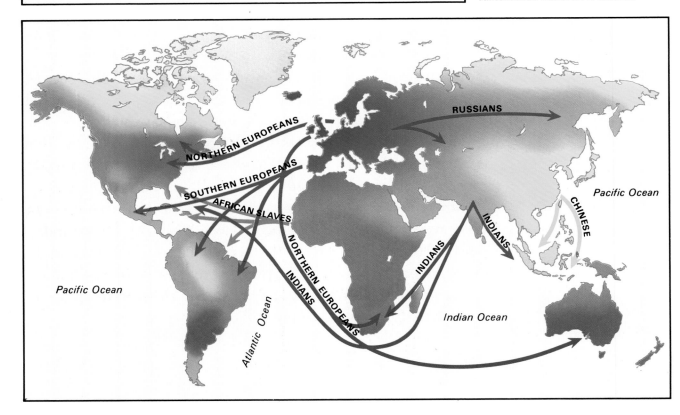

seems probable that between two-thirds and three-quarters of the total population was concentrated in the relatively small area which had been brought under the plough.

This concentration of both people and wealth closely matches the location of the major Eurasian civilisations. The comparative fragility of the Aztec and Inca civilisations in the Americas, and of the African kingdoms immediately south of the Sahara, which were outstanding in many respects, may be partly explained: first, by their geographic isolation and lack of external stimulus, which bred retardation; and second, by their dependence on hand cultivation. After 1500, when the expansion of Europe brought all continents for the first time into direct contact with each other, these non-Eurasian civilisations often found themselves unable to put up more than a feeble resistance.

It is nevertheless important not to exaggerate the tempo of change. Although in America the Aztec and Inca civilisations were destroyed by 1521 and 1535 respectively, elsewhere the political impact of Europe was extremely limited before the second half of the 18th century. China and Japan remained intact, and in India the Europeans were kept at arm's length for 250 years following the arrival of Vasco da Gama in 1498. There, as in west Africa and south-east Asia, the European presence was largely confined to trading stations along the coast. The cultural influence of Europe was even more negligible, and Christianity made little headway, except where it was imposed by the Spanish conquerors in the Philippines and Latin America, until it was backed by the resources of western technology in the 19th century.

On the other hand, the European discoveries not only opened up new global horizons but also led to a new global redistribution of races, and to a diffusion of animals and plants which

was of first-rate importance. The diffusion of races involved a corresponding diffusion of religions and of animals (e.g. horses, cattle and sheep from the Old World to the New World), plants and food crops. The spread of food plants – almost all domesticated by prehistoric man in various parts of the world – had proceeded slowly until 1500, when they were transplanted to every continent. In addition, the American Indians were responsible for two major cash crops: tobacco and cotton (derived largely in its commercial form from varieties they had domesticated, though other species were known and used in the Orient before 1500). Cane sugar, introduced by Europeans into Brazil and the West Indies about 1640, also quickly became a staple of foreign trade.

This interchange of plants produced an enormous increase in food supplies, which made possible the unprecedented increase of human populations in modern times. It also initiated a corresponding increase in intercontinental trade. Before 1500, this trade had been limited to Eurasia and Africa, and involved mostly luxury goods; after 1500, the combination of regional economic specialisation and improvements in sea transport made possible the gradual transformation of the limited mediaeval luxury trade into the modern mass trade of new bulky necessities – hence the flourishing 'triangular trade' of rum, cloth, guns and other metal products from Europe to Africa, slaves from Africa to the New World, and sugar, tobacco and bullion from the New World to Europe.

It was not until the 19th century, with the opening of the Suez and Panama canals and the construction of transcontinental railways in Canada, the United States, Siberia and Africa, that areas and lines of commerce which had previously been separate finally dissolved into a single economy on a world scale, but the first stages of global integration were completed in the period of just over two centuries beginning in 1500.

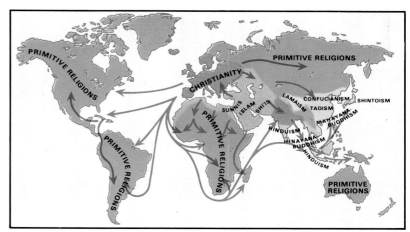

4/The diffusion of world religions (above) In 1500 Christianity was almost entirely a European religion, but the great Catholic powers, Spain and Portugal, imposed it, by prayer and the sword, wherever their vessels touched land, and the Anglo-Saxon Protestants soon followed suit.

5/The diffusion of plants (below) Wheat, originating in the Near East, had spread across Africa and Eurasia; now it spanned the globe, and was soon joined by bananas, yams, rice and the sugar cane, all from Asia, and by maize, and both sweet and ordinary potatoes, from the Americas.

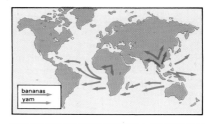
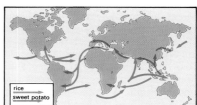

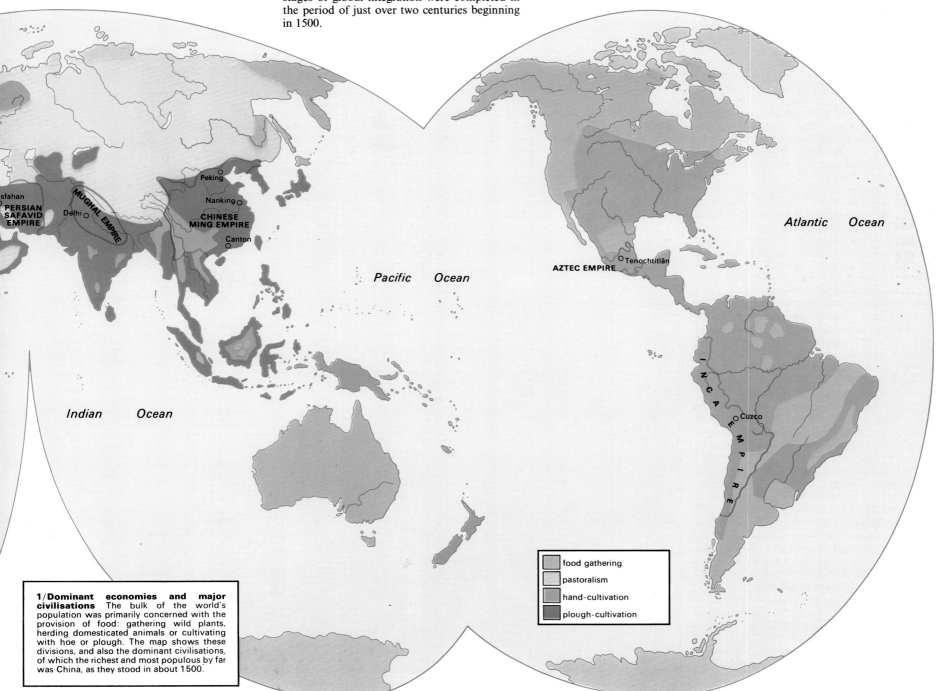

1/Dominant economies and major civilisations The bulk of the world's population was primarily concerned with the provision of food: gathering wild plants, herding domesticated animals or cultivating with hoe or plough. The map shows these divisions, and also the dominant civilisations, of which the richest and most populous by far was China, as they stood in about 1500.

food gathering
pastoralism
hand-cultivation
plough-cultivation

The European voyages of discovery
1487 to 1780

THE European voyages of discovery heralded a new era in world history. In 1480 the principal seafaring peoples of the world were separated not only by great expanses of uncharted sea but also by continental landmasses whose extent and shape were unknown. Regular European shipping was still mainly confined to the North Atlantic, the Mediterranean and the Baltic. The West African coast had been explored cursorily, and only very recently, by Europeans, but from the Gaboon to Mozambique the coast was unknown to any shipping. In the Americas, there were limited areas of raft-and canoe-borne navigation on the Pacific coasts of Ecuador and Peru and in the Caribbean, but no communication with Europe nor – so far as is known – with other parts of the Pacific. In the East several seafaring peoples overlapped. Indian, Persian and Arab shipping plied in the northern Indian Ocean. Chinese shipping – which in the past had sailed intermittently to East Africa – in 1480 usually went no farther west than Malacca, but shared the shallow seas of the Malay archipelago with local shipping, chiefly Javanese. No shipping used the southern Indian Ocean; Javanese contacts with Madagascar had long ceased. Chinese shipping, dense in the China Seas and the archipelago, went no further east than the Philippines. The great areas of the central Pacific were crossed only occasionally and perilously by Polynesian canoes. In the north Pacific, except in Japanese coastal waters, there was no shipping at all.

In the course of three centuries, approximately between 1480 and 1780, European seaborne explorers linked together the separate areas of maritime communication, and opened all seas, except in the regions of circumpolar ice, to European ships. In this long process of discovery, several distinct stages can be distinguished: initially, in the late 15th century, two series of voyages intended to find a sea passage to southern Asia, in the hope of opening direct trade for spices. One series, based on Portugal, sailing by a south-eastern route, and employing local navigators in the East, soon reached its declared destinations: the entrance to the Indian Ocean (1488), Malabar (1498), Malacca (1511), and the Moluccas (1512). The other series, based on Spain, sailing by a western or south-western route, was less successful in its immediate purpose but more fruitful in incidental discovery. The Spaniards hit upon the West Indian islands (1492) and the Spanish Main (1498). Eventually (1521) they reached south-eastern Asia, but by a route too long and arduous for commercial use. In the process of search they proved the Pacific to be a great ocean and not, as some respected authorities had supposed, a mere arm of the Indian Ocean. To reach the Pacific they had to circumvent an immense landmass, which they believed initially to be a peninsula of Asia, but which by the 1520s they accepted as a New World; though its complete separation from Asia was not proved until the 18th century. They immediately began to settle their new world, and for more than a hundred years kept it effectively an Iberian preserve.

The combined effect of Spanish and Portuguese discovery was to show that all the oceans of the world, at least in the southern hemisphere, were connected. For a hundred years or so Spain and Portugal, by the use of force and threat of force, prevented other Europeans from using the connecting passages, except for occasional raids. The third great series of voyages, therefore, mostly English, French or Dutch in inception, looked for corresponding passages to Asia in the northern hemisphere, in the west, north-west or north-east. Unsuccessful in their primary purpose, they revealed another continental landmass with a continuous coast from the Caribbean to the Arctic, and opened the way for the exploration and settlement of eastern North America

by northern Europeans.

After 1632 the search for the northern passages was abandoned. By that time influential groups in England and the Netherlands had defied the Iberian monopoly and opened trade with Asia by the south-eastern route. The last three-quarters of the 17th century and the first quarter of the 18th century was a period of settlement and of commercial consolidation rather than of new discovery; the brief encouragement which the Dutch East India Company gave to Tasman was exceptional, and was openly regretted by the directors of the Company. A series of circumnavigations by buccaneers or privateers, shortly before and shortly after the turn of the century, was similarly barren of practical results.

A second, a Silver Age of discovery began in the 18th century, inspired as much by scientific curiosity as by hope of commercial advantage. The voyages were organised by governments rather than by private investors, and were made by warships commanded by naval officers, often accompanied by scientists and painters. The objects were, in general, the exploration of the Pacific; in particular the location of a great southern continent believed, on the authority of Ptolemy, Ortelius and others, to extend north of the Tropic of Capricorn in the southern Pacific; and the discovery of a strait between north-eastern Asia and north-western America leading to the Arctic Ocean and thence, possibly, round to the Atlantic – the old North-west Passage from the opposite side. The results, in part at least, were negative: there is no habitable southern continent, other than Australia; the passage to the Arctic, though it exists, is choked with ice. On the other hand, many unknown island groups were discovered; the insularity of New Zealand was established and its coasts charted; the attractive and habitable east coast of Australia was explored, and shortly afterwards settled; the general configuration of the American and Asian coasts of the North Pacific was revealed; and the old problem of keeping men alive and healthy on long ocean voyages was, in large measure, solved. After Cook's death in 1779 – as La Pérouse complained – few of the world's coastlines remained to be explored.

Voyages in the Caribbean:
29/Bastidas & La Cosa 1501-02 explored coast from Gulf of Maracaibo to Gulf of Urabá.
30/Pinzón & Solís 1508 sent from Spain to find strait to Asia, coasted E. coast of Yucatán.
31/Ponce de León 1512-13 sailed from Puerto Rico, explored coast of Florida from N. of Cape Canaveral to (possibly) Pensacola. May have sighted Yucatán on return. First explorer to note force of Gulf Stream.
32/Hernández de Córdoba 1516 sailed from Cuba, explored N. and W. coasts of Yucatán. First report of Maya cities.

33/Grijalva 1517 followed S. and W. coasts of Gulf of Mexico as far as River Pánuco.
34/Pineda 1519 explored N. and W. coasts of Gulf of Mexico from Florida to River Pánuco. Finally ended hope of strait to Pacific in that region.

2/Voyages in the Caribbean, 1493 to 1519
(below) Spanish expeditions explored the Caribbean searching for a seaway to China, India and the Golden Chersonese. They found it landlocked on the west; took to slaving, pearling and plunder; encountered settled, city-building peoples; and founded a European empire.

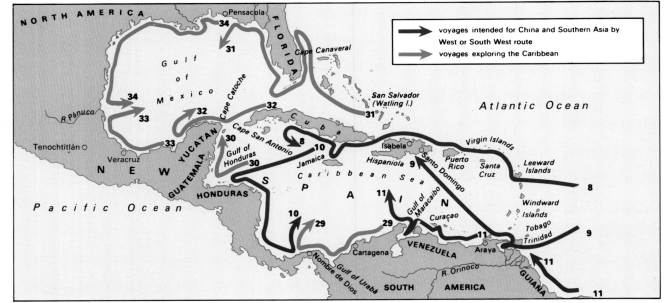

voyages intended for Southern Asia by South East route

voyages intended for China and Southern Asia by West or South West route

voyages intended for Asia by North West and North East routes

approximate prevailing winds (shown for the first quarter of the year)

alternating monsoons

voyages intended for China and Southern Asia by West or South West route

voyages exploring the Caribbean

1/Major European voyages of discovery from about 1480 to 1630 *(below)* Explorers seeking sea routes to Asia found, in addition, a continent hitherto unknown to Europe, and an ocean of unsuspected extent. They proved that all the oceans were connected, and that the world was much bigger than accepted authorities had taught.

Voyages intended for S. Asia by S.E. Route:
1/Dias 1487-88 (outward) discovered open water S. of Cape Agulhas; entered Indian Ocean; reached Great Fish River.
2/Vasco da Gama 1497-99 (outward) discovered best use of Atlantic winds on way to Cape of Good Hope; reached India, navigated by local pilot.

3/Cabral 1500 (outward) the second Portuguese voyage to India, sighted coast of Brazil at Monte Pascoal, probably accidentally.
4/First Portuguese voyage to Malacca, 1509.
5/Abreu 1512-13 visited Moluccas.
6/First Portuguese visits to Canton River, 1514.

Voyages intended for China and S. Asia by W. or S.W. Route:
7/Columbus 1492-93 (outward and homeward) discovered islands in Bahama group; explored N. coasts of Cuba and Hispaniola; interpreted discoveries as part of Asia; found best return route.
8/Columbus 1493-94 (outward) explored S. coast of Cuba; reported it as peninsula of mainland China.
9/Columbus 1498 (outward) discovered Trinidad and coast of Venezuela; recognised coast as mainland, surmised it to be terrestrial paradise.
10/Columbus 1502-04 explored coast of Honduras, Nicaragua and the Isthmus. Believed Honduras to be Indo-China.
11/Ojeda & Vespucci 1499-1500 (outward) reached Guiana coast, failed to round Cape São Roque, coasted W. to Cape de la Vela. First report of Amazon.
12/Coelho & Vespucci 1501 (outward) coasted S. from Cape São Agostinho to (possibly) 35°S.
13/Solís 1515 entered River Plate estuary and investigated N. bank.
14/Magellan & Elcano 1519-22 discovered Strait of Magellan, crossed Pacific, reached Moluccas via Philippines. Revealed Pacific as separate ocean of immense size. First circumnavigation.
15/Saavedra 1527 discovered route from coast of

Mexico across Pacific to Moluccas.
16/Urdaneta 1565 found feasible return route Philippines to Mexico in 42°N. using W. winds.
17/Schouten & Le Maire 1616 discovered route into Pacific via Le Maire Strait and Cape Horn.

Voyages intended for Asia by Northern Route:
18/Cabot 1497 (outward) rediscovered Newfoundland, first sighted by Norsemen in 11th century; took it for N.E. extremity of Asia.
19/Corte-Real 1500 rediscovered Greenland.
20/Verrazzano 1524 traced E. coast of N. America from (probably) 34°N. to 47°N.; revealed continental character of N. America.
21/Cartier 1534 and 1535 explored Strait of Belle Isle and St. Lawrence as far as Montreal.
22/Willoughby & Chancellor 1553 rounded North Cape and reached Archangel.
23/Frobisher 1574 reached Frobisher Bay in Baffin Island, which he took for a 'strait'; diverted from further exploration by spurious gold strike.
24/Davis 1587 explored W. coast of Greenland to the edge of the ice in 72°N.
25/Barents 1596-97 discovered Bear Island and Spitsbergen and wintered in Novaya Zemlya.
26/Hudson 1610 sailed through Hudson Strait to the S. extremity of Hudson Bay, which he and others took to be the Pacific.
27/Button 1612 explored W. coast of Hudson Bay, concluded Bay landlocked on the W.
28/Baffin & Bylot 1616 explored whole coastline of Baffin Bay and came to the conclusion that no navigable N.W. passage existed in that area.

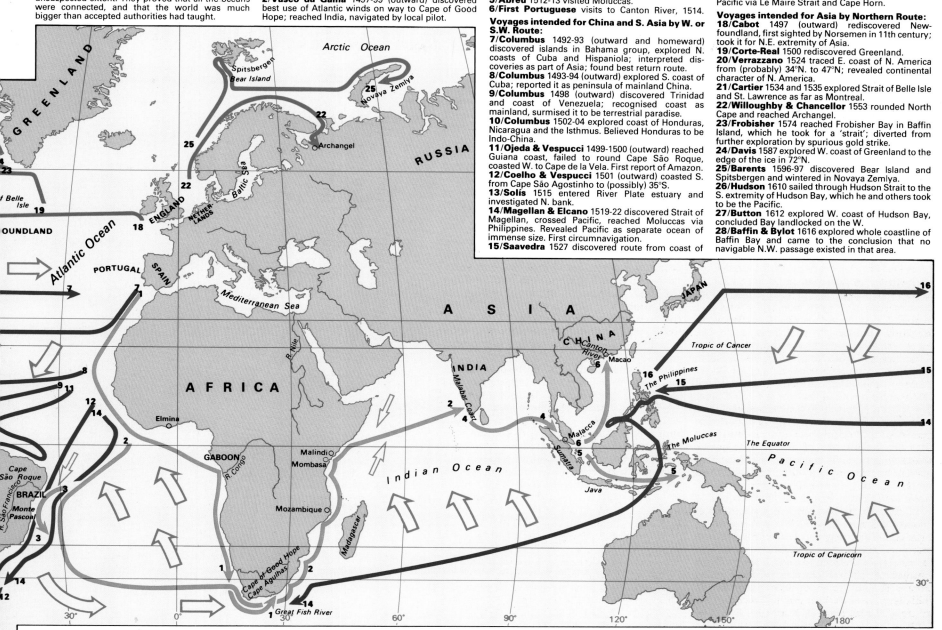

The ships of the discoverers *(below)* The outstanding characteristics of European ships employed in exploration were a stout pre-constructed frame to which carvel planking was fastened; and a rig combining square and lateen sails in the same vessel, giving driving power when running, adequate performance on a wind, and manoeuvrability. The engraving shows Elmina Castle, two lateen caravels, and a ship with the combined rig.

3/European exploration of the Pacific, 1720 to 1780 *(right)* Most 18th-century voyages of discovery were searches for a habitable southern continent or for a usable northern strait. Both proved imaginary. The expeditions revealed instead an insular New Zealand, a habitable eastern Australia, many attractive islands and a valuable whale fishery.

Voyages in the Pacific:
35/Roggeveen 1721-22 discovered Easter Island and some of the Samoan group. Circumnavigation.
36/Bering 1728 sailed from Kamchatka, discovered strait separating N.E. Asia from N.W. America.
37/Wallis 1766-68 discovered Society Islands (Tahiti), encouraged hope of habitable southern continent. Circumnavigation.
38/Cook 1768-71 charted coasts of New Zealand, explored E. coast of Australia, confirmed existence of Torres Strait. Circumnavigation.
39/Cook 1772-75 made circuit of southern oceans in high latitude, charted New Hebrides, discovered many islands, ended hope of habitable southern continent. Circumnavigation.
40/Cooke & Clerke 1776-80 discovered Sandwich Islands (Hawaii), explored N.W. coast of N. America from Vancouver Island to Unimak Pass, sailed through Bering Strait to edge of pack ice, ended hope of navigable passage through Arctic to Atlantic.

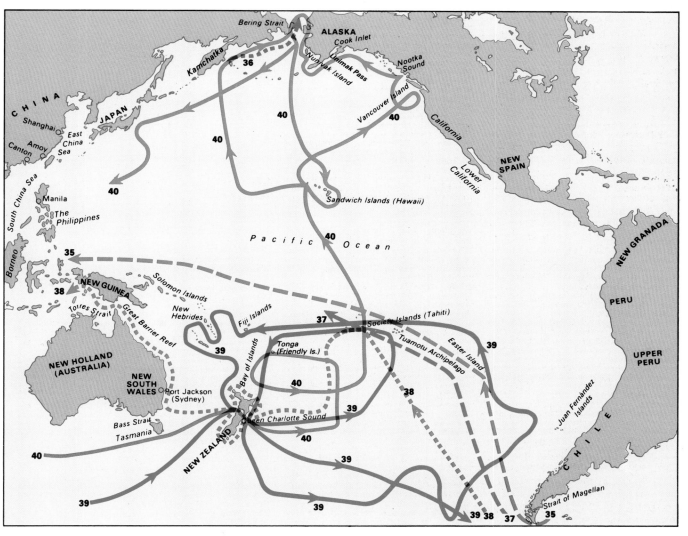

European expansion overseas: Spain and Portugal 1500 to 1600

AT the end of the 15th century Portuguese possessions outside Europe included several island groups in the Atlantic and the Gulf of Guinea, and a few trading stations on the west coast of Africa, of which the fortress-factory of Elmina was the most important. At these stations cloth and hardware were bartered for slaves and gold dust, a dozen or so ships making the voyage between Portugal and Guinea every year.

After the discovery of the sea route to India the Portuguese, in their endeavour to become suppliers of spices to Europe, quickly acquired, by capture or lease, trading posts and fortified bases on the east coast of Africa, round the northern shores of the Indian Ocean, and in the Malay archipelago. By the middle of the 16th century they had more than fifty forts and factories, in a tenuous string from Sofala to Nagasaki. Strategically the most important bases were Mozambique, on the east coast of Africa opposite Madagascar; Goa (1510) on the west coast of India, headquarters of the Portuguese governor-general in the East; Ormuz island (1515) at the mouth of the Persian Gulf, a major port of trans-shipment in the international spice trade; and Malacca (1511), also a major spice market, on the strait connecting the Indian Ocean with the shallow seas of the archipelago. All these were outright Portuguese possessions. East of Malacca, the position of the Portuguese was precarious and their activity purely commercial. Their settlement at Macao was first occupied in 1557, through the connivance or indifference of Chinese officials. From there they traded to Nagasaki, where they were welcomed as carriers of Chinese goods, since the Chinese government forbade its own subjects to trade directly with the Japanese. At Ternate they maintained a fortified warehouse, built to collect cloves produced in the Moluccas (and at that time nowhere else) but a league of Muslim princes expelled them and restored the site to the local ruler in 1575.

All these Far Eastern trades, and the trade in the gold of the Zambezi drainage through Sofala, provided means of paying for the cargoes of pepper and other spices shipped annually from Goa to Lisbon, for distribution to western Europe. The Portuguese never achieved anything like monopoly. Large quantities of pepper, carried across the Indian Ocean in Arab, Persian and Indian ships, still reached Europe through the Red Sea, Cairo and Alexandria. Portuguese attempts to control this route, by seizing Aden as a base, were unsuccessful. Nevertheless, the Portuguese were formidable enough at sea, throughout the Indian Ocean, to channel much of the trade of the area through harbours under their control, and to extort tolls or duties from the local shipping by threat of sinking or plundering those who refused to pay. If they could not fully control the trade of the Indian Ocean, the Portuguese successfully preyed upon it, and for a hundred years they had no European rivals.

The Spaniards, like the Portuguese, moved quickly to exploit their late 15th-century discoveries. The settlement of Hispaniola began in 1493, partly in the hope of finding gold, partly with the intention of developing a base for trade with China, supposedly nearby. The discovery of the Main coast opened alternative opportunities, for slaving and for acquiring pearls and gold trinkets by trade or plunder. Mainland settlement began in 1509-10, on both shores of the Gulf of

1/Iberian trade, establishments and settlement by c.1600 (below right)   In the East, the Portuguese 'empire' consisted of fortified bases and trading posts, few of them bigger than a single city and its immediate surrounding country, some of them mere warehouse compounds; by 1600 there were more than fifty such establishments. In the West, however, because of the considerable numbers of Spanish and Portuguese who emigrated to the Americas during the 16th century, they had by 1600 occupied all the areas of dense native population, had built impressive cities and towns, and had created an elaborate territorial administration centred in Europe.

3/The Spanish invasion of Peru 1531-33 (above) showing Tumbes, where Pizarro landed; Cajamarca, where Atahuallpa was seized at his first meeting with Pizarro; Jauja, the site of the first serious battle; Vilcaconga, where Soto was ambushed; and Cuzco, the Inca highland capital.

route of Francisco Pizarro's army to Cajamarca and Cuzco
route of Hernando Pizarro to Pachácamac and Jauja
× battles

Acapulco   Small, unhealthy harbour town, sheltered anchorage. Terminus of annual Manila Galleon voyages.
Aden   Major harbour at entrance to Red Sea; successfully resisted an attack by Portuguese fleet 1513.
Arequipa   Principal Spanish city of southern Peru, founded 1540 by Pizarro.
Arica   The port for Arequipa and Potosí.
Asunción   Capital of province of Paraguay; the earliest surviving Spanish settlement in Plate River drainage, founded 1535.
Bahia   Capital of Bahia province and of vice-royalty of Brazil; founded 1549.
Buenos Aires   Founded 1580 by Juan de Garay, governor of Paraguay, to provide access to the sea.
Calicut   First town in Malabar visited by Portuguese 1498.
Callao   Port for Lima.
Cartagena   Strongly fortified harbour and naval base. Founded 1533 by Pedro de Heredia.
Cochin   Portuguese *feitoria*, occupied 1502, fortified 1503. Early allied with Portuguese against Calicut.
Colombo   Portuguese *feitoria*, occupied 1517, fortified 1520. Principal centre for collection of cinnamon. 1600 Portuguese controlled most of Ceylon coast.
Cuzco   Inca capital of Peru, captured and occupied by Spaniards 1533.
Diu   Island. Portuguese *feitoria* and major base, heavily fortified; acquired 1535 by treaty with ruler of Gujerat.
Elmina   Principal Portuguese settlement on Gulf of Guinea, founded and fortified 1481. Centre for collection and shipment of Ashanti gold. By 1600 important as slave barracoon.
Goa   Administrative, commercial and spiritual headquarters of Portuguese in east.
Guadalajara   Capital of New Galicia, Spanish foundation 1531.
Guatemala   Founded 1542 by Pedro de Alvarado.
Guayaquil   Harbour for Quito region; principal ship-building centre on Pacific coast.
Havana   Assembly point for combined annual convoys for return to Spain. Good, almost land-locked harbour, heavily fortified.
Hooghly   Portuguese *feitoria*; occupied 1537, subsequently fortified; important centre for collection of Bengal silk.
Lima (Ciudad de los Reyes)   Capital of vice-royalty of Peru; Spanish city, founded 1535 by Francisco Pizarro.
Luanda   Principal centre for export of slaves from Angola to Brazil, founded 1576.

Macao   Portuguese town and *feitoria*, established c. 1557 with tacit permission of local Chinese authorities. Unfortified. Collection centre for Chinese silk.
Malacca   Portuguese *feitoria*; captured and occupied 1511; fortified; principal centre of spice trade.
Malindi   First Swahili town to welcome Portuguese (1498).
Manila   Spanish town and fortress in Luzon, Philippines. Founded 1571; by 1600 a major commercial harbour and administrative centre. Connected by annual sailings with Acapulco, with silver westbound, silk eastbound.
Mérida   Spanish capital of province of Yucatán, founded 1542 by Francisco de Montejo on site of antecedent Maya town.
Mombasa   Island; Portuguese *feitoria* occupied 1505; before and after occupation a major trading centre; persistently resisted Portuguese: sacked 1505, 1529, 1587. Major fortress (Fort Jesus) constructed 1593-95.
Mozambique   Major Portuguese base, occupied 1507; port of call for outbound fleets of *Carreira da India*.
Nagasaki   Only Japanese port where Portuguese had permission to trade.
Nombre de Dios   Shanty town on north coast of Isthmus of Panama, important as terminus of convoys from Spain and as starting point of portage to Panama.
Olinda   Capital of Pernambuco province, founded c. 1535. Recife, the port for Olinda, was already in 1600 a larger town.
Ormuz   Portuguese *feitoria*, and major strategic base, occupied 1515. A major market and port of trans-shipment in spice trade.
Potosí   Principal silver mining centre of vice-royalty of Peru; silver discovered 1545; in 1600 probably the biggest concentration of Europeans in the Americas.
Puebla   Prosperous Spanish city, founded 1532, by 1600 important for provisioning convoys returning from Vera Cruz to Seville.
Quito   Indian city occupied by Benalcázar 1533; Spanish city incorporated 1541.
Saltillo   Capital of province of Nuevo León; Spanish foundation 1586; cattle town.
San Agostín   Small, isolated fortress on south-east coast of Florida, founded 1565 to cover passage of convoys through Straits.
San Juan del Puerto Rico   Windward defence of Spanish Caribbean and of trans-Atlantic convoys. Immense fortifications were planned and started by Antoneli in 1591.
Santa Fe de Bogotá   Province capital New Granada; founded 1538.

Santa Marta   Prosperous port and base for hinterland expeditions. Founded 1525.
Santiago   Capital of captaincy-general of Chile. Founded 1541 by Pedro de Valdivia.
Santo Domingo   Founded 1496 by Bartholomew Columbus; capital of Hispaniola, administrative centre for Spanish Caribbean.
São Tomé   Portuguese island plantation; important source of sugar and of provisions.
Sofala   Portuguese *feitoria*, occupied 1505; port of outlet for gold of Zambezi drainage (Monomatapa) mostly shipped to Mozambique, thence to Goa.
Spice Islands (Moluccas)   Portuguese *feitorias* with light fortification in Ternate (1513) Tidore . (1529), Amboina and the Banda islands; collection centres for cloves, nutmeg and mace; all still occupied with local permission in 1600, except Ternate from which the Portuguese were expelled in 1575.
Tenochtitlán   Capital of vice-royalty of New Spain. Large Spanish and Indian city, captured 1521.
Timor   Portuguese *feitoria*, in 1600 administrative centre, and collection centre for sandalwood destined for sale in China.
Veracruz   Most important harbour on Gulf of Mexico. Terminus of annual convoys from Spain; founded by Cortés 1519.
Zacatecas   Principal silver mining centre, Spanish foundation 1546.

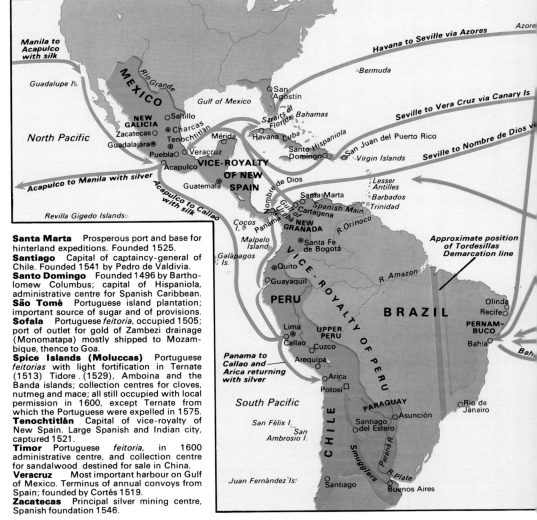

Urabá and along the Isthmus coast. Panama, the first Pacific settlement, was established in 1519. In the 1520s the news of Cortés' conquest of central Mexico, and descriptions of the elaborate culture and dense population he encountered there, attracted a rush of emigrants to Mexico both from Spain and from the islands. A similar rush followed the conquests of Pizarro in Inca Peru in the early 1530s, though Peru was less accessible than Mexico and could be reached only by trans-shipment and a troublesome portage across the Isthmus of Panama. Hispaniola had been the base for the settlement of central America, Cuba for that of Mexico, Panama for that of Peru; each in turn was to some extent depopulated by emigration to the new conquests. Mexico and Peru became the chief centres of Spanish population in the New World, initially because they were, before the Spaniards arrived, the chief centres of settled, organised native population; and subsequently because they were the areas where precious metals were chiefly found. None of the other major conquests – Guatemala (1523-42), New Granada (1536-39) or central Chile (1540-58) – compared with them in either respect. Their pre-eminence was recognised: a vice-regal administration was formally established in Mexico in 1535. Administrative organisation in Peru was delayed by faction among the conquerors, but there too vice-regal government was firmly established by the middle of the century.

Spanish population in the New World was largely concentrated in towns and initially wholly parasitic upon Indian society; but Spaniards soon developed characteristic economic activities, chiefly ranching and mining, employing Indian labour. Immensely productive silver mines were discovered, both in Mexico and in Peru, in the 1540s. Potosí in Upper Peru became, and for a hundred years remained, the biggest single source of silver in the world. By the 1560s silver had become the chief export to Spain, with cochineal, hides, tallow, and sugar a long way behind. These immensely valuable shipments necessitated, from 1564, a rigid system of trans-Atlantic convoys, escorted by warships, and later in the century heavy fortification of principal harbours and strategic points: Cartagena, Veracruz, Havana, San Juan del Puerto Rico. From 1564 also, Spaniards established themselves in Cebu and Luzon in the Philippines, and large quantities of silver began to be shipped annually from Mexico to Manila, chiefly to purchase Chinese silk, of which some was used in Mexico, some re-exported to Peru, and some even, after portage across Mexico, carried to Spain.

At the end of the 16th century the whole vast, cumbersome empire was at the height of its power and prosperity. French, English and latterly Dutch raids harassed its harbours, its shipping and its colonial outposts; but none had yet succeeded in causing major damage.

The line of demarcation established by the Treaty of Tordesillas in 1494, though its precise position could not be determined, clearly excluded Spaniards from a great area in eastern South America. The Portuguese did nothing to settle Brazil until the 1530s, when they were impelled to it by fear of being forestalled by the French. Bahia was founded as an administrative capital in 1549; the first slave-worked sugar plantations and mills, on a pattern already familiar in São Tomé in the Gulf of Guinea, were established shortly afterwards. Between 1575 and 1600 coastal Brazil became the foremost sugar-producing territory in the western world, and attracted many land-hungry emigrants from Portugal and the Azores. The Brazilian demand for slave labour gave new importance to the Portuguese trading stations in West Africa, where the gold trade had dwindled as the gold became exhausted, and caused the Portuguese slavers to extend their operations from Guinea south to Angola. The Portuguese town and barracoon of Luanda was founded in 1575. Slave ships shuttled directly between Angola and Brazil, since the slaves were paid for in low-grade tobacco grown in Brazil. Any surplus of slaves could easily be disposed of in Spanish America, as the Spaniards had no direct access to the source of slaves, and were able to pay in silver; and because from 1580 Spain and Portugal were united under a common crown. Thus the Iberian crown in those years ruled not one overseas empire, but three: the silver empire of Spanish America, the spice empire of the Indian Ocean, and the sugar empire of the South Atlantic. No other European group had achieved anything permanent in the field of overseas settlement.

2/The Spanish invasion of Mexico 1519-20 *(above and left)* showing old Vera Cruz, the first Spanish 'city'; Cempoala, whose ruler was encouraged by Cortés in revolt against the Mexica; Tlaxcala, home of Cortés' principal allies; and Tenochtitlán, capital of the Mexica, on its island in Lake Texcoco.

Aztec ceremonial shield *(above)* with feather design on a woven fibre backing. Such mosaics, often incorporating thousands of feathers, were cherished works of art in ancient Mexico. Few now survive. This example was sent, with other loot, to Charles V by Cortés in 1520. The coyote was the personal emblem of the war chief Ahuitzotl, Moctezuma's predecessor. The shield is now in the Museum für Völkerkunde, Vienna.

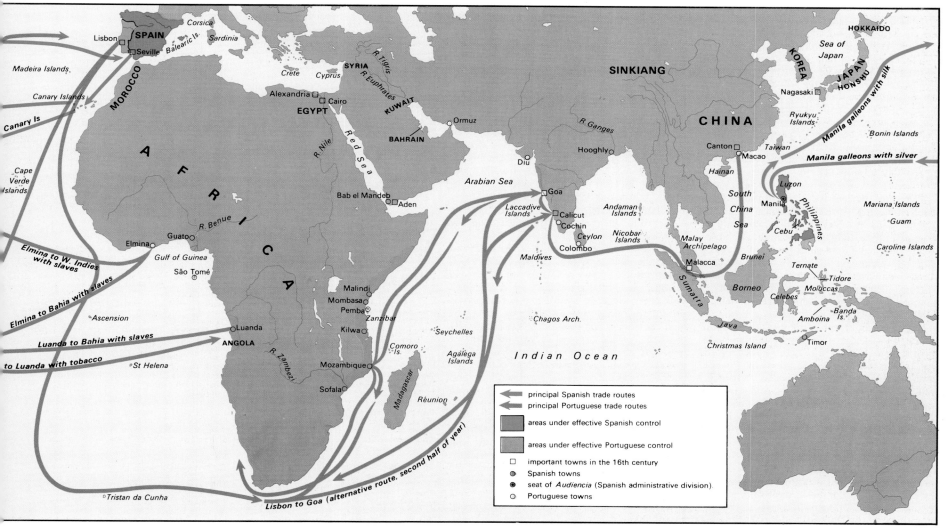

principal Spanish trade routes
principal Portuguese trade routes
areas under effective Spanish control
areas under effective Portuguese control
important towns in the 16th century
Spanish towns
seat of *Audiencia* (Spanish administrative division)
Portuguese towns

European expansion overseas: Holland, Britain and France 1600 to 1713

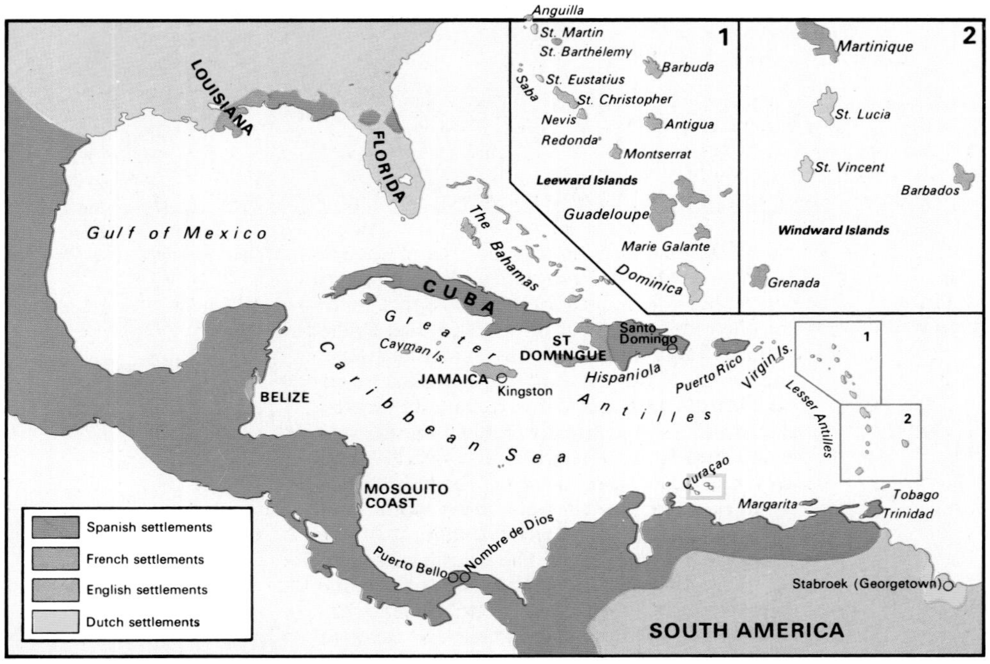

3/European settlement in the West Indies *(above)* Sugar was the most profitable of all the exotic products imported into Europe in early modern times. From the middle of the 17th century until after the end of the 18th, sugar-producing islands in the West Indies were considered by Europeans the most desirable of all overseas possessions.

Bahamas English from 1670 (Treaty of Madrid).
Belize Acknowledged as Spanish territory, but occupied c. 1660 by English logwood cutters.
Curaçao Captured from Spaniards by Dutch, 1634, formally ceded 1648 (Treaty of Münster).
Jamaica Captured from Spain by English 1655. Formally ceded 1670 (Treaty of Madrid).
Leeward Islands Anguilla (1650), Barbuda (1628), Antigua (1632) and Nevis (1628) were continuously English from first settlement. Monserrat (1632), taken by French in 1664, restored in 1668. St Christopher, shared by English and French settlers, 1625-1713, wholly English in Treaty of Utrecht. St Barthélemy, Guadeloupe and Marie Galante, French from first settlement (1648, 1635, 1648). St Eustatius (1632), Saba (1640) and St Martin (1648) confirmed to the Netherlands in 1648 (Treaty of Münster), though subsequently changed hands several times. Dominica, claimed by both England and France, inhabited only by Caribs in 1713.
Mosquito Coast English alliance with local Indians; a few English settlers; claimed by Spain.
Saint-Domingue Evacuated by Spaniards c. 1605; occupied by French buccaneers; formally ceded to France 1697 (Treaty of Ryswick).
Tobago French from 1677.
Virgin Islands Tortola English from 1666; St Thomas Danish from 1671.
Windward Islands Martinique continuously French since first settlement (1635); Grenada claimed by France 1650, in 1713 had a few French settlers; St Lucia and St Vincent, disputed between England and France, inhabited in 1713 only by Caribs.

In the early 17th century northern Europeans, already experienced in Caribbean smuggling, in raids on Spanish shipping and minor harbours, and in attempts, occasionally successful, on returning Portuguese Indiamen, began to establish permanent colonies of their own in the Americas and to develop eastern trades on their own account. In competing with the traditional Iberian enemy in these fields of activity, they possessed important advantages: fewer political commitments and less dispersed interests in Europe; easier access to sources of ship-building material, especially in the Baltic; thus, cheaper ships and, increasingly as the century progressed, more and better ships; a more strictly commercial attitude towards overseas endeavour; and more sophisticated devices for concentrating investment capital and spreading financial risk. The organisation which they used most commonly for distant trade or settlement, or both combined, was the chartered joint-stock company, a device earlier developed on a limited scale in northern Italy, but virtually unknown in Spain and Portugal. The companies might be empowered to trade, settle, conquer, administer and defend.

In the East, the most formidable European group throughout the 17th century was the Dutch East India Company, first formally incorporated in 1602. In 1619 this huge concern, the biggest trading corporation in Europe, established its eastern headquarters at Batavia, well to windward of Malacca and Goa, so acquiring a permanent strategic advantage. Its captains pioneered a direct route to Batavia, provisioning (after 1652) at the new Dutch settlement at the Cape, then running east before the prevailing wind in the forties of south latitude, and entering the archipelago by way of the Sunda Strait. The company never became in the 17th century – nor did its directors wish it to become – a major territorial power; but by acquiring bases in strategic locations, by bringing pressure on local rulers, and by squeezing other Europeans out, it established a monopoly of the more valuable trades of the archipelago. Elsewhere in the East it traded, as all Europeans did, in competition with other merchants, native and European, on terms laid down by Asian rulers; but throughout the 17th century it held its own against all European rivals.

The English East India Company, incorporated in 1600, was a somewhat smaller concern, rarely able to resist Dutch pressure in the archipelago, principally engaged in trade in cotton goods and pepper from India, first at the Mughal port of Surat, subsequently at stations of its own at Madras, Bombay and Calcutta. In 1685 it began a modest trade to China, purchasing tea and porcelain at Amoy, and later at Canton, where from 1698 its factors found themselves in competition with the French *Compagnie de Chine*.

As a result of the commercial competition and naval aggression of these corporations, which continued irrespective of formal war or peace in Europe, the Portuguese *Estado da India* shrank both in territorial possession and in commercial profit; and many native trades, by sea or by land caravan, which the Portuguese had hardly touched – or had touched only to the extent of levying tolls – also began to dry up. The Red Sea and the Persian Gulf both became commercial backwaters as the companies gathered more and more of the trade between Europe and Asia into their own capacious, well-armed ships.

In America the Portuguese fared better. The Dutch West India Company – less well entrenched than its eastern counterpart, but formidable nonetheless – conquered Pernambuco in 1630 and in the next few years seized the Portuguese slaving stations in West Africa, without which the Brazilian plantations were unworkable; but in the 1640s the Portuguese, having made themselves independent of Spain, recovered the Angola barracoons, and in 1654 they drove the Dutch from Brazil. The West India Company turned to the West Indies, though many Dutch private merchants continued its trade, and much Brazilian sugar continued to flow through Amsterdam. Brazil, however, was not wholly dependent on sugar; in the 1690s a series of gold strikes in Minas Gerais made it a principal supplier of gold as well.

For Spaniards the 17th century was a period of industrial, commercial and financial debility, of faltering government and of repeated military defeat. The weight of misfortune fell much more heavily on Spain itself than upon the Spanish Indies, which remained relatively prosperous and – outside the Caribbean sea lanes – relatively peaceful. In the 1620s and 1630s a powerful offensive by the Dutch West India Company against Spanish shipping in the Caribbean interrupted the flow of silver to Spain and provided a screen for English and French settlements in unoccupied islands in the Lesser Antilles. These settlements in a few decades became prosperous sugar plantations, using Brazilian methods, employing African slave labour, and initially selling their crop to Dutch carriers. In the second half of the century, buccaneering raids, often undertaken with the connivance of French and English colonial governors, caused much damage to minor Spanish harbours, and some islands actually in Spanish possession changed hands. By the end of the century, a long string of modest but growing colonies, English, French and Dutch, stretched intermittently along the American seaboard from Barbados to Quebec. Many of them, the sugar islands especially, had themselves become objects of contention between the metropolitan governments. Every major European war was reflected by fighting in the Americas. The treaties of Münster (1648), Breda (1667), Nijmegen (1678), Ryswick (1697) and Utrecht (1713) all included cessions of American territory. Mainland colonies were less esteemed by governments and by orthodox economists in France and England

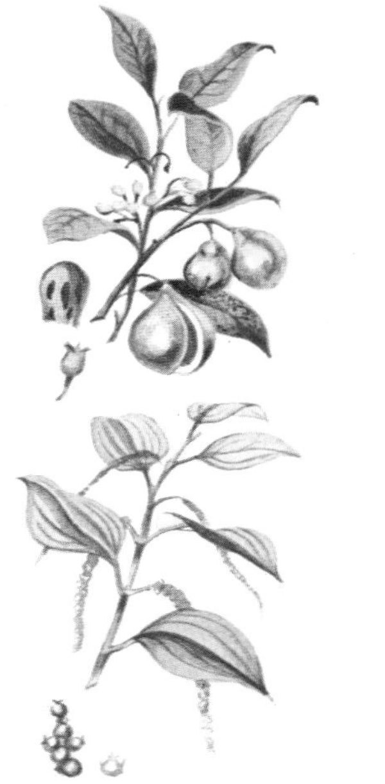

The importance of spices *(above)* In northern Europe, before the development of winter feed for cattle in the late 17th century, many beasts had to be slaughtered every autumn and the meat preserved for winter eating. Hence the eager demand for spices, both as condiments and as preservatives, and the large profits to be made by importing them to Europe. Of the most important spices, pepper *(above)* grew in many places in southern Asia; cinnamon was virtually confined to Ceylon, cloves to the Moluccas and nutmeg *(top)* to Amboina and the Banda Islands. In the 16th century, the Indian Ocean trade in these commodities had been shared between Malay, Indian, Persian, Arab and Portuguese merchants. In the course of the 17th century the Dutch East India Company, by a combination of force and diplomacy, seized control of the sources of the most valuable spices, and established a virtual monopoly of their shipment to Europe.

1/Commercial expansion to the East *(below right)* During the 17th century northern European commercial companies – Dutch, French, English and others – established trading stations throughout the East. The Portuguese lost much of their former trade and some territory; and the overland caravan trade between Europe and Asia almost disappeared.

Achin Early visited by Europeans (Dutch 1577, English 1602, French 1623) but resisted European penetration. Important commercial harbour and source of gold, but decayed by 1713.
Amoy First Chinese port visited by English traders, 1685.
Bassein (Baçain) Economic capital of Portuguese Province of the North. Still prosperous in 1713.
Bandar Abbas (Gombroon) Successor to Persian trade of Ormuz. Dutch and English East India Companies maintained factories there.
Bantam Dutch factory established 1598, English 1602; Dutch expelled English 1682, reduced sultan to vassalage 1683.
Batavia Eastern headquarters of Dutch East India Co., established 1619 on site of small town of Jakarta, acquired by conquest from Bantam.
Bombay Principal English station in western India, acquired by treaty from Portuguese 1660. Fortified.
Calcutta Principal English station in Bengal, founded 1690 on uninhabited site, after English withdrawal from Hooghly; fortified.
Canton Principal Chinese harbour in which (after 1684) Europeans were allowed to trade. All the East India Companies maintained factories there.
Cape of Good Hope Settlement begun by Dutch East India Co. 1652; victualling station for its ships.
Chandernagore Principal French station in Bengal; acquired 1688; in 1713 still very small.
Chinsura Principal Dutch station in Bengal, acquired 1656 after Dutch withdrawal from Hooghly.
Cochin Principal harbour of Malabar. Taken by Dutch from Portuguese 1663.
Colombo Principal harbour of Ceylon. Taken by Dutch from Portuguese 1656.
Macao Portuguese settlement. After loss of Malacca to Dutch, Macao merchants altered business, becoming chief suppliers of silk to Manila for export in the galleons.
Macassar Taken by Dutch fleet 1669; sultan remained as Dutch vassal.
Madras Principal English station on Coromandel coast; occupied 1640 by treaty with local ruler; successor to Masulipatam (occupied 1611); fortified.
Malacca Taken from Portuguese by Dutch with Achinese help, 1641.
Manila Only significant Spanish harbour in the East, terminus of Acapulco-Manila galleons and administrative centre of Spanish Philippines.
Mocha Harbour for Beit el Fakih, marketing centre for Arabian coffee.
Mombasa Major harbour; Portuguese defeated and expelled by forces of Imam of Oman, 1698 (see page 158).
Mozambique Portuguese town and factory; repelled Dutch attempts at conquest in early 17th century.
Nagasaki Only Japanese port in which Europeans were allowed to trade; privilege restricted to Dutch East India Co. from 1639.
Negapatam Principal Dutch station on Coromandel Coast, taken from Portuguese by Dutch 1660.
Ormuz Portuguese expelled by Shah Abbas with help of English fleet, 1622. In 1713 almost deserted.
Pondicherry Principal French station in India, occupied 1683 by treaty with local ruler.
Spice Islands (Moluccas, Amboina, Banda Islands) Dutch East India Co. held some islands, having expelled Portuguese early in 17th century, and monopolised spice trade in all.
Surat Major harbour of Mughal Empire. All East India Companies had factories there.
Tellicherry Principal English station on Malabar coast; small fortified factory, outside native town, built 1683. Centre for collection of pepper.
Tenasserim Disputed territory between Ayutthaya (Siam) and Pegu (Burma), with several good harbours and busy trade.
Zanzibar Portuguese island, town and factory.
Zeelandia Dutch factory in Formosa, operated from 1624 to 1683, when island occupied by Ming forces and Dutch expelled.

than were the islands. Colbert was almost alone among leading statesmen in actively encouraging North American settlement, by making *seigneuries* conditional on occupation, by granting land, on the St Lawrence river and elsewhere, to demobilised soldiers, by assisting passages and providing tools, seed and stock. As a result of his efforts the population of New France, though never more than a tenth of that of the English colonies, was militarily very formidable. Nova Scotia (Acadia) in French hands was considered a serious threat to New England; it was the object of repeated attack and counter-attack, especially during King William's War and the War of the Spanish Succession; even after its annexation in 1713 the English hold on it was precarious. The chain of French trade forts on the Great Lakes and in the Ohio-Mississippi valleys, because it threatened to block westward expansion, alarmed the English colonists and their metropolitan government. The emergence of French explorers on the shore of the Gulf of Mexico in 1682 caused grave concern in Spain.

The major Spanish colonies, however, despite widespread foreign smuggling and occasional interruption of communications, were never seriously threatened. They owed their safety partly to their inaccessibility, partly to their own capacity for resistance, partly to increasing fear of French domination which towards the end of the century caused both English and Dutch to seek insurance by accommodation with Spain.

This re-grouping of colonial forces was frustrated by the extinction of the Spanish Habsburg dynasty and its bequest to France, which included the most extensive, most populous and most productive of the European colonial empires, an empire whose subjects bitterly opposed any scheme of dismemberment. The War of the Spanish Succession arose from the insistence of the Austrian, Dutch and English governments upon a partition, in order to prevent the whole empire falling under French control. Twelve years of destructive war produced, in Europe, a limited success for the allies, and in America, a number of territorial gains and commercial concessions for England. The Treaty of Utrecht of 1713 embodied these changes, and established a pattern of colonial territories which was to survive intact for a generation or more.

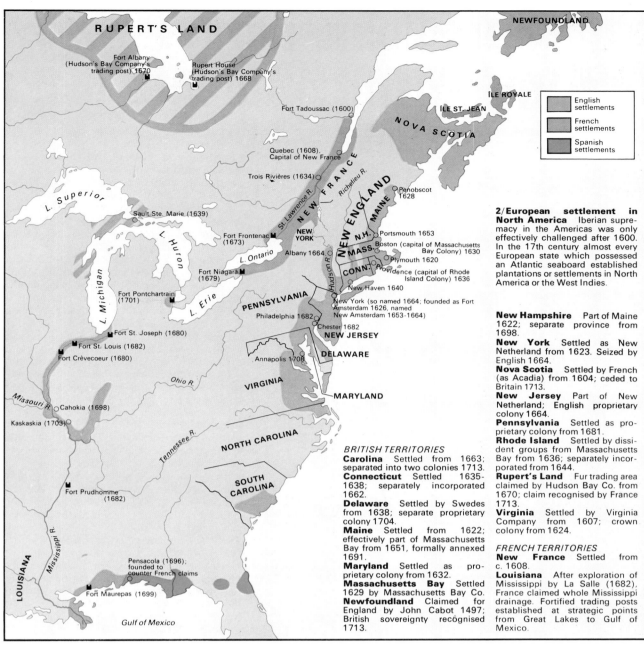

English settlements
French settlements
Spanish settlements

2/European settlement in North America Iberian supremacy in the Americas was only effectively challenged after 1600. In the 17th century almost every European state which possessed an Atlantic seaboard established plantations or settlements in North America or the West Indies.

New Hampshire Part of Maine 1622; separate province from 1698.
New York Settled as New Netherland from 1623. Seized by English 1664.
Nova Scotia Settled by French (as Acadia) from 1604; ceded to Britain 1713.
New Jersey Part of New Netherland; English proprietary colony 1664.
Pennsylvania Settled as proprietary colony from 1681.
Rhode Island Settled by dissident groups from Massachusetts Bay from 1636; separately incorporated from 1644.
Rupert's Land Fur trading area claimed by Hudson Bay Co. from 1670; claim recognised by France 1713.
Virginia Settled by Virginia Company from 1607; crown colony from 1624.

FRENCH TERRITORIES
New France Settled from c. 1608.
Louisiana After exploration of Mississippi by La Salle (1682), France claimed whole Mississippi drainage. Fortified trading posts established at strategic points from Great Lakes to Gulf of Mexico.

BRITISH TERRITORIES
Carolina Settled from 1663; separated into two colonies 1713.
Connecticut Settled 1635-1638; separately incorporated 1662.
Delaware Settled by Swedes from 1638; separate proprietary colony 1704.
Maine Settled from 1622; effectively part of Massachusetts Bay from 1651, formally annexed 1691.
Maryland Settled as proprietary colony from 1632.
Massachusetts Bay Settled 1629 by Massachusetts Bay Co.
Newfoundland Claimed for England by John Cabot 1497; British sovereignty recognised 1713.

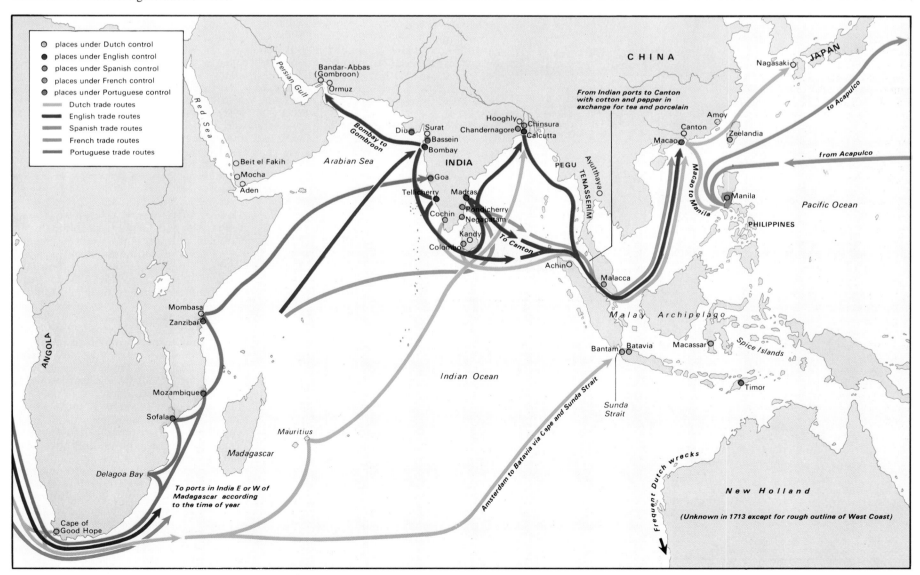

places under Dutch control
places under English control
places under Spanish control
places under French control
places under Portuguese control
Dutch trade routes
English trade routes
Spanish trade routes
French trade routes
Portuguese trade routes

Russian expansion in Europe and Asia 1462 to 1815

2/Economic activity in 1600, 1725, 1815 *(above)* By 1600 industry had concentrated in and around Moscow consisting mainly of the processing of animal and vegetable products. By 1725, thanks to Peter the Great's initiative, the extensive smelting of copper and iron was established in the Urals. By 1815 a third industrial area had arisen around St Petersburg.

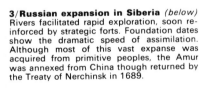

3/Russian expansion in Siberia *(below)* Rivers facilitated rapid exploration, soon reinforced by strategic forts. Foundation dates show the dramatic speed of assimilation. Although most of this vast expanse was acquired from primitive peoples, the Amur was annexed from China though returned by the Treaty of Nerchinsk in 1689.

Master and serfs *(above)* From 1497 to 1861 Russian peasants were tied to the land. Initially they had two weeks of free movement each November. This was withdrawn under Godunov (1593). A 1648 decree then removed all limits to forcible reclamation of runaway serfs.

THE state created by the Grand Princes of Moscow in the north-eastern part of the Russian territory and known as Muscovy was destined not only to recover the lands lost to Swede, Pole, German, Lithuanian, Tartar and Turk in the west and south, but also to expand across the whole of northern Asia. The most noteworthy aspect of this state's international position in 1462 was its extraordinary degree of isolation: it was cut off from almost all contact with the outside world by the hostility of its immediate neighbours. In particular it was unable to share in the scientific and cultural advances of Europe and became relatively more and more backward. But by 1815 Russia had become a powerful participant in the European political system.

After the Mongol invasions of the 13th century, the Russian lands formerly ruled from Kiev were split into eastern and western parts. The east became subject to Mongol overlordship, under the shadow of which the principality of Moscow rose to dominate its neighbours and eventually to throw off the Tartar yoke. The west formed the major part of the Lithuanian kingdom and was afterwards absorbed by Poland.

The growing power of Muscovy, which finally gained its independence from the Mongols under Ivan III in 1480, was at first exerted in the east and south-east. Novgorod had already been subjugated in 1478 and Pskov soon followed. The Russian conquest of the khanate of Kazan (1552) opened the way to advance across the Urals and into Siberia; the conquest of the khanate of Astrakhan (1556) gave the control of the Volga all the way to the Caspian Sea. But there were substantial setbacks. Under Ivan IV (the Terrible) the debilitating Livonian Wars dragged on inconclusively for twenty-five years on the Polish and Swedish frontiers, and in 1571 Moscow itself was sacked by an invading force of Crimean Tartars.

It was the lucrative fur trade that tempted enterprising Russians deeper and deeper into Siberia, until the Pacific coast was reached (1639) and the Russian hold established over the whole of northern Asia. The opening of the Volga route led to the rapid growth of the silk trade with Persia.

In 1613, after the 'time of troubles' that followed the deaths of Ivan the Terrible and Boris Godunov, Michael, the first of the long-lasting Romanov dynasty, was elected Tsar. During the remainder of the 17th century the Muscovites turned their attention to the recovery of West Russia from Poland, and although there were initial losses caused by the internal chaos and disunity of the earlier years, substantial gains were made between 1640 and 1686: Kiev and the middle Dnieper lands were acquired. In the Ukraine the Cossacks of the lower Dnieper transferred their allegiance from Poland to Muscovy in 1654, and their territory, known as Zaporozh'ye, was henceforth claimed by the Russians.

During the late 16th and 17th centuries Russian colonisation spread southwards across the Oka and Ukrainians migrated eastwards from Poland into the forest-steppe zone. Many towns in the zone began their existence as frontier outposts at this time, e.g. Orel (1564), Voronezh (1586), Kursk (1586).

Isolation remained Russia's problem. There was great potential demand for the products of the Russian forest among the maritime powers of the west, but Muscovy could not profit from this because hostile Swedes, Poles and Turks blocked oversea and overland communication with Europe. British merchants had opened up the difficult northern route to the White Sea and Ivan IV founded the port of Archangel in 1584, but this outlet for Russian produce was available only during the brief summer season. Peter I made it his chief task to break through to the Baltic, wresting Livonia and Estonia from Sweden, thus acquiring the ancient port of Riga and founding the new one of St Petersburg (1703). What was done by Peter I for the Baltic was achieved in the south under Catherine II. Fiercely fought wars (1768-1792) led to the final destruction of the Tartar khanate in the Crimea and the substitution of Russian for Turkish control along the north shores of the Black Sea, in the Crimean Peninsula, around the Sea of Azov, and across the adjoining steppes. Odessa, founded in 1794, rapidly became for the Black Sea what Archangel had been for the White Sea and St Petersburg for the Baltic – the main outlet for Russian exports.

The period from 1772 to 1815 saw the Russian land frontier advanced 600 miles at the expense of Poland. By the partitions of 1772, 1793 and 1795 Russia obtained much of the former Polish state, and after the interlude of Napoleon's Grand Duchy of Warsaw, the Congress of Vienna agreed to the Tsar becoming king of a reconstituted Polish kingdom.

Economic growth was rapid during the 18th century. The wars fought to gain access to the Baltic and Black Seas and to push the frontiers of the Empire westwards into Poland required a large armaments industry and a correspondingly productive metallurgical base. This was established by Peter I, mainly in the Urals, which abounded in iron and copper ores and were clad in extensive forests suitable for charcoal making. Peter I founded factories, gave investment incentives, encouraged new management, and established a form of industrial serfdom. The textile and animal fat industries of central Russia continued to grow, and a new industrial centre arose at St Petersburg.

The population of the empire was swollen both by territorial acquisition and by prolific natural increase. The total for East Russia or Muscovy is estimated at 10 million for 1600, and 15.5 million for 1725. The census of 1811-12 gave the greatly enlarged Russian empire a population of 42.75 million; in this total were included many peoples of diverse origin, both European and Asian. The population of Siberia had grown from about half a million in 1720 to nearly 1,400,000 in 1811. Only 4 per cent of the total population was urban, of which a third lived in St Petersburg and Moscow.

the expansion of Muscovy

- boundary of Russian territories in 1462
- boundary of Lithuania in 1462

Moscow territory at end of 13th century
1478 date of acquisition by Muscovy
acquisitions to 1462
acquisitions under Ivan III 1462-1505
acquisitions during 16th century (1505-86)
acquisitions during 17th century
acquisitions during 18th century
acquisitions 1801-15
territory ceded to Sweden 1617 and Poland 1618
recovered from Poland 1634
recovered from Poland 1667
area affected by Pugachev uprising 1773-74
route of Pugachev rebels
Orel 1564 date of foundation of new town

Barents Sea

Kola Peninsula

R. Pechora

Obdorsk 1595

PECHORA

R. Mezen

R. Pechora

White Sea

1478

Berezov 1593

1501

YUGRA

Archangel 1584
Kholmogory

NOVGOROD   TERRITORY

R. Onega

Kargopol *1478*

Solvychegodsk
Ustyug

R. Vychegda

R. Sukhona

1472

R. Kama

Solikamsk

FINLAND
1809

L. Onega

1478

1478

1393-1425

Nizhniy Tagil 1724

Åland Is.

1743 *1721*
Vyborg

L. Ladoga

Kronstadt 1704

Gulf of Finland

Narva

St Petersburg 1703

1362-89

Vologda

1393-1425

Soligalich

1364
Galich

Vyatka

R. Vyatka

Perm 1724

Kungur

Yekaterinburg
1725

ESTONIA
1721

1478 Novgorod

L. Ilmen

1389-1425

1364

Kostroma

Yaroslavl

1489

MARI

SIBERIA

*Baltic
Sea*

LIVONIA
Pskov

1510

R. Lovat

R. Volga

1302

1364

1451

Nizhniy Novgorod

**KHANATE
OF
KAZAN**

Kazan

R. Belaya

Ufa 1586

BASHKIRS

Riga

1772

Western Dvina

1503
Velikiye Luki

1389-1425

Tver

Dmitrov

Vladimir

1364 *1393-1425*

Murom

Arzamas

CHUVASHI
1552

Simbirsk 1648

COURLAND

LITHUANIA

Memel

R. Niemen

Kovno

Vilna

1514-21
Polotsk
Vitebsk
Smolensk

1494
Vyazma

Mozhaysk

Moscow
1301

1364
1393

MESHCHERA

1393

MORDVA

Penza 1650

R. Sura

Samara 1586

Syzran 1683

R. Volga

Grodno

Minsk

Mogilev

1772

1634

Serpukhov

Kaluga

1353-59

1425-62
Tula

Ryazan

1521

Tambov 1636

R. Khoper

Saratov
1590

**NOGAI
TARTARS**

R. Ural

1807

POLAND
1815

Warsaw

Kalish

R. Vistula

1795

Pinsk

1793

R. Pripet

Lublin

1772

Bryansk
Orel 1564

1503
Gomel

Chernigov

R. Desna

R. Seym

Kursk
1586

1503

1634

Yelets
1592

Voronezh 1586

Belgorod 1593

R. Don

1589
Tsaritsyn

Kamyshin

**KHANATE OF
ASTRAKHAN**
1556

KALMYKS

Guryev 1645

*Caspian
Sea*

Lvov

Novograd-
Volynskiy

1793

Kiev

Pereyaslavl

1667

Kharkov 1654

Poltava

Kamenets

R. Dniester

R. Prut

Bratslav

ZAPOROZH'YE

Yekaterinoslav
(Kodak)
1786

Sech

R. Dnieper

R. Donets

**DON
COSSACKS**
1739

R. Don

KALMYKS

Astrakhan

MOLDAVIA

Kishinev

1791
Ochakov

Nikolayev 1789

1774

Kherson 1774

1783

Taganrog

Azov

1783

**KUBAN
COSSACKS**

Yekaterinodar
1792

Stavropol

R. Kuma

OTTOMAN EMPIRE

Odessa 1794

1812

R. Danube

Akkerman

**KHANATE OF
CRIMEA**

Yevpatoriya

Karasubazar

Bakhchisaray

Simferopol
(Ak-Mechet) 1784

Sevastopol 1783

Kerch

Feodosiya (Kaffa)

Sea of Azov

Black Sea

Sukhum-Kale

Poti

1810

1804

1801

Kutaisi

GEORGIA

Tiflis

1806

Vladikavkaz

R. Terek

Pyatigorsk

1784

DAGHESTAN

Derbent

1806

1805

R. Kura

AZERBAIJAN

Baku

1813

ceded temporarily by Persia 1723-32

1/The evolution and expansion of Muscovy
(above) This map portrays the division of Russia after the Mongol conquest, into West Russia or Lithuania, and East Russia. It shows how East Russia, as a result of the increasing preponderance of Moscow, came to be known as Muscovy. Finally, it demonstrates the expansion of Muscovy in all directions: westwards, to absorb Lithuania and much of Poland; eastwards into Siberia; south-eastwards to the Caspian Sea; southwards to the Black Sea; and north-westwards to the Baltic Sea and into Finland.

Map1

Map2

Map3

Colonial America
1535 to 1783

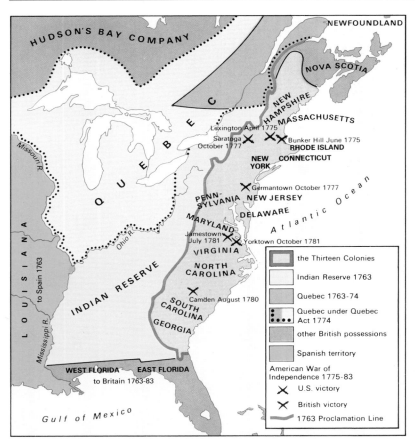

3/British North America *(above)* With the Capitulations of Montreal, 1760, France abandoned her vast American territories to Britain. But the resulting Proclamation of 1763, failing either to halt encroachment on Indian land or to impose acceptable rule, helped to trigger the American Revolution. By 1783 the original Thirteen Colonies had decisively established themselves as the new United States.

the Thirteen Colonies

Indian Reserve 1763

Quebec 1763-74

Quebec under Quebec Act 1774

other British possessions

Spanish territory

American War of Independence 1775-83

U.S. victory

British victory

1763 Proclamation Line

A rich inhabitant *(below)* of Bahia, the capital of colonial Brazil until the mid-18th century, being carried in a litter by Negro slaves.

THE foundation of the city of Lima, capital of Peru, in 1535 marked the end of the first, dramatic phase of colonisation in America. The task of pushing forward frontiers into unexplored territory was to continue, however, throughout the colonial period.

Until the 17th century the initiative lay primarily with the Iberian nations. Spain rapidly built up an impressive presence in America on the basis of the silver mines of Peru and New Spain, although her settlers showed less interest in territory which contained neither civilised Indians nor precious metals, a factor which allowed Portuguese adventurers to extend the frontiers of Brazil well beyond the line established at Tordesillas in 1494. Portugal, in her turn, faced threats to her authority from the French and the Dutch. Determined defensive measures ultimately succeeded, however, in pushing these intruders away from northern Brazil to the less important Guiana region. By the mid-17th century the maritime nations of northern Europe had adopted the new strategy of seizing Spanish islands in the Caribbean – thus providing themselves with bases for buccaneering and contraband trade, and eventually with the means of producing their own sugar and tobacco. This competition harmed Brazil's economy, but the damage was more than balanced by rich gold and diamond strikes in the early 18th century. Despite the stagnation of her imperial economy, Habsburg Spain succeeded in defending the territorial integrity of her major American possessions and in the 18th century a more positive strategic and commercial policy led her to create two new viceroyalties – New Granada (1739) and Rio de la Plata (1776) – and to liberalise trade.

In North America, too, Spain adopted a more vigorous policy in this period. As her miners, soldiers and priests gradually moved further into the savage, semi-desert lands of the American south-west, new military governments were organised: in Texas (1718), Sinaloa (1734), New Santander (1746) and California (1767). By then Spanish authority extended as far east as the Mississippi, and northward to Monterrey and San Francisco, halting only where it came face to face with the Russians, now probing south from Alaska along the Pacific coast.

Meanwhile the French, whose first explorers, like Cartier, had already penetrated far up the St Lawrence river by 1535, were extending their North American territories in a vast sweep from the harsh northern shores of Acadia (later Nova Scotia) beyond the Great Lakes and down the eastern banks of the Mississippi to the Gulf of Mexico and the new settlement of New Orleans (founded 1718). In quest of skins and furs, New France's trappers, soldiers and Catholic missionaries thrust far into the forest wilderness, fighting and converting the Indians and starting future cities (Quebec, 1608; Ville-Marie, later Montreal, 1642; Detroit, 1701).

The French, like the Spaniards, were few and widely dispersed. The highly profitable fur trade not only discouraged formal colonisation but inevitably brought conflict: first with the Dutch and their Indian allies, the Iroquois; then, after the fall of New Amsterdam (New York) to the English in 1664, with the far more numerous Anglo-Saxon colonists of the eastern seaboard.

After a false start in the 1580s, serious development had begun here with the founding of Jamestown, Virginia (1607) and the Mayflower landing in Massachusetts Bay (1620). By the end of the 17th century the twelve so-called 'continental colonies' (Georgia was added in 1733) already possessed a prosperous agricultural, commercial and fishing economy, with the beginnings of a manufacturing industry and a population of some 250,000 souls. Fifty years later British North America, including its well over 100,000 Negro slaves, was almost one-third as populous as England itself, with Massachusetts alone having as many settlers as the whole of 'New France'.

The Anglo-French struggle for continental supremacy began very early. Quebec was first stormed by the English in 1629, and Acadia changed hands many times, even before 1700. Hostility deepened as England, starting in 1670, built up her own formidable fur-trading empire, based on the rich hunting grounds around Hudson Bay; and each major European war of the period had its parallel beyond the Atlantic. The peace of Utrecht in 1713 gave Britain Nova Scotia, Newfoundland and a clear field for the Hudson's Bay Company; but it was the French and Indian War of 1754-60, pre-dating and then forming part of the near-global Seven Years War (1756-63) between the two powers, which finally extinguished France's American ambitions. With the Treaty of Paris (1763) all Canada and the land east of the Mississippi were ceded to Britain, while Louisiana went to Spain in compensation for France's earlier transfer, to England, of the once-Spanish area of Florida.

Three new British colonies were now created: East Florida, roughly matching the present state; West Florida, stretching along the Gulf; and a much-shrunken Quebec. But the policies devised in London to administer and defend these and the vast new territories beyond were to contribute directly to the outbreak of the American Revolution in 1775.

The English colonial attitude to the Indians had always been ambivalent. Where the Spaniards willingly assimilated and intermarried – hence their extensive native and *mestizo* populations, especially in Peru and Mexico – Anglo-Americans preferred to eliminate or expel to make way for farms and plantations. Now, in 1763, the Crown established the so-called Proclamation Line, near the crest of the Allegheny mountains, and declared all land to the west to be a huge Indian reserve. But the line, lacking any geographical reality, had little effect in stemming the westward surge of the settlers and land-speculators: it merely irritated the independent-minded colonists, thus compounding their already mounting resistance to English tax demands and trade controls. By 1768 the line had been radically revised to open up large new areas,

2/Population and Settlement *(below)* Three main strands have created the ethnic pattern of the Americas: the settlers, primarily west European; the negro slaves, from west and east Africa; and the indigenous Indian races, some savage, some civilised. The map shows the frontier between European settlement and Indian land. The colours on the colonies are explained in the key to map 1 *(right)*.

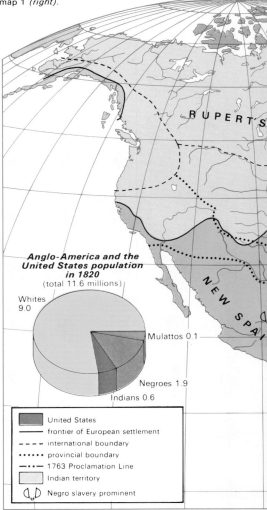

Anglo-America and the United States population in 1820
(total 11.6 millions)

Whites 9.0

Mulattos 0.1

Negroes 1.9

Indians 0.6

United States

frontier of European settlement

international boundary

provincial boundary

1763 Proclamation Line

Indian territory

Negro slavery prominent

but this still did not satisfy demand; in 1774 the Quebec Act, re-expanding the boundaries of the new Canadian colony to the Mississippi and Ohio rivers, was interpreted as seriously harming the interests of Virginia and Pennsylvania. Coinciding with the bitterly resented Coercive Acts, this move helped light the fuse for the American War of Independence (1775-83).

Fighting began at Lexington and Concord, Massachusetts, in April 1775. In June the colonies' Continental Congress created a Continental Army under General Washington. Despite several defeats, and the loss of New York in September 1776, Washington hung on, and at Christmas 1776, with the successful crossing of the Delaware, inaugurated a series of victories, culminating in Saratoga (1777). Final triumph was only assured, however, with the signing of a Franco-American alliance in 1778 (joined by Spain the next year). Reinforced by French troops and naval support, Washington forced the British to surrender at Yorktown on 19 October, 1781. The resulting Treaty of Versailles in 1783 recognised the Great Lakes in the north and the Mississippi in the west as the frontiers of the newly-born United States.

1/Colonial America (above) Two great empires and three only relatively smaller ones flourished in the western hemisphere in the 16th to 18th centuries. Richest by far were the Spanish conquests, whose bullion directly or indirectly (through contraband trade and piracy) financed most European governments of the period; but England too grew wealthy on her American and Caribbean trade, as Holland and France faded and Portugal remained content with Brazil.

Trade and empire in Africa 1500 to 1800

THREE main processes dominate the history of Africa during the period from 1500 to 1800. One was the growth of large political units, which gathered momentum in much of black Africa. During these three centuries, independent African political and cultural achievements reached their zenith. Across the Sudanic belt of west Africa, these states were the successors of those established much earlier, such as Ghana and Mali (see page 136). In 1464 one of Africa's most renowned kings and military heroes, Sunni Ali, became ruler of the Songhay people who lived along the eastern part of the Niger bend, around the city of Gao. Sunni Ali conquered far and wide, and built up a huge Songhay Empire; but his son was deposed as ruler by an even greater leader, Askia the Great, who reigned from 1493 to 1528. This was a time of flourishing trade – especially that carried across the Sahara. The Songhay Empire incorporated a number of great commercial cities, including Timbuktu and Jenne as well as Gao, which also became centres of learning and Muslim piety.

Trading communities from the rich Hausa city states, and others of the Manding people called Dyola, from Mali and Songhay, were instrumental in the rise of a series of states in the savannah and forest country to the south of the Niger. These were the Mossi-Dagomba states on the one hand, and the Akan-Asante states on the other. By 1500 Oyo and Benin, two of the great states of present-day Nigeria, had emerged in the woodlands to the west of the Niger delta. It was in this region that the supreme examples of the plastic arts of Africa were produced, such as the famous Ife and Benin terracottas and bronzes.

Elsewhere in black Africa similar processes were at work, leading to the emergence of powerful kingdoms out of societies of iron-working agriculturalists and cattle-keepers. In favourable environments, the number of people (and their

2/The growth of the slave trade (below) In the 15th century a few hundred slaves were taken from west Africa to Europe and the Atlantic islands. From the 1520s, slaves began to be transported by Europeans to the New World. The trans-Atlantic trade was at its peak during the 18th century, when between six and seven million slaves were shipped to the Americas; it came to an end in 1870.

cattle) increased, their economies became more diverse, giving rise to trade in iron and copper goods and other wares, all of which provided the basis for stronger political control over a larger area. When the Portuguese arrived off the coast south of the estuary of the Congo (Zaire) river in 1484, they found the brilliant Kongo kingdom just inland. South of the Congo basin forests was a string of Bantu-speaking African states, such as the Luba and Lunda kingdoms. Likewise in the fertile lands between the lakes of east Africa — the interlacustrine region — there developed a whole series of states, the most prominent of which were Rwanda and Buganda. Another prosperous region was the plateau of present-day Rhodesia, with kingdoms based upon Zimbabwe; the Mwenemutapa empire, well known to the Portuguese and other early Europeans, was centred upon the area to the north-east of modern Salisbury. In between these great kingdoms, and over much of southern Africa lived numerous peoples slowly evolving smaller, less flamboyant states.

The first occupation of Zimbabwe can be traced back to early Iron Age farmers around the 4th century AD. It was reoccupied in the 10th century by people who traded in copper and gold. Two hundred years later stone was being used for the buildings of Zimbabwe. There was then a great fire, and the site had to be rebuilt from about the middle of the 14th century. These are the ruins which are so impressive now, and which have given their name to the African version of Rhodesia. In the valley there is a huge palace with a girdle wall more than 30 feet high, constructed of dressed stone. On the hill overlooking the palace is a massive temple or acropolis. Zimbabwe was the political and religious centre of a mighty trading state with connections as far distant as China.

The second predominating historical process was the continual expansion of Islam. Not only was northern Africa fully Islamised, but during the period 1500 to 1800 Islam consolidated its position in the Sudanic lands, and spread even further south and down the coast of east Africa. In the Horn of Africa what started as a trading rivalry between Christian Ethiopia and the

1/Developments in trade and empire (right) During the 300 years from 1500 to 1800, the course of African history developed along both well-established lines and in new ways. The interaction between Mediterranean and Sudanic Africa, which had begun in pre-Roman times, continued with Islam making deeper inroads into tropical Africa. African states and cultures, generally deep in the interior of the continent, also continued their mainly slow and steady – but sometimes most dynamic – growth. However, many parts of Africa came increasingly under the economic influence of western European states; coastal peoples were affected by this both politically and economically.

Muslim coastal states, especially Adal, became a long, bitter religious and political conflict. The sultan of Adal, Ahmad Gran, launched a fierce attack in the 1520s, and Muslim armies pushed into the heartlands of Ethiopia; the exhausted Christian empire was then invaded and settled by pagan Galla from the south and east, as indeed was Adal itself. Meanwhile in 1517 the Ottomans conquered the Mamelukes in Egypt, and subsequently Ottoman control was extended over Tripoli and Tunis; Algiers was ruled by the Corsairs, who owed allegiance to the Ottomans. Only Morocco remained independent, ruled during much of this period by factions of the Sharifian dynasty. In the 16th century much of coastal north Africa was the scene of a prolonged religious and economic conflict between the Christian powers, especially Spain and Portugal, and the Ottoman Empire and Morocco. In 1590, when at the height of its power, Morocco invaded the Songhay Empire, and set up a client state in the Sudan; this invasion disrupted the economic life of the whole region. By the beginning of the 18th century the politics and commerce of Muslim west Africa were being revived by a burst of Islamic proselytising which reached its zenith with the great Holy Wars of the 1790s.

The last great historical movement was the trade in human beings from Africa to the New World. This terrible trade was inaugurated by the Portuguese explorers of the western coast of Africa (see page 147); but the Dutch, British, French and other European nations soon joined in, setting up trading 'factories' along the coast. During the 400 years of the trade – from about 1450 to 1870 – over ten million Africans were transported to the Americas, from all over the western part of the continent as far south as Angola and, by the 19th century, from much of east Africa and Madagascar as well. At the same time, African slaves were carried across the Sahara and from east Africa to the Muslim world.

The effects of this vast, forced demographic change are hotly debated. Certainly a number of African states engaged in the trade gained in political importance and power — Asante, Dahomey and Benin are examples. Certainly the European slave traders and their countries made huge profits from the exploitation of human beings. Certainly what was the Americas' gain was Africa's loss. But all these gains and losses are difficult to quantify, and none of them overrides the cruelty and indignity inflicted on the slaves themselves. Later, after the abolition of the trade and the emancipation of the slaves in the 19th century, many of the ideas generated by blacks in the New World, such as the concept of Black Power, became crucial ingredients of modern African nationalism.

In spite of the shadow of the slave trade which falls over so much of the history of Africa in this period, the peoples of Africa had made tremendous political and cultural strides by 1800. The greater part of the continent still remained independent of external control, if not of influence. Only parts of north Africa, some scattered factories in west Africa, a few Portuguese outposts, and the Dutch East India Company settlement at the Cape (established in 1652) were occupied by foreigners. Elsewhere, particularly in the interior, political and social development followed its own established pattern.

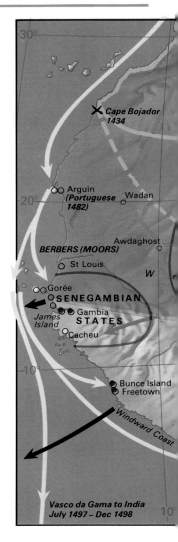

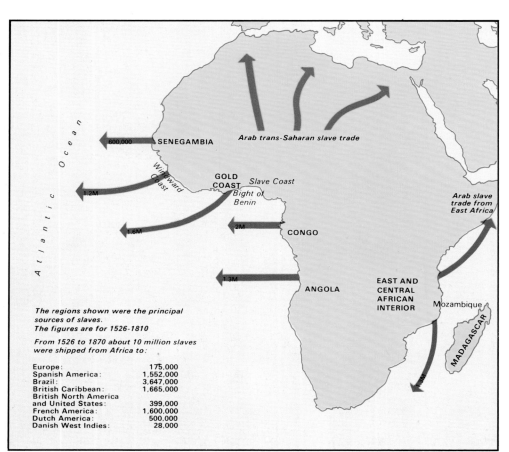

The regions shown were the principal sources of slaves.
The figures are for 1526-1810

From 1526 to 1870 about 10 million slaves were shipped from Africa to:

Europe:	175,000
Spanish America:	1,552,000
Brazil:	3,647,000
British Caribbean:	1,665,000
British North America and United States:	399,000
French America:	1,600,000
Dutch America:	500,000
Danish West Indies:	28,000

Ife sculpture (above) During the golden age of African kingdoms, art forms, especially that of sculpture, flourished. Some of the most sublime African sculpture came from the forest kingdoms of Ife and Benin, in present-day Nigeria. The Ife terracotta and bronze heads began to be made in the 13th century, and the tradition continued for several hundred years. In nearby Benin, the bronze sculptures produced in the 16th and 17th centuries were more powerful and robust than the beautifully refined and naturalistic Ife figures.

East Asia at the time of the Ming Dynasty 1368 to 1644

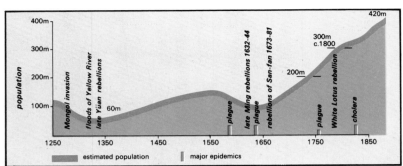

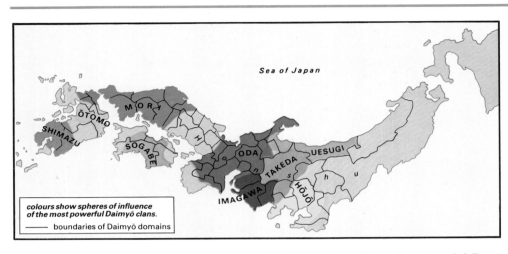

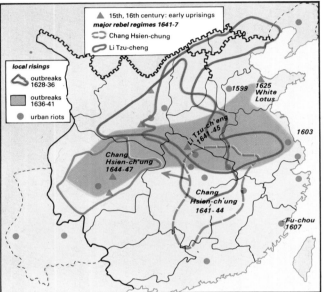

4/Japan's century of civil war. 1467 to 1590 *(above)* The powerful centralised regime established by the Kamakura shōguns was destroyed in the 1330s, to be replaced by the Ashikaga, a new dominant military family, until 1400, when their power declined. The Onin War (1467-77) began a century of strife between the feudal lords. The map shows the political fragmentation of the country in about 1560; Oda Nobunga and Hideyoshi Shigekuni gradually reunified Japan by 1590, preparing the way for the powerful state of the Tokugawa, set up in 1603.

3/Rebellions under the Ming *(left)* Rural distress produced a number of rebellions during the 15th century, mostly in central and south-eastern China. In the early 17th century taxation and economic pressures produced urban risings in the great cities, and from the 1620s great numbers of peasant rebellions in central and northern China. In the 1640s two rebels, Li Tzu-ch'eng and Chang Hsien-chung, became contenders to found a new dynasty.

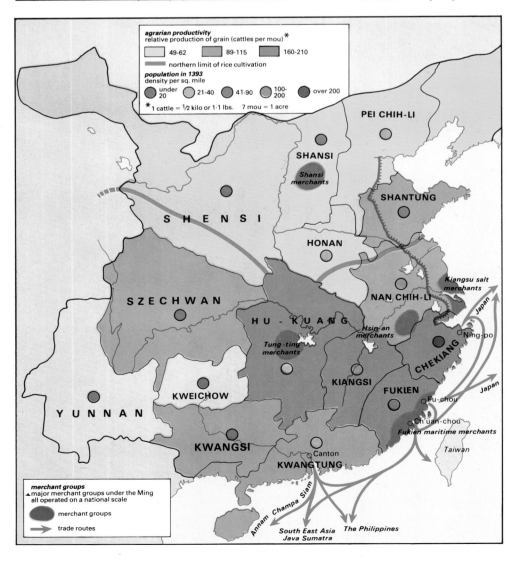

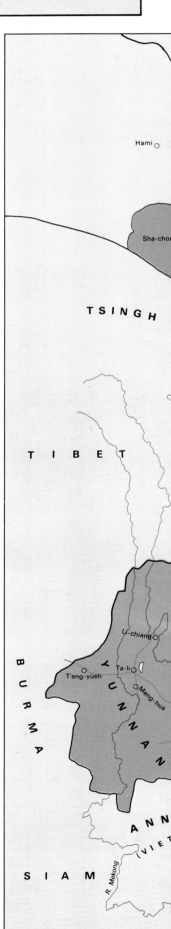

THE Mongols caused immense destruction in China, especially during the conquest of northern China before 1241. Much of the land went out of cultivation, its cities and industries were largely destroyed. Countless numbers died, many more were enslaved. In the south Mongol rule was less harsh after 1279, but during the Mongol (Yüan) dynasty (1280-1367) the Chinese were ruthlessly exploited, productivity fell, and commerce was badly disrupted. Popular resentment erupted in a wave of popular risings from 1335 onwards. In 1354-59 disastrous floods in the eastern plain caused further distress, and major rebellions flared up in Chekiang, the Yangtze valley, Shantung and Honan. One of the rebel leaders, Chu Yüan-chang, gradually overcame his rivals and established his new dynasty, the Ming, in Nanking in 1368. It was not until 1387 that all of China was conquered, and the Mongols were finally defeated in 1388.

Until the end of the 14th century the Ming were preoccupied with the restoration of normal life. The first priority was the revival of agriculture: irrigation and drainage works were rebuilt in great numbers, reafforestation carried out on a grand scale, and vast numbers of people moved to repopulate the devastated areas of the north. An attempt was made to break the power of the large landowners and encourage small peasants. Unlike the Sung, who had relied heavily on trade and merchants as sources of revenue, the Ming reverted to the ancient system of reliance on agriculture for revenues. They also attempted to revive the ancient concept of a self-sufficient army, and established a class of hereditary military families settled in 'military colonies' on the frontiers and in other strategic places. A new canal system was built linking Peking with the Yangtze valley, and the capital was moved to Peking in 1421.

In 1393 the Chinese population was just over 60,000,000, 40 per cent less than in the late Sung. With peace and internal stability it began again to increase, and by 1580 was probably about 130,000,000, although a drastic reduction was caused by major plagues in the late 16th century and again in the 1640s. Improved agricultural techniques enabled China to feed this growing population. New crops were introduced; cotton had become common under the Mongols and was widely grown in the Yangtze valley and the north of Chiang-su (Kiangsu). In the dry west and north-west sorghum became a common grain crop. In the 16th and 17th centuries Spanish and Portuguese traders reached the Chinese coast and introduced more new crops: sweet potato, maize, peanuts, Irish potato and tobacco, which could be grown on soils unsuited to traditional crops.

The Ming government took a negative attitude towards trade. It abandoned the use of paper money, by the misuse of which the Mongols had seriously damaged the economy. The government itself monopolised some important industries. Nevertheless industry boomed, and the great cities of the Yangtze delta, Nanking, Su-

2/The Ming economy *(left)* Chinese silk and cotton textiles and ceramics were exchanged in Manila for Spanish silver from the New World; and from the early 17th century tea was exported to Europe via Dutch traders. China imported silver, spices, sulphur, sandalwood, and copper from Japan.

Ming naval power (above) As this detail from a painting showing the defence of Korea illustrates, the Ming were a considerable naval power, capable of intervening in the affairs of distant nations.

Population fluctuations (left) At the beginning of the Ming, China still suffered from the effects of Mongol rule. Population had fallen drastically, especially in the north. With extensive reconstruction, population rose steadily, and agriculture became more productive. Outbreaks of plague in the 1580s and the 1640s, however, again reduced the population in many areas.

chou, Wu-hsi, Sung-chiang and Hang-chou became major industrial centres, particularly for textiles. They were supplied with grain and raw cotton from the north, by the grand canal, and from Hunan and Hupeh by the Yangtze. Large movements of goods were also needed to supply Peking and the garrisons on the northern borders, for the system of self-sufficient military colonies soon decayed. To handle this huge volume of trade several powerful groups of merchants arose (see map 2). In the late 16th century commerce was stimulated by the inflow of silver from the New World, used to pay for extensive Chinese exports of tea, silk and ceramics.

The Ming state reverted to the institutions of T'ang times, abandoning many Sung innovations. Government was simple; control over the vast population was effected largely through a new social group, the 'gentry' (shen-shih), degree-holders who had been through the examination system and shared the values of the officials without holding office. The new system discouraged innovation and was over-centralised. The abolition of the post of chief minister made all decisions dependent upon the emperor.

At first the Ming engaged in an aggressive foreign policy. Campaigns against the Mongols in the far north, the restoration of Korea to vassal status in 1392, the occupation of Annam from 1407 to 1427 and a series of immense sea-borne expeditions (see page 146) extended Chinese power to new limits. These ventures proved extremely costly, and after an attempted invasion of Mongolia in 1449 ended in the emperor's capture, the Ming reverted to a defensive strategy. In the 16th century they were under constant pressure from revived Mongol power under Altan Khan (1550-73) and from attacks from the sea. Japanese pirates constantly harassed the coasts, and after 1550 invaded coastal districts in force, sailed up the Yangtze, and attacked major cities. The Portuguese, by comparison a minor irritant, first appeared in 1514 and from 1557 were permanently established in Macao.

The threat from Japanese pirates was diminished when, in 1590, Japan was reunified after over a century of civil war and political disunion. But this Japanese revival brought new dangers. In 1592 the Japanese under Hideyoshi invaded Korea, and the Chinese had to send huge armies to aid the Koreans. Another expedition against Korea, in 1597-98, again caused terrible destruction, and again required heavy Chinese involvement.

These major threats coincided with a decline in Ming government. After 1582 the emperors refused to conduct court business or even to see their ministers. Power passed into the hands of the eunuchs who, with their own army and secret police, were able to terrorise officials and populace alike, and to extort heavy taxes. Reformist officials attempted to counter them, but this led to purges and factional discord.

The Ming had suffered rebellions before. An uprising in Fukien and Chekiang in 1448-49 had led to a million deaths. After 1627, however, a wave of rebel movements broke out, following repeated crop failures in the north-west. By 1636 much of central, northern and north-western China was in rebellion. The main contenders for power were Chang Hsien-cheng, who ravaged the eastern plain and the Yangtze valley before setting up a kingdom in Szechwan, and Li Tzu-ch'eng in Shan-hsi, Hupeh and Honan. Li Tzu-ch'eng took Peking in 1644, and the last Ming emperor committed suicide. But Li's ambition to found a dynasty was thwarted by the intervention of the Manchus, who in the previous quarter century had established a powerful state in Liao-tung with the aid of Chinese defectors.

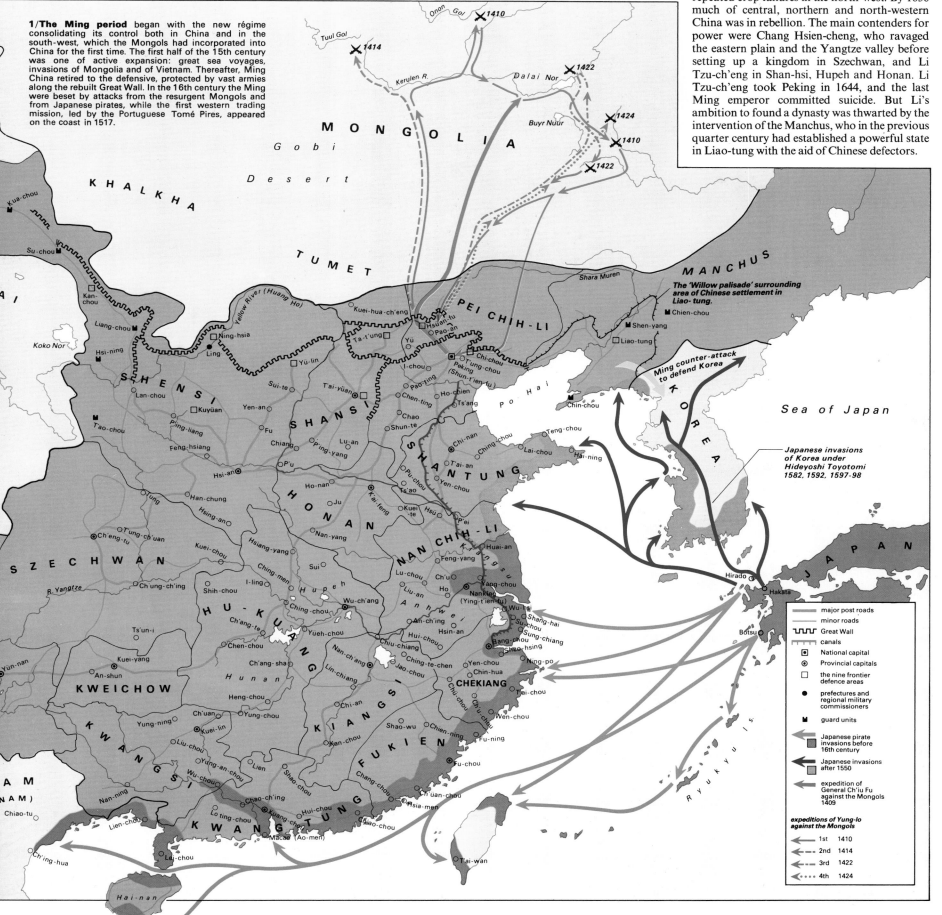

1/The Ming period began with the new régime consolidating its control both in China and in the south-west, which the Mongols had incorporated into China for the first time. The first half of the 15th century was one of active expansion: great sea voyages, invasions of Mongolia and of Vietnam. Thereafter, Ming China retired to the defensive, protected by vast armies along the rebuilt Great Wall. In the 16th century the Ming were beset by attacks from the resurgent Mongols and from Japanese pirates, while the first western trading mission, led by the Portuguese Tomé Pires, appeared on the coast in 1517.

Japanese invasions of Korea under Hideyoshi Toyotomi 1582, 1592, 1597-98

Ming counter-attack to defend Korea

The 'Willow palisade' surrounding area of Chinese settlement in Liao-tung.

	major post roads
	minor roads
	Great Wall
	canals
	National capital
	Provincial capitals
	the nine frontier defence areas
	prefectures and regional military commissioners
	guard units
	Japanese pirate invasions before 16th century
	Japanese invasions after 1550
	expedition of General Ch'iu Fu against the Mongols 1409

expeditions of Yung-lo against the Mongols

	1st	1410
	2nd	1414
	3rd	1422
	4th	1424

The resurgence of Muslim power 1520 to 1639

1 / The Ottoman, Safavid and Mughal Empires *(right)* The great Muslim victories of Mohács on the Danube and Panipat in the Ganges basin took place in the same year, 1526. Subsequently, the Ottoman frontier advanced still further into Europe, and the Mughals in India extended their domains southwards until the end of the 17th century. The Ottoman triumph was less enduring; weakened by internal revolts, and challenged by the Habsburgs in Europe, Muscovy in southern Russia and the Safavids in Iran, they gradually retreated from Hungary, the Caucasus and Iraq; by the end of the 17th century many of the gains realised in the reign of Suleiman the Magnificent (1520-66) had been lost.

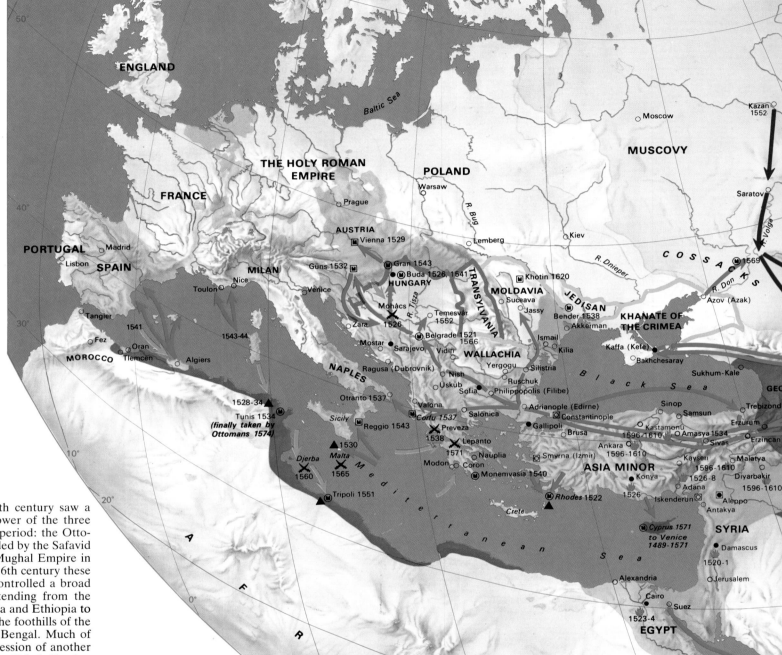

THE first half of the 16th century saw a great advance in the power of the three major Muslim states of the period: the Ottoman Empire, the state founded by the Safavid dynasty in Persia, and the Mughal Empire in India. In the middle of the 16th century these three polities occupied or controlled a broad belt of lands and seas, extending from the frontiers of Morocco, Austria and Ethiopia to the fringes of central Asia, the foothills of the Himalayas, and the Bay of Bengal. Much of central Asia was in the possession of another dynasty of Turkish origin, the Uzbek Shayba-nids, who ruled in Bukhara. Khanates with Muslim rulers still existed in the Crimea and on the Volga at Kazan and Astrakhan, and continued to do so for many generations in the lands along the ancient Silk Road. All these states were the creation of Turkish-speaking Muslim dynasties of a strongly military character. All, with the exception of the Safavid state in Persia, affirmed their adherence to orthodox (Sunni) Islam; the Safavids, however, followed Shi'ism, a fact which encouraged bitter rivalry and intermittent warfare between them and their Ottoman and Uzbek neighbours throughout the 16th and early 17th centuries.

By the death of Mehmed II (1481) the Ottomans had conquered Constantinople and overrun the Balkans. Thereafter the sudden revival of Persia under Ismail I (1500-24) drew them back to Asia. Ismail was defeated in 1514, Syria and Egypt conquered in 1516-17. With the accession of Suleiman I (1520-66) the assault on Europe was renewed. After the battle of Mohács (1526) Hungary was overrun and Vienna besieged (1529); but Persia still remained independent. Nevertheless the Ottoman Empire, buttressed by the wealth acquired from the conquest of Egypt, was indisputably the greatest Muslim power of the

age. In the early years of Suleiman's reign the subjects of the Sultan numbered perhaps 14 million (Spain at this time had 5 million inhabitants; England had 2.5 million). The population of Constantinople itself, which at the time of the Ottoman conquest had been no more than 40,000, increased tenfold, and Ottoman and European writers alike testified to the splendour of its public works, the impressiveness of the imperial mosques and the outstanding quality of administrative, charitable and educational institutions. To European observers, such as the Habsburg Emperor's ambassador Busbecq, the magnificence of the Ottoman state, and the strength and discipline of the Ottoman army, were matters for admiration — and concern.

Persia, also, under the new dynasty enjoyed a remarkable revival of art, architecture and trade, which reached its culmination in the reign of Abbas I (1587-1629), while in India Babur, an adventurer from central Asia who had seized power in Afghanistan in 1504,

Suleiman I at Mohács *(right)* The military might, order and discipline of the Ottoman army in the first half of the 16th century are vigorously depicted in this miniature. Suleiman I is shown surrounded by his vezirs, sipahis and janissaries and the heads of the decapitated Hungarians he defeated at the Battle of Mohács in 1526.

swept aside the effete sultanate of Delhi and founded the Mughal Empire in 1526. Here again (see page 172) there was a great efflorescence of culture, which reached its peak during the reign of Akbar (1556-1605). But the vast extension of Muslim power and influence concealed a number of flaws. Most serious was the continuing clash between Sunni Turkey and Shi'i Persia — which drove a wedge into the Muslim world. Just as the Ottomans allied with France against the Habsburgs, so the Persians allied with Austria against the Turks. Secondly, the Mughal and

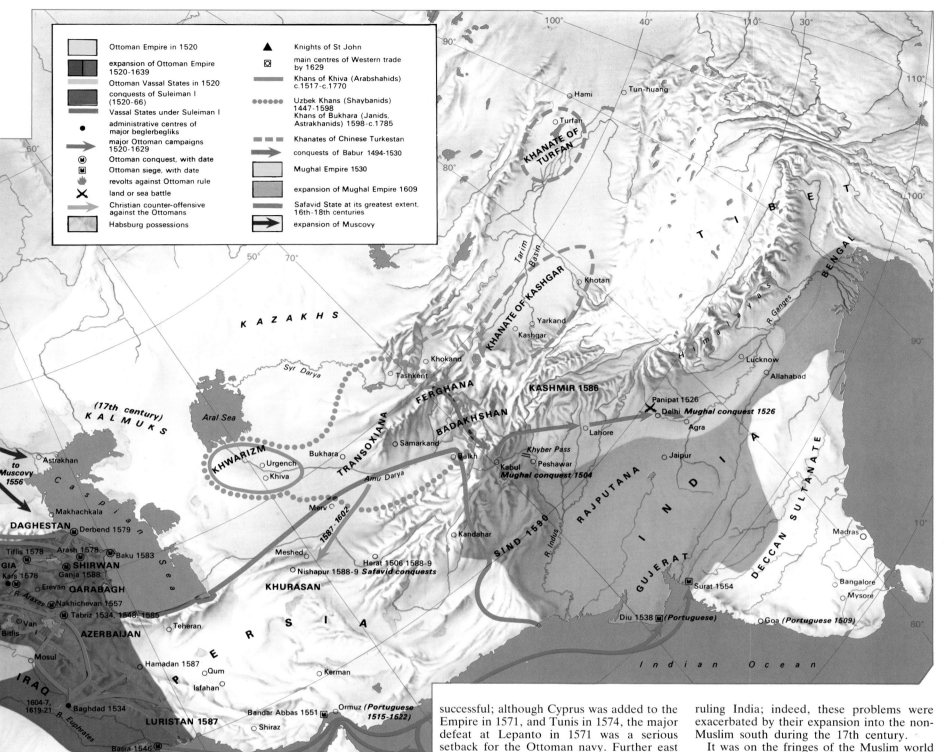

Ottoman Empire in 1520

expansion of Ottoman Empire 1520-1639

Ottoman Vassal States in 1520

conquests of Suleiman I (1520-66)

Vassal States under Suleiman I

● administrative centres of major beglerbegliks

➤ major Ottoman campaigns 1520-1629

Ⓜ Ottoman conquest, with date

Ⓜ Ottoman siege, with date

🔥 revolts against Ottoman rule

✕ land or sea battle

➤ Christian counter-offensive against the Ottomans

Habsburg possessions

▲ Knights of St John

⧇ main centres of Western trade by 1629

Khans of Khiva (Arabshahids) c.1517-c.1770

Uzbek Khans (Shaybanids) 1447-1598 Khans of Bukhara (Janids, Astrakhanids) 1598-c.1785

Khanates of Chinese Turkestan

➤ conquests of Babur 1494-1530

Mughal Empire 1530

expansion of Mughal Empire 1609

Safavid State at its greatest extent, 16th-18th centuries

➤ expansion of Muscovy

---

successful; although Cyprus was added to the Empire in 1571, and Tunis in 1574, the major defeat at Lepanto in 1571 was a serious setback for the Ottoman navy. Further east they had been unable to prevent the capture of Socotra (1507) and Ormuz (1515) by the Portuguese, still less the establishment of a Portuguese presence in India itself.

For the Ottomans, the year 1538, when the armies and fleets of the Sultan in one season reduced Moldavia to vassal status, defeated a poorly-led Christian armada at Preveza, and appeared against the Portuguese under the walls of Diu, was certainly an *annus mirabilis*. However, the conflicts on the Hungarian and Persian frontiers began to lose their momentum in the last two decades of Suleiman's reign. In the second half of the 16th century, the wars against the Safavids (1578-90 and 1603-19) and against the Habsburgs (1593-1606) ended in the loss of the Caucasus territories and the Habsburgs' last payment of tribute for Hungary. Furthermore, during these wars the lifeblood of the Empire, its traditionally-recruited ruling class and army, was drained away. The changing conditions of war, the effects of inflation after 1584, and the insoluble problem of a rising population, a shrinking economy, and a static frontier, had by the early decades of the 17th century produced a crisis in the Ottoman state.

In Persia the political weakness of the Safavids in the latter part of the 16th century was redressed by Abbas I, but after his death in 1629 the Safavid dynasty, too, entered a period of weakness, leading to ultimate demise. Similarly, in India the administrative reorganisation and religious experimentation under Akbar were ultimately unable to solve the problems which faced the Mughals in

ruling India; indeed, these problems were exacerbated by their expansion into the non-Muslim south during the 17th century.

It was on the fringes of the Muslim world that the changes in this period were the most ominous. At sea, the Portuguese circumnavigation of Africa and their attempt to put a stranglehold on the indigenous trade of the Indian Ocean had not gone unnoticed by the Ottomans; as successors to the Mamelukes they were able at least to hold the Portuguese at bay during the 16th century. However, the arrival of the English, and later the Dutch, brought into the region powers economically stronger and politically more ruthless than the Portuguese. Their effect was increasingly felt during the remainder of the 17th century. Meanwhile, to the north, the Muslim successor states of the Mongol Empire had by the middle of the 16th century for the most part entered on the last stages of decay. The khanates of Kazan and Astrakhan were annexed by Muscovy in 1552 and 1556. This brought Russian forces to the mouth of the Volga, thus driving a wedge between the Ottomans and the Uzbeks. On the other hand, the khanate of the Crimea, another successor state of the Golden Horde, continued in existence and was at times a useful military auxiliary of the Ottomans as well as a barrier closing off the Black Sea from hostile Christian states to the north. By the 1620s, however, Cossack raiders were appearing on the Black Sea and ravaging its shores. Within less than a hundred years the Islamic world had passed from the offensive to the defensive, and the great Islamic empires, which had seemed so formidable in the 16th and 17th centuries, failed to make the transition to the modern world.

Safavid were essentially land empires, and when the Portuguese appeared in the Indian Ocean, hitherto a Muslim lake, they were unable to cope. After their conquest of Egypt, the Ottomans assumed the defence of their territories against the seapower of Spain and the Italian city states in the Mediterranean, and of Portugal in the Red Sea and the Persian Gulf. Here they were only partially

The Mughal Empire and the growth of British power in India

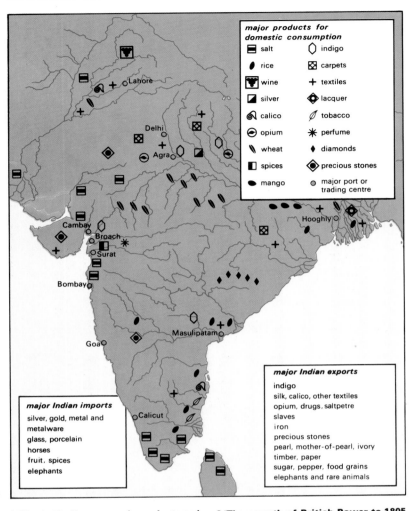

2/Mughal India: economic products and trade *(above)* Textiles from Bengal, Gujerat and Coromandel were India's main export; also sugar to Japan and Persia and pepper and saltpetre to Europe. The main imports were gold and silver.

major products for domestic consumption

▣ salt	◇ indigo
◗ rice	⊠ carpets
▼ wine	✛ textiles
◩ silver	◈ lacquer
◔ calico	∅ tobacco
◔ opium	✳ perfume
↘ wheat	◆ diamonds
▯ spices	◈ precious stones
● mango	○ major port or trading centre

major Indian exports
indigo
silk, calico, other textiles
opium, drugs, saltpetre
slaves
iron
precious stones
pearl, mother-of-pearl, ivory
timber, paper
sugar, pepper, food grains
elephants and rare animals

major Indian imports
silver, gold, metal and metalware
glass, porcelain
horses
fruit, spices
elephants

3/The growth of British Power to 1805 *(below)* **and principal Maratha States in 1795** *(below right)* After Tipu's death at Seringapatam (1799) the Marathas represented the only major obstacle to British supremacy, largely achieved by 1805.

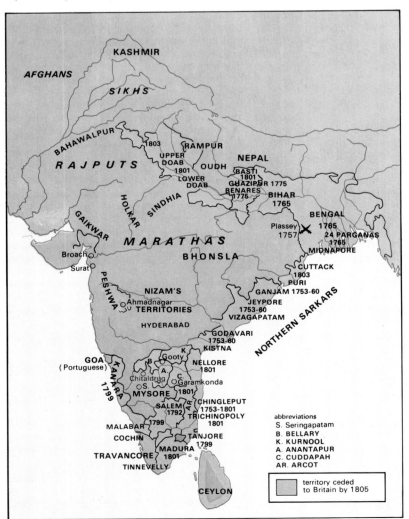

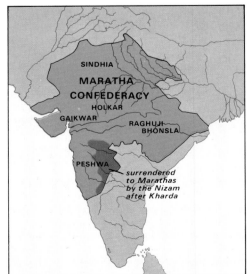

BABUR, fifth in line from Tamerlane, entered India in 1523 from Afghanistan. With his victory at Panipat in 1526 he established the Mughal Empire, but it took some time to make the foundations firm. After his death, the Mughals were expelled by the Afghans of South Bihar, under their leader Sher Shah, and it took a full-scale new invasion, brilliantly consolidated by Babur's grandson, Akbar (1556-1605), to restore their rule. This now extended to Bengal in the east and Godavari in the south, as well as Kashmir, Baluchistan, Sind and Gujerat. Most of the Rajput princes became tributary allies, and the empire, divided into *subahs* (provinces) was administered by a new class of bureaucrats, the *mansabdars,* ranked in a military hierarchy on lines first planned by Sher Shah. A standardised tax system, and tolerance towards the non-Muslim majority, helped to foster one of the great flowerings of Indian civilisation, particularly in painting and architecture. The reign of Akbar is considered one of the golden ages in India's past. Unlike his descendants, who, thanks to his policy of marriage alliances with the Rajput princely families were half Indian, Akbar was entirely a foreigner in India. Yet his sense of identification with the life and culture of the country he reconquered was total. The popular acclaim, *'Dillisvaro va jagadisvaro va'* – 'the Ruler of Delhi is the same as the Lord of the Universe' – testified to the masses' enthusiastic acceptance of his benevolent autocratic rule. The artists and savants at his court recalled, in popular imagination, the glories of the mythical Vikramaditya's court with its 'nine jewels' *(navaratna)*. The Mughal school of miniature painting, which combined the traditions of the Persian and Rajput schools, flourished under his patronage. His red sandstone capital at Fatehpur Sikri similarly expressed a striking synthesis of Hindu and Islamic traditions of architecture. The new style reached its climax in the days of his grandson, Shahjahan, the builder of the Taj Mahal.

Akbar's political inheritance included a ceaseless thrust towards territorial expansion, especially towards the south. New territories were added under Shahjahan (1627-56) and the Mughal domains reached their furthest extent under Aurangzeb (1656-1707), who had seized the throne after a fratricidal war. Bijapur and Golconda were annexed, Assam briefly occupied, and Chittagong wrested from Arakan. But the southern conquests led to confrontation with a new Hindu power, the Marathas, who under Sivaji (1627-80) had established an independent kingdom on the Konkan coast, with outposts in Coromandel and Mysore. The execution of Sivaji's son in 1689 failed to check the Maratha depredations, and by now religious intolerance and administrative decay were stirring up opposition on all sides. By 1700 the Marathas were ravaging the Deccan and the eastern provinces, the former Rajput allies were at war, and near the capital Sikhs, Jats and Satnamis were all in revolt.

During the previous 150 years of Mughal peace and prosperity, foreign trade had attracted new, and increasingly powerful European interest in India. Following Vasco da Gama's first landfall at Malabar in 1498, the spice-seeking Portuguese soon acquired territories – Goa, Daman and Diu Island – from which they tried to monopolise spice and textile sales, as well as the pilgrim voyages to Mecca. In the 17th century they were joined by less unpopular Dutch, English, French and Danish companies, all eager to set up coastal trading centres, exporting textiles, sugar, indigo and saltpetre to markets as far away as Japan and the New World.

Shortly after Aurangzeb's death, Oudh, the Deccan and the eastern provinces became effectively independent, owing only nominal allegiance to Delhi. The Peshwas, officially the chief ministers of Sivaji's house, presided over a confederacy of Maratha chiefs, the Sindhias, Gaikwars, Holkars and Bhonslas. Their territories stretched deep into north, west, central and eastern India, while in the south, Mysore, under Haidar and Tipu, had grown into a formidable power. By the late 18th century, the Mughal emperor had become a Sindhia protégé. The Marathas at this time seemed destined to succeed the Mughals. Such hopes were effectively destroyed at the Third Battle of Panipat (1761) where the Afghan Ahmad Shah Abdali decisively defeated the Peshwa's forces.

The War of the Austrian Succession (1740-48) saw the French and English trading companies in armed conflict along the Carnatic coast. With the death of the local ruler, the Nizam, this developed into open war (1744-63), ending in British victory and the eclipse of France's Indian ambitions. Robert Clive's triumph at Plassey in 1757 brought effective control of Bihar, Orissa and Bengal (where the East India Company had established its new trading centre of Calcutta in 1690). By 1768 the Northern Sarkars were secured from the Nizam. Benares and Ghazipur were wrested from Oudh in 1775. But British supremacy was only assured after a series of battles with the Marathas and Mysore, of which the outcome was frequently uncertain. However, the company's possessions were steadily expanding – particularly with the victory over Tipu in 1792 and his fall in 1799 – and by the turn of the century they formed a continuous block from Malabar to Coromandel.

In Britain, the Regulating Act of 1773 and the Younger Pitt's India Act in 1784, had placed these new Indian acquisitions firmly under English parliamentary control (and also led to the impeachment of Warren Hastings, the first Governor-General of Bengal). Now, under Richard Wellesley, brother of the Duke of Wellington, they were to be consolidated into the beginnings of an imperial realm.

Wellesley, given a virtually free hand by the Napoleonic Wars at home, swiftly defeated Tipu, the most effective of the Indian leaders, and embarked on the Second Maratha War. Both these produced large accretions of territory, alongside important but subsidiary annexations in Gooty, Garamkonda, Surat, Tanjore, the Carnatic, and large parts of Oudh and Chitaldrug. The Maratha defeats delivered the Upper Doab, Rajputana, Broach, Ahmadnagar and the south-west Deccan, while subsidiary alliances, another important policy instrument, won recognition of British suzerainty from nearly all the major Indian rulers. In 1803, the Mughal emperor himself accepted Wellesley's protection, and when he left India in 1805, the Company's supremacy was an acknowledged fact.

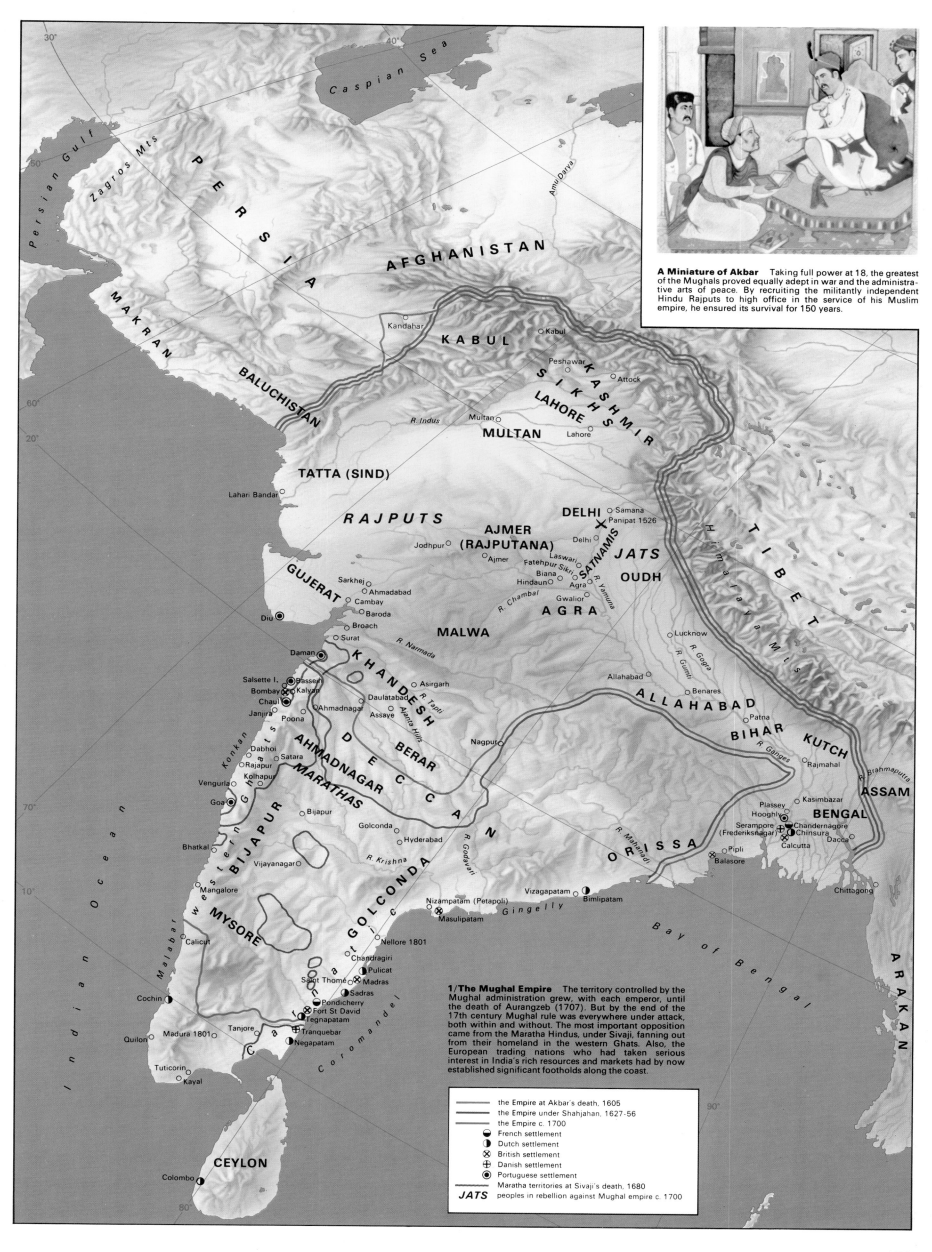

Caspian Sea

Persian Gulf

Zagros Mts

P E R S I A

MAKRAN

BALUCHISTAN

AFGHANISTAN

o Kandahar

KABUL

o Kabul
Peshawar o
o Attock

KASHMIR

SIKHS

LAHORE

R. Indus

Multan o
o Lahore

MULTAN

TATTA (SIND)

Lahari Bandar o

DELHI
o Samana
Panipat 1526

Amu Darya

T I B E T

Himalaya Mts

R A J P U T S

AJMER
(RAJPUTANA)

Jodhpur o

Ajmer o

o Delhi

SATNAMIS

JATS

OUDH

Laswari
Fatehpur Sikri o
Biana o
Hindaun o
Agra o

R. Yamuna

R. Goera

R. Gumti

o Lucknow

GUJERAT

Sarkhej o
o Ahmadabad
o Cambay
o Baroda
Diu ⊕
o Broach
o Surat

Daman o

MALWA

R. Chambal

R. Narmada

AGRA

Gwalior o

Allahabad o

o Benares

ALLAHABAD

Salsette I. ⊙ Bassein
Bombay ⊙ Kalyan
Chaul ⊙
Janjira ⊙

Poona o

KHANDESH

D
E
C
C
A
N

BERAR

o Ahmadnagar
Daulatabad o
Assaye o
Ajanta Hills

R. Tapti

Asirgarh o

Nagpur o

BIHAR

KUTCH

o Patna

R. Ganges

o Rajmahal

R. Brahmaputra

ASSAM

AHMADNAGAR

MARATHAS

Dabhoi o
Rajapur o Satara o
Kolhapur o

Vengurla o

Goa ⊙

Western Ghats

Konkan

BIJAPUR

Bijapur o

MYSORE

Bhatkal o

Mangalore o

Vijayanagar o

Calicut o

Cochin ◐

Quilon o

Tuticorin o

GOLCONDA

Golconda o
o Hyderabad

R. Krishna

R. Godavari

R. Mahanadi

ORISSA

Nizampatam (Petapoli) o
Masulipatam ⊗

Vizagapatam o ◐

Bimlipatam ◑

Gingelly

Plassey o
Hooghly o
Serampore
(Frederiksnagar) ⊕
o Kasimbazar
Chandernagore
Chinsura
Calcutta ⊗
Dacca o

BENGAL

Pipli ⊗
o Balasore

Bay of Bengal

Chittagong o

A R A K A N

Nellore 1801 o
Chandragiri o
Pulicat ◑
Saint Thomé o
Madras ⊗
Sadras ◑
Pondicherry ◐
Fort St David ⊗
Tegnapatam ⊗
Tranquebar ⊕
Negapatam ◑

Coromandel

Madura 1801 o

Tanjore o

Kayal o

Indian Ocean

Malabar

CEYLON

Colombo ◐

A Miniature of Akbar Taking full power at 18, the greatest of the Mughals proved equally adept in war and the administrative arts of peace. By recruiting the militantly independent Hindu Rajputs to high office in the service of his Muslim empire, he ensured its survival for 150 years.

1/The Mughal Empire The territory controlled by the Mughal administration grew, with each emperor, until the death of Aurangzeb (1707). But by the end of the 17th century Mughal rule was everywhere under attack, both within and without. The most important opposition came from the Maratha Hindus, under Sivaji, fanning out from their homeland in the western Ghats. Also, the European trading nations who had taken serious interest in India's rich resources and markets had by now established significant footholds along the coast.

———	the Empire at Akbar's death, 1605
———	the Empire under Shahjahan, 1627-56
———	the Empire c. 1700
◐	French settlement
◑	Dutch settlement
⊗	British settlement
⊕	Danish settlement
⊙	Portuguese settlement
———	Maratha territories at Sivaji's death, 1680
JATS	peoples in rebellion against Mughal empire c. 1700

East Asia at the time of the Ch'ing Dynasty

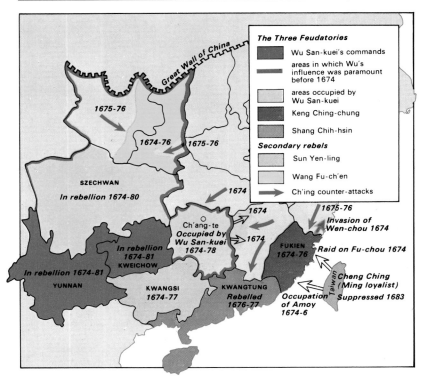

2/Rebellion of the Three Feudatories *(above)* The southern provinces, where resistance to the Ch'ing continued, were allowed to become the personal domains of various generals. Most important of these was Wu San-kuei, governor of Yunnan and Kweichow, who exercised great power over all the western provinces. In 1674 the Ch'ing government attempted to reassert control over Kwangtung. As a result the governors of all the southern and western provinces rose in a rebellion which lasted until 1681. For a time most of southern and western China was in rebel hands, but by 1677 only the south-west remained. After Wu San-kuei's death in 1678 the government slowly reduced the remaining rebels, and in 1683 occupied Taiwan, whose Ming loyalist leader Cheng Ching had supported the rebels.

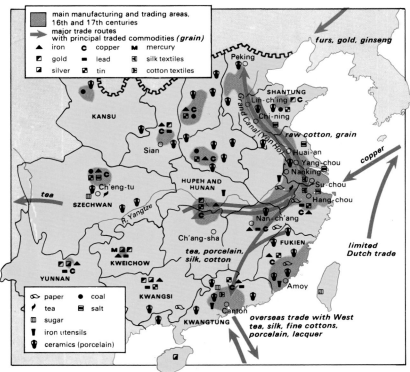

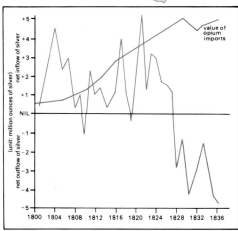

3/The Ch'ing economy *(above)* By the 17th century China had developed considerable regional specialisation and a nation-wide marketing system. Some cities in the lower Yangtze sustained large and varied handicraft industries. These industries drew their raw materials, and food for their populations, from great distances by the Yangtze and by the Grand Canal, which also supplied food and manufactured goods to the capital city, Peking.

The Chinese economy in the 19th century *(left)* Chinese exports of tea increased by over 50% in the period shown. Silk exports were increased fourfold. But ever-increasing imports of opium converted a net inflow of silver into a net outflow from the mid-1820s, with serious effects on the Chinese internal economy.

THE Ch'ing dynasty (1644-1911) was established by a non-Chinese people, the Manchus. From their homeland in the mountains of south-eastern Manchuria they gradually expanded, in the first decades of the 17th century, into the modern provinces of Liaoning and Kirin. With the aid of many Chinese, they established a stable Chinese-style state with its capital at Mukden (modern Shenyang) from 1625 to 1644; from this base they invaded Korea, reducing it to vassal status in 1637, and Inner Mongolia, which became a Manchu dependency in 1629-35. When the Ming were toppled by the rebel Li Tzu-ch'eng in 1644, the Manchus invaded China, proclaiming a new dynasty. In spite of Ming loyalist resistance in the south, most of the country was under Manchu control by 1652. Resistance continued in the south-west until 1659, and on the south-east coast Ming loyalists in 1662 occupied Taiwan (never previously under Chinese control), where they remained until 1683.

After the suppression of the rebellion of the Three Feudatories (see map 2), the Ch'ing enjoyed more than a century of internal peace and prosperity under a succession of very able rulers. The Manchus maintained their predominant place in government, and above all in the military. But they established a good working relationship with their Chinese officials, and by the end of the 18th century, deeply influenced by Chinese education and culture, had begun to lose their sharp identity. There was a number of risings of minority peoples, who were harshly exploited by Chinese and Manchus alike. There were tribal risings in Yunnan in 1726-9, among the Miao people of Kweichow in 1795-7 and again in 1829, among the Yao people of Kwangsi in 1790. The Chinese Muslim minority in Kansu rebelled in 1781-4. Most serious were the massive Chin-ch'uan tribal rebellions in western Szechwan. These first broke out in 1746-9, and after simmering for years were renewed in 1771-6, when order was finally restored after ruinously expensive military operations. A further rising occurred in the newly-occupied territory of Taiwan in 1787-8. All these risings were, however, in peripheral areas and posed no major threat to the dynasty.

At the end of the 18th century, rebellion took on a new form. By this time, although China remained immensely powerful, productive and populous, a major economic crisis loomed ahead. The area available for agriculture, which had been expanded by the introduction of new crops (maize (corn), sweet potato, groundnuts, tobacco) in the 16th and 17th centuries, was now almost totally occupied. The only vacant area suitable for Chinese-style agriculture was Manchuria, which was deliberately preserved as a Manchu homeland, and Chinese settlement in it banned. Meanwhile the population, held in check by the epidemics of the late 16th and the 17th centuries, and by the rebellions and hostilities of the late Ming and early Ch'ing, had trebled, from 100 million to 300 million, between 1650 and 1800, and continued to increase at a headlong pace. By 1850 it was 420 million. This constantly growing population had to be fed by ever more intensive cultivation of a limited area, and by the end of the 18th century population pressure was beginning to generate widespread hardship and impoverishment.

This hardship began to produce risings and rebel movements, usually inspired by secret societies, among the Chinese population. The first major outbreak was the series of risings known as the White Lotus rebellion, which erupted in the mountainous borderlands of Szechwan, Shensi and Hupeh in 1795-1804, and again on a lesser scale some years later. In Shantung a rebellion of the Eight Trigrams sect broke out in 1786-8, and in 1811 a large-scale rising of the sect of the Heavenly Principle broke out in Honan, Hopeh (Chihli) and Shantung, which was accompanied by an attempted coup in Peking before its final suppression in 1814. More risings occurred among the border peoples: the Tibetans near Koko Nor in 1807, the Yaos in Kweichow in 1833, and in Sinkiang, where the oases of Yarkand and Kashgar were in open rebellion from 1825 to 1828.

The basic economic problems of the country were made more severe by government policies of external expansion, which placed a great strain on the empire's very inefficient financial administration. Another factor was foreign trade. During the 17th and 18th centuries extensive export trades, mostly in tea, silk, porcelain and handicraft goods, were built up under government licence at Canton and with the Russians at Kyakhta. Since the Chinese economy was largely self-sufficient, these exports were paid for mostly in silver, the standard medium of currency in China. Late in the 18th century the foreign powers began to import opium into China from India and the Middle East to pay for exports. By the 1830s opium imports had outstripped the Chinese exports of tea and silk, and a drain of silver out of China began, which had increasingly serious effects upon the Chinese economy, and further impoverished the state finances.

Moreover, the quality of Ch'ing government began sharply to decline. In the late 18th century corruption became rife at every level of government from the court downwards, affecting both the civil administration and the Manchu armies, whose demoralisation, lack of supplies and equipment were shown up by the White Lotus rising. Moreover, the administration did not increase to keep pace with the vast growth of population; by the early 19th century the bureaucracy was grossly understaffed, and government came to delegate more and more power to the members of the local gentry, who acted as their unpaid agents.

By the 1820s, Manchu China was the world's largest and most populous empire, directly controlling vast territories in inner Asia, and treating as tributary states still larger areas: Korea, Indochina, Siam, Burma, Nepal. But within this huge empire, effective Ch'ing administrative and military control was gradually declining, while inexorable economic pressures built up which could be cured only by large-scale technological innovation and radical re-organisation. Neither was likely to be forthcoming, and in the meantime China faced new pressures from the expansionist Western powers.

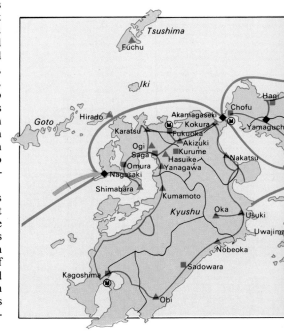

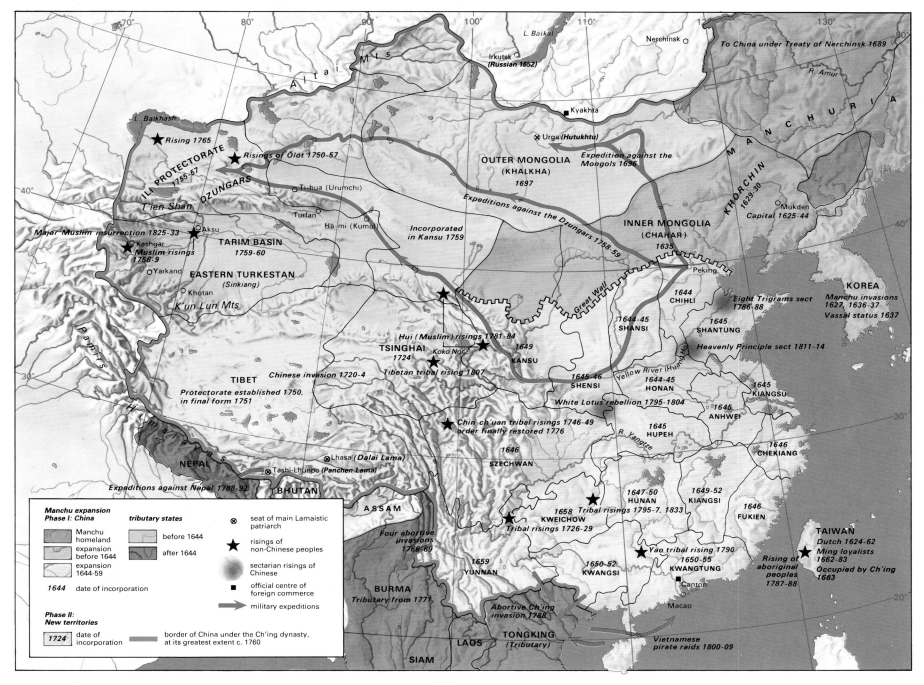

1/Chinese imperial expansion (above) Throughout the late 17th and the 18th centuries the Manchus pursued an expansionist policy, which left them in control of the Amur region in the north-east, Mongolia, Dzungaria, the Tarim Basin, the Ili region east of Lake Balkhash, and Tibet. Only a small part of these vast regions was incorporated under Chinese administration, and apart from military garrisons few Chinese or Manchus settled there. But these campaigns of conquest, triggered off in part by the fear of Russian expansion into Siberia and of British and French expansion into India, were immensely expensive. Chinese military expeditions went still further. Four abortive invasions of Burma were mounted in 1766-69, an expedition into Nepal in 1788-92, and a large-scale invasion of Tongking was undertaken in 1788, only to end in failure. There was a series of widespread peasant rebellions in the late 18th and early 19th centuries, usually inspired by millenarian sects. In almost every case they broke out in areas severely affected by the economic problems caused by population pressure.

4/Japan in isolation (below) In 1603 Tokugawa Ieyasu, who had established military dominance over the Japanese state reunified in 1590 by Hideyoshi, was made Shogun (Military Leader) by the powerless imperial court. The shogunate he founded lasted until 1868 and gave Japan a much-needed period of political stability. A complex government emerged in which the many fiefs (han) of feudal lords (daimyo) – some 250 in number – were dominated and regulated by the Shogun's government (Bakufu) in Edo. Society was organised in a hierarchy of classes, and a legal code enacted. The Christian missionaries active in the late 16th century were banned after 1612, and Christians systematically persecuted in the 1630s. Japanese were forbidden to travel abroad, and foreign contacts were limited to the Dutch, who maintained a post at Nagasaki, the Chinese and Koreans. Despite this isolation, Tokugawa Japan was extremely prosperous. Trade and cities grew rapidly. The population rose from about 20 million in 1600 to about 30 million in the 18th century. By the 19th century Japan was prosperous, well governed, had a high standard of literacy, and was far better prepared than China to meet the challenge of Western expansion.

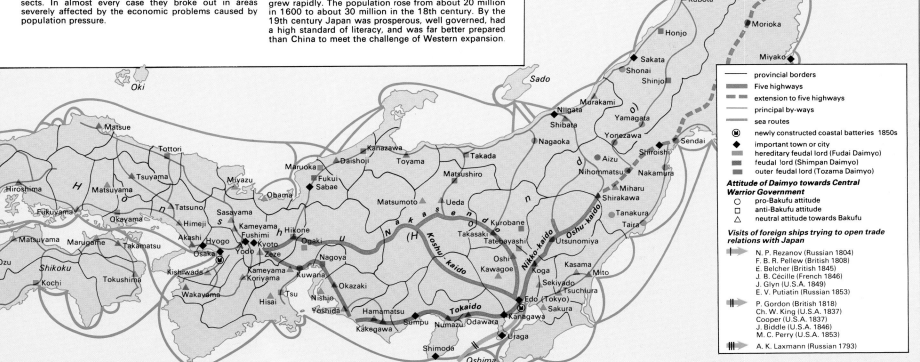

South-East Asia and the European powers 1511 to 1826

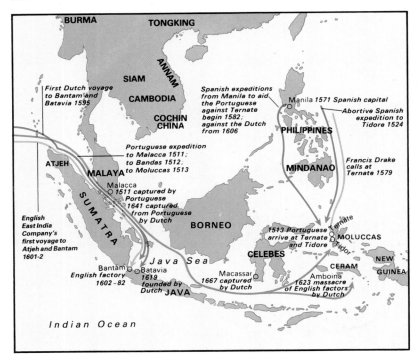

2/**The spice routes** (*above*) The Portuguese first appeared in the Moluccas and Bandas in 1512-13. Francis Drake visited Ternate in 1579. The Dutch began to trade with them in 1599; though the Anglo-Dutch treaty of 1619 provided for joint trading, the Dutch forced their partners out. The Spaniards of Manila came to the aid of the Portuguese in the Moluccas, and there was a long struggle before the Dutch gained full control.

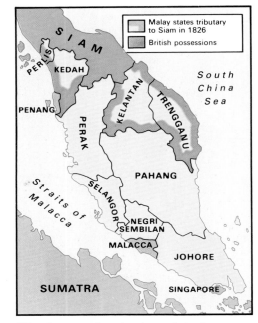

4/**The Malay states in 1826** (*left*) By the Treaty of London (1824) the Dutch withdrew from the Malay peninsula. The British settlements there — Penang, Singapore and Malacca — were bound by the doctrine of non-intervention laid down in Pitt's India Act. The immediate danger to the independence of the Malay states in 1826 lay in Siamese expansionism; the Burney Treaty in that year halted Siam's pressure upon them, though only after two incidents in which the Penang government safeguarded Perak's independence.

3/**Dutch expansion in Java** (*below*) Dutch territorial expansion in Java began through Sultan Agung of Mataram's attempts to capture Batavia. After his death in 1646 the Dutch East India Company, by intervening in succession disputes, gradually became the strongest political force in the island, with the ruling houses coming under its control and paying their debts by cessions of territory. The maintenance of its trade monopoly played a vital part in this expansion.

WHEN the 16th century dawned, the present Union of Burma consisted of four monarchies: Arakan (capital Myohaung), Burmese Ava, dominating the main Irrawaddy valley, Burmese Toungoo, dominating the Sittang valley, and Mon Pegu, dominating the Irrawaddy delta and Tenasserim. To the north and east of Ava a number of formidable Shan states threatened Burmese independence. Half a century later the Toungoo dynasty was to conquer both Shans and Mons. In the valley of the Chao Phraya the ruler of Ayutthaya headed a powerful Thai kingdom which controlled much of the eastern coast of the Malay peninsula. The Laos kingdom of Luang Prabang stretched along the upper and middle Mekong. The Vietnamese of Tongking and northern Annam had in 1471 annexed Cham territories down to Qui Nhon. Later they were to absorb the remaining Cham lands to the south and wrest the Mekong delta from Cambodia. Phnom Penh, not Angkor, was the capital of the much reduced Khmer kingdom. In the Malay archipelago the Javanese empire of Majapahit was little more than a memory; there were hundreds of small states with little cohesion. Islamisation was proceeding in Sumatra, Java and Borneo, chiefly from Malacca, which was the capital of an empire which included the Malay states of the peninsula and of Sumatra's east coast.

In 1511 Albuquerque conquered the great emporium of Malacca for the king of Portugal. Its ruling family escaped and established the sultanate of Johore further south, with much the same territorial sway as Malacca had exercised over the mainland Malay states and those of the Sumatran coast opposite. The Portuguese objective was to dominate the spice trade through a chain of forts linked by naval power.

Had they united, the Malay states might have driven out the invaders, but Atjeh in Sumatra strove against Johore for the leadership of the Malay world, and it was left to the Dutch East India Company, formed in 1602, to conquer the Portuguese settlements. Before then, the Spaniards had established themselves in the Philippines, making Manila, captured in 1571, their capital. From their centre at Batavia in western Java the Dutch controlled the Moluccas and Banda islands, the 'Spice Islands', making the local rulers their pensioners. They captured Malacca in 1641, but their many attempts to take Manila all failed. At the time of the Spanish occupation, the Philippines had no political organisation except for the Muslim states on Mindanao; these, in alliance with the sultans of the Sulu archipelago, maintained their independence until the 19th century.

Like the Portuguese, the Dutch empire began as one of fortified trading posts based upon sea power. But Sultan Agung of Mataram (1613-46), campaigning for supremacy over Java, failed twice to conquer Batavia, and from the 1670s his successors became dependent upon Dutch aid in their constant succession struggles, and paid for it by cessions of territory. The sultanate of Bantam, with its immensely valuable pepper trade, came under Dutch control in the same way in 1684. This involved the expulsion of the staff of the weaker rival of the Dutch, the English East India Company, from its factory there, and the transfer of its settlement to the pepper port of Benkulen on the west coast of Sumatra. After the 'Massacre of Amboina' in 1623 it had abandoned direct trade to the Spice Islands and relied upon obtaining spices indirectly through Macassar in Celebes (Sulawesi); in 1667 that source was dammed up through the Dutch conquest of the port.

The mainland monarchies of Arakan, Burma, Siam, Cambodia, Luang Prabang and Annam had little interest in European trade. They employed Portuguese adventurers as mercenaries in the 16th century, but the attempts of the latter to seize power in Lower Burma and Cambodia at the end of the century caused strong xenophobia. This increased in the next century as a result of the behaviour of the Portuguese freebooters (*feringhi*) and the attempts of the Dutch to monopolise Siam's foreign trade. To check the Dutch, King Narai (1661-88) and his Greek adviser, Constant Phaulkon, made the mistake of invoking French aid. Louis XIV's takeover bid, involving the planting of French garrisons at Bangkok and Mergui, stirred up strong popular reaction which led both to a change of dynasty at Ayutthaya and to the expulsion of the French, with heavy loss. Burma became the scene of dramatic events when the Mons rebelled in 1740 and set up a king of their own at Pegu. Their capture of the Burmese capital Ava in 1752 brought a new Burmese leader, Alaungpaya, to the fore. Josef Dupleix at Pondicherry intervened on the side of the Mons, and the English East India Company at Madras in reply seized the island of Negrais at the mouth of the Bassein river as a naval base. Alaungpaya defeated the Mons and their French allies, founding Rangoon in 1755 as the southern port of a reunited Burma. In 1759 he captured Negrais and the British left Burma.

By that time the English East India Company's expanding trade with China was causing it to look for a more southerly site for a naval station: ultimately in 1786 Penang was acquired for this purpose from the Sultan of Kedah. The conquest of Holland in 1795 by French revolutionary armies led to the British occupation of Malacca and of a number of Dutch settlements in the archipelago. In 1811 Java was conquered. After the fall of Napoleon in 1815, however, the British restored their possessions in South-East Asia to the Dutch. Trouble arose with the Dutch when Raffles acquired Singapore for the British, which was only settled by the Anglo-Dutch treaty of 1824 which drew a dividing line through the Straits of Malacca. As a result the British abandoned their west Sumatran settlements and the Dutch handed over Malacca and recognised British possession of Singapore. Borneo, omitted from the treaty, was to become the subject of further disagreement between the two parties when, in the 1840s, James Brooke became Rajah of Sarawak.

The aggressive dynasty founded by the Burmese leader Alaungpaya, after failing to make good its conquest of Siam in 1767, switched its efforts westwards to Arakan, Manipur and Assam, which it conquered and from which it threatened Bengal. Hence the first Anglo-Burmese war of 1824-26, which resulted in the annexation of Assam, Arakan and Tenasserim to British India and measures to stabilise India's north-eastern frontier. Arakan's once-famous rice industry revived through contact with India, but the great development of Burma's rice production only began after the British occupa-

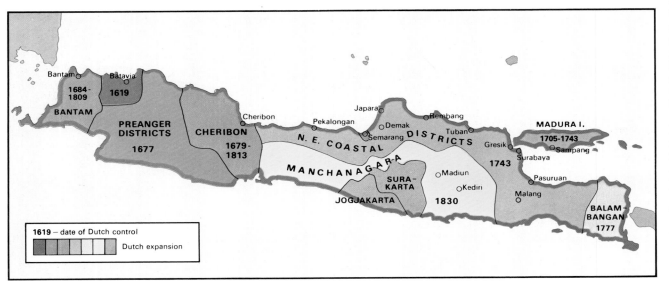

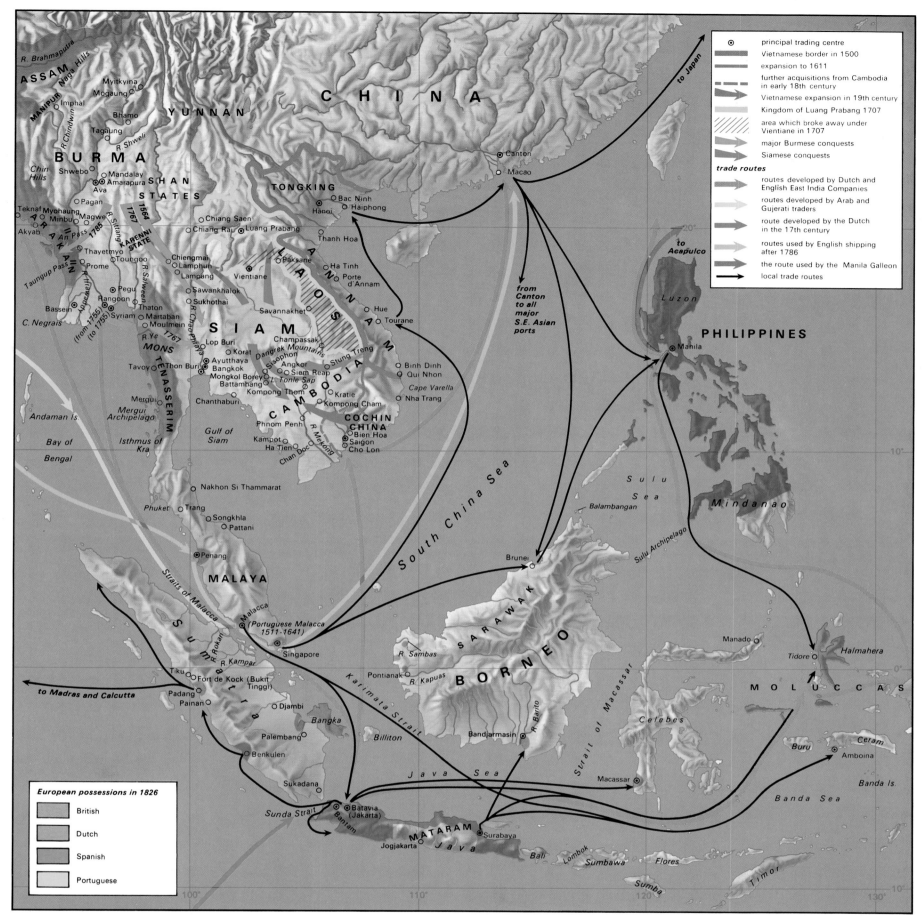

1/The Europeans in South-East Asia *(above)* The increasing European demand for spices and pepper led the maritime powers to seek direct trade with the islands producing them, thereby opening new fields for the missionary and the adventurer. The Dutch drove all their rivals out of the spice trade; Spain took over the Philippines. European activities made little impact upon the mainland monarchies, but in the 18th century brought coffee, China tea and chinoiserie into European social life.

tion of the Irrawaddy delta region after the second Anglo-Burmese war of 1852, as did the systematic exploitation of its teak forests.

European activities had comparatively little effect upon the economies of the South-East Asian states before the 19th century, when the Industrial Revolution created an increasing demand for raw materials, markets and openings for capital investment. Great Britain's impact was minimal until the foundation of Singapore in 1819 as a free trade port. Earlier, the Spaniards had sought to keep the Philippines *incommunicado*, but the Manila Galleon, trading with

Acapulco (Mexico), brought the silver dollar into the international trade of the western Pacific. After the British occupation of 1762-64 had temporarily opened Manila to world commerce, the Spaniards began to foster the cultivation of tobacco, sugar, hemp and other commercial products, some of which became important in world markets, though not until 1834 was Manila officially opened to foreign traders.

At an earlier stage the Portuguese and the Dutch had forced their way into the long-established spice and pepper trades and their counterpart, the import of Indian textiles into South-East Asia. In the 18th century the Dutch introduced coffee cultivation into the parts of Java they directly controlled, but their policy of 'buy cheap, sell dear' bore heavily upon the peasantry. Nevertheless the principle of free peasant cultivation was maintained until 1830 when, with the introduction of the so-called 'Culture System', the Javanese were compelled to devote one-fifth of their land to export crops designated by the government.

Raffles *(right)* Appointed at the age of thirty as lieutenant-governor of British-occupied Java (1811-16), Raffles determined, after the restoration of the island empire of the Dutch, to seek a new focus for British power 'within its gates'. In 1819 he founded Singapore, permanently breaking the Dutch trading monopoly.

The European economy: agriculture and agricultural society 1500 to 1815

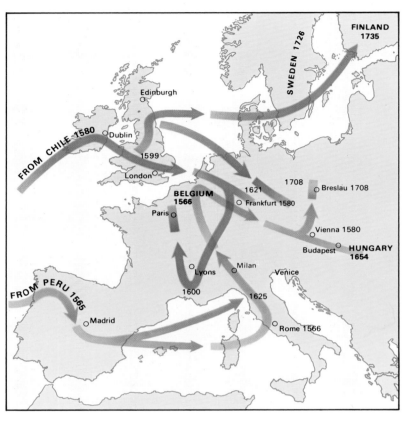

2/The introduction of the potato to Europe (above) Yielding four times as much carbohydrate per acre as wheat, this South American import spread rapidly after its arrival in 1525 – first in gardens and small farms, then as a key field crop after 1700.

3/Land Reclamation in the Netherlands (left) Between 1540 and 1715 the people of Friesland, Zeeland and Holland wrested 364,565 acres from the sea, mainly around the river estuaries, and another 84,638 acres from around the edges of their inland lakes. Their capital-intensive methods, based on widespread use of windmills and pumps, were adapted, with great success, to draining the English Fenlands, and also more patchily in France, Italy and North Germany.

DURING this period Europe's agricultural economy as a whole improved only slowly, mainly in response to the needs of the steadily rising population. This is estimated to have grown from 69 to 188 million between 1500 and 1800, mainly in the towns and cities. But there were sharp regional contrasts. Whereas the majority of European farmers were subsistence peasants on smallholdings of from 2 to 10 hectares, the situation in north-west Europe, especially Belgium, Holland and Britain, was quite different. There an agricultural revolution, beginning in the 16th century, had produced a highly efficient, commercialised farming system by 1800. Most farms elsewhere, though, still consisted of many small parcels of ground distributed throughout the village lands. Each farm usually had a small adjacent enclosed paddock and sometimes an orchard. Techniques and levels of productivity had hardly changed since Roman times. Most peasants probably produced only about 20 per cent more each year than they needed to feed their families, their livestock and to provide for next year's seed. Consequently, in most countries about 80 per cent of the people worked on the land. But in Britain and the Low Countries, this fell rapidly in the 19th century. By 1811 the British proportion was already down to 33 per cent, releasing a huge workforce for the new mines, iron works and textile factories.

Most improvements in this period, apart from Britain and the Netherlands, came from the introduction of new, more productive crops, mainly from America. Thus the potato became a basic staple in western Europe. In Ireland it allowed so massive an increase in population (from 2.5 to 8 million) that disaster struck when the crop failed in 1846.

American maize, similarly introduced into southern Europe, gave a far higher yield per hectare than the old regional cereals – barley, millet and sorghum. Buckwheat, useful on poor

soils, entered northern Europe from Russia. In the Mediterranean, sugar cane, rice and citrus fruits had arrived from Asia before 1500. Sugar production declined after 1550 in face of competition from Madeira, the Canaries and, after 1600, the West Indies and Brazil.

These slow crop changes contrasted strongly with the rapidly developing north-west. The Dutch began the process by pouring capital into reclaiming land from the sea. Naturally wishing to avoid leaving land fallow every third year (as under the old system), they discovered that fertility could be maintained by an elaborate rotation of crops, each removing different chemicals from the soils. Specially important were turnips (on which sheep could be grazed in winter, giving manure as well as mutton and wool), and peas, beans and clovers which actually restored nitrogen to the soil (though no one understood this at the time). England took these innovations much further. English farming was transformed by improved farm implements such as iron ploughs and Jethro Tull's seed drill, and such projects as extensive liming to neutralise soil acidity, irrigation and massive drainage. By 1750, 17 per cent of England's exports were foodstuffs and the old fear of famine had been banished.

Such techniques gradually spread as the growth of towns encouraged more specialisation in food production. Holland concentrated on dairy products and was exporting 90 per cent of her cheese by 1700. The Danes were sending 80,000 head of cattle a year to Germany, and the Dutch, German and Italian cloth industries were sustained by massive imports of Spanish wool. Spain, with 3 million sheep in the 16th century, gradually lost her lead to German wool and imported cotton. Trade grew between the cereals and timber of northern Europe and the

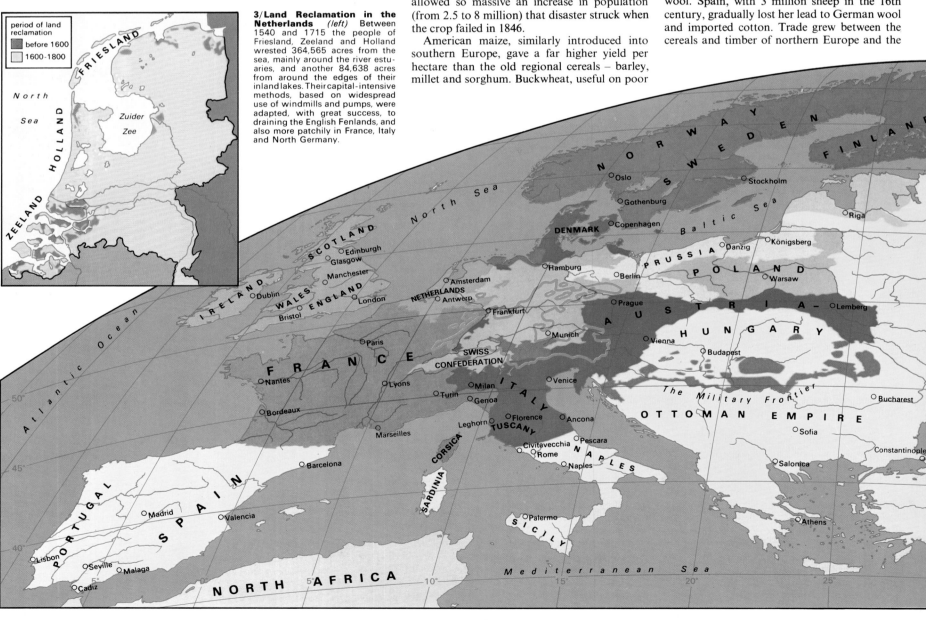

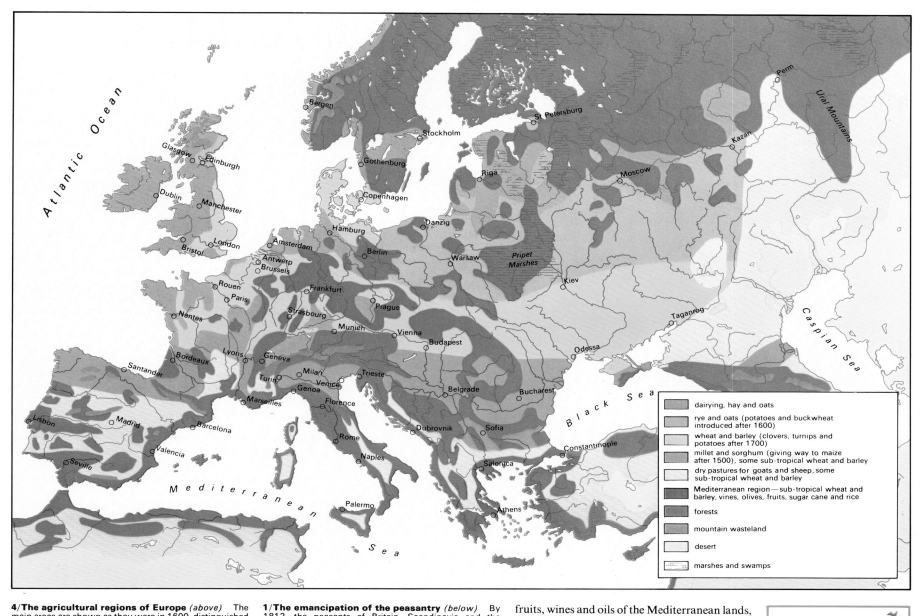

4/The agricultural regions of Europe *(above)* The main areas are shown as they were in 1600, distinguished by predominant activity or crops. Boundaries are only approximate. Potatoes gradually took over from cereals in many parts of northern and central Europe, while maize in the south replaced millet and sorghum.

Legend for map 4:

- dairying, hay and oats
- rye and oats (potatoes and buckwheat introduced after 1600)
- wheat and barley (clovers, turnips and potatoes after 1700)
- millet and sorghum (giving way to maize after 1500), some sub-tropical wheat and barley
- dry pastures for goats and sheep, some sub-tropical wheat and barley
- Mediterranean region—sub-tropical wheat and barley, vines, olives, fruits, sugar cane and rice
- forests
- mountain wasteland
- desert
- marshes and swamps

1/The emancipation of the peasantry *(below)* By 1812, the peasants of Britain, Scandinavia and the Netherlands had long been free. Those of Denmark and the Habsburg's Austrian Empire, were encouraged in their efforts by the revolution of 1789, which unshackled the French peasantry and revivified emancipation movements in Poland and Germany, scene of the most famous peasant revolt (1525). Only Russia, Spain, Portugal and Southern Italy remained fully under the landlords' yoke.

fruits, wines and oils of the Mediterranean lands, with Danzig becoming a great export port, as did Leghorn, handling wine and fruit. Better farming not only released labour for industry but also helped to provide both capital and markets. In the 18th century, 15 per cent of British iron production was for horseshoes.

All improvements in productivity depended on breaking the old feudal relationships which oppressed the peasants. Here there was a sharp east-west cleavage. Prior to 1500 feudalism had been stronger in the older settled areas of western Europe than in the still sparsely peopled lands of eastern Europe and Russia, where nomadic herdsmen still roamed. After 1500 this was completely changed. Peasants in north-west Europe exchanged the old labour services on the lords' land for a money rent (especially in England and the Netherlands) or for share-cropping tenancies *(métayage)* in France and further south. They also gradually freed themselves from burdensome personal services and dues, though this required revolutionary action, inspired by France in 1789, before it was complete.

In total contrast feudal power grew and spread in eastern Europe till it became almost slavery. Feudal lords increased their power, halting migration to empty lands further east (as in Russia) and increasing grain-export profits (as in eastern Germany and Poland-Lithuania). Free peasants only survived in newly conquered lands, when they agreed to perform military service instead of paying rent. Notable examples were the Volga Cossacks around Saratov and the settlers on the 'military frontier' in Hungary after it was freed from the Turks c. 1700-1710.

The peasants of western Germany occupied a middle position. They had tried to win complete freedom in a great revolt in 1525, partly inspired by Luther and the Swiss example. For a short time they controlled most of southern Germany before their revolt was savagely crushed. Yet the worst east European excesses were averted, and the peasants gradually moved towards greater freedom between 1600 and 1800. Their slow emancipation was, however, an important reason for the German industrial revolution coming so late.

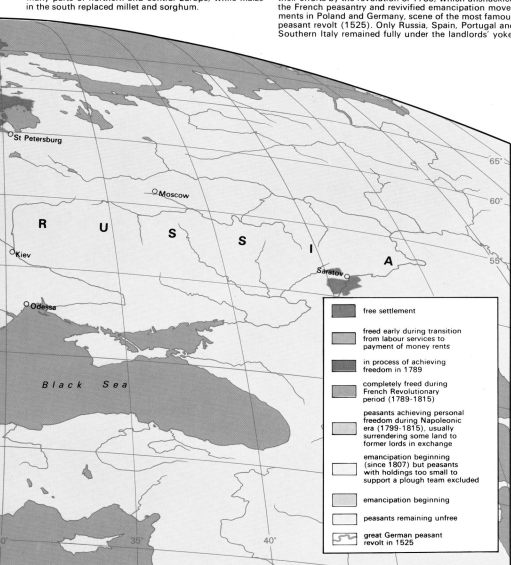

Legend for map 1:

- free settlement
- freed early during transition from labour services to payment of money rents
- in process of achieving freedom in 1789
- completely freed during French Revolutionary period (1789-1815)
- peasants achieving personal freedom during Napoleonic era (1799-1815), usually surrendering some land to former lords in exchange
- emancipation beginning (since 1807) but peasants with holdings too small to support a plough team excluded
- emancipation beginning
- peasants remaining unfree
- great German peasant revolt in 1525

Jethro Tull's Seed Drill *(above)* Described in Tull's *Horse Hoeing Husbandry* (1733) this machine gradually ousted the wasteful hand-scatterer.

Developments in Animal Breeding *(above)* Robert Bakewell's New Leicester long-wool sheep and greatly improved shire horses. John Ellman's short-wool breeds and the Colling brothers' shorthorn cattle started a new world industry.

Crop Rotation *(above)* Fields, once left fallow one year out of two or three, now produced continuous yields.

The European economy: trade and industry 1550 to 1775

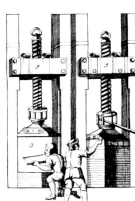

Baling press *(above)* from a German textile mill was used for preparing cloth for transportation. Even before 1700 expanding woollen and linen industries in Saxony and Bohemia began to encroach on the old English and Flemish markets.

3/Atlantic trade in the 18th century *(left)* Slaves and tropical produce from the new colonial empires made fortunes for all the main west European ports, from Cadiz to Glasgow shown here according to the size of their trade.

EUROPE'S population, expanding fast in the 16th century, was retarded by famine, plague and large-scale war in the 17th, and rapid growth was not resumed before the middle of the 18th century. The total nearly doubled overall during this period, and towns and cities grew even faster. In 1500 only four cities – Paris, Milan, Naples and Venice – had more than 100,000 inhabitants. By 1700 this number had trebled, and London, Paris and Constantinople had passed the half-million mark.

Increased complexity of government, a marked stepping-up of trade and finance, a growing taste for organised pleasure and conspicuous consumption, and a feeling that survival was better assured in the cities, all helped to hasten this trend. The resulting problems, particularly the need to guarantee large and reliable urban food supplies, also created new opportunities. Most notably, they generated a massive demand for eastern Europe's wheat and rye. In the century down to 1650, great quantities were going to western Europe, reaching even as far as Portugal, Spain and Italy. This trade fed the burgeoning economic strength of Holland, now nearly monopolising the Baltic carrying trade.

The Netherlands, whose shipbuilders, merchants and manufacturers consistently maintained a leading position in this period, formed the hinge for a gradual but decisive shift in commercial power. In 1500 industry remained largely concentrated in the narrow corridor running from Antwerp and Bruges, through Ulm and Augsburg, thence to Florence and Milan. Although English woollens, French linens and Spanish iron all possessed international reputations and markets, the main non-agricultural activity, whether it was in textiles and weapons, or in newer developments like paper, glass, printing and cloth-making, all lay along this north-south line. By 1700 this north-south axis had swung almost through ninety degrees. At one end stood England and Holland, not merely the greatest textile producers of Europe, but also owners of the greatest merchant fleets, the most active traders, and with fast-developing manufacturers of ships and metalwares; eastward the line extended through the metal and woollen districts of the lower Rhine to the great industrial concentrations in the hills of Saxony, Bohemia and Silesia. Even huge and backward Russia was beginning to build up, for the first time since the Mongols, its own industrial base. But the great trading cities of northern Italy and the southern Netherlands, dominant two centuries earlier, were mostly stagnant after a severe decline.

The advance of technology was patchy and intermittent. The power-driven silk mills of the Po valley were the mechanical wonders of the 17th century, but produced little imitation. The spread of watch-making in the early 18th

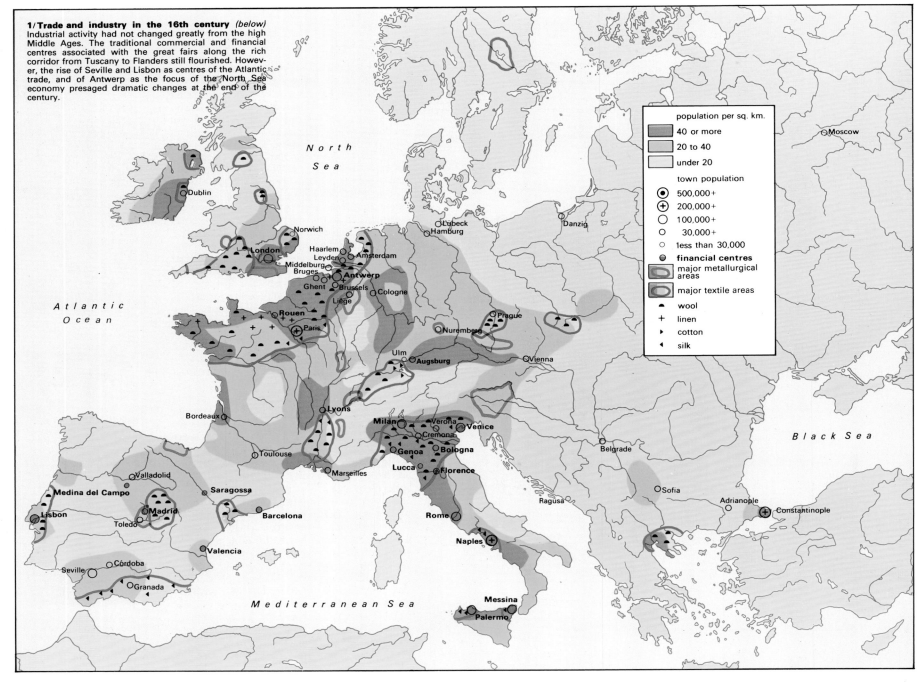

1/Trade and industry in the 16th century *(below)* Industrial activity had not changed greatly from the high Middle Ages. The traditional commercial and financial centres associated with the great fairs along the rich corridor from Tuscany to Flanders still flourished. However, the rise of Seville and Lisbon as centres of the Atlantic trade, and of Antwerp as the focus of the North Sea economy presaged dramatic changes at the end of the century.

population per sq. km.
- 40 or more
- 20 to 40
- under 20

town population
- 500,000+
- 200,000+
- 100,000+
- 30,000+
- less than 30,000
- financial centres
- major metallurgical areas
- major textile areas
- wool
- linen
- cotton
- silk

century created a repository of precision skills, and Newcomen's mine pump opened the way to the advance of the steam engine. But the crucial breakthrough to the age of steam, James Watt's separate condenser (1769), made its industrial impact only in the last years of the century. Industrial expansion was achieved by the flooding of a great number of workers into industrial occupations using the old methods. Even this, however, made it possible to improve industrial organisation, by splitting up production processes, developing production in rural areas free of urban restriction, and drawing on the cheap part-time labour of peasant families. Wool, linen and much metal manufacture was controlled by traders who organised a scattered cottage labour force. By the 18th century this had become the typical form of all but local and luxury industry.

Much more impressive, however, than the slow and erratic spread of industry was the striking increase in international trade. No longer confined to Europe, the maritime powers, with their colonies and trading ports established all over Asia and the Americas, attracted a fast-growing stream of new exotic tropical products: tea, coffee, sugar, chocolate, tobacco. They were paid for with European manufactures – the British linen and metalware industries particularly thrived on the expanding colonial markets – and with the shipping, insurance and merchanting services that built up the wealth of the western ports, all the way from Bordeaux up to London and Glasgow and even Hamburg. All these became the seats of wealthy merchant firms and great shipping interests.

Governments assisted the sectors of economic activity they favoured. Holland and England waged wars to protect and expand their shipping and trading interests, but did not consistently aid industry. The governments of France and

central European states established new industries and gave protection and subsidies to old ones. Increasingly costly wars, however, had an influence even more powerful than explicit economic policies. They called for heavy taxation, with the burdens falling largely on the producing classes, and large borrowings that undermined the precarious stability of Europe's gradually evolving monetary systems. These were ruinous to Spain and damaging to France and many smaller states; only Holland and England kept their military commitments within bounds that they could realistically finance.

Trade and war also generated an unprecedented demand for money. After being desperately short, gold and silver were amply – for a time, more than amply – supplied from Spanish Mexico and Peru after 1550, supported from the 1690s by Brazilian gold. This bullion was rapidly redistributed all over Europe by merchants and by Spanish government transactions, and much of it went to finance large trade deficits with the East Indies and the Levant. The money supply was supplemented by the growth of banking in western Europe. Breaking away from the older banking methods of Italy and the German towns, which were heavily engaged in government lending, Dutch and English banks served private interests with giro and foreign exchange facilities and short-term credits. For a century, almost from its opening in 1609, the Amsterdam Exchange Bank, with its links in every important commercial centre, was the undisputed focus of continental trade; England could compete with it only when, in 1694, the Bank of England provided a focus for older private banking firms. With low interest rates, free capital movement, secure international payments and an assured savings flow, the foundations of modern finance were now firmly laid in England and Holland.

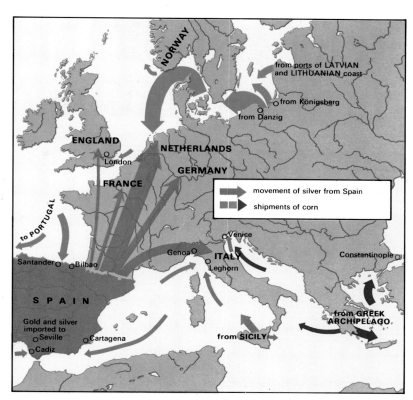

4/ Grain trade and silver flows within Europe 1550-1650 *(above)* The bullion-bearing galleons from the Indies brought a flood of liquid funds to the Spanish treasury. But it flowed out as fast as it arrived, to finance the Habsburgs and to pay for the Baltic grain now needed to victual a Mediterranean no longer able to feed itself.

2/ Trade and industry in the 18th century *(below)* Even before the Industrial Revolution, there has been a dramatic change. Italy and Spain have fallen back, while England, with major metal-working and mining interests, Holland, building ships for the whole of Europe, France behind a high protective wall, and Sweden, exploiting her mineral resources, are all developing fast.

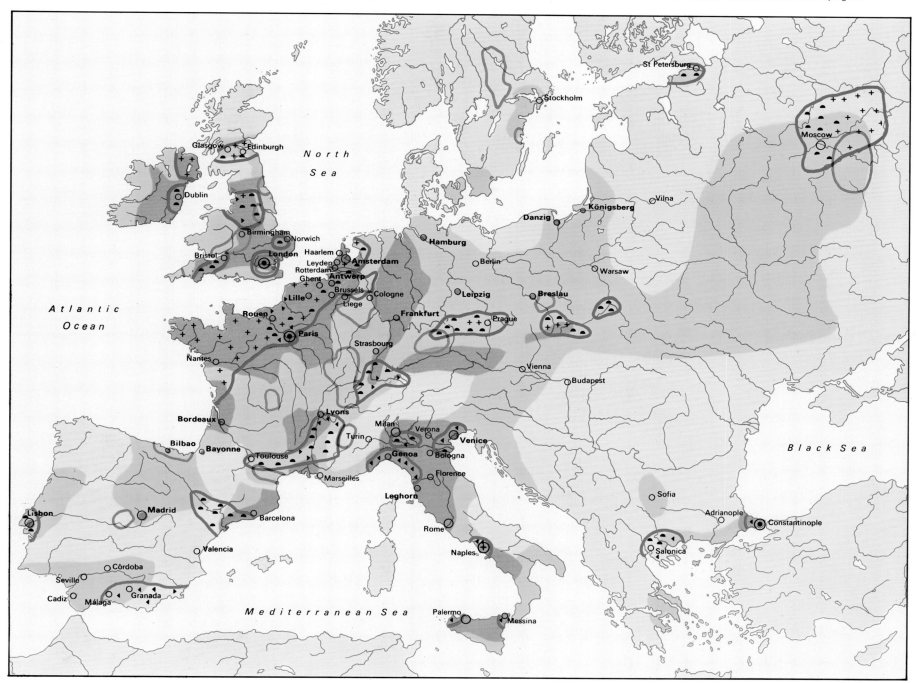

Reformation and counter-reformation: the wars of religion in Europe 1517 to 1648

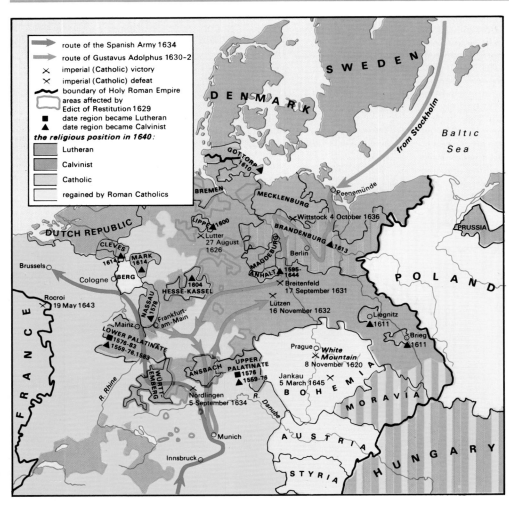

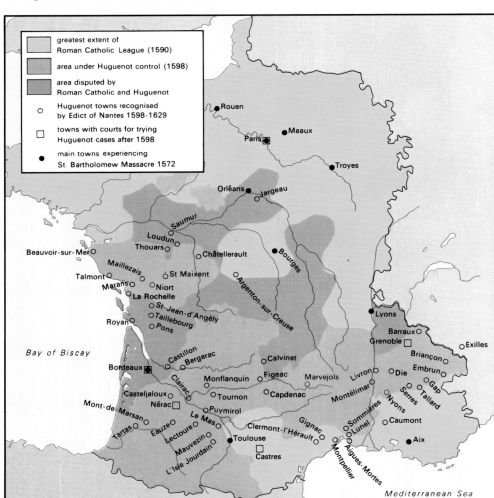

2 and 3/Religious conflict to 1640 By 1640, the Protestant hold on Europe had weakened. Although the Mediterranean lands were still Catholic and the countries on the northern periphery were still Protestant, there were major changes in France (*below*) and the Holy Roman Empire (*above*). In the former, four decades of intermittent civil war and occasional massacres reduced the Huguenots, as French Protestants were called, to a small area around La Rochelle and a rather larger area in the south. Another period of war, from 1621-29, reduced their territories even further and in 1685 Protestantism was forbidden. The Thirty Years War (*above*) extirpated Protestantism in the Habsburgs' patrimonial lands, but not in north Germany, thanks to military intervention by Denmark (1624-29), Sweden (after 1630) and France (after 1635) on the side of the Protestants.

RELIGION held a central place in the lives of the people of early modern Europe. It elevated and dignified every major action in their lives, from birth and baptism to death and burial, and it held out the hope of salvation. The need for reassurance about the after-life appears to have been particularly acute in the years around 1500.

At first this spiritual revival was contained within the existing churches: Roman Catholic in the west and Greek Orthodox in the east, with the frontier running through Poland-Lithuania (two-fifths Orthodox) and to the south of Hungary to reach the Adriatic just south of Ragusa. The only important groups outside these two monolithic communities were the Jews, the Lollards (a small and fragmented group of English dissenters), a few Moors in southern Spain, and the Hussites (including over half the population of Bohemia and Moravia). 'Heresy' was thus virtually dead in 1500 and, faced by no substantial rivals, the Roman Catholic church became complacent and failed to deploy its wealth adequately to satisfy the 'spiritual hunger' of the early 16th century. Absenteeism, for example, was growing among the clergy and there were enough ignorant and immoral priests to discredit the Church in the eyes of many laymen. It was the conjuncture of a spiritually bankrupt yet materially acquisitive church at a time of heightened religious awareness which explains why a religious revolution occurred in the 16th century.

Within only fifty years almost 40 per cent of the inhabitants of Europe observed a 'Reformed' theology. The first reformers came from Germany and German-speaking Switzerland, led by Martin Luther (1483-1546) in Saxony and north Germany, and Huldreich Zwingli (1484-1531) in Zurich (the first state to renounce allegiance to Rome, in 1520) and the surrounding towns of south Germany. By 1570, out of every ten subjects of the Holy Roman Emperor, seven were Protestants. The Protestants already held Scandinavia, Baltic Europe, and England. There was a limited penetration of France, Spain, Italy and the Netherlands, and of the German settlements in eastern Europe.

Then came a new wave of Protestantism, the work of John Calvin (1509-64), a Frenchman, who implemented his ideas from 1541 in the city-state of Geneva. Calvinism made swift progress: in France there were over a hundred Calvinist churches by 1559 and perhaps 700 by 1562; in the Netherlands, there were perhaps 20 Calvinist churches by 1559 and over 150 by 1566; in Germany, several Lutheran states (most notably the Palatinate and Brandenburg) changed their official religion to Calvinism; and in Scotland a complete reformed polity was established by act of Parliament in 1560. Calvin's church also achieved some striking successes in eastern Europe, especially in Poland and Transylvania, two countries which also tolerated the existence of other minority groups in some numbers: Unitarians, Bohemian Brethren, Anabaptists and Jews. In Hungary and in other areas under Ottoman control, Catholic worship was prohibited and Calvinism received official protection. Calvinism also won more adherents among the Slavs, both noble and middle class, than Lutheranism.

The toleration of Protestantism was often fragile, however. In many countries, including the Holy Roman Empire, it was the product of weakness rather than strength, and it only occurred in countries where the state was not strong enough to impose the religious uniformity which in early modern times was considered essential to political survival. It was inevitable that the 'states without stakes' would perish as soon as their governments became powerful enough to enforce the chosen faith on all their subjects. What was not inevitable was that the

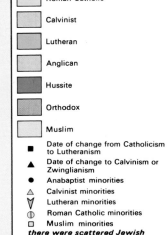

	Roman Catholic
	Calvinist
	Lutheran
	Anglican
	Hussite
	Orthodox
	Muslim
■	Date of change from Catholicism to Lutheranism
▲	Date of change to Calvinism or Zwinglianism
●	Anabaptist minorities
△	Calvinist minorities
⩔	Lutheran minorities
⊕	Roman Catholic minorities
□	Muslim minorities

there were scattered Jewish communities in the Ottoman Empire, Hungary, Poland, Portugal, Bohemia and Italy

chosen faith after 1570 should so often have been Catholicism.

Not all the men who wished to reform the Church in the earlier 16th century rejected the authority of the Pope. St Ignatius Loyola (1491-1556), who founded the Jesuit order, was just one of the many who decided that the best way to achieve salvation was to remain obedient to Rome and to persuade others to do the same. From 1540 onwards, even the Papacy began to accept the need for some reforms, and a General Council of the Church was summoned to meet at Trent, on the border between Italy and Germany. There were three sessions (1545-47, 1551-52 and 1562-63) which achieved three things: the worst clerical abuses (absenteeism and the like) were condemned; the correct doctrine of the Church was defined (the *professio fidei tridentina*); and an efficient system of ecclesiastical supervision, to maintain clerical standards, was established. In addition, an educational offensive was mounted to promote orthodoxy among the laity.

With the aid of this revitalised organisation, the Catholic church began to regain some of its

losses. The Protestant 'share' of the European continent fell from 40 to 20 per cent between 1570 and 1650. In Poland, the largest country of eastern Europe, a succession of Catholic kings actively favoured Catholicism, and the number of Protestant churches in the country fell from around 560 in 1572 to only 240 in 1650. Much the same happened in the Habsburg lands further south: the Protestants were expelled from Austria (1597) and from Styria (1600). In France, the crown waged war for decades in order to beat off the Protestant challenge. Although there were perhaps 1¼ million Protestants in France in 1562, by 1629 there were only 1 million and by 1685, when the remainder was forced to choose between conversion to Catholicism or expulsion, there were scarcely 500,000.

The decisive phase of the struggle between Protestants and Catholics took place in the Holy Roman Empire. It began in 1618-21 when the Emperor, Ferdinand II, with the aid of troops and treasure from Spain, the German Catholics and the Papacy, defeated the Bohemian Protestants. Catholicism soon became the only

permitted religion in Bohemia and Moravia. Encouraged by this success, the Emperor tried to reduce the power of the Protestant princes in Germany. Despite the aid sent to them by England, Denmark and the Dutch, in 1629 the Emperor's forces were victorious and an 'Edict of Restitution' was issued which reclaimed large areas of Church land held by the Protestants. The German Protestants were only saved from collapse by the arrival of substantial military aid from King Gustavus Adolphus of Sweden: the Emperor's forces were defeated at Breitenfeld (1631) and Lützen (1632). Spain soon intervened to help the Emperor; France to help his enemies. The war had become a free-for-all with fighting spreading to almost the whole continent. The political as well as the religious rivalries of over a century were settled at the great battles of Nördlingen (1634), Wittstock (1636), Rocroi (1643) and Jankau (1646), and at the peace of Münster-Westphalia which followed. The religious and political frontiers of central Europe which were then agreed lasted unchanged for a hundred years.

Spreading the word of God *(above)* Of the 250,000 or so works printed in Europe between 1447 (the date of the earliest surviving printed book) and 1600, about three-quarters were written about religion. The Reformation would have been impossible without printing-presses like this one, which graced the cover of a book printed in Paris in 1511.

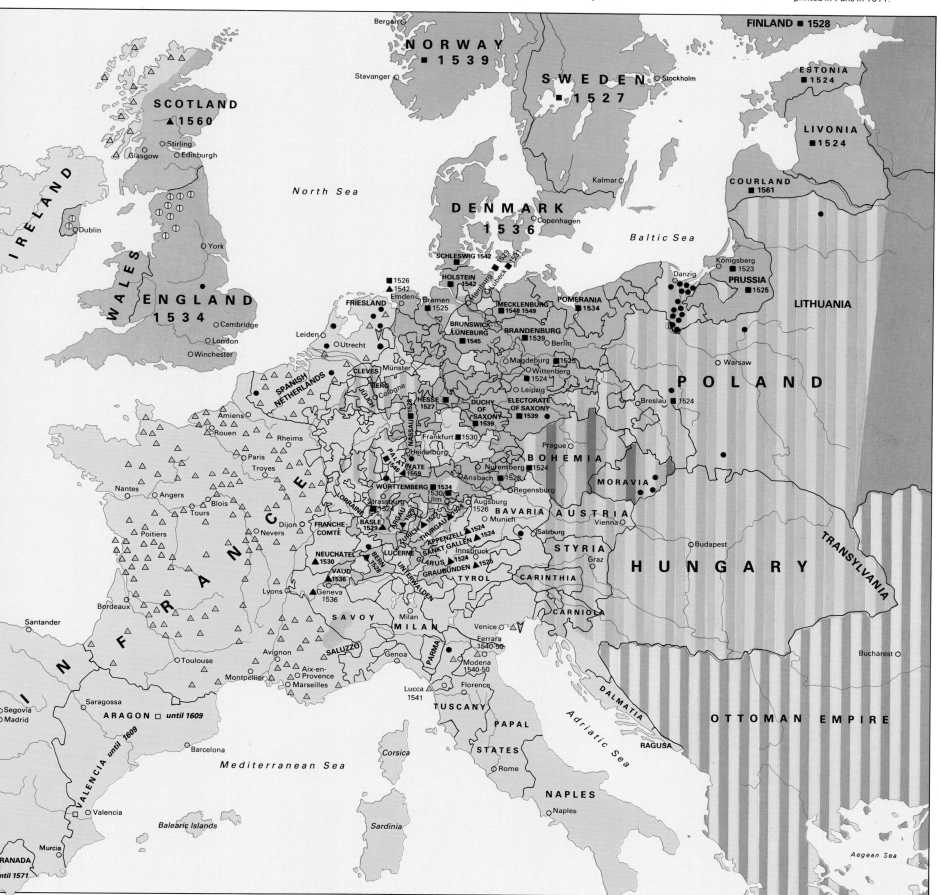

The rise of the modern state in north-west Europe 1500 to 1688

The Universal Soldier (above) This cartoon, first printed in the 1640s as propaganda against the English Parliamentary army in Ireland, reflects the civilians' hatred of the ill-fed soldier who enforced government policies while taking everything he needed from the local people — down to the sausages of his shoe buckles!

DESPITE their apparent strength, until 1660 the 'new monarchies' of Europe (see page 150) never entirely escaped from the framework of government which they inherited from earlier times. Their wealth, bureaucracies, control of religion and standing armies were not sufficient to break the patterns of personal dependence which had characterised monarchy in the feudal period (see page 124). The state still relied on the goodwill of its nobles for the enforcement of its policies (in England, for example, the Tudors depended upon unpaid Justices of the Peace, always local landowners, to apply their laws), and failure to retain the support of the landed classes could provoke major revolts. The French aristocracy staged several rebellions against the crown, culminating in the Fronde (1648-53); a section of the English aristocracy rebelled against Elizabeth I in 1569-70 (the 'Northern Rising') and many English peers supported Parliament's stand against Charles I after 1640; nobles of the Netherlands opposed their 'natural prince', Philip II of Spain, in 1566 and 1576.

The Fronde, the English Civil War and the Dutch Revolt were only the most important of the rebellions which threatened the 'new monarchies' of north-western Europe: uprisings against the state were a continuing fact of life throughout the 16th and 17th centuries. Some revolts arose from attacks on the privileges of the 'estates'; others were caused by economic hardship – from taxes imposed at a time of high prices and widespread unemployment, as was the case in most French popular revolts, or from the enclosing of common land, which caused the revolts of 1549 and 1607 in England; other uprisings (the Pilgrimage of Grace in England in 1536 and the Covenanting Movement in Scotland in 1638) were triggered off by unpopular

religious policies. In all cases the revolts were a response to attempts at innovation. Governments everywhere were endeavouring to create, in the words of James VI of Scotland soon after he became king of England in 1603: 'one worship to God, one kingdom entirely governed, one uniformity of laws'. The problem, however, was one of means, not ends. Neither James nor any of his fellow sovereigns had the resources to enforce such ambitious new policies. They lacked the revenues and the officials required. Even in France, which had the largest civil service in Europe, most of the 40,000 royal officials bought their offices or acquired them by hereditary succession and could pursue a course independent of the crown. They became a distinct aristocratic caste – the *noblesse de robe*.

The barriers to centralisation in early modern times were formidable. Many subjects did not speak the same language as their government (Breton and Provençal in France, Cornish and Welsh in England, Frisian in the Netherlands); there were many 'dark corners of the land' which were too inaccessible to be effectively governed; certain 'corporations', notably the Church, possessed privileges which protected them against state interference; and provinces recently annexed by the crown (see page 150) were protected by charters guaranteeing their traditional way of life. It was when the state tried to erode or remove these privileges that the most serious political upheavals occurred. The Dutch rebelled in 1566, 1572 and 1576 largely because they believed that the central government, controlled from Spain, threatened their traditional liberties; and they continued their armed opposition until in 1609 Spain in effect recognised the independence of the seven provinces still in rebellion. The Dutch Republic was born (see map 1). In England, Parliament

began a civil war against, Charles I in 1642 because it believed that he intended to destroy the established rights of 'free-born Englishmen': they too maintained their armed resistance, with the help of the Scots, until the power of the king was shattered in battle, and Charles himself was tried and executed in 1649 (see map 2). The English Republic, which survived for eleven years under the Lord Protector, Oliver Cromwell, immediately set about reducing the independence of Scotland and Ireland. Although Charles's son was restored in 1660 with full powers and even a small standing army, another revolt in 1688, supported by the Dutch, drove James II into exile and ensured that the power of the crown in England would never again be absolute. Although opposition in France did not go to such lengths, the absolutist policies and fiscal exactions of Cardinal Mazarin (1602-61), chief minister of Louis XIV, so alienated the crown's officials, the nobles and the people of Paris that in 1649 they drove the king from his capital and forced him to make major concessions. Royal control was not fully restored until 1655.

In all three countries, however, the structure of the state survived. None of the rebels seriously questioned the need for strong government, only the location of that strength. 'The question was never whether we should be governed by arbitrary power, but in whose hands it should be,' wrote an English republican in 1653, and in England the 'great rebellion' gave rise to a really modern state. After 1660, even more after 1688, power was shared between Parliament, representing merchants and landowners, and the crown; but the power was absolute, even after 1707, when Scotland was incorporated to form Great Britain. In France, the failure of the Fronde cleared the way for the absolutism of Louis XIV (see page 192). In both France and England the last major effort to resist the rise of the central power and defend local autonomy had failed; there was to be no further 'great rebellion' for over a century. The Dutch Revolt, however, did protect local independence against central encroachment. Despite the preponderance of Holland within the Republic, the other six provinces retained a large measure of autonomy. But this decentralised system, reminiscent of the 15th century, seriously weakened the Dutch, particularly in commercial competition with France and Britain. The Dutch were at a permanent disadvantage in a world which permitted no profit without power and no security without war. No sooner had they broken free of Spain (the independence asserted in 1609 was formally recognised in 1648) than they were attacked on land by France (1672-78 and 1689-1713), and at sea by England (1652-3, 1665-7 and 1672-4). The strain and expense of these wars proved too much, and Dutch strength declined. The 18th century and its profits – particularly in the colonial world – would belong to the newly arisen modern states, France and Great Britain.

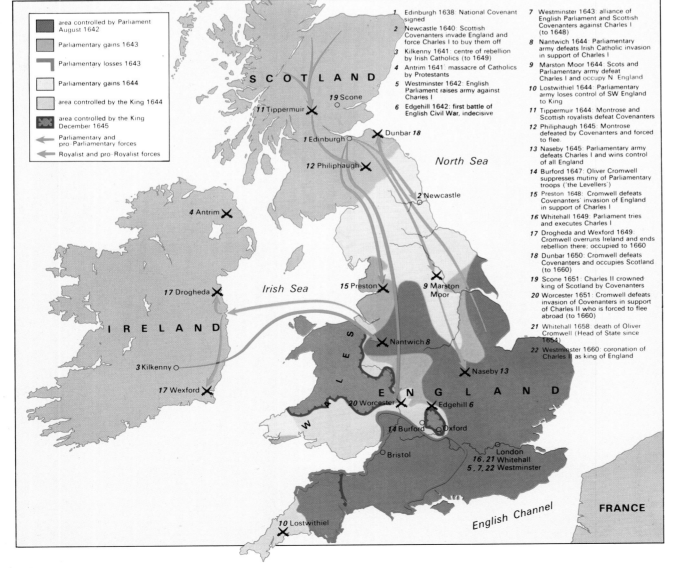

1 Edinburgh 1638: National Covenant signed
2 Newcastle 1640: Scottish Covenanters invade England and force Charles I to buy them off
3 Kilkenny 1641: centre of rebellion by Irish Catholics (to 1649)
4 Antrim 1641: massacre of Catholics by Protestants
5 Westminster 1642: English Parliament raises army against Charles I
6 Edgehill 1642: first battle of English Civil War, indecisive
7 Westminster 1643: alliance of English Parliament and Scottish Covenanters against Charles I (to 1648)
8 Nantwich 1644: Parliamentary army defeats Irish Catholic invasion in support of Charles I
9 Marston Moor 1644: Scots and Parliamentary army defeat Charles I and occupy N. England
10 Lostwithiel 1644: Parliamentary army loses control of SW England to King
11 Tippermuir 1644: Montrose and Scottish royalists defeat Covenanters
12 Philiphaugh 1645: Montrose defeated by Covenanters and forced to flee
13 Naseby 1645: Parliamentary army defeats Charles I and wins control of all England
14 Burford 1647: Oliver Cromwell suppresses mutiny of Parliamentary troops ('the Levellers')
15 Preston 1648: Cromwell defeats Covenanters' invasion of England in support of Charles I
16 Whitehall 1649: Parliament tries and executes Charles I
17 Drogheda and Wexford 1649: Cromwell overruns Ireland and ends rebellion there; occupied to 1660
18 Dunbar 1650: Cromwell defeats Covenanters and occupies Scotland (to 1660)
19 Scone 1651: Charles II crowned king of Scotland by Covenanters
20 Worcester 1651: Cromwell defeats invasion of Covenanters in support of Charles II who is forced to flee abroad (to 1660)
21 Whitehall 1658: death of Oliver Cromwell (Head of State since 1653)
22 Westminster 1660: coronation of Charles II as king of England

2/The English Civil War, 1642-5 (left) At first, most of the north and west of England rallied to Charles I, most of the east and south supported Parliament, and Scotland stayed neutral. The campaigns of 1642 brought small Parliamentary gains in the north-west but heavy losses in the south-west, and the king seemed likely to win until in 1644 Parliament secured the support of the Scottish Covenanters (who had signed the National Covenant in 1638 to protect Scotland against the 'popish practices' imposed by Charles I). In 1645 Charles was decisively defeated at Naseby and his Scottish lieutenant, Montrose, was routed at Philiphaugh, but the king managed to ally with the Covenanters against Parliament. In 1647 the Parliamentary army was weakened by mutinies in favour of a more democratic government (the 'Leveller' movement) but the troubles were suppressed swiftly and the army moved on to defeat the Covenanters at Preston (1648), Dunbar (1650) and Worcester (1651) and to subjugate Ireland (1649). Charles I was tried and executed (1649) and the army established a Republic which controlled the entire British Isles until 1660 when monarchy was restored.

Map legend:
- area controlled by Parliament August 1642
- Parliamentary gains 1643
- Parliamentary losses 1643
- Parliamentary gains 1644
- area controlled by the King 1644
- area controlled by the King December 1645
- Parliamentary and pro-Parliamentary forces
- Royalist and pro-Royalist forces

SCOTLAND
19 Scone
11 Tippermuir
1 Edinburgh
Dunbar 18
12 Philiphaugh
North Sea
2 Newcastle
4 Antrim
Irish Sea
15 Preston
9 Marston Moor
17 Drogheda
IRELAND
Nantwich 8
3 Kilkenny
Naseby 13
17 Wexford
WALES
20 Worcester
Edgehill 6
ENGLAND
14 Burford
Oxford
Bristol
London
16, 21 Whitehall
5, 7, 22 Westminster
English Channel
FRANCE
10 Lostwithiel

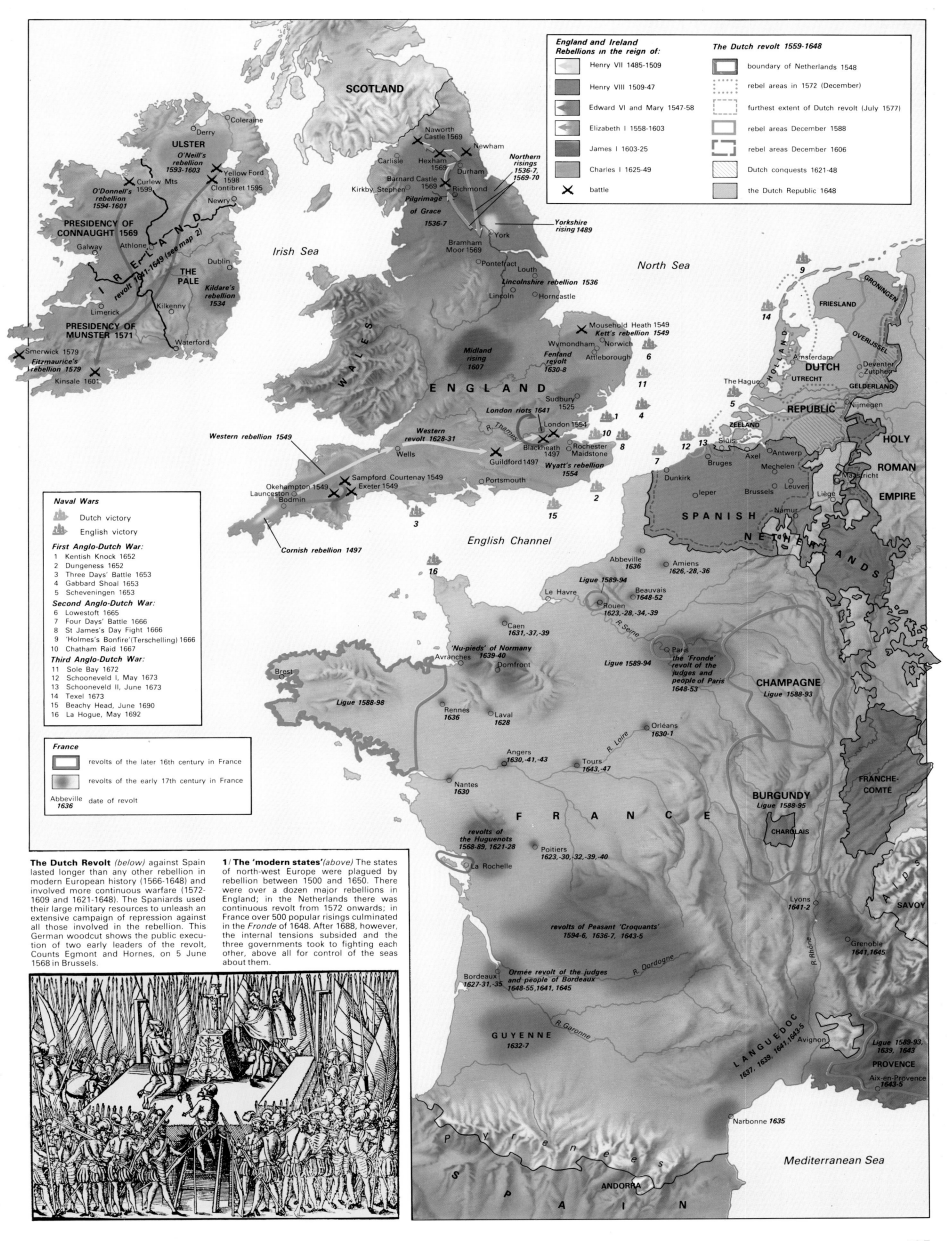

SCOTLAND

Coleraine

Derry

ULSTER
O'Neill's rebellion 1593-1603
Curlew Mts 1599
Yellow Ford 1598
Clontibret 1595
Newry
O'Donnell's rebellion 1594-1601

PRESIDENCY OF CONNAUGHT 1569
Galway
Athlone

I R E L A N D
revolt 1641-1649 (see map 2)
Dublin

THE PALE
Kildare's rebellion 1534

Limerick
Kilkenny

PRESIDENCY OF MUNSTER 1571
Waterford

Smerwick 1579
Fitzmaurice's rebellion 1579
Kinsale 1601

Irish Sea

Naworth Castle 1569
Newham
Carlisle
Hexham 1569
Durham
Barnard Castle 1569
Richmond
Kirkby Stephen

Northern risings 1536-7, 1569-70

Pilgrimage of Grace 1536-7
York
Yorkshire rising 1489
Bramham Moor 1569

Pontefract
Louth
Lincolnshire rebellion 1536
Lincoln
Horncastle

North Sea

Mousehold Heath 1549
Kett's rebellion 1549
Wymondham
Norwich
Fenland revolt 1630-8
Attleborough

E N G L A N D
Midland rising 1607

Sudbury 1525
London riots 1641
R. Thames
London 1554
Blackheath 1497
Rochester Maidstone
Wyatt's rebellion 1554
Guildford 1497

Western revolt 1628-31
Wells
Western rebellion 1549
Sampford Courtenay 1549
Exeter 1549
Okehampton 1549
Launceston
Bodmin
Cornish rebellion 1497
Portsmouth

English Channel

W A L E S

England and Ireland
Rebellions in the reign of:
- Henry VII 1485-1509
- Henry VIII 1509-47
- Edward VI and Mary 1547-58
- Elizabeth I 1558-1603
- James I 1603-25
- Charles I 1625-49
- ✕ battle

The Dutch revolt 1559-1648
- boundary of Netherlands 1548
- rebel areas in 1572 (December)
- furthest extent of Dutch revolt (July 1577)
- rebel areas December 1588
- rebel areas December 1606
- Dutch conquests 1621-48
- the Dutch Republic 1648

Naval Wars
- Dutch victory
- English victory

First Anglo-Dutch War:
1. Kentish Knock 1652
2. Dungeness 1652
3. Three Days' Battle 1653
4. Gabbard Shoal 1653
5. Scheveningen 1653

Second Anglo-Dutch War:
6. Lowestoft 1665
7. Four Days' Battle 1666
8. St James's Day Fight 1666
9. 'Holmes's Bonfire'(Terschelling) 1666
10. Chatham Raid 1667

Third Anglo-Dutch War:
11. Sole Bay 1672
12. Schooneveld I, May 1673
13. Schooneveld II, June 1673
14. Texel 1673
15. Beachy Head, June 1690
16. La Hogue, May 1692

France
- revolts of the later 16th century in France
- revolts of the early 17th century in France
- Abbeville 1636 date of revolt

9
14
FRIESLAND
GRONINGEN
OVERIJSSEL
HOLLAND
Amsterdam
DUTCH
Deventer
Zutphen
UTRECHT
GELDERLAND
The Hague
5
REPUBLIC
Nijmegen
ZEELAND
Sluis
12 13
Axel
HOLY
Antwerp
Bruges
Mechelen
Maastricht
ROMAN
Dunkirk
Brussels
Leuven
Namur
Liège
EMPIRE
SPANISH
NETHERLANDS
ieper

1
4
5
6
7
8
10
11
12
13
15
2
3
16

Abbeville 1636
Amiens 1626,-28,-36
Ligue 1589-94
Le Havre
Beauvais 1648-52
Rouen 1623,-28,-34,-39
Caen 1631,-37,-39
'Nu-pieds' of Normandy 1639-40
Avranches
Domfront
Paris
the 'Fronde' revolt of the judges and people of Paris 1648-53
Ligue 1589-94
CHAMPAGNE
Ligue 1588-93
Brest
R. Seine
Rennes 1636
Laval 1628
Ligue 1588-98
Angers 1630,-41,-43
Tours 1643,-47
Orléans 1630-1
R. Loire
Nantes 1630

F R A N C E

BURGUNDY
Ligue 1588-95
CHAROLAIS
FRANCHE-COMTÉ

revolts of the Huguenots 1568-89, 1621-28
La Rochelle
Poitiers 1623,-30,-32,-39,-40

revolts of Peasant 'Croquants' 1594-6, 1636-7, 1643-5

Ormée revolt of the judges and people of Bordeaux 1648-55,1641, 1645
Bordeaux 1627-31,-35

GUYENNE 1632-7

R. Dordogne
R. Garonne

Lyons 1641-2
SAVOY
Grenoble 1641,1645
R. Rhône

LANGUEDOC 1637, 1639, 1641,1643-5
Avignon
Ligue 1589-93, 1639, 1643
PROVENCE
Aix-en-Provence 1643-5
Narbonne 1635

S P A I N
ANDORRA
P y r e n e e s
Mediterranean Sea

The Dutch Revolt (below) against Spain lasted longer than any other rebellion in modern European history (1566-1648) and involved more continuous warfare (1572-1609 and 1621-1648). The Spaniards used their large military resources to unleash an extensive campaign of repression against all those involved in the rebellion. This German woodcut shows the public execution of two early leaders of the revolt, Counts Egmont and Hornes, on 5 June 1568 in Brussels.

1/ The 'modern states' (above) The states of north-west Europe were plagued by rebellion between 1500 and 1650. There were over a dozen major rebellions in England; in the Netherlands there was continuous revolt from 1572 onwards; in France over 500 popular risings culminated in the *Fronde* of 1648. After 1688, however, the internal tensions subsided and the three governments took to fighting each other, above all for control of the seas about them.

The Mediterranean world
1494 to 1797

2/Spain in the Maghreb (left) Spanish conquests in North Africa were originally an extension of the Christian 'Reconquest'. After the capture of Granada (1492) this 'crusade' against the Moors was carried across the straits, and successive fortresses in Morocco and Algeria were taken. But after 1510 the process was halted as Spain became more deeply involved in its Aragonese inheritance in Italy. The expeditions against Tunis in 1535, after the victory in Italy, and in 1573 after Lepanto, were distinct in character: they were designed to defend the western Mediterranean against the Turks. The crusade against the Moors was now left to Portugal, which pursued it to disaster at Alcazarquivir in 1578. However, this renunciation brought its revenge: the Turks were able to extend their protection over the 'Barbary states' of Tunis and Algiers; the coastal fortresses were recovered; and the city of Algiers, under the rule of the famous corsair Barbarossa, became the capital of piracy. It was to chastise these pirates that an English fleet, under Blake, entered the Mediterranean in 1655. Blake bombarded Tunis and coerced the Bey of Algiers. This was the beginning of English naval intervention in the Mediterranean, which culminated in the capture and retention of Gibraltar (1704).

The Lion of Venice (above) appears on Venetian fortresses throughout the eastern Mediterranean. This flag shows the Lion standing on land as well as on water, symbolising the Republic's dominance of its hinterland as well as of the Adriatic.

IN the three centuries from 1495 to 1797 the Mediterranean world underwent two drastic changes. First, the primacy of the Italian cities was lost as the sea became the theatre of a power-struggle between two multi-national empires whose interests were only partly Mediterranean: the Spanish Habsburgs and the Ottoman Turks. Second, in the 17th century the whole area lost significance as initiative and sea-power, even in the Mediterranean, passed to the Atlantic nations.

The loss of Italian primacy was precipitated by the French invasion of Italy in 1494. In the ensuing Franco-Spanish struggle France was defeated and thereafter, by the Treaty of Cateau-Cambrésis (1559) and the French wars of religion (1562-98), effectively excluded from Italy, which was dominated by Spain. Milan was ruled by a Spanish governor; Naples, Sicily and Sardinia by Spanish viceroys. Genoa, with its colony of Corsica, was tied economically to Spain. The central Italian states, pressed between Spanish Milan and Spanish Naples, had limited freedom. There were Spanish naval bases in Tuscany, a Spanish garrison in Piacenza. Venice, which sought to preserve independence by neutrality, was nevertheless threatened by Spanish land-power in Milan and Spanish sea-power at Brindisi. As the front line of defence against the Turks, Italy was protected, and therefore dominated, by the opposite power of Spain.

While Spain pushed along the northern coast to the straits of Otranto, the Turks reached along the southern coast towards the straits of Gibraltar. At first the Spaniards made the pace here too. The Catholic kings destroyed the last Muslim kingdom in Spain, the kingdom of Granada, in 1492, and Spanish coastal garrisons were established in Morocco and Algeria. In 1535 Charles V captured Tunis and installed a puppet ruler. But Spanish resources were increasingly diverted to Italy and the north, and meanwhile Ottoman power steadily advanced. Syria and Egypt were conquered in 1517, Tripoli, Tunisia and Algeria gradually vassalised, and Spanish conquests east of Oran reversed. In 1560 Philip II's expedition against Djerba failed. In 1565 the Turks besieged Malta, to which the Knights Hospitallers of St John had

been driven back from Rhodes in 1522. However, Malta was relieved; in 1571 the great Spanish-Venetian victory of Lepanto broke Turkish sea-power in the central Mediterranean; and in 1609 the expulsion of the Moriscos (nominally converted Moors) from Spain removed a potential Turkish fifth column. By this time the Turks, engaged in Persia and on the Danube, were content to hold the eastern Mediterranean, leaving the western area as a Spanish lake. To Spain this control was now doubly necessary, for Anglo-Dutch sea-power in the Atlantic had made the traditional route from Spain to the Netherlands too dangerous. The Mediterranean route from Barcelona through Genoa to Milan was now the lifeline of the Spanish Empire in Europe: by it, troops and bullion were sent to the Spanish governors of the Netherlands and the Habsburgs of Austria.

The victims in this long struggle were the Italian mercantile republics of Genoa and Venice. Genoa lost the last of its eastern colonies, Chios and Samos to the Turks in 1566. Venice lost its last positions in the Morea – Monemvasia and Nauplia – in 1540, Naxos in 1566, Cyprus in 1571. Genoa retained its western colony of Corsica, but only after a long revolt (1552-69), in which the insurgents received help from the Turks. Venice clung to Crete till 1669, and temporarily recovered the Morea in 1685, but was effectively reduced to an Adriatic city. Meanwhile commercial interest was bringing other powers into the Mediterranean. France had had an informal alliance with the Turks since 1525, and Marseilles grew on eastern trade; the English Levant Company established itself in Constantinople in 1581; and from 1590 Dutch fleets brought Baltic corn, Norwegian timber and colonial wares into the Mediterranean. To profit by this trade, the Grand Duke of Tuscany declared Leghorn a free port in 1593. To prey on it, international pirates invaded the sea and joined the 'Barbary corsairs' who made Algiers into a great pirate city, the Croatian Uskoks who terrorised Adriatic shipping, and the Turkish corsairs of Albania, the Morea and Anatolia. In time of war, local rulers invested in privateering and increased the need of trading nations for political stability in the sea.

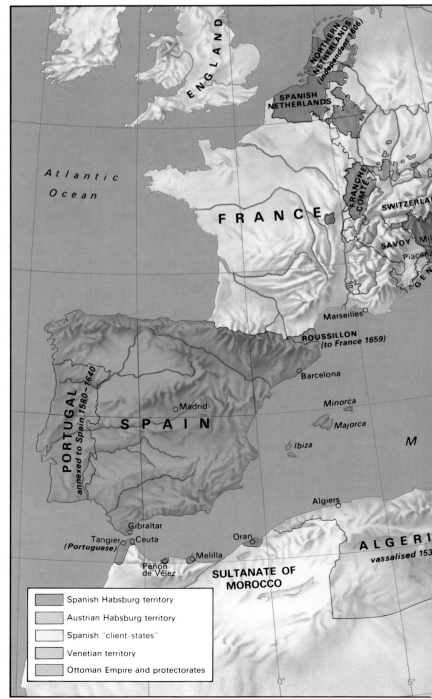

In general, they achieved it. In the 17th century Spanish control was challenged in detail by France, but the effective changes were dynastic, not territorial. When a French dynasty was established in Spain (1700-14), the balance of power was preserved in the Mediterranean. The Austrian Habsburgs secured Milan. After some shuffling, a branch of the Spanish Bourbons received Naples and Sicily, and Sardinia was neutralised in the hands of Savoy. Tuscany fell, in 1737, to a branch of the Habsburgs. Lesser principalities were similarly shared out. The republics of Venice, Genoa and Lucca remained undisturbed. Venice retained its Adriatic possessions and Genoa its rule over Corsica (though challenged by another long revolt, 1755-68) till the late 18th century.

The guardian of this 18th-century stability was England. English fleets had first entered the Mediterranean in force under Cromwell, to pursue royalist vessels and to chastise the Barbary pirates. From 1662 to 1683 England held Tangier, guarding the entrance to the Mediterranean; in 1704 it took Gibraltar from Spain. Sardinia was a British base from 1708 to 1714, Minorca from 1708 to 1783. But generally the British preferred diplomacy to direct control, until Napoleon's invasion of Italy and annexation of Egypt and Malta convulsed eastern and western Mediterranean alike and brought in the British navy to dominate both.

1/The struggle for power 1495 to 1620 (below)
The expanding power of Spain in the West and of the Ottoman Empire in the East frequently clashed in the Mediterranean. Spain was enriched by its new Atlantic acquisitions in the Americas, and the Ottomans by their Middle Eastern and Balkan gains. The turning point which broke the Ottoman westward advance was the Battle of Lepanto (1571), after which the central Mediterranean was left to the power of Spain.

3/The Adriatic, life-line of Venice The most critical areas in the Mediterranean, during the struggle for its control in the 16th century, were the stretch between Tunisia and Sicily and the Adriatic Sea. Here the great confrontations took place: Tunis 1535, 1571, 1574; Djerba 1559-60; Malta 1565; Preveza 1538; Lepanto 1571. The Adriatic was the life-line of the Venetian Empire, and control of the narrow straits of Otranto was a vital Venetian interest; but with the Turks on one side and the Spaniards on the other, it was always in danger, and Venice would give up its neutrality to defend it. The Turks had seized Otranto in 1480, but could not keep it. After the victory of Lepanto in 1571, Turkish warships were excluded from the Adriatic, but the Spaniards then sought to strangle Venice by the same means. They also encouraged the Uskoks, who preyed on Venetian (and other) ships from Senj. Venice was forced to make war on the Uskoks, 1613-18, and clung to its positions guarding the entry to the Adriatic — Cattaro, Corfu, Levkas, Cephalonia, Zante — until the extinction of the Venetian Republic by Napoleon (1797).

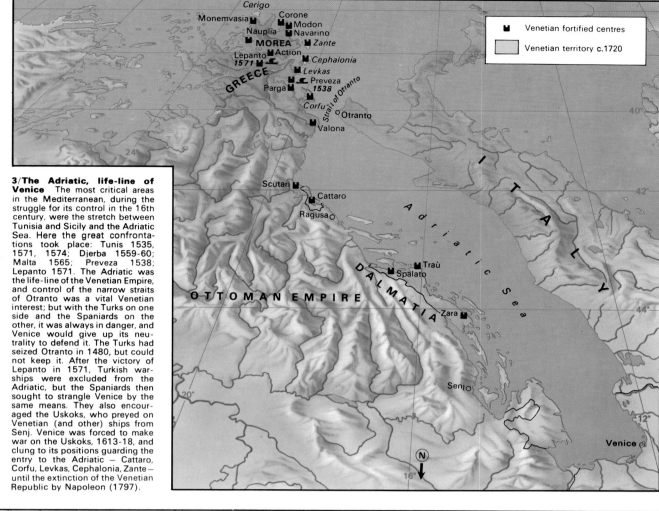

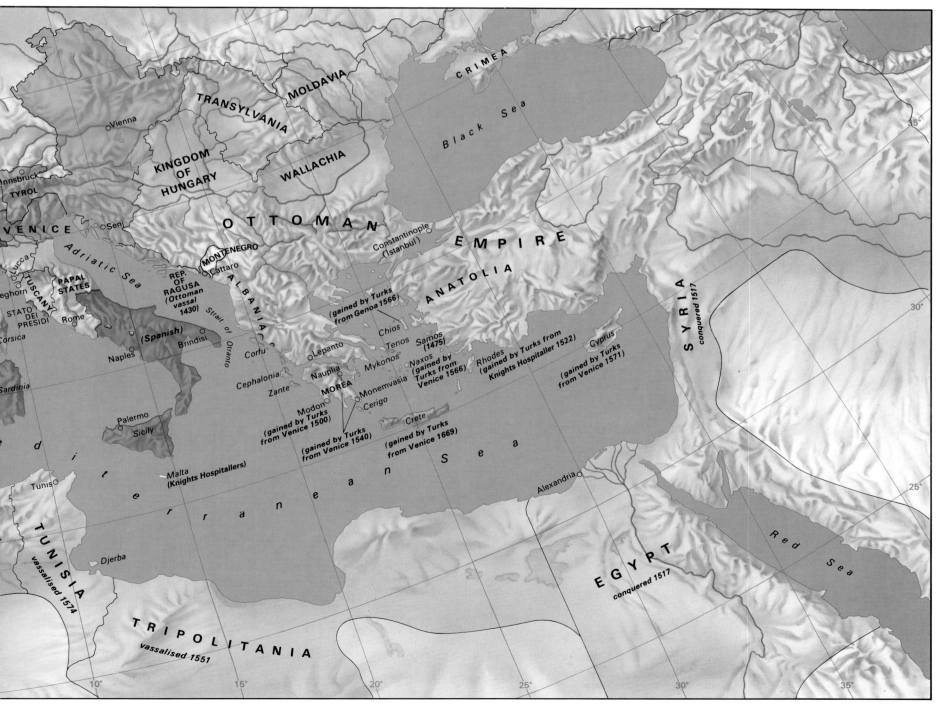

The struggle for the Baltic 1523 to 1721

1561 Reval, an independent Hanseatic port, threatened by the commercial rivalry of Viborg and Narva and the ambitions of Poland and Denmark to control Livonia, put itself under Swedish protection.

1595 Peace of Teusina added Narva and effectively the whole of Estonia, turned the Gulf of Finland into a Swedish waterway and pushed the northern borders across the Arctic Circle.

1617 Peace of Stolbovo confirmed possession of Estonia, added Ingermanland, Karelia and the river Neva, and cut off Russia, including its great trading city of Novgorod, (sacked 1616) from all access to the Baltic.

1645 All Livonia became Swedish through the Armistice of Altmark (1629); the Peace of Brömsebro transferred Ösel, Gotland, Jämtland, Härjedalen and a 30-year control over Halland from Denmark-Norway.

1648 With the Peace of Westphalia ending the Thirty Years War, Sweden gained West Pomerania, including the important port of Stettin, Wismar in Mecklenburg, and the bishoprics of Bremen and Verden.

1658 Peace of Roskilde brought Scania, Blekinge, Bohuslän, Trondheim and Bornholm; but additional Swedish demands created a Danish-Dutch alliance; renewed war, rebellion in Scania and defeat at Funen (1660).

1660 After the death of Charles X, fighting ceased. The treaty of Copenhagen returned Trondheim and the island of Bornholm to Denmark, and formally abandoned Sweden's earlier attempts to close the Baltic to foreign warships.

1721 The treaties ending the Great Northern War (1700-21) marked the effective break-up of the Swedish Empire. In the east, Karelia and the Baltic provinces were lost, and in Germany, Bremen-Verden and most of West Pomerania.

THE Baltic is a vast, almost land-locked, frequently ice-bound area of water covering over 166,000 square miles. In early modern times it provided the great bulk of the timber, tar, pitch, hemp and flax for the ships with which England, Holland, France, Spain and Portugal were building their world trading empires; also much of the grain needed to insure the rest of the continent against poor harvests, and the copper for its everyday money. The Sound Tolls, imposed on most of the commerce passing between the Baltic and the North Sea, gave Denmark (which usually controlled the narrow exit passages) a formidable source of wealth and power, but created at the same time a source of bitter rivalry with her neighbours. The resulting local struggles, with their threats to security of supply, constantly interlocked with wider European affairs – the maritime jealousies of Britain, France and the Netherlands, the dynastic confrontation of Bourbon and Habsburg, the religious conflicts between Catholic and Protestant. There was thus a much more than parochial significance in the complex Baltic power shifts of these 200 years, which saw the final decline of the Hanseatic League, Sweden's dramatic rise and eclipse, the dwindling of Denmark, the virtual elimination of Poland and the advance of Russia and Brandenburg-Prussia.

From 1397 to 1523, Denmark, Norway and Sweden were united under one crown in the Union of Kalmar. Early in the 16th century, Sweden finally broke away and re-established its independence under Gustavus Vasa (1523-60). Gustavus also promptly broke with Rome, adopted Lutheranism, and set about improving the country's economic, naval and military strength. Its position was initially extremely fragile. Its only ice-free outlet to the North Sea consisted of an eleven-mile strip of coast between the Danish province of Halland and the Norwegian province of Bohuslän, and although this was defended by the fortress of Älvsborg, it fell several times into the hands of Danish invading forces. Denmark also controlled the southern shores adjoining the Sound, and a string of strategic islands, while the Hanseatic port of Lübeck had been given, in return for its help in the wars of independence, a near-monopoly of Swedish foreign trade. This was broken, by a temporary alliance of Sweden and Denmark, as early as 1525, but the possibility of economic strangulation remained a constant threat. In the east, too, there was danger from the rising power of Muscovy, which openly coveted both Finland, under Swedish control since the 14th century, and the rapidly-disintegrating territories of the Teutonic Knights to the south of the Gulf of Finland, which represented a major trading outlet for Gustavus Vasa's new port of Helsingfors. Gradually rising tensions under Gustavus's sons, Eric XIV (1560-8) and John III (1568-92), finally erupted in the Seven Years' War of the North (1563-70). On balance Sweden held her own in this struggle, although she had to pay a crippling ransom to Denmark for the return of Älvsborg, and by 1581 she was becoming a significant force even beyond the Baltic region.

Her precise role was complicated by dynastic and religious considerations. John III had married a Polish (and Roman Catholic) princess, and his son ascended the Polish throne in 1587 as Sigismund III. A major constitutional crisis followed when he also became King of Sweden on his father's death in 1592. He was deposed in 1599 with his Lutheran uncle ultimately taking the crown as Charles IX; Poland and Sweden, already deeply at odds over their opposing interests in Livonia, remained open enemies for fifty years. Indeed, at the accession in 1611 of Charles's seventeen-year-old son, Gustavus Adolphus, Sweden was ringed by hostile states, and her own internal weaknesses, both constitutional and financial, appeared to make a mock-

ery of her long-held aim to make the Baltic a Swedish lake. Amazingly, by 1660 the dream had almost become reality.

The young monarch's reign started with a serious setback. At the Peace of Knäred (1613) Sweden had to make further sacrifices to regain her fort of Älvsborg, lost to Denmark again two years before. The years from the Peace of Stolbovo to the Peace of Westphalia (1617-48) brought large new territories (see maps on left), although Gustavus was killed in 1632. Sweden was now a great international power.

Even before Westphalia, fear of Sweden's growing might had again brought war to Scandinavia. In 1643-45 Sweden fought Denmark, and in the resulting Peace of Brömsebro, Denmark lost Gotland and Ösel, together with Halland for a period of thirty years, and Norway too had to part with substantial lands. Renewed Danish attacks, while the Swedes under Charles

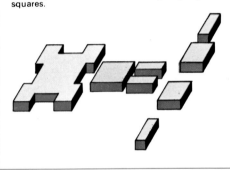

The military revolution Gustavus Adolphus created a modern army of small, tactical units under professional commanders. He also introduced greater concentrations of light, mobile field guns for support in battle. Co-operation between infantry, cavalry and gunners made possible the victory of the wedge-shaped Swedish army formations over the traditional massed pikemen and musketeers fighting in great squares.

X were embroiled with Russia, Brandenburg and Poland, led to further humiliation. Charles, attacking from the south, occupied Jutland, led his troops across the frozen waters of the Great Belt in the winter of 1658 and threatened Copenhagen. At the Peace of Roskilde, Sweden won Scania, Blekinge, Bornholm, Bohuslän and Halland in perpetuity.

This was the climax. From then on, Sweden's foes formed an increasingly effective alliance against her. When Denmark invaded Scania and started the Scanian War (1676-79). Sweden was saved from territorial loss only by her French ally Louis XIV, and after a pause during the cautious reign of Charles XI (1660-97) the tide began, disastrously, to turn. The old king was succeeded by his brilliant, impetuous 15-year-old son, Charles XII, and three years later, in 1700, the Great Northern War broke out, which in twenty years was to lay the foundations for the greatness of modern Russia and to erase Sweden and Poland from the ranks of the major powers.

The war started with the deceptively crushing victory of Narva, when Charles' troops decisively defeated a Russian army five times its size. But events in Poland (see page 196) side-tracked the Swedish forces. Peter the Great recaptured Narva (1704), annihilated the Swedes at Poltava (1709), and in the final peace treaties (1719-21) gained Livonia, Estonia, all of Ingermanland, Karelia and south-eastern Finland. With minor exceptions, former Swedish areas of Germany were divided between Hanover and the newly-emergent state of Brandenburg-Prussia. Most other naval powers, for whom a prime objective had always been to prevent the Baltic becoming a 'closed sea', regarded the decay of the short-lived Swedish Empire with relief.

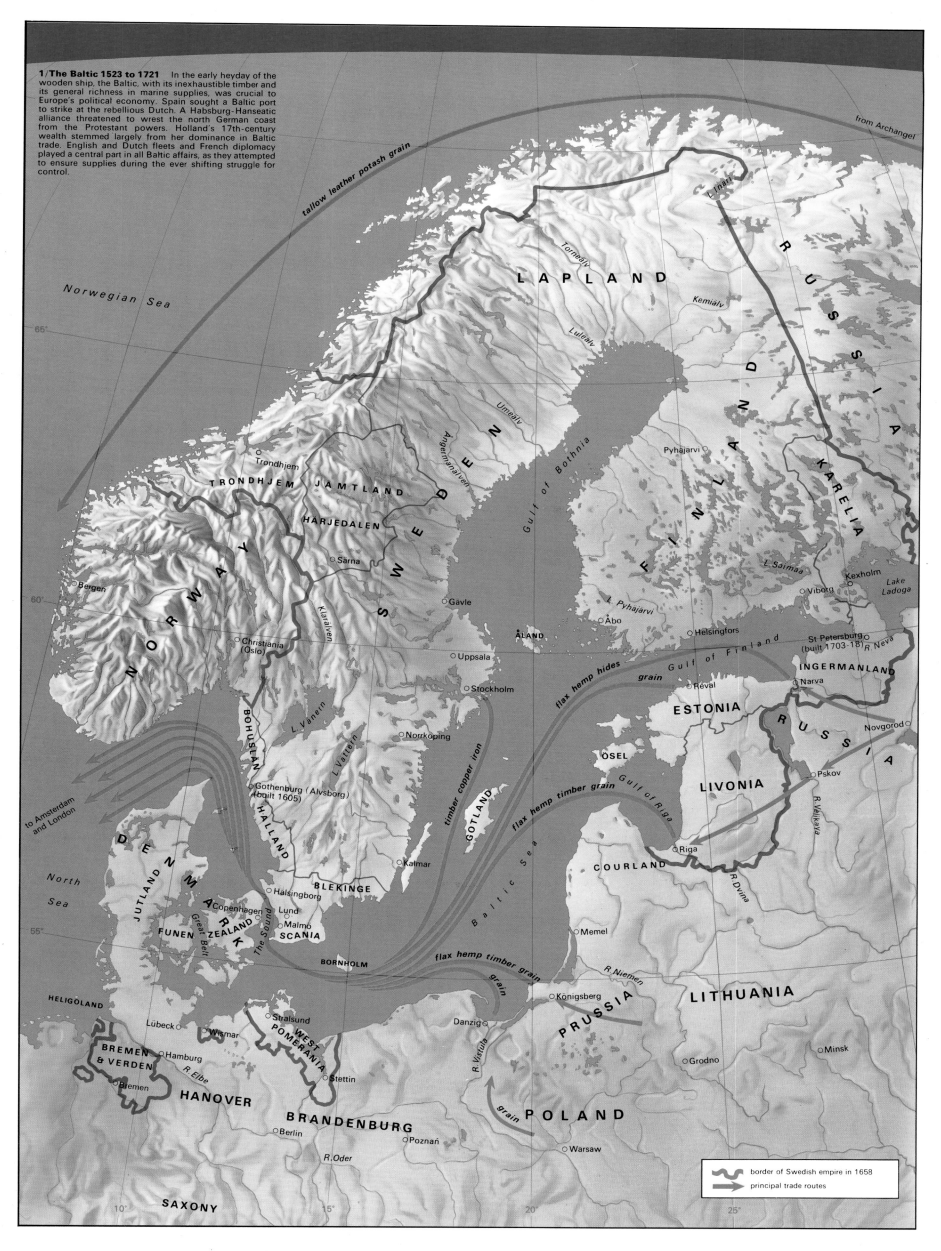

1/The Baltic 1523 to 1721 In the early heyday of the wooden ship, the Baltic, with its inexhaustible timber and its general richness in marine supplies, was crucial to Europe's political economy. Spain sought a Baltic port to strike at the rebellious Dutch. A Habsburg-Hanseatic alliance threatened to wrest the north German coast from the Protestant powers. Holland's 17th-century wealth stemmed largely from her dominance in Baltic trade. English and Dutch fleets and French diplomacy played a central part in all Baltic affairs, as they attempted to ensure supplies during the ever shifting struggle for control.

Norwegian Sea

tallow leather potash grain

from Archangel

LAPLAND

Torneälv

Kemiälv

Luleälv

RUSSIA

Umeälv

Trondhjem

TRONDHJEM JÄMTLAND

HÄRJEDALEN

Särna

S W E D E N

Ångermanälven

FINLAND

KARELIA

Pyhäjärvi

Gulf of Bothnia

L. Saimaa

Kexholm

Lake Ladoga

Viborg

Bergen

Klarälven

Gävle

L. Pyhäjärvi

Åbo

Åland

Helsingfors

St Petersburg (built 1703-18) R. Neva

INGERMANLAND

Christiania (Oslo)

N O R W A Y

Uppsala

Stockholm

Gulf of Finland

Réval

Narva

Novgorod

flax hemp hides   grain

ESTONIA

RUSSIA

Norrköping

B O H U S L Ä N

L. Vänern

L. Vättern

ÖSEL

LIVONIA

Pskov

R. Velikaya

timber copper iron

GOTLAND

flax hemp timber grain

Gulf of Riga

Gothenburg (Älvsborg) (built 1605)

H A L L A N D

Kalmar

Riga

COURLAND

R. Dvina

to Amsterdam and London

Baltic Sea

BLEKINGE

Hälsingborg

Lund

Malmö

SCANIA

D E N M A R K

JUTLAND

FUNEN

ZEALAND

Copenhagen

Great Belt

The Sound

BORNHOLM

Memel

North Sea

flax hemp timber grain

grain

Königsberg

R. Niemen

PRUSSIA

LITHUANIA

HELIGOLAND

Lübeck

Wismar

Stralsund

WEST POMERANIA

Danzig

R. Vistula

Minsk

BREMEN & VERDEN

Hamburg

R. Elbe

Stettin

grain

Grodno

Bremen

HANOVER

BRANDENBURG

POLAND

Berlin

Poznań

Warsaw

R. Oder

SAXONY

	border of Swedish empire in 1658
	principal trade routes

Germany disunited
1648 to 1806

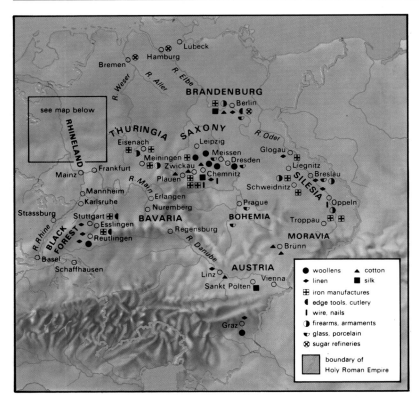

Meissen Merchant *(above)*
The first Meissen factory opened near Dresden in 1710, after Böttger, an alchemist employed by the Elector of Saxony, succeeded in reproducing the translucency of Chinese porcelain with local clay. This piece, dated 1765, is now in New York's Metropolitan Museum of Art.

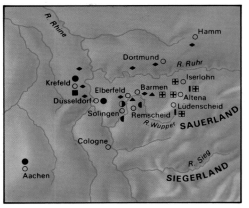

2/Industrial growth in the 18th century *(above)* Urban development centred on Vienna, Berlin, Hamburg and Bremen; textiles and iron enriched Saxony, Silesia and the lower Rhineland.

T HE Peace of Westphalia, which in 1648 finally ended the Thirty Years War, left Germany ravaged, impoverished and little more than a geographical expression. The might of the Emperor was irretrievably ruined; his domains, whose political fragmentation had begun as early as the 14th century, were now split into some 300 separate principalities, bishoprics and Free Cities, with each ruler, Catholic or Protestant, lay or ecclesiastical, rich or poor, interested solely in exploiting his own sovereign power. The Empire still had common institutions, including a Diet, or *Reichstag,* which sat permanently at Regensburg (where the most important delegate was probably the French ambassador) but their effectiveness was minimal.

Among the mosaic of small, petty and 'duodecimo' states only Austria remained a major force. This was due mostly, however, to the extent of the ruling Habsburgs' possessions in Hungary, the Netherlands and Italy, rather than to those in Germany. The few other princes of any importance derived their strength – and often their titles – from outside the Empire. The Elector of Brandenburg, raised to royal dignity in 1701, took his title from Prussia (outside the imperial boundary, under Polish overlordship, from 1461 to 1657). The Elector of Hanover became King of England in 1714, and the Elector of Saxony, King of Poland (1697). Sweden ruled over Bremen and Western Pomerania, and Denmark over Holstein; while France, always alert to extending its territories at German expense, annexed Burgundy (1678), Strassburg (1681), the rest of Alsace (1697), and Bar and Lorraine (1766). Only the jealous vigilance of England, Holland, Sweden and Russia prevented her from seizing much more.

The population of Germany, between twenty and twenty-five million on the eve of the thirty-year struggle, was savagely reduced. The loss of life, variously estimated at one-third, one-half and in some regions seventy per cent, was not made good until the second half of the 18th century. War also accelerated the economic decline which had set in towards the close of the 16th century. The great south German commercial cities, Nuremberg and

Augsburg (where the Fuggers had gone bankrupt in 1627) suffered, like Venice, from the rise of the Ottoman Empire and the shift in trade from the Mediterranean to the Atlantic. The Hanseatic ports, once dominant in the Baltic and the North Sea (see page 144), failed to stem the growing power of Holland, and dissolved their League in 1669.

The rise of Prussia, begun under the Great Elector (1640-88) and continued by Frederick William I (1713-40) and his son Frederick the Great (1740-86), disguised the fragility of the Prussian state which was quickly shown by its collapse in 1806. Its real rise to great power status belongs essentially to the 19th century (see page 216). Certainly its rulers evolved a significant armoury of administrative and military institutions, as well as a highly characteristic set of social attitudes in the course of imposing order on their widely-scattered territories. However, down to 1700, Brandenburg-Prussia was outstripped by Bavaria, and until the middle of the 18th century by Saxony, in wealth and population. Though the bare framework of a kingdom existed by the end of the 17th century, it was only with the acquisition of Silesia in 1742 and the successful conclusion of the war which had been fought over it with Austria in 1763 that Prussia really began to affect the balance of power within the Empire. Not until the partitions of Poland was it possible to create a continuous Prussian territory from Memel to Magdeburg.

3/The rise of Prussia The 1648 Peace, the weakening of Poland, inheritance, the Northern Wars (1655-60, 1700-21), and the War of the Austrian Succession (1740-48) enabled the Hohenzollern to extend and consolidate the territories of Brandenburg-Prussia.

	Brandenburg in 1648
	Prussian acquisitions 1648-1707
	acquisitions 1715, 1720
	acquisitions 1742, 1744, 1772

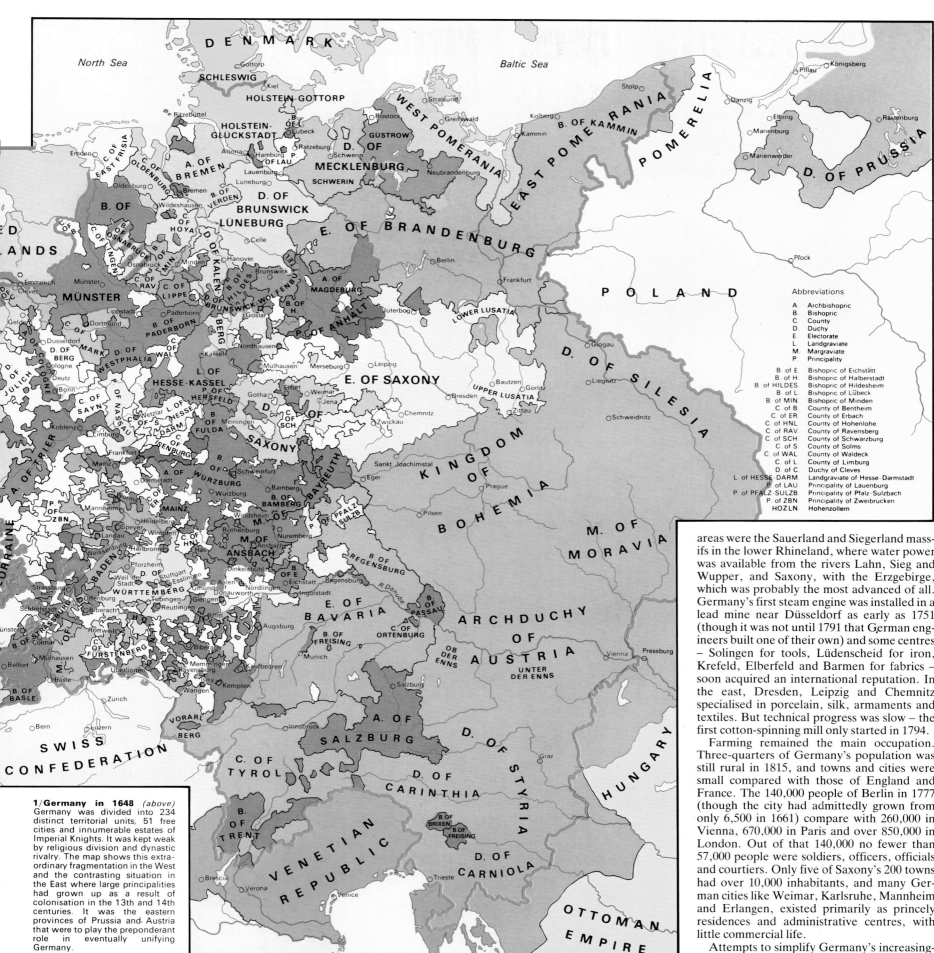

1/Germany in 1648 (above)
Germany was divided into 234 distinct territorial units, 51 free cities and innumerable estates of Imperial Knights. It was kept weak by religious division and dynastic rivalry. The map shows this extraordinary fragmentation in the West and the contrasting situation in the East where large principalities had grown up as a result of colonisation in the 13th and 14th centuries. It was the eastern provinces of Prussia and Austria that were to play the preponderant role in eventually unifying Germany.

Abbreviations

A.	Archbishopric
B.	Bishopric
C.	County
D.	Duchy
E.	Electorate
L.	Landgraviate
M.	Margraviate
P.	Principality
B. of E.	Bishopric of Eichstätt
B. of H.	Bishopric of Halberstadt
B. of HILDES.	Bishopric of Hildesheim
B. of L.	Bishopric of Lübeck
B. of MIN.	Bishopric of Minden
C. of B.	County of Bentheim
C. of ER.	County of Erbach
C. of HNL.	County of Hohenlohe
C. of RAV.	County of Ravensberg
C. of SCH.	County of Schwarzburg
C. of S.	County of Solms
C. of WAL.	County of Waldeck
C. of L.	County of Limburg
D. of C.	Duchy of Cleves
L. of HESSE-DARM.	Landgraviate of Hesse-Darmstadt
P. of LAU.	Principality of Lauenburg
P. of PFALZ-SULZB.	Principality of Pfalz-Sulzbach
P. of ZBN.	Principality of Zweibrucken
HOZLN.	Hohenzollern

areas were the Sauerland and Siegerland massifs in the lower Rhineland, where water power was available from the rivers Lahn, Sieg and Wupper, and Saxony, with the Erzgebirge, which was probably the most advanced of all. Germany's first steam engine was installed in a lead mine near Düsseldorf as early as 1751 (though it was not until 1791 that German engineers built one of their own) and some centres – Solingen for tools, Lüdenscheid for iron, Krefeld, Elberfeld and Barmen for fabrics – soon acquired an international reputation. In the east, Dresden, Leipzig and Chemnitz specialised in porcelain, silk, armaments and textiles. But technical progress was slow – the first cotton-spinning mill only started in 1794.

Farming remained the main occupation. Three-quarters of Germany's population was still rural in 1815, and towns and cities were small compared with those of England and France. The 140,000 people of Berlin in 1777 (though the city had admittedly grown from only 6,500 in 1661) compare with 260,000 in Vienna, 670,000 in Paris and over 850,000 in London. Out of that 140,000 no fewer than 57,000 people were soldiers, officers, officials and courtiers. Only five of Saxony's 200 towns had over 10,000 inhabitants, and many German cities like Weimar, Karlsruhe, Mannheim and Erlangen, existed primarily as princely residences and administrative centres, with little commercial life.

Attempts to simplify Germany's increasingly anachronistic pattern of tiny states were first made by the Austrian Emperor, Joseph II (1780-90). They were frustrated by Prussia, now powerful enough to block anyone else's unificatory moves but not to initiate one of her own. It was only under the impact of France's post-revolutionary wars that the redrawing of the political map seriously began. The 64 ecclesiastical principalities, with their 3 million inhabitants, were secularised in 1803; 45 of the 51 Free Cities (75,000 people) and the remaining Imperial Knights, with 450,000 subjects, were absorbed into larger units.

These changes marked the end of the old Reich, providing a springboard for the developments of the 19th century. Their significance was formally recognised in 1806, when Francis II of Austria (1792-1806) finally abdicated his sonorous, though now almost meaningless title. He was the last Holy Roman Emperor, in a line that had lasted 850 years.

Frederick the Great's forced industrialisation programme, largely based on Silesia's iron and coal, was only a modest success. Many of his state-sponsored enterprises failed even in his own lifetime, and few survived the French occupation of 1806. Nevertheless, 18th-century Germany was not an economic backwater. Although the older cities stagnated, new industries sprang up in rural districts where they could escape the crippling guild restrictions. Apart from Silesia, where the large landowners combined with government to invest in mining, iron and textiles, the main

4/Germany in 1806 (left)
Napoleon and his armies drastically simplified the German map. Petty states were amalgamated wholesale with larger entities; new middle-sized territories emerged including Prussia, though after 1806 it had to surrender its western provinces; and France took firm control of the left bank of the Rhine.

Confederation of the Rhine 1806
1 Württemberg
2 Baden
3 Wurzburg
4 Thuringian states
5 Electorate of Hesse
6 Swedish Pomerania
7 Oldenburg
8 Duchy of Hesse
9 Berg

The ascendancy of France 1647 to 1715

DURING the reign of Louis XIV France became so influential in Europe that other powers feared her ascendancy, regarding her – to use a contemporary expression – as an 'exorbitant' state, dangerous for the very balance of the Continent and threatening the religious as well as the political freedom of individual states and princes. Louis was suspected of plans to oust the Austrian Habsburgs from their traditional position as elected emperors of the Holy Roman Empire of the German Nation, and of spearheading a second Catholic counter-reformation. He was generally held to aim at French hegemony over Europe.

There were some solid grounds for such fears. Although war, civil and international, had for more than a century impeded progress in manufactures, in trade, overseas expansion, and in ship-building, the relatively peaceful years between 1661 and 1672 gave Louis XIV and his able ministers and administrators a chance to catch up with France's rivals in all three fields. At the same time the French army and navy were greatly expanded. The richness of French resources, including a population estimated at twenty million, played a significant part in these developments, but so did conscious effort and directives from the centre.

Louis' military objectives were, however, limited and concerned the security of France's northern and eastern frontiers. The Habsburg ring, forged by the family compacts of the Austrian and Spanish Habsburgs, was still felt to be pressing round France though the Peace of Westphalia (1648) brought sovereignty over Metz, Toul and Verdun (occupied by the French since 1552) and possession of the landgravates of Upper and Lower Alsace, and the Peace of the Pyrenees (1659) plugged the gap in these southern frontier: Spain ceded Roussillon and northern Cerdagne. Yet many *portes* (gates) remained through which France could be invaded, from

the Spanish Netherlands in the north, through Lorraine and the Belfort Gap, right down to the Barcelonette valley from Italy. Spain still held Franche-Comté on the eastern border, and Louis' hold over Alsace was weakened by imperial suzerainty over its ten principal towns. The near-certainty, after 1665, that the Spanish king Carlos II would die without heirs of his own body and leave his possessions to the Austrian Habsburgs raised the spectre of a resurrection of the empire of Charles V. This helps to explain the two aggressive wars of Louis' reign: the War of Devolution, fought to lay claim to part of the Spanish Netherlands in 1667-78, and the attack on the Dutch Republic in 1672. The latter, much to Louis' discomfiture, escalated into a European-wide war which was not settled till 1678-79.

Louis did his best to avoid large-scale war after 1679 by resort to arbitration and multilateral treaties to settle European problems, but the memories of his early wars and the enormous power of France made the rest of Europe suspicious of his intentions. Indeed, he preferred brief campaigns or the diplomatic isolation of those who opposed him by the use of subsidies to rulers and presents to influential ministers. His conquest of Spanish Netherlands territory (1668) and of Franche-Comté (1678) might be forgiven, but his 'reunion' policy to expand his control of German border areas was vigorously opposed; and he lost the sympathy of all Protestant powers once his anti-Huguenot measures in France began to bite. The deleterious economic effects of the exodus of over 200,000 French Huguenots in the 1670s and 1680s have been greatly exaggerated. The political consequences abroad of Louis' revocation of the Edict of Nantes (1685) were far-reaching, however, and contributed both to the Nine Years' War (1689-97) and the War of the Spanish Succession (1701-14).

The defensive element in Louis' foreign policy is still disputed among historians, but can be demonstrated in various ways: by the construction of a *barrière de fer* of Vauban fortresses around the whole of France, thickest on the ground in the north and east; by the decision, put into effect by 1696, to pull out of Italy (thus abandoning a cornerstone of the policies of Richelieu and Mazarin) to permit concentration of resources on the defensive *barrière*; by the clauses in the second partition treaty of 1700 which – while giving Spain, the Spanish Netherlands and Spain overseas to an Austrian archduke – ceded the Spanish possessions in Italy to France, but with specific provisions and plans for 'exchanges' to strengthen the eastern frontier: the duchy of Milan was to be exchanged for Lorraine, and Naples and Sicily, it was hoped, for Savoy and Piedmont.

Parallel to the preoccupation with the northern and eastern frontiers went an intense concern to catch up with the Maritime Powers (England and the Dutch Republic) in overseas settlements and commerce, and especially to have a share in the illicit trade with Spanish America. Here Louis aroused such resentment and fear that the English and the Dutch would only contemplate one of Louis' younger grandsons inheriting the Spanish throne, if they themselves were given territories and strongpoints in the West Indies, on the Spanish Main, in Spanish North Africa, on Spain's Balearic Islands and in Spain itself. The Maritime Powers were well aware that no union of the two dynasties, that of Spain and that of France, was intended; but unless they received compensation of the kind mentioned above they feared that French ascendancy in overseas trade would become a corollary of French ascendancy in Europe. They could no more free themselves from such fears than could Louis from his conviction that the Austrian Habsburgs, who between 1683 and 1699 made such vast re-conquests from the Turks in Hungary, would

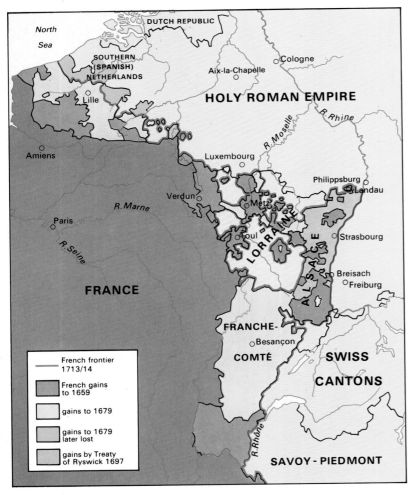

2/The North-East Frontier *(above)* Louis expanded into the Spanish Netherlands. He conquered Franche-Comté, widened his hold on Alsace, and in 1681 annexed Strasbourg.

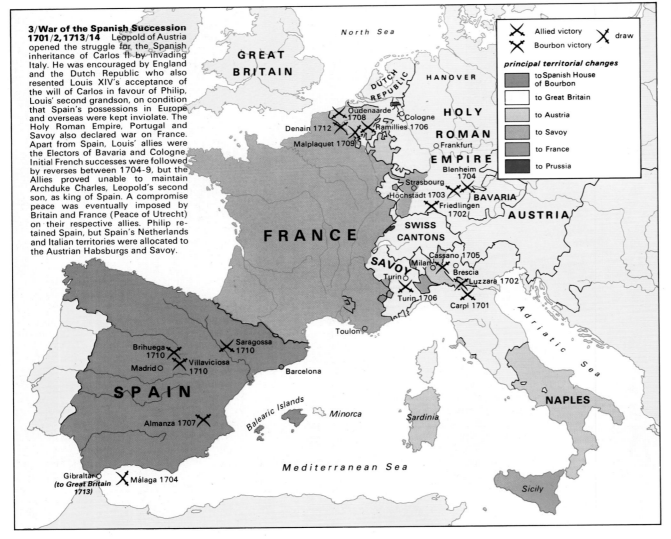

3/War of the Spanish Succession 1701/2, 1713/14 Leopold of Austria opened the struggle for the Spanish inheritance of Carlos II by invading Italy. He was encouraged by England and the Dutch Republic who also resented Louis XIV's acceptance of the will of Carlos in favour of Philip, Louis' second grandson, on condition that Spain's possessions in Europe and overseas were kept inviolate. The Holy Roman Empire, Portugal and Savoy also declared war on France. Apart from Spain, Louis' allies were the Electors of Bavaria and Cologne. Initial French successes were followed by reverses between 1704-9, but the Allies proved unable to maintain Archduke Charles, Leopold's second son, as king of Spain. A compromise peace was eventually imposed by Britain and France (Peace of Utrecht) on their respective allies. Philip retained Spain, but Spain's Netherlands and Italian territories were allocated to the Austrian Habsburgs and Savoy.

sooner or later turn west to regain, as they loudly proclaimed, everything lost to France by their dynasty between 1552 and 1678.

French ascendancy between 1661 and 1715 was not, it should be remembered, only in the political fields which can be illustrated in an historical atlas. Indeed, in the perspective of cultural and intellectual history, Louis' work for French literature, architecture, learning, and science and the arts in general, and his pensions paid to a great number of European poets, artists and scholars, whether they studied in France or not, may seem more important than his wars. His Versailles building programme and his support for academies became models for other princes; French became the language of the educated classes all over Europe and helped to create the cosmopolitan civilisation of the late 17th and the early 18th centuries. France also

made progress during his reign in the number of colleges and hospitals (a combination of what we would call hospitals, workhouses and houses of correction), in codification of laws, in administrative procedures and efficiency, and in all kinds of practical improvements from the street lighting and policing of Paris to the digging of the Languedoc canal (completed by 1684) which gave cheap and efficient communication between the Atlantic and the Mediterranean.

Taken as a whole, the reign fixed the French frontiers in Europe (though colonial cessions had to be made to Great Britain) and foreshadowed the exchange which in 1738 brought the certainty of Lorraine being incorporated with France (achieved by 1766); while, in the history of French civilisation, the reign is traditionally and deservedly honoured with the title *Le Grand Siècle*.

Versailles Louis XIV's vast palace at Versailles, the centre of his government and his court, was built in 'envelope' form round three sides of his father's hunting château, preserved at the king's insistence for his private apartments. Gardens and park were enlarged and embellished. Symbolism abounded in indoor decorations and outdoor statues and sculpture. The Coysevox Vase 'War', shown here, celebrated French victories of the reign up to the Truce of Regensburg (1684).

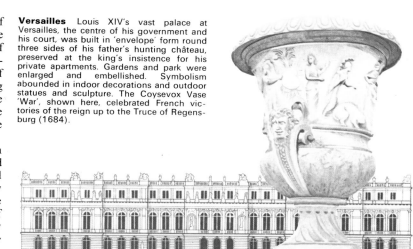

frontiers and administration

⟋ frontier of France 1713-14

administrative units of Louis XIV's reign, the *généralités* (generalities)

⊙ seat of intendants, Louis XIV's royal commissioners

⊕ *parlement* (law courts)

defence

◼ fortifications (the so-called *barrière* or *frontière de fer*)

▣ fortifications built by Vauban but ceded during reign of Louis XIV

➤ fortification gap, possible invasion route *(porte)*

⚓ galley port

⊞ naval port

economic

‡ commercial harbours

major manufactures

◻ brandy

🐚 cloth

▢ glass

⊞ iron

◧ madder dye

◗ paper

♟ pottery

▤ printing

◕ salt

◔ silk

◉ soap

⊠ tapestry and carpets

♥ wine

1/Administrative units and defensive fortification system This map indicates those provinces of France which had *parlements* (law courts) and delineates the administrative units of the reign, the 'generalities'. It shows the towns where the intendants, the royal commissioners appointed by the king 'at his pleasure' (and thus not able to buy or sell their offices), resided. The fortresses in the iron belt round France, built or improved by Vauban from 1679 onwards, are indicative of the increasingly defensive stance of the monarchy.

The struggle for empire 1713 to 1815

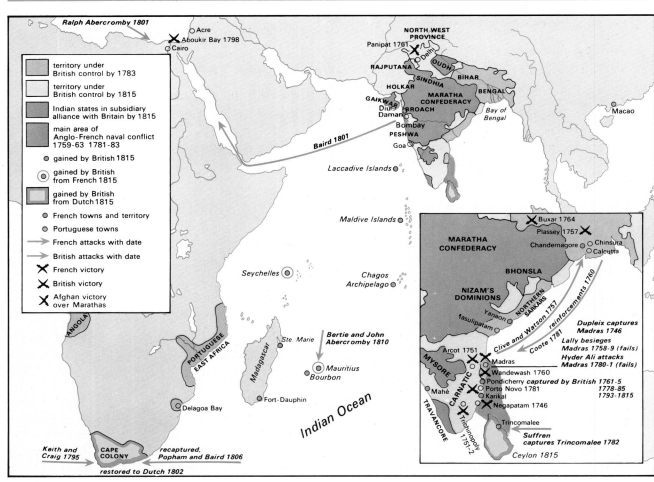

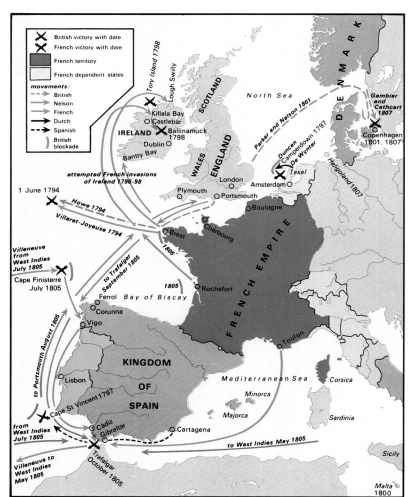

2/The Franco-British struggle for India *(above)* The capture of Madras by Dupleix in 1746 began the struggle for India. As in America, British seapower proved decisive. Dupleix was checked at Trichinopoly in 1752, and after the capture of Bengal in 1757 the British could reinforce the Carnatic at will. The capture of Pondicherry in 1761 destroyed French power, and with local resources and control of the sea the British were able to hold off all subsequent challenges.

3/The British triumph in home waters, 1794-1805 *(below)* In the final confrontation between Great Britain and France the decisive battles were fought in European waters. Weakened by the French Revolution, the French fleet was no match for the British, and as successive invasion attempts foundered against British superiority at sea, Britain occupied its rival's possessions. By 1815 British possession of the key strategic colonies left it the supreme imperial power.

British expansion. But the key to colonial victory was control of the lines of communication, and thus seapower. The outbreak of the Seven Years War in Europe transformed the local struggle; in the wider conflict of 1756-63, while France was handicapped by its continental commitments, Great Britain took control of the Atlantic and isolated the French forces in North America. Cut off from reinforcements, Louisbourg fell in 1758, Quebec in 1759. The capture of Montreal in 1760, following British naval victories at Quiberon Bay and Lagos, completed the fall of French Canada. In the West Indies, by 1763 the British were in control of Spanish Havana and all the French islands

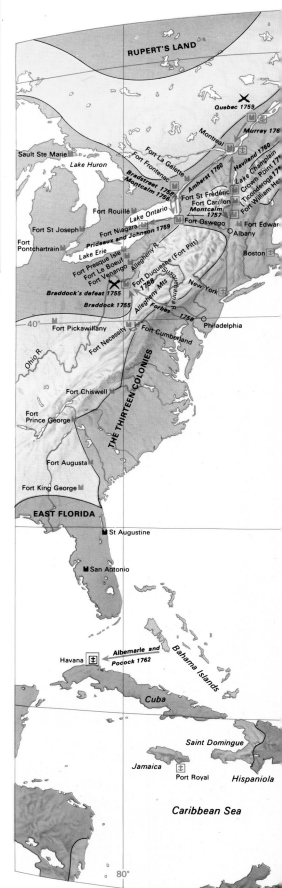

BY leaving the Spanish empire and its trading monopolies substantially intact, the Treaty of Utrecht (1713) sought to establish a stable state system in Europe and overseas based upon the balance of power. Instead, it perpetuated the principal causes of colonial conflict. Territorial expansion continued throughout the 18th century, and led to serious clashes between Portugal and Spain in the Banda Oriental (Uruguay), between Spain and Great Britain in Georgia, and between Great Britain and France in North America. Trading monopolies proved an even greater source of friction. Illegal trade with the Spanish empire flourished, and Spanish attempts to suppress British and Dutch smugglers from Jamaica, St Eustatius and Curacao reduced the Caribbean to a state of undeclared war. Further north, British efforts to enforce similar restrictions upon its American colonists provoked resistance and finally open revolt.

But although dissension originated in the unsettled situation overseas, the outcome depended upon the actions of the European powers. During 1739-40 the fragile peace collapsed as Great Britain and Spain went to war in defence of their trading rights, and Frederick the Great's invasion of Silesia began the mid-century struggle for supremacy in eastern Europe (see page 196). The outbreak of war between Great Britain and France in 1744 brought the war for Caribbean trade and the war for Silesia together into a single global conflict that extended from North America to India, and from the West Indies to Russia. This struggle, which lasted intermittently until 1815, rapidly became a duel between Great Britain and France for global supremacy. European powers, American settlers, North American Indian chiefs and Indian princes all fought as subsidised and dependent allies of these two great powers. Local factors determined the nature of local struggles, but all were subordinated to the larger conflict.

The Treaty of Aix-la-Chapelle (1748) settled none of the outstanding questions, and fighting began again in North America in 1754. By 1756 France had achieved local military superiority, its strategically sited forts preventing further except St Domingue. These were restored at the Treaty of Paris (1763), but Great Britain retained the North American mainland east of the Mississippi, including Florida which was ceded by Spain.

The British triumph was short-lived. Between 1763 and the American War of Independence (1776-83), France rebuilt both its navy and its alliances in pursuit of revenge. By 1781, confronted by a hostile coalition of France, Spain and the Dutch Republic, threatened by the 'armed neutrality' of the Baltic powers, and overstrained by the need to defend an empire stretching from Canada to India, Great Britain was forced to surrender control of North American waters. The French blockade of Yorktown forced Cornwallis to surrender, and although Rodney's victory off the group of islands known as The Saints in 1782 saved British possessions in the West Indies, Great Britain was obliged to recognise American independence at the Treaty of Versailles (1783). Nevertheless, the triumph of 1763 ensured that the new United States developed as an English-speaking nation. Trading contacts quickly revived, and despite occasional differences, the cultural link between the two countries exercised a profound influence on subsequent history.

During these same years the British found a new empire in India. The emergence of independent princes upon the ruins of the Mughal Empire forced both French and British East India Companies to intervene in local politics to protect their commerce. Here again seapower was decisive. Thus, after early French successes, Great Britain's ability to reinforce its position by sea enabled it to check Dupleix's ambitious designs for a French empire in the Carnatic. But the real foundation of the British empire in India followed Clive's victory at Plassey (1757) which, assisted by the victory of the Afghans over the Marathas at Panipat (1761), gave the British control of the rich province of Bengal (see page 172). During the Seven Years War reinforcements from Bengal enabled the British to eliminate French influence in the Carnatic. Henceforth, despite a French challenge in 1781-83, Great Britain was the predominant European power in India.

The French Revolution of 1789 shattered the French navy and, despite a partial recovery after 1794, France never regained the position as a naval power it held in 1783. This alone ruined Napoleon's plans for the invasion of Great Britain. By 1815, the French, Spanish, Dutch and Danish fleets were defeated, their colonies mostly in British hands. With the acquisition of the Cape, Ceylon and Mauritius, Great Britain secured the route to India and the East, and laid the foundations for the second British empire. It occupied a position of unrivalled power throughout large areas of the world, and its influence was to be a decisive factor in their evolution.

Nelson's Victory (left) A British ship of the line carrying 102 guns and 850 men, HMS Victory became famous as the flag ship of Admiral Nelson. Ships such as the Victory were used throughout the 18th century. Nelson was the supreme tactician of the age of sail, and his victory over the combined French and Spanish fleets at Trafalgar in 1805 finally ensured British triumph in the long struggle for empire.

1/The struggle in the North Atlantic and North America, 1754-63 (below) After 1748 France built up its forces in North America to encircle the British colonies from the west. But its position there, and in the West Indies, depended upon constant reinforcement from Europe. Isolated by the British blockade in European waters, that position deteriorated rapidly after 1758, and the French overseas empire collapsed before determined British attacks. The sugar islands of the Caribbean were returned in 1763, but the fall of Montreal ended French power in North America.

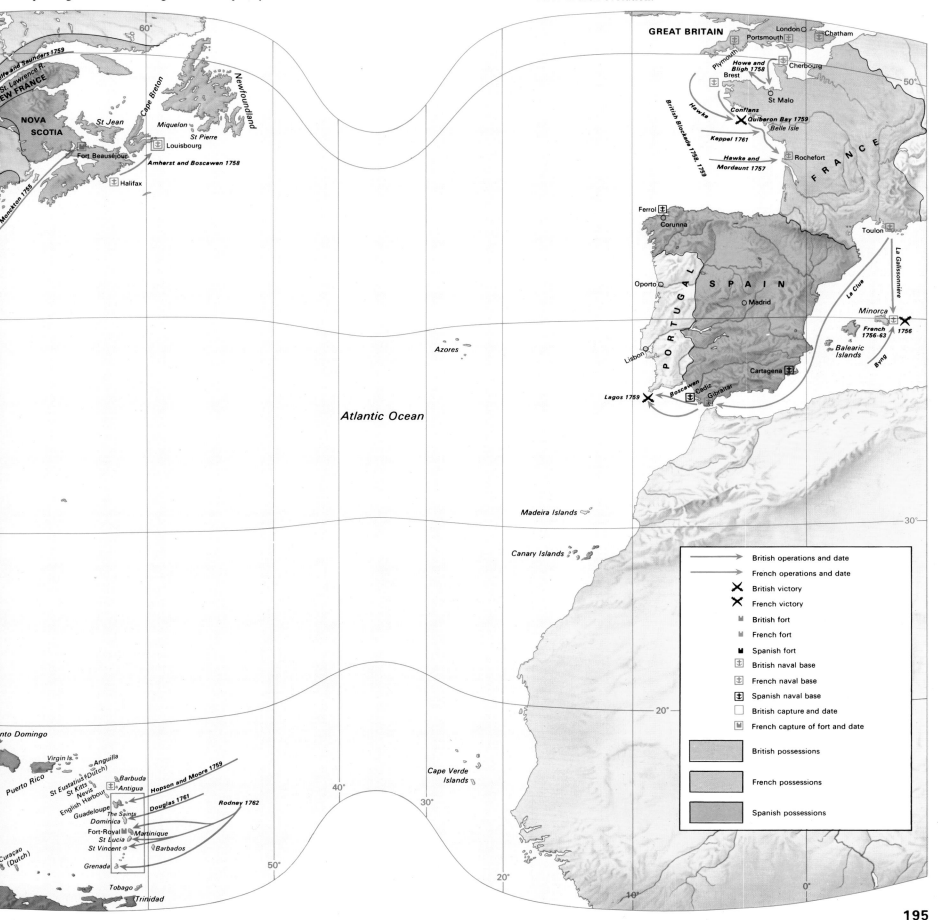

The Ottoman Empire, Austria and Russia: Eastern Europe from 1648 to 1795

Russian conquests from Poland 1667-1795
Russian conquests from Sweden 1700-43
Russian conquests from Turkey 1768-92
Prussian conquests from Austria 1740-41
Prussian conquests from Sweden 1721
Prussian conquests from Poland 1772-95
Habsburg conquests from Turkey 1683-1775
Habsburg conquests from Poland 1772-95
Turkish conquests from Venice 1669-1718

1/Territorial Gains and Losses in Eastern Europe 1648-1795 *(above)* During this period the western powers began to realise that the Ottoman Empire, once the terror of Europe, was no longer an invincible force and had indeed become dangerously weak. As Austria and Russia sought advantage from the Turkish disintegration, Prussia expanded, while France and Sweden tried to maintain the traditional balance. With France increasingly paralysed, and Britain's attention concentrated beyond Europe, the eastern powers were able to contrive the Partitions of Poland (see map 5).

4/The Silesian Wars *(below)* The intensive struggle began when the Prussians first won Silesia, at Mollwitz. Hohenfriedberg ended the first Austrian attempt at reconquest. In the Seven Years War, Prussians occupied Saxony and Bohemia as far as Prague (1757). Austrian victory at Kolin freed Bohemia, but recovery of Silesia was foiled at Leuthen. Though the Russians did occupy Berlin after Kunersdorf (1759) they failed to inflict a decisive defeat on Frederick II's highly mobile forces. Russian withdrawal after Peter III's accession (1762) forced Austria to renounce Silesia for good.

battles between Austria and Prussia
battle between Saxony and Prussia
battles between Russia and Prussia
battle between Austria with Russia and Prussia

SULTAN Mehmed IV, in whose reign the Ottoman Empire launched its last major military onslaught on the west, came to the throne in 1648, just as the Treaty of Westphalia ended the Thirty Years' War. Between then and the final partition of Poland in 1795, an almost continuous series of wars, frontier changes, alliances and population movements profoundly altered the European balance of power.

Under Mehmed, and a capable dynasty of grand viziers recruited from the Köprülü family, the Turks undertook an energetic expansionist policy designed to relieve the social, religious and generally disruptive pressures that had been building up internally since the days of Suleiman the Magnificent. But Ottoman methods of warfare, triumphant in the 15th and 16th centuries, failed to take account of technical and organisational developments which had begun to transform their traditional enemies' fighting power. They achieved some naval success with the conquest of Crete at the end of a long war with Venice (1645-69), but the failure of the last vizier, Kara Mustapha, to overwhelm the defences of Vienna in 1683, started a period of spectacular decline.

The siege having been successfully raised by an anti-Ottoman coalition led by the Polish king, John III Sobieski (1674-96), the Turkish domains now came under sustained attack from all sides. The Austrian Habsburgs reconquered Hungary in 1699, and went on, in 1718, to occupy the Banat of Temesvar and part of Serbia, including Belgrade. Venice renewed her attempts to establish naval bases in the Adriatic and the Morea. Russia redoubled her efforts to break through to the Black Sea. Altogether, although there was some occasional recovery – Serbia, for example, was regained in the encounters of 1737-39 – the Turks were at war for forty-one of the 109 years between the siege of Vienna and the Treaty of Jassy (1792); most of the results were disastrous. After the peace settlements of Carlowitz (1699), the Pruth (1711), Passarowitz (1718), Belgrade (1739), Küçük Kaynarca (1774) and Jassy itself, they found themselves shorn of Hungary, the Banat, Transylvania and Bukovina. To Russia, similarly, they had lost the north coast of the Black Sea from Bessarabia to the Caucasus, including the Crimea. They also had to grant Russia and Austria the legal right to intervene on behalf of the Empire's many Christian subjects, a concession carrying the seeds of much future conflict (see page 214).

The reconquest of Hungary, with the acquisitions that followed the War of the Spanish Succession, promoted the Austrian Habsburgs to the ranks of the recognised 'great powers'. But territory alone did not signify strength. Resistance by the Hungarian nobility to the extension of absolutist control hampered the full development of the country's resources. Large areas had been devastated and depopulated during the Turkish wars, and the main economic achievement of this period was the recolonisation of this land by hard-working immigrants, many from south-west Germany. Though the first settlements were unsuccessful, almost 50,000 immigrants arrived in the 1760s and 1770s, with a further 25,000 in the 1780s. Their skills and crafts made possible a more intensive and diversified agriculture.

The real weakness of the Habsburgs was revealed when the male line died out in 1740. This was the signal for Frederick II of Prussia to occupy Austria's highly-industrialised province of Silesia. He crushed the Austrian forces sent against him at Mollwitz (1741), and although Maria Theresa vigorously reformed her army and administration, encouraged economic development and entered into alliances with France and Russia, many years of bitter fighting failed to win her back the lost territory. Prussia had emerged as a rival, challenging the traditional pre-eminence of the Habsburg dynasty in Germany.

John Sobieski's successful participation in the alliance against the Turks had temporarily masked the growing disintegration of Poland, but in fact this process continued almost throughout the 17th and 18th centuries. The disastrous reign of John II Casimir Vasa (1648-68) saw the rebellion of the Ukrainian Cossacks, the establishment of an independent Cossack state, and a Russian-Cossack invasion detaching most of eastern Poland. The Swedes, under Charles X Gustav, then occupied northern Poland and Lithuania (1655), until their brutality inspired a successful counter-attack. The Russians were also expelled (although they retained Smolensk and the eastern Ukraine). Civil war and more Cossack unrest followed, and even John Sobieski's successes did more to help the emergence of Austria and Russia than to strengthen his own country.

At Sobieski's death in 1696, eighteen candidates sought the votes of the nobles who had the right to elect a monarch for the Republic of Poland. The winner was Augustus the Strong of Saxony, who as Augustus II reigned until 1733. His ambition to annex Livonia sparked off the Great Northern War (1700-21), in which the Swedes, under Charles XII, again devastated Poland, destroying a third of its cities and forcing Augustus's temporary abdication before being defeated at Poltava, in the Ukraine, in 1709. The real victor was Peter the Great of Russia, who restored Augustus to the throne but seized Livonia for himself, thus opening Russia's long-sought window to the Baltic. A marsh was drained to found St Petersburg as a warm-water port, and the new city became Russia's capital in 1715.

From then on, Russia played an increasingly important part in Europe's affairs, while Poland, once her most formidable foe, declined to the status of a satellite.

In 1733, a French-supported candidate was elected king, but Russian and Saxon troops put Augustus's son on the throne as Augustus III (1733-63). With Prussia's seizure of Silesia, Frederick II (the Great) controlled Poland's western boundaries and all its key trade outlets to central Europe. Russia based its armies in Danzig, Thorn and Posen during the Seven Years' War. Apart from these incursions, 1716-68 was a period of peace and prosperity.

Russia might have been content with the degree of control already achieved, but in 1768, four years after the election of King Stanislaw II Poniatowski (1764-95), Catherine the Great, using religious divisions as a political lever, provoked civil war. The Turks, seeing an opportunity to oppose Russia's steady, but so far sporadic, expansion to the south, intervened to stiffen Polish resistance. The resulting war (1768-74) revealed the full extent of Russia's new-found power. Her armies advanced through the Danubian principalities; her navy, making its first appearance in the Mediterranean, destroyed the Turkish fleet at Chesmé (1770) and the total collapse of the Ottoman Empire appeared a distinct possibility. From then on 'the eastern question' became a central issue in European affairs, as each great power tried to ensure that the Ottoman realms should not fall intact into one of the other's hands.

The presence of Russian forces near the mouth of the Danube aroused the determined opposition of Austria, who tried to involve Prussia in an anti-Russian block. Frederick II, with much to lose and little to gain from a Balkan conflict, proposed the first Polish partition thus shifting the great-power conflict to an area where he had most to gain. Hence Poland paid the price for Russia's initial moderation in relation to Turkey. But further gains were in any case soon to follow. After the occupation of the Crimea in 1783, the

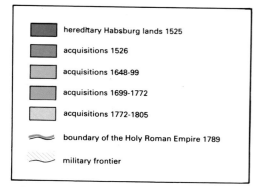

	hereditary Habsburg lands 1525
	acquisitions 1526
	acquisitions 1648-99
	acquisitions 1699-1772
	acquisitions 1772-1805
	boundary of the Holy Roman Empire 1789
	military frontier

3/Growth of the Habsburg Empire *(right)* The Austrian branch of the Habsburg dynasty was founded by Charles V's brother Ferdinand, who took advantage of a marriage tie to have himself elected king of Bohemia and Hungary in 1526. But for nearly two centuries he and his successors had to dispute possession of Hungarian territory with the Ottomans. After the Turkish collapse following the siege of Vienna (map 2), the Habsburgs were able to expand rapidly down the Danube. Their gains were consolidated at the treaties of Carlowitz (1699) and Passarowitz (1718), though some land was lost again by the treaty of Belgrade (1739). Another consequence of the contest with the Turks was the establishment from the 16th century of a frontier area under the direct control of military authorities in Vienna, which survived until the 1870s. Austria's largest 18th-century acquisitions resulted from the First and Third Partitions of Poland (map 5), but her gains from the latter proved short-lived.

exodus of the Crimean Tartars, who preferred to live under Turkish rule, opened up all their vast, fertile, lands to Russian colonisation. Russia's next offensive against Turkey (1787-92) for the first time provoked British opposition. Though she was able to acquire all the land between the Dniester and the Bug rivers, the final dismemberment of Poland was now only a matter of time. The outbreak of the French Revolution in 1789 temporarily eclipsed France's traditionally pro-Polish influence, and Russia, Austria and Prussia took the opportunity to complete the Second and Third Partitions. Ironically it was the jealousies aroused by the Partitions which prevented an effective anti-French combination among the powers, and thus to a large extent enabled the Revolution to survive.

2/Siege of Vienna *(below)* The Turks, advancing from the east, laid siege to the city in July 1683. The garrison and citizens held out long enough for the slow-moving German and Polish relief forces to cross the Danube and traverse the hilly country to the north and west. They finally swept down the slopes of the Wiener-wald on 12 September and destroyed the Turkish positions. The relief of Vienna marked the beginning of the Habsburg Empire's rise to great power status.

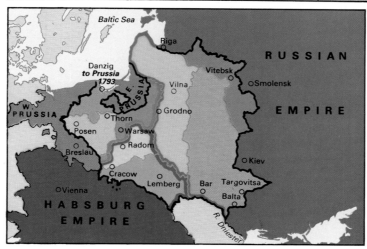

5/The Partitions of Poland *(left)* In the First Partition (1772), Russia made relatively modest gains, Prussia annexed the territory dividing Pomerania from East Prussia except for Danzig, Austria annexed a large area to the north of Hungary including Lemberg. In the Second Partition (1793), Russia annexed the entire eastern territory inhabited by Ukrainians and White Russians, while Prussia gained Danzig, Thorn and Posen, and pushed her frontier eastwards close to Warsaw. In the final Partition (1795) Prussia annexed Warsaw itself, Austria West Galicia, including Cracow, and Russia the remaining Polish territory, including modern Lithuania.

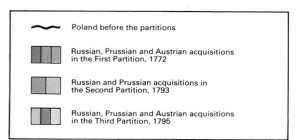

	Poland before the partitions
	Russian, Prussian and Austrian acquisitions in the First Partition, 1772
	Russian and Prussian acquisitions in the Second Partition, 1793
	Russian, Prussian and Austrian acquisitions in the Third Partition, 1795

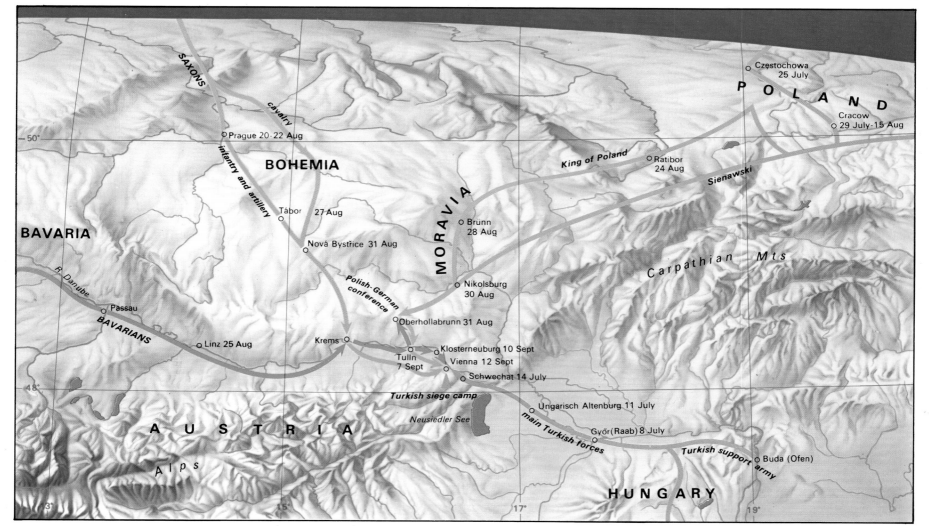

The emerging global economy 1775

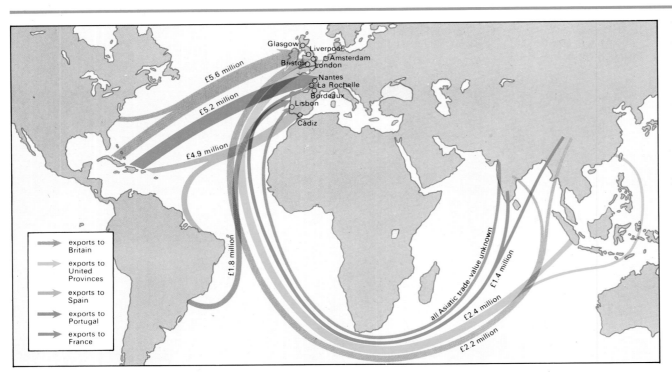

- exports to Britain
- exports to United Provinces
- exports to Spain
- exports to Portugal
- exports to France

Glasgow, Liverpool, Amsterdam, Bristol, London, Nantes, La Rochelle, Bordeaux, Lisbon, Cádiz

£5.6 million
£5.2 million
£4.9 million
£1.8 million
all Asiatic trade, value unknown
£1.4 million
£2.4 million
£2.2 million

3/The main trading flows (above) In the 1770s Britain's total trans-Atlantic imports stood slightly ahead of France. Both now topped Spain, where over 80 per cent consisted of silver and gold. In Asia the Dutch retained their leadership, thanks mainly to the East Indies, but overall they were beginning to fall behind their larger rivals. Both Britain and France were now doing as much business with India as with China.

4/The fur trade in the North (below) The Russians pressed east into Siberia with even more systematic determination than the French and English into the Canadian north-west. By 1745, when there were still only isolated trading posts west of Hudson Bay, the Cossacks who had crossed the Urals 'in search of the sable' had explored the Bering Strait, established bases in the Aleutian Islands, and were beginning to penetrate Alaska.

Pacific Ocean
Aleutian Islands
Petropavlovsk 1740
Bolsheretsk 1703
R. Amur
Alaska
Bering Strait
CANADA
SIBERIA
Yakutsk 1631
Fort La Reine (Portage la Prairie) 1738
Cumberland House (the English break away from shores of Hudson Bay) 1774
R. Lena
beyond Lake Baikal 1638-50
Fort Bourbon 1742
Fort Orléans (Missouri) 1718
Fort Charles (Lake of the Woods) 1732
Fort Pierre (Rainy Lake) 1718
from Yenisey and Yakutsk to R. Uda and R. Anadyr basins 1648-56 into Amur basin, penetrating to its mouth, 1643, but in 1689 Russians were forced by Chinese to withdraw from Amur
Fort St Louis 1682
Fort York 1684
Fort Kaministikwia 1679
R. Yenisey
Yeniseysk 1619
Fort Albany 1679
Turukhansk 1607
Krasnoyarsk
mouth of Yenisey 1619
Mangazeya 1601
Ketsk 1602
Fort Niagara 1679
Tomsk 1604
Kuznetsk 1618
R. Ob
Surgut 1594
Berezov 1593
Tara 1594
Loz'va 1590
Pelym 1590
Tobolsk 1587
Turinsk 1600
Tyumen 1586

- French Fort
- British Fort

Atlantic Ocean

BY the second half of the 18th century, Europe's trading connections with America and Asia were making an important contribution to its prosperity. They had begun to offer large markets for manufactures in exchange for the exotic foods and materials that Europe herself could not produce. Although the commercial links with the two distant continents were very different, the circle of trade was bound together by the transmission of South and Central American silver to Asia via western Europe.

In the Americas settlement had taken three main forms, each with its corresponding social and economic structures. In Peru (then occupying a much greater area than today) and Mexico the Spaniards had settled in small numbers as rulers over large native peasant populations; as races and skills mingled some industry grew up, and by 1700 Spanish America was essentially self-sufficient. On the outskirts of this rural economy, which engaged most of the population, were the great silver mines of northern Mexico and the Bolivian Andes, whose produce enabled the colonists to buy, at highly profitable prices, large quantities of European manufactures.

Second, there were the Caribbean and the Brazilian coastal strip, providing Europe with most of its sugar, coffee, cacao, rice, cotton and other tropical products. Here the large Indian population had almost been exterminated by conquest and disease, necessitating the massive importation of African slaves to build up the plantations. By 1775 five and a half million slaves had been brought to America; but as only a million and a half of them survived, a large replacement trade was needed to recruit scores of thousands more each year. These colonies, with their cheap tropical produce, were seen as Europe's most valuable overseas possessions.

Third, the North American mainland settlements were populated almost entirely by Europeans – English, Scots, Irish, Germans, Dutch – all breeding rapidly to a point where the original few hundred thousand immigrants had increased their numbers to over two million. Apart from the slave plantations in the southern colonies, which produced tobacco and rice, these were lands of small, independent farmers, whose grain, meat and butter duplicated those of the lands from which they had come. Unable to sell their surpluses in Europe, they found a large, rapidly-growing market in the West Indies, which now concentrated almost entirely on export crops. The bills of exchange they received in payment allowed them to buy Scots linen, Birmingham hardware and other imported manufactures. Similarly, but on a much smaller scale, Spanish farmers and ranchers in the Plate river basin supplied the plantations of Brazil.

The first three-quarters of the 18th century saw enormous developments, both in the absolute size of world trade and in its geographical distribution, even before there was any real sign of the Industrial Revolution. Between 1702 and 1772, England's already healthy foreign commerce almost trebled, while that of France, starting from a much lower base, increased more than eightfold in value from 1715 to 1771 and virtually caught up. Even more significantly, Britain's trading pattern, in 1700 still largely directed towards its continental neighbours, had spread almost throughout the world by the outbreak of the American Revolution, with approximately two-thirds involving sources and destinations outside Europe.

A complex series of exchanges now tied the American colonies to Europe, to each other, and to Asia. Most of the silver brought by the Spanish bullion fleets to Cádiz, which was the monopoly port of entry until 1778, flowed out again in the ships of the Portuguese, English, Dutch and French East India Companies, or travelled overland through Turkey and Russia to China, India or the Indonesian archipelago.

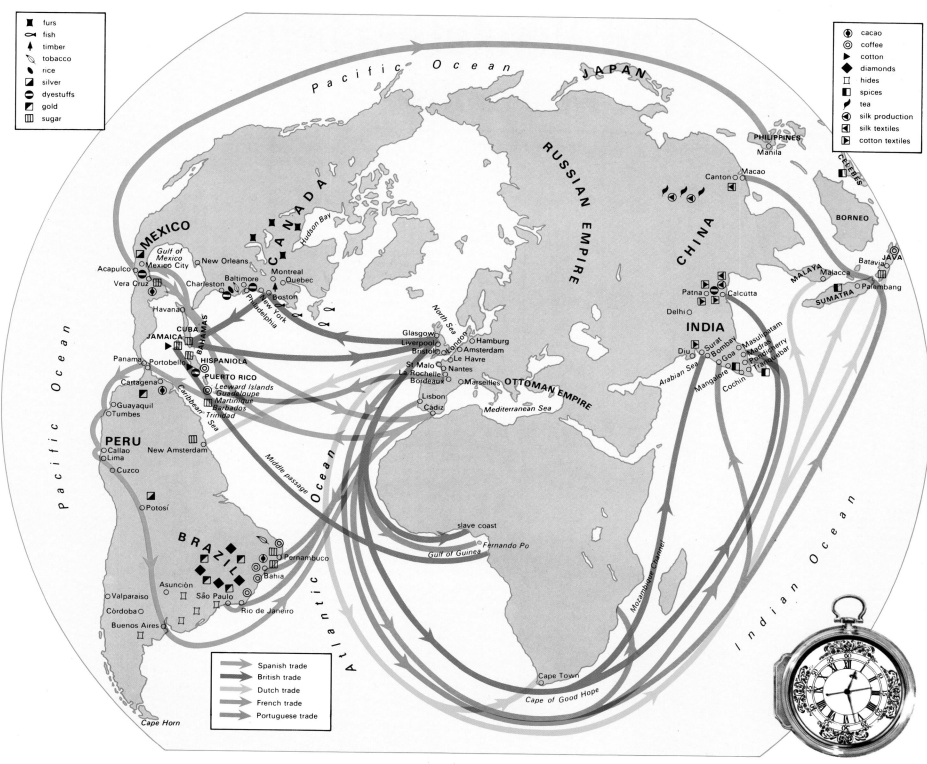

furs		cacao
fish		coffee
timber		cotton
tobacco		diamonds
rice		hides
silver		spices
dyestuffs		tea
gold		silk production
sugar		silk textiles
		cotton textiles

Spanish trade
British trade
Dutch trade
French trade
Portuguese trade

1/The pattern of world trade *(above)* As the 18th century progressed, a world-wide network of trade developed. Caribbean cotton, bought with American silver, woven in France or Spain, was sold in Lima or Mexico for silver, returning to pay for more cotton.

2/The exports of the Americas *(below)* Silver, gold and foodstuffs dominated the west-to-east leg of the Atlantic trade. Only in shipbuilding did the colonies have an industry whose products were wanted in Europe.

Harrison's Chronometer *(above)* Accurate measurement of time is essential for calculation of longitude. In 1762 the Yorkshireman Harrison won the British Government's prize for his invention.

South India's spices, China's tea (in which trade was said to be more profitable than in gold) and many other commodities were increasingly in demand, as were the cotton and silk textiles that could be better and more cheaply produced in Asia than in Europe. The industries of India and China were still at least as advanced as those in the west and European manufactures made little headway; what little European export trade there was at this time was mainly involved with supplying home comforts for the small, but increasingly well-established English and Dutch trading communities. Asia wanted silver, not goods, and American silver alone made it possible to develop a large east-west trade. Even England, becoming steadily more committed to the gold standard at home (an evolution largely completed by 1774) had to spend about £30 million between 1733 and 1766 on silver bullion to cover her purchases in India and the Far East.

A handful of port cities prospered mightily on this international trade. London, greatest of them all, was the biggest sugar-handler and monopolised Britain's Asian commerce. Liverpool rose rapidly to dominate the slave business and much general North American commerce. Glasgow became the leading tobacco importer. In France, Bordeaux drew ahead of the other Biscay ports, though Nantes still had the largest slave trade. Amsterdam was the centre of the Dutch trade with Asia and America, and like Hamburg combined its world-wide commerce with a large intermediary business, processing and forwarding French and English colonial produce into central Europe. Lisbon and Cádiz dominated the world trade of Portugal and Spain.

European expansion was not wholly by sea. In thinly-populated North America and northern Asia, pioneering fur traders travelled vast distances to find native trappers and the sites for future forts and trading posts. Russian expansion across Siberia, starting in the 1580s, finally established its borders in the Amur region with the first formal agreement between China and a European nation, the Treaty of Nerchinsk, in 1689, followed in 1727 with the founding of a Russian trading station in Peking.

This extra-European trade required the shipment of bulky goods over long distances, the provision of very long-term credit, the financing of large stocks and large-scale capital investment. It was responsible for making most of the great new individual fortunes of the period (apart from those of the war-financiers). This commercial revolution dominated economic thought in the hundred years prior to Adam Smith's *Wealth of Nations* in 1776.

For a century at least the merchant class was outstanding, and its importance declined only when the Industrial Revolution, with its new processes, profits, capital needs and social relationships, transformed the British economy.

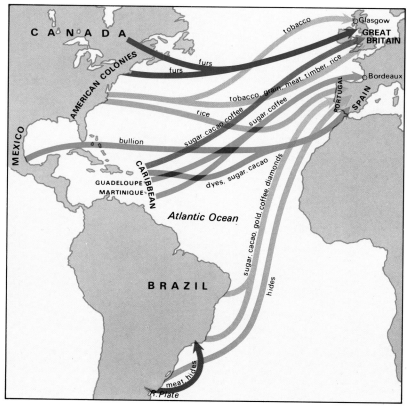

199

The Industrial Revolution begins: Great Britain 1760 to 1820

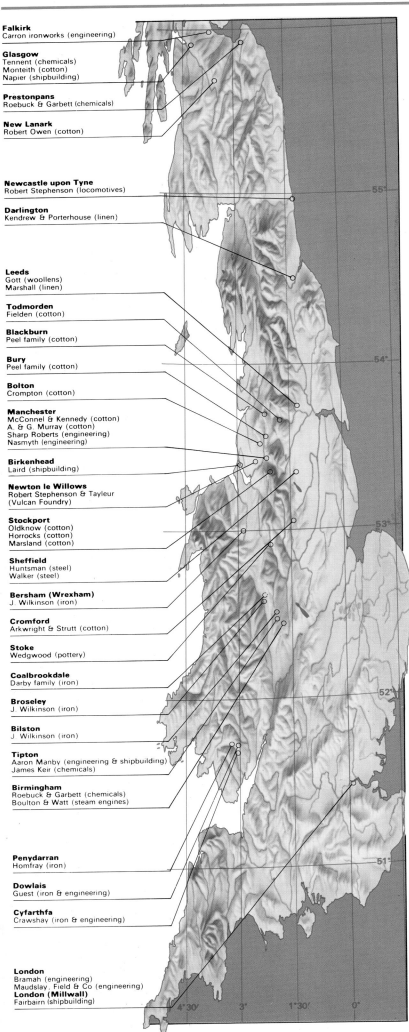

Falkirk
Carron ironworks (engineering)

Glasgow
Tennent (chemicals)
Monteith (cotton)
Napier (shipbuilding)

Prestonpans
Roebuck & Garbett (chemicals)

New Lanark
Robert Owen (cotton)

Newcastle upon Tyne
Robert Stephenson (locomotives)

Darlington
Kendrew & Porterhouse (linen)

Leeds
Gott (woollens)
Marshall (linen)

Todmorden
Fielden (cotton)

Blackburn
Peel family (cotton)

Bury
Peel family (cotton)

Bolton
Crompton (cotton)

Manchester
McConnel & Kennedy (cotton)
A. & G. Murray (cotton)
Sharp Roberts (engineering)
Nasmyth (engineering)

Birkenhead
Laird (shipbuilding)

Newton le Willows
Robert Stephenson & Tayleur
(Vulcan Foundry)

Stockport
Oldknow (cotton)
Horrocks (cotton)
Marsland (cotton)

Sheffield
Huntsman (steel)
Walker (steel)

Bersham (Wrexham)
J. Wilkinson (iron)

Cromford
Arkwright & Strutt (cotton)

Stoke
Wedgwood (pottery)

Coalbrookdale
Darby family (iron)

Broseley
J. Wilkinson (iron)

Bilston
J. Wilkinson (iron)

Tipton
Aaron Manby (engineering & shipbuilding)
James Keir (chemicals)

Birmingham
Roebuck & Garbett (chemicals)
Boulton & Watt (steam engines)

Penydarran
Homfray (iron)

Dowlais
Guest (iron & engineering)

Cyfarthfa
Crawshay (iron & engineering)

London
Bramah (engineering)
Maudslay, Field & Co (engineering)
London (Millwall)
Fairbairn (shipbuilding)

3/Pioneer entrepreneurs *(above)* In the manufacturing regions that developed after 1750 there were men who stood out: some like Huntsman, Crompton, Arkwright and Stephenson, as inventors, while others (McConnel and Kennedy, Gott, Marshall) are remembered as founders of great firms. The large pioneer enterprises shown on the map played a significant role in the Industrial Revolution; but in some industries – textiles and cutlery, for example – the firms were mostly small.

THE Industrial Revolution – as the rapid transition from a predominantly agrarian to a predominantly industrial economy is generally called – was the starting point of a new period in world history. Even in Europe, however, its impact was limited before 1820, and in many countries before the middle of the 19th century; in the wider world (see page 218) its revolutionary consequences were felt only much later. Nevertheless it is important to trace its beginnings in 18th century England, which in less than a century made Great Britain the workshop of the world. In the reign of George III (1760-1820) the structure of the British economy and of British society underwent fundamental changes in a very short period. There was an unprecedented rise in the output of coal, pig iron, engineering products and textiles. The first revolution of its kind in the world, it occurred in Great Britain and not on the continent of Europe for a variety of reasons. Great Britain had valuable resources, such as coal, iron, tin, copper, stone and salt; her farms supplied food for the growing population and raw materials to cloth manufacturers, leatherworkers, millers, and brewers. The transport facilities with which the country was endowed by nature – navigable rivers (Clyde, Thames, Severn, Trent, Ouse, Humber), good harbours (London, Bristol, Liverpool, Newcastle upon Tyne), and the sea – were supplemented by networks of new canals, toll roads and colliery railways. It was much cheaper to send goods, particularly heavy, bulky goods, by water than by land, and England's economic growth in the second half of the 18th century was stimulated by the heavy traffic on her inland waterways and along her coasts. A striking example was the movement of large quantities of coal from the Tyne and Wear to London. Again, nature had provided Lancashire with a climate which proved to be particularly suitable for the manufacture of cotton cloth, and this was the great growth industry in England at the time of the Industrial Revolution. The remarkable growth of London was significant in providing an expanding market for manufactured goods.

While continental Europe was plagued by one campaign after another in the 18th century, Great Britain fought her wars abroad and was free from internal strife except for two brief Jacobite revolts in 1715 and in 1745. The Wars against the French (see page 194) enabled the British to extend their empire – and to expand their overseas markets – in Canada and India. The loss of the American colonies did not, for many years, lessen the importance of the United States as a market for British manufactured goods. Again, the temporary loss of continental markets suffered during the revolutionary and Napoleonic wars was counterbalanced by the opening up of new trading opportunities in South America. The stimulus of war helped the iron, engineering, shipbuilding and textile industries which supplied the armed forces.

At a time when commerce in continental Europe was strangled by a multiplicity of customs barriers, river tolls and local taxes, men and goods had moved freely all over Great Britain since the union of England and Scotland in 1707. The government played its part in maintaining law and order, providing a stable currency, protecting industry from foreign competition, and taking special measures to foster shipping, overseas trade and the woollen industry. In negotiations with foreign countries British ministers showed considerable skill in opening up markets for manufactured goods.

With a few important exceptions – such as mining and shipbuilding – only a modest initial capital was required to set up a new industrial enterprise. In the cotton industry, for example, a small workshop and relatively inexpensive machines were all that the pioneer entrepreneur

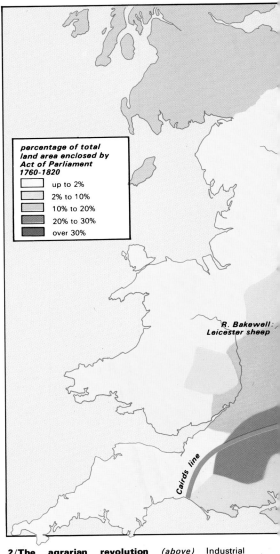

percentage of total land area enclosed by Act of Parliament 1760-1820

- up to 2%
- 2% to 10%
- 10% to 20%
- 20% to 30%
- over 30%

R. Bakewell: Leicester sheep

Caird's line

2/The agrarian revolution *(above)* Industrial growth is generally preceded by an agrarian revolution; in England after 1750 the completion of enclosure of old commons and open fields together with scientific farming increased the output of food for a growing population and of raw materials for expanding industries. Increased prosperity enabled the agricultural community to buy more manufactured goods and to invest in new industries and public works. 'Caird's Line' indicates the division between grazing and dairy lands (to the west) and the chief grain districts (to the east).

needed. Robert Owen had to borrow only £200 to get started. An industrialist could often expand his undertaking by ploughing back some of his profits into the business. Although the family business or partnership which financed its own expansion was very common, a number of enterprises were established with capital derived from land or from commerce. Short-term loans were often available from the country (provincial) banks at low rates of interest.

A series of inventions and technical innovations in the second half of the 18th century greatly increased the output of both consumer and capital goods. They included new spinning machines and looms, the coke-smelting process, puddling, and the introduction of crucible cast steel. Above all, the steam engine provided industry with a new source of power and made possible the replacement of small workshops by large factories.

Social conditions, too, were favourable to economic progress. The class structure in England was less rigid than in continental Europe. No social stigma prevented the landed gentry from engaging in industry or trade; no legal impediments prevented an artisan from rising in the social scale. In spite of some sporadic violent opposition to the new order – machinebreaking (the Luddite riots in the north of England) and rick-burning – a labour force was set up which eventually accepted factory discipline.

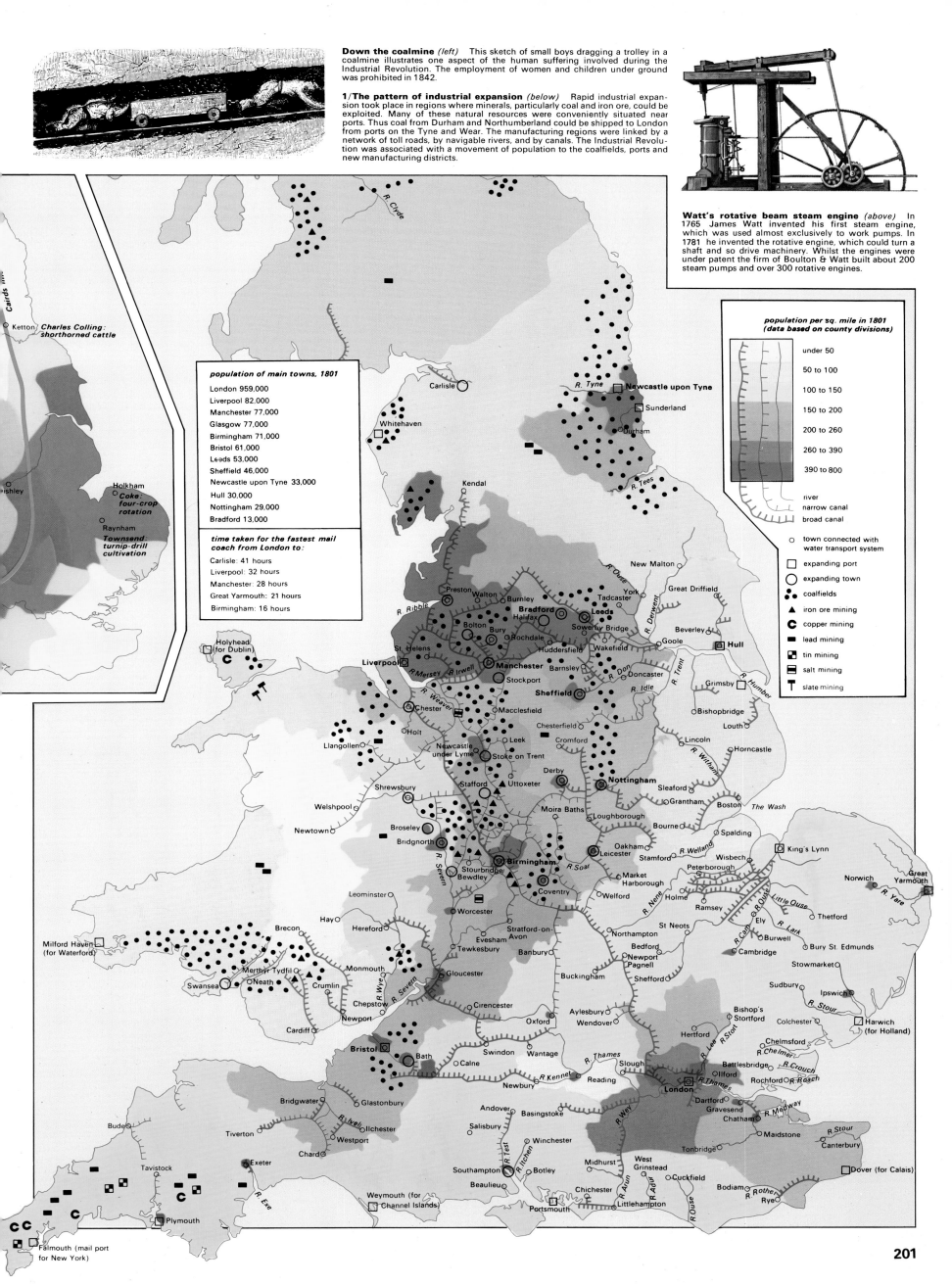

Down the coalmine *(left)* This sketch of small boys dragging a trolley in a coalmine illustrates one aspect of the human suffering involved during the Industrial Revolution. The employment of women and children under ground was prohibited in 1842.

1/The pattern of industrial expansion *(below)* Rapid industrial expansion took place in regions where minerals, particularly coal and iron ore, could be exploited. Many of these natural resources were conveniently situated near ports. Thus coal from Durham and Northumberland could be shipped to London from ports on the Tyne and Wear. The manufacturing regions were linked by a network of toll roads, by navigable rivers, and by canals. The Industrial Revolution was associated with a movement of population to the coalfields, ports and new manufacturing districts.

Watt's rotative beam steam engine *(above)* In 1765 James Watt invented his first steam engine, which was used almost exclusively to work pumps. In 1781 he invented the rotative engine, which could turn a shaft and so drive machinery. Whilst the engines were under patent the firm of Boulton & Watt built about 200 steam pumps and over 300 rotative engines.

population per sq. mile in 1801
(data based on county divisions)

- under 50
- 50 to 100
- 100 to 150
- 150 to 200
- 200 to 260
- 260 to 390
- 390 to 800

— river
— narrow canal
— broad canal
○ town connected with water transport system
□ expanding port
◎ expanding town
:• coalfields
▲ iron ore mining
C copper mining
■ lead mining
tin mining
salt mining
T slate mining

population of main towns, 1801

London 959,000
Liverpool 82,000
Manchester 77,000
Glasgow 77,000
Birmingham 71,000
Bristol 61,000
Leeds 53,000
Sheffield 46,000
Newcastle upon Tyne 33,000
Hull 30,000
Nottingham 29,000
Bradford 13,000

time taken for the fastest mail coach from London to:

Carlisle: 41 hours
Liverpool: 32 hours
Manchester: 28 hours
Great Yarmouth: 21 hours
Birmingham: 16 hours

Charles Colling: shorthorned cattle

Coke: four-crop rotation

Townsend: turnip-drill cultivation

The age of revolution
1773 to 1814

THE late 18th century was a time of upheaval in many parts of the western hemisphere, upheaval which can be attributed, directly or indirectly, to the ferment of ideas known as the Enlightenment. These ideas, themselves a reflection of the needs and tensions of a changing society, were based on the new scientific knowledge of the 17th century, which bred a new faith in reason and progress. On the one hand, this led to a rejection of authority and an assertion of the Rights of Man, expressed in Rousseau's famous statement that man is born free, but is everywhere in chains. On the other hand, the new ideas provided inspiration for monarchs who had already, at the close of the 17th century (see page 184), begun to draw power into their own hands and to govern through bureaucratic agents of their own choice. Centralising, enlightened rulers such as Joseph II of Austria (1780-90) or Frederick II of Prussia (1740-86) derived their ideas from rationalist philosophers such as the Encyclopaedists, for whom government was a science leading to the efficient satisfaction of needs. But their centralising activities were opposed by all those with a vested interest in the old régime – churches, guilds and corporations, and above all the aristocracy, whose leaders drew upon the theories of Montesquieu and Burke to prove that society was an organic growth, and that its traditional groupings not only conferred inalienable rights upon their members but resulted in a balance of power which guaranteed the individual against tyranny. This, and the natural desire of provinces for autonomy, was the origin of unrest. But it soon became clear that the ferment could not stop at this point.

Open revolt was most likely to occur in areas where the aristocracy could obtain support from the peasantry; but in eastern Europe (see page 178) peasants were still serfs, and were unlikely to rebel in support of the landlords who were their immediate oppressors. However, peasants also disliked innovation and would sometimes fight

1/The age of revolution (left and below)
1755, 1793 Corsica Local clans led by Paoli rebelled against Genoese rule and established independent democratic government. France bought island from Genoa in 1768, crushed revolt. Second attempt by Paoli to secure independence from (revolutionary) France, 1793, led to brief British occupation; rise of Bonaparte, himself a Corsican, put an end to separatist movement.
1768 Geneva Middle-class citizens of small city-state rebelled against domination by few patrician families; with French support the latter reasserted predominance 1782.
1773 South-East Russia Serfs, Cossacks and Asiatic tribes rebelled in Volga and Ural region under leadership of Pugachev, a Don Cossack. After fierce fighting Russian army put down revolt at the end of 1774.
1775 America Prolonged resistance by Britain's Thirteen Colonies to financial policies of mother country resulted in open warfare and Declaration of Independence, 1776 (see page 164).
1784 Dutch Netherlands Three-cornered struggle for power between Stadtholder, patrician families who controlled Estates General, and middle-class Patriot party which aimed to democratise government. In 1787 Prussian troops defeated Patriot army and restored Stadtholder with greater powers.
1787 Austrian Netherlands (Belgium) Revolt against centralising policy of Emperor Joseph II, leading to proclamation of the Republic of the United Belgian Provinces (1790). Faction fights broke out between aristocratic and middle-class rebels; Austrian Emperor reconquered area end 1790.
1789 France The States-General, summoned by Louis XVI to solve his financial difficulties, turned itself into a National Assembly, proclaimed Rights of Man, and issued constitution (1791). Risings by peasantry and Parisians overthrew feudal social and political order; Louis XVI's opposition, and attempted flight, led to abolition of monarchy (1792). King and Queen were guillotined as traitors (1793). Threat of invasion by a coalition under Austria led under the Jacobins to 'reign of terror', ended by fall and execution of Robespierre (1794). Following weak and corrupt rule of Directory (1795-99) power passed to Napoleon Bonaparte.

1789 Liège Middle-class citizens supported by workers and peasants expelled prince-bishop and abolished feudalism. Bishop restored by Austrian troops, 1790.
1790 Hungary Magyar nobles rejected edicts of Austrian emperor and demanded greater independence for Hungary within Habsburg Empire; later, frightened by peasant disturbances, accepted compromise with the monarchy.
1791 Poland King, supported by lesser nobles, adopted new constitution designed to strengthen Poland against Russian encroachment. Catherine II of Russia, at invitation of greater nobles, invaded, destroyed constitution and divided large areas of Polish territory between Russia and Prussia. Attempt by Kościuszko and lesser nobles to strengthen surviving Polish state (1794) crushed by Russia and Prussia; Poland partitioned and ceased to exist as separate state.
1791 Haiti Slave rising in western (French) part of island (Saint Domingue) resulted in rise of Negro leader, Toussaint l'Ouverture; by 1801 had conquered rest of island from Spaniards and secured virtual independence. Island then seized by the French, rising suppressed, and independence not fully secured until 1825.
1793 Sardinia In return for expelling French revolutionary invaders, islanders demanded autonomy within combined kingdom of Piedmont-Sardinia. King re-asserted his authority when French threat subsided in 1796.
1798 Ireland Rebellion of United Irishmen seeking independence from England, put down by British army. Leading conspirator, Wolfe Tone, committed suicide.
1804 Serbia Revolt against Ottoman atrocities led to demands for autonomy within the Ottoman Empire and later for independence. Rebels under Kara George fought until, the Ottoman reoccupation of Serbia in 1813.
1808 Spain After Napoleon placed his own brother, Joseph, on throne, a large-scale peasant rebellion gave valuable assistance to British expeditionary force under Wellington. Middle-class intellectuals proclaimed constitution, but it did not survive restoration of Bourbon king in 1814.
1809 Tyrol After Austria renewed war against Napoleon, the peasants of Tyrol, whose territory had been taken from Austria by Napoleon in 1805 and given to Bavaria, rebelled against new rulers. In spite of brave stand under Andreas Hofer, an innkeeper, revolt was crushed by Bavarian and French troops.
1810 Spanish America Discontent against mother country increased after 1808, when colonists faced prospect of new imperialist policies from either Napoleon or Spanish liberals; beginning of revolutionary movement which secured independence of entire sub-continent during following two decades (see page 226).

fiercely to retain their traditional way of life, as they did in Russia under Pugachev and in Hungary against Joseph II. In western Europe, a similar peasant reaction to foreign rule played a part in the Belgian revolution. But the Polish peasants had little inducement to support the gentry in the Polish revolts of 1791 and 1794, and in Ireland also middle-class nationalists who relied on peasant unrest against English landlords were disappointed and quickly succumbed to British armed force when support from France failed to arrive. On the other hand, the peasants of Serbia, who rose in 1804 in the first nationalist revolt in the Balkans, held out for three years until overwhelmed by the reorganised armies of the Sultan.

Revolution on a large scale first appeared in England's American colonies. Appealing to Locke's philosophy of natural right, the colonists refused to be taxed by a parliament in London in which they were not represented. By 1775 the dispute had led to open war (see pages 164 and 194). Moderate men, who would have retained the old structure of society, were superseded by men with more democratic aims, and the war for national independence attracted support from all classes of the population, including small farmers, town labourers, and a numerous bourgeoisie. The American example was an inspiration to rebels in the Netherlands as well as in France (whose troops had fought on the American side in the war), but in Holland and Belgium factions were too much divided between reactionary and progressive aims to succeed in face of foreign intervention.

In France, also, the revolution began as an aristocratic reaction to the centralising monarchy. But this soon proved to be merely a prelude to widespread popular revolt. This began in 1789 when the middle class took advantage of a financial crisis to establish a parliamentary type of government on a basis of wealth. This assertion of middle-class preponderance was challenged when the peasants, exploited as much by bourgeois as by aristocratic landlords, rose in a vast wave of rioting which brought about the destruction of feudal society. At the same time, the labouring population of Paris, impelled by food shortage, seized the strategic fortress of the Bastille and made it impossible for the king, Louis XVI, to recover despotic power by overawing the city. For two years the middle class retained control of the political scene and used its power to reorganise France's civil, military and religious institutions. They intended to co-operate with the king and with liberal sections of the aristocracy; but this became impossible when counter-revolutionary forces gathered strength both inside and outside the country. In 1792 the revolutionaries, confronted with the threat of armed invasion, declared war on Austria, and were soon at war with Prussia and the greater part of Europe. Early defeats produced panic measures, including the deposition and subsequent execution of the king and the slaughter of political suspects. This unification of the nation against external threat was the work of Danton, Carnot and the Girondins; but they were displaced by a more extreme set of revolutionaries, the Jacobins, who rallied support by placing government on a more democratic basis and by terrorist action against dissidents. A total call-up of the nation for war produced enthusiastic armies, superbly organised by Carnot, and the French not only expelled the foreign invaders but also attacked in their turn. Belgium and other territories were annexed to secure France's 'natural frontiers'. Army officers who owed their advancement to the revolutionary doctrine of 'careers open to talent' extended French power into Holland, Switzerland and Italy. Outstanding among them was Napoleon Bonaparte who, after a brilliant campaign in Italy, led an expedition across the Mediterranean and carried revolutionary institutions to Malta and Egypt. Only the assault on the British Isles proved unsuccessful. A raid on Wales in 1797 failed to win local support, and three expeditions to Ireland failed to meet up with local rebels.

At home, victory produced a revulsion against the Robespierrist terror, and France reverted once more to middle-class government (1794). But the corruption of the Directory and the relaxation of national effort soon led to economic

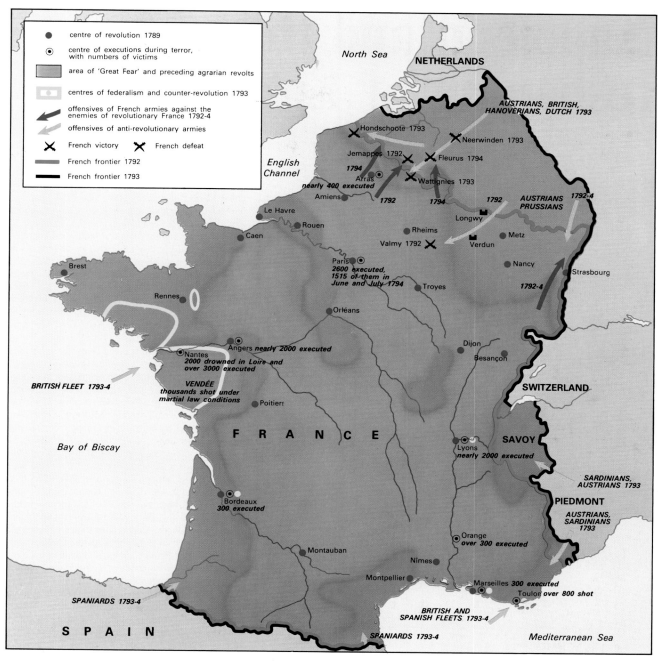

- centre of revolution 1789
- centre of executions during terror, with numbers of victims
- area of 'Great Fear' and preceding agrarian revolts
- centres of federalism and counter-revolution 1793
- offensives of French armies against the enemies of revolutionary France 1792-4
- offensives of anti-revolutionary armies
- French victory   French defeat
- French frontier 1792
- French frontier 1793

2/The revolution in France (above) The French Revolution proceeded by violence and war. In 1789 a Paris rising secured the overthrow of the government, and peasant revolt destroyed feudalism. Both were to some extent caused by food shortage at a time of political excitement. In 1792-93 fear of counter-revolution led to war with the reactionary forces in Europe, led by Austria. Economic distress and military defeat encouraged royalist revolt in Vendée and federalist revolt in large towns, but the Jacobins suppressed opponents and achieved military victory.

3/The expansion of revolutionary France (right) The French Revolution produced successful armies which extended France's power and influence. Territory was annexed to secure 'natural frontiers', and beyond them 'sister republics' were established. French armies remained in occupation, but administration was in the hands of local democrats. These were too few to sustain the republics when French military power temporarily waned in 1799, but the experience of revolutionary institutions had a lasting effect.

crisis, political discontent and military defeat. These were the dangers from which France was rescued by Napoleon when he seized power in 1799. Napoleon not only re-established revolutionary institutions in France – even if in a modified form – but also carried them by military conquest to many other parts of Europe.

The French Revolution was a decisive turning point in European history. At the same time its vigorous assertion of personal dignity, regardless of birth or creed, was an inspiration to people as far away as Haiti, and made a lasting impact upon ideas and institutions in all quarters of the globe. Nevertheless, French attempts to impose Enlightenment by force caused resentment. Peasant resistance began in France itself at an early stage and was repeated, with nationalist implications, in the Tyrol and in Spain in Napoleonic times. Meanwhile, Spain's American colonists (see page 226) were even more determined to resist interference from a reformed mother country than from the pre-revolutionary régime, and revolutionary movements which themselves owed much to the Enlightenment eventually secured the independence of Latin America.

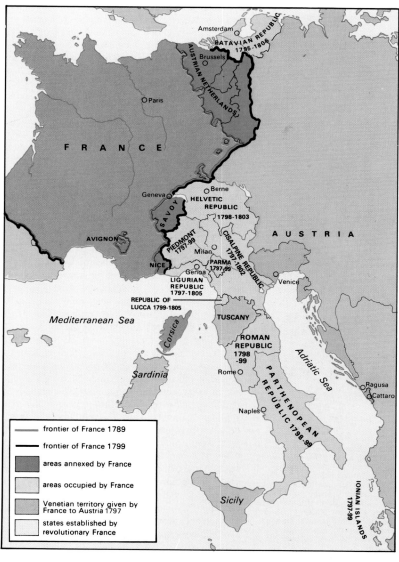

- frontier of France 1789
- frontier of France 1799
- areas annexed by France
- areas occupied by France
- Venetian territory given by France to Austria 1797
- states established by revolutionary France

Napoleon and the reshaping of Europe

IN 1799 the 31-year-old General Napoleon Bonaparte seized power in France. Born in Corsica, he had risen to prominence by leading French Revolutionary armies in a descent on northern Italy and an attack on Egypt. His autocratic rule as First Consul (1799-1804) and as Emperor (1804-14) was acceptable to the French people after the chaos of the last few years of the Revolution, and during his first few years of power he justified their hopes of sound government by introducing measures which were to form a lasting basis for most of France's institutions. An administrative law of 1800 reorganised the *départements* into which France had been divided by the Revolution, reducing the power of their locally elected councils and giving them prefects to carry centralised authority to every part of the country. A Concordat of 1801 brought an end to the quarrel that had broken out between revolutionary France and the Church, allowing the state to control the temporalities of the Church while the Pope confined himself to spiritual direction. An educational law of 1801 set up state grammar schools (*lycées*) for which scholarships were available and in which education was directed towards providing well-trained civil servants and army officers. More welcome still to the majority of Frenchmen was the civil code of 1804, later known as the *Code Napoléon*, which confirmed the legal equality and the property rights that had emerged from the Revolution. Members of the old nobility were allowed to share the benefits of this legislation provided they accepted the new regime. Napoleon thus consolidated the more concrete achievements of the Revolution to such an extent that they proved unshakeable even after his downfall, though in doing so he substituted efficiency for individual liberty as the goal of human endeavour. The functions of parliament were reduced to a minimum, and administrative activity took the place of politics. France became a nation of peasant farmers and landed proprietors, with a heavy top-dressing of bureaucracy in which men of talent could compete for jobs and rewards.

The bureaucrats were soon joined by a military élite, for the general peace which Bonaparte secured at the outset of his career lasted only a short time, and from 1803 to 1814 war was continuous. France's armies, which had already shown their potential during the Revolution, reached the height of their achievement as a result of Napoleon's administrative genius and brilliant generalship. Abandoning the siege warfare of an earlier age, Napoleon aimed at defeating the enemy's forces in the field, after outmanoeuvring them in such a way that they were divided and thus outnumbered. Shattering defeats were inflicted on Austria at Austerlitz (1805), on Prussia at Jena (1806), and on Russia at Friedland (1807), leaving Napoleon supreme in western Europe. A lightning invasion of Spain in 1808 drove a British expeditionary force to the sea at Corunna, and renewed hostilities by Austria in 1809 produced another rapid victory for the French at Wagram. Military success was accompanied by ruthless diplomacy. Territories on the borders of France were annexed; Switzerland came under French 'protection'; the princely rulers of western Germany allied with Napoleon in return for aggrandisement of their states; Spain, north-east Italy, Naples and Westphalia became satellite kingdoms under members of the Bonaparte family; and Polish lands taken from Austria and Prussia received a Napoleonic nominee as Grand Duke. Only Austria and Prussia, greatly reduced in size, remained in precarious independence alongside the enigmatic power of Russia.

Napoleon insisted that even the remotest of his puppet rulers should establish French-style institutions if at all possible, and adopt the *Code Napoléon*. His intention was partly to carry out a social revolution in the more backward areas such as Poland, and partly to harness the resources of the whole Empire to the needs of France. The success of the new institutions in creating a society based on wealth and merit rather than on prescription and privilege was greatest in the Netherlands, the Rhinelands and north-east Italy, where feudalism had long been breaking down and where French Revolutionary armies had already laid a foundation of French ideas, but the result was nowhere negligible. Nor

was Napoleon's influence confined to the continent of Europe. His reforms, which were secular in inspiration and therefore not tied to Christianity, were adopted as a pattern by both Mohammed Ali of Egypt and the Ottoman Sultan Mahmud II later in the 19th century, and the *Code Napoléon* became a model for legal reform in South America and Japan.

Fortunately for Napoleon, national feeling at this time was almost non-existent in Germany and Italy. In spite of grievances created by France's economic exactions, many young men in annexed or allied territories appreciated the career opportunities opened up to them by Napoleonic institutions and by the fusion of petty states into larger territorial units. The only serious popular resistance to French encroachment came from Spain, where peasant guerrilla warfare encouraged a British army under Sir Arthur Wellesley (later the Duke of Wellington) to land in Portugal in 1809 and fight its way through Spain into southern France by 1813. Napoleon's chief enemies on the continent of Europe were the dynastic rulers of Austria, Prussia and Russia. All three at one time or another allied with Napoleon for the sake of expediency, but his insatiable ambition finally led him to invade Russia in 1812, and his defeat there encouraged all three monarchs to ally against him. The money for their military efforts came chiefly from Great Britain, France's most persistent enemy.

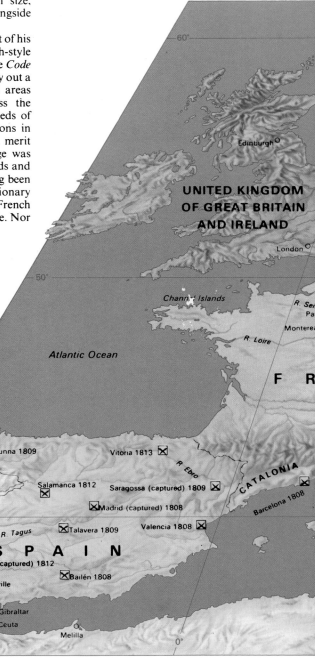

Great Britain's hostility arose from strategic and economic reasons. It had never been in her interest to allow France to dominate the whole of the Channel coast. French governments had long excluded British trade from France's territories: in an effort to bring ruin and revolution to Britain, Napoleon attempted in his Continental System to close the whole of Europe to British goods. Nelson thwarted Napoleon's invasion schemes by destroying the French and Spanish fleets at Trafalgar (1805), and British naval power in the Baltic and the Mediterranean continually undermined the Continental System, but Britain would never have been able to destroy the Napoleonic Empire without help from the eastern European powers on land. This led to the curious situation in which Britain, politically and industrially the most advanced nation in the world, allied with reactionary powers to defeat the only other modernising force in Europe.

In France, Napoleon's wars were popular for some years. Conscription could be avoided by anyone wealthy enough to buy a replacement, and for men without capital or education the army provided a welcome career in which advancement could be rapid for anyone showing courage and initiative. Only in 1814, when France was invaded by Russian, Prussian, Austrian and British armies, did the French people begin, vainly, to urge Napoleon to make peace. He was defeated and exiled to Elba. In 1815 he escaped and ruled France again for a hundred days, but he was defeated by Wellington at Waterloo and sent as a prisoner to St Helena, where he died in 1821.

3/The overseas world *(right)* Napoleon frequently toyed with world-wide schemes which might have threatened the British Empire had he succeeded in controlling the colonies of Spain and Holland.

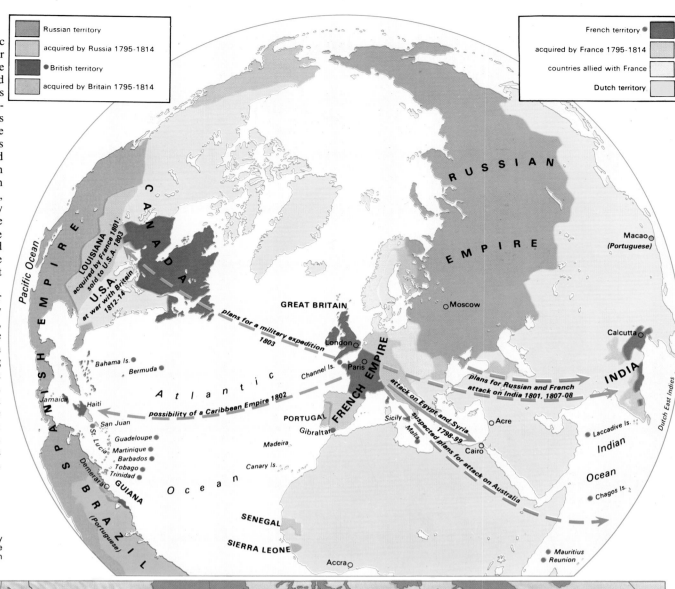

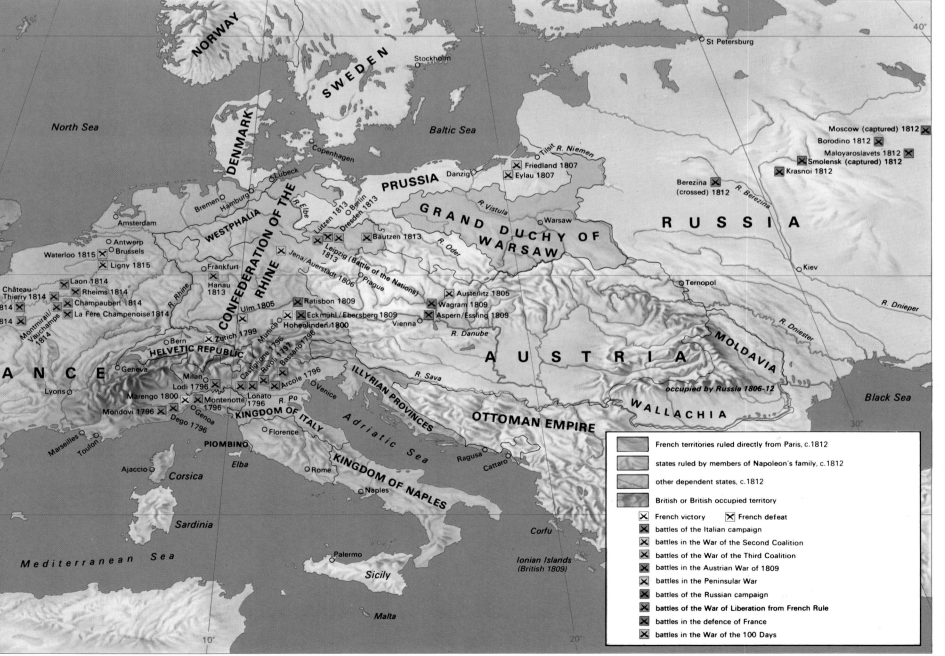

6 The age of

European dominance

Between 1815 and 1914 Europe thrust out into the world, impelled by the force of its own industrialisation. Millions of Europeans poured overseas and into Asiatic Russia, seeking and finding new opportunities in the wider world. Between 1880 and 1900 Africa, a continent four times the size of Europe, was parcelled out among the European powers. And when in 1898 the United States of America, following the European lead, annexed Puerto Rico, the Philippines and other islands of the Pacific, and asserted a controlling voice in Latin American affairs, it seemed as though European expansion was turning into the domination of the white race over the coloured majority. But expansion carried with it the seeds of its own destruction. Even before European rivalries plunged the continent into the war of 1914-18, the beginnings of anti-European reaction were visible in Asia and Africa, and no sooner had the United States occupied the Philippines than they were met by a nationalist uprising under the great Philippine leader, Aguinaldo.

Today, in retrospect, we can see that the age of expansive imperialism was a transient phase of history; while it lasted, it left a European imprint on the world. The world in 1914 was utterly different from the world in 1815, the tempo of change during the preceding century greater than previously during whole millennia. Though industry in 1914 was only beginning to spread beyond Europe and North America, and life in Asia and Africa was still regulated by age-old traditions, the nineteenth century inaugurated the process of transformation which dethroned agricultural society as it had existed through the ages, and replaced it with the urban, industrialised, technocratic society which is spreading – for good or for ill – like wildfire through the world today.

Population growth and movements 1815 to 1914

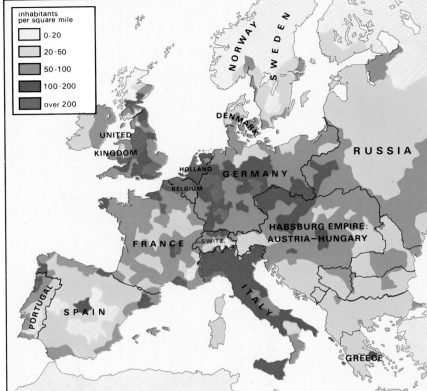

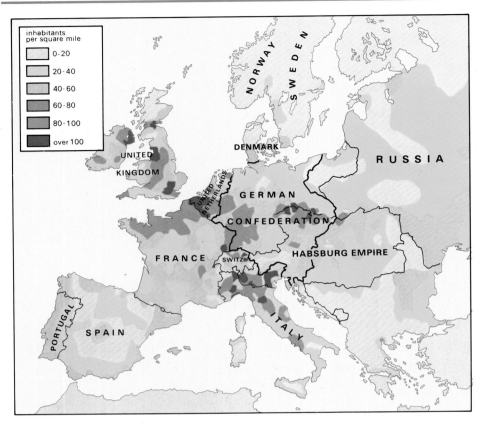

3/Europe's population in 1820 *(above)* The major centres were the industrialised regions of the United Kingdom and a few major cities and ports (London, Paris, St Petersburg, Liverpool, Bordeaux, Hamburg, Marseilles).

4/Europe's population by c. 1900 *(above)* was concentrated in the main industrial British centres: the Midlands, Yorkshire, Lancashire, south Wales, Tyneside, Clydeside; in Belgium, France and Germany (the Ruhr, Rhineland, Upper Silesia).

New York *(above)* By 1810 New York had outstripped its rivals to become the most dynamic urban centre in the New World. In 1810 the population was only 100,000, but passed 1,000,000 by 1871.

Immigration *(below)* During the 19th century more than two-thirds of the immigrants to the United States passed through the port of New York where the Statue of Liberty symbolised their hopes.

IT has been estimated that in the 19th century the population of the world expanded more rapidly than in any previous period, from about 900 million to 1600 million. (During the 20th century it was to grow four times faster.) The population of Europe increased from 190 million to 423 million; at the same time, European peoples – emigrants and their descendants – settled in North and South America, South Africa, Australia, New Zealand and Siberia, and the population of these regions grew from 5,670,000 to 200,000,000 between 1810 and 1910. In the three countries which were the leading industrial states in 1914 – the United Kingdom, Germany and the United States – the population had increased nearly five-fold in the previous hundred years. The distribution of the world's population at the beginning of the 20th century was estimated to be as follows (again in millions): Europe 423, Asia 937, Africa 120, North and South America 144, and Australia 6. There were, however, exceptions to the general growth in population. Ireland, for example, had a declining population: it fell from 8,175,000 in 1841 to 4,390,000 in 1911.

Various factors promoted the growth of the population during the 19th century. In Europe, in the United States, and in the colonies and spheres of influence of European states, the greatly improved methods of industrial and agricultural production, coupled with more efficient communications, provided work and food for expanding populations. The colonial powers established mines and plantations in their overseas territories which supplied manufacturing countries with increased quantities of raw materials and foodstuffs. Advanced industrial regions were free from the food shortages which were all too common in backward countries. There was no parallel in England, France or Germany to the famines that afflicted Ireland in 1847, India in 1866 and 1877, China in 1878 and Russia in 1891. Advances in medicine, improved sanitation and higher standards of personal hygiene resulted in a dramatic reduction in mortality from cholera, tuberculosis, smallpox, typhus and typhoid.

Population growth was not spread evenly over urban and rural districts. The expansion of old cities and the founding of new towns were characteristic features of the industrial age. The population of some cities with a history going back to mediaeval times – London, Cologne, Lyons, Moscow and many others – increased rapidly in the 19th century. Towns which had been mere villages, or had not even existed, in the previous century sprang to life as great centres of industry, commerce or mining. Middlesbrough and Barrow in England; Gelsenkirchen, Oberhausen and Königshütte in Germany; Lodz in Poland; and a host of towns in the United States and in the English colonies were examples of this type of mushroom urban growth. In industrial countries more and more people worked and lived in towns while fewer lived in the country.

Populations not only grew more rapidly in the 19th century than ever before but also moved on a considerable scale. Millions of people moved from Europe to the United States or to British colonies in North America, South Africa, Australia and New Zealand, building up new communities of white settlers which produced foodstuffs and raw materials for the countries they had left behind. The 'Europeanisation' of vast territories overseas was a significant factor in increasing the political influence of the major European states throughout the world. Migrations within states or regions included movements of workers from one district to another, seeking employment either on the land during the harvest, or in towns where job opportunities existed in factories and mines or in public works such as railway building. Irishmen sought work in Liverpool, Manchester and Glasgow; Poles moved to the coalmines in the Ruhr. Some migration was temporary in character. Irishmen who went to England or Scotland to dig potatoes generally returned home when the harvest was over. From Italy, there were seasonal labourers who worked in France, Germany and Switzerland – and even in the Argentine – and it has been estimated that in 1914 there were no less than three million of these migrant workers. In Russia there were peasants who secured jobs in factories in towns for the winter and then returned to work in their villages during the summer. However, emigration from one country to another – especially when long distances were involved –

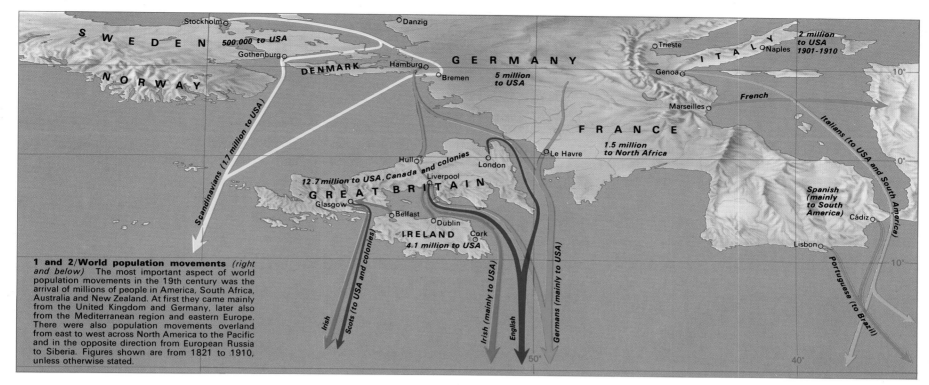

1 and 2/World population movements (right and below) The most important aspect of world population movements in the 19th century was the arrival of millions of people in America, South Africa, Australia and New Zealand. At first they came mainly from the United Kingdom and Germany, later also from the Mediterranean region and eastern Europe. There were also population movements overland from east to west across North America to the Pacific and in the opposite direction from European Russia to Siberia. Figures shown are from 1821 to 1910, unless otherwise stated.

was more usually permanent.

Some of those who left their native land had no choice in the matter. The convicts transported from England to Australia up to 1867, or from France to Devil's Island, did not go of their own accord. Nor were the Russian political prisoners who were exiled to Siberia willing migrants. Negro slaves shipped from West Africa to the Americas or from Zanzibar to Arabia were forced to leave their homes. The Atlantic slave trade, though prohibited by international agreements shortly after the Napoleonic wars, survived (though on a much reduced scale) until after the middle of the 19th century; it was not until the 1890s that the Arab slave trade on the east coast of Africa was at last stamped out.

Two factors influenced the timing of emigration and the destination of the migrants. One was the fact that conditions at home were unsatisfactory, the other that the United States, Canada, Australia and New Zealand had much to offer new settlers. Some emigrated because they were persecuted on account of their religious or political beliefs. German liberals who were harassed by Metternich's police, or Russian Jews who feared for their lives, found sanctuary in the United States. But most emigrants from Europe sought a new home. And in the first half of the 19th century they braved great dangers and hardships to cross the Atlantic to North America. The Irish who emigrated at the time of the great famine of 1847, and the German peasants who gave up their smallholdings in Baden and Württemberg a year or two later because they could no longer make ends meet, had nothing to lose and everything to gain by leaving home. Whenever there was a trade slump in the industrial regions of Europe some of the unemployed emigrated. Cheap – even free – land for farmers, good prospects for employment in mines and factories and democratic institutions made the United States a promised land for those who crossed the Atlantic. The hope of making a fortune quickly brought tens of thousands of immigrants to America and Australia during the celebrated gold rushes to California (1849) and Victoria (1851).

In the first half of the 19th century the bulk of the European emigrants came from the United Kingdom (2,369,000) and Germany (1,130,000). In the second half of the century those from the United Kingdom (9.5 million) and Germany (5 million) were joined by others from Italy (5 million), the Scandinavian countries (1 million), Belgium, Spain and the Balkans. The British settled in the United States and in British colonies while the Germans went to the United States (Pennsylvania and the mid-West) and to South America (Rio Grande do Sul in Brazil). French emigrants settled in Algeria, Italians in Tunis and Argentina, and Russians in Siberia.

There were also considerable population movements in Asia and across the Indian Ocean and the Pacific. From China – particularly from

the southern provinces – there was a continuous flow of settlers to Siam, Java and the Malay peninsula. Chinese also emigrated to California, British Columbia and New South Wales. From India emigrants crossed the Indian Ocean to Natal and East Africa. In British East Africa they eventually surpassed the white settlers in numbers and probably in aggregate wealth. (It has been estimated that the white element in world population grew from 22 per cent in 1800 to 35 per cent in 1930.) Some of the Chinese and Indian emigrants were coolies who were engaged by contractors for a fixed term to work on plantations, in mines, and on public works. This system of indentured labour was open to grave abuses which were only gradually eradicated.

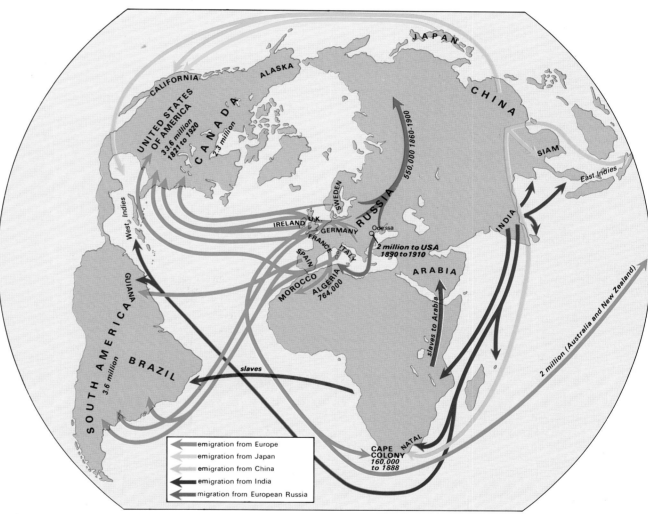

Urban growth: Berlin (right) A typical example of the expansion of a European city brought about by the construction of railways and the development of consumer industries. The court, the administration, the army and the university also contributed to population growth.

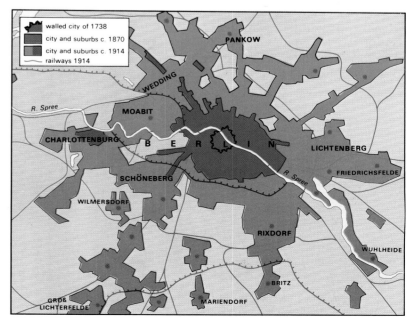

The Industrial Revolution in Europe
1815 to 1870

IN the first half of the 19th century the United Kingdom was the leading manufacturing country in the world. But modern factories, with machines driven by steam, were also to be found in some regions on the continent of Europe. As early as 1809 a visitor to the valleys of the Ruhr and the Wupper described them as a 'miniature England'. On the Continent, as in Britain, the coalfields were the most important centres of industrial growth. The largest coal measures were those situated in the Nord *département* of France, the valleys of the Sambre and the Meuse in Belgium, and the valley of the Ruhr in Germany. Here modern industries developed in the first half of the 19th century. Elsewhere on the Continent progress towards industrialisation was largely confined to capital cities (Paris, Berlin), to centres of communications (Lyons, Cologne, Frankfurt am Main, Cracow, Warsaw), to major ports (Hamburg, Bremen, Rotterdam, Le Havre, Marseilles) and to a few isolated districts such as the textile regions of Lille, Roubaix, Mulhouse, Barmen-Elberfeld (Wuppertal), Chemnitz, Lodz and Moscow, and the iron and engineering districts on the coalfields of the Loire basin, the Saar, and Upper Silesia.

Although in certain important respects the Industrial Revolution on the Continent followed a somewhat similar pattern to that in Britain, there were also significant differences. As England was the first country to become industrialised, her entrepreneurs were pioneers who could not draw upon the experiences of manufacturers elsewhere. But in the early 19th century the continental countries could benefit from earlier English experience. English blueprints, machinery and steam engines were installed in continental factories, and some English skilled artisans crossed the Channel to show local workers how to operate the machines. Moreover, English entrepreneurs and financiers helped to found new industrial enterprises on the Continent. In France, Aaron Manby and Daniel Wilson founded the Charenton ironworks, Humphrey Edwards was a partner in the Chaillot engineering plant, Richard Roberts planned the layout of a cotton mill for André Koechlin at Mulhouse, while Thomas Brassey and W. and E. Mackenzie built many French railways. In Germany, W. T. Mulvany, the founder of the Shamrock and Hibernia collieries, played a leading part in promoting the expansion of the Ruhr industrial region. In time, continental countries ceased to rely upon Britain for new machines. In France, for example, several important inventions were made, such as the Jacquard loom, the Seguin multi-tubular boiler, and the Heilmann mechanical comb. And native entrepreneurs, like Alfred Krupp of Essen, showed that they had the initiative and skill to build up large enterprises without assistance from abroad. Krupp eventually became one of the largest manufacturers of armaments in Europe – a reminder that wars and preparations for war were a significant factor in the expansion of the iron and steel industries.

While in England private investors were generally able to raise the capital to found new business undertakings and public works without government assistance, pioneer entrepreneurs on the Continent frequently had difficulty in securing the funds to build factories and to buy modern machines. Consequently the state played a more important role than it did in England in fostering industrial expansion. In Prussia, for example, the Overseas Trading Corporation (*Seehandlung*), a nationalised undertaking, was engaged in wholesale trade, operated steamships on the Brandenburg waterways, and owned or controlled textile mills, engineering plants, paper factories and chemical works. In Belgium and in some German states (Hanover, Brunswick, Baden) railways were built and operated by the state, while in France most lines were constructed

jointly by the state and by private companies.

In central Europe many tariff barriers, which had long hampered economic progress, were removed between 1815 and 1870. In Germany the customs union (*Zollverein*), established in 1834, was gradually extended so that by 1870 only Hamburg and Bremen retained their tariff independence. In the Habsburg dominions the customs frontier between Austria and Hungary was abolished in 1850. In Russia the customs frontier with Congress Poland was abolished in the following year. In Switzerland the tariff barriers between the *cantons* were removed between 1848 and 1874, while Italy achieved both political and economic unity in the 1860s.

Another factor which promoted economic expansion on the Continent was the improvement in communications. Navigation on the great rivers – the Seine, Loire, Rhine, Elbe, Oder, Vistula and Danube – was improved and numerous tolls were reduced or abolished. Transport by inland waterways was of particular significance in certain regions such as Holland, Brandenburg, and the basin of the Seine. In France the reign of Louis Philippe (1830-48) saw

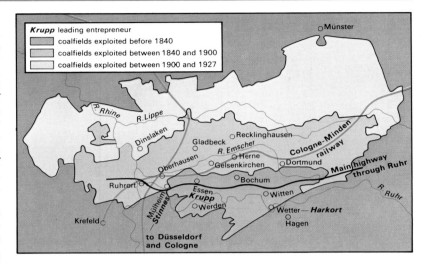

3/The expansion of the Ruhr *(above)* The exploitation of the Ruhr coalfield began in the valley of the river Ruhr. During the 19th century deeper seams to the north of the Ruhr were gradually opened up. The establishment of the Ruhrort as a coal port and the construction of the Cologne-Minden railway stimulated expansion. Mulvany established new collieries (Shamrock at Herne and Hibernia at Gelsenkirchen) while Krupp of Essen was the leading ironmaster in the district.

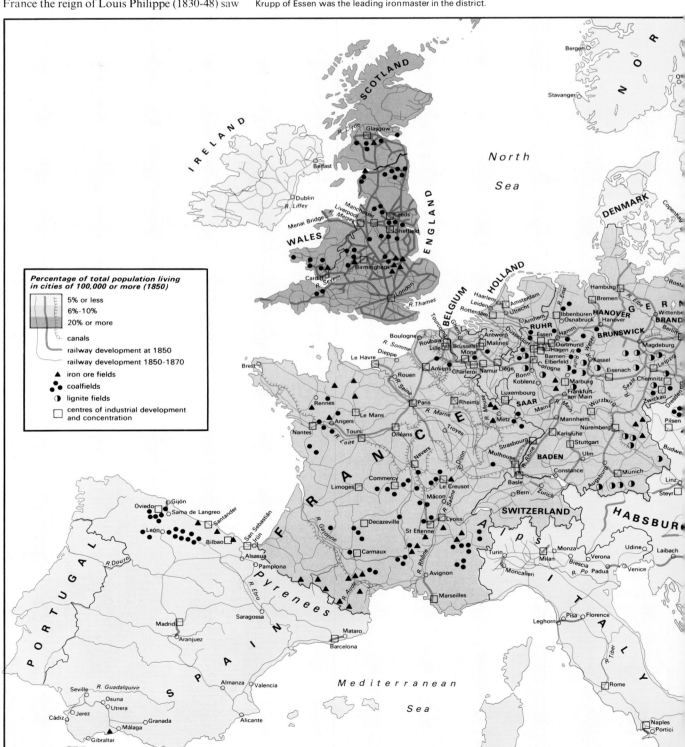

the construction of several canals, while in Germany the Main-Danube and the Saar canals were undertakings of some importance. But it was the railways which really propelled the states on the Continent into the industrial age. By 1850 the railway networks of Britain and Belgium were virtually complete, and in Germany most of the main lines had been built except for one linking Berlin and Danzig. In France, however, many main lines were still only in the planning stage, though Paris was connected by rail with Lille, Le Havre and Orléans.

On the Continent, as in Britain, a feature of the Industrial Revolution was the concentration of manufactures in particular districts. The growth of industries in the Ruhr coalfield illustrates the expansion of such a region; but even in Germany industrialisation had not proceeded very far by 1870. The greatest surge forward, there and elsewhere, came later.

2/Customs unions in Europe in the 19th century *(right)* In the 18th century, trade in Europe had been hampered by tariffs. France abolished internal tariffs in 1790; German states in the early 19th century. The German customs union, founded in 1834, linked independent states and preceded political unification (1871) (see page 217).

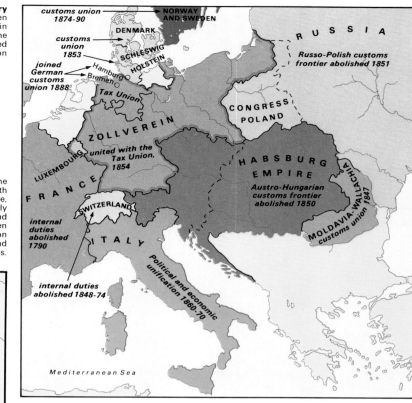

1/Industrialisation of Europe to 1850 *(below)* The early industrial areas in Europe were mainly regions with deposits of coal or iron ore, such as Lancashire, Yorkshire, the Ruhr, and France's Nord *département.*. Relatively isolated coalfields or ironfields, such as Upper Silesia and the Donets basin, could be developed only when railways had been built. Urbanisation and industrialisation went hand in hand; except for some capital cities and ports all the large towns were in manufacturing regions.

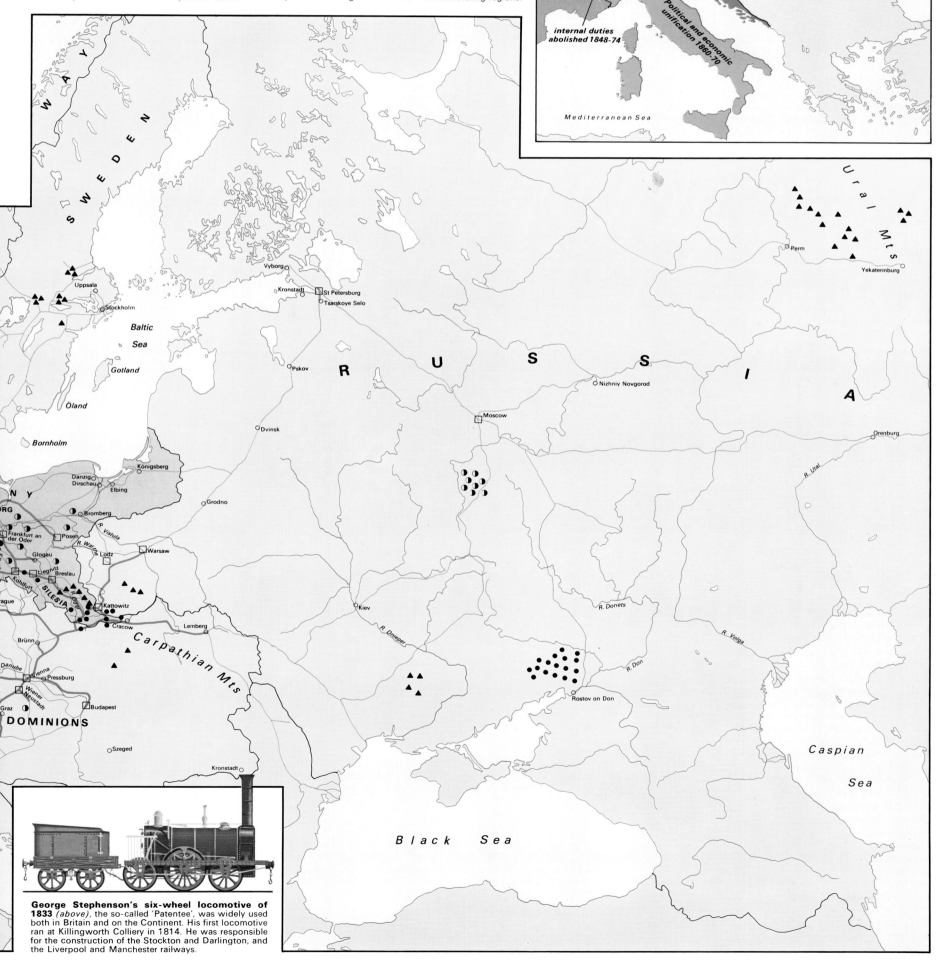

George Stephenson's six-wheel locomotive of 1833 *(above)*, the so-called 'Patentee', was widely used both in Britain and on the Continent. His first locomotive ran at Killingworth Colliery in 1814. He was responsible for the construction of the Stockton and Darlington, and the Liverpool and Manchester railways.

The Industrial Revolution in Europe 1870 to 1914

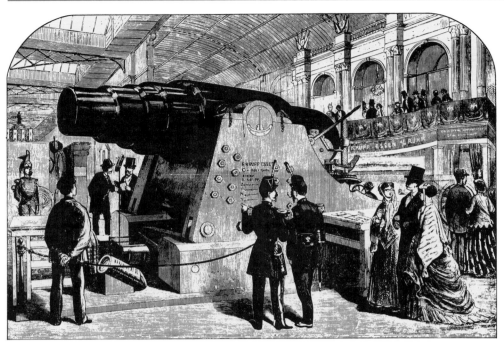

Krupp's gun at the Paris exhibition of 1867 *(above)*
In his search for new outlets for steel, Alfred Krupp of Essen had begun to experiment with armaments in the 1840s and had shown a six-pounder cannon with a cast steel barrel at the Great Exhibition in the Crystal Palace, London, in 1851. It was not until 1859 that he received an order from the Prussian military authorities for 300 steel barrels. In 1863 Krupp was awarded a large contract for steel guns from the Russian government. At the Paris Exhibition of 1867 Krupp, now established as a leading manufacturer of armaments, showed a 50-ton steel cannon; it was presented to the King of Prussia.

BETWEEN 1870 and 1914 Europe and the United States experienced a second industrial revolution. By 1850 Great Britain had become the leading manufacturing country in the world. Through the initiative and skill of its inventors and entrepreneurs Britain had been transformed from a predominantly agrarian country into a predominantly manufacturing country. During this second industrial revolution Britain remained one of the leading manufacturing states but it was Germany, united in 1871, which now set the pace in the race for industrial supremacy. In addition to expanding its established industries – coal, iron, textiles – Germany took the lead in the development of new industries such as chemicals and electricity. At the same time there was a remarkable expansion of Germany's exports of manufactured products and of its invisible exports (banking, insurance, shipping).

In the second – as in the first – industrial revolution important new machines and processes were invented in the United Kingdom. Perkin's synthetic mauve dye (the first aniline dye), the Bessemer steel converter, the Gilchrist-Thomas basic steel process, and Parsons' steam turbine were English inventions. But the invention and the development of the internal combustion engine, the diesel engine, the automobile, the electric dynamo and electric traction largely occurred in Germany, while the ring frame, the sewing machine, the typewriter, the filament lamp and the telephone were invented in the United States.

The first industrial revolution has been called a 'revolution of coal and iron', the second a 'revolution of steel and electricity'. In the first half of the 19th century steel was almost a semi-precious metal, costing between £50 and £60 a ton, compared with £3 to £4 a ton for pig iron. Initially, steel was made by the cementation process, or, alternatively, by Huntsman's crucible method. In the second half of the 19th century the new Bessemer and Siemens-Martin processes – improved by Gilchrist and Thomas – enabled the production of steel to be greatly increased. World output rose from a mere 540,000 tons in 1870 to 14,600,000 in 1895 – and there was a dramatic fall in price.

The electrical industry provided the world with a new source of energy with which to supplement steam power. When efficient dynamos were built in the 1860s electric power was used to drive machinery and trams and to light streets, factories and homes. Water power – one of the oldest sources of energy in the world – found a new use in hydro-electric power stations. Italy, in particular, with no national coal resources, turned increasingly to hydro-electric

coal by-products, nitrogen and phosphates. The soap and glass industries used soda made from ammonia (a coal by-product) while the textile industries used synthetic (aniline) dyes made from coal tar. Nitrates from natural sources and 'synthetic' nitrogen and phosphates were the raw materials for the production of explosives and fertilisers. Other branches of the chemical industries were the production of drugs, insecticides, perfumes, cosmetics, and photographic accessories. Plastics, made from resins prepared from coal tar acids, were used to make a wide variety of products while synthetic textiles, such as artificial silk, were also increasingly used in the early 20th century.

In the development of these new branches of industry – electricity and chemicals – Germany played a leading part. In the electrical industry two large cartels were formed, the Siemens-Schuckert group and the *Allgemeine Elektrizitäts Gesellschaft*, at the head of which were the two pioneers who dominated the industry: Werner Siemens and Emil Rathenau. The expansion of the chemical industry owed much to the invention of synthetic dyes and new drugs in the laboratories of great German firms. Two

power as a source of energy after 1905. Another new form of energy in the second half of the 19th century was produced by the internal combustion engine, which used petrol as its fuel. Franz Reuleau's prophecy of 1875 that this engine would one day become 'the real power-machine of the masses' came true in the 20th century. A new petroleum industry which exploited and refined the oil resources of the United States, Russia and the Middle East enabled stationary gas engines, motor vehicles and ships to be driven by petrol or diesel oil. Without the electric generating stations and the internal combustion engine the rapid industrial progress of Europe and the United States after 1870 would not have been possible.

The expansion of new chemical industries was another significant aspect of the development of manufactures after 1870. For centuries chemicals had been extracted from natural substances – alkalis from vegetable ashes and dyes from madder root, indigo and so forth. Now more and more chemical substances were produced from

1/The industrialisation of Europe 1870-1914 *(below)*
The industrial regions which had been developed in the first half of the 19th century – such as Lancashire, Yorkshire, south Wales, Clydeside, the Ruhr, the Saar, the Nord *département*, and the Sambre-Meuse region in Belgium – continued to expand after 1870; they were now joined by new industrial regions, such as the Donets basin, which were opened up when railways were developed. The construction of the Berlin-Baghdad railway as far as Ras el'Ain, and the completion of the Trans-Siberian railway, extended Europe's economic links with the Near East and the Far East, while the opening of the Kiel Canal stimulated the trade of the Baltic region. After 1870 old-established industries (coal, iron, textiles) were joined by new branches of manufacture such as the chemical and electrical industries.

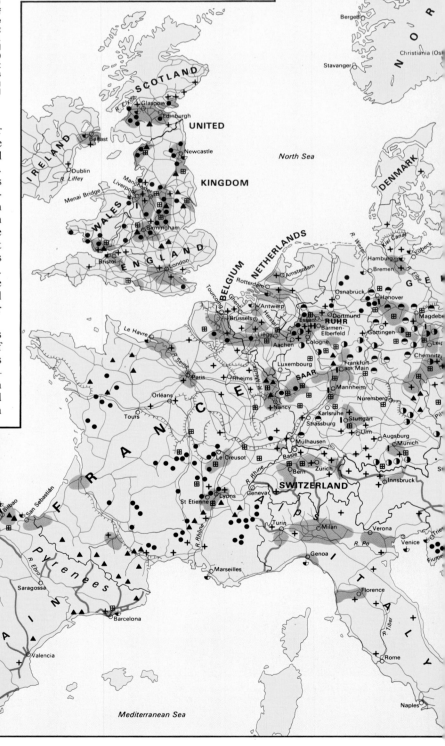

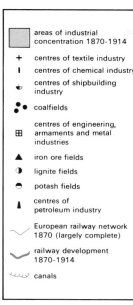

- areas of industrial concentration 1870-1914
- + centres of textile industry
- ∣ centres of chemical industry
- ⚓ centres of shipbuilding industry
- ●● coalfields
- ⊞ centres of engineering, armaments and metal industries
- ▲ iron ore fields
- ◑ lignite fields
- ◐ potash fields
- ◮ centres of petroleum industry
- European railway network 1870 (largely complete)
- railway development 1870-1914
- canals

chemical cartels were formed which united in 1925 to form the German Dye Trust (*I. G. Farben*). Germany's production of coal, iron and steel also expanded; by 1914 it produced twice as much steel and nearly as much coal as Britain. Germany's shipbuilding industry and mercantile marine both expanded in a spectacular fashion. By the outbreak of the First World War Germany's shipyards could build 400,000 tons of merchant ships a year in addition to warships and river craft, while its mercantile marine of 2,400,000 tons included some of the finest liners on the Atlantic run.

In Russia, too, striking industrial progress occurred between 1870 and 1914. The textile industries used raw materials – flax, wool and cotton – largely produced at home. At the end of this period the cotton industries had 745 mills employing 388,000 operatives and turning out products valued at 589 million roubles. The linen industry expanded rapidly in the last quarter of the 19th century with the aid of foreign capital. At the same time the woollen

industry, with major centres at Moscow, St Petersburg and Lodz, had 700,000 spindles, 4500 looms and 150,000 operatives. Moreover, an important new industrial region, based on coal and iron ore resources, had developed in the basin of the Donets. Here great iron and steel works were established. The opening of the railway to Krivoy Rog in 1886 enabled high-grade iron ore to be sent from Krivoy Rog to the ironworks in the Donets basin. The exploitation of Russia's oil wells at Baku and Groznyy was another factor which stimulated Russia's economic development after 1880. The Nobel brothers from Sweden were the pioneer entrepreneurs of this new industry. They built refineries at Baku and launched an oil tanker on the Caspian in 1878 to ply between Baku and Astrakhan. Again, the construction of the Trans-Siberian and Trans-Caucasian railways made it possible for Russia to tap some of the vast natural resources of its territories in Asia. Despite many handicaps Russia had been able to create a number of large and efficient industrial

enterprises by the eve of the First World War. But, unlike the industrial states of western Europe, Russia also had a very large number of small domestic workshops which had survived side by side with modern plants and factories.

Nevertheless, at the end of the 19th century even in highly industrialised countries in Europe a high proportion of the population was still engaged in agriculture. In Germany, for example, the agricultural population in 1895 amounted to 18.5 million, which was just over one-third (35.5 per cent) of the total population. Most of eastern Europe (Poland, Romania, Bulgaria) and much of southern Europe (Spain, Greece, southern Italy) was still, by modern standards, under-developed. In France, industry as late as the end of the century was still with few exceptions small in scale; in countries such as Poland and Spain industrialisation was confined to a few small areas (Lodz; Bilbao, Barcelona) and the way of life of the bulk of the population had virtually been untouched by the great upsurge of industry elsewhere between 1870 and 1914.

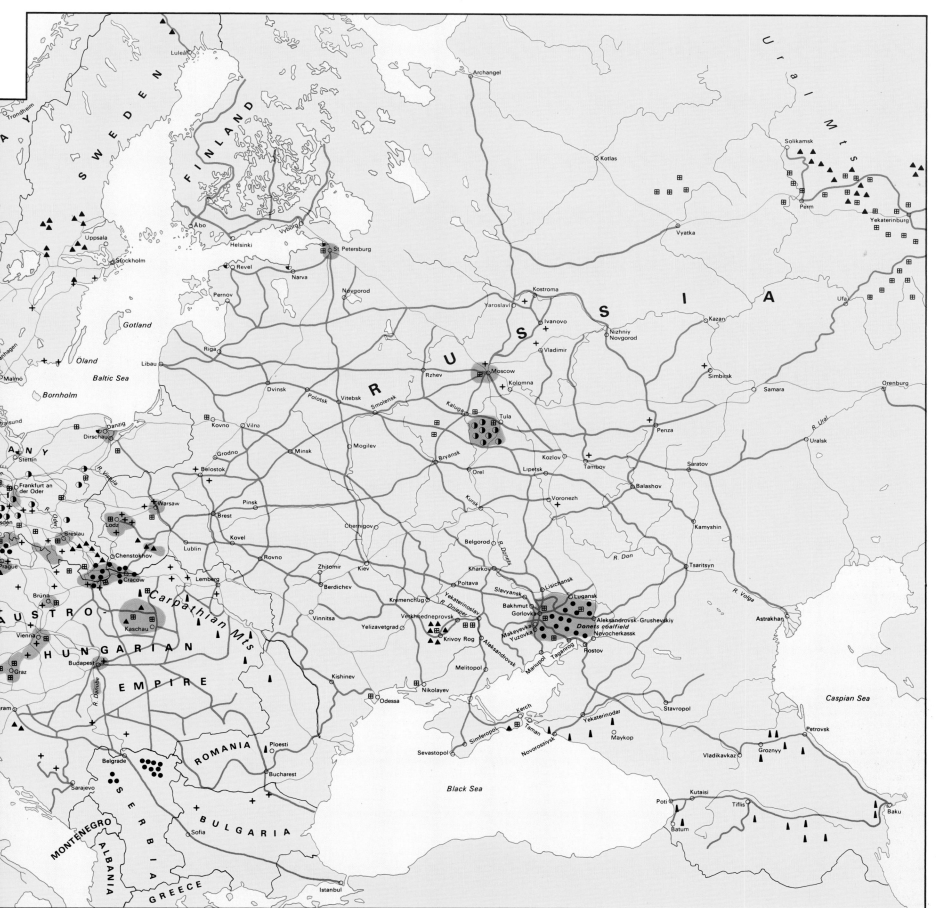

The rise of nationalism in Europe 1800 to 1914

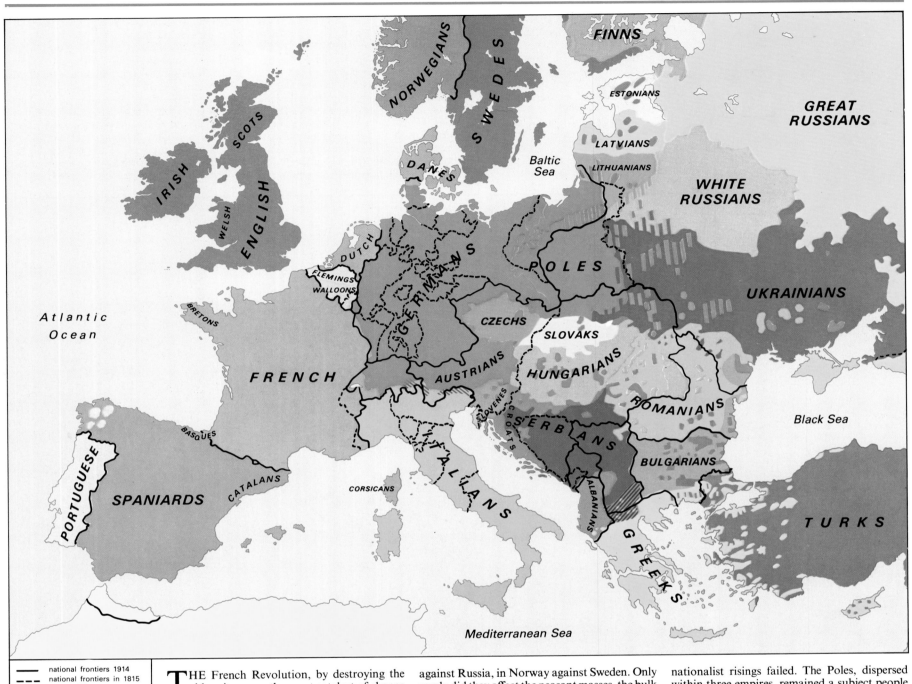

1/Languages, peoples and political divisions of Europe (above) This map of 19th century Europe shows the boundaries at the time of the Vienna Settlement of 1815 and the changes which took place between then and 1914. Linguistic boundaries were rarely precise and political frontiers often left linguistic minorities, and even majorities, under alien rule. The map shows the major languages, but some are too scattered to be included: Sorb (or Wendish, Lusatian) in Prussia and Saxony; Masurian in East Prussia; Vlach in Macedonia, Epirus and Transylvania; Gallego, a dialect of Portuguese, in Galicia, Spain; and Yiddish: there were some five million Jews, many living in the large European towns, but most in the Pale of Settlement (Lithuania, Russia, Poland, the Ukraine, Bessarabia and the Crimea).

THE French Revolution, by destroying the old regime, was the great catalyst of change in Europe. The revolutionary armies carried with them not only the slogan of 'liberty, equality and fraternity' but also the ideas of liberalism, self-government and nationalism, which were to be the central themes of 19th-century European history. Already before 1789, in reaction against the rational spirit of the Enlightenment, writers such as Herder (1744-1803) had emphasised the sense of national identity. But the state was still regarded as a dynastic patrimony, an estate to which owners of lesser estates owed allegiance and service. This conception was challenged by the French revolutionary governments, which called upon oppressed peoples to rise against their landlords and rulers. But French oppression under Napoleon produced nationalist reactions in Spain, in Russia, in the Tyrol, eventually (after 1807) in Germany. This was one source of the nationalism of the later 19th century.

Nevertheless, the strength of nationalism in the first half of the 19th century can easily be exaggerated. Down to 1866 most Germans and Italians were more attached to their provincial rulers and cultures (Bavarian, Hessian, Tuscan, Emilian) than to the ideal of national unity. Only where there was alien rule were there loud protests, chiefly from the middle classes (lawyers, teachers, businessmen), in Italy against Austria, in Ireland against England, in Belgium against Holland, in Greece against Turkey, in Poland against Russia, in Norway against Sweden. Only rarely did they affect the peasant masses, the bulk of the European population at this time. Even in the Ottoman Empire, in spite of the corrupt, oppressive and increasingly incompetent Turkish government and the resentment of Christians against Muslim overlordship, there was little active national opposition, except in the region which during the 1820s became the core of modern Greece. In the far-flung Austrian Empire, ruling over a score of nationalities, only the Czechs and the Hungarians, both peoples with proud memories of an independent past, were restive, though they sought autonomy within the Empire, not national independence.

Furthermore, after the defeat of Napoleon in 1815, the victorious powers were hostile to nationalist aspirations, which they saw, correctly, as associated with liberalism and therefore a threat to constituted authority. At the Congress of Vienna, under the influence of Talleyrand and Metternich, the powers had adopted the principle of 'legitimacy' as a basis for redrawing the map of Europe. Metternich believed that any concessions to nationalism would be fatal to Austria, and he resisted them on all fronts down to 1848. In this period only Greece and Belgium (1830) achieved independence, and in both cases special factors – notably the rivalry of the Great Powers – were involved. Elsewhere, in Poland (1831, 1846), Germany (1848), Italy (1848) and Hungary (1849), owing to internal dissensions and the solidarity of the conservative powers,

nationalist risings failed. The Poles, dispersed within three empires, remained a subject people until 1918-19. The Hungarians, however, exploiting Austrian weakness in its war with Prussia, managed to win equal status with the German-speaking population by the *Ausgleich* (Compromise) of 1867.

In Italy and Germany provincialism and apathy were overcome by the expansionist policies of Piedmont and Prussia (see page 216). After 1854 a new generation of European statesmen no longer upheld the old order, and industrial and commercial expansion gave a new impetus to the desire for national unity. Nationality was now seen as a stabilising force; that is to say, it was thought that unified national states would have no further ambitions, and apostles of nationalism such as Mazzini (1805-72) predicted a new age when satisfied national states would co-operate peacefully in a democratic federation of peoples. After 1870 it quickly became clear that this was an illusion. Though it is true that the Czechs of Bohemia never aspired, before 1918, to more than autonomy within the Habsburg Empire, and the Slavs of Bosnia and Herzegovina were content to exchange Turkish for Austrian rule, nationalist ideas spread rapidly, particularly among the Balkan peoples. Though the standard criterion of nationality was language, linguistic groups were so mixed that a division on the basis of language was impracticable, particularly in the Balkan Peninsula. Moreover, language was

The Balkans map showing national frontiers after the Balkan wars 1912–13, the frontier of the Ottoman empire 1800, and proposed Bulgaria under the Treaty of San Stefano 1878.

Legend:
- - - - frontier of Ottoman empire 1800
- —— proposed Bulgaria under Treaty of San Stefano 1878
- ▬▬ national frontiers after the Balkan wars 1912 - 13
- —— railway

GERMAN EMPIRE

RUSSIAN EMPIRE

AUSTRO-HUNGARIAN EMPIRE

Vienna
Budapest

BESSARABIA

Jassy

MOLDAVIA
semi-independent 1829

Banja Luka

BOSNIA
administered by Austria-Hungary 1878
annexed 1908

Sarajevo

HERZEGOVINA

Mostar

R. Sava

Belgrade
Požarevac

SERBIA
principality 1817; independent 1878

Nish

ROMANIA

Craiova
Ploieşti
Bucharest
united 1859; independent 1878;
Kingdom 1881

Galatz
Brăila

WALLACHIA
semi-independent 1829

Vidin

Turtukaia
Silistria

R. Danube

DOBRUJA

Constantsa

MONTENEGRO

Kotor (Cattaro)
Podgorica
Cetinje

SANJAK OF NOVIBAZAR

Ipek (Peć)
to Serbia 1878

Mitrovica

Pirot

principality 1878

Slivnitsa

Plevna

BULGARIA
independent 1908

Ruschuk

Shumla

Balchik

L. Scutari
Scutari

Prizren
to Serbia 1913

Usküb (Skoplje)

Kumanovo

Sofia
Küstendil

Trnovo

EASTERN RUMELIA
to Bulgaria 1885

Varna

Black
Sea

Tirana

ALBANIA
principality 1913

L. Ochrida
L. Prespa
Koritsa

Monastir

R. Vardar

Kočani

to Bulgaria 1913

Strumitsa

Philippopolis
R. Maritsa

Burgas

Saseno I.
Valona
Argyrokastron

MACEDONIA

Salonica

to Bulgaria 1913

Adrianople

Cape Stylos
Corfu

EPIRUS

to Greece 1913

R. Aliakmon

Kavalla

Thasos
Dede-Agach

THRACE

Bosporus
San Stefano
Constantinople

Ionian
Sea

IONIAN ISLANDS

Yannina
Arta
Preveza

THESSALY
to Greece 1881

Larissa
Volos

Aegean
Sea

Samothrace

to Greece 1913

Lemnos
Imbros

Dardanelles

Tenedos

Lesbos

OTTOMAN
EMPIRE

Patras

KINGDOM OF GREECE
independent 1830

Tripolis
Nauplia

Athens
Piraeus

Chios

Samos

Nikaria

to Greece 1864

Canea
Suda Bay

Candia

CRETE independent 1898

to Greece 1913

Dodecanese
(occupied by Italy 1912;
ceded by Turkey 1920)

Rhodes

---

not always recognised by those wishing to redeem their long lost brothers, as the sole criterion of nationality. In Macedonia, Greeks, Serbians and Bulgarians made conflicting nationalistic claims and, like nationalists within the Habsburg Empire, expressed them in terms of folklore, literature, and national history as well as those of linguistic and racial theory. The result of their endeavours was that by 1913 the Turks had lost almost all their possessions in Europe. Nor was nationalist unrest confined to the Turkish and Habsburg Empires. Great Britain was faced with troubles in Ireland and Norway demanded separation from Sweden.

The activities of Serbian nationalists in Bosnia and the determination of Austria-Hungary to resist them became the immediate cause of war in 1914. This war led to the disruption of the Habsburg, German and Russian Empires and led to the formation of the states of Czechoslovakia, Poland, Yugoslavia, Hungary, Estonia, Latvia and Lithuania. Although established in recognition of the principle of 'national self-determination', two of these states, Czechoslovakia and Poland, contained large German

minorities, the redemption of which became one of the aims of German policy.

2/The Balkans (above) From the later 18th century onwards the Russians encouraged uprisings in the Turkish Balkan provinces. The Great Powers, fearing Russian domination of the Near East and wishing to preserve the Ottoman Empire as a viable power, endeavoured to pacify the Balkans by extracting concessions to the Slavs, Greeks and Romanians. Following the Crimean War, in 1856 they imposed a settlement on Russia and Turkey and in 1878 at the Congress of Berlin they recognised the complete independence of Serbia, Montenegro and Romania, but reduced the territory which the Pan Slav Treaty of San Stefano had allocated to the new Principality of Bulgaria.

This upheaval made the Powers aware of the complexity of the rivalries between the races inhabiting the Balkan peninsula, and of the dangerous incompatibility of their own ambitions there. For the next thirty years, despite growing racial and religious strife in Macedonia and the Greco-Turkish war in 1897, the Powers clung stubbornly to the territorial *status quo*, seeking to pacify the Balkan Christians by a programme of administrative reforms under Austro-Russian supervision. But the Austro-Hungarian annexation of Bosnia (1908) revived the fires of nationalism and destroyed the unity of the Powers. In 1912 the Balkan states formed a league to expel the Turks from Macedonia; but after their victory over the Turks the old rivalries over the spoils re-emerged. The Second Balkan War left Serbia and Greece in possession of most of Macedonia and parts of Albania.

3/Scandinavia (right) The Treaty of Nystad (1721) marked the decline of Sweden as a great Northern and Baltic power.

In 1809 Sweden had ceded Finland to Russia. In 1815 her new dynasty received Norway, formerly a Danish possession, under an arrangement ensuring considerable autonomy and a separate government. During the nineteenth century, the pan-Scandinavian movement, which aimed at a close union between Denmark, Sweden and Norway, came to nothing and in 1905 Norway became completely independent with its own dynasty.

NORWAY
SWEDEN
FINLAND
(Part of Sweden 1154-1809;
Russian 1809-1917;
Independent 1917)

United 1814-1905
United 1397-1814

Trondheim
Bergen
Stavanger
Christiania

Tammerfors (Tampere)
Åbo (Turku)
Helsingfors (Helsinki)
Uppsala
Stockholm
Gothenburg

KARELIA
Viborg
St. Petersburg

RUSSIA

DENMARK
SCHLESWIG 1866-70 Prussia
HOLSTEIN
Kiel

Copenhagen
Malmö

SWEDISH POMERANIA
to Prussia 1815

Stettin

Germany and Italy: the struggles for unification 1815 to 1871

The Bismarck tower *(above)* Towering sculptures of Bismarck, the chief architect of German unity, were erected in Germany during the 1890s. Their mediaeval style recalls the period of the Teutonic Knights and the heyday of German expansion in the Middle Ages.

EVEN before the defeat of Napoleon and the Congress of Vienna (1815), demands for national unity were stirring in Germany and Italy, but they were largely confined to literary and academic circles and had no widespread appeal. Only Stein in Prussia aspired to translate them into a political programme, but he was swept aside in 1808, and after 1815 Metternich, the Austrian chancellor, had no difficulty in restoring the traditional rulers. Although during the period of the 'Restoration' (1815-48) there was some unrest, fomented chiefly by ex-military personnel and officials formerly employed in the Napoleonic administration, the revolts of 1820 and 1821 (in Naples and Piedmont) and those of 1830-31 (in Parma, Modena and Romagna) had no national aims, while the liberals in Hanover, Brunswick, Hesse-Kassel and Saxony were satisfied with moderate constitutional changes. Not until 1848 did the national question, both in Germany and in Italy, come to the fore, and then only to reveal cross-purposes within nationalist ranks. In Italy, uprisings in Venice, Rome, Messina, Palermo, Reggio and Milan ended in failure, and in July 1848 Charles Albert of Piedmont was decisively beaten by the Austrians at Custozza. In Germany, a national assembly of liberals met at Frankfurt in May 1848 and embarked on the self-appointed task

of drawing up a constitution for Germany which they hoped to unite by consent, but they soon became divided between *Grossdeutsche* (those who wanted a federal Germany, including Austria and extending from the Baltic and the Adriatic) and *Kleindeutsche* (those who wanted a smaller Germany, excluding Austria, under Prussian leadership). The Prussian liberals denounced the provisional government of United Germany, of which the Austrian Archduke John had been proclaimed Regent, and demanded a Prussian constitution. By a small majority the Frankfurt liberals offered the German crown to the king of Prussia. The south German liberals made separately a similar offer. Both offers the Prussian king contemptuously turned down.

After the failure of the revolutions of 1848-9 Germany reverted to an Austro-Prussian condominium with Prussia as the junior partner (Treaty of Olmütz 1850), and Italy remained divided. However, with the appointment of Cavour as prime minister of Sardinia-Piedmont (1852) and of Bismarck as chief minister in Prussia (1862), liberal nationalists in Italy and Germany showed some readiness to support the expansionist aims of Piedmont and Prussia. The policies of Napoleon III, a 'revisionist' with nationalist inclinations, gave encouragement to these aims, as did the weakening of Austria, which

lost the support of Russia. After the Crimean War (1854-56), Napoleon favoured a strong Prussia in northern Germany and a relatively powerful Sardinia-Piedmont in northern Italy within an Italian federation including Tuscany, the kingdom of Naples, and the Papal States, under the presidency of the Pope. Both powers, he hoped, would be the natural allies of France. He hoped, moreover, to create a Rhineland kingdom which would be a client state of France.

Prussia had for long been an expansionist power. Despite losses during the Napoleonic Wars, in 1815 she had been awarded a part of Saxony and territory in western Germany with the object of raising a bulwark against France and of buttressing Holland. Thereafter it was her policy to weld together her eastern and western territories. From 1828 she formed a series of customs unions *(Zollvereine)*. In 1834 the German Zollverein was created and subse-

3/The unification of Germany *(below)* The political unification of Germany involved wars against Denmark in 1864, against Austria in 1866 and against France in 1870. Austria was excluded from the North German Confederation of 1867 which comprised the German states north of the river Main. Any influence that remained to Austria in Germany as a relic of the dualism that had obtained before 1866 was finally destroyed in 1871, when the German Southern States joined the German Empire.

	Prussia in 1815
	acquired by Prussia 1815-66
	boundary of German Confederation of 1815
	boundary of North German Confederation of 1866
	Imperial territory of Alsace-Lorraine 1871
	boundary of German Empire 1871
	Austro-Prussian forces attack Denmark 1864
	Prussian armies in the war with Austria 1866
	German armies in the Franco-Prussian war 1870-71

quently expanded under the impact of the development of German railways and industrialisation. By the 1850s (the *Gründerjahre*) Prussia had gained an economic preponderance over Austria, but it was not until Bismarck came to power that she challenged Austria's political leadership. This challenge arose over the question of Schleswig and Holstein. In 1864 Austria and Prussia, acting on behalf of the German Confederation, went to war with Denmark, defeated her, and took over the administration of those two duchies (Convention of Gastein, 1865). When Austria attempted to follow a separate policy in Holstein and to deprive Prussia of her rights under the traditional dualistic arrangements, Bismarck made war on Austria, defeated her at Sadowa (1866), excluded her from Germany, and formed the North German Confederation (1867) under Prussian control. Following Prussia's defeat of France at Sedan (1870) and her annexation of Alsace and Lorraine, the German States south of the Main, through sheer economic necessity, joined the new German Reich.

In Italy, Cavour, realising that Piedmont's expansion depended on foreign support, allied with France (Plombières, 1858) against Austria, and in June 1859 the two allies won decisive victories at Magenta and Solferino. Fearing, however, the formation of a hostile European combination and the creation of a too-powerful Piedmont, Napoleon III hastily concluded preliminaries at Villafranca. At the definitive Peace of Zürich (November 1859) only Lombardy went to Piedmont but, on being offered compensation in Nice and Savoy, Napoleon agreed to plebiscites in Tuscany, Parma and Modena, where spontaneous revolutions had broken out. These plebiscites favoured union with Piedmont, which

was doubled in size. In June 1860 the patriot Garibaldi and his 'thousand' volunteers took Sicily and, in September, Naples. Cavour, fearing that the final stages of unification might militate against Piedmont, sent troops to the Papal States, brought Garibaldi to heel, and organised plebiscites which resulted in the union of Sicily, Naples, Umbria, Romagna and the Marches with Piedmont-Sardinia. In 1861, an Italian parliament met in Turin and proclaimed Victor Emmanuel II king of united Italy. In April 1866 Cavour's successors made a treaty with Prussia and, following Austria's defeat at Sadowa in the Austro-Prussian war, Italy acquired Venetia from Austria. In 1870 it obtained Rome, the French having been obliged to withdraw their occupation forces as a result of defeat by Prussia.

The making of modern Italy and the creation of the German Empire, had not only changed the European balance of power but had fostered a spirit of realpolitik and militarism. Neither power was fully satisfied with its achievements. Italy had hopes of obtaining the Alto Adige, Trieste and Fiume. The new Reich, despite Bismarck's claim that Germany was a 'satiated' state, revived the idea of a Greater Germany. In the period 1871-1914, however, the policy of immediate expansion in Europe was not practical politics. Both powers were compelled to devote attention to internal problems, to improve and expand their armed forces and to seek markets and raw materials outside Europe in competition with the other powers. While Italy remained tied to Germany and Austria by the treaty of triple alliance she was debarred from her *irredenta* and so long as Germany clung to her alliance with the Austrian-Hungarian monarchy any hopes of a Greater Germany had to be abandoned.

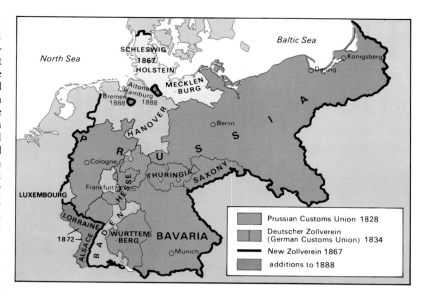

1/The economic unification of Germany (above) Well before the diplomatic skill of Bismarck and the military genius of Moltke were brought into play, the way had been prepared for the political unification of Germany by the officials responsible for the creation of the German *Zollvereine*, the developers of German roads, railways and canals, the pioneers in industry, shipping and banking.

2/The unification of Italy (below) The rapid expansion of Piedmont-Sardinia, which began with the acquisition of Lombardy in 1859, led, at the expense of the loss of Nice and Savoy, to the creation of the United Italy of 1861. The new kingdom acquired Venetia in 1866 and in 1870 Rome, which was made the capital.

The Industrial Revolution in the wider world 1850 to 1929

AFTER the middle of the 19th century the Industrial Revolution, which had radiated out from Great Britain to north-western Europe and the eastern seaboard of the United States, was spreading further afield in ever-widening circles. It did so at very different rates, depending largely on the economic, social and cultural preparation of the receiving territories.

Societies modelled on the West and formed or dominated by European settlers adopted industrialisation with no greater difficulty than the home country; the Anglo-Saxon areas of settlement being, as in Europe, well ahead of those of the Spanish and Portuguese. In most other, non-settler societies, industrialisation was a foreign transplant rather than an indigenous growth. Economic as well as political control

tended to pass to Europeans, and this limited industrialisation to certain enclaves, hardly touching the lives of the majority of inhabitants.

India and China exhibited as late as 1930 all the features of such enclave industrialism. In India, 69 per cent of all cotton workers in 1919 were in Bombay Province, two-thirds of them in Bombay City. Much of the sub-continent's steel capacity was concentrated in a single firm, the Tata Iron and Steel Co. at Tatanagar in Bihar, which produced in 1926-27 650,000 tons of pig iron and 600,000 tons of steel. China was opened up in the late 19th century mainly along the lines of the railway concessions granted to foreign groups, capitalists who had no interest in the development of the country as a whole. Of the foreign-owned firms in China between 1895 and

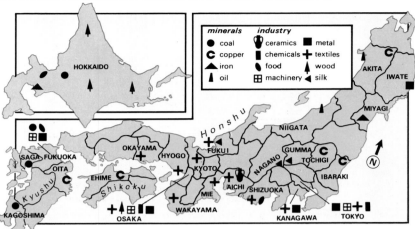

2/Japan's industrialisation *(above)* began after the Meiji restoration (1868). In spite of its poor natural endowment in such key resources as coal, iron ore and oil, it was the only non-Western society to have built a broad and varied industrial base by 1929.

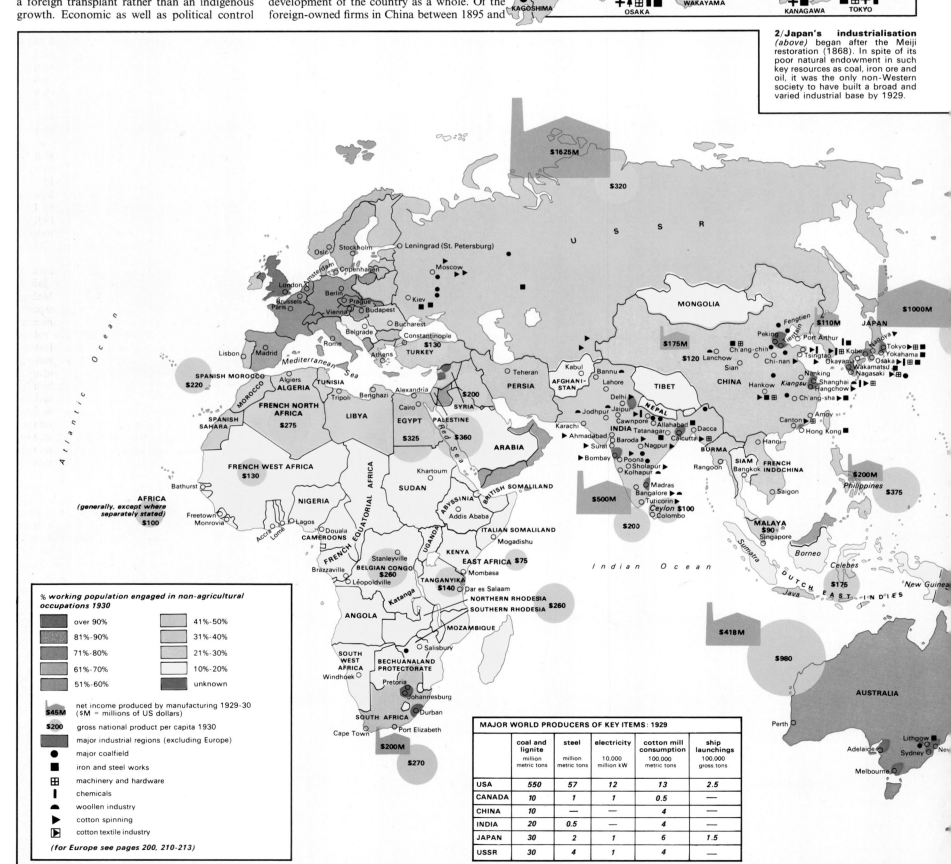

% working population engaged in non-agricultural occupations 1930

- over 90%
- 81%-90%
- 71%-80%
- 61%-70%
- 51%-60%
- 41%-50%
- 31%-40%
- 21%-30%
- 10%-20%
- unknown

$45M net income produced by manufacturing 1929-30 ($M = millions of US dollars)

$200 gross national product per capita 1930

major industrial regions (excluding Europe)

● major coalfield

■ iron and steel works

⊞ machinery and hardware

| chemicals

woollen industry

► cotton spinning

cotton textile industry

(for Europe see pages 200, 210-213)

MAJOR WORLD PRODUCERS OF KEY ITEMS: 1929

	coal and lignite (million metric tons)	steel (million metric tons)	electricity (10,000 million kW)	cotton mill consumption (100,000 metric tons)	ship launchings (100,000 gross tons)
USA	550	57	12	13	2.5
CANADA	10	1	1	0.5	—
CHINA	10	—	—	4	—
INDIA	20	0.5	—	4	—
JAPAN	30	2	1	6	1.5
USSR	30	4	1	4	—

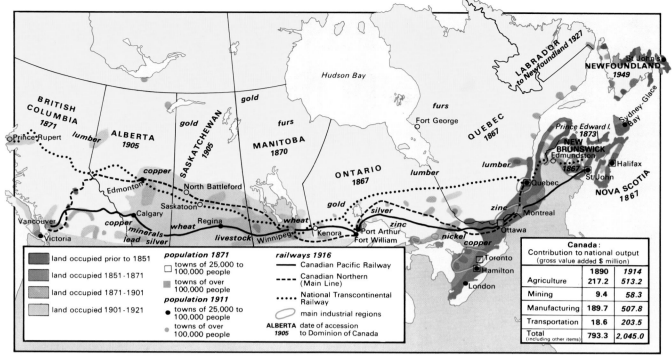

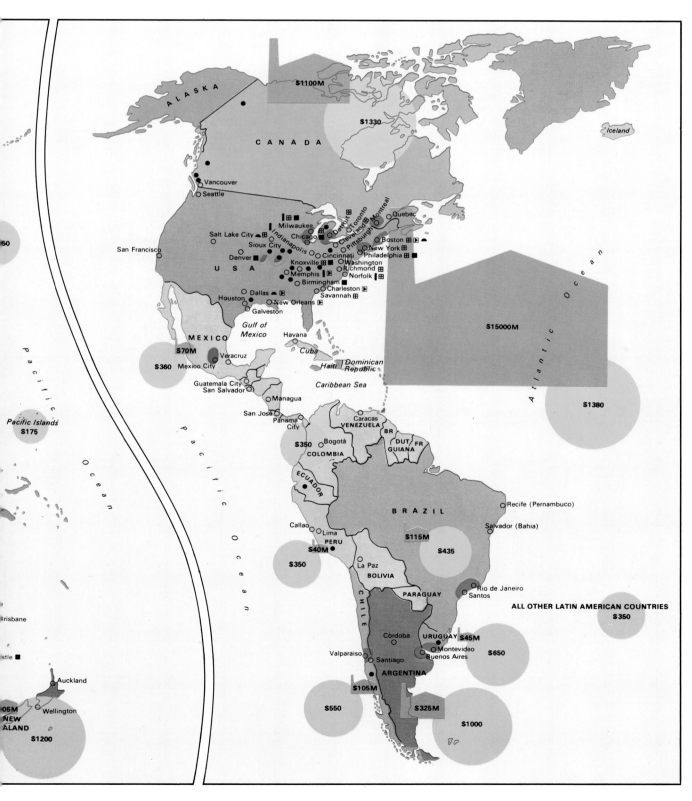

3/Canada in 1915 *(above)* after a quarter of a century of rapid economic development. Hard on the heels of expanding exports of wheat and timber, after 1890 there followed an influx of people and capital. Mining was well under way by 1914; manufacturing grew mainly after that date.

1917, 60 per cent, owning 40 per cent of the capital, were in only two provinces, Kiangsu and Fengtien.

Industrial development overseas occurred generally in three overlapping stages. In the first, it was entirely directed by westerners, usually to exploit some valuable primary product such as metallic ores, agricultural produce or oil. Virtually the whole world had reached that stage by 1930.

The second stage developed out of the need for servicing and repairing the major plants focussed on export production. In addition there was a growth of businesses supplying the needs of a more demanding population, but since these firms frequently merely replaced and destroyed existing traditional native handicraft industries, the proportion of the population engaged in manufacture did not necessarily grow, and may even have declined. For this reason, rather than registering the proportion engaged in manufactures, the main map shows the comparative non-agricultural population as a more sensitive indicator of the stage of development. Latin America, North Africa and many parts of Asia had reached this stage by 1930.

Such growth could sometimes be extremely fast. In Canada, which became the classic 'wheat economy' after all the land in the United States had been occupied in the early years of the 20th century, 73 million acres of land were occupied in 1900-16, and $400 million of foreign investment a year were attracted, together with a large stream of immigrants. The mining of coal, gold, lead, zinc, nickel and copper followed, and the country was well on the road to industrialisation.

In South Africa, gold was discovered on the Witwatersrand in 1886; by 1900, the gold fields employed 100,000 workers, and Johannesburg, a place of under 100 inhabitants in 1885, had 237,000 in 1911. Katanga, where copper deposits were first recognised in 1900, produced by 1914 10,722 metric tons of copper, and by 1930 its output, together with that of Northern Rhodesia, had risen to 305,000 tons, employing 30,000 African miners.

In Malaya, tin production was first encouraged on a large scale by the abolition of the British import duties on tin in 1853. By 1900, Malaya furnished nearly half the world's tin exports. Rubber was first grown on a few experimental acres in 1894; 50,000 acres were under rubber trees in 1905, and 300,000 acres in 1910. Most tin, however, was produced neither by European nor by native enterprise but by the Chinese, and apart from the port of Singapore, the effects of the large new industries were limited and localised. In China itself, where pig iron production rose from a derisory 477,000 tons in 1928 to 5.9 million tons in 1937, steel from 30,000 tons to 5.3 million tons and coal from 25 million tons to 124 million tons in the same period, the effects on the economy were even more circumscribed.

The third stage was the development of industries which competed with manufactured goods entering world markets. Iron and steel, textiles and machinery are always the most important of such commodities, and have therefore been emphasised in the map. As the map shows, Australia and New Zealand, Japan and some very limited areas in China and Manchuria, India, the Mediterranean coastline and Latin America had reached this stage. Among them, Japan stands out as the only wholly independent non-European society which had successfully embraced the western type of industrialism before the Depression of 1929. Nevertheless, the changes since 1850 in many, if scattered, parts of the globe had been scarcely less remarkable than those in Europe and the United States a hundred years earlier.

1/Industrialisation outside Europe and North America *(left)* was still the exception rather than the rule in 1929. Even after the opening of Africa in the 1880s and 1890s, the amount of European capital which flowed into the colonial world was small, and colonial governments were disinclined to invest in the infrastructure of ports, roads and railways, except in India. Even by the end of the period such transport and industry as did exist were either focussed on the ports trading with Europe or worked by European settler communities.

The making of the United States: westward expansion 1783 to 1890

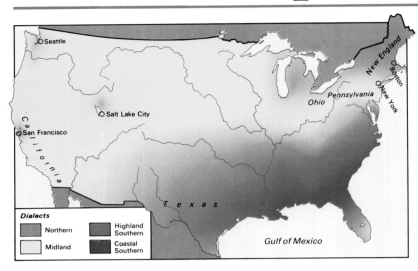

2/Migration and settlement (above) The American population flowed west in several distinct migration streams. The best guide to their location is the study of linguistic geography, which still preserves the history of the westward movement in the different spatial patterns of American speech. One migration stream led westward from New England to New York, Ohio and the northern plains. Another went by sea from Boston and New York to San Francisco and Seattle. Still a third went overland from Vermont and western New York to Salt Lake City. The largest migration stream rose in Pennsylvania and spread westward through the middle of the continent to California. Two southern streams flowed side by side, one south-west through the mountains, the other along the coast. They met and merged in Texas.

1/Westward expansion (below) There were several separate frontiers in American history—the frontier of the explorer, the fur trader, the miner, the cattleman and sheepherder, and finally the domestic frontier with which the Wild West ended. Each of those westward movements had its own special rhythm, its own settlements and routes.

IN 1783, the American republic was small and weak. Its population was a little more than three million people. Half its territory was held by hostile neighbours. Its colonial economy was still tributary to the mother country, and its polity was dangerously disordered. In less than a hundred years, the new nation had become a giant. By 1890 its population had grown larger than that of any European nation except Russia. Its economy was the most productive in the world. Its territory had grown to continental proportions. And its republican government had become strong, centralised, and highly stable.

The expansion of the American republic was sustained by its vast abundance of physical resources. As the great powers of Europe pursued their imperial dreams in Africa and Asia, the United States enjoyed the luxury of a built-in empire. The westward movement may be understood as a type of domestic imperialism, with many of the same motives as the imperialist movement in Europe but with profoundly different results. The native culture of North America was not merely conquered but destroyed; an integrated capitalist democracy developed in its place.

In 1783 the United States had an area of approximately 800,000 square miles, much of it rich arable land. That immense territory was soon enlarged by other tracts, even larger and more fertile. The Louisiana Purchase (827,000 square miles) was a mighty windfall which dropped into the hands of an astonished

President Thomas Jefferson in 1803. West Florida was taken by force during James Madison's administration and East Florida (60,000 square miles) by purchase, with the threat of force, during the presidency of James Monroe.

A second set of acquisitions in the period 1845-53 completed the contiguous area of the continental United States. Protracted negotiations for the territory of Oregon (285,000 square miles) finally ended with a compromise in 1846. The Texas republic (390,000 square miles) was annexed in 1845, and the vast Mexican cession (529,000 square miles) was a spoil of war in 1848. Finally, there was the Gadsden Purchase in 1853, bought from Mexico to control a promising railroad route. Compared with other acquisitions, it was trivial in size – a

3/Land cessions and density of settlement (below) In 1783, the new nation occupied a space between the Atlantic coast and the Mississippi river. Its territory was enlarged in only two great expansionist movements. During the first (1803-19), three Jeffersonian presidents acquired Louisiana and the Floridas. The second (1845-53) added Texas, Oregon and California.

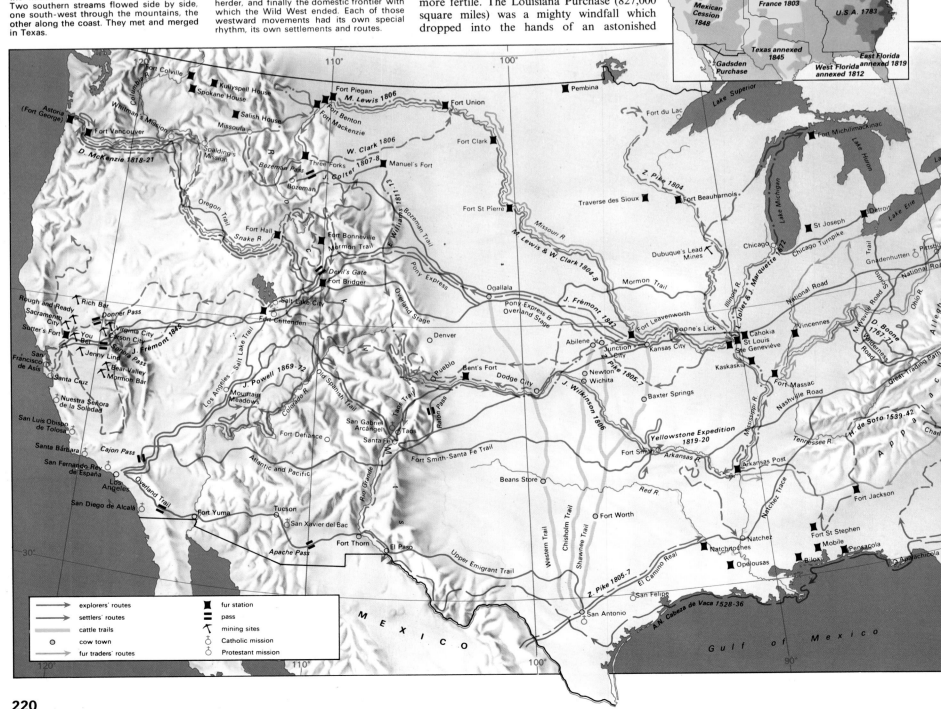

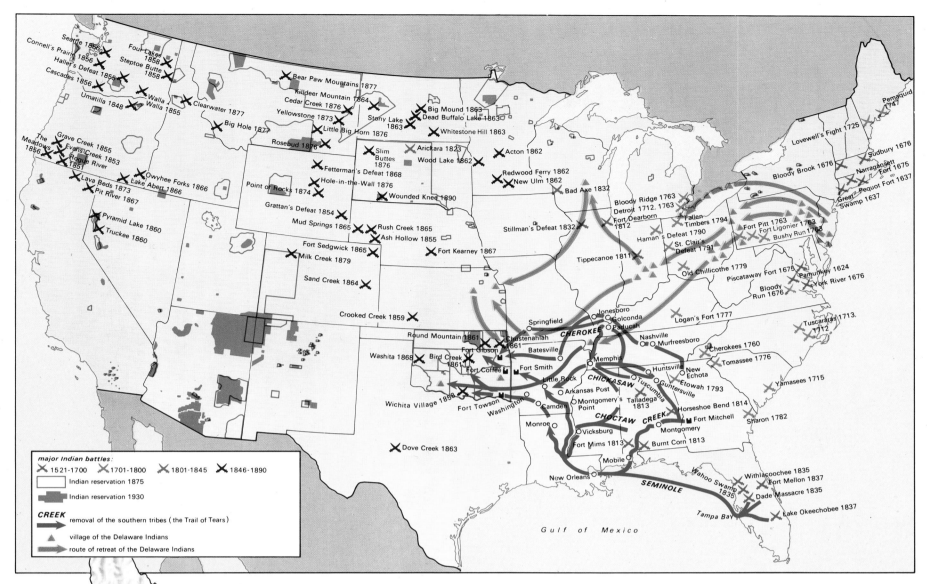

major Indian battles
- ✕ 1521-1700
- ✕ 1701-1800
- ✕ 1801-1845
- ✕ 1846-1890

☐ Indian reservation 1875

■ Indian reservation 1930

CREEK → removal of the southern tribes (the Trail of Tears)

▲ village of the Delaware Indians

⬛⬛⬛ route of retreat of the Delaware Indians

mere 30,000 square miles, approximately the area of Scotland.

This enormous landmass was occupied almost as swiftly as it was acquired. Before 1776, the Americans had been slow to settle the interior, which they called the 'back-country'. After 1800, the 'back-country' became 'frontier' in American speech, and the line of settlement advanced westward with astonishing speed. By its conventional definition, the 'frontier' is commonly understood to be the outer edge of the area with a population density of at least two persons per square mile. Before 1783 that line was still largely east of the Appalachian mountains except for a small settlement on the dark and bloody ground of Kentucky. Thirty years later, the great centre of the continent was occupied. By 1820 the frontier had crossed the Mississippi. And by 1840, it had reached the 100th meridian. The plains beyond were subdued after 1865 with the aid of a new technology – the steel plough, the six-shooter, and the barbed wire fence. After the census of 1890, the superintendent of the census observed that for the first time in American history, a single frontier-line was no longer visible on his map. The frontier, in that sense, had come to an end.

But as an experience, myth and symbol, the frontier continues to dominate American thought even today. The movement, progress, energy, expectation, confidence, prosperity and hope which it engendered still remain central to American culture. The unique experience of a built-in empire made it especially difficult for Americans to understand the conditions of other less fortunate people, and for others to understand America as well.

4/The fate of the Indians (above) For the indigenous Indians, every American cliché ran in reverse: expansion became contraction, democracy became tyranny, prosperity became poverty, and liberty became confinement. Before 1600, a million Indians lived north of the Rio Grande, speaking 2000 languages and subsisting in small villages on maize, game and fish. The coming of the Europeans caused a flowering of Indian culture. From whites, the Sioux obtained their horses; the Navajo, their sheep; the Iroquois, their weapons. But destruction quickly followed. The New England tribes, hard hit by disease, were broken in the Pequot War (1636) and King Philip's War (1675-6). In the middle colonies, the great Delaware nation was defeated by the Dutch in the Esopus Wars (1660), disgraced by the Iroquois (who made all the Delaware into 'honorary women'), and cheated by Quakers. The Delaware began a great diaspora; today they are scattered from Canada to Texas. For the southern tribes another fate was in store. Planters, led by Andrew Jackson obtained a law for their 'removal'. Despite the opposition of the Supreme Court, some 50,000 Cherokee were collected in concentration camps, and sent on a winter march to Oklahoma in 1838. Many died. The Choctaw, Creek and Chickasaw suffered equally. Only the Seminole resisted for long in the Florida swamps.

5/The buffalo (right) On the plains, the economic base of Indian herd was broken when the buffalo herd was cut in two by the railroad (1869). Twenty years later the buffalo, like the Indians, survived only in protected reservations.

6/Indian culture after the conquest (below right) As the material base of Indian culture crumbled, its spiritual structure was also destroyed. Many Indians created new systems of belief. The Ghost Dance was a religion of resistance, first developed in non-violent form c. 1870 by the Paiute prophet Woroke. The Sioux made it a warrior's faith; the inevitable result was the battle of Wounded Knee (1890). The Peyote drug cult, on the other hand, was a religion of accommodation, a syncretist faith which drew its doctrines from Indian and European sources, and which served as a spiritual bridge from one culture to another.

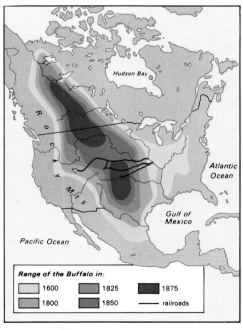

Range of the Buffalo in:
- 1600
- 1800
- 1825
- 1850
- 1875
- railroads

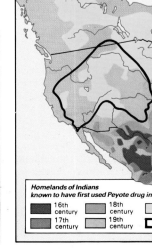

Homelands of Indians known to have first used Peyote drug in:
- 16th century
- 17th century
- 18th century
- 19th century
- 20th century
- approximate area of Ghost Dance, c.1890

Westward migration (right) by covered wagon started at the end of the 18th century and gathered pace after the breaching of the Allegheny mountains and the entry of immigrants to the mid-west by way of the great lakes and the Mississippi. The immigrants were opposed by Indian tribes driven westward by the ever increasing pressure.

The making of the United States: civil war and economic growth

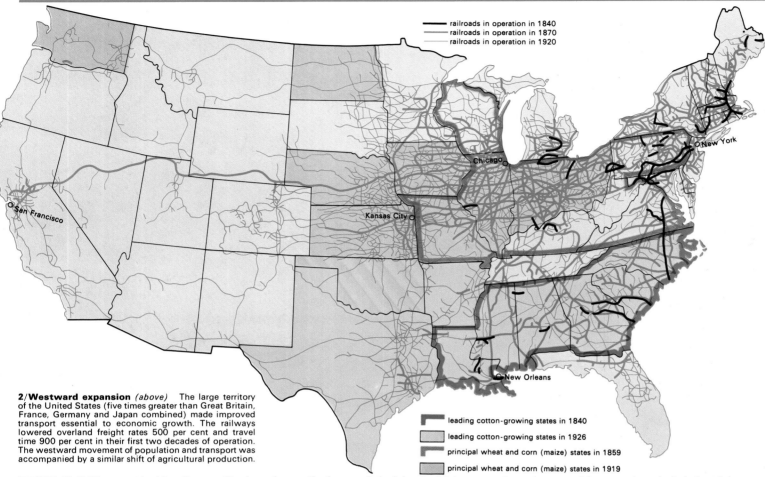

railroads in operation in 1840
railroads in operation in 1870
railroads in operation in 1920

leading cotton-growing states in 1840

leading cotton-growing states in 1926

principal wheat and corn (maize) states in 1859

principal wheat and corn (maize) states in 1919

2/Westward expansion (above) The large territory of the United States (five times greater than Great Britain, France, Germany and Japan combined) made improved transport essential to economic growth. The railways lowered overland freight rates 500 per cent and travel time 900 per cent in their first two decades of operation. The westward movement of population and transport was accompanied by a similar shift of agricultural production.

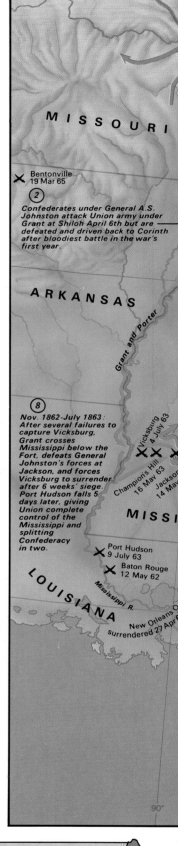

Bentonville
19 Mar 65

Confederates under General A.S. Johnston attack Union army under Grant at Shiloh April 6th but are defeated and driven back to Corinth after bloodiest battle in the war's first year.

Nov. 1862-July 1863: After several failures to capture Vicksburg, Grant crosses Mississippi below the Fort, defeats General Johnston's forces at Jackson, and forces Vicksburg to surrender after 6 weeks' siege. Port Hudson falls 5 days later, giving Union complete control of the Mississippi and splitting Confederacy in two.

Champions Hill 16 May 63
Jackson 14 May 63

Port Hudson 9 July 63

Baton Rouge 12 May 62

New Orleans surrendered 27 Apr 62

THE Civil War was the bloodiest conflict in American history. More Americans died than in all the nation's other wars combined. And the consequences equalled the cost – four million slaves emancipated, central government strengthened, and northern hegemony established.

Soon after the election of Lincoln, South Carolina left the Union. She was followed by the other six states of the lower South, which combined to form the Confederate States of America on 8 February 1861. After fighting began at Fort Sumter on 12 April, the states of Virginia, North Carolina, Tennessee and Arkansas joined their departing sisters. Although the South seceded to forestall a felt threat to slavery, the North fought at first only for the Union and not for the freedom of slaves. But by 1863 the revolutionary social and military momentum of the war, coupled with the growing power of radical Republicans in Congress, made emancipation a second Union war aim.

The massive volunteer armies mobilised by both sides were little more than armed mobs in 1861. The only major battle of the war's first year was fought at Bull Run on 21 July 1861, when the southern mob turned back a northern invasion of Virginia. Serious military operations began in the spring of 1862. Northern strategy was to deny the South vital resources by a naval blockade, to gain control of key river routes and forts in the west, and to capture the Confederate capital of Richmond. In view of the North's overwhelming superiority in manpower and resources, it may seem surprising that Union victory took four years. There were two main reasons for this: first, the South enjoyed superior generalship during the first two years of war; second, the North's war aims required occupation of the South and destruction of its armies, whereas the southern goal of independence required a primarily defensive strategy. In the east, General Robert E. Lee turned back two invasions of Virginia in 1862 and carried the war into the North. But he was stopped at Antietam, Maryland in September 1862 and decisively defeated at Gettysburg, Pennsylvania in July 1863. By the latter date the Northern strategy in

the west had succeeded, giving the Union control of the Mississippi and Tennessee rivers and opening the way for invasion of the lower South. By 1864 the Union blockade was effective, and General Grant began his invasion of Virginia which, combined with General Sherman's march through Georgia and South Carolina, destroyed the South's armies by the spring of 1865.

Northern victory was a triumph not only for the political and social goals of union and emancipation, but for economic modernisation as well. Before the war the contrasting economic systems of plantation slavery and free-labour capitalism had generated bitter ideological conflict between pro-slavery and anti-slavery partisans that was finally resolved on the battlefield. The North won the war mainly because its modernising economy could better mobilise the resources for war than could the agricultural South. Although many of the criteria for modernisation – per capita increase of agricultural and industrial output, technological innovation, urbanisation, expansion of education – were present before the war, these developments were confined mainly to the North. The war crippled the Southern ruling class and liberated its labour force, thereby removing the chief obstacle to the triumph of competitive free-labour capitalism.

From 1825 to 1910 the output of the American economy grew at an average annual rate of 1.6 per cent per capita. At the same time the population, through natural increase and immigration, doubled every twenty-seven years, giving the United States the fastest economic growth rate in the world.

Most important to this result was the growth of agricultural output. A population moving westward onto virgin lands, increased mechanisation and use of fertilisers, new strains of cotton, maize and wheat, and more efficient farm management made the United States the leading agricultural producer in the world.

Dramatic improvements in transport from 1790 to 1840 – turnpikes, bridges, canals, high-pressure steamboats and railways – lowered costs, raised volume, and created new markets for farm products. Because of the large size of the

country and because America's industrial revolution coincided with the great age of railway building, railways played a more important part in American economic development than in any other country. By 1890 the rail network was larger in the United States than in all Europe, including the British Isles and Russia.

These developments in agriculture and transport, combined with abundant resources, a literate population, technological innovation, managerial expertise, large-scale capital investment, political stability and a widely-shared entrepreneurial ethic, promoted the rapid industrialisation of the United States in the 19th century. The greatest industrial growth occurred from 1877 to 1892, when American factories tripled their output. By 1890 the United States was the world's leading industrial power.

In the 19th century the United States was an importer of capital, and much of the country's economic growth was fuelled by British and European investment. During the First World War that balance changed. After 1918 the United States became an exporter of capital.

3/Union states and Confederate states (below) This was a sectional Civil War, with geography determining the separation between the slave plantation and free labour economies. The five most northerly slave states remained in the Union, though part of their population supported the Confederacy.

Union States

Confederate States

slave states that stayed in the union

1/The Civil War, 1861-65 (below) began when the Confederate States of America fired on United States troops in Fort Sumter (Charleston, South Carolina) 12 April 1861, and ended when the main Confederate armies surrendered in April 1865. Nearly three million Americans served in the Union and Confederate armed forces. Two hundred thousand of the Union soldiers were Negroes, most of them emancipated slaves fighting for their freedom. More than 21 per cent of the Civil War soldiers lost their lives, a much higher proportion of deaths than in any of the armies of the First World War. In the Civil War armies about twice as many men died of disease as were killed in battle.

Civil War: enlistments and casualties

	UNION	CONFEDERACY
Men enlisted	2,200,000	800,000
Total deaths	360,222	258,000
Total wounded	275,175	125,000
Total casualties	635,397	383,000

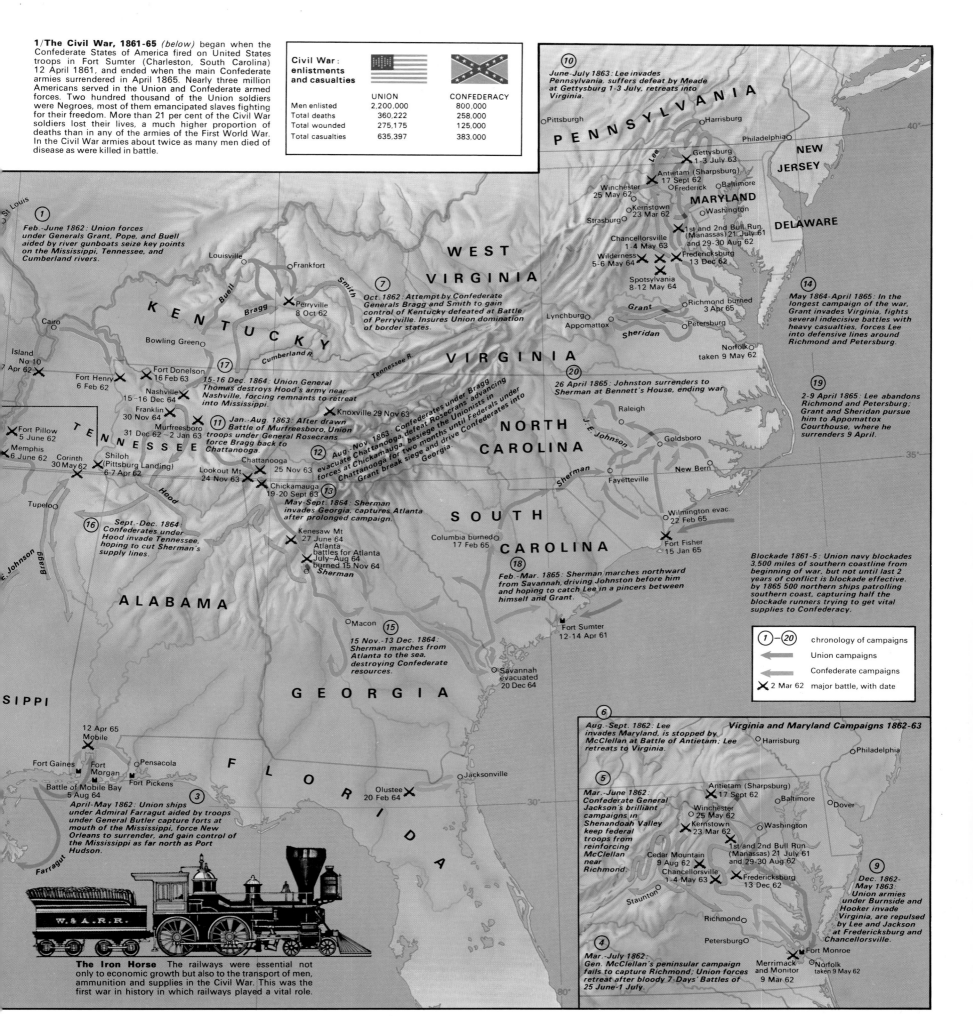

10 June-July 1863: Lee invades Pennsylvania, suffers defeat by Meade at Gettysburg 1-3 July, retreats into Virginia.

7 Oct. 1862: Attempt by Confederate Generals Bragg and Smith to gain control of Kentucky defeated at Battle of Perryville. Insures Union domination of border states.

1 Feb.-June 1862: Union forces under Generals Grant, Pope, and Buell aided by river gunboats seize key points on the Mississippi, Tennessee, and Cumberland rivers.

17 15-16 Dec. 1864: Union General Thomas destroys Hood's army near Nashville, forcing remnants to retreat into Mississippi.

11 Jan.-Aug. 1863: After drawn Battle of Murfreesboro, Union troops under General Rosecrans force Bragg back to Chattanooga.

12 Aug.-Nov. 1863: Confederates under Bragg evacuate Chattanooga, defeat Rosecrans at Chickamauga, besiege the Unionists in Chattanooga for two months until Federals under Grant break siege and drive Confederates into Georgia.

13 May-Sept. 1864: Sherman invades Georgia, captures Atlanta after prolonged campaign.

16 Sept.-Dec. 1864: Confederates under Hood invade Tennessee, hoping to cut Sherman's supply lines.

15 15 Nov.-13 Dec. 1864: Sherman marches from Atlanta to the sea, destroying Confederate resources.

18 Feb.-Mar. 1865: Sherman marches northward from Savannah, driving Johnston before him and hoping to catch Lee in a pincers between himself and Grant.

20 26 April 1865: Johnston surrenders to Sherman at Bennett's House, ending war.

14 May 1864-April 1865: In the longest campaign of the war, Grant invades Virginia, fights several indecisive battles with heavy casualties, forces Lee into defensive lines around Richmond and Petersburg.

19 2-9 April 1865: Lee abandons Richmond and Petersburg; Grant and Sheridan pursue him to Appomattox Courthouse, where he surrenders 9 April.

Blockade 1861-5: Union navy blockades 3,500 miles of southern coastline from beginning of war, but not until last 2 years of conflict is blockade effective. by 1865 500 northern ships patrolling southern coast, capturing half the blockade runners trying to get vital supplies to Confederacy.

3 April-May 1862: Union ships under Admiral Farragut aided by troops under General Butler capture forts at mouth of the Mississippi, force New Orleans to surrender, and gain control of the Mississippi as far north as Port Hudson.

Key
1-20 chronology of campaigns
← Union campaigns
← Confederate campaigns
✕ 2 Mar 62 major battle, with date

6 Aug.-Sept. 1862: Lee invades Maryland, is stopped by McClellan at Battle of Antietam; Lee retreats to Virginia.

Virginia and Maryland Campaigns 1862-63

5 Mar.-June 1862: Confederate General Jackson's brilliant campaigns in Shenandoah Valley keep federal troops from reinforcing McClellan near Richmond.

9 Dec. 1862-May 1863: Union armies under Burnside and Hooker invade Virginia, are repulsed by Lee and Jackson at Fredericksburg and Chancellorsville.

4 Mar.-July 1862: Gen. McClellan's peninsular campaign fails to capture Richmond; Union forces retreat after bloody 7-Days' Battles of 25 June-1 July.

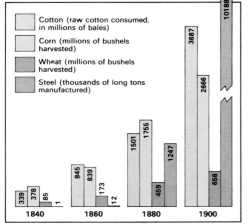

The Iron Horse The railways were essential not only to economic growth but also to the transport of men, ammunition and supplies in the Civil War. This was the first war in history in which railways played a vital role.

Economic growth, 1840-1900 (left) The growth of American agriculture and industry reflected in this graph resulted from technological innovations (especially reapers and threshing machines, and the Bessemer and open-hearth steel-making processes) as well as population growth and the settlement of new land.

Comparative resources, Union and Confederate states, 1861 (right) Because the South lacked the North's industrial capacity, the Confederacy was obliged to import or capture most of its arms. As the Union blockade tightened and the Confederate transport system broke down owing to inability to replace equipment, the agricultural South experienced difficulty even in feeding itself.

Legend (graph):
- Cotton (raw cotton consumed, in millions of bales)
- Corn (millions of bushels harvested)
- Wheat (millions of bushels harvested)
- Steel (thousands of long tons manufactured)

1840: 339, 378, 85, 1
1860: 845, 839, 173, 12
1880: 1501, 1755, 459, 1247
1900: 3687, 2666, 658, 10188

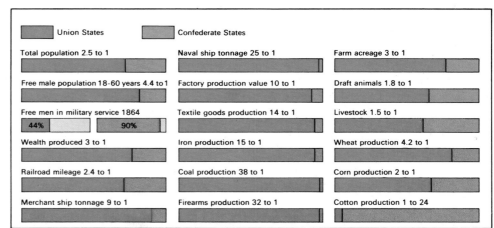

Union States / Confederate States

Total population 2.5 to 1
Free male population 18-60 years 4.4 to 1
Free men in military service 1864 — 44% / 90%
Wealth produced 3 to 1
Railroad mileage 2.4 to 1
Merchant ship tonnage 9 to 1
Naval ship tonnage 25 to 1
Factory production value 10 to 1
Textile goods production 14 to 1
Iron production 15 to 1
Coal production 38 to 1
Firearms production 32 to 1
Farm acreage 3 to 1
Draft animals 1.8 to 1
Livestock 1.5 to 1
Wheat production 4.2 to 1
Corn production 2 to 1
Cotton production 1 to 24

The making of the United States: politics and society 1776 to 1930

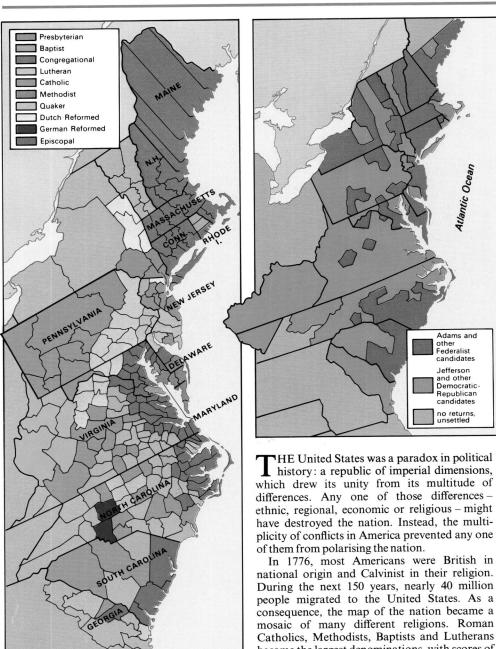

MAINE

N.H.

MASSACHUSETTS

CONN.

RHODE I.

NEW JERSEY

PENNSYLVANIA

DELAWARE

MARYLAND

VIRGINIA

NORTH CAROLINA

SOUTH CAROLINA

GEORGIA

Atlantic Ocean

Adams and other Federalist candidates

Jefferson and other Democratic-Republican candidates

no returns, unsettled

1/The election of 1800 (above and above right) In the election of 1800, power passed from the ruling Federalist party to its Jeffersonian challengers. That peaceable revolution provided a foundation for stable republicanism in North America. Voting patterns reflected the distribution of ethnic and religious groups.

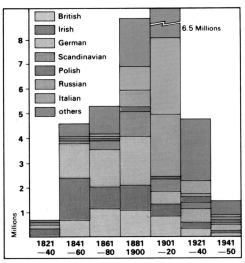

British
Irish
German
Scandinavian
Polish
Russian
Italian
others

6.5 Millions

8

7

6

5

4

3

2

1

Millions

1821 –40 | 1841 –60 | 1861 –80 | 1881 1900 | 1901 –20 | 1921 –40 | 1941 –50

Immigration in the 19th century (above) Economic change, population surplus, and famine sent millions of Europeans to North America, where scarcity of labour and virgin agricultural land provided economic opportunity. In the 1890s there was a fundamental shift in the

THE United States was a paradox in political history: a republic of imperial dimensions, which drew its unity from its multitude of differences. Any one of those differences – ethnic, regional, economic or religious – might have destroyed the nation. Instead, the multiplicity of conflicts in America prevented any one of them from polarising the nation.

In 1776, most Americans were British in national origin and Calvinist in their religion. During the next 150 years, nearly 40 million people migrated to the United States. As a consequence, the map of the nation became a mosaic of many different religions. Roman Catholics, Methodists, Baptists and Lutherans became the largest denominations, with scores of smaller rivals. The ethnic map of American Society thus became more complex too.

As the country expanded, its regions also became more diverse. The difference between North and South – between a system of wage labour and bond labour – became the most dangerous difference, as it was at once economic, political and racial. Before 1860 more than 90 per cent of the black population lived below the Mason-Dixon line. Race was a regional problem. Not until the First World War did significant numbers of blacks move north. And as the economy developed the distribution of wealth became increasingly unequal between both individuals and regions. Rich and poor concentrated in urban areas, while the middling classes remained predominantly rural. With the growth of economic inequality came a corresponding growth of class consciousness.

American presidential elections reflected the interplay of these patterns of ethnicity, religion, region and class. The 1800 campaign, in which the Republican candidate Thomas Jefferson beat the Federalists' John Adams, saw a coalition of New England Congregational elites, Dutch burghers in New York, Free Blacks in the middle states lining up against the northern Baptist yeomen, Virginia Episcopalian planters, Irish immigrants in the cities and German farmers in Pennsylvania. The peaceful transfer

sources of immigrants from north-western to southern and eastern Europe. Russian Jews and subject nationalities of the Austro-Hungarian Empire as well as Poles and Italians now constituted the majority of immigrants.

of power was made possible by the complexity of those electoral patterns.

By 1828 the Federalist party had disappeared and the Jeffersonians had divided into the National-Republicans, headed by John Quincy Adams, and the Democratic-Republicans led by Andrew Jackson. This election prefigured the evolution of the Whig and Democratic parties. Jackson ran strongly among the common people of northern cities and the southern countryside; his opponents in 1828 and later were strongest in rural New England and the Old North-West, and among the commercial and planter elites of both North and South. National Republicans/ Whigs found their greatest support among Unitarians, Congregationalists, Presbyterians and Episcopalians; Jacksonians were strongest among Baptists and Catholics; Methodists and Lutherans were divided.

Although many of these patterns persisted in 1860, the sectional conflict over slavery overshadowed them. The Democratic party, which had traditionally united different ethnic and economic groups across sectional lines, broke into two parties, one southern, one northern, which ran John C. Breckinridge and Stephen A. Douglas respectively for the presidency. Battered remnants of the Whigs formed the Constitutional Union party, with John Bell as its candidate, to try to unite conservatives in both sections, but Bell ran well only in the border states. The anti-slavery Republicans, entirely a northern party, nominated Abraham Lincoln on a platform of slavery containment. Carrying every county in New England and most of the counties in the other free states (but only two counties in all the south), Lincoln won the presidency with only 39 per cent of the popular vote. His election precipitated the secession of eleven slave states, and brought on the Civil War.

For a generation after the war, ethnic, religious and sectional patterns dominated American elections. As the party of Union, emancipation, and reform, the Republicans won the votes of most evangelical Protestants in the North and Negroes in the South. The Democrats were supported by most whites in the South, and many non-evangelical Protestants in the North. Class was only a minor factor in determining party allegiance, but since an increasing percentage of unskilled working men in the North were immigrants and Catholics, there appeared to be a relation between class and party in some northern cities.

In the election of 1896, economic issues jolted old ethnic and religious patterns. William Jennings Bryan and the Democrats, campaigning for an inflationary policy of expanded silver coinage, carried all but three counties in the silver states of the West, as well as the farm states of Kansas, Nebraska and the South. Fearing the impact of inflation on real wages, and attracted by McKinley's repudiation of traditional Republican anti-Catholicism, northern working men of Catholic as well as Protestant faiths joined native-born middle-class Protestants in voting Republican. The Democratic party, in power when the Panic of 1893 began, became stigmatised as the party of depression. The sectional and rural/ urban divisions in this election were striking: McKinley carried every county in New England (despite the region's large Catholic population), all but one county in New York, and all but two in New Jersey. He was the only Republican candidate in the 19th century to carry New York City. For twenty years before 1896 the two major parties had been evenly balanced in national elections; McKinley's success in winning many immigrant and urban votes while losing only the farmers and miners of thinly-populated Western states moved the Republican party in a more urban, cosmopolitan and progressive direction and ensured its domination until the 1930s.

Seattle Spokane

WASHINGTON

Portland

OREGON

Sacramento

San Francisco

CALIFORNIA

NEVADA

Los Angeles

1896 Electoral results

McKinley, Republican

Bryan, Democrat, Populist, and National Silver

no returns, unsettled etc.

Wealth per capita

below $500 income, rest of U.S.A. over $500

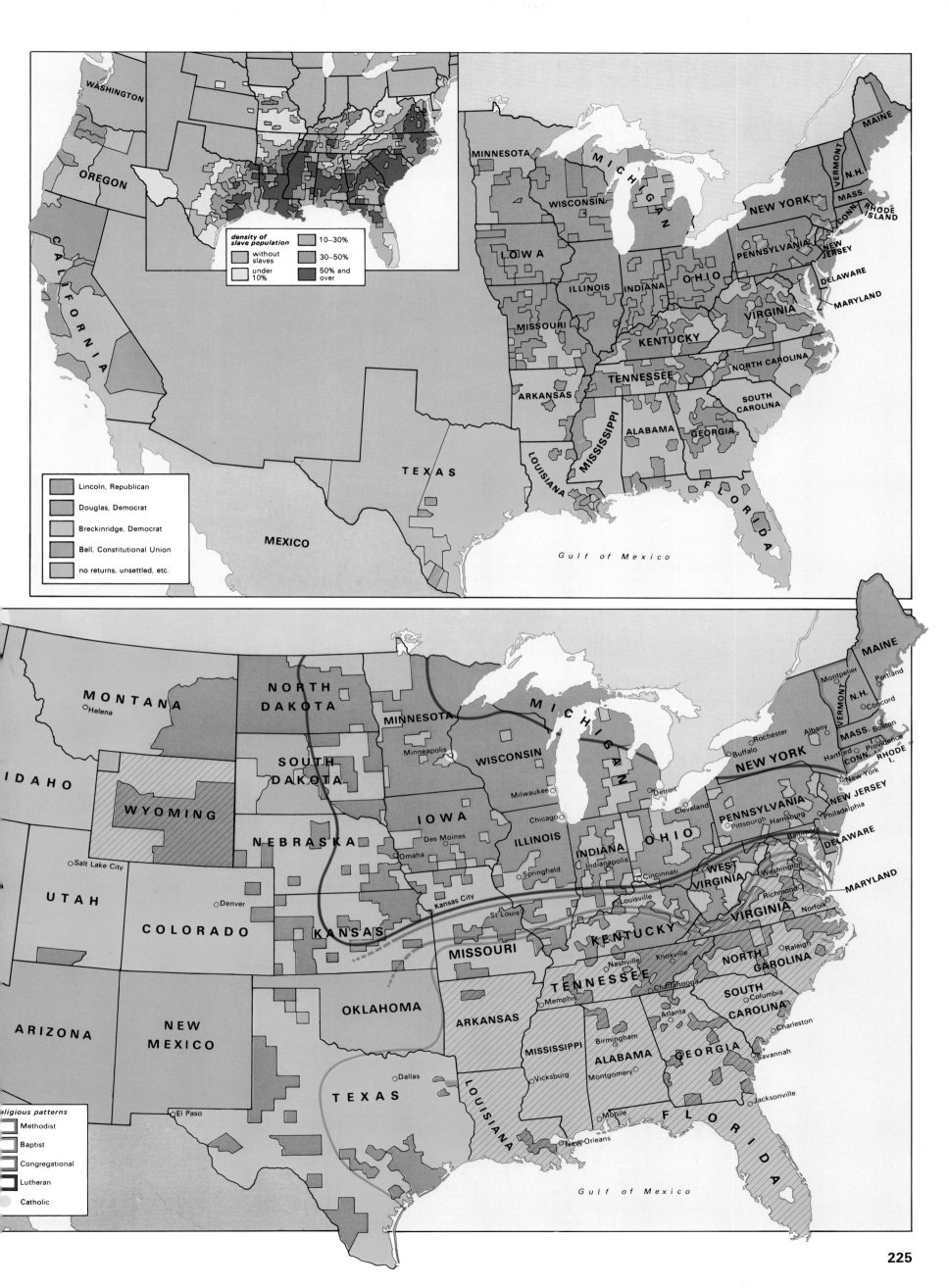

density of
slave population
without
slaves
under
10%
10–30%
30–50%
50% and
over

Lincoln, Republican
Douglas, Democrat
Breckinridge, Democrat
Bell, Constitutional Union
no returns, unsettled, etc.

WASHINGTON
OREGON
CALIFORNIA
MEXICO
TEXAS
MINNESOTA
MICHIGAN
WISCONSIN
IOWA
ILLINOIS
INDIANA
OHIO
MISSOURI
KENTUCKY
ARKANSAS
TENNESSEE
MISSISSIPPI
ALABAMA
GEORGIA
LOUISIANA
FLORIDA
SOUTH CAROLINA
NORTH CAROLINA
VIRGINIA
MARYLAND
DELAWARE
PENNSYLVANIA
NEW JERSEY
NEW YORK
VERMONT
MAINE
N.H.
MASS.
CONN.
RHODE ISLAND

Gulf of Mexico

religious patterns
Methodist
Baptist
Congregational
Lutheran
Catholic

MONTANA
IDAHO
WYOMING
NORTH DAKOTA
SOUTH DAKOTA
MINNESOTA
MICHIGAN
WISCONSIN
NEBRASKA
IOWA
UTAH
COLORADO
KANSAS
MISSOURI
ILLINOIS
INDIANA
OHIO
WEST VIRGINIA
VIRGINIA
KENTUCKY
TENNESSEE
NORTH CAROLINA
SOUTH CAROLINA
ARIZONA
NEW MEXICO
OKLAHOMA
ARKANSAS
MISSISSIPPI
ALABAMA
GEORGIA
TEXAS
LOUISIANA
FLORIDA
NEW YORK
PENNSYLVANIA
NEW JERSEY
DELAWARE
MARYLAND
MAINE
VERMONT
N.H.
MASS.
CONN.
RHODE I.

Helena
Salt Lake City
Denver
Minneapolis
Des Moines
Omaha
Kansas City
St. Louis
Chicago
Springfield
Milwaukee
Detroit
Cleveland
Indianapolis
Cincinnati
Louisville
Pittsburgh
Harrisburg
Washington
Baltimore
Philadelphia
Rochester
Buffalo
Albany
Hartford
Providence
Boston
New York
Montpelier
Concord
Portland
Nashville
Knoxville
Chattanooga
Memphis
Atlanta
Birmingham
Montgomery
Vicksburg
Mobile
New Orleans
Jacksonville
Savannah
Charleston
Columbia
Raleigh
Richmond
Norfolk
Dallas
El Paso

Gulf of Mexico

Latin America: independence and national growth 1810 to 1910

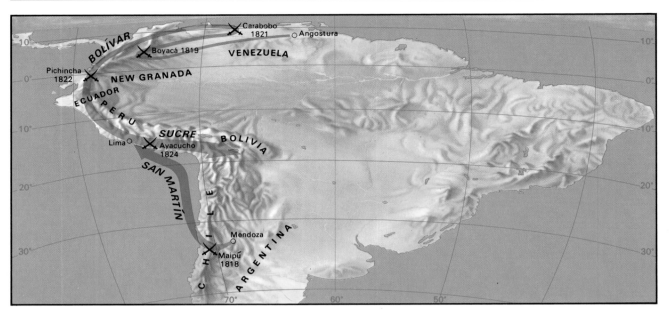

2 / Independence campaigns 1810 to 1826 *(above)* Latin America's main wars of liberation, against Spain, lasted until 1826. They involved two major forces: one, led by the Venezuelans, Bolívar and Sucre, converging on Peru, the central Spanish bastion; the other, the Army of the Andes, with San Martín's Argentines and Bernardo O'Higgins' Chileans, attacking the Peruvian capital, Lima.

3/Export economies and foreign investment *(below)* The new nations of Latin America were classic export economies, exploiting cheap land and labour to produce raw materials for a world market. Foreign competition and small, subsistence-level domestic markets held back development of national industries; characteristic economic institutions were the plantation, the ranch and the mine. From the 1880s, a massive immigration of foreign manpower and capital, reinforced by railways and improved ocean transport, accelerated economic growth.

THE emancipation of Latin America between 1808 and 1826 was precipitated by the Napoleonic subjection of Spain and Portugal, which effectively cut off the colonies from their motherlands. This merely released a long dormant nationalism, now able to express itself in demands for political freedom, administrative autonomy and economic self-determination. The Portuguese royal family met these demands by adopting them and leading Brazil peacefully into nationhood as an independent empire, with its own crown and a minimum of social change. Spain, on the other hand, sought to crush its colonies' pretensions at their source. Spanish American independence then swept across the sub-continent in two violent movements: the southern revolution advanced across the pampas from Buenos Aires and was carried by San Martín's Army of the Andes to Chile and beyond; the northern revolution, more vigorously harassed by Spanish troops, was led by Bolívar from Venezuela to the mountainous battlefield of Boyacá in Colombia (then called

New Granada) and back to its birthplace. Both converged on Peru, the fortress of Spain in America. In the north, Mexican insurgency followed a course of its own – first frustrated social revolution, then prolonged counter-revolution and finally a successful power-seizure by the conservative commander Iturbide, enthroned as Emperor Agustín I. Independence everywhere was essentially a political movement, involving a transfer of authority but only marginal social and economic change.

The wars caused great loss of life and property; terror and insecurity provoked a flight of capital and labour, making it difficult to organise recovery. The first decades of freedom were occupied with violent political debate – between centre and regions, between free trade and protection, between agriculturists, mine-owners and industrialists, and between supporters of cheap imports and defenders of national production. In Colombia the civil war between 'liberals' and 'conservatives' lasted well over a hundred years. On the whole, policies of primary export and

cheap imports won the day, and British (and later French and North American) merchants, bankers and shippers were ready and eager to fill the entrepreneurial vacuum left by Spain.

Prospects of national economic development were really defeated by the social structure of the new states, where impoverished rural populations offered little support for local industry. The old colonial division between a privileged minority, monopolising land and office, and a barely subsisting mass of peasants and workers, survived independence and grew even sharper. The new power base was the *hacienda*, the great landed estate; this was a social rather than an economic investment, utilising too much land and too little capital, and was ultimately carried on the back of cheap labour, seasonal or servile. The slave trade did not long survive independence, and slavery itself was abolished in all Spanish-speaking republics by the 1850s – though not in Brazil, where it lasted until 1888. But the Negro, like the majority of *mulattos* and *mestizos*, remained at the foot of the economic ladder. Such groups often became tied *peons*, allowed a strip of land on the *hacienda* in return for arduous labour service. After the wars, the new rulers sought to reduce tension by abolishing socio-racial discrimination – at least in law. They also sought to integrate the Indians into the nation by forcing them to participate in the economy; this involved dividing their communal lands among individual owners, theoretically benefiting the Indians themselves, but in practice only strengthening their powerful white neighbours.

The independence movement was a war, and inevitably nurtured warriors, giving a prepon-

4/Population and immigration *(below)* Latin America inherited a complex racial structure. Spanish American societies were composed in varying proportions of a great mass of Indians, a lesser number of mestizos, and a minority of whites. The Indian base of this pyramid was extensive in Peru, Mexico and Guatemala, less so in the Río de la Plata and Chile. The slave trade from Africa had also added the Negro, from whom were descended Mulattos and other mixed groups. Brazil was a slave society until 1888, blacks and mixed bloods occupied the lower part of the social scale. Both Argentina and Brazil received massive immigration from Europe in the late 19th century.

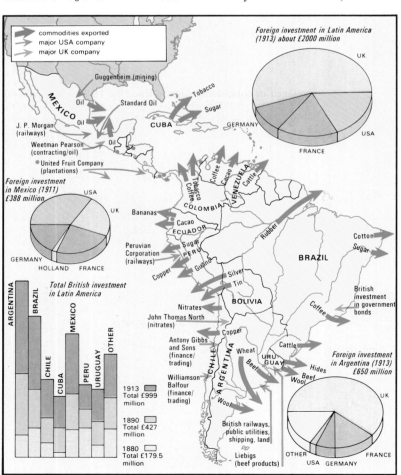

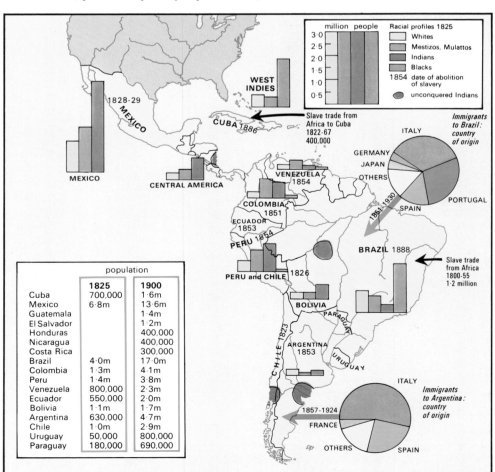

population		
	1825	**1900**
Cuba	700,000	1·6m
Mexico	6·8m	13·6m
Guatemala		1·4m
El Salvador		1·2m
Honduras		400,000
Nicaragua		400,000
Costa Rica		300,000
Brazil	4·0m	17·0m
Colombia	1·3m	4·1m
Peru	1·4m	3·8m
Venezuela	800,000	2·3m
Ecuador	550,000	2·0m
Bolivia	1·1m	1·7m
Argentina	630,000	4·7m
Chile	1·0m	2·9m
Uruguay	50,000	800,000
Paraguay	180,000	690,000

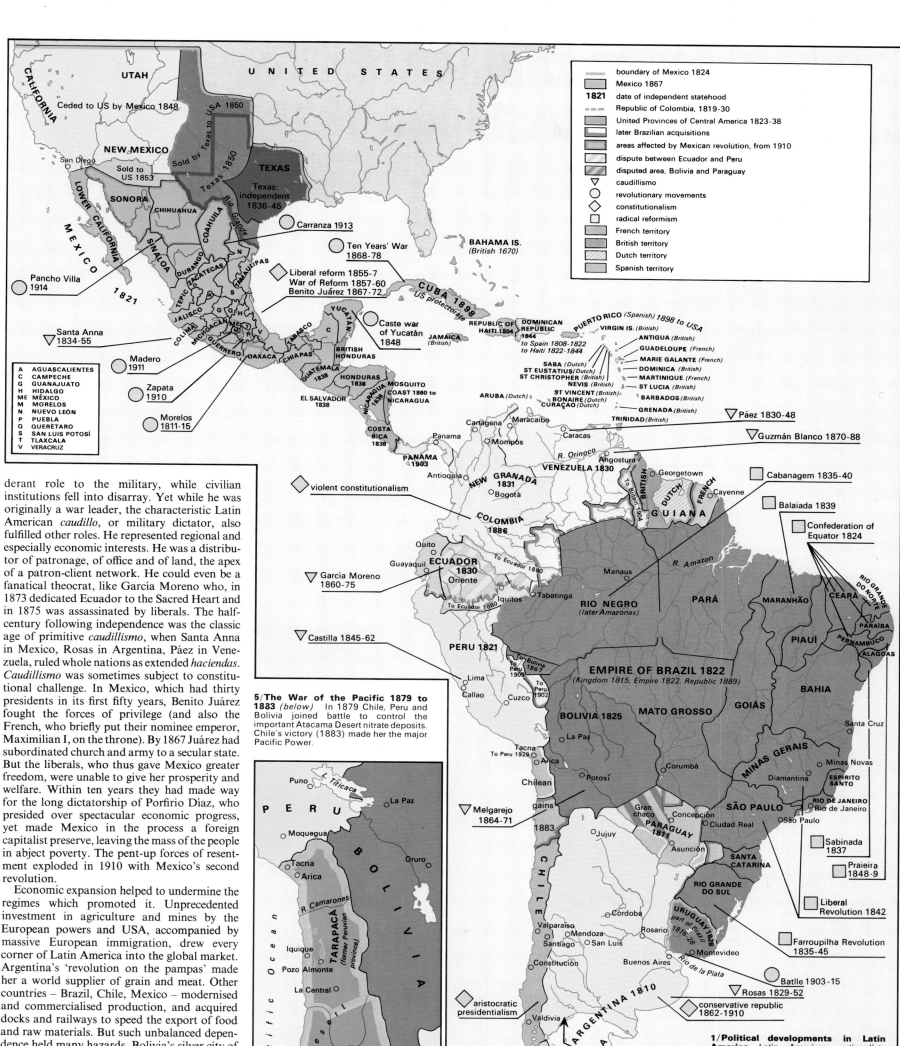

Map labels and annotations

Legend (top right):
- boundary of Mexico 1824
- Mexico 1867
- **1821** date of independent statehood
- Republic of Colombia, 1819-30
- United Provinces of Central America 1823-38
- later Brazilian acquisitions
- areas affected by Mexican revolution, from 1910
- dispute between Ecuador and Peru
- disputed area, Bolivia and Paraguay
- ▽ caudillismo
- ○ revolutionary movements
- ◇ constitutionalism
- □ radical reformism
- French territory
- British territory
- Dutch territory
- Spanish territory

Mexico / North America:
UTAH — Ceded to US by Mexico 1848
CALIFORNIA
NEW MEXICO — Sold to US 1853
Sold by Texas to USA 1850
TEXAS — Texas: independent 1836-45
UNITED STATES
San Diego
LOWER CALIFORNIA
SONORA
CHIHUAHUA
SINALOA
DURANGO
ZACATECAS
TEPIC
JALISCO
COLIMA
MICHOACÁN
GUERRERO
OAXACA
CHIAPAS
COAHUILA
NUEVO LEÓN
TAMAULIPAS
Rio Grande
MEXICO 1821
YUCATÁN
TABASCO
CAMPECHE
VERACRUZ

○ Carranza 1913
○ Pancho Villa 1914
▽ Santa Anna 1834-55
○ Madero 1911
○ Zapata 1910
○ Morelos 1811-15
◇ Liberal reform 1855-7 / War of Reform 1857-60 / Benito Juárez 1867-72
○ Ten Years' War 1868-78
○ Caste war of Yucatán 1848

State abbreviation key:
- A AGUASCALIENTES
- C CAMPECHE
- G GUANAJUATO
- H HIDALGO
- ME MÉXICO
- M MORELOS
- N NUEVO LEÓN
- P PUEBLA
- Q QUERÉTARO
- S SAN LUIS POTOSÍ
- T TLAXCALA
- V VERACRUZ

Central America / Caribbean:
GUATEMALA 1838
HONDURAS 1838
EL SALVADOR 1838
NICARAGUA 1838
COSTA RICA 1838
BRITISH HONDURAS
MOSQUITO COAST 1860 to Nicaragua
PANAMA 1903
BAHAMA IS. (British 1670)
CUBA 1898 US protectorate
JAMAICA (British)
REPUBLIC OF HAITI 1804
DOMINICAN REPUBLIC 1844 to Spain 1808-1822 to Haiti 1822-1844
PUERTO RICO (Spanish) 1898 to USA
VIRGIN IS. (British)
ANTIGUA (British)
GUADELOUPE (French)
MARIE GALANTE (French)
DOMINICA (British)
MARTINIQUE (French)
ST LUCIA (British)
ST VINCENT (British)
BARBADOS (British)
GRENADA (British)
TRINIDAD (British)
SABA (Dutch)
ST EUSTATIUS (Dutch)
ST CHRISTOPHER (British)
NEVIS (British)
ARUBA (Dutch)
BONAIRE (Dutch)
CURAÇAO (Dutch)

South America:
Cartagena, Maracaibo, Mompós, Caracas, Antioquia, Panama
R. Orinoco, Angostura
NEW GRANADA 1831, Bogotá
COLOMBIA 1886
VENEZUELA 1830
BRITISH GUIANA To Britain 1904
DUTCH GUIANA
FRENCH GUIANA, Cayenne
Georgetown
Quito, Guayaquil
ECUADOR 1830, Oriente
To Ecuador 1880
Tabatinga, Iquitos
R. Amazon
Manaus
RIO NEGRO (later Amazonas)
PARÁ
MARANHÃO
CEARÁ
RIO GRANDE DO NORTE
PARAÍBA
PERNAMBUCO
ALAGOAS
PIAUÍ
BAHIA
EMPIRE OF BRAZIL 1822 (Kingdom 1815, Empire 1822, Republic 1889)
MATO GROSSO
GOIÁS
MINAS GERAIS
Diamantina, Minas Novas
ESPÍRITO SANTO
RIO DE JANEIRO, Rio de Janeiro
SÃO PAULO, São Paulo
SANTA CATARINA
RIO GRANDE DO SUL
PERU 1821, Lima, Callao, Cuzco
To Bolivia 1867, To Peru 1909, To Peru 1902
BOLIVIA 1825, La Paz, Potosí
Santa Cruz, Corumbá, Concepción, Ciudad Real
Gran Chaco
PARAGUAY 1811, Asunción
Tacna, To Peru 1929, Arica, Chilean gains 1883
URUGUAY 1828 (part of Brazil 1816-28), Montevideo
Jujuy, Córdoba, Rosario, Río de la Plata, Buenos Aires
CHILE, Valparaíso, Santiago, Mendoza, San Luis, Constitución
Valdivia
ARGENTINA 1810
PATAGONIA
FALKLAND IS. (Islas Malvinas) claimed by Spain to 1811, subsequently claimed by Argentina; colonised by Britain 1765-1774; 1833 British

○ Battle 1903-15
▽ Páez 1830-48
▽ Guzmán Blanco 1870-88
◇ violent constitutionalism
▽ García Moreno 1860-75
▽ Castilla 1845-62
▽ Melgarejo 1864-71
□ Cabanagem 1835-40
□ Balaiada 1839
□ Confederation of Equator 1824
□ Sabinada 1837
□ Praieira 1848-9
□ Liberal Revolution 1842
□ Farroupilha Revolution 1835-45
▽ Rosas 1829-52
◇ conservative republic 1862-1910
◇ aristocratic presidentialism
War of the Desert 1880-81

5/The War of the Pacific 1879 to 1883 (below)
In 1879 Chile, Peru and Bolivia joined battle to control the important Atacama Desert nitrate deposits. Chile's victory (1883) made her the major Pacific Power.

War of the Pacific inset map:
PERU, Puno, L. Titicaca, La Paz, Moquegua, Tacna, Arica, R. Camarones, Oruro
BOLIVIA
TARAPACÁ (former Peruvian province), Iquique, Pozo Almonte, La Central
Atacama Desert
ANTOFAGASTA (former Bolivian province), Calama, Miraflores, Taltal
ARGENTINA
Pacific Ocean
CHILE
- Chilean gains
- nitrates

Body text

derant role to the military, while civilian institutions fell into disarray. Yet while he was originally a war leader, the characteristic Latin American *caudillo*, or military dictator, also fulfilled other roles. He represented regional and especially economic interests. He was a distributor of patronage, of office and of land, the apex of a patron-client network. He could even be a fanatical theocrat, like García Moreno who, in 1873 dedicated Ecuador to the Sacred Heart and in 1875 was assassinated by liberals. The half-century following independence was the classic age of primitive *caudillismo*, when Santa Anna in Mexico, Rosas in Argentina, Páez in Venezuela, ruled whole nations as extended *haciendas*. *Caudillismo* was sometimes subject to constitutional challenge. In Mexico, which had thirty presidents in its first fifty years, Benito Juárez fought the forces of privilege (and also the French, who briefly put their nominee emperor, Maximilian I, on the throne). By 1867 Juárez had subordinated church and army to a secular state. But the liberals, who thus gave Mexico greater freedom, were unable to give her prosperity and welfare. Within ten years they had made way for the long dictatorship of Porfirio Díaz, who presided over spectacular economic progress, yet made Mexico in the process a foreign capitalist preserve, leaving the mass of the people in abject poverty. The pent-up forces of resentment exploded in 1910 with Mexico's second revolution.

Economic expansion helped to undermine the regimes which promoted it. Unprecedented investment in agriculture and mines by the European powers and USA, accompanied by massive European immigration, drew every corner of Latin America into the global market. Argentina's 'revolution on the pampas' made her a world supplier of grain and meat. Other countries – Brazil, Chile, Mexico – modernised and commercialised production, and acquired docks and railways to speed the export of food and raw materials. But such unbalanced dependence held many hazards. Bolivia's silver city of Potosí declined in the 19th century to a sleepy little Andean town. The Chilean nitrate boom of 1880 to 1919 collapsed with peace and the advent of synthetic substitutes. Rubber forced Iquitos in Peru, and Manaus on the Amazon, into hectic but temporary world prominence, while Venezuela's oil discoveries in 1914 soon promoted dramatic extremes of wealth and poverty. These events promoted social change, with increased urbanism and the appearance of new groups, neither landlords nor peasants, whose livelihoods depended directly or indirectly on modern trade and technology, and provided the material for fresh political movements. Latin America's middle classes were emerging.

1/Political developments in Latin America
Latin American nationalists fought not only Spain and Portugal but also each other; except for Brazil fragmentation swiftly followed emancipation, leading to the eventual emergence of today's 20 republics. Boundary disputes were the occasion, though not necessarily the cause, of several major wars, including the Mexican and United States war, 1846-8, following the secession of Texas, which cost Mexico California and altogether 40% of her original territory; the Paraguayan war, 1864-70, in which Atlantic-facing Argentina, Uruguay and Brazil defeated and despoiled Paraguay, the one country whose Indians had successfully preserved their identity, and the war of the Pacific, 1879-83 (see inset). Bloody international conflicts (the Paraguayan struggle alone cost 330,000 lives) were matched almost everywhere by prolonged civil strife.

The disintegration of the Ottoman Empire 1800 to 1923

3/The Greco-Turkish War, 1920-1922 *(above)* After the First World War, the Allies proposed to dismember Turkey under the Treaty of Sèvres (1920). Nationalist opposition crystallised around the country's only unbeaten general, Mustapha Kemal, and erupted after the Greek occupation of Smyrna (1920). Turkish resistance, centred on Ankara, was at first unable to counter the Greek advance towards central Anatolia. However, the Turks rallied and drove the Greeks back after two important battles at Inönü (1921). The tide gradually began to turn in the Nationalists' favour; they concluded a border agreement with the Soviet Union (1921), and made separate pacts with France and Italy, which withdrew from the Turkish mainland. In 1922, Turkish forces reoccupied Smyrna, massacring many of the Greek population. Advancing towards the Dardanelles, they met a British detachment at Çanakkale, and confrontation appeared inevitable. Eventually, Turkish demands were met, and the Treaty of Lausanne (1923), recognised Turkish sovereignty.

Turkey's national flag provides a link with both the Ottoman and Byzantine Empires. Legend tells that the Greek city of Byzantium was saved from Philip of Macedon by the brightness of the crescent moon, which was adopted as the symbol of the later Christian Byzantine Empire and by its Muslim Ottoman conquerors.

B ETWEEN the beginning of the 19th century and the end of the First World War, the Ottoman Empire disintegrated, despite extensive efforts to reform and modernise its structure. Steady European commercial and colonial penetration into the Near East and North Africa undermined its fragile economy, and growing demands for national independence among the subject peoples caused large areas either to break away or to fall effectively under foreign control.

The Napoleonic expedition to Egypt in 1798 was the first indication of the Great Powers' new concern with the area. In spite of his defeat by Britain, Napoleon's invasion marked the beginning of an extensive period of acculturation between East and West, which brought European technical, political and philosophical ideas to an area which had known neither the Renaissance nor the Enlightenment. In Egypt itself, 1798 marked the end of effective control from Constantinople; the Ottoman commander in Egypt, Mohammed Ali, sent in 1802 to restore order, founded a dynasty in 1805 which lasted until the revolution of 1952. Mohammed Ali's son, Ibrahim Pasha, led expeditions to Nejd, to subdue the Wahabis, adherents of a puritanical form of Islam, who had challenged Ottoman authority in the Hejaz and in Iraq. Ibrahim Pasha also conquered the whole area between Egypt and what is now Turkey between 1831 and 1839, and was only dissuaded from attempting to overthrow the central authority of the Empire itself under pressure from Britain and France. Egyptian

pretensions were subsequently confined to Egypt itself and Sudan, which had been ruled from Cairo since 1821.

Faced with this and other challenges to its authority, the Empire embarked on a series of major reforms, in the armed forces, and in the fields of law, education, religion and administration. Previous efforts at reform had generally foundered on the intransigence of the traditional military forces, the janissaries, in the face of what they correctly perceived as a threat to their own position; Mahmud II (1808-1839) had dissolved the janissaries in a bloody battle in 1826, which meant that this obstacle no longer existed. Two edicts, in 1839 and 1856, stressed the subjects' rights to security of life and property, equitable taxation, and limited military service, and emphasised complete equality between Muslim and Christian subjects in the Empire. Here, as in other spheres, the gap between the ideal and the reality was apparent, and opposition to the reforms soon developed. In addition, the stress on Muslim/Christian equality provided a ready excuse for the intervention of the European powers on behalf of their Christian and other protégés: the Orthodox, supported by Russia; the Maronites and other Catholics, protected by France; and the Druzes and Jews, under British

1/The Middle East and North Africa 1798-1923 *(right)* The Ottoman Empire and the regions adjoining it broke up into a large number of political units in the course of the 19th and early 20th centuries:

Afghanistan Independent state under Durrani dynasty 1747-1842, power gradually assumed by Barakzais (c.1819-1973); remained independent in spite of Russian invasions and wars with Britain 1839-42, 1878-90, 1919.

Albania Ottoman province until independence secured late 1912 after fierce fighting; pro-Italian regime of King Zog 1928-39, followed by Italian occupation.

Armenia Western part in Ottoman Empire, eastern in Persia; east part occupied by Russia 1804; briefly a united independent republic 1918-20; autonomy promised but not given due to non-ratification of Treaty of Sèvres (1920); subsequently absorbed by Turkey and USSR.

Azerbaijan Persian until early 19th century; partly occupied by Russia 1803-1828; briefly independent 1918-20, thereafter incorporated into USSR; Azeri speakers roughly equally divided between USSR and Iran.

Bahrain Independent sheikhdom under al-Khalifa family since 1783; British protection from 1820, formalised in agreements of 1880 and 1892.

Bessarabia Ceded to Russia by Ottomans under Treaty of Bucharest (1812); southern part returned to (Ottoman) Moldavia under terms of settlement after Crimean War (1856); recovered by Russia 1878. Incorporated into Romania 1918.

Bosnia-Herzegovina Ottoman; Austrian administration from 1878; incorporated into Austro-Hungarian Empire, 1908; part of Yugoslavia after 1918.

Bukhara Independent khanate; Russian protectorate 1868; incorporated into Soviet Union, 1924.

Bulgaria Ottoman province since 14th century; unsuccessful national rising 1875-76; given autonomy but partitioned 1878; united with Eastern Rumelia 1885; independent kingdom 1908; gained Macedonia and Western Thrace 1913; present (1983) boundaries from 1919.

Crete Ottoman province since 1669; autonomous 1898; incorporated into Greece 1913.

Daghestan Persian; Russian occupation complete by 1859; formally incorporated into USSR 1921.

Eastern Rumelia Ottoman province since 14th century; privileged province 1878; incorporated into Bulgaria 1885.

Georgia Independent kingdom under intermittent Persian control; incorporated into Russia 1801; briefly independent 1918-20; thereafter incorporated into USSR.

Greece Ottoman rule since 14th century; independent state after revolts of 1821, 1833; enlarged by additions of Crete (1913), Macedonia (1913) and Dodecanese (1947).

Iraq Formed out of three former Ottoman provinces of Basra, Baghdad and Mosul, 1920, unified as kingdom under Hashemite monarchy, 1921-58; under British mandate. 1920-32.

Kars and Ardahan Fortress of Kars occupied by Russia, 1828; returned to Ottomans after

Crimea, 1856; to Russia after San Stefano, 1878; incorporated in Armenian Republic, 1918-20; re-occupied by Turkey after 1920.

Khiva Independent khanate; Russian occupation after 1873.

Kokand Independent khanate; Russian occupation after 1876.

Kuwait Autonomous sheikhdom under al-Sabah family since c.1756; treaty of protection with Britain, 1899-1961.

Lebanon Ottoman conquest, 1516-17; Mount Lebanon ruled by Ma'n princes (12th century-1697), then Shihab princes (1697-1840), both generally independent of Istanbul; 'double qaimaqamate' established after re-assertion of Ottoman control, 1840-1861; given privileged status after civil war of 1860-61 under Christian governors, 1861-1914; French occupation 1918-20; enlarged and given republican status under French mandate, 1920-46.

Macedonia Ottoman province; divided between Greece, Serbia and Bulgaria 1913.

Montenegro Autonomous region within Ottoman Empire (prince-bishops until 1851, then princes); independent 1878; kingdom 1910; incorporated into Yugoslavia after 1918.

Palestine Ottoman conquest, 1516-17; ruled by provincial governors and/or local dynasts until 1917; British conquest 1917-18, assigned to Britain as mandate (1920-47) with British obligation to facilitate creation of Jewish national home.

Persia Independent kingdom under Qajar Shahs 1779-1924; Constitutional Revolution, 1905-11; British and Russian agreement on partition into spheres of influence, 1907; under Pehlevi dynasty, 1924-79.

Qatar Autonomous sheikhdom under al-Thani family since late 18th century; treaty of friendship and protection with Britain, 1916-71.

Romania Formerly Ottoman provinces of Moldavia and Wallachia under local rulers; autonomous 1861; independent kingdom, 1878, enlarged by the addition of Bessarabia, 1918.

Serbia Ottoman province; autonomous from c.1817; independent kingdom, 1878; incorporated into Yugoslavia after 1918.

Syria [Name formerly applied to whole area of modern Syria, Israel-Palestine, Lebanon, Jordan] Ottoman conquest 1516-17; British conquest/occupation 1918; independent Arab state 1918-20; French occupation 1920, French mandate within present geographical boundaries (Sanjak of Alexandretta ceded to Turkey, 1939) 1920-46.

Transjordan Formerly part of Ottoman province of Damascus; princedom (Hashemite family) under British mandate for Palestine 1921-23; separate administration created 1923.

Trucial Oman Small sheikhdoms under British protection, 1820s-1971.

Tunisia Ottoman conquest, 1574; virtually independent under Husainid dynasty, 1705 to French occupation in 1881; French protectorate, 1881-1956.

Yemen Local rulers belonging to Za'idi (Shi'i) sect; nominally incorporated into Ottoman Empire, 1517; Aden occupied by Britain 1839; declaration of independence, 1918; loss of part of Asir, Najran and Tihama to Saudi Arabia, 1934.

protection. Foreign intervention contributed in particular to the Crimean War (1853-1856) and the Lebanese crisis of 1860-1861, while Russian and Austrian pressures were vitally important in securing the independence of Bulgaria, Montenegro, Serbia and Romania by 1878.

Thus by the outbreak of the First World War, the Ottoman Empire had been reduced to what is now Turkey, a small corner of south-eastern Europe, and the Arab provinces in Asia. Further west, North Africa was completely dominated by the Powers; the French invaded Algeria in 1830, and by 1900 there were some 200,000 French settlers installed there. Similar developments took place on a smaller scale in Tunisia after the French invasion in 1881, in Morocco – itself never a part of the Ottoman Empire – after 1912, and in Libya, invaded and colonised by Italy after 1911. In Egypt, the rise of nationalism and the dangers which this posed to some £100 million of foreign investment served as the excuse for the British occupation in 1882.

In the other Arab provinces, there were stirrings of discontent, particularly during the long and oppressive reign of Abdul-Hamid II (1876-1909). Ideas of autonomy, encouraged by the revival of Arabic literature and campaigns to reform the Arabic language, gradually gained wider currency. Abdul-Hamid had prorogued the Ottoman parliament, itself one of the major achievements of the second wave of Ottoman reformers, in 1878, and opposition to his rule culminated in the Young Turk revolution of 1908-09, which was supported by members of most of the ethnic groups in what was left of the Empire. After the revolution, however, the Turkish element in the government proceeded to 'Turkify' all administrative, legal and educational

institutions, a step which succeeded in alienating many Arabs and contributed in considerable measure to their willingness to seek an accommodation with Britain in the course of the war. In this they were to be disappointed, since the effect of the peace settlememt was to put most of the Middle East firmly under British and French colonial control. After Turkey's defeat, her new leader, Mustapha Kemal (Atatürk) abolished the caliphate and attempted to construct a purely secular state.

As the process of disintegration continued, new forms of trade and communications, largely funded by foreign capital had begun to transform the empire. By 1914, Turkey and Egypt had substantial rail networks, with banks and mines and public utilities such as ports, tramways, water and electricity companies. North Africa and the Middle East became important markets for European goods, and Algeria began to export wine, Lebanon to produce silk, and perhaps most spectacularly, Egypt to export cotton. Starting in 1822, demand for Egyptian cotton soared tenfold during the American civil war and almost trebled again, to £27 million, before 1914.

Parallel developments were taking place in Iran. The Qajars (1779-1924) had suffered constant British and Russian interference in their internal affairs, which culminated in the partition of the country into the spheres of influence of the two powers in 1907. However, the Tobacco Rebellion of 1896-98 and the Constitutional Revolution of 1905-11 served to arouse national consciousness and political awareness, although the Qajars were eventually to be overthrown by a military coup led by Reza Khan Pehlevi in 1924. In the interwar period it was to be oil, discovered in the Arabian peninsula, Iran and Iraq, which was to become the region's most precious and most sought after natural asset.

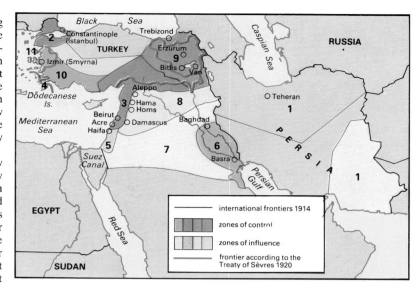

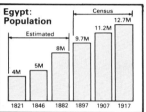

Egypt: Population

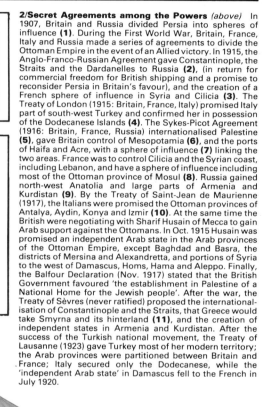

2/Secret Agreements among the Powers *(above)* In 1907, Britain and Russia divided Persia into spheres of influence **(1)**. During the First World War, Britain, France, Italy and Russia made a series of agreements to divide the Ottoman Empire in the event of an Allied victory. In 1915, the Anglo-Franco-Russian Agreement gave Constantinople, the Straits and the Dardanelles to Russia **(2)**, (in return for commercial freedom for British shipping and a promise to reconsider Persia in Britain's favour), and the creation of a French sphere of influence in Syria and Cilicia **(3)**. The Treaty of London (1915: Britain, France, Italy) promised Italy part of south-west Turkey and confirmed her in possession of the Dodecanese Islands **(4)**. The Sykes-Picot Agreement (1916: Britain, France, Russia) internationalised Palestine **(5)**, gave Britain control of Mesopotamia **(6)**, and the ports of Haifa and Acre, with a sphere of influence **(7)** linking the two areas. France was to control Cilicia and the Syrian coast, including Lebanon, and have a sphere of influence including most of the Ottoman province of Mosul **(8)**. Russia gained north-west Anatolia and large parts of Armenia and Kurdistan **(9)**. By the Treaty of Saint-Jean de Maurienne (1917), the Italians were promised the Ottoman provinces of Antalya, Aydin, Konya and Izmir **(10)**. At the same time the British were negotiating with Sharif Husain of Mecca to gain Arab support against the Ottomans. In Oct. 1915 Husain was promised an independent Arab state in the Arab provinces of the Ottoman Empire, except Baghdad and Basra, the districts of Mersina and Alexandretta, and portions of Syria to the west of Damascus, Homs, Hama and Aleppo. Finally, the Balfour Declaration (Nov. 1917) stated that the British Government favoured 'the establishment in Palestine of a National Home for the Jewish people'. After the war, the Treaty of Sèvres (never ratified) proposed the internationalisation of Constantinople and the Straits, that Greece would take Smyrna and its hinterland **(11)**, and the creation of independent states in Armenia and Kurdistan. After the success of the Turkish national movement, the Treaty of Lausanne (1923) gave Turkey most of her modern territory; the Arab provinces were partitioned between Britain and France; Italy secured only the Dodecanese, while the 'independent Arab state' in Damascus fell to the French in July 1920.

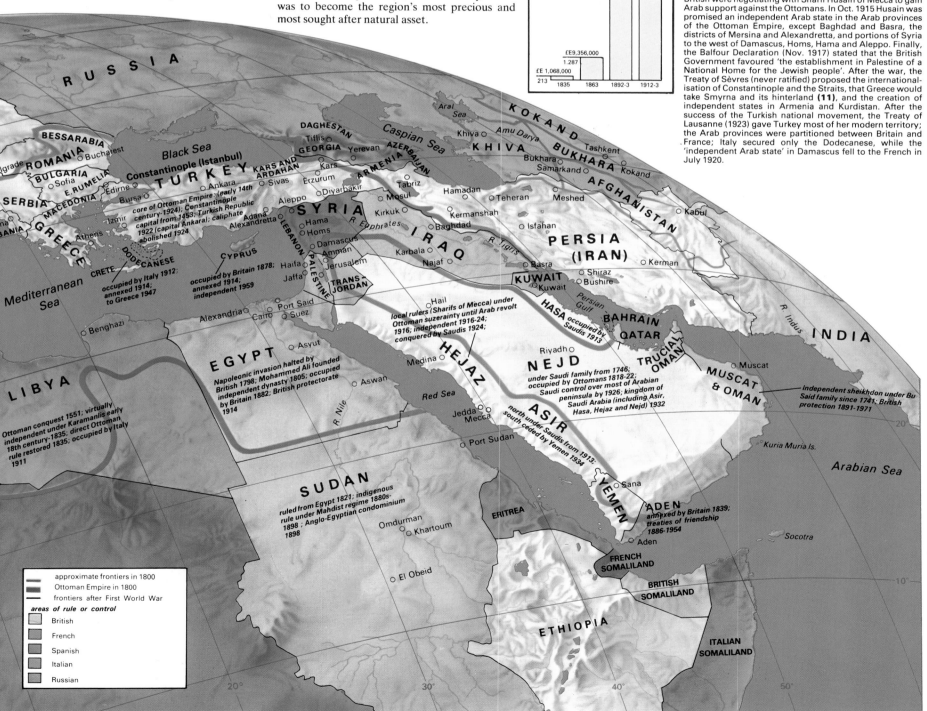

The Russian Empire: expansion and modernisation 1815 to 1917

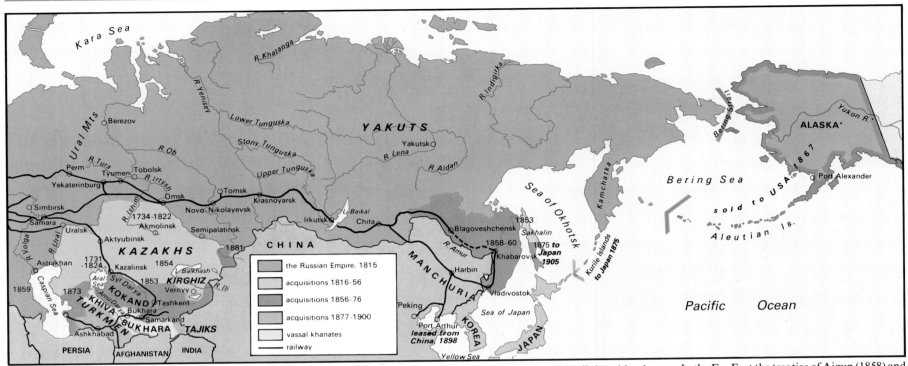

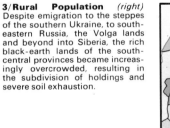

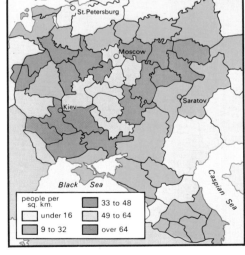

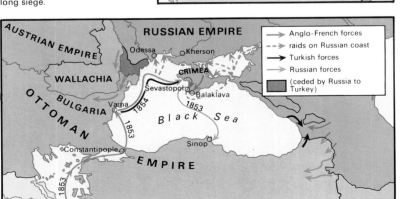

2/Russia in Asia *(above)*
During the 19th century, Russian authority was extended southwards across the deserts of central Asia inhabited by nomadic Kazakhs, Turkmen and others, to embrace the irrigated areas at the foot of the central Asian mountains and along the Amur river. In the Far East, acquisition of the Amur territory and Sakhalin was followed by penetration of Manchuria and Korea, but the war with Japan (1904-5) expelled Russian influence from these provinces, and southern Sakhalin was abandoned.

3/Rural Population *(right)*
Despite emigration to the steppes of the southern Ukraine, to southeastern Russia, the Volga lands and beyond into Siberia, the rich black-earth lands of the south-central provinces became increasingly overcrowded, resulting in the subdivision of holdings and severe soil exhaustion.

4/The Crimean War *(below)*
resulted from the determination of Britain and France, abetted by Austria, to prevent Russia benefiting from the impending dissolution of the Ottoman Empire. The war centred on the allied attempt to take the naval base of Sevastopol, which fell in September 1855 after a year-long siege.

FOR forty years after the Congress of Vienna, Russia remained the strongest military power in Europe, and she used her strength to maintain the order established in 1815. In this she was associated with Austria and Prussia, but Britain and France drifted away from the principles which had inspired the Congress. British public opinion became increasingly antagonistic towards the absolutism and repression which characterised the Russian system, while from France emanated the revolutionary impulses that threatened established monarchies everywhere.

Russian interests after 1815 focussed on the Balkans and on the straits leading from the Black Sea to the Mediterranean. The Turkish subjects of the Balkan countries were mostly Slavs and Orthodox, and the Russians therefore saw themselves as their natural protectors; because

Turkey lay athwart Russia's link with the Mediterranean it seemed essential that Constantinople should be amenable only to Russian influence. But France, Austria and Prussia also had imperial ambitions in the Balkans or in the eastern Mediterranean, while Great Britain was opposed to any further Russian aggrandisement anywhere and regarded the maintenance of a Turkey independent of Russia as equally essential. In 1841 an international Straits Convention closed the Bosporus to Russian warships. In 1853 the Russians invaded Turkey's Danubian provinces and also gained control of the Black Sea by sinking the Turkish fleet. In 1854 Britain and France declared war, while Austria insisted on the withdrawal of Russian troops replacing them with her own. Britain and France then invaded the Crimea, and the Russians, unable to dislodge them, accepted the humiliating terms of the Peace of Paris in 1856, undertaking to keep no navy on the Black Sea and to maintain no bases on its shores.

In the 1870s spontaneous revolts of the Balkan Slavs and their ferocious repression by the Turks provoked another Russian invasion of the Balkans (1877) but, faced with the united opposition of the great powers, Russia again had to give way at the Congress of Berlin (1878). Russia, having at great cost fought what seemed to her people a thoroughly justifiable war, and having liberated fellow Slavs and co-religionaries from intolerable oppression, had to stand by while the fruits of victory were either transferred to Austria or handed back to Turkey.

Russia had meanwhile completed the acquisition of the whole of northern Asia as far as – and sometimes into – the great mountain chains which separate it from Persia, Afghanistan, India and China. Military domination over the Kazakh nomads to the east of the Caspian was secured by the building of forts, beginning with that of Akmolinsk in the north in 1830 and ending with the foundation of Vernyy (now Alma-Ata) in 1854. Mountain campaigns between 1857 and 1864 completed Russian control of the Caucasus, and the armies thus set free were used to reduce central Asia. Here the Uzbek khanates of Kokand, Bukhara and Khiva, the Turkmen nomads and the Tajik and Kirghiz mountaineers were all in turn subdued.

In the late 18th century Russian colonisation spilled over into Alaska and early in the 19th century forts were built as far south as Fort Ross in California (1812). This penetration was short-lived, but Alaska was held until 1867, when it was sold to the United States.

In the Far East the treaties of Aigun (1858) and Peking (1860) brought the Russian frontier south to the Amur river and, in the coastal region, to south of Vladivostok (founded in 1860); the southern part of Sakhalin was acquired from Japan in exchange for the Kurile Islands. In 1891 the Trans-Siberian railway was begun; but northern Manchuria stood in the way of a direct route to Vladivostok. In 1896 the Chinese conceded a strip of land for the building of the railway across Manchuria, and two years later leased Port Arthur in the Yellow Sea, giving Russia a warm-water port unimpeded by winter ice. This was also connected by railway to the main trans-Siberian line.

These advances conflicted with Japanese designs. Encouraged by the Anglo-Japanese alliance, Japan began hostilities in 1904. Russia, handicapped by fighting at such a distance from her main centres of industry and population, was compelled in the Treaty of Portsmouth (1905) to give up the concessions she had won, to leave Manchuria, and to return southern Sakhalin to Japan.

At home, serfdom was abolished in 1861 by Alexander II (1855-1881), the 'Tsar Liberator', one of a series of measures to remedy the backwardness exposed by the Crimean War. Yet the peasants were in some ways worse off, having to buy by instalments the land they had always worked, a tax they could ill afford to pay. They became increasingly impoverished and, bound still to remain in their village communes, more and more overcrowded. Unrest became widespread, culminating in violent uprisings during the revolution of 1905, which forced Tsar Nicholas II (1894-1917) to grant a parliament or *duma*. Prime Minister Stolypin's agricultural reforms (1906-11) came too late. Gradually, however, the commune lost its grip on the peasant population and during the last two decades of the 19th century and up to the Revolution, there was a mass exodus from the Russian countryside into Siberia and to the towns. With labour cheap and abundant, the Russian industrial revolution could at last begin. Railways were built and factories arose in the towns: Petersburg and Moscow became textile and metal-working centres while the metal-lurgical industry developed in the Ukraine. Towns grew rapidly, the urban population more than trebling – rising from 6 million to 18.6 million – between 1863 and 1914. Thus the urban proletariat, whose hardships and grievances the revolutionaries were quick to exploit, was formed (see page 258).

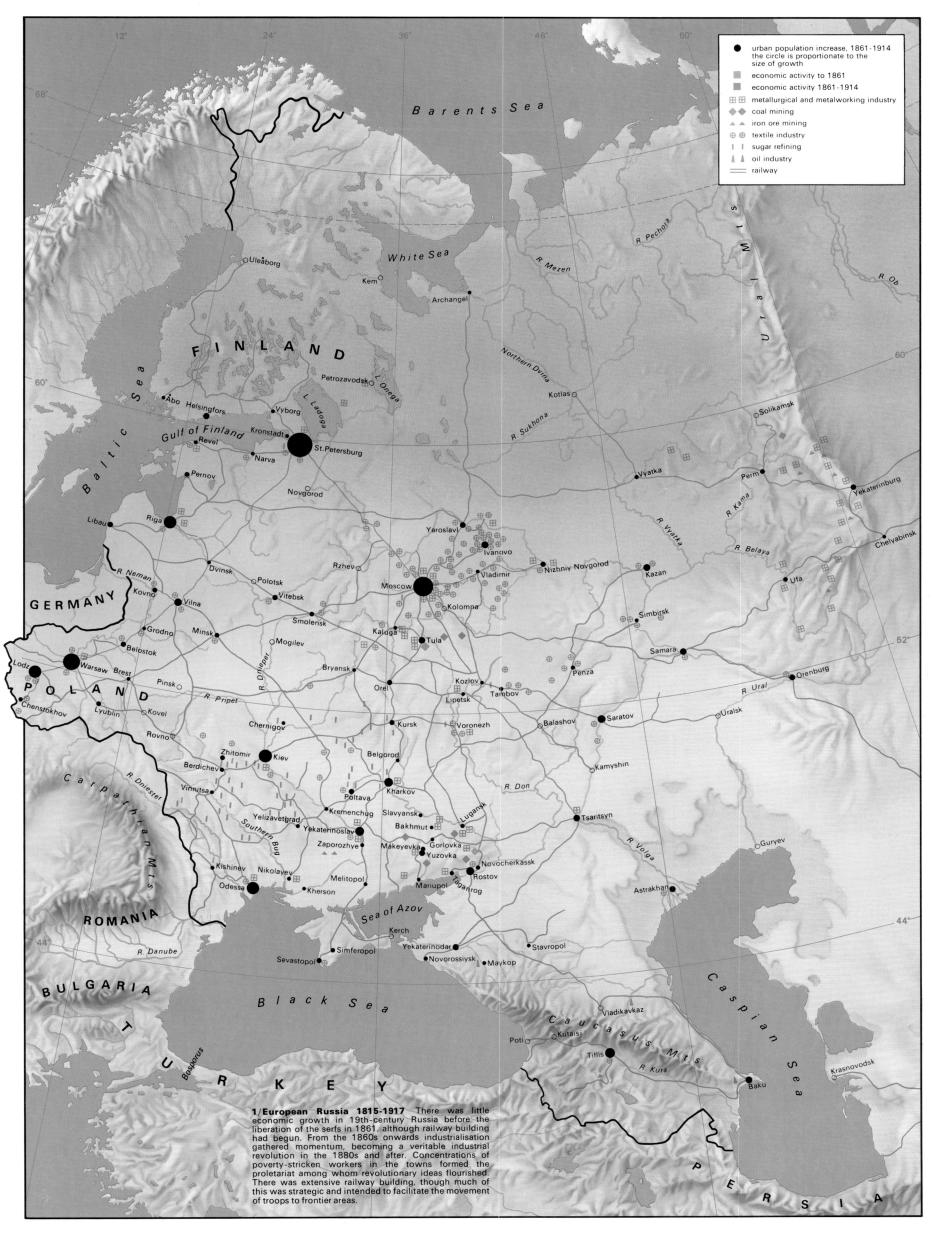

	urban population increase, 1861-1914 the circle is proportionate to the size of growth
	economic activity to 1861
	economic activity 1861-1914
	metallurgical and metalworking industry
	coal mining
	iron ore mining
	textile industry
	sugar refining
	oil industry
	railway

Barents Sea

White Sea

F I N L A N D

R. Pechora

R. Mezen

R. Ob

Uleåborg

Kem

Archangel

Petrozavodsk

L. Onega

Northern Dvina

Kotlas

R. Sukhona

Solikamsk

Åbo Helsingfors

Vyborg

L. Ladoga

Kronstadt

St. Petersburg

Vvatka

Perm

Yekaterinburg

Revel

Narva

Novgorod

R. Vyatka

R. Kama

R. Belaya

Chelyabinsk

Pernov

Baltic Sea

Gulf of Finland

Libau

Riga

Dvinsk

Rzhev

Yaroslavl

Ivanovo

Nizhniy Novgorod

Kazan

Uta

R. Neman

Polotsk

Vladimir

Simbirsk

GERMANY

Kovno

Vilna

Vitebsk

Smolensk

Moscow

Kolomna

R. Dnieper

Samara

Grodno

Minsk

Kaluga

Tula

Penza

Belostok

Mogilev

Pinsk

Bryansk

R. Pripet

Orel

Kozlov

Lipetsk

Tambov

Saratov

Orenburg

Lodz

Warsaw Brest

R. Ural

Uralsk

P O L A N D

Kovel

Chernigov

Kursk

Voronezh

Balashov

Kamyshin

Chenstokhov

Lyublin

Rovno

Zhitomir

Kiev

Belgorod

R. Don

Berdichev

Vinnitsa

Poltava

Kharkov

Slavyansk

Lugansk

Tsaritsyn

Yelizavetgrad

Kremenchug

Bakhmut

Yekaterinoslav

Makeyevka Gorlovka

Zaporozhye

Yuzovka

Novocherkassk

R. Volga

Guryev

Kishinev

Nikolayev

Melitopol

Mariupol Taganrog

Rostov

Astrakhan

ROMANIA

Odessa

Kherson

Sea of Azov

Caspian Sea

R. Danube

Kerch

Simferopol

Yekaterinodar

Stavropol

Sevastopol

Novorossiysk

Maykop

B U L G A R I A

Black Sea

Vladikavkaz

T U R K E Y

C a u c a s u s   M t s

Kutaisi

Poti

Tiflis

R. Kura

Krasnovodsk

Baku

P E R S I A

1/European Russia 1815-1917 There was little economic growth in 19th-century Russia before the liberation of the serfs in 1861, although railway building had begun. From the 1860s onwards industrialisation gathered momentum, becoming a veritable industrial revolution in the 1880s and after. Concentrations of poverty-stricken workers in the towns formed the proletariat among whom revolutionary ideas flourished. There was extensive railway building, though much of this was strategic and intended to facilitate the movement of troops to frontier areas.

The collapse of the Chinese Empire 1842 to 1911

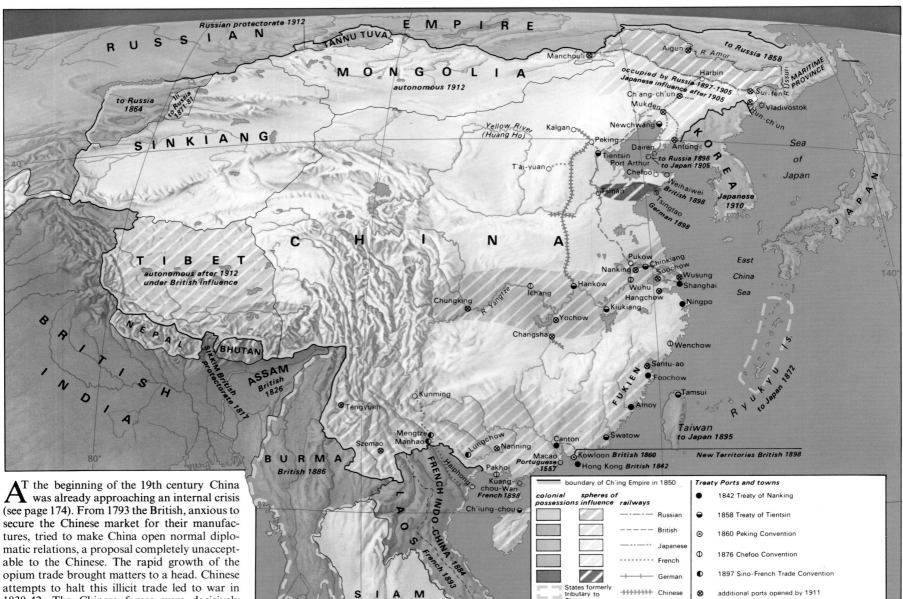

(see page 174)

AT the beginning of the 19th century China was already approaching an internal crisis (see page 174). From 1793 the British, anxious to secure the Chinese market for their manufactures, tried to make China open normal diplomatic relations, a proposal completely unacceptable to the Chinese. The rapid growth of the opium trade brought matters to a head. Chinese attempts to halt this illicit trade led to war in 1839-42. The Chinese forces were decisively defeated. The result was the cession of Hong Kong and the opening of five Treaty Ports in which foreign residents were permitted to trade and were freed of Chinese jurisdiction. French and American treaties followed. Shanghai soon replaced Canton as the centre of foreign trade and influence. Exports of tea and silk flourished, and the opium trade continued to expand.

The Chinese failed to understand the new challenge the western powers presented. Until the 17th century China had remained superior to the West in many ways. During the 18th century the Manchu empire achieved a peak of prosperity and stability, while its armies conquered a vast new empire in inner Asia. But during this period of great success, China had been overtaken by the rapid growth of Europe. Although the empire remained self-sufficient, it was now forced to deal with expansionist Western powers enjoying technological superiority and the wealth and capacity for organisation resulting from the Industrial Revolution. As the 19th century progressed, China's ruling class, nurtured in a tradition of unquestioned Chinese cultural supremacy, proved unable to understand this new challenge, or to modernise the country. Consequently, China fell further and further behind.

Even had the Manchu government responded to this new situation and been willing to modernise the empire it could have done little, for internal developments now involved it in a desperate struggle for survival. The Chinese defeat in the Opium War weakened imperial authority, and switching the export trade from Canton to Shanghai exacerbated the economic problems of the south. In 1850 a rebellion broke out in Kwangsi, which rapidly grew into a full-scale dynastic revolt, the T'ai-p'ing T'ien-kuo (Heavenly Kingdom of Great Peace). Moving north to the Yangtze valley the rebels took Nanking in 1853 and established control over much of central China. The rebellion was not suppressed until 1864.

The T'ai-p'ing rebellion was only the most serious of the major rebellions which erupted in the 1850s and 1860s, affecting a large part of the empire. The last of them was not finally suppressed until 1878. The Manchu armies and government again proved inadequate to deal with these internal threats. The suppression of the rebellions was largely the work of a few far-sighted provincial governors who built up modern armies, founded modern arsenals and trained experts in Western technology. They were a minority, however. Most of the court and the bureaucracy remained intent on the restoration of traditional institutions rather than on change.

The rebellions caused terrible suffering. The T'ai-p'ing and Nien rebellions alone left 25 million dead, while the Muslim risings depopulated vast tracts of Yunnan and the northwest. The wealthy region around Nanking did not recover for decades. In 1877-79 there followed a terrible famine in the north during which at least ten millions starved to death.

These grave disorders favoured the foreign powers, which had still failed to open normal relations with China. When their attempts to negotiate were refused, the British and French began another war in 1856, which ended with the occupation of Peking. The ensuing peace settlement finally secured diplomatic representation in Peking, opened more treaty ports and allowed foreign missionaries freedom of movement throughout China. Meanwhile, the Russians took advantage of the situation to occupy the Amur river region in 1858 and the Maritime Province in 1860. In 1871 they occupied the Ili valley in Turkestan, only withdrawing in 1881 when the Chinese paid an indemnity. A further defeat came in a war with France over Indo-China in 1884-85. The final humiliation came from Japan, which, faced with the same challenge, had begun to transform itself into a modern industrialised power. Japan had already intervened in Taiwan, in the Ryukyu Islands and in Korea. Finally, in 1894-95 Japan overwhelmed the modernised Chinese forces in a full-scale war. As a result, Taiwan was annexed.

This defeat finally convinced many Chinese that radical changes were inevitable. In 1898 the young Emperor and a group of reformers attempted a sweeping reform programme, but the conservative Manchus, led by the Empress Dowager, carried out a coup to prevent its implementation. Meanwhile, the foreign powers, believing China on the point of collapse, joined in a scramble for further rights and concessions, carving out spheres of influence and leasing territories as bases. This produced a wave of xenophobia which inspired the Boxer Rising in north-east China. The rebels attacked first missionaries, and then the foreign legations in Tientsin and Peking. The western powers sent troops into north China, while Russia occupied most of Manchuria. The final settlement wrung

2/The dismemberment of the Ch'ing Empire (above) During the 19th century China was forced to cede Hong Kong to Great Britain, and to open ever more ports to foreign trade, in which foreigners enjoyed extra-territorial rights. At the same time she lost extensive territories in the north and north-east to the expansionist Russian empire, and was challenged in the peripheral states like Nepal, Burma, Laos, Tongking, the Ryukyus and Korea, which had been her tributary states. With the collapse of the Ch'ing Empire in 1912 China lost control of Tibet and Mongolia.

Japan defeats China (above) In the Sino-Japanese war of 1894-5 the carefully modernised western-style Japanese army disastrously routed the ill-led Chinese forces.

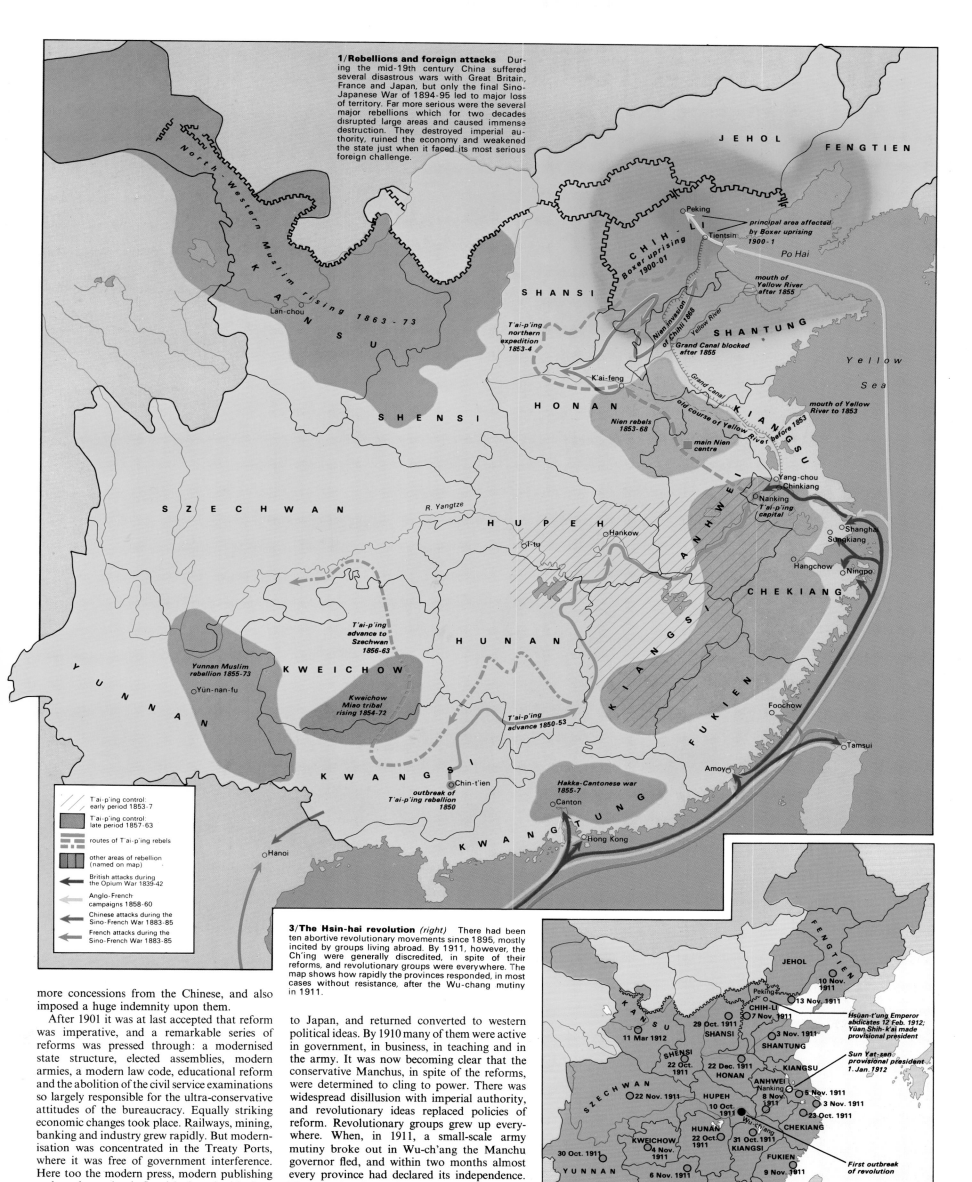

1/Rebellions and foreign attacks During the mid-19th century China suffered several disastrous wars with Great Britain, France and Japan, but only the final Sino-Japanese War of 1894-95 led to major loss of territory. Far more serious were the several major rebellions which for two decades disrupted large areas and caused immense destruction. They destroyed imperial authority, ruined the economy and weakened the state just when it faced its most serious foreign challenge.

T'ai-p'ing control:
early period 1853-7

T'ai-p'ing control:
late period 1857-63

routes of T'ai-p'ing rebels

other areas of rebellion
(named on map)

British attacks during
the Opium War 1839-42

Anglo-French
campaigns 1858-60

Chinese attacks during the
Sino-French War 1883-85

French attacks during the
Sino-French War 1883-85

3/The Hsin-hai revolution (right) There had been ten abortive revolutionary movements since 1895, mostly incited by groups living abroad. By 1911, however, the Ch'ing were generally discredited, in spite of their reforms, and revolutionary groups were everywhere. The map shows how rapidly the provinces responded, in most cases without resistance, after the Wu-chang mutiny in 1911.

Hsüan-t'ung Emperor
abdicates 12 Feb. 1912;
Yüan Shih-k'ai made
provisional president

Sun Yat-sen
provisional president
1. Jan. 1912

First outbreak
of revolution

8 Nov. 1911 revolt, with date of province's independence

more concessions from the Chinese, and also imposed a huge indemnity upon them.

After 1901 it was at last accepted that reform was imperative, and a remarkable series of reforms was pressed through: a modernised state structure, elected assemblies, modern armies, a modern law code, educational reform and the abolition of the civil service examinations so largely responsible for the ultra-conservative attitudes of the bureaucracy. Equally striking economic changes took place. Railways, mining, banking and industry grew rapidly. But modernisation was concentrated in the Treaty Ports, where it was free of government interference. Here too the modern press, modern publishing and modern schools flourished, and with them the political movements of revolutionary and reformist parties.

From the 1890s ever-increasing numbers of young men were sent to study abroad, especially

to Japan, and returned converted to western political ideas. By 1910 many of them were active in government, in business, in teaching and in the army. It was now becoming clear that the conservative Manchus, in spite of the reforms, were determined to cling to power. There was widespread disillusion with imperial authority, and revolutionary ideas replaced policies of reform. Revolutionary groups grew up everywhere. When, in 1911, a small-scale army mutiny broke out in Wu-ch'ang the Manchu governor fled, and within two months almost every province had declared its independence. There was hardly any fighting. The revolutionary T'ung-men-hui party set up a provisional government at Nanking, where its leader Sun Yat-sen was proclaimed president on 1 January 1912.

India under British rule
1805 to 1931

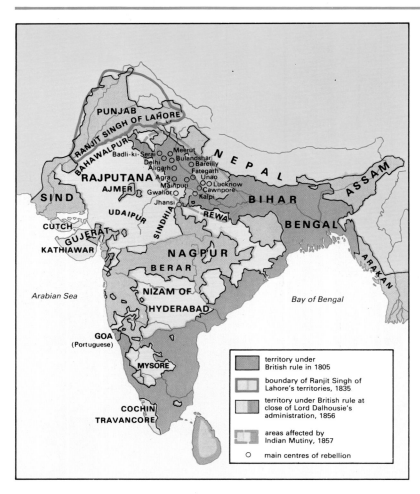

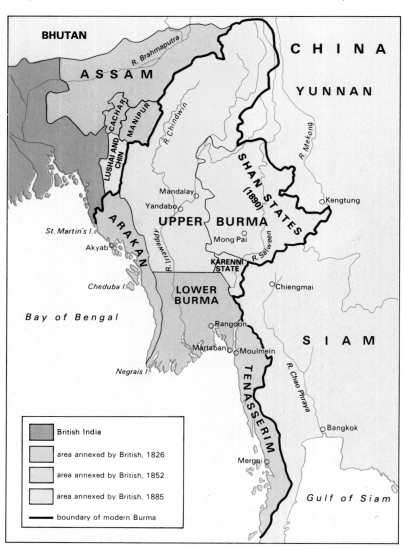

1/India in 1857 *(above)* The Mutiny began at Meerut on 10 May, spread swiftly to other parts of northern India, involving Hindus and Muslims. Sikh loyalty in the Punjab, and passivity in the Deccan and south, turned the tide in favour of the British.

2/The acquisition of Burma *(below)* Part of Britain's Indian dominion until 1935, Burma was annexed, along with her dependencies of Arakan, Manipur and Assam, as a result of three wars fought in 1826, 1852 and 1885. The Shan States were acquired in 1890.

BY 1805 the English East India Company's hegemony was an established fact in the Indian sub-continent. In another fifty years the Company emerged as the paramount power. The Third Anglo-Maratha War (1813-23) marked the end of the most serious threat to the Company's supremacy. With the conquest of Sind (1843) and the Sikh kingdom of the Punjab (1849), the empire became coterminous with the country's natural frontiers in the north-west, while in the north a war with Nepal (1814-16) had extended it to the Himalayan foothills. To the east, the British clashed with the Burmese empire and, by 1885, annexed all its territories including Assam. Within the empire, Dalhousie's Doctrine of Lapse (1848-56) led to the absorption of autonomous but dependent states like Oudh and several Maratha kingdoms into the directly administered territories.

The hostility of dispossessed rulers and agrarian classes who shared their discontent, as well as suspicions of intended assaults on India's traditional faiths – aroused by innovations including the prohibition of *suttee* and the introduction of cartridges greased with the fat of tabooed animals for the use of the Indian sepoys – found a violent outlet in the rebellion of 1857. Beginning as a mutiny of the Company's sepoys, it soon involved princes, landlords and peasants in northern and central India and was only crushed after fourteen months of bitter fighting. The government of India was now taken over by Britain (1858).

India soon acquired a pivotal position in the British imperial system and became involved in European rivalries, particularly after the Russian advance in central Asia (see page 230). The attempt to stabilise Afghanistan as a buffer state under friendly Amirs generated a series of wars fought with Indian armies and increasing India's debts. The last Anglo-Burmese War (1885) had as its background the growing rivalry with France in South-East Asia. Security of the Indian empire was also a major concern in Great Britain's involvement in the partition of Africa (see page 240). From Abyssinia to Hong Kong, the Indian army was freely deployed to protect British interests.

India was absorbed into the world economy as a colony of Great Britain. The Company's monopoly over the Indian market was abolished in 1833 through persistent pressure from British commercial and business interests, which also pressed for the development of modern transport in India to facilitate the import of British manufactures and export of raw materials. By 1853, India had lost its world-wide market for textiles and was importing the products of Lancashire. The Lancashire cotton famine, generated by the American Civil War, led to a cotton boom in the Deccan and thus to regional specialisation in cropping patterns in India. Railway development, financed by British capital, and the opening of the Suez Canal in 1869, contributed to a sevenfold increase in India's foreign trade between 1869 and 1929. Despite severe British competition, a range of modern industries developed, including textiles and iron and steel under Indian entrepreneurs; but neither the character of the economy nor traditional agriculture experienced any basic change. The gross national product increased very slowly, but with sustained population growth from 1921 onwards, per capita income declined. In short, India developed the typical characteristics of an under-developed economy while contributing substantially to the British balance of payments.

Administrative developments also contributed to India's absorption into a world order dominated by Europe. English civil servants inspired by Benthamite ideas abandoned earlier hesitations regarding interference with the indigenous social order. Tenurial systems guaranteeing property rights in land, a network of modern irrigation in parts of the country, prohibition of social customs abhorrent to humanistic ideas, and the development of a modern judiciary and civil service, were among the chief expressions of the new spirit. The net results of such policies are still a matter of debate. Probably the rural propertied classes benefited but often at the cost of the mass of producers. Periodic famines continued to take heavy tolls of life until 1899, while commercial agriculture flourished.

Professional groups, employees of the colonial administration, and landed proprietors created by the new tenurial systems constituted the new élite of colonial India. Western-style education – officially supported only from 1835 – is traceable to the material and cultural urges of these new social groups. Knowledge of the West generated social and literary movements influenced by western models but looking back, selectively, to India's past traditions. The Brahmo Samaj founded by Rammohan Roy (1819), aiming at restoring Hindu monotheism, and the frankly revivalist Arya Samaj, represent two extremes of this new consciousness.

The new awareness of an Indian identity, reinforced by the Anglo-Indians' overt racism, soon acquired a political dimension first expressed through local political associations and public agitation over specific issues. The Indian National Congress, the first all-India political organisation, was founded in 1885 with official blessing as a safety valve for the growing disaffection. Beginning as a tame annual gathering of affluent public men, it soon developed an extremist wing which began to question the alien's right to rule India. In 1905, the first mass agitation – anticipating Gandhi's non-violent

4 and 5/Population: social and economic change *(below)* Between 1881 and 1931 population rose from 253.9 million to 352.8 million, with a slight acceleration following the First World War. Over the same period the proportion of literates grew only from 35 to 80 per thousand; 101 people in every 10,000 were able to read and write in English. Nevertheless, the beginnings of a modern economy were emerging.

inhabitants per sq. km.

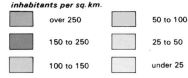

over 250	50 to 100
150 to 250	25 to 50
100 to 150	under 25

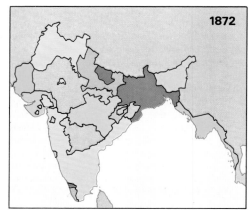

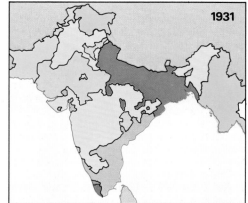

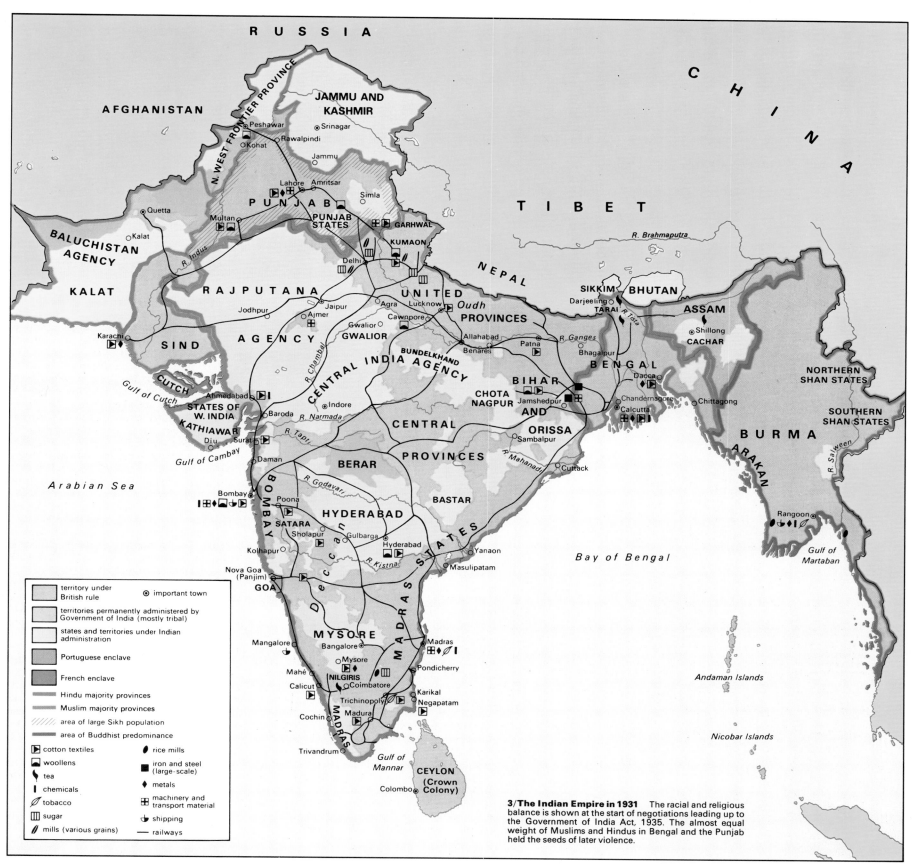

RUSSIA

AFGHANISTAN

JAMMU AND KASHMIR

N. WEST FRONTIER PROVINCE

Peshawar
Kohat
Rawalpindi
Srinagar
Jammu

CHINA

Quetta

BALUCHISTAN AGENCY

KALAT

Kalat

Multan
Lahore • Amritsar
Simla
PUNJAB
PUNJAB STATES
GARHWAL
KUMAON
Delhi

TIBET

R. Brahmaputra

SIKKIM BHUTAN
Darjeeling
TARAI R. Tista

ASSAM

Shillong
CACHAR

NORTHERN SHAN STATES

SOUTHERN SHAN STATES

RAJPUTANA AGENCY

Jodhpur
Jaipur
Ajmer

R. Indus

Karachi

SIND

CUTCH
Gulf of Cutch

STATES OF W. INDIA
KATHIAWAR
Ahmedabad
Diu Surat
Baroda
Daman
Gulf of Cambay

Arabian Sea

Bombay
Poona
BOMBAY
SATARA
Sholapur
Kolhapur

Nova Goa (Panjim)
GOA

Mangalore

Mahé
Calicut
Cochin

Trivandrum

Gulf of Mannar

CEYLON (Crown Colony)
Colombo

GWALIOR
Agra
Gwalior

UNITED
Lucknow Oudh
PROVINCES

Cawnpore
Allahabad
Benares

CENTRAL INDIA AGENCY
BUNDELKHAND
Indore
R. Narmada
R. Tapti
BERAR
R. Godavari

CENTRAL PROVINCES

HYDERABAD

Gulburga
Hyderabad

R. Kistna

BASTAR

NEPAL

Patna
R. Ganges
Bhagalpur

BIHAR AND
ORISSA
CHOTA NAGPUR
Jamshedpur
Sambalpur
R. Mahanadi
Cuttack

BENGAL
Dacca
Chandernagore
Calcutta

Bay of Bengal

Andaman Islands

BURMA
ARAKAN
R. Salween

Rangoon

Gulf of Martaban

DECCAN

MADRAS STATES

Bangalore
MYSORE
Mysore
NILGIRIS
Coimbatore
Trichinopoly
Madura
MADRAS

Madras

Pondicherry

Karikal
Negapatam

Masulipatam
Yanaon

Nicobar Islands

Legend:

- territory under British rule
- territories permanently administered by Government of India (mostly tribal)
- states and territories under Indian administration
- Portuguese enclave
- French enclave
- Hindu majority provinces
- Muslim majority provinces
- area of large Sikh population
- area of Buddhist predominance

⊙ important town

▶ cotton textiles
▬ woollens
↘ tea
| chemicals
∅ tobacco
▥ sugar
⫽ mills (various grains)
● rice mills
■ iron and steel (large-scale)
◆ metals
⊞ machinery and transport material
⚓ shipping
— railways

3/The Indian Empire in 1931 The racial and religious balance is shown at the start of negotiations leading up to the Government of India Act, 1935. The almost equal weight of Muslims and Hindus in Bengal and the Punjab held the seeds of later violence.

non-cooperation and propagating *swaraj* (self-rule) – was launched to resist the decision to partition the province of Bengal, while revolutionary groups adopted terror as the means to attain the same goal (see page 248). Political awareness and expectations were quickened by the First World War and a Royal Proclamation (1917) which declared the realisation of responsible government to be the goal of British rule in India, while the Montagu-Chelmsford reforms (1919) set up elective provincial councils. But repressive legislation enacted in 1919 authorising detention without trial seemed to conflict with this goal. Against it, Gandhi deployed his weapon of *satyagraha* or non-violent mass action, first developed in his fight against racist laws in South Africa. The official response included the massacre at Amritsar, which provoked intense racial bitterness. Indian Muslims were further incensed by the Allies' treatment of the Turkish sultan, their khalifa or spiritual head. The Non-Cooperation Movement (1920-22), aimed at redressing the 'Khalifat wrong' and winning *swaraj*, was the first all-Indian mass movement, involving sections of the peasantry as well. But the Hindu-Muslim unity achieved during the movement did not long

survive its suspension. Elections to the newly created provincial councils with their communal electorates further embittered relations.

While communal riots undermined national unity in the mid-twenties, a radical wing within Congress under the leadership of the young Jawaharlal Nehru and Subhas Bose pressed for renewed militant action against the Raj, and induced Congress to adopt complete independence as its goal (1929). When in 1930 Gandhi launched the Civil Disobedience Movement (1930-34) for the attainment of *Purna Swaraj* (complete independence), he himself and some 60,000 of his followers were arrested. Nevertheless the movement was a watershed. Suspended briefly in 1931 as a result of an agreement with Viceroy Irwin, it was resumed when Gandhi returned from the abortive constitutional discussions at the Round Table Conference in London. Negotiation had failed, and the policy of confrontation espoused by the younger leaders was reinforced.

The 1911 Durbar *(right)* King George V had his coronation as King Emperor of India at a Durbar, or assembly of notables, held in Delhi in 1911. A decision to annul the unpopular partition of Bengal was announced at this Durbar.

The development of Australia and New Zealand

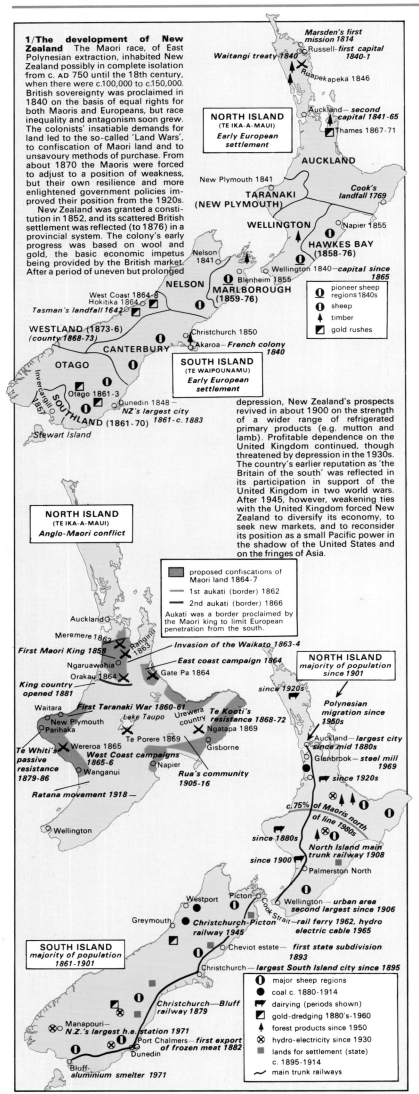

1/The development of New Zealand The Maori race, of East Polynesian extraction, inhabited New Zealand possibly in complete isolation from c. AD 750 until the 18th century, when there were c.100,000 to c.150,000. British sovereignty was proclaimed in 1840 on the basis of equal rights for both Maoris and Europeans, but race inequality and antagonism soon grew. The colonists' insatiable demands for land led to the so-called 'Land Wars', to confiscation of Maori land and to unsavoury methods of purchase. From about 1870 the Maoris were forced to adjust to a position of weakness, but their own resilience and more enlightened government policies improved their position from the 1920s.

New Zealand was granted a constitution in 1852, and its scattered British settlement was reflected (to 1876) in a provincial system. The colony's early progress was based on wool and gold, the basic economic impetus being provided by the British market. After a period of uneven but prolonged depression, New Zealand's prospects revived in about 1900 on the strength of a wider range of refrigerated primary products (e.g. mutton and lamb). Profitable dependence on the United Kingdom continued, though threatened by depression in the 1930s. The country's earlier reputation as 'the Britain of the south' was reflected in its participation in support of the United Kingdom in two world wars. After 1945, however, weakening ties with the United Kingdom forced New Zealand to diversify its economy, to seek new markets, and to reconsider its position as a small Pacific power in the shadow of the United States and on the fringes of Asia.

NORTH ISLAND (TE IKA-A-MAUI) Early European settlement

Marsden's first mission 1814
Russell- first capital 1840-1
Waitangi treaty 1840
Ruapekapeka 1846
Auckland – second capital 1841-65
Thames 1867-71
AUCKLAND
New Plymouth 1841
Cook's landfall 1769
TARANAKI (NEW PLYMOUTH)
WELLINGTON
Napier 1855
HAWKES BAY (1858-76)
Nelson 1841
Wellington 1840 –capital since 1865
Blenheim 1855
NELSON
MARLBOROUGH (1859-76)
West Coast 1864-8
Hokitika 1864
Tasman's landfall 1642
WESTLAND (1873-6) (county 1868-73)
Christchurch 1850
Akaroa – French colony 1840
CANTERBURY
SOUTH ISLAND (TE WAIPOUNAMU) Early European settlement
OTAGO
Invercargill 1857
Otago 1861-3
Dunedin 1848 – NZ's largest city 1861-c.1883
SOUTHLAND (1861-70)
Stewart Island

- ◑ pioneer sheep regions 1840s
- ● sheep
- ▲ timber
- ◪ gold rushes

NORTH ISLAND (TE IKA-A-MAUI) Anglo-Maori conflict

proposed confiscations of Maori land 1864-7
— 1st aukati (border) 1862
— 2nd aukati (border) 1866
Aukati was a border proclaimed by the Maori king to limit European penetration from the south.

Auckland
Meremere 1863
First Maori King 1858
Rangiriri 1863
Invasion of the Waikato 1863-4
Ngaruawahia
East coast campaign 1864
Orakau 1864
Gate Pa 1864
King country opened 1881
Waitara
First Taranaki War 1860-61
New Plymouth
Parihaka
Lake Taupo
Urewera country
Te Kooti's resistance 1868-72
Ngatapa 1869
Te Porere 1869
Te Whiti's passive resistance 1879-86
Wereroa 1865
West Coast campaigns 1865-6
Gisborne
Wanganui
Napier
Rua's community 1905-16
Ratana movement 1918 –
Wellington

NORTH ISLAND majority of population since 1901

since 1920s
Polynesian migration since 1950s
Auckland – largest city since mid 1880s
Glenbrook – steel mill 1969
since 1920s
c. 75% of Maoris north of line 1980s
since 1880s
North Island main trunk railway 1908
since 1900
Palmerston North

Westport
Picton
Wellington – urban area second largest since 1906
Cook Strait –rail ferry 1962, hydro electric cable 1965
Greymouth
Christchurch-Picton railway 1945
Cheviot estate – first state subdivision 1893
Christchurch – largest South Island city since 1895

SOUTH ISLAND majority of population 1861-1901

- ◑ major sheep regions
- ● coal c. 1880-1914
- ⛏ dairying (periods shown)
- ◪ gold-dredging 1880's-1960
- ▲ forest products since 1950
- ⊗ hydro-electricity since 1930
- ■ lands for settlement (state) c. 1895-1914
- ∿ main trunk railways

Christchurch—Bluff railway 1879
Manapouri – N.Z.'s largest h.e. station 1971
Port Chalmers – first export of frozen meat 1882
Dunedin
Bluff – aluminium smelter 1971

BEFORE European discovery in the seventeenth century there was neither contact nor similarity between Australia and New Zealand, and their development since white settlement has been distinct, if parallel. The Maoris of New Zealand shared the civilisation of their island neighbours (see map 1). The Aboriginal inhabitants of Australia retained only tenuous contact with Asia (from which they had originally migrated) after the rising of the seas made their continent an island. Dispersed in a hot, dry habitat, they hunted and gathered plants but did not herd, cultivate or build settlements, and identified their destinies with the natural features of the land they wandered. They remained free from European interference until late in the period of European expansion.

Winds and currents guarded their isolation. Spaniards rounding the Horn sailed north-west into the Pacific and did not beat against the prevailing westerlies, while the Portuguese turned towards India from the Cape of Good Hope. The Portuguese may have discovered Australia before 1542, as the Dutch did after 1600 when they exploited the westerlies for a fast route to the East Indies. In 1642-3 Tasman discovered Van Diemen's Land (later Tasmania) and New Zealand, but otherwise the Dutch encountered only the inhospitable north and west coasts.

Scientific curiosity was a motive in Cook's Pacific exploration, and his discovery in 1770 of Australia's more fertile eastern coast, with its extraordinary animals and plants, excited European scientists and artists more than traders or colonists. He claimed the coast for Britain, and strategy and trade were at least subordinate motives when George III's government decided in 1786 to found a penal colony in New South Wales. Sydney Cove was settled in 1788, and the need for subsidiary jails, and outposts against the French, led to further settlements at Norfolk Island (1788), Newcastle (1801), Hobart (1804) and Brisbane (1824). The naval officers who charted the southern coasts were followed by a marauding tribe of whalers and sealers. In 1829 Britain annexed the whole continent.

The small settlement at Sydney Cove was hemmed by mountains, and free settlers were attracted only when access to the inland plains was won after 1813. Squatters followed the explorers, settling large areas of south-eastern Australia, while private ventures at Perth (1829), Melbourne (1835), and Adelaide (1836) established bridgeheads for settlement which became the capitals of the separate colonies of Western Australia, Victoria, and South Australia which, with Tasmania, Queensland and the remnant of New South Wales gained responsible government between 1855 and 1890. Despite inter-colonial rivalry, regional differences were never great enough to destroy a sense of common destiny, and the federation of the colonies into the Commonwealth of Australia in 1901 had a logic which only the far west continued intermittently to deny.

Unlike New Zealand, where the wars between European and Maori led to co-existence, if not equality, of old inhabitant and new, European settlement in Australia destroyed Aboriginal civilisation. The tribes fell before European diseases and weapons, and their lands were expropriated by European law. Aboriginal institutions survived only in the centre and north, damaged even there. The settler society which seized and transformed the land was predominantly British in origin, though spiced by having a different admixture of Irish and Scots, and a higher proportion of dissidents and outlaws, than at home. These factors made for a remarkable social homogeneity. Its politics have been rancorous in tone but democratic in process.

The Australian colonies, like New Zealand, had to seek self-sufficiency through trade. Farming was commercial, with little subsistence agriculture. The growing world market for wool caused the inland grasslands to be settled before the richer forested eastern coastlands, which awaited the development of dairying and sugar cultivation in Queensland. Wheat cultivation expanded after the 1860s and the development of the frozen meat trade after 1880 gave impetus to meat production. But settlement in dry areas proved hazardous and intermittent, and although most of Australia was explored and much nominally settled by 1890, effective exploitation was restricted to areas of adequate rainfall. Even irrigation scarcely succeeded outside the river systems of the south-east.

The commercial nature of Australia's primary industry strengthened the dominance of the major ports over the inland cities, and the transport systems consolidated their power after the railway supplanted the bullock dray and the river boat. Spectacular mineral discoveries, especially of gold in the 1850s and 1880s, brought new wealth and a more polyglot immigration, but although the gold rushes at first took population inland, the eventual beneficiaries in wealth and people were the cities, especially Melbourne and Sydney. By 1890 some two-thirds of Australians lived in urban areas. Nevertheless isolation persisted; Melbourne, when Australia's largest city, faced neither Asia nor the Pacific as its true neighbours, but London and Liverpool. Isolation bred concern about national identity and exaggerated fears of foreign threats. Free (until 1942) from war at home, Australians met its realities only when they crossed the world to fight in other peoples' battles.

This predominantly British society persisted until the middle of the twentieth century, dependent on primary exports despite the growth of secondary industry, particularly in the decades following the beginning of steel production in 1908. The Second World War, and Australia's appeal to the United States rather than Britain for protection against the Japanese, signalled major changes in her situation and policies. Post-war governments fostered non-British immigration from Europe, and gradually abandoned the White Australia Policy to admit an increasing number of Asians. Sharing the economic growth of the West, Australia expanded her secondary and service industries behind tariff barriers, sustained externally by buoyant agricultural exports, a large new export trade in iron ore and coal to Japan, and local discoveries of oil and gas. Her new dependence on Pacific trading partners was confirmed after Britain joined the European Economic Community in 1973. The world recession of the Seventies hit Australia later and perhaps less than most other countries, but the combination of natural resources, basic prosperity and political stability brought gradual revival, so that the nation approached its bicentenary celebrations due in 1988 in a new buoyant mood of confidence.

5/Settlement and Development (right) After 1820 settlement spread inland from scattered coastal towns, but vast arid areas of the continent remained sparsely populated, and the total population did not reach 5 million until 1918. Exports of wool, wheat and minerals enabled Australians to enjoy the highest per capita income in the world by 1900, a position not maintained despite recent extensive mineral discoveries. Most Australians depend on urban employment; in 1980, 70 per cent of the population of 14.7 million lived in 12 cities, including 3.2 million in Sydney and 2.8 million in Melbourne. Canberra, federal capital since 1927 and largest inland city, had a population of 245,500 in 1980.

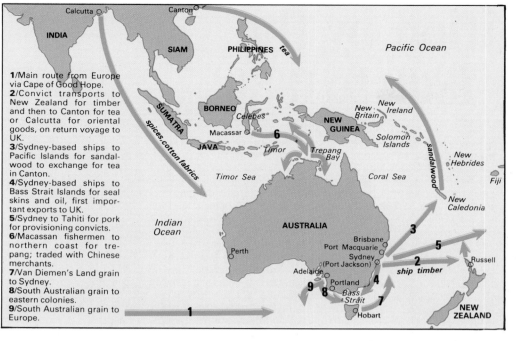

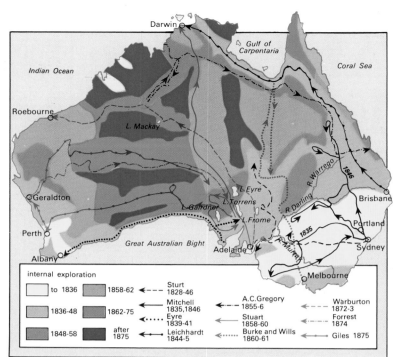

1/Main route from Europe via Cape of Good Hope.
2/Convict transports to New Zealand for timber and then to Canton for tea or Calcutta for oriental goods, on return voyage to UK.
3/Sydney-based ships to Pacific Islands for sandalwood to exchange for tea in Canton.
4/Sydney-based ships to Bass Strait Islands for seal skins and oil, first important exports to UK.
5/Sydney to Tahiti for pork for provisioning convicts.
6/Macassan fishermen to northern coast for trepang; traded with Chinese merchants.
7/Van Diemen's Land grain to Sydney.
8/South Australian grain to eastern colonies.
9/South Australian grain to Europe.

internal exploration

to 1836	1858-62	←--- Sturt 1828-46
1836-48	1862-75	←--- Mitchell 1835,1846
1848-58	after 1875	←--- Eyre 1839-41
		←····· Leichhardt 1844-5

A.C.Gregory 1855-6
Stuart 1858-60
Burke and Wills 1860-61
Warburton 1872-3
Forrest 1874
Giles 1875

4/**Early Trade** (above) Problems of establishing agriculture in an alien environment hampered the development of the first settlement, which had to rely on imported food supplies. The settlers traded sealskins, seal oil and sandalwood to pay for imports, but it was only when wool exports developed in the 1820s that the Australian colonies ceased to drain the British treasury.

2/**The Discovery of Australia** (right) Although the north-west and south coasts were discovered in the 17th century and the east coast in the 18th, detailed charting by Matthew Flinders and Philip Parker King came in the early 19th century.

3/**Exploration** (above) Because the navigators failed to discover river mouths, inland explorers searched first for an inland sea, then made attempts to reach the centre of the continent and to cross it from south to north, and finally traversed the western part between the coast and the Overland Telegraph Line (built 1870-72, see map 5).

Westward navigation by sail impeded by winds and current

Dutch discoveries to 1644
coasts charted by 1802

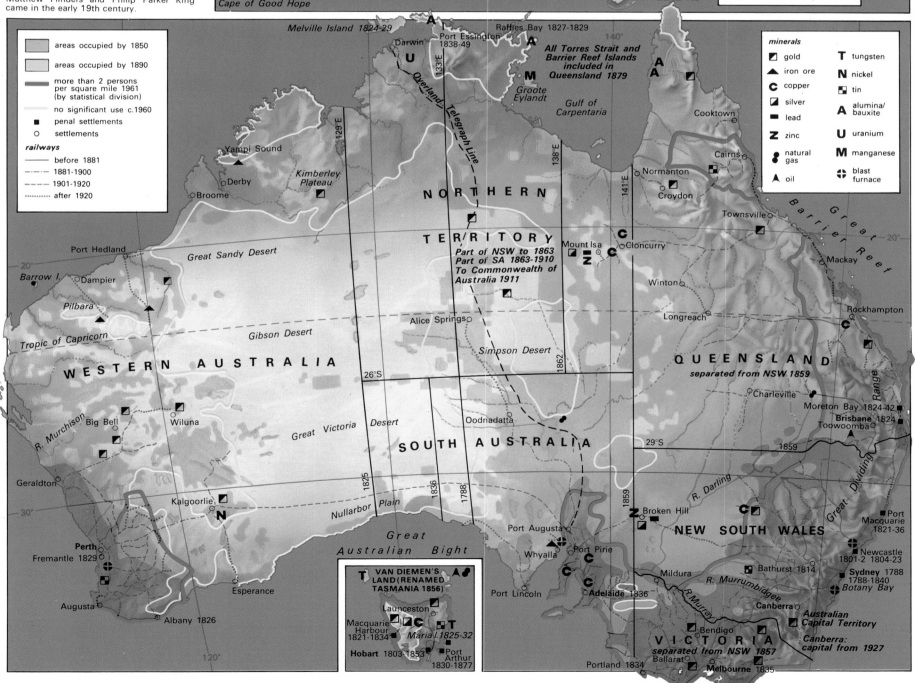

areas occupied by 1850
areas occupied by 1890
more than 2 persons per square mile 1961 (by statistical division)
no significant use c.1960
■ penal settlements
○ settlements

railways
before 1881
1881-1900
1901-1920
after 1920

minerals

	gold		T	tungsten
▲	iron ore		N	nickel
C	copper		⊟	tin
	silver		A	alumina/bauxite
▬	lead		U	uranium
Z	zinc		M	manganese
☗	natural gas		⊕	blast furnace
▲	oil			

Melville Island 1824-29
Raffles Bay 1827-1829
Port Essington 1838-49
All Torres Strait and Barrier Reef Islands included in Queensland 1879
Darwin
Groote Eylandt
Gulf of Carpentaria
Overland Telegraph Line

NORTHERN TERRITORY
Part of NSW to 1863
Part of SA 1863-1910
To Commonwealth of Australia 1911

Cooktown
Cairns
Normanton
Croydon
Townsville
Mount Isa
Cloncurry
Winton
Great Barrier Reef

Yampi Sound
Kimberley Plateau
Derby
Broome

Port Hedland
Great Sandy Desert
Barrow I.
Dampier
Pilbara
Tropic of Capricorn
Gibson Desert

Alice Springs
Simpson Desert
Longreach
Mackay

WESTERN AUSTRALIA
Great Victoria Desert

Oodnadatta
QUEENSLAND separated from NSW 1859
Rockhampton
Charleville

Moreton Bay 1824-42
Brisbane 1824
Toowoomba

R. Murchison
Big Bell
Wiluna

SOUTH AUSTRALIA

Geraldton
Kalgoorlie
Nullarbor Plain
Great Australian Bight

Broken Hill
NEW SOUTH WALES
R. Darling
Port Macquarie 1821-36

Perth
Fremantle 1829
Esperance
Augusta
Albany 1826

Port Augusta
Whyalla
Port Pirie
Port Lincoln
Adelaide 1836

Mildura
R. Murrumbidgee
Newcastle 1801-2 1804-23
Bathurst 1814
Sydney 1788 1788-1840
Botany Bay
Canberra
Australian Capital Territory

VAN DIEMEN'S LAND (RENAMED TASMANIA 1856)
Launceston
Macquarie Harbour 1821-1834
Maria I. 1825-32
Hobart 1803-1853
Port Arthur 1830-1877

Portland 1834
VICTORIA separated from NSW 1857
Bendigo
Ballarat
Melbourne 1835

Canberra: capital from 1927

Bass Strait

Africa before partition by the European powers 1800 to 1880

DURING the eighty years prior to the European partition of the continent, much of west Africa was dominated by a Muslim religious revival, which took the form of holy wars (jihads) waged mainly against backsliding Muslim (or partly Muslimised) communities. The great warriors of the jihad were the Fulani cattle-keepers, widely scattered among the agricultural communities of the Sudanic region. Though the Fulani were largely pagan, a section of them became Muslims, fervent in the faith of the newly converted. In the 18th century they set up theocracies in the far west – Futa Toro and Futa Jallon – and at Masina, in the former Mali and Songhay empires on the upper Niger. It was the Muslim Fulani in Hausaland, however, who set up the largest Muslim state of the 19th century. In 1804 a Fulani religious leader, Uthman dan Fodio, was proclaimed Commander of the Faithful (Amir al-Mu'minin), and declared a jihad against the infidel. Within a few years his formidable army of horsemen (many of them drawn from the pagan Fulani) conquered all the Hausa city states, and struck east into Adamawa and south-west into Nupe and Yorubaland. Uthman dan Fodio's son became the Sultan of Sokoto, an empire still in existence when the British invaded Nigeria in the 1890s.

An even fiercer jihad was conducted by another holy man, al-Hajj Umar from Futa Jallon, whence he conquered the Bambara kingdoms and Masina, and was only prevented from reaching the Atlantic by the French on the Senegal river. In the 1870s and 1880s a Mandingo Muslim leader, Samori, carved out another empire south of the Niger valley; he was finally defeated by the French only in 1898.

South of the area of the jihads, African states, among which Ashanti and Dahomey were outstanding, responded to the change in the trading requirements of the Europeans on the coast, from slaves to products such as palm oil and groundnuts, and became more wealthy and powerful. Other states, in modern southern Nigeria, such as Oyo and Benin, tended to

disintegrate – partly because this was a region where the economic changeover was uneven, illegal slaving continuing there until the 1870s. By and large, much of west Africa experienced increasing instability and violence during the first three-quarters of the century.

Another huge area where new patterns of trading and political developments were disruptive and violent was central and East Africa. The western world evinced an almost insatiable appetite for ivory in the 19th century (middle class males playing billiards and females playing the piano), and the hunting of elephants and trading of their tusks became a major economic activity in much of this part of the continent. Many states and peoples grew rich on the proceeds of this activity – the Chokwe and King Msiri in central Africa, for instance, and Buganda and the Nyamwezi in East Africa. In central Africa the foreign traders were often Portuguese, from their settlements in Angola and Mozambique; in East Africa, Swahili-Arabs from Zanzibar, the island state of the Omani Sultan, made contact with the states in the interior, in many instances bringing their Muslim religion with them. Some peoples – particularly around Lakes Nyasa and Tanganyika – suffered severely from the Arab slave trade, which often went hand in hand with that in ivory.

In north-east Africa the territorial expansion of Egypt, ruled after Napoleon's invasion at the beginning of the century by Mohammed Ali, nominally viceroy of the Ottoman Sultan, brought a foretaste of the later European partition. Mohammed Ali's armies conquered the northern Nilotic Sudan, founding Khartoum as the capital of the province in 1830. Mohammed Ali had refused to sanction the Suez Canal, but after his death in 1849 construction went ahead. His grandson, the Khedive Ismail, consolidated the Egyptian hold over much of the littoral of the Red Sea and Horn of Africa. He also pushed south up the Nile towards the Great Lakes in an attempt to create a great African empire. Partly in response to this Egyptian activity, there was a

revival of Ethiopian political power under the emperors Theodorus and Johannes.

Two areas of Africa were being colonised by European powers before the partition. In 1830 the French invaded Algeria (nominally part of the Ottoman Empire), and in the course of a long and bitter struggle, conquered and settled the territory. At the other end of the continent, the British had taken over the Cape from the Dutch during the Napoleonic Wars. Coincidentally in time, but unrelated in cause, there was a major political and demographic revolution among the peoples of the interior of southern Africa, initiated by the formation of the Zulu kingdom by Shaka in 1818. Large numbers of Nguni and Sotho-speaking peoples moved away from the troubled area (the period is known as the Mfecane, or the Time of Troubles), the Ndebele (Matabele) into present-day Zimbabwe, the Nguni as far north as Zambia, Malawi and Tanzania, where their presence created even more disruption, and the Sotho (Kololo) into Barotseland (Zambia). No sooner had southern Africa begun to settle down after the Mfecane than another event disrupted the region. This was the Great Trek of Dutch or Afrikaner colonists, known as Boers (farmers) who, dissatisfied with British rule, left the Cape colony after 1836 and marched north to found settlements which became the republics of the Orange Free State and Transvaal. By 1880 whites had appropriated the greater part of the habitable land of South Africa.

MAURITANIA

French advance up Sénégal R. Sénégal river 1860-80

St Louis · Kayes
FUTA TORO
Dakar · BONDU
KAARTA
Bathurst · FUTA JALLON

Freetown
SIERRA LEONE founded as a colony for liberated slaves c.1800 (British colony 1808)
LIBERIA

Liberia established by former Negro slaves from America 1820s

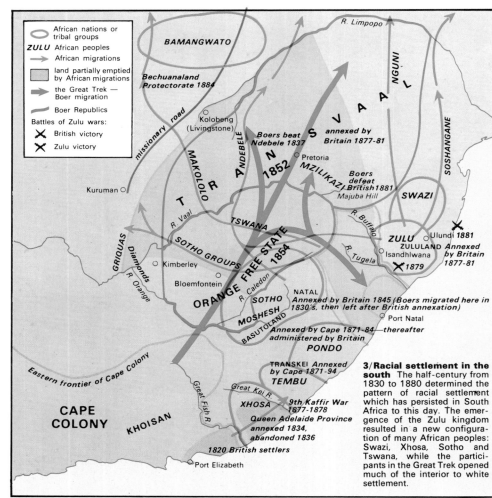

African nations or tribal groups
ZULU African peoples
→ African migrations
land partially emptied by African migrations
the Great Trek — Boer migration
Boer Republics
Battles of Zulu wars:
✗ British victory
✗ Zulu victory

R. Limpopo
BAMANGWATO
Bechuanaland Protectorate 1884
missionary road
Kolobeng (Livingstone)
MAKOLOLO
Kuruman
ANDEBELE
TRANSVAAL
MZILIKAZI 1852
Pretoria
Boers beat Ndebele 1837
annexed by Britain 1877-81
Boers defeat British 1881 Majuba Hill
SWAZI
NGUNI
SOSHANGANE
R. Vaal
TSWANA
SOTHO GROUPS
ORANGE FREE STATE 1854
R. Buffalo
ZULU ZULULAND Annexed by Britain 1877-81
Ulundi 1881
Isandhlwana ✗ 1879
R. Tugela
GRIQUAS
Diamonds R. Orange
Kimberley
Bloemfontein
R. Caledon
NATAL Annexed by Britain 1845 (Boers migrated here in 1830's, then left after British annexation)
SOTHO
MOSHESH
BASUTOLAND
Annexed by Cape 1871-84 — thereafter administered by Britain
PONDO
Port Natal
Eastern frontier of Cape Colony
Great Kei R.
TRANSKEI Annexed by Cape 1871-94
TEMBU
Great Fish R.
XHOSA
9th Kaffir War 1877-1878
Queen Adelaide Province annexed 1834, abandoned 1836
1820 British settlers
CAPE COLONY
KHOISAN
Port Elizabeth

3/Racial settlement in the south The half-century from 1830 to 1880 determined the pattern of racial settlement which has persisted in South Africa to this day. The emergence of the Zulu kingdom resulted in a new configuration of many African peoples: Swazi, Xhosa, Sotho and Tswana, while the participants in the Great Trek opened much of the interior to white settlement.

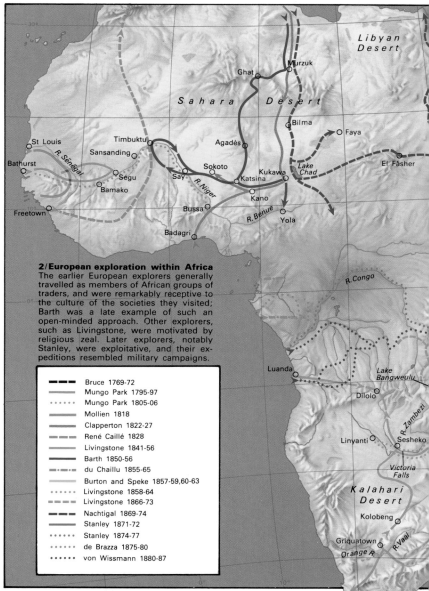

Libyan Desert
Murzuk
Ghat
Sahara Desert
Bilma
St Louis
Timbuktu
Agadès
Faya
R. Senegal
Sansanding
Bathurst
Ségu
Say
Sokoto
Katsina
Kukawa
Lake Chad
El Fàsher
Bamako
R. Niger
Kano
Freetown
Bussa
R. Benue
Yola
Badagri
R. Congo
Luanda
Lake Bangweulu
Dilolo
R. Zambezi
Linyanti
Sesheko
Victoria Falls
Kalahari Desert
Kolobeng
Griquatown
Orange R.
R. Vaal

2/European exploration within Africa The earlier European explorers generally travelled as members of African groups of traders, and were remarkably receptive to the culture of the societies they visited; Barth was a late example of such an open-minded approach. Other explorers, such as Livingstone, were motivated by religious zeal. Later explorers, notably Stanley, were exploitative, and their expeditions resembled military campaigns.

Bruce 1769-72
Mungo Park 1795-97
Mungo Park 1805-06
Mollien 1818
Clapperton 1822-27
René Caillé 1828
Livingstone 1841-56
Barth 1850-56
du Chaillu 1855-65
Burton and Speke 1857-59,60-63
Livingstone 1858-64
Livingstone 1866-73
Nachtigal 1869-74
Stanley 1871-72
Stanley 1874-77
de Brazza 1875-80
von Wissmann 1880-87

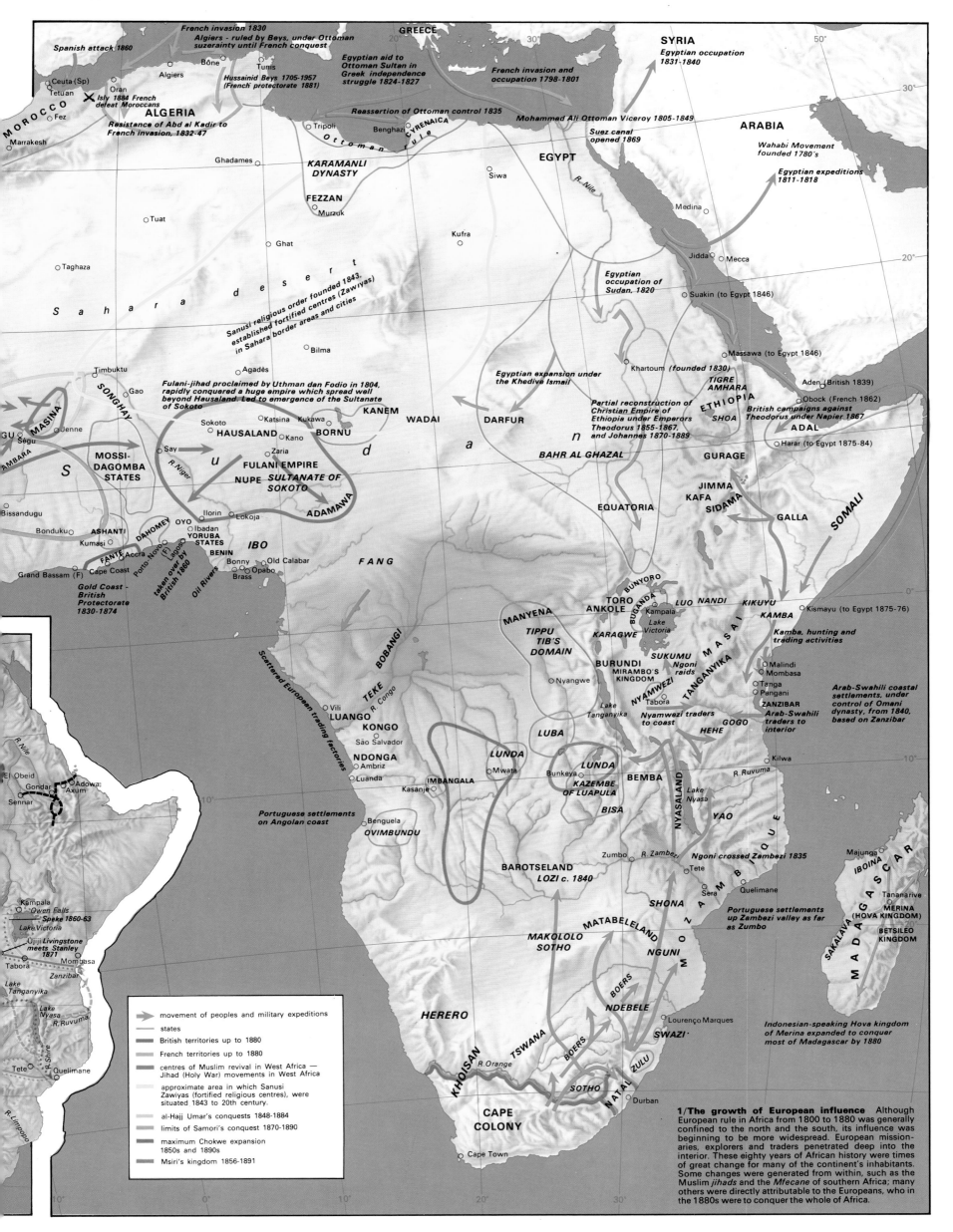

GREECE

SYRIA
Egyptian occupation 1831-1840

French invasion 1830
Algiers - ruled by Beys, under Ottoman suzerainty until French conquest

Spanish attack 1860

Bône
Tunis
Algiers
Ceuta (Sp)
Tetuán

Hussainid Beys 1705-1957 (French protectorate 1881)

Egyptian aid to Ottoman Sultan in Greek independence struggle 1824-1827

French invasion and occupation 1798-1801

ARABIA

Oran
Isly 1884 French defeat Moroccans

ALGERIA
Resistance of Abd al Kadir to French invasion, 1832-47

Reassertion of Ottoman control 1835

Mohammed Ali Ottoman Viceroy 1805-1849

Wahabi Movement founded 1780's

Fez
Marrakesh

Tripoli
Benghazi
CYRENAICA

Ott om an rule

EGYPT

Suez canal opened 1869

Egyptian expeditions 1811-1818

MOROCCO

Ghadames

KARAMANLI DYNASTY

Siwa

R. Nile

Medina
Jidda
Mecca

Taghaza

FEZZAN
Murzuk

Kufra

Egyptian occupation of Sudan, 1820

Suakin (to Egypt 1846)

Tuat

Ghat

S a h a r a   d e s e r t

Bilma
Agadès

Sanusi religious order founded 1843, established fortified centres (Zawiyas) in Sahara border areas and cities

Massawa (to Egypt 1846)

Aden (British 1839)

Timbuktu
Gao

SONGHAY
MASINA

Fulani-jihad proclaimed by Uthman dan Fodio in 1804, rapidly conquered a huge empire which spread well beyond Hausaland. Led to emergence of the Sultanate of Sokoto

KANEM
WADAI

KARTHOUM (founded 1830)

Egyptian expansion under the Khedive Ismail

TIGRE
AMHARA

Obock (French 1862)

Jenne
Ségu

Sokoto
Katsina
Kukawa
BORNU

DARFUR

Partial reconstruction of Christian Empire of Ethiopia under Emperors Theodorus 1855-1867, and Johannes 1870-1889

ETHIOPIA
SHOA

British campaigns against Theodorus under Napier 1867

ADAL

MOSSI-DAGOMBA STATES

Say
R. Niger
HAUSALAND
Kano
Zaria

FULANI EMPIRE
NUPE

SULTANATE OF SOKOTO

BAHR AL GHAZAL

GURAGE

Harar (to Egypt 1875-84)

Bissandugu

Ilorin
Lokoja
ADAMAWA

JIMMA
KAFA
SIDAMA

Bonduku
ASHANTI

Kumasi
FANTE
DAHOMEY
OYO
Ibadan
YORUBA STATES
BENIN

Accra
Porto-Novo (F)
Lagos
taken over by British 1860

IBO

EQUATORIA

GALLA

SOMALI

Grand Bassam (F)
Cape Coast

Bonny
Old Calabar
Opabo
Brass
Oil Rivers

Gold Coast - British Protectorate 1830-1874

FANG

Kismayu (to Egypt 1875-76)

Scattered European trading factories

BUNYORO
TORO
ANKOLE
BUGANDA
LUO NANDI
KIKUYU
KAMBA

MANYEMA

Kampala
Lake Victoria

Kamba, hunting and trading activities

TIPPU TIB'S DOMAIN

KARAGWE

Malindi
Mombasa

BOBANGI
TEKE

Vili
LUANGO
R. Congo

BURUNDI
MIRAMBO'S KINGDOM
SUKUMU
NYAMWEZI
Tabora
TANGANYIKA
MASAI

Ngoni raids

Tanga
Pangani

ZANZIBAR
Arab-Swahili traders to interior

GOGO
HEHE

Arab-Swahili coastal settlements, under control of Omani dynasty, from 1840, based on Zanzibar

KONGO
São Salvador

Nyangwe

Lake Tanganyika

Nyamwezi traders to coast

LUBA

NDONGA
Ambriz
Luanda

LUNDA

Mwata

LUNDA

Bunkeya
KAZEMBE OF LUAPULA

BEMBA

Kilwa

R. Ruvuma

IMBANGALA
Kasanje

BISA

NYASALAND

YAO

Lake Nyasa

MOZAMBIQUE

Portuguese settlements on Angolan coast

Benguela

OVIMBUNDU

BAROTSELAND
LOZI c. 1840

Zumbo
R. Zambezi
Ngoni crossed Zambezi 1835

Tete
Sena
Quelimane

Majunga
IBOINA

Portuguese settlements up Zambezi valley as far as Zumbo

SHONA

MADAGASCAR
MERINA (HOVA KINGDOM)

MATABELELAND

MAKOLOLO
SOTHO

NGUNI

Lourenço Marques

SAKALAVA
BETSILEO KINGDOM

HERERO

Indonesian-speaking Hova kingdom of Merina expanded to conquer most of Madagascar by 1880

KHOISAN
TSWANA
R. Orange

BOERS
NDEBELE

SWAZI

BOERS
ZULU
NATAL

SOTHO

Durban

CAPE COLONY

Cape Town

1/The growth of European influence Although European rule in Africa from 1800 to 1880 was generally confined to the north and the south, its influence was beginning to be more widespread. European missionaries, explorers and traders penetrated deep into the interior. These eighty years of African history were times of great change for many of the continent's inhabitants. Some changes were generated from within, such as the Muslim *jihads* and the *Mfecane* of southern Africa; many others were directly attributable to the Europeans, who in the 1880s were to conquer the whole of Africa.

(Inset map, lower left)

El Obeid
Gondar
Axum
Adowa
Sennar

Kampala
Owen Falls
Speke 1860-63
Lake Victoria
Ujiji Livingstone meets Stanley 1871

R. Nile

Tabora
Mombasa
Zanzibar

Lake Tanganyika

Lake Nyasa
R. Ruvuma

Tete
R. Shire
Quelimane

R. Limpopo

Legend:

→ movement of peoples and military expeditions

— states

▬ British territories up to 1880

▬ French territories up to 1880

▬ centres of Muslim revival in West Africa — Jihad (Holy War) movements in West Africa

▬ approximate area in which Sanusi Zawiyas (fortified religious centres), were situated 1843 to 20th century

▬ al-Hajj Umar's conquests 1848-1884

▬ limits of Samori's conquest 1870-1890

▬ maximum Chokwe expansion 1850s and 1890s

▬ Msiri's kingdom 1856-1891

The partition of Africa 1880 to 1913

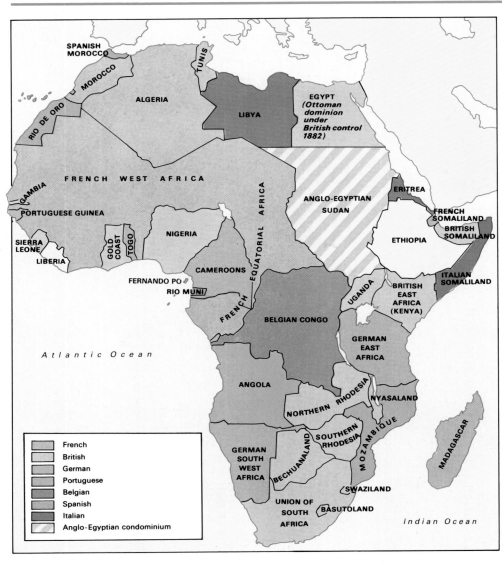

2/Alien rule in Africa in 1913 *(above)* Once the partition of Africa among the European powers got under way, the whole continent was carved up in a remarkably short period: in thirty years the scramble was complete.

AFRICA, as late as 1879, remained almost unknown territory to the European powers; an intricate kaleidoscope of tribal kingdoms and traditional hunting grounds. Before 1880 the areas of Africa under direct European control were few. In the north, the French had been engaged in conquering Algeria since the 1830s. There were small French and British colonies in West Africa – Senegal, Sierra Leone, the Gold Coast, Lagos and Gabon – and old-established but moribund Portuguese settlements in Angola and up the Zambezi valley in Mozambique; but only in the south, where the British colonists of the Cape were already locked in rivalry with the Afrikaners of the Transvaal and the Orange Free State, was penetration at all deep. Elsewhere, apart from French Algeria and the debt-ridden regimes of Egypt and Tunis, occupation and even influence were restricted to a handful of trading posts, military stations and the offshore islands of Madagascar and Zanzibar. Yet within two decades the entire continent had been seized, annexed, fought over and partitioned. Of the forty political units into which it had been divided – often with little more than a ruler and pencil, wielded in London, Paris or Berlin – direct European control extended to thirty-six. Only Ethiopia, which had fought off the Italians, and Liberia, with its financial links to the United States, claimed real independence. France, the largest beneficiary, controlled nearly 4 million out of Africa's 11.7 million square miles.

Many ingredients contributed to this imperialistic explosion. The progress of industrialisation in Europe created a demand for new markets and also set up new social tensions, for which some politicians at least (e.g. Joseph Chamberlain) saw colonisation as an outlet. The rivalries between the European states were transferred to the extra-European world, and to Africa in particular. This meant that often trivial incidents between competing European traders in Africa achieved the status of major international crises, and that initiatives undertaken locally by European agents, occurring in rapid succession, set in motion the undignified scramble for possession of the continent. To a large extent the partition of Africa resulted from the backing given by the metropolitan countries to the unco-ordinated activities of their men on the spot, who decided that the best way out of minor confrontations, either with African states or with other Europeans, was to take a little more African territory under their control.

In West Africa, it was mainly the French who took these local initiatives. The most important were the exploits of the French army attempting to advance up the Senegal river towards the upper Niger. French officers, denied the chance of avenging the defeat of 1870, sought glory in the dusty savannahs south of the Sahara (the Sudan region). This brought them into conflict with the British in Gambia and Sierra Leone, and with African states such as the empires of Samory and al-Hajj Umar (see page 238). Along the West African coast there was intense Anglo-French rivalry in the regions of the Gold Coast, Togo, Dahomey and Yorubaland. French attitudes towards Great Britain hardened after the unilateral British invasion and occupation of Egypt in 1882, but it was the intervention of other European powers that exploded these squabbles all over the continent.

After the explorer Stanley's epic journey down the Congo river in 1877, the ambitious King Leopold of the Belgians took him into his personal service. In 1879 Stanley returned to the lower Congo and laid the foundations of the huge private domain the king carved out for himself in the Congo basin. Stanley's activities stimulated others in the same area. The Italian de Brazza concluded some vital treaties with African chiefs, and on his return to Europe, France readily took up his claims. The action of France brought an immediate British and Portuguese response, though this came to nothing because of pressure exercised by Bismarck. Bismarck bought off French thoughts of revenge over the loss of Alsace by allowing France a free hand in Africa: this he was able to do by blackmailing Great Britain over Egypt. Then Germany itself, under Bismarck, entered the race by grabbing territory in four widely separated regions: in Togoland, the Cameroons, South-West Africa and East Africa. French and German initiatives in West Africa led Great Britain to intervene actively, especially in securing the lands which became Nigeria. The far interior was left to the French, who by 1900 had swept right across the western Sudan region.

The German presence in southern Africa revived Portuguese ambitions, and the threat of Afrikaner expansion led to British thrusts into the interior of central Africa, into what later became Rhodesia, Zambia and Malawi. The initiative for these drives came largely from the Cape industrialist and politician Cecil Rhodes. Likewise, German colonisation in East Africa (Tanganyika) produced its British counterpart when the Prime Minister, Lord Salisbury, laid claim to the region of the Great Lakes (Uganda) and the intervening territory down to the coast, which later became Kenya. The British were also drawn from their position in Egypt to intervene in the affairs of the Sudan, which had rebelled against Egypt in 1881 under the Islamic religious leader, the Mahdi. At the same time, French successes in the west – the occupation of Gabon in the western Congo, the conquest of the ancient kingdom of Dahomey (1893) and a three-pronged drive towards Lake Chad – caused Great Britain to mobilise the resources of the Royal Niger Company, to seize the emirates of Nupe and Ilorin, and to embark on a series of armed clashes not only with the French but also, for the first time, with the African states within its trading sphere. The tension reached its height in 1898, when France's Commandant Marchand, after a two-year march from Gabon, faced the British troops at Fashoda on the White Nile, and the two countries only just averted open war.

Partition, which had begun as a fairly peaceful process, was now causing more and more bloodshed. Ethiopia inflicted a heavy defeat on the Italians at Adowa in 1896. Some 20,000 Sudanese died during the British suppression of the Mahdist state. Rhodes' settler forces engaged in bitter battles with the Matabele and Mashona as they moved north, and the white colonists everywhere came to rely increasingly on the repeating rifle and the Maxim gun.

Conflict reached its climax with the Boer War (1899-1902) in which the British, with great difficulty, won control of the Transvaal gold mines (discovered on the Witwatersrand in 1886) and absorbed the Afrikaner republics. Hostilities opened with the abortive Jameson Raid in 1896, which destroyed Rhodes' political reputation, but Chamberlain, the British Colonial Secretary, and Milner, the High Commissioner in Cape Town, continued to push Rhodes' policies to the point of war. The Africans, on the other hand, though they bitterly opposed the 'forward moves' of the European powers (see page 248), never offered concerted resistance, and were fairly easily dealt with piecemeal. Of the handful of African states still precariously independent in 1902, Libya was invaded by Italy in 1911, and Morocco survived until 1912 before being divided between France and Spain. Elsewhere there was barely a flagpole from which one of the European colonial standards did not fly.

	Belgian territories
	British territories
	French territories
	German territories
	Italian territories
	Portuguese territories
	Spanish territories
⇨	strategic plans of the colonial powers

3/Colonial strategy in Africa *(above)* All the major powers involved in the scramble for Africa had wide-reaching ambitions. The Germans hoped to absorb the Portuguese colonies and at least part of the Congo, and in this way to form a solid empire extending across the centre of the continent. France had similar ambitions in the north. To counter them, the British pushed north through Bechuanaland and south from the Sudan, hoping to form a continuous belt of British territory from the Cape to Cairo. These conflicting aims brought the British and French face to face at Fashoda in 1898 and nearly led to a major war.

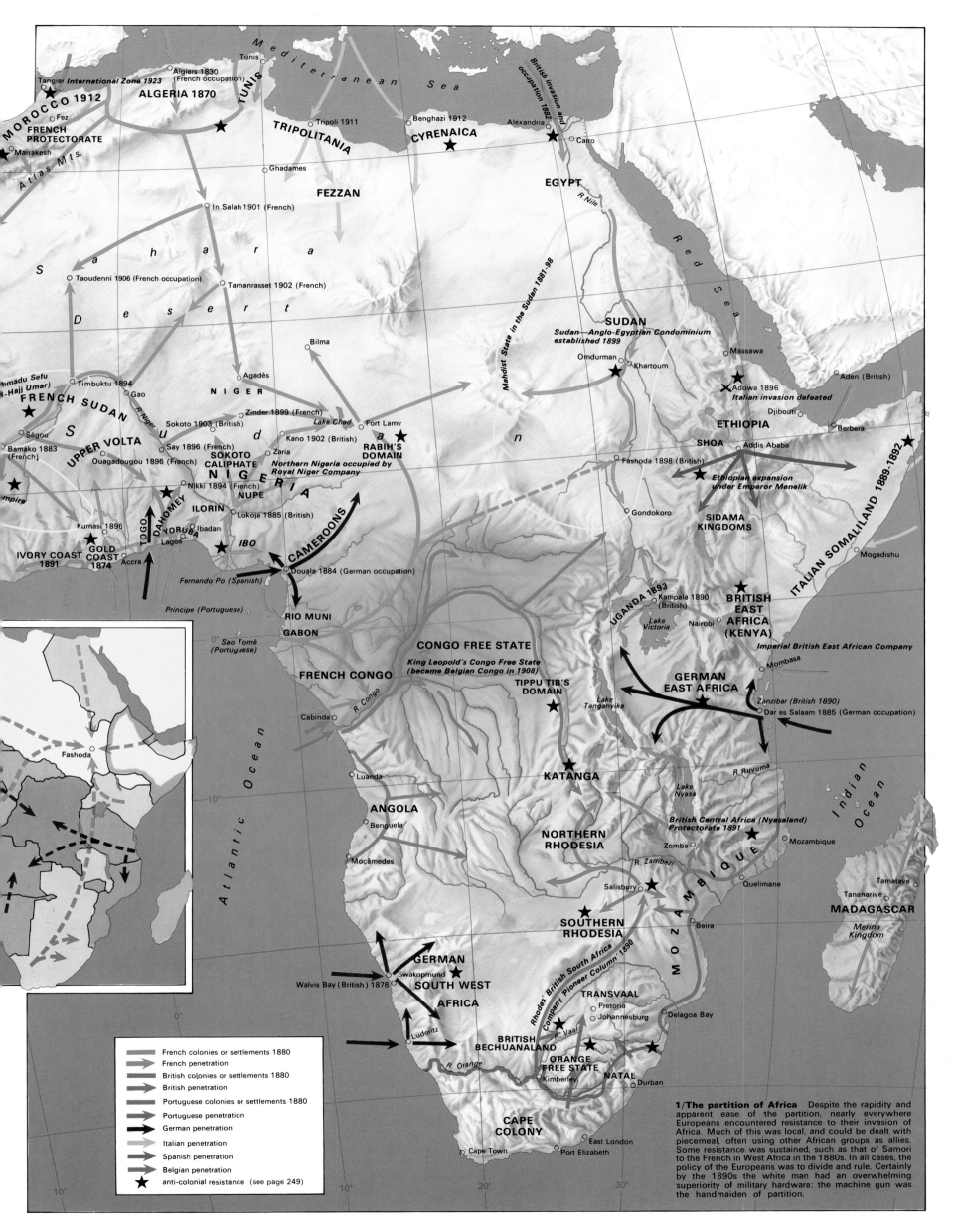

Mediterranean Sea

Tangier *International Zone 1923*
★ MOROCCO 1912
FRENCH PROTECTORATE
Fez
★ Marrakesh
Atlas Mts.

Algiers 1830 (French occupation)
ALGERIA 1870
★ TUNIS
Tunis

TRIPOLITANIA
Tripoli 1911

Benghazi 1912
CYRENAICA ★

Alexandria ★
Cairo
EGYPT

British invasion and occupation 1882

R. Nile

Red Sea

Ghadames

FEZZAN

Sahara Desert

In Salah 1901 (French)

Taoudenni 1906 (French occupation)

Tamanrasset 1902 (French)

Bilma

Ahmadu Sefu (al-Hajj Umar)
Timbuktu 1894
FRENCH SUDAN
Gao
NIGER
Ségou
Agadès
UPPER VOLTA
Bamako 1883 (French)
...empire
Sokoto 1903 (British)
Zinder 1899 (French)
Lake Chad
Fort Lamy
Ouagadougou 1896 (French)
Say 1896 (French)
Kano 1902 (British)
RABIH'S DOMAIN ★
NIGERIA
Zaria
Northern Nigeria occupied by Royal Niger Company
Nikki 1894 (French)
NUPE
Kumasi 1896 ★
SOKOTO CALIPHATE
ILORIN
Lokoja 1885 (British)
DAHOMEY
YORUBA
Ibadan
IVORY COAST 1891
GOLD COAST 1874
Accra
Lagos
IBO ★
CAMEROONS
Douala 1884 (German occupation)
Fernando Po (Spanish)
Principe (Portuguese)
RIO MUNI
GABON
Sao Tomé (Portuguese)

Mahdist State in the Sudan 1881-98

SUDAN
Sudan — Anglo-Egyptian Condominium established 1899
Omdurman
Khartoum ★

Massawa

Aden (British)

Adowa 1896 ✕
Italian invasion defeated
ETHIOPIA
SHOA
Addis Ababa
Fashoda 1898 (British) ★
Ethiopian expansion under Emperor Menelik ★
SIDAMA KINGDOMS
Djibouti
Berbera

ITALIAN SOMALILAND 1889-1892

Gondokoro

Mogadishu

Atlantic Ocean

FRENCH CONGO
R. Congo
Cabinda

CONGO FREE STATE
King Leopold's Congo Free State (became Belgian Congo in 1908)

TIPPU TIB'S DOMAIN ★

Lake Tanganyika

UGANDA 1893
Kampala 1890 (British)
Lake Victoria
Nairobi
BRITISH EAST AFRICA (KENYA)
Imperial British East African Company
Mombasa
GERMAN EAST AFRICA
Zanzibar (British 1890)
Dar es Salaam 1885 (German occupation)

KATANGA ★

Luanda

ANGOLA
Benguela
Moçâmedes

NORTHERN RHODESIA

Lake Nyasa
R. Ruvuma

British Central Africa (Nyasaland) Protectorate 1891 ★
Zomba
R. Zambezi
Mozambique
Quelimane

Indian Ocean

MADAGASCAR
Tamatave
Tananarive
Merina Kingdom

GERMAN SOUTH WEST AFRICA
Walvis Bay (British) 1878
Swakopmund ★
Lüderitz

Salisbury ★
SOUTHERN RHODESIA
Rhodes' British South Africa Company 'Pioneer Column' 1890
Beira

MOZAMBIQUE

BRITISH BECHUANALAND
R. Orange

TRANSVAAL
Pretoria ★
Johannesburg
R. Vaal
ORANGE FREE STATE ★
Kimberley
Delagoa Bay

NATAL ★
Durban
East London
CAPE COLONY
Cape Town
Port Elizabeth

Legend:
- French colonies or settlements 1880
- French penetration
- British colonies or settlements 1880
- British penetration
- Portuguese colonies or settlements 1880
- Portuguese penetration
- German penetration
- Italian penetration
- Spanish penetration
- Belgian penetration
- ★ anti-colonial resistance (see page 249)

1/The partition of Africa Despite the rapidity and apparent ease of the partition, nearly everywhere Europeans encountered resistance to their invasion of Africa. Much of this was local, and could be dealt with piecemeal, often using other African groups as allies. Some resistance was sustained, such as that of Samori to the French in West Africa in the 1880s. In all cases, the policy of the Europeans was to divide and rule. Certainly by the 1890s the white man had an overwhelming superiority of military hardware: the machine gun was the handmaiden of partition.

Fashoda

The expansion and modernisation of Japan 1868 to 1918

JAPAN is of major importance in considering the expansion of Western power and civilisation to the rest of the world in the 19th and 20th centuries. First, it is the outstanding example of Western-induced political and economic modernisation in the non-Western world; second, its response was not only to modernise, but also to create an imperialism of its own, making Japan as much an influence on its neighbours as the West was on Japan.

The process began in the 1850s. Two centuries of self-imposed isolation, during which feudalism had been gradually undermined by the growth of a money economy, ended when the powers, led by the United States, demanded access to Japanese ports for trade. The 'unequal treaties' concluded under threat in 1858 aroused hostile reactions, which contributed to the overthrow of the ruling Tokugawa house in January 1868. Direct imperial rule was then restored in the name of the Meiji emperor (1867-1912).

These events brought to power new leaders, men who saw their main task as the pursuit of national wealth and strength in order to assert Japan's international independence and equality. They abolished the feudal domains (1871), creating a system of prefectures and a centralised bureaucracy. By the 1880s the pattern of official recruitment and promotion, previously based on traditional Chinese models introduced in the 7th century, had become much more comparable with those in continental Europe, especially in France and Germany, and from about 1900 staffing was increasingly from graduates of Japan's new universities. A Western-style peerage (1884), cabinet government (1885) and a bicameral legislature (1889), laid a foundation of political unity and stability on which was soon erected a modern social, economic and military structure. Samurai privilege was abolished and a conscript army created (1873). A navy was founded, equipped with modern ships. A national education system was instituted (1872), providing teaching for 90 per cent of school-age children by 1900. Legal codes, largely based on French and German models (except in traditional areas like the family system) were introduced, beginning in 1882. Land tax was reformed (1873), furnishing a regular cash revenue to replace feudal dues. Official encouragement was given to commerce and industry by a wide variety of measures: quality control of export goods such as silk; subsidies or direct government investment for strategic and import-saving industries; technical training schemes; tax advantages; the development of transport and communications.

Economic modernisation was not easy, even though Japan started with greater advantages than most Asian countries. In 1868 she already had an extensive domestic commerce. Moreover, despite a shortage of arable land – over four-fifths of the country is mountain and upland – there was a highly developed intensive agriculture, capable of supporting a population of 30 million. Japan, for several centuries a major copper producer, also had adequate coal deposits, some already in use, and enough accessible ore to supply an iron industry in its initial stages (though not beyond). Japanese scholars had begun to study and experiment with Western science and technology, learning at first from books imported through the Dutch, then after 1858 directly from foreigners or in foreign countries. By 1860 they had built a Western-style ship, which crossed the Pacific with a Japanese crew. From then on, many students were sent abroad, sometimes for short training visits to Europe or America, sometimes for longer periods at Western universities. This provided knowledge not only of technical skills, but also of political and economic affairs. Later development depended heavily on Japan's ability to adopt such institutions as the joint stock company and banks, as well as on the government's success in providing a stable social and financial environment.

Within this framework capitalism made rapid headway, quickly making Japan the outstanding example of large-scale industrialisation in the non-Western world. By the late 1880s there were beginnings in textiles, and after 1895 heavy industry also began to develop on a considerable scale. Further impetus came from Japan's increased penetration of foreign markets during the first world war. Foreign trade rose sharply from the 1890s, as Japan exploited major outlets in China (cotton textiles) and the United States (silk). The trade structure changed strikingly as she became a large-scale importer of raw materials and exporter of finished goods.

Predictably, these developments were reflected in considerable changes in the country's way of life. Population rose from 35 million in 1873 to 55 million in 1918. By then, although half the population was still engaged in agriculture, nearly a third lived in towns of 10,000 persons or more, especially in the major industrial areas of Honshu and northern Kyushu, and along the coastal belt that joined them. Moreover, these areas were linked to most parts of the country, even remote ones, by a railway system totalling 10,000 kilometres of government trunk routes (nationalised in 1906) connecting a network of

3/The Russo-Japanese War *(above)* After surprising Tsarist ships at Port Arthur (8 February 1904), Japan's forces achieved a series of victories, culminating in the fall of Port Arthur (January 1905), the Battle of Mukden (February-March), and the destruction of Russia's Baltic Fleet in the Tsushima Straits (May). Adults and children *(left)* study together in a typical Meiji period classroom scene.

1/Industrial Japan *(below)* By 1918 the country's first major phase of modern economic growth was completed. Urban population had substantially increased. Port cities and installations had expanded to meet changes in the scale and structure of foreign trade. The main railway network, nationalised in 1906, connected all major centres. World War I, diverting the energies of all significant competitors, opened large new markets for manufactured exports. Japanese shipping was now operating worldwide.

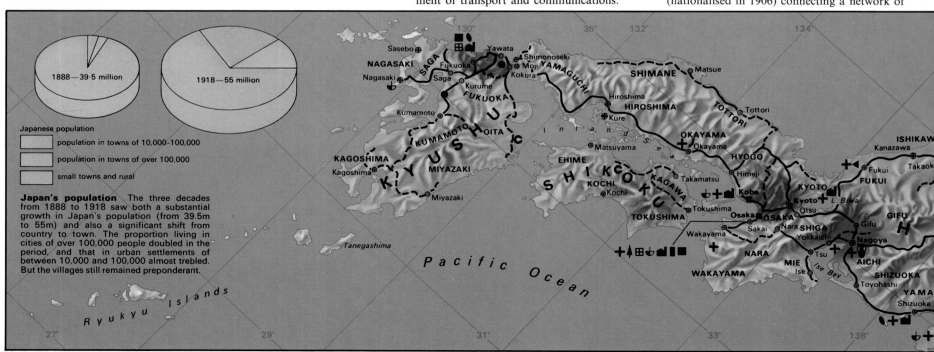

Japan's population The three decades from 1888 to 1918 saw both a substantial growth in Japan's population (from 39.5m to 55m) and also a significant shift from country to town. The proportion living in cities of over 100,000 people doubled in the period, and that in urban settlements of between 10,000 and 100,000 almost trebled. But the villages still remained preponderant.

Japanese population

population in towns of 10,000-100,000

population in towns of over 100,000

small towns and rural

privately-owned local lines.

National strength, military and industrial, brought expansion overseas. Initially, foreign policy was preoccupied with problems of defence. The nearby islands of the Ryukyu archipelago were claimed in 1872 and were made a Japanese prefecture in 1879 despite Chinese protests. The Bonin (Ogasawara) islands were taken over by agreement with Britain and the United States in 1873. The Kuriles had been partitioned between Japan and Russia by a treaty of 1855, but in 1875 Japan relinquished a claim to part of Sakhalin in return for all the Kurile chain.

As Japan's strength and confidence grew, so did nationalist and imperialist ambitions. The 'unequal treaties' were revised in 1894, though the revisions were not fully implemented until 1911. In 1894-5 a victorious war against China, arising from disputes in Korea, led to the treaty of Shimonoseki in 1895, granting Formosa (Taiwan) to Japan. A claim to the Liaotung Peninsula was made in the treaty, but had to be withdrawn under pressure from Russia, France and Germany. From then on, Japan and Russia were in rivalry over their respective interests in Korea and South Manchuria, a rivalry culminating in war in 1904-5. Again Japan was successful. She gained land victories in Manchuria, notably at Port Arthur and Mukden, and defeated the Russian fleet in the Tsushima Straits in May 1905. The Treaty of Portsmouth (1905) gave her a lease of Liaotung (Kwantung Leased Territory), plus extensive rights in South Manchuria and a colony in southern Sakhalin (Karafuto). Korea was made a protectorate and later annexed (1910). Finally, the outbreak of war in Europe in 1914 gave Japan an opportunity to extend her rights on the Chinese mainland, this time in the former German sphere in Shantung, as well as in Manchuria and Fukien. In the Twenty-one Demands she made sweeping claims in these areas, most of which were incorporated in treaties with China in 1915. Bitterly resented by many Chinese, they were nevertheless acquiesced in by Japan's allies in a series of separate agreements which also recognised her claims to captured German islands in the northern Pacific. Most of these gains were confirmed at the Versailles Conference in 1919, when Japan emerged as a major power, with a permanent seat on the Council of the League of Nations.

There was another side to the story. The era of reform on which international success was founded had also helped to destroy the basis of stability at home. The removal by death and retirement of the Meiji generation of leaders opened the way for a power struggle between fresh contenders. By 1918 the army was already showing a willingness to act independently of civil control in operations against Soviet Russia in Siberia. Party politicians, appealing to Western parliamentary ideas, sought power through the support of businessmen. Finally, cutting across previous patterns of political development, were those who rejected the whole trend of Japan's modern history: traditionalists, offended by the sacrifice of Japanese to Western-style habits and institutions; and representatives of the tenant farmer and the factory labourer, who resented the capitalist structure. Following the end of the war in 1918, Japan suffered a wave of strikes in major industrial centres, followed by widespread rural unrest. In 1921 Hara Kei, prime minister and party leader, was assassinated by a young right-wing fanatic. In these events were the seeds of future disruption, presaging a new phase of international conflict.

Nevertheless, with the rise of Japan, Asia had returned to the forefront of world history; although Japan itself continued to be divided between its Asian past and its future as one of the world's leading industrial powers.

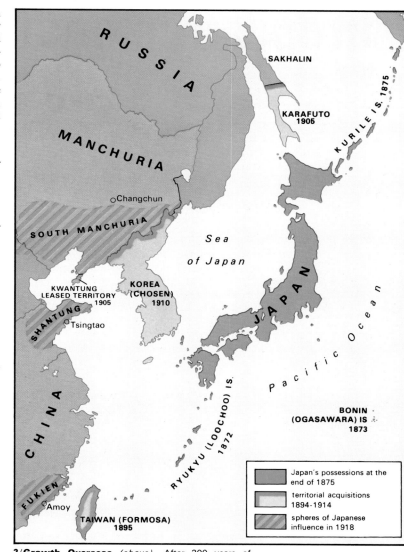

2/Growth Overseas (above) After 200 years of isolation, 1868 brought an explosion of Japanese interest both in the West and in her neighbours. By the end of 1875 Japan had successfully asserted rights in several nearby islands. Thereafter three wars (1894-95, 1904-5 and 1914-18) extended her holdings north and south and established an empire on the mainland.

The dramatic growth of Japanese trade (below right) The growth of imports and exports is shown in yen. The yen was first issued in 1871 at parity with the dollar, but it declined steadily until 1894, when the exchange rate stabilised at 2 yen to the dollar, where it remained, with small variations, until 1931.

Japan's trading partners (right) The United States had already become Japan's major trading partner 1918-22, with imports and exports roughly in balance. China was more important as a customer than as a supplier, and India the reverse. Britain's dominance of China was not duplicated in Japan.

Japan's trading partners 1918-1922
□ exports   ▨ imports

The structure of Japan's foreign trade (above) changed strikingly between 1878-82 and 1918-22. In the earlier period manufactured goods represented almost half of all imports, but only 7.2 per cent of exports. Within 40 years the ratio had reversed; finished manufactures now accounted for over 40 per cent of sales and only 15 per cent of purchases.

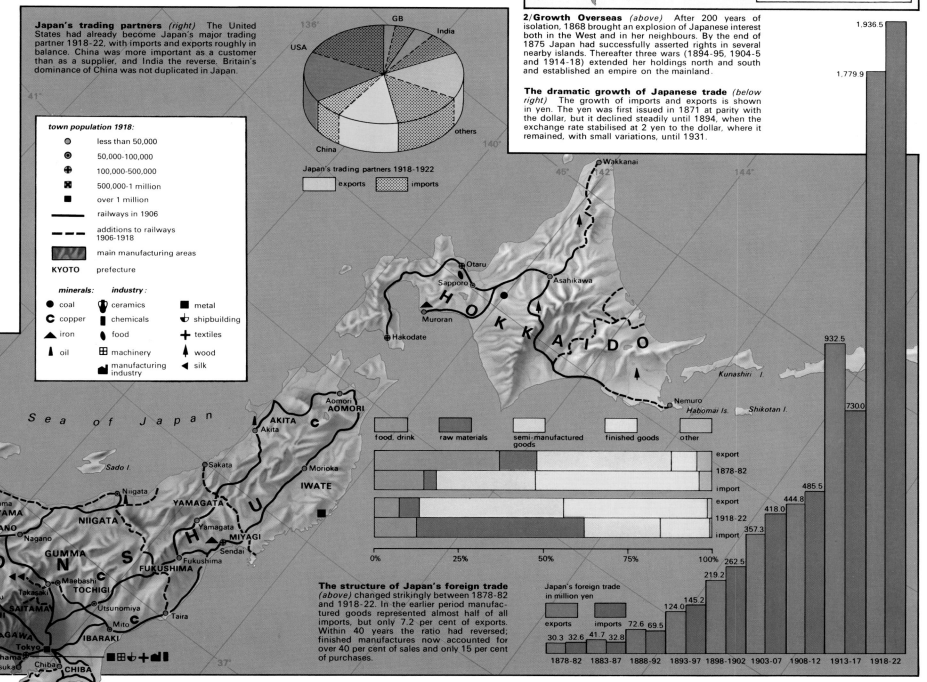

town population 1918:
- ● less than 50,000
- ◉ 50,000-100,000
- ⊕ 100,000-500,000
- ⊠ 500,000-1 million
- ■ over 1 million
- railways in 1906
- additions to railways 1906-1918
- main manufacturing areas
- **KYOTO** prefecture

minerals:	industry:	
● coal	⚱ ceramics	■ metal
C copper	▯ chemicals	⚓ shipbuilding
▲ iron	▯ food	✚ textiles
⌇ oil	⊞ machinery	◀ wood
	▮ manufacturing industry	◀ silk

food, drink | raw materials | semi-manufactured goods | finished goods | other

export / 1878-82 / import

export / 1918-22 / import

Japan's foreign trade in million yen

exports   imports

period	exports	imports
1878-82	30.3	32.6
1883-87	41.7	32.8
1888-92	72.6	69.5
1893-97	124.0	145.2
1898-1902	219.2	262.5
1903-07	357.3	418.0
1908-12	444.8	485.5
1913-17	932.5	1,779.9
1918-22	730.0	1,936.5

European colonial empires
1815 to 1914

THE 19th century is often seen as the great age of European expansion or 'imperialism', and one of the main themes of 20th century history has been the anti-colonialist reaction it has provoked among the peoples of Asia and Africa. In fact the creation of large new empires occupied only the last quarter of the century. As late as 1871, apart from the possessions of Great Britain in India and South Africa, of Russia in Siberia and central Asia, and of France in Algeria and Indo-China, the European stake in Asia and Africa was confined to trading stations and strategic posts. Colonial struggles had played an important part in European politics in the 18th century (see page 194), but by the mid-19th century empire-building seemed to have lost its attractions. On a theoretical level, its mercantilist justification had been demolished by Adam Smith and the Manchester School of economists. More practically, Great Britain's flourishing trade with both the United States and South America appeared to show that political control was not necessary for commer-

cial success. The future British prime minister, Benjamin Disraeli, expressed the prevailing orthodoxy when he said, in 1852, 'the colonies are millstones round our neck'.

Nevertheless, the European powers were in no hurry to abandon their existing possessions. Spain and Portugal lost their empires in the western hemisphere as they became weaker at home. By 1830 their former colonies in South and Central America were virtually all independent (see page 226). Russia too surrendered her North American territories, selling Alaska to the United States in 1867. But France, who had lost most of her first empire by 1815, gradually built a new one, conquering Algeria in the 1830s and 1840s, expanding her colony of Senegal in the 1850s, taking various Pacific islands (Tahiti, the Marquesas) in the 1840s, and annexing Saigon in 1859. Great Britain also steadily acquired new territories. By the peace settlements of 1815 she retained the Cape of Good Hope and the maritime provinces of Ceylon from the Dutch, Malta from the Knights of St. John,

Mauritius and the Seychelles from France and some West Indian islands from France and Spain. Fearing a French challenge, she extended her claim to sovereignty over the whole of Australia in the 1830s and over New Zealand in 1840. Her power continued to expand in India (see page 234), and by 1858 the boundaries of British India and of the Princely States under British tutelage had assumed roughly the positions they were to retain until independence in 1947. Elsewhere she acquired Singapore in 1819, Malacca in 1824, Hong Kong in 1842, Natal in 1843, Labuan in 1846, Lower Burma in 1852, Lagos in 1861 and Sarawak in 1888. Many of these acquisitions were strategic points, commanding sea routes. Great Britain was particularly sensitive about the route to India, her most valuable overseas possession. This apparent paradox between theory and practice is explained by the fact that the British felt that their prosperity and survival depended on trade and, although they preferred to safeguard this by 'influence', they never ruled out direct political

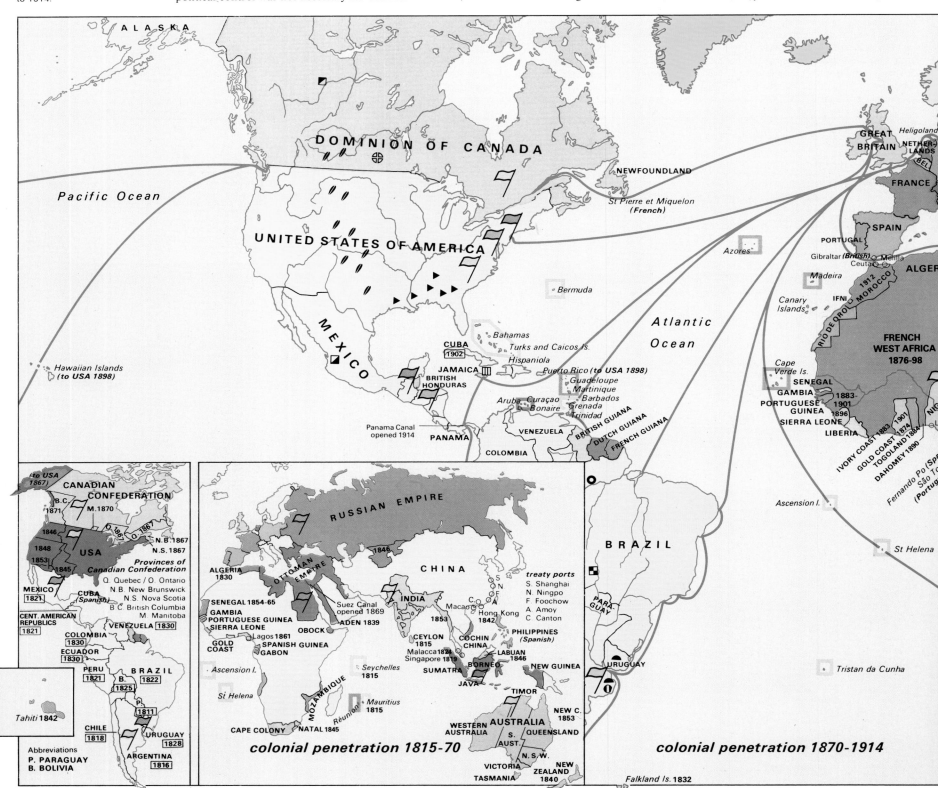

colonial penetration 1815-70

colonial penetration 1870-1914

or military intervention.

The late 19th century saw a new imperial outburst of an intensely competitive kind. In the scramble for territory, resources, markets and outlets for capital investment, an immense part of the world's total land area passed under European control. But many desirable areas were already pre-empted: the Monroe Doctrine discouraged further European involvement in the western hemisphere; latecomers such as Germany and Italy had to look to Africa, the Pacific or China. Great Britain, France, and even Portugal re-entered the lists. The United States seized former Spanish territory in the war of 1898. Japan, emerging as a great Pacific power, began to covet Korea, Formosa and even mainland China. Of the great trading nations, the Netherlands almost alone remained content with their existing (and prosperous) possessions in the East Indies. Between 1871 and 1914 the French empire grew by nearly 4 million square miles and nearly 47 million people. Her new empire was mainly in north and west Africa and Indo-China, where Laos and Tongking were added to Cambodia and Cochin China, but she also secured Madagascar and some Pacific territories. Germany acquired an empire of 1 million square miles of territory and 14 million colonial subjects in South-West Africa, Togoland, the Cameroons, Tanganyika and the Pacific islands. Italy obtained Libya, Eritrea and Italian Somaliland but failed to secure Abyssinia. Leopold II of the Belgians got international recognition for his

Congo State (later the Belgian Congo). Portugal extended her territory in Angola and Mozambique. Great Britain made the greatest gains of all in Africa, controlling *inter alia* Nigeria, Kenya, Uganda, Northern and Southern Rhodesia, Egypt and the Sudan, and in the Pacific, where she took Fiji, parts of Borneo and New Guinea, and other islands. She added 88 million subjects to her empire and, by 1914, exercised authority over a fifth of the world's land surface and a quarter of its peoples.

Africa was completely partitioned (see page 240). Russia joined the other European powers in competing for influence here. Her land empire in central Asia and Siberia had grown enormously since the 1860s and over 7 million Russians had emigrated from European to Asiatic Russia between 1801 and 1914. In China, the late 19th century was the time of the 'battle of the concessions', when the leading contenders manoeuvred for commercial advantage and financial and railway concessions. But the Chinese state, although debilitated, was stronger and more centralised than the divided polities of Africa. The Chinese held the West at bay until the First World War which was a watershed. Although the British empire actually grew in size after the war, with the addition of the former German colonies, indiscriminate landgrabbing was no longer considered acceptable conduct in a world supposedly ruled by the League of Nations.

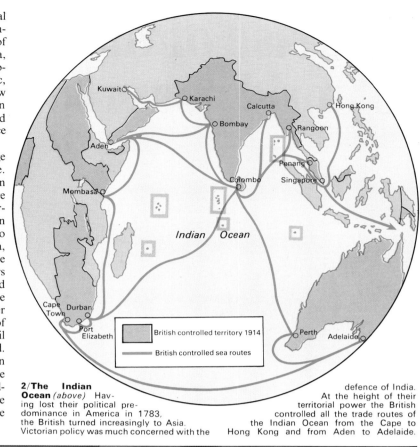

2/The Indian Ocean (*above*) Having lost their political predominance in America in 1783, the British turned increasingly to Asia. Victorian policy was much concerned with the defence of India. At the height of their territorial power the British controlled all the trade routes of the Indian Ocean from the Cape to Hong Kong and from Aden to Adelaide.

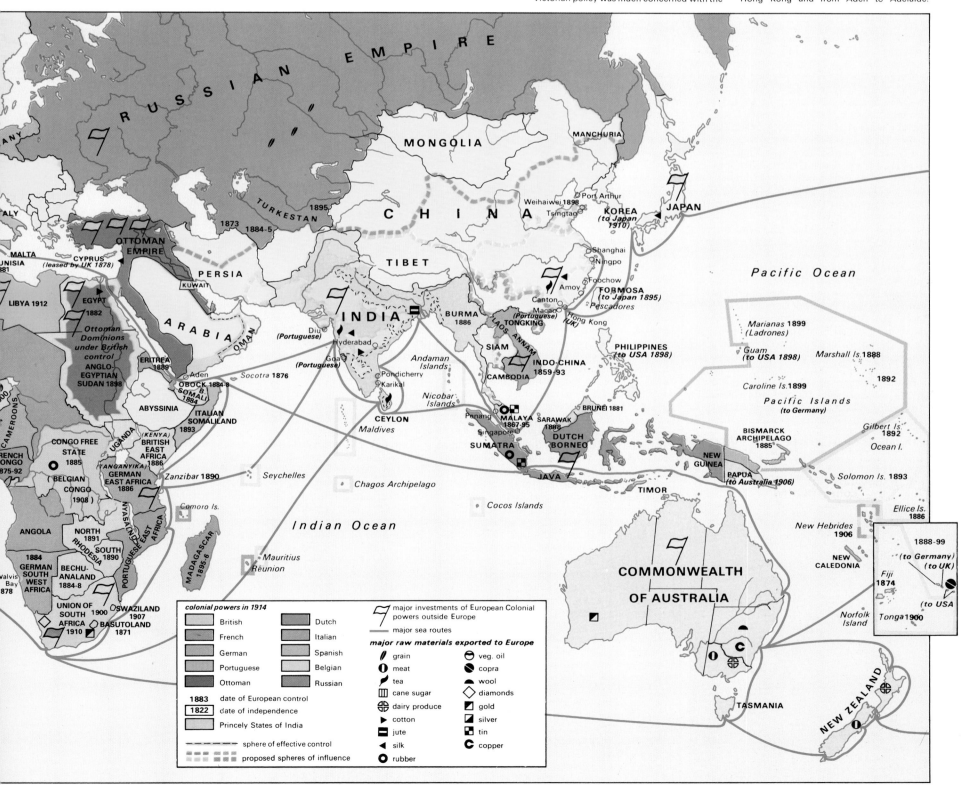

colonial powers in 1914

- British
- French
- German
- Portuguese
- Ottoman
- Dutch
- Italian
- Spanish
- Belgian
- Russian

1883 date of European control
1822 date of independence
Princely States of India

━ ━ ━ sphere of effective control
▪▪▪▪ proposed spheres of influence

major investments of European Colonial powers outside Europe

━━ major sea routes

major raw materials exported to Europe

- grain
- meat
- tea
- cane sugar
- dairy produce
- cotton
- jute
- silk
- rubber
- veg. oil
- copra
- wool
- diamonds
- gold
- silver
- tin
- copper

The rise of the United States to world power 1867 to 1917

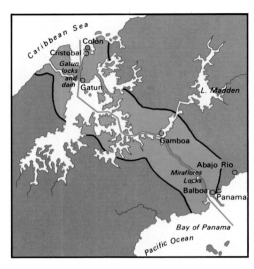

2/The Panama Canal zone *(above)* Under the treaty with Panama (1903) the US leases this zone in perpetuity but also possesses it as 'if it were sovereign'. Such contradictory language has caused endless argument. The zone, 10 miles wide, is bisected by the Canal which, unlike Suez, has locks.

THE United States emerged onto the world stage in 1867, followed by Germany in 1870. Between them these two imperial powers exerted a decisive influence in transforming the modern world. In 1917, by entering the war on the side of Great Britain and France, the United States brought about a decisive German defeat and thereby made itself the world's greatest power.

The preceding half-century, from 1867 to 1917, was a period of intense international rivalries, of which the United States took full advantage. American ambitions had manifested themselves since the 18th century, but dissension between the northern and southern states, culminating in the Civil War of 1861 to 1865, slowed expansion to a halt. When the forward movement was resumed, industrialism and later finance capitalism appeared as potent forces superimposed upon the earlier type of empire-building which had stressed commerce and territory. This new imperialism vented itself in war against Spain in 1898, a watershed year when the United States plunged into world politics; meanwhile, it had been strengthening its navy and occupying strategic outposts before claiming supremacy in the Caribbean and the Pacific.

The first step in the resumption of this new forward movement was the acquisition of Alaska in 1867 as the result of a deal with Russia. To Americans Alaska was both the back door to Canada and a 'finger pointed at Asia'. Many

3/The Alaska border dispute *(below)* The rush to the Klondike gold fields in 1897 brought this dispute near the boiling stage. Canada feared the loss of the north-west, but a politically-oriented tribunal, a British judge holding the casting vote, favoured the boundary demanded by the US (1903).

land claimed by US
land claimed by Canada
boundary agreed 1903

Americans believed that British North America, encircled in this way, would be forced into the Union, thus fulfilling the dream of a continent-wide empire. But the Canadians frustrated these hopes, first by federation (1867), then by the purchase of Rupert's Land from the Hudson's Bay Company (1869). Finally they attracted Manitoba (1870) and British Columbia (1871) into the new Dominion, thus blunting the northward thrusts of the United States. Tensions with Britain stemming from the American Civil War were eased by the Treaty of Washington (1871).

With the Aleutian island chain stretching out toward Japan, Alaska was the natural bridge to north-east Asia. Since the mid-19th century, however, Hawaii had been the main entrepôt to the Orient. A three-power rivalry involving Britain and France had kept American relations with this native kingdom in an unsettled state, but by annexing Midway Island (1867) the United States moved ahead of the other two powers. A commercial treaty in 1875 made Hawaii a virtual American protectorate, and in 1887 the United States obtained Pearl Harbor as a coaling station and future naval base. Annexation entered its final stage in 1893, when a group of sugar planters and Honolulu businessmen, aided by American officials, overthrew the native monarchy and established a republic. The outbreak of war with Spain in 1898 furnished the impetus for formal annexation. Wake Island followed in 1899. Earlier, in 1878, a foothold had been established at Pago Pago in the Samoan group, where the British and Germans were also involved. Friction resulted in a treaty (1899) partitioning the group, but the Germans lost their share to New Zealand in 1914.

The chief fruits of the Spanish-American war in the Pacific were the Philippines and the island of Guam, formally ceded by Spain in the peace treaty of 1898. The United States now had its 'stepping stones' to China, already the focus of international rivalry as a field for capital investment (see page 232). Backed by the government, American bankers and entrepreneurs expected to get their share. They would secure the 'Open Door', a phrase already in current use to describe the unlimited opportunities China was supposed to offer. A secret move in 1900 to obtain a lease over Samsah Bay in Fukien province, opposite Formosa, proved unsuccessful. Nevertheless, the United States was determined to outpace the European powers in the scramble. Its attention was concentrated particularly on Manchuria. Promoters like Willard Straight, who was consul-general in Mukden, conceived of Manchuria as America's 'new West', to be gridironed by railways owned and managed from the United States. These designs were thwarted by Russia and Japan, who effectively divided Manchuria between themselves by treaty in 1907 and 1910 respectively.

The other principal area of American expansion took in Mexico and the Caribbean. From Mexico the United States had wrested the provinces of Texas, New Mexico and California between 1846 and 1848. Land, mining and oil companies, competing with European interests, penetrated the country after 1880 but were checked by the revolution of 1911, which adumbrated a far-reaching programme of nationalisation. President Wilson reacted with two armed interventions: an occupation force to Veracruz in 1914, and a punitive expedition across the Rio Grande in 1916. But these actions stimulated the Mexicans to resist, and helped the initiation of a German intrigue which came to a head in 1917. Meanwhile, the war on Spain in 1898 had led to the conquest of Puerto Rico and the conversion of Cuba into a protectorate (1903). Britain, the other power chiefly interested in the Caribbean, recognised the changed situation and, in the Hay-Pauncefote treaty of 1901, gave the United States a free hand. From this

agreement followed the building of the Panama Canal (opened in 1914) under the sole ownership and control of the United States.

The ideological basis for this hegemony was the Monroe Doctrine which, even when first set forth in 1823, implied an intention to treat Latin America as a United States sphere of influence. However, with the outbreak of the Civil War (1861), expansionist ambitions were temporarily dropped, although the Monroe Doctrine was by no means forgotten. The French attempt to erect a puppet empire in Mexico (1862-67) offered it a fresh challenge, and in actually beginning work on a canal across Panama the French engineer, Ferdinand de Lesseps, builder of the Suez Canal, caused further objections. As President Hayes put it, any such canal must be regarded as 'virtually a part of the coastline of the United States' (1879).

Interfering in a British dispute with Venezuela over a boundary question, the United States, through Secretary of State Olney, in 1895 declared itself 'practically sovereign on this continent', and the British dropped the argument. Obstinacy on the part of Colombia in failing to bow to American demands for canal rights across Panama led to an insurrection accompanied by the forcible detachment of that country from Colombia. The United States then guaranteed the 'independence' of Panama but under terms that made it a protectorate. This period of dominance in the Caribbean survived under difficulties till about 1945. Mexican resistance stiffened into open defiance (1934-38), tactics had to be altered to appease the larger South American countries, intense diplomacy was undertaken to offset the activities of Nazi Germany. Interventions that occurred from time to time in the affairs of the Caribbean republics were covert or indirect, on the surface the Monroe Doctrine was transformed into the 'Good Neighbour' policy, and a battle of wits ensued to convince Latin America of US good intentions. But obviously new forces were at work, and the Monroe Doctrine continued to recede farther into the background.

An American view *(above)* of the relative importance of Uncle Sam and John Bull, from *The New York Journal* in 1898. *The Times* of London predicted, after America's crushing victory over Spain, that she would henceforth play a prominent role in world affairs.

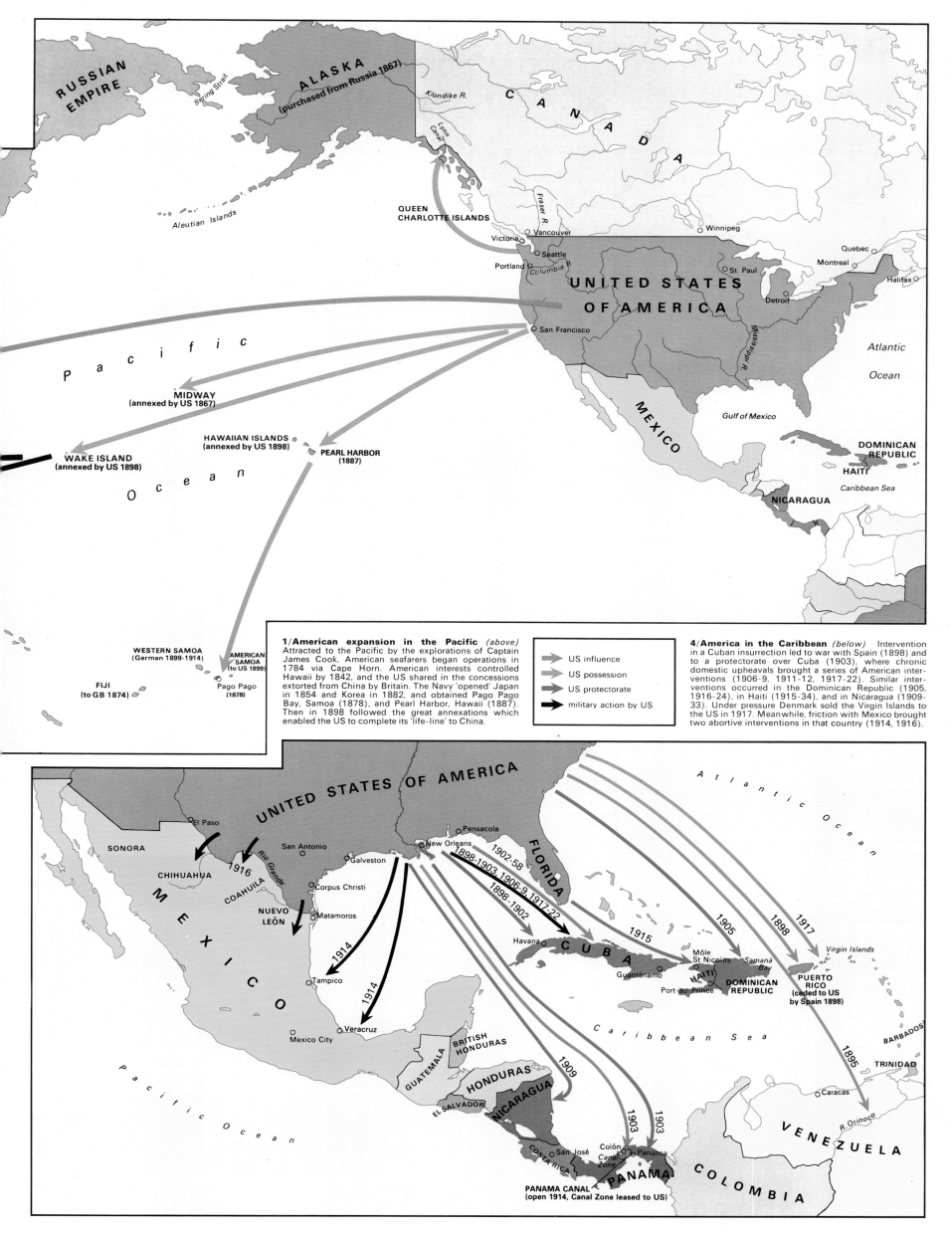

RUSSIAN EMPIRE

Bering Strait

ALASKA (purchased from Russia 1867)

Klondike R.

C A N A D A

Aleutian Islands

Lynn Canal

QUEEN
CHARLOTTE ISLANDS

Fraser R.

Victoria ○ ○ Vancouver

Winnipeg ○

Quebec ○

Seattle ○
Portland ○ *Columbia R.*

St. Paul ○

Montreal ○

Halifax ○

Detroit ○

**UNITED STATES
OF AMERICA**

P a c i f i c

San Francisco ○

Mississippi R.

Atlantic

Ocean

MIDWAY
(annexed by US 1867)

MEXICO

Gulf of Mexico

**DOMINICAN
REPUBLIC**

WAKE ISLAND
(annexed by US 1898)

HAWAIIAN ISLANDS
(annexed by US 1898)

PEARL HARBOR
(1887)

O c e a n

HAITI

Caribbean Sea

NICARAGUA

WESTERN SAMOA
(German 1899-1914)

**AMERICAN
SAMOA**
(to US 1899)

FIJI
(to GB 1874)

Pago Pago
(1878)

1/American expansion in the Pacific *(above)*
Attracted to the Pacific by the explorations of Captain James Cook, American seafarers began operations in 1784 via Cape Horn. American interests controlled Hawaii by 1842, and the US shared in the concessions extorted from China by Britain. The Navy 'opened' Japan in 1854 and Korea in 1882, and obtained Pago Pago Bay, Samoa (1878), and Pearl Harbor, Hawaii (1887). Then in 1898 followed the great annexations which enabled the US to complete its 'life-line' to China.

→ US influence
→ US possession
→ US protectorate
→ military action by US

4/America in the Caribbean *(below)* Intervention in a Cuban insurrection led to war with Spain (1898) and to a protectorate over Cuba (1903), where chronic domestic upheavals brought a series of American interventions (1906-9, 1911-12, 1917-22). Similar interventions occurred in the Dominican Republic (1905, 1916-24), in Haiti (1915-34), and in Nicaragua (1909-33). Under pressure Denmark sold the Virgin Islands to the US in 1917. Meanwhile, friction with Mexico brought two abortive interventions in that country (1914, 1916).

UNITED STATES OF AMERICA

Atlantic Ocean

El Paso ○

SONORA

Pensacola ○

San Antonio ○

New Orleans ○

FLORIDA

1902-58

CHIHUAHUA

1916

Rio Grande

Galveston ○

1898-1903 1906-9 1917-22

COAHUILA

Corpus Christi ○

1898-1902

M E X I C O

**NUEVO
LEÓN**

Matamoros ○

1915

1905

1898

1917

Havana ○

C U B A

Virgin Islands

Môle
St Nicolas

Samaná Bay

1914

Tampico ○

Guantánamo ○

HAITI

**DOMINICAN
REPUBLIC**

**PUERTO
RICO**
(ceded to US
by Spain 1898)

1914

Port-au-Prince ○

Mexico City ○

Veracruz ○

**BRITISH
HONDURAS**

Caribbean Sea

BARBADOS

GUATEMALA

1909

HONDURAS

TRINIDAD

Pacific Ocean

EL SALVADOR

NICARAGUA

1903

1903

1895

COSTA RICA

San José ○

Colón ○
Canal
Zone

Panama ○

Caracas ○

PANAMA

COLOMBIA

V E N E Z U E L A

R. Orinoco

PANAMA CANAL
(open 1914, Canal Zone leased to US)

247

The anti-colonial reaction 1881 to 1917

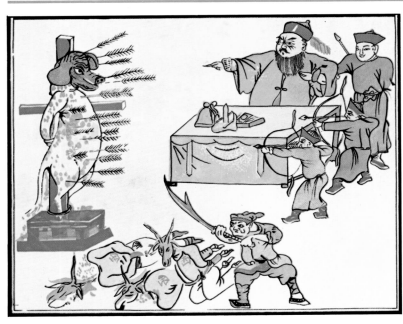

Shooting the Pig and Decapitating the Sheep *(above)* This detail from a popular Chinese woodcut of the 1890s illustrates graphically the intensity of anti-western feeling in the colonial and semi-colonial world. The pig is Christ, the sheep are the Christians. This was the sentiment behind the Boxer rising of 1900, but it was duplicated in many other parts of the world.

THE 'new imperialism', beginning with the French occupation of Tunis in 1881 and the British occupation of Egypt in 1882, unleashed an anti-colonial reaction throughout Asia and Africa, the extent, intensity and significance of which have rarely been fully appreciated. In Tunisia French intervention provoked a large-scale Islamic rising, followed by spasmodic warfare in the south; in Egypt the British faced a national revolt under Arabi Pasha. Independence was not passively surrendered either in Africa or in Asia. The Italians were decisively defeated by the Abyssinians at Adowa in 1896. In Annam the emperor, Ham Nghi, took to the mountains in 1883 and resisted French occupation until 1888. The British suffered repeated setbacks in the Sudan at the hands of the Mahdi and his successor, the Khalifa, including the annihilation of the garrison of Khartoum under General Gordon in 1885. Russia, fanatically opposed in the Caucasus from 1834 to 1859 by Shamil, 'ruler of the righteous and destroyer of the unbeliever', encountered further Muslim resistance when it invaded central Asia; and when the United States occupied the Philippines in 1898, the Americans also found themselves involved in a costly war with nationalist forces under Emilio Aguinaldo, which cost them some 7000 casualties and dragged on until 1902.

Even after occupation, the European powers had to face almost continuous unrest. After the capture of Aguinaldo, the Moros of Mindanao carried on resistance in the Philippines. In Indo-China the 'Black Flags' took up the struggle after the capture of Emperor Ham Nghi in 1888, and after 1895 a new leader appeared in the person of De Tham, who resisted the French until 1913. In Africa the British met equally determined resistance from the Ashanti, Matabele, Zulu and other African tribes, and oppressive German rule provoked the great Herero and Maji-Maji revolts in South-West Africa and Tanganyika in 1904 and 1905.

Much of this resistance was a negative explosion of resentment, xenophobia and despair; it was also conservative and backward-looking, with a strong traditionalist and religious bias. In Egypt and North Africa nationalists such as Afghani and Mohammed Abduh called for an Islamic revival to expel the infidel, and the Mahdiyya, which effectively controlled the Sudan from 1881 to 1898, was a Muslim revivalist movement, directed at once against Egyptians and Europeans. A similar role in fomenting resistance was played by Hinduism in India and by Confucianism in China. But this conservative, traditionalist reaction to European imperialism, which had little prospect of success in view of the immense military preponderance of the colonial powers, was accompanied elsewhere by a more positive response, particularly in countries such as Turkey, Egypt, China and India where

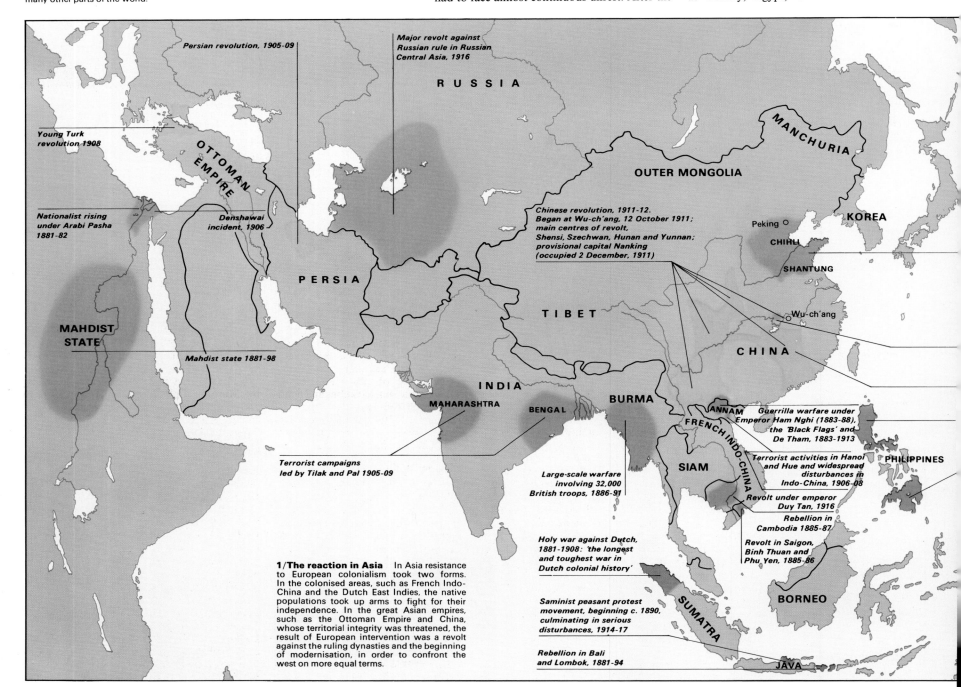

Persian revolution, 1905-09

Major revolt against Russian rule in Russian Central Asia, 1916

RUSSIA

MANCHURIA

Young Turk revolution 1908

OTTOMAN EMPIRE

OUTER MONGOLIA

Nationalist rising under Arabi Pasha 1881-82

Denshawai incident, 1906

Chinese revolution, 1911-12. Began at Wu-ch'ang, 12 October 1911; main centres of revolt, Shensi, Szechwan, Hunan and Yunnan; provisional capital Nanking (occupied 2 December, 1911)

Peking ○

KOREA

CHIHLI

SHANTUNG

PERSIA

TIBET

Wu-ch'ang

MAHDIST STATE

CHINA

Mahdist state 1881-98

INDIA

MAHARASHTRA

BENGAL

BURMA

ANNAM

Guerrilla warfare under Emperor Ham Nghi (1883-88), the 'Black Flags' and De Tham, 1883-1913

FRENCH INDO-CHINA

Terrorist activities in Hanoi and Hue and widespread disturbances in Indo-China, 1906-08

PHILIPPINES

Terrorist campaigns led by Tilak and Pal 1905-09

SIAM

Revolt under emperor Duy Tan, 1916

Rebellion in Cambodia 1885-87

Large-scale warfare involving 32,000 British troops, 1886-91

Revolt in Saigon, Binh Thuan and Phu Yen, 1885-86

1/The reaction in Asia In Asia resistance to European colonialism took two forms. In the colonised areas, such as French Indo-China and the Dutch East Indies, the native populations took up arms to fight for their independence. In the great Asian empires, such as the Ottoman Empire and China, whose territorial integrity was threatened, the result of European intervention was a revolt against the ruling dynasties and the beginning of modernisation, in order to confront the west on more equal terms.

Holy war against Dutch, 1881-1908: 'the longest and toughest war in Dutch colonial history'

Saminist peasant protest movement, beginning c. 1890, culminating in serious disturbances, 1914-17

BORNEO

SUMATRA

Rebellion in Bali and Lombok, 1881-94

JAVA

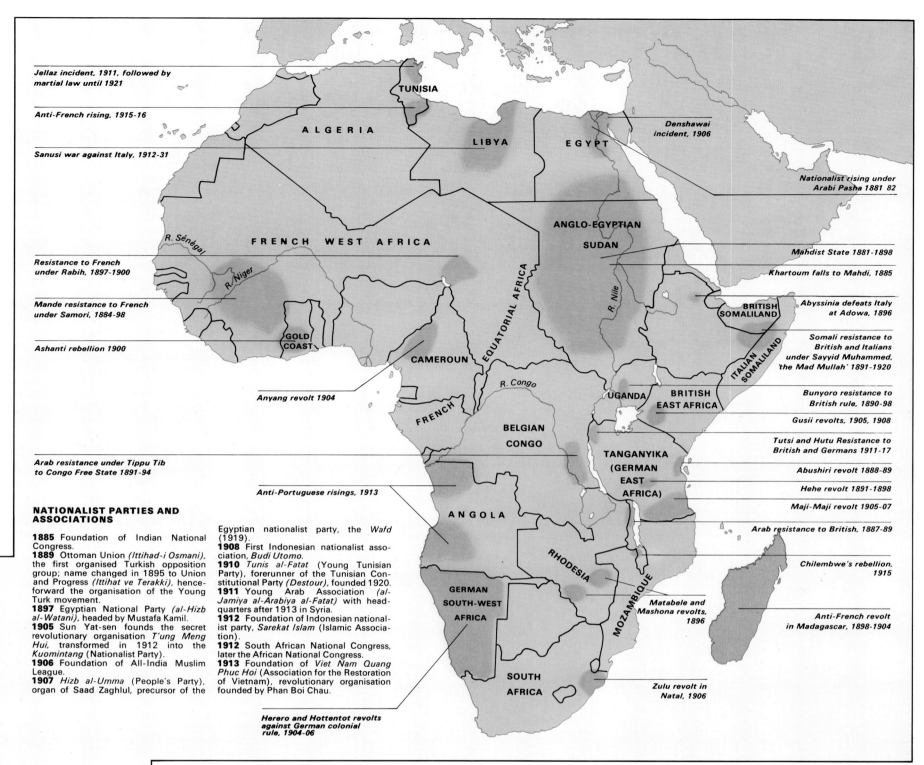

Jellaz incident, 1911, followed by martial law until 1921

Anti-French rising, 1915-16

Sanusi war against Italy, 1912-31

Denshawai incident, 1906

Nationalist rising under Arabi Pasha 1881 82

Mahdist State 1881-1898

Khartoum falls to Mahdi, 1885

Resistance to French under Rabih, 1897-1900

Abyssinia defeats Italy at Adowa, 1896

Mande resistance to French under Samori, 1884-98

Somali resistance to British and Italians under Sayyid Muhammed, 'the Mad Mullah' 1891-1920

Ashanti rebellion 1900

Bunyoro resistance to British rule, 1890-98

Gusii revolts, 1905, 1908

Anyang revolt 1904

Tutsi and Hutu Resistance to British and Germans 1911-17

Abushiri revolt 1888-89

Arab resistance under Tippu Tib to Congo Free State 1891-94

Hehe revolt 1891-1898

Maji-Maji revolt 1905-07

Anti-Portuguese risings, 1913

Arab resistance to British, 1887-89

Chilembwe's rebellion, 1915

Anti-French revolt in Madagascar, 1898-1904

Matabele and Mashona revolts, 1896

Zulu revolt in Natal, 1906

Herero and Hottentot revolts against German colonial rule, 1904-06

Map place names: TUNISIA, ALGERIA, LIBYA, EGYPT, FRENCH WEST AFRICA, ANGLO-EGYPTIAN SUDAN, R. Sénégal, R. Niger, GOLD COAST, CAMEROUN, FRENCH EQUATORIAL AFRICA, R. Congo, R. Nile, BRITISH SOMALILAND, ITALIAN SOMALILAND, UGANDA, BRITISH EAST AFRICA, BELGIAN CONGO, TANGANYIKA (GERMAN EAST AFRICA), ANGOLA, RHODESIA, MOZAMBIQUE, GERMAN SOUTH-WEST AFRICA, SOUTH AFRICA

NATIONALIST PARTIES AND ASSOCIATIONS

1885 Foundation of Indian National Congress.
1889 Ottoman Union (Ittihad-i Osmani), the first organised Turkish opposition group; name changed in 1895 to Union and Progress (Ittihat ve Terakki), henceforward the organisation of the Young Turk movement.
1897 Egyptian National Party (al-Hizb al-Watani), headed by Mustafa Kamil.
1905 Sun Yat-sen founds the secret revolutionary organisation T'ung Meng Hui, transformed in 1912 into the Kuomintang (Nationalist Party).
1906 Foundation of All-India Muslim League.
1907 Hizb al-Umma (People's Party), organ of Saad Zaghlul, precursor of the

Egyptian nationalist party, the Wafd (1919).
1908 First Indonesian nationalist association, Budi Utomo.
1910 Tunis al-Fatat (Young Tunisian Party), forerunner of the Tunisian Constitutional Party (Destour), founded 1920.
1911 Young Arab Association (al-Jamiya al-Arabiya al-Fatat) with headquarters after 1913 in Syria.
1912 Foundation of Indonesian nationalist party, Sarekat Islam (Islamic Association).
1912 South African National Congress, later the African National Congress.
1913 Foundation of Viet Nam Quang Phuc Hoi (Association for the Restoration of Vietnam), revolutionary organisation founded by Phan Boi Chau.

Boxer uprising 1899-1900 - Shantung and Chihli

Anti-western riots, 1891

Large-scale republican rising, 1906-07 - Hunan, Kiangsi, Kwangtung

Nationalist revolt under Aguinaldo 1898-1902

Continuing resistance of Moros, 1898-1913

western interference had already undermined the old order. The bankruptcy of Turkey in 1875 and of Egypt in 1879 drove home the lesson that the only hope of halting western encroachment was to get rid of archaic institutions and decadent, semi-feudal dynasties and carry through a programme of modernisation and reform. In Turkey the Russian assault in 1877 and the dismemberment of the Ottoman Empire by the European powers at the Congress of Berlin in 1878 fanned the patriotism of the Young Turks, who were to rise in revolution in 1908. In China the disastrous war with Japan in 1894-95, and the threat of partition which was its immediate consequence, led to the abortive Hundred Days' Reform of 1898 and, after its failure, to the bitterly anti-foreign Boxer rising. In Egypt the revolt of Arabi Pasha, directed first against the khedive Tewfik, a pliant tool of European interests, turned against the foreigner after the British occupation in 1882. In India the National Congress, founded in 1885, which pursued a moderate policy of constitutional reform, was overtaken after 1905 by a militant, Hindu-inspired, terrorist movement led by the Maharashtrian Brahmin, Bal Gangadhar Tilak.

All these movements were 'proto-nationalist' rather than nationalist in character; the disparate elements they brought together lacked unity and clearly defined objectives, and none achieved lasting results. In the Ottoman Empire the Young Turks deposed Sultan Abdul Hamid in 1908, but their attempts at reform floundered. In China the republic proclaimed in 1912 gave way a year later to the dictatorship of Yüan Shih-k'ai. In Persia

strikes and riots in 1906 forced the Shah to convoke a national assembly, the majlis, which drew up a liberal constitution, and when his successor attempted to revoke it, he was deposed in 1909; but only two years later Mohammed Ali was restored and the majlis was suppressed. In spite of these and other setbacks the movement of protest and resistance should not be written off as a failure. Though xenophobic and anti-foreign in origin, already before 1914 it was being transformed into a modern nationalist movement. The clearest evidence of this change is the appearance of nationalist associations and political parties. Many of these were small groups of the disaffected intelligentsia; but a few already had a mass following. The membership of Sarekat Islam, the first politically-based Indonesian nationalist organisation, founded in 1912, was 360,000 in 1916 and had risen to over two million by the end of the First World War.

The First World War gave new impetus to the incipient nationalism stirring in Asia and Africa before 1914. Even earlier the flame of resistance had been fanned by the Japanese victory in the Russo-Japanese war of 1904-5, which showed that the European powers were not invincible. Chinese nationalists, Sun Yat-sen later recalled, 'regarded the Russian defeat by Japan as the defeat of the West by the East', and the repercussions were felt throughout Asia from Persia to Indo-China, where it sparked off the Chieu conspiracy against France in 1906. By diverting the imperialist powers' attention from their colonies, the outbreak of war in Europe in 1914 created new opportunities. When in 1914 the

2/The reaction in Africa (above) The partition of Africa among the European powers, inaugurated at the Berlin Conference of 1884, provoked a movement of resistance among the African peoples, which was never quelled, in spite of harsh repression. The map shows how widespread and continuous rebellion was during the whole period from 1887 to 1917.

British proclaimed a protectorate over Egypt, they united Egyptian opposition and gave the final impetus to anti-British sentiment, already inflamed by the notorious Denshawai incident of 1906. In Russia a major revolt broke out among the Muslim peoples of central Asia in 1916. In North Africa there were risings against the French in Tunisia in 1915-16, supported by the Sanusi tribesmen of the Sahara who had been waging war against the Italians ever since the Italian occupation of Tripolitania and Cyrenaica in 1911 and 1912. France also had to face disaffection in Annam in 1916, and in Nyasaland the withdrawal of regular troops to fight the Germans on the northern frontier made it possible for Chilembwe to stage a revolt against the British settlers in 1915. The remarkable fact is the persistence of opposition in spite of disheartening setbacks and harsh repression. None of the powers which had launched the scramble for colonies in 1884 was secure in its possessions; nowhere was the finality of European rule accepted. The tangible achievements of nationalists in this period were negligible; but by keeping the flame of resistance alive, they inaugurated the process which led, a generation later, to the collapse of the European empires and the emancipation of the colonial peoples.

European rivalries and alliances
1878 to 1914

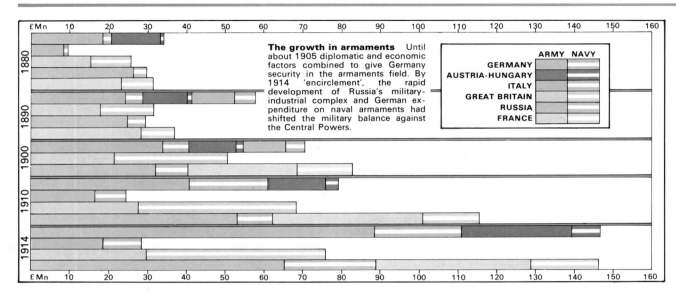

The growth in armaments Until about 1905 diplomatic and economic factors combined to give Germany security in the armaments field. By 1914 'encirclement', the rapid development of Russia's military-industrial complex and German expenditure on naval armaments had shifted the military balance against the Central Powers.

	ARMY	NAVY
GERMANY		
AUSTRIA-HUNGARY		
ITALY		
GREAT BRITAIN		
RUSSIA		
FRANCE		

1a/The Dual Alliance: October 1879 *(below)* recognised the fact that Germany could never afford to let Austria-Hungary succumb to a Russian attack, but Germany, as a military-aristocratic agrarian state engaged in suppressing Polish nationalism, still had more in common with Russia than with any other Power. Bismarck sympathised with Russia's efforts to consolidate its position in Bulgaria, and even exploited Germany's new role as an ally to force Austria-Hungary into line, pouring scorn on its attempts to enlist the support of the UK, Italy and Germany against Russia.

1b/Bismarck's system at its zenith: 1883 *(below)* Austria-Hungary, rebuffed by Gladstone, fell back on co-operation with Germany and Russia in the Three Emperors' Alliance (1881). But the Dual Monarchy still reinsured itself with the Triple Alliance (1882), which assured it of Italy's neutrality in a war with Russia; while its dynastic alliances with Serbia and Romania lessened the risk of Russia exploiting Serbian and Romanian irredentism against it. The Triple Alliance was worth more to Germany, providing for Italy's assistance in the event of a French attack.

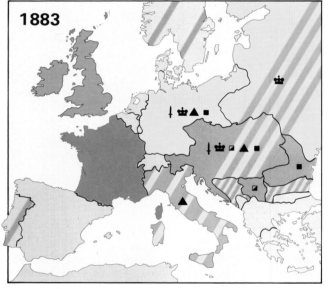

1c/The 'Mediterranean' Entente: 1887 *(below)* The Three Emperors' Alliance survived the crisis over the union of Bulgaria and E. Rumelia in 1885, but the Austro-Russian contest for control of Bulgaria (1886-7) destroyed it. Bismarck had promised the Russians his continued support in the Reinsurance Treaty, but the 'Mediterranean' agreements of Feb.-March and Dec. 1887 between the UK, Italy and Austria-Hungary (Spain acceding in May), to resist supposed French and Russian designs in the Mediterranean and at the Straits, annihilated Russian influence in Bulgaria.

1d/The 'New Course' in Germany: 1891 *(below)* Italy acceded to the Austro-German-Romanian alliance in 1888, and between 1889 and 1894 Germany, with a new emperor and chancellor, swung into line behind the Mediterranean Entente. Already, before the Reinsurance Treaty was dropped after Bismarck's fall in 1890, Russo-German relations had deteriorated sharply as a result of disputes over tariffs and loans after 1887. France drew steadily closer to Russia: the first of a series of loans was concluded in 1888 and a military convention was signed in 1894.

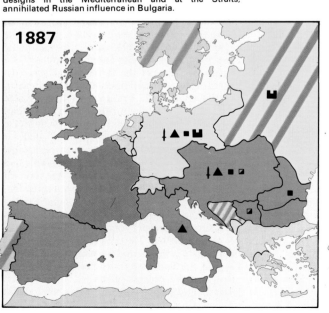

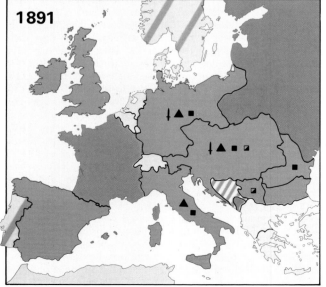

THE years 1871 to 1914 saw the apogee of the European state system. The Great Powers established their control of the non-European world to an extent never witnessed before or since; within Europe they sought security in a multi-faceted system of diplomatic alignments and alliances. Although always implying threats of war, as long as it remained flexible the system made for the peaceful adjustment of rivalries.

Four wars in a dozen years had solved the Italian and German questions and revised the map of Europe from Denmark to Sicily; for four decades after 1871 there were no more wars between the Great Powers, and although irredentist and nationalist grievances continued to fester, territorial questions had ceased to be an issue for most governments.

Of the Great Powers, only France was unable to reconcile itself to the rise of the new German Empire, which had robbed it of the primacy of Europe; this, rather than the cession of Alsace-Lorraine in 1871 was the basic cause of Franco-German estrangement. This was the one fixed point in the shifting alignments of the Great Powers during the armed peace of 1871 to 1914, but in itself it was not a threat to peace. France was in no position to challenge a Germany which had developed by the end of the century into the strongest military-industrial power in the world; nor for the first half of the period could it find an ally to provide even a diplomatic counterweight to German power.

The other five powers of Europe all accepted the changed balance of power set up in 1871. Neither Austria-Hungary nor Russia was inclined to support France because all the three eastern empires were united by a common conservative ideology of co-operation against the threat of proletarian revolution which they discerned in the Paris commune of 1871, the activities of the Second International after 1889, and the progress of social democracy consequent upon the progress of industrialisation. In 1882 even the Italian government joined the conservative camp, and clamped down firmly on irredentist propaganda about Italians still languishing under Habsburg rule. Nor could France find support elsewhere. By the 1880s a variety of economic, social, political and strategic factors was driving the European powers (except Austria) to intensify their 'imperialist' activities outside Europe; and disputes over Tunis (1881) and Egypt (1882) ensured that France's relations not only with Italy but also with Britain became as cool as her relations with Germany. Finally, dynastic links between the Hohenzollerns and the Romanovs and a community of interest in suppressing Polish nationalism, still counted for much in Russo-German relations. Altogether, Germany succeeded for twenty years after 1871 in convincing most of Europe of her conservative and pacific intentions, and France remained safely isolated.

Less intractable than the Franco-German estrangement, but equally permanent and sometimes threatening to combine with it, was the potential clash of Austro-Hungarian and Russian interests in south-east Europe, where a combination of misgovernment and insurgent nationalism threatened to destroy the Ottoman Empire (see page 214). For Russia, it was essential to ensure that no other power achieved a position from which it could control the Straits at Constan-

↓	Austro-German alliance 1879-1918
♔	three Emperors' alliance 1881-7
◨	Austro-Serbian alliance 1881-95
▲	triple alliance 1882-1915
■	Austro-German-Romanian alliance 1883-1916
⬛	reinsurance treaty 1887-90
◯	Franco-Russian alliance 1894-1917
⟋	Russo-Bulgarian military convention 1902-13

Stripes, similar and identical colours indicate an entente or community of interests.

tinople – through which passed much of that grain export trade on which Russia's economy and Great Power status depended. Russia's fundamental aim was therefore defensive; but its tactics varied from trying to bolster up and influence the Ottoman government, to assisting its Christian subjects against it in the hope of replacing the empire by a string of docile satellites.

To Austria-Hungary, Russia's efforts to achieve security by extending its influence in the Ottoman Empire seemed dangerous and offensive, either as threatening Austria-Hungary's 'colonial' markets in the Balkans, or as portending the encirclement of the Habsburg monarchy by a crowd of irredentist states under Russian protection. Nevertheless, for most of the period the Austrians were able to achieve a conservative understanding with the Tsarist government against revolutionary nationalism in both Russia and the Ottoman Empire. But when these agreements broke down (1878, 1886, 1908) Austria-Hungary sought salvation in trying to establish its own economic and diplomatic control of the Balkan states; and in building up blocs to oppose Russia.

In this policy Austria-Hungary could usually count on support from the United Kingdom, where many people regarded Russia's interest in the Ottoman Empire as a threat to the overland and Suez routes to India, already threatened (as they thought) by Russian expansion towards Persia and Afghanistan. Until the Anglo-Russian agreement of 1907 removed these fears, Anglo-Russian rivalry in the Near East, in central Asia and, in the 1890s, in China, was perhaps the chief determinant of diplomatic relations between the island empire and the continental Powers. The Anglo-Italo-Austrian entente of 1887-97 against Russia (and France) was, Salisbury told Queen Victoria, 'as close an alliance as the Parliamentary character of our institutions will permit'.

In the early 1890s even Germany lent her support to this combination. Already in 1887 Bismarck had increased the tariffs against Russian grain exports in order to protect the economic interests of Prussian landowners, and it was he who put a stop to Russia borrowing on the Berlin stock exchange the money to finance potentially threatening armaments and strategic railways. When France made the Paris *bourse* available the foundations were laid for the Franco-Russian alliance of 1894. Germany's attempts to parry this by co-operating with Russia in the Far East after 1895 were only partially successful; but Russia's concentration at this period on its Far Eastern interests at least allowed the Austrians to re-establish the conservative entente in 1897. By the end of the 1890s, therefore, there were three groups of Powers in Europe: the British Empire; its chief opponent, the Franco-Russian alliance, and the Triple Alliance (Germany, Austria-Hungary, Italy) – an unstable equilibrium which allowed for endless diplomatic manoeuvring and was therefore probably conducive to peace.

The dangerous simplification of alignments into a bi-polar system started with the development of German *Weltpolitik*, a challenge to all three established imperial Powers, and one which convinced Great Britain in particular that Germany was out to dominate the European continent. By 1907 Great Britain had made up its differences with France and Russia, and joined with them in a Triple Entente to contain – or in Berlin's view to 'encircle' – Germany. By 1914 the Germans and their Austrian allies were deeply concerned about this 'encirclement', particularly in the Balkans, the one area of Europe where frontier questions were still an explosive issue. The breakdown of the Austro-Russian entente when Austria-Hungary annexed Bosnia and the Herzegovina in 1908, and the Balkan wars of 1912 and 1913 which replaced Turkey-in-Europe by a complex of dissatisfied and mutually antagonistic Balkan states, created a highly unstable situation, and when, in 1914, it looked as though Serbian ambitions were reopening the issue, Vienna decided that it was now or never. When Berlin, impelled by the fear of 'encirclement', decided to support Vienna far beyond the terms of the defensive alliance of 1879, the fuse was lit which exploded in the First World War.

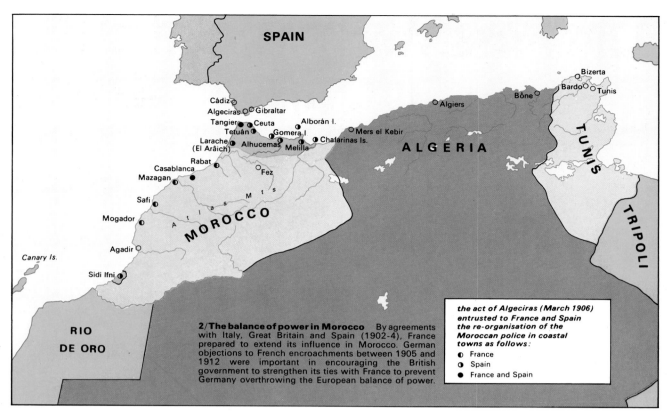

2/The balance of power in Morocco By agreements with Italy, Great Britain and Spain (1902-4), France prepared to extend its influence in Morocco. German objections to French encroachments between 1905 and 1912 were important in encouraging the British government to strengthen its ties with France to prevent Germany overthrowing the European balance of power.

the act of Algeciras (March 1906) entrusted to France and Spain the re-organisation of the Moroccan police in coastal towns as follows:
◑ France
◐ Spain
● France and Spain

1e/The Austro-Russian Entente: 1897 *(below)* The Germans now abandoned the 'New Course', ceasing to underwrite Austria-Hungary in the Balkans and co-operating in the Far East with Russia and France. The UK, after the Armenian massacres, refused to promise to fight for the Sultan. Austria-Hungary, torn by domestic strife, and with its Balkan alliances in decay, settled for an entente with Russia to put Balkan problems 'on ice' (1897). Russia still improved its position in Bulgaria, signing a military convention (1902); and in Serbia, after a coup by nationalist army officers in 1903.

1f/The Anglo-French Entente: 1904 *(below)* By 1902 France – partly to weaken the Triple Alliance – had settled the 20-year dispute with Italy; in 1904 it reached agreements about Egypt and Morocco with the UK. Meanwhile, Russia and Austria-Hungary extended their entente. Germany's clumsy efforts to exploit Russia's embarrassments over Japan in order to renew formal ties with St Petersburg and to browbeat France out of recent agreements with the United Kingdom failed; the Anglo-French link was even strengthened when Russia settled its own extra-European disputes with the UK in 1907.

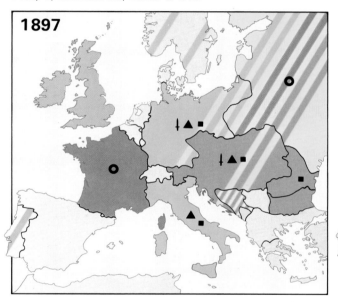

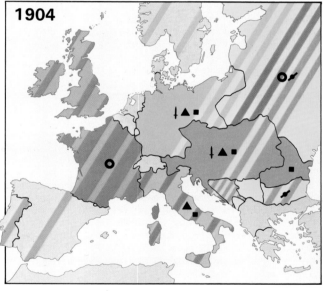

1g/Europe after the Bosnian crisis: 1909 *(below)* Between the Moroccan crises of 1905-6 and 1911, Anglo-German relations, complicated by the naval issue, reached their nadir. Friction between Russia and Austria-Hungary over the Austro-Serbian 'Pig War' (1906-11), the Sanjak railway project and the annexation of Bosnia and the Herzegovina put an end to the entente of 1897 and severely strained Russo-German relations (although the Potsdam agreement over Persia and the Baghdad railway in Nov. 1910 showed that the German 'wire to St Petersburg' had not been broken).

1h/Europe on the eve of war: 1914 *(below)* Between 1911 and 1914 the fronts between Triple Alliance and Triple Entente hardened, the grudging attitude of the latter towards Italy's ambitions in Tripoli and Albania helping restore links between Italy and her allies. In 1912-13 Austria-Hungary watched in alarm while a Russian-sponsored Balkan League expelled the Turks from Europe. The Austro-Romanian alliance was a dead letter. Although there were signs of Anglo-German co-operation on Balkan and colonial issues, Russo-German relations deteriorated sharply.

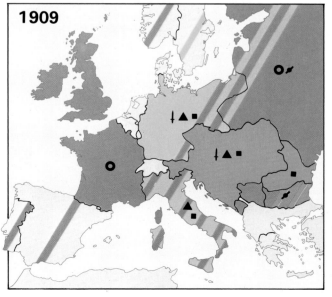

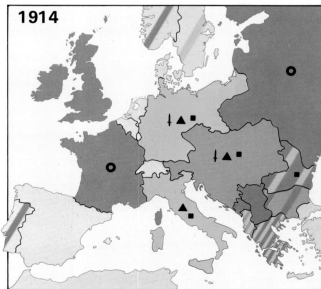

The First World War
1914 to 1918

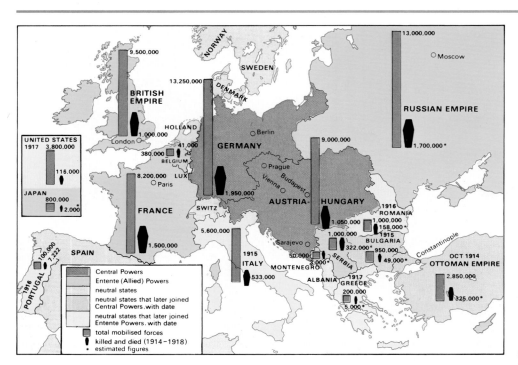

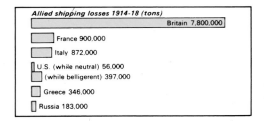

The naval war (above) After the battle of Jutland (1916) in which the Germans inflicted heavier losses but the British retained command of the North Sea, both sides used naval means to cut the other's supply lines in a war of attrition. The British instituted an open blockade of the Central Powers which became effective by the end of 1916. In that year, there were fifty-six food riots in German cities. In reply, the Germans resorted to unrestricted submarine warfare in February 1917 and one out of every four ships leaving British ports was sunk (above). This assault was only checked by the convoy system, first used in May 1917.

THE war which began in August 1914–to contemporaries the 'Great War', to posterity the 'First World War'–marked the end of one period of history and the beginning of another. Starting as a European war, it turned in 1917 into a world war, and thus can be seen as a bridge between the age of European predominance and the age of global politics. The spark that triggered it off was the assassination of the Austrian heir-presumptive, Archduke Franz Ferdinand, by Bosnian terrorists at Sarajevo on 28 June 1914. In the ensuing crisis, none of the powers was prepared to accept diplomatic defeat; war replaced diplomatic manoeuvre.

Everyone expected a short war, over by Christmas 1914. The Germans knew that their chances in a long war on two fronts were slender. Their war plan, drawn up by Schlieffen in 1905, was to trap and annihilate the French army by a great encircling movement through Belgium, before the Russians had time to mobilise. But the Russians mobilised unexpectedly quickly, invaded East Prussia, defeated the German 8th Army at Gumbinnen (20 August), and drew off German reserves from the west. However, the Germans defeated the Russian invasion at Tannenberg (26-29 August), but were not strong enough to exploit their victory. In the west the Allies outmanoeuvred the Germans in the Battle of the Marne (see map 2), 5-8 September. The Schlieffen Plan was always a gamble; when it failed the Germans had no alternative strategy. On 8-12 September the Russians won a crushing victory over Austria at Lemberg. A last, mutual, attempt, by the German and Allied armies to outflank each other in Flanders failed in November, and both sides dug in on a line 400

1/The line-up of the Powers (above) By 1914 the European powers were already divided into two rival camps (see page 251). After the outbreak of war both groups sought allies. Germany and Austria-Hungary were joined by Turkey and Bulgaria. Russia, France and Great Britain sought, and gained the support of Japan, Italy, Romania and, after a long struggle, Greece. By far the most important adherent to the Allied cause was the United States, which declared war on Germany on 6 April 1917. In Europe, the price in terms of human life and material destruction changed men's conception of war; it is estimated that over eight million combatants were killed.

miles long from the Channel to the Swiss frontier. In the east, mobile warfare was still possible because of the far lower density of men and guns–a possibility brilliantly exploited by the Germans at Gorlice-Tarnow in 1915, and by the Russian general Brusilov in 1916.

In the west, from the beginning of 1915 the dominant factors were trenches, barbed wire, artillery, machine-guns and mud. The war of mobility gave way to a war of attrition. One entrenched man with a machine-gun was more than a match for a hundred advancing across open country. Railways could bring up defenders faster than slowly-moving troops could advance into the front-line gaps which they had created at such high human cost.

Yet the German occupation of Belgium and northern France made it inevitable that the Allies should seek to expel them. This meant repeated French offensives in Artois and Champagne in 1915, assisted by small British offensives at Neuve Chapelle and Loos. For 1916 the Allies planned a joint offensive on the Somme, but the Germans struck first, at Verdun, with the intention of bleeding the French army to death. On 1 July 1916, the British launched their first mass offensive of the war, on the Somme. The fighting lasted until November; each side suffered some 600,000 casualties. It failed to break the stalemate.

By now the conflict was becoming a total war demanding the mobilisation of industry, carried out in Germany by Rathenau and in Britain by Lloyd George. Answers to the trench stalemate were sought in technology; poison gas was first used by the Germans at Ypres in April 1915; the British invented the tank and fielded 32 of them in the closing stages of the Somme battle, but owing to manufacturing difficulties it was only in November 1917, at Cambrai, that the first mass tank attack took place–also proving indecisive.

The struggle spread to the skies, where the handful of reconnaissance aircraft of 1914 gave place to fighters, bombers and artillery-spotters. With the Zeppelin airship and the Gotha long-range bomber the Germans introduced strategic

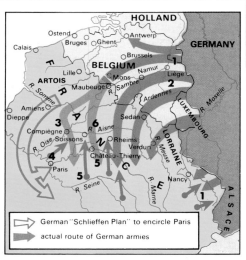

2/The German attack in the west and the battle of the Marne (left) 1 Germans invaded Belgium, successfully taking Liège on 16 August; the French offensive in Alsace was defeated with heavy loss. 2 A further French offensive towards the Ardennes was defeated, and the British and one French army were forced to retreat from the Mons area to avoid encirclement. 3 The Germans were too weak to go west of Paris as they planned, and passed north-east of Paris to cross the Marne. 4 The exposed German army north of Paris was attacked by the French army on 5 September, and in manoeuvring to oppose the French attack left a gap on its own eastern flank. 5 British and French advanced into the gap. 6 The German army retired to the Aisne to regroup.

bombing of enemy towns. By means of naval blockade the Allies sought to starve the industries and peoples of the Central powers; Germany riposted by U-boat attacks on British shipping.

Confronted by failure in the west, the Allies sought successes on other fronts: the Dardanelles (April 1915-January 1916); an offensive in Mesopotamia against the Turks; a landing at Salonika to help the Serbs. All ended in failure. Italy, which entered the war on the Allied side on 23 May 1915, likewise failed to break the Austrian front on the Isonzo.

On the Eastern Front, too, there was no decision, despite the German-Austrian offensive at Gorlice-Tarnow in 1915 and a far-reaching Russian advance under General Brusilov in 1916. Serbian resistance was crushed, but the Germans were now embedded in the prolonged two-front war they had dreaded. By the end of 1916 all the combatants recognised that victory was far off. There were peace feelers, but annexationist German demands ruled out a compromise peace. The war went on–under new and ruthless leaders: the soldiers Hindenburg and Ludendorff in Germany, the civilians Lloyd George in Britain and later Clemenceau in France. On 1 February 1917 Germany declared unrestricted U-boat warfare, in the hope of bringing Britain to her knees. This was narrowly averted by the introduction of the convoy system in May 1917. But the U-boat offensive brought the United States into the war on 6 April 1917–a potentially decisive help to the Allies.

In March, revolution broke out in Russia, sparked by heavy losses, war-weariness and economic dislocation. On 15 March 1917 the Tsar abdicated. The future of Russia as an ally lay in doubt. By May France was in deep trouble too. An offensive by the new Commander-in-Chief, Nivelle, failed to achieve his promised

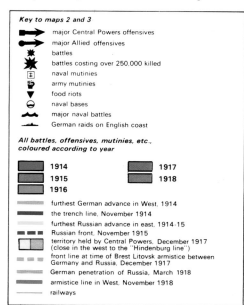

Munitions factory in England (above) As a result of the labour shortage, the British used women to do men's work in offices, factories and behind the front lines in France. Political emancipation came immediately after the war.

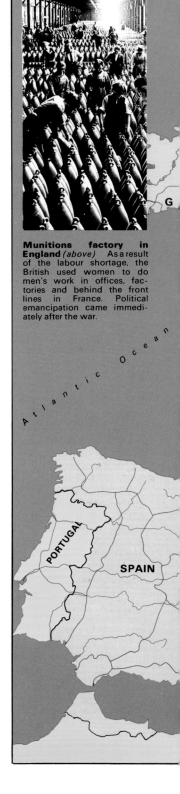

object of a breakthrough leading to peace. Widespread mutinies erupted in the French army with parallel civilian unrest on the home front. The British planned an offensive at Ypres as the best means of keeping German pressure off the French and encouraging Russia. The "Passchendaele" offensive, dogged by bad weather, failed to break the German front; each side suffered some 250,000 casualties.

In November 1917 the Bolsheviks seized power in Russia (see page 258) and in December sued for peace at Brest-Litovsk. At last the Germans could concentrate the bulk of their strength on the Western Front. On 21 March 1918 Hindenburg and Ludendorff launched a series of offensives aimed at victory in the West before the Americans could arrive in strength. They failed, despite impressive initial success. On 18 July the new Allied generalissimo, Foch, launched a French counterstroke. On 8 August Haig followed with a brilliant success on the Somme. From then on the Allies hammered the enemy without respite, breaking the Hindenburg Line on 27-30 September. Meanwhile Germany's allies, Austria Turkey and Bulgaria were beginning to collapse under Allied offensives. On 29 September Ludendorff acknowledged defeat and urged his government to ask for an immediate armistice. In October the German fleet mutinied; revolution and the abdication of the Kaiser followed,

and the new German government accepted the Allies' armistice terms. Fighting stopped on 11 November 1918.

The material and human cost of the war had been immense; the political and social consequences were incalculable. The Europe of 1914 had vanished.

4/The war in the Middle East (right) The war was not confined to Europe. In order to protect the Persian oil wells an Anglo-Indian force occupied Basra (22 Nov. 1914), and marched on Baghdad (Oct. 1915); they were forced to retreat and surrendered to the Turks at Kut (April 1916). Meanwhile, the British had repelled a Turkish attempt to cross the Suez Canal (1915), and a counter-offensive force entered Palestine in 1916. Here they were assisted by the British-sponsored Arab revolt against Ottoman rule, which broke out in June 1916 under Sherif Hussein of Mecca, but they were checked by the Turks at Gaza in 1917. To the north, the Russians occupied Turkish Armenia (July 1916), and held it until the Russian revolution restored initiative to the Ottomans. In Autumn 1917, British forces under General Allenby rallied, and pushed through Gaza to Jerusalem (11 Dec.). In Mesopotamia Kut was retaken, and Baghdad was finally captured (10 March 1917); Mosul was occupied shortly after the Anglo-Turkish Armistice (29 Oct. 1918), while Damascus had fallen to British and Arab troops at the beginning of the same month.

The war spilled over into Africa and the Far East where Germany quickly lost its colonial possessions (see page 244). The South Africans conquered German South-West Africa in July 1915; the British and French took the Cameroons and Togoland. In German East Africa the British had a far more difficult task because of the determined German defence under General von Lettow-Vorbeck. In the Pacific, Australian, New Zealand and Japanese troops captured the German colonies within four months of the outbreak of war, and the concessions in China also fell to Japanese and British forces.

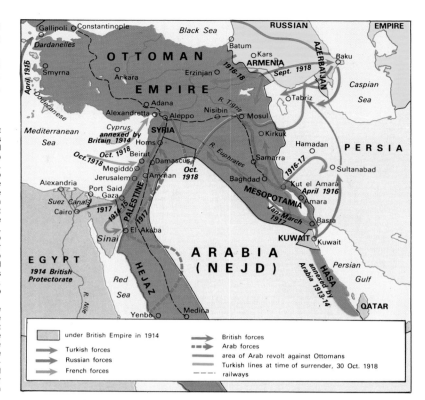

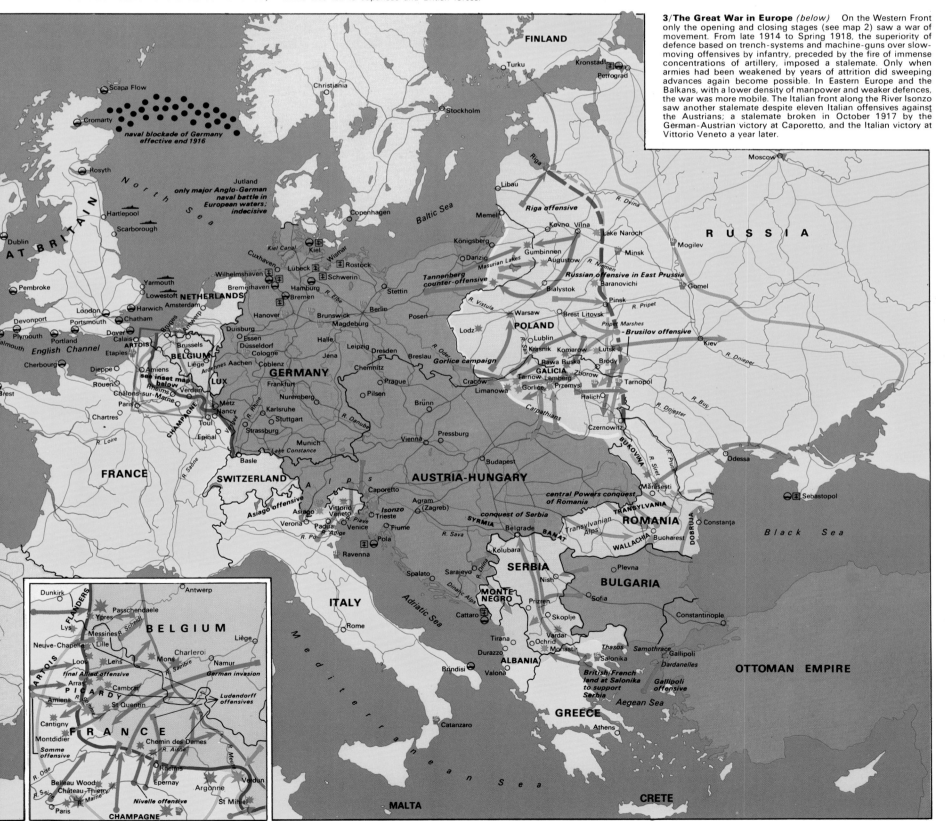

3/The Great War in Europe (below) On the Western Front only the opening and closing stages (see map 2) saw a war of movement. From late 1914 to Spring 1918, the superiority of defence based on trench-systems and machine-guns over slow-moving offensives by infantry, preceded by the fire of immense concentrations of artillery, imposed a stalemate. Only when armies had been weakened by years of attrition did sweeping advances again become possible. In Eastern Europe and the Balkans, with a lower density of manpower and weaker defences, the war was more mobile. The Italian front along the River Isonzo saw another stalemate despite eleven Italian offensives against the Austrians; a stalemate broken in October 1917 by the German-Austrian victory at Caporetto, and the Italian victory at Vittorio Veneto a year later.

7 The age

of global civilisation

The date at which the European age was succeeded by the age of global civilisation is a matter of debate. Some historians have picked out 1917 as a year of destiny. Others have seen 1947, the year of Indian independence, and 1949, the year of the Chinese revolution, as decisive turning points. The United States' declaration of war in 1917 turned a European conflict into a world war; the Bolshevik revolution in Russia, challenging the existing social and political order, split the world into two conflicting ideological camps; the independence of India and the revolution in China symbolised the resurgence of Asia and the gathering revolt against the west. All were important events in world history; but even earlier a single world economy was in existence, and the rise of the United States to world power between 1867 and 1917 was an omen of things to come.

Today it is obvious that we are in a post-European age. By making the whole world one, the European powers stirred up forces which spelled their own eclipse. The European civil war – or what has been called the second Thirty Years War, from 1914 to 1945 – whittled away the resources of the European powers, and only the healing of the wounds, symbolised by the formation of the European Economic Community in 1957, restored their fortunes. The residuary legatees, when the Second World War ended in 1945, were the Soviet Union and the United States, the two superpowers on the eastern and western flanks, whose rivalry seemed for twenty years to herald an age of bipolarity. But bipolarity may prove to be a temporary phenomenon. The recovery of Europe, the emancipation of Asia and Africa, and the rise of Japan to the first rank among the industrial powers, brought a new constellation into being, and with it the threat of a confrontation between rich nations and poor nations, and between the white and coloured peoples. Whether this is the shape of things to come, no one can foretell. All this section can do is to show, in historical perspective, how the world balance changed during the past fifty or sixty years, and the new factors in the situation.

The formation of a world economy 1870 to 1914

ONE of the main features of the period between 1870 and 1914 was the way in which the world's economy became knitted together into a single interdependent whole, to an extent inconceivable in earlier ages. The focus of this process was Europe, with the United States as a subsidiary centre, and it was from there that the impulses went out which opened up the last unknown landmasses of the globe to European exploration and penetration, as well as linking the continents, settled and unsettled, colonial and independent, with the industrial and commercial capitalism which had conquered most of Europe and North America in the preceding age.

Three closely interrelated aspects of this process are illustrated here. One was the development of means of communication, with railways and shipping taking a main share, but canals and river navigation as well as roads also playing a significant part in some areas of the globe. The basic technical problems of railways had been solved well before 1870, though improvements in speed, capacity, safety, reliability and comfort were continuously being made afterwards. Yet at that date they were limited almost wholly to Europe and the United States, and even there complete networks could be said to have existed only in north-western Europe and in the eastern states of the USA: indeed, the first United States 'transcontinental' link between the Pacific and Atlantic oceans had been forged only in 1869, though others were to follow in 1881, 1883 and 1893. In 1870, Europe had 60,400 miles of track open, the United States and Canada 56,300 miles, and the rest of the world 9,100 miles – most of which had been built by European or North American engineers. By 1911 the world's network of tracks had increased to 657,000 miles, the areas outside Europe, the United States and Canada now accounting for 175,000 miles. Among the most striking achievements were the completion of transcontinental lines in Canada (1886), in Russia to the Pacific coast at Vladivostok (1904) and in South America, to cross the Andes, in 1910. Railways also breached many other mountain barriers which had hitherto inhibited traffic flows between adjacent countries: the main lines and tunnels across the Alps are illustrated here in map 2. Yet it will be noticed that despite its relatively rapid growth, the rest of the world's mileage still largely consisted of single trunk lines instead of the dense network of the industrialised countries. This reflected the differing role of the railways in regions outside Europe and North America, where they were often built primarily as strategic lines, or as a means of tapping certain exportable primary products, rather than as an integral part of an industrialised community.

The expansion of world shipping was equally striking. It was in fact greater than the statistics indicate, as in 1870 most of the world's tonnage, apart from the British, still consisted of sailing vessels, whereas by 1913 it was composed mostly of steamers. Because of the higher speed and greater regularity obtainable in powered ships, one steam ton was generally reckoned to be the equivalent of four sailing tons, while steamers themselves greatly increased in speed and efficiency. For passengers, comfort and safety also improved. The diagram (far right) contrasts the conditions and amenities available in one of the earliest passenger liners with one of the finest vessels of the immediate pre-war years. By such developments the hardships of the crossing, which once held back emigration except among the poor and desperate, were largely removed for the millions who now flocked to North and South America, while for first-class passengers crossings on regular liners became indulgences of luxury. Again, it will be observed, the main shipping traffic was to be found among the advanced countries and the white dominions, or

between them and their producers of raw materials. The traffic among the latter had grown but little.

Canals were also built in this period, particularly in Europe. Those of the greatest significance for world trade were the ship canals that broke through important land barriers. The Suez Canal, completed in 1869, carried 437,000 net register tons in 1870 and 20,034,000 net tons in 1913; the Panama Canal, opened in August 1914, carried 4,900,000 tons of cargo in its first year. The savings in miles achieved by these two canals were particularly significant for the journeys from Europe to India, and for the routes from the east coast to the west coast of the United States.

These developments in transport reflected the concurrent developments in trade. Foreign trade, as a proportion of world output, increased from 3 per cent to 33 per cent between 1800 and 1913. It grew some threefold in volume between 1870 and 1914, and again we observe its concentration on the links among the industrialised countries, or between them and their suppliers of primary materials, and the varied markets now opening up for their manufactures: only 11 per cent of the world's trade was carried on among the primary producers themselves in 1913. Among industrial nations, trade permitted specialisation, with some advantages to consumers' choice and a very considerable contribution to furthering large-scale production. But trade between them and the primary producers was of a different nature. While in a sense it 'opened up' the latter to receive western influences of all kinds, it was not in any way directed by them, nor did it reflect their needs, except accidentally. The initiative came from entrepreneurs in the West, looking for markets, food and raw materials.

The operation of a single multi-national system of world trade, pivoting on London, was made possible by the adoption of a gold standard

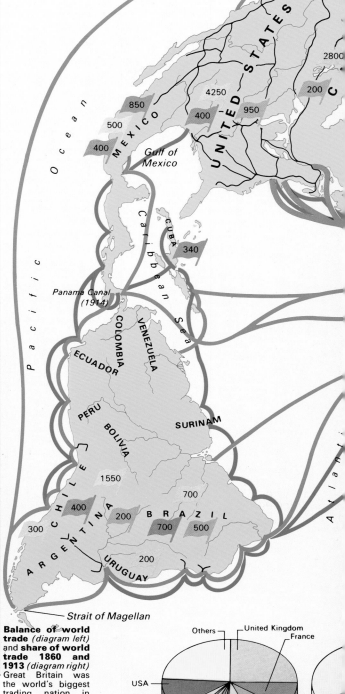

		Europe	N. America	S. America	Asia	Africa
UNITED KINGDOM	imports 1860	419	252	96	143	80
	exports 1860	358	132	74	139	36
	imports 1913	1,548	848	393	458	220
	exports 1913	917	265	272	620	248
USA	imports 1860	217	—	80	29	—
	exports 1860	249	—	46	11	—
	imports 1913	893	199	381	298	26
	exports 1913	1,479	469	294	140	29
FRANCE	imports 1860	234	47	41	16	34
	exports 1860	293	49	53	3	45
	imports 1913	880	187	183	192	148
	exports 1913	937	89	94	36	181
HOLLAND	imports 1860	92	5	3	32	—
	exports 1860	87	2	1	14	—
	imports 1913	624	190	87	274	14
	exports 1913	1,131	57	9	73	14
GERMANY	imports 1913	1,402	423	290	250	118
	exports 1913	1,828	184	183	130	50
RUSSIA	imports 1913	556	—	—	—	—
	exports 1913	719	—	—	—	—

figures in million dollars US

Suez and Panama (above) Not until the advent of the commercial aeroplane was the world again so significantly shrunk as by the opening of these two great canals.

Balance of world trade (diagram left) and **share of world trade 1860 and 1913** (diagram right) Great Britain was the world's biggest trading nation in 1860 but by 1913 Germany had twice the exports to Europe and America was catching up just as fast. British, Dutch and French networks in the wider world were still predominant.

Strait of Magellan

1860 share of world trade

total $8 billion

for the currencies of the chief European nations between 1863 and 1874. It was also intimately connected with the third type of international linkage shown here: foreign investment. Normally flowing from the more advanced to the poorer regions, the transfer of capital had earlier in the 19th century been largely a phenomenon occurring within Europe and North America, and indeed much of it was still of this kind in 1914. In this setting, the process undoubtedly assisted and speeded economic advancement, especially when devoted to building up the costly infrastructure, such as railways and other public works, for developing nations which could then ultimately repay their international debts. But increasingly, as these investments flowed into the non-industrial regions of Europe such as Russia, the Balkan countries and the Ottoman Empire, and then to overseas territories which were without either the knowledge or the power to direct the capital flow, it did not help to develop them, but rather to colonise them, often

destroying what native industry there was. Where the loans were made to governments, or to enterprises guaranteed by government, as many inevitably were, they raised serious questions of political control, and as rival European powers fought for concessions and controls in overseas areas, the rivalries and conflicts engendered thereby became part of the drive to 'imperialism' and to war.

Britain was the largest source of foreign investment, and London a highly important centre of banking. British overseas assets in 1914 totalled nearly £4000 million. France and Germany were the other chief lenders, but the total foreign investments of France, Germany, Belgium, Holland and the United States put together amounted to less than £5500 million. The United States and Russia were still, in fact, net borrowers of foreign capital.

Closely associated with the movement of capital was the large-scale migration of labour illustrated on page 208.

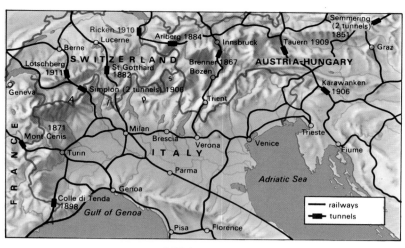

2/Alpine tunnels and railways *(above)* Only two rail routes pierced the Alps in 1870, but in the next forty-one years they were joined by another ten, many of them involving feats of tunnel-building and civil engineering on a previously unparalleled scale.

1/The development of the world economy *(below)* Between 1870 and 1914 the whole world became closely connected by an intricate web of transport routes, communication channels, trading relationships and financial flows. The major benefits, however, remained concentrated where the network was at its most dense – among the industrial nations of Europe and North America.

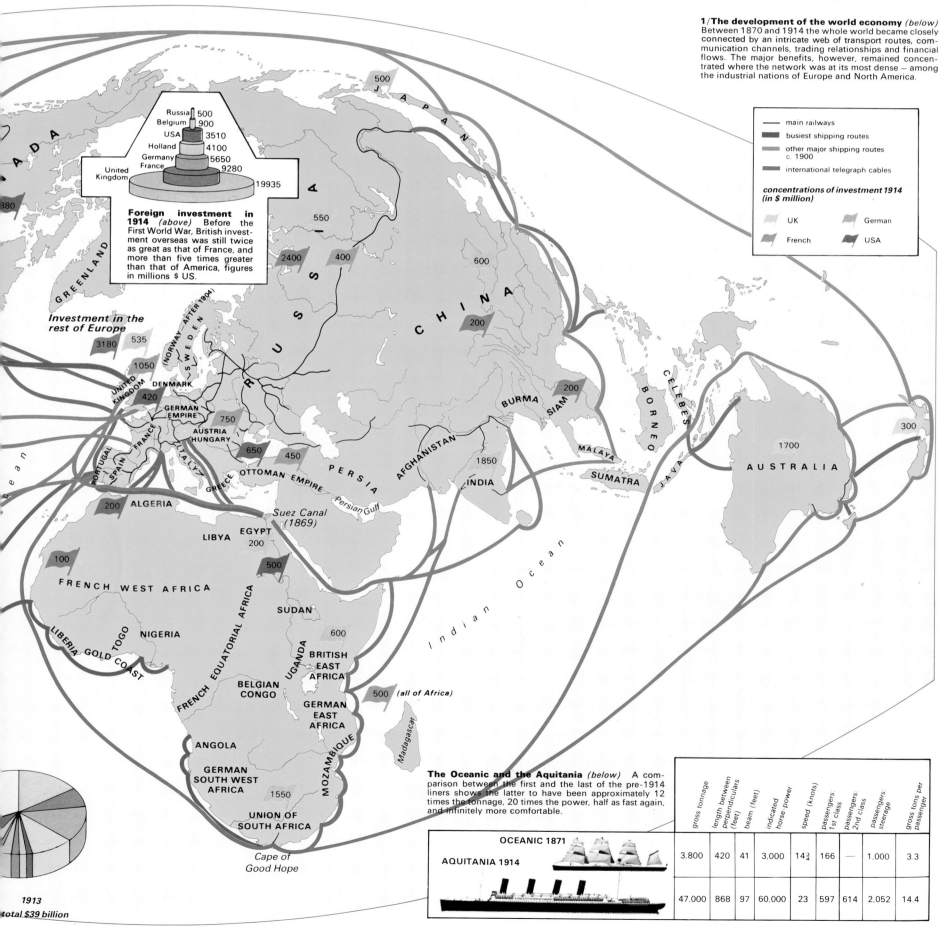

Foreign investment in 1914 *(above)* Before the First World War, British investment overseas was still twice as great as that of France, and more than five times greater than that of America, figures in millions $ US.

The Oceanic and the Aquitania *(below)* A comparison between the first and the last of the pre-1914 liners shows the latter to have been approximately 12 times the tonnage, 20 times the power, half as fast again, and infinitely more comfortable.

	gross tonnage	length between perpendiculars (feet)	beam (feet)	indicated horse-power	speed (knots)	passengers 1st class	passengers 2nd class	passengers steerage	gross tons per passenger
OCEANIC 1871	3,800	420	41	3,000	14¾	166	—	1,000	3.3
AQUITANIA 1914	47,000	868	97	60,000	23	597	614	2,052	14.4

The Russian Revolution 1917 to 1925

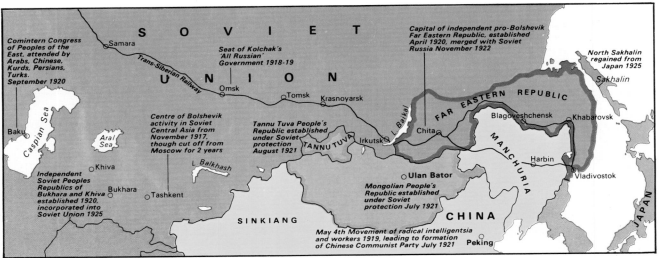

3/Red Star over Asia (left) '...the east has been definitely drawn into the revolutionary movement...In the last analysis, the outcome of the struggle will be determined by the fact that Russia, India, China, etc. account for the overwhelming majority of the population of the globe.' (From Lenin's last article, March 1923). As the prospects of revolution dimmed in the west, Lenin looked eastwards to the backward countries colonised by the great powers. Here the struggle for national independence might be combined with the fight for socialism. Victory, though perhaps far off, would fatally weaken the capitalist world.

Architect of revolution (left) From its foundation in 1903, Lenin dominated the Bolshevik party. His combination of theoretical originality, political decisiveness and passionate dedication to the socialist cause made him the greatest revolutionary leader of modern times. Trotsky (bottom right of picture), the only other Bolshevik whose stature approached Lenin's during the revolution and civil war, himself acknowledged that without Lenin the Bolshevik revolution would have been impossible.

2/Red Star over Europe (below) 'If we come out now, we shall have all proletarian Europe on our side.' (Lenin, October 1917). The Bolsheviks seized power firmly convinced that socialist revolution was imminent in advanced western countries. These, they believed, would come to the aid of backward Russia. At first events in central and eastern Europe seemed to justify their optimism. By 1921, however, revolution was on the retreat, and Soviet Russia isolated.

NO other single event has had such decisive impact upon the modern world as the Russian Revolution of 1917. It opened a new epoch in Russia's history, transforming an underdeveloped country into an industrial and military superpower, fundamentally altering the pattern of international relations. Above all, it inaugurated the age of modern revolutions. By showing that Marxists could gain power and begin the construction of a socialist society, the Bolsheviks inspired revolutionaries everywhere to emulate their victory. After 1917 the world could never be the same again.

By March 1917 the strain of war had fatally weakened the Tsarist government. Liberals, socialists, businessmen, generals, nobles–all were plotting its overthrow. Yet the disturbances in Petrograd which in four days destroyed the regime owed little to organised opposition. Sheer hunger turned wage demands into a general strike and bread queues into anti-government demonstrations. Ordered to disperse the crowds, the garrison mutinied. Nicholas II set out for the capital from his headquarters at Mogilev, but was prevented by railway workers from arriving. On 15 March at Pskov he abdicated. Authority now passed to a Provisional Government established by prominent Duma politicians. But its power was limited by the existence of the Petrograd Soviet (or Council) of Workers' and Soldiers' Deputies. The latter, looked to for leadership by Soviets throughout Russia, effectively constituted an alternative government. At first, however, the instability of 'dual power' was not apparent. The Soviet's moderate, Menshevik and Socialist-Revolutionary leaders supported the Government, and in May entered it. Even the Bolsheviks initially gave their qualified support.

Their policy was dramatically reversed in April when Lenin returned to Petrograd. All Europe, he declared, was on the brink of socialist revolution. Marxists should therefore destroy the Provisional Government and transfer all power to the Soviets. This was a crucial turning-point. The Government, struggling to maintain order amid mounting chaos, was now faced with outright opposition. As the war dragged on, the desire for peace spread, and desertions from the army escalated. Impatient with official procrastination over agrarian reform, the peasants began to seize the land. Urban workers, discontented about failures to improve their conditions, became increasingly militant. Support grew for the Bolsheviks, with their promise of peace, land and bread. In September they won control of the Petrograd and Moscow Soviets, and in October gained a majority at the Second All-Russian Congress of Soviets. The outcome was inevitable – a coup by Left or Right. In September the Commander-in-Chief, General Kornilov, marched on the capital, only to be abandoned by his troops. Two months later, on 7 November (25 October according to the old calendar), the Bolsheviks struck. Organised by Trotsky, they seized strategic points in Petrograd, arrested the Provisional Government, and in the name of the Soviets assumed power.

But could they retain it? Few people thought so. Even the Bolsheviks believed only revolution in western Europe could guarantee survival. When Germany demanded humiliating territorial concessions in return for peace, a majority wanted to fight on, however hopelessly, rather than capitulate. Nevertheless, Lenin's determination to gain time prevailed, and the Treaty of Brest-Litovsk was signed. Almost immediately, White Russian armies, assisted by foreign powers, attacked the young Soviet republic. After three years of brutal civil war, the Bolsheviks emerged victorious – but at enormous cost. Thirteen million people perished in the war and subsequent famine. The economy was shattered, with industrial production in 1920 at only a seventh of its 1913 level. Money lost significance and was replaced by a barter system which, combined with an attempt at state direction of the economy, was dignified by the title 'War Communism'. In the battle with counter-revolution democracy vanished, dictatorial power exercised by the Communist Party replacing rule by Soviets in all but name. As the war ended, a wave of strikes and riots broke out, culminating in mutiny at the Kronstadt naval base in February 1921. The regime was in no mood for political concessions, and ruthlessly suppressed rebellion. Economic concessions, however, were granted. In March 1921, Lenin announced the New Economic Policy (NEP). Food requisitioning was replaced by a 'tax in kind', with peasants allowed to sell surplus produce on the free market. Private firms were freed from government control; the retail trade largely returned to private hands. In effect, a market economy was restored.

Again the Bolsheviks won a breathing-space. The economy rapidly revived. By late 1925, industrial production had virtually regained its pre-war level. Relative prosperity created a more relaxed atmosphere, reflected especially in cultural life. Despite the failure of revolutionary movements elsewhere, greater security resulted from resumption of relations with the outside world. A trade agreement with Britain in 1921 was followed by the Rapallo Treaty of 1922 with Germany, and by diplomatic recognition in 1924 from Britain, France and other European countries.

This new-found stability could only be short-term. Soviet Russia was still isolated, still surrounded by hostile capitalist powers. The majority of its population were still peasants, wedded to their land, sharing few of their rulers' socialist aims. How could Russia advance? Was NEP a short pause before renewal of the socialist offensive, or a long-term programme for acquiring the economic preconditions for socialism? Lenin provided no answer before his death in January 1924. During the struggle for the succession, two distinct lines emerged: Trotsky's policy of encouraging revolution abroad and industrialising rapidly at home, and Stalin's strategy of gradual economic growth plus recognition of capitalism's temporary stabilisation – 'permanent revolution' versus 'socialism in one country'. Labelled an extremist, by 1925 Trotsky had been manoeuvred out of high government office. Stalin and Bukharin now dominated Soviet politics. Moderation, it seemed, had triumphed.

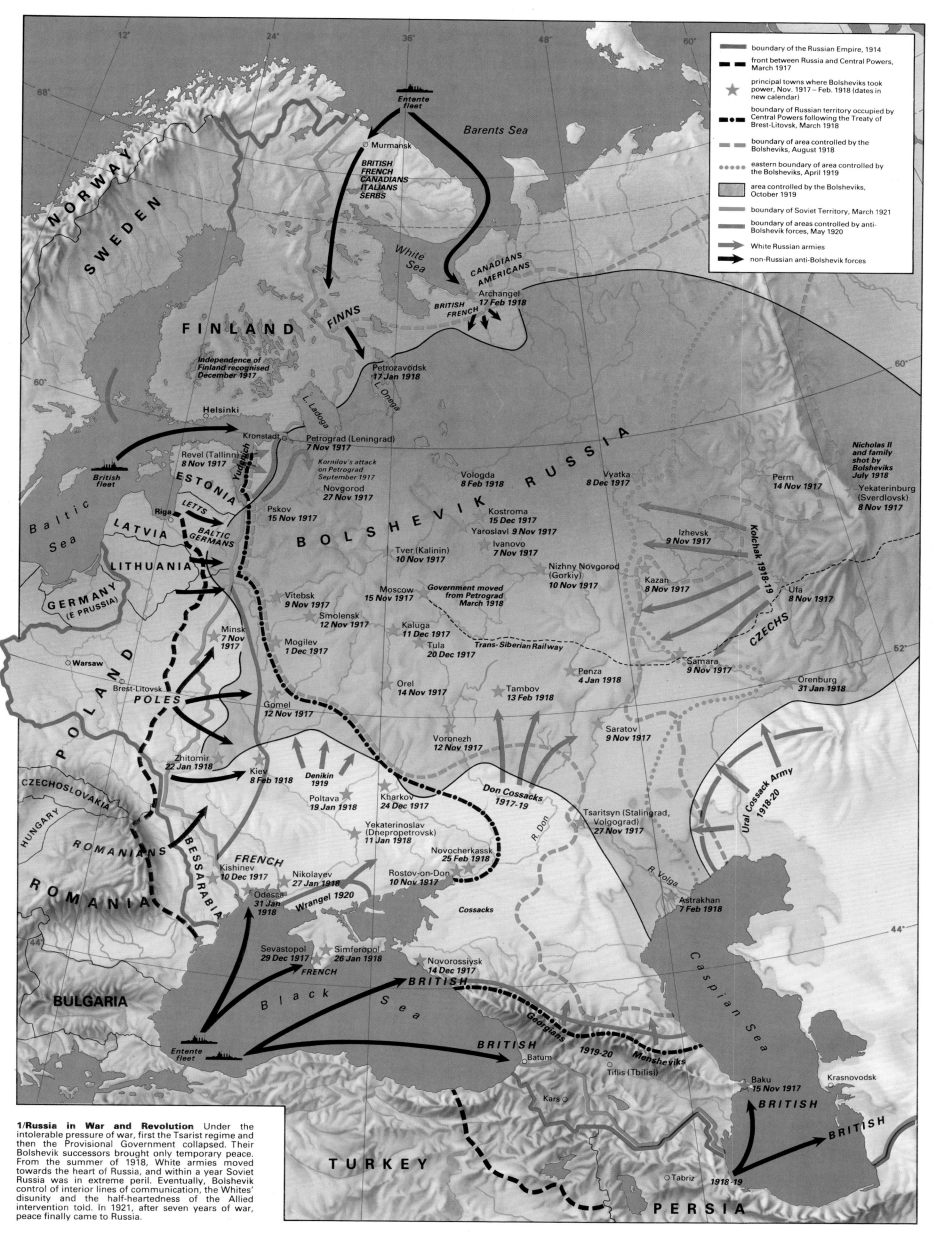

1/Russia in War and Revolution Under the intolerable pressure of war, first the Tsarist regime and then the Provisional Government collapsed. Their Bolshevik successors brought only temporary peace. From the summer of 1918, White armies moved towards the heart of Russia, and within a year Soviet Russia was in extreme peril. Eventually, Bolshevik control of interior lines of communication, the Whites' disunity and the half-heartedness of the Allied intervention told. In 1921, after seven years of war, peace finally came to Russia.

Imperialism and nationalism 1919 to 1941

BY the 1920s the European empires in Asia and North Africa had reached their greatest extent. At the end of the First World War, France gained control of Syria and Lebanon. Iraq, Palestine and Transjordan were drawn into the area of British control which already included Egypt, the Sudan, the southern and eastern fringes of Arabia, India, Burma, Ceylon and the Malay states. The Dutch remained in the East Indies, the Spaniards consolidated their control over the northern zone of Morocco, and the Italians theirs over Libya. After this, the only important addition was Ethiopia, conquered by Italy in 1936. Turkey, Persia, Saudi Arabia, Yemen, Afghanistan and Siam were independent, but only within limits: the military power of Europe and the domination of world markets by the industrial states of the West were facts which even independent countries had to take into account. Moreover, this situation began to assume a new dimension with the increasing demand for oil for armies and industry, and the discovery and exploitation of large oil resources in the Middle East, especially in Persia and Iraq.

The position of the imperial powers was weaker than it seemed, however. The exhaustion of the victors in the First World War; the growth of a new conception of imperial rule as something temporary and limited, expressed both in the British idea of progress towards 'dominion status' and in the mandate system of the League of Nations; criticism and challenges coming from the United States, the USSR and later from Nazi Germany: all these limited the freedom of action of Great Britain and France. The countries of Asia and North Africa were for the most part also countries of ancient literate civilisation, with a tradition of independence or participation in their own government; in some of them, several generations of modern education had produced an élite which was playing some part in colonial administration and wished to obtain greater autonomy as a step towards independence.

Thus the colonial powers were faced with increasing opposition in Asia and North Africa, though not yet in sub-Saharan Africa. Reaction to it was a mixture of repression and concession. Opposition was of two kinds either led by traditional rulers or élites making use of indigenous social forces. Thus in Morocco first Spanish and then French rule was threatened by a revolt in the Rif mountains, led by Abd el-Krim and only suppressed with difficulty (1921-26); and in Cyrenaica, the Italian conquest met with prolonged resistance from the Sanusi tribesmen. The ruler of Afghanistan, long dependent on British India in foreign affairs, threatened the British position on the troubled North-West Frontier in 1919, and secured his independence by the treaty of 1921.

In other places, the new educated élite espoused the idea that each nation (whether defined in territorial or in ethnic terms) should have its own independent state. But in this period nationalist movements could only present a serious challenge in countries where they were able to mobilise wider support. This occurred first in Turkey, where the nationalists, led by Mustafa Kemál (Atatürk), were able to defeat Anglo-French plans for the partition of the Ottoman Empire, to abolish their own traditional system of government, and to create an independent Turkish republic in 1923.

In the former Arab regions of the Ottoman Empire similar attempts to secure independence had less success. In Syria, a nation-wide revolt beginning in the Jebel Druze was eventually suppressed (1925-27), and the French made only minor concessions before the end of the Second World War. In Iraq, a revolt in 1920 helped to persuade the British to create an autonomous government under an Arab king, Faisal, of the Hashemite dynasty of the Hejaz, which some nationalists were willing to accept as a first step; by 1932, Iraq had secured formal independence and membership of the League of Nations, but the British military presence continued under the new treaty. In Palestine, the conflict resulting from Britain's support for the creation of a Jewish national home led to disturbances in the 1920s, and opposition to the rise in Jewish

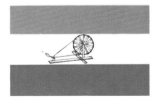

The Indian national flag *(above)*, adopted by the Congress Party in 1930, showed a spinning wheel, the symbol of Gandhi's appeal to Indians to revive their traditional way of life and win economic independence. It was first hoisted by Nehru as President of Congress on 1 January 1930 to launch the civil disobedience campaign.

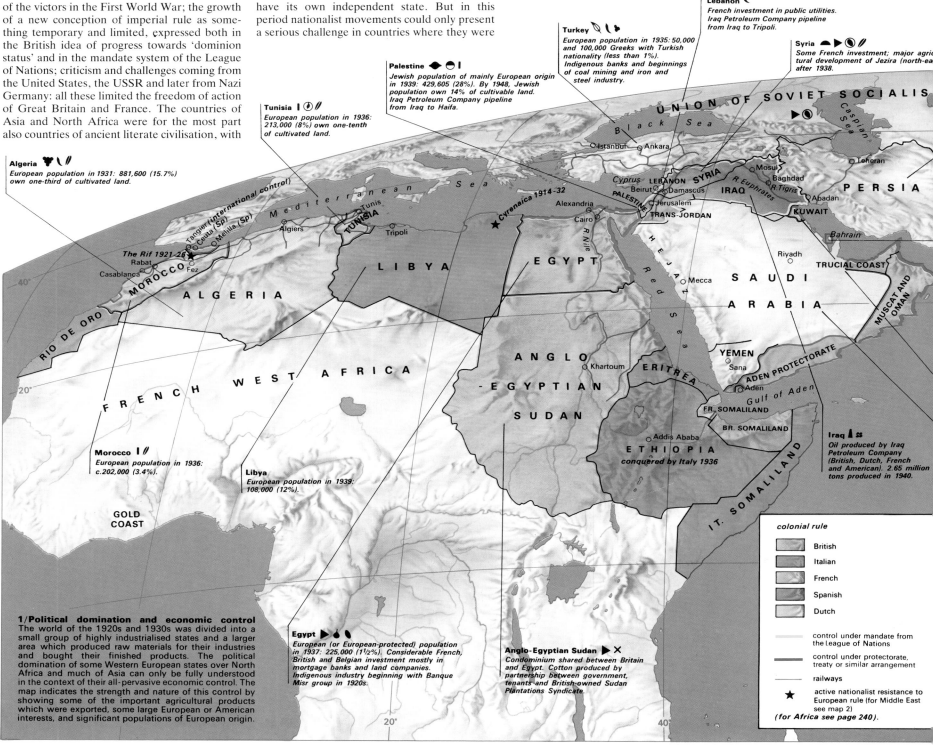

Turkey 🖋 \ ➤
European population in 1935: 50,000 and 100,000 Greeks with Turkish nationality (less than 1%). Indigenous banks and beginnings of coal mining and iron and steel industry.

Palestine ◆ ◐ ▮
Jewish population of mainly European origin in 1939: 429,605 (28%). By 1948, Jewish population own 14% of cultivable land. Iraq Petroleum Company pipeline from Iraq to Haifa.

Lebanon ↳
French investment in public utilities. Iraq Petroleum Company pipeline from Iraq to Tripoli.

Syria ➤ ◐ ⁄⁄
Some French investment; major agricultural development of Jezira (north-east) after 1938.

Tunisia ▮ ◐ ⁄⁄
European population in 1936: 213,000 (8%) own one-tenth of cultivated land.

Algeria ♥ \ ⁄⁄
European population in 1931: 881,600 (15.7%) own one-third of cultivated land.

Morocco ▮ ⁄⁄
European population in 1936: c.202,000 (3.4%).

Libya
European population in 1939: 108,000 (12%).

Egypt ➤ ◐ ◐
European (or European-protected) population in 1937: 225,000 (1½%). Considerable French, British and Belgian investment mostly in mortgage banks and land companies. Indigenous industry beginning with Banque Misr group in 1920s.

Anglo-Egyptian Sudan ➤ ✕
Condominium shared between Britain and Egypt. Cotton produced by partnership between government, tenants and British-owned Sudan Plantations Syndicate.

Iraq ▮ ▤
Oil produced by Iraq Petroleum Company (British, Dutch, French and American). 2.65 million tons produced in 1940.

1/Political domination and economic control
The world of the 1920s and 1930s was divided into a small group of highly industrialised states and a larger area which produced raw materials for their industries and bought their finished products. The political domination of some Western European states over North Africa and much of Asia can only be fully understood in the context of their all-pervasive economic control. The map indicates the strength and nature of this control by showing some of the important agricultural products which were exported, some large European or American interests, and significant populations of European origin.

colonial rule

British
Italian
French
Spanish
Dutch

control under mandate from the League of Nations

control under protectorate, treaty or similar arrangement

railways

★ active nationalist resistance to European rule (for Middle East see map 2)

(for Africa see page 240).

immigration after Hitler's seizure of power in Germany in 1933 led to a widespread Arab revolt between 1935 and 1939. In Egypt, the main nationalist party, the Wafd under Saad Zaghlul, succeeded in mobilising considerable popular support. A national revolt in 1919 ultimately led to Britain conceding independence in 1922, although a number of important matters were 'absolutely reserved to the discretion of His Majesty's Government'. In 1936 an Anglo-Egyptian treaty gave Egyptians wider control over their affairs, but military control and the management of the Suez Canal remained outside Egyptian hands. Further west, in the European colonies of North Africa, nationalist feeling was less developed; the Moroccan and Algerian movements were only beginning in the 1930s, and the pressures exerted on the French by the Néo-Destour in Tunisia were insufficient to change basic policies.

In India, too, the main nationalist party, the Indian National Congress, was by now gathering wide popular support, thanks largely to the leadership of Mahatma Gandhi. By linking the idea of nationalism with traditional Hindu thought and action, Gandhi propelled India into the age of mass politics. His first civil disobedience campaign in 1920 misfired, and was followed by a period of repression. But in 1930, profiting from the unrest caused by unemployment and the world economic depression, he launched a second campaign which went on for some years and played a part in inducing the British to introduce the Government of India Act in 1935. This provided a framework of participation, in central and still more in provincial governments, which the more conservative elements in Congress were able to accept, but was less to the liking of more radical nationalists such as Jawaharlal Nehru; in 1937 Congress controlled the majority of the fourteen provin-

cial governments. This phase, however, came to an end with the Second World War; Congress decided not to participate in the war effort, and its ministers resigned. By this time, moreover, leaders of the Muslim population were developing their own movements; in 1940 their most powerful group, the Muslim League, which aimed at a special status for the Muslim parts of India, passed a resolution calling for an autonomous Pakistan.

In other areas of the colonial world the distress of the 1930s was a catalyst, providing nationalist leaders with the popular support hitherto for the most part lacking. This was the case in the Gold Coast, where the cocoa farmers, hit by falling world prices, were stirred into action; and throughout the West Indies, beginning in St Kitts in 1935, there were riots and strikes. In some cases, the result was concessions which created a temporary balance of forces, as in Ceylon, where a new constitution was in force from 1931, and in Burma, which was separated from India and given a limited kind of responsible government in 1935. In the Dutch East Indies a phase of revolutionary movements, beginning with the Communist revolt of 1926, was suppressed with only limited changes in provincial government, and the Dutch were able to ride out the storm until the arrival of the Japanese in 1941. In French Indo-China no concessions were made, and the policy of retaining firm French control led to outbreaks in the 1930s, and the creation of the Viet Minh by Ho Chi Minh in 1941. But the period as a whole saw the rise of new, more radical nationalist leaders — Azikiwe in West Africa, Ho Chi Minh in Vietnam, Nehru in India, Sukarno in Indonesia, Bourguiba in Tunisia — who understood better than their predecessors how to manipulate popular forces and who were destined to make their mark after the end of the Second World War.

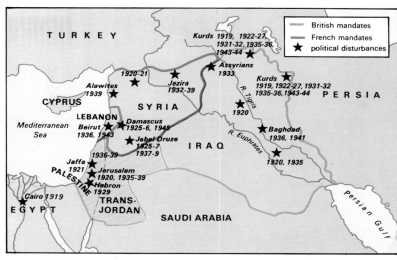

2/Disturbances in Egypt and the mandated territories of the Middle East, 1919 to 1945 *(above)* These included instances of opposition to British and French imperialism and also attempts by rural or minority populations to resist the newly-created central governments.

Egypt 1919 Nation-wide revolt, organised by the Wafd Party, against British refusal to consider an Egyptian request for independence and the end of the British protectorate.

Palestine 1920, 1921, 1929, 1935-39 Riots and disturbances and Arab Revolt (1935-39): expressions of opposition by indigenous Arab population to Jewish immigration, land purchase and exclusivist labour policy. Nation-wide strikes and rural rising 1936-39. Jewish agitation for increased immigration.

Syria/Lebanon 1920-21, 1925-27, 1936-39, 1943-45 Local rebellions (Aleppo 1920-21, Jebel Druze 1925-27) against French adminis-

tration; national risings against the mandate (1925-27); further revolt against French failure to grant independence (1943-45). Local revolts against centralised government in Jebel Druze (1937-39), Jezira (1937-39) and Alawite area (1939). Local disturbance in Beirut in 1936 between anti-French Muslims, and pro-French Armenian Christians.

Iraq 1920, 1933, 1935, 1936, 1941 Revolt of rural tribes against British military rule (1920); massacre of Assyrian Christians (community closely associated with British rule) (1933); major tribal rising in the Euphrates basin against centralised government (1935); military coup (1936); attempted seizure of power by pro-Axis politico-military group (Baghdad 1941).

Iraqi Kurdistan 1919, 1922-27, 1931-32, 1935-36, 1943-44 Kurds promised (and subsequently denied) autonomy under unratified Treaty of Sèvres (1920); revolts in northern Iraq led by Sheikh Mahmud Barzinji, later by Mulla Mustafa Barzani.

Anti-colonial uprisings *(below)*
Afghanistan 1919 Anglo-Afghan war May-June 1919 precipitated by King Amanullah's declaration of Afghan independence, following recognition by Soviet Russia; British acquiescence, August 1919.

The Rif 1921-26 Attempt by Berber tribesmen under Abd el-Krim to establish state independent of Spanish, and later French, rule.

Cyrenaica 1914-32 Long, drawn-out attempt by Arabs of Cyrenaica, within the framework of the Sanusi religious brotherhood, to resist Italian occupation.

India 1919-41 Most populous and complex society to be wholly colonised, its nationalist movement was the most articulate and highly

organised. General disturbances, characterised by Gandhi's civil disobedience campaigns: first in 1920, called off in 1922 after violence and bloodshed; second in 1930, inaugurated by famous 'march to the sea', called off in 1934. Important disturbances took place in Amritsar (1919) when British troops dispersed urban demonstration with considerable loss of life, and in Bengal (1923-32) which had a long period of intermittent terrorist activity.

Dutch East Indies 1926 Attempted rebellion by the Communist party in support of nationalist demand for self-rule.

Indo-China 1930 Urban strikes and rural rebellion, aiming at national independence and mainly organised by the Communist party led by Ho Chi Minh.

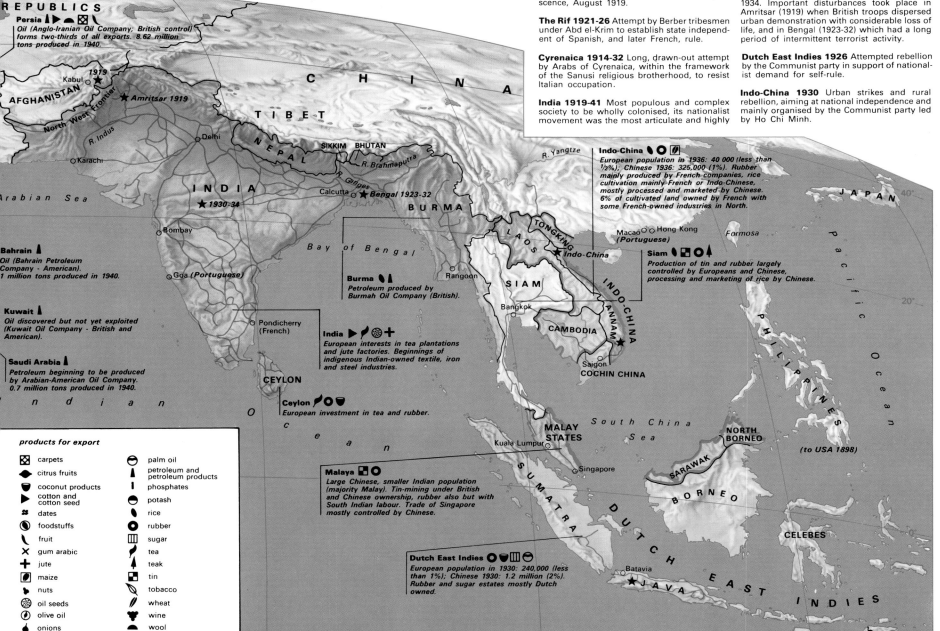

products for export

- carpets
- citrus fruits
- coconut products
- cotton and cotton seed
- dates
- foodstuffs
- fruit
- gum arabic
- jute
- maize
- nuts
- oil seeds
- olive oil
- onions
- palm oil
- petroleum and petroleum products
- phosphates
- potash
- rice
- rubber
- sugar
- tea
- teak
- tin
- tobacco
- wheat
- wine
- wool

Persia
Oil (Anglo-Iranian Oil Company; British control) forms two-thirds of all exports. 8.62 million tons produced in 1940.

Bahrain
Oil (Bahrain Petroleum Company - American). 1 million tons produced in 1940.

Kuwait
Oil discovered but not yet exploited (Kuwait Oil Company - British and American).

Saudi Arabia
Petroleum beginning to be produced by Arabian-American Oil Company. 0.7 million tons produced in 1940.

Burma
Petroleum produced by Burmah Oil Company (British).

India
European interests in tea plantations and jute factories. Beginnings of indigenous Indian-owned textile, iron and steel industries.

Ceylon
European investment in tea and rubber.

Malaya
Large Chinese, smaller Indian population (majority Malay). Tin-mining under British and Chinese ownership, rubber also but with South Indian labour. Trade of Singapore mostly controlled by Chinese.

Dutch East Indies
European population in 1930: 240,000 (less than 1%); Chinese 1930: 1.2 million (2%). Rubber and sugar estates mostly Dutch owned.

Indo-China
European population in 1936: 40 000 (less than ½%); Chinese 1936: 325,000 (1%). Rubber mainly produced by French companies, rice cultivation mainly French or Indo-Chinese, mostly processed and marketed by Chinese. 6% of cultivated land owned by French with some French-owned industries in North.

Siam
Production of tin and rubber largely controlled by Europeans and Chinese, processing and marketing of rice by Chinese.

The Chinese Revolution
1912 to 1949

1/The Northern Expedition 1926-27 In 1926 the Kuomintang and their Communist allies launched a major expedition to unify the country. Their government was moved to Wuhan, which became the centre of the Left. In April 1927 Chiang Kai-shek carried out a purge of the Communists, and transferred the capital to Nanking. Subsequent operations against the Feng-tien faction in the north were joined by Yen Hsi-shan, warlord of Shansi, and Feng Yu-hsiang leader of the Kuo-min-chün faction. Although the Kuomintang now claimed to control China, many areas remained outside their effective control.

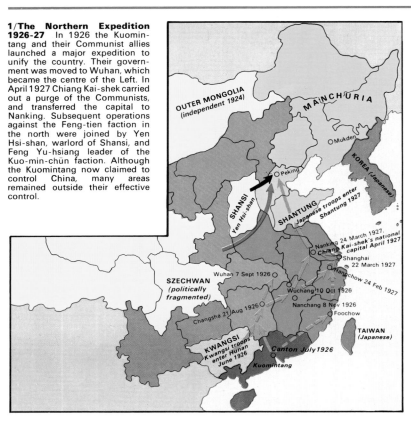

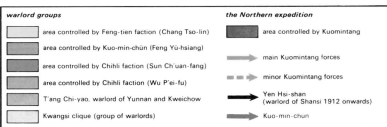

warlord groups	the Northern expedition
area controlled by Feng-tien faction (Chang Tso-lin)	area controlled by Kuomintang
area controlled by Kuo-min-chün (Feng Yü-hsiang)	
area controlled by Chihli faction (Sun Ch'uan-fang)	main Kuomintang forces
area controlled by Chihli faction (Wu P'ei-fu)	minor Kuomintang forces
T'ang Chi-yao, warlord of Yunnan and Kweichow	Yen Hsi-shan (warlord of Shansi 1912 onwards)
Kwangsi clique (group of warlords)	Kuo-min-chun

2/The Nationalist (Kuomintang) regime (1928-37) only controlled part of China. The north-east was occupied by Japan from 1931 and the Japanese constantly attempted to gain complete control of northern China. Warlords remained in control of many provinces; other areas were in a state of anarchy. Large areas of Kiangsi were under a Communist regime from 1931 to 1934, and by 1936 the Communists had a new base in the north-west at Yenan.

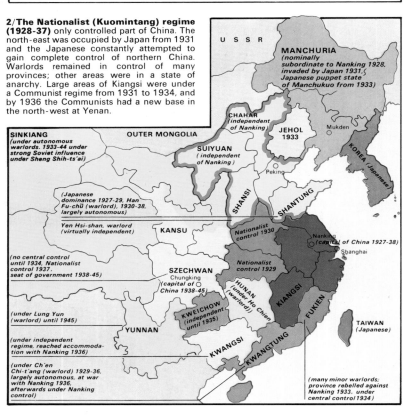

occupied by Japan by 1933	
area in which Japan attempted to establish a puppet North China state 1935	
area under effective control of Chiang Kai-shek's Nationalist government at Nanking 1928	
brought under Nanking control 1929-34	
brought under Nanking control 1935-37	
brought under Nanking influence 1935-37	

THE foundation of the Republic in 1912 failed to produce a lasting political solution for China's problems. Within weeks Sun Yat-sen, the revolutionary who had been elected China's first president, was replaced by Yuan Shih-k'ai, China's most powerful military figure under the old order. Yuan and the revolutionary leaders were soon involved in bitter political struggles; Yuan suppressed a 'Second Revolution' that broke out in the provinces in 1913, and by 1914 was a virtual dictator.

China's position was seriously weakened. The government was forced to borrow huge sums abroad to offset the lack of a modern revenue system, and the whole customs revenue passed into foreign hands. Tibet and Mongolia broke away, becoming autonomous, but under British and Russian dominance respectively, and in 1924 Mongolia finally became independent. More serious were the expansionist plans of Japan. When the outbreak of the First World War diverted the attention of the Western powers from Asia, Japan seized the German leased territory and sphere of influence in Shantung, and then presented China with a set of demands which would have reduced her to a Japanese dependency. Yuan resisted the more extreme demands, but in 1915 a treaty was signed establishing Japanese dominance in Shantung, Manchuria and Inner Mongolia. This provoked a massive upsurge of nationalist feeling.

Yuan died in 1916, after attempting unsuccessfully to have himself made emperor. His regime left China with a weak and unstable central government, and real authority in the provinces passed increasingly into the hands of the generals. For the next decade, although the government in Peking claimed to govern China, it was the puppet of one group of generals or another, and the country was divided between rival warlords. Some of these, as in Shansi, Kwangsi and Manchuria, established relatively stable regimes, sometimes instituting reformist programmes. In other areas, such as Szechwan, anarchy prevailed, with a host of petty generals living off the countryside. Even some of the most powerful warlord leaders, such as Feng Yü-hsiang, never found a permanent territorial base. In the 1920s there was a series of devastating wars between the major warlord coalitions, which not only destroyed orderly civil government but also caused millions of casualties and untold physical damage and disruption. Only the Treaty Ports were secure under foreign protection.

The early 1920s saw an upsurge of revolutionary activity. Both the revolutionaries and the nascent Communist party benefited from widespread popular reaction against foreign interference, the grossly unfair terms of the Paris Peace Conference, which reinforced Japan's position in Shantung, and economic exploitation. In 1919 this upsurge of nationalism erupted in the 4 May Movement, in which a new generation of Western-orientated students and intellectuals, together with urban workers, first made themselves a force in politics, forcing the government to refuse to sign the Treaty of Versailles.

Sun Yat-sen's revolutionary party had established a regional regime in Canton. From 1923 Sun reorganised the Nationalist (Kuomintang) Party and its army, with aid and advice from the Comintern, and entered into an alliance with the still minuscule Communist Party. Sun died suddenly in 1925, and in that year anti-foreign feeling reached a new peak with widespread strikes and boycotts in which both organised labour and the merchant class joined. Communist influence rapidly gained ground in the industrial cities. In 1926 Chiang Kai-shek, the principal general of the Kuomintang army, led a 'Northern Expedition' aimed at the elimination of the warlords and the unification of the nation. At the end of 1926 the Nationalist government moved to Wuhan, while its armies moved into

the lower Yangtze, taking Nanking and Shanghai in April 1927. Chiang Kai-shek now instigated a purge of his Communist allies, and set up a regime of his own in Nanking. Communist troops rose against Chiang in Nanchang in August 1927, but were easily put down, as was a peasant rising in Hunan. In 1928 Chiang's armies again turned north and took Peking.

Although the Nationalists now dominated China, and were recognised as the national government, the warlords were not eliminated. Even after the most powerful warlords, Yen Hsi-shan and Feng Yü-hsiang, were defeated in a major war in 1929-30, many provinces retained a great degree of autonomy, and warfare with provincial armies repeatedly broke out. Chiang's government held firm centralised control only over the rich provinces of the lower Yangtze, where they modernised the administration and the army, built a road system and railways, and established new industry in spite of world depression and constant Japanese pressure. But much of this development was concentrated in the cities, particularly in Shanghai and Nanking.

In addition to continued warlord power, Chiang had to face the far more serious threat of Japanese expansion. The Japanese had constantly intervened in warlord politics, especially in the north-east. In 1931 they occupied Manchuria, in 1933 establishing there a puppet state of Manchukuo under the last Manchu emperor. They then occupied the neighbouring province of Jehol, and in 1935 unsuccessfully attempted to establish a puppet regime controlling all northern China. In Manchuria they rapidly built up the basis of a modern economy, with a dense railway network and various heavy and light industries, on a scale unmatched elsewhere in China. This economic growth was intensified after the outbreak of war in 1937.

The second threat to Chiang's position was the Communists. After the purges of 1927 and a series of abortive insurrections, the power of the Communist Party in the cities was systematically broken, and the Communist leaders retreated to remote mountain areas where they established local regimes. Most important of these was the Kiangsi soviet, based at Jui-chin, where from 1929-34 the Communist Party controlled an area with several million people and developed reform programmes as a peasant-based party rather than a party based on an urban proletariat on the Russian model. Chiang's armies repeatedly attacked Kiangsi, and in 1934 the Communist leaders decided to abandon the area. The ensuing Long March led them to the north-west, where another minor Communist base had been established since 1930 in Pao-an. At the Tsunyi conference during the Long March, the party's peasant-based wing, led by Mao Tse-tung, finally established its leadership. His policies were put into practice in the new Communist base area centred on Yenan.

Even now, Chiang's first priority was to crush the Communists and his provincial rivals, rather than resist the Japanese, but in 1936 he was forced, under threat of deposition if not of assassination, to form a united front against the common enemy. The Japanese response was to invade China in force, and by the end of 1938 they had occupied most of north and central China, together with the main coastal ports and all the centres of modern industry. The Nationalists retreated into the impregnable mountains of Szechwan and the south-west, and the fighting subsided until the Japanese offensives of 1944, which led to further areas falling into their hands.

Although they occupied a large part of China, the Japanese actually controlled only the major cities and lines of communication. In the occupied zones there were many centres of Chinese resistance, often dominated by Communists who gained widespread credibility as the party actively pursuing guerrilla warfare,

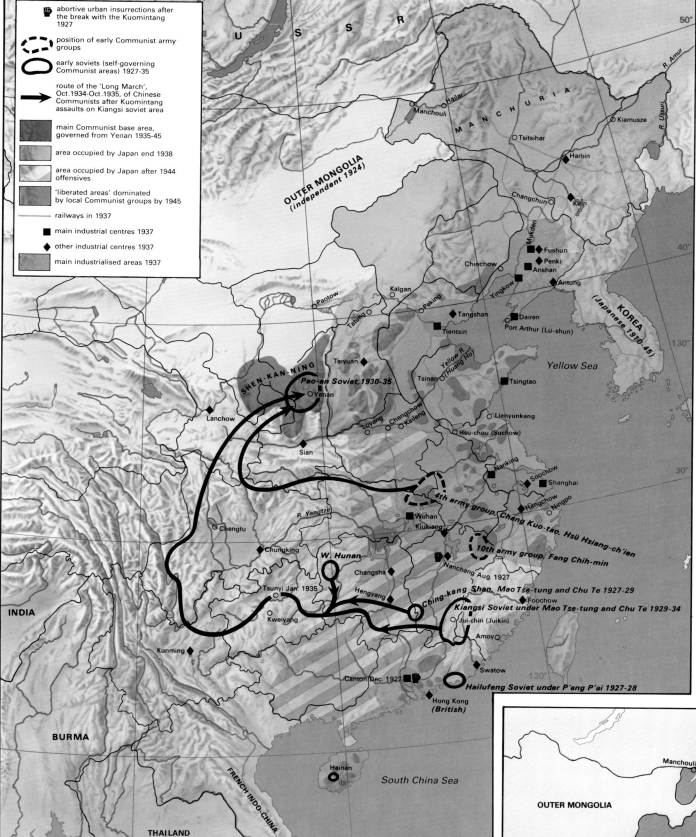

3/The Chinese Communist movement to 1945 *(left)* After the break with the Kuomintang (KMT) in 1927 there were abortive risings in Nanchang and Canton. The first Communist regime was that at Hailufeng, 1927-28. Various small bases emerged in remote mountain areas in central China in 1927-1930. Most important was Mao Tse-tung's base at Ching-kang shan. In 1929 he moved to southern Kiangsi where a stable soviet government survived repeated KMT campaigns until 1934 when the Communist forces withdrew from their southern bases and travelled to the north-west on the famous Long March. From 1937, during the Japanese war the Chinese Communist regime in Yenan and the Nationalist government in Chungking were at least nominally united in resistance to the Japanese. By the end of 1938 Japan had occupied a very large part of north and central China, including all the major industrial centres and ports. However, Japanese control was only fully effective in the cities and along the main rail lines. In rural areas many centres of resistance grew up, many of them Communist-organised. Only a few of the centres had any real territorial control, but all were centres of Communist political influence among the rural population. In 1937 China's industries, poor and largely foreign-owned, were concentrated in the Treaty Ports: Shanghai alone had about 60 per cent of all industrial plant. Much of the rail network and well-planned industry was built up in Japanese-controlled Manchuria. By 1945, in spite of some wartime development in the west (Chungking, Kunming), the industrial situation had changed little.

4/Communist victory in the Civil War 1945-49 *(below)* After the defeat of Japan, Manchuria was occupied by Russian armies; in the rest of China, Communist and Nationalist forces competed in guerrilla operations for control of former Japanese territory. By 1947 the Communists controlled most of the north apart from the Peking-Tientsin area, some major cities and rail-lines. After 1948 the Communists were strong enough to engage the Nationalists in major battles: the main Nationalist armies were destroyed in Manchuria in 1948 and at Hsü-chou in 1948-9, and after the rapid fall of northern China no serious attempt was made to hold China south of the Yangtze.

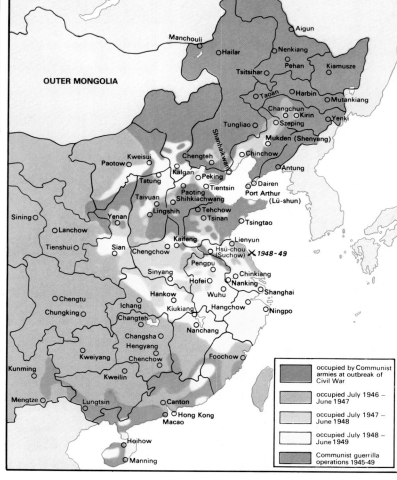

and won the sympathy of the peasant farmers by the reform programmes practised in their base area around Yenan. By 1945 the Communists claimed to control numerous 'liberated areas', but only in a few of these did they have real administrative power.

When the Second World War ended in 1945 the Nationalist government returned to Nanking. During the war years it had become increasingly dependent upon American aid and finance, more and more reactionary and corrupt. By 1945 it was widely discredited; inflation was rampant, its armies were demoralised. After the Japanese surrender the Nationalist and Communist forces raced to take possession of former Japanese-held territory; the Communists gained control of much of the north and most of Manchuria, which had been occupied by the Russians in 1945. For some time negotiations went on in an attempt to reach a political settlement and to create a national government, but hostilities continued between Nationalist and Communist forces, and in 1947 this broke into open civil war. By 1948 the initiative had passed

to the Communists, who defeated the crack Nationalist armies in Manchuria and entered Tientsin and Peking in January 1949. Further south a major battle around Hsü-chou raged from November 1948 to January 1949 with half a million troops engaged on each side. The Nationalists were defeated; Nanking fell in April, Shanghai in May, Canton in October 1949. On 1 October 1949 the People's Republic of China was founded. By May 1950 the Nationalist government had fled to Taiwan.

The civil war completed the destruction that had taken place during the warlord period and the Japanese war. In 1949 most of the Chinese industrial plant was in ruins; the Japanese industrial base in Manchuria had been systematically looted by the Russians; much of the rail system was inoperative. Years of hyper-inflation had destroyed the currency, the banking system and urban business. But for the first time since 1911 a strong regime controlled all Chinese territory, and moreover had plans, already tested in limited areas, for the regeneration of the economy and the transformation of the country.

European political problems
1919 to 1934

THE collapse of the Central Powers in the autumn of 1918 and the subsequent peace treaties of Versailles (28 June 1919) between the Allies and Germany, of St Germain (10 September 1919) with Austria, of Neuilly (27 November 1919) with Bulgaria, and of Trianon (4 June 1920) with Hungary, brought about major frontier changes, the emergence of a number of new states and the enlargement of others fortunate enough to be on the victorious side. New states included Finland, Estonia, Latvia and Lithuania (all now independent of their former Russian overlords); Poland (reconstituted from the three empires which had shared in its partition at the end of the 18th century); Czechoslovakia, comprising the old Habsburg 'crown lands' of Bohemia, Moravia and Silesia, together with Slovakia and Carpathian Ruthenia from former Hungarian territory; and Yugoslavia, comprising the territories of the former independent kingdoms of Serbia and Montenegro, the former crown land of Croatia, the former Turkish provinces of Bosnia and the Herzegovina, and the Habsburg provinces of Slovenia and Dalmatia. Romania enlarged itself greatly, taking Transylvania from Hungary, Bukovina from Austria and Bessarabia from Russia. Italy took the South Tyrol (Alto Adige) and the Triestino, the former Habsburg province of Istria. France recovered Alsace-Lorraine, and Belgium the small frontier areas of Eupen and Malmédy. Plebiscites held in the disputed areas of Upper Silesia, Marienwerder, Allenstein and Schleswig resulted in more or less satisfactory solutions on ethnic lines, although the Poles did their best to annex Upper Silesia by force of arms.

The ethnic elements in the other settlements were far from satisfactory, *irredenta* being scattered wholesale across the map of eastern Europe, save only on the boundary between Greece and Turkey, where at the end of the Greco-Turkish war of 1920-22 (see page 228) a wholesale exchange of populations was negotiated. Danzig and the Saarland were set up under League of Nations High Commissioners, the Saarland reverting to Germany by plebiscite in January 1935. Peace with Turkey was delayed until the Treaty of Lausanne (24 July 1923), owing to the inability of the Allies to impose their terms on a renascent Turkish national movement despite their enlisting the help of the Greeks. On Europe's eastern frontiers settlement had to await the victory of the Bolsheviks in the Russian civil war, and the repulse first of the Polish invasion of Russia and then of the Soviet invasion of Poland. The Western Powers proposed a mediated frontier along the Curzon Line (Spa Conference, July 1920). The frontier finally settled at the Treaty of Riga (Oct. 1920) gave Poland a large minority of White Russians and Ukrainians.

The destruction of the Habsburg Empire, the disarmament of Germany and the effects of the Russian Revolution and the civil war completely altered the balance of power in Europe. Potentially Germany, in terms of population and industrial strength, was now without any counterbalance in central Europe. The only hope of those powers who stood to lose by a revision of the peace treaties was the maintenance of overwhelming military strength in alliance against any revival of German power. France tried to restrain Germany by signing alliances with the new states of Poland and Czechoslovakia, and by using the issue of reparations to hold Germany down. But France's efforts to promote a separatist movement in the Rhineland, and its occupation of the Ruhr to enforce reparations deliveries in 1923, proved disastrous. Thereafter Germany and France came much closer together, and the Treaty of Locarno (1925) established a system of guarantees along the Franco-German and Belgian-

German frontiers. Germany joined the League of Nations (1926), but at the same time signed a pact of friendship and non-aggression with the USSR; French and British forces occupying the Rhineland were steadily withdrawn, and the European powers began discussions intended to lead to a world disarmament agreement.

Superficially, Europe in 1929 presented the appearance of a stable system secured against war by the sanctions clauses of the Covenant of the League of Nations. But the illusory nature of that security had been shown when Italy's naval action against the Greek island of Corfu in 1923, and Poland's seizure of Vilna from Lithuania in 1920, went unpunished. Another weakness was the lack of stability in the domestic politics of many European powers, particularly in Eastern Europe, and the weakness of the economic underpinning of the international system. The strains of the war of 1914-18 and the defects of the peace settlements, coupled with the major and occasionally disastrously inflationary strains of economic adjustment, combined to strengthen anti-parliamentary (see page 258) and revolutionary groups, parties and movements of both left and right throughout Europe. The Russian Revolution led to the setting up of a new Third Socialist International (the Comintern). Russian insistence that all parties and movements affiliating themselves to it should follow its leadership and organisational model split the socialist parties of Europe into rival parliamentary socialist and revolu-

tionary Communist sections, and made their defeat by the right inevitable. Some of the new regimes 'and movements were organised on nationalist totalitarian lines on the model of Italian Fascism, which achieved power in 1922. Others (Poland, Yugoslavia, Greece) were simply military-bureaucratic tyrannies. In Germany armed risings and major breakdowns of public order created an atmosphere of incipient civil war until the economic recovery of 1924. Great Britain experienced a series of strikes, culminating in the General Strike of 1926; and in Ireland from 1919 to 1922 violent guerrilla-style warfare ranged between the forces of the Irish nationalists, who set up their own underground government in 1919, and the British forces. The settlement of 1921 preserved the Loyalist (and Protestant) stronghold of Ulster under British rule, made Ireland a Dominion of the Empire, but led to a bitter conflict within the new Irish Free State between radicals and moderates, settled in 1923.

The stabilisation of 1925-29 was more apparent than real, and with the onset of the Depression (see page 266), financial and economic chaos returned to Europe. Unemployment mounted drastically in Germany and Great Britain. In Germany after 1930 the anti-parliamentary movements of right and left, Nazis and Communists, increased their strength enormously. In Great Britain a 'national' government, with a huge majority in the 1931 general election, maintained parliamentary con-

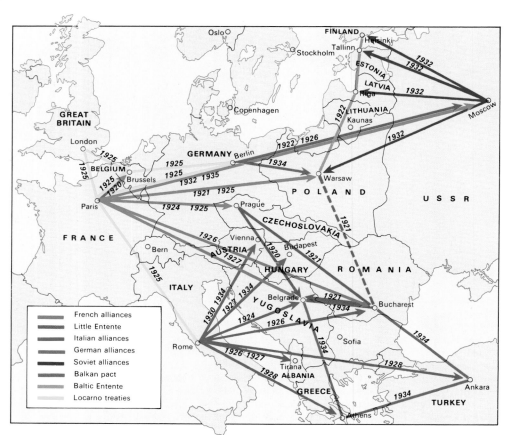

French alliances
Little Entente
Italian alliances
German alliances
Soviet alliances
Balkan pact
Baltic Entente
Locarno treaties

1920 Franco-Belgian military convention.
1920 Czechoslovak-Yugoslav defensive alliance (against Hungarian revisionism), converted **1921** into 'Little Entente' by alliances between Czechoslovakia and Romania and between Romania and Yugoslavia. The system further cemented by Franco-Polish alliance (19 February 1921) and alliance between Poland and Romania (against U.S.S.R.), later by treaties between France and Czechoslovakia (1924), France and Romania (1926), and France and Yugoslavia (1927).
1922 Baltic Entente between Poland, Estonia, Latvia and Finland (defensive alignment against U.S.S.R.).
1922 Rapallo Treaty between Germany and Soviet Union, consolidated by Treaty of Berlin, **1926.**
1924 Adriatic Treaty (Italy and Yugoslavia) confirming *status quo* in Adriatic.
1925 Locarno treaties: Germany, France, Belgium, Great Britain, Italy guarantee frontiers in West. Treaties of mutual assistance in event of German aggression between France and Poland and France and Czechoslovakia.
1926 Pact between Italy and Albania, converted into

alliance (1927).
1926 Treaty of Friendship between Italy and Romania.
1927 Italian-Hungarian treaty (putting Italy on side of revisionist powers).
1928 Treaties between Italy and Turkey and Italy and Greece.
1930 Treaty of Friendship between Italy and Austria.
1932 Non-aggression Pact between France and U.S.S.R., leading to Franco-Russian Mutual Assistance Treaty, **1935.** Further non-aggression treaties concluded between U.S.S.R. and Finland, Estonia, Latvia and Poland (to protect Russia's western frontier).
1934 Balkan Pact (Yugoslavia, Romania, Turkey, Greece) to forestall German and Russian revisionist pressures.
1934 Rome Protocols (Italy, Austria, Hungary) to strengthen Italy's position in Danubian region in face of National Socialist pressures.
1934 German-Polish Non-Aggression Treaty (beginning of collapse of French security system in Eastern Europe).
1936 Germany denounces Locarno treaties.

2/The European Security System, 1921-34 (left) The peace settlements of 1919 were supported by a series of pacts and alliances with three main purposes: to prevent Germany from seeking to reverse the verdict of the First World War; to build up a *cordon sanitaire* against Bolshevik Russia; to maintain the territorial settlement in Eastern Europe and forestall treaty revision, particularly on the part of Hungary. The map shows clearly the key position of France, in alliance with Poland, as the main support of the Little Entente, and the comparative isolation of the two 'outsiders', Germany (which only recovered freedom of manoeuvre after 1934) and the Soviet Union. It also shows the ambition of Italy under Mussolini to play a major role in the Mediterranean and in the Danubian basin. Nevertheless, the French security system operated effectively until the onset of Depression (see page 266), which weakened France and after 1936, if not before, undercut its alliances in Eastern Europe. The decisive change came with the German-Polish Neutrality Pact (1934), which knocked the lynch-pin out of France's defensive system. After 1936, when Germany repudiated the Locarno treaties of 1925, a new period began, leading to the outbreak of war in 1939 (see page 268).

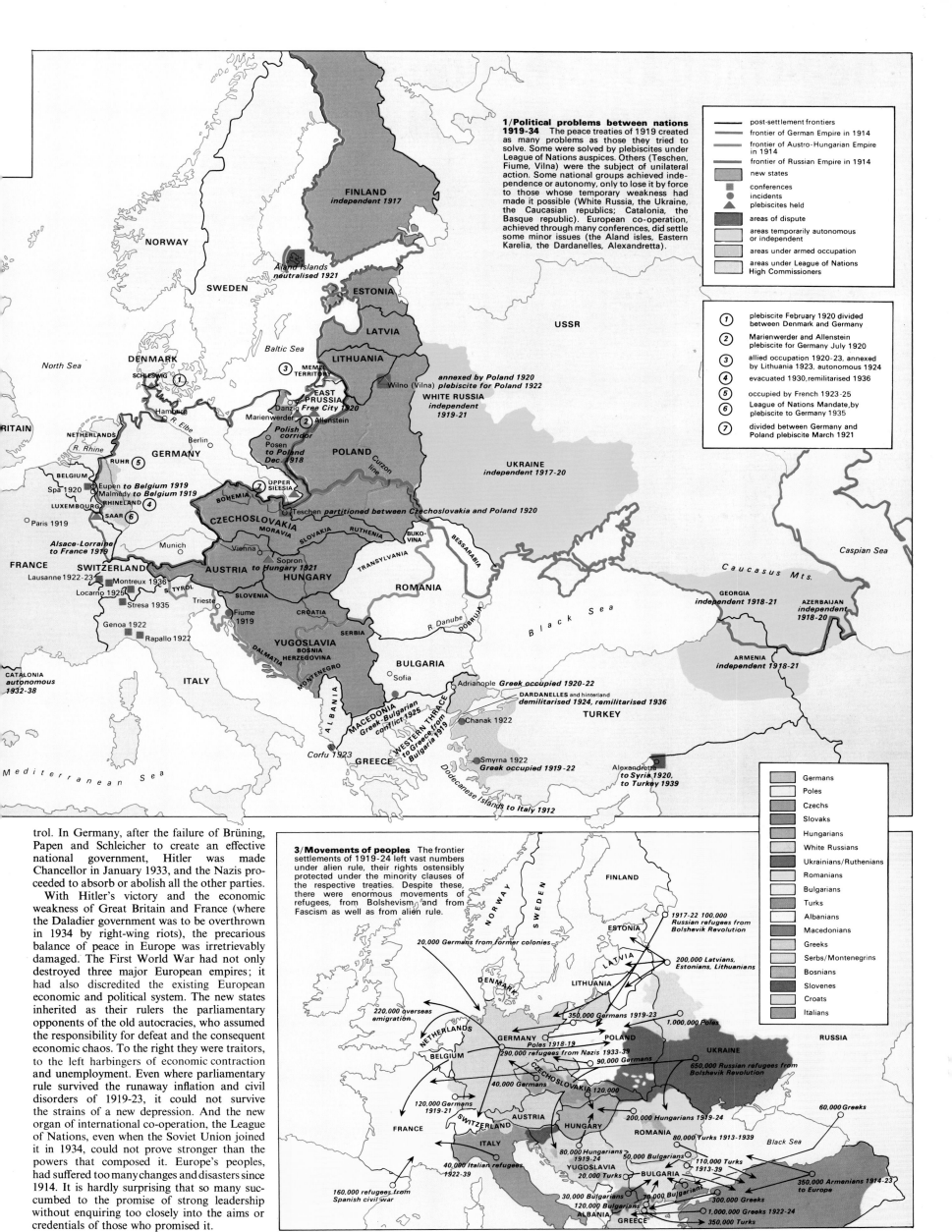

1/Political problems between nations 1919-34 The peace treaties of 1919 created as many problems as those they tried to solve. Some were solved by plebiscites under League of Nations auspices. Others (Teschen, Fiume, Vilna) were the subject of unilateral action. Some national groups achieved independence or autonomy, only to lose it by force to those whose temporary weakness had made it possible (White Russia, the Ukraine, the Caucasian republics; Catalonia, the Basque republic). European co-operation, achieved through many conferences, did settle some minor issues (the Aland isles, Eastern Karelia, the Dardanelles, Alexandretta).

post-settlement frontiers
frontier of German Empire in 1914
frontier of Austro-Hungarian Empire in 1914
frontier of Russian Empire in 1914
new states
conferences
incidents
plebiscites held
areas of dispute
areas temporarily autonomous or independent
areas under armed occupation
areas under League of Nations High Commissioners

1 plebiscite February 1920 divided between Denmark and Germany
2 Marienwerder and Allenstein plebiscite for Germany July 1920
3 allied occupation 1920-23, annexed by Lithuania 1923, autonomous 1924
4 evacuated 1930, remilitarised 1936
5 occupied by French 1923-25
6 League of Nations Mandate, by plebiscite to Germany 1935
7 divided between Germany and Poland plebiscite March 1921

NORWAY
SWEDEN
FINLAND *independent 1917*
DENMARK
North Sea
Baltic Sea
ESTONIA
LATVIA
LITHUANIA
USSR
Aland Islands neutralised 1921
SCHLESWIG
Hamburg
R. Elbe
Berlin
MEMEL TERRITORY
East Prussia
Danzig *Free City 1920*
Marienwerder
Allenstein
Polish corridor
Posen *to Poland Dec. 1918*
Wilno (Vilna) plebiscite for Poland 1922
annexed by Poland 1920
WHITE RUSSIA *independent 1919-21*
NETHERLANDS
R. Rhine
GERMANY
RUHR
BELGIUM
Spa 1920
Eupen to Belgium 1919
Malmédy to Belgium 1919
RHINELAND
LUXEMBOURG
SAAR
Paris 1919
Alsace-Lorraine to France 1919
Munich
FRANCE
SWITZERLAND
Lausanne 1922-23
Montreux 1936
Locarno 1925
Stresa 1935
Genoa 1922
Rapallo 1922
S TYROL
Trieste
Fiume 1919
BOHEMIA
UPPER SILESIA
Teschen partitioned between Czechoslovakia and Poland 1920
CZECHOSLOVAKIA
MORAVIA
SLOVAKIA
RUTHENIA
BUKOVINA
BESSARABIA
Vienna
AUSTRIA
Sopron to Hungary 1921
HUNGARY
SLOVENIA
CROATIA
POLAND
Curzon line
UKRAINE *independent 1917-20*
TRANSYLVANIA
ROMANIA
R. Danube
DOBRUJA
Black Sea
Caucasus Mts.
Caspian Sea
GEORGIA *independent 1918-21*
AZERBAIJAN *independent 1918-20*
ARMENIA *independent 1918-21*
CATALONIA *autonomous 1932-38*
ITALY
DALMATIA
BOSNIA HERZEGOVINA
YUGOSLAVIA
SERBIA
MONTENEGRO
ALBANIA
MACEDONIA *Greek-Bulgarian conflict 1925*
BULGARIA
Sofia
WESTERN THRACE to Greece from Bulgaria 1919
Adrianople *Greek occupied 1920-22*
DARDANELLES and hinterland demilitarised 1924, remilitarised 1936
Chanak 1922
TURKEY
Smyrna 1922
Greek occupied 1919-22
Corfu 1923
GREECE
Dodecanese Islands to Italy 1912
Alexandretta *to Syria 1920, to Turkey 1939*
Mediterranean Sea

trol. In Germany, after the failure of Brüning, Papen and Schleicher to create an effective national government, Hitler was made Chancellor in January 1933, and the Nazis proceeded to absorb or abolish all the other parties.

With Hitler's victory and the economic weakness of Great Britain and France (where the Daladier government was to be overthrown in 1934 by right-wing riots), the precarious balance of peace in Europe was irretrievably damaged. The First World War had not only destroyed three major European empires; it had also discredited the existing European economic and political system. The new states inherited as their rulers the parliamentary opponents of the old autocracies, who assumed the responsibility for defeat and the consequent economic chaos. To the right they were traitors, to the left harbingers of economic contraction and unemployment. Even where parliamentary rule survived the runaway inflation and civil disorders of 1919-23, it could not survive the strains of a new depression. And the new organ of international co-operation, the League of Nations, even when the Soviet Union joined it in 1934, could not prove stronger than the powers that composed it. Europe's peoples, had suffered too many changes and disasters since 1914. It is hardly surprising that so many succumbed to the promise of strong leadership without enquiring too closely into the aims or credentials of those who promised it.

3/Movements of peoples The frontier settlements of 1919-24 left vast numbers under alien rule, their rights ostensibly protected under the minority clauses of the respective treaties. Despite these, there were enormous movements of refugees, from Bolshevism and from Fascism as well as from alien rule.

Germans
Poles
Czechs
Slovaks
Hungarians
White Russians
Ukrainians/Ruthenians
Romanians
Bulgarians
Turks
Albanians
Macedonians
Greeks
Serbs/Montenegrins
Bosnians
Slovenes
Croats
Italians

NORWAY
SWEDEN
FINLAND
DENMARK
ESTONIA
LATVIA
LITHUANIA
20,000 Germans from former colonies
1917-22 100,000 Russian refugees from Bolshevik Revolution
200,000 Latvians, Estonians, Lithuanians
220,000 overseas emigration
NETHERLANDS
BELGIUM
GERMANY
350,000 Germans 1919-23
1,000,000 Poles
Poles 1918-19
290,000 refugees from Nazis 1933-39
90,000 Germans
POLAND
RUSSIA
UKRAINE
650,000 Russian refugees from Bolshevik Revolution
40,000 Germans
CZECHOSLOVAKIA
120,000
SWITZERLAND
AUSTRIA
120,000 Germans 1919-21
FRANCE
ITALY
HUNGARY
200,000 Hungarians 1919-24
ROMANIA
80,000 Turks 1913-1939
Black Sea
60,000 Greeks
40,000 Italian refugees 1922-39
80,000 Hungarians 1919-24
50,000 Bulgarians
110,000 Turks 1913-39
YUGOSLAVIA
20,000 Turks
BULGARIA
160,000 refugees from Spanish civil war
30,000 Bulgarians
120,000 Bulgarians
70,000 Bulgarians
ALBANIA
GREECE
300,000 Greeks
1,000,000 Greeks 1922-24
350,000 Turks
350,000 Armenians 1914-23 to Europe

265

The Great Depression 1929 to 1939

THE chronology of the 'Slump' is by now well known, but its causes are still debated. What is certain is that the stock market crash of 1929, and the ensuing world-wide financial collapse, were only the manifestation of deeper weaknesses in the world economy. The sources of instability were several: the First World War caused a dramatic increase in productive capacity, especially outside Europe, but there was no corresponding increase in demand. Above all, there was a world-wide imbalance between agriculture and industry. The rewards of growth accrued disproportionately to the industrialised countries and, within these countries, to their industrial and financial sectors. Increased production allowed food and raw material prices to decline throughout the 1920s, worsening the terms of trade for countries dependent on the export of such commodities, and decreasing their ability to buy the industrial products of Europe and the United States. Within the latter, wages lagged behind profits, impairing the development of domestic markets, and limiting the potential of new industries, such as automobiles, to replace declining ones, like textiles. International finance never fully recovered from the dislocations of the First World War. The pre-war system of fixed exchange rates and free convertibility (see page 256) was replaced by a compromise – the Gold Exchange Standard – which never achieved the stability necessary to rebuild world trade.

The slump was touched off by financial crisis. The great Bull Market of 1928 – itself a sign of weakness, of shrinking opportunities for investment – gave way to a precipitous fall in stock prices in October 1929. In the ensuing scramble for liquidity, funds flowed back from Europe to America, and the shaky European prosperity collapsed. In May 1931, the Austrian Credit-Anstalt defaulted. When England left the Gold Standard, allowing sterling to depreciate in September 1931, virtually the entire world was affected.

In many industrial countries, over a quarter of the labour force was thrown out of work. Industrial production fell to 53 per cent of its 1929 level in Germany and the United States, and world trade sank to 35 per cent of its 1929 value. For many the Depression seemed endless:

as late as 1939, the world average of unemployment was over 11 per cent. But the impact of the slump was uneven. Some economies rebounded relatively quickly; others languished throughout the decade. In retrospect, it is evident that considerable structural changes took place in the 1930s. New industries continued to progress, consumption patterns shifted, peripheral areas increased their output of industrial goods, and real wages rose. A new economic world order, anchored on Wall Street and Detroit, was struggling to be born. But even by 1939 the lynchpin of this new system had not yet regained the level of industrial output of 1929, and it ultimately required a Second World War to pull the United States out of depression.

Government reactions to the Depression were unenlightened. The first response was to deflate and to try to preserve the value of the currency. Soon, however, the dire consequences led one government after another to attempt to stimulate the domestic economy by reflation (e.g. public works), devaluation (in the hope of increasing exports), protective and preferential tariff arrangements (e.g. the Ottawa Agreements, 1932), or by some combination of these policies. Even the most economically conservative regimes were forced to abandon *laissez faire* in favour of some degree of state intervention.

These measures achieved mixed results. Success hinged on the consistency and firmness with which the stimulants were applied and, more importantly, on how soon and how thoroughly rearmament was undertaken. Germany and the United Kingdom rearmed early, stimulating their own economies and those of the Commonwealth, Scandinavia and eastern Europe. France and the United States rearmed late, and suffered much more severely in the recession of 1937-38. Internationally, government policies led to a decrease and redirection of trade. By 1935, much of the world had divided into five currency blocs: the sterling and dollar areas, the gold and yen blocs, and the German-dominated exchange control area. Though plagued by instability, these groupings corresponded roughly to the new patterns of trade and influence.

The revival of economic nationalism was

paralleled by a new intensity in international politics. The Japanese export offensive had its political reflex in military aggression against China. Hitler, Mussolini and the Japanese exploited the disarray which the economic collapse had brought about, and gradually the world polarised into two armed camps, the Axis (Germany, Italy and Japan) and the 'democracies' (led by the United Kingdom, France and the United States). In between stood the Soviet Union, the one country which, isolated from the world market, had managed to sustain economic growth throughout the 1930s, and which both sides tried, alternately, to ally with or to isolate.

Few countries emerged from the Depression without undergoing some dramatic domestic transformation. In Africa, Asia and Latin America, nationalist and revolutionary movements gained new bases of support, as the crisis radicalised urban workers, poor peasants and agricultural labourers. The developed world followed one of two patterns. The first was liberal and democratic, typified by Roosevelt's New Deal in the United States, and by the Popular Front government in France. In both countries, the election of left- or liberal-minded administrations unleashed enormous waves of strikes and trade union organisation, and stimulated numerous efforts at reform. Much more common was the path to the right. The resignation of the Hamaguchi Cabinet in 1931 marked the effective end of Japan's weak experiment in constitutional democracy. With the coming of the Depression, fascist movements spread throughout Europe, carrying Hitler to power in Germany in January 1933, followed two months later by Dollfuss in Austria. Most of eastern Europe quickly followed suit. Even in France, the United Kingdom and the USA, fascist movements arose, pressuring governments from the right and harassing reform movements.

In summary, the Great Depression brought the collapse not only of economic liberalism, but also of liberal political institutions. Yet the triumph of the authoritarian regimes proved short-lived. They were incapable of restoring the old order, or of establishing a stable new one, and ultimately perished in the Second World War.

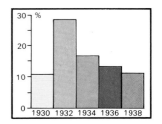

World unemployment *(above)*
In the early 1930s unemployment reached record levels in just about every industrialised country, and many workers remained jobless throughout the decade.

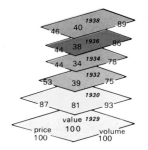

Indices of world trade *(above)*
A drastic drop in the level of prices, coupled with a moderate decrease in volume, produced a sharp decline in the value of world trade.

Farm workers begin organising 1934

San Francisco general strike, May–July 1934

Dr Townsend founds Townsend Clubs Jan. 1934 under slogan '$200 a month at sixty'

1934 Upton Sinclair, leader of End Poverty in California (EPIC) movement, wins 38% of vote as Democratic candidate for Governor

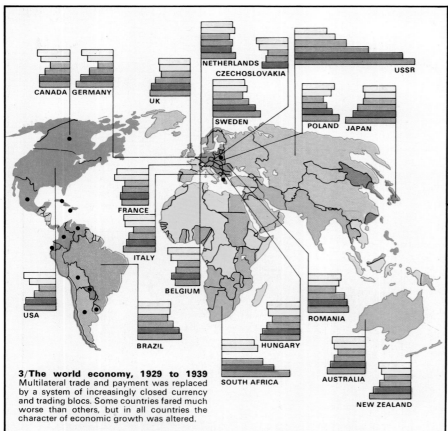

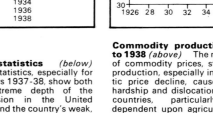

major currency blocs
- gold bloc
- yen bloc
- German-dominated exchange control area
- dollar area
- sterling area
- areas of shifting or dubious allegiance due to German–American rivalry
- • areas of loose currency bloc allegiance

production indices
- 1929 = 100
- 1930
- 1932
- 1934
- 1936
- 1938

3/The world economy, 1929 to 1939
Multilateral trade and payment was replaced by a system of increasingly closed currency and trading blocs. Some countries fared much worse than others, but in all countries the character of economic growth was altered.

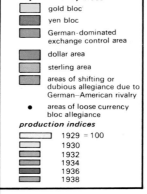

Commodity production 1926 to 1938 *(above)* The movement of commodity prices, stocks and production, especially in the drastic price decline, caused severe hardship and dislocation in many countries, particularly those dependent upon agricultural and raw materials exports.

US statistics *(below)*
These statistics, especially for the years 1937-38, show both the extreme depth of the Depression in the United States and the country's weak, slow and halting recovery.

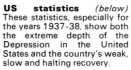

	unemployment (no. in 000's)	Federal budget surplus + or deficit – (millions of $)	days lost through strikes (000's)	no. of union members (000's)
1930	4340	+737	3320	3632
1932	12060	–2,735	10500	3226
1934	11340	–3,689	19600	3249
1936	9030	–4,424	13900	4164
1938	10390	–1,176	9150	8265

1/The depression in the US
1929 Oct. Wall Street Crash.
1930 Hawley-Smoot Tariff passed.
1931 Hoover declares moratorium on war debts.
1932 Jan. Reconstruction Finance Corporation established, with power to use $2 billion to underwrite banks and businesses. **July** Federal Home Loan Bank Act provided $125 million to prevent foreclosures. **Nov.** Roosevelt elected president promising 'New Deal'.
1933 4 Mar. Roosevelt inaugurated. **9 Mar.** to **16 June** 'Hundred Days' of reform:
Bank Holiday. Glass-Steagull Act (reform of banking). Federal Securities Act. US goes off gold.

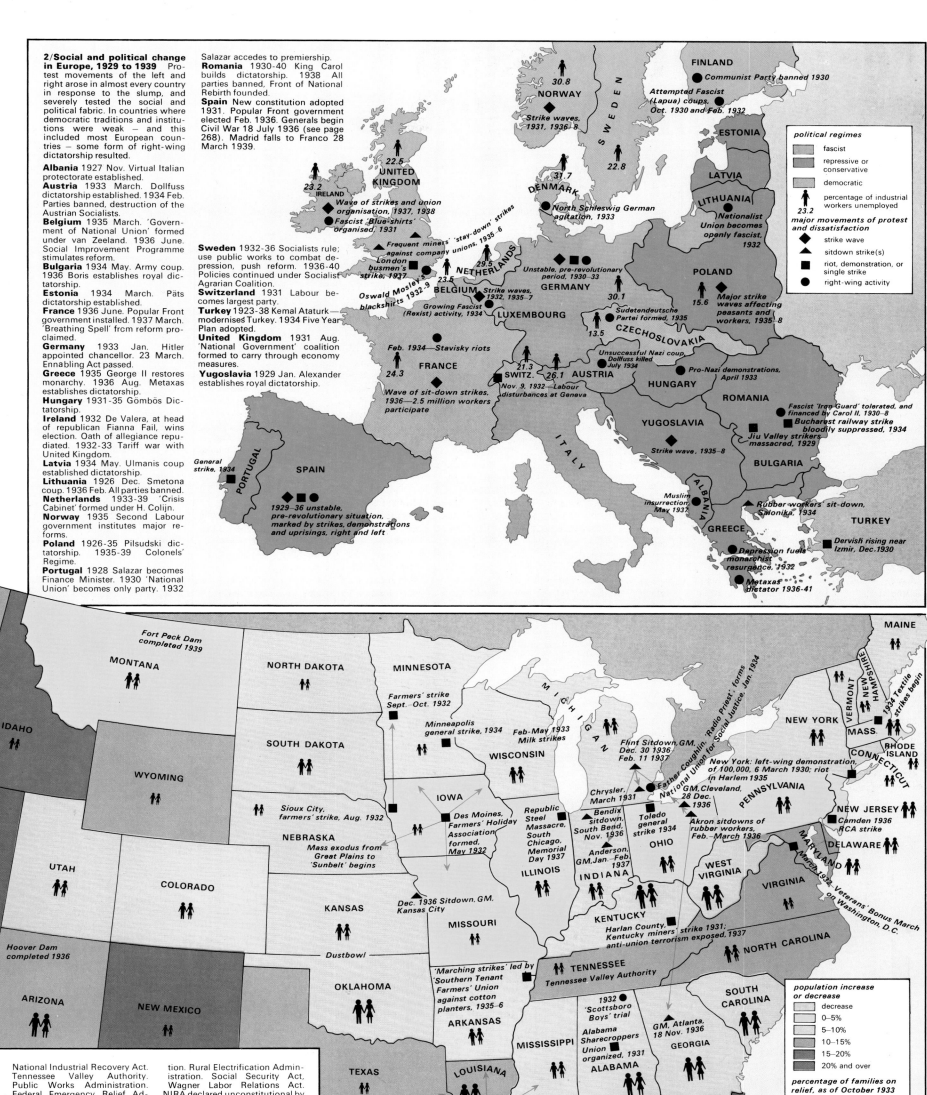

2/Social and political change in Europe, 1929 to 1939 Protest movements of the left and right arose in almost every country in response to the slump, and severely tested the social and political fabric. In countries where democratic traditions and institutions were weak – and this included most European countries – some form of right-wing dictatorship resulted.

Albania 1927 Nov. Virtual Italian protectorate established.

Austria 1933 March. Dollfuss dictatorship established. 1934 Feb. Parties banned, destruction of the Austrian Socialists.

Belgium 1935 March. 'Government of National Union' formed under van Zeeland. 1936 June. Social Improvement Programme stimulates reform.

Bulgaria 1934 May. Army coup. 1936 Boris establishes royal dictatorship.

Estonia 1934 March. Päts dictatorship established.

France 1936 June. Popular Front government installed. 1937 March. 'Breathing Spell' from reform proclaimed.

Germany 1933 Jan. Hitler appointed chancellor. 23 March. Ennabling Act passed.

Greece 1935 George II restores monarchy. 1936 Aug. Metaxas establishes dictatorship.

Hungary 1931-35 Gömbös Dictatorship.

Ireland 1932 De Valera, at head of republican Fianna Fail, wins election. Oath of allegiance repudiated. 1932-33 Tariff war with United Kingdom.

Latvia 1934 May. Ulmanis coup established dictatorship.

Lithuania 1926 Dec. Smetona coup. 1936 Feb. All parties banned.

Netherlands 1933-39 'Crisis Cabinet' formed under H. Colijn.

Norway 1935 Second Labour government institutes major reforms.

Poland 1926-35 Pilsudski dictatorship. 1935-39 'Colonels' Regime.

Portugal 1928 Salazar becomes Finance Minister. 1930 'National Union' becomes only party. 1932

Salazar accedes to premiership.

Romania 1930-40 King Carol builds dictatorship. 1938 All parties banned, Front of National Rebirth founded.

Spain New constitution adopted 1931. Popular Front government elected Feb. 1936. Generals begin Civil War 18 July 1936 (see page 268). Madrid falls to Franco 28 March 1939.

Sweden 1932-36 Socialists rule; use public works to combat depression, push reform. 1936-40 Policies continued under Socialist Agrarian Coalition.

Switzerland 1931 Labour becomes largest party.

Turkey 1923-38 Kemal Ataturk modernises Turkey. 1934 Five Year Plan adopted.

United Kingdom 1931 Aug. 'National Government' coalition formed to carry through economy measures.

Yugoslavia 1929 Jan. Alexander establishes royal dictatorship.

political regimes
- fascist
- repressive or conservative
- democratic
- percentage of industrial workers unemployed 23.2

major movements of protest and dissatisfaction
- strike wave
- sitdown strike(s)
- riot, demonstration, or single strike
- right-wing activity

Europe map labels:

FINLAND — Communist Party banned 1930
Attempted Fascist (Lapua) coups, Oct. 1930 and Feb. 1932
NORWAY 30.8 — Strike waves, 1931, 1936-8
SWEDEN 22.8
DENMARK 31.7 — North Schleswig German agitation, 1933
ESTONIA
LATVIA
LITHUANIA — Nationalist Union becomes openly fascist, 1932
UNITED KINGDOM 22.5 — IRELAND 23.2 — Wave of strikes and union organisation, 1937, 1938; Fascist 'Blue-shirts' organised, 1931; London busmen's strike, 1937; Oswald Mosley's blackshirts 1932-9
NETHERLANDS 29.5 — Frequent miners' 'stay-down' strikes against company unions, 1935-6
BELGIUM 23.5 — Strike waves, 1932, 1935-7; Growing Fascist (Rexist) activity, 1934
LUXEMBOURG
POLAND 15.6 — Major strike waves affecting peasants and workers, 1935-8
GERMANY 30.1 — Unstable, pre-revolutionary period, 1930-33
CZECHOSLOVAKIA 13.5 — Sudetendeutsche Partei formed, 1935
FRANCE 24.3 — Feb. 1934—Stavisky riots; Wave of sit-down strikes, 1936—2.5 million workers participate
SWITZ. 21.3 — Nov. 9, 1932—Labour disturbances at Geneva
AUSTRIA 26.1 — Unsuccessful Nazi coup, Dollfuss killed July 1934; Pro-Nazi demonstrations, April 1933
HUNGARY
ROMANIA — Fascist 'Iron Guard' tolerated, and financed by Carol II, 1930-8; Bucharest railway strike bloodily suppressed, 1934
YUGOSLAVIA — Jiu Valley strikers massacred, 1929; Strike wave, 1935-8
BULGARIA
ITALY
PORTUGAL — General strike, 1934
SPAIN — 1929-36 unstable, pre-revolutionary situation, marked by strikes, demonstrations and uprisings, right and left
ALBANIA — Muslim insurrection, May 1937
GREECE — Depression fuels monarchist resurgence, 1932; Metaxas dictator 1936-41
TURKEY — Rubber workers' sit-down, Salonika, 1934; Dervish rising near Izmir, Dec. 1930

National Industrial Recovery Act. Tennessee Valley Authority. Public Works Administration. Federal Emergency Relief Administration.

1934 Jan. Return to gold at new level. Federal Housing Administration. Reciprocal Trade Agreements Act. Political Polarisation: Major strikes in textiles, city-wide strikes in Minneapolis, Toledo, and San Francisco. Father Coughlin, Huey Long, and Dr Townsend gain mass followings. Ku Klux Klan revitalised. Democratic gains in Congressional elections.

1935 'Second Hundred Days': Public Utilities Holding Company Act. Works Progress Administration. Rural Electrification Administration. Social Security Act, Wagner Labor Relations Act. NIRA declared unconstitutional by Supreme Court. Committee for Industrial Organisation formed, led by John L. Lewis.

8 Sept. Huey Long assassinated.

1936 Agricultural Adjustment Act declared unconstitutional. **June** Coughlin, Townsend, and remnants of Long movement propose W. Lemke for President. **Nov.** Roosevelt wins re-election by landslide.

1937 Sitdown strikes, begun late 1936, spread throughout country; 400,000 'sitting down' by **1 March.** 477 sitdown strikes in 1937 lead to victory of CIO in steel and automobile industries. **Aug.** Renewed business downturn. Neutrality Act.

1938 Roosevelt cuts public works spending by half as recession deepens. Wages and Hours Act. **Nov.** Republicans make gains in Congressional elections.

1939 $552 million appropriated for defence. Neutrality Act reaffirmed by Congress.

US map labels:

MONTANA — Fort Peck Dam completed 1939
NORTH DAKOTA
MINNESOTA — Farmers' strike Sept. – Oct. 1932; Minneapolis general strike, 1934
MICHIGAN — Feb-May 1933 Milk strikes; Flint Sitdown, GM, Dec. 30 1936 – Feb. 11 1937
IDAHO
SOUTH DAKOTA
WYOMING
WISCONSIN
IOWA — Sioux City, farmers' strike, Aug. 1932; Des Moines, Farmers' Holiday Association formed, May 1932
NEBRASKA — Mass exodus from Great Plains to 'Sunbelt' begins
NEW YORK — New York: left-wing demonstration of 100,000, 6 March 1930; riot in Harlem 1935
Father Coughlin, 'Radio Priest', forms National Union for Social Justice, Jan. 1934
MAINE — 1934 Textile strikes begin
VERMONT / NEW HAMPSHIRE / MASS. / RHODE ISLAND / CONNECTICUT
PENNSYLVANIA — Chrysler, March 1931; Bendix sitdown, South Bend, Nov. 1936; Anderson, GM, Jan.—Feb. 1937; Akron sitdowns of rubber workers, Feb.—March 1936; GM, Cleveland, 28 Dec. 1936; Toledo general strike 1934
NEW JERSEY — Camden 1936 RCA strike
DELAWARE
UTAH
COLORADO
KANSAS
MISSOURI — Dec. 1936 Sitdown, GM, Kansas City
ILLINOIS — Republic Steel Massacre, South Chicago, Memorial Day 1937
INDIANA
OHIO
WEST VIRGINIA
VIRGINIA
MARYLAND — March 1932 Veterans' Bonus March on Washington, D.C.
KENTUCKY — Harlan County, Kentucky miners' strike 1931; anti-union terrorism exposed, 1937
ARIZONA
NEW MEXICO
OKLAHOMA
ARKANSAS — 'Marching strikes' led by 'Southern Tenant Farmers' Union against cotton planters, 1935-6
TENNESSEE — Tennessee Valley Authority
NORTH CAROLINA
SOUTH CAROLINA
TEXAS
LOUISIANA — Huey Long, Governor 1933-5. Launches National Share-the-Wealth Society, 1934
MISSISSIPPI
ALABAMA — 1932 'Scottsboro Boys' trial; Alabama Sharecroppers Union organized, 1931
GEORGIA — GM, Atlanta, 18 Nov. 1936
FLORIDA
Hoover Dam completed 1936
Dustbowl

population increase or decrease
- decrease
- 0–5%
- 5–10%
- 10–15%
- 15–20%
- 20% and over

percentage of families on relief, as of October 1933
- below 8%
- 8–15%
- over 15%

GM General Motors
- sitdown strike
- riot, demonstration, strike, or other protest action
- right-wing political activity

The approach of the Second World War 1931 to 1941

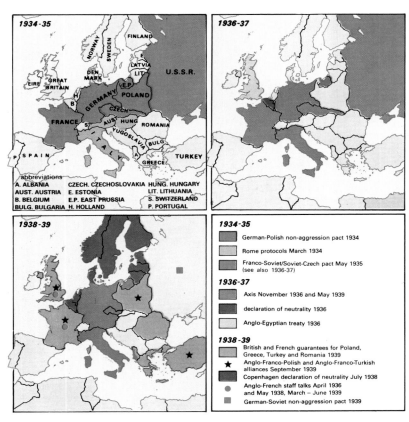

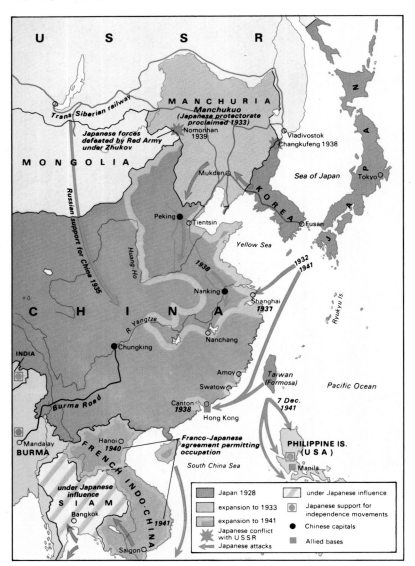

1/European alliances and alignments *(above)* France and Great Britain sought associates to deter German or Italian aggression. Hitler tried either to isolate or, as with the Axis and the Anti-Comintern Pact, to distract potential opponents. Mussolini hoped to control Hitler's rate of expansion to match Italy's capabilities. Other countries concluded non-aggression pacts with Hitler or joined in the 'neutralist' Declaration of Copenhagen, hoping to contract out of war.

2/The expansion of Japan, 1931-41 *(below)* Japanese expansion in Manchuria and northern China before 1936 was designed to control China's potentialities and eliminate British, American and Soviet influence. From 1937 to 1940 Japan sought victory in China through isolating China from external aid. American economic counter-pressure led in 1941 to the decision to conquer and hold 'Greater East Asia', seen as a self-sufficient, defensible empire.

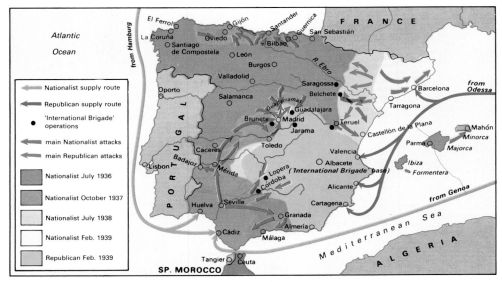

THE events of the years 1931 to 1941 marked the breakdown of the international security system set up in 1919. This system, centred round the League of Nations, was designed to prevent a dispute between two states escalating, as in 1914, into a general war. It could not rely on American support, and the Soviet Union, though a member of the League from 1934 to 1939, never played a major role. Leadership therefore fell to Great Britain and France. Italy alone, and possibly Japan, might have been deterred or dissuaded from expansion, but Germany under Hitler was, in the last resort, irrationally set on world power or defeat. When all three joined together in the Anti-Comintern Pact and then in the Tripartite Pact, the democratic powers were thrown on to the defensive.

Japanese expansionism was fuelled by exclusion from vital markets and by a sense of racial discrimination on the part of the 'whites'. The ruling groups were also driven by fear of conspiracies among nationalist extremists, especially in the officer corps, such as those who provoked the expulsion of Chinese authority from Manchuria in 1931 and mutinied in 1936. Japanese expansion began with pressure on northern China, continued with open conquest of central China and the Chinese coastline in 1937-39, spread into northern Indo-China and finally, under the pressure of the American economic embargo imposed in July 1941, culminated in the attack on Pearl Harbor and the seizure of the central Pacific and South-East Asia. Japanese expansion was opposed by the Soviet Union, Great Britain and the United States, at first in the form of aid to China; after 1939 the United States steadily escalated economic pressure on Japan and refused to discuss anything but total Japanese withdrawal. Japan sought German assistance, in the Anti-Comintern Pact of 1936, against the Soviet Union. After the Nazi-Soviet pact (1939), and the Soviet defeat of Japan at Nomonhan in Mongolia, in 1941 Japan signed a non-aggression pact with the Soviets. German aid was now sought, in the Tripartite Pact of 1940, against the United Kingdom and the United States.

Italian expansionism was inspired by Mussolini's need to fulfil the nationalist ambitions his democratic predecessors had failed to meet and to maintain his prestige as a world leader. This led him to build up Italy's position in central Europe and seek a colonial empire in Ethiopia in 1935. British and French resistance, and the anti-Fascist Popular Front victory in France, induced him to intervene in Spain, and to turn to Hitler in the Rome-Berlin Axis of 1936. Thereafter imitation of Hitler inspired him to claim French territory in 1938, annex Albania in April 1939 and, after the defeat of France, attack Greece in 1940. But military and economic weakness stultified his efforts to match Hitler's

3/The Spanish Civil War, 1936-39 *(above)* The Civil War grouped the military, the political right and the Roman Catholic Church (with German and Italian 'volunteers' and military aid) against the 'Popular Front' government, republicans, anti-clericals, anarchists, socialists and Communists, Basque and Catalan autonomists (with Soviet military aid). Against widespread criticism, Great Britain and France initiated an international Non-Intervention Agreement to prevent escalation into a Mediterranean conflict with Italy.

achievements, and tied him to Hitler in the Pact of Steel of 1939.

Hitler's expansionism embraced German nationalist desires to recover the losses of 1919, and looked to dominion over Europe, including European Russia, with a colonial empire in Africa and elsewhere to follow. He took advantage of Anglo-French disagreement and the Ethiopian crisis to ensure recovery by plebiscite of the Saarland and remilitarise the Rhineland. Thereafter, in the annexation of Austria, the Czech crisis and the occupation of Bohemia and Moravia in 1939, he relied on British and French unreadiness for and fear of war. Against Poland his miscalculation involved him in war, not only with Poland but also, despite his conclusion of the Nazi-Soviet pact, with Great Britain and France. Conquest of Denmark and Norway and the defeat of France in 1940 failed to bring him the compromise peace with Great Britain he desired. He ordered preparations for the invasion of England, but the defeat of his preliminary air offensive in the Battle of Britain led him to postpone the invasion - as it happened, for good. Instead he decided to attack Soviet Russia. The directive for "Operation Barbarossa" was issued in December 1940. The invasion of Russia was launched on 22 June 1941, after a delay caused by the need to conquer Yugoslavia and Greece. "Barbarossa" precluded a major German effort in the Mediterranean and Middle East.

Before 1939 British and French opinion on Hitler was far from united. Their governments were inhibited by the need to repair the military, economic and financial weaknesses caused by the Depression (see page 266). Furthermore, Hitler's authoritarianism, anti-Bolshevism and anti-Semitism were widely admired, and the propertied classes in France and other European countries were not averse to co-operation with Nazi Germany. After the League's failure over Ethiopia, Belgium and other smaller European states tried to preserve their neutrality, uniting in 1938 in the Declaration of Copenhagen. It was a vain attempt, and by 1941 only Spain, Portugal, Turkey, Switzerland and Sweden remained inviolate. Meanwhile, Britain and France sought to avoid conflict by appeasing Hitler; but after the sacrifice of Czechoslovakia at Munich in 1938, this no longer seemed possible. Deterrence by a system of guarantees failed too, bringing war over Poland. The Soviets preferred to make a deal with Hitler (Aug

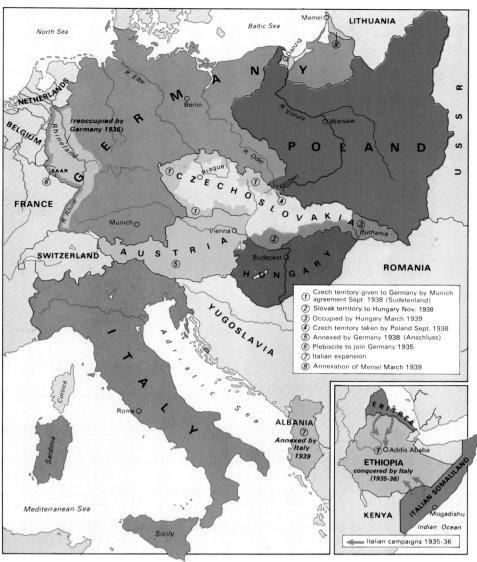

4/German and Italian expansion 1934-39 *(left)* Hitler first eliminated the restrictions of Versailles (the recovery of the Saarland by plebiscite, re-militarisation of the Rhineland, annexation of Austria). Then, pretending to advocate self-determination for German minorities, he turned on France's allies, Czechoslovakia and Poland. Czechoslovakia's multi-racial composition facilitated, with British and French acquiescence at Munich, its progressive partition. Polish resistance to German claims (Danzig, the 'Corridor') led to war with Great Britain and France earlier than planned despite Hitler's agreement with the USSR to divide Poland and the Baltic States.
Mussolini's colonial ambitions (Ethiopia) changed into emulation of Hitler (Albania, Greece).

① Czech territory given to Germany by Munich agreement Sept. 1938 (Sudetenland)
② Slovak territory to Hungary Nov. 1938
③ Occupied by Hungary March 1939
④ Czech territory taken by Poland Sept. 1938
⑤ Annexed by Germany 1938 (Anschluss)
⑥ Plebiscite to join Germany 1935
⑦ Italian expansion
⑧ Annexation of Memel March 1939

← Italian campaigns 1935-36

1939), by dividing Poland with him rather than defending it in alliance with a Great Britain and France they distrusted. Their reward was eastern Poland, the Baltic states and Bessarabia. Finland resisted; after victory, Stalin contented himself with limited gains.

President Roosevelt only began to take Hitler seriously after Munich. Until 1941 he thought economic pressure alone could restrain Japan. French defeat and British financial exhaustion brought him to advance his naval power into mid-Atlantic and give lend-lease aid for Great Britain. American opinion, was at first both isolationist and anti-Hitler; Pearl Harbor united America in war.

The European collapse, placing the French, Dutch and British colonies in south-east Asia at Japan's mercy, turned a war which had begun in eastern Europe into a world war.

5/The campaigns in Europe 1939-41 *(right)* In September 1939 Hitler overran Poland; in 1940 Denmark, Norway, the Low Countries and the defeat of France followed. Great Britain, its army in France evacuated from Dunkirk, rejected Hitler's peace offers and defeated his *Luftwaffe*. Mussolini's abortive attack on Greece, British intervention and an anti-Axis coup in Yugoslavia led to German occupation of Yugoslavia, Greece and Crete (May 1941). In June 1941 Hitler attacked the Soviet Union.

Propaganda Following the rise of National Socialism, propaganda took on a new dimension. *Above*: protest against bombing of Madrid, 1937, during Spanish Civil War; *below*: exhortation to vote for Hitler in 1938 plebiscite.

■ Axis territory 1 September 1939
□ Axis satellites   ■ Axis occupied
← German advances   ⚓ airborne landings
← Italian advances
← Soviet forces
← Allied forces   ←--- retreat and withdrawal
⚓ cities severely damaged by bombing
■ Soviet occupied territory 1939-40
■ British Empire   □ neutral powers

The war in Asia and the Pacific 1941 to 1945

THE Great Depression (see page 266) fell heavily upon Japan. The great majority of the Japanese people became deeply disillusioned with party government. They believed that their army's conquest of Manchuria and advances in Inner Mongolia and northern China indicated their nation's predestined role to become the new leader of east Asia. They were convinced that the exploitation of those regions would ease the economic stresses resulting both from a rapidly growing population and from military expenditures which absorbed half of the national budget.

Chiang Kai Shek, supported by the United States and other powers with special interests in China, refused to acquiesce in Japan's advances. With Japan's foreign policy largely determined by the military, any minor incident between Chinese and Japanese troops became potentially explosive. In July 1937, skirmishes began near Peking and quickly erupted into a full-scale war. Chiang's troops were no match for the Japanese. In December China's capital, Nanking, was ravaged by the Japanese army and Chiang's government fled into the interior. Within the next year, Japan completed its conquest of eastern and central China, and proclaimed a New Order in which the western powers would be driven from eastern Asia.

The United States and the United Kingdom replied by sending aid to Chiang over the Burma Road, strengthening his will not to capitulate. In February 1939 Japan occupied Hainan Island, and in July blockaded British and French concessions in Tientsin, prompting the United States to denounce its treaty of commerce with Japan. The rulers of Japan were convinced that its destiny depended on the acquisition of petroleum, bauxite and rubber in the Philippines, Burma, Malaya and the Indies. By joining the

Tripartite Alliance, Japan secured the approval of the Axis for its New Order in east Asia. Unable to obtain its objectives through diplomacy, Japan used the opportunity provided by the German attack on Russia in June 1941 to occupy Indo-China. In October, an expansionist, General Hideki Tojo, became Prime Minister and supported plans for simultaneous surprise attacks on the Americans at Pearl Harbor and on the British in Malaya. The aim was to force the capitulation of South-East Asia within four months, and to create an impregnable Greater East Asia Co-Prosperity Sphere within two years.

The die was cast on 7 December 1941. Pearl Harbor was attacked and the American Pacific Fleet was temporarily crippled. On the same day, Japan attacked the Philippines. By the end of March, all Malaya was conquered, the Netherlands East Indies had surrendered and Burma was overrun. In May 1942 the American fortress at Corregidor fell and Allied resistance ended in the western Pacific. Japan had completed the first stage of its conquest with a minimum of loss. Prime Minister Churchill and President Roosevelt, with a war on two fronts, gave first priority to the defeat of Germany. But they also took steps to prevent the extension of the Japanese perimeter by sending American forces to occupy the Fiji Islands and New Caledonia. In May 1942 a Japanese fleet heading for Port Moresby was intercepted by an American task force in the Coral Sea. Neither side won a decisive victory.

Then suddenly the tide turned. A great Japanese fleet was sent against the Americans at Midway Island in June 1942. It was brought to battle and in a single afternoon four Japanese aircraft carriers were sunk and the momentum of war reversed. Before the Battle of Midway, Japan never lost a major battle in the Pacific; afterwards, it never won another.

In late 1942 the Allies seized the initiative, advancing against the Japanese in four separate lines. The South-West Pacific Forces under General MacArthur began their amphibious drive against the Japanese perimeter. At Guadalcanal the Americans successfully challenged Japanese landings and reinforcements while the Australians halted an overland threat to Port Moresby. Henceforth, these South-West Pacific Forces moved north from the Bismarck Archipelago and New Guinea to the Philippines and eventually to Okinawa.

In November 1943 the Pacific Ocean Area Forces under Admiral Nimitz began successful amphibious assaults on the Gilbert Islands, the first of a series of co-ordinated advances across the central Pacific to cut Japan's supply lines, and to provide forward American bases for the next selected target as well as airfields for bombing Japan's home islands. The fanatical stands of the Japanese defenders on their island strongholds were ineffective against the prodigious Allied sea, air and land attacks. After the great battle of Leyte Gulf (larger than Jutland in the number of ships involved), the Japanese navy no longer posed a threat to Allied advances. Their air force became so diminished that after March 1945 it was powerless against the devastating incendiary air raids on principal metropolitan areas.

At the same time, British and Indian troops stopped the Japanese advance through Burma at Imphal and began the liberation of South-East Asia. American assistance was despatched to the Chinese nationalists, and the American air force began bombing the Japanese homeland from China. The American submarines, guided to their targets by American crypto-analysts, inflicted severe damage on Japan's merchant marine and slowly strangled its island economy. At Cairo in 1943, the Allies announced that they would fight until Japan's unconditional surrender, stripping it of all territories acquired after 1895. Even though Japan showed no signs of giving up, post-war policy planners in the US Department of State believed that Japan might stop its fanatical resistance if it knew what the Allies really meant by 'unconditional surrender', and prepared a policy statement defining unconditional surrender in specific terms. Simultaneously, the secret work on a nuclear weapon, which Churchill and Roosevelt had sanctioned in 1942, was nearing completion. In July 1945 a special commission recommended to President Truman that the bomb be used against Japan. The American Secretary of War, Henry Stimson, argued instead that Japan should be given a chance to surrender before the bomb was used. But at Potsdam that month, the Allied leaders approved the Potsdam Declaration appealing to Japan to surrender or face destruction, confirmed the territorial limits set at Cairo, called for an Allied occupation of Japan, the elimination of its armed forces and the establishment of a peacefully inclined and responsible government. When Japan failed to reply positively to this offer, President Truman ordered the first atomic bomb to be dropped on Hiroshima on 6 August 1945. Three days later a second bomb was dropped, on Nagasaki, and Russia entered the war against Japan. Early the next morning, at an Imperial Conference attended by the leading military and civilian authorities, the Emperor decided for peace. The following week he publicly announced his nation's capitulation, and on 2 September 1945, on board USS Missouri in Tokyo Bay, General MacArthur, the Allied Supreme Commander, accepted Japan's surrender.

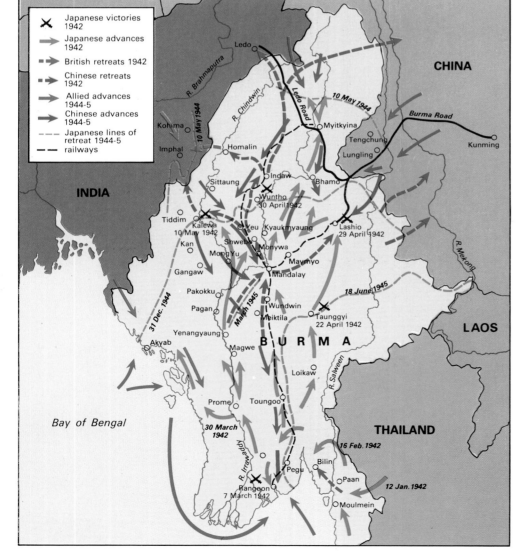

S.E. Asian Forces

Chungki...

Chinese counter-offensive April...

Imphal
Kunming

BURMA
Mandalay
Lao Cai
Hanoi
Gulf of Tongki...
Hain...

Rangoon
Moulmein
Tengchung
THAILAND
Bangkok

FRENCH INDO-CHINA

Recaptured 5 May 1945

Phnom Penh
Gulf of Thailand
Saigon

Japanese land on Malay coast 8 Dec 1941

Penang

MALAY
Sabang
Kuala Lumpur
Medan
STATES

Singapore
Japanese take Singapore 15 Feb 194...

Sumatra
Netherlands East...
Palembang

Java Sea

Batavia

HMS Prince of Wales and Repulse sunk by Japanese 10 Dec 1941

Battle of the Java Sea 27 Feb 1942 unsuccessful attempt to halt Japanese invasion of Java

2/The Burma Campaigns *(left)* Shortly after the attack on Pearl Harbor the Japanese simultaneously attacked the Dutch East Indies and Burma, aiming to cut the Burma Road, by which aid was reaching China. Within four months Burma was overrun, with heavy Allied losses. In May 1944 Allied troops, advancing from Imphal, began the gradual reconquest of Burma, finally reaching Rangoon on 3 May 1945.

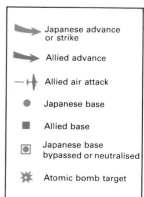

→ Japanese advance or strike
→ Allied advance
‑I‑ Allied air attack
● Japanese base
■ Allied base
◉ Japanese base bypassed or neutralised
✳ Atomic bomb target

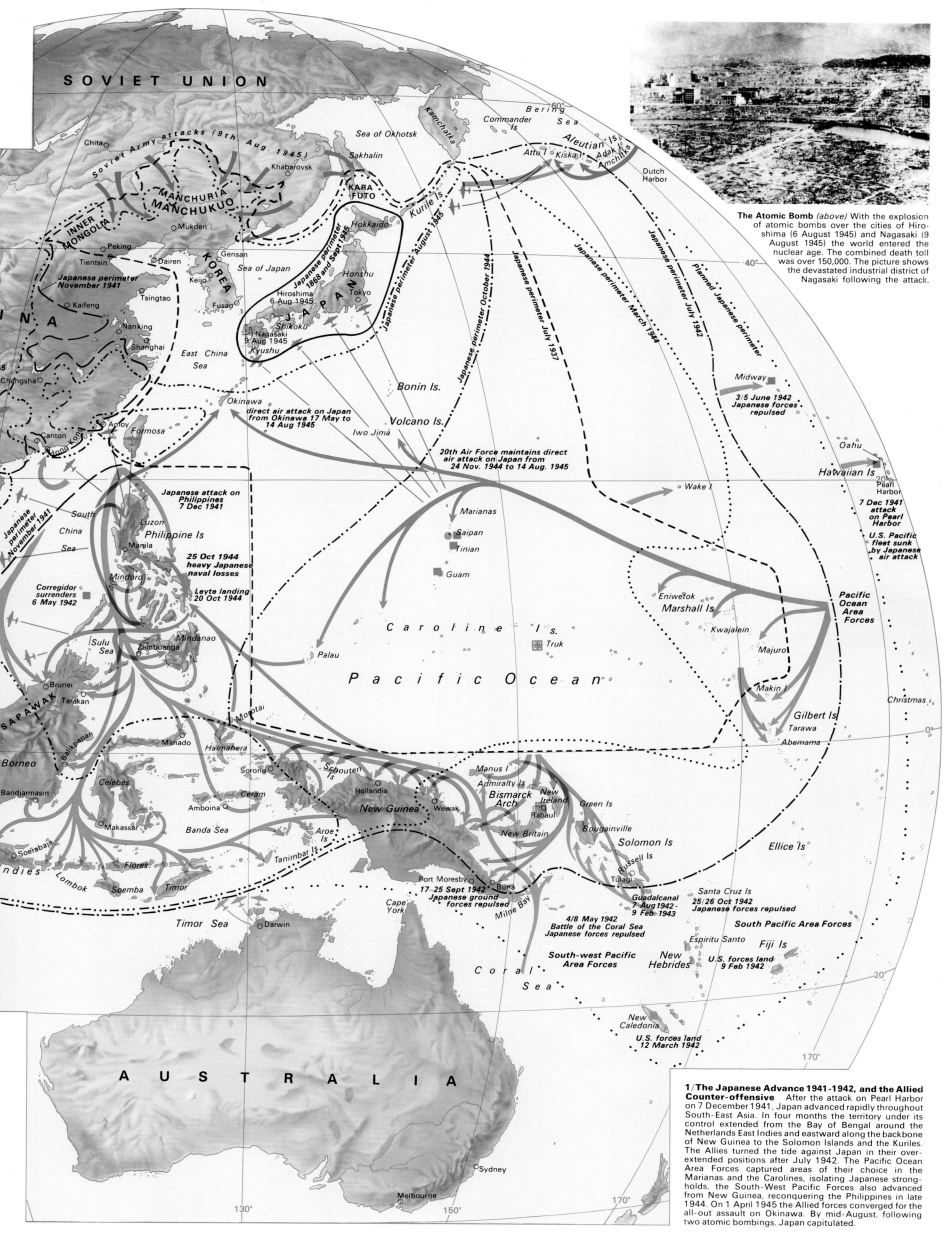

SOVIET UNION

Chita

Soviet Army attacks (9th Aug. 1945)

Khabarovsk

Sakhalin

Sea of Okhotsk

Commander Is

Bering Sea

Kamchatka

Aleutian Is

Attu I Kiska I Adak I Amchitka

Dutch Harbor

MANCHURIA
MANCHUKUO

INNER
MONGOLIA

Mukden

KARA
FUTO

Hokkaido

Kurile Is

Peking

Tientsin

Dairen

KOREA

Gensan

Sea of Japan

Japanese perimeter
Sept 1945
1868 and

Japanese perimeter August 1945

Japanese perimeter August 1945

Japanese perimeter October 1944

Japanese perimeter July 1937

Japanese perimeter March 1944

Japanese perimeter July 1942

Planned Japanese perimeter

CHINA

Japanese perimeter
November 1941

Kaifeng

Tsingtao

Keijo

Fusap

Shanghai

Nanking

Chingsha

45

JAPAN

Hiroshima
6 Aug 1945

Honshu

Shikoku

Tokyo

Midway

3/5 June 1942
Japanese forces
repulsed

East China
Sea

Nagasaki
9 Aug 1945

Kyushu

Okinawa

direct air attack on Japan
from Okinawa 17 May to
14 Aug 1945

Bonin Is.

Volcano Is.

Iwo Jima

20th Air Force maintains direct
air attack on Japan from
24 Nov. 1944 to 14 Aug. 1945

Wake I

Oahu

Hawaiian Is

Pearl
Harbor

7 Dec 1941
attack
on Pearl
Harbor

U.S. Pacific
fleet sunk
by Japanese
air attack

Formosa

Amoy

Canton

Hong Kong

Japanese
perimeter
November 1941

South
China
Sea

Japanese attack on
Philippines
7 Dec 1941

Luzon

Philippine Is

Manila

25 Oct 1944
heavy Japanese
naval losses

Leyte landing
20 Oct 1944

Marianas

Saipan

Tinian

Guam

Eniwetok

Marshall Is

Kwajalein

Majuro

Pacific
Ocean
Area
Forces

Christmas I

Corregidor
surrenders
6 May 1942

Mindoro

Sulu
Sea

Zamboanga

Mindanao

Caroline   Is.

Truk

Palau

Pacific   Ocean

Makin I

Gilbert Is

Tarawa

Abemama

0

SARAWAK

Brunei

Tarakan

Balikpapan

Borneo

Bandjarmasin

Morotai

Manado

Halmahera

Sorong

Celebes

Ceram

Amboina

Makassar

Banda Sea

Schouten
Is

Hollandia

Wewak

New Guinea

Aroe
Is

Tanimbar Is

Manus I

Admiralty Is

Bismarck
Arch

New
Ireland

Rabaul

New Britain

Green Is

Bougainville

Solomon Is

Russell Is

Ellice Is

Indies

Soerabaja

Flores

Lombok

Timor

Soemba

Timor Sea

Port Moresby

17-25 Sept 1942
Japanese ground
forces repulsed

Buna

Milne Bay

Cape
York

Darwin

Tulagi

Guadalcanal
7 Aug 1942-
9 Feb 1943

Santa Cruz Is

25/26 Oct 1942
Japanese forces repulsed

South Pacific Area Forces

4/8 May 1942
Battle of the Coral Sea
Japanese forces repulsed

South-west Pacific
Area Forces

New
Hebrides

Espiritu Santo

Fiji Is

U.S. forces land
9 Feb 1942

Coral   Sea

AUSTRALIA

New
Caledonia

U.S. forces land
12 March 1942

Sydney

Melbourne

130°   150°   170°   20°

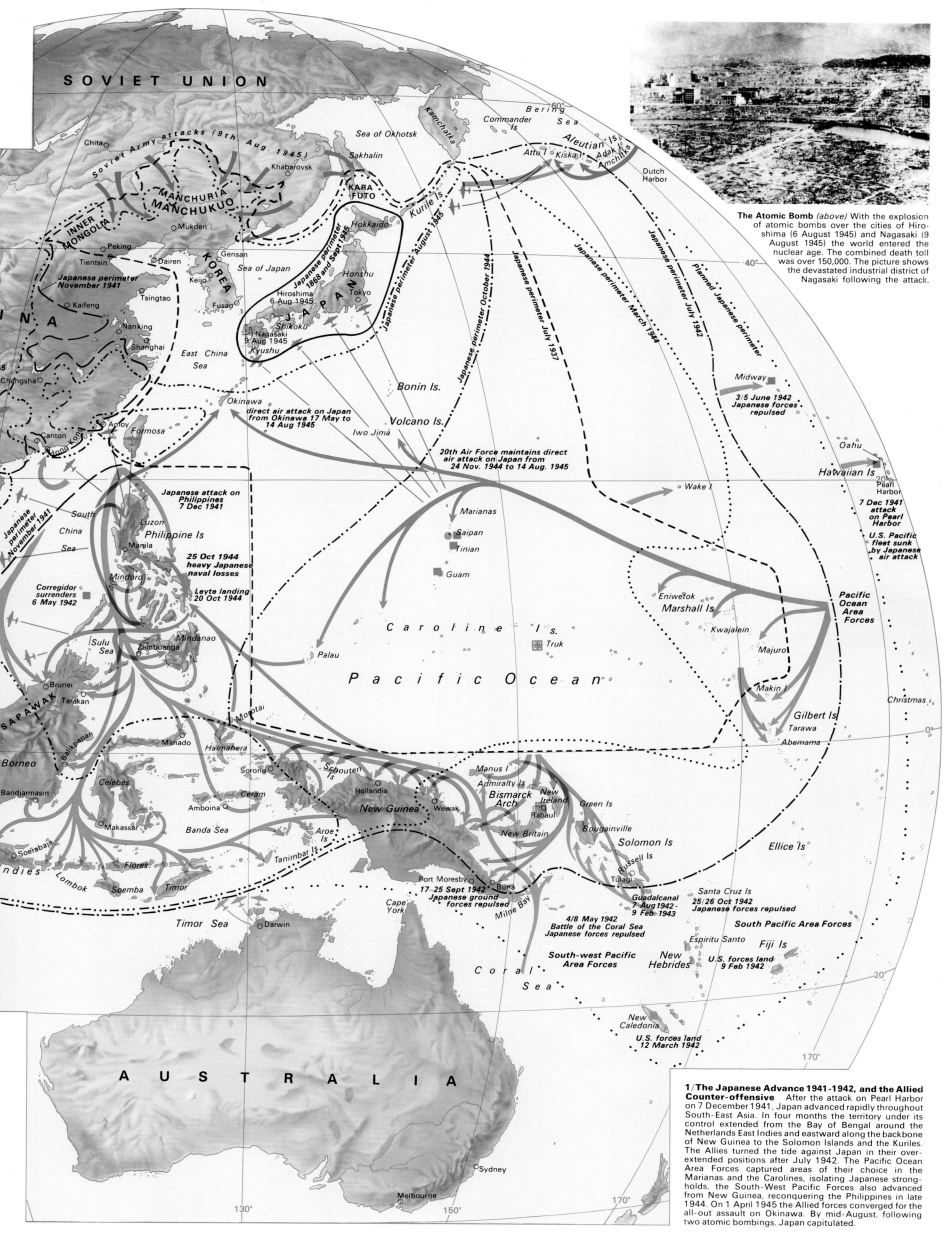

The Atomic Bomb *(above)* With the explosion of atomic bombs over the cities of Hiroshima (6 August 1945) and Nagasaki (9 August 1945) the world entered the nuclear age. The combined death toll was over 150,000. The picture shows the devastated industrial district of Nagasaki following the attack.

1/The Japanese Advance 1941-1942, and the Allied Counter-offensive   After the attack on Pearl Harbor on 7 December 1941, Japan advanced rapidly throughout South-East Asia. In four months the territory under its control extended from the Bay of Bengal around the Netherlands East Indies and eastward along the backbone of New Guinea to the Solomon Islands and the Kuriles. The Allies turned the tide against Japan in their over-extended positions after July 1942. The Pacific Ocean Area Forces captured areas of their choice in the Marianas and the Carolines, isolating Japanese strongholds, the South-West Pacific Forces also advanced from New Guinea, reconquering the Philippines in late 1944. On 1 April 1945 the Allied forces converged for the all-out assault on Okinawa. By mid-August, following two atomic bombings, Japan capitulated.

The war in the West 1941 to 1945

THE German attack on the Soviet Union in June 1941 was to be followed by fourteen months of German victory, interrupted by the Soviet winter offensive of December 1941 which drove the invaders, frozen and unprepared for the Russian winter, back from Moscow, and by a British offensive in November 1941 in Cyrenaica. The tide of victory turned against Germany in November 1942 with the British victory at El Alamein, the Anglo-American landings in French North Africa and the Soviet break through the German front at Stalingrad. After massive withdrawals, heroic German efforts temporarily stabilised the various fronts. Vichy France was occupied. But by February 1943 the Germans had lost their Sixth Army, surrounded near Stalingrad, and all North Africa with a quarter of a million men. In July 1943 the Allies invaded Sicily and the Russians defeated the last major German offensive at Kursk. In Italy the Fascist Grand Council deposed Mussolini (July 25th) who was arrested. The new Premier sued in secret for an armistice, which was announced on September 8th. In swift reaction, Germany seized northern and central Italy, rescued Mussolini to head a puppet Fascist Republic and disarmed Italian occupation forces in Greece and Yugoslavia. Allied landings in southern Italy met bitter resistance, and they took eleven months to reach Rome. Soviet forces met equally bitter resistance, reaching the Vistula only in August 1944.

In June 1944, Anglo-American forces landed

in northern France, creating the Second Front so often promised to Stalin over the two previous years. The differing political aims of the Big Three – the United States, Great Britain and the Soviet Union – were already apparent, despite the conference of the Allied leaders at Teheran (November 1943). Soviet offensives led to the conquering of all southeastern Europe. Romania surrendered in August, 1944, Bulgaria in September. A German coup prevented Hungary from doing likewise. Churchill, failing to secure a Western invasion of south-east Europe, agreed at Moscow in October to divide the area with the Soviet Union on a percentage basis. In Poland the Russians made little effort to intervene when the Germans suppressed a rising in Warsaw by the non-Communist Polish underground army. In April 1943 to 1944 they had broken relations with the Polish government in exile, recognising instead their own creation, the Lublin Committee. They also prepared a Free German movement, to work for Soviet victory in post-war Germany.

The Allied forces in northern France aimed for victory in 1944, but they failed. France and Belgium were liberated, the German border reached; but the drive for northern Germany ended with the failure to capture the Rhine bridges by airborne assault at Arnhem. Hitler chose the west for his final offensive in the Ardennes in December 1944. The major Soviet offensive against East Prussia opened in January. In February, Roosevelt, Churchill and Stalin met at Yalta. Both Roosevelt and Churchill, particularly the former, put the need to secure Russian membership of the new United Nations before everything else, accepting Soviet primacy in Poland and major changes in Poland's frontiers. By April Berlin was under assault and Hitler committed suicide on the 30th. On 7 May,

Admiral Doenitz, his successor, surrendered unconditionally.

Until June 1944, the main Anglo-American attack on Germany had been by air against the cities. German air defences had gained the upper hand by late 1943, but were unable to withstand its resumption in late 1944 despite Germany's lead in developing jet engines. German guided and ballistic missiles, used from June 1944 against south-east England, came too late to be effective. At sea, the German submarine blockade, operating in mid-Atlantic beyond the range of Allied land-based aircraft, brought the Allies close to disaster, until the advent of long range aircraft and escort carriers from May 1943 onwards closed the unpatrolled 'gap'.

In German-occupied Europe, resistance forces fought against German occupation and, where they were ideologically divided, against each other. In Yugoslavia, Tito's Communist partisans won British backing. In Greece the Communist EAM rose against the British when the latter decided to restore the monarchy. In Slovakia a Communist rising was defeated by the Germans. In Italy, partisans caught and killed Mussolini in April 1945.

The conduct of war was 'total', embracing and mobilising everyone. Great Britain and the Soviet Union achieved total mobilisation, including severe food rationing, from 1940 onwards. Germany only adopted full mobilisation in 1944, led by Josef Goebbels and Albert Speer. United States' unused productive capacity was so great that the American economy enjoyed boom conditions where Europe and the western USSR saw major destruction and massive movements of population. Several millions of slave and contract labourers were drawn into Germany; German settlers were sent into the Baltic states and then withdrawn. Over ten

The Russian flag hoisted on the ruins of the Reichstag *(above)* Russian forces under Koniev and Zhukov took Berlin in May 1945. The Soviet Union bore the lion's share of all land fighting from 1941 to 1944, suffering seven and a half million military deaths alone and untold devastation throughout European Russia.

1/Hitler's 'New Order' in Europe *(below)* Hitler divided Europe into four: pure Aryan areas annexed to or occupied by Germany and integrated into the German economy; occupied 'non-incorporated' areas; puppet and satellite states; the occupied and despoiled Slavic east, earmarked for German colonisation, whose native population would become illiterate helots.

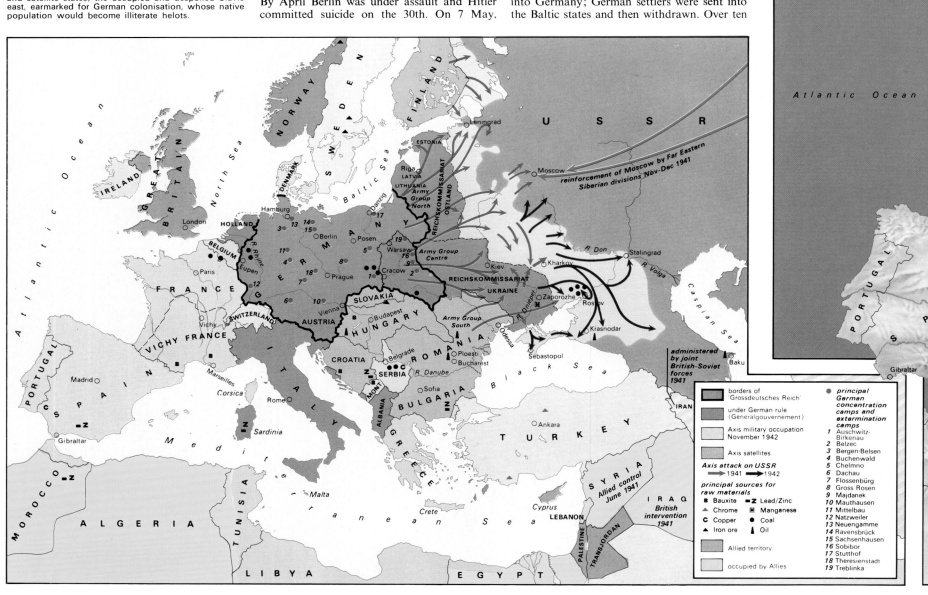

■	borders of 'Grossdeutsches Reich'	● principal German concentration camps and extermination camps
■	under German rule (Generalgouvernement)	1 Auschwitz-Birkenau
□	Axis military occupation November 1942	2 Belzec
■	Axis satellites	3 Bergen-Belsen
		4 Buchenwald
	Axis attack on USSR	5 Chelmno
	→ 1941 ➡ 1942	6 Dachau
	principal sources for raw materials	7 Flossenbürg
■ Bauxite	⊠ Lead/Zinc	8 Gross Rosen
▲ Chrome	⊞ Manganese	9 Majdanek
C Copper	● Coal	10 Mauthausen
▲ Iron ore	▲ Oil	11 Mittelbau
		12 Natzweiler
		13 Neuengamme
		14 Ravensbrück
■	Allied territory	15 Sachsenhausen
		16 Sobibor
□	occupied by Allies	17 Stutthof
		18 Theresienstadt
		19 Treblinka

million Germans were expelled from Eastern Europe or fled the Russian advance. Germany rounded up Europe's Jewish and Gipsy minorities for slaughter in the death-camps. Stalin deported sixteen minority peoples from the Crimea and Caucasus for alleged collaboration with the Germans. One hundred million men and women were mobilised to fight. The dead have been estimated at fifteen million military and thirty-five million civilians (twenty million of these being Soviet citizens, six million Jews, four and a half million Poles). There are no reliable estimates of the wounded. When the war ended, the leaders of the so-called Big Three countries led the United Nations. But Great Britain and

Europe were bankrupt, and European Russia was in ruins. Only the United States, whose money and industries had through 'lend lease' sustained and augmented the war economies of her allies, seemed the immediate and real victor.

2/The Battle of the Atlantic (right) The German campaign against British shipping began in the western approaches to Britain, moving in April 1941 to the mid-Atlantic 'gap', then beyond the range of British air-cover. The entry of the United States into the war opened further killing-grounds in US waters and the Caribbean to the new German long-range U-boats. After May 1943, patrolling of the 'gap' by very long range aircraft, with airborne radar acting on deciphered U-boat radio traffic, destroyed the existing U-boats' effectiveness.

3/The defeat of Germany (below) Hitler's failure to defeat Great Britain in the Blitz and the Atlantic and to overthrow Stalin's regime in the Soviet Union made his own defeat inevitable, as irreconcilable ideologies ruled out a compromise peace. The German armies were defeated in detail on the eastern front, the British and Americans knocked out Italy and invaded France, making German collapse under attack from east, west and south only a question of time.

6/The Normandy landings (inset below) On 6 June, 1944 American, British and Canadian armies landed in Normandy, breaching the German fortifications ('Atlantic Wall'). Allied air attack on German communications prevented German counter-attack. Artificial 'Mulberry' harbours turned the beaches into ports adequate for all necessary supplies.

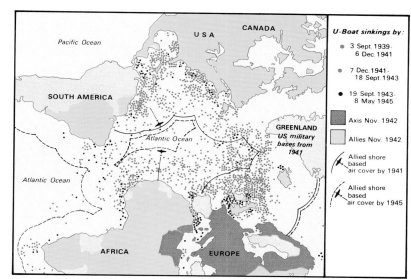

U-Boat sinkings by:
- 3 Sept. 1939 – 6 Dec. 1941
- 7 Dec. 1941 – 18 Sept. 1943
- 19 Sept. 1943 – 8 May 1945

Axis Nov. 1942
Allies Nov. 1942
Allied shore based air cover by 1941
Allied shore based air cover by 1945

4/The Battle of Stalingrad (inset below) In November 1942 the Russians encircled the German Sixth Army near Stalingrad, broke a rescue attempt and rolled the German front back to the Kharkov-Taganrog line.

5/The Battle of Kursk (inset bottom) in July 1943 was Hitler's last major offensive on the eastern front. It failed because of his own hesitation, superior Russian firepower and fears of an Italian collapse following the Allied invasion of Sicily.

invasion beaches
A Utah (American)
B Omaha (American)
C Gold (British)
D Juno (British)
E Sword (British/Canadian)

Russian attacks
front, 19 Nov. 1942
front, 12 Dec. 1942
trapped Axis armies

planned German attack, 5 July 1943
limits of German advance
Russian counter offensive 23 July – 23 August 1943

'Grossdeutsches Reich' 1942
Axis attacks
Axis withdrawal
cities under heavy air attack
Allied attacks
commando raids
airborne landings
partisan/resistance movements
V1 launching sites
V2 launching sites

273

The aftermath of the War in Europe

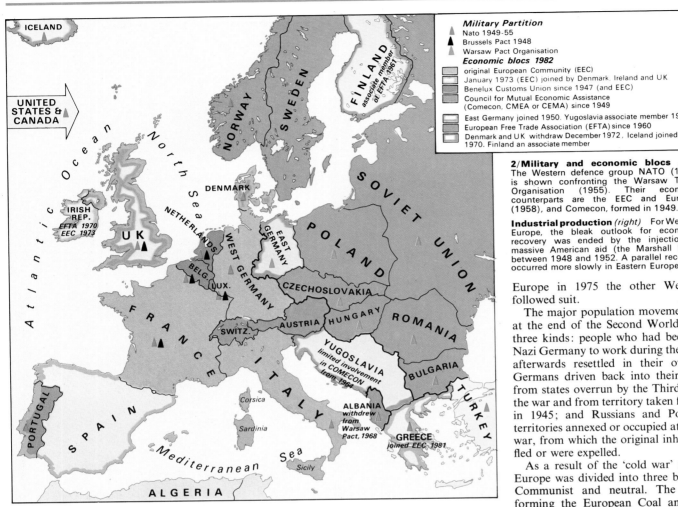

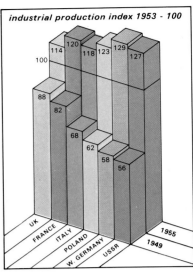

2/Military and economic blocs *(left)* The Western defence group NATO (1949) is shown confronting the Warsaw Treaty Organisation (1955). Their economic counterparts are the EEC and Euratom (1958), and Comecon, formed in 1949.

Industrial production *(right)* For Western Europe, the bleak outlook for economic recovery was ended by the injection of massive American aid (the Marshall Plan) between 1948 and 1952. A parallel recovery occurred more slowly in Eastern Europe.

THE war left Europe in 1945 not only politically disorganised but also in a state of economic prostration, greatly exacerbated by large-scale population movements. In 1946 pig iron output in Western Europe was just over 19 million tons, less than half the 1939 volume; in France, Germany, Italy and the Benelux countries output was less than 10 million tons, less than one-third the 1939 volume. West European crude steel production in 1946 was under 10 million tons, less than one-third the 1939 figure. Coal output in Western Europe in 1945 was 292 million tons as compared with 490 million tons in 1939. Agriculture suffered even more severely than industry, and the breakdown of the communications network (especially railways) was crippling. Until 1949 the outlook was bleak, and political uncertainty, fostered by the antagonism between the USA and the USSR, hampered recovery.

Meanwhile, the dismantling of the German New Order and the political reconstruction of Europe were taking place under the shadow of Russian-American conflict. The political frontiers of Europe were established at the Yalta and Potsdam conferences of the Soviet Union, the United Kingdom and the United States in February and July-August 1945 respectively. The agreement reached at those meetings was that Germany as it was in 1937, less East Prussia (which was divided between Poland and the Soviet Union) and German territory between the 1937 frontier with Poland and the Oder and Western Neisse rivers (which was placed under Polish administration pending a peace treaty with Germany), should be divided into American, British and Soviet occupation zones. The two French occupation zones were later formed from parts of the American and British zones. Sovereignty in Germany, pending a peace treaty, was exercised by the three (later four) commanders-in-chief of the occupying forces, each in his own zone, and, in respect to Germany as a whole, by an inter-Allied Control Council in Berlin. Berlin itself was similarly divided into

three (later four) sectors, each commander-in-chief likewise having full authority in his own sector, while matters concerning Berlin as a whole were decided, until 1949, by an inter-Allied council called the *Kommandatura*. The exceptional position of Berlin, some hundred miles within the Soviet zone of occupation, created problems for the western powers during the 'airlift' crisis of 1948-49 and again in 1958-61, when the Soviet government sought to have the Western sectors of Berlin incorporated in a demilitarised Free City. The latter crisis ended with the building of the Berlin Wall by the East Germans in August 1961.

The division of Austria for occupation purposes was somewhat similar, with Vienna also divided into four sectors. The *Anschluss* (unification) of Austria and Germany in March 1938 was nullified. In May 1955 the Soviet government, after ten years' disagreement with the Western powers, at length dropped its objections to the draft state treaty with Austria. As a result, the four-Power occupation was ended and Austria re-emerged as an independent though permanently neutralised state.

Another point of contention was the position of Trieste and its hinterland at the head of the Adriatic Sea (see map 4).

In 1955 the occupation of the three Western zones of Germany, which had formed the Federal Republic of Germany since 1949, was ended, and sovereignty was fully restored. The Federal Republic joined the European Coal and Steel Community (ECSC) in 1952 and the North Atlantic Treaty Organisation (NATO) in 1955. The conversion of the Soviet zone of occupation into a separate state, the German Democratic Republic (DDR) occurred in 1949, and in 1955 the new state joined the newly-founded Warsaw Treaty Organisation. The Western Powers refused for many years to recognise the DDR, but in 1972 the West German government reversed its policy and accorded recognition, and at the Helsinki Conference on Security and Co-operation in

Europe in 1975 the other Western Powers followed suit.

The major population movements in Europe at the end of the Second World War were of three kinds: people who had been forced into Nazi Germany to work during the war and were afterwards resettled in their own countries; Germans driven back into their own country from states overrun by the Third Reich during the war and from territory taken from Germany in 1945; and Russians and Poles settled in territories annexed or occupied at the end of the war, from which the original inhabitants either fled or were expelled.

As a result of the 'cold war' (see page 292) Europe was divided into three blocs: Western, Communist and neutral. The six countries forming the European Coal and Steel Community in 1952 – the Benelux group (Belgium, Luxembourg and the Netherlands), West Germany, France and Italy – joined together to form the European Economic Community (EEC) and Euratom in 1957. These three Communities became the European Community and were joined by Denmark, Ireland and the United Kingdom in January 1973. It was envisaged that eventually this economic grouping would form a political unit. According to the planned timetable the European Assembly, the parliamentary element in the Community, was to be directly elected by 1978 and the Community would form a single monetary unit. But problems arising over the common agricultural policy and exchange rate fluctuations suggested that these objectives might prove optimistic.

At the Helsinki Conference on Security and Co-operation in Europe, held in 1975, frontiers in Europe were accepted as inviolable, though revision by peaceful agreement was not ruled out. Yugoslavia, expelled from the Soviet-led Cominform in 1948, remained non-aligned; so did Spain, where the monarchy was restored under King Juan Carlos in 1975 after the death of General Franco; and Portugal remained in NATO, though the political future there was still uncertain after the fall of the Caetano dictatorship in 1974. On the southern flank of NATO, hostility between Greece and Turkey over Cyprus, a country populated by a Greek four-fifths majority and a Turkish minority, remained unsolved.

1/Post-war population movements *(right)* The collapse of Hitler's Third Reich in 1945 released millions of prisoners of war and slave-workers incarcerated in Germany during the war. Furthermore, some 5 million Russian prisoners, refugees and servicemen were forcibly repatriated. A more lasting shift of population was the expulsion of Germans from some of their pre-war territories, especially in eastern Europe, and from lands they had annexed in the late 1930s. A further movement at the end of the war was the result of the westward expansion of the Soviet Union, especially the annexation of the Baltic states, Estonia, Latvia and Lithuania.

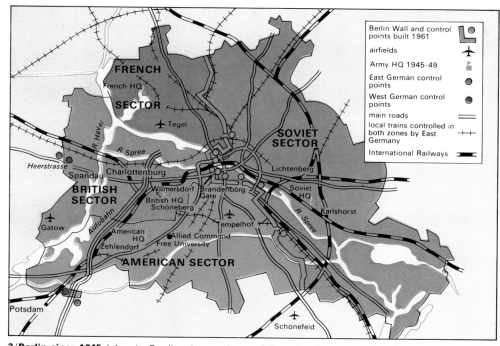

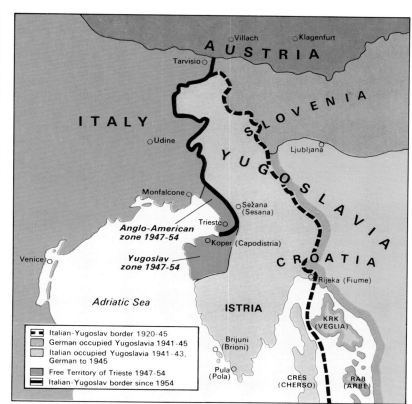

3/Berlin since 1945 (above) Pending the reunification of Germany, its pre-war capital, situated in the present German Democratic Republic (East Germany), remained under four-power Allied occupation. In August 1961 the famous 'Berlin Wall' was built, dividing the Soviet from the three Western sectors.

4/Trieste since 1945 (right) The city of Trieste and its hinterland, Venezia Giulia, passed from the Austro-Hungarian Empire to Italy in 1920. After Italy's defeat in the Second World War the city and territory were claimed by Yugoslavia. The dispute lasted until 1954, when the territory was divided.

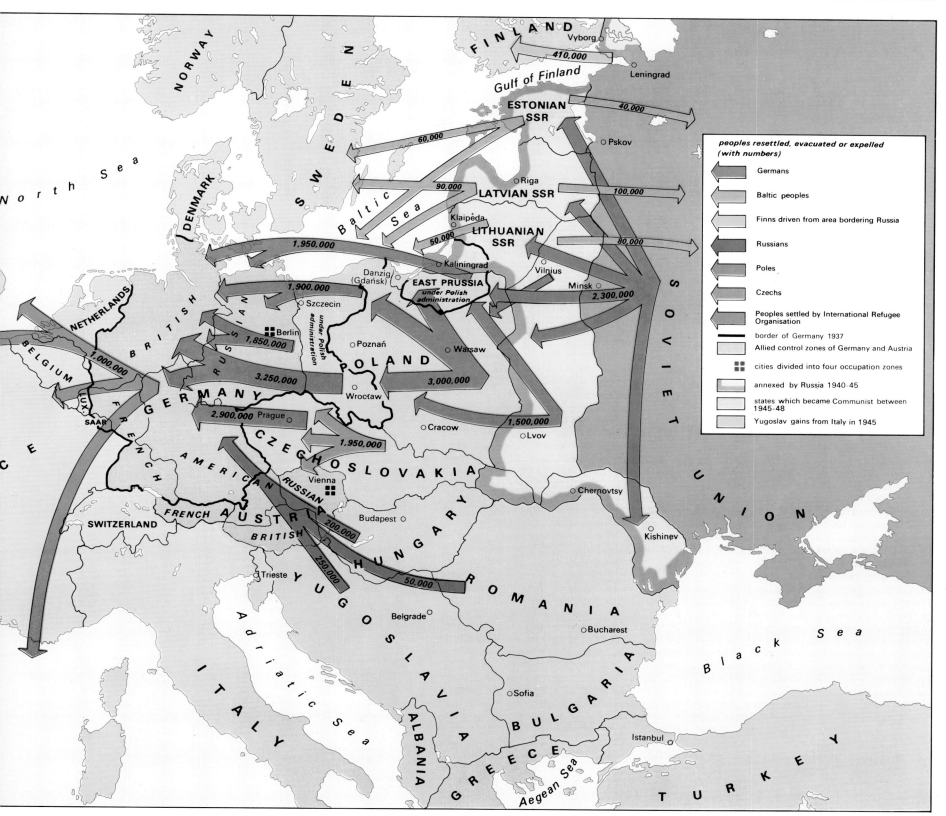

Retreat from empire 1939 to 1983

IN 1939 the European powers with colonial possessions were Great Britain, France, the Netherlands, Italy, Belgium, Spain and Portugal. The first three powers were, to varying degrees, committed to the evolution of their colonial territories towards self-government, and this commitment was reinforced, in the case of Great Britain and France, by the terms under which they had been granted mandates by the League of Nations over territories formerly part of the German and Ottoman empires. Great Britain alone conceived the ultimate goal as going beyond self-government to independence, within a loose framework of attachment to the Commonwealth (established by the Statute of Westminster, 1931), a goal already reached in 1939 by Canada, South Africa, Australia and New Zealand, and towards which India was considered to be moving. The continental powers thought more in terms of evolution towards a common citizenship, and saw their colonies largely as overseas parts of the metropolitan territory. These commitments were, however, complicated both by the resistance of sizeable minorities of European settlers, with consequent inter-racial tensions, and by clashes between the European ideal of evolution along western lines (e.g. in education and in economic development) and the powerful Islamic, Hindu, Buddhist and Confucian cultures of their colonial subjects.

The need to raise western-educated élites from the colonial peoples to man at least the lower ranks of colonial administrations had already resulted in the growth of important local nationalist movements, some of which also were inspired by Soviet, Chinese or Japanese models. The unwillingness of metropolitan legislatures or electorates to finance full-scale European-manned administrations also encouraged the colonial powers to rely on indigenous local authorities wherever these were powerful enough to be used by the European governments.

The events of the Second World War had revolutionary effects on the slow processes of development within the main colonial empires. In Europe the metropolitan territories of Belgium, France and the Netherlands were overrun by Germany. The governments of Belgium and the Netherlands took refuge in England; that of France accepted defeat and compromise with Germany and Italy so completely that in part of the overseas territories an anti-capitulation movement, the Free French, sprang up, while the British and Americans felt obliged to take over Vichy-held territories in the Middle East and North Africa. Italy's African colonies passed under British occupation. In South-East Asia, Germany's Japanese ally expelled the colonial powers from Malaya, the East Indies and Burma, and established governments based on local nationalist movements in Burma in 1942 and the East Indies and Indo-China in 1945. After the surrender of Japan these governments, enlarged or superseded by anti-Japanese nationalist elements, won much popular backing and were strong enough to force the colonial power – in the case of Burma with only minimal violence, in the East Indies and Indo-China after prolonged conflict – to recognise their independence.

The war years were marked by a political impasse in India. The ill-timed Cripps' Mission, sent by a reluctant Churchill under American pressure, failed to resolve it. In 1942, Gandhi and his associates were imprisoned and the subsequent mass uprising was suppressed with great firmness. The radical leader, Subhas Bose, escaped and organised an Indian National Army under Japanese auspices. When, after the war, the unrest spread to the main army, the newly-elected Labour government in England decided to break with the tradition of holding on to the essence of power. Meanwhile the Indian Muslim demand for an autonomous region had grown strong and in 1947 power was transferred to the

two states of India and Pakistan (see page 280).

In France, the Fourth Republic, by its constitution promulgated in 1946, replaced the old Empire by a new *Union française* consisting of metropolitan France with its overseas *départements* and territories, and a group of associated states, among which were Laos, Cambodia and a French-inspired Republic of Vietnam. But in Vietnam the French 'satellite' adminstration was opposed by the forces of the Democratic Republic of Vietnam which were committed to independence, and after the defeat of Dien Bien Phu the French were forced, in 1954, to withdraw. In 1957 Great Britain took the first major step towards conferring independence in Africa, with the grant of independence to Ghana.

Attempts to solve the problem posed by white settler minorities in central Africa by the creation of a Central African Federation broke down in 1963, and Rhodesia, which had enjoyed white settler self-government since 1923, declared its independence, without British agreement, in 1965. In the case of France, after the collapse of the Fourth Republic in 1958, the *Union française* was replaced by the *Communauté française*, but this was unacceptable to Guinea, which opted for complete independence; thirteen others followed its example in 1960, leaving Algeria the only French possession in Africa.

In the French territories in the Middle East and North Africa, the effects of British or American occupation and protection had helped to revitalise the independence movements. Italy's two main colonial possessions, Libya and Somalia, placed under UN mandate in 1945, became independent in 1951 and 1960; Eritrea, was absorbed uneasily into Ethiopia.

At the same time, Britain hoped to maintain her links with the Arab world after the ending of the mandates system by encouraging the formation of the Arab League, and later by the Baghdad Pact, a military alliance intended to incorporate the US, Britain, Pakistan and various pro-Western Middle Eastern states. However, Zionist victories in Palestine leading to the creation of Israel in 1948, Nasser's seizure of power in 1952, and the Anglo-French-Israeli invasion of Egypt in 1956 combined to diminish British and French influence and credibility in the region. Bitter conflicts in Cyprus and Aden led Britain to withdraw in 1960 and 1967, and the British presence east of Suez was gradually abandoned; many of the smaller Gulf sheikhdoms combined to form the United Arab Emirates in 1971. For its part France realised its inability to sustain prolonged conflict in more than one of its North African territories; Morocco and Tunisia became independent in 1956, while Algeria suffered 8 years of war and over a million dead until the French capitulated in 1962.

Since the powers had tended to endow their colonial territories with political institutions with little or no indigenous roots, it is not surprising that colonial withdrawal was frequently accompanied – or soon followed – by acts of revolutionary violence, and the setting up of repressive regimes. In other cases, ethnic or tribal units extended across frontiers: Indonesian claims over all Malay-speaking areas in the 1950s and 1960s led to conflict with Malaysia, and Somalia laid claim to areas of Kenya and Ethiopia. After Belgium abandoned the Congo in 1960, most of the new African states were united against the remaining Portuguese colonial territories and supported guerrilla liberation movements which brought independence to Angola and Mozambique a year after the collapse of the dictatorship in Portugal in 1974. Spain continues to occupy a few tiny enclaves in Morocco, but abandoned the Sahara to Morocco and Mauritania in 1976. After 13 years of guerrilla warfare, white minority rule ended in Rhodesia, which became Zimbabwe in 1980, leaving South Africa as the last remaining 'colonial' state in the African continent in 1983.

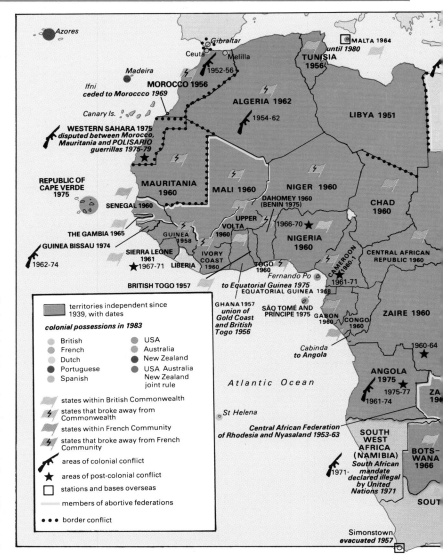

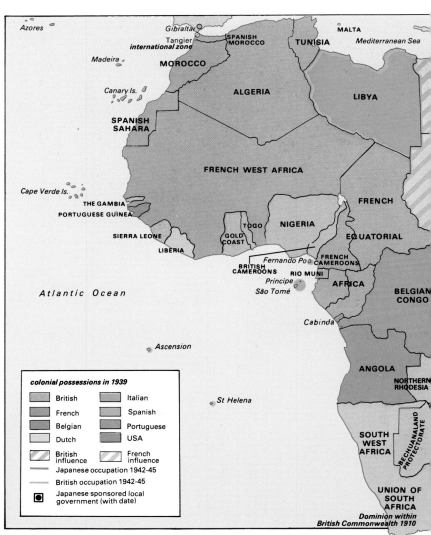

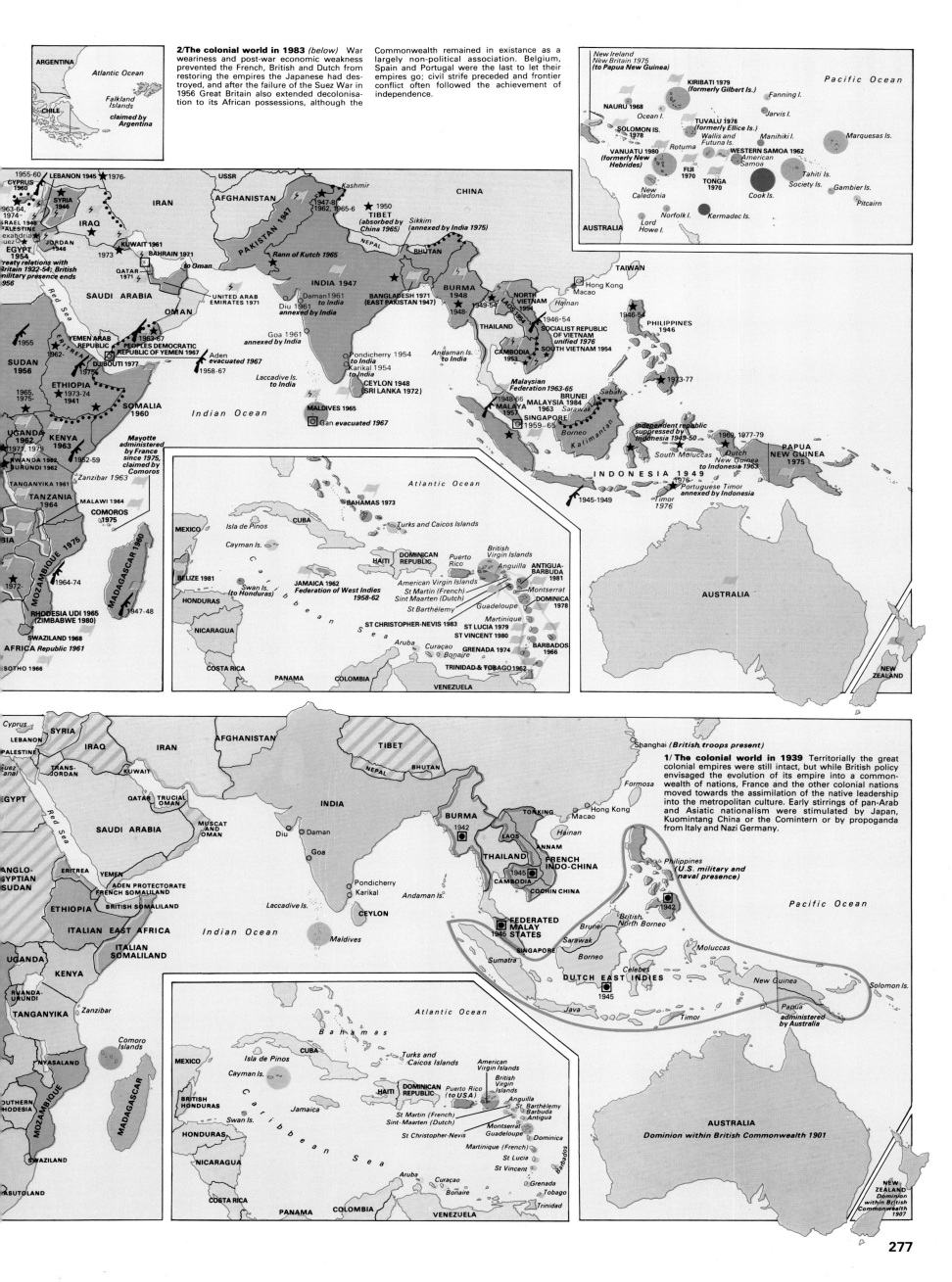

2/The colonial world in 1983 (below) War weariness and post-war economic weakness prevented the French, British and Dutch from restoring the empires the Japanese had destroyed, and after the failure of the Suez War in 1956 Great Britain also extended decolonisation to its African possessions, although the Commonwealth remained in existence as a largely non-political association. Belgium, Spain and Portugal were the last to let their empires go; civil strife preceded and frontier conflict often followed the achievement of independence.

1/ The colonial world in 1939 Territorially the great colonial empires were still intact, but while British policy envisaged the evolution of its empire into a commonwealth of nations, France and the other colonial nations moved towards the assimilation of the native leadership into the metropolitan culture. Early stirrings of pan-Arab and Asiatic nationalism were stimulated by Japan, Kuomintang China or the Comintern or by propaganda from Italy and Nazi Germany.

277

The new states of East and South-East Asia 1945 to 1983

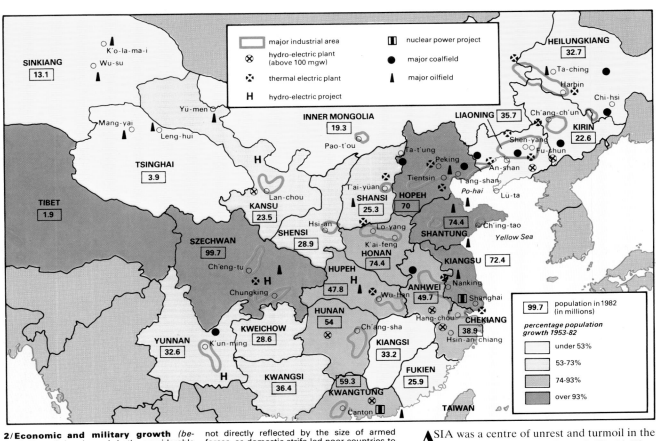

3/The development of China *(left)* The world's most populous country, China developed rapidly in the period after the end of the civil war in 1949. The People's Republic established an industrial infrastructure, growing petroleum sector and nuclear capabilities. China's increased grain and industrial expansion was slowed by the Cultural Revolution and her economy remains far below the spectacular growth levels of Japan, Hong Kong, Taiwan and Singapore.

aftermath of the attempted coup in Indonesia in 1965 brought deaths reportedly ranging from 100,000 to 750,000. Coups have been primarily led by the military, with new states often maintaining large standing armies. In part they derived from the low levels of economic growth in a region in which – in spite of high growth rates in Japan, Singapore, Malaysia and South Korea – most countries remained extremely poor.

While outside forces were involved in domestic disputes and insurgency activities in South-East Asia, territorial disputes frequently occurred between Asian states themselves. Most of these took a legal rather than a violent form. Fighting did occur in the dispute between China and South Vietnam over the Spratly and Paracel Islands, during Indonesia's successful effort to incorporate West Irian (formerly Dutch New Guinea) and Portuguese Timor and during the 'confrontation' between Indonesia and Malaysia over the Borneo territories. The conflict over Taiwan is a carry-over from the Chinese civil war. Other areas that have been in dispute are Cochin China, and surrounding waters claimed by Cambodia; the temple of Preah Vilhear acquired by Cambodia after a legal dispute with Thailand; Sabah, incorporated into Malaysia but claimed by the Philippines; the southern Kurile Islands and southern Sakhalin, taken by the Soviet Union after the Second World War and the object of Japanese irredentism; Okinawa, held by the United States after the War and finally brought under full Japanese control in 1972; Takeshima Island (Tok-do) claimed by Japan and South Korea, and three small areas on the Sino-Burmese border ceded by China to Burma in 1960. China's borders with her neighbours have been areas of contention with both Communist and Nationalist regimes producing maps claiming large areas, allegedly lost to imperialist countries.

The most serious tensions in the region followed the establishment of the new governments in Indo-China in 1975. Internally, this led to the flight of over one million refugees from Cambodia, Laos and Vietnam. More serious were the deaths of over one million Cambodians during the rule of the Communist Pol Pot from 1975 to early 1979. Internationally, tensions and border clashes led to the invasion of Cambodia by Vietnamese forces in 1978 and a new Cambodian leadership friendly to Hanoi. Since then, there have been continuous clashes between Vietnamese troops in Cambodia and opposition Communist and non-Communist insurgents. Hanoi's increased power, alleged ill-treatment of its Chinese citizens and the emerging alliance between Vietnam and the Soviet Union brought tensions between Vietnam and China to a head in 1979.

The post-war years did not only bring turmoil. Asia in 1984 had a higher standard of living than in 1947, Japan had become the third largest industrial power in the world, China had revived from decades of war, and countries such as Malaysia, Taiwan, Singapore and the Koreas had developed strong economies. On the international scene, old enemies had begun efforts to form regional organisations, the most successful being the Association of South-East Asian Nations, ASEAN. By 1984 there also appeared to be increasing stability in the region. In China the government turned to a more moderate course following the turmoil of the Cultural Revolution, while most of South-East Asia displayed strong continuities in leadership. However, after decades of colonial rule and civil and international strife, in 1984 competitive democracy only flourished in three of the region's sixteen states.

2/Economic and military growth *(below)* East Asia showed both considerable economic growth and imbalance in the post-war years. By 1983, per capita GNP varied from under $100 in Laos to over $9000 in the more developed nations, such as Japan. GNP was not directly reflected by the size of armed forces, as domestic strife led poor countries to develop large armies. In recent years, the developing nations of South-East Asia have become polarised between the ASEAN countries and an Indo-Chinese bloc.

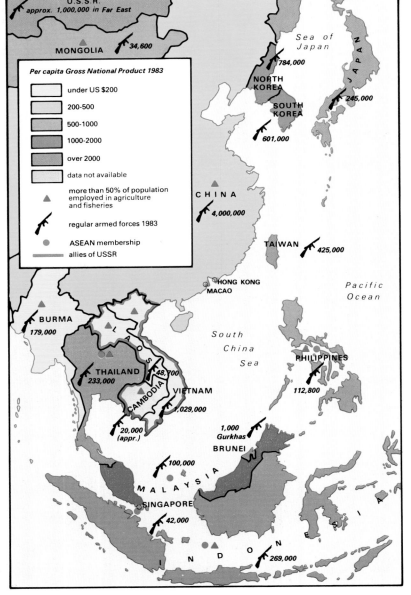

ASIA was a centre of unrest and turmoil in the generation since the Second World War, with violence and instability at many levels. Civil war developed in China, Burma, Indo-China and Korea. The Communist-Nationalist conflict in China had begun in the 1920s, coming to a head after 1945 when the Communists began the drive that brought them control of China (apart from Taiwan and Tibet) by the end of 1949. In 1950 war between North and South Korea, brought China into the battle against South Korea and the UN forces. Negotiations brought peace in 1953. Burma still suffers civil strife, on both communal and ideological issues. In 1984 this series of conflicts was in its thirty-seventh year and showed no sign of ending. The most intense war began in Vietnam in 1948-49. It was a war which combined conflict between internal groups with anti-colonial resistance to France, and after the defeat of France in 1954 turned into a struggle between the US-sponsored Ngo Dinh Diem in Saigon and the National Liberation Front. Ultimately, the civil war brought in North Vietnamese and US armed forces and spread to other areas of Indo-China. Although a formal ceasefire was established in 1973 and US forces withdrew, in 1975 Cambodia fell to the Khmer Rouge and South Vietnam to the Viet Minh.

Clashes between Communist-led insurgents and government forces were widespread, beginning in 1947-48 with rebellions in Malaya, Burma, Indonesia and the Philippines. By 1984 there was still small-scale insurgency in Malaysia, Thailand, Burma, the Philippines, and Indo-China. Communal violence based on religious, racial, regional and linguistic issues was endemic, with incidents including clashes between Christians and Muslims in the southern Philippines; Thai Buddhist government forces and Muslim Malays in southern Thailand; Burmese and Kachins, Mons, Shans, Karens and Arakanese in Burma; Vietnamese and Montagnards in southern Vietnam; Vietnamese and Cambodians; the Java-based government and dissidents in the outer islands of Indonesia; Malays and Chinese in Malaysia and Singapore; and Chinese and Tibetans in Tibet.

The post-war era saw the successful revolution in an independent China, and later victories of communist forces in Indo-China. Elsewhere, revolts and coups were increasingly frequent. Most coups were relatively non-violent, but the

The economic recovery of Japan *(right)*. Japan's progress, after regaining its independence in 1951, was phenomenal. Maintaining close relations with the United States, successive governments concentrated on industrial development and new technology until in the 1970s Japan emerged as the world's third industrial nation.

1/East Asia after independence *(below right)*. Post-independence East Asia experienced severe domestic and international strife. Coups and unconstitutional changes in government were rife, and lengthy civil wars with heavy casualties took place in China, Burma, Indo-China and Korea. Major territorial disputes involved almost every state in the region.

Independent countries and colonies 1983

Brunei Oil-rich Islamic state, under British protection from 1888; internally self-governing 1959; independent 1984.

Burma Independent from Britain in 1948. Military coups 1958-62; military government since then. Insurgencies among ethnic minorities and Communists continue. Economically stagnant.

Cambodia (Kampuchea; Khmer Republic) French protectorate 1862-1953. Prince Sihanouk ousted by Lon Nol, 1970; gave way to Khmer Rouge regime of Pol Pot in 1975; invaded by Vietnam in 1978; ruled by "puppet" regime of Heng Samrin. Active Khmer-Rouge-Sihanouk insurgency on Thai border. Degree of economic recovery.

China Communist regime under Mao Tse-tung from 1949. Death of Mao in 1976 led to modernisation and a revival of a degree of private sector trade and production.

Hong Kong Vigorous private sector produced flourishing trade and light industry and a busy financial centre 1950-83. Negotiations since Sept. 1982 for the reunification with China have led to dislocation of economy.

Indonesia Declared independence 1945; negotiated end to Dutch control 1949; rebellions in 1950s. Military became dominant after abortive Communist coup of 1965. "New order" of President Suharto suppressed political opponents, but social policies have ameliorated authoritarian excesses.

Japan Following end of US military rule in 1952, conservative, pro-business government policies led to spectacular economic growth. Low profile in international politics.

Korea Japanese empire, 1905-45; North Korea became a "Peoples Democracy" (Communist) 1948. South Korea established constitutional government with elections 1948. War between north and south, 1950-53, involving UN and Chinese forces ended in stalemate. Economic growth in South Korea under strong rule with military backing.

Laos French protectorate 1893-1953; coups and civil wars between Communist and non-Communist forces, with outside military involvement, until 1975 when Pathet Lao abolished monarchy. Measure of economic recovery since 1979.

Macao Former Portuguese colony now "Chinese territory presently administered by Portugal".

Malaysia Under British protection 1874-1958; joined with Sabah and Sarawak to form Malaysia Federation 1963. Multi-racial; political stability and economic growth.

Mongolia "People's Republic" under Soviet influence from 1921; gradually modernising.

Philippines Independent 1946. Continuing Communist and Muslim insurgencies. Strong-man rule under President Marcos from 1965; martial law 1972-81. Respectable degree of economic growth.

Singapore Part of Malaysia 1963; independent 1965. Economic planning brought prosperity.

Taiwan Japanese colony 1895 – 1945; the KMT forces retreated to Taiwan in 1949 and maintain their regime as the Republic of China. Economically prosperous.

Thailand Absolute monarchy succeeded by constitutional monarchy in 1932; governments then military. Several coups 1932-76; continuing Communist insurgency. Slow economic growth.

Timor Portuguese colony 1586-1976 when it was annexed to Indonesia; smouldering insurgency.

Vietnam Under French colonial administration 1862-1954 when North Vietnam became Communist state. South Vietnam became a republic in 1955 when monarchy ended. North-South war from late 1950s with outside military involvement. North invaded south 1975: Unified Vietnam has extended power over Indo-China.

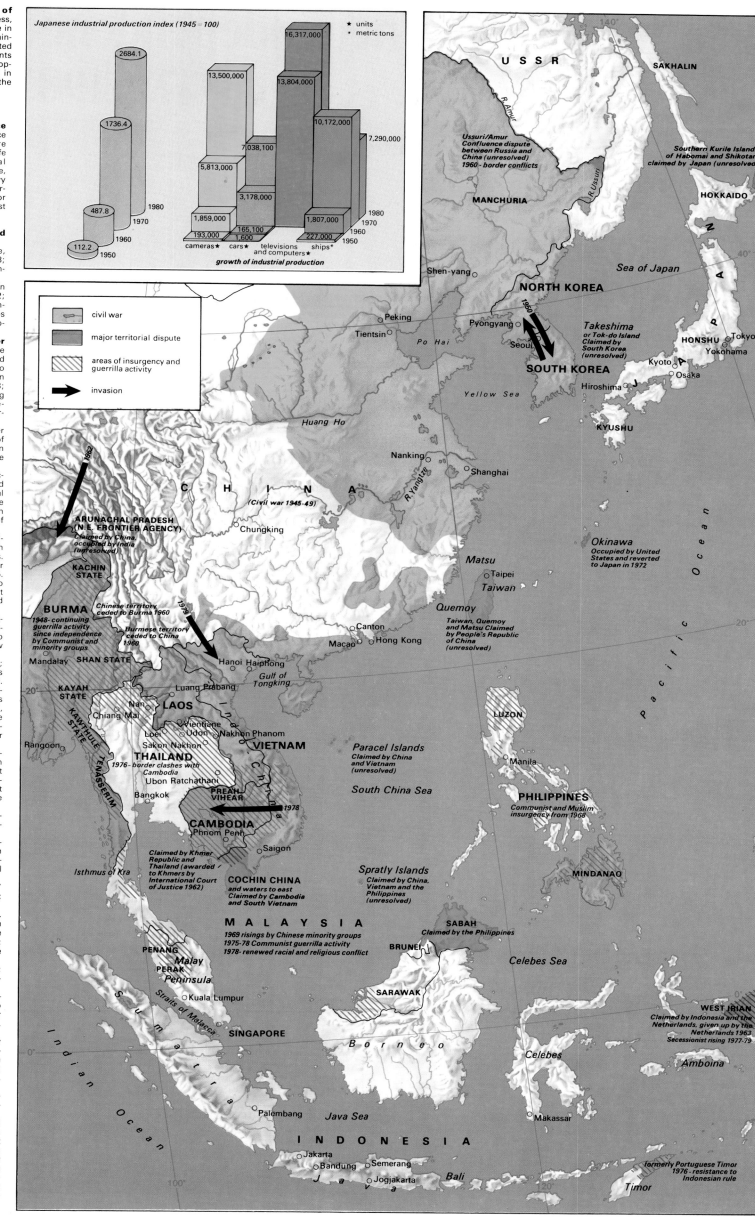

Japanese industrial production index (1945 = 100)

★ units
• metric tons

cameras ★ — 2684.1, 1736.4, 487.8, 112.2 (1980, 1970, 1960, 1950)

cars ★ — 1,859,000; 193,000 (1950)

televisions and computers ★ — 13,500,000; 5,813,000; 7,038,100; 3,178,000; 1,600; 165,100

ships • — 16,317,000; 13,804,000; 10,172,000; 7,290,000; 1,807,000; 227,000 (1980, 1970, 1960, 1950)

growth of industrial production

civil war

major territorial dispute

areas of insurgency and guerrilla activity

invasion

USSR

SAKHALIN

MANCHURIA

Ussuri/Amur Confluence dispute between Russia and China (unresolved) 1960 - border conflicts

Southern Kurile Islands of Habomai and Shikotan, claimed by Japan (unresolved)

HOKKAIDO

Shen-yang

NORTH KOREA

Pyongyang

Sea of Japan

Takeshima or Tok-do Island Claimed by South Korea (unresolved)

HONSHU Tokyo

Peking

Tientsin

Seoul

SOUTH KOREA

Po Hai

Yellow Sea

Hiroshima

Kyoto Osaka

KYUSHU

Huang Ho

Nanking

Shanghai

R. Yangtze

C H I N A

(Civil war 1945-49)

Chungking

Matsu Taipei

Taiwan

Okinawa *Occupied by United States and reverted to Japan in 1972*

Quemoy

Taiwan, Quemoy and Matsu Claimed by People's Republic of China (unresolved)

ARUNACHAL PRADESH (N.E. FRONTIER AGENCY) *Claimed by China, occupied by India (unresolved)*

KACHIN STATE

BURMA *1948- continuing guerrilla activity since independence by Communist and minority groups*

Chinese territory ceded to Burma 1960

Burmese territory ceded to China 1960

Canton

Macao Hong Kong

Mandalay SHAN STATE

Hanoi Haiphong

Gulf of Tongking

KAYAH STATE

Luang Prabang

KAWHULE STATE

Nan LAOS

Chiang Mai Vientiane

Loei Udon Nakhon Phanom

VIETNAM

Paracel Islands Claimed by China and Vietnam (unresolved)

LUZON

Manila

Rangoon THAILAND *1976- border clashes with Cambodia* Sakon Nakhon

Ubon Ratchathani

South China Sea

PHILIPPINES *Communist and Muslim insurgency from 1968*

TENASSERIM

Bangkok PREAH VIHEAR 1978

CAMBODIA Phnom Penh

Saigon

Claimed by Khmer Republic and Thailand (awarded to Khmers by International Court of Justice 1962)

COCHIN CHINA *and waters to east Claimed by Cambodia and South Vietnam*

Spratly Islands Claimed by China, Vietnam and the Philippines (unresolved)

MINDANAO

Isthmus of Kra

M A L A Y S I A

SABAH *Claimed by the Philippines*

BRUNEI

Celebes Sea

PENANG

Malay PERAK Peninsula

1969 risings by Chinese minority groups 1975-78 Communist guerrilla activity 1978- renewed racial and religious conflict

SARAWAK

S u m a t r a

Kuala Lumpur

Straits of Malacca

SINGAPORE

B o r n e o

Celebes

WEST IRIAN *Claimed by Indonesia and the Netherlands, given up by the Netherlands 1963 Secessionist rising 1977-79*

Amboina

Indian Ocean

Palembang Java Sea

Makassar

I N D O N E S I A

Jakarta Bandung Semerang

Jogjakarta Bali

J a v a

Timor *formerly Portuguese Timor 1976 - resistance to Indonesian rule*

279

Southern Asia since independence 1947 to 1983

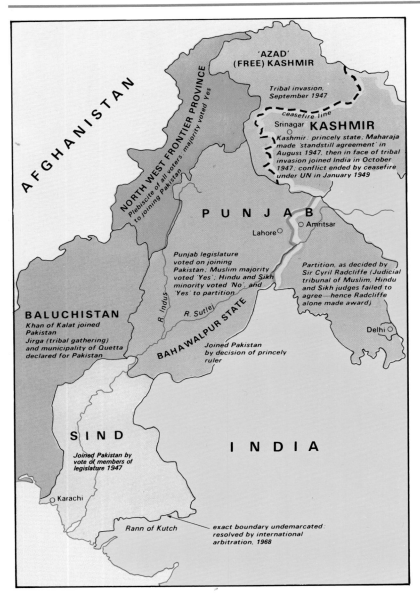

'AZAD' (FREE) KASHMIR

Tribal invasion, September 1947

AFGHANISTAN

NORTH WEST FRONTIER PROVINCE
Plebiscite of all voters: majority voted Yes to joining Pakistan

ceasefire line
Srinagar KASHMIR
Kashmir: princely state. Maharaja made 'standstill agreement' in August 1947, then in face of tribal invasion joined India in October 1947; conflict ended by ceasefire under UN in January 1949

PUNJAB

Lahore   Amritsar

Punjab legislature voted on joining Pakistan: Muslim majority voted 'Yes', Hindu and Sikh minority voted 'No', and 'Yes' to partition

R. Indus
R. Sutlej

Partition, as decided by Sir Cyril Radcliffe (Judicial tribunal of Muslim, Hindu and Sikh judges failed to agree – hence Radcliffe alone made award)

BALUCHISTAN
Khan of Kalat joined Pakistan Jirga (tribal gathering) and municipality of Quetta declared for Pakistan

BAHAWALPUR STATE
Joined Pakistan by decision of princely ruler

Delhi

SIND
Joined Pakistan by vote of members of legislature 1947

INDIA

Karachi

Rann of Kutch
exact boundary undemarcated: resolved by international arbitration, 1968

1 and 2/The partition of Punjab *(above)* **and Bengal** *(below)* The division of the Indian sub-continent in 1947 particularly affected Punjab and Bengal. The result of partition was a great exodus. Some 6 million Muslims migrated from Punjab to the new

Pakistan and about 4.5 million Sikhs and Hindus to the areas between Amritsar and Delhi. In Bengal about 1.6 million Hindus left the eastern sector (now Bangladesh); thousands of Muslims from Bihar, Calcutta and elsewhere sought shelter in east Bengal.

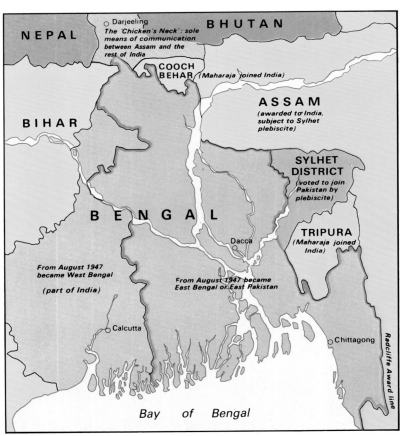

NEPAL

Darjeeling
The 'Chicken's Neck': sole means of communication between Assam and the rest of India

BHUTAN

COOCH BEHAR *(Maharaja joined India)*

BIHAR

ASSAM
(awarded to India, subject to Sylhet plebiscite)

SYLHET DISTRICT
(voted to join Pakistan by plebiscite)

BENGAL

Dacca

TRIPURA
(Maharaja joined India)

From August 1947 became West Bengal (part of India)

From August 1947 became East Bengal or East Pakistan

Calcutta

Chittagong

Radcliffe Award line

Bay of Bengal

INDEPENDENCE came to India and Pakistan in August 1947, to Burma in January 1948, and to Ceylon in February 1948. In India it was fraught with problems from the beginning. The major part of the Indian sub-continent wished to remain united under the leadership of Nehru and the Indian National Congress, but the explosive situation and the impossibility of securing agreement between Congress and the Muslim League led by Jinnah forced the hand of the Viceroy, Lord Mountbatten, and on 14 August 1947, the sub-continent was partitioned and the new state of Pakistan came into existence. The Princely states, over 500 in number, were left to the individual decisions of their rulers, who could in effect join either India or Pakistan, if their boundaries marched with the new partition lines.

For India and Pakistan the first question was the delimitation of frontiers between the new states. This particularly affected the provinces of Punjab and Bengal, where the populations were so mixed that partition seemed the only feasible solution. But the boundary award cut through areas which in Punjab were occupied by rich farmlands populated by Sikhs, Muslims and Hindus as neighbours. Communal riots followed, and a two-way exodus began, with Muslims moving west and Sikhs and Hindus moving east. The partition of Bengal produced similar results. Overall some 500,000 people lost their lives. In addition to the resettlement of the refugees, the governments had to integrate the 500 princely states. Most princes were persuaded to accede, promptly, to either India or Pakistan. Hyderabad resisted and was absorbed only after a 'police action'; Kashmir's ruler also hesitated, and an invasion of tribesmen from Pakistan's N.W.F. Province followed. The Maharaja then acceded to India, subject to a plebiscite of the Kashmir people, but Pakistan supported the tribal invaders and the situation was only stabilised by United Nations mediation in 1949.

Burma's start in independence was even more troubled. Revolts by different communist groups and by minorities demanding separation almost led to the overthrow of the government in the first two years, 1948-49. Subsequently the country settled into some kind of stability under prime minister U Nu, but the army commander, General Ne Win, intervened in 1958 and the army again took over in 1962. Ne Win declared that the country must establish 'The Burmese Way to Socialism' on Marxist lines, and in January 1974, following a referendum, the Socialist People's Republic of Burma was inaugurated. Ceylon's first decade was marked, on the contrary, by evolutionary, conservative government. But in 1956, S.W.R.D. Bandaranaike came to power with a populist programme designed to appeal to the rural masses. After a conservative interlude (1965-70) a radical government led by Mrs Sirimavo Bandaranaike (widow of the premier assassinated in 1959) initiated constitutional reforms which involved recognising the special position of the Buddhist religion and insisting that the Sinhala name of the country - Sri Lanka - be its official title (1972).

All the countries of South Asia have been troubled by the special position of minorities and of regional groups, to say nothing of the persistent social problems arising from untouchability which still dominate Indian society, in spite of legislation to the contrary. The Indian government's attempt to foster Hindi was soon faced by demands for a new structure of states on linguistic lines, and from the 1950s onward state boundaries were realigned. But linguistic feeling remained strong, especially in south India in Madras State, which was renamed Tamil Nadu. In Assam, groups among the Nagas claimed independence. In Pakistan linguistic and regional demands were initially resisted, and the separate provinces of West Pakistan were amalgamated as One Unit. But regional loyalties forced a return to the old

provinces, representing linguistic regions, in 1970. In East Pakistan, the strength of Bengal culture and grievances against the dominant West Pakistan elite fostered a demand for autonomy. In Burma, the frontier peoples resisted the central government, and among the Karens, Shans and Kachins the separatist movements were able to take control of large areas. Ceylon also witnessed the emergence of strong separatist movements among the Tamil, Hindu population. The workers on the tea estates, whose fathers and grandfathers had arrived from India, were mostly disenfranchised and rendered stateless; those recognised as Ceylon Tamils campaigned for autonomy within a loose federal state leading to attacks by the Sinhalese in 1983.

Conflicts in South Asia have periodically led to hostilities. The growing deterioration on the frontiers between India and China led to the outbreak of war in 1962 and a humiliating defeat for India. As Sino-Indian relations deteriorated, so Sino-Pakistan relations became closer. In 1965 Pakistan attempted to infiltrate troops in Kashmir. In the fighting which ensued India made some gains, but in the agreement afterwards reached at Tashkent under Soviet auspices both countries agreed to return to the status quo. Relations continued tense, however, and rapidly worsened in 1971 when Pakistan's military president, Yahya Khan, cruelly repressed the demands for autonomy in the East, which led to 10 million refugees crossing over into India. Finally, in December 1971 India supported the Bangladesh guerrillas with powerful military forces which defeated the Pakistan army within two weeks. After the Pakistan surrender, the new state of Bangladesh emerged under the leadership of Sheikh Mujib Rahman.

All the states in South Asia have attempted to function under democratic, parliamentary forms of government but gradually parliamentary institutions have been eroded. Pakistan and Burma both came under military rule in 1958. Bangladesh soon discarded parliamentary democracy after the murder of Sheikh Mujib in 1975. Pakistan, after a brief period of civilian government under Bhutto's leadership is once more under a military dictator. In India, prime minister Indira Gandhi ruled by emergency decree from 1975 to 1977, but allowed elections to take place leading to her defeat. Her party was reelected in the next election. Despite occasional outbreaks of intercommunal violence and Sikh demands for autonomy in the Punjab, India remains the world's largest functioning democracy. In Ceylon, as in India, the parliamentary form of government has survived though in both countries the power exercised by a single political party inhibits democratic processes. In India and Pakistan, industrial development has been substantial. India is one of the major industrial powers today, but income per head remains low and maldistribution keeps vast numbers in abject poverty.

Since independence, the main emphasis in economic development was placed upon increased industrialisation, though Ceylon and Burma remained heavily dependent on the export of raw materials. India put great emphasis upon periodic Five Year Plans and upon the establishment of a vast new public sector in heavy industry: hydro-electricity, steel, fertilisers, tractors and military hardware. Pakistan's industrial expansion emphasised the private sector and consumer goods. But over the period unemployment rose more rapidly than new production, and 80 per cent of the population was still dependent on agriculture. During the 1960s governments began to lay greater emphasis on better yields from the soil. Though the rate of growth remains slow, both India and Pakistan have attained self-sufficiency in food. Yet some 50% of the rural population remain undernourished because their income is very low.

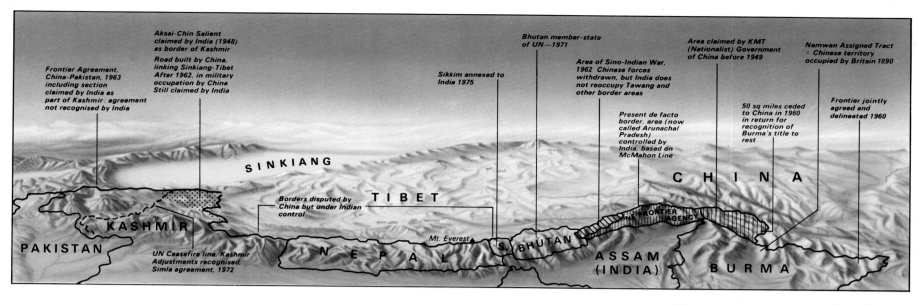

Frontier Agreement, China-Pakistan, 1963 including section claimed by India as part of Kashmir: agreement not recognised by India

Aksai-Chin Salient claimed by India (1948) as border of Kashmir
Road built by China, linking Sinkiang-Tibet After 1962, in military occupation by China Still claimed by India

Sikkim annexed to India 1975

Bhutan member-state of UN—1971

Area of Sino-Indian War, 1962 Chinese forces withdrawn, but India does not reoccupy Tawang and other border areas

Area claimed by KMT (Nationalist) Government of China before 1949

Namwan Assigned Tract = Chinese territory occupied by Britain 1890

Present de facto border, area (now called Arunachal Pradesh) controlled by India, based on McMahon Line

50 sq miles ceded to China in 1960 in return for recognition of Burma's title to rest

Frontier jointly agreed and delineated 1960

SINKIANG

TIBET

CHINA

PAKISTAN

KASHMIR

Borders disputed by China but under Indian control

Mt. Everest

NEPAL

S BHUTAN

ASSAM (INDIA)

BURMA

UN Ceasefire line, Kashmir Adjustments recognised. Simla agreement, 1972

FRONTIER AGENCY

4/Boundary disputes *(above)* When China lost control over Tibet the British pushed forward the frontiers of India to the McMahon Line (1914). In 1962, China defeated the Indian army, and imposed rectifications. Similar boundary disputes with Burma, Nepal and Pakistan were settled peaceably.

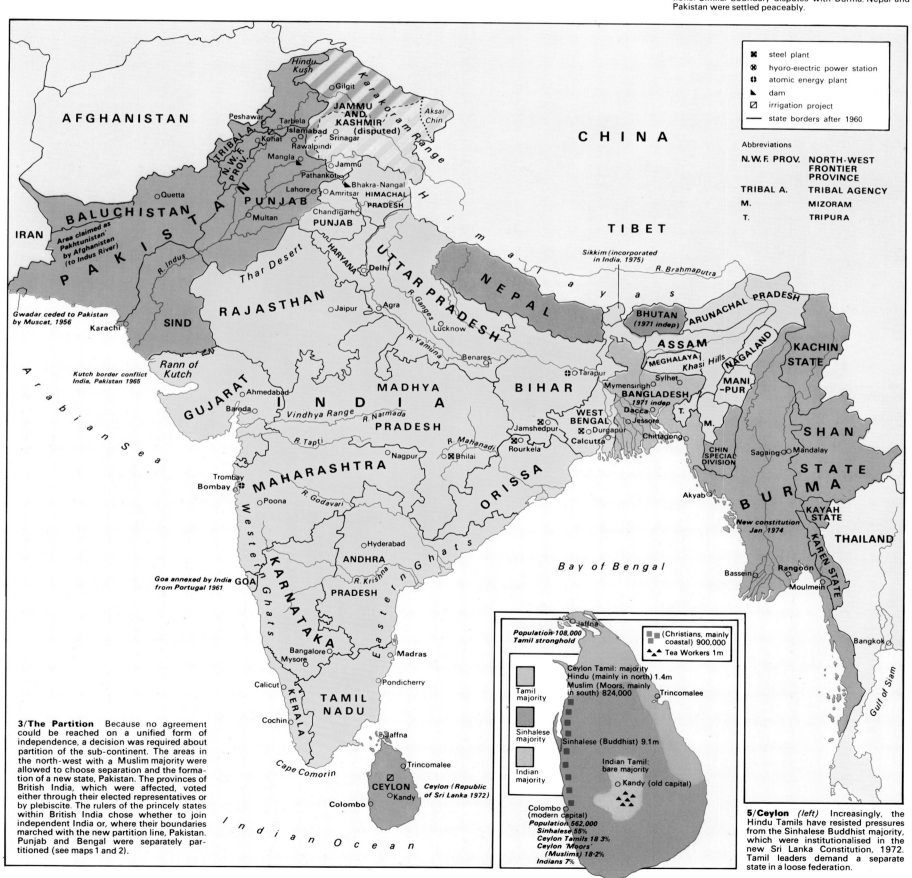

steel plant
hydro-electric power station
atomic energy plant
dam
irrigation project
state borders after 1960

Abbreviations
N.W.F. PROV.   NORTH-WEST FRONTIER PROVINCE
TRIBAL A.   TRIBAL AGENCY
M.   MIZORAM
T.   TRIPURA

AFGHANISTAN

Hindu Kush

Gilgit

Karakoram Range

JAMMU AND KASHMIR (disputed)

Aksai Chin

CHINA

Peshawar

Tarbela

Islamabad

Kohat

Srinagar

Rawalpindi

Mangla

Jammu

TRIBAL A.

N.W.F. PROV.

Pathankot

HIMACHAL PRADESH

Bhakra-Nangal

Quetta

Lahore

Amritsar

BALUCHISTAN

PUNJAB

Multan

Chandigarh

PUNJAB

TIBET

IRAN

Area claimed as 'Pakhtunistan' by Afghanistan (to Indus River)

P A K I S T A N

R. Indus

Thar Desert

HARYANA

Delhi

Himalayas

Sikkim (incorporated in India, 1975)

R. Brahmaputra

Gwadar ceded to Pakistan by Muscat, 1956

Karachi

SIND

RAJASTHAN

Jaipur

Agra

R. Ganges

UTTAR PRADESH

Lucknow

NEPAL

BHUTAN (1971 indep)

ARUNACHAL PRADESH

NAGALAND

KACHIN STATE

Kutch border conflict India, Pakistan 1965

Rann of Kutch

GUJARAT

Ahmedabad

Baroda

R. Yamuna

Benares

I N D I A

MADHYA PRADESH

Vindhya Range

R. Narmada

Tarapur

BIHAR

ASSAM

MEGHALAYA

Khasi Hills

Sylhet

Mymensingh

BANGLADESH 1971 indep

Dacca

MANI-PUR

T.

M.

SHAN

A r a b i a n   S e a

R. Tapti

Nagpur

R. Mahanadi

Jamshedpur

Bhilai

Rourkela

WEST BENGAL

Durgapur

Calcutta

Jessore

Chittagong

CHIN SPECIAL DIVISION

Sagaing

Mandalay

STATE

B U R M A

Trombay

Bombay

MAHARASHTRA

Poona

R. Godavari

ORISSA

Akyab

New constitution Jan 1974

KAYAH STATE

Goa annexed by India from Portugal 1961

Western Ghats

GOA

Hyderabad

ANDHRA PRADESH

R. Krishna

Eastern Ghats

KARNATAKA

Bangalore

Mysore

Madras

Bay of Bengal

Bassein

THAILAND

KAREN STATE

Rangoon

Moulmein

Calicut

KERALA

Pondicherry

TAMIL NADU

Bangkok

Cochin

Jaffna

Cape Comorin

Trincomalee

CEYLON

Colombo

Kandy

Ceylon (Republic of Sri Lanka 1972)

I n d i a n   O c e a n

Gulf of Siam

3/The Partition Because no agreement could be reached on a unified form of independence, a decision was required about partition of the sub-continent. The areas in the north-west with a Muslim majority were allowed to choose separation and the formation of a new state, Pakistan. The provinces of British India, which were affected, voted either through their elected representatives or by plebiscite. The rulers of the princely states within British India chose whether to join independent India or, where their boundaries marched with the new partition line, Pakistan. Punjab and Bengal were separately partitioned (see maps 1 and 2).

Population 108,000 Tamil stronghold

Jaffna

(Christians, mainly coastal) 900,000
Tea Workers 1m

Tamil majority

Ceylon Tamil: majority Hindu (mainly in north) 1.4m
Muslim (Moors, mainly in south) 824,000

Sinhalese majority

Sinhalese (Buddhist) 9.1m

Indian Tamil: bare majority

Trincomalee

Indian majority

Kandy (old capital)

Colombo (modern capital)

Population 562,000
Sinhalese 55%
Ceylon Tamils 18 3%
Ceylon 'Moors' (Muslims) 18·2%
Indians 7%

5/Ceylon *(left)* Increasingly, the Hindu Tamils have resisted pressures from the Sinhalese Buddhist majority, which were institutionalised in the new Sri Lanka Constitution, 1972. Tamil leaders demand a separate state in a loose federation.

The emancipation of Africa 1946 to 1983

IN 1939 control over most of the African continent appeared secure; within 40 years white control was confined to a South African *laager*. The necessary impetus for change was provided by the Second World War, consequent social changes, often accompanied by heightened political consciousness, strengthening the hands of African leaders committed to the social and political advancement of their nations.

Equally important were changes external to Africa. Allied victory greatly increased the prestige of the USSR, while the USA emerged determined to prevent the colonial powers from impeding the extension of American influence. In France and Britain, liberals and socialists sympathetic to African claims initiated programmes of social improvement and political reform (though these ran into difficulty in territories where they threatened the interests of white settler populations). But even reformers appreciated that colonial empire might assist Britain and France to recover some of their economic strength and political influence. From about 1947 the onset of the Cold War, and the continuing dollar famine, pointed towards a certain reassertion of colonial control; France's fierce repression of rebellion in Madagascar was only the most striking demonstration of this.

Some nationalist movements nevertheless effectively challenged these policies. In 1948 riots in Accra and other Gold Coast towns constrained the British government to initiate constitutional reforms which three years later enabled the Convention Peoples' Party of Kwame Nkrumah to achieve a striking electoral success. Meanwhile disturbances in the Ivory Coast led the French government to seek reconciliation with the *Rassemblement Democratique Africain*, hitherto distrusted because of Communist influence. By 1960 both British and French governments had concluded that in their West African colonies wise policy required them to transfer responsibility to elected governments.

In Muslim North Africa longer-established nationalist movements received great stimulus from the overthrow of the Egyptian monarchy in 1952, and the subsequent rise of Gamal Abdel Nasser. In 1953-54 Britain agreed to withdraw her troops from the Suez Canal zone and to accelerate the independence of Sudan; in 1956 France accepted the independence of the protectorates of Tunisia and Morocco. But

in Algeria, which was considered part of Metropolitan France, French determination to maintain control had been clear since their repression of a popular rising in 1945; in November 1954 the Front de Libération Nationale began a war which continued with increasing ferocity until 1962 (see map 3). In 1956 Britain and France attempted to protect their interests in the Suez Canal and reassert their power in the region by invading the Suez Canal zone; but strong opposition from the USA, the USSR, and the UN showed that such methods were no longer practicable.

In the south and east, the crucial event of the post-war years was the election of a Nationalist government in South Africa under D. F. Malan, dedicated to the establishment of an Afrikaner Republic and policies of racial *apartheid*, even though British post-war policies in east and central Africa had been directed towards the encouragement of multi-racial "partnership" in government. Settlers in Kenya, though numbering only about 40,000, at one time hoped for ascendency in an East African dominion; but these hopes perished after 1952, when the British government assumed responsibility for combatting the Mau Mau insurrection. In Central Africa the British in 1953 enacted the federation of Nyasaland and Northern and Southern Rhodesia, with Rhodesian whites in a dominant position; but after 1960 this too collapsed under the force of what the British Prime Minister Harold Macmillan called the "wind of change." Ghanaian independence provided a great stimulus to African nationalists; from a pan-African conference in Accra in 1958 Dr Hastings Banda returned to lead the anti-Federation movement in Nyasaland (Malawi), while Patrice Lumumba's enthusiasm accelerated the drive to independence in the Congo (see map 2). With the achievement of independence in Nigeria and most of the former French colonies, 1960 appeared to be Africa's year.

During the 1960s this euphoria largely evaporated. The African economy proved fragile, and the ethnic rivalries and political disorders of Zaire were reproduced in other states; military coups and takeovers became more common, and in Nigeria led in 1967 to a destructive civil war. While the Algerian revolutionaries achieved independence in 1962 after a bitter eight-years war, the Portuguese government failed to learn its lesson; nationalists were driven into revolutionary warfare in

Angola, Mozambique and Guinea-Bissau. In 1965 Ian Smith illegally declared the independence of white-dominated Rhodesia; the British government failed to repress this rebellion, and during the 1970s African nationalists resorted to armed rebellion here also. Behind these surviving colonial regimes stood the growing economic and military power of South Africa, since 1961 a Republic outside the Commonwealth and committed to repressive measures against militant African nationalists.

In 1976 the overthrow of the Portuguese dictatorship opened the way to independence for her African colonies. By 1980 the armed struggle of nationalist guerrillas, the support of the Organisation of African Unity (united on this as on nothing else), and international pressures through the British government, interacted to replace the rebel regime in Rhodesia by the Republic of Zimbabwe. South Africa, increasingly isolated, sought to protect itself by tightening its illegal control of Namibia, by military incursions into neighbouring states, and by conceding to the impoverished labour reserves known as "Bantustans" a spurious independence which was not recognised internationally.

For the new states, whether capitalist or socialist in orientation, immediate economic prospects remained poor. For some, the exploitation of petroleum and other minerals offered short-term relief, though often at the cost of diverting resources from producing food for rapidly growing populations. Increasingly, elected governments proved unable to control problems of poverty, corruption and ethnic rivalry and were replaced by military dictatorships or single-party regimes, often with populist leanings. Almost everywhere, the fruits of political emancipation proved less sweet than had been expected.

Polisario government recognised by a majority of OAU, but occupied by Morocco since Spanish withdrawal, 1976

1960

MAURITAN

War with Polisario 1976-79
Military rule 1978
Slavery officially abolished 1980

Senegambian Confederation formed following Gambian rising 1981

1960

SENEGAL

1965

Cape Verde Islands

REPUBLIC OF CAPE VERDE

1974

1975

1958

GUINEA
1953-1984 Sekou Touré President

1961

SIERRA LEONE

1963-74 PAIGC war against Portuguese

President Tolbert overthrown by Master Sergeant Doe 1980

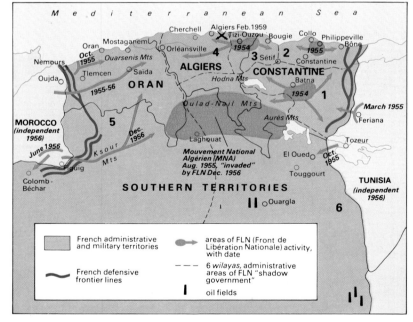

2/The Congo crisis, 1960-65 *(left)* Tribal and regional factions in the Congo (independent 30 June 1960) led to demands for a federal constitution. However, the federalist leader, Kasavubu, of the Bakongo tribal party (ABAKO) was opposed by Lumumba's centralist Mouvement National Congolais (MNC). After a compromise a central government was formed, but the army, left under Belgian officers, mutinied on 4 July. Belgium flew in troops to protect her civilians and interests. On 11 July the mineral-rich province of Katanga seceded under Moise Tshombe. Lumumba and Kasavubu, convinced that Belgium wished to regain control, called in the UN. Following the dismissal of Lumumba, and his murder in Katanga, the UN intervened with US support, but attempts to reach a compromise with Katanga were abandoned. By 1963 Katanga was overrun by the UN. Tshombe, who had withdrawn to Angola, was recalled as President in 1964 and, with Belgian and US aid, suppressed a new revolt backed by the OAU. But both he and Kasavubu were overthrown by the army under Mobutu in November 1965.

3/The Algerian Civil War, 1954-62 *(above)* In 1945 the French assumed Algeria would be re-incorporated into the Fourth Republic. However, this assumption was challenged by nationalist demonstrations which were followed by violent repression. Subsequent reforms did not satisfy the more nationalist Algerians; in 1954 they formed the Front de Libération Nationale (FLN) and launched attacks on 1 November on French positions throughout Algeria. The French were committed to protecting oil and gas resources, but faced a formidable underground army—a revolutionary movement of socialist inspiration, capable of eliminating its rival the Mouvement Nationaliste Algérien(MNA). In 1958 the threat of a military coup by the frustrated French army brought de Gaulle to power. Holding Algeria was only possible at an unacceptable price and the FLN could not be broken, refusing offers to negotiate peace without independence. In the Evian agreements of March 1962 de Gaulle finally recognised their sovereignty, though with provision to safeguard continuing French interests.

area of Katanga secession 1960-63

maximum area of rebel advance 1964

BALUBA main tribes

UN troops base

railways

Belgian intervention 1961

centres of 1963-4 rebellion

Belgian paratroop intervention 1964

state borders

diamonds

gold

tin

manganese

coal

copper

zinc

cobalt

uranium

iron ore

CENTRAL AFRICAN REPUBLIC

BAMONGO

ORIENTALE

BANGALA

BANGALA

Paulis

Stanleyville

EQUATEUR

Coquilhatville

CONGO

R. Congo

BAMONGO

BAMBALA

BATETELA

BALUBA (KASAI)

Kindu

KIVU

BAKUSU

RWANDA

BURUNDI

Brazzaville

Port Francqui

Léopoldville

BAKONGO

Matadi

KASAI

BENALULA

Luluabourg

BASONGE

Albertville

Lake Tanganyika

TANGANYIKA (Tanzania 1961)

Gungu

BAPENDE

BALUBA (KATANGA)

BALUNDA KATANGA

BATSHOKWE

Kamina

ANGOLA (Portuguese colony)

BALUNDA

NORTHERN RHODESIA (Zambia 1964)

Elisabethville

Atlantic Ocean

Benguela

Lobito

French administrative and military territories

French defensive frontier lines

areas of FLN (Front de Libération Nationale) activity, with date

6 *wilayas*, administrative areas of FLN "shadow government"

oil fields

Mediterranean Sea

Cherchell

Algiers Feb.1959

Collo

Philippeville

Oran

Mostaganem

Tizi-Ouzou

Bougie

Bône

Nemours

Oct. 1955

Orléansville

4

1954

3

Sétif

2

Constantine

Tlemcen

Ouarsenis Mts

ALGIERS

Hodna Mts

CONSTANTINE

Batna

Oujda

Saida

1955-56

ORAN

1954

1

March 1955

MOROCCO (independent 1956)

Ksour Mts

Dec. 1956

Oulad-Naïl Mts

Aurès Mts

Feriana

June 1956

Laghouat

Mouvement National Algérien (MNA) Aug. 1955, "invaded" by FLN Dec. 1956

El Oued

Oct. 1955

Tozeur

Colomb-Béchar

Figuig

SOUTHERN TERRITORIES

Ouargla

Touggourt

TUNISIA (independent 1956)

6

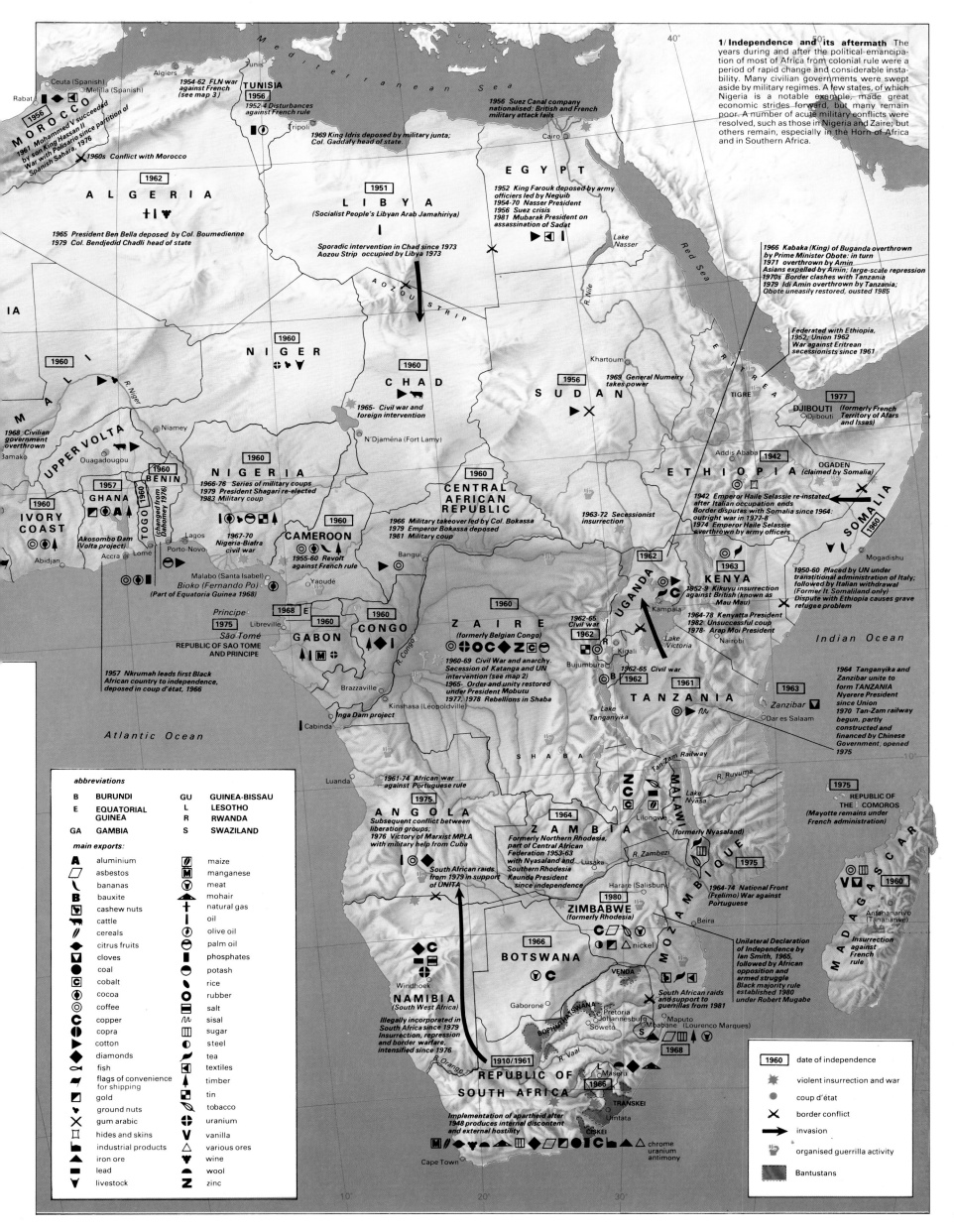

1/ Independence and its aftermath The years during and after the political emancipation of most of Africa from colonial rule were a period of rapid change and considerable instability. Many civilian governments were swept aside by military regimes. A few states, of which Nigeria is a notable example, made great economic strides forward, but many remain poor. A number of acute military conflicts were resolved, such as those in Nigeria and Zaire; but others remain, especially in the Horn of Africa and in Southern Africa.

Ceuta (Spanish)
Melilla (Spanish)
Rabat
Algiers
Tunis
TUNISIA 1956
1954-62 FLN war against French (see map 3)
1952-4 Disturbances against French rule
Tripoli
1956 Suez Canal company nationalised: British and French military attack fails
Cairo

MOROCCO 1956
1961 Mohammed V succeeded by son King Hassan II
War with Polisario since partition of Spanish Sahara, 1976
1960s Conflict with Morocco

1969 King Idris deposed by military junta; Col. Gaddafy head of state

E G Y P T
1952 King Farouk deposed by army officers led by Neguib
1954-70 Nasser President
1956 Suez crisis
1981 Mubarak President on assassination of Sadat

A L G E R I A 1962
1965 President Ben Bella deposed by Col. Boumedienne
1979 Col. Bendjedid Chadli head of state

L I B Y A 1951
(Socialist People's Libyan Arab Jamahiriya)
Sporadic intervention in Chad since 1973
Aozou Strip occupied by Libya 1973

Lake Nasser
Red Sea

1966 Kabaka (King) of Buganda overthrown by Prime Minister Obote: in turn 1971 overthrown by Amin Asians expelled by Amin; large-scale repression 1970s Border clashes with Tanzania 1979 Idi Amin overthrown by Tanzania; Obote uneasily restored, ousted 1985

N I G E R 1960

R. Nile

Khartoum

C H A D 1960
1965- Civil war and foreign intervention

S U D A N 1956
1969 General Numeiry takes power

Federated with Ethiopia, 1952; Union 1962 War against Eritrean secessionists since 1961

E R I T R E A

TIGRE

DJIBOUTI 1977 (formerly French Territory of Afars and Issas)

Niamey

N'Djaména (Fort Lamy)

Addis Ababa
E T H I O P I A 1942
OGADEN (claimed by Somalia)
1942 Emperor Haile Selassie re-instated after Italian occupation ends Border disputes with Somalia since 1964: outright war in 1977-8 1974 Emperor Haile Selassie overthrown by army officers

UPPER VOLTA 1960
1968 Civilian government overthrown
Ouagadougou
Bamako

M A L I 1960

R. Niger

1950-60 Placed by UN under transtitional administration of Italy; followed by Italian withdrawal (Former It. Somaliland only) Dispute with Ethiopia causes grave refugee problem

N I G E R I A 1960
1966-76 Series of military coups
1979 President Shagari re-elected
1983 Military coup

GHANA 1957
BENIN 1960 (changed from Dahomey 1976)
TOGO 1960
IVORY COAST 1960
Akosombo Dam (Volta project)
Accra
Lagos
Porto-Novo
Lomé
Abidjan

CENTRAL AFRICAN REPUBLIC 1960
1966 Military takeover led by Col. Bokassa
1979 Emperor Bokassa deposed
1981 Military coup

Bangui

UGANDA 1962
Kampala

KENYA 1963
1852-9 Kikuyu insurrection against British (known as Mau Mau)
1964-78 Kenyatta President
1982 Unsuccessful coup
1978 Arap Moi President
Nairobi

Lake Victoria

CAMEROON 1960
1967-70 Nigeria-Biafra civil war
1955-60 Revolt against French rule
Yaoundé

1957 Nkrumah leads first Black African country to independence, deposed in coup d'état, 1966

Malabo (Santa Isabel)
Bioko (Fernando Po) (Part of Equatoria Guinea 1968)

Principe
São Tomé
Libreville
REPUBLIC OF SAO TOME AND PRINCIPE 1975
GABON 1960
E 1968
CONGO 1960
Brazzaville
R. Congo
Kinshasa (Léopoldville)
Inga Dam project
Cabinda

Z A I R E 1960
(formerly Belgian Congo)
1960-69 Civil War and anarchy. Secession of Katanga and UN intervention (see map 2)
1965- Order and unity restored under President Mobutu
1977, 1978 Rebellions in Shaba

1962-65 Civil war 1962

Kigali
Bujumbura
R 1962
B 1962
1962-65 Civil war

T A N Z A N I A 1961
Lake Tanganyika
Zanzibar
Dar es Salaam

1964 Tanganyika and Zanzibar unite to form TANZANIA Nyerere President since Union 1970 Tan-Zam railway begun, partly constructed and financed by Chinese Government; opened 1975

Indian Ocean

1963-72 Secessionist insurrection

S H A B A

Tan-Zam Railway
R. Ruvuma
Lake Nyasa

1975
REPUBLIC OF THE COMOROS 1975 (Mayotte remains under French administration)

Luanda

1961-74 African war against Portuguese rule

A N G O L A 1975
Subsequent conflict between liberation groups; 1976 Victory of Marxist MPLA with military help from Cuba

ZAMBIA 1964
Formerly Northern Rhodesia, part of Central African Federation 1953-63 with Nyasaland and Southern Rhodesia Kaunda President since independence

MALAWI 1964 (formerly Nyasaland)
Lilongwe
Lusaka
R. Zambezi

M O Z A M B I Q U E 1975
1964-74 National Front (Frelimo) War against Portuguese

South African raids from 1979 in support of UNITA

Windhoek

NAMIBIA (South West Africa)
Illegally incorporated in South Africa since 1979 Insurrection, repression and border warfare, intensified since 1976

Harare (Salisbury)
ZIMBABWE 1966 (formerly Rhodesia)
Unilateral Declaration of Independence by Ian Smith, 1965, followed by African opposition and armed struggle Black majority rule established 1980 under Robert Mugabe

BOTSWANA 1966
Gaborone
VENDA 1980

Beira

South African raids and support to guerrillas from 1981

MADAGASCAR 1960
Antananarivo (Tananarive)
Insurrection against French rule

BOPHUTHATSWANA
Pretoria
Johannesburg
Soweto
Mbabane
S 1968
Maputo (Lourenço Marques)

L 1966
Maseru

REPUBLIC OF SOUTH AFRICA 1910/1961
R. Orange
R. Vaal

Implementation of apartheid after 1948 produces internal discontent and external hostility

TRANSKEI
Umtata
CISKEI
Cape Town

283

---

abbreviations

B	BURUNDI	GU	GUINEA-BISSAU
E	EQUATORIAL GUINEA	L	LESOTHO
GA	GAMBIA	R	RWANDA
		S	SWAZILAND

main exports:

A	aluminium		maize
	asbestos	M	manganese
	bananas		meat
B	bauxite		mohair
	cashew nuts		natural gas
	cattle		oil
	cereals		olive oil
	citrus fruits		palm oil
	cloves		phosphates
	coal		potash
C	cobalt		rice
	cocoa		rubber
	coffee		salt
C	copper		sisal
	copra		sugar
	cotton		steel
	diamonds		tea
	fish		textiles
	flags of convenience for shipping		timber
	gold		tin
	ground nuts		tobacco
X	gum arabic		uranium
	hides and skins	V	vanilla
	industrial products		various ores
	iron ore		wine
	lead		wool
	livestock	Z	zinc

1960	date of independence
	violent insurrection and war
	coup d'état
X	border conflict
→	invasion
	organised guerrilla activity
	Bantustans

The Middle East
1945 to 1983

IN the years since 1945, the Middle East has been in a state of almost continuous upheaval, and the last decade in particular has seen an enormous increase in the level of violence and human suffering which now appears almost endemic to the region. Most of the regimes in the area are either highly autocratic, or little more than military dictatorships; almost all are brutally repressive of minority communities, political dissidents, even of political organisations.

In the immediate post-war period, a combination of war weariness, financial pressure and local opposition gradually led to Britain and France abandoning formal control over the area. These changes were accompanied by the growing nationalist ferment of the time, which continued into the 1950s, and the ending of Soviet isolation after the death of Stalin in 1953, all factors which encouraged the US to take a more active interest in the region's affairs. Thus the Eisenhower doctrine (1957) promised US assistance to regimes apparently threatened by Soviet aggression, and covert and overt threats by the US, notably in Jordan in 1957 and Lebanon in 1958, had the effect of encouraging other states in the region to seek closer political and military ties with the USSR and with each other.

In the 1950s and 1960s, the US became the most powerful external influence in the Middle East, using the fear of Soviet expansion to increase its support to Israel, which, with Saudi Arabia, and Iran until 1979, functioned as the principal surrogates of American interests in the area. The inherent instability of the 'revolutionary states' (Egypt, Iraq, Syria) meant that they proved unreliable partners for the Soviet Union, and while the spokesmen and leaders of these and other local regimes would reiterate their passionate verbal commitment to anti-imperialism, Arab unity, the Palestinian cause and revolutionary socialism, the practical reality was very different.

The Arab countries were unable to combine effectively against Israel, partly – as, for instance, in Iraq in 1967 – because their crack troops had to be kept in the capitals in times of crisis to maintain what were often highly unpopular regimes in power. Israel naturally thrived on inter-Arab differences, especially as it became increasingly clear in the 1970s – to Egypt in particular – that the Soviet Union was not prepared to risk a major confrontation with Israel by supplying her Arab allies with weapons of the appropriate degree of sophistication. The Soviet Union's major military undertaking in the area, the invasion of its neighbour Afghanistan in 1979, is probably more correctly analysed as a costly aberration than as indicative of a more wide-ranging policy trend.

The Arab-Israeli conflict has dominated Middle Eastern politics since 1948, and has profoundly influenced events inside and relations between the states in the area. As well as the four main wars between the various Arab states and Israel, the conflict has also spilled into Lebanon, because of the large numbers of Palestinians living there, and because of the Palestine Liberation Organisation's use of Lebanese territory as a base for guerrilla operations against Israel since 1968. Since its inception, Israel has expanded beyond its 1948 boundaries into the West Bank and Gaza (1967), Sinai (1956, 1967-1981), the Golan Heights (1967: incorporated officially into Israel in 1981), and has been firmly in control of large parts of south Lebanon since 1978. President Sadat's visit to Israel in 1977, and the bilateral treaty between Egypt and Israel which followed, resulted in the return of the Sinai peninsula to Egypt in 1981. Israel has justified this expansion, and the creation of large numbers of settlements on the occupied West Bank, on the grounds that it needs to secure its borders and to protect its citizens from guerrilla attacks. It is a matter of record that some 300 Israeli civilians

were killed in such attacks between 1967 and 1982, some in particularly horrifying incidents such as the Country Club massacre in March 1978, in which 37 Israeli civilians and six Israeli commandos were killed. However, in the invasion of south Lebanon which this attack apparently prompted, 2000 Lebanese and Palestinian civilians were killed, and the operations surrounding the attack on Beirut in June-August 1982 resulted in the deaths of between 15,000 and 20,000 Lebanese and Palestinians, most of whom were non-combatants.

Over the past decades, especially since the oil boom, attempts have been made to overcome some of the problems of poverty and underdevelopment in the region. Although great strides have been made in the provision of health, education and welfare services in a number of states, government policies have generally tended to increase the gap between rich and poor. The rapidity of change, the intractability of social and economic problems, the belief that the West and 'modernisation' bear a heavy responsibility for many contemporary ills, and the moral and ideological bankruptcy of most of the regimes have combined to produce a sense of bewilderment and despair. It is thus not surprising that many of the young, and the recent migrants to the cities, often living in slums, should find new fulfilment in a renewed commitment to Islam.

One of the most visible manifestations of this reassertion of commitment to Islam was the revolution in Iran in 1978-79, which overthrew a regime with particularly close ties to the West. The ruler of the new Islamic Republic of Iran, Ayatollah Khomeini, proclaimed a new form of Islamic government, in which the Shi'i religious authorities exercised a special theocratic function. Other features of the regime included the 'reintroduction' of the Islamic legal system, attempts to purge Iran of influences and institu-

1/ The Middle East since independence *(below)* With the exception of the smaller states of the Arabian peninsula (which had all become independent by 1971) most of the nations of the Middle East had obtained formal independence from Britain or France by 1950, although both sought to maintain their influence through military and other alliances. During the 1950s many of the constitutional monarchies and republics established by Britain and France in the 1920s and 1930s were overthrown by nationalist-inspired military coups, ushering in regimes of varying degrees of permanence and stability. For many in the Arab world, the success of Nasser in Egypt provided a model for their aspirations for true independence, especially after his successful nationalisation of the Suez Canal in 1956. However, pan-Arab nationalism and calls for Arab unity have proved largely powerless to resolve any settlement of the outstanding problems in the area: the glaring contrasts between rich and poor, the virtual absence of democracy, and economic dependence on the outside world. Almost all the poorer states (particularly Jordan, Syria, Egypt and Turkey) suffer from chronic inflation and massive migration from rural areas to cities, and most, even the most fertile, are net importers of food.

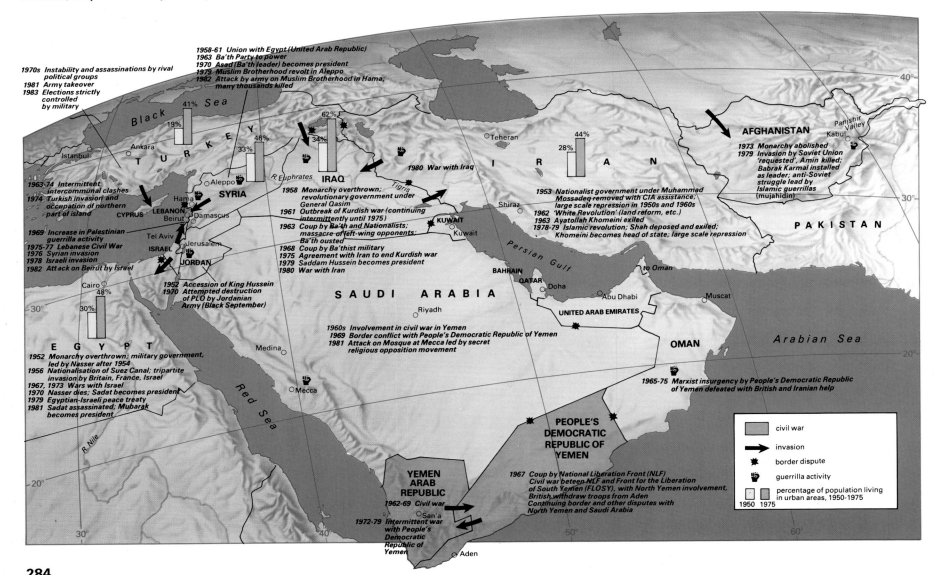

2/Israel and Palestine *(right)* For many centuries Palestine had an Arabic-speaking Muslim majority and Christian and Jewish minorities, but in the late 19th century the proportions began to change as Jews from Eastern Europe began to emigrate, under the pressure of Russian persecution and of the new 'Zionist' ideal of the recreation of a Jewish national state. In 1917, during the First World War, the British government stated that it looked with favour on the establishment of a Jewish National Home in Palestine, provided that the position of the non-Jewish population was not harmed. These two obligations were embodied in the mandate under which Great Britain administered the country, subject to supervision by the League of Nations, but they proved difficult to reconcile, particularly after the rise of Hitler, when Jewish emigration from Europe increased sharply (in 1922, Jews formed 11 per cent of the population; in 1936, 29 per cent; in 1946, 32 per cent). Arab fears led to a serious revolt before the Second World War; after the war and the holocaust of European Jewry, the Jewish demand that the survivors be allowed to immigrate, American pressure in support of it, and Arab fear that such immigration would lead to their subjection or dispossession, caused the British government to declare its intention of withdrawing. A plan to partition Palestine into a Jewish and an Arab state, while Jerusalem would be under international control, was adopted by the United Nations General Assembly on 29 Nov. 1947, but was rejected by the Arabs. On the day of British withdrawal 14 May 1948, David Ben Gurion proclaimed the state of Israel and a war ensued between the Jews and the Palestinian Arabs, supported by the neighbouring Arab states, in which the Arab armies were defeated. The greater part of Palestine became the Jewish state of Israel, most of the rest was amalgamated with Transjordan to become Jordan, and the Gaza Strip was occupied by Egypt. During and after the fighting, two-thirds of the Arabs left their homes and became refugees in Jordan, Gaza, Syria and Lebanon. After 1948, the wish of the refugees to return to their homes and of the Palestinians in general to have their own state, the refusal of Israel to accept Palestinian claims and of the Arab states to recognise Israel, and intervention by external forces, led to three further wars: in 1956 the Israelis, following increasing *Fedayeen*, or guerrilla raids, attacked Egypt in secret agreement with Great Britain and France, but were compelled to withdraw under pressure from the United States and the Soviet Union; in June 1967, with the Six-Day War, the Israelis moved to prevent what they saw as a threat to their existence when the Straits of Tiran were closed to Israeli shipping by Nasser, and occupied the west bank of the Jordan, Sinai and the Golan Heights in Syria; in 1973 an Egyptian and Syrian attack on Israel had a limited military success (it led to Egyptian occupation of an area east of the Suez Canal, but to Israeli occupation of an area west of it as well as a further part of Syria), and opened a new phase of negotiations; it gradually became clear that Egypt under President Sadat had little desire to continue the struggle. Sadat's visit to Jerusalem (Nov. 1977), followed by the Egyptian-Israeli Camp David accords (1978), confirmed this. However, Begin's Likud government now began to take a harder line on the West Bank (which it claimed as an integral part of biblical Israel) by greatly increasing the settlements begun by its Labour predecessors. The focus of conflict shifted when, in 1978, Israel invaded southern Lebanon to counter Palestinian guerrilla (PLO) activity and advanced as far as Beirut in the summer of 1982 (see map 4), opening a new front of Arab-Israeli tension. Meanwhile, Israel fulfilled part of its commitment to the Camp David agreement by withdrawing from Sinai in 1981.

tions contrary to the spirit of Islam, and the persecution, imprisonment and execution of large numbers of political detainees. Since 1980, Iran has been engaged in what seems to be an unwinnable war with Iraq, whose almost equally repressive regime (thousands of political prisoners have been executed since 1978) started the war in the hope of securing its own position by installing a more moderate regime in Teheran. Casualties on both sides have been extremely high, but all attempts at mediation have so far proved unsuccessful. It is only the latest eruption of many violent tensions in the region, the implications of which extend far beyond the Middle East itself.

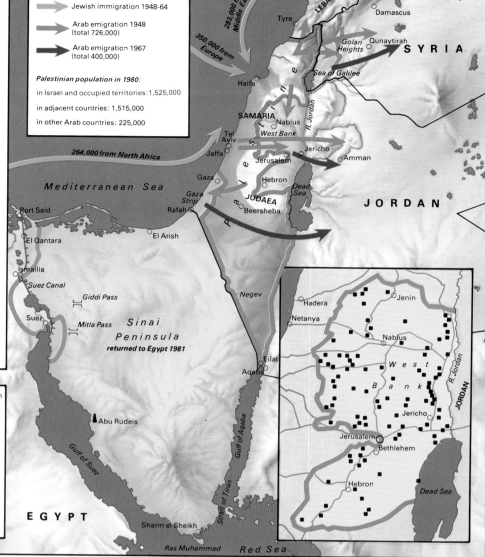

Jewish immigration 1948-64
Arab emigration 1948 (total 726,000)
Arab emigration 1967 (total 400,000)

Palestinian population in 1980:
in Israel and occupied territories: 1,525,000
in adjacent countries: 1,515,000
in other Arab countries: 225,000

returned to Egypt 1981

Jewish state under UN partition plan for Palestine 1947
Israel after Arab invasion and War of Independence 1948
Israel conquests 1967
Egyptian re-conquests and Israel conquests 1973
Israeli settlements on the West Bank (see inset right)
main roads
■ Israeli settlements in 1983

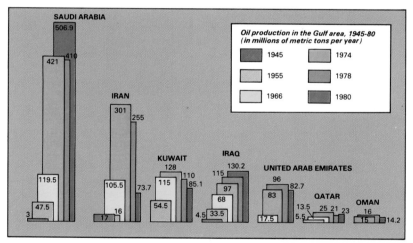

Oil production *(above)* Oil is the region's most valuable natural asset, and production and revenues have increased dramatically in recent years, most notably since the OPEC price rise in 1973. However, later figures show the impact of the war between Iran and Iraq.

Ironically, the wealth which oil has created has contributed to serious inflation in the poorer states; also, the lack of indigenous skilled labour has made large-scale labour immigration and the presence of a high proportion of foreign workers permanent features of the area.

Oil production in the Gulf area, 1945-80 (in millions of metric tons per year)
1945 · 1974 · 1955 · 1978 · 1966 · 1980

4/ The Lebanon crisis *(right)* The Lebanese political system is based on the distribution of offices between the various communities (Maronite, Orthodox, Catholic and Armenian Christians, Sunni and Shi'i Muslims and Druzes) in a way which ensured the pre-eminence of the Maronites, although by the 1970s they were no longer the largest single community. Opposition forces joined with the Palestinian (PLO) guerrillas in the mid-1970s in an attempt to force the Maronites to agree to a secular democratic Lebanon, but were both checked by Syrian intervention in 1976. Lebanon then became the principal arena of the Arab-Israeli conflict with Syrian troops in permanent occupation and the Israeli invasion of the south in 1978. A major invasion by Israel in 1982 succeeded in expelling PLO forces from Beirut, but in spite of the presence of US and European peace-keeping troops, the opposition forces managed to prevent the government from concluding permanent agreements with Israel.

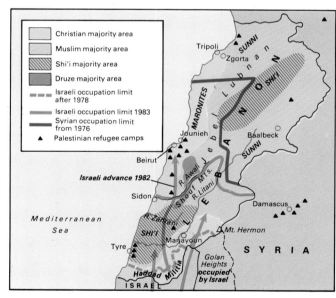

Christian majority area
Muslim majority area
Shi'i majority area
Druze majority area
Israeli occupation limit after 1978
Israeli occupation limit 1983
Syrian occupation limit from 1976
▲ Palestinian refugee camps
Israeli advance 1982

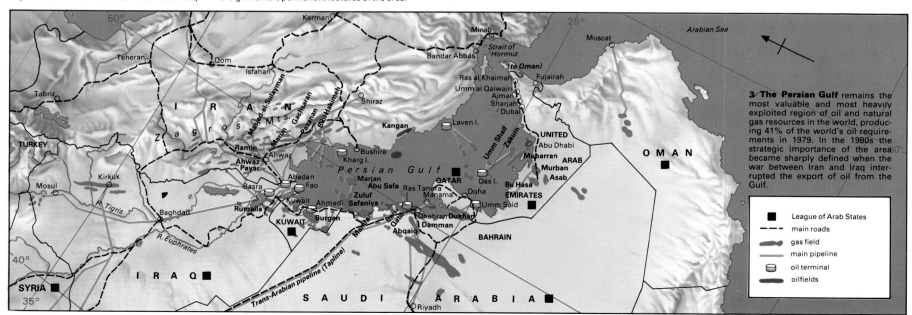

3/ The Persian Gulf remains the most valuable and most heavily exploited region of oil and natural gas resources in the world, producing 41% of the world's oil requirements in 1979. In the 1980s the strategic importance of the area became sharply defined when the war between Iran and Iraq interrupted the export of oil from the Gulf.

■ League of Arab States
- - - main roads
gas field
main pipeline
oil terminal
oilfields

Latin America: revolution and reaction 1930 to 1983

2/Economic development (below) Latin America's traditional primary-export economy was modified, though not transformed, by the great depression and the Second World War. The search for economic development and independence met with some success in some countries and impetus was given to import substitution. But the area continued to depend upon the developed world for markets for its raw material exports, for imports of industrial capital goods, for technology, and for finance.

THE Great Depression of 1929 struck Latin America a shattering blow, cutting off supplies of foreign capital and lowering the price of its primary products in the world markets. In the long run this forced the area to look to its own resources and to undertake a programme of industrialisation. But it caused great immediate distress, especially among those who lacked the political power to protect themselves. Urban workers lost faith in the middle-class liberal or radical parties which had hitherto wooed them, and began to look to the strong man who offered immediate relief. Governments emerged appealing directly to the masses, basing themselves on the support of organised labour, and offering accelerated industrialisation. Such was the regime of Vargas in Brazil (and later that of Perón in Argentina). Instead of the vote he offered security, improved working conditions, stronger – though state-controlled – trade unions. However populist dictators could not escape their military origins or desert the interests of the armed forces and their civilian allies. Perón, as well as Vargas, was made to realise this. Peronism rested not only on the support of urban workers, to whom it offered higher wages, a new unionism, and more jobs, but also on the acquiescence of a nationalist and development-minded military. And when, in 1955, the military decided that the rival power base had become a threat to their own interests they overthrew Perón.

The prospects of further reform began to grow dim, even in Mexico, the homeland of revolution. In the 1930s, it is true, there was a radical shift to the left under Cárdenas, who expanded the distribution of land to the peasants, increased the power of organised labour and nationalised the foreign oil companies. But from 1940 land distribution and social reform declined; there was a new emphasis on industrialisation, foreign investment was encouraged and closer economic relations with the US were developed.

In the rest of Latin America, too, the first wave of change had spent itself. In some countries – Uruguay, Mexico, Brazil and Argentina – it had produced noticeable results. In most it had hardly been felt. The result was frustration, and it was stimulated by two things. Population growth, especially from the 1950s, outstripped economic development and further worsened the prospects of the under-privileged. Meanwhile, during the Second World War, Latin America was cut off from foreign sources of consumer goods and forced to industrialise still further; this brought great profit, but little went to the working-class sector, widening the gulf between the wealthy and the poor.

By this time, people were looking for new answers to economic and social problems; some found inspiration in Marxism and the example of the Soviet Union. Communist parties had existed in Latin America since the 1920s. In 1935 the Brazilian Communist Party launched an open revolution against the Vargas regime. Most of them eschewed violence, preferring to operate by constitutional means and the formation of popular fronts. They had few convinced adherents. The Guatemalan revolution of 1944 inaugurated basic social change. When, from 1951, President Arbenz undertook a programme of agrarian reform, only the Communists could give him the ideas and the political machine he needed. In the event the Communists overreached themselves, for they gained political influence without acquiring any military power, and they were unable to defend the revolution against the conservative rebellion organised, with US connivance, from Honduras in 1954. The Guatemalan revolution also underlined a common problem – at what point does investment in social welfare hinder rather than promote economic growth? The dilemma of creating a welfare state without having the economic resources to sustain it was seen above all in Bolivia, one of the worst examples of under-development in the region. In 1952 left-wing forces led a violent revolution of civilians over the military junta. The new regime nationalised the tin mines, enfranchised the Indians and imposed agrarian reform. But wage increases, productivity decline, and enormous inflation eroded many of the social accomplishments of the revolution and brought it to a halt in the 1960s.

From 1959, however, another revolution, that in Cuba, sought to achieve social change and economic growth simultaneously. This involved a decision to adopt Communism, a decision reinforced by the hostility of the US as well as by the need for an ideology and a political machine. Land was collectivised, businesses were nationalised, and education was given a Marxist orientation. While this led to greater social equality and to some improvement in the prospects of the rural workers, it was procured at the cost of political freedom and did not resolve the problem of how to impose social change at an early stage of economic development; the Cuban economy remained rooted in sugar and dependent on an outside metropolis.

Nevertheless, Castro and his followers were convinced that it was their mission to extend the revolution throughout Latin America. There was some response; rural guerrilla movements in a number of countries posed a serious threat to security forces, culminating in the expedition of Guevara to Bolivia and his death there in 1967. An alternative revolutionary focus was then provided by urban guerrillas, but these had too narrow a political base to succeed. Meanwhile, left of centre democratic parties, including Christian Democracy, sought to prove that change could be accomplished in liberty. Their record in Venezuela and Chile was criticised for producing too little and proceeding too slowly. The election of Allende in Chile in 1970 at the head of Popular Unity brought Marxism to power and the chance to prove that structural change could be made by constitutional means. In 1973 military intervention terminated the experiment.

Meanwhile, the Latin American economies had been undergoing major structural change. Investments in mining and agriculture (though not in oil) had lost their traditional dynamism, while investments in manufacturing and commerce were expanding dramatically. This shift from the primary-export model to industrialisation by import substitution represented a new stage of modernisation and brought in its wake important social and economic changes. New social and political groups replaced or challenged the traditional landed oligarchy, explosive urbanisation · took place, further concentration of income was encouraged, and acute social tensions appeared. At the same time industrialisation made Latin America dependent upon imported capital goods, raw materials, technology and finance, creating enormous foreign debts, which neither the traditional exports nor the new manufactured exports could meet. The penetration of foreign subsidiaries into national industries, the appearance of new forms of economic control such as the multi-national corporation, caused many Latin American governments to impose constraints on foreign investments and to re-define their international relations. Social tensions arose from income concentration, unemployment, lack of opportunities and the presence of foreign interests. By the early 1970s the most dynamic political alternatives in Latin America were militarism of the right and of the left.

As the 1970s advanced the military governments of the south combined political conservatism with economic liberalism, and enjoyed some support from the upper and middle sectors. The alternative model was that of democracy and regional integration, exemplified in the Andean Pact, some of whose member countries could claim economic and social gains, especially with the dramatic rise of oil revenues from 1973. In the late 1970s democracies such as Mexico and Venezuela appeared to be stable and prosperous, but the impermanence of the oil boom and excessive state expenditure cast a shadow over their future development and by 1982 Mexico was in deep trouble. The authoritarian regimes, meanwhile, saw their free market economies challenged by world recession and, in the case of Argentina, by growing political opposition. When, in 1976, the Argentine military ended the second Peronist regime they replaced populism by dictatorship, economic protection by market forces, and non-alignment by a commitment to the West. The policy failed and society was further divided. The invasion of the Falklands was intended to rally the country behind a national cause, but it discredited the military and led to a return to democracy in 1983. Elsewhere democratisation was a hesitant process, and Central America continued to be polarised between the Nicaraguan Revolution and the presence of the United States.

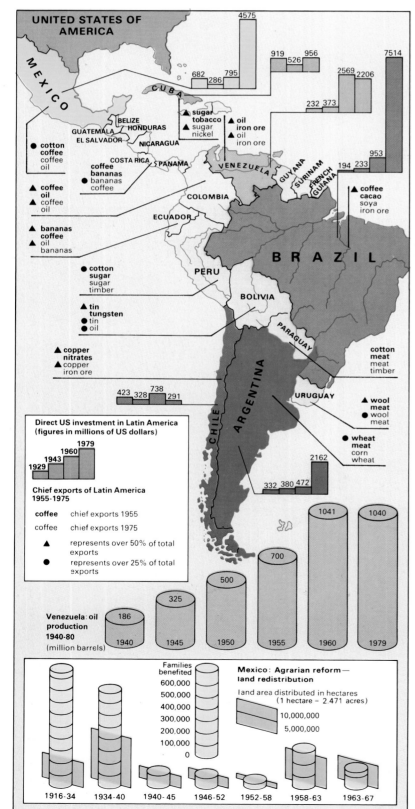

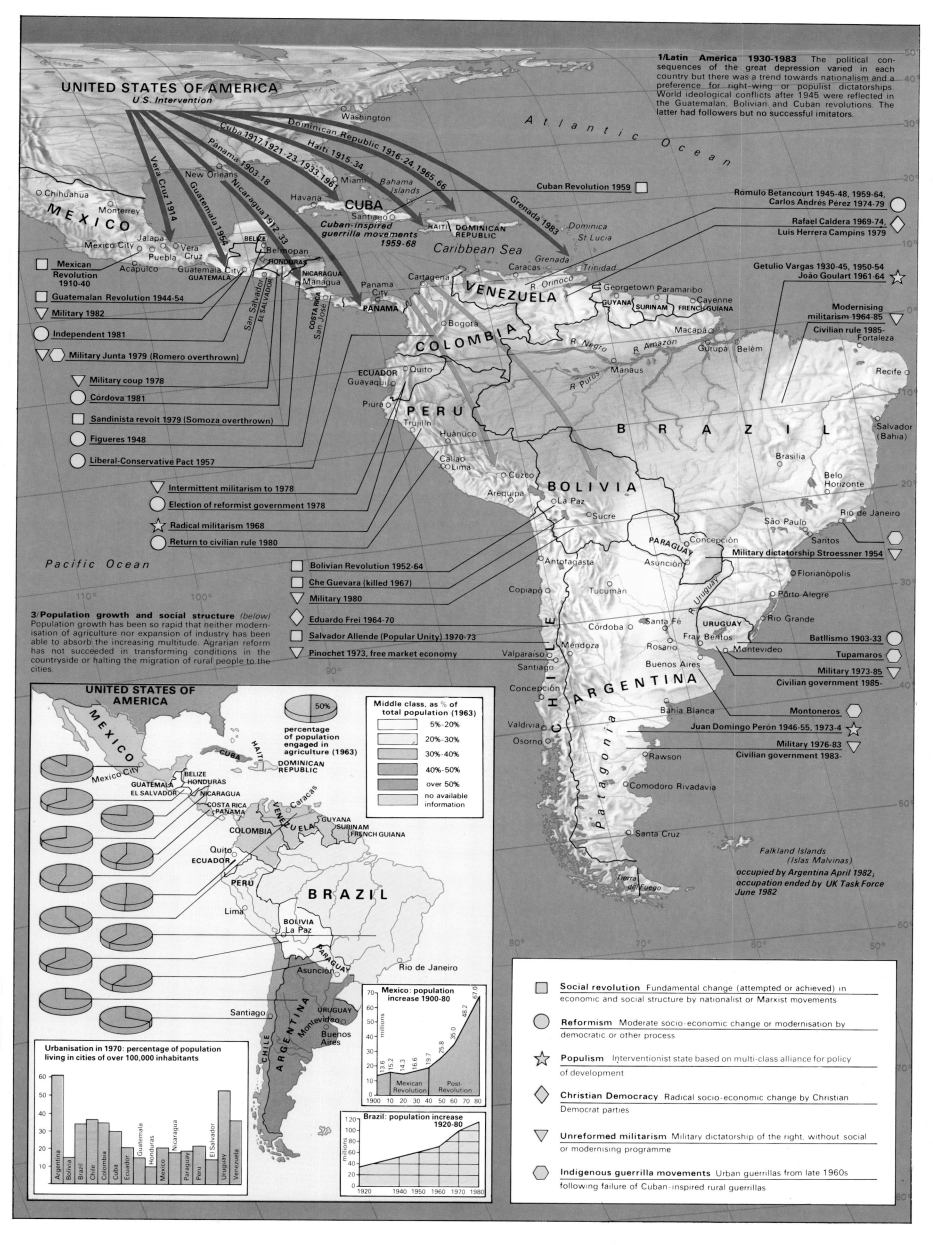

1/Latin America 1930-1983 The political consequences of the great depression varied in each country but there was a trend towards nationalism and a preference for right-wing or populist dictatorships. World ideological conflicts after 1945 were reflected in the Guatemalan, Bolivian and Cuban revolutions. The latter had followers but no successful imitators.

UNITED STATES OF AMERICA
U.S. Intervention

Vera Cruz 1914
Guatemala 1954
Panama 1903-18
Nicaragua 1912-33
Cuba 1917, 1921-23, 1933, 1961
Haiti 1915-34
Dominican Republic 1916-24, 1965-66
Grenada 1983

Washington

Chihuahua
Monterrey
MEXICO
Mexico City Jalapa
Puebla Vera Cruz
Acapulco
New Orleans
Miami *Bahama Islands*
Havana CUBA Santiago
Cuban-inspired guerrilla movements 1959-68
HAITI DOMINICAN REPUBLIC
Caribbean Sea
Dominica St Lucia
Grenada
Trinidad

Cuban Revolution 1959 ☐

BELIZE
Belmopan
Guatemala City GUATEMALA
HONDURAS
San Salvador EL SALVADOR
NICARAGUA Managua
COSTA RICA San José
Panama City PANAMA

Cartagena
Caracas
VENEZUELA
Bogota
COLOMBIA
R. Orinoco
Georgetown Paramaribo
GUYANA SURINAM Cayenne FRENCH GUIANA

Rómulo Betancourt 1945-48, 1959-64, Carlos Andrés Pérez 1974-79 ○
Rafael Caldera 1969-74, Luis Herrera Campins 1979 ◇

Getulio Vargas 1930-45, 1950-54, João Goulart 1961-64 ☆

☐ Mexican Revolution 1910-40
☐ Guatemalan Revolution 1944-54
▽ Military 1982
○ Independent 1981
▽⬡ Military Junta 1979 (Romero overthrown)

▽ Military coup 1978
○ Córdova 1981
☐ Sandinista revolt 1979 (Somoza overthrown)
○ Figueres 1948
○ Liberal-Conservative Pact 1957

▽ Intermittent militarism to 1978
○ Election of reformist government 1978
☆ Radical militarism 1968
○ Return to civilian rule 1980

ECUADOR Quito
Guayaquil
PERU Piura
Trujillo
Huánuco
Callao Lima
Cuzco
Arequipa
BOLIVIA
La Paz Sucre
Antofagasta
PARAGUAY Concepción Asunción
Copiapó
Tucumán
Córdoba
Santa Fé
URUGUAY Fray Bentos
Rosario Montevideo
Valparaíso
Santiago
Mendoza
Buenos Aires
Concepción ARGENTINA
Valdivia
Osorno
Bahia Blanca
Rawson
Comodoro Rivadavia
Santa Cruz

R. Negro R. Amazon
Macapá
Gurupá Belém
R. Purus Manaus
BRAZIL
Brasília
Belo Horizonte
São Paulo Rio de Janeiro
Santos
Florianópolis
Pôrto Alegre
Rio Grande
Recife
Salvador (Bahia)

Modernising militarism 1964-85 ▽
Civilian rule 1985- Fortaleza

Military dictatorship Stroessner 1954 ▽

Batllismo 1903-33 ○
Tupamaros ⬡
Military 1973-85 ▽
Civilian government 1985-

Montoneros ⬡
Juan Domingo Perón 1946-55, 1973-4 ☆
Military 1976-83 ▽
Civilian government 1983-

☐ Bolivian Revolution 1952-64
☐ Che Guevara (killed 1967)
▽ Military 1980
◇ Eduardo Frei 1964-70
◇ Salvador Allende (Popular Unity) 1970-73
▽ Pinochet 1973, free market economy

Pacific Ocean
Atlantic Ocean

Falkland Islands (Islas Malvinas)
occupied by Argentina April 1982; occupation ended by UK Task Force June 1982

Tierra del Fuego
Patagonia

3/Population growth and social structure *(below)*
Population growth has been so rapid that neither modernisation of agriculture nor expansion of industry has been able to absorb the increasing multitude. Agrarian reform has not succeeded in transforming conditions in the countryside or halting the migration of rural people to the cities.

UNITED STATES OF AMERICA
MEXICO
Mexico City
CUBA HAITI DOMINICAN REPUBLIC
BELIZE HONDURAS
GUATEMALA NICARAGUA
EL SALVADOR
COSTA RICA PANAMA
VENEZUELA Caracas
COLOMBIA GUYANA SURINAM FRENCH GUIANA
Quito ECUADOR
PERÚ Lima
BRAZIL
BOLIVIA La Paz
PARAGUAY Asunción
Rio de Janeiro
CHILE ARGENTINA URUGUAY Montevideo
Santiago Buenos Aires

50%
percentage of population engaged in agriculture (1963)

Middle class, as % of total population (1963)
5%-20%
20%-30%
30%-40%
40%-50%
over 50%
no available information

Urbanisation in 1970: percentage of population living in cities of over 100,000 inhabitants
(bar chart: Argentina, Bolivia, Brazil, Chile, Colombia, Cuba, Ecuador, Guatemala, Honduras, Mexico, Nicaragua, Paraguay, Peru, El Salvador, Uruguay, Venezuela)

Mexico: population increase 1900-80
(millions) 13.6 15.2 14.3 16.6 19.7 25.8 35.0 48.2 67.0
Mexican Revolution Post-Revolution
1900 10 20 30 40 50 60 70 80

Brazil: population increase 1920-80
(millions) 1920 1940 1950 1960 1970 1980

☐ **Social revolution** Fundamental change (attempted or achieved) in economic and social structure by nationalist or Marxist movements

○ **Reformism** Moderate socio-economic change or modernisation by democratic or other process

☆ **Populism** Interventionist state based on multi-class alliance for policy of development

◇ **Christian Democracy** Radical socio-economic change by Christian Democrat parties

▽ **Unreformed militarism** Military dictatorship of the right, without social or modernising programme

⬡ **Indigenous guerrilla movements** Urban guerrillas from late 1960s following failure of Cuban-inspired rural guerrillas

The development of the United States 1940 to 1983

RECOVERY from the Great Depression only came with the Second World War. In 1939 industrial production was still below the 1929 level, but by 1943 it was more than twice as high and the unemployment rate had fallen from 17.2 per cent to 1.9 per cent. President Roosevelt had been unwilling to use deficit spending to cure the Depression, but the war did it for him and the federal debt rose almost tenfold between 1939 and 1945.

The quarter-century after the war was a period of growth unmatched in American history; in real terms, gross national product nearly trebled between 1950 and 1980 and income per head almost doubled. A number of factors brought this about: population increase, technological advances and the emergence of new things to buy, as well as the stimulus given to the economy by the Korean War (1950-53) and the Cold War that followed it. Furthermore, there was no major recession. But the 1960s saw increasing instability in the economy culminating in the recession beginning in 1973, the worst since the 1930s, with national income actually falling in real terms for two years. Inflation, already at 5 per cent per annum in the late 1960s, was pushed still higher by the tripling of world prices after the oil embargo of November 1973, reaching 11 per cent in 1974, then falling back slightly, but rising to 13.5 per cent again in 1980.

A significant feature of American life in these years was the baby boom, which started late in the war and reached its peak in 1956. In 1960 nearly 22 per cent of the population was under ten years of age, but by 1980 this proportion had fallen to 14.6 per cent. The average annual increase in population, which was 0.7 per cent during 1935-39, reached 1.7 per cent in the 1950s but was back to 1 per cent by 1975-79. The total population rose from 132 million in 1940 to 226 million at the end of 1980. There was also a second great migration of people to the west — mostly, but by no means entirely, to California, and Los Angeles

replaced Chicago as the second most populous city after New York. Meanwhile, immigration, which dropped to very low levels during the Depression, rose steadily after 1945. The new immigration law of 1965 changed the quotas that since 1924 had favoured immigration from north-western Europe, with the result that much greater numbers of immigrants in this period entered from southern Europe, the Far East, and from Central and South America (map 1).

While wealth and output increased, the pattern of economic activity changed rapidly. The farming population shrank, though capital investment and technological change greatly raised its productivity. The leading sectors in industry were those dominated by new technologies or by defence needs. Beginning with the introduction of the transistor by the Bell laboratories in 1948, the United States led the way in electronics. Much of the initial growth in this sector came from military requirements, including the missile race and the successful moon landing programme. IBM quickly came to dominate the world computer industry and a host of smaller firms concentrated in 'Silicon Valley' near Palo Alto in California and near Cambridge, Massachusetts, produced a remarkable succession of new products both for civil and military use. The aircraft industry enjoyed a continuous boom in orders for military aircraft and on the basis of this support built up an overwhelming superiority throughout the world in the manufacture of civil aircraft. The rapid development of the interstate highways (map 3) and the growth of air travel left all but a few railways hopelessly bankrupt, and the splendid days of transcontinental passenger trains came to an end. However, whereas a notable feature of American industry for decades was a remarkable rise in productivity, since 1965 a sharp decrease in the rate of growth set in, especially compared with progress in other advanced countries. The automobile industry lost ground to competi-

tors in sales, productivity and design. The steel industry lagged seriously in the adoption of new techniques, but mining, construction and public utilities all contributed to the relative decline, due in part to a fall in investment and in research.

This age of mass consumption was accompanied by a more equal distribution of income and a greater concern for the under-privileged, even though in 1969 some 20 million Americans were described as living below the poverty line. President Truman launched his Fair Deal campaign in 1949 but not a great deal of legislation actually got through. The Eisenhower administration was a sterile interlude, and President John F. Kennedy, though he had the benefit of a rapidly expanding economy, had little success with his request to 'get the country moving' on a road to reform. President Johnson's shrewd relationship with Congress produced better results — above all, Medicare, Civil Rights and the Education Act of 1965. Wealth and success had created a belief in the universal validity of the American way of life; with Johnson's unexpected decision not to run for re-election in 1968, however, the conflicts and divisions building up in American society since 1945 came to a head. The protests of blacks and other minorities against discrimination, the militancy of students, disillusionment over the Vietnam War, combined with concern over the threat to the quality of life posed by the headlong pace of economic growth, all played a part. After the withdrawal from Vietnam (1973) protests became more muted — except for the powerful and largely successful campaign against nuclear power — though the problems of the inner city areas seem to be ever more insoluble. The Presidential election of 1980 revealed a nation divided, and how far these trends will be affected in the long run by the taxpayers' revolt in many states during the late 70s and by the unsympathetic attitude of the Reagan administration, remains to be seen.

The superior technology (above) and management techniques which helped maintain her position as the world's most sophisticated industrial power were shown by the speed with which the US responded to the early Soviet lead in rocketry. The first men to walk on the moon (20 July 1969) were launched by the Saturn V rocket.

3 and 4/Urban growth (below and right) Suburban growth has seen great development, and in several areas this has had the effect of joining up formerly separate urban areas to create "super cities", nowhere more dramatically than in the Los Angeles region (map 4). In the '70s, however, perhaps for the first time in US history the population in rural areas grew as fast as the population as a whole. An interstate system of highways totalling about 40,000 miles by 1980 facilitated long-distance movement of people and the rise of complex networks of residence and work (map 3).

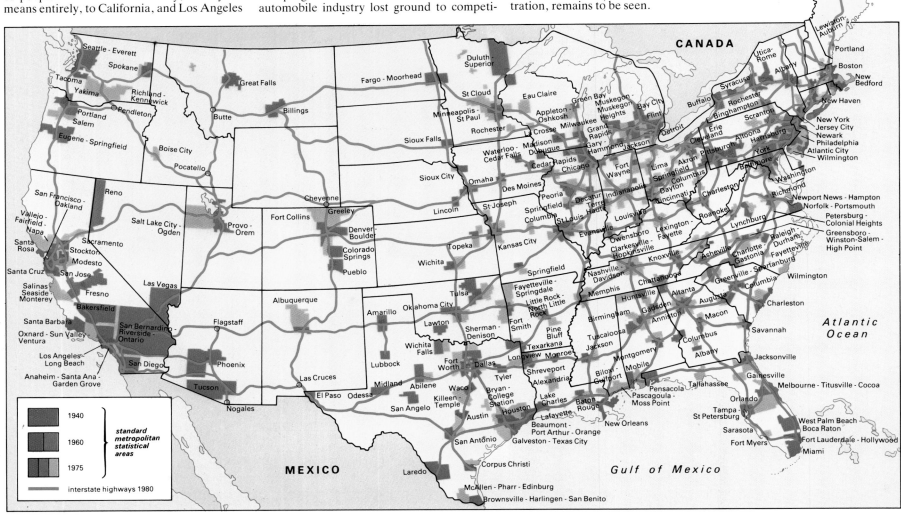

standard metropolitan statistical areas
- 1940
- 1960
- 1975
- interstate highways 1980

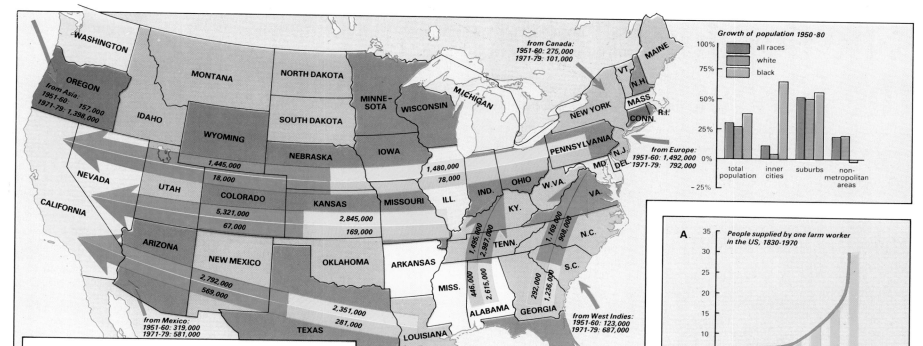

from Canada:
1951-60: 275,000
1971-79: 101,000

from Europe:
1951-60: 1,492,000
1971-79: 792,000

from Asia:
1951-60: 157,000
1971-79: 1,398,000

WASHINGTON
OREGON
MONTANA
NORTH DAKOTA
MINNE-SOTA
WISCONSIN
MICHIGAN
MAINE
VT
N.H.
NEW YORK
MASS.
CONN.
R.I.
IDAHO
SOUTH DAKOTA
WYOMING
IOWA
PENNSYLVANIA
N.J.
NEBRASKA
MD
DEL
NEVADA
UTAH
COLORADO
KANSAS
MISSOURI
ILL.
IND.
OHIO
W.VA.
VA.
CALIFORNIA
KY.
N.C.
ARIZONA
NEW MEXICO
OKLAHOMA
ARKANSAS
TENN.
S.C.
MISS.
ALABAMA
GEORGIA
TEXAS
LOUISIANA
FLORIDA

1,445,000
18,000
1,480,000
78,000
5,321,000
67,000
2,845,000
169,000
2,987,000
1,495,000
2,792,000
569,000
2,615,000
446,000
2,351,000
281,000
1,169,000
908,000
292,000
1,236,000

from Mexico:
1951-60: 319,000
1971-79: 581,000

from Central America:
1951-60: 45,000
1971-79: 111,000

from South America:
1951-60: 123,000
1971-79: 245,000

from West Indies:
1951-60: 123,000
1971-79: 687,000

Gulf of Mexico

income per head 1970

1930-60 / 1965-79	movement of white population
1930-60 / 1965-79	movement of black population
→	immigrants

- under $3000
- $3000-3500
- $3500-4000
- $4000-4500
- $4500-4750
- over $4750

(USA average $3943)

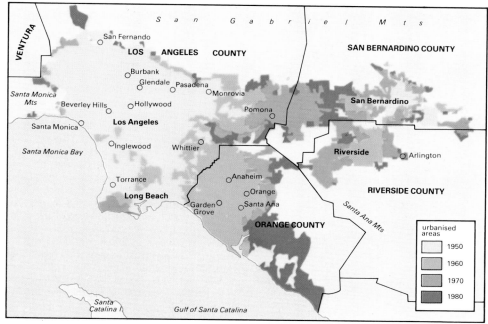

VENTURA

San Gabriel Mts

LOS ANGELES COUNTY
SAN BERNARDINO COUNTY

San Fernando
Burbank
Glendale
Pasadena
Monrovia
Beverley Hills
Hollywood
Pomona
San Bernardino
Santa Monica Mts
Santa Monica
Inglewood
Whittier
Los Angeles
Santa Monica Bay
Torrance
Long Beach
Anaheim
Orange
Santa Ana
Garden Grove
Riverside
Arlington
RIVERSIDE COUNTY
ORANGE COUNTY
Santa Ana Mts

Santa Catalina I

Gulf of Santa Catalina

urbanised areas
- 1950
- 1960
- 1970
- 1980

2 Wealth and population *(above)*
Since the Second World War there has been a striking migration of population to the far West; California is now the most populous state. The industrial states have the highest average incomes and the Dakotas, Arkansas and Mississippi have fared worst as regards both income and population growth. The black population has grown faster than the white (see graph) and the blacks have moved heavily into the big cities.

Farm efficiency *(right)* The farming population fell from 30.5 million in 1940 to 9 million in 1974, yet because of remarkable increases in productivity the US remain the world's greatest food supplier (see graphs A, B, C).

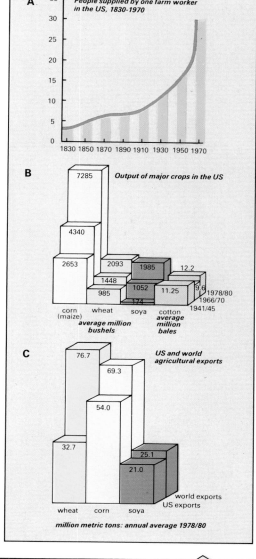

A
35
30
25
20
15
10
5

People supplied by one farm worker in the US, 1830-1970

1830 1850 1870 1890 1910 1930 1950 1970

B

7285
4340
2653
2093
1985
12.2
1448
1052
11.25
9.6
985
985
774
21.0

Output of major crops in the US

corn (maize) | wheat | soya | cotton

average million bushels

average million bales

1978/80
1966/70
1941/45

C

76.7
69.3
54.0
32.7
25.1
21.0

US and world agricultural exports

wheat | corn | soya

world exports
US exports

million metric tons: annual average 1978/80

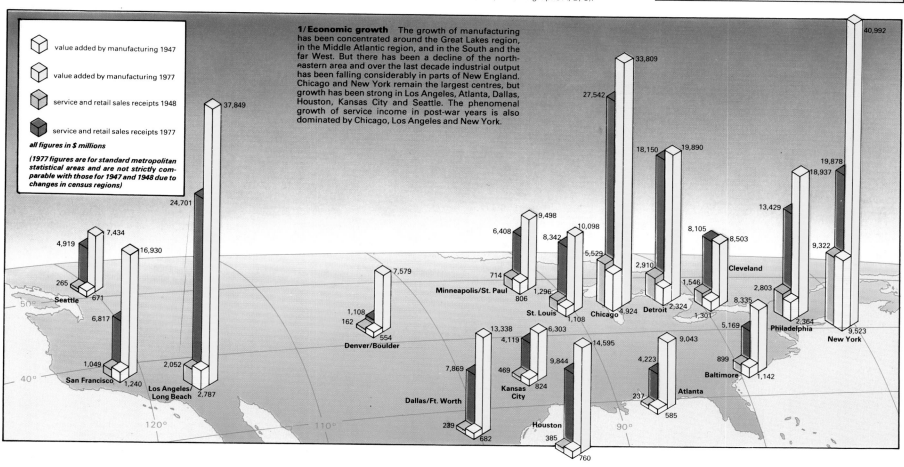

1 / Economic growth The growth of manufacturing has been concentrated around the Great Lakes region, in the Middle Atlantic region, and in the South and the far West. But there has been a decline of the north-eastern area and over the last decade industrial output has been falling considerably in parts of New England. Chicago and New York remain the largest centres, but growth has been strong in Los Angeles, Atlanta, Dallas, Houston, Kansas City and Seattle. The phenomenal growth of service income in post-war years is also dominated by Chicago, Los Angeles and New York.

☐	value added by manufacturing 1947
☐	value added by manufacturing 1977
☐	service and retail sales receipts 1948
◼	service and retail sales receipts 1977

all figures in $ millions

(1977 figures are for standard metropolitan statistical areas and are not strictly comparable with those for 1947 and 1948 due to changes in census regions)

Seattle: 4,919 / 7,434 / 265 / 671
San Francisco: 24,701 / 16,930 / 6,817 / 1,049 / 1,240
Los Angeles/Long Beach: 37,849 / 2,052 / 2,787
Denver/Boulder: 7,579 / 1,108 / 162 / 554
Minneapolis/St. Paul: 9,498 / 6,408 / 8,342 / 714 / 806 / 1,296
St. Louis: 10,098 / 5,529 / 1,108
Chicago: 33,809 / 4,924 / 2,910
Detroit: 18,150 / 19,890 / 1,546 / 2,324
Cleveland: 8,105 / 8,503 / 1,301
Philadelphia: 27,542 / 13,429 / 2,803 / 8,335 / 2,364
New York: 40,992 / 19,878 / 18,937 / 9,322 / 9,523
Baltimore: 5,169 / 899 / 1,142
Atlanta: 9,043 / 4,223 / 585 / 237
Houston: 14,595 / 9,844 / 385 / 760
Kansas City: 6,303 / 4,119 / 469 / 824
Dallas/Ft. Worth: 13,338 / 7,869 / 239 / 682

50°
40°
120°
110°
90°

The development of the Soviet Union 1926 to 1980

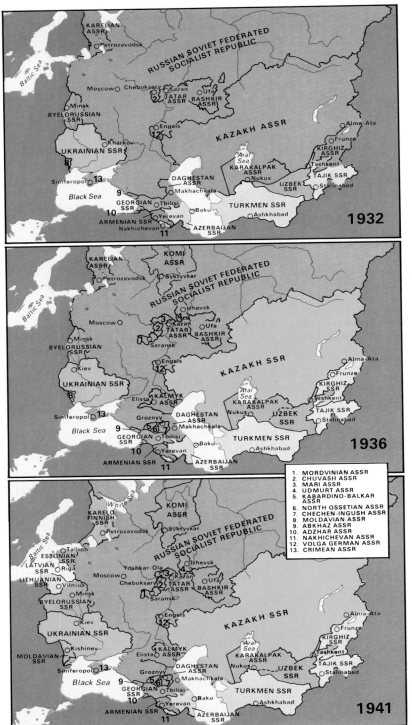

1932

1936

1. MORDVINIAN ASSR
2. CHUVASH ASSR
3. MARI ASSR
4. UDMURT ASSR
5. KABARDINO-BALKAR ASSR
6. NORTH OSSETIAN ASSR
7. CHECHEN-INGUSH ASSR
8. MOLDAVIAN ASSR
9. ABKHAZ ASSR
10. ADZHAR ASSR
11. NAKHICHEVAN ASSR
12. VOLGA GERMAN ASSR
13. CRIMEAN ASSR

1941

BY 1926 it was clear that the Bolshevik regime was going to survive, in spite of the immense problems still facing it. Civil war, foreign intervention, chaos and famine followed the Revolution, and Russia became again an isolated nation, as it had been in the 16th century. After Lenin's death in 1924, Trotsky and Stalin both struggled for the leadership, which was decided by Trotsky's expulsion from the Communist Party in 1927. Trotsky's aim had been to spread communism to other countries; Stalin's triumph meant, instead, concentration on domestic problems, and the first five-year plan of industrialisation was introduced in 1928. Russia looked inwards to the resources of her own vast territories: self-sufficiency was to be the new economic goal. But industrialisation could not be achieved while eighty per cent of the labour force was engaged in primitive and inefficient peasant agriculture; an agricultural revolution was therefore an essential prerequisite. It took the form of collectivisation and mechanisation: the peasants were compelled to merge their holdings into large collective farms which were to be mechanised. Hence the first great industrial enterprises were the tractor works at Kharkov, Stalingrad (Volgograd) and Chelyabinsk. Collectivisation and mechanisation began in 1928, and by 1934 three-quarters of peasant holdings had been collectivised and 278,000 tractors were in use. The surplus labour resulting from these changes was drafted to industrial construction sites. The terror which accompanied compulsory collectivisation and the famine which followed it, resulted in enormous loss of life. This, together with the arbitrary requisition by the State of farm produce at low prices, led to bitter resentment in the countryside, and agricultural productivity was slow to grow.

Heavy industry made immense strides. Between 1928 and 1940 production of coal increased from 36 to 166 million tons, of electricity from 5 to 48 billion kwh, and of steel from 4 to 18 million tons. In 1928 there had been an obsolescent iron industry in the Ukraine and an obsolete one in the central Urals. By 1940

2/Changes in republican status (left) Autonomous Soviet Socialist Republics (ASSRs) were created for important nationalities within Union Republics (SSRs). Since 1941 the Karelo-Finnish Republic has become an ASSR, the Crimean ASSR has been incorporated in the Ukrainian SSR and the Volga-German ASSR has been dissolved. Although these maps cover only the western part of the country, all the Union Republics (SSRs) are shown. The eastern regions not included on the maps are wholly within the Russian Soviet Federated Republic (RSFSR), but they contain two Autonomous Republics — the Buryat-Mongolian ASSR (capital Ulan Ude) and the Yakutian ASSR (capital Yakutsk).

both had been expanded and modernised. Two new large iron and steel bases were established: one near a massive iron ore deposit in the southern Urals at the new town of Magnitogorsk; the other on the Kuzbass coalfield at Stalinsk (Novokuznetsk).

Much of the industrialisation of the first five-year plans had taken place in eastern regions beyond the reach of the Germans in the 1941-45 war, and this was a vital factor in Soviet survival. During the war the industrialisation of these strategically safe regions was greatly speeded up, but the western parts of the country were devastated. Agriculture suffered from the destruction of farm buildings and equipment. Many of the better farmers had been Germans, settled along the Volga and elsewhere, who were now uprooted and exiled to Siberia, harming agricultural production. After the war there was further mass transportation of nationalities thought to be disloyal.

The first five post-war years were taken up by reconstruction. After 1950 the output of heavy industry continued to grow, and light industry, neglected during the Stalinist period (1928-53), also progressed. Siberian reserves of oil, gas and mineral ores were discovered and exploited, and powerful hydro-electric and coal-fired generating stations built in eastern Siberia and Kazakhstan. The Soviet economy was largely integrated with those of the countries of eastern Europe which came under Soviet control after the war, and their high-quality engineering products proved to be of immense value to the USSR's technological progress.

Stalin's successors were forced to recognise the immensity of the agricultural problem. A growing population was expecting the oft-promised increase in the level of living, but agriculture was scarcely more productive than before the revolution. Khrushchev, in the late 1950s, organised the ploughing up of the virgin steppes of northern Kazakhstan; although there were bad harvests in 1963 and 1965, this led to an increase in average annual grain production from 100 million tons in the 1950s to 190 million tons in the 1970s. Since 1965 much was done under Brezhnev to improve the collective farmer's lot.

Industrialisation was accompanied by rapid urbanisation. In 1922 only 16 per cent of the total population of 136 million was classified as urban; by 1940 this had doubled to 33 per cent (of 194 million). In 1980 it was 63 per cent of 264 million. Regionally, population grew most rapidly in Kazakhstan where the steppes were colonised under Khrushchev, and in central Asia, where the rate of natural increase was extremely high. In 1922 the central Asian republics accounted for only 5 per cent of the total population, a proportion that had risen to 10 per cent by 1980.

By 1980 the Soviet Union was generally recognised as a 'superpower', a distinction shared only with the USA, and attributable in the main to a comparable degree of military strength, especially in nuclear weapons. This military prowess had a rapidly expanding industrial base. Although Soviet gross national product still fell well short of America's, the USSR had already overtaken the USA in the production of iron ore, cement, steel and oil, and was rapidly developing the world's largest reserves of natural gas. But agriculture nevertheless remained the weak link in the economic chain. And over all this past achievement and future promise lay the shadow of a resurgent and hostile China.

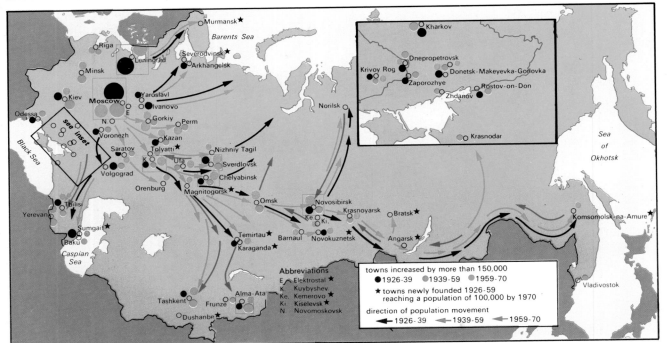

3/The movement of population (left) From 1926 to 1939 major population growth was in Moscow and Leningrad; early Soviet industrial expansion was concentrated here. The second period (1939-59) included the war, and reflects the eastward movement of industry and urban population. More urban growth took place in the west during the years 1959-70.

Abbreviations
E. Elektrostal
K. Kuybyshev
Ke. Kemerovo
Ki. Kiselevsk
N. Novomoskovsk

towns increased by more than 150,000
● 1926-39 ● 1939-59 ● 1959-70
★ towns newly founded 1926-59 reaching a population of 100,000 by 1970
direction of population movement
← 1926-39 ← 1939-59 ← 1959-70

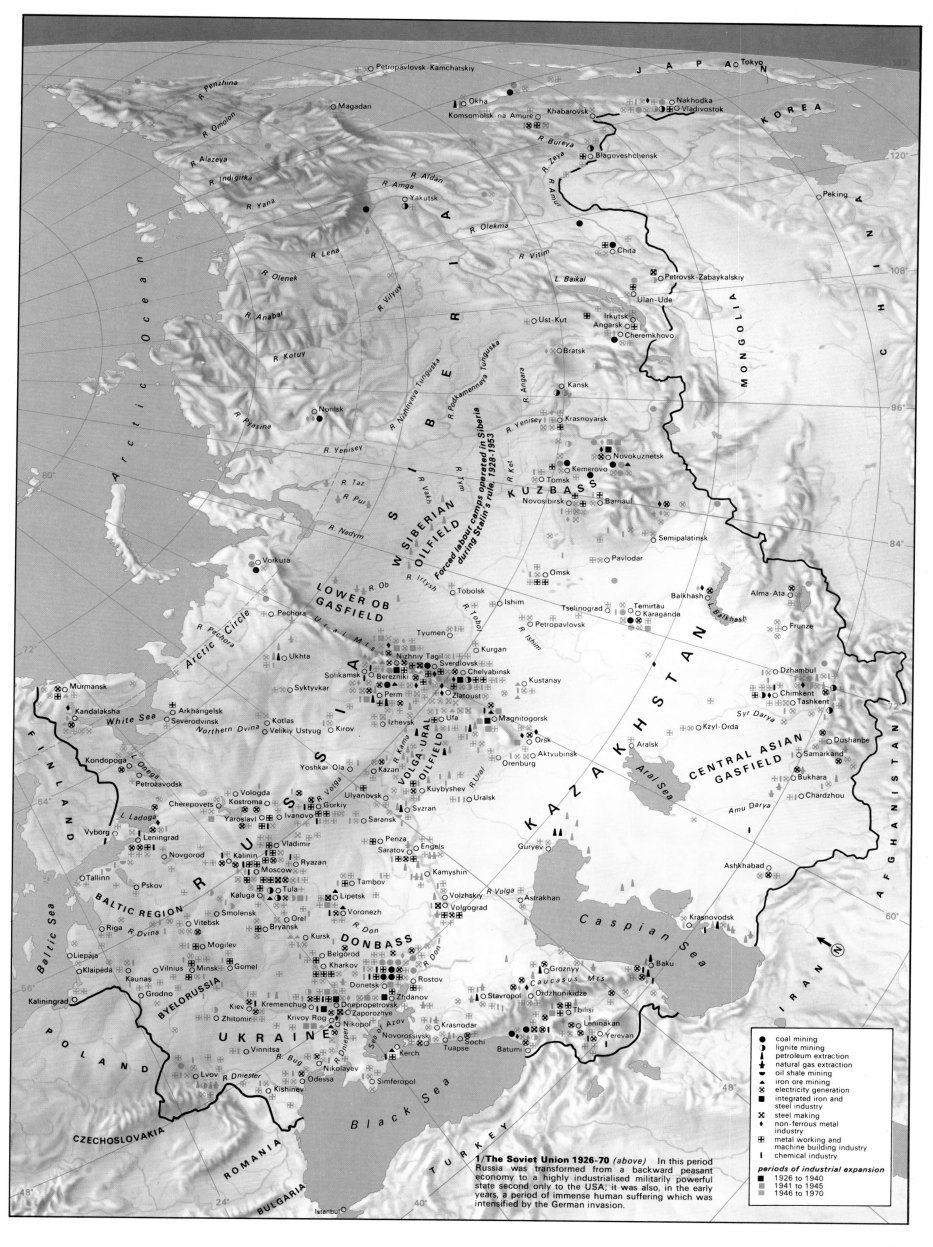

1/The Soviet Union 1926-70 (above) In this period Russia was transformed from a backward peasant economy to a highly industrialised militarily powerful state second only to the USA; it was also, in the early years, a period of immense human suffering which was intensified by the German invasion.

coal mining
lignite mining
petroleum extraction
natural gas extraction
oil shale mining
iron ore mining
electricity generation
integrated iron and steel industry
steel making
non-ferrous metal industry
metal working and machine building industry
chemical industry

periods of industrial expansion
1926 to 1940
1941 to 1945
1946 to 1970

The Cold War
1949 to 1973

2/Europe (left) Soviet control in eastern Europe was established gradually between 1945 and 1948. Although it was evident that Allied victory over Germany would bring a major westward expansion of Soviet influence, Stalin at first proceeded cautiously. 'Bourgeois' parties were tolerated and elections in 1945 and 1946 were relatively free, but by February 1948 eastern Europe was ruled by communist or communist-controlled 'socialist unity' parties. Subsequently 'national communists' (Gomulka 1949, Kádár 1950) were removed, thus assuring full Soviet control, except in Yugoslavia, where Marshal Tito broke with Moscow in 1948.

3/Korea (left) The Korean War carried the Cold War to the Far East. Occupied in 1945 by Soviet and American troops, the country was already divided *de facto* by 1948. In 1950, after the withdrawal of the American and Russian occupation forces, the North Koreans attacked the South. The United States and the United Nations immediately intervened. After initial North Korean successes, the Americans counter-attacked under General MacArthur and advanced to the Chinese frontier. This resulted in Chinese intervention (October 1950) and a stalemate, which was ended by the armistice of Panmunjom (1953) and the partition of Korea around the 38th parallel.

WITH the elimination of Germany, Japan and Italy and the weakening of Great Britain and France in the Second World War, the United States and the Soviet Union emerged as the two 'super-powers'. The Cold War was the expression of their political and ideological confrontation.

Already visible at the Yalta Conference (February 1945), their conflict of interests became more acute after the death of Franklin D. Roosevelt and the succession of Harry S. Truman as President of the United States (12 April 1945). The American monopoly of the A-bomb, first successfully detonated on 16 July 1945, increased tension, and after the inconclusive Potsdam Conference of July-August 1945, the Soviet Union under Stalin decided to consolidate Communist control of eastern Europe. In 1947 Soviet-dominated governments were set up in Hungary, Poland, Bulgaria, Romania, and finally (in February 1948) in Czechoslovakia; only Yugoslavia retained some independence. When civil war and an attempted Communist takeover occurred in Greece in December 1947, and the Russians threatened in April 1948 to freeze out the western sectors of Berlin and incorporate the whole city in the German Democratic Republic (established on 7 October 1949), the United States reacted vigorously. Even earlier, the Truman Doctrine and Marshall Plan (1947) had been established as the American reply to the alleged Russian threat.

Starting as a conflict over central Europe and divided Germany, the Cold War spread to Asia following the Communist victory in China (1949), and soon developed into a global conflict. For the United States, the Korean War (1950) was evidence of a world-wide Communist conspiracy. Actually China and the USSR were not acting in unison, and the Chinese only intervened in the Korean War (October 1950) when the American advance to the Yalu river seemed to threaten their territorial security. Even then, the USSR remained in American eyes the main threat, and though Japan was built up as an American bastion against China (1951) and Okinawa retained as an American missile base, the main aim of United States policy was to 'contain' the USSR by a series of encircling alliances and bases around its frontiers from west to east. First was NATO (North Atlantic Treaty Organisation, 1949), followed by SEA-TO (South-East Asia Treaty Organisation, 1954) and CENTO (Central Treaty Organisation, 1959, replacing the Baghdad Pact of 1955). By this time the United States had over 1400 foreign bases in 31 countries, including

275 bases for nuclear bombers. For its own defence, after the USSR had acquired nuclear weapons (A-bomb 1949, H-bomb 1953), it constructed the so-called 'DEW line' (a Distant Early Warning system of radar posts across the Arctic Circle from Alaska through Canada to Baffin Island). But this became obsolete after the Soviet launching of the satellite Sputnik in 1957 and the advent of the intercontinental ballistic missile (ICBM).

The most intensive phase of the Cold War occurred during the period 1949-59, when Dean Acheson and John Foster Dulles were United States secretaries of state. After 1955 (Baghdad Pact) it spilled over into the Middle East (Eisenhower Doctrine, 1957; United States intervention in Lebanon, 1958), where it proved a divisive force, some countries seeking Soviet, others American, support. But by this time conditions were changing, the two monolithic blocks were showing signs of strain. Uprisings in Hungary and Poland (1956) shook Soviet self-confidence; unrest in Latin America and Soviet attempts to strike up relationships there (1958) were scarcely less disturbing for the United States. Both parties seem to have concluded that they had more to lose than to gain by the conflict, and after the settlement of the Cuban crisis in 1962, Soviet-American tension gradually relaxed. A first sign of this was the signature of a nuclear test treaty in 1963.

The focus of the Cold War now shifted to South-East Asia, where the United States had been increasingly involved in Indo-China since 1954. The greater moderation of Soviet policy after the fall of Khrushchev in 1964, accumulating evidence of Sino-Soviet conflict, and the Chinese acquisition of nuclear potential (1964), all seemed to point to China as the centre of militant Communism. The 'Domino Theory' led the United States to ever-increasing military intervention in Laos, Cambodia, and particularly Vietnam, which reached its peak under President Johnson (1963-68), until ultimately more than 543,000 American troops were committed.

At this stage a revulsion set in. The failure to destroy Vietnamese resistance without recourse to nuclear weapons, involving the possibility of Chinese intervention and the outbreak of a third world war, but above all American over-commitment and the financial strain imposed both by the war and by the costly American system of alliances, imposed a halt. The new Republican President, Richard M. Nixon, promised in 1969 to reduce and finally (1973) to withdraw United States ground troops from Vietnam. When in 1971 he followed up this reversal by overtures to Communist China and later visited Peking and Moscow, the relaxation of tension seemed to mark the beginning of a new era in international relations; and a similar change occurred in Europe with the conclusion of a Four-Power Agreement on Berlin in 1971 and détente between East and West Germany. But the underlying tensions and suspicions remained unresolved, particularly in the field of nuclear armaments, and in spite of continuing discussion of limitation and control in the so-called SALT negotiations of 1972 and later, both the Soviet Union and the United States continued to build up new and more powerful strategic weapon systems. Down to

4/Indo-China (above) From 1945 to 1954 Indo-China struggled against French colonial rule. After defeat at Dien Bien Phu (1954) the French withdrew, but the United States refused to subscribe to the Geneva agreements. And it built up a counter-revolutionary government at Saigon under Ngo Dinh Diem. The second Indo-Chinese war, 1957 to 1973 resulted. In spite of saturation bombing and the commitment of over half a million ground troops, the United States failed to break North Vietnamese resistance. A compromise settlement in 1973 led eventually to the collapse of Saigon in 1975, when the United States finally evacuated the country.

1979 the atmosphere of détente, or 'thaw', created in 1971 was at least outwardly maintained; but from the beginning of the 1980s the unresolved tensions came to the surface again, and a marked deterioration in Soviet-American relations seemed to point to a recrudescence of the Cold War.

members of Baghdad Pact

countries opposed to Baghdad Pact

major pipelines of the Iraq Petroleum Company and Aramco

major oil fields

areas occupied by Israel after the 1967 war

decline of British influence:
(1) evacuation of Canal Zone 1954
(2) dismissal of General Glubb 1956
(3) Iraqi revolution, assassination of Nuri es-Said 1958
(4) withdrawal from Aden 1968

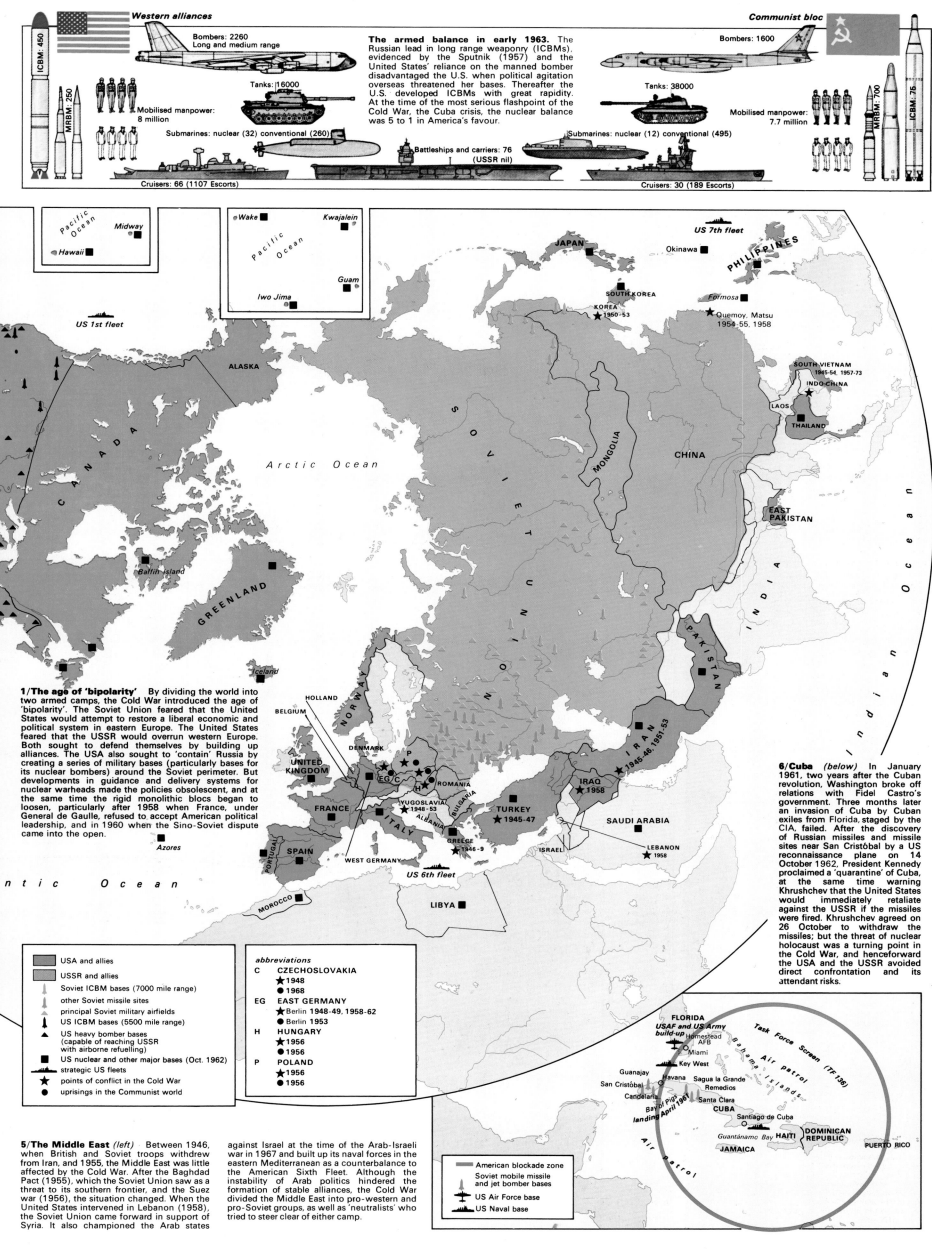

Western alliances

ICBM: 450
MRBM: 250

Bombers: 2260
Long and medium range

Tanks: 16000

Mobilised manpower:
8 million

Submarines: nuclear (32) conventional (260)

Battleships and carriers: 76
(USSR nil)

Cruisers: 66 (1107 Escorts)

The armed balance in early 1963. The Russian lead in long range weaponry (ICBMs), evidenced by the Sputnik (1957) and the United States' reliance on the manned bomber disadvantaged the U.S. when political agitation overseas threatened her bases. Thereafter the U.S. developed ICBMs with great rapidity. At the time of the most serious flashpoint of the Cold War, the Cuba crisis, the nuclear balance was 5 to 1 in America's favour.

Communist bloc

Bombers: 1600

Tanks: 38000

Mobilised manpower:
7.7 million

Submarines: nuclear (12) conventional (495)

Cruisers: 30 (189 Escorts)

MRBM: 700
ICBM: 75

1/The age of 'bipolarity' By dividing the world into two armed camps, the Cold War introduced the age of 'bipolarity'. The Soviet Union feared that the United States would attempt to restore a liberal economic and political system in eastern Europe. The United States feared that the USSR would overrun western Europe. Both sought to defend themselves by building up alliances. The USA also sought to 'contain' Russia by creating a series of military bases (particularly bases for its nuclear bombers) around the Soviet perimeter. But developments in guidance and delivery systems for nuclear warheads made the policies obsolescent, and at the same time the rigid monolithic blocs began to loosen, particularly after 1958 when France, under General de Gaulle, refused to accept American political leadership, and in 1960 when the Sino-Soviet dispute came into the open.

6/Cuba (below) In January 1961, two years after the Cuban revolution, Washington broke off relations with Fidel Castro's government. Three months later an invasion of Cuba by Cuban exiles from Florida, staged by the CIA, failed. After the discovery of Russian missiles and missile sites near San Cristóbal by a US reconnaissance plane on 14 October 1962, President Kennedy proclaimed a 'quarantine' of Cuba, at the same time warning Khrushchev that the United States would immediately retaliate against the USSR if the missiles were fired. Khrushchev agreed on 26 October to withdraw the missiles; but the threat of nuclear holocaust was a turning point in the Cold War, and henceforward the USA and the USSR avoided direct confrontation and its attendant risks.

Legend:

- USA and allies
- USSR and allies
- Soviet ICBM bases (7000 mile range)
- other Soviet missile sites
- principal Soviet military airfields
- US ICBM bases (5500 mile range)
- US heavy bomber bases (capable of reaching USSR with airborne refuelling)
- US nuclear and other major bases (Oct. 1962)
- strategic US fleets
- ★ points of conflict in the Cold War
- ● uprisings in the Communist world

abbreviations

C   CZECHOSLOVAKIA
★1948
●1968

EG   EAST GERMANY
★Berlin 1948-49, 1958-62
●Berlin 1953

H   HUNGARY
★1956
●1956

P   POLAND
★1956
●1956

Cuba inset legend:

- American blockade zone
- Soviet mobile missile and jet bomber bases
- ✈ US Air Force base
- ⚓ US Naval base

5/The Middle East (left) Between 1946, when British and Soviet troops withdrew from Iran, and 1955, the Middle East was little affected by the Cold War. After the Baghdad Pact (1955), which the Soviet Union saw as a threat to its southern frontier, and the Suez war (1956), the situation changed. When the United States intervened in Lebanon (1958), the Soviet Union came forward in support of Syria. It also championed the Arab states against Israel at the time of the Arab-Israeli war in 1967 and built up its naval forces in the eastern Mediterranean as a counterbalance to the American Sixth Fleet. Although the instability of Arab politics hindered the formation of stable alliances, the Cold War divided the Middle East into pro-western and pro-Soviet groups, as well as 'neutralists' who tried to steer clear of either camp.

Rich nations and poor nations: the world in the 1980s

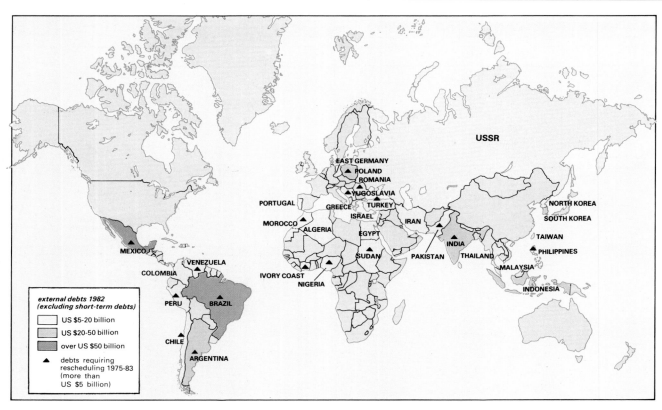

was more than a postponement of the day of reckoning was an open question.

The onset of the 1980s saw a world in disarray, and despite a measure of economic revival in 1984 (which, however, in real terms did not restore the position before 1979), the disarray tended to increase rather than diminish. Poverty and economic stringency fed the flames of civil war and guerrilla activity in Central America, in which the United States became increasingly involved, and the revolution in Iran (1979), followed by war between Iran and Iraq, threw the whole area of the Persian Gulf, with its vitally important oilfields, into turmoil. More threatening in some respects, because of Great Power involvement, was the continuing instability in Lebanon, in which large Israeli and Syrian forces remained entrenched. In these circumstances it is understandable that two-thirds of the arms trade carried on between 1977 and 1981 ($120-140 billion) was with developing countries, always ready, in spite of mounting economic difficulties, to spend on armaments to guard against internal unrest and external threats.

Characteristic of the international situation in

2/International debts *(left)* The world recession of the 1970s left many developing countries attempting, with decreasing earnings, to service increased interest payments on loans. By 1983 many were forced to reschedule these loans, and to introduce austere economic programmes which would nevertheless avoid severe social and political upheavals.

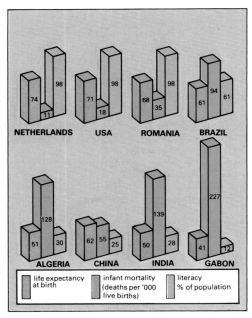

IN the wider perspective of world history the outstanding development of the years following the end of the Second World War was an unparalleled expansion of wealth and productivity. In the United States industrial output increased two and three-quarter times between 1938 and 1955, and gross national product (GNP) rose from $100 billion (or $770 a head) in 1940 to $1,140 billion (or $5,420 a head) in 1971. But this era of growth and prosperity, in which all the Western industrial nations and Japan participated, came to an end in the 1970s, and by 1980 the major industrialised countries were beset by mounting unemployment and acute economic strains. Moreover, the economic upsurge had been marked from the beginning by gross inequalities. In theory, the prosperity of the West was supposed to 'trickle down' to the less developed countries. In a few instances (Taiwan, South Korea, Brazil) it did so for a time. But overall the gap between rich and poor, instead of closing, continued to widen. By 1980 GNP per head in the United States was $10,820, in India it was $190, and even in oil-producing Nigeria no more than $670.

By 1972 the gap between the rich and poor nations had become an issue in international politics. Once the Third World countries had won independence and secured a voice in the United Nations, it was only a matter of time until they challenged the unequal distribution of the world's wealth. The issue came to a head in October 1973 when a cartel of petroleum exporting countries (OPEC) quadrupled the price of oil. The success of OPEC was the signal for a general assault on the West, led by the so-called 'Group of 77', and a demand for a New International Economic Order (NIEO), which was formally endorsed by the United Nations in 1974. But with the onset of world depression in 1979 the initial impact of NIEO quickly petered out. By 1983 the developing countries faced a third successive year of declining per capita incomes, and the fall in commodity prices to their lowest level for 30 years confronting many of them (including newly industrialised countries such as Brazil and Argentina) with a desperate shortage of foreign currency. By this time their debts exceeded $600 billion, and about 30 developing and Eastern block countries, unable to service their debts, were forced to seek renegotiation and re-scheduling. Whether this

The gap between nations *(above)* The graphs illustrate the gross discrepancies between developed and poor countries in literacy, life expectancy and infant mortality. Nevertheless, in spite of an infant mortality eight times higher and a life expectancy one-third lower, the population of the poor countries is still growing three to four times as fast as that of the rich countries, thus compounding all their problems.

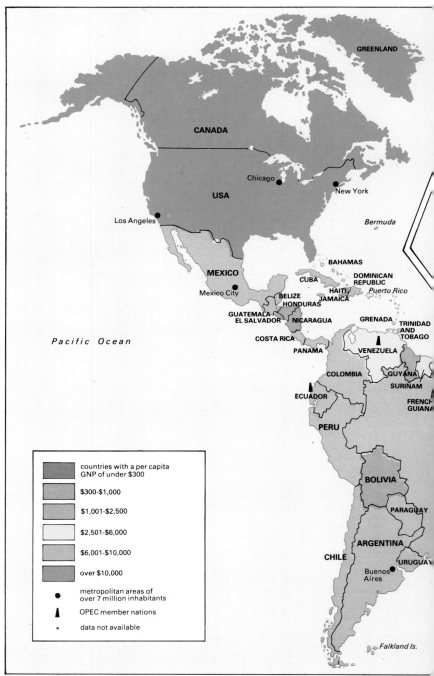

the 1980s more generally, was the fact that an increasing amount of global GNP, rising to $600 billion in 1982, was being spent on defence. In the United States alone the military budget increased from $126 billion in 1979, President Carter's last year, to $274 billion in 1984. The 1970s had seen some effort, beginning with the Strategic Arms Limitation Agreement of 1972 (SALT I) to control offensive weapons, but a second agreement (SALT II) in 1979 came to nothing when the United States declined to ratify it following the Soviet invasion of Afghanistan in December 1979. From that time forward the arms race was stepped up, the result being the basing of a new generation of Soviet SS-20 missiles in eastern Europe and American Cruise and Pershing missiles in western Europe in 1984. Not surprisingly, as the 1980s progressed, an increasing number of voices was heard expressing doubt whether the world would survive.

In addition to the long-term conflict of interests between the Third World and the West and deepening antagonism between the United States and the Soviet Union, the 1980s were marked by growing disagreements within the different alliances. Politically the Western European countries were reluctant to follow the United States in its anti-Soviet stance. Economically they blamed many of their difficulties on its fiscal policies. Furthermore, competition for markets injected additional strains into the Western alliance. In the East, the suppression of the Solidarity movement and the imposition of martial law in Poland in December 1981 pinpointed the instability of the Soviet block at the end of the Brezhnev era, and the short-lived Andropov regime (1982-84) and that of Andropov's successor, Chernenko, brought no apparent change. People spoke of a retreat to nationalism, but overt nationalism was less apparent than cross-purposes and lack of direction.

The era which followed the Second World War opened with great promise. The inauguration of a Welfare State in Great Britain and elsewhere seemed to presage a wide-reaching redistribution of wealth and increasing benefits in health and education for ordinary men and women, and for many years the promise was fulfilled. Endemic unemployment, the curse of the pre-war years, was banished, and the upsurge of prosperity in Europe following the formation of the EEC in 1957 carried the process still further. The ex-colonial countries, in control of their own destinies, were poised to forge ahead. But the onset of depression dashed these hopes, and the picture which emerged in the 1980s was very different. Although there were exceptions, economic stringency brought with it a marked trend to conservative governments, and to a questioning, if not dismantling, of the social achievements of the preceding generation. The result was strikes, lockouts and turbulence, from which no country was exempt.

From this point of view and others, the 1980s marked a watershed in the history of the contemporary world, with the prospect of going forward or going backward almost equally balanced. Taking into account as well the heightened international tensions and the build-up of nuclear armaments, all lines of development pointed to a precarious, unsettled future. But more serious in the long run were the gross disbalances in the world economy, setting poor nations against rich nations. With 5 thousand million out of an anticipated world population of 6 thousand million in the year 2000 crowded in impoverished Third World countries, disbalances of this magnitude could give rise, if nothing were done to correct them, to an explosion capable of tearing apart the world as we know it. But the signs of anything being done are few and far between.

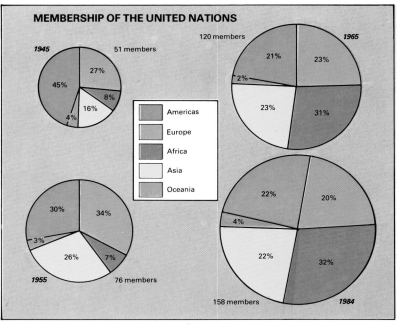

3/Membership of the United Nations *(above)* In 1945 the UN had 51 member states; by 1984 it had 158. At the same time, the distribution of voting power changed. In 1945 the United States, with the support of the Latin American members and Western Europe, had an absolute majority. In 1955 membership rose from 60 to 76 and the balance shifted in favour of the Afro-Asian bloc. In 1961, with the addition of 17 new (mostly African) members, it shifted further. By 1970 the Third World had an absolute majority, and the Latin American delegations, which formerly were found supporting the US position, normally voted with the Afro-Asian bloc, as members of the 'Group of 77', whose number had actually increased to 104 by 1975.

1/Rich nations and poor nations *(below)* The peoples of the world are here divided into categories according to Gross National Product per head. Per capita GPN is a useful but inaccurate index of wealth which often hides gross inequalities between different segments of the population within a single country. Nevertheless there is a close correlation between low per capita GNP and other indices of poverty and deprivation. Anything below $1000 indicates poverty.

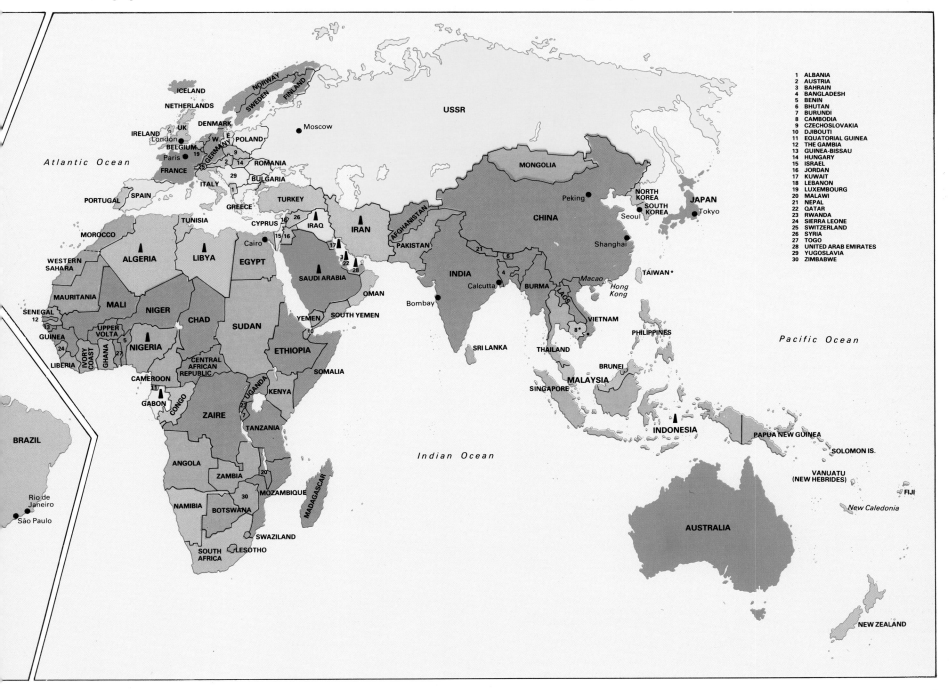

Acknowledgements

Acknowledgements and Bibliography: Maps

We have pleasure in acknowledging the following: Map 4, page 37, is based, with kind permission, on Professor P.A. Martin *American Population Explosion* Science Magazine 1973.

Map 4, page 55, is based, with permission, on a map on page 51 in W.H. McNeill, M.R. Buske, A.W. Roehm, *The World . . . . . its History in Maps*, Chicago 1969 © Denoyer-Geppert

Among the large number of works consulted by contributors, the following contain valuable maps and other data that have been particularly useful:

I. History Atlases

Atlas zur Geschichte 2 vols. Leipzig 1976
Bazilevsky, K.V., Golubtsov, A., Zinoviev, M.A. *Atlas Istorii SSR*, Moscow 1952
Beckingham, C.F. *Atlas of the Arab World and the Middle East*, London 1960
Bertin, J. (et al) *Atlas of Food Crops*, Paris 1971
Bjørklund, O., Holmboe, H., Røhr, A. *Historical Atlas of the World*, Edinburgh 1970
Cappon, L. (et al) *Atlas of Early American History*, Chicago 1976
Darby, H.C., Fullard, H. (eds.) *The New Cambridge Modern History* vol. XIV: Atlas, Cambridge 1970
Davies, C.C. *An Historical Atlas of the Indian Peninsula*, London 1959
Engel, J. (ed.) *Grosser Historischer Weltatlas* 3 vols. Munich 1953–70
Fage, J.D. *An Atlas of African History*, London 1958
Gilbert, M. *Russian History Atlas*, London 1972
Gilbert, M. *Recent History Atlas 1860–1960*, London 1966
Gilbert, M. *First World War Atlas*, London 1970
Gilbert, M. *Jewish History Atlas*, London 1969
Hazard, H.W. *Atlas of Islamic History*, Princeton 1952
Herrmann, A. *Historical and Commercial Atlas of China*, Harvard 1935
Herrmann, A. *An Historical Atlas of China*, Edinburgh 1966
Jedin, H., Latourette, K.S., Martin, J. *Atlas zur Kirchengeschichte*, Freiburg 1970
Joppen, C., Garrett, H.L.O. *Historical Atlas of India*, London 1938
Kinder, H., Hilgermann, W. *DTV Atlas zur Weltgeschichte* 2 vols. Stuttgart 1964 (published in English as *The Penguin Atlas of World History*, London 1974 & 1978)
Matsui and Mori *Ajiarekishi chizu*, Tokyo 1965
May, H.G. (ed.) *Oxford Bible Atlas*, Oxford 1974
McNeill, W.H., Buske, M.R., Roehm, A.W. *The World . . . . . its History in Maps*, Chicago 1969
Nelson's Atlas of the Early Christian World, London 1959
Nelson's Atlas of the Classical World, London 1959
Nelson's Atlas of World History, London 1965
Nihon rekishi jiten Atlas vol., Tokyo 1959
Palmer, R.R. (ed.) *Atlas of World History*, Chicago 1965
Paullin, C.O. *Atlas of the Historical Geography of the United States*, Washington 1932
Ragi al Faruqi, I. *Historical Atlas of the Religions of the World*, New York 1974
Roolvink, R. *Historical Atlas of the Muslim Peoples*, London 1957
Shepherd, W. R. *Historical Atlas*, New York 1964
Toynbee, A.J., Myers, E.D. *A Study of History, Historical Atlas and Gazetteer*, Oxford 1959
Treharne, R.F., Fullard, H. (eds.) *Muir's Historical Atlas*, London 1966
Van der Heyden, A.M., Scullard, H.H. *Atlas of the Classical World*, London 1959
Wesley, E.B. *Our United States . . . . . its History in Maps*, Chicago 1977
Westermann *Grosser Atlas zur Weltgeschichte*, Brunswick 1976
Whitehouse, D. & R. *Archaeological Atlas of the World*, London 1975
Wilgus, A.C. *Latin America in Maps*, New York 1943

II. General Works

Ahzweiler, H. *L'Asie Mineure et les Invasions Arabes*, Revue Historique 1962
Ajayi, J.F.A., Crowder, M. *History of West Africa* vols. 1 & 2 London 1974
Allchin, B. & R. *The Birth of Indian Civilisation*, London 1968
Australia, Commonwealth of, Department of National Development, *Atlas of Australian Resources*
Barraclough, G. *Medieval Germany*, Oxford 1938
Basham, A.L. *The Wonder that was India*, London 1967
Beresford, M. *New Towns of the Middle Ages*, London 1967
Berney, M. (ed.) *Australia*, Sydney 1965
Bloch, M. *Les Caractères Originaux de l'Histoire Rurale Française*, Oslo 1931
Boisselier, J. *La Statuaire du Champa*, Paris 1963
Braudel, F. *The Mediterranean and the Mediterranean World at the time of Philip II*, London 1972
Bury, J.B., Cook, S.A., Adcock, F.E. (eds.) *The Cambridge Ancient History*, Cambridge 1923–
Bury, J.B. Gwatkin, H.M., Whitney, J.P. (eds.) *The Cambridge Medieval History*, Cambridge 1911
Bussagli, M. *Paintings of Central Asia*, Geneva 1963
Chang, K.C. *The Archaeology of Ancient China*, New Haven & London 1968
Cheng Te-k'un *Archaeology in China*, Cambridge 1959
Churchill, Winston S. *The Second World War*, London 1948–53
Coedès, G. *Les Etats Hindouisés de l'Indochine et d'Indonésie*, Paris 1964
Cook, M.A. (ed.) *A History of the Ottoman Empire to 1730*, Cambridge 1974
Cresswell, K.A.C. *A Short Account of Early Muslim Architecture*, Oxford 1958
Crowder, M. *West Africa under Colonial Rule*, London 1968
Cumberland, K.B. *Aotearoa Maori: New Zealand about 1780*, Geographical Review no. 39
Curtin, P. de A. *The Atlantic Slave Trade*, Wisconsin 1969
Dalton, B.J. *War and Politics in New Zealand 1855–1870*, Sydney 1967
Darby, H.C. (ed.) *An Historical Geography of England before AD 1800*, Cambridge 1936 & 1960
Despois, J., Raynal, R. *Géographie de l'Afrique du Nord*, Paris 1967
Dyos, H.J., Aldcroft, D.H. *British Transport*, Leicester 1969
East, W.G. *The Geography behind History*, London 1965
East, W.G. *An Historical Geography of Europe*, London 1966
Edwardes, M. *A History of India*, London 1961
Evans, B.L. *Agricultural and Pastoral Statistics of New Zealand 1861–1954*, Wellington 1956
Ferguson, J. *The Heritage of Hellenism*, London 1973
Fisher, C.A. *South-East Asia*, London 1964
Fletcher, A. *Tudor Rebellions*, London 1968
Fowler, K. *The Age of Plantagenet and Valois*, New York 1967
Fourquin, G. *Histoire Economique de l'Occident Médiéval*, Paris 1969
Ganshof, F.L. *Etude sur le Développement des Villes entre Loire et Rhin au Moyen Age*, Paris–Brussels 1943
Geelan, P.J.M., Twitchett, D.C. (eds.) *The Times Atlas of China*, London 1974
Gernet, J. *Le Monde Chinois*, Paris 1969
Grousset, R. *The Empire of the Steppes: A History of Central Asia*, New Brunswick N.J. 1970
Guillermaz, J. *Histoire du Parti Communiste Chinois*, Paris 1968
Hall, D.G.E. *A History of South-East Asia*, London 1968
Harlan, J.R. *The Plants and Animals that Nourish Man*, Scientific American 1976
Harlan, J.R., Zohary, D. *The Distribution of Wild Wheats and Barleys*, Science 1966
Hatton, R.M. *Europe in the age of Louis XIV*, London 1969
Henderson, W.O. *Britain and Industrial Europe 1750–1870*, Liverpool 1954
Hopkins, A.G. *Economic History of West Africa*, London 1973
Inalcik, H. *The Ottoman Empire: The Classical Age 1300–1600*, London 1973
Jeans, D.N. *An Historical Geography of New South Wales to 1901*, Sydney 1972
Kennedy, J. *A History of Malaya 1400–1959*, London 1962
Kjölstad, T., Rystad, G. *5000 år: Epoker och utvecklingslinjer*, Lund 1973
Konigsberger, H., Mosse, G.L. *Europe in the sixteenth century*, London 1968
Laird, C.E. *Language in America*, New York 1970
Langer, W.L. *An Encyclopedia of World History*, London 1972
La Roncière (et al) *L'Europe au Moyen Age*, Paris 1969
Lattimore, O. *Inner Asian Frontiers of China*, New York 1951
Lyashchenko, P.I. *History of the National Economy of Russia to the 1917 Revolution*, New York 1949
Majumdar, R.C. *The Vedic Age*, Bombay 1951
Majumdar, R.C. *History and Culture of the Indian People, Age of Imperial Unity*, Bombay 1954
Macmillan's Atlas of South-East Asia, London 1964
McBurney, C.B.M. *Proceedings of the British Academy LXI* 1975
McIntyre, W.D., Gardner, W.J. *Speeches and Documents on New Zealand History*, Oxford 1970
McNeill, W.H., *A World History*, New York 1971
Meinig, D.W. *On the Margins of the Good Earth*, New York 1962, London 1963
Mellaart, J. *The Neolithic of the Near East*, London 1975
Ministry of Works *A Survey of New Zealand Population*, Wellington 1960
Miquel, A. *L'Islam et sa Civilisation*, Paris 1968
Morrell, W.P., Hall, D.O.W. *A History of New Zealand Life*, Christchurch 1957
Moss, H. St. L.B. *The Birth of the Middle Ages*, Oxford 1935
Mulvaney, D.J. *The Prehistory of Australia*, London 1975
Musset, L. *Les Invasions: Les Vagues Germaniques*, Paris 1965
Musset, L. *Les Invasions: Le Second Assaut contre l'Europe Chrétienne*, Paris 1971
The National Atlas of the United States of America, Washington DC 1970
Neatby, H. *Quebec, The Revolutionary Age 1760–1791*, London 1966
New Zealand Official Yearbook, Wellington 1893–
Ogot, B.A. (ed.) *Zamani, A Survey of East African History*, London 1974–1976
Oliver, R., Fagan, B. *Africa in the Iron Age c.500BC – AD 1400*, Cambridge 1975
Oliver, R., Atmore, A. *Africa since 1800*, Cambridge 1972
Ostrogorsky, G. *History of the Byzantine State*, Oxford 1956
Parker, W.H. *An Historical Geography of Russia*, London 1968
Piggott, S. *Prehistoric India to 1000 BC*, London 1962
Pitcher, D.E. *An Historical Geography of the Ottoman Empire*, Leiden 1973
Roberts, J.M. *The Hutchinson History of the World*, London 1976
Sanders, W.T., Marino, J. *New World Prehistory: Archaeology of the American Indian*, Englewood Cliffs, N.J. 1970
Saum, L.O. *The Fur Trader and the Indian*, London 1965
Seltzer, L.E. (ed.) *The Columbia Lippincott Gazetteer of the World*, New York 1952
Simkin, C.F. *The Traditional Trade of Asia*, Oxford 1968
Smith, C.T. *An Historical Geography of Western Europe before 1800*, London & New York 1960
Smith, W.S. *The Art and Architecture of Ancient Egypt*, London 1965
Snow, D. *The American Indians: their Archaeology and Prehistory*, London 1976
Stavrianos, L.S. *The World to 1500*, Englewood Cliffs, N.J. 1975
Stein, Sir Aurel *Travels in Central Asia*, London 1935
Stoye, J. *The Siege of Vienna*, London 1964
Stratos, A.N. *Byzantium in the seventh century*, Athens 1965
Tarn, W.W. *Alexander the Great*, Cambridge 1948
Tate, D.J.M. *The Making of South-East Asia*, Kuala Lumpur 1971
Thapar, R. *A History of India*, London 1967
The Times Atlas of the World, Comprehensive Edition, London 1976
Toynbee, A.J. (ed.) *Cities of Destiny*, London 1967
Toynbee, A.J. *Mankind and Mother Earth*, Oxford 1976
U.S. Strategic Bombing Survey, Summary Report (Pacific War), Washington 1946
Van Alstyne, R.W. *The Rising American Empire*, Oxford 1960
Van Heekeren, H.R. *The Stone Age of Indonesia*, The Hague 1957
Wadham, S., Wilson, R.K., Wood, J. *Land Utilization in Australia*, Melbourne 1964
Watters, R.F. *Land and Society in New Zealand*, Wellington 1965
Wheatley, P. *The Golden Khersonese*, Kuala Lumpur 1961
Wheeler, M. *Early India and Pakistan to Ashoka*, London 1968
Willey, G. *An Introduction to American Archaeology* vols. 1 & 2 Englewood Cliffs, N.J. 1970
Williams, M. *The Making of the South Australian Landscape*, London 1974
Wilson, M., Thompson, L. *Oxford History of South Africa* vols. 1 & 2 Oxford 1969, 1971

Acknowledgements: Illustrations

Unless stated to the contrary all the illustrations in this book are the work of the following artists: Peter Sullivan, David Case, John Grimwade, Tom Stimpson, Chris Fen, Chee Chai, Chris Burke, Ken Tan.

The publishers would like to thank the following museums, publishers and picture agencies for permission to base illustrations upon their photographs or to reproduce them. Where there is no such acknowledgement we have been unable to trace the source, or the illustration is a composition by our illustrators and contributors.

p.32 illustration based on a cave painting at Gargas, France
p.34 from K.P. Oakley *Man the Tool-Maker*, reproduced with kind permission of the Trustees of the British Museum (Natural History), London
p.35 from Cueva de los Caballos, near Castellón, Spain
p.37 The Times Picture Library
p.40 National Archaeological Museum, Athens
p.42 Hungarian National Museum, Budapest
p.47 University Museum, Philadelphia
p.53 a reconstruction by Seton Lloyd, *The Art of the Ancient Near East*, London 1961
p.55 Archive Photographique, Musée du Louvre, Paris
p.56 reproduced courtesy of the Trustees of the British Museum, London
p.59 The Cooper-Bridgeman Library, London (photograph)
p.63 *The Genius of China*, London 1973
p.65 National Museum of Pakistan, Karachi
p.70 Musée Guimet, Paris
p.75 National Archaeological Museum, Athens
p.81 *The Genius of China*, London 1973
p.86 Professor H.H. Scullard
p.102 from The Arch of Titus, Rome
p.106 Bibliothèque Municipale Classée de Cambrai, France
p.109 from Bernet Kempers *Ancient Indonesian Art*, Harvard University Press, 1959
p.116 Nationalmuseet, Copenhagen, Denmark
p.132 from D.G.E. Hall *A History of South-East Asia* London 1968
p.134 Kunsthistorisches Museum, Vienna
p.136 from Abraham Cresques *Catalan Atlas* 1375 (Bibliothèque Nationale, Paris)
p.138 Turkish miniature from the *Hünername*
p.141 from a woodcut from Schedel's *World Chronicle of 1493*, provided courtesy of the Czech Embassy, London
p.142 John Freeman, London
p.144 *Archiv der Hansestadt*, Lübeck 1256
p.145 Fugger Museum, Babanhausen, Germany
p.146 courtesy of Dr. P. Whitehouse, British School of Archaeology, Rome
p.148 top: reproduced courtesy of the Trustees of the British Museum, London
middle: American Museum of Natural History, New York
bottom: from L.C. Wyman *Sandpaintings of the Navaho Shootingway and the Walcott Collection*, Washington 1970, courtesy of the Department of Anthropology, Smithsonian Institution, Washington DC
p.157 The Cooper-Bridgeman Library, London
p.159 Museum für Völkerkunde, Vienna
p.162 from *Istoriya SSSR*, vol. 3, Moscow 1967
p.164 from A.F. Frezier *A Voyage to the South Seas and along the Coasts of Chile and Peru*, 1717
p.166 Holle Bildarchiv, Baden-Baden, Germany
p.170 Topkapi Saray Museum, Istanbul
p.173 The Chester Beatty Library and Gallery of Oriental Art, Dublin
p.177 National Portrait Gallery, London
p.180 *Scripta Mercaturae*, Munich 1972
p.183 Radio Times Hulton Picture Library, London
p.185 Larousse, Paris
p.190 Metropolitan Museum of Art, New York
p.201 left: Radio Times Hulton Picture Library, London
right: by courtesy, Science Museum, London
p.208 from *The Illustrated London News*, 1892
p.211 by courtesy, Science Museum, London
p.212 from *The Illustrated London News*, 1867
p.216 Statue, Hamburg, Germany
p.221 from a contemporary American painting
p.235 from Hutchinson's *Story of the British Nation*, London 1924/5?
p.242 provided by the Historiographical Institute, Tokyo
p.246 from *The New York Journal*, 1898 (Radio Times Hulton Picture Library)
p.248 Church Missionary Society, London
p.252 Imperial War Museum, London (photograph)
p.258 Popperfoto, London
p.269 top: Musée de l'Affiche, Paris
bottom: Museo Civico Luigi Bailo, Salce Collection, Treviso, Italy
p.272 based on a photograph by Yevgeni Khaldei
p.288 photograph by NASA/Space Frontiers

For the revised edition: Maps

We have pleasure in acknowledging the following:

Map 3, page 278, is based with permission on material reproduced from *Population Change in China* by Paul White, page 3, The Geographical Magazine, London, January 1984.

Map 4, page 289, is based with permission on *The Slowing of Urbanization in the US* by Larry Long and Diana DeAre, page 35, Scientific American, July 1983.

Illustrations

p.271 Keystone Press Agency, London

Glossary

This glossary is intended to provide supplementary information about some of the individuals, peoples, events, treaties, etc. which, because of lack of space, received only brief mention on the maps or in the accompanying texts. It is not a general encyclopaedia: only names mentioned in the atlas proper are included.

Names printed in **bold** type have their own glossary entries.

ABBAS I, THE GREAT (c.1557–1629) Shah of Persia. Attaining the throne in 1587, he reorganised and centralised the **Safavid** state. His reign was marked by cultural efflorescence and territorial expansion. Having crushed the rebellious **Uzbeks** (1597) he drove the **Ottomans** from their possessions in western Iran, Iraq and the eastern Caucasus (1603–7), and extended Safavid territories (temporarily) from the Tigris to the Indus. He moved the capital to Isfahan.

ABBASIDS Second major dynasty in Islam, displacing the **Umayyads** in 750. It founded a new capital, Baghdad, 762; its political control over the Islamic world, almost complete in the 9th and early 10th centuries, gradually decayed. Its rulers frequently became figureheads for other regimes: the last true caliph was killed by Mongols, 1258; later Abbasid caliphs, nominally restored in 1260, were merely court functionaries to Egypt's **Mameluke** sultans.

ABD AL KADIR (1808–83) (also known as Abd el-Kader and Abdal-Qadir). Algerian independence leader. He was elected in 1832 to succeed his father as leader of a religious sect; as emir, he took control of the Oran region, successfully fought the French, and in 1837 concluded the Treaty of Tafna; he extended his authority to the Moroccan frontier; renewed hostilities (1840–7) ended with his defeat and imprisonment, though he was freed in 1852.

ABD ALLAH (1846–99) Khalifa, or religious and political leader, in the Sudan after the death of the Mahdi in 1885. In 1880 he became a disciple of the **Mahdi Mohammed Ahmed**, whom he succeeded. As leader of the Mahdist movement he launched attacks on Egypt and Ethiopia; he consolidated power within the Sudan, building up an effective centralised state, until invaded by Anglo-Egyptian forces under Kitchener. He lost the battle of Omdurman in 1898, and was killed the following year while resisting Anglo-Egyptian troops.

ABD EL-KRIM (1882–1963) Founded Republic of the Rif (1921–26), the North African precursor of many 20th-century independence movements. His forces defeated major French and Spanish armies until overwhelmed, in May 1926, by 250,000 Franco-Spanish troops. He was exiled to Réunion, but escaped to Egypt where he was given political asylum in 1947.

ABDUL HAMID II (1842–1918) Last important Ottoman sultan, 1876–1909. He carried further some lines of modernisation already begun, and used Islamic sentiment to resist European encroachments. The revolt by **Young Turks** in 1908 against his autocratic rule led to his deposition, 1909; he was imprisoned at Salonika, 1910, and died in Istanbul eight years later.

ABRAHAM First of three patriarchs of the **Jews** (Abraham, his son Isaac, Isaac's son Jacob). Born in Ur, he flourished in the early 2nd millennium BC. He journeyed to Canaan (Palestine), the land promised by God to his descendants. According to much later tradition, he was considered to be the progenitor of the Arabs through his other son, Ishmael.

ABREU, ANTONIO DE 16th-century Portuguese navigator, who in 1512 discovered the Banda Islands, Indonesia, during an exploratory voyage to the Moluccas.

ABU BAKR (c.573–634) Close friend and adviser to **Mohammed**, and said to have been the first male convert to Islam. He became Mohammed's father-in-law, and accompanied him on the historic journey to Medina in 622. Accepted after Mohammed's death as caliph –

'deputy of the Prophet of God'; under his two-year rule central Arabia accepted Islam and the Arab conquests began, with expansion into Iraq and Syria.

ABUSHIRI REVOLT An insurrection in 1888–9 by the Arab population of those areas of the East African coast which were granted by the sultan of Zanzibar to Germany in 1888. It was eventually suppressed by an Anglo-German blockade of the coast.

ACHAEMENIDS Ancient Persian dynasty of Fars province. **Cyrus II the Great**, a prince of the line, defeated the **Medes** and founded the Achaemenid Empire, 550–330 BC. Descended traditionally from Achaemenes (7th century BC), the senior line of his successors included Cyrus I, Cambyses I, Cyrus II and **Cambyses II**, after whose death in 522 BC the junior line came to the throne with **Darius I**. The dynasty was extinguished with the death of Darius III after defeat by **Alexander the Great** in 330 BC.

ACHESON, DEAN (1893–1971) US Secretary of State, 1949–53. He was responsible for many important policy initiatives under President **Truman**, including the implementation of the **Marshall Plan**, the **North Atlantic Treaty Organisation**, non-recognition of Communist China and the rearming of West Germany.

ADAMS, JOHN (1735–1826) Second President of the United States, 1797–1801. A leading advocate of resistance to British rule before the American War of Independence, in 1776 he seconded the Declaration of Independence. He was American envoy to Britain, 1785–8, and author of *Thoughts on Government* (1776).

ADAMS, JOHN QUINCY (1767–1848) Sixth President of the United States, 1825–9. The son of **John Adams** he was Secretary of State, 1817–25; in this post he contributed to the shaping of the **Monroe Doctrine**. In 1843 he led the opposition to the annexation of Texas.

AESCHYLUS (525/4–456 BC) Athenian dramatist, who also fought at the **battle of Marathon**, 490 BC. He wrote at least eighty plays, mostly tragedies, of which seven survive in full: *The Persians, The Seven against Thebes, The Suppliants, The Oresteia* trilogy and *Prometheus Bound*. He was the creator of tragic drama.

ÆTHELRED II (d.1016) King of Wessex, England, from 978. His reign was marked by a steady increase in Danish influence; in 1013 he fled to Normandy and the English recognised the Danish king, **Sven Forkbeard**, as their ruler.

AFGHANI, JAMAL AD-DIN AL- (1838–97) Muslim agitator, reformer and journalist. Born in Persia, he was politically active in Afghanistan, Istanbul and Cairo. Exiled from Egypt in 1879 for political reasons, he published (1884) *The Firmest Bond*, a periodical attacking British imperialism and advocating Islamic reform. Exiled from Persia in 1892, he spent his remaining years in Istanbul; he instigated the assassination of the Shah in 1896.

AGHLABIDS Muslim Arab dynasty, ruling much of North Africa from 800 to 909. They controlled Tunisia and eastern Algeria, conquered Sicily in 827 and invaded southern Italy. They were finally defeated and replaced by the **Fatimids**.

AGIS IV (c.262–239 BC) King of Sparta who attempted to introduce a 'communist' programme of land redistribution and debt cancellation in 243 BC. Tricked by an unscrupulous uncle and unable to complete his reforms quickly enough, he was forced to

leave the country for war with the Aetolians in 241; in his absence a counter-revolution put his enemies in power, and after a mock trial he was executed.

AGUINALDO, EMILIO (1869–1964) President of the short-lived Philippine Republic (1898–1901). Of mixed Chinese and Tagalog ancestry, he fought Spanish rule as leader of the revolutionary Katipunan Society. Exiled in 1897, he returned, first to co-operate with US forces, and then to lead a three-year insurrection. He was captured and deposed in 1901. In 1945 he was briefly imprisoned for supporting Japanese occupation. He became a member of the Philippine Council of State in 1950.

AGUNG, SULTAN Third ruler of Mataram, the Muslim kingdom which in the 17th century dominated central and much of eastern Java. He sought an alliance against Bantam, and when this was refused attacked Batavia (now Jakarta), founded in 1619 by the **Dutch East India Company**. Defeated there in 1629, he undertook the Islamisation of eastern Java by force; but failed in all attempts to conquer Bali, which remained loyal to traditional Hindu-Buddhist culture.

AGUSTÍN I Emperor of Mexico: *see* Iturbide.

AHMADU SEFU (c.1835–97) Son and successor of **al-Hajj Umar** (d.1864), a Tukolor chief whose kingdom was on the upper Niger. He came to power some years after his father's death, but his kingdom was eventually destroyed by the French in the 1890s.

AHMED GRAN (c.1506–42) Muslim conqueror in 16th-century Ethiopia. He gained control of the Somali Muslim state, Adal, and declared a *jihad* (holy war) against Christian Ethiopia. By 1535, with help from Turkish troops and firearms, he had seized three-quarters of the country, and in 1541 defeated a Portuguese relief force. He was killed in battle against the new Ethiopian leader, Galawdewos.

AHMOSE see **Amosis I**

AIDAN, ST (d.651) Born in Ireland, he trained as a monk at Iona, off the Isle of Mull, West Scotland. He was consecrated bishop of the newly-converted Northumbrians in 635; he established his church and monastery on Lindisfarne, off the north-east coast of England, from where evangelists set out to convert large areas of northern England, under the protection of kings Oswald and Oswin of Northumbria.

AIGUN, TREATY OF Agreement reached in 1858 by which China ceded the north bank of the Amur river to Russia. Together with further gains under the **Treaty of Peking** (1860), this gave Russia access to ice-free Pacific waters; the port of Vladivostok was founded in 1860.

AIX-LA-CHAPELLE, TREATY OF Agreement reached in 1748 which concluded the War of the Austrian Succession; Austria ceded Silesia to Prussia, Spain made gains in Italy, and **Maria Theresa** was confirmed as Empress of Austria.

AKBAR (1542–1605) Greatest of India's **Mughal** emperors. Born in Umarkot, Sind, he succeeded his father, Himayun, in 1556. During his reign he consolidated Mughal rule throughout the sub-continent, winning the loyalty of both Muslims and Hindus; at his death he left superb administrative and artistic achievements, including the fortress-palace at Agra and the magnificent but now deserted city of Fatehpur Sikri.

AKHENATEN XVIIIth Dynasty Egyptian pharaoh, reigning 1379–62 BC; the son of Amenhotep III, he took the throne as Amenhotep IV. He promoted the monotheistic cult of Aten, the god in the sun disc; changed his name c.1373 BC and transferred the capital from Thebes to the new city of Akhetaten (El-Amarna). With his wife, Nefertiti, and six daughters, he devoted the rest of his reign largely to the cult of Aten, dangerously neglecting practical affairs.

AKKADIANS Name given to a wave of Semitic-speaking immigrants from the west, of increasing prominence in Mesopotamia from the first third of the 3rd millennium. **Sargon** of Agade was of Akkadian origin.

AKKOYUNLU Turcoman tribal federation, ruling eastern Anatolia, Azerbaijan and northern Iraq from c.1378 to 1508. The dynasty, whose name means 'white sheep', was founded by Kara Yüllük Osman (ruled 1378–1435), who was granted control over the Diyarbakir region of Iraq by **Timur** in 1402. Under Uzun Hasan (1453–78) they expanded at the expense

of the **Karakoyunlu** ('black sheep') but were defeated by the Ottomans in 1473; they finally succumbed to internal strife and to pressure from the **Safavids**.

AL- For all Arabic names prefixed by al-, see under following element.

ALANS Ancient people, first noted in Roman writings of the 1st century AD as warlike, nomadic horse-breeders in the steppes north of the Caucasus Mts. They were overwhelmed by the **Huns** in 370; many Alans fled west, reaching Gaul with the **Vandals** and **Suebi** in 406, and crossing into Africa with the **Vandals** in 429.

ALARIC I (c.370–410) **Visigothic** chief and leader of the army that captured Rome in AD 410. Born in Dacia, he migrated south with fellow-tribesmen to Moesia, and briefly commanded a Gothic troop in the Roman army. Elected chieftain in 395, he first ravaged the Balkans and then, in 401, invaded Italy; the 'sack' of Rome, following a decade of intermittent fighting, negotiation and siege, was in fact relatively humane and bloodless, as Alaric's main aim was to win land for the settlement of his people.

ALARIC II (d.507) King of the **Visigoths**. From his accession in AD 484 he ruled Gaul south of the Loire and all Spain except Galicia. He issued a code of laws known as the Breviary of Alaric. He died after defeat by **Clovis**, king of the Franks, at the Battle of Vouillé, near Poitiers.

ALAUDDIN KHALJI (d.1316) Sultan of Delhi who usurped the throne in 1296 from the sons of Jalaluddin. His was a unifying rule in northern India, with heavy taxes and a standing army; he began the Muslim penetration of the south, and repelled a series of Mongol invasions between 1297 and 1306.

ALAUNGPAYA (1752–60) King of Burma known as Alaungpaya the Victorious, and founder of the Konbaung dynasty which ruled until the British annexation of 1886. He rose from the position of village headman to lead resistance against invading Mons of Lower Burma; recaptured the Burmese capital, Ava, in 1753, finally seizing Pegu, the Mon capital, in 1757; massacred staff of the **English East India Company's** trading settlement on the island of Negrais, 1759. He was mortally wounded during the siege of the Siamese capital, Ayutthaya.

ALBIGENSIANS (Albigenses) Members of a heretical Christian sect, following the **Manichaean** or **Cathar** teaching that all matter is evil. Strongly entrenched in southern France around the city of Albi in the 12th century, they were subjected to violent attack by northern French nobles in the Albigensian Crusade.

ALBUQUERQUE, AFONSO DE (1453–1515) Portuguese empire-builder. Appointed Governor-General of Portuguese India in 1509, he seized Goa and several Malabar ports, 1510; Malacca and the coast of Ceylon, 1511.

ALEMANNI Germanic tribe which in the 5th century AD occupied areas now known as Alsace and Baden; defeated in 496 by the Franks under **Clovis**.

ALEXANDER THE GREAT (356–23 BC) Most famous conqueror of the ancient world. The son of **Philip II of Macedon** he was taught by **Aristotle**. Succeeding his father in 336, he reaffirmed Macedonian dominance in Greece and between 334 and 323 BC led his armies all but 'through to the ends of the earth'. He was only thirty-two when he died in Babylon. His victories, though never consolidated into a world empire, spread Greek thought and culture throughout Egypt, northern India, central Asia and the eastern Mediterranean. His body, sealed in a glass coffin and encased in gold, was preserved in Alexandria, the city he founded as his own memorial, but the tomb has never been located.

ALEXANDER I (1888-1934) King (1921–34) of the Serbo-Croat-Slovene state whose name he changed to Yugoslavia in 1929. Prince Regent of Serbia, 1914–21, enthroned in 1921, he established a royal dictatorship in 1929; he was assassinated.

ALEXANDER II (1818–81) Tsar of Russia. The son of Nicholas I, he succeeded in 1855. He emancipated the serfs in 1861, and introduced legal, military and local government reforms; he extended the Russian frontiers into the Caucasus (1859) and Central Asia (1865–8), and defeated Turkey in the last of the Russo-Turkish wars (1877–8). He was assassinated.

ALEXANDER II (1198–1249) King of Scotland, son of William I the Lion. He succeeded to the throne in 1214, and sided with the rebel English barons against **King John** in the following year. He paid homage to Henry III in 1217, and in 1221 married his sister Joan. Under the Peace of York, which he concluded in 1237, Scotland abandoned English land claims and the border was fixed in more or less its present position.

ALEXANDER III (d.1181) Pope 1159–81. Distinguished canon lawyer, at one time professor at the University of Bologna. As Pope, he opposed secular authority over the Church, allying successfully with the cities of Lombardy against Emperor **Frederick I Barbarossa** imposed a penance on **Henry II** of England for the murder of Thomas Becket, Archbishop of Canterbury.

ALEXIUS I COMNENUS (1048–1118) Byzantine emperor who seized the imperial throne in 1081. He was victorious over the Normans of Italy and the **Pecheneg** nomads; revived the Byzantine economy; founded the Comnene dynasty, and reluctantly accepted the arrival of the First **Crusade** in the East (1096–7).

ALFONSO X, THE WISE (1221–84) King of Castile and León, succeeding to the throne in 1252. He promulgated the *Siete Partidas*, Spain's great mediaeval code of laws; captured Cádiz and the Algarve from the Moors.

ALFRED THE GREAT (849–99) King of Wessex, England, succeeding his brother, Aethelred I, in 871. The early part of his reign was spent in hard struggle against Danish (Viking) invaders, in which he was gradually successful; Wessex itself was freed by 878, London retaken in 885, and the country divided on the line London-Chester. A notable lawgiver, he encouraged learning, vernacular translations of Latin classics and the compilation of an historic record, the Anglo Saxon Chronicle; he also created many fortifications, a fast, mobile army and the beginnings of a fleet.

ALI (c.600–61) Mohammed's cousin, second convert and son-in-law (married to the Prophet's daughter, **Fatima**), who became fourth caliph after the murder of Othman in 656. His accession led to civil war; he was murdered by a dissident supporter, Ibn Muljam. His descendants' claim to be imams, heirs of the Prophet as leaders of the community, still divides Islam (see **Shi'is**).

ALLENBY, EDMUND HENRY HYNMAN (1861–1936) 1st Viscount; British field marshal. After service in France he commanded British forces in Palestine, 1917–18; he conducted a successful campaign against the Ottoman Turks culminating in the capture of Jerusalem (9 December 1917), victory at Megiddo (September 1918), and the capture of Damascus.

ALLENDE GOSSENS, SALVADOR (1908–73) Chilean statesman, elected president, 1970, becoming the world's first democratically-chosen Marxist head of state. He instituted a major programme of political, economic and social change, but ran into increasing opposition both at home and abroad, and was killed during the successful right-wing military *coup d'état* which brought to power General **Pinochet**.

ALMOHADS Berber dynasty ruling North Africa and Spain, 1130–1269, inspired by the religious teachings of Ibn Tumart. It defeated the **Almoravids**, 1147, and established its capital at Marrakesh; captured Seville, 1172. Its control over Islamic Spain was largely destroyed by the Christian victory of Las Navas de Tolosa in 1212.

ALMORAVIDS Saharan Berbers who built a religious and military empire in north-west Africa and Spain in the 11th and 12th centuries, after halting the advance of Castilian Christians near Badajoz, 1086; they ruled all Muslim Spain except El Cid's Christian Kingdom of Valencia. Their sober, puritanical style of art and architecture replaced the exuberant work of the **Umayyads** whose Córdoba government collapsed in 1031.

ALTAN KHAN (1507–82) Mongol chieftain who terrorised China during the 16th century. He became leader of the Eastern Mongols in 1543; in 1550 he crossed the Great Wall into northern China, and established his capital, Kuku-khoto (Blue City) just beyond the Wall; he concluded a peace treaty with China in 1570. In 1580 he converted the Mongols to the *Dge-bugs-pa* (Yellow Hat) sect of Lamaism, a mystical Buddhist doctrine originating in Tibet, and gave the head of the sect the title of Dalai ('all-embracing')Lama.

ALTMARK, ARMISTICE OF Truce concluded in May 1629 ending the war (since 1621) between Sweden and Poland. Sweden won the right to levy tolls along the Prussian coast, but renounced this when the agreement was renewed for twenty-six years in 1635.

AMBROSE, ST (c.339–97) He served as governor of Aemilia-Liguria, in northern Italy, c.370–4; appointed bishop of Milan in 374, he was frequently in conflict with imperial authority. His writings laid the foundation for mediaeval thinking on the relationship between Church and state.

AMHARIC The most widely spoken language of Ethiopia, of Semitic origin, derived from Geez, a southern Arabian tongue related to Arabic and Hebrew, and still used in the liturgy of the Ethiopian Orthodox Church. It displaced and partially absorbed the indigenous Cushitic languages of the western highlands.

AMIN DADA, IDI (1925–) President of Uganda. He joined the British army in 1946, and was promoted to commander of the Ugandan army in 1965. He seized power in 1971 during the absence of President Milton Obote. He expelled all Asians (1972) and most Britons (1973). Having survived revolts against his repressive regime, in 1979 Ugandan exiles seized power and (1980) restored Dr. Obote.

AMORITES Nomads of the Syrian desert, who settled in Mesopotamia and took over political supremacy from the **Sumerians** at the beginning of the 2nd millennium BC.

AMOSIS I Founder of Egypt's XVIIIth Dynasty. He completed the expulsion of **Hyksos** after the death of his brother, Kamose, Reigned c. 1570–46 BC; with the aid of his mother, Queen Ahhotep, who may have acted as co-regent early in his reign, he extended Egyptian control into Palestine and Nubia, and reopened trade with Syria. He died leaving the country prosperous and reunited.

AMSTERDAM EXCHANGE BANK Important early financial institution founded in 1609 with an official monopoly of foreign currency dealings in the city. It played a key part in the development of monetary instruments and commercial credit in western Europe.

ANAXAGORAS (c.500–c.428 BC) Greek philosopher. He taught a theory of cosmology based on the idea that the universe was formed by Mind; his particulate theory of matter opened the way to atomic theory. He was exiled as part of a political attack on his friend **Pericles**, perhaps c.450 BC, after suggesting that the sun was an incandescent stone.

ANGEVINS Dynasty of English kings, often known as the Plantagenets, beginning with **Henry II** (reigned 1154–89). Descended from Geoffrey, Count of Anjou, and Matilda, daughter of Henry I; the direct line ended with **Richard II** (reigned 1377–99).

ANGLO-SAXONS Term originally coined to distinguish the Germanic tribes ruling England from 5th to 11th centuries AD, from the Saxons of continental Europe, the Angles and the Saxons being the most prominent of the invaders; later extended to mean 'the English' and their descendants all over the world.

AN LU-SHAN (703–57) Rebel Chinese general. Of Sogdian and Turkish descent, in 742 he became military governor of the north-eastern frontier districts. After the death of his patron, the emperor's chief minister Li Lin-fu, in 752, great rivalry developed between him and the courtier Yang Kuo-chung; in 755 he turned his 160,000-strong army inwards and marched on the eastern capital, Lo-yang, proclaiming himself emperor of the Great Yen dynasty in 756 and capturing the western capital, Ch'ang-an. He was murdered by the next year. The rebellion petered out by 763, but resulted in the serious weakening of the authority of the **T'ang** dynasty.

ANSKAR or Ansgar (801–65) Frankish saint, known as 'the Apostle of the North', who conducted missions to the Danes (826) and Swedes (829); first archbishop of Hamburg, 834.

ANTI-COMINTERN PACT Joint declaration by Germany and Japan, issued on 25 November 1936, that they would consult and collaborate in opposing the **Comintern** or Communist International. It was acceded to by Italy in 1937, and later became the instrument by which Germany secured the loyalty of its Romanian, Hungarian and Bulgarian satellites and attempted to bind Yugoslavia.

ANTIGONUS III DOSON (c.263–21 BC) King of Macedonia from 227 BC, who created and led the Hellenic League (founded 224 BC) which defeated **Cleomenes III** of Sparta.

ANTIOCHUS III (242–187 BC) Seleucid king of Syria, who succeeded his brother, Seleucus III, in 223. After an inconclusive war with Egypt, he conquered Parthia, northern India, Pergamum and southern Syria, and invaded Greece (192), but was decisively driven back by the Romans at Thermopylae and defeated at Magnesia in Asia Minor (190). By his death the empire had been reduced to Syria, Mesopotamia and western Persia.

ANTONY (c.82–31BC) Marcus Antonius, best known as Mark Antony. A member of a prominent Roman family, he became joint consul with **Julius Caesar** in 44 BC; after Antony's defeat of Caesar's murderers, Brutus and Cassius, at Philippi, he controlled the armies of the Eastern Empire; started liaison with **Cleopatra**; war broke out between him and Octavian, 32 BC. He committed suicide after naval defeat at Actium.

APACHE Indian hunters and farmers, located in the North American south-west. They probably originated in Canada, reaching their main hunting grounds, west of the Rio Grande, some time after the year 1000. The main groupings were the Western Apache, including the Mescalero and Kiowa tribes, and the Eastern Apache, including the Northern and Southern Tonto. In the colonial period they proved an effective barrier to Spanish settlement, and under such leaders as Cochise, Geronimo and Victorio in the 19th century figured largely in the frontier battles fought in the American advance westward. After Geronimo's surrender in 1886 the remaining survivors became prisoners of war in Florida and Oklahoma; after 1913 they were allowed to move to reservations in Oklahoma and New Mexico.

APAMEA, PEACE OF Agreement ending the Syrian War between Rome and Seleucia; signed after the battle of Magnesia in 190 BC. The Seleucid king, **Antiochus III**, paid an indemnity of 15,000 talents, surrendered his elephants and ships, and ceded all Asia Minor west of the Taurus Mts.

APOLLONIUS (c.295–c.230 BC) Poet and director of the library at Alexandria in the 3rd century BC; known as 'Rhodius' because he chose to retire to the island of Rhodes. His four-book epic, the *Argonautica*, tells the story of Jason's quest for the Golden Fleece.

ARABIAN AMERICAN OIL COMPANY (ARAMCO) Joint venture, set up in 1936 by **Standard Oil** of California and Texaco to exploit petroleum concessions in Saudi Arabia. It is now among the most powerful oil groups in the world, with additional partners Exxon and Mobil. In 1974 the Saudi Arabian government acquired a 60 per cent stake in the company and in 1979 took complete control. The services of the four US companies were retained to operate the production facilities on behalf of the government. ARAMCO has the ability to produce over 11 million barrels of oil a day.

ARABI PASHA (1839–1911) Egyptian military leader. After service in the Egyptian-Ethiopian War, 1875–6, he was made a colonel; he joined the officers' mutiny, 1879, against **Ismail Pasha**, and in 1881 led the movement to oust Turks and Circassians from high army posts. Minister of War, 1882, he quickly became a national hero with his slogan *Misr lil Misriyin* ('Egypt for the Egyptians'); he was commander-in-chief, 1882, when the British navy bombarded Alexandria, and was defeated on 13 September at Tell-el-Kebir by British troops under Sir Garnet Wolseley. He was captured and sentenced to death, but instead was exiled to Ceylon.

ARAB LEAGUE Association of Arab states, with its headquarters in Tunis. Founded in 1945 by Iraq, Trans-Jordan, Lebanon, Saudi Arabia, Egypt, Syria and Yemen (now the Arab Republic of Yemen), it was later joined by other states as they became independent: Algeria, Bahrain, Djibouti, Kuwait, Libya, Mauritania, Morocco, Oman, Qatar, Somalia, Sudan, Tunisia, United Arab Emirates, People's Democratic Republic of Yemen. The PLO has also been a full member since 1976, and Egypt was expelled in 1978.

ARAUCANIANS (sometimes known as the Mapuche). A warlike Indian tribe in southern Chile which successfully resisted many Inca and Spanish incursions. The first native group to adopt the Spaniards' horses, they became brilliant cavalry fighters, and in 1598 three hundred mounted Araucanians wiped out a major Spanish punitive expedition. They retained effective independence, despite numerous Spanish and Chilean attempts to subdue them, until the late 19th century.

ARBENZ GUZMÁN, JACOBO (1913–71) Guatemalan political leader of Swiss immigrant parentage. He rose to the rank of colonel in the Guatemalan army; played a leading role in the democratic revolution of 1944, becoming Minister of Defence, 1945, and President of Guatemala, 1951; he inaugurated a radical left-wing land reform programme. He was overthrown in a United States-backed military coup in 1954.

ARCHILOCHUS Greek satirical poet, writing about 700 BC; many fragments of his work survive.

ARCHIMEDES (c.287–12 BC) Greek mathematician and scientist. Born in Syracuse, he studied in Alexandria. He calculated the upper and lower limits for the value of π; devised a formula for calculating the volume of a sphere; invented, among many other things, Archimedes' Screw, for raising large quantities of water to a higher level, and also Archimedes' Principle, which enabled him to discover, with a cry of 'Eureka!' the impurity in King Hiero's crown by weighing it in and out of water in comparison with pure gold and pure silver. He returned to Sicily to design weapons and defence strategies for King Hiero, and was killed during the Roman siege of his native city.

ARDASHIR I (d.241) Founder of the Sasanian Empire of Persia; born in the late 2nd century AD. Ardashir took the crown of Persis in 208. He rapidly extended his territory, defeating his Parthian overlords at Hormizdagan in 224, and occupying their capital, Ctesiphon. He made Zoroastrianism the state religion.

ARIANISM see Arius

ARISTOPHANES (c.450–c.380 BC) Athenian comic dramatist. Eleven of some forty plays survive, including *The Frogs, The Birds* and *Lysistrata;* they are highly political, brilliant in language and verse, dramatic situation, parody, satire, wit and farce, sparing neither men nor gods.

ARISTOTLE (384–22 BC) Greek philosopher and scientist. Born in Thrace, he studied in Athens under Plato. He taught the young **Alexander the Great**, then established his Lyceum in Athens, 335, and founded the Peripatetic school of philosophy. He was an outstanding biologist. His voluminous works, covering almost every aspect of knowledge, survive mainly in the form of lecture notes, edited in the 1st century AD.

ARIUS (c.AD250–336) Originator of the Christian doctrine known as Arianism, later condemned as the Arian heresy. A pupil of Lucian of Antioch, he taught that the son of God was a creature, not consubstantial or coeternal with the Father. He was excommunicated for these views by the provincial synod of Alexandria in 321, unsuccessfully defended his belief in 325 before the **Council of Nicaea** and was banished. He died on the point of being reinstated by the Emperor **Constantine**. His controversial teachings divided the Church for many centuries.

ARKWRIGHT, SIR RICHARD (1732–92) English inventor and pioneer of the factory system, who invented the water-frame (1769) and other mechanised spinning processes.

ARMENIANS Indo-European people occupying in ancient times the area now comprising north-eastern Turkey and the Armenian Soviet Socialist Republic. They were converted to Christianity in the late 3rd century. Armenians boast a highly distinctive culture, which flowered particularly during periods of national independence and reached a peak in the 14th century. In 1915 the entire Armenian population of Asia Minor (about 1,750,000 people) was deported by Turkey to Syria and Mesopotamia – almost 600,000 died.

ARMINIUS (c.18 BC–AD 21) German tribal chief and early national hero, known also as Hermann. He became leader of the Cherusci after service and honour with Roman forces; in AD 9 he defeated and massacred three Roman legions at the battle of Teutoburg Forest; held off Roman attacks, 16–17 AD, but was murdered by his own people during a war with the Marcomanni, another German tribe. Described by Tacitus as *liberator haud dubie Germaniae* ('undoubtedly the liberator of Germany').

ARNOLD OF BRESCIA (c.1100–55) Radical theologian and religious reformer who studied under Peter Abelard and was condemned with him at the Council of Sens in 1140. He later moved to Italy where, in alliance with the citizens of Rome, he strongly attacked Pope **Eugenius III** and forced him to leave the city. He was captured and executed at pope's request by **Frederick Barbarossa**. His leading anti-clerical argument was that spiritual persons should not possess temporal goods.

ÁRPÁD Magyar dynasty, ruling Hungary from late 9th century to 1301; named after Árpád, who was chosen in 889 to lead seven Magyar tribes westward from their homeland on the river Don. Under Béla III (1172–96), Hungary was established as a major central European power, but was later weakened by the Mongol invasion (1241–42); the dynasty died out with Andrew III (1290–1301), who left no heir.

ARTAXERXES II MNEMON (c.436–358 BC) King of Persia, son of Darius II (reigned 423–404); he changed name from Arsaces on his accession in 404. He was challenged by his brother, Cyrus the Younger (c.430–401), but defeated and killed him at Cunaxa, near Babylon, 401.

ARTEVELDE, JACOB VAN (c.1295–1345) Flemish leader during the early phases of the **Hundred Years War.** In 1338 he emerged as one of five 'captains' governing the town of Ghent; formed an alliance with the English king, **Edward III,** against France and the Count of Flanders; ruled as chief captain until killed in a riot.

ARYA SAMAJ Hindu reform movement; its followers reject all idolatrous and polytheistic worship and insist on the sole authority of the **Vedas.**

ARYAN Contentious term used at various times to describe (1) a member of the Caucasian race from which the Indo-European peoples supposedly sprang; (2) in **Hitler's** Germany, a member of the so-called 'master' or 'Nordic' race. Correctly applied to the Indo-Iranian branch of the eastern Indo-European group of languages, and at one time to the hypothetical parent language of that group.

ASHANTI (Asante) One of several states of Akan-speaking peoples of southern Ghana, Togo and Ivory Coast. Also an independent kingdom in southern Ghana in the 18th and 19th centuries, taking an active part in the Atlantic slave trade. Ultimately failing to resist British penetration, it was annexed in 1901, and is now an administrative region of Ghana.

ASHANTI WARS Engagements fought in 1824–7, 1873–4, 1893–4 and 1895–6 between the West African kingdom of Ashanti, which originated in the 17th century, and the British, at first to prevent Ashanti expansion into the British (coastal) colony of the Gold Coast, and subsequently as resistance by the Ashanti to the attempted imposition of British rule over them. Final annexation of Ashanti came in 1901; it is now a province of independent Ghana.

ASHKENAZIM From the Hebrew word *Ashkenaz*, meaning Germany. It refers to the Jews of the Germanic lands, many of whom emigrated eastward in the Middle Ages. Today it represents most of the Jews of Europe, the British Commonwealth, the United States, the USSR, South America and approximately half the Jewish population of Israel. The word is used in distinction to **Sephardim,** who have slightly different customs and rites.

ASHOKA *see* **Asoka**

ASHURNASIRPAL II (d.858 BC) King of Assyria, 884–858 BC, who began the 1st millennium expansion of the Assyrian Empire to the Mediterranean. Monuments and inscriptions describe with great frankness the harsh treatment of conquered peoples in ancient warfare. He created Calah (Nimrud) as his new capital.

ASIENTO Monopoly granted to an individual or company for the exclusive supply of Negro slaves to the Spanish colonies in America. The first asiento was signed by the Spanish court with Genoese entrepreneurs in 1517, later it passed mainly to the Portuguese until 1640, and then in succession to the French Royal Guinea Company and to the British South Sea Company (until 1750). It was finally extinguished in 1793, when all Spanish colonial trade was freed from central control.

ASKIA THE GREAT (d.1538) Founder of the Askia dynasty, rulers of the Songhay Empire, centred round the capital of Gao in present day Mali, from 1492-1591. He rose to power in 1493, reigning as Mohammed I Askia; he promoted the spread of Islam in his domains and made a pilgrimage to Mecca in 1495–7. He was deposed in 1528 by his sons, led by Askia Musa.

ASOKA (Ashoka) (d. 232 BC) Greatest of the Mauryan emperors of early India, succeeding his father, **Bindusara**, in 272 BC. In 260 BC, he inflicted a crushing defeat on Kalinga (modern Orissa) the last major independent Indian state. He was converted to **Buddhism**, and developed a policy of toleration and non-violence, renouncing conquest.

ASSASSINS European name given to the Nizari branch of the Ismailis, organised by the leader of the 'new preaching', Hadan-i Sabbah (died 1124). They ruled parts of northern Persia and coastal Syria from strongholds of which Alamut in Persia was the most important, and played a part in the general history of Persia and Syria, partly because of their practice of killing opponents (hence 'assassination'). The leader of the Syrian group was known to Crusaders as the 'Old Man of the Mountains'. Their political power was ended by the Mongols in Persia, and by the **Mamelukes** in Persia.

ASSYRIANS Warlike people of northern Mesopotamia, remarkable for fighting prowess, administrative efficiency (after 745 BC) – which made possible the control of an empire of unprecedented size – and for the magnificent bas-reliefs in their palaces. They formed an independent state in the 14th century BC, and under the Neo-Assyrian Empire dominated much of the Near East until destroyed by a Chaldaean-Mede coalition in 612 BC. In modern times the term is applied to an ancient Christian sect, found chiefly in Iraq and Iran, whose members claim to be descended from the ancient Assyrians.

ASTURIAS, KINGDOM OF Founded in 718 in the extreme north of Spain by a group of Visigothic nobles after the Muslim invasions. Expanded and established on a firm basis under Alfonso I (739–57), it included north-western Spain and northern Portugal. For almost two hundred years it remained the sole independent Christian bastion in Iberia; it survived many attacks and, particularly under Alfonso III (866–910), began to push its frontier further south. After 910 it was continued as the kingdom of León.

ATAHUALLPA (c.1502–33) Last independent ruler of the **Inca** Empire in Peru. He was given the subsidiary kingdom of Quito on the death of his father, **Huayna Capac**; he fought a war with his brother **Huascar**, and deposed him in 1532, just before the Spaniards invaded the Inca realms. Taken prisoner by **Francisco Pizarro,** he was accused of complicity in his brother's murder and was executed.

ATATÜRK (1881–1938) Founder and first President of the republic of Turkey. Originally named Mustapha Kemal, he was born in Salonika; he graduated from Istanbul Military Academy, 1902. He resigned from the army in 1919 to support the Turkish independence movement, and in the same year was elected president of the National Congress. After British and Greek occupation (1920), he opened the first Grand National Assembly, was elected first President and Prime Minister, and directed operations in the Greco-Turkish War of 1920–22. After the peace treaty of 1923 he abolished the Ottoman caliphate and began a far-reaching reform and modernisation programme. He took the name Atatürk, 'Father of the Turks', in 1934.

ATHANASIUS (c.296–373) Theologian, statesman and saint, born in Alexandria (Egypt). He attended the **Council of Nicaea,** 325, and was appointed bishop of Alexandria in 328. He became both Egyptian national leader and the chief defender of orthodox Christianity against the heresy of Arianism. His major writings include a *Life of St Antony*, a short treatise *On the Incarnation of the Word*, and *Four Orations against the Arians*.

ATTALUS III (d.133 BC) Last independent king of Pergamum, reigning 138–133 BC. On his deathbed be bequeathed his kingdom to Rome, which then (129) organised it into the province of Asia.

ATTILA (c.406–53) Sole ruler of the vast **Hun** empire after the murder of his brother Bleda c.445. He overran much of the Roman Empire, reaching Orléans in Gaul, 451, and the river Mincio in Italy, 452; his empire collapsed after his death.

ATTLEE, CLEMENT (1883–1967) British Prime Minister. Educated at Oxford University, he briefly practised law, then spent 1907–22 (apart from war service) working among the poor in London's East End. He became Mayor of Stepney, 1919 and a Member of Parliament, 1922; a junior minister in the Labour governments of 1924 and 1929–31; and was a member of **Churchill's** War Cabinet. As Prime Minister, 1945–51, he presided over the establishment of the Welfare State in Britain and the granting of independence to India, Pakistan, Burma and Ceylon; he relinquished British control of Egypt and Palestine. He was created Earl Attlee in 1955.

AUGUSTUS (63 BC – AD 14) First Emperor of Rome, born Gaius Julius Caesar Octavianus; great-nephew, adopted son and heir of **Julius Caesar.** With **Antony** and Lepidus he emerged victorious in the civil war against Brutus and Cassius, after Caesar's murder. He broke with Antony and defeated him at Actium in 31 BC; offered sole command in Rome, he brought peace and prosperity to the empire, over which he effectively ruled from 27 BC until his death.

AUGUSTINE OF HIPPO, ST (354–430) Leading thinker of the early Christian Church. After a restless youth, recorded in his *Confessions*, he was converted in 386, baptised by **St Ambrose** the following year, and in 396 appointed Bishop of Hippo, in North Africa. His greatest work, *The City of God*, was written between 413 and 426 as a philosophic meditation on the sack of Rome by the **Visigoths** in 410.

AURANGZEB (1618–1707) Last of India's great Mughal emperors. Son of the emperor **Shahjahan;** he succeeded in 1658 after a struggle with his brothers. Up to 1680 he successfully consolidated power over Hindu and Muslim subjects, but later his empire began to disintegrate through rebellions, wars with the **Rajputs** (erstwhile allies) and the **Marathas;** his reversal of the traditional policy of tolerance towards the Hindus contributed to his difficulties.

AUSTRIAN WAR After making peace with France in 1805, Austria re-entered the Napoleonic Wars in 1809, but after a few months was totally defeated by France at Wagram.

AUSTRO-SERBIAN 'PIG WAR' Tariff conflict in 1906–11 between Austria-Hungary and Serbia, which also fomented anti-Habsburg agitation in Montenegro (occupied by Austria in 1878) and Bosnia (occupied in 1908).

AVVOCATI (or Avogadro) Prominent family of mediaeval Vercelli, Italy. Supporters of the **Guelph** (anti-imperial) party, they were engaged in a semi-permanent feud with their Ghibelline (pro-imperial) rivals until in 1335 the city came under the control of the **Visconti** of Milan.

AXUM Ancient city and kingdom of northern Ethiopia, an offshoot of one of the Semitic states of southern Arabia in the last millennium BC. By the start of the Christian era it was the greatest ivory market of north-east Africa. Converted to **Christianity** in the 4th century AD, it was gradually transformed, after the Muslim conquest of the Red Sea littoral in 10th century, into the modern Amhara state of Ethiopia.

AYYUBIDS Sunni Muslim dynasty, founded by **Saladin.** It ruled Egypt, Upper Iraq, most of Syria and Yemen from Saladin's death in 1193 until the **Mameluke** rise to power (1250).

BABUR (1483–1530) Founder of the **Mughal** dynasty of Indian emperors. Son of the ruler of Ferghana, central Asia, he lost this territory while seeking to conquer Samarkand (1501–4). He captured Kandahar, strategic point on the northern road to India, 1522; occupied Delhi, 1526, and established himself on the imperial throne. He wrote poetry and his memoirs.

BACSONIAN AND HOABINHIAN Stone Age cultures of South-East Asia, characterised by the fact that their typical implements and artefacts are worked on one side only. They were named after two provinces of northern Vietnam, Bac Son and Hoa Binh, where the largest concentrations of examples have been found.

BAFFIN, WILLIAM (c.1584–1622) English navigator; sailed (1612) with Captain James Hall's expedition in search of the North-West Passage; in 1615 and 1616, with **Captain Robert Bylot,** he penetrated the waters between Canada and Baffin Island, and deep into Baffin Bay, both named after him; working for the **East India Company** he surveyed the Red Sea and the Persian Gulf.

BAGHDAD PACT *see* **Central Treaty Organisation.**

BAIBARS (1223–77) Mameluke sultan, ruling Egypt and Syria, 1260–77. Born among the **Kipchak** Turks north of the Black Sea, he was sold as a slave to an Egyptian soldier. He fought and held both Crusaders and Mongols before seizing the throne.

BAKEWELL, ROBERT (1725–95) English animal-breeder who revolutionised the development of meat-bearing strains in sheep and cattle. His successes included the Leicester Longhorn cow (now superseded by the Shorthorn) and the heavy, barrel-shaped Leicester sheep. He was the first man to commercialise large-scale stud-farming.

BALAIADA Revolutionary uprising, 1838–41, in Maranhão province, Brazil; it was finally suppressed by the imperial general, Duque de Caxias.

BALBAN (1207–87) Sultan of Delhi, originally a junior member of the Forty, made up from personal slaves of Iltutmish, who divided the kingdom after his death. He acted as deputy to Sultan Nasiruddin Mahmud (reigned 1246–66), whom he succeeded; he ably consolidated Muslim power, despite continual war with **Rajputs,** Mongols and Hindu states.

BALFOUR DECLARATION Letter from Britain's Foreign Secretary, Arthur Balfour, dated 2 November 1917, to Lord Rothschild, a leader of British Jewry, stating British support for the establishment in Palestine of a national home for the Jewish people, provided that the rights of the non-Jewish communities be respected. Approved at the San Remo Conference in 1920, it was incorporated into the mandate over Palestine granted to Britain by the **League of Nations** in 1922.

BALKAN LEAGUE The outcome of bilateral agreements made by Bulgaria with Serbia, Greece and Montenegro, leading to the Balkan Wars against Turkey, 1912-13. It collapsed completely in June 1913 when Bulgaria attacked Greece and Serbia in the hopes of preventing them from acquiring the bulk of Macedonia.

BALKAN WAR, FIRST War that largely expelled the Ottomans from Europe. Montenegro, Bulgaria, Greece and Serbia attacked the Ottoman Empire in October 1912; by December only the fortresses of Adrianople, Scutari (Shkodër) and Janina (Yannina) remained in Turkish hands, and they too were lost to Turkey by the Treaty of London (May 1913) which also, at Austrian insistence, created the Albanian state to keep Serbia from the Adriatic.

BALKAN WAR, SECOND War among the victors of the First Balkan War over the division of Macedonia, June-August 1913. Romania intervened on the side of Greece and Serbia against Bulgaria, which suffered heavy defeat recorded in the Treaty of Bucharest (10 August 1913); meanwhile, the Turks took the opportunity of regaining Adrianople from Bulgaria.

BALKE, HERMANN (d. 1239) Provincial master of the **Teutonic Order,** who began the conquest of the pagan Prussians in 1231, at the head of a crusading army.

BAMBARA Also known as Banmana. West African people from the Upper Niger region of the Republic of Mali. Their spoken language is derived from the **Mande** group, but their method of writing is distinctive, as is its associated cosmological system. The Bambara states, Segu (founded c.1600) between the Senegal river and the Niger, and Kaarta (c.1753) on the Middle Niger, flourished until the mid-19th century.

BANDARANAIKE, SOLOMON (1899–1959) Prime Minister of Ceylon, 1956-9. He resigned from the Western-orientated United National Party in 1951 to form the nationalist Sri Lanka Freedom Party; in 1956 his People's United Front, an alliance of four nationalist-socialist groups, won a sweeping electoral victory. As Prime Minister he replaced English with Sinhala as the official language, fostered **Buddhism,** and established diplomatic relations with Communist states. He was assassinated, and succeeded by his widow.

BANK OF ENGLAND Central financial institution of Great Britain. It was founded in 1694 with the initial object of lending King William III £1,200,000 at 8 per cent. Originally a private, profit-making institution, its public responsibilities were extended and defined by Bank Charter Acts of 1833 and 1844; it was finally transferred to public ownership in 1946.

BANTU A large group of closely related languages, spoken by the majority of the black inhabitants in Africa south of the Equator. By association, the term is sometimes applied to the people themselves, especially in South Africa.

BAPTISTS Members of a Christian Protestant movement dating from the 16th century. They are now represented by many churches and groups of churches throughout the world, organised in independent congregations. Many follow the practice of baptism by total immersion, and insist that the rite should take place only when the initiate is old enough to appreciate its significance.

BARAKZAI Tribal group from which emerged Afghanistan's ruling dynasty, from 1837 to 1973. The brothers who founded the dynasty seized control of the country in 1826 and divided it between them; Dost Mohammed Khan consolidated and unified the family rule, c.1837, and his direct descendants held the throne until 1929 when, after the abdication of the reigning monarch, succession passed to a cousin's line; the military coup of 1973 overthrew the monarchy and a republic was declared.

BARBAROSSA Name of two Greek brothers, famous as Algerian Muslim pirates. Barbarossa I (c.1473–1518), was killed by the Spaniards after a series of raids on the Spanish coast; Barbarossa II, also known as Khair ed-Din (c.1466–1546) took over command on his brother's death and in 1519 became a vassal of the Ottoman sultan, for whom he repulsed an invasion by the emperor **Charles V** in 1541.

BARDI Important Florentine family, established there in the 11th century, which flourished in trade and finance, especially from the mid-13th to the mid-14th century. It became the greatest merchant and banking company in Europe at that time, and exercised considerable political influence. Defaults on debt payments by **Edward III** of England and by Florence finally led to bankruptcy and collapse in 1345.

BARENTS, WILLEM (c.1550–97) Dutch explorer of the Arctic, who in 1594 and 1595 rounded northern Europe to reach the Novaya Zemlya archipelago. He is remembered particularly for his charting of northern waters; the Barents Sea is named after him.

BARTH, HEINRICH (1821–65) German geographer and explorer. After travels in Tunisia and Libya (1845–7), he set off on a British-sponsored expedition across the Sahara. Returning after 10,000 miles, he wrote *Travels and Discoveries in North and Central Africa* (1857–8), still one of the richest sources of information on the area. He became Professor of Geography at Berlin in 1863.

BASIL I (d.886) Byzantine emperor. Of peasant stock, he was the founder of the Macedonian dynasty, so called from his place of origin. He rose to be co-emperor with Michael III in 866, but murdered Michael in 867. He began formulating the legal code (completed by his son, **Leo VI**) known as the Basilica.

BASIL II (958–1025) Most powerful of Byzantium's Macedonian emperors. He was crowned co-emperor with his brother Constantine in 960; claimed sole authority, 985; extended Byzantine rule to the Balkans, Mesopotamia, Georgia and Armenia. His conquest of the Bulgarian Empire earned him the nickname 'Bulgar Slayer'.

BASTIDAS, RODRIGO (1460–1526) Spanish explorer who discovered the mouths of the Magdalena river in modern Colombia, and founded the Colombian city of Santa Marta.

BATLLE Y ORDÓÑEZ, JOSE (1856–1929) President of Uruguay. He founded a newspaper, *El Día*, 1886; elected President in 1903, by a narrow margin, he emerged victorious from the ensuing civil war (1904–5), and was re-elected, 1905–7, and again, after freely stepping down, 1911–15. He inaugurated a wide-ranging programme of social and economic reform; defeated over constitutional reform in 1918, he went on to serve as president of the national executive council in 1920 and 1926.

BATU KHAN (d.1255) Leader of the Golden Horde. The grandson of **Genghis Khan**, in 1235 he was elected western commander-in-chief for the Mongol Empire, and entrusted with the invasion of Europe. By 1240 he had conquered all Russia; by 1241, after defeating Henry II, Duke of Silesia, and the Hungarians, he was poised to advance further west. However, on hearing of the death of **Ogedei** (December 1241) he withdrew his forces to take part in the choice of successor. He later established the Kipchak khanate, or the **Golden Horde,** in southern Russia.

BAYEZID I, YILDIRIM (c.1360–1403) Known as 'the Thunderbolt'. Ottoman ruler. Succeeding to the throne in 1389, he claimed the title of sultan and attempted to establish a strong centralised state based on Turkish and Muslim institutions. He conquered large areas of the Balkans and Anatolia; blockaded Constantinople, 1391–8; invaded Hungary, 1395, and crushed at Nicopolis in 1396 the Crusaders sent to repel him. He was defeated by **Timur's** Mongol armies at Ankara in 1402, and died in captivity, with his empire poised between his sons and the restored Anatolian principalities.

BAYEZID II (c.1447–1512) Ottoman sultan, succeeding to the throne in 1481. His reign marked a reaction from the policies of his father **Mehmed II**. The conquest of Kilia and Akkerman (1484–5) gave the Ottomans control over the mouth of the Danube and the land route from Constantinople to the Crimea; the later years of Bayezid's reign were taken up by war with Venice (1496–1503), by growing social unrest in Anatolia connected with the rise of the **Safavids** under their leader Ismail, and by the struggle among the sons of Bayezid for the succession to the Ottoman throne.

BEAUMANOIR, PHILIPPE DE RÉMI, SIRE DE (c.1246–96) French administrator and jurist; wrote *Coutumes du Beauvoisis* (c.1280–3), one of the earliest codifications of French law.

BELGAE Ancient Germanic and Celtic people, inhabiting northern Gaul; some emigrated to southern Britain in the first century BC. Gallic Belgae were conquered by **Julius Caesar** in 57 BC, the British in 55–54 BC.

BELGRADE, TREATY OF Peace agreement of 1739 ending the Turkish-Austrian war of 1737-9. Austria surrendered most of its gains under the **Treaty of Passarowitz,** and thus re-established the line of the rivers Danube and Save as the frontier between the two empires.

BELISARIUS (c.494–565) Byzantine general. Under Emperor Justinian I he swept the **Vandals** out of North Africa and **Ostrogoths** out of Italy (533–40); repulsed Persian assaults (541–2).

BELL, JOHN (1797–1869) Nominee for President of the United States on the eve of the American Civil War. He entered Congress, 1827; became Secretary for War, 1841, and a US senator, 1847–59. He opposed the extension of slave-holding, though a large owner himself; nominated on a Constitutional Union ticket, 1860, he was classed as a rebel after advocating Southern resistance to war.

BENEDICT OF NURSIA, ST (480–546) Founder of a Christian monastic order. He became a hermit, but c.529 decided to form a monastic community, which he established at Monte Cassino in Italy, and for which, in the 530s, he composed the Benedictine Rule (a relatively short document of 73 chapters) which has served as the basic of Christian monastic organisation.

BEN GURION, DAVID (1886–1973) Israeli labour leader, politician and statesman; born in Poland. He became active in **Zionist** affairs; emigrated to Palestine in 1906 and became secretary-general of the labour movement in 1921. In the struggle to found an independent Jewish state he cooperated with the British during the Second World War but led political and military struggle against them, 1947-48. He was the first Prime Minister (and also Minister of Defence) of the new state of Israel, 1948-53, and again 1955-63. He continued to exert an influence as its founding father and elder statesman in retirement from the Negev Kibbutz of Sede Boker until his death.

BENTHAMITE Follower of the English utilitarian philosopher Jeremy Bentham (1748–1832). Benthamite thinking, summed up in the concept of the Pleasure Principle ('men seek pleasure and avoid pain') and the belief that institutions should be judged by their ability to promote 'the greatest happiness of the greatest number', influenced many later legal and political reforms.

BERBERS Original peoples of North Africa, who were colonised by Rome. Invaded by the Arabs in the 7th century AD, they were converted to Islam after some resistance. Those in or near cities were gradually absorbed into Arabic culture, but Berber languages continue to be spoken, particularly in mountain and pastoral regions of Morocco and Algeria.

BERING, VITUS JONASSEN (1681–1741) Danish navigator and discoverer of Alaska. After a voyage to the East Indies, he joined the Russian navy of **Peter the Great**; in 1724 he was appointed by the tsar to establish whether Asia was joined to North America, and in 1728 sailed through the strait which now bears his name, into the Arctic Ocean. He died when his ship was wrecked on Bering Island, east of the Kamchatka peninsula.

BERLIN, CONGRESS OF Meeting of European statesmen in June-July 1878 under the presidency of **Bismarck** to revise the Treaty of **San Stefano** (1878), concluded by Russia and Turkey. Bulgaria, greatly reduced in extent, was constituted as an autonomous principality. The independence of Romania, Serbia and Montenegro was confirmed. Austro-Hungary was given the right to occupy Bosnia and Herzegovina, and Russia was confirmed in its possession of Ardahan, Kars and Batum.

BERNARD, ST (c.1090–1153) He entered the Cistercian Order in 1113, only fifteen years after the foundation of the monastery of Citeaux, and soon became its leading light. Two years later he founded the monastery of Clairvaux, also in south- eastern France, and remained its abbot for the rest of his life. Through personal influence, teaching and voluminous writings he dominated the theological and to a large extent also the political life of his times, particularly by securing the recognition of Innocent II as Pope in 1130, by advice to his former pupil **Eugenius III** (Pope 1145–53), and by preaching the second **Crusade** in 1147.

BESANT, ANNIE (1847–1933) Theosophist, social reformer and Indian independence pioneer. She was a Fabian Socialist, with George Bernard Shaw, in the late 1880s, and was converted to the theosophic ideas of Helen Blavatsky, 1889–91. She spent much of her remaining life in India, jointly founding the Indian Home Rule League in 1916.

BESSEMER, SIR HENRY (1813–98) British inventor of the Bessemer steel-making process. He developed various mechanical devices, including a movable date stamp, and in the Crimean War the first rotary shell. In 1856 he announced a process for purifying molten iron with a blast of air; with contributions from other innovators, his work made possible the Bessemer converter and the mass production of cheap steel.

BETANCOURT, RÓMULO (1908–81) Venezuelan political leader. Imprisoned while a student, and exiled to Colombia, he returned in 1936 to lead the anti-Communist left-wing underground movement; again exiled, 1939–41, in 1941 he organised Acción Democrática (AD), and became president of the revolutionary governing junta after the overthrow of President Medina Angarita, 1945. Forced yet again into exile by the Pérez Jiménez regime, 1948–58, he became President of Venezuela, 1959–64.

BHONSLAS Dynasty of **Maratha** rulers in western India, founded by the family of **King Sivaji.** They were leaders in the 18th-century Maratha confederacy formed to resist the British; later they became British clients (1816–53).

BINDUSARA (d.272 BC) Early Indian emperor, succeeding his father, **Chandragupta Maurya,** in 297 BC. He campaigned in the Deccan, as far south as Mysore, and brought most of the sub-continent under Mauryan control.

BISMARCK, PRINCE OTTO VON (1815–98) German statesman, known as 'the Iron Chancellor'. He was appointed Minister-President of Prussia, 1862; after wars against Denmark (1864) and Austria (1866), he formed the North German Confederation (1867), and after the **Franco-Prussian War** (1870–1) inaugurated the German Empire (1871–1918). As German Chancellor (1871–90) he instituted important social, economic and imperial policies and played a leading role in the European alliance systems of the 1870s and 1880s.

BLACK FLAGS Chinese bandits and mercenary groups active in Annam and Tongking, 1873-5, led by Liu Yung-fu, a former T'ai-p'ing rebel. Called on by the mandarins of Hanoi to oppose the French (1873), they were responsible for the defeat and death of several French commanders during a decade of bitter guerilla war.

BLACKFOOT INDIANS A group of Indian tribes of Algonquin stock. They were one of the strongest Indian confederations in the early 19th century but were gradually defeated and subdued by the US settlers. Their name derived from the colour of their moccasins.

BLAKE, ROBERT (1599–1657) English admiral; he commanded **Cromwell's** navy in the English Interregnum, and defeated the Dutch and the Spanish.

BLIGH, WILLIAM (1754–1817) British vice-admiral. He served on Captain **James Cook's** last voyage; he was commanding the *Bounty* when the crew mutinied in 1789 in the South Seas and set him adrift in an open boat. On his voyage of exploration of 1791 he made discoveries in Tasmania, Fiji and the Torres Straits. He fought at Gibraltar (1782), Camperdown (1797) and Copenhagen (1801). He was governor-general of New South Wales, 1805-8, from which post he was deposed by force and imprisoned until 1810.

BLITZ Second World War term for a sudden attack, particularly from the air; derived from the German word *Blitzkrieg*, or lightning war.

BOETHIUS (c.480–524) Early mediaeval scholar and statesman, born in Rome. He was appointed consul under **Theodoric** the Ostrogoth in 510. He translated **Aristotle's** *Organon* and helped to preserve many classical texts; he wrote on music, mathematics and astronomy. His **Christianity,** clear from some short treatises, does not inform his larger works. After falling from favour with Theodoric, he wrote in prison his *De consolatione philosophiae*. He was executed on charges of treason.

BOGOMILS Balkan religious sect, flourishing from the 10th to the 15th century. It inherited **Manichaean** doctrines from the **Paulicians;** believed the visible world was created by the devil; rejected baptism, the Eucharist, the Cross, miracles, churches, priests and all orthodox Christianity. Its leader, Basil, was publicly burned in Constantinople c.1100. Adopted by the ruling class in Bosnia, it also directly influenced the **Cathars** in Italy and **Albigensians** in France; it died out after the Ottoman conquest of south-east Europe.

BOLESLAV I CHROBRY, 'THE BRAVE' (966–1025) First fully-accepted king of Poland, son of **Miesko I.** He inherited the principality of Greater Poland, 992; reached the Baltic, 996, and seized control of Cracow and Little Poland; crowned by Emperor **Otto III,** 1000, he was embroiled in wars, 1002–18, with Emperor Henry II over lands seized in Lusatia, Meissen and Bohemia. He defeated Grand Prince Yaroslav I of Kiev (1018), and placed his son-in-law on the Kievan throne.

BOLÍVAR, SIMON (1783–1830) Venezuelan soldier-statesman who freed six South American countries from Spanish rule. He participated in Venezuela's declaration of independence in 1811, fleeing to Haiti after the Spanish counter-revolution; liberated New Granada (Colombia) in 1819; Venezuela, 1821; Ecuador, 1822; Peru, 1824; and Upper Peru, renamed Bolivia, in 1825. A liberal political thinker but an autocratic ruler, he failed in his real ambition to establish a union of Spanish-American peoples: most of the nations he had helped to create were in turmoil or conflict when he died.

BOLSHEVIKS Named from *Bolsheviki*, Russian for 'those of the majority', the name adopted by **Lenin**'s supporters in the Russian Social-Democratic Workers' Party at the 1903 Congress when, advocating restriction of membership to professional revolutionaries, they won a temporary majority on the central committee. From 1912 they constituted a separate party. Seizing control of Russia in October 1917, in March 1918 they adopted the name 'Communists'

BONAPARTE *see* **Napoleon I**

BONIFACE VIII (c.1235–1303) Pope, 1294–1303. He reasserted papal claims to superiority over temporal powers; his Bull *Clericis laicos* (1296) led to conflict with **Edward I** of England, and particularly with **Philip IV** of France, over taxation of the clergy, but the dispute soon widened to cover the whole relationship of Church and state. He was briefly kidnapped at Anagni by the French, 1303, but soon released; to escape repetition of such treatment, the papacy took up residence at Avignon – the so-called 'Avignon Captivity'.

BONIFACE, ST (c.675–754) Often called the Apostle of Germany. Born in Wessex, England; ordained priest c.705 under his original name of Wynfrith; he left England (716) to evangelise the Saxons. He was sent first into Hesse and Thuringia by Pope Gregory II (722–35), and then by Gregory III into Bavaria. He became Archbishop of Mainz, 751; organised German and reformed Frankish churches. He was martyred by pagan **Frisians**.

BOONE, DANIEL (1734–1820) American frontiersman, explorer and fighter in Kentucky and Missouri. He created the wilderness road, north-west of the Appalachians.

BOSE, SUBHAS CHANDRA (1897–1945) Indian nationalist leader. Educated Calcutta and Cambridge, England; he was imprisoned (1924–7) for his part in **Gandhi's** non-cooperation movement; on his release was elected president of Bengal's provincial congress. Most of the next decade was spent in prison or exile, but he became head of the Indian National Congress in 1938; under house arrest (1940), he escaped to Germany. He formed an Indian volunteer force to attack the Western allies, and in 1943, with Japanese support, invaded India from Rangoon. He died two years after his defeat, in an air crash in Taiwan.

BOURBONS European ruling family. Descended from Louis I, Duc de Bourbon (1279–1341), grandson of King **Louis IX** of France (reigned 1226–70), the Bourbons themselves held the thrones of France (1589–1791 and again 1814–48), Spain (more or less from 1700 to 1931), and Naples and Sicily (1735–1860).

BOURGUIBA, HABIB (1903–) Tunisian politician. He became a journalist in 1930 on a paper which advocated self-government for Tunisia. He founded his own Neo-Déstour party in 1934 to achieve independence from France, but was imprisoned 1934–6, 1938–45 and 1952–4, and in exile 1945–9. He became first Prime Minister of independent Tunisia in 1956–7, and its first President from 1957 onwards.

BOXER REBELLION Chinese peasant uprising in 1900, aiming to drive out all foreign traders, diplomats and particularly missionaries. The name is derived from a secret society, the I-ho-ch'üan (Right and Harmonious Fists), which had earlier violently opposed the ruling **Ch'ing** (Manchu) dynasty, but in 1899 began to attack westerners. On 18 June 1900, as hostilities grew, the Empress Dowager ordered all foreigners killed; hundreds were besieged in the Peking legation quarter until relieved on 14 August by an international expeditionary force, which then looted the capital. Peace and reparations were finally agreed in September 1901.

BRACTON, HENRY DE (died c.1268) Mediaeval English jurist, judge of King's Court under Henry III (1247–57). Author of *De legibus et consuetudinibus Angliae* ('On the laws and customs of England'), one of the oldest and most influential treatises on common law.

BRADDOCK, EDWARD (1695–1755) English general who in 1754 was appointed to command all British land forces in North America; he was ambushed (with his army) and killed by mixed French and Indian forces while leading an expedition against Fort Duquesne.

BRAHMA Hindu creator of the universe who, with **Vishnu** and **Shiva**, forms the leading trinity of Hindu gods.

BRAHMO SAMAJ Hindu theistic society, founded in 1830 by the religious reformer, **Rammohan Roy**. It split into two in 1865, when the philosopher Keshub Chunder Sen (author of *The Brahmo Samaj Vindicated*) founded a separate branch known as 'Brahmo Samaj of India'. It was the earliest modern reform movement in India, reflecting nationalist ideas.

BRASSEY, THOMAS (1805–70) English railway contractor; trained as a surveyor, in 1835 he built the Grand Junction line, and later helped to the finish the London-Southampton link. Starting with the Paris-Rouen line (1841–3), he went on to build railway systems all over the world, including the 1100-mile Grand Trunk in Canada (1854–9).

BRAZZA, PIERRE SAVORGNAN DE (1852–1905) Piedmontese explorer and coloniser who made pioneering journeys through equatorial Africa, 1873–7. He negotiated treaties with African chiefs which were then taken up by the French, whose service Brazza subsequently entered, governing for France the region north of the Congo, 1887–97.

BRECKINRIDGE, JOHN CABELL (1821–75) Unsuccessful Southern Democrat candidate for the United States presidency on the eve of the American Civil War (1861–5). Born in Kentucky, he entered the US Congress in 1851; Vice-President to James Buchanan, 1857–61; US Senator, 1861; expelled after joining the Confederate army. He served as brigadier, major-general and later, Secretary for War in the Confederacy; fleeing to England at the end of hostilities, he returned in 1868.

BREDA, TREATY OF Inconclusive agreement, signed 31 July 1667, ending the Second Anglo-Dutch War (1665–7). France, which had supported Holland, gave up Antigua, Montserrat and St Kitts, in the West Indies, to Britain, but recovered Acadia (now Canada's Maritime Provinces); England acquired New York and New Jersey from the Dutch; Holland won valuable sea-trading concessions.

BREST-LITOVSK, TREATY OF Peace agreement, signed March 1918, between Russia and the Central Powers. Russia recognised the independence of Poland, Georgia, the Baltic States and the Ukraine, and agreed to pay a large indemnity. The treaty was declared void under the general armistice of 1918.

BREZHNEV, LEONID ILICH (1906–82) Soviet leader. He joined the Communist party, 1931; became Red Army political commissar, major-general, 1943; a member of the Communist Party Central Committee, 1952. He succeeded **Khrushchev** as First Secretary of the Party, 1964; enunciated the Brezhnev Doctrine to justify invasion of Czechoslovakia, 1968, by Warsaw Pact forces; replaced Podgorny as President of the USSR, 1977–82.

BRIAN BORUMA (c.941–1014) High King of Ireland. He succeeded as ruler of a small Irish kingdom, Dal Cais, in 972, and also of Munster. Brian defeated Ivar, the Norse king, in Inis, Cathaig in 977; attacked Osraige (982); was recognised as ruler of southern Ireland (997) and by 1005 claimed his position as king of all Ireland. He was killed after the Battle of Clontarf.

BRITAIN, BATTLE OF Series of aerial encounters between the German Luftwaffe and the British Royal Air Force, mainly over southern England, fought between July and October 1940. As a result of Germany's failure to win air mastery, plans for a seaborne invasion of Britain were abandoned.

BRONZE AGE In the Old World, the first period of metal-use, based on copper and its alloys. Beginning in the Near East and Europe after 2000 BC, and independently in south-eastern Asia at the same time, this technology spread among both peasant and urban societies – Bronze Age civilisations included Sumer, Egypt, the Indus, and Shang China.

BROOKE, SIR JAMES (1803–68) Founder of a dynasty of 'white rajahs' in Sarawak, north-west Borneo. He served with the **English East India Company's** army in the Burma War 1824–6; assisted the Rajah of Brunei in suppressing various rebellions, and in 1843 was made Rajah of Sarawak.

BRUCE see **Robert I** of Scotland

BRUNHILDE (c.545–613) Twice regent of Austrasia and for a period the most powerful ruler in **Merovingian** France. The daughter of Athanagild, Visigothic king in Spain, she married Sigebert, son of Lothar, king of the Franks. The murder of her sister, Galswintha, precipitated a forty-year civil war in Gaul; the deaths of her husband and her son, **Childebert II**, placed her at the head of affairs. She was driven from Austrasia by palace officials in 599, and in 613 executed by being tied to a wild horse.

BRÜNING, HEINRICH (1885–1970) German statesman. He became leader of the Catholic Centre Party, 1929, and formed a conservative government in 1930 without a Reichstag majority. After parliamentary rejection of his major economic plans, he began to rule by presidential emergency decree. He resigned the chancellorship in May 1932 after the failure of both his foreign and his domestic policies.

BRUSATI Prominent family of mediaeval Novara, Italy. Supporters of the **Guelph** (anti-imperial) party, they enjoyed a brief supremacy in the city 1305–15, but were overcome by their Ghibelline (pro-imperial) rivals, supported by the **Visconti** family in neighbouring Milan.

BRUSILOV, ALEKSEY ALEKSEYEVICH (1853–1926) Russian general who led the famous Russian offensive against Austria-Hungary in June-August 1916; he became the supreme Russian commander in 1917. Under the **Bolsheviks** he directed the war against Poland, 1920; he retired in 1924 as inspector of cavalry.

BRUSSELS PACT Defensive alliance of 1948 providing for military, economic and social co-operation, signed by France, Great Britain and the Benelux countries.

BRYAN, WILLIAM JENNINGS (1860–1925) Three times unsuccessful candidate for the presidency of the United States. Entering politics in 1888, he quickly won a reputation as a Populist orator; he was elected to Congress in 1890. He won his first presidential nomination in 1896, at the age of thirty-six; defeated then, and again in 1900 and 1908, he remained a leading political figure; and was appointed Secretary of State to **Woodrow Wilson** in 1913. As a pacifist, he resigned in 1915 when the US protested to Germany over the sinking of the *Lusitania*.

BUDDHA, GAUTAMA (c.563–483 BC) Founder of the world religion known as **Buddhism**. Born on the modern border between India and Nepal, the son of a nobleman of the Hindu Kshatriya caste, traditionally he was inspired to change his life at the age of twenty-nine by the sight of an old man, a sick man, a corpse and an itinerant ascetic. In the Great Renunciation he gave up his privileges and for six years practised extreme asceticism, then abandoned it in favour of deep meditation, receiving enlightenment as he sat under a tree. The remainder of his life was spent teaching and serving the order of beggars which he founded.

BUDDHISM Religious and philosophic system based on the teachings of Gautama, the **Buddha**, who rejected important features of his native **Hinduism** in the 6th century BC. In his first sermon at Benares he preached the Four Noble Truths and the abandonment of desire and sorrow by systematic pursuit of the Noble Eightfold Path, the ultimate end of which is Nirvana, the destruction of all desire and anguish. This remains the basis for the Dharma or Teaching, carried out through the Samgha or monastic Order. Since the Buddha's death the religion has developed along two distinct and sometimes conflicting lines: Theravada (or Hinayana), in South-East Asia, stressing monasticism and avoiding any taint of theism or belief in a god; and Mahayana, in China, Japan, Tibet and Korea, which embraces more personal cults.

BUGANDA Former kingdom and later administrative region, occupying 44,835 km² of present-day Uganda, inhabited largely by the Baganda tribe. It was an important independent power from the 17th to the 19th century, becoming a British protectorate in 1894; limited self-government, under British rule, was granted in 1900.

BUKHARIN, NICOLAI IVANOVICH (1888–1938) Bolshevik economist and theoretician. He lived in exile in New York until the Revolution, when he returned to Russia (Nov. 1918) and became leader of the Communist Party's Right faction, which advocated cautionary progress to full socialism through the continuation of the New Economic Policy (NEP). A member of the Politburo, 1918–29, and head of the Third International, 1926–9, he was expelled from the Party in 1929 because of his association with Trotskyist opposition to **Stalin**. He was restored to Party membership in 1934, when he became editor of *Izvestia*. He was executed after the last of the Great Purge Trials.

BUNYORO One of the earliest East African kingdoms, founded in the 16th century and occupying territory now part of Uganda. It prospered until the 19th century, when it lost ground and power to neighbouring **Buganda**. Its last ruler, Kabarega, was deposed by the British in 1894, and his kingdom absorbed into the British protectorate in 1896.

BUONACOLSI Prominent family of mediaeval Mantua, Italy. They rose to dominance in the late 13th century; confirmed as lords of the city by Emperor Henry VII in 1311, they were overthrown in a coup by their rivals the Gonzaga family in 1328.

BUONSIGNORI Italian banking house, founded in Siena in 1209, which became the foremost company in Europe. It began to collapse in 1298 and finally closed its doors in 1309.

BURGUNDIANS Germanic people, originally from the Baltic island of Burgundaholm, 1st century AD. In the 5th century they established a powerful kingdom in the Saône and Rhône valleys, extending to the Rhine; they were defeated and absorbed by the **Franks** in 534.

BURKE, EDMUND (1729–97) British statesman, orator and political theorist. He entered Parliament in 1765, and made a reputation with eloquent speeches and writings on the American question and on the arbitrary government of George III. He sought abolition of the slave trade; in his *Thoughts on the revolution in France* (1790) he bitterly condemned the outbreak of revolution and predicted increasing violence.

BURTON, SIR RICHARD FRANCIS (1821–90) Explorer and English translator of *The Thousand and One Nights*. He visited Mecca in 1853 and was the first European to reach Harar, Ethiopia, in 1854; with **Speke** he discovered Lake Tanganyika in 1858.

BUSHMEN see **San**

BUTTON, SIR THOMAS (d.1634) English navigator, and the first to reach the western shores of Hudson Bay (1612–13). He also discovered the Nelson River, which rises in Manitoba and runs into Hudson Bay.

BUWAYHIDS (Buyids) Dynasty originating in northern Persia. They occupied Baghdad, capital of the **Abbasid caliphate**, in 945; though Shi'is, they ruled the central lands of the caliphate in the name of the Abbasid caliph. Their power was ended by the occupation of Baghdad in 1055 by the **Seljuks**.

BUYIDS see **Buwayhids**

BYLOT, ROBERT English navigator and discoverer of Baffin Bay (1615); because he was suspected of disloyalty the bay was named after his lieutenant, **William Baffin**.

BYNG, JOHN (1704–57) English admiral, remembered mainly for an epigram by the French writer Voltaire, who said that he was shot *'pour encourager les autres'* after failing to relieve Minorca.

CABANAGEM Revolutionary uprising, 1835–40, in the Pará region of Brazil. The term was coined from *cabana* or cabin, perhaps an allusion to the lowly origins of the insurgents.

CABOT, JOHN (c.1450–c.1499) Italian explorer (real name Giovanni Caboto) largely instrumental in establishing England's claim to Canada. Precise details of his travels are much in dispute, but around 1484 he moved from Italy to London, and in 1496 was given authority by **Henry VII** to search for unknown lands; after one abortive attempt, he left Bristol in 1497 in a small vessel, the *Mathew*, and made landfall, probably in the region of Cape Breton, Nova Scotia. The fate of his second, larger expedition in 1498 remains unknown.

CABOT, SEBASTIAN (1476–1557) Explorer, cartographer and navigator. In 1512 he worked as map-maker for **Henry VIII** of England; seconded to assist Spain against the French, he was appointed in 1518 as pilot-major to the Spanish *Casa de la Contratación*; in 1525 he led an expedition intended for the Moluccas via the Magellan Straits, but diverted it to the Río de la Plata and spent three years exploring Paraná and Paraguay. He published a celebrated but unreliable world map 1548, and organised an expedition to seek the North-West Passage.

CABRAL, PEDRO ALVARES (1467/8–1520) Reputed discoverer of Brazil, commissioned by the Portuguese king, Manuel I, to sail to India; he sighted the Brazilian coast, 1500, before continuing voyage in which he lost nine out of his thirteen ships by stress of weather; he bombarded Calicut, established a Portuguese factory at Cochin, and returned to Portugal with his four remaining ships loaded with pepper. He was not subsequently employed at sea.

CAINOZOIC Geological era, starting c.65 million years ago, during which all surviving forms of mammal life (including Man) first evolved, and the earth's surface assumed its present form.

CALDERA RODRIGUEZ, DR RAFAEL (1916–) Venezuelan political leader. He was secretary of the Venezuelan Catholic youth organisation, 1932–4, and in 1936 founded the country's national union of students. In 1946 he founded the Committee of Independent

Political Electoral Organisations (COPEI); an unsuccessful presidential candidate in 1947, 1958 and 1963, he finally became President, as the candidate of COPEI, in 1969, holding the post until 1974, in which year he was appointed senator for life.

CALIPHATE The office of caliph, regarded by **Sunnis** as successor to the Prophet **Mohammed** in his capacity as leader of the community. The first four caliphs ('patriarchal', 'right-guided' or 'orthodox' caliphs) ruled from Medina; they were succeeded first by **Umayyads** ruling from Damascus, 661–750; then by the **Abbasids** of Baghdad, whose dynasty continued until 1258, although effective power was held by various dynasties of sultans – **Buwayhids, Seljuks.** In the 10th century two other dynasties took the title of caliph: a branch of the Umayyads in Spain, and the **Fatimids** in Cairo. The last Abbasid caliph was killed by the Mongol conquerors of Baghdad in 1258, and the caliphate virtually came to an end. The title was revived by the Ottoman sultans in the 19th century, but abolished by the Turkish Republican government in 1924.

CALLIMACHUS (c.305–c.240 BC) Poet from Cyrene who worked in Alexandria, compiling a 120-volume critical catalogue of the great Library; only fragments of his 800 recorded works survive, but his *Aetia* (*'Origins'*) and his shorter poems had a profound influence on Roman authors, including Catullus and Propertius. He refused to write long epics, saying that 'a large book is a great evil'.

CALVIN, JOHN (1509–64) French theologian who established strict Presbyterian government in Geneva, and spread his own version of the Protestant Reformation throughout France and Switzerland. He wrote *Institutes of the Christian Religion* (1536) setting out his teachings – that the state should support the Church, that biblical authority should override Church tradition, and that the sacraments, though valuable, are not essential to true religion. He strongly influenced the **Huguenots** in France, the Protestant churches in Scotland and the Netherlands, and the Puritan movement in England and North America.

CAMBYSES II (d.522 BC) Second **Achaemenid** Persian emperor, the eldest son of **Cyrus,** whom he represented in Babylon, 538–530 BC; he succeeded on Cyrus' death in 530. He invaded Egypt, taking Memphis in 525, and was returning home when he heard of the usurpation by his brother **Smerdis,** and died soon afterwards.

CAMINO, DA Mediaeval Italian family, prominent in the affairs of the city of Treviso. It first gained power through Gherado (c.1240–1306), a noted soldier of fortune. His sons wavered between the rival **Guelph** and Ghibelline factions in Italian politics, resulting in the murder of one and the expulsion of the other from Treviso in 1312.

CANUTE *see* **Cnut the Great**

CÃO, DIOGO 15th century Portuguese navigator who explored much of the west coast of Africa. He was the first European to reach the mouth of the Congo (1482).

CAPETIANS Ruling dynasty of France, 987–1328. It was founded by Hugh Capet, elected king in 987 to replace the previous **Carolingian** line; gradually he and his successors extended their control, initially limited to the area around Paris, to cover the larger part of present-day France; they also began to develop many of the country's main political institutions, such as the *Parlements* (royal law courts) and the States General (representative assemblies). Notable Capetian kings included **Philip II Augustus** (reigned 1180–1223), (St) **Louis IX** (1226–70), and **Philip IV** the Fair (1285–1314).

CARACALLA (188–217) Roman emperor, born Marcus Aurelius Antoninus at Lugdunum (modern Lyons). Son of Emperor Septimius Severus, he gained the imperial throne, 211; murdered his wife, Fulvia Plautilla, and younger brother, Geta; he extended Roman citizenship to virtually all inhabitants of the Empire, 212. He was assassinated at Carrhae, Mesopotamia, while preparing his second campaign against Parthia.

CÁRDENAS, LÁZARO (1895–1970) Mexican soldier and radical leader. Governor of home state of Mihoacán, 1928–32; Minister of the Interior, 1931; President of Mexico, 1934–40. During his term of office he launched a Six-Year Plan, a land redistribution programme, the expropriation of foreign-owned oil companies (1938) and a renewed attack on the Catholic Church; he was Minister of Defence, 1942–5.

CARLOWITZ, TREATY OF A truce agreement, signed on 26 January 1699, ending hostilities (1683–99) between the Ottoman Empire and the Holy League (Austria, Poland, Venice and Russia). Under its terms Transylvania and much of Hungary was transferred from Turkish control to Austrian, making Austria the dominant power in eastern Europe. In 1700 the armistice was confirmed by the Treaty of Constantinople.

CARNOT, LAZARE NICOLAS MARGUERITE (1753–1823) French military engineer and statesman who directed the early successes of French revolutionary armies (1793–5); he was a member of the Directory, the five-man group ruling France, 1795–9. Although opposed to **Napoleon**'s rise to power as emperor, he joined in the campaign to resist invasion, 1814, and was Minister of the Interior during the **Hundred Days,** 1815; he died in exile.

CAROL II (1893–1953) King of Romania who supplanted his son Michael as legitimate ruler in 1930, and created a royal dictatorship. He was deposed in 1940.

CAROLINGIANS Royal dynasty descended from Pepin of Landen (died AD 640), chief minister to the **Merovingian** king, Chlothar II. Pepin's illegitimate grandson was **Charles Martel,** after whom the dynasty was named. His great-great grandson was the emperor **Charlemagne.**

CARRACK Large round sailing ship developed in the Middle Ages for both trade and naval warfare, particularly by the Genoese and Portuguese. Deep-keeled and high in the water, with two or three masts, castles fore and aft, and usually well armed with cannon, larger versions were used by the Portuguese in trade to the East Indies and Brazil in the 16th century.

CARRANZA, VENUSTIANO (1859–1920) President of Mexico. The son of a landowner, he was active in politics from 1877; as governor of Coahuila, in 1910, he supported **Madero,** and in 1913 led the opposition to Madero's successor, Victoriano Huerta. He set up a provisional government, defeated the armies of **Pancho Villa,** and was installed as first President of the Mexican Republic (1917). He fled during an armed uprising in 1920, was betrayed and murdered in the mountains near Vera Cruz.

CARREIRA DA INDIA The round voyage between Portugal and India, inaugurated with **Vasco da Gama's** pioneering expedition of 1497–8 and continuing until the age of steam. Under sail it averaged eighteen months, including the stay at Goa.

CARRON Pioneer Scottish ironworks, established by John Roebuck. Founded with capital of £12,000 in 1760, it was the first to use a cast-iron blowing-cylinder to increase air-blast. Technicians trained there started iron-making in Russia and Silesia.

CARTIER, JACQUES (1492–1557) Explorer of Canada, commissioned by **Francis I** of France to sail in search of gold, spices and a new route to Asia; he entered the Gulf of St Lawrence in 1534, and on subsequent expeditions established a base at Quebec and reached Montreal.

CASIMIR I, THE RESTORER (1016–58) King of Poland. He ascended the throne in 1039; he recovered the former Polish provinces of Silesia, Masovia and Pomerania, lost by his father **Miesko II;** he restored central government and revived the Catholic church, but failed to throw off German suzerainty.

CASIMIR III THE GREAT (1310–70) King of Poland. He succeeded to the throne in 1333. He concluded a favourable peace with the **Teutonic Order** in 1343, and annexed the province of Lwów from Lithuania during the 1340s. The last ruler of the **Piast** dynasty, he agreed in 1339 to the union of Poland and Hungary after his death. At home he unified the government, codified laws and founded new towns and the first university in eastern Europe at Cracow in 1364.

CASIMIR IV (1427–92) King of Poland. A member of the **Jagiello** dynasty, he succeeded to the Grand Duchy of Lithuania in 1440 and to the throne of Poland in 1447. He defeated the Teutonic Knights and recovered West Prussia for Poland by the Treaty of Toruń, 1466; thereafter he sought to create a Polish empire stretching from the Baltic to the Black Sea, but was checked by the Turks and, at time of his death, by **Ivan III** of Russia.

CASTILLA, RAMÓN (1797–1867) President of Peru. Born in Chile, he fought for the Spaniards until captured by Chilean patriots; changing sides, he fought in Peru with **Bolívar** and **San Martín.** The first elected President, 1845–51 and again 1855–62, he built up Peru's economic strength by the exploitation of newly-discovered guano and sodium nitrate deposits.

CASTRO, FIDEL (1926–) Prime Minister of Cuba. Law graduate, 1950; after failure to win power by a coup, 1953, he led the guerrilla group '26th of July Movement'; invaded Cuba in 1956 but failed to raise a revolt and fled to the mountains; regrouped, and finally displaced the Batista regime in 1959. He was boycotted by the United States after his **Marxist** aims became apparent; survived the Bay of Pigs invasion of 1961, and the Cuban missile crisis, 1962; with Soviet aid he promoted a programme of land and economic reform. In 1976 he sent troops to Angola, and embarked on an increasingly active African and Central American policy.

CATEAU-CAMBRÉSIS, TREATY OF Agreement signed in 1559 to end the war between France, Spain and England. Spain's claims in Italy were recognised by France, making the former the dominant power in southern Europe; France gained the bishoprics of Toul, Metz and Verdun; England finally surrendered Calais.

CATHARS (CATHARISM) A doctrinal heresy descended from the **Manichaeism** of the early Church and having non-Christian roots, which from the mid-11th century spread rapidly in western Europe, throughout northern Italy and southern France (where the Cathars were known as **Albigensians** from their centre at Albi). Their chief tenet was the dualism of good and evil, which was contrary to Catholic belief although in some respects resembling it. They also devoted themselves to poverty and evangelism, in these respects resembling both the **Humiliati** and the monastic orders. **Innocent III** launched the Albigensian Crusade against them in 1209 and his successors combated them with the **Inquisition.**

CATHERINE II, THE GREAT (1729–96) Empress of Russia, 1762–96. She advanced Russia's status as a great power but greatly extended serfdom among the peasantry. Born a princess of the German principality of Anhalt-Zerbst, in 1744 she married Peter of Holstein-Gottorp, who became Tsar **Peter III** in 1762. Six months later she usurped his throne with the aid of her lover, Orlov. She ruled with the help of the statesman Potemkin, recovering Russia's Black Sea provinces from Turkey, 1783–92, and with Austria and Prussia partitioned Poland in 1795.

CATHOLIC LEAGUE Union of German Catholic princes, formed in 1609 in opposition to the Protestant Union of 1608, and headed by Maximilian I of Bavaria. Its armies, under Tilly (1559–1632), played an important part in the early stages of the Thirty Years' War (1618–48), in which they conquered Bohemia, 1619–22, and defeated Denmark, 1624–9.

CAVALCABO Prominent family of mediaeval Cremona, Italy. Supporters of the **Guelph** (anti-imperial) party, they gained control of the city in the second half of the 13th century, retaining power until 1312; they were driven out by Emperor Henry VII. In 1314 they returned, but were driven out permanently by the **Visconti** of Milan in 1344.

CAVOUR, COUNT CAMILLO BENSO (1810–61) Italian statesman. He abandoned court and an army career, visited England and then embarked on a career in finance, agriculture, industry and radical politics. In 1848 he founded the newspaper, *Il Risorgimento,* to champion monarchical and liberal aims, and promote democratic reforms; entered the Piedmontese cabinet, 1850; given control of government, 1852, by the new king, **Victor Emmanuel II.** He was primarily responsible for creating the United Kingdom of Italy of 1861.

CELTS Ancient people of western Europe, called by the Greeks *Keltoi* and by the Romans *Celtae.* Now more generally used of speakers of languages descended from these, notably Breton in France, Welsh, Cornish, Gaelic (Scots and Irish), and Manx in the British Isles. Archaeologically often used as synonymous with **La Tène** style.

CENOZOIC *see* **Cainozoic**

CENTRAL TREATY ORGANISATION (CENTO) Defence alliance, originally known as the Baghdad Pact, between Iran, Iraq, Pakistan, Turkey and the United Kingdom, signed in 1955. The headquarters were moved from Baghdad to Ankara in 1958, and the name changed with the withdrawal of Iraq in 1959. The Pact was weakened from the first by the refusal of the United States, which had sponsored it, to become a full member. It aroused the hostility of **Nasser;** an ill-judged attempt to recruit Jordan led to riots which nearly caused the fall of King Hussein.

CHALCEDON, COUNCIL OF Fourth ecumenical council of the Christian Church, called in 451 to pronounce on the nature of Christ; it condemned the heresy of **Monophysitism.**

CHALDEANS A group of Semitic tribes, related to the Aramaeans, who settled in the marsh areas of southern Babylonia c.1000 BC. They eventually spread up the Euphrates, infiltrating into territories of many of the major cities of Babylonia, almost to Babylon. By the late 8th century BC, Chaldean chieftains, notably Ukin-zer and Marduk-apal-iddina (Merodach-baladan of the Bible) sought the kingship of Babylonia, producing endemic disturbance. A Chaldean dynasty, whose best-known ruler was Nebuchadnezzar, succeeded to the kingship from 625 to 539 BC. In the Hellenistic and Roman period the term 'Chaldeans' was used to describe Babylonian astrologers generally, without any ethnic basis.

CHAMBERLAIN, JOSEPH (1836–1914) British political leader. Mayor of Birmingham, 1873–6, and a pioneer of radical local government, he became a Member of Parliament in 1876. He was Colonial Secretary in the Conservative government, 1895–1903, during the last, and for Great Britain vital, stages of the partition of Africa; he was responsible for sending Kitchener to the Sudan, for declaring a protectorate over Uganda, and – most important – for the Anglo-Boer War of 1899–1902. He resigned to campaign for Imperial Preference (*see* **Ottawa Agreement**) and tariff protection for British industry.

CHAMPA Ancient kingdom of Indo-China, originally occupying most of the central coastal region of modern Vietnam, and inhabited by the Chams, a people of Malay affinity. Founded c.AD 192, according to Chinese sources, it had close tributary relations with China down to the 16th century, but avoided a Chinese attempt at conquest in 1285. Frequent wars against the Vietnamese led to piecemeal loss of territory, and then to annexation of the main part of Champa by 1471; the kingdom disappeared completely c.1700, apart from Cham communities surviving near Phan Thiet and Phan Rang. Its Hindu temples survive at various places, indicating Indian cultural influence.

CHANAK INCIDENT (1922) Landing of British troops at Çannakale (Chanak) on the Dardanelles to oppose a Turkish takeover of the straits. **Lloyd George,** the British Prime Minister, was accused of recklessness and his government fell.

CHANCA Andean tribe occupying land in Andahuaylas, Peru. In 1440 they attacked but were heavily defeated by the neighbouring, previously insignificant, **Incas.**

CHANCELLOR, SIR RICHARD (d.1556) Navigator and pioneer of Anglo-Russian trade. In 1553 he was appointed pilot-general to Sir Humphrey Willoughby's expedition seeking a north-east passage to China; separated from them by bad weather, he continued into the White Sea and overland to Moscow; warmly received by Tsar **Ivan IV,** he returned to England in 1554 after negotiating the formation of the Muscovy Company.

CHANDELLAS Rajput warrior clan, ruling Bundelkhand, northern India, from the 9th to the 11th century. Defeated in 1001 by Muslim armies of **Mahmud of Ghazni** and expelled from their great fortress of Kalinjar (1023), they were reduced to vassalage by Prithviraja of Ajmer in 1082.

CHANDRAGUPTA II Indian king of the Gupta dynasty, reigning c.375–415, son of Samudragupta. Traditionally renowned for his valour and chivalry, he fought a long campaign against the Sakas (388–409); extended Gupta power, by war in northern India and by marriage in the Deccan; and took title *Vikramaditya,* Sun of Prowess.

CHANDRAGUPTA MAURYA Founder of the first Indian empire, he usurped the throne of the Ganges Valley kingdom of Magadha, 321 BC; exploited the power vacuum left by the retreat of **Alexander the Great** from northwestern India; defeated the forces of **Seleucus I Nicator**, 305–303 BC; acquired Trans-Indus province (now part of **Afghanistan**). He is said to have been converted to **Jainism** at the end of his life, abdicating in 297 in favour of his son **Bindusara**, and dying, as a monk, by deliberate starvation.

CHANG CH'IEN (d.114 BC) Chinese diplomat and explorer, sent in 138 BC by the **Han** emperor **Wu-ti** to establish contact with the **Yüeh-chih** tribes, and the first man to bring reliable reports of central Asia back to China. He was captured and held for ten years by the **Hsiung-nu** tribes but still completed his mission, returning after thirteen years. He made many other journeys, his travels taking him as far as the Tarim Basin, Ferghana, Bactria, Sogdiana and the Hellenic outpost-states established by **Alexander the Great**. Besides information, his efforts gave China its first access to such valuable products as large, fast horses, grapes and alfalfa grass.

CHANG HSIEN-CHUNG (c.1605–47) Chinese rebel leader in the last days of the **Ming** dynasty. Trained as a soldier, he was dismissed from the imperial army and started bandit raids in northern Shensi, 1628; he moved into Honan and Hupeh, 1635; forced to surrender in 1638, he was nevertheless allowed to retain his forces, and rebelled again in 1639. In 1643 he failed to set up administrations in Wuchang and Changsha; he retreated into Szechwan, but captured Cheng-tu in 1644 and took the title of King of the Great Western Kingdom. His government disintegrated in a reign of terror in 1646, and he was killed the following year.

CHANG KUO-T'AO (1897–1979) A founder of the Chinese Communist Party (CCP). After playing a minor role in the May 4 Movement, he represented Peking Marxists at the first CCP Congress at Shanghai in 1921. He helped to found the CCP-sponsored Labour movement, and developed close ties with the **Comintern**. From 1929 he played a major role in Communist base areas on the borders of Honan, Anhwei and Hupeh, and led his forces through Szechwan on an important leg of the Long March. From 1935 he engaged in bitter debates with **Mao Tse-tung**; attempting to set up an independent base in the far north-west, his troops were disastrously defeated in Kansu. After 1938 he defected to the Nationalists and lived in semi-retirement, moving to Hong Kong in 1949, and writing his autobiography.

CHANG TSO-LIN (1873–1928) Chinese warlord known as 'the Old Marshal'. Originally an officer in a Manchurian army, he built up control of southern Manchuria, and from 1917 increasingly dominated Manchuria and much of northern China until 1928. After 1921 he controlled Inner Mongolia. Attempts to control the Peking government led to war with **Wu P'ei-fu** in 1922, in which Chang was initially defeated. In 1924 he concluded a pact with the Soviet Union which recognised his regime in Manchuria as independent, and later that year he invaded northern China, seriously defeating Wu P'ei-fu and driving south almost to Shanghai. His power was backed by the tacit support of the Japanese, who supported him in Manchuria as a buffer against Soviet influence, and to whom he granted major concessions in Manchuria. Unable to counter the growing power of the **Kuomintang** (Nationalist Party) armies under **Chiang Kai-shek**, which invaded his territories in 1927, he abandoned Peking to them. He was killed when Japanese extremists blew up his private train.

CHARLEMAGNE (742–814) Emperor of the **Franks**, son of **Pepin the Short**. Succeeded as joint king, 768; sole ruler from 771. He conquered most of the Christian territory in western Europe, defeating the Lombards and converting the pagan Saxons, and he allied with the papacy to counter dominance of Byzantium. He was anointed as emperor in 800.

CHARLES I, OF ANJOU (1226–85) Angevin king of Naples and Sicily, younger brother of **Louis IX** of France. He acquired the county of Provence, 1246; defeated the last **Hohenstaufen** in 1266 and 1268 to conquer Naples and Sicily, and in 1277 became heir to the kingdom of Jerusalem. Transferring his capital

from Palermo to Naples he set off the revolt of the Sicilian Vespers, 1282; and was defeated by the alliance of the Sicilians and Peter III of Aragon in the Bay of Naples, 1284.

CHARLES I (1600–49) King of England, Scotland and Ireland, son of **James VI (and I)**. Succeeding in 1625, he came increasingly into conflict with Parliament over religion, foreign policy and taxation. After being forced to sign the Petition of Right (1628), he ruled without Parliament until 1640; civil war broke out in 1642, after the King's attempt to arrest five Members of Parliament. Captured in 1647 by the English army under **Cromwell**, he was tried and beheaded.

CHARLES IV (1316–78) King of Bohemia, 1346–78, and ruler of the mediaeval German Empire from 1355, son of John of Luxembourg and Elizabeth, sister of last native Bohemian king. He reformed the finances and legal system, and built up the power of the monarchy in Bohemia, but left Germany largely to the princes; in 1356 he issued the **Golden Bull**, laying down a permanent constitution for the Empire.

CHARLES V (1500–58) Holy Roman Emperor. He was the son of Philip I (died 1506), heir to the Burgundian states, and of Joanna (declared insane in 1506), heiress to Castile and Aragon, to which he succeeded in 1516. Elected emperor in 1519, he annexed Lombardy (1535), and several Netherlands provinces, but was eventually defeated (1551–5) by an alliance of Turks, French and German Lutherans. He abdicated in 1556, leaving his German possessions to his brother Ferdinand (elected emperor in 1558), and the rest to his son Philip II. He retired to a monastery in 1557.

CHARLES IX (1550–1611) Effective ruler of Sweden from 1599, and king 1604–11. The third son of **Gustavus I Vasa**; in 1568 he helped his brother, then crowned as **John III**, to depose their half-brother **Eric XIV**. A strong Lutheran, he first broke with John over religion and then, after the accession of John's Catholic son, **Sigismund III**, called the Convention of Uppsala, 1593, to demand the acceptance of **Lutheranism** as the state religion. Appointed regent in Sigismund's absence, he precipitated a civil war and deposed the king, 1599. He died after strengthening Sweden's metal-based economy and provoking the Kalmar War with Denmark, 1611–13.

CHARLES X GUSTAV (1622–60) King of Sweden, son of John Casimir, Count Palatine of Zweibrücken, and Catherine, eldest daughter of **Charles IX**. He fought with the Swedish armies in Germany, 1642–5, and his cousin Queen Christina of Sweden appointed him commander of the Swedish forces in Germany and also her official successor. He was crowned in 1654, invaded Poland in 1655 and Denmark in 1657–8, and won an advantageous peace.

CHARLES XI (1655–97) King of Sweden, succeeding his father, **Charles X Gustav**, in 1660. He was kept in tutelage by aristocratic regents until Sweden's defeat by Brandenburg at Fehrbellin in 1675; from then on, he established absolute rule, expanding the royal estates to cover 30 per cent of Sweden and Finland and rebuilding the armed forces to match those of Denmark. In 1693, the Swedish Diet granted him unrestricted powers to ensure his reforms.

CHARLES XII (1682–1718) Warrior king of Sweden, eldest son of **Charles XI**, succeeding to the throne in 1697. Brilliantly defeated the anti-Swedish coalition (formed in 1699 to crush Sweden's Baltic hegemony) of Denmark, Russia, Poland and Saxony, invading each in turn (1700–1706). He invaded Russia again with Cossack help in 1708 but was routed at Poltava, taking refuge in Turkey which he succeeded in turning against Russia. Forced to leave Turkey in 1714, he was killed fighting in Norway.

CHARLES ALBERT (1798–1849) King of Sardinia-Piedmont. Son of the Prince of Carignano, he was exiled from Italy and brought up in revolutionary Paris and Geneva, succeeding his father in 1800. He was involved in an abortive plot to displace his cousin as king of Piedmont, 1821, but ascended the throne on his cousin's death in 1831. He sought to lead the unification of Italy; granted representative government; declaring war on Austria in 1848, he was defeated at Custozza, 1848, and Novara, 1849; he abdicated and died in Portugal.

CHARLES THE BOLD (1433–77) Duke of Burgundy, son of **Philip the Good**, inheriting the title in 1467. He attempted to conquer the lands dividing his territories of Luxembourg, Burgundy, the Low Countries and Franche-Comté; but was defeated and killed in battle. Soon after this, in the year 1483, Burgundy passed to the French crown, and Charles' other domains became part of the **Habsburg dominions**.

CHARLES MARTEL (c.688–741) Reunifier of the **Franks**. The illegitimate son of Pepin of Herstal, mayor of the Palace of Austrasia, he emerged, after a five-year struggle, as his father's successor and as effective ruler of all the **Franks**, 719. He defeated the Muslims, advancing north from Spain, near Poitiers, 732; subdued Burgundy, 733, the Frisians, 734, and Bordeaux, 735. He retired, and died the same year.

CH'EN CHI-T'ANG (1890–1954) Military officer in Kwangtung army, commander during the Northern Expedition, taking command in Canton in 1931 and although overtly loyal, consolidating his control of Kwangtung. He began a three-year economic plan in 1933, with a considerable measure of success. In 1936 he invaded Hunan, was defeated and dismissed; after exile abroad he returned to China.

CHEOPS (Khufu) Second king of Egypt's IVth Dynasty (early 26th century BC), succeeding his father, Snefru. He built the Great Pyramid of Giza and three subsidiary pyramids for his principal wives.

CHEPHREN (Khafre) Fourth king of Egypt's IVth Dynasty (late 26th century BC). The son of **Cheops**, he succeeded his brother, Djedefre. He built the second of the three pyramids of Giza and the granite valley temple linked to it by a causeway.

CH'I Large and powerful Chinese state in the period 771–221 BC, located on the eastern edge of the North China Plain (modern Shantung and Hopeh). In the 7th and 6th centuries BC Ch'i began to expand, absorbing its smaller neighbours; during this period it was also the most technologically advanced state in China. Under the semi-legendary Duke Huan in 651 it gained short-lived hegemony over all Chinese territories. In the 3rd century BC a new ruling house again attempted to impose sole dominance on China, but it failed, and in 221 Ch'i was absorbed by **Ch'in**.

CHIANG KAI-SHEK (1887–1975) Chinese general and political leader. He took control of the **Kuomintang** in 1926; established a stable republican government in Nanking, 1928–37; fought war lords, Japanese invaders and the Chinese Communist Party (with occasional periods of alliance) until finally defeated in 1949. He withdrew to Taiwan (Formosa) to form the Chinese Nationalist Government, of which he remained President until his death.

CHIBCHA (also known as Muisca). South American Indians, at the time of the Spanish conquest occupying the high valleys near today's Bogotá and Tunja, Colombia. Their tightly centralised political structure, based on intensive agriculture, was crushed in the 16th century, and since the 18th century (when their language ceased to be spoken) they have been fully assimilated with the population of Colombia.

CHICHIMECS Barbarian and semi-civilised Indian groups who invaded central Mexico from the north in the 12th and 13th centuries and ended the rule of the **Toltecs**; the Aztecs originated as one of the Chichimec tribes.

CHILDEBERT II (570–95) King of Austrasia, son of Sigebert and **Brunhilde**. He began to rule on Christmas Day, 575, after the murder of his father; was seized and forcibly adopted by his uncle, Chilperic, 581; led an expedition to Italy, 584; was re-adopted by another uncle, Gontran, 585, and controlled two-thirds of Gaul after Gontran's death in 593.

CHILDERIC (d.481) Chieftain of the Salian Franks, occupying territory between the rivers Meuse and Somme with their capital at Tournai. He helped the Romans to defeat the Visigoths, near Orléans in 463, and again in 469; cleared the Saxon pirates from along the coast near Angers. He was succeeded by **Clovis**.

CHILEMBWE, JOHN (1860–1915) Nyasaland missionary and rebel leader, now regarded as one of the spiritual forebears of modern Malawi. He worked closely with the European

fundamentalist Joseph Booth, 1892–5; in 1897 received a degree from the United States Negro theological college; returned to Nyasaland in 1900, founding the Providence Industrial Mission with Negro Baptist finance. He protested in 1914 against economic oppression and the use of Nyasa troops in the First World War; he was shot after leading a suicidal revolt against British rule.

CHIMÚ South American Indians, famous for their goldware and pottery, whose rule immediately preceded that of the **Inca** in Peru. Their comparable, though small-scale, civilisation, centred at Chanchán in the Moche valley about 300 miles north of Lima, was conquered by **Pachacuti** in 1465–70.

CHIN Dynasty ruling northern China from 1122 to 1234. Rising from the nomadic Jurchen tribes of northern Manchuria who destroyed their overlords, the **Khitan** dynasty of the Liao, in 1125, it went on to defeat the Sung and to establish control of the territory north of the Huai river. It was destroyed, in turn, by the Mongols in 1234.

CH'IN First great Chinese imperial dynasty: founded by **Shih Huang-ti**; *see page 80.*

CHIN-CH'UAN RISINGS Series of risings of the aboriginal peoples of western and north-western Szechwan in 1745–9, flaring up intermittently again until 1776. In difficult mountain terrain, the risings tied down large Manchu armies, and their suppression was extremely costly.

CHIN FU (1633–92) Chinese official responsible for major water improvements under the early **Ch'ing** dynasty. From 1677 he dredged and banked up the frequently flooding Yellow River (Huang Ho), and made large-scale repairs to the Grand Canal.

CH'ING Last imperial dynasty in China. *See pages 174–5, 232–3.*

CHOKWE (Bajokwe) People occupying the southern region of Zaire, north-eastern Angola and north-western Zambia, formed by a mixture of aboriginal groups and **Lunda** invaders; they were famous ivory-hunters in the 19th century.

CHOU Chinese dynasty, c.1122–221 BC. The Western Chou (c.1122–771 BC) were originally semi-nomadic barbarians from west of the North China Plain; they conquered the lands ruled by the previous Shang dynasty and extended them. Their territory was organised in a 'feudal' system of virtually independent fiefs; in 771 central authority finally broke down. During the Eastern Chou (771–221 BC), China became one of the world's most advanced regions; its greatest philosophers, **Confucius** and **Lao-tzu**, lived at this time, and from this period date many of its most characteristic innovations.

CHREMONIDES' WAR The last flicker of Athenian aggression. In 267 BC a citizen called Chremonides called for a Greek league of liberation with the support of Egypt against the Macedonian king, Antigonus Gonatus; few others joined, and after an intermittent siege Gonatus captured the city in 262. Athens never again sought political leadership in classical times.

CHRISTIANITY Religion of those who have faith in **Jesus**. In the central traditions of Christianity the single God is nonetheless a Trinity – the Father, the Son (incarnate in the human life of Jesus of Nazareth) and the Holy Spirit. Christianity spread despite persecution, and in the 4th century was adopted by the Roman ruling class. Despite divisions it has remained one of the great world religions, sending its missionaries all over the world.

CH'U One of the Chinese states which, with **Ch'i**, **Ch'in** and later Chin, contended in the period 771–221 BC for the domination of China. Based on present-day Hupeh, in the fertile Yangtze Valley of southern China, Ch'u had a completely distinctive culture of its own. It expanded very rapidly into Anhwei and Hunan, and eventually controlled all central China. In 223 BC it was finally absorbed by Ch'in, but fifteen years later, when Ch'in collapsed, a Ch'u aristocrat, Hsiang Yü, briefly became emperor of China; but his reign only lasted a few months before the advent of the Han dynasty.

CHURCHILL, SIR WINSTON LEONARD SPENCER (1874–1965) British statesman and author. The son of Lord Randolph Churchill, he served as a soldier and journalist in Cuba, India, the Sudan and South Africa, became a Conservative Member of Parliament in 1900 and a minister in both the Tory and Liberal governments between 1908 and 1929, serving as First Lord of the Admiralty 1911 to 1915. During the 1930s he warned of the growing threat from **Nazi** Germany, and later directed Britain's war effort as First Lord of the Admiralty in 1939–40, then as premier and Minister of Defence 1940–5. He was Prime Minister again in 1951–5. His works, written while out of office, include *The World Crisis, 1916–18* (1923–9), *The Second World War* (1948–53) and *A History of the English-speaking Peoples* (1956–8); he won the Nobel Prize for literature in 1953.

CHU TE (1886–1976) 'Father' of the Chinese Red Army. Originally a military officer in Yunnan and Szechwan, he went to Shanghai in 1921 and joined the Chinese Communist Party in 1922. After studying in Germany (1922–6) he took part in the abortive rising in Nan-ch'ang in 1927. With **Mao Tse-tung** he built a famous fighting unit in the Kiangsi Soviet, took part in the Long March, commanded Communist forces in the Sino-Japanese War and became commander-in-chief during the civil war with the Nationalists. During the 1930s and 1940s he played a major role in developing Communist policies in rural areas, and in strategic planning; in 1949 became vice-chairman of the central people's government and by 1958 was looked on as natural successor to Mao as head of state. However, in 1959 he was passed over in favour of Liu Shao-ch'i, and had little real power after that time.

CHU YÜAN-CHANG (1328–98) Chinese emperor, founder of the **Ming** dynasty. Born in Anhwei province, he joined a monastery, but between 1356 and 1364 led insurgent forces, gradually gaining control of the region north of the Yangtze, being proclaimed Prince of Wu in 1364. Driving out the Mongols in 1368, he established the Ming dynasty with its capital at Nanking and reigned for thirty years under the reign-title Hung Wu.

CIMMERIANS Indo-European people, originally living in the area of southern Russia. Driven from their homelands, north of the Caucasus and the Sea of Azov, by the closely-related **Scythians** in the 8th century BC; turned aside into Anatolia; conquered Phrygia, 696–5; routed by Alyattes of Lydia, c.626, after which they were absorbed by surrounding groups.

CISTERCIAN Religious Order founded at Citeaux, in south-eastern France, in 1098. It rose to great prominence under the influence of **St Bernard**; by the end of the 12th century it had more than 500 monasteries all over Europe. The motive of the foundation was the re-establishment of the primitive rigour of the Rule of St Benedict, which had lately been neglected.

CLAPPERTON, HUGH (1788–1827) Scottish explorer of West Africa. He joined an expedition journeying south from Tripoli across the Sahara; in 1823 he reached Lake Chad, and travelled in what is now northern Nigeria. He made a second expedition to southern Nigeria; he died near Sokoto after crossing the Niger.

CLARK, WILLIAM (1770–1838) American explorer. With Meriwether Lewis he led a momentous expedition up the Missouri river and over the Rocky Mountains to the Pacific, opening vast territories to westward expansion.

CLAUDIUS I (10 BC–AD 54) Fourth Roman emperor, born Tiberius Claudius Drusus Nero Germanicus, nephew of the emperor **Tiberius**. He achieved power unexpectedly in AD 41, after the murder of his elder brother's son, Caligula; annexed Mauretania, North Africa, 41–2; invaded Britain, 43, and extended the Empire in the east. He had his third wife, Messalina, killed on suspicion of conspiracy, and was almost certainly poisoned by his fourth, his niece Agrippina.

CLEMENT OF ALEXANDRIA (c.AD 150–c.213) Saint, and principal reconciler of early Christian beliefs with the mainstream of Graeco-Roman cultural tradition. Born in Athens, he settled in Egypt, and became head of the Catechetical School, Alexandria. He taught many future theologians (e.g. Origen) and church leaders (Alexander, Bishop of Jerusalem), and wrote important ethical and theological works.

CLEMENT OF ROME Saint, first Apostolic Father of the Christian Church and Bishop of Rome at the end of the first century AD. Author of the *Letter to the Church of Corinth*,

an important source for the Church history of the period.

CLEMENT IV (d.1268) Pope 1265–8. A Frenchman who had been in the service of **Louis IX**, his pontificate signified the growth of French influence in the Church which became so great during the next hundred years. He allied with **Charles of Anjou** to drive the **Hohenstaufen** out of Italy.

CLEOMENES III (d.219 BC) King of Sparta, succeeding his father, Leonidas, in 235 BC. He successfully fought the Achaean League, 228–226; usurped the constitutionally jointly-held Spartan throne to establish virtual autocracy, 227; reintroduced many of the 'communist' ideas of **Agis IV**. His predominance in the Peloponnese was challenged by the Macedonian, **Antigonus Doson**; defeated by Doson at Sellasia in 222, he escaped to Egypt and was interned by Ptolemy IV. He committed suicide after an abortive attempt at revolution in Alexandria.

CLEOPATRA (c.70–31 BC) Last Ptolemaic ruler of Egypt, the daughter of King Ptolemy Auletes. Joint heir with her brother, she was made queen by **Julius Caesar** in 48 BC. She went to Rome as his mistress, but transferred her affections to **Antony**, who then left for four years, but returned after breaking with Octavian. She committed suicide after the Egyptian fleet was defeated at Actium and her ally Antony's troops refused to fight.

CLIVE, ROBERT (1725–74) Conqueror of Bengal and founder of British power in India. He arrived in India in 1743 as a clerk in the **English East India Company**; fought French, and later (1757) Indian forces to establish British control in Bengal, where he was twice Governor (1757–60 and 1765–7). His rule was marred by corruption scandals; despite successful Parliamentary defence in 1773, he committed suicide the following year.

CLOVIS I (c.466–511) Founder of the kingdom of the **Franks**, succeeding his father, **Childeric**, as Frankish chieftain in 481. He defeated **Syagrius**, 486, and by 494 had conquered all northern Gaul; was converted to Christianity, 497; defeated the **Burgundians** and drove the **Visigoths** from Toulouse; he established his capital at Paris.

CLUNIAC The monastery of Cluny (near Mâcon, Burgundy) was founded in 910 by the Duke of Aquitaine, and wielded a tremendous influence on the life of the Church for the next two centuries. The respect in which the Cluniacs were held through their many foundations all over western Europe, the statesmanlike activity of their leaders and the monarchical organisation of the Order under the abbot of Cluny, combined to make it one of the foundation stones of the general reform of the Church led by Pope **Gregory VII.**

COELHO, DUARTE (c.1485–1554) Portuguese soldier. He was granted the captaincy of Pernambuco in 1534, and developed it into the most flourishing colony in Brazil.

CNUT THE GREAT (c.995–1035) King of England (where he is remembered as Canute), Denmark and Norway. The son of **Sven Forkbeard**, he went to England with his father in 1013; he divided the country with Edmund II in 1016, and then assumed rule over all the country on Edmund's death in the same year; succeeded to the Danish throne, 1019; invaded Scotland, 1027.

COLBERT, JEAN BAPTISTE (1619–83) Minister of Finance to **Louis XIV** of France. Personal assistant to Cardinal **Mazarin**, he became a dominant member of Louis' Council of Finance, and in 1665 was made Controller-General. He reformed taxes, founded state manufactures, created the French merchant fleet and laid the basis for France's economic dominance in late 17th century Europe.

COLIJN, HENDRIKUS (1869–1944) Dutch statesman. Fought in Sumatra where he was later colonial administrator. He entered the Dutch parliament in 1909; became war minister, 1911–13; finance minister, 1923–5; Prime Minister, 1925–6 and 1933–9; instituted successful anti-depression policies. He was forced to resign, 1939; arrested by the Germans in 1941, he died three years later in a concentration camp.

COLLA People of the high Andes who in pre-Columbian times occupied the area south of Lake Titicaca. They were conquered by the **Incas** in the early 15th century.

COLLING BROTHERS English 18th century stockbreeders, farming near Darlington, who

developed the shorthorn cow, c.1780, into an animal equally good for milk and meat.

COLTER, JOHN (c.1775–1813) United States trapper and explorer, who in 1807 discovered the area now known as Yellowstone National Park; he was also a member of the Lewis & Clark expedition.

COLUMBA (521–97) Irish saint, famous as the missionary who carried Christianity to **Picts** in Caledonia (Scotland); founded monastery at Iona, 563, the mother house of numerous monasteries on the Scottish mainland.

COLUMBUS, CHRISTOPHER (1451–1506) Spanish navigator, discoverer of America and founder of the Spanish empire in the Americas. Born in Genoa; in 1492 he obtained finance from the Spanish court to seek the east by sailing west; his three ships, the *Pinta*, *Niña* and *Santa María*, sighted San Salvador, 12 October 1492. During his second voyage, in 1493, he founded Isabela, the first European city (now deserted) in the New World, in the Dominican Republic. His third journey, 1498–1500, revealed the mainland of South America. He was embittered when administrative disasters and lack of political sense made the king of Spain reluctant to trust his governorship. His last voyage, 1502–4, coasted Honduras, Nicaragua and the isthmus of Panama, and ended with his ships beached off Jamaica.

COMINTERN The Third Socialist International, set up in 1919 to replace the **Second International** by those who condemned it for its failure to prevent the First World War. Captured immediately by the leadership of Bolshevik Russia, it split the world socialist movement between evolutionary and revolutionary parties, fomenting a number of uprisings in Europe and in the European colonies in South-East Asia in the 1920s. Extensively purged by **Stalin**'s secret police in the 1930s, it was formally dissolved in 1943.

COMNENES Byzantine dynasty holding the imperial throne, 1081–1185. Isaac I, son of Manuel Comnenus, a Paphlagonian general, became emperor briefly from 1057 to 1059, but his nephew, **Alexius I** (reigned 1081–1118) consolidated the family power. The elder line died out in 1185, but after the sack of Constantinople by Crusaders (1204) relatives founded the Empire of Trebizond, lasting until 1461, when David Comnenus was deposed.

CONFEDERATION OF THE RHINE Created by **Napoleon I** in 1806 after the dissolution of the Holy Roman Empire, to gather his client states into a federation of which he was 'protector'. Excluding Austria and Prussia, it formalised French domination over German territory, and lasted until Napoleon's defeat.

CONFLANS, TREATY OF Agreement concluded in 1465 between **Louis XI** of France and the League of the Public Weal, under which Louis agreed to return land captured on the Somme to the League's leader, **Charles the Bold**, Duke of Burgundy, and promised him the hand of his daughter, Anne of France, with the territory of Champagne as dowry.

CONFUCIUS Chinese philosopher. He served as a public administrator, c.532–c.517 BC, then spent the rest of his life teaching and editing the ancient Chinese classics. His sayings, collected after his death as *The Analects*, formed the basis for Chinese education and social organisation until the 20th century. His philosophy was conservative: he advocated submission to one's parents and of wives to husbands, loyalty of subjects to ruler, conformity to established social forms. He advocated the supremacy of ethical standards and rule by 'humanity' and moral persuasion rather than brute force, and laid great stress on ritual observance. Confucianism has been deeply influential in Japan, Korea and Vietnam as well as in China.

CONGREGATIONALIST Member of one of the independent Protestant churches established in the 16th and 17th centuries in the belief that each congregation should decide its own affairs. Among its famous followers were John Winthrop, founder of the Massachusetts Bay Colony in 1629, and **Oliver Cromwell**, Lord Protector of England, 1649–60. Congregationalism became the established religion in 17th century New England; many such churches still survive in North America and in Great Britain.

CONSTANTINE I (c.287–337) Roman emperor, known as 'the Great'. Born at Naissus, now Niš, Yugoslavia, he was brought up at the

court of **Diocletian**, and became Western emperor in 312 and sole emperor in 324. Committed to Christianity, he issued the **Edict of Milan**, 313, extending toleration to the members of this much-persecuted faith; addressed the **Council of Nicaea**, 325, called to resolve some of its crucial theological disputes; founded many churches and was baptised shortly before his death. He built Constantinople as a New Rome on the site of Byzantium, 324, as his permanent capital, and was largely responsible for the evolution of the empire into a Christian state.

CONSTANTINOPLE, COUNCILS OF The first council, an ecumenical gathering of the Christian Church held in AD 381, reaffirmed the teaching of the **Council of Nicaea** and defined the doctrine of the Holy Trinity. The second, in 553, rejected the Nestorian version of Christianity and defined the unity of the person of Christ in his two natures, human and divine. This was reasserted in the third council in 680–1. The fourth, summoned in 869–70, excommunicated Photius, Patriarch of Constantinople (he was reinstated ten years later) and forbade lay interference in the election of bishops.

COOK, JAMES (1728–79) Explorer of the Pacific Ocean. Appointed 1768 to take members of the British Royal Society to Tahiti and locate *Terra Australis Incognita*, or Unknown Southern Continent, he instead charted the coasts of New Zealand and established its insular character, explored the east coast of Australia, navigated the Great Barrier Reef (1770); on his second voyage of circumnavigation, 1772–5, he finally disposed of the notion of an inhabited southern continent; on the third voyage, 1776–80, he discovered the Sandwich (Hawaiian) Islands and proved that no navigable passage connected the north Pacific and north Atlantic. He was famous for his radical dietary methods, which protected all his men from the previously unavoidable scourge of scurvy. He was killed in Hawaii.

COPT Member of the Coptic Church, an ancient **Monophysite** branch of **Christianity**, founded in Egypt in the 5th century. Persecuted by Byzantines and intermittently during the Arab conquest after 640, the Church, with its strong monastic tradition, survived, and in the 19th century achieved relative security in the Muslim world. Its 3 to 4 million followers today still use the Coptic language, derived from ancient Egyptian, for their version of the Greek liturgy.

CORFU INCIDENT Italian bombardment and temporary occupation of the island in September 1923, in retaliation for killing of Italian officers in Greece.

CORNISH REBELLION English uprising in 1497 against the heavy taxes levied by **Henry VII** to pay for his Scottish wars. The rebels killed a tax collector at Taunton (Devon) and marched on London, but they were attacked and defeated in their camp at Blackheath by government troops; 2000 rebels died and the leaders were hanged.

CORNWALLIS, CHARLES (1738–1805) British general during the American War of Independence, forced to surrender at Yorktown, 1781; he was Governor-General of India, 1786–93, and Viceroy of Ireland, 1798–1801.

CORREGGIO, DA Italian family, prominent in the affairs of the Emilian city of Correggio from the 11th century until 1634, and of Parma in the 14th century. Its territories were sold to the House of **Este** in 1634; the dynasty finally died out in 1711.

CORSAIRS Pirates, particularly on the Barbary Coast of North Africa.

CORTE-REAL, GASPAR and MIGUEL Portuguese explorer brothers who made a series of voyages in the late 15th and early 16th centuries under royal commission to discover lands in the north-west Atlantic within the Portuguese domain. Gaspar travelled along the coast of south-east Greenland and crossed the Davis Strait to Labrador; Miguel in 1502 visited Newfoundland and possibly the Gulf of St Lawrence. Both were lost at sea.

CORTÉS, HERNAN (1485–1547) Conqueror of Mexico. At the age of nineteen he settled in Hispaniola; in 1511 sailed with Diego de Velásquez to conquer Cuba; from there, in 1518 he headed an expedition to colonise the Mexican mainland, and achieved a complete and remarkable victory over the Aztec Empire. In 1524 he led an arduous and profitless expedition to Honduras. The rest of his life was spent fighting political enemies and intriguers both in New Spain and at home in Spain.

COSA, JUAN DE LA (c.1460–1510) Spanish geographer and traveller. He owned **Columbus'** flagship, the *Santa Maria*, and served as his pilot. He compiled a celebrated map, dated 1500, showing Columbus' discoveries, **Cabral**'s landfall in Brazil, **Cabot**'s voyage to Canada, and **da Gama**'s journey to India. Sailed with **Bastidas** in 1500; explored Darien, 1504; he died during an expedition to central America and Colombia.

COSSACKS Bands of warlike adventurers, recruited mainly from Ruthenian and Russian peasant fugitives. Renowned for their horsemanship, courage and ruthlessness in war, they were active on the frontiers of Russia from the 14th century onwards; helped secure Ruthenian independence from Poland; aided Muscovy in its wars with the Poles and Turks; under Yermak they conquered Siberia for **Ivan the Terrible** in the 1580s, and formed cavalry regiments in the Tsar's service. They survived as semi-autonomous societies into the Soviet period, when they set up short-lived local anti-Bolshevik governments.

COUGHLIN, FATHER CHARLES EDWARD (1891–1979) Populist and anti-semitic Catholic priest. Born in Canada; from 1930 he broadcast weekly to large audiences in the United States; at first he supported President **F. D. Roosevelt,** but then dropped him in 1936. He edited an increasingly right-wing journal, *Social Justice*, until publication ceased in 1942 after the magazine was banned from the mails for infringing the Espionage Act.

COVENANTERS Those who signed the Scottish National Covenant in 1638, pledging to defend Presbyterianism against all comers. Covenanting armies entered England in 1640, 1644 and 1651; they were defeated by **Cromwell** at Dunbar (1650) and Worcester (1651). The Westminster Confession (1643), drawn up after agreeing the Solemn League and Covenant with the English Parliamentarians, defined the worship, doctrines and organisation of the Church of Scotland. The movement faded away after 1690, when the official Scottish religion became episcopalian.

COVILHÃ, PERO DE 15th century Portuguese explorer sent by the crown in 1487 to see whether the Indian Ocean connected with the Atlantic. His reports from Ethiopia, which he reached after travels in India and Arabia, were important in the Portuguese decision to send the fleet of **Vasco da Gama** to India in 1497–8. Covilhã reached the court of the emperor of Ethiopia, whom he thought was a descendant of **Prester John.**

CRASSUS, MARCUS LICINIUS (c.112–53 BC) Wealthy Roman, third member of the First Triumvirate with **Julius Caesar** and **Pompey.** He sought power and prestige to equal his political colleagues; invaded Mesopotamia; he was ignominiously defeated and killed by Parthians at the battle of Carrhae.

CRIPPS, SIR STAFFORD (1889–1952) British lawyer and politician. He became a member of the Labour Party in 1929, and served in the Cabinet 1930–1. A leading left-wing MP during the 1930s, he was ambassador to Moscow, 1940–42, and headed missions sent to India with plans for self-government in 1942–3 and 1946 (both plans were rejected by the Indian leaders). He held Cabinet office 1942–50, including the post of Chancellor of the Exchequer, 1947–50.

CROATS East European people who migrated in the 6th century from White Croatia, now in the Ukraine, to the Balkans. Their conversion to Roman Catholicism in the 7th century has continued to divide them from their Orthodox neighbours, the **Serbs.** The first Croatian kingdom, formed in the 10th century, was united by marriage with the crown of Hungary in 1091. In 1918 an independent Croatia was proclaimed, but it immediately entered the union of Slav states known as Yugoslavia; a Fascist-led independent state of Croatia, under Ante Pavelič, lasted from 1941 to 1945 before reunification with Yugoslavia under the Communist partisans.

CROMPTON, SAMUEL (1753–1827) British inventor who pioneered the automatic spinning mule, 1779, so called because it combined the principles of the jenny and the water frame.

CROMWELL, OLIVER (1599–1658) Head of republican England. Elected to Parliament in 1640; he led the 'New Model' army to victory in the Civil War, and supported the execution of **Charles I** in 1649. He crushed uprisings by the **Levellers**, 1649, and by royalists in Ireland and Scotland, 1649–51. Appointed Lord Protector (effectively dictator) by army council in 1653; he declined the offer of the monarchy in 1657.

CROQUANTS Peasants who rose in large-scale and well-organised revolts in the Saintonge, Angoumois and Périgord regions of France in 1593–5, 1636–7 and 1643–5. The colloquial meaning of the name is 'clodhopper' or 'nonentity'.

CRUSADES The First Crusade, a holy war waged from 1096 until 1099 by Christian armies from western Europe against Islam in Palestine and Asia Minor, was inspired by a sermon of Pope **Urban II** in 1095. Its leaders included Robert of Normandy, Godfrey of Bouillon, Baldwin and Robert II of Flanders. Nicaea and Antioch were successfully besieged, Jerusalem stormed in 1099, and the Christian kingdom of Jerusalem established by Godfrey of Bouillon.

The Second Crusade, 1147–9, was inspired by **St Bernard.** It was led by the emperor, Conrad III, and by **Louis VII** of France, but foundered on quarrels between its leaders and the barons of the kingdom of Jerusalem, who were in alliance with Muslim Damascus, which the newly-arrived Crusaders wished to attack. The Crusade petered out fruitlessly, and the Latin kingdom was soon weaker than ever.

The Third Crusade, 1189–92, was led by Emperor **Frederick I Barbarossa** (who died before reaching Palestine), King Richard I of England and King **Philip II Augustus** of France. It aimed to regain Jerusalem, which had been captured by the Muslim leader **Saladin** in 1187. It failed to do so, but the coast between Tyre and Jaffa was ceded to Christians and pilgrimage to Jerusalem was allowed.

The Fourth Crusade (1202–04) was originally intended to attack Egypt, centre of Muslim power in the late 12th century. The crusading armies, heirs to a long hostility towards Byzantium, were diverted by Venice, which provided the transport first to Zara in Yugoslavia, and then to Constantinople, which fell on 13 April 1204 and was subjected to three days of massacre and pillage. A horrified Pope **Innocent III**, who had called the Crusade, was unable to re-establish control, and his legate absolved the Crusaders from their vow to proceed to the Holy Land.

CULTURE SYSTEM A system of land cultivation introduced in the Dutch East Indies in the 19th century by the governor-general, van den Bosch, whereby each cultivator set aside an agreed portion of his land for the cultivation of certain cash crops – primarily coffee, tea, sugar, indigo and cinnamon – to be delivered at fixed prices to the government in lieu of land rent. It was such a success that all the safeguards against exploitation of labour gradually broke down; Javanese agriculture benefited in various ways, but at the price of oppression and, in places, famine. The system was strongly attacked by the Dutch Liberals, who came to power in 1848, and abolition began in the 1860s; coffee, the most profitable item in the system, was removed from it only in 1917.

CURZON LINE Ethnically-defined frontier between the USSR and Poland, proposed in 1919 by the British Foreign Secretary Lord Curzon (1859–1925). At the time it was not accepted by either party (after victory in the Russo-Polish war of 1919–20, Poland, as a result of the **Treaty of Riga,** 1921, retained over 50,000 square miles east of the line). The Russo-Polish frontier as settled in 1945 in some respects conforms to the Curzon recommendations.

CUSHITIC Group of languages, related to Egyptian and Berber, spoken originally in the western highlands of Ethiopia; many elements are now partially absorbed into **Amharic,** the official national language. The most widely used Cushitic dialects today include Galla, Somali and the much-divided Sidamo group.

CYNICS Followers of the way of life of Diogenes of Sinope (c.400–325 BC), nicknamed the Dog (hence Cynic, i.e. dog-like), who pursued non-attachment or self-sufficiency by a drastic attack on convention, and by renouncing possessions, nation and social obligations, and choosing self-discipline and a simple life. Cynicism returned to prominence in the early Roman Empire.

CYNOSCEPHALAE, BATTLE OF First decisive Roman victory over a major Greek army, fought in Thessaly in 197 BC against **Philip V of Macedon**, who commanded 25,000 troops.

CYPRIAN, ST (c.200–58) Early Christian theologian. He practised law in Carthage, and was converted to **Christianity** c.246. Elected Bishop of Carthage, c.248, in 250 he fled from Roman persecution, but regained his authority on his return the following year. He was exiled in 257 in a new persecution under Emperor **Valerian**. After attempting to return, he was tried and executed – Africa's first martyr-bishop.

CYRIL (826–69) and METHODIUS (816–85) Brother saints, known as 'the apostles of the Slavs'. They worked to convert the **Khazars**, north-east of the Black Sea; were sent by Byzantine Emperor Michael III into Greater Moravia, 863; translated the scriptures into the language later known as Old Church Slavonic, or Old Bulgarian, inventing for the task the Cyrillic alphabet still used in modern Russia and Bulgaria.

CYRUS II, THE GREAT (d.529 BC) Known as 'the Elder' or 'Cyrus the King' in the Old Testament. Founder of the Persian **Achaemenid** Empire. Originally a vassal king to the **Medes** in Anshan (Fars province), 559 BC, he rebelled, captured the Median capital Ecbatana in 550, conquered and in most cases liberated Babylonia, Assyria, Lydia, Syria and Palestine, where he ordered the rebuilding of the Temple in Jerusalem.

DALHOUSIE, JAMES ANDREW BROUN-RAMSAY, 1st Marquis (1812–60) British colonial administrator. In 1847 he was appointed the youngest-ever Governor-General of India; during his nine-year term he annexed vast territories, including the Punjab and Lower Burma, built railways, roads and bridges, installed a telegraph and postal system, opened the Ganges Canal, acted against thuggee (murder and robbery), dacoity (armed robbery) and the slave trade, and opened the Indian Civil Service to native Indians.

DANEGELD Tax levied in Anglo-Saxon England by King **Æthelred II** (978–1016), to finance the buying-off of Danish invaders; it was preserved as a revenue-raising device by the Anglo- Norman kings who last made use of it in 1162. The name itself is Norman, replacing the earlier, Old English *gafol* (tribute).

DANELAW Region of eastern England, north and east of a line from the Dee to the Tee rivers, governed in the 9th and 10th centuries under the Danish legal code. Some of its legal and social elements survived the **Norman Conquest,** gradually dying out in the course of the 12th century.

DANTE ALIGHIERI (1265–1321) Italian poet, born in Florence. He was sentenced to death in 1301 on political charges, but escaped; the remainder of his life was spent in exile. His greatest work, the *Commedia* (written c.1308–20, known since the 16th century as the *Divina Commedia*), is the earliest masterpiece written in Italian. It traces an imaginary journey through Hell, Purgatory and Heaven, and symbolically describes the progress of the soul from sin to purification.

DANTON, GEORGES-JACQUES (1759–94) French revolutionary who helped to found the Cordeliers Club, 1790; as Minister of Justice, 1792, he organised the defence of France against the Prussians; he was a member of the Committee of Public Safety 1793, but was overthrown by his rival, **Robespierre,** and guillotined.

DARBY Family of English iron-masters whose enterprise helped to create the Industrial Revolution. Abraham Darby I (c.1678–1717) was the first man to smelt iron ore successfully with coke instead of charcoal. His son, Abraham II, built over a hundred cylinders for the **Newcomen** steam engine. His grandson Abraham III built the world's first iron bridge, over the Severn at Coalbrookedale, 1779, and the first railway locomotive with a high-pressure boiler (for Richard Trevithick, 1802). The new smelting process had a slow start, but in the second half of the 18th century developed rapidly, leading to a great increase in the output of pig-iron and of cast-iron goods.

DARIUS I (c.550–486 BC) King of ancient Persia (reigned 522–486 BC). Son of Hystaspes, satrap of Parthia and Hyrcania; he extended Persian control in Egypt and western India; invaded Scythia across the Bosporus, 513. His attack on Greece was defeated at **Marathon,** 490; he died while preparing a second Greek expedition.

DAVID (died c.972 BC) King of the Israelites, son of Jesse. Reared as a shepherd boy, he slew the giant Goliath, champion of the Philistines. He was disaffected from Saul, king of Israel, but was accepted as king after Saul's death; he established his capital at Jerusalem. Traditionally believed to have composed many of the Biblical Psalms. Christian tradition claims that **Jesus** was among his descendants, as a member of the House of David, from which, according to Jewish belief, the Messiah must spring.

DAVIS, JOHN (c.1550–1605) English sea captain, who in 1585 made the first of three unsuccessful attempts to find a North-West Passage through Canadian Arctic – detailed in his later treatise, *The World's Hydrographical Description*, 1595; fought against Spanish Armada, 1588; discovered Falkland Islands, 1592; sailed with Walter Raleigh to Cádiz and the Azores, 1596–7. He was killed by Japanese pirates on last of three voyages to East Indies.

DELIAN LEAGUE Confederation of ancient Greek states, with its headquarters on the sacred island of Delos, originally created under the leadership of Athens in 478 BC to oppose **Achaemenid** Persia. Initially successful; however, freedom to secede was not permitted. In 454 BC the Treasury was transferred to Athens, and the League became effectively an Athenian empire.

DEMOSTHENES (384–322 BC) Ancient Greek statesman and orator. He led the democratic faction in Athens; engaged in bitter political rivalry with his fellow-orator Aeschines; roused the Athenians to oppose both **Philip of Macedon** and **Alexander the Great.** He died by self-administered poison.

DENIKIN, , ANTON IVANOVICH (1872–1947) Russian general. After the revolution in 1917 he joined the anti-Bolshevik armies in south Russia; promoted to commander in 1918, in 1919 he led an unsuccessful advance on Moscow and in 1920 resigned and went into exile.

DENSHAWAI INCIDENT Anti-British episode in Egypt in 1906. Several British officers on a pigeon-shooting expedition were attacked by Egyptians and one was killed; punishment of the culprits provoked strong demonstrations against the British.

DESCRIPTION OF THE WORLD Original title for the work later known in English as *The Travels of Marco Polo.*

DE THAM (c.1860–1913) Vietnamese freedom fighter. He joined a local pirate band and started organising formidable attacks on the French colonists. As 'the tiger of Yen Tri' he built up a large guerrilla army, including the great-uncle of **Ho Chi Minh;** he attacked the French railway, 1894, and temporarily ran Yen Tri district as an autonomous empire. In 1906–7 he linked with the other main anti-French group under **Phan Boi Chau;** implicated in the abortive 'Hanoi Poison Plot' in 1908, he was later assassinated.

DIARMAT, MAC MAEL (1010–71) King of Leinster, Ireland, between 1040 and 1071. He extended his authority over much of the Scandinavian kingdom of Dublin (1071) and planned to make himself High King, but he died first and Ireland disintegrated into warring sub-kingdoms until the Norman invasion of 1170.

DÍAZ, PORFIRIO (1830–1915) Dictatorial President of Mexico. He joined the army fighting against the United States (1846–8), in the War of the Reform (1857–60), and in opposition to the French (1862–7). Involved in unsuccessful revolts in 1871 and 1876, he returned later in 1876 from the US and defeated the government at the Battle of Tecoac. Elected President in 1877, he gradually consolidated power; he was re-elected in 1884 and effectively ruled the country until 1910, modernising its economy at great social cost. He was forced by the military supporters of **Madero** to resign in 1911, and died in exile in Paris.

DIESEL, RUDOLF (1858–1913) Inventor of the heavy oil internal combustion engine bearing his name. Trained at Technische Hochschule, Munich; worked two years at the Swiss Sulzer Machine Works, and then in Paris at Linde Refrigeration Enterprises. He started work on his engine in 1885, making his first working model in 1893.

DIOCLETIAN (245–316) Roman emperor, born Aurelius Valerius Diocletianus, in Dalmatia. Acclaimed by his soldiers as emperor in 284, at a time of deep economic, political and military trouble, he took sole control of affairs in 285 and forced through an immense programme of legal, fiscal and administrative reform, restoring much of Rome's former strength. He abdicated in 305.

DIODOTUS I Founder of the ancient Greek kingdom of Bactria, originally subject to the **Seleucid** kings, Antiochus I and II. He rebelled and made himself king (250–230); he was succeeded by his son, Diodotus II Soter.

DISRAELI, BENJAMIN (1804–81) First Earl of Beaconsfield, statesman, novelist and twice British Prime Minister; born of a Jewish family but baptised as a Christian. He first stood for Parliament as a radical, but was elected as Conservative MP for Maidenhead in 1837. Quarrelled with Sir Robert **Peel** over the repeal of the Corn Laws, 1846, and emerged as a leader of the rump of the Conservative Party. He succeeded Lord Derby as Prime Minister for a few months in 1868; and became Prime Minister again 1874–80. He incorporated concern for the Empire into the Conservative programme in his Crystal Palace speech of 1872 and saw a link between imperialism and social reform at home; his real concern was for India and the route to India. Represented Britain at the **Congress of Berlin** in 1878; his ministry was associated with forward policy in Afghanistan and South Africa.

DOENITZ, KARL (1891–1981) German naval commander and briefly head of state. In the First World War he served as a submarine officer. After the succession of **Hitler** he supervised the clandestine construction of a new U-boat fleet; he was appointed commander of submarine forces in 1936, head of the German navy in 1943 and head of the northern military and civil command in 1945. Named in Hitler's political testament as the next President of the Reich, he assumed control of the government for a few days after Hitler's suicide on 2 May 1945. Sentenced to ten years' imprisonment as a Nazi war criminal in 1946, he was released in 1956.

DOLLFUSS, ENGELBERT (1892–1934) Chancellor of Austria, 1932–4, who effectively made himself dictator until he was assassinated by Austrian Nazis.

DOMINICANS *see* **Friars**

DOMITIAN (AD 51–96) Roman emperor, born Titus Flavius Domitianus, son of Emperor **Vespasian**; succeeded his brother, **Titus**, in AD 81. He is remembered for his financial rapacity and the reign of terror (particularly 93–6) waged against his critics in the Senate; he was murdered by conspirators, including his wife, Domitia Longina.

DONATUS (died c.355) Leader of the Donatists, a North African Christian group named after him, who broke with the Catholic church in 312 after a controversy over the election of Caecilian as Bishop of Carthage; Donatus, appealing against the appointment, was overruled by a council of bishops, 313, by another at Arles, 314, and finally by Emperor **Constantine**, 316. The dissidents were persecuted, 317–21, then reluctantly tolerated; they continued to gain strength (perhaps through African nationalist feeling); in 347 Donatus was exiled to Gaul, where he died. The movement continued; thanks to the teachings of St. Augustine, and to state persecution, it had disappeared by c.700.

DORIANS Last of the Hellenic invaders to press into Greece from the north, c.1100 BC, perhaps from Epirus and south-western Macedonia, traditionally via Doria in central Greece. They recognised three 'tribes', the Hylleis, perhaps coming down the east, the Dymanes down the west, and the Pamphyloi covering minor groupings. They spread through the Peloponnese and to the islands of Cythera, Melos, Thera, Crete, Rhodes, Cos, and into southern Anatolia. Many problems about them still challenge archaeologists.

DOUGLAS, STEPHEN ARNOLD (1813–61) United States Senator. He was elected to Congress in 1843, and to the Senate in 1846. He strongly supported 'popular sovereignty' (local option) on the question of slavery. In 1858 he engaged in a series of highly-publicised debates with **Abraham Lincoln,** to whom he lost in the presidential election. He condemned secession on the outbreak of the Civil War.

DRAKE, SIR FRANCIS (c.1540–96) English seaman who led slave-trading and buccaneering expeditions to west Africa and the Spanish West Indies, 1566–75. He circumnavigated the globe in his ship the *Golden Hind*, 1577–80; raided Spanish fleet in Cádiz, 1587, and fought against the Spanish Armada, 1588.

DRAVIDIAN Group of seven major and many minor languages, including Tamil, Telugu, Kanarese, Malayalam, Gondi and Tulu, spoken mainly by some 110 million people in southern India (also known collectively as Dravidians); characteristically these are darker, stockier, longer-headed and flatter-faced than the Indic or Aryan races of northern India.

DRUID Member of a pre-Christian religious order in Celtic areas of Britain, Ireland and Gaul. It has been retained as a name for officers in the modern Welsh Gorsedd.

DUAL MONARCHY OF AUSTRIA-HUNGARY Political system, 1867–1918, established by the Compromise of 1867 which granted a large measure of autonomy to the Hungarian lands of the former Austrian Empire.

DULLES, JOHN FOSTER (1888–1959) US lawyer and statesman. He began legal practice in 1911; became counsel to the US commission to negotiate peace after the First World War, 1918–19, and to other government bodies. He was special adviser to the Secretary of State, 1945–51, and filled that post himself, 1953–9. He was associated with a vigorously anti-Communist US foreign policy.

DUMA Lower house of the Russian parliament, established by Tsar **Nicholas II** in 1905; on the collapse of tsarism in March 1917 leading Duma politicians formed the Provisional Government, which never in fact met.

DUPLEIX, JOSEPH FRANÇOIS (1697–1763) French administrator, Governor-General of Chandernagore 1731–41, and of Pondicherry 1741–54. His expansionist ambitions in southern India were checked by **Robert Clive,** 1751–2; he was recalled in 1754.

DUTCH EAST INDIA COMPANY (Vereenigde Oostindische Compagnie, VOC) Powerful trading concern set up in 1602 to protect Dutch merchants in the Indian Ocean and to help finance the war of independence with Spain. Under able governors-general, such as Jan Pieterszoon Coen, 1618–23, and Anthony van Diemen, 1636–45, the company effectively drove both British and Portuguese out of the East Indies, and established Batavia (now Jakarta) as its base for conquering the islands. Growing corruption and debt led to the company's dissolution in 1799.

DUY TAN (1888–1945) Emperor of Annam, the son of Emperor Thanh Thai, whom he succeeded in 1907. His reign was a period of revolt against the French colonial power; after one revolt, which sought to make him a real emperor, he was deposed and exiled to Réunion in 1916. Later he served with the Free French forces in the Second World War; he died in an air crash.

EADGAR (c.943–75) English king; younger son of Edmund I. He became king of Mercia and Danelaw, 957, on the deposition of his brother Eadwig, and in 959 succeeded to the throne of West Saxons and effectively all England. He reformed the Church in England.

EAM (Initials in Greek for National Liberation Front). One of the Greek resistance movements, formed in 1941 to fight the German and Italian armies. By 1944, when the Germans evacuated, it controlled two-thirds of the country. It rejected Allied orders to disarm in December 1944, but accepted the Varkiza Peace Agreement, 1945; it participated in large-scale civil war, 1946–9.

EAST INDIA COMPANY *see* **English East India Company** and **Dutch East India Company.**

EDEN TREATY Trade agreement between England and France, negotiated in 1786–7 by William Eden, 1st Baron Auckland (1744–1814). It gave the English free access to French markets; because it encouraged the export of French corn to England it contributed to popular tension during the food crisis preceding the French Revolution.

EDWARD THE CONFESSOR (c.1003–65) King of England, son of **Æthelred II** the Unready. Exiled after Æthelred's death (1016) when the Danes again seized power in England, he returned from Normandy, 1041, and succeeded to the throne of his half-brother, Harthacnut, 1042; however, the main power in the kingdom remained first with Godwin, earl of the West Saxons, then with his son, Harold, named as king on Edward's death. Claims that Edward had previously promised the throne to Duke William of Normandy led to the **Norman Conquest** (1066).

EDWARD I (1239–1307) King of England; the son of Henry III. He led the royal troops to victory in the Barons' War (1264–6); succeeded to the throne, 1272; conquered Wales (1277–83); established suzerainty over Scotland and defeated the Scottish revolt under **William Wallace,** 1298. His consistent utilisation of Parliament in wide-ranging legislation consolidated its institutional position. He died on an expedition to suppress the revolt of **Robert Bruce** of Scotland.

EDWARD II (1284–1327) King of England, son of **Edward I,** whom he succeeded in 1307. He ruled, weakly and incompetently, through favourites such as Piers Gaveston (murdered 1312) and the Despensers (executed 1326); he was heavily defeated by the Scots at Bannockburn, 1314; strongly opposed by the barons, who in 1311 tried to subject him to control by committee of 'lords ordainers', he was deposed and put to death when his queen, Isabella, invaded from France with her ally, Roger Mortimer.

EDWARD III (1312–77) King of England, son of **Edward II,** succeeding in 1327. By 1330 he had freed himself from subjection to his mother, Isabella, and her ally, Roger Mortimer. Defeated the Scots, 1333 and 1346; at the start of the **Hundred Years War** he defeated the French fleet at Sluys, 1340, and invaded France; his notable victories at Crécy, 1346, and Calais, 1347, with that of his son at Poitiers, 1356, were consolidated by the Peace of Brétigny in 1360. He resumed war in 1369, and by 1375 had lost all his previous gains except Calais, Bordeaux, Bayonne and Brest.

EIGHT TRIGRAMS Secret north Chinese sect, part-religious, part-political. It flourished, particularly in Chihli, Shantung and Honan, in the 19th century, and was involved in the palace revolution in Peking of 1814.

EISENHOWER, DWIGHT DAVID (1890–1969) 34th President of the United States, 1953–61. He was commander of the American forces in Europe, and of the Allies in North Africa, 1942; directed the invasions of Sicily and Italy, 1943; became Supreme Allied Commander, 1943–5, and Commander, NATO land forces, 1950–2. Under his presidency, the Korean War was ended, 1953, **SEATO** formed, and federal troops were ordered (1957) to enforce racial desegregation of US schools at Little Rock, Arkansas.

EISNER, KURT (1867–1919) German socialist leader. In 1914 he opposed German aid to Austria-Hungary, and became leader of the pacifist Independent Social Democratic Party in 1917; he was arrested as a strike-leader the following year. After his release he organised the overthrow of the Bavarian monarchy and proclaimed an independent Bavarian republic; he was assassinated by a right-wing student.

ELCANO, JUAN SEBASTIÁN DE (d. 1526) First captain to make a complete circumnavigation of the earth. A Basque navigator, he sailed in 1519 as master of the *Concepción* under **Magellan**; after Magellan's death he took command of the three remaining ships and returned to Spain, 1522, with one ship, the *Victoria*. Henceforth his family coat-of-arms carried a globe and the motto *Primus circumdedisti me* ('You were the first to encircle me').

ELECTOR Historically, one of the small group of princes who, by right of heredity or office, were qualified to elect the Holy Roman Emperor. Originally, in the 13th century, there were six; from 1356 to 1623 there were seven – the archbishops of Mainz, Trier and Cologne, the King of Bohemia, the Count Palatine of the Rhine, the dukes of Saxony and the margrave of Brandenburg. By 1806, when the Empire ended, there were ten.

ELIZABETH I (1533–1603) Queen of England. The daughter of **Henry VIII** and Anne Boleyn, she succeeded to the throne in 1558. In 1559 she returned England's official religion to Protestant (Anglican); she was deposed by the Pope in 1571, but survived a Spanish attempt to put the sentence into effect (Spanish Armada, 1588). She made English authority effective in Ireland (1601).

ELLMAN, JOHN English 18th century sheep-breeder, farming at Glynde, Surrey, who in about 1780 began developing short wool varieties, a process which eventually transformed the Southdown sheep from a light, long-legged animal into one solid, compact, and equally good for mutton and for wool.

ENCYCLOPAEDISTS Group of French writers, scientists and philosophers connected with the influential *Encyclopédie ou dictionnaire raisonné des sciences, des arts et des métiers*, edited 1751–72 by Denis Diderot (1713–84) assisted by d'Alembert (1717–83); the work and its contributors powerfully expressed the new spirit of 18th century rationalism.

ENGLISH EAST INDIA COMPANY Founded in 1600 to trade with the East Indies, but excluded by the Dutch after the Amboina Massacre in 1623. The company negotiated concessions in Mughal India and won control of Bengal in 1757, but its political activities were curtailed by the Regulating Act of 1773 and the India Act of 1784. Its commercial monopoly with India was broken in 1814, and that with China in 1833. It ceased to be the British government's Indian agency after the Mutiny in 1857; its legal existence ended in 1873.

ENTREPÔT Commercial centre, specialising in the handling, storage, transfer and dispatch of goods.

EON OF STEILA (d.1148) Christian heretic. He preached opposition to the wealth and organisation of the Roman church, gaining followers in Brittany and Gascony before being imprisoned by Pope **Eugenius III** at the Synod of Rheims. He died in prison; his followers, like the **Henricians** and **Petrobrusians**, faded away.

EPICUREANS Followers of the Greek philosopher Epicurus (341–271 BC). To Epicurus happiness ('pleasure') is all; it consists in freedom from disturbance. So the wise man will free himself from fear, through scientific understanding, and from desire, by 'doing without'. The structure of the universe is atomic; death is annihilation; gods exist but do not intervene in human affairs. The Epicureans fostered friendship and discouraged ambition. The system is expounded by the Roman poet Lucretius (c.94–55 BC).

EPIRUS, DESPOTATE OF Byzantine principality in southern Albania and north-western Greece, organised as a rival principality during the Western occupation of Constantinople after the Fourth Crusade. Founded in 1204 by Michael Angelus Ducas, it was continually attacked by Nicaea, Bulgaria and later, after the restoration of Michael VIII Palaeologus, by Byzantium itself. In the 13th century it was a pre-Renaissance centre for classical studies; it was reannexed to Byzantium in 1337.

EPISCOPALIAN Member of the Protestant Episcopal Church of Scotland and the United States, a believer in the principle that supreme authority in the Church lies with the bishops assembled in council, rather than with a single head.

ERATOSTHENES (c.276–c.194 BC) The first systematic geographer. He directed the Library at Alexandria, c.255 BC; wrote on astronomy, ethics and the theatre; compiled a calendar, showing leap years, and a chronology of events since the Siege of Troy; calculated the earth's circumference with remarkable accuracy. He was known as Beta, because he was good without being supreme in so many fields; he is said to have starved himself to death after going blind.

ERIC XIV (1533–77) King of Sweden, 1560–68, the son of **Gustavus I Vasa.** He seized strategic territory in Estonia, prompting Denmark and Norway to initiate the Seven Years War of the North; he was accused of insanity and deposed by his half-brothers, 1568, after failing to win the war and after defying the Swedish nobility in order to make his commoner mistress, Karin Mansdotter, queen; he died in prison.

ERIK BLOODAXE (d.954) King of Norway and of York in the 10th century, named to commemorate his murdering seven of his eight brothers. The son of **Harald Finehair,** he was expelled from Norway, 934; by 948 he was king of York and ruled there until expelled in 954. He was killed at Stainmore.

ESKIMOS People of the western Arctic region, thinly spread in small settlements across the northern coasts of North America, from Alaska to Greenland. Of closely related physical type, language and culture, these groups, totalling some 50,000 people, share a common adaptation to the harsh living and hunting conditions of the Arctic tundra.

ESSENE Member of an ancient Jewish sect founded between the 2nd century BC and 2nd century AD. It was characterised by stern asceticism, withdrawal, communistic life, ceremonial purity, a rigorous novitiate lasting three years, identification of Yahweh with the Sun, and a mystic belief in immortality. The Dead Sea Scrolls, found in the Qumran between 1947 and 1956, probably belonged to an Essene community; attempts to link **Jesus** to them are implausible.

ESTE Italian family which presided over an unusually brilliant court, ruling as princes in Ferrara from the 13th century until 1598, and as dukes in Reggio and Modena from 1288 until the mid-19th century. The dynasty was founded by the margrave Albert Azzo II (d.1097); their connection with Ferrara ended when Clement VIII imposed direct papal rule.

ETRUSCANS A people in Italy inhabiting Etruria, the land between the Tiber and Arno rivers, west and south of the Apennine hills. Their origins are unknown, but they possibly came from Asia Minor. From 800 BC to their decline in the 5th century BC they developed an elaborate urban civilisation, particularly notable for its tombs; they were ultimately absorbed by Rome. The Etruscan language is still largely undeciphered.

EUGENIUS III (d.1153) The first Cistercian Pope (1145–53), a pupil of **St Bernard**, whose *De Consideratione* presented his views on how the Pope should lead the Church. Forced to leave Rome because of conflict with the city and with **Arnold of Brescia**, he was finally re-established by the Treaty of Constance (1153) with **Frederick I Barbarossa**.

EURIPIDES (480–406 BC) Last of the three great Athenian tragic dramatists; 19 of his 92 plays survive, distinguished by their concentration on real human problems expressed in contemporary language. He left Athens in 408, moved to Thessaly and then Macedon, where he wrote *The Bacchae;* he died at the court of King Archelaus.

EUSEBIUS (c.265–340) Bishop of Caesarea. His *History of the Church* is the first scholarly work on the early institutions of Christianity.

EXARCHATE Under the Byzantine and the Holy Roman Empires, it referred to the governorship of a distant province; in the eastern Catholic church, to the area of responsibility of certain high-ranking ecclesiastics known as exarchs (approximate equivalents of patriarchs or archbishops).

FAIRBAIRN, SIR WILLIAM (1789–1874) Victorian authority on factory design who wrote the classic treatise, *Mills and Millwork*. A builder of ships and bridges, he constructed many iron ships at Millwall, London, between 1835 and 1849, and also invented the rectangular tube used on **Robert Stephenson's** Menai Bridge.

FANG CHIH-MIN (1900–1935) Early leader of the Chinese Communist Party. He became prominent in Communist and **Kuomintang** affairs in Kiangsi during the 1920s; helped to found the Communist base in north-eastern Kiangsi, which developed into the Fukien-Chekiang-Kiangsi Soviet in the early 1930s. He led the 10th Army Corps when encircled by the Nationalist Army in mid-1934, and the following year was captured and executed by the Nationalists.

FAROUK I (1920–65) King of Egypt. The son of Fuad I, he succeeded to the throne in 1936. He was involved in the long struggle for power with the nationalist party, the **Wafd;** during the Second World War Britain, then in occupation of Egypt, forced him to appoint a Wafdist government. He was deposed and exiled after the military *coup d'état* organised by **Neguib** and **Nasser**.

FARROUPILHA REVOLUTION Provincial uprising in Rio Grande do Sul, southern Brazil; it flared intermittently, 1835–45, until finally suppressed by the armies of Pedro II under the Duque de Caxias. The name means 'rags', alluding to the rebels' lack of uniforms.

FASCISM Originally the anti-democratic and anti-parliamentarian ideology adopted by the Italian counter-revolutionary movement led by **Mussolini;** characterised by advocacy of the corporate, one-party state, to which all aspects of life are subordinated. It was later extended to describe any extreme right-wing political creed that combines absolute obedience to the leader with a willingness to use brute force to gain power and suppress opposition.

FATIMA (c.616–33) Mohammed's daughter, and first wife of **Ali**. The imams recognised by the **Shi'is** are her descendants, and Shi'is have a special reverence for her; her descendants led a moderate wing of the Shi'is, the second major division of Islam, and ultimately founded the **Fatimid** dynasty.

FATIMIDS North African dynasty claiming descent from **Fatima, Mohammed's** daughter, founded in 908 in Tunisia by the imam, Ubaidallah. Muizz, the fourth Fatimid caliph, conquered Egypt and founded Cairo, 969. In the 11th century, they supplanted the **Abbasids** as the most powerful rulers in Islam, but were finally abolished by **Saladin** (1171).

FEDERALISTS Name, first used in 1787, to denote the supporters of the newly-written United States Constitution; and later for a conservative party which was hostile to the Revolution in France, favourable to an alliance with Great Britain and generally supportive of central authority in America. From 1791 to 1801 Federalists controlled the national government, organised the new nation's administrative and tax machinery, and formulated a policy of neutrality in foreign affairs. In 1801 they were displaced by an opposition group led by **Thomas Jefferson,** and never again held national office.

FEITORIA Fortified factory or trading post, established by the Portuguese during their period of maritime dominance.

FENG YÜ-HSIANG (1882–1948) Chinese warlord, nicknamed 'the Christian general'. At first an officer in the Hwai army under **Yüan Shih-k'ai**, he served in the Peiyang army after the 1911 revolution. From 1918 he created a private army, controlling a large part of north-west China, 1912–20; he was involved in a series of *coups d'état* and civil wars, 1920–8, but never acquired a permanent territorial base. To relieve chronic financial pressures he sought the help of Russia, but in 1929 was forced to relinquish control of his troops to **Chiang Kai-shek**. His army, joined by **Yen Hsi-shan**, attempted to form a northern coalition against Chiang, and in 1929–30 they fought a bitter war. When it ended he joined the Nationalist government, but never again had any real power.

FENLAND REVOLT Prolonged local opposition, 1632–8, to government-sponsored measures to drain and enrich the fens of eastern England, thus depriving the local population of common rights. **Oliver Cromwell** was one of the leaders of the revolt.

FERDINAND II *see* **Ferdinand of Aragon**

FERDINAND III (c.1199–1252) Saint and king of Castile (1217–52) and León (1230–52). He united the crowns of Castile and León, and completed the conquest of all Moorish dominions in Spain except **Granada**.

FERDINAND OF ARAGON (1452–1516) By marriage to Isabella of Castile, 1469, he united Spain into a single power. The son of John II of Aragon, he became king of the two largest states of Spain, Castile and Aragon, adding Navarre (1512). In 1504 he also conquered Naples, which remained Aragonese until 1713. He established the **Inquisition** in Spain, 1478; conquered Granada, the last Muslim area of Spain, 1492, and backed **Columbus'** voyage to the New World. He ordered the expulsion of **Jews** and Moors from Spain, 1492.

FEUDALISM Political system of mediaeval Europe, based on the mutual obligations of vassal and superior, linked by the granting of land (the feud, or fee) in return for certain services. The feudal lord normally had rights of jurisdiction over his tenants, and held a feudal court. Similar systems (sometimes also termed 'feudal' by analogy) are found in other parts of the world (e.g. early China and Japan) at a similar stage of development.

FIANNA FÁIL Irish political party; founded in 1926 by **de Valera** to espouse republican nationalism and erase all English influence from Irish public life.

FIELDEN, JOSHUA (d.1811) Cotton industry pioneer. In 1780 he was still a peasant farmer, operating two or three weaving looms; by 1800 he owned a five-storey cotton mill in Todmorden, Yorkshire. After his death his sons developed the business – Fielden Brothers, Waterside Mills – into one of the largest cotton mills in Britain.

FIGUERES FERRER, JOSÉ (1906–) Costa Rican political leader. He worked as a coffee planter and rope-maker; exiled to Mexico

1942–4, he became Junta President of the Republic, 1948, but resigned in 1949; he was President of Costa Rica 1953–8 and 1970–4.

FISSIRAGA Prominent family of mediaeval Lodi, Italy. Supporters of the **Guelph** (anti-imperial) party, they rose to prominence in the 1280s; in 1311 their leader, Antonio Fissiraga, was captured by the **Visconti** of Milan and died in prison (1327).

FIUME INCIDENT Unsuccessful attempt to seize the Adriatic sea port in September 1919, by a private Italian army, led by the poet Gabriele d'Annunzio, to forestall its award to Yugoslavia at the Paris Peace Conference.

FIXED EXCHANGE RATES Regime under which the value of one currency bears a constant relationship to that of another: e.g. the pound sterling in the period 1949–67, when it was always worth US $2.80. Such relations linked most major currencies in the period 1947–71, under the so-called Bretton Woods System, but that then gave place to a period of mainly 'floating' rates.

FLAMININUS (c.227–174 BC) Principal Roman general and statesman during the period when Greece became a Roman protectorate. He defeated **Philip V of Macedon** at **Cynoscephalae** in 197 BC; declared that all Greeks should be free and governed by their own laws in 196; and supported Greek autonomy in Asia Minor during Rome's wars with the **Seleucids**.

FLAVIANS Dynasty ruling the Roman Empire from AD 69 to 96. It was founded by **Vespasian** (69–79) and continued by his sons, **Titus** (79–81) and **Domitian** (81–96).

FLINDERS, MATTHEW (1774–1814) Maritime explorer of Australia, born in Lincolnshire, England. He entered the Royal Navy in 1789, from 1795 to 1799 he charted much of Australia's east coast between Fraser Island and Bass Strait, and circumnavigated Tasmania, in 1801–2, as commander of the *Investigator*, he surveyed the whole southern coast, and in 1802–3 circled the entire continent. He was interned by the French in Mauritius, 1803–10; his *Voyage to Terra Australis* was finally published about the time of his death.

FOCH, FERDINAND (1851–1929) French soldier, Marshal of France, a teacher of military history and author of many standard works. Appointed a general in 1907, he won distinction during the First World War in the first battle of the Marne, 1914, the first battle of Ypres, 1915, and the battle of the Somme, 1916. He was appointed as commander-in-chief of the French armies in 1917, and after the onset of the German offensive in spring 1918 was appointed to command all French, British and American forces.

FORREST, JOHN (1847–1918) 1st Baron Forrest. Australian explorer and statesman. He led several expeditions across Western Australia from 1869; became Surveyor-General of Western Australia, 1883–90, and its first premier, 1890–1901. He held Cabinet office in several ministries in the federal government of the new Commonwealth of Australia between 1901 and 1918.

FOURTEEN POINTS Programme put forward by United States President **Woodrow Wilson** in 1918 for a peace settlement following the First World War. Several of the Points related to the right of self-determination of peoples; although statesmen at the Peace Conference were thinking of the rights of the successor states of Austro-Hungarian and Ottoman empires, the principle was noted by colonial peoples in Asia and Africa. The final proposal for a 'general association' to guarantee integrity of 'great and small states alike' led to the setting up of the **League of Nations**.

FRANCIS I (1494–1547) King of France; he succeeded his cousin, **Louis XII**, in 1515. In 1520 he attempted unsuccessfully to win the support of the English king, **Henry VIII,** for his struggles with the **Habsburgs;** he pursued his rivalry alone in a series of Italian wars (1521–5, 1527–9, 1536–7, 1542–4), but finally abandoned Italian claims in 1544. He was a noted patron of Renaissance art.

FRANCIS II (1768–1835) The last Holy Roman Emperor. The son of Leopold II, he succeeded to the imperial title in 1792, and held it until dissolution of the Empire by **Napoleon** in 1806. He continued to reign as the first Emperor of Austria, under the title Francis I; through his chancellor, **Metternich,** he made Austria a leading European power.

FRANCISCANS *see* **Friars**

FRANCO, FRANCISCO (1892–1975) Spanish dictator. A general in the Spanish army, he organised the revolt in Morocco in 1936 which precipitated the Spanish Civil War of 1936–9, from which he emerged as head of state ('El Caudillo'). He was named regent for life in 1947. In 1969 he proposed that Prince Juan Carlos of Bourbon should ultimately take the throne, as indeed he did at Franco's death.

FRANCO-PRUSSIAN WAR Struggle provoked by rivalry between France and the growing power of Prussia, reaching a head over the candidacy of Leopold of Hohenzollern for the throne of Spain. Prussian armies under von Moltke invaded France and quickly won victories at Wörth, Gravelotte, Strasbourg, Sedan and Metz between August and October 1870. **Napoleon III** abdicated, and the Third French Republic was declared on 4 September 1870; Paris, under siege for four months, surrendered on 28 January 1871. Under the Treaty of Frankfurt (May 1871) France ceded Alsace and East Lorraine to the newly-established German Empire, and agreed to pay an indemnity of 5 billion francs.

FRANKS Germanic peoples who dominated the area of present-day France and West Germany after the collapse of the West Roman Empire. Under **Clovis** (481–511) and his **Merovingian** and **Carolingian** successors they established the most powerful Christian kingdom in western Europe. Since the disintegration of their empire in the 9th century the name has survived in France and Franconia.

FRANZ FERDINAND (1863–1914) Archduke of Austria, nephew of, and from 1896 heir to, the Emperor Franz Joseph I (1830–1916). He was assassinated on 28 June 1914 at Sarajevo, an incident which provoked the Austrian ultimatum to Serbia that led directly to the outbreak of the First World War.

FREDERICK THE GREAT (1712–86) King of Prussia, son of **Frederick William I,** whom he succeeded, as Frederick II, in 1740. He entered the War of the Austrian Succession, won the Battle of Mollwitz, 1741, and acquired the economically valuable province of Silesia, which he retained through the **Seven Years War** (1756–63). He annexed West Prussia in the First Partition of Poland, 1772; formed the Fürstenbund (League of German Princes), 1785. He patronised writers and artists, including Voltaire; wrote *L'Antimachiavel*, 1740, and *History of the House of Brandenburg*, 1751.

FREDERICK I BARBAROSSA (c.1123–90) King of Germany, 1152, emperor 1155; second of the **Hohenstaufen** dynasty. In 1154 he launched a campaign to restore royal rights in Italy; captured Milan, 1162, and Rome, 1166; supported the anti-pope against the powerful Pope **Alexander III,** but was defeated by the **Lombard League** (Legnano 1176); reached a *modus vivendi* with the papacy and Italian cities at the Peace of Venice (1177) and Peace of Constance (1183). He was drowned in Syria while leading the Third **Crusade**.

FREDERICK II (1194–1250) Last great **Hohenstaufen** ruler. He was elected German king in 1212, after civil war and disorder in Germany, Italy and Sicily following the early death of his father, **Henry VI,** in 1197. He left Germany for Italy in 1220 to concentrate his energies on restoring royal authority in Sicily (Constitution of Malfi, 1231); he was crowned emperor by Pope Honorius III in 1220, and led the Fifth Crusade, 1228–9, but his Italian ambitions brought him into conflict with Honorius' successors, Gregory IX and **Innocent IV;** he was excommunicated and deposed at the Council of Lyons (1245), and forced to make lasting concessions to German princes to win their support against the papacy and the Lombard cities. The conflict was continuing at the time of his death, and was only resolved when **Charles of Anjou** defeated Frederick's son and grandson at Benevento (1266) and Tagliacozzo (1268).

FREDERICK II OF PRUSSIA *see* **Frederick the Great**.

FREDERICK AUGUSTUS I (1670–1733) Elector of Saxony (1694–1733) and, as Augustus II, King of Poland, 1697–1733. He succeeded as Elector of Lutheran Saxony in 1694, then became a Catholic in order to be elected king of Poland in 1697; elected by a minority of Polish nobles, he used his Saxon army to secure his coronation. He entered the **Great Northern War** and was defeated by

Charles XII of Sweden (1702). Deposed in 1706, and his kingdom occupied until 1709 by Stanislas Leszczynski, a rival Polish king, he was restored at the Treaty of Stockholm, 1719. He was succeeded by **Frederick Augustus II,** his son (Augustus III of Poland).

FREDERICK AUGUSTUS II (1696–1763) Elector of Saxony (1733–63) and, as Augustus III, King of Poland (1735–63). The only legitimate son of **Frederick Augustus I** of Saxony. He married Maria Josepha, daughter of the Emperor Joseph I, in 1719. In 1733 he succeeded as Elector of Saxony, and in the same year drove his rival Stanislas I Leszczynski into exile and was elected king of Poland (as Augustus III) by a minority vote. He supported Austria against Prussia in the War of the Austrian Succession (1740–48) in 1742, and again in 1756 in the **Seven Years' War.** He failed to counter the growing influence of the Czartoryski and Poniatowski families, or the intervention of the Russian empress, **Catherine the Great,** in Polish affairs.

FREDERICK WILLIAM (1620–88) Elector of Brandenburg, known as the Great Elector. He succeeded in 1640 and successfully reconstructed his domain after the ravages of the Thirty Years War; created a standing army after agreement with the Estates; fought France and Sweden, 1674; defeated the Swedes at Fehrbellin, 1675, and concluded the **Peace of Nimwegen.**

FREDERICK WILLIAM I (1688–1740) King of Prussia. Son of Frederick I, and father of **Frederick the Great.** He succeeded in 1713; reorganised the administration and economy to sustain an army of 83,000 men, and won most of Pomerania from Sweden under the Treaty of Stockholm, 1720.

FREI, EDUARDO (1911–82) Chilean political leader, and a founder member, in 1935, of the National Falange, later renamed the Christian Democrat Party. He edited a daily newspaper, *El Tarapacá,* 1935–7; he held office as Minister of Public Works, and was President of Chile from 1964 until 1970, when the Christian Democrats were defeated by **Allende** in the presidential election.

FRÉMONT, JOHN CHARLES (1813–90) United States explorer and mapmaker who headed expeditions to survey the Des Moines River (1841), the route west to Wyoming (1842), the mouth of the Columbia River (1843), and California (1845). He was the Republican Party's nominee for President of the United States, 1856; he was Governor of Arizona, 1878–83.

FRIARS During the first decade of the 13th century St Francis (1181–1226) and St Dominic (1170–1221) were independently moved to raise the standard of religious life in Europe by instructing the populace (particularly in the towns) through preaching and example, in order to counteract the growing menace of heresy. The Franciscans (Order of Friars Minor, or Grey Friars) were informally recognised by Pope **Innocent III** in 1209 and formally established in 1223; the Dominicans (Order of Preachers, or Black Friars) were formally established in 1216. The Franciscan St Bonaventura (1221–74) and the Dominican St Thomas Aquinas (1226–74) were among their most prominent early members. Friars took the monastic vows of poverty, chastity and obedience, but differed from monks in two main respects: their convents were bases for preaching tours, not places of permanent residence like monasteries, and they sought education at the newly-founded universities. Other 13th-century Orders of friars were the Austin Friars and the Carmelites.

FRISIANS Germanic people. They first entered the coastal provinces of western Germany and the Netherlands in prehistoric times, ousting the resident Celts; after the collapse of Rome, the territory was infiltrated by Angles and **Jutes** on their way to England. The Frisians were conquered and converted to Christianity by **Charlemagne.**

FROBISHER, SIR MARTIN (c.1535–94) Explorer of Canada's north-east coasts, who sailed in 1576 with three ships in search of a North-West Passage to Asia; he reached Labrador and Baffin Island, but failed to find gold or establish a colony. He became vice-admiral to **Drake** in the West Indies, 1585, was prominent in fighting the Spanish Armada, and was mortally wounded fighting Spanish ships off the coast of France.

FRONDE Complex revolt against the French government under **Mazarin** during the minority of **Louis XIV.** Leaders of the Paris *parlement* were imprisoned in 1648 after violent protests against taxation; they were freed by popular revolt in Paris, supported by a separate rebellion of the nobility in alliance with Spain, but the revolt was defeated by royal armies by 1653.

GADSDEN PURCHASE Sale to the United States of some 30,000 square miles (78,000 sq.km) of land along the Mexico-Arizona border, required by the US to provide a low pass through mountains for railway construction. The purchase was negotiated by US minister to Mexico James Gadsden in 1853 at a cost of $10 million.

GAIKWARS Powerful **Maratha** family which made its headquarters in the Baroda district of Gujarat, west-central India, from 1734 to 1947. In 1802 the British established a residency in Baroda to conduct relations between the **East India Company** and the Gaikwar princes.

GAISERIC (428–77) King of the **Vandals,** also known as Genseric. He transported his whole people, said to number 80,000 people, from Spain to North Africa in 429; sacked Carthage, 439, after defeating the joint armies of Rome's Eastern and Western Empires, and declared independence. By sea he attacked, captured and looted Rome, 455; and fought off two major Roman expeditions (460 and 468).

GALLA Large ethnic group in Ethiopia. Cushitic-speaking camel nomads, in a series of invasions from their homelands in the south-east of the country they migrated north and east, and by the end of the 16th century had reached almost to Eritrea. Since then they have largely been assimilated into, and dominated by, the rival Amharic and Tigrean cultures.

GALLEON Powerful sailing ship developed in the 15th and 16th centuries for Mediterranean and ocean navigation. Larger than the galley, with a ratio of beam to length of 1 to 4 or 5, usually with two decks and four masts – two square-rigged and two lateen, it was heavily armed and used in particular by Spain in fleets across the Atlantic and in the annual voyage from Acapulco to Manila.

GALLIC WARS The military campaigns in which the Roman general, **Julius Caesar,** won control of Gaul. As described in his account, *De Bello Gallico,* the conquest took eight years, from 58 to 50 BC; in the first phase, 57–54, Roman authority was fairly easily established, but a large-scale revolt in 53, led by the Gallic chieftain, Vercingetorix, required all Caesar's skill to suppress it.

GAMA, VASCO DA (1462–1524) First discoverer of a continuous sea route from Europe to India via the Cape of Good Hope, Mombasa and Malindi. In 1497–9 he led a Portuguese expedition round Africa to India; a second voyage in 1502 established Portugal as controller of the Indian Ocean and a world power. He died shortly after his arrival to take up an appointment as the Portuguese viceroy in India.

GANDHI, MAHATMA (1869–1948) Indian independence leader. Born in a strict Hindu community, he studied law in England 1889–92, then worked in South Africa as a lawyer and subsequently as a leader of the civil rights movement of Indian settlers, 1893–1914. Entering politics in India in 1919, he turned the previously ineffectual Indian National Congress into a potent mass organisation; perfected the disruptive techniques of mass disobedience and non-violent non-cooperation; during an attack on the Salt Tax (1930) 60,000 followers were imprisoned. Three major campaigns, in 1920–22, 1930–34 and 1940–2, played a major part in accelerating India's progress to dominion status in 1947. He bitterly opposed partition, and worked incessantly to end the Hindu-Muslim riots and massacres accompanying the emergence of independent India and Pakistan. He was assassinated by a Hindu fanatic.

GANDHI, INDIRA (1917–84) Indian Prime Minister and head of state, 1966–77. The daughter of **Nehru,** she was elected to the premiership in 1966, and won the national elections in 1967 and 1971; she led India in war against Pakistan, 1971. She declared a national emergency in 1975, after an adverse legal decision on her own election. Defeated in 1977, returned as leader of Congress I party in 1980. Assassinated by Sikh extremists.

GARCÍA MORENO, GABRIEL (1821–75) Theocratic president of Ecuador, 1860–75. He based his regime on ruthless personal rule and forcible encouragement of the Roman Catholic church. All education, welfare and much state policy were turned over to clerics; political opposition and alternative religions were suppressed; he encouraged agricultural and economic reform, and Ecuadorian nationalism. He was assassinated.

GARIBALDI, GIUSEPPE (1807–82) Italian patriot and member of **Mazzini**'s Young Italy movement. He led an abortive revolt in Piedmont, 1834; became a guerrilla leader in South America; commanded the Italian Legion in Uruguay's war against Argentina; was a national hero during the Italian revolution of 1848–9. In 1860 he led the expedition of 'The Thousand' in a successful invasion of Sicily, and later captured Naples, thus ensuring the unification of Italy under **Victor Emmanuel II;** he was wounded fighting against the Papal States, 1862, and later routed by the French at Mentana.

GAUGAMELA Battlefield near the river Tigris, scene of **Alexander the Great**'s most notable victory, in 331 BC, when, greatly outnumbered, his Macedonian cavalry and Thracian javelin-throwers routed the Persian armies of Darius III by brilliant tactics, and opened the way to Babylon and Susa for him.

GAULLE, CHARLES DE (1890–1970) French soldier and statesman. He escaped to London after the French surrender to Germany, 1940; organised the Free French forces and led the French government-in-exile from Algiers, 1943–4. He was first head of the post-war provisional government, 1944–6. He withdrew from public life, 1953, but returned, 1958, to resolve the Algerian crisis; established the Fifth Republic, becoming its first President, 1959; ended the Algerian war, 1963, and presided over his country's spectacular economic and political recovery. Resigned in 1969 after an adverse referendum vote.

GEDYMIN (c.1275–1341) (or Giedymin) Grand Duke of Lithuania, ancestor of the **Jagiellonian** dynasty. Came to power in 1316, ruling a vast pagan principality based on Vilna. He built the strongest army in eastern Europe to hold his empire in the east and south, while repelling the advances of the Knights of the **Teutonic Order** against the Prussians, who were one of his Lithuanian tribes.

GENERAL MOTORS World's largest industrial manufacturing corporation; sales in 1983 exceeded $74,000 million.

GENERAL PRIVILEGE Legal document, compiled in 1293, setting out limits of royal power in Aragon and Valencia. Approved, under protest, by King **Peter III** of Aragon, it was a source of continuous acrimony between king and subjects until abolished in 1348 by Peter IV, the Ceremonious, after defeating his nobles at the battle of Epila.

GENGHIS KHAN (c.1162–1227) Mongol conqueror. According to the anonymous *Secret History of the Mongols* Temujin (his personal name) first became leader of an impoverished Central Asian clan. He overcame all rivals, gathering a fighting force of 20,000 men, and by 1206 was acknowledged as Genghis Khan, meaning universal ruler, by all the people of the Mongol and Tartar steppes. He invaded northern China, capturing Peking in 1215, and destroyed the Muslim empire of **Khwarizm,** which covered part of modern Soviet Central Asia and Iran, between 1216 and 1223.

GEORGE II (1890–1947) King of Greece, 1922–3, but exiled on the formation of the republic in 1923. Restored in 1935, he was again exiled during the Second World War. He returned to Greece in 1947.

GERMAN CONFEDERATION A grouping of thirty-eight independent German states under the presidency of Austria, set up at the **Congress of Vienna** (1815). Superseded by the Frankfurt Parliament in 1848, it was re-established in 1851, and then dissolved by Prussia after the Seven Weeks' War of 1866.

GHAZNAVIDS Afghan dynasty, founded by Sebuktigin, father of **Mahmud of Ghazni,** in 977. At its greatest extent the empire stretched from the Oxus river in central Asia to the Indus river and the Indian Ocean. Under Mahmud's son, Masud (reigned 1037–41), much northern territory was lost to the **Seljuks;** the last Indian possessions were conquered by **Muizzudin Muhammad** in 1186.

GHURIDS Dynasty ruling north-western Afghanistan from the mid-12th to the early 13th century. Under **Muizzudin Muhammad** the empire was extended into northern India, helping the establishment of Muslim rule in the sub-continent.

GIBBS, ANTONY & SONS London trading and banking house, founded in 1808. Active in South American trade during the 19th century, it now operates as an international merchant bank, with extensive timber interests, under the name Antony Gibbs Holdings.

GIRONDINS Members of a moderate republican party during the French Revolution, so named because the leaders came from the Gironde area. Many were guillotined, 31 October 1793, after the group had been overthrown by the rival **Jacobins** in June 1793.

GLADSTONE, WILLIAM EWART (1809–98) British Prime Minister. Entered Parliament in 1832 as a Tory; President of the Board of Trade, 1843–5, and Colonial Secretary, 1845–6; he resigned after repeal of the Corn Laws; later became Chancellor of the Exchequer, 1853–5 and 1859–66. He led the newly-formed Liberal party to victory, 1868, and was four times Prime Minister, 1868–74, 1880–5, 1886 and 1892–4. He was responsible for many military, educational and civil service reforms, and for the Reform Act of 1884; he was repeatedly defeated over attempts to bring about Irish Home Rule.

GODUNOV, BORIS FYODOROVICH (c.1551–1605) Tsar of Muscovy. He rose in power and favour at the court of **Ivan IV, the Terrible,** and was appointed guardian of Fyodor, the Tsar's retarded son, when Fyodor succeeded in 1584. Godunov banished his enemies and became effective ruler, and was himself elected tsar when Fyodor died without heirs in 1598. Plagued by war, pestilence, famine and constant opposition from the boyars (the old Russian nobility), he was unable to fulfil his desired programme of social, legal, diplomatic and military reforms. His sudden death during civil war with a pretender known as 'the false Dmitri' precipitated Russia into a devastating 'time of troubles'.

GOEBBELS, PAUL JOSEPH (1897–1945) **Hitler's** Minister of Propaganda. He entered journalism in 1921, and in 1926 was appointed by Hitler as district administrator of the National Socialist German Workers' Party (NSDAP), becoming its head of propaganda in 1928. On Hitler's accession he was appointed Minister for Public Enlightenment and Propaganda, controlling the press, radio, films, publishing, theatre, music and the visual arts. He committed suicide, with his wife and six children, in Hitler's besieged Berlin bunker.

GOETHE, JOHANN WOLFGANG VON (1749–1832) Most famous of all German poets, novelists and playwrights. Minister of state to the Duke of Saxe-Weimar, 1775, and one of the outstanding figures of European literature. His early novel, *The Sorrows of Young Werther,* 1774, expressed the reaction against the Enlightenment, the sensation of 'emotion running riot' and the conflict between the artist and society, but after a visit to Italy, 1786–88, which affected his whole life and work, he returned to classicism; from this period onwards his work (*Faust,* part I and part II, 1808, 1832, *Wilhelm Meister,* 1791–1817, *Tasso,* 1789) has a philosophical content which lifts it out of time and place and gives it a universal quality.

GOKHALE, GOPAL KRISHNA (1866–1915) Indian independence leader. He resigned in 1902 from a professorship of history and political economy at Ferguson College, Poona, to enter politics; advocated moderate protest and constitutional reform. He was President of the Indian National Congress, 1905, and founder of the Servants of India Society, dedicated to the alleviation of poverty and service to the underprivileged.

GOLDEN BULL OF 1356 Constitution of the Holy Roman Empire, promulgated by the Emperor **Charles IV;** confirmed, *inter alia,* that succession to the German throne would continue to be determined by seven electors, convened by the Archbishop of Mainz, but that henceforth the electoral lands and powers would be indivisible, and inheritable only by the eldest son, thus removing confusion over the right to vote; it sanctioned the primacy of the territorial princes under loose imperial suzerainty. It also rejected traditional papal claims to rule during periods when the throne was vacant.

GOLDEN HORDE Western portion of the Mongol Empire, also known as the Kipchak khanate. Founded by **Batu** c.1242, it dominated Southern Russia to end of the 14th century. It was finally broken up by **Timur** to form three **Tartar** khanates: Kazan, Astrakhan and the Crimea.

GOLD EXCHANGE STANDARD Device evolved at the Genoa monetary conference, 1922, after the collapse of the **Gold Standard** during the First World War, to maintain the stability of currency exchange rates. Under this system central banks redeemed their currency not in gold, as before, but in a currency that is convertible into gold. The system collapsed 1931–33, but was revived after the Second World War, and during the period 1958–71 most European treasuries adopted this approach, treating the US dollar as the main unit in which they accumulated reserves.

GOLD STANDARD Monetary system in which the value of currency in issue is legally tied to a certain quantity of gold. During the last quarter of the 19th century virtually all major trading nations adopted this policy and most attempted to return to it after the break caused by the First World War; this attempt was abandoned, in all important cases, with the onset of world economic slump in 1931.

GÖMBÖS, GYULA (1886–1936) Hungarian Prime Minister. In 1919 he organised the counter-revolutionary network dedicated to the overthrow of the Communist government, and became Minister of Defence (1932–6). Szeged government. At first he opposed the conservative premier, István Bethlen (1921–31), but joined his administration in 1929 and in 1932 was swept to power by the 'right radical' movement. He advocated a reactionary, anti-Semitic programme and alliance with Germany and Italy; but he failed.

GOMES, FERNÃO 15th century Portuguese merchant who in 1469 was granted a monopoly to explore the West African coast and keep all trading profits. Gomes and his captains explored as far as the Congo river, and prepared the way for the voyage to India of **Vasco da Gama** in 1497–9.

GOMULKA, WLADYSLAW (1905–82) Polish Communist leader. A youth organiser for the banned Communist Party, 1926, and a wartime underground fighter, he was stripped of Party membership in 1949 after incurring the displeasure of Stalin, but readmitted in 1956 to become First Secretary of the Central Committee. Resistance to his regime erupted in riots in 1968; he was deposed and retired in 1970.

GORDON, CHARLES GEORGE (1833–85) British general, first distinguished for bravery in the Crimean War (1854–6). He volunteered for service in China, where his exploits in the 'Arrow' war, the T'ai-p'ing Rebellion and the burning of the emperor's Summer Palace earned him the nickname 'Chinese Gordon'. In 1884 he was sent to the Sudan (where he had earlier been Governor-General) to evacuate British troops from Khartoum; he was besieged and killed by Sudanese followers of **Mohammed Ahmed al-Mahdi.**

GORGIAS OF LEONTINI (c.483–c.376 BC) Ancient Greek rhetorician, noted for his poetic language and carefully balanced clauses. In his treatise *On Nature* he argued the essential non-existence, unknowability and incommunicability of Being. He was portrayed with respect by **Plato** in *Gorgias*.

GORM King of Denmark, father of **Harald Bluetooth;** died after 935.

GOTHIC Relating to the art and language of the **Ostrogoths** and **Visigoths**; by extension, also to the culture of mediaeval Europe, and particularly to the style of church architecture, with characteristic pointed arches, predominant from the 12th to the 15th century.

GOTT, BENJAMIN (1762–1840) English manufacturer of woollen cloth and philanthropist. In 1793 he established a woollen mill in Leeds, introducing an improved mechanical cloth-cutting device in spite of much hostility.

GOTTFRIED VON STRASSBURG German mediaeval poet, author of *Tristan*, the classic version of the story of Tristan and Isolde. He lived and worked in the late 12th and early 13th centuries.

GOULART, DR JOÃO (1918–76) Brazilian political leader. He joined the Brazilian labour party, Partido Trabalhista, in 1945 and became national party director in 1951, Minister of Labour and Commerce, 1953–4, Vice-President of Brazil, 1956, was re-elected in 1961 and became president that year. He was deposed in a military *coup d'état*, 1964.

GOVERNMENT OF INDIA ACT British Act of Parliament of 1935 embodying a number of constitutional reforms, including 'provincial autonomy' and a federal structure at the centre. Only the provisions relating to the provinces were implemented, the proposals for federation being rejected by the Indian political parties.

GRANADA, KINGDOM of Last foothold of the Muslims in Spain. Ruled by the **Nasrid** dynasty, 1238–1492, it prospered by welcoming Moorish refugees from Seville, Valencia and Murcia; it built one of Islam's most famous architectural achievements, the Alhambra (Red Fortress). It was finally conquered by Christian forces, 1492.

GRANT, ULYSSES SIMPSON (1822–85) Eighteenth President of the United States, 1869–77. He was commander-in-chief of the Union armies during the American Civil War. His administration (Republican) was marked by corruption and bitter partisanship between the political parties.

GREAT ELECTOR *see* **Frederick William,** Elector of Brandenburg.

GREAT FEAR Series of rural panics, spreading through the French countryside between 20 July and 6 August 1789, at the onset of the French Revolution. Following a series of peasant disorders, during which stores of grain were looted and châteaux burned, rumours of invasion by armed brigands spread in five main currents covering the greater part of the country, which stimulated further disorders that petered out as suddenly as they had begun.

GREAT NORTHERN WAR Struggle between Sweden and Russia, 1700–21, mainly for control of the Baltic. **Charles XII** of Sweden at first defeated an alliance of Russia, Denmark, Poland and Saxony (1700–6), but was heavily defeated by **Peter the Great** of Russia in 1709. This advantage was lost when Turkey declared war on Russia in 1710, and fighting continued in Poland and Scandinavia until Charles' death in 1718. In the final settlement Sweden lost Livonia and Karelia to Russia (which gained permanent access to the Baltic Sea), and abandoned its claims to be a great power.

GREAT PEASANT REVOLT 14th-century uprising in the English countryside and towns of villeins, free labourers, small farmers and artisans. Initially in protest against the Poll Tax of 1381 and stringent labour regulations imposed after the Black Death, it was concentrated mainly in East Anglia and the south-east. Under the leadership of Wat Tyler, a vast mob invaded London, executing royal ministers and destroying the property of supposed enemies of the common people, extracting promises of redress from the young king, **Richard II.** However, the insurgents were dispersed, Tyler was slain, and insurgent action in other areas was vigorously suppressed; the reforms and royal pardons were revoked.

GREAT SCHISM A political split in the Catholic Church, lasting from 1378 to 1417, during which rival popes – one in Rome, the other in Avignon – attempted to exert authority. The result of a serious split among cardinals and high churchmen on ecclesiastical reform, and the political influence of the French monarchy. The Schism was resolved by the Council of Constance, 1414–17.

GREGORY I 'THE GREAT' (c.540–604) Pope, saint and one of the Fathers of the Christian Church. During his papacy (590–604), he strengthened and reorganised church administration, reformed the liturgy, promoted monasticism, asserted the temporal power of the papacy, extended Rome's influence in the west and sent St Augustine of Canterbury on his mission to convert the British.

GREGORY VII (c.1020–85) Pope and saint, born in north Italy and given the name Hildebrand. He served under Pope Gregory VI during the Pope's exile in Germany after deposition by the Emperor **Henry III.** He was recalled to Rome by Pope **Leo IX,** and thereafter was often the power behind the papal throne. He was made a cardinal by **Alexander II** (1061–73), and elected by acclaim as his successor. From 1075 he was engaged in the contest over **lay investiture** with Emperor **Henry IV**, whom he excommunicated in 1076; after absolving him at Canossa in 1077, he re-excommunicated him after fresh attacks. Gregory was driven from Rome in 1084. He was canonised in 1606.

GRIJALVA, JUAN DE (c.1489–1527) Spanish explorer. Sailing along the coast of Mexico, where he discovered the river Grijalva (named after him) in 1518, he was probably the first of the *conquistadores* to hear of the rich Aztec civilisation of the interior.

GRUFFYDD AP LLEWELYN (d.1063) Briefly king of all Wales. He challenged the authority of existing dynasties holding power over Welsh kingdoms; seized control in Gwynedd in the north-west, Deheubarth in the south-west, and for a short period the whole country; he devastated the borderland with England.

GUELPH and GHIBELLINE The two great rival political factions of mediaeval Italy, reflecting the rivalry of Guelph dukes of Saxony and Bavaria and the **Hohenstaufen.** The names Guelph and Ghibelline came to designate support for the papal (Guelph) side against the imperial (Ghibelline) side in the struggle between the **papacy** and the **Holy Roman Empire.**

GUEST, SIR JOSIAH (1785–1852) British industrialist. He created an improved smelting process at the family ironworks at Dowlais (near Merthyr Tydfil, Wales) and raised its annual iron production to 75,000 tons, mostly in the form of rails for the new railways.

GUEVARA, ERNESTO 'CHE' (1928–67) South American revolutionary leader, born in Argentina. He qualified as a doctor of medicine, 1953; became chief aide to **Fidel Castro** in his successful Cuban revolution, 1959; wrote *Guerrilla Warfare*, 1960, and *Episodes of the Revolutionary War*, 1963. He was killed in Bolivia, trying to establish a guerrilla base there.

GUGGENHEIM, MEYER (1828–1905) Founder of modern American metal-mining industry, born in Switzerland he emigrated to the United States in 1847. In the early 1880s he bought control of two Colorado copper mines, and quickly built up a worldwide network of mines, exploration companies, smelters and refineries. With his son Daniel (1856–1930) he merged all the family interests in 1901 into the American Smelting & Refining Company.

GUPTA Imperial dynasty, ruling in northern India from the 4th to the 6th centuries AD. It first rose to prominence under Chandragupta I, ruling over Magadha and parts of Uttar Pradesh, c.319–335. Its power was extended and reinforced under **Samudragupta** (reigned c.335–75), **Chandragupta II** (c.375–415) and Kumaragupta (c.415–54). The dynasty was later weakened by domestic unrest and **Hun** invasion, and effectively eliminated as a major political force by 510.

GURJARAS Central Asian tribe, reaching India with the **Hun** invasions of the 4th and 5th centuries AD. They settled in Rajasthan, in western India, and were reputed ancestors of the **Pratiharas.**

GUSTAVUS I VASA (c.1496–1560) King of Sweden (1523–1560), founder of the Vasa dynasty. He fought in Sweden's 1517–18 rebellion against Denmark, was interned, but returned in 1520 to lead another rebellion against Denmark. He was elected king of Sweden in 1523, thus breaking up the **Union of Kalmar.** He introduced the **Lutheran** Reformation; and in 1544 persuaded the Diet to make the monarchy hereditary in his Vasa family line.

GUSTAVUS II ADOLPHUS (1594–1632) King of Sweden, grandson of **Gustavus I Vasa.** he succeeded to the throne in 1611, and made Sweden a major political and military power. He entered the Thirty Years War on the side of the Protestants, 1630, and conquered most of Germany; he was killed at the Battle of Lützen.

GUTIANS (Guti) Ancient mountain people from the Zagros range, east of Mesopotamia. They destroyed the empire of Akkad, c.2230 BC, and exercised sporadic sovereignty over much of Babylonia for the next century. Traditionally they were eclipsed as a historical force after the defeat of the last king, Tirigan, by Utu-Khegal of Uruk, c.2130 BC. The Gutians were primarily remembered in later tradition as barbarians.

GUZMÁN BLANCO, ANTONIO (1829–99) President of Venezuela. He was appointed special finance commissioner to negotiate loans from Great Britain; seized control of the government in 1870; as head of the Regeneration party was elected constitutional president, 1873; ruled as absolute dictator until 1877, and again 1879–84 and 1886–88, laying the main foundations of modern Venezuela, and accumulating a vast personal fortune. Ousted by a *coup d'état* during one of his frequent visits to Europe, he died in Paris.

HABSBURGS Major European royal and imperial dynasty from the 15th to the 20th century. The ascendancy of the family began in Austria, c. 1276. Frederick V, Habsburg king of Germany, was crowned Holy Roman Emperor in 1452, as Frederick III; the title remained a family possession until the Empire was dissolved in 1806. At their peak, under **Charles V** (Charles I of Spain), Habsburg realms stretched from eastern Europe to the New World; after Charles' death, the house split into the Spanish line, which died out in 1700, and the Austrian line, which remained in power — after 1740 as the House of Habsburg-Lorraine — until 1918.

HADRIAN IV (c.1100–59) Pope 1154–59. Born Nicholas Breakspear, and the only English Pope, he renewed the initiative of the papacy in the spirit of **Gregory VII,** notably in the incident of Besançon, when he claimed that the imperial crown was held from the Pope. He expelled the heretic **Arnold of Brescia** from Rome.

HADRIAN, PUBLIUS AELIUS (AD 76–138) Roman emperor. Adopted as his son by **Trajan,** whom he succeeded in 117. He abandoned the policy of eastern expansion in order to consolidate frontiers and initiate far-reaching military, legal and administrative reforms; his fortifications in Britain and Syria still stand. He travelled widely in the Empire, encouraging the spread of Greco-Roman civilisation and culture.

HAFSIDS Dynasty of **Berber** origin, ruling Tunisia and eastern Algeria c.1229–1574. The most famous ruler, Mustansir (1249–77), used the title of caliph; his diplomacy averted danger from the Crusade of **Louis IX** and extended his influence into Morocco and Spain.

HAIDER ALI (1722–82) Muslim ruler of Mysore, southern India. He created the first Indian army equipped with European firearms and artillery. He deposed the local rajah and seized the throne, c.1761; he defeated the British several times between 1766 and 1780 but finally lost in the three battles of Porto Novo, Pollilu and Sholinghar. Before his death he implored his son **Tipu** to make peace with the invaders.

HAIG, DOUGLAS (1861–1928) 1st Earl Haig. British field marshal, commander-in-chief of the British forces in Flanders and France 1915–18, during the First World War. His strategy of attrition on the Somme (1916) and in Flanders (1917), especially at the third battle of Ypres (or Passchendaele), resulted in enormous British casualties.

HAILE SELASSIE I (1892–75) Emperor of Ethiopia. A close relative of Emperor **Menelik II** (1889–1913), he was appointed to provisional governorships from 1908, became regent and heir apparent to Menelik's daughter Zauditu in 1916. He took Ethiopia into the **League of Nations** in 1923, and became emperor in 1930, introducing bicameral Parliament the following year. He was driven out by the Italian occupation of 1936–41; he led the reconquest, with British aid, and began to modernise the country. He survived a serious plot in 1960, but in 1974 news of the famine in the Wallo district and an armed mutiny provoked a revolution which deposed him, and he died under house arrest.

HAJJ UMAR, AL- (1794–1864) West African Tukolor warrior-mystic, founder of the Muslim empire based on Masina in the western Sudan (now in the republic of Mali). He became a member of the newly-founded militant religious order, the Tijanyya. He made a pilgrimage to Mecca in 1826, and returned inspired to propagate Islam in the western Sudan; in 1852 he embarked upon a great and bloody *jihad* (holy war), and conquered much of the western Sudan, coming into violent conflict with the French, who were expanding up the Senegal river. He was killed in battle; his empire was finally conquered by the French by the end of the 19th century.

HAKKA North Chinese people who migrated south under the Sung dynasty (1126–1279) to Kwangtung and Fukien where they remained a distinct social group, living in separate communities, usually in poor uplands. They were involved in many bitter communal feuds in the 18th and 19th centuries, culminating in the

Hakka-Punti war in the 1850s. Many emigrated after the T'ai-p'ing rebellion, and they are now widely spread throughout east Asia.

HALLSTATT Early Celtic Iron Age culture, flourishing in central Europe c.700–500 BC, named after an Austrian village in the Salzkammergut, where an archaeologically important cemetery was found in the 19th century. The culture was notable for elaborate burials, in which the dead person was placed in a four-wheeled chariot, of which examples have been found from the Upper Danube region to Vix in Burgundy.

HAMAGUCHI, OSACHI (1870–1931) Japanese statesman. Official of the finance ministry, 1895–1924, and Finance Minister 1924–6, in 1927 he was elected leader of the new Rikken Minseitō (Constitutional Democratic) Party, and became Japanese Prime Minister in 1929. He decreed drastic deflationary policies, but was assassinated before they could take effect. The army forced his colleagues to resign, thus bringing democratic government to an end.

HAMDANIDS Bedouin dynasty controlling Mosul and Aleppo, 905–1004; renowned warriors and patrons of Arab art and learning.

HAMMADIDS North African Berber dynasty, a branch of the **Zirids**. In the reign of the Zirid leader Badis Ibn al-Mansur (995–1016) they gained control of part of Algeria; in 1067, under attack from the **Fatimids** and their Bedouin allies, they established themselves in part of Bejaia (Bougie), and developed a successful trading empire until conquered by the **Almohads** in 1152.

HAMMARSKJÖLD, DAG (1905–61) Swedish and international statesman. Son of a Swedish Prime Minister, he entered politics in 1930 and became Deputy Foreign Minister in 1951. Elected as Secretary-General of the **United Nations** in 1953, he greatly extended the influence both of the UN and of its secretary-general, striving to reduce the tensions caused by decolonisation in Africa, particularly in the Congo (1960–1), where he was killed in an air crash.

HAMMURABI King of Babylon, reigning 1792–1750 BC. He succeeded his father, Sin-Mabullit, and extended his small kingdom (originally only 80 miles long and 20 miles wide) to unify all Mesopotamia under Babylonian rule. He published a collection of laws on a basalt stele, 8ft high, now in the Louvre Museum.

HAM NGHI (1870–c.1940) Emperor of Vietnam. He reached the throne in 1884 after intense intrigue following the death of his uncle, the emperor Tu Duc; at the instigation of his regents, Nguyen Van Tuong and Thou That Thuyet, he led a revolt against the French, 1885; he fled after its failure, was deposed in 1886, captured and exiled to Algeria.

HAN Chinese imperial dynasty, ruling from 206 BC to AD 9, (Former Han), and AD 25–220, (Later Han); see page 81.

HAN FU-CHÜ (1890–1938) Military officer who served under **Feng Yü-hsiang**, 1912–28. He was appointed governor of Honan in 1928; defecting from Feng in his confrontation with **Chiang Kai-shek**, in 1929, he controlled Shantung from 1930 to 1938 and brought it under the control of Nanking. In 1937 the Japanese invaded Shantung; he put up only token resistance, and was executed for dereliction of duty the following year.

HANNIBAL (247–183 BC) Most famous Carthaginian general, son of another great soldier, Hamilcar Barca. He was commander-in-chief in Spain aged 26; after the beginning of the Second **Punic War** against Rome (218–201) he led 40,000 troops, with elephants, over the Alps to smash the Roman armies at Lake Trasimene, 217, and Cannae, 216. Forced to abandon Italy in 203 as Rome had attacked Carthage itself, he was finally defeated at Zama in 202 and later driven into exile. He committed suicide.

HANSEATIC LEAGUE Association of mediaeval German cities and merchant groups which became a powerful economic and political force in northern Europe. With a centre for meetings in the city of Lübeck, the members established an important network of Baltic trade, and a string of commercial bases stretching from Novgorod to London and from Bergen to Bruges. In its heyday during the 14th century the Hansa included well over a hundred towns; its influence gradually faded with the emergence of powerful competitor states, and the last meeting of the Diet was held in Lübeck in 1669.

HARALD BLUETOOTH (died c.985) King of Denmark from c.940. He accepted the introduction of Christianity into his kingdom, and strengthened its central organisation; he successfully defeated German and Norwegian attacks on Denmark, unifying its disparate elements.

HARALD I FINEHAIR (c.860–c.940) First king claiming sovereignty over all Norway, in the 2nd half of the 9th century, the son of Halfdan the Black, ruler of a part of south-east Norway and a member of the ancient Swedish Yngling dynasty, whom he succeeded when very young. His conquests culminated in the Battle of Hafrsfjord, c.900; many defeated chiefs fled to Britain and possibly Iceland. The best account is given in Snorri Sturlson's 13th century saga, the *Heimskringla*.

HARALD II GREYCLOAK (died c.970) Norwegian king, son of **Erik Bloodaxe**. He overthrew his half-brother, Haakon the Good, c.961, ruling oppressively, with his brothers, until c.970. He is credited with establishing the first Christian missions in Norway. He was killed in battle against an alliance of local nobles and his former supporter, **Harald Bluetooth**.

HARKORT, FRIEDRICH (FRITZ) (1793–1880) Pioneer entrepreneur in the German engineering industry. In 1819 Harkort and Kamp, in partnership with Thomas (an English engineer), established works producing textile machinery and steam engines at Wetter in the Ruhr district. The plant was later expanded to include the puddling process. Harkort twice visited England to recruit skilled mechanics. He was a pioneer in the construction of steamships on the Weser and the Rhine, and was also a leading advocate of railway building in Germany.

HARA TAKASHI (1856–1921) First 'commoner' (i.e. untitled) Prime Minister of modern Japan. Graduated from Tokyo university into journalism, and then entered foreign service in 1882. He became ambassador to Korea in 1897, chief editor of the Osaka *Mainichi* newspaper in 1899. He helped to found the Rikken-Seiyukai (Friends of Constitutional Government) Party, 1900, and built it into an American-style party machine, meanwhile rising to ministerial, and finally prime ministerial rank in 1918. He was assassinated by a right-wing fanatic after opposing the use of Japanese troops in Siberia.

HARSHA (c.590–c.647) Indian ruler, second son of a king in the Punjab. He ultimately exercised loose imperial power over most of northern India. Converted from **Hinduism** to **Buddhism**, he was the first to open diplomatic relations between India and China (c.641); his court, at Kanauj, his early years, and his model administration are described in Bana's poem *The Deeds of Harsha*, and the writings of the Chinese pilgrim, **Hsüan Tsang**.

HARUN AL-RASHID (c.763–806) Fifth caliph of the **Abbasid** dynasty, immortalised in *The Thousand and One Nights*. He inherited the throne in 786, ruling territories from northwest India to the western Mediterranean; his reign saw the beginning of the disintegration of the **caliphate**.

HASHEMITES Direct or collateral descendants of the prophet **Mohammed**, who was himself a member of the house of Hashem, a division of the Quraysh tribe. In the 20th century, Hussein ibn Ali, descendant of a long line of Hashemite *sharifs* or local rulers of Mecca, and King of Hejaz, 1916–24, founded the modern Hashemite dynasty, carried on by his sons, King Feisal of Iraq and King Abdullah of Jordan.

HASSAN II (1929–) King of Morocco, 17th monarch of the Alaouite dynasty. The son of **Mohammed V**, he became commander-in-chief of the Royal Moroccan Army in 1957. Succeeding to the throne in 1961, he held the posts of Prime Minister, 1961–3 and 1965–7, Minister of Defence, 1972–3, and commander-in-chief of the army from 1972. He established strong monarchical government, and was the main force in the partition of the former Spanish Sahara between Morocco and Mauritania.

HASTINGS, FRANCIS RAWDON-HASTINGS, (1754–1826) 1st Marquis. Early Governor-General of Bengal. He landed in India, 1813; defeated the Gurkhas, 1816; conquered the Maratha States and cemented British control east of the Sutlej river. He purchased Singapore, 1819, but resigned under a financial cloud, 1823; he was Governor of Malta 1824.

HASTINGS, WARREN (1732–1818) First Governor-General of British India, 1774–85. He carried out important administrative and legal reforms, but was impeached on corruption charges, 1788; he was finally acquitted, after a long and famous trial, in 1795.

HAUSA West African people, organised from about the 11th century into a loose grouping of states centred to the west of Lake Chad. In the 16th century Kano became the greatest of the Hausa cities, but the Hausaland region only came under unified control after conquest by the Fulani in the early 19th century. They are now one of the largest ethnic groups in Nigeria.

HAWLEY-SMOOT TARIFF United States tariff, passed in 1930, which set the highest import duties in American history, attracted immediate retaliation from European governments, and is considered to be one of the factors responsible for deepening the Great Depression.

HAY-PAUNCEFOTE TREATY Composite name for two Anglo-American agreements, signed in 1900 and 1901, freeing the US from a previous commitment to international control of any projected Central American canal. It freed US hands for the building of the Panama Canal, which was completed in 1914.

HAYES, RUTHERFORD B. (1822–93) 19th President of the United States, and the first chief executive to say openly that an isthmian canal must be American-owned. This pronouncement correlates with the beginning of a programme of naval expansion.

HEAVENLY PRINCIPLE SECT (T'ien-li chiao) Secret sectarian movement connected with the White Lotus society, with a large following during the late 18th century in northern China (Hopei, Honan, Shantung), led by Lin Ch'ing and Li Wen-ch'eng, who began a rebellion in Honan in 1813. A small group infiltrated Peking and entered the palace.

HEGIRA Arabic word for 'emigration', and the starting date of Muslim era. By order of **Omar** I, the second caliph, in AD 639, Islamic letters, treaties, proclamations and events were to be dated by reference to the day, 16 July 622, on which the Prophet **Mohammed** migrated from Mecca to Medina.

HELLENISM Culture, philosophy and spirit of ancient Greece, spread across Asia, and across Europe through the Roman adoption of Greek models; through thought and art it touched Buddhism, Christianity, Hinduism and Islam. It was revived in the western world in the Renaissance and other renaissances. It is often associated with humanism, rationality and beauty of form, though these are by no means a complete picture of Greek civilisation.

HELLENISTIC The era from 323 to 30 BC, when the eastern Mediterranean and the Near East were dominated by dynasties and state governments founded by the successors of **Alexander the Great**.

HENRICIANS Followers of Henry of Lausanne, an itinerant preacher of southern France in the 12th century, whose criticisms of the Church followed those of the **Petrobrusians** and were transmitted to the more numerous and better organised **Waldensians**.

HENRY II (1333–79) King of Castile, 1369–79. The natural son of Alfonso XI, Henry drove his brother Pedro (1356–69) from the throne with French aid and founded the Trastámara dynasty, which continued until 1504.

HENRY II (1133–89) King of England. Grandson of Henry I, he became Duke of Normandy in 1150 and Count of Anjou in 1151. He married Eleanor of Aquitaine in 1152 after her repudiation by **Louis VII** of France. He succeeded to the English throne in 1154; in his own right and that of his wife he ruled over domains extending from Ireland to the Pyrenees and Mediterranean. He was noted for his expansion of the judicial and administrative authority of the English crown; his generally successful reign was marred by quarrels with Thomas Becket, Archbishop of Canterbury, and with his own family.

HENRY IV (1367–1413) King of England, 1399–1413, son of John of Gaunt and grandson of **Edward III**. He was banished in 1398 by **Richard II**, but returned in 1399 to depose his cousin and seize the throne. He put down baronial rebellions under Owen Glendower and Sir Henry Percy in 1403, and under Thomas de Mowbray in 1405; he was the subject of two plays by Shakespeare.

HENRY V (1387–1422) King of England, son of Henry IV, whom he succeeded in 1413. In 1415 he reopened the **Hundred Years War** in support of his claims to the French throne; won the Battle of Agincourt, 1415, and conquered Normandy, 1419. Under the Treaty of Troyes he married Catherine of Valois and became heir to the French king, Charles VI. Renewed war, 1421, the year before his death.

HENRY VII (1457–1509) King of England. He became head of the royal House of Lancaster which challenged their cousins, the House of York, for the crown of England; exiled until 1485, when he defeated and killed the Yorkist, Richard III, he then became king and ended the civil war (**Wars of the Roses**). He founded the **Tudor** dynasty (which lasted until 1603), creating a strong central government in England after almost a century of disruption.

HENRY VIII (1491–1547) King of England, son of **Henry VII**, succeeding in 1509. His desire for a male heir caused his search for a means to declare his first marriage, to Catherine of Aragon, invalid; after papal refusal, and non-recognition of his second marriage in 1533 to Anne Boleyn, Parliament passed the Act of Supremacy, 1534, declaring Henry head of the English Church; monasteries were suppressed (1536, 1539). Wales was brought into legal union with England, 1534–6.

HENRY IV (1533–1610) King of France, 1589–1610, son of Antoine, king of Navarre. He married Marguerite of Valois, daughter of the French king, Henry II, in 1572. He emerged as Protestant leader in the French wars of religion, and was excommunicated, 1585. Reconciled with King Henry III in 1589, he abjured the Protestant faith in 1593 and was crowned king in 1594. He drove the Spaniards out of Paris, and declared war on the Spanish king, **Philip II**, in 1595. In 1598 he signed the **Edict of Nantes**, granting toleration to French Protestants. He married Marie de' Medici, 1600; authorised **Jesuits** to reopen colleges in Paris, 1603. He was assassinated.

HENRY III (1017–56) German king 1039–56, and emperor 1046–56. He brought Church reform to Rome at the **Synod of Sutri**, 1046, and appointed a succession of Germans – notably **Leo IX** – to the papacy.

HENRY IV (1050–1106) German Emperor, son of Henry III and Agnes of Poitou. He succeeded in 1056 under his mother's regency. He broke with Pope **Gregory VII** over the investiture issue in 1075, was excommunicated and declared deposed by him, but restored after performing penance to the Pope at Canossa in 1077; he was excommunicated again in 1080. He appointed Clement III as anti-Pope in 1084, but was outmanoeuvred by Pope **Urban II** and his position was weakened by the revolts of his sons Conrad and the future emperor, Henry V. He died after defeating Henry at Visé, near Liège.

HENRY VI (1165–97) Son of **Frederick I Barbarossa**, he was chosen as German king in 1169; married Constance, daughter of **Roger II** of Sicily in 1186, and inherited Roger's kingdom in 1189; crowned emperor, in 1191, after Frederick's death on the Third **Crusade**. The ransom of Richard I, whom he held prisoner, 1193–4, enabled him to overcome internal opposition in the Lower Rhineland and Saxony led by **Duke Henry**, and then to finance his conquest of Sicily after the death of the rival claimant, King Tancred, in 1194. He died of malaria while preparing a crusade. Because his son **Frederick II** was then aged only two years, his death caused a succession dispute in the Empire.

HENRY, DUKE OF SAXONY (c.1130–95) Known as 'the Lion'. He spent his early years fighting for his father's duchies. He was granted Saxony in 1142 but had to wait until 1156 for Bavaria; founded Munich in 1157 and Lübeck in 1159. Stripped of his lands after breaking with **Frederick I Barbarossa**, 1179–80, he was twice exiled, 1181–5 and 1189–90, but was reconciled with Emperor **Henry VI** in 1194.

HENRY THE NAVIGATOR (1394–1460) Portuguese prince, third son of John I and Philippa of Lancaster. He helped in the capture of Ceuta, Morocco, in 1415, and at the age of twenty-six was made Grand Master of Portugal's crusading Order of Christ. Thereafter, he devoted much of his life to the encouragement of maritime trade and discovery, to the organisation of voyages to west

Africa, and to occasional crusading operations in Morocco.

HERACLIANS Byzantine dynasty, ruling from AD 610 to 711, founded by Emperor **Heraclius** (610–41) and ending with Justinian II (685–95, and again 705–11).

HERACLIUS (c.575–641) Eastern Roman Emperor. He landed at Constantinople in 610 and seized the crown from Emperor Phocas; fought and defeated the Persians, 622–8; restored the True Cross to Jerusalem, 630; persecuted the **Jews,** 632. His armies were beaten by Muslim Arabs in 636, and Syria and Palestine (640) and Egypt (642) were lost to Islam; in the meantime he reformed the administration of the remaining provinces and laid the foundations for the mediaeval Byzantine state.

HERDER, JOHANN GOTTFRIED VON (1744–1803) German critic, linguist and philosopher who wrote on the origins of language, poetry and aesthetics. He was a leading figure in the literary movement known as *Sturm und Drang*. He made a famous collection of German songs (*Volkslieder*, 1778–9), wrote the *Essay on the Origin of Language* (1772), and at Weimar, where he became superintendent of schools in 1776, *Outlines of a Philosophy of the History of Man* (1784–91).

HEREDÍA, PEDRO DE (c.1500–54) Spanish soldier who founded Cartagena in Central America in 1533, and several other New World cities; he amassed a vast fortune through his many expeditions to the interior. He was drowned in Spain.

HERERO Bantu-speaking peoples of south-west Africa, mostly in central Namibia and Botswana.

HERERO REVOLT A protest which broke out in 1904 against German colonial oppression of the Herero and other peoples of south-west Africa. In 1907, when the risings ended, over 65,000 Hereros out of an original 80,000 had been killed, starved in concentration camps or driven into the Kalahari Desert to die.

HERNÁNDEZ DE CÓRDOBA, FRANCISCO Name of two Spanish soldier-explorers active in the New World at the beginning of the 16th century. The first, born c.1475, went in 1514 to the Isthmus of Panama with Pedro Arias de Ávila, and in 1524 was sent to seize Nicaragua from its rightful discoverer, Gil González de Ávila; after founding the towns of Granada and León and exploring Lake Nicaragua he defected to **Cortés**, and was executed by Pedrarias in 1526. His namesake went to Cuba with Velázquez in 1511 and later commanded the expedition that coasted Yucatán and made the first recorded European contact with **Mayan** civilisation; he died in 1517.

HEROD ANTIPAS (21 BC–AD 39) Tetrarch of Galilee during the lifetime of **Jesus**. The son of Herod the Great, he inherited part of his father's kingdom under the Romans, c.4 BC; he was goaded into beheading John the Baptist, and later refused to pass judgement on Jesus himself.

HERODOTUS (c.484–c.420 BC) Greek writer, known as 'the father of history'. He travelled widely in Asia, Egypt and eastern Europe; his *Histories*, a history of the Greco-Persian wars and the events preceding them, is one of the world's first major prose works, incorporating many vivid and, to contemporaries, almost incredible travellers' tales; modern research has sometimes shown even the wildest of them to contain an element of truth.

HIDEYOSHI TOYOTOMI (1536–98) Unifier of 16th century Japan. He served as a chief lieutenant to the feudal general, Oda Nobunaga (1534–82), and after his death became the Emperor's chief minister (1585). In 1590 he conquered the islands of Shikoku and Kyushu to integrate the country; he energetically promoted internal peace, economic development and overseas expansion. He died after an unsuccessful invasion of Korea.

HINDENBURG, PAUL VON (1847–1934) German soldier, President of Germany 1925–34. Recalled from retirement in 1914 to take command in east Prussia after the Russian invasion, he won the victory of Tannenberg, and the first and second battles of the Masurian Lakes (1914–15). Appointed a field-marshal and supreme commander of all German armies, 1916, he became virtual dictator of German domestic policy too. As President he appointed **Hitler** as Chancellor in 1933.

HINDENBURG LINE Fortified line on the Western Front in the First World War, taken up by German armies following the battle of the Somme in 1916. A formidable defence system, it was eventually pierced in September 1918 by the British and French forces.

HINDUISM Predominant religion of India; all-embracing in its forms, capable of including external observances and their rejection, animal sacrifice and refusal to take any form of life, extreme polytheism and high monotheism.

HIPPOCRATES (c.460–c.377 BC) Ancient Greek physician, traditionally regarded in the West as the father of medicine. He believed in the wholeness of the body as an organism, in the close observation and recording of case-histories, and in the importance of diet and climate. The works making up the Hippocratic Collection, forming the library of the medical school at Cos, where he taught, reflect the continuing effects of his work. The Hippocratic Oath is still used as a guide to conduct by the medical profession.

HIPPODAMUS Ancient Greek architect who flourished in the 5th century BC. He is best known for the grid system of street planning, developed for the Athenian port of Piraeus, the pan-Hellenic settlement of Thurii, and perhaps the new city of Rhodes.

HIROHITO (1901–) Emperor of Japan, supposedly the one hundred and twenty-fourth direct descendant of Jimmu, Japan's legendary first ruler. An authority on marine biology, and the first Japanese crown prince to travel abroad (1921), he succeeded his father in 1926; he tried, ineffectually, to avert war with the United States, and broke political deadlock in 1945 to sue for peace. He ended centuries of public imperial silence to broadcast Japan's announcement of surrender on 15 August 1945. He is now a constitutional monarch, with greatly restricted powers.

HITLER, ADOLF (1889–1945) German dictator. Born in Austria, he moved to Munich in 1913, served in the German army, joined the National Socialist German Workers' Party and reorganised it as a quasi-military force. He tried unsuccessfully to seize power in Bavaria, 1923; wrote *Mein Kampf* (*My Struggle*) in prison, elaborating his theories of Jewish conspiracy and **Aryan** superiority. Appointed Chancellor, 1933; in 1936 he remilitarised the Rhineland, in 1938 invaded Austria and Czechoslovakia and in 1939, Poland. His sweeping initial successes in the Second World War were followed by defeats in Russia and North Africa, 1942–3. He survived an assassination plot in 1944, but committed suicide in 1945 as the Russians entered Berlin.

HITTITES A people speaking an Indo-European language who had occupied central Anatolia by the beginning of the 2nd millennium BC, quickly absorbing the older population. The Old Hittite kingdom, c.1750–1500 BC, later expanded into the Hittite Empire, c.1500–1190, which at its greatest extent controlled all Syria and briefly much of northern Mesopotamia. After the collapse of the empire, various neo-Hittite kingdoms survived in the region for a further 500 years.

HOABINHIAN *see* **Bacsonian**

HOCHE, LOUIS-LAZARE (1768–97) French Revolutionary general. He enlisted in the French Guards, 1784, was appointed a corporal, 1789; as commander of the army of the Moselle (1793) he drove Austro-Prussian forces from Alsace. He suppressed the **Vendée** counter-revolution, 1794–6, and commanded an expedition to Ireland to help rebels against England which failed due to storms at sea.

HO CHIEN (1887–1956) Warlord who controlled Hunan province, 1929–37. He played a major role in the campaigns against the Communists, 1930–5, supported by Kwangsi and Kwangtung. On the outbreak of the Japanese war he became a minister in the Nationalist government. He resigned in 1945.

HO CHI MINH (1890–1969) President of the Democratic Republic of Vietnam (North Vietnam), 1945–69. He was a founding member of the French Communist Party, 1920; and founded the Indo-Chinese Communist Party, 1930. He escaped to Moscow, 1932, but returned to Vietnam, 1940. Imprisoned in China, 1942–3, he emerged as leader of the **Viet Minh** guerrillas; he declared Vietnam independent, 1945, and played a dominant role in both the first and the second Indo-China wars, 1946–52, and from 1959 until his death.

HOHENSTAUFEN German royal dynasty, ruling Germany and the **Holy Roman Empire**, 1138–1254, and Sicily, 1194–1268. It restored German power and prestige after the setbacks during the Investiture Contest (see **Lay Investiture**); it became increasingly embroiled with the papacy for control of Italy following the marriage of **Henry VI** to the Sicilian heiress in 1186. The extirpation of the dynasty by the French allies (**Charles of Anjou**) of Pope **Clement IV** in 1268 continued a period of disunity and territorial fragmentation in Germany and Italy. The Hohenstaufen period marked the high point of German courtly culture (Wolfram von Eschenbach, **Gottfried von Stassburg**, Walther von der Vogelweide).

HOHENZOLLERN German dynastic family, ruling in Brandenburg-Prussia, 1415–1918, and as German emperors from 1871–1918. They were originally descended from Burchard I, Count of Zollern, in Swabia (d.1061); a subsidiary branch, the Hohenzollern-Sigmaringens, held the throne of Romania from 1866 to 1947.

HOLKARS Ruling dynasty of Indore, southern India, founded by Malhar Rao Holkar, a **Maratha** soldier who at his death in 1766 had become virtual king in the region of Malwa. Power crystallised during the long reign of his son's widow, Ahalyabai (1767–95); family forces were defeated by the British in 1804, and princely power ended with Indian independence in 1947.

HOLY ROMAN EMPIRE Name first bestowed in 1254 to denote the European lands ruled by successive dynasties of German kings. It was used retrospectively to include the empire of **Charlemagne**, on whom Pope Leo III conferred the title of Roman Emperor in 800; and also applied to the domains held by **Otto II** (d. 983) and his successors. At its fullest extent the Empire included modern Germany, Austria, western Czechoslovakia, Switzerland, eastern France, the Netherlands, and much of Italy. The title lapsed with the renunciation of imperial dignity by Francis II in 1806.

HOMER Putative author of the two great Greek national epic poems, *The Iliad* (or *The Wrath of Achilles*) and *The Odyssey*. The poems stand in a bardic tradition, using verse formulas, but each suggests composition by a single mind. Homer may have composed *The Iliad* in the 8th century BC in the eastern Aegean; *The Odyssey* is less certain.

HOMFRAY family British industrialists. They built an ironworks at Penydarren, near Merthyr Tydfil, Wales, and built the first true railway from there to the sea; in 1804 Richard Trevithick made the first journey in a locomotive engine there, pulling truckloads of iron.

HOMINID Man, considered from the point of view of zoology; a member of the mammalian family *Hominidae*, which includes only one living species, *Homo sapiens*.

HOMINOID Animal resembling man, or with the form of a man.

HOMO SAPIENS Biological genus and species incorporating all modern human beings. It is characterised by a two-legged stance, high forehead, small teeth and jaw, and large cranial capacity; it dates back some 350,000 years.

HONORIUS (384–423) Roman emperor, son of **Theodosius I**. He succeeded to the western half of the Empire when it was divided after his father's death in 395.

HOOVER, HERBERT CLARK (1874–1964) 31st President of the United States. He organised American relief to Europe after the First World War; he was elected Republican President, 1929–33, but bitterly criticised for his failure to combat the Depression. He opposed **Roosevelt's New Deal**; he sat as Chairman of the Hoover Commission, 1947–9 and 1953–5, on simplification of government administration.

HORROCKS, JOHN (1768–1804) Cotton manufacturer. In 1786 he erected a cotton mill at Preston, Lancashire. He was appointed by the **English East India Company** to be the sole supplier of cotton goods to India.

HOTTENTOTS *see* **Khoi**

HOUPHOUET-BOIGNY, FELIX (1905–) President of the Ivory Coast. A planter and doctor, in 1945 he formed his own political party and was elected to represent the Ivory Coast in the French National Assembly, 1945–58. He entered the French Cabinet, 1956–9, working closely after 1958 with **General de Gaulle** to achieve peaceful decolonisation. He became the first Prime Minister of the Ivory Coast in 1959, and was elected its first President after independence in 1960.

HOWE, WILLIAM (1729–1814) 5th Viscount Howe. British general who, after a distinguished career in the **Seven Years War** (1756–63) commanded British forces during the American War of Independence (1775–8).

HOYSALAS Central Indian dynasty, ruling territory centred on Dorasamudra, near modern Mysore. It was founded by Vishnuvardhana in the first half of the 12th century, consolidated under his grandson, Ballala II, who won control of the southern Deccan, but overthrown in the 14th century by the Turkish sultans of Delhi.

HSIEN-PI Group of tribes, probably of Turkic origin but according to some scholars of mixed Tungusic and Mongolian race. They first emerged as one of the Eastern Hu peoples in southern Manchuria, becoming vassals of the **Hsiung-nu** after 206 BC. From the late 1st century AD they developed into a powerful tribal federation which dominated south Manchuria and Inner Mongolia. With the final collapse of Chinese power in the early 4th century they invaded north China repeatedly. Individual Hsien-pi tribes established several short-lived dynasties during the 4th century, and from that time Hsien-pi royal families ruled the dynasties Northern (Toba) Wei, Western Wei, Northern Chou, Eastern Wei and Northern Ch'i, which unified and controlled all of north China.

HSIUNG-NU Chinese name for the vast alliance of nomad tribes that dominated much of central Asia from the late 3rd century BC to the 4th century AD. They were first identified in the 5th century BC, when their constant raids prompted construction of the fortifications which later became the Great Wall of China. Their power was largely broken by the emperor **Wu-ti**; around 51 BC the tribes split into two great groups: the eastern horde, more or less submitting to Chinese control, and the western, which migrated to the steppes. Later, after the collapse of the **Han** dynasty, Hsiung-nu generals, hired as mercenaries, founded the short-lived Earlier Chao and Later Chao dynasties in northern China, c.AD 316–330. No reference to them after the 5th century is extant; the theories linking them with the European **Huns** or the early Turkish empire of central Asia remain unsubstantiated.

HSÜAN-T'UNG (1906–67) Last Emperor of China, succeeding at the age of three on the death of his uncle. He reigned under a regency for three years before being forced to abdicate in 1912 in response to the success of the 1911 revolution. He continued to live in the palace at Peking under the name of Henry Pu-yi until 1924, when he left secretly for a Japanese concession in Tientsin. He ruled as puppet emperor of Manchukuo, 1936–45, was tried as a war criminal in 1950 and pardoned in 1959, when he went to work as a gardener.

HSÜ HSIANG-CH'IEN (1902–) Commander in Chinese Communist Army, a subordinate of **Chang Kuo-t'ao**, during the Long March, and commander of the Eighth Route Army troops in the early part of the Sino-Japanese War. He was a leading general in Shansi in the late 1940s during the civil war with the Nationalists, and a member of the Communist Party Central Committee in 1945. He re-emerged as a leading figure in the Cultural Revolution of 1966, and became a member of the CCP Politburo the following year.

HUARI Early Andean civilisation (c. AD 600–1000), named after its most characteristic archaeological site, in the highlands of present-day Peru. Its distinctive motif, the 'doorway god' with its rectangular face and rayed headdress, is also found among the vast ruins of Tiahuanaco, on the southern shore of Lake Titicaca, with which it appears to have been linked in its period of imperial expansion.

HUASCAR (d. 1533) Son of **Huayna Capac**, on whose death (probably in 1525) he succeeded to the southern half of the Inca Empire, based on Cuzco. He was soon involved in a succession war with his half-brother **Atahuallpa**, who had inherited the northern half of the empire and ruled from Quito. Huascar fled from Cuzco after a series of defeats, but he was captured and forced to watch his family and supporters being murdered. He was himself assassinated by Atahuallpa on the arrival of the Spanish invaders under **Pizarro**, for fear they would restore him to power.

HUAYNA CAPAC (died c. 1525) Inca emperor, youngest son of the principal wife (and sister) of the Inca **Topa**, whom he succeeded in 1493. He reigned mostly peacefully after an initial succession struggle. He conquered Chachapoyas, in north-western Peru, and later northern Ecuador, returning home on hearing that an epidemic (probably measles or smallpox, brought by Spanish settlers at La Plata) was sweeping his capital, Cuzco; he died after contracting the disease. (Scholars now suggest that his death may have occurred as late as 1530, but that the earlier date was given by the Cuzco Incas in an effort to 'legitimise' **Huascar**'s rule.)

HUDSON, HENRY (c.1550–1611) English seaman, after whom Hudson River, Hudson Strait and Hudson Bay are all named. He explored the islands north of Norway, 1607–8, in search of a North-East Passage to Asia; in 1609, commissioned by the **Dutch East India Company** to find a North-West Passage, he sailed up the Hudson River. In 1610, working again for the English, he passed through Hudson Strait and Hudson Bay, but died the following year after being abandoned by his mutinous crew.

HUDSON'S BAY COMPANY Incorporated in England, 1670, to seek a North-West Passage to the Pacific, to occupy land around Hudson Bay, and to engage in profitable activities. The Company concentrated on fur-trading for two centuries; armed clashes with competitors led to a new Charter, 1821. It lost its monopoly, 1869, as territories were transferred to the Canadian government; it is still one of the world's major fur-dealing and general retailing organisations.

HUGUENOTS French followers of the Swiss religious reformer, **John Calvin**. Huguenot rivalry with the Catholics erupted in the French Wars of Religion, 1562–98; under the **Edict of Nantes**, 1598, the two creeds were able to co-exist, but when this edict was revoked by **Louis XIV** in 1685 many Huguenots preferred to flee the country; they settled, to the great benefit of the host states, in Great Britain, the United Provinces, north Germany and in those colonies overseas in which Protestants were tolerated.

HÜLEGÜ (c.1217–65) Mongol leader, grandson of **Genghis Khan** and younger brother of **Möngke**, who led the epic campaign from east Asia to capture Baghdad in 1258; on the disruption of the Mongol Empire after the death of Möngke, he remained to found the Ilkhan Empire, dominating Persia and the Middle East.

HUMILIATI A society of penitents in 12th century Europe who followed a life of poverty and evangelism. This brought them into conflict with the hierarchy of the Church, and they were condemned as heretics by Pope Lucius III in 1184. They were in some respects similar to the **Cathars**, but unlike the latter did not originally hold doctrines at variance with the Catholic faith. They were finally suppressed in the late 16th century.

HUNDRED DAYS, WAR OF THE Napoleon's attempt, after being defeated and exiled in 1814, to re-establish his rule in France. It began with his return to Paris from Elba in 1815 and ended with his defeat by Great Britain and Prussia at the Battle of **Waterloo**.

HUNDRED YEARS WAR Prolonged struggle of England and France, beginning in 1337 and ending in 1453. English forces twice came close to gaining control of France: once under **Edward III** (victories at Crécy, 1346, and Poitiers, 1356; Treaty of Brétigny, 1360), and again under **Henry V** (victory at Agincourt, 1415; Henry was recognised as heir to French throne, 1420). England's resources were insufficient to consolidate these gains, however, and by 1453 the only remaining English possession in France was Calais, lost in 1558.

HUNS Mounted nomad archers who invaded south-eastern Europe across the Volga, c.370, and dominated lands north of the Roman frontier until the defeat of their most famous leader, **Attila**, in Gaul at the battle of the Catalaunian Fields in 451. Their empire broke up and disappeared from history, c.455. The Huna who attacked Iran and India in the 5th and 6th centuries, and the **Hsiung-nu** of central Asia, may have been related to the Huns, but this is unproven.

HUNTSMAN, BENJAMIN (1704–50) English steelmaker who invented the crucible process for making high-quality cast steel, c. 1750.

HURRIANS Near Eastern people, possibly from the region of Armenia, who briefly controlled most of northern Syria and northern Iraq in the 15th century BC. The principal Hurrian political unit was the kingdom called Mitanni, centred on the Khabur.

HUS, JAN (1372/3–1415) Czech religious reformer, born in Husinec, Bohemia. In 1402 he was appointed rector of a Prague church; he was fatally involved in the struggles of the **Great Schism**: tricked by a promise of safe conduct into attending the Council of Constance, he was tried and burned for heresy. His death sparked off a Czech national revolt against the Catholic church and its German supporters, particularly the Emperor Sigismund.

HUSSEIN (d.1931) Hashemite sherif of the Hejaz, eastern Arabia. In 1915 he agreed to join the war of Great Britain against his Ottoman overlords; he proclaimed himself king of the Arabs in 1916 and began the war, aided by T. E. Lawrence, a British agent (Lawrence of Arabia), but his title was challenged by **Ibn Saud**, sultan of Nejd, after 1919. Hussein was forced to abdicate in 1924 and by 1926 Ibn Saud had conquered all of Arabia, although Hussein's sons ruled in Iraq and Transjordan.

HUSSEIN-McMAHON CORRESPONDENCE Letters exchanged in 1915 between Sir Henry McMahon, British High Commissioner in Cairo, and Hussein, sherif of Mecca and later king of Hejaz, setting out the area and terms in which Great Britain would recognise Arab independence after the First World War. Unpublished for decades, they remained a potent source of controversy and tension in the Middle East, especially in their ambiguous references to the future of Palestine.

HUSSITES Followers of **Jan Hus**. They broke with the papacy, used the Czech liturgy, and made many converts in Bohemia. From 1420 they repelled numerous attacks by Catholic neighbours, retaining freedom of worship until the battle of the White Mountain in 1620 restored Roman Catholicism and forced the Hussites (and others) into exile.

HYKSOS Asiatic invaders, sometimes known as the Shepherd Kings, who overran northern Egypt c.1674 BC, and established the XVth Dynasty. Their capital, Avaris, was located in the eastern delta of the Nile. They were said to have introduced the horse and chariot into Egypt. Their rule collapsed c.1570 BC.

HYWEL DDA (d.950) Also known as Hywel the Good, and to chroniclers as 'King of all Wales'. On the death of his father, Cadell, c.910, he succeeded as joint ruler of Seisyllwg (roughly, modern Cardiganshire and the Towy valley) and from 920 ruled alone following the death of his brother Clydog; he acquired Dyfed (south-west Wales) and Gwynedd (north-west Wales) by marriage and inheritance. His reign was noted for its peacefulness, both internally and with England.

IBALPIEL II An Amorite dynast, King of Eshnunna (modern Tell Asmar) in the Diyala region of ancient Iraq. He reigned from 1790 to 1761 BC, when he was overthrown by **Hammurabi** of Babylon.

IBO (now Igbo) People (and language) of south-east Nigeria; they were associated with the attempt to secede from Nigeria and set up the state of Biafra in the 1960s.

ICONOCLASM the policy of banning, and often destroying, religious images, officially imposed in 8th and 9th century Byzantium. Veneration of icons, previously encouraged, was first prohibited by **Leo III** in 730; the resulting persecutions reached their peak in 741–75. The policy was reversed, 787–814, but then reimposed until the death of Emperor Theophilus, 842; the final restoration of iconveneration, promulgated in 843, is still celebrated as the Feast of Orthodoxy in the Eastern Church.

ICTINUS Ancient Greek architect working in the 5th century BC. He was largely responsible for the Parthenon at Athens, the Temple of the Mysteries at Eleusis and the Temple of Apollo Epicurius at Bassae; he was joint author of a lost treatise.

IDRIS (1890–1983) Former king of Libya. Leader of the Sanusi Order, 1916; he was proclaimed king of Libya at independence in 1950. He was deposed in a coup by the army in 1969, fled the country for exile in Egypt and in 1971 was sentenced to death *in absentia*.

IDRISI, ABU ABD ALLAH MUHAMMAD AL-(1100–c.1166) Mediaeval geographer. After travel in Spain and North Africa, he entered the service of **Roger II** of Sicily in about 1145; he became a leading mapmaker and scientific consultant to the court of Palermo. He constructed a silver planisphere showing the world, a seventy-part world map and a great descriptive work completed in 1154, *The Pleasure Excursion of One Who is Eager to Traverse the Regions of the World.*

IDRISIDS Islamic dynasty, ruling a kingdom occupying the northern part of what is now Morocco from 789 to 926. It was founded by Idris I, a descendant of the Prophet **Mohammed**'s son-in-law, **Ali**; after his death in 791 his son, Idris II, reigned until 828, when the kingdom split into a number of principalities. The Idrisids founded the important city of Fez.

IEYASU *see* Tokugawa

IGNATIUS OF LOYOLA, ST (1491–1556) Founder of the order of Jesuits. A page and soldier of **Ferdinand of Aragon**, he made a barefoot pilgrimage to Jerusalem, 1523–4; studied at Alcalá, Salamanca and Paris, where in 1534 he planned a new religious order, the Society (or Company) of Jesus, devoted to converting the infidel and counteracting the Protestant Reformation. His Society was approved by the Pope in 1540, and he was appointed its first Superior, or general, in 1541. He was canonised in 1622.

IGOR SVYATOSLAVICH (1151–1202) Russian warrior who succeeded to the title of Prince of Novgorod-Seversk in 1178, and that of Prince of Chernigov in 1198. He led an ambitious but unsuccessful campaign against the Kuman or Polovtsy nomads, ending in total defeat in 1185; escaping from captivity in 1186, he returned to resume his rule.

ILIAD Ancient Greek epic poem in twenty-four books, better called *The Wrath of Achilles,* describing an episode in the Trojan War; attributed to **Homer**.

ILKHANIDS Mongol rulers of Iran, 1256–1353. The dynasty was founded by **Hülegü** after he seized Persia with an army of 13,000 men; captured Baghdad by 1258. They lost contact with the Chinese Mongols after the conversion of **Mahmud of Ghazni** (1255–1304) to Sunni Islam; the dynasty was later weakened by divisions between **Sunni** and **Shi'is**.

ILTUTMISH Founder of the Delhi Sultanate, son-in-law and successor of **Qutbuddin Aibak** as ruler of the Muslim conquests in India. During his reign, 1211–36, Delhi established itself as the largest, strongest state in northern India.

IMHOTEP Chief minister to **Zoser**, second king of Egypt's IIIrd Dynasty (27th century BC); later worshipped as the god of medicine in Egypt. He was architect of the world's oldest hewn-stone monument, the step pyramid at Saqqara, the necropolis of Memphis.

INCA Name for the Indian group which dominated the central Andes region in the 15th and 16th centuries; also for their emperor and any member of the royal dynasty. From the capital, Cuzco in Peru, they controlled in the 16th century a region extending from Ecuador to north Chile; although lacking either knowledge of the wheel or any form of writing, their society reached a high level of civilisation before being destroyed by the Spaniards in 1533. Occasional Inca uprisings occurred until the 19th century.

INDULF King of Alba (Scotland), 954-62. He captured Edinburgh from the Angles of Northumbria before being killed in battle by Danes.

INNOCENT III (1160–1216) Pope 1198–1216. In conflicts with the Empire, France and England he asserted superiority of spiritual over temporal power as **Gregory VII**, **Urban II** and **Alexander III** had done, but more widely and more successfully. With him the mediaeval papacy reached its highest point of influence over European life. He claimed to dispose of the imperial crown, and excommunicated **King John** of England. His methods were mainly but not entirely political; he reconciled some heretics as well as launching the Albigensian Crusade against them, showed favour to St Francis at the beginning of his mission, and in the Fourth **Lateran Council** (1215) imposed spiritual regulations on the whole Church. The Fourth **Crusade** was the major blemish on his career as Pope.

INNOCENT IV (c.1190–1254) Pope, 1243–54. Continued the struggle of previous Popes to establish superiority of spiritual over temporal power in bitter conflicts with the Emperor **Frederick II**.

INÖNÜ, ISMET (1884–1973) Turkish soldier and statesman, succeeding **Atatürk** as President of the Turkish Republic (1938–50). He commanded the 4th Army in Syria, 1916, became Under-Secretary for War in 1918, joined the independence movement and in 1921 led the Turks to victory in the two battles of Inönü (1921), from which he took his name. He successfully negotiated the **Treaty of Lausanne** and was the first Republican Prime Minister, 1923–38; he advocated one-party rule, 1939–46, but later, in opposition, ardently advocated democratic reform.

INQUISITION Established by Pope Gregory IX in 1233 as a supreme Church court to repress heresy following the Albigensian Crusade, it brought about a considerable reduction in the number of heretics. Torture was permitted in 1252, though used less in the 13th century than later. The Inquisition was reorganised as the 'Sacred Congregation of the Roman and Universal Inquisition or Holy Office' in 1542, again as the 'Congregation of the Holy Office', 1908, and as the 'Sacred Congregation for the Doctrine of the Faith', 1965. Established in 1478, abolished in 1820, it played an important part in imposing religious and civil obedience.

INVESTITURE CONTEST *see* Lay Investiture

IRON AGE The final period among archaeological periods of the prehistoric and early historic Old World, it takes in the barbarian tribes which were contemporaries of the classical civilisations of the Mediterranean, and much of Africa down to colonial times. Iron began increasingly to replace bronze after 1000 BC, and can still be considered as one of the world's most important materials.

IRAQ PETROLEUM COMPANY US-British consortium, set up to exploit oil concessions in Iraq under an agreement signed in 1925. In 1952 a fifty-fifty share agreement was reached with the government; in 1961, 99 per cent of the group's undeveloped concessions were nationalised, including the rich North Rumaila field. Under the arrangement finally agreed in 1975, IPC paid £141 million in a tax settlement, receiving 15 million tons of crude oil and the right to continue operating in South Rumaila.

IROQUOIS American Indians living round the lower Great Lakes. The Iroquois League, founded between 1570 and 1600, united five tribes – the Mohawk, Oneida, Onondaga, Cayuga and Seneca – as 'the People of the Long House', playing a key part in early American history. After defeating their native enemies, they turned on the French; when joined by the Tuscarora in 1722, they became the 'Six Nations'; split during the American Revolution, the League disbanded under the Second Treaty of Fort Stanwix, 1784.

ISAIAH Old Testament prophet, son of Amoz, who stood alongside the kings of Judah in the last part of the 8th century BC. The book that bears his name falls into three parts; there is glorious poetry and profound insight in all, and many passages are taken by Christians to presage the coming of Christ.

ISAURIAN emperors Dynasty of Byzantine (East Roman) emperors, 717–802.

ISMAIL (1830–95) Khedive, or viceroy, of Egypt under Ottoman sovereignty, grandson of **Mohammed Ali**. He studied in Paris, and became viceroy in 1863; in 1867 he persuaded the Ottoman sultan to grant him the title of khedive. He opened the Suez Canal in 1869 and expanded Egyptian rule in the Sudan; he carried further the process of economic and educational change begun by Mohammed Ali, but in doing so incurred a large foreign debt (£100 million by 1876) which ultimately led to British occupation in 1882. He was deposed in 1879 by the Ottoman sultan, in favour of his son.

ISMAIL I (c.1487–1524) Shah of Persia (1501–24) and founder of the **Safavid** dynasty. In 1501 he established what some historians have regarded as the first truly Iranian dynasty since the Arab conquests, although the dynasty was Turkish-speaking and religious affiliation to **Shi'ism** provided the prime focus of loyalty to it. The strength of the state, resting on the Kizilbash (Turcoman tribes owing allegiance to the shah) enabled it to hold off serious threats from the Ottomans and the **Uzbeks** in 1510, and to stabilise its power on the Iranian plateau.

ISMAILIS Branch of the **Shi'i** division of Islam, which split from other branches over the question of succession to the sixth imam, and gradually developed theological doctrines of its own. Some Ismaili groups were politically active from the 9th to the 13th centuries; they established local rule in Bahrain and eastern Arabia; then, on a larger scale, in Tunisia and Egypt (**Fatimid** caliphate); from there a further group, the 'new preaching' led by Hasan-i Sabbah, established itself in northern Persia (see **Assassins**). Ismailis of different groups still exist in Syria, Iran, Yemen, Pakistan and India, where the Aga Khan is head of the most important group.

ISMET see **Inönü**

ISOCRATES (436–338 BC) Athenian orator and pamphleteer. Too nervous to speak, he nevertheless composed eloquently for others. He preached in favour of enlightened monarchy and Greek unity in face of the threat from Persia.

ITURBIDE, AGUSTÍN (1783–1824) First emperor of independent Mexico. An officer in the Spanish colonial army, 1797; in 1810 he rejected an invitation to join anti-Spanish revolutionaries, and successfully defended Valladolid for the royalists. After 1820, he led a conservative independence movement; crowned himself Emperor Augustín I in 1822, but in 1823 abdicated in the face of mounting opposition. Returning from Europe, unaware of the death sentence passed in his absence, he was captured and shot.

IVAN III (1440–1505) Grand Duke of Moscow, succeeding his father, Vasily II, in 1462. By defeating Novgorod in 1478 he made Moscow supreme among the principalities of west Russia, known henceforth as Muscovy. He declared the Muscovite independence of the Mongols and stopped tribute payments to the **Golden Horde**.

IVAN IV VASILIEVICH 'THE TERRIBLE' (1530–84) Grand Duke of Moscow, 1533–84, and from 1547 Tsar of Russia. He conquered Kazan in 1552, Astrakhan in 1554, destroyed the free city of Novgorod in 1570, and annexed much of Siberia, to create a unified Russian state. He killed his elder son in anger in 1581.

JACKSON, ANDREW (1767–1845) Seventh President of the United States, 1829–37. A lawyer, planter and general, he defeated the British attack at New Orleans in 1815. He was elected as the champion of individual freedom and the common man in 1828; in 1832 he vetoed a bill for establishing a national bank, but otherwise supported strong federal government. He is credited – unjustly – with the introduction of the 'spoils system', the dispensing of official jobs as rewards for political support, into American public life.

JACKSON, THOMAS JONATHAN 'STONEWALL' (1824–63) Confederate general in the American Civil War, best known for his mobile tactics in the Virginia theatre, 1861–3.

JACOBINS Members of a French Revolutionary club, founded in May 1789 among the deputies at Versailles. It was named from the former Dominican monastery where early meetings were held. Under the leadership of **Robespierre** the group became increasingly extreme, overthrowing the moderate **Girondins** in 1793 and instituting the Terror. The movement was eliminated after the *coup d'état* of July 1793.

JACQUARD, JOSEPH-MARIE (1752–1834) French textile-machinery inventor. He started work on the Jacquard loom in 1790, broke off to fight in the French Revolution, and completed his designs in 1801. The machine, working on a punch-card system, was capable of duplicating all traditional weaving motions: it replaced all previous methods of figured silk-weaving. In 1806 his invention was declared public property, winning him a pension and a royalty on all sales. At first his looms were burned and he himself attacked by the handweavers of Lyons, fearing loss of employment, but by 1811, 11,000 looms were installed in France.

JACQUERIE Popular uprising in north-east France in 1358, named from the contemporary nobles' habit of referring to all members of the lower classes as 'Jacques'. Unrest began near Compiègne and quickly spread; peasant armies destroyed numerous castles and killed their inmates; under their leader, Guillaume Cale (or Carle) they joined forces with the Parisian rebels under **Étienne Marcel**, but

Cale's forces were crushingly defeated at Clermont-en-Beauvaisis on 10 June, and a general massacre followed.

JADWIGA (1371–99) Queen of Poland in her own right. Her marriage to **Wladyslaw II Jagiello** linked the thrones of Poland and Lithuania (1386).

JAGIELLO, GRAND DUKE OF LITHUANIA see **Wladyslaw II Jagiello**

JAGIELLONIAN dynasty East European ruling family, prominent from the 14th to the 16th century. It was founded by Jagiello, Grand Duke of Lithuania (see **Wladyslaw II**), grandson of **Gedymin**, who married Queen **Jadwiga** of Poland in 1386, thus uniting the two crowns.

JAINISM Early Indian religion, emphasising non-violence, frugality, and the purification of the soul; it regards the existence of God as irrelevant. Much practised among merchants, traders and moneylenders. Shaped and organised in the 6th century BC by the prophet **Mahavira**, its basic doctrines, at first transmitted orally, were finally codified in the 5th century AD. It is followed today by several million people in western and northern India and around Mysore.

JAMES I OF ARAGON (1208–76) Known as 'the Conqueror'. Born in France, he was acknowledged as king of Aragon and Catalonia in 1214, taking full power in 1227. He conquered the Balearic Islands, and in 1233 began a successful campaign to recover Valencia from the Moors. He renounced his French territories in 1258. He formulated an important code of maritime law, and established the Cortes as a parliamentary assembly.

JAMES VI and I (1566–1625) King of Scotland, Ireland and England. The son of Mary Queen of Scots, he succeeded to the throne of Scotland, as James VI, on his mother's enforced abdication in 1567, and to that of England and Ireland, as James I, in 1603 on the death of **Elizabeth I**. In Scotland he created a strong government for the first time, but in England his absolutist policies, extravagant court spending and High Church and pro-Spanish attitudes made him unpopular.

JAMESON RAID Abortive attack launched from Bechuanaland into the South African Republic (Transvaal) in 1895–6, led by Dr (later Sir) Leander Starr Jameson, a colleague of **Cecil Rhodes**. It was intended to overthrow the Afrikaner government of Paul Kruger (1825–1904), but it resulted in the resignation of Rhodes, the worsening of Anglo-Boer relations and Jameson's imprisonment. Jameson, however, returned to public life as Prime Minister of Cape Colony (1904–8).

JASSY, TREATY OF Pact signed on 9 January 1792 to end the Russo-Ottoman war of 1787–92. It confirmed the **Treaty of Küçük Kaynarca** (or Kuchuk Kainarji) advanced the Russian frontier to the Dniester river, and reinforced Russian naval power in the Black Sea.

JATAKA A popular tale, relating one of the former lives of **Buddha**. The largest collection, the Sinhalese *Jatakatthavannana*, contains 547 stories; other versions are preserved in all branches of Buddhism, and some reappear in non-Buddhist literatures, such as *Aesop's Fables*.

JEFFERSON, THOMAS (1743–1826) Third President of the United States, 1801–9. He trained as a lawyer; opposed British colonial rule; became a member of the Continental Congress (1775–6), and chairman of the committee which drafted the Declaration of Independence. He was minister to France, 1785–9; Secretary of State in Washington's administration, 1790–3; Vice-President, 1797–1801. As President he defended states' rights and completed the **Louisiana Purchase**. In his old age he founded the University of Virginia.

JEM (d. 1495) Claimant to the Ottoman sultanate, the younger son of **Mehemmed II**. On his father's death in 1481 he attempted to seize the succession, but was pre-empted by his elder brother **Bayezid II**. He declared himself sultan but was defeated at Yenisehir (1481); after a further vain assault on Konya in 1482 he fled, first to Rhodes, then to France. In 1489 he came under the control of Pope Innocent VIII, who received a pension from Bayezid for keeping him safe. For fourteen years he was the centre of European intrigues and schemes to invade the Ottoman realms.

Charles VIII of France was making plans to use him in a **Crusade** when he died.

JEROME, ST (c.342–419/20) Born at Stridon, now in Yugoslavia, and educated at Rome, he was baptised c.366. He retired for two years as a desert hermit in 375, was ordained priest in Syria in 378 and in 382 returned to Rome as secretary to Pope Damasus. In 385 he left for Palestine, and established a monastery at Bethlehem. He wrote voluminously, including his influential Latin translation of the Bible and numerous controversial polemics.

JESUIT Member of the Society of Jesus, a Roman Catholic order founded in 1540 by **St Ignatius of Loyola**. Organised to support the papacy, to fight heresy and to conduct overseas missionary activity, it quickly established a dominant influence in the Church. Though suppressed, 1773, by Pope Clement XIV and expelled by many European countries in the 18th century, it was restored by Pope Pius VII in 1814, and is now widely entrenched, particularly in education, with schools and universities all over the world.

JESUS OF NAZARETH (8/4 BC–c. AD 29) Jewish teacher whose preaching, personal example and sacrificial death provide the foundations for the religion of Christianity. The name is the Greek form of Joshua, Hebrew for 'Jehovah is salvation'; to this is often added Christ, from the Greek *Christos*, the Hebrew *Messiah*, or anointed one. Born near the end of the reign of Herod the Great, his ministry and Passion are recounted in the four Gospels of the New Testament. He was crucified, but is believed by his followers to have risen from the dead and ascended to heaven as the Son of God.

JEW Originally a member of the tribe of Judah, the fourth son of Jacob, one of the twelve tribes of Israel which took possession of the Biblical Promised Land of Palestine; later a member of the kingdom of Judah, as opposed to the more northerly kingdom of Israel. After the Assyrian conquest in 721 BC, it applied to all surviving adherents of **Judaism**. In modern times it refers to an adherent of the Jewish religion whether by birth or by conversion, or to the child of a Jewish mother.

JEWISH UPRISING First of two major revolts, AD 66–73, against Roman rule in Judaea. The Romans were expelled from Jerusalem, 66, and the country rose in revolt; a revolutionary government was set up. Jewish forces finally succumbed to the Roman armies of **Vespasian** and **Titus**; Jerusalem was stormed, the Temple burned and Jewish statehood ended in 70, and the Jews' last outpost, Masada, fell in 73. A second revolt, in 132–5, in the days of Emperor **Hadrian**, was suppressed with difficulty by the Romans after three years.

JINNAH, MOHAMMED ALI (1876–1948) Hailed as *Qaid-i-Azam*, 'Great Leader', by Indian Muslims, he was founder and first Governor-General of Pakistan. Born in Karachi, he became a highly successful barrister, and in 1906 entered the Indian National Congress. He supported Hindu-Muslim unity until the rise of **Gandhi**. As President of the Muslim League, which he transformed into a mass movement, he adopted the demand for separate Muslim states in 1940, and headed the Muslims in their independence negotiations, 1946–7, securing the partition of India.

JOHANNES IV (d. 1889) Christian emperor of Ethiopia. Originally a *ras*, or prince, of Tigre in northern Ethiopia, his strong, militaristic policies were largely thwarted by external threats – from Egypt, Italy and the Mahdist Sudan – and by the internal rivalry of Menelik, ruler of Shoa. Successful against Egypt, 1857–6, and Italy, 1887, Johannes was finally killed at the battle of Matama in a retaliatory invasion against the khalifa **Abd Allah** of the Sudan.

JOHN (1167–1216) King of England, youngest son of **Henry II**. He tried to seize the throne in 1193 while his brother Richard I was away on **Crusade**. He succeeded in 1199 on Richard's death; lost Normandy and other English possessions to the French; was excommunicated, 1209, in a quarrel with Pope **Innocent III**. In 1215, after six years of strife with his barons, he was forced to accept **Magna Carta**, a charter confirming feudal rights and limiting abuses of royal power; he died during renewed civil war.

JOHN II (1455–95) King of Portugal, nicknamed 'the Perfect Prince'. Succeeded his

father, Alfonso V, in 1481; he broke the power of the richest family in Portugal, the Braganzas; organised expeditions to explore west and central Africa.

JOHN II CASIMIR VASA (1609–72) King of Poland, son of **Sigismund III**. He fought with the **Habsburgs** in the Thirty Years' War and was imprisoned by the French 1638–40. Created a cardinal in 1647, he was elected in 1648 King of Poland on the death of his brother Wladyslaw IV; he fled in the face of the Swedish invasion of 1655. He lost large areas of Polish territory to Sweden at the Peace of Oliva (1660) and to Russia at the Treaty of Andrusovo (1667). He abdicated in 1668, retiring to France as titular abbot of St-Germain-des-Prés.

JOHN II COMNENUS (1088–1143) Byzantine emperor, 1118–43. He fought unsuccessfully to end Venetian trading privileges, 1122; defeated **Pecheneg**, Hungarian, Serbian and Norman threats to the Empire; attempted to confirm Byzantine suzerainty over the Norman kingdom of Antioch.

JOHN III (1537–92) King of Sweden, 1568–92. The elder son, by his second marriage, of **Gustavus I Vasa**, he overthrew his half-brother, **Eric XIV** in 1568 to seize the throne. A learned theologian, he hoped to reconcile the beliefs of **Lutheranism** and Roman Catholicism, and fought hard but unsuccessfully to impose his own liturgy, known as *The Red Book*, on the Protestant Swedes. He died bitter and frustrated, leaving an impoverished and divided kingdom to his son **Sigismund III**.

JOHN III SOBIESKI (1624–96) King of Poland and Grand Duke of Lithuania. In 1655–60 he fought in the Swedish war; he became commander-in-chief of the Polish army in 1668 and won victories over **Tartars**, Turks and **Cossacks**; he was elected king in 1674. In 1683 he led the army which drove the Turks back from the gates of Vienna, but failed in a long campaign (1684–91) to extend Poland's influence to the Black Sea.

JOHN XXII (1249–1334) Second Avignon Pope, elected 1316. A lawyer and administrator, he was accused of financial extortion and involvement in politics and lowered the reputation of the papacy as a religious force. He contested the election of Louis of Bavaria as German emperor (1324); declared a heretic by Louis and by the Spiritual Franciscans, whom he had criticised, in return he excommunicated and imprisoned Louis' candidate, the anti-Pope, Nicholas V (1328).

JOHN OF AUSTRIA (1545–78) Spanish military commander, often known as Don John, the illegitimate son of Emperor **Charles V**. He commanded a Christian fleet against the Turks in the Mediterranean, 1570–6, winning the Battle of Lepanto in 1571. He was commander of the Spanish army against the Dutch Revolt until his death.

JOHN CHRYSOSTOM, ST (c.347–407) Father of the Christian Church. He became a hermit-monk, and was ordained priest in 386. A renowned preacher, he was appointed Archbishop of Constantinople in 398. In 403 he was indicted on twenty-nine theological and political charges, was deposed and banished.

JOHNSON, LYNDON BAINES (1908–73) 36th President of the United States, 1963–9. Elected to Congress, 1937; Senator for Texas, 1949; majority Senate leader, 1955–61; largely instrumental in passing civil rights bills of 1957 and 1960. He was elected Vice-President in 1960, and succeeded after **John F. Kennedy**'s assassination in 1963. He inaugurated the Great Society programme, but came under increasing criticism over the US involvement in the Vietnam War; he refused renomination in 1968.

JOHNSTON, ALBERT SIDNEY (1803–62) Confederate general in the American Civil War. He was appointed a second-ranking Confederate commander in 1861, and in the following year was mortally wounded leading a surprise attack at the Battle of Shiloh.

JOINT-STOCK System of business finance in which the capital is contributed jointly by a number of individuals, who then become shareholders in the enterprise in proportion to their stake. It is usually, though not necessarily, combined with the principle of limited liability, under which the shareholders cannot be legally held responsible for any debts in excess of their share-capital.

JOLLIET, LOUIS (1645–1700) French Canadian explorer and cartographer. He led French parties of exploration from Lake Huron to

Lake Erie, 1669, and down the Mississippi, 1672 (this expedition reached the junction of the Mississippi and Arkansas rivers, but all Jolliet's maps and journals were lost when his canoe overturned; only the diary of the expedition's chaplain, **Jacques Marquette,** survived). He explored the coast of Labrador, 1694, and in 1697 was appointed Royal Hydrographer for New France.

JOSEPH II (1741–90) Holy Roman Emperor. Son of **Maria Theresa** and the Emperor Francis I, he succeeded to the Empire in 1765, and to **Habsburg** lands in 1780. He continued his mother's attempts to reform and modernise the Habsburg dominions; introduced a new code of criminal law, 1787; suppressed the Catholic contemplative orders; agreed to the partition of Poland. He was harassed by disaffection in Hungary and the Austrian Netherlands which compelled him to revoke some reforms.

JUAN-JUAN (also called Avars). Central Asian nomad people, controlling the north-western border areas of China from the early 5th to the mid-6th century and spreading to Europe, where they were finally destroyed by **Charlemagne** at the end of the 8th century.

JUÁREZ, BENITO (1806–72) National hero of Mexico. Of Indian parentage, he studied law and entered politics in 1831; exiled to the United States in 1853, he returned in 1858 and fought in the civil war. Elected Mexico's first Indian President in 1861, he instituted large-scale reforms, led opposition to the French-imposed **Emperor Maximilian** and defeated him in 1867. He was re-elected President in 1867 and again in 1871.

JUDAH Hebrew patriarch, fourth son of Jacob; also the Israelite tribe to which he was ancestor, and the kingdom established by this tribe in southern Palestine, c.932–586 BC.

JUDAH HA-NASI (c.135–c.220) Jewish sage, known as 'the rabbi' or 'our saintly teacher', son of Simeon ben Gamaliel II. He succeeded his father as patriarch (head) of the Jewish community in Palestine. He codified the Jewish Oral Law (supplementing the Written Law, found in the Pentateuch of Moses), and set down his findings in the **Mishnah** (Teaching), which includes regulations for all aspects of Jewish life.

JUDAH MACCABEE (d.161 BC) Third son of the priest Mattathias the Hasmonean, who initiated the revolt against the **Seleucid** king, Antiochus IV, and his decrees against **Judaism.** He succeeded his father and recaptured most of Jerusalem, rededicating the temple in 164 BC; he was killed in battle. Eventually, under his brother Simon, an independent Judaea emerged in 140 BC.

JUDAISM Religion of the Jewish people, distinguished by its pure monotheism, its ethical system and its ritual practices, based on the Pentateuch as interpreted by the rabbis of the Talmudic period (first five centuries AD) and their successors up to the present.

JULIAN (c.331–63) Roman emperor, known as 'the Apostate'. He was educated as a Christian but reverted to paganism and tried to make the Empire pagan again after his election as emperor in 360.

JULIUS CAESAR (c.100–44 BC) Dictator of Rome. He was a patrician, general, statesman, orator, historian – one of the greatest men produced by the Roman Republic. He wrote vivid accounts of his conquest of Gaul and his civil war with **Pompey**. He was murdered by Brutus and other conspirators.

JUPITER *see* **Zeus**

JUSTINIAN I (483–565) Byzantine emperor, born in what is now Yugoslavia, Flavius Anicius Justinianus. Went to Constantinople, where his uncle was the Emperor Justin I. Became co-emperor and then emperor in 527. He was most successful as a legal reformer (Codex Justinianus, 534) and a great builder (the Santa Sophia). His foreign policy, directed at defending and re-extending the imperial frontiers, achieved the reconquest of North Africa, Italy, southern Spain and western Yugoslavia, but the victories proved fragile.

JUTES Germanic people inhabiting Jutland; with the Angles and Saxons they invaded Britain in the 5th century AD, settling mainly in Kent, Hampshire and the Isle of Wight.

KABIR (1440–1518) Indian mystic and founder of the **Sikh** faith, who attempted to combine what he regarded as the best elements in **Hinduism** and Islam, a project completed by his disciple **Nanak**. Kabir's thinking, much of it incorporated into the *Adi Granth*, the sacred book of the Sikhs, also contributed to the development of several Hindu cults, notably the Kabirpanth, with its total rejection of caste.

KACHINS Rice-farming tribesmen in northern Burma. They total some 500,000 people, with their own Kachin state, capital Myitkyina.

KÁDÁR, JÁNOS (1912–   ) Hungarian statesman. He became a member of the then illegal Communist Party in 1932, was elected to the Central Committee in 1942 and to the Politburo in 1945. Post-war Minister of the Interior; he was expelled in 1950. Rehabilitated in 1954 he joined Imre Nagy's government, forming a new administration after the suppression of the Hungarian Revolution in 1956. Premier 1956–8 and 1961–5, and later First Secretary of the Hungarian Socialist Workers Party.

KALMAR, UNION OF An agreement, concluded in 1397, under which Norway, Sweden and Denmark shared a single monarch. It broke down in 1523 with the rebellion of Sweden led by **Gustavus I Vasa.**

KALMYKS Buddhist Mongolian nomads, now mainly occupying the Kalmyk Autonomous Soviet Socialist Republic located in the steppes around the delta of the Volga.

KAMOSE Last king of Egypt's XVIIth Dynasty (c.1650–1567 BC). He ruled the southern part of the country after the death of his father, Seqenenre II; he began the expulsion of the **Hyksos** from the northern part. He was succeeded by his brother, **Amosis I**, founder of the XVIIIth Dynasty.

KARAKHANIDS Turkic dynasty ruling the central Asian territory of Transoxania from 992 to 1211. In 992 they occupied Bukhara, capital of the then disintegrating Samanid dynasty. Split by internal rivalries, the land fell under the domination of the **Seljuks** in the late 11th century and then under the Kara Khitai. After a brief resurgence under Uthman (ruled 1204–11) the dynasty was extinguished in battle with the **Khwarizm**-shah.

KARAKOYUNLU (Black Sheep) Turcoman tribal confederation, ruling Azerbaijan and Iraq c.1375–1467. They seized independent power in Tabriz under Kara Yusuf (ruled 1390–1400 and 1406–20); were routed by **Timur** in 1400; captured Baghdad, 1410; annexed much of eastern Arabia and western Persia under Jihan Shah (ruled 1437–66). They were finally defeated in 1466 and absorbed by the rival **Ak Koyunlu** (ruler Uzun Hasan).

KARENS Agricultural tribesmen occupying a mountainous area in south-eastern Burma.

KASAVUBU, JOSEPH (c.1910–69) First President of independent Congo. He entered the Belgian Congo civil service, 1942; he became an early leader of the Congo independence movement, and in 1955 president of Abako (Alliance des Ba-Kongo). Joined with **Lumumba** in an uneasy alliance to share government power in 1960. He dismissed Lumumba in September 1960; he was deposed by **Mobutu** in 1965.

KAUNDA, KENNETH (1924–   ) First President of independent Zambia. A school headmaster from 1944–7, he became in 1953 secretary-general of the North Rhodesia branch of the African National Congress, and in 1958 broke away to form the Zambia African National Congress. He became Prime Minister of Northern Rhodesia, and President of Zambia, 1964.

KAZAKHS Traditionally pastoral nomads occupying a semi-arid steppe region in Soviet Central Asia to the east of the Ural River and extending into China. Their territory was incorporated into the Russian Empire between 1830 and 1854. Russian colonisation encroached on their best grazing land before the Revolution, and during the 1930s they were settled on collective farms. There are now over 5 million Kazakhs in the USSR, most of whom live in the Kazakh SSR (Kazakhstan).

KEIR, JAMES (1735–1820) Scottish chemist. A retired army officer, he opened a glass factory in Stourbridge in 1775. Three years later he was placed in charge of the Boulton & Watt engineering works at Soho (Birmingham). In 1779 he patented an alloy capable of being forged or wrought when red hot or cold. In partnership with Alexander Blair he set up a chemical plant to make alkali products and soap.

KEMAL, MUSTAPHA *see* **Atatürk**

KENG CHING-CHUNG (d.1682) Chinese general, son of Keng Chi-mao (d.1671) who became provincial governor of Fukien after 1660. On Chi-mao's death he succeeded him and in 1674 joined in the rebellion of the **Three Feudatories** to prevent loss of his control over the province. After initial successes in southern Chekiang, he was attacked by superior forces and surrendered in 1676. For a time restored to his province, he was later taken to Peking and was executed.

KENNEDY, JOHN FITZGERALD (1917–63) 35th President of the United States, 1961–3. Member of the House of Representatives 1947–53, Senator for Massachusetts 1953–61. He was the youngest candidate and the first Roman Catholic to be elected to the White House. He confronted the USSR in 1962 and successfully insisted that Russian missiles be withdrawn from Cuba. During his administration, the US launched its first manned space flights. He was assassinated on 22 November 1963 in Dallas, Texas.

KENYATTA, JOMO (1891-1978) First President of independent Kenya. He returned from studying in London, 1946, and became president of the Kenya African Union the following year. Convicted and imprisoned for allegedly running Mau Mau revolt in 1953, he was released in 1959 under restriction. He was leader of the Kenyan delegation to the London constitutional conference of 1962; became Prime Minister, 1963–4, and President, 1964.

KEPPEL, AUGUSTUS (1725–86) British admiral and politician. He served in the British navy from the age of ten. During the **Seven Years War** (1756–63) he captured Belle Isle in 1761; he participated with **Pocock** and his brother Albemarle in the capture of Havana; he commanded the Channel fleet in 1776. He was court martialled after an indecisive battle with the French off Ushant, 1778, during the American War of Independence. A Member of Parliament from 1761, he became First Lord of the Admiralty, 1782–3.

KETT'S REBELLION English uprising in protest against the enclosure of common land. It was named after Robert Kett, a Norfolk smallholder who led the revolt and stormed Norwich in 1549. He was soon defeated by government forces and was executed.

KHALIFA *see* **Abd Allah**

KHANATE State, region or district governed by a khan; the title 'khan' or 'kaghan' was first assumed by the chiefs of a tribe – perhaps of Mongol speech and origin – inhabiting the pastures north of the Gobi desert in the 5th century AD, and known to the Chinese as **Juan-Juan**. The title was destined later to adorn half the thrones of Asia.

KHAZARS Turkic and Iranian tribes from the Caucasus, who founded a major trading empire in southern Russia in the 6th century AD. In 737 they moved the capital north to Itil, near the mouth of the Volga, adopted the Jewish religion, and started massive westward expansion. At their peak in the late 8th century they ruled a huge area, from Hungary and beyond Kiev almost to Moscow. Two Byzantine emperors, Justinian II (in 704) and Constantine V (in 732) took Khazar wives. The Khazars were crushed by **Svyatoslav** in 965.

KHITAN Nomadic tribes who, under the Liao dynasty (947–1125), controlled most of present-day Manchuria, Mongolia and part of north-east China. During the Five Dynasties, when China was weak and divided, they destroyed the Po-hai state in Manchuria and invaded north-east China before establishing a Chinese-style dynasty in 947 and adopting many Chinese administrative techniques. They carried on a border war with the Sung dynasty for control of northern China, which was settled in 1004 when the Sung agreed to pay an annual tribute. The dynasty was destroyed in 1125 by one of its subsidiary peoples, the Jurchen (see **Chin**).

KHMER The predominant people of Cambodia; there are also communities of them in eastern Thailand and the Mekong Delta region of Vietnam. Their ancient civilisation is exemplified by the remarkable, mainly Hindu temple complex of the Angkor area, dating from the 9th to the 13th century. After the 14th century most lowland Khmers became Theravada Buddhists; the conflicts with the neighbouring Thai and Vietnamese led to wars in the 17th to 19th centuries, and have re-emerged during and since the Cambodian war of 1970–5 (*see also* **Khmer Rouge**).

KHMER ROUGE Ruling Communist regime in Cambodia since 1975. Originally organised to oppose the right-wing government of **Lon Nol**, President 1970–5; after defeating him and depopulating the capital Phnom Penh, it subjected the country to a reign of terror. Resisting Vietnamese invasion since 1978.

KHOI (HOTTENTOTS) A nomadic pastoral people, and their click language, from Namibia, Botswana and the Northern Cape. Probably related to the **San**.

KHOISAN Relating to the Stone Age Bushmen (**San**) and Hottentot (**Khoi**) inhabitants of southern Africa.

KHOSRAU I ANOHSHIRVAN (d. 579) Known as 'the Just', ruler of **Sasanian** Persia 531–79; succeeded his father Kavadh, whom he helped to suppress the Mazdakite heretics. He also reorganised the bureaucracy and religious establishment, fought back against Byzantium, and restored the dynasty's flagging fortunes. He patronised both Greek and Sanskrit learning, and is reputed to have brought the game of chess to the West from India.

KHOSRAU II 'THE VICTORIOUS' (d. 628) (also known as Chosroes) The last great **Sasanian** king of Persia. He made a bid for power on the assassination of his father, Hormizd IV, in 590, but was expelled. He fled to Byzantine territory, and after being provided with forces by the Emperor Maurice (582–602) gained the Persian throne in the following year. When in 601 Maurice was murdered by the usurper Phocas, Khosrau pledged vengeance against the whole Byzantine people, and invaded the empire with vast forces. Eventually he captured Antioch, Jerusalem and Alexandria, and camped repeatedly along the Bosporus opposite Constantinople, but for lack of ships was never able to cross. Phocas had been overthrown by **Heraclius**, a capable general whose brilliant successive seaborne expeditions to Cilicia and Trebizond, and long march through Armenia and Azerbaijan, finally threatened the Sasanian capital at Ctesiphon. Khosrau was compelled to return home, but by this time both empires were exhausted, and social unrest at Ctesiphon forced his son Shiruya (Siroes) to acquiesce in the killing of his father, and the ending of the war, in 628.

KHRUSHCHEV, NIKITA SERGEYEVICH (1894–1971) Soviet leader. He joined the Communist Party, 1918, and its Central Committee, 1934; became a member of the Politburo, 1939. Victorious in the succession struggle with Malenkov after the death of **Stalin**, he was made First Secretary, 1953 and launched the de-stalinisation campaign, 1956. Forced to back down in the Cuban missile crisis in 1962, he was removed by increasingly powerful opposition, 1964.

KHWARIZM Ancient central Asian territory along the Amu Darya (river Oxus) in Turkestan; part of **Achaemenid** Persia, 6th to 4th centuries BC. Conquered for Islam in the 7th century AD; it was ruled by an independent dynasty, the Khwarizm-shahs, from the late 11th to the early 13th century; successively conquered by Mongols, Timurids and **Shaybanids,** in the early 16th century it became centre of khanate of Khiva, under the **Uzbeks**. After repelling many invasions, it was absorbed as a Russian protectorate in 1873; after the 1917 Revolution became the short-lived Khorezm Peoples' Soviet Republic (1920–4), but is now split between the Turkmen and Uzbek SSRs.

KIKUYU Bantu-speaking people of Kenya and their language; they were associated with the Mau Mau revolt against the British in the 1950s.

KILLIAN, ST (d.697) Irish bishop, known as the Apostle of Franconia; he was martyred at Würzburg.

KING, PHILIP PARKER (1791–1856) British naval officer, explorer of Australia and South America. He conducted surveys of Australia's tropical and western coasts from 1818 to 1822, and of the coasts of Peru, Chile and Patagonia from 1826 to 1830.

KING PHILIP'S WAR Savage conflict between Indians and English settlers in New England, 1675–6. King Philip (Indian name, Metacom) was chief of the Wampanoag tribe; during the fighting six hundred white men died and entire Indian villages were destroyed.

KING WILLIAM'S WAR North American extension of the War of the Grand Alliance (1689–97) between William III of England, supported by the **League of Augsburg**, and **Louis XIV**'s France. The British captured parts of eastern Canada but failed to take Quebec; France penetrated into present-day New England but failed to seize Boston. The *status quo* was restored under the **Treaty of Ryswyck.**

KIPCHAKS *see* **Polovtsy**

KIPCHAK KHANATE *see* **Golden Horde**

KIRGHIZ Turkic-speaking people of central Asia. They were widely dispossessed of their traditional nomad grazing lands during Russia's 19th century expansion; their protest revolt in 1916 was bloodily suppressed, with more than a third of the Kirghiz survivors fleeing to China. The remainder now live mostly in the Kirghiz SSR.

KLONDIKE Tributary of the Yukon river, Canada. It became world-famous in 1896, when gold was found in Bonanza Creek; 30,000 prospectors swarmed in from all over the world. By 1910 the main deposits had been worked out and the population reduced to a thousand; all mining ceased in 1966.

KNARED, PEACE OF Treaty concluding the Kalmar War of 1611–13, fought between Denmark and Sweden over the control of north Norway. It was provoked by Sweden's king, **Charles IX**, claiming sovereignty over the region. The Danes took the Swedish port of Kalmar (1611) and Älvsborg's vital western harbour (1612). The ignominious peace, including the payment of a massive ransom for the return of Älvsborg, was signed by Charles' son and successor, **Gustavus II Adolphus.**

KNIGHTS HOSPITALLERS OF ST JOHN Members of a military and religious order, the Hospital of St John of Jerusalem, founded in the 11th century to help poor and sick pilgrims to the Holy Land. The Order was recognised by the papacy in 1113; it became active in the **Crusades** but was driven from Palestine in 1291. It conquered Rhodes in 1310, and as the Knights of Rhodes grew in wealth and power until expelled by the Turks in 1522. The Order was moved by **Charles V** to Tripoli (to 1551), and thereafter to Malta until it was deposed by **Napoleon** in 1798, after which it took refuge in Russia. Reformed in 1879 as the charitable order of St John, its English branch is now widely known for its ambulance and first aid work.

KOLCHAK, ALEXANDER VASILYEVICH (1874–1920) Russian counter-revolutionary admiral. He led a *coup d'état* in Siberia in 1918, and was recognised as ruler of Russia by the Western allies; but he was betrayed to the **Bolsheviks** and shot.

KONIEV, IVAN STEPANOVICH (1897–1973) Marshal of the Soviet Union. He was a front commander, 1941–3; senior commander in the liberation of the Ukraine, the Soviet drive into Poland (1944), and the attack on Berlin and liberation of Prague, 1945. Between 1956 and 1960 he was commander-in-chief of the **Warsaw Pact** forces.

KÖPRÜLÜS (also spelled Kuprili) Family of pashas and generals of Albanian origin, who held high office in the Ottoman state in the second half of the 17th century. The founder of the family's fortunes, Köprülü Mehmed Pasha, was called to the grand vizierate in 1656 by **Mehemmed IV** at the age of eighty, being succeeded as grand vizier by his son Fazil Ahmed Pasha in 1661, and by his son-in-law Kara Mustafa Pasha (1676–83). The last significant member of the family was Köprülüzade Mustafa Pasha, grand vizier 1689–91. Their military and administrative reforms did much to arrest the decline of the Ottoman house (final reduction of Crete, 1669; conquest of Podolia, 1672), but the over-confident policies of Kara Mustafa Pasha, culminating in his failure before Vienna in 1683, severely damaged the fabric of the state and sowed the seeds of future defeat.

KORAN Holy book of Islam, believed by Muslims to be the word of God communicated to the Prophet, **Mohammed.** The text is said to have been definitely fixed by order of the third caliph, **Othman;** containing 114 chapters of different lengths and content, it serves as a basis of law and social morality as well as of doctrine and devotion.

KORNILOV, LAVR GEORGIYEVICH (1870–1918) Russian general. An intelligence officer during the Russo-Japanese war of 1904–5, and military attaché in Peking 1907–11, he was captured by the Austrians in 1915, escaping the following year. He was placed in charge of Petrograd military district after the February Revolution, 1917; he was appointed commander-in-chief by Kerensky. Accused of attempting a military *coup d'état*

he was imprisoned, but escaped and took command of the anti-Bolshevik ('White') army in the Don region. He was killed at the battle for Yekaterinodar.

KOSCIUSKO, TADEUSZ (1746–1817) Polish general and patriot. After military training in Warsaw, he went to America to join the 'struggle for liberty' there (1777–80). He fought Russia and Prussia in 1792–3 in an unsuccessful attempt to save Poland from a second partition; led a national uprising against Russia and Prussia in 1794 which failed, and led to the final partition of Poland the following year. He spent much of the rest of his life in exile, attempting to enlist foreign support for the recreation of a Polish state.

KRUM (d. 814) Khan of the Bulgars, 802–14. After **Charlemagne's** defeat of the Avars in 796, he greatly extended the power and territory of the Pannonian Bulgars. His early forays against Byzantium were repulsed, but he decisively defeated Emperor Nicephorus I in 811, and besieged Constantinople in 813, though he died during a second siege the following year.

KRUPP, ALFRED (1812–87) German industrialist and arms manufacturer. He was the son of Friedrich Krupp (1787–1826), founder of the family's cast-steel factory at Essen in 1811. Alfred perfected techniques to produce first railway track and locomotive wheels, then armaments. The **Franco-Prussian War** (1870–1) was won largely with Krupp field-guns, and the firm became the largest weapon manufacturer in the world, at one time supplying the armies of forty-six nations.

KUBLAI KHAN (1215–94) Mongol emperor of China, founder of the Yüan dynasty. Grandson of **Genghis Khan**, he was proclaimed Great Khan in 1260 in succession to his brother **Möngke**. He reunited China, divided since the eclipse of the T'ang dynasty. His court was first described to the West by the Venetian, **Marco Polo.**

KÜÇÜK KAYNARCA, TREATY OF (also known as Kuchuk Kainarji). A pact signed on 21 July 1774 to end the Russo-Ottoman war of 1768–74. Under its terms the Ottomans renounced their previously undisputed control of the Black Sea and allowed Russia the privilege of representing the interests of the Greek Orthodox Christians in Moldavia, Wallachia and the Aegean islands; this provided the basis much later for Russian interference in the affairs of the Ottoman Empire.

KU KLUX KLAN American anti-Negro secret society, founded in 1866 to assert white supremacy and oppose the rule of the 'carpet-baggers' in the Southern states. It was declared illegal in 1871, but was relaunched in 1915, and broadened to attack not only Negroes but also Jews, Roman Catholics and foreigners. Violently active during the early 1920s in the mid-West and South, and again in the South in the 1960s, it came under increasing attack as a result of Federal enforcement of the Civil Rights Acts of 1964 and 1965.

KUMANS *see* **Polovtsy**

KUN, BELA (1886–?1937) Hungarian revolutionary leader. He led the Communist insurgents who overthrew the Karolyi regime in 1918; became premier in 1919, and attempted to reorganise the country on Soviet principles, but was forced into exile four months later.

KUO-MIN CHÜN (People's Army) Group of warlord armies led by **Feng Yü-hsiang**, 1924–8.

KUOMINTANG (Also known as Chinese Nationalist Party) Political party, ruling mainland China from 1928 to 1949, and since then (from Taiwan) claiming to be the only legitimate Chinese government. It evolved from a revolutionary group formed after the Chinese Republican Revolution of 1911. It was outlawed in 1913; established three short-lived governments under **Sun Yat-sen**, 1917–23; allied with the Chinese Communist Party, 1923; jointly they conquered most of the country, but split, 1927–8; co-operation was renegotiated in face of a Japanese invasion, 1937. Civil war was resumed in 1946, ending with Communist victory in 1949.

KURDS A Sunni Muslim people of Aryan stock of about seven million people, mostly in the mountains where Iran, Iraq and Turkey meet. Many are nomadic, others farmers; they are tribal, with no loyalty beyond their immediate group. With Russian support, a Kurdish Republic was declared in 1946, but this collapsed when Soviet backing was with-

drawn. In Iraq they revolted in 1961 and two-thirds of the Iraqi army was soon deployed against them; fighting continued until 1970, when an agreement gave them autonomy, but was resumed in 1974. When Persian support of the Kurds was withdrawn, following an Iraqi-Iranian agreement in March 1975, the revolt was finally liquidated. In 1979 they again demanded autonomy, supporting opponents of the Iranian revolutionary government. The Kurds are not recognised as a separate ethnic group by the Turkish government, which refers to them as 'Mountain Turks'.

KUSHANS Imperial dynasty, ruling in central Asia and northern India from the late 1st to the mid-3rd century AD, and traditionally founded by Kanishka, who succeeded to the throne of a kingdom extending from Benares in the east to Sanchi in the south, somewhere between AD 78 and 144. The Kushan Empire lasted about 150 years, until its kings in Taxila and Peshawar were reduced to vassals of the Persian **Sasanians.**

KYANZITTHA (1084–1112) One of the first great kings of Burma, responsible for the expansion of **Buddhism.**

LA For all personal names prefixed by la, le, etc., see under following element.

LAIRD, MACGREGOR (1808–61) Scottish explorer, shipbuilder and trader. He designed the first ocean-going iron ship, the 55-ton paddle-steamer *Alburkah*, and in it accompanied in 1832 an expedition to the Niger delta. He ascended the river's principal tributary, the Benue, developed West African commerce in an attempt to undermine the slave trade, and pioneered transatlantic shipping routes. He promoted a second major expedition, penetrating 150 miles further up the Niger than any previous European, in 1854.

LAMAISM Form of **Buddhism** established in Tibet c.750. It is derived from Mahayana beliefs, combined with elements of erotic Tantrism and animistic Shamanism. In 1641 the Mongols inaugurated the appointment of the Dalai Lama, to rule Tibet from Lhasa, while the Panchen Lama from the Tashi Lhunpo monastery near Shigatse became spiritual head of the religion. The last Dalai Lama, 14th in a line claiming descent from Bodhisattva Avalokiteshvara, ancestor of the Tibetans, accepted exile in India in 1959. In Tibet Lamaism temporarily lost its hold, but again now has widespread support.

LANGOSCO Prominent family of mediaeval Pavia, Italy. Supporters of the **Guelph** (anti-imperial) party, they gained control of Pavia in 1300–15 and 1357–9, but lost it to their rivals, the **Visconti** of Milan.

LAO-TZU Originator of the Chinese Taoist philosophy. Little definite is known of his life, though he is traditionally said to have met Confucius during the 6th century BC. His authorship of the *Tao-te Ching*, one of the central Taoist texts, is unproven, and it certainly dates from a later period (probably 3rd century BC). Since his death he has been venerated as a philosopher by Confucians, as a saint or god by many Chinese, and as an imperial ancestor during the T'ang dynasty (AD 618–907).

LAPPS Inhabitants of northern Scandinavia and the Kola Peninsula of Russia. The origin of these people is obscure, but their history goes back at least 2000 years; the best known, but smallest, group are nomadic reindeer herders; their forest and coastal cousins rely on a semi-nomadic hunting and fishing economy.

LA TÈNE Celtic Iron Age culture, flourishing in central Europe from c.500 BC until the arrival of the Romans, and in remote areas such as Ireland and northern Britain until the 1st century AD. It was named after an archaeological site excavated near Lake Neuchâtel, Switzerland. Most surviving Celtic art – weapons, jewellery, tableware, horse and chariot decoration – is characteristically La Tène in motif and design.

LATERAN COUNCILS Four Church Councils were held at the Lateran Palace in Rome during the Middle Ages. The first (1123) confirmed the **Concordat of Worms** which ended the Investiture Contest; the second (1139) reformed the Church after the schism at Innocent II's election; the third (1179) marked the end of the conflict with **Frederick I Barbarossa** and introduced a two-thirds majority rule for papal elections; the fourth, (1215) the high water mark of **Innocent III's**

pontificate, inaugurated large-scale reform to deal with the recent widespread dissatisfaction with the Church, and proclaimed a **Crusade.**

LATIN EMPIRE OF CONSTANTINOPLE From 1204 to 1261 the Byzantine capital, Constantinople, was ruled by a succession of western European crusaders after its capture by the Venetian-backed armies of the Fourth **Crusade**; its wealth was systematically pillaged before it was recaptured by Michael VIII Palaeologus, the Greek Emperor of Nicaea, in 1261.

LAUSANNE, TREATY OF Agreement signed on 24 July 1923 by First World War Allies with Turkish nationalists. It recognised the territory and independence of the new Turkish Republic which had replaced the Ottoman Empire. Turkey abandoned claims to its former Arab provinces, recognised British and Italian rights in Cyprus and the Dodecanese Islands, and opened to all shipping the Turkish straits (Dardanelles) linking the Aegean and the Black Sea.

LAY INVESTITURE The right claimed by many mediaeval rulers to appoint and install their own bishops. The denial of this right by the papacy gave rise to the Investiture Contest (1075–1122); a form of settlement was reached at the **Concordat of Worms.**

LEAGUE OF NATIONS Organisation set up by the Allies for international co-operation at the Paris Peace Conference in 1919 following the end of the First World War. Weakened by the non-membership of the United States, it failed to halt German, Japanese and Italian aggression in the 1930s. Moribund by 1939, it was replaced in 1946 by the **United Nations**.

LEE, ROBERT E. (1807–70) Commander-in-chief of the Confederate (Southern) army in the American Civil War, 1861–5. He graduated top cadet from West Point military academy, 1829; fought in the Mexican War of 1846–8. In 1861 he resigned his commission to lead the Virginian forces; he was military adviser to Jefferson Davis, commander of the Army of Northern Virginia, and General-in-Chief of the Confederate Armies. He surrendered at Appomattox Court House on 9 April 1865. After the war he served as President of Washington College (later Washington and Lee University), Virginia.

LEGALISM Ancient school of Chinese thought, advocating institutional rather than ethical solutions in politics, and teaching that governments should rule by rigid and harshly enforced laws, irrespective of the views of their subjects. It was first adopted as a state ideology by the **Ch'in** dynasty (221–206 BC) and regularly revived since, particularly during periods of national crisis.

LENIN (1870–1924) Architect of the Russian Revolution. Born Vladimir Ilyich Ulyanov. Converted to Marxism while training to be a lawyer, he was exiled to Siberia, 1897–1900; he led the Bolshevik wing of the Social Democratic Party from 1903. He returned from Switzerland in 1917 at the outbreak of revolution and overthrew Kerensky's government to become first head of the Soviet government, 1917–24. His influential writings include *What Is To Be Done?*, *Imperialism, the Highest Stage of Capitalism*, *The State and Revolution* and *The Development of Communism.*

LEO I, THE GREAT (d. 461) He succeeded to the papacy in 440, and was the founder of papal primacy. As a theologian he defined Catholic doctrine, and secured the condemnation of the **Monophysites** at the **Council of Chalcedon** (451). He asserted the primacy of the Roman see against Constantinople. In 452 he saved Rome from the **Huns.**

LEO III (675–741) Byzantine emperor, founder of the Isaurian, or Syrian, dynasty. He seized the throne in 717, defeated the Arab attack on Constantinople, and went on to drive them from Anatolia. He launched the policy of **iconoclasm**, which opened deep religious conflict in the Empire.

LEO VI (866–912) Byzantine emperor, known as 'the Wise' or 'the Philosopher'. Son of Basil I the Macedonian, he became co-emperor in 870, and attained full power in 886. He issued a set of imperial laws, the *Basilica*, which became the accepted legal code of Byzantium.

LEO IX (Bruno of Egisheim) (1002–54) Pope and saint. He became Bishop of Toul in 1026, and in 1048 was appointed Pope by **Henry III** of Germany, a relation. He showed his reforming spirit by demanding also to be elected by the clergy of Rome; and also by condemning simony and clerical marriage, and by travelling widely in order to spread reforming ideas. He was defeated and briefly held captive by the Normans of southern Italy. His assertion of papal supremacy led to the great schism of 1054 between the Eastern and Western churches.

LEOPOLD II (1835–1909) King of the Belgians. The son of Leopold I, he succeeded in 1865. He was instrumental in founding the Congo Free State, 1879, over which he secured personal control in 1885. Under his guidance, Belgium became a significant industrial and colonial power. He handed over sovereignty in the Congo to his country in 1908.

LETTOW-VORBECK, PAUL VON (1870–1964) German general. He served in the South-West Colonial Forces, helping to suppress the Herero and Hottentot rebellions; as commander of the (German) East African Colonial Forces he repelled a British landing in Tanganyika, in 1914, and with less than 17,000 troops pinned down British, Portuguese and Belgian forces of over 300,000 in East Africa, 1914–18. He led the right-wing occupation of Hamburg, 1919. He became a member of the Reichstag, 1929–30 and tried without success to organise conservative opposition to **Hitler**.

LEVELLERS Members of a radical movement both in the Parliamentary army and in London during the English Civil War. It advocated total religious and social equality among 'freeborn Englishmen', and sought an extreme form of republican government based on the pamphlet *The Agreement of the People* (1648) written by its leader, John Lilburne (c.1614–57). It was suppressed by **Oliver Cromwell** at Burford, Oxfordshire in 1649.

LEWIS, JOHN LLEWELLYN (1880–1969) United States labour leader. In 1905 he became legal representative to the United Mine Workers of America, and its president from 1920 to 1960. With the American Federation of Labour (AFofL), he encouraged the organisation of mass production workers into industrial unions. Expelled from the AFofL, these unions then set themselves up in 1935 as the Congress of Industrial Organisations (CIO), with Lewis as president. He himself resigned from CIO in 1940, and withdrew the mineworkers in 1942.

LEWIS, MERIWETHER (1774–1809) American explorer; *see under* **Clark, William**

LIBERATION FROM FRENCH RULE, WAR OF Penultimate struggle of the Napoleonic Wars, when the French armies, after their retreat from Russia in 1812, suffered a series of setbacks against a new coalition of Britain, Prussia, Sweden and Austria, culminating in defeat at the Battle of the Nations (1813). The allies then advanced to Paris, Napoleon abdicated, peace was made with France and the **Congress of Vienna** was called (1814) to make a settlement for the rest of Europe.

LIGUE *see* **Catholic League**

LILIUOKALANI (1838–1917) Queen of Hawaii, 1891–5; born in Honolulu. She opposed the renewal of the Reciprocity Treaty, 1887, under which her brother, King Kalakaua, granted the US commercial rights and Pearl Harbor; she supported Oni Pa's party, whose motto was 'Hawaii for the Hawaiians' Deposed by the US-inspired provisional government in 1893, she abdicated in 1895 after a loyalist revolt. In 1898 she composed the famous Hawaiian song *Aloha Oe*.

LINCOLN, ABRAHAM (1809–65) 16th President of the United States, 1861–5. Raised in the backwoods of Indiana, he was a self-taught lawyer. He entered Congress in 1847, eventually being elected President, on an anti-slavery platform. He fought the Civil War (1861–5) to preserve national unity; proclaimed the emancipation of slaves in 1863, and was assassinated in 1865 by John Wilkes Booth, a fanatical Southerner.

LI TZU-CH'ENG (c.1605–45) Chinese rebel leader, born in Shensi. He was a bandit chieftain, 1631–45, during the final disturbed years of the **Ming** dynasty. After first operating in Shensi, in 1639 he overran parts of Honan and Hupeh, and captured Kaifeng (1642) and all of Shensi (1642–4). In 1644 he also invaded Shansi, and in April seized Peking and proclaimed himself emperor. He was defeated by the combined tribes of General **Wu San-kuei** and the **Manchus**, and was driven from Peking, retreating first to Sian and then into Hupeh.

LIVINGSTONE, DAVID (1813–73) Scottish missionary and explorer. He started his mission career in the Botswana region in 1841; crossed the Kalahari Desert; reached the Zambezi, 1851; reached Luanda, 1853; discovered the Victoria Falls, 1855; explored the basin of Lake Nyasa and the Upper Congo. He was feared lost in early 1870, but was found by **Stanley** in 1871 near Lake Tanganyika.

LIVONIAN ORDER Society of German crusading knights, also known as Brothers of the Sword, or Knights of the Sword. They conquered and Christianised Livonia (covering most of modern Latvia and Estonia) between 1202 and 1237, but were reprimanded by both pope and emperor for their brutal approach to conversion. They were destroyed by pagan armies at the Battle of Saule in 1236, and the following year were disbanded and reorganised as a branch of the **Teutonic Order**. After secularisation (1525) the last Grand Master of the Order became Grand Duke of Courland. a fief of the Polish crown.

LLOYD GEORGE, DAVID (1863–1945) British statesman. Born into a poor Welsh family, he was elected a Liberal Member of Parliament in 1890, and entered the Cabinet as President of the Board of Trade (1905–8) and Chancellor of the Exchequer (1908–15), introducing an ambitious welfare and pension programme. When a coalition Cabinet was formed during the First World War, he became Minister of Munitions (1915–16), and Minister of War (1916), replacing the Liberal Party leader, H.H. Asquith, as Prime Minister later the same year. In 1918 the coalition won a General Election and Lloyd George represented Great Britain at the **Paris Peace Conference**, where he exercised a moderating influence on his allies. In 1922 the Conservative Party withdrew its support from the coalition and the Liberals, divided between Asquith and Lloyd George, were heavily defeated in a new General Election. Although Lloyd George became party leader, 1926–31, and remained in Parliament almost until his death, he became an increasingly isolated political figure, and the Liberal Party steadily declined as a political force.

LOCARNO PACT A treaty, signed 1 December 1925, between Great Britain, France, Germany, Italy and Belgium. Under its terms Britain and Italy agreed to guarantee the frontiers of Germany with Belgium and France and the continued demilitarisation of the Rhineland. **Hitler** repudiated it on 7 March 1936, stationing troops on both sides of the Rhine and refortifying it.

LOCKE, JOHN (1632–1704) English philosopher. His most important political work, the second *Treatise of Civil Government* (1690) provided the theoretical justification for government with only limited and revocable powers; his main philosophical work, *An Essay concerning Human Understanding* (1690) was the basis for most 18th century European thought on the function of reason and the importance of environment in life.

LOESS Fine, yellowish, often very fertile soil, carried by the wind; large deposits are found in Europe, Asia and North America.

LOLLARDS Members of a reforming religious movement, influential in the 14th and 15th centuries in Europe, especially in England under **John Wyclif**. It was widely popular for its attacks on Church corruption and its emphasis on individual interpretation of the Bible as the basis for a holy life, but was repressed under the English king Henry IV.

LOMBARDS German people ruling northern Italy, 568–774. Originally one of the tribes forming the **Suebi**, they migrated south from north-western Germany in the 4th century. By the end of the 5th century they occupied approximately the area of modern Austria north of the Danube, and in 568 crossed the Julian Alps into Italy. They were defeated and absorbed by the **Franks** in 774.

LOMBARD LEAGUE Association of north Italian cities, established in the 12th and 13th centuries to resist the authority of the **Holy Roman Empire**. The League was originally founded in 1167, with sixteen members and the blessing of Pope **Alexander III** to defy **Frederick I Barbarossa**, hostilities ending in 1177 with the Peace of Venice and in 1183 with the Peace of Constance. In 1226 the League was revived and strengthened to avert new imperial ambitions by **Frederick II** but was dissolved after Frederick's death in 1250.

LONDON RIOTS Popular demonstrations in 1641 by Londoners outside the Houses of Parliament and **Charles I**'s palace at Whitehall, demanding that the king's chief minister, Strafford, should be sentenced to death. He was.

LONG, HUEY PIERCE (1893–1935) United States Senator and Governor of Louisiana. He was elected governor in 1928 after a noisy demagogic campaign for the redistribution of wealth, and became a senator in 1932. He was assassinated.

LON NOL (1914–85) President of Cambodia, 1970–5. He became a general in the army, then Prime Minister, 1966–7, and again in 1969. He seized power from Prince **Sihanouk** in a right-wing coup in 1970, but was ousted and fled to Bali in 1975 when the Communist **Khmer Rouge** overran the country.

LOUIS I, THE GREAT (1326–82) King of Hungary, 1342–82. He succeeded his father, Charles Robert, a member of the Neapolitan dynasty of Anjou, who was invested with the kingdom after the extinction of the **Árpád** dynasty in 1301. Louis fought wars against Naples and Venice; in 1370 he acquired the Polish crown, but with little power, and won most of Dalmatia in 1381. One of his daughters, Maria, became Queen of Hungary; the other, **Jadwiga**, Queen of Poland.

LOUIS THE PIOUS (778–840) Emperor of the Franks, son of **Charlemagne**. He was crowned co-emperor in 813, was twice deposed by his four sons and twice restored (830 and 834); his death preceded the break-up of the empire.

LOUIS VI (1081–1137) King of France, also known as Louis the Fat. Son of Philip I, he was designated his successor in 1098, and crowned in 1108. He made substantial progress in extending French royal power; fought major wars against Henry I of England (1104–13 and 1116–20); he arranged an important dynastic marriage between his son, **Louis VII** and Eleanor, heiress of Aquitaine.

LOUIS VII (c.1120–80) Known as Le Jeune (the Young). King of France, succeeding his father, **Louis VI**, in 1137, after marrying Eleanor, heiress to the dukedom of Aquitaine, and thus effectively extending his lands to the Pyrenees. He repudiated Eleanor for misconduct in 1152, upon which she married his great rival, **Henry II** of England, who took over the claim to Aquitaine. The later years of his reign were marked by continual conflict with the English.

LOUIS IX (1214–70) Capetian king of France, canonised as St Louis. He was crowned at the age of thirteen. In 1228 he founded the Abbey of Royaumont, and in 1248 led the Sixth **Crusade** to the Holy Land. He sought peace with England by recognising Henry III as Duke of Aquitaine. He died on a second Crusade, to Tunisia.

LOUIS XI (1423–83) King of France, son of Charles VII. He succeeded in 1461; in 1477 he defeated a rebellion of nobles, led by **Charles the Bold**, Duke of Burgundy. By 1483 he had united most of France with the exception of Brittany.

LOUIS XII (1462–1515) King of France. Son of Charles, Duke of Orléans, he succeeded his cousin, Charles VIII, in 1498. He embarked on fruitless Italian wars (1499–1504, 1508–13), and was finally driven out by the Holy League – an alliance of England, Spain, the Pope and the Holy Roman Empire – in 1513.

LOUIS XIV (1638–1715) The Sun King (*Le Roi Soleil*), ruler of France without a First Minister, 1661–1715, hence looked upon as the archetype of an absolute monarch. The son of Louis XIII and Anne of Austria, he succeeded in 1643 but remained under **Mazarin**'s tutelage until the cardinal's death. He extended and strengthened France's frontiers, built the palace of Versailles and set a European-wide pattern for courtly life. He founded or refashioned academies, supported artists and craftsmen, writers, musicians, playwrights and learned men, French and non-French. He was hated by Protestants for his revocation of the **Edict of Nantes**; and opposed by the maritime powers and the Austrian Habsburgs, who feared that he aimed at European hegemony.

LOUIS XVI (1754–93) King of France, grandson of Louis XV. He married the Austrian Archduchess Marie-Antoinette in 1770, and succeeded to the throne, 1774. The early years of his reign saw France in a state of progressive financial and political collapse;

with the outbreak of the French Revolution in 1789 the royal family became virtual prisoners of the Paris mob. Their attempted flight in 1791 led to deposition, trial for treason and execution by guillotine in 1793.

LOUIS-PHILIPPE (1773–1850) King of France, son of Louis-Philippe Joseph, Duke of Orléans. Exiled, 1793–1815, during the French Revolution and the Napoleonic period, he succeeded to the throne in 1830 after the reactionary regime of Charles X had been ended by the July Revolution. His reign was characterised by financial speculation, the ostentatious affluence of the emerging middle class, and growing failure in foreign policy. He abdicated in 1848 after renewed revolutionary outbreaks, and fled to England.

LOUISIANA PURCHASE The western half of the Mississippi Basin, bought from Napoleon in 1803 by President **Thomas Jefferson** for under 3 cents an acre. It added 828,000 square miles to the United States, at the time doubling its area, and opened up the West.

LUBA Also known as Baluba. Bantu-speaking peoples, widespread in south-eastern Zaire. The main present-day groups all trace their history back to the Luba empires which flourished, but finally broke down, in the 16th and 17th centuries. With the **Lunda** they established a series of satellite states, trading with and buying firearms from the Portuguese in Angola until colonised by the Belgians in the late 19th century.

LUDDITE Machine-smasher, orginally a member of one of the bands of workers who systematically broke looms, textile plant and machine tools in Lancashire, Yorkshire and the east Midlands of England during the early Industrial Revolution (1811–16). Traditionally named after Ned Ludd, a – possibly mythical – leader of the rioters.

LUDENDORFF, ERICH VON (1865–1938) German soldier. Chief of staff to **Hindenburg** throughout the First World War, he was increasingly influential in German military and (after 1916) domestic policies. After the failure of the offensives on the Western Front of March 1918 he insisted upon an immediate armistice. He fled to Sweden at the end of the war, but returned in 1919 to take part in the Kapp Putsch (1920) and Munich Beer-Hall Putsch (1923). An early supporter of **Hitler**, he sat as a Nazi deputy in the Reichstag, 1924–8.

LUMUMBA, PATRICE (1925–61) First Prime Minister of Congo (later Zaire). He was educated at a Protestant mission school; became local president of the Congolese trade union, 1955; founded the Mouvement National Congolais, 1958, to work for independence from Belgium. Imprisoned in 1959, he was asked to form the first independent government in 1960. He was removed from office after opposing the Belgian-backed secession of Katanga province. He was murdered.

LUNDA Bantu people, originating in the Katanga-Shaba district of the former Congo (the central Lunda kingdom) and now spread widely over south-eastern Zaire, eastern Angola, north-western Zambia and the Luapula valley. The Lunda of Kazembe were famous as ivory and slave traders throughout central Africa, especially with the Portuguese.

LUNG YÜN (1888–1962) Chinese warlord. A member of the Lolo minority peoples, he trained as a military officer and joined the staff of **T'ang Chih-yao** in Yunnan. In 1915 he joined the rebellion of Yunnan against **Yüan Shih-k'ai**, which left T'ang in control of the province. In 1927 Lung Yün ousted T'ang, and ruled the Yunnan region as an independent satrapy until 1945. He fostered the cultivation of the opium poppy and inflicted savage taxes on the population. He collaborated unwillingly with **Chiang Kai-shek** during the Japanese War 1937–45, but in 1944 joined a group opposed to the Nationalist government. In 1945 Chiang organised a coup which deposed him, but Lung was given a government post, and Yunnan was placed under his close relative Lu Han. In 1950 Lung went to Peking as a member of the Communist government, and served until he was purged in 1957.

LUPACA Andean people in the Lake Titicaca region of South America. In alliance with the **Incas** in the early 15th century they defeated their neighbouring rivals, the **Colla**, but were in turn overthrown and absorbed by the Incas in the 1470s.

LUTHER, MARTIN (1483–1546) German theologian and initiator of the Protestant Reformation. He was ordained priest in 1507, and taught at the University of Wittenberg from 1508–46. In 1517 his Ninety-Five Theses, attacking papal abuses, provoked excommunication, but Luther advanced an alternative theology which was adopted by many states of northern Europe (the Lutheran Reformation).

LUTHERANISM A system of theology, originated by **Martin Luther** (1483–1546) and expressed in *The Book of Concord* (1580), which incorporated the three traditional Creeds, the Augsburg Confession, Luther's two Catechisms and the Formula of Concord (1577). The main tenets of Lutheranism are that justification is by faith alone and that the scriptures are the sole rule of faith. The Lutherans have traditionally made a sharp distinction between the kingdom of God and the kingdom of the world, so that the state has sometimes seemed autonomous in its own field.

LUVIANS (LUWIANS) A people established in southern Anatolia by the beginning of the 2nd millennium BC, speaking a language closely related to that of the **Hittites**. Many inscriptions are extant in the Luvian language, written in hieroglyphs commonly called 'hieroglyphic Luvian'.

LUXEMBOURGS European ruling dynasty. Initial line, founded by Count Conrad (d.1086) held the lordship of Luxembourg but became extinct in 1136; a collateral descendant, Henry II, Count of Luxembourg, founded a second line including four emperors of the **Holy Roman Empire**: Henry VII, **Charles IV**, Wenceslas and Sigismund; on the death of Sigismund in 1438 the family was replaced on the imperial throne by Albert II of Habsburg and his descendants.

LYNN RIOTS Popular revolt at King's Lynn, Norfolk, England in 1597 against the high price of food and the high taxes imposed by the government of **Elizabeth I** to pay for the war against Spain and for the conquest of Ireland.

MACARTHUR, DOUGLAS (1880–1964) American general who commanded the defence of the Philippines, 1941–2. From 1942–5 he was Commander, United States Forces in the Pacific. He headed United Nations forces in the Korean War (1950–1) until dismissed by President **Truman** after a policy disagreement.

McCLELLAN, GEORGE BRINTON (1826–85) American general, commander-in-chief of the Union forces in 1861–2 during the American Civil War.

McCONNEL & KENNEDY Machinery manufacturers for the rapidly expanding English cotton industry in the late 18th and 19th centuries. For many years the firm was virtually the sole supplier of spinning mules to the industry. John Kennedy (1769–1855) made several improvements in the machines used to spin fine yarns.

McKINLEY, WILLIAM (1843–1901) 25th President of the United States. He served in the Civil War under Colonel (later President) **Rutherford Hayes**. He was a member of Congress, 1877–91, and Governor of Ohio in 1891–5. He defeated the Populist candidate, **William Jennings Bryan**, in the presidential election of 1896 without ever leaving his front porch. He led the country into the Spanish-American war, 1898, and in the suppression of the subsequent Filipino revolt (1899–1902). Re-elected in 1900 with a huge majority, he was shot the following year by an anarchist at the Pan-American Exhibition in Buffalo.

MACEDONIAN DYNASTY Family of Byzantine emperors, founded by Basil I (867–86) and ruling, with some interruptions, until the death of Theodora (1056). Originally peasant marauders, murdering their way to power, they presided over almost two centuries of Byzantium's highest military, artistic and political achievements.

MACHIAVELLI, NICCOLÒ (1469–1527) Florentine statesman, historian and political theorist. In response to foreign invasions and the anarchic state of Italy in his time, he wrote his most famous work, *Il Principe (The Prince)* in 1513, advocating the establishment and maintenance of authority by any effective means.

MACMILLAN, HAROLD (1894–) British statesman. A Conservative MP 1924–9 and 1931–64, he was noted for progressive social views and for opposition to the policy of appeasement of the dictators, voting against his party on abandonment of sanctions against Italy in 1936; he was British Minister Resident at Allied headquarters in north-west Africa, 1942–5; he entered the Cabinet in 1951 and held various offices before becoming Prime Minister, 1957–63, and presiding over the peaceful decolonisation of British Africa.

MADERO, FRANCISCO (1873–1913) President of Mexico 1910–13. He inspired, organised and eventually led the movement to displace the dictator *Porfirio Díaz*. He was arrested in 1909, released and escaped to Texas. In 1910 he declared himself the legitimate President, and was elected in 1911 after the military successes of his supporters, Pascual Orozco and **Pancho Villa**. He failed to implement democracy or stem corruption; he was betrayed by an army commander, Victoriano Huerta, in the course of a military revolt in 1913 during which he was arrested and assassinated.

MADISON, JAMES (1751–1836) Fourth President of the United States, 1809–17. A member of the Continental Congress (1780–3 and 1787–8), he played a leading role in framing the US Constitution (1787). He broke with the **Federalists** and helped to found the Democratic-Republican party; served **Thomas Jefferson** as Secretary of State, 1801–9; during his presidency war broke out between America and Great Britain (1812–14).

MADRID, TREATY OF Agreement signed 14 January 1526 between Emperor **Charles V** and the French king, **Francis I**, taken prisoner after the Battle of Pavia (1525). To secure his release, Francis promised to cede certain territories, but once he was back in France he refused to ratify the treaty.

MADRID, TREATY OF Agreement, also known as 'Godolphin's Treaty', between England and Spain in 1670 to end piracy in American waters; Spain also confirmed the English possession of Jamaica, captured in 1655.

MAGELLAN, FERDINAND (c.1480–1521) (Portuguese name, Fernão de Magalhães). First European to navigate in the Pacific Ocean. He was prominent in Portuguese naval and military expeditions to Africa, India and the east, 1505–16. In 1518 he was commissioned by Spain to find a south-west route to the Spice Islands; after sailing through the strait later named after him between South America and Tierra del Fuego, he crossed the Pacific and reached Guam in 1521, with three of his five original ships, but their crews in a state of near-starvation; the round-the-world voyage (the first) was completed by **Elcano** with one ship and eighteen survivors, of an original 270 men, after Magellan had been killed by local people near Mactan in the Philippines.

MAGGI Prominent family of Brescia, Italy, which gained control of the city in the later 13th century until the siege by Emperor Henry VII in 1311, after which other families replaced them.

MAGNA CARTA The Great Charter issued under duress by King **John** of England in 1215. Though its provisions, promptly repudiated by John, concerned primarily the relationships of a feudal ruler with vassals, subjects and the Church, revisions and reconfirmations in 1216, 1217, 1225 and most notably by **Edward I** in 1297 asserted the supremacy of the laws of England over the king. Thus it came to be regarded as a keystone of British liberties.

MAGNUS OLAFSSON 'THE GOOD' (1024–47) King of Norway and Denmark, illegitimate son of Olaf Haraldsson (St Olaf). He was exiled to Russia, with his father, at the age of four by **Cnut the Great**. Elected as king in 1039 by Norwegian chieftains, he gained sovereignty over Denmark in 1042. He was unsuccessfully challenged by Cnut's nephew, Sweyn; agreed to share thrones with his uncle, Harald Hardrada, in 1045; he was killed in a Danish battle while planning to claim the English crown.

MAHABHARATA 'The Great Epic of the Bharata Dynasty'. This vast work of early Indian literature, running to 100,000 couplets (seven times as long as *The Odyssey* and *The Iliad* combined) relates the struggle between two families, the Kauravas and the Pandavas, as well as incorporating a mass of other romantic, legendary, philosophic and religious material from the heroic days of early **Hinduism**. Traditionally ascribed to the sage Vyasa, it was more probably the result of 2000 years of constant accretion and reshaping before reaching its present form c.AD 400. Included in it is the *Bhagavadgita (The Lord's Song)*, probably Hinduism's most important single text.

MAHAVIRA Indian religious teacher of the 6th century BC, principal founder of **Jainism**. At the age of thirty he renounced his family and became an ascetic, wandering for twelve years in the Ganges valley seeking enlightenment; he shaped and organised the Jaina sect, named from his honorific title of *Jina*, the Conqueror.

MAHDI Islamic concept of the messianic deliverer, who will one day fill the earth with justice, faith and prosperity. The title has been frequently adopted, since Islam's 7th and 8th century upheavals, by social revolutionaries – notably Ubaidallah, founder of the **Fatimid** dynasty in 908, Mohammed ibn Tulart, leader of the 12th century **Almohad** movement, and in 1881 by **Mohammed Ahmed al-Mahdi** on declaring rebellion against the Egyptian administration in the Sudan.

MAHDI, MOHAMMED AHMED AL- (d.1885) Mystic founder of a vast Muslim state in the Sudan. He gathered a growing band of supporters through his increasingly intense interpretation of Islam; in 1881 he proclaimed a divine mission to purify Islam under the title of al-Mahdi, the Right-Guided One. He swiftly mastered virtually all territory once occupied by Egypt; captured Khartoum in 1885, and created the theocratic state of the Sudan. He died in that year at his new capital, Omdurman; the theocratic state fell to forces under the British general Kitchener in 1898.

MAHMUD of GHAZNI (971–1030) Muslim warrior and patron of the arts. He was the son of Sebuktigin, a Turkish slave who became ruler of Ghazni (comprising most of modern Afghanistan and north-eastern Iran). He succeeded to the throne in 998, and from 1001 to 1026 led seventeen invading expeditions to India, amassing an empire including the Punjab and most of Persia. His capital, Ghazni, became an Islamic cultural centre rivalling Baghdad.

MAHMUD II (1785–1839) Reforming Ottoman sultan, nephew of Sultan Selim III. He was brought to the throne in 1808 in a coup led by Bayrakdar Mustafa Pasha, later his grand vizier. He was heavily defeated in wars with Russia, Greece, France and Britain, and by **Mohammed Ali's** insurgents in Syria. He destroyed the moribund Janissary corps in 1826, establishing a modern, European-style army in 1831 and a military academy in 1834. He introduced cabinet government, postal services, compulsory education and European dress.

MAIRE, JAKOB LE (1585–1616) Dutch navigator and South Sea explorer. With **Willem Schouten**, in 1615–16 he sailed through Le Maire Strait, rounded Cape Horn for the first time, and discovered some of the Tuamotus, the northernmost islands of the Tonga group, and the Hoorn islands.

MAJAPAHIT Last of the Javanese Hindu-Buddhist empires, founded after the defeat of the Mongol seaborne expedition against Java in 1292. It rose to greatness under Gaja Mada (d.1364), chief minister of King Hayam Wuruk, with whose death in 1389 its decline began. Its size is a matter for dispute; its effective sway was probably limited to east and central Java, Madura, Bali and Lombok, while its powerful fleets ensured the allegiance and tribute of the Spice Islands and the chief commercial ports of southern Sumatra and southern Borneo.

MAJI-MAJI East African revolt against German colonialism which broke out in 1905 and was suppressed in 1907.

MALATESTA Italian family, ruling Rimini from the late 13th century until 1500. They first became lords of the city in 1295, when the **Guelph** leader, Malatesta di Verruchio (d.1312) expelled his Ghibelline rivals. Sigismondo Malatesta (1417–68) is often represented as the ideal Renaissance prince – a soldier who also cultivated the arts; in 1461 he was the subject of a **Crusade** launched by Pope Pius II which deprived the family of most of its powers. Sigismondo's son, Roberto il Magnifico (d.1482), recovered Rimini in 1469, but the dynasty was finally driven out by Cesare Borgia in 1500.

MALFANTE, ANTONIO 15th-century Genoese merchant, sometimes known, exaggeratedly, as 'the first explorer of the Sahara'.

MALINKE People of the ancient West African empire of Mali. As the Dyula, or travelling merchants, their traders have remained a potent factor in the economy of the region since the 13th century.

MAMELUKES Generically, military slaves or freedmen, mainly from the Caucasus or central Asia, and employed by many mediaeval Muslim states. A group of them established a sultanate which ruled Egypt and Syria 1250–1517, until defeated by the **Ottomans**.

MANBY, AARON (1776–1850) English engineer. In 1821 he patented his design for an oscillating steam engine, widely used for marine propulsion, and in 1822 launched the first practical iron ship, the *Aaron Manby*, sailing from London to Paris. He also founded an iron works at Charenton (1810) which made France largely independent of English engine-builders, and in 1822 formed the first company to supply gas to Paris. He returned to England in 1840.

MANCHESTER SCHOOL Group of 19th century British political economists advocating free trade and *laissez-faire*, led by Richard Cobden (1804–65) and John Bright (1811–89).

MANCHUS People of Manchuria (north-eastern China) who in 1644 founded the imperial dynasty known as the **Ch'ing**.

MANDATE Former colonial territory, assigned by the **League of Nations** to a victorious Allied power after the First World War under supervision of the League, and in some cases with the duty of preparing it for independence. Great Britain thus assumed responsibility for Iraq, Palestine (from the Ottoman Empire) and Tanganyika (from Germany); France for Syria and Lebanon; and Belgium for Ruanda-Urundi. The arrangement was replaced by the **United Nations'** Trusteeship System in 1946, except for South-West Africa (Namibia), for which South Africa refused to give up its mandate (the situation remains in dispute).

MANDE A West African language group, the Mande-speaking people, found primarily in the savannah plateaux of the western Sudan, where they developed such complex civilisations as the Solinke state of Ghana, around 900 to 1100, and the empire of Mali which flourished in the 14th and early 15th centuries. Today the most typical Mande groups are the **Bambara**, the **Malinke** and the Solinke, speaking characteristic Mande versions of the Niger-Congo group of languages.

MANDINGO West African people, related to the larger **Mande** language group, occupying parts of Guinea, Guinea-Bissau, Ivory Coast, Mali, Gambia and Senegal. The many independent tribes are dominated by a hereditary nobility, which in one case, the Kangaba, has ruled uninterruptedly for thirteen centuries: starting as a small state in the 7th century, Kangaba (on the Mali-Senegal boundary) became the focus for the great **Malinke** empire of Mali, reaching its peak around 1450.

MANICHAEISM Dualist religion founded in Persia in the 3rd century AD by Mani, 'the Apostle of Light', who tried to integrate the messages of **Zoroaster, Buddha** and **Jesus** into one universal creed. It is often regarded, wrongly, as a Christian heresy: properly it is a religion in its own right, and has influenced many other sects, Christian and otherwise, in both east and west. It became extinct in the Middle Ages, but some scriptures have been recovered in this century in Egypt and Chinese Turkestan.

MANSA MUSA Most famous of the emperors of ancient Mali, who reigned 1312–37. He pushed the frontiers of the empire out to the edges of the Sahara, the tropical rain forest, the Atlantic and the borders of modern Nigeria. He made a lavish pilgrimage to Mecca and actively promoted Islam among his subjects; he also developed Saharan trade, introduced brick buildings and founded Timbuktu and Jenne as world centres of Muslim learning.

MANSUR, ABU AMIR AL- (c.938–1002) ('Almanzor' in mediaeval Spanish and Latin texts). Chief minister and effective ruler of the **Umayyad** caliphate in Córdoba, 978–1002. He overthrew and succeeded his vizier in 978, and fought fifty campaigns against the Christians of northern Spain, including an expedition against the great shrine of Santiago de Compostela in 997.

MANSUR, ABU JAFAR AL- (c.710–75) Second caliph of the **Abbasid** dynasty, great-grandson of Abbas, **Mohammed's** uncle; he succeeded to the caliphate in 754 on the death of his brother as-Saffah. He completed the elimination of the deposed **Umayyad** dynasty, and founded the city of Baghdad, begun in 762.

MANUEL I COMNENUS (1122–80) Emperor of Byzantium, son of **John II Comnenus,** he succeeded in 1143. He tried but ultimately failed to build alliances in the West; was defeated in 1156 at Brindisi and expelled from Italy. He forced Jerusalem to recognise Byzantine sovereignty in 1159, in 1167 added Dalmatia, Bosnia and Croatia to his empire, and broke ties with Venice in 1171. His armies were destroyed by the Seljuk Turks at Myriocephalon in 1176.

MANZIKERT, BATTLE OF Held near the town in Turkish-held Armenia (today Malazgirt, Turkey) in 1071; the **Seljuks**, under Sultan Alp-arslan (1063–72) decisively defeated the Byzantine armies under Emperor Romanus IV Diogenes (1068–71). The victory led to Seljuk conquest of almost all Anatolia, and fatal weakening of Byzantine power.

MAORI Member of the aboriginal Polynesian people inhabiting New Zealand at the time of its European discovery.

MAO TSE-TUNG (1893–1976) First Chairman of the People's Republic of China (1949–77). He helped to found the Chinese Communist Party in 1921, and until 1926 organised peasant and industrial unions. After the Communist split with the **Kuomintang** in 1927 he set up Communist bases in Hunan, and later in Kiangsi, and in 1934–5 led the Long March of the Red Army from Kiangsi to Yenan. He became the dominant figure in the Party after 1935, establishing it as a peasant-based party. During the second Sino-Japanese War (1937–45) he worked for national unity, and after a bitter civil war in 1949 expelled Nationalist forces from mainland China. In 1966 he launched the Cultural Revolution.

MARATHAS Hindu people of western India, famous in 17th and 18th century history for their warlike resistance to the **Mughal** emperors. Now the term covers the 10 million or so members of the Maratha and Kunbi castes in the region bounded by Bombay, Goa and Nagpur, or more loosely the 40 million speakers of the Marathi language.

MARATHON, BATTLE OF A famous victory in 490 BC won on the coastal plain north-east of Athens by the Greeks, under the Athenian general Miltiades, over an invading army of Persians. It is remembered *inter alia* for the feat of the runner Phidippides, who raced 150 miles in two days to warn the Spartans and to return with the news that their forces would be delayed by a religious festival.

MARCEL, ÉTIENNE (c.1316–58) Provost of merchants of Paris, a member of the States General (the French national assembly). He proposed in 1355–6 that the States should control royal revenues and purge crown officials; he led Paris in a revolt against the crown in 1357–8, and supported the **Jacquerie**. He was assassinated in 1358 after the revolt collapsed.

MARCHAND, JEAN-BAPTISTE (1863–1934) French explorer and general, who in 1897 led a remarkable eighteen-month-long march from Libreville, in Gabon, to the Upper Nile, occupying Fashoda in 1898. He withdrew after a prolonged confrontation with Kitchener which provoked an international diplomatic crisis.

MARCION (c.100–160) Originator of a religious sect challenging Christianity throughout Europe, North Africa and western Asia from the 2nd to the 5th century. Possibly the son of a bishop of Sinope, he went to Rome c.140, formed separate communities and was excommunicated in 144. He preached the existence of two gods: the Old Testament Creator or Demiurge, i.e. the God of Law, and the God of Love revealed by Jesus, who would overthrow the first. He compiled his own version of the New Testament (the *Instrumentum*), largely based on St Luke and St Paul's Epistles. After his death the Marcionite sect survived many persecutions and remained significant, particularly in Syria, until the 10th century.

MARGARET (1353–1412) Queen of Norway. The daughter of Valdemer III of Denmark, she married Haakon VI of Norway (1343–80), and became effective ruler of Norway and Denmark, c.1387, and of Sweden, 1389. She was regent on behalf of her great-nephew, Eric of Pomerania, who was crowned ruler of Sweden, Denmark and Norway at the **Union of Kalmar** in 1397.

MARI (Cheremiss) Finno-Ugrian speaking peoples now living mainly in the Autonomous Soviet Socialist Republics of Mari, on the middle Volga, and Bashkir.

MARIA THERESA (1717–80) Eldest daughter of the Emperor Charles VI, and one of the most capable **Habsburg** rulers. She was Archduchess of Austria and Queen of Hungary and Bohemia in her own right, and always overshadowed her husband, the elected Emperor Francis I (1745–65). She died after fifteen years of widowhood and a troublesome co-regency with her son, Joseph II.

MARINIDS Berber dynasty, ruling in Morocco and elsewhere in North Africa from the 13th to the 15th centuries, replacing the **Almohads** on the capture of Fez (1248) and Marrakesh (1269). They launched a holy war in Spain which lasted until the mid-14th century. Despite many attempts, they failed to re-establish the old Almohad empire; after a period of internal anarchy, the related Wattasids assumed control of Morocco in 1465, but were finally expelled, by the **Saadi** sharifs, in 1549.

MARQUETTE, JACQUES (1637–75) French Jesuit missionary and explorer, the first Frenchman to sail on the Mississippi (1673); he explored much of its length with **Jolliet.**

MARRANO Spanish term for a **Jew** who converted to **Christianity** in Spain or Portugal to avoid persecution but secretly continued to practise **Judaism**; also used to designate the descendants of such a person.

MARSHALL PLAN Popular name given to the European recovery programme, proposed in 1947 by US Secretary of State General George C. Marshall (1880–1959), to supply US financial and material aid to war-devastated Europe. Rejected by Eastern European countries under Soviet pressure, it came into force in Western Europe in 1948 and was completed in 1952.

MARSHALL, WILLIAM (1745–1818) Agriculturalist and leading improver, famous for his twelve-volume *General Survey, from personal experience, observation and enquiry, of the Rural Economy of England* (1787–98). He proposed setting up a governmental Board of Agriculture, put into effect by Parliament in 1793.

MARTIN IV (c.1210–85) Pope from 1281 to 1285. He supported Charles I of Naples and Sicily, and opposed the Aragonese claims after the **War of the Sicilian Vespers**.

MASON-DIXON LINE Originally a boundary line between the American states of Pennsylvania and Maryland named after the English surveyors, Charles Mason and Jeremiah Dixon, who first delineated it, 1763–7. It later became a symbolic frontier between slave and free states in the American Union.

MARXIST Follower of the social, political and economic theories developed by Karl Marx (1818–83). Characteristic beliefs include dialectical materialism, the collapse of capitalism through its internal contradictions, the dictatorship of the proletariat and a withering away of the state after the achievement of a classless society.

MATABELE (also known as Ndebele). Southern African people, breaking away from the **Nguni** of Natal in the early 19th century. Under **Mzilikazi** they migrated to the High Veld area of modern Transvaal, and later the Marico Valley. In 1837, after confrontation with Dutch settlers in the Transvaal, they crossed the river Limpopo into Matabeleland (southern Rhodesia). The resulting state grew powerful under the leadership of Mzilikazi's successor, Lobengula. They were finally defeated in 1893 by settlers of the British South Africa Company.

MATACOS South American Indians, forming the largest and most important group of the Chaco Indians in the Gran Chaco region of north-west Argentina. They were first encountered by Europeans in 1628, and resisted Christianity and colonisation, suffering large-scale massacre, before being placed on reservations and in Spanish government colonies. They are now gradually being incorporated into the *mestizo* (mixed blood) population of the Chaco.

MATILDA (1046–1115) Countess of Tuscany. She was a strong supporter of Pope **Gregory** XII. Having acknowledged (c.1080) papal overlordship of her lands, strategically placed across the route of German invasions of Italy, she eventually made Emperor Henry V her heir, thus giving rise to much conflict between the Empire and the Papacy.

MATTHIAS CORVINUS (1440–90) Elected King of Hungary (1458) and Bohemia (1469). He acquired Moravia, Silesia and Lusatia in 1478, Vienna in 1485, and built up the most powerful kingdom in central Europe. He was also a patron of science and of literature.

MAURYAS First Indian dynasty to establish rule over the whole sub-continent. The dynasty was founded in 321 BC by **Chandragupta Maurya**, and steadily extended under his son Bindusara and grandson **Asoka**. Power was gradually eroded under Asoka's successors, finally dying out c.180 BC.

MAXIMILIAN I (1459–1519) Holy Roman Emperor, son of Frederick III. He married Mary of Burgundy in 1477; was crowned king of Germany in 1486 and emperor in 1493. He attempted unsuccessfully to reform the imperial administration, and in 1499 to subjugate the Swiss cantons. He was succeeded by **Charles V**.

MAXIMILIAN (1832–67) Emperor of Mexico. Younger brother of the Austrian emperor, Francis Joseph I, in 1863 he accepted the offer of the Mexican throne as an unwitting pawn in the plot by Mexican opponents of **Juárez** and the French emperor, **Napoleon III**. He was installed by French troops and crowned, 1864; his attempts at liberal reform were nullified by local opposition and lack of funds. He was deserted by the French in 1867, surrounded, starved and tricked into surrender by the armies of Juárez, and shot in June that year.

MAYA Indian people of the Yucatán peninsula and the adjoining areas of southern Mexico, Guatemala and Honduras. The Classic period of Maya civilisation (marked by fine buildings, magnificent art and an advanced knowledge of mathematics and astronomy) falls between the 3rd and 9th centuries AD. Archaeologically it is best represented at the southern cities of Tikal, Copán, Uaxactún, Quiriguá and Piedras Negras. In the 9th century, for reasons still poorly understood, Classic Maya civilisation declined. Mexican (see **Toltec**) influence became important, and the main centres of power shifted to Chichén Itzá and Mayapán in northern Yucatán. Although the Spanish conquest destroyed much of the political and religious life, the Maya still exist as a linguistic and cultural unit in their original homelands.

MAYFLOWER Famous ship that carried the 102 Pilgrims of the later United States from England to found the first permanent New England colony at Plymouth, Massachusetts, in 1620. Her precise size is not recorded, but she was probably about 180 tons and some 90 foot long. Originally she set out for Virginia, but was blown north first to Cape Cod and then to Plymouth.

MAZARIN, JULES (1602–61) Italian-born French statesman. He pursued a career in papal service, 1625–36, was brought into the service of Louis XIII by **Richelieu** in 1639 and, on French nomination, was made a cardinal in 1641. He inherited Richelieu's position as Louis XIII's First Minister. The king made him godfather to the future **Louis XIV**, over whose training for kingship he had a good deal of influence. He showed skill both in handling the civil wars of the **Fronde** and in negotiating gains for France under the treaties of **Westphalia** (1648) and the Pyrenees (1659).

MAZZINI, GIUSEPPE (1805–72) Italian revolutionary and patriot. He founded the Young Italy movement and a journal of that name in 1831. Following the failure of the invasion of Savoy in 1834, and banished from Switzerland, he went to London in 1836, returning to Italy in 1848. He was angered by the emergence in 1861 of an Italian kingdom instead of the republic he had always favoured.

MEADE, GEORGE GORDON (1815-72) Union general in the American Civil War, best remembered for his victory in the Battle of Gettysburg (1863).

MEDES The branch of the Iranian invaders of present-day Iran who settled in the north-west of Iran. Under Cyaxares (c.625 BC) the Medes became a major military power which, once it had settled accounts with the Scythian invaders of northern Iran, made an alliance with Babylon to destroy the hated **Assyrian** Empire. Under the last king, Astyages, the Medes were defeated by the Persian **Cyrus II the Great** in 550 BC, in whose empire the 'Medes and Persians' were held in equal honour. Thereafter, especially under the **Sasanians**, the Medes became effectively merged with the other groupings which came to constitute the Iranian nation-state.

MEDICI Most important of the great families of Florence. Their origins are obscure, but they were established in 13th century in the cloth trade and in finance, and soon exercised considerable political influence. The family developed three lines: that of Chiarissimo II, who failed to gain power in Florence in the 14th century; Cosimo the Elder (1389–1464) who became the hereditary, although uncrowned, monarch of Florence; Cosimo, who became Grand Duke of Tuscany in 1569, the line ending with death of Gian Gastone, 1737. The family provided many rulers and patrons, and three Popes, including Clement VII.

MEGALITH Monument constructed of large undressed stones or boulders, usually as a ritual centre (e.g. a stone circle) or burial monument (e.g. chambered cairn). Of many different kinds, these were erected by simple agricultural communities in many parts of the world, most notably in **Neolithic** Europe during the 3rd millennium BC.

MEHMED I, CHELEBI (d.1421) Younger son of **Bayezid I** and reunifier of the Ottoman state after the defeat of Ankara (1402), the death of his father and the civil war (1403–13) with his brothers. Mehemmed, from a territorial base at Amasya, moved to defeat successively Isa in Brusa, Suleiman in Edirne (1403–11), and Musa in Rumeli (1411–13), while maintaining nominal allegiance to the Timurids, and later overcoming both dangerous social revolts and Byzantine-inspired attempts to place his brother Mustafa on the throne (1415–16). By his death the prestige, if not the full authority, of the sultanate was restored, enabling it to survive the further shocks of the first years of **Murad II**'s reign.

MEHMED II, FATIH ('the Conqueror') (1432–81) By the conquest of Constantinople in 1453 Mehemmed II obtained for the Ottoman state a fit site for the capital of a would-be universal world empire. His reign is a record of unceasing warfare: against Hungary, Venice, the **Akkoyunlu** and the Knights of St John. The last vestiges of Greek rule disappeared (in the Morea 1460, in Trebizond 1461); Serbia (1459), Bosnia (1463) and Karaman (1466) were annexed; Moldavia (1455) and the khanate of the Crimea (1475–8) rendered tributary.

MEHMED IV AUJI ('the Hunter') (1642–93) Ottoman sultan, succeeding on the deposition of his eccentric father in 1648. His reign was most notable for the emergence in 1656 of the grand vizierate as the dominating institution of the state under the ministerial family of **Köprülü**. His reign was one of incessant and not altogether unsuccessful warfare in the Mediterranean (reduction of Crete, 1644–69, ended by the thirteen-year siege of Candia); and on the northern frontiers of the empire (invasion of Transylvania 1654, conquest of Podolia 1672). Against the **Habsburgs** Mehemmed IV and his advisers were less successful (St Gotthard campaign 1663, second unsuccessful siege of Vienna 1683). The subsequent loss of Hungary (1684–7) fuelling popular resentment, and exacerbated by the Sultan's withdrawal from matters of state and notorious obsession with hunting, precipitated his deposition in 1687 and detention until his death.

MEIJI Name meaning 'enlightened rule' by which the Japanese emperor, Mutsuhito, was known during his long reign. Mutsuhito (1852–1912) came to the throne in 1867; within a year the 'Meiji Restoration' ended two and a half centuries of feudalism and isolation in Japan under the **Tokugawa** shogunate. Under his rule, industrialisation and modernisation began, and a Western democratic constitution was adopted (1889). By the time of his death, Japan was widely accepted as a world power; his role was largely symbolic, new political leaders being more directly responsible for the reshaping of the nation.

MELGAREJO, MARIANO (1818–71) Bolivian dictator. A general in the Bolivian army, he deposed José Maria Achá in 1864 to become President. He conceded to Chile some of Bolivia's claim to the rich nitrate deposits of the Atacama desert. He was deposed, and assassinated in the same year.

MENELIK II (1844–1913) Emperor of Ethiopia. He was enthroned in 1889, and in 1896 defeated an Italian invasion at Adowa to ensure his country's independence and consolidate its power. He greatly expanded the boundaries of Ethiopia by conquering Galla lands in the south-west and Ogaden in the east.

MENES Traditionally, the first king to unite Upper and Lower Egypt, c.3100 BC; he may also have founded the royal capital of Memphis. He is said by the historian Manetho to have ruled for sixty-two years and to have been killed by a hippopotamus.

MENSHEVIKS Moderate faction in the Russian Social Democratic Party, which generally supported the **Bolshevik** regime during the civil war, after which most Mensheviks were either liquidated or absorbed into the Russian Communist Party, or emigrated.

MENTUHOTEP I Governor of the Theban province who, according to tradition, became the first king of the XIth Dynasty and the founder of the Middle Kingdom, c.2120 BC.

MENTUHOTEP II (died c.2010 BC) King of Egypt's XIth Dynasty. He acceded c.2060 to the throne of Upper Egypt; in 2046 he launched a campaign against the Heracleopolitan kingdom of Lower and Middle Egypt and by c.2040 had reunited the country.

MERCANTILISM Economic theory much favoured in the 16th and 17th centuries, under which a country's prosperity was held to depend on its success in accumulating gold and silver reserves. It favoured a strict limitation of imports and the aggressive promotion of export trade.

MEROVINGIANS Frankish dynasty, ruling much of Gaul from the time of **Clovis** to their replacement by the **Carolingians** in 751.

MESOLITHIC The middle part of the **Stone Age** in Europe, representing hunting and collecting groups in the period of present-day climatic conditions after the end of the last glaciation, 10,000 years ago. It succeeded the reindeer-hunting groups of the **Palaeolithic**, and was gradually displaced by the incoming farmers of the **Neolithic**.

METAXAS, IOANNIS (1871–1941) Greek military leader. After reaching the rank of general he emerged as dictator of Greece in 1936; he defeated the Italians when they invaded the country in 1940.

METHODIST Member of one of the several Protestant denominations which developed after 1730 from the Church of England revival movement led by John and Charles Wesley. It emerged as a separate church in 1791 with supporters in North America and Great Britain.

METHODIUS, ST *see* **Cyril**

METHUEN TREATY Commercial agreement signed in 1703 between England and Portugal. It was named after John Methuen (c.1650–1706), at that time British ambassador to Lisbon. The treaty gave a preferential tariff on Portuguese wine in exchange for freer import of English woollens, and helped to promote the drinking of port in England.

METTERNICH, PRINCE KLEMENS WENZEL LOTHAR VON (1773–1859) Austrian statesman. He was ambassador to various nations, and Minister of Foreign Affairs, 1809; following a period of collaboration with France, he then joined the victorious alliance against **Napoleon.** He was a leading figure at the **Congress of Vienna**, 1814–15, during which he restored the Habsburg Empire to a leading place in Europe. He continued to be dominant in the Austrian government until the revolution of 1848.

MEWAR Independent state in northern India, first prominent in the 8th century under the Rajput clan of the Guhilas. Under Hamir in the 14th century it defied the Muslim armies of **Alauddin**; enriched by the discovery of silver and lead, it continued to battle with the Delhi sultanate and their **Mughal** successors. The state was in decline after Rana Sanga's defeat by **Babur** in 1527; **Akbar's** long war against Rana Pratap was inconclusive, but Pratap's son accepted Mughal suzerainty.

MEZZOGIORNO Name for the region of Italy south of Rome, covering roughly the area of the former kingdom of Naples. Its long-standing backwardness, unemployment and low standard of living (half the per capita income of the north) have made it a perpetual preoccupation of Italian governments and planners.

MIAO Mountain-dwelling people of China, Vietnam, Laos and Thailand. Divided into more than a hundred groups distinguished by dress, dialect and customs, its members all share a heritage of Sino-Tibetan language. In China they are concentrated in the provinces of Kweichow, Hunan, Szechwan, Kwangsi and Yunnan and Hainan island.

MIDLAND RISING Peasant rebellion in 1607 in several shires of the English east Midlands, caused mainly by the enclosure of common land by landlords which deprived the local population of grazing rights.

MIESKO (Mieszko) I (d.992) First ruler of united Poland, a member of the **Piast** dynasty. He succeeded as Duke of Poland c.963; he expanded his territories into Galicia and Pomerania. In 966 he accepted (Roman) **Christianity** from Bohemia, and placed his country under the protection of the Holy See (mainly in the hope of securing papal protection against the 'crusade' of the Germans against the Slavs).

MIESKO II (990–1034) King of Poland, succeeding to the throne in 1025. He lost much territory to Bohemia and the **Holy Roman Empire.**

MILAN, EDICT OF Proclamation issued in AD 313, granting permanent religious toleration for Christians throughout the Roman Empire. It was jointly promulgated by the emperors Licinius in the Eastern and **Constantine I** in the Western Empire.

MILNER, ALFRED (1854–1925) 1st Viscount Milner. British statesman and imperialist. As High Commissioner for South Africa, 1897–1905, he was responsible for the reconstruction of the Transvaal and Orange River Colony after the Boer War. He was a member of the War Cabinet, 1916–18, War Secretary, 1918, and Colonial Secretary, 1919–21.

MILITARY FRONTIER The Habsburg frontier *(Militärgrenze)* consisted at the end of the 16th century of a long strip of southern Croatia in which immigrants, holding land in return for military service, manned a line of forts. The system was later extended to Slavonia and subsequently to Transylvania, thus covering the whole frontier with the Ottoman Empire. Highly unpopular among the Croats and Hungarians, it was finally abolished in 1872.

MING Chinese imperial dynasty ruling 1368 to 1644; *see page* 168.

MINISTERIALES Originally of servile status, from the 11th century onwards they served as stewards, chamberlains and butlers to kings and other lords in Germany. Gradually, as they assumed military, administrative and political functions, their social status improved until, in the 14th century, their estates and offices became hereditary, and they were accepted as members of the nobility.

MINOS Early king of Crete, referred to by **Homer** and Thucydides. According to legend he was the son of Zeus and Europa, and husband of Pasiphaë. Knossos was said to have been his capital and the focus of his vast sea-power. The 'Minoan' civilisation of Crete (c.3000–1500 BC) was named after him by Sir Arthur Evans, excavator of Knossos.

MISHNAH Compilation of the oral interpretations of the legal portions of the Bible by the **Pharisees** and Rabbis; codified by **Judah ha-Nasi,** in Palestine around AD 200, it served as the basis for the **Talmud.**

MITCHELL, SIR THOMAS LIVINGSTONE (1792–1855) Australian explorer. Born in Scotland, he joined the British army in 1811 and served in the Peninsular War. As surveyor-general of New South Wales (from 1828) he surveyed the province, constructed roads and (1831–47) led four major expeditions to explore and chart the Australian interior. He produced *Australian Geography* (1850) for use in schools – the first work to place Australia at the centre of the world – and published his expedition journals.

MITHRAISM Worship of Mithra or Mithras, ancient Indian and Persian god of justice and law; in pre-Zoroastrian Persia a supporter of Ahura Mazda, the great god of order and light. In the Roman Empire Mithraism spread as a mystery-cult with Mithras as a divine saviour, underground chapels, initiation rites, a common meal, and the promise of a blessed immortality. The adherents were men only, mostly soldiers, traders and civil servants. In the 4th century it was ousted by **Christianity.**

MITHRIDATES (120–63 BC) King of Pontus, in Asia Minor. He assumed the throne as Mithridates VI, known as 'the Great'. He fought three wars with Rome, finally being defeated by **Pompey**.

MOBUTU SESE SEKO (1930–) President of Zaire (formerly Congo). He enrolled as a clerk in the Belgian Congolese army in 1949; in the mid-1950s he edited a weekly newspaper *Actualités Africaines*. He joined **Lumumba** in 1958 as a member of *Mouvement National Congolais;* and became chief of staff of the Force Publique after Congo gained independence in 1960. He supported **Kasavabu** and then ousted him in a coup in 1965, put down a white mercenary uprising in 1967 and nationalised the Katanga copper mines. In 1977 he defeated an invasion of Shaba province (Katanga) from Angola.

MOHAMMED (Muhammad) (c.570–632) Prophet and founder of Islam, born in Mecca in western Arabia (now part of Saudi Arabia). When aged about twenty-five he married Khadija, widow of a wealthy merchant (later he made several other marriages, some for political reasons). In about 610 he received a religious call, regarded by himself and his followers as revelations from God, later written down in the **Koran**. He was forced by opposition in Mecca to emigrate to Medina in 622 at the invitation of some Arab groups there; this emigration, or **Hegira**, is the starting point of the Muslim calendar. In Medina he became first arbitrator, then ruler of a new kind of religious and political community, the Umma; he conquered Mecca in 630 and then unified much of Arabia under his leadership. After his death he was succeeded as leader of the Umma, but not as prophet, by **Abu Bakr,** first of the line of caliphs.

MOHAMMED ABDUH (1849–1905) Islamic religious reformer, born in Egypt. In 1882 he was exiled for his political activity after the British occupation of Egypt. Returning, he was appointed appellate judge in 1891. He suggested many modernising liberal reforms in Islamic law, education, ritual and social thought.

MOHAMMED ALI (1769–1849) Founder of modern Egypt. Born in Macedonia, he was appointed Ottoman viceroy in Egypt, 1805; challenged the sultan and invaded Syria, 1831; after European intervention (1840) he gave up Syria, but was appointed hereditary ruler of Egypt and the Sudan the following year.

MOHAMMED V (1910–61) King of Morocco. He succeeded his father as sultan of Morocco in 1927, then under French tutelage which he worked to remove. Deposed and exiled by the French, 1953–5, he was first reinstated as sultan and then recognised as sovereign (1956) and first king of Morocco (1957).

MÖNGKE (d.1259) Mongol leader, grandson of **Genghis Khan**. He played a prominent part in the great Mongol drive into western Asia and Europe. Elected Great Khan in 1251, he planned a world conquest, from China to Egypt.

MONISM Philosophic doctrine that asserts the single nature of phenomena and denies duality or pluralism (i.e. the separateness of mind and matter). Religiously, it is also the doctrine that there is only one Being, not an opposition of good and evil, or a distinction of God from the world.

MONOPHYSITES Those who followed Eutyches and Dioscorus, Patriarch of Alexandria (d.454), who taught that there was only one nature, not two, in the person of **Jesus** Christ. This doctrine was condemned by the **Council of Chalcedon** (451). Modern churches which grew out of Monophysitism are orthodox in belief though they retain some Monophysite terminology, notably the Coptic, Syrian and Armenian variations.

MONROE, JAMES (1758–1831) Fifth President of the United States. He negotiated the **Louisiana Purchase** (1803). During his presidency, 1817–25, he drew up with his Secretary of State, **John Quincy Adams,** the Monroe Doctrine, which has aimed at excluding foreign influence from the Western Hemisphere ever since.

MONTAGNARDS Hill-dwellers in Indo-China. In Vietnam they cultivate rice on burned-out forest land, live in longhouses or huts raised on piles, trace their descent through the female line, and speak a variety of Mon-Khmer and Malayo-Polynesian languages.

MONTANIST Follower of the heretical Christian sect founded in Phrygia by Montanus and by two women, Prisca and Maximilla, in the 2nd century AD. The group was ecstatic and prophetic, restoring belief in the present power of the Spirit; there was mystical identification with the divine and ascetic practice. **Tertullian** was a notable convert, but by the 3rd century the sect was under condemnation; it persisted in Phrygia until the 5th century.

MONTCALM, LOUIS, MARQUIS DE (1712–59) French general who as commander-in-chief of the French Canadian forces defended Canada against the British in the French and Indian War (1756–60). He was killed during the battle for Quebec on the Heights of Abraham.

MONTESQUIEU, BARON DE (1689–1755) French political philosopher. His main works included *Lettres Persanes* (1721), satirising French life and politics, and *L'Esprit des Lois* (1748), his masterpiece, which first set out many of the key ideas in modern democratic and constitutional thought, characteristic of the Enlightenment and of rationalism.

MONTFORT, SIMON DE (c.1160–1218) Baron of Montfort (near Paris). He became a leader of the Albigensian Crusade and Count of Toulouse after the Battle of Muret, 1213; he extended north French and Catholic influence in the south of France. He was the father of Simon de Montfort, Earl of Leicester, the opponent of Henry III of England.

MORDAUNT, SIR JOHN (1697–1780) British general. In 1756 he commanded the army assembled in Dorset to repel an expected French invasion; in 1757 he led an unsuccessful expedition (with Admiral Hawke) to attack the French naval base at Rochefort, and was court-martialled for his failure.

MORELOS, JOSÉ MARÍA (1765–1815) Mexican priest and revolutionary. He joined Hidalgo's insurrection against the Spanish colonial government, 1811, and took command in southern Mexico after Hidalgo's death, leading a successful guerrilla army but with too few men to consolidate his victories. In 1813 he called the Congress of Chilpancingo, which declared Mexican independence, but two years later was captured, defrocked and shot as a traitor after directing a heroic rearguard action against the Spaniards.

MORENO, MARIANO GARCÍA (1778–1811) Argentine independence leader. He practised as a lawyer in Buenos Aires; in 1809 published his 'Landowners' petition' (*Representación de los hacendados*) attacking restrictive Spanish trade laws, and in 1810 joined the revolutionary junta which replaced the Spanish administration. He became secretary for military and political affairs; founded Argentina's national library and official newspaper, *La Gaceta de Buenos Aires*; he was forced to resign after prematurely advocating complete separation on a diplomatic mission to London.

MORGAN, JOHN PIERPONT (1837–1913) United States financier. In 1871 he joined the New York firm of Drexel, Morgan & Co. (renamed J. P. Morgan & Co. in 1895); under his guidance this became one of the world's greatest financial institutions, deeply involved in US government borrowing, reorganisation of the US railways and the formation of such massive industrial groups as US Steel, International Harvester and the General Electric Company. By the time of his death his name was accepted everywhere as a symbol of 'money power'; he had also formed a great art collection.

MOSES Israelite leader, prophet and lawgiver who flourished somewhere between the 15th and 13th centuries BC. According to the Old Testament, he was born in Egypt; he led the Israelites out of slavery, and travelled forty years in the Sinai desert seeking Canaan, the land promised to the descendants of **Abraham**. He received the Ten Commandments, the basis of Jewish law; he died within sight of the promised land.

MOSLEY, SIR OSWALD (1896–1980) Leader of the British Union of Fascists. He served as a Member of Parliament, successively as a Conservative, Independent and Labour representative. He left the Labour Party in 1930 to found the right-wing 'New Party' and, later, the BUF or Blackshirts. He was imprisoned by the British government during the Second World War, and subsequently lived in France.

MOSSADEQ, MOHAMMED (?1880–1967) Iranian politician. As Prime Minister, 1951–3, he nationalised the Anglo-Iranian oil company; after a struggle for power with the Shah and his supporters, and with Western oil interests, he was overturned by a *coup d'état* in 1953 and imprisoned until 1956.

MOUNTBATTEN, LOUIS, EARL (1900–79) British military commander. A grandson of Queen **Victoria**, he entered the Royal Navy in 1913. He was Allied Chief of Combined Operations, 1942–3; Supreme Commander South-East Asia 1943–6; last Viceroy (1947) and first Governor-General (1947–8) of India; commanded the Mediterranean fleet (1948–9 and 1952–4); became First Sea Lord (1955–9), Chief of UK Defence Staff and Chairman of Chiefs of Staff Committee (1959–65); and personal aide-de-camp to the British sovereign from 1936. Killed by Irish terrorists 1979.

MSIRI (d.1891) African king, also known as Ngetengwa and Mwendo. Born near Tabora, now in Tanzania, in 1856 he settled in southern Katanga (Shaba); with a handful of Nyamwezi supporters, he seized large parts of this valuable copper-producing region, and by 1870 had largely displaced the previous Lunda rulers. His rejection of overtures from the British South Africa Company in the 1880s resulted in the Copper Belt being divided between Great Britain (Zambia) and Belgium (Zaire). He was shot while negotiating with emissaries from **Leopold II** of Belgium's Congo Free State.

MUGHALS Dynasty of Muslim emperors in India; *see page* 172.

MUHAMMAD BIN TUGHLUQ (c.1290–1351) Indian empire-builder, who succeeded his father in 1325 as ruler of the Delhi sultanate. He extended the frontiers far into southern India, fighting many campaigns to consolidate his gains; he failed, however, to impose coherent control, and saw his domains begin to crumble before he died.

MUIZZUDIN MUHAMMAD (d.1206) Greatest of the **Ghurids**. He helped his brother to seize power in Ghur, north-western Afghanistan, c.1162, expelled Turkish nomads from Ghazni, 1173; invaded northern India, 1175; annexed the **Ghaznavid** principality of Lahore, 1186. He was defeated by a **Rajput** coalition at Tara, 1191, but returned to rout them in 1192; he was assassinated.

MUKDEN, BATTLE OF Main land engagement of the Russo-Japanese War (1904–5). Mukden (Shen-yang), the industrial centre of Manchuria, became a tsarist stronghold after Russia obtained extensive railway building rights in the region (1896). The battle lasted over two weeks, starting in late February 1905 and ending with Japanese occupation of the city on 10 March.

MULVANY, WILLIAM THOMAS (1806–85) Irish industrialist. An engineer and civil servant 1833–49, he went to the German Ruhr district in 1854 and directed the opening of coalmines and ironworks there. In 1858 he organised an association of Ruhr industrialists (the *Bergbauverein*) which transformed the Ruhr into the largest coalfield and industrial complex on the European continent.

MÜNSTER, TREATY OF An agreement signed in January 1648 as part of the arrangements known collectively as the **Peace of Westphalia**, which ended the Thirty Years War. It brought Spanish recognition of the independence of the Dutch Republic and brought to an end the Dutch Revolt.

MURAD I (c.1326–89) Third ruler of the Ottoman state, succeeding **Orkhan** in 1362. He controlled (or profited from) the continuing Turkish expansion in the Balkans which brought Thrace and later Thessaly, the south Serbian principalities and much of Bulgaria under Ottoman control. Byzantium, Bulgaria and Serbia were successively reduced to vassalage after the defeat of hostile coalition forces at Chirmen (Chermanon) in 1371 and Kossovo in 1389; Murad was killed during the latter battle. Ottoman territory was also expanded in Anatolia (acquisition of Ankara, 1354; hostilities with the Karaman in the 1380s).

MURAD II (1404–51) Ottoman sultan, son of **Mehemmed I**. Succeeding to the throne in 1421, he spent the early years of his reign overcoming rival claimants backed by Byzantium or Karaman. After a seven-year war with Venice, Murad took Salonika in 1430. The later years of his reign were dominated by the struggle with Hungary for the lands of the lower Danube, Serbia and Wallachia. Murad gained control over Serbia in 1439 but in 1440 failed to take Belgrade; by 1443 the **Ottomans** were forced on to the defensive at Izladi, and in the following year, having made an unfavourable peace with Hungary and Karaman, Murad abdicated in favour of his twelve-year-old son **Mehemmed II**. Following the penetration of the Balkans by a Christian army, Murad led the Ottoman forces to a crushing victory at Varna in 1444. Two years later he reassumed the throne; in 1448 he defeated the Hungarians once more at Kossovo.

MUSSOLINI, BENITO (1883–1945) Italian dictator. He practised as a schoolteacher and journalist; having been expelled in 1914 from the Socialist party for advocating support of the Allied powers, in 1919 he organised the Fascist party, advocating nationalism, syndicalism and violent anti-Communism, backed up by a paramilitary organisation, the Blackshirts. He organised a march on Rome in 1922. He was appointed Prime Minister and then, as Il Duce (the Leader), established himself as totalitarian dictator. He invaded Ethiopia in 1935, formed the Rome-Berlin Axis with **Hitler** the following year, and in 1940 declared war on the Allies. He was defeated in 1943, installed by Hitler as head of a puppet state (Republic of Salo) in northern Italy and shot by Italian partisans in 1945.

MWENEMUTAPA (later Mashonaland). Kingdom of south-eastern Africa between the 14th and 18th centuries, with its capital probably at Zimbabwe; famous for its gold deposits, which attracted Portuguese traders, based in Mozambique, from 1505 onwards.

MYCENAEAN Ancient Greek civilisation flourishing c.1600–1100 BC, culturally influenced by Minoan Crete. It was centred on the city of Mycenae, in Argolis, where the most famous surviving monuments include the citadel walls with the Lion Gate, and the Treasury of Atreus.

MZILIKAZI (d.1870) Matabele (Ndebele) chief. He fled from Zululand to set up a new kingdom north of the Vaal river, but was defeated by the Boers, 1836; he withdrew across the Limpopo river and established the Matabele kingdom.

NABOPOLASSAR (d.605 BC) King of Babylon and destroyer of Assyria, a notable of one of the Kaldu (Chaldaean) tribes of southern Babylonia. While governor of the Sea-land province, he assumed leadership of an insurrection against the Assyrians in 627 BC. He founded the last native Babylonian dynasty, the Chaldaean, in 626, quickly gaining control of much of Babylonia. He unsuccessfully besieged Ashur, 616, formed an alliance with the **Medes**, 614, and made a joint assault on Nineveh which was completed in 612. He was succeeded by his son, Nebuchadnezzar.

NANAK (1469–1539) Founding guru of the **Sikh** faith, combining Hindu and Muslim beliefs into a single doctrine. The son of a merchant, he made an extended pilgrimage to Muslim and Hindu shrines throughout India, returning to the Punjab in 1520 and settling in Kartarpur. His teaching, spread by a large following of disciples, advocated intensive meditation on the divine name; many of his hymns still survive.

NANKING TREATY *see* **Opium War**

NANTES, EDICT OF Order, issued in 1598 by **Henry IV** of France guaranteeing freedom of worship to French Protestants. Its revocation in 1685 by **Louis XIV** forced many non-Catholics to flee the country, weakening the French economy and creating much international friction.

NAPIER, SIR CHARLES JAMES (1782–1853) British general and prolific author. He served under **Wellington** in the Peninsular War; he led the British conquest of Sind, 1841–3.

NAPOLEON I (NAPOLEON BONAPARTE) (1769–1821) Emperor of the French; *see pages* 204–5.

NAPOLEON III (CHARLES LOUIS NAPOLÉON BONAPARTE) (1808–73) Emperor of the French, son of Louis Bonaparte and nephew of **Napoleon I.** He was exiled, like his uncle, after 1815. He wrote *Les Idées Napoléoniennes* in 1839, was involved in two unsuccessful insurrections, in 1836 and 1840, and returned to France after the 1848 revolution, to be elected President by a huge majority, and to become Emperor in 1852. During his highly prosperous reign, central Paris was rebuilt, Cochin China was acquired and the Suez Canal opened. He was defeated by **Bismarck** in the **Franco-Prussian War** (1870–1), and after the collapse of his regime in 1871 went into exile in England.

NARAI (d.1688) (also Narayana). King of Siam from 1657 until his death. In his struggle to free his country's foreign trade from Dutch control he sought the help of the **English East India Company**'s factors at Ayutthaya. Their inability to help caused him to turn to the French, whose cause was espoused by his Greek adviser, **Constant Phaulkon** a convert to Catholicism. After an exchange of missions between Versailles and Lopburi, Narai's up-country residence, **Louis XIV** sent a naval expedition which seized the then village of Bangkok and the port of Mergui (now in Burma) with the declared aim of converting Siam to **Christianity.** The resulting national uprising, led by Pra Phetraja, forced the French to withdraw; Pra Phetraja became regent, and on Narai's death a few months later his successor.

NARAM-SIN The last great ruler of Sumer and Akkad, in ancient Mesopotamia, and grandson of **Sargon**. He reigned c.2291–2255 BC, and was a famous warrior whose victories are commemorated in several extant carvings and monuments, including the impressive stele found at Susa, now in the Louvre Museum.

NASRIDS The last Muslim dynasty in Spain, which rose to power under Muhammad I al-Ghalib (died 1272) and ruled Granada from 1238 until its conquest by the Christians in 1492.

NASSER, GAMAL ABDEL- (1918–70) Egyptian politician. As an army officer he became the leading member of the group which overthrew King **Farouk** in 1952, under the nominal leadership of General **Neguib**. In 1954, after a power struggle with Neguib, he became Prime Minister, and in 1956 President until his death. His regime was marked by socio-economic changes – reform of land-tenure, building of the Aswan High Dam – and a foreign policy of neutralism between the great powers, and of providing leadership for the Arab nationalist movement, which led to the short-lived union with Syria in the United Arab Republic (1958–61), two wars (with Israel, Great Britain and France, 1956, with Israel, 1967), and increasing dependence on the USSR.

NATO *see* **North Atlantic Treaty Organisation**

NAVAJO North American Indian tribe which probably emigrated from Canada to the region of the south-western United States between 900 and 1200. After a long history of raids against white settlers in New Mexico, 8000 Navajo were captured by a force under Colonel Kit Carson (1863–4) and interned for four years in New Mexico; in 1868 they were released and sent to a reservation. Today some 100,000 Navajo survive, many still occupying the 24,000 square mile reservation in New Mexico, Arizona and Utah. They form the largest Indian tribe in the United States.

NAZISM Term formed from the abbreviation for the National Socialist German Workers' Party – leader **Adolf Hitler**. Its creed covered many of the features of **Fascism.** Its special characteristics were (1) a belief in the racial superiority of the **'Aryan** race' and of the German people who, as the purest carriers of Aryan blood, constituted a master race destined to dominate the sub-human Slav peoples of eastern Europe and Russia; (2) virulent anti-semitism expressed in the systematic extermination of the Jewish population throughout Europe, the Jews being accused of an insatiable desire to corrupt and destroy Aryan purity and culture; (3) anti-urbanism and anti-intellectualism, the peasant being held to be purified by his contact with the land; (4) the personality and ruthless political leadership of Hitler, who believed himself destined to risk all to lead the German people to the empire which would last for a thousand years.

NAZI-SOVIET PACT (also known as Molotov-Ribbentrop Pact). Mutual non-aggression pact signed on 24 August 1939 between Germany and Soviet Russia, containing secret protocols which divided Eastern Europe between the signatories: eastern Poland, Latvia, Estonia, Finland and Bessarabia to Russia; western Poland and Lithuania (later transferred to the Russian sphere) to Germany. The Russians invaded Poland seventeen days after the Germans, on 17 September 1939.

NDEBELE *see* **Matabele**

NEGUIB, MOHAMMED (1901–84) Egyptian soldier and President. He was second in command of Egyptian troops in Palestine in the first Arab-Israeli war in 1948. Adopted as their titular head by the Egyptian officers who made the revolution of 1952, after the revolution he became Prime Minister and President of the republic, 1953–4. He was deprived of office after a struggle for power with the real leader of the officers, **Nasser.**

NEHRU, JAWAHARLAL (1889–1964) First Prime Minister of independent India, 1947–64. Educated in England, in 1920 he joined the nationalist movement led by **Gandhi**, and was imprisoned eight times between 1920 and 1927. He was four times President of the Indian National Congress Party: 1929–30, 1936–7, 1946 and 1951–4.

NELSON, HORATIO (1758–1805) 1st Viscount Nelson. British naval hero, who rose to the rank of admiral in 1797 during the French Revolutionary Wars, winning decisive victories at the Nile (1798) and at Copenhagen (1801). He was killed in 1805 during his most famous battle, Trafalgar, which effectively ended the threat of a French invasion of England.

NEOLITHIC The last part of the **Stone Age,** originally defined by the occurrence of polished stone tools, but now seen as more importantly characterised by the practice of agriculture, for which polished stone axes were essential forest-clearing equipment. Such cultures emerged in the Near East by 8000 BC, and appeared in Europe from 6000 to 3000 BC.

NERCHINSK, TREATY OF Peace agreement signed in 1689 between Russia and China, as a result of which Russia withdrew from lands east of the Stanovoiy Mts and north of the Amur river. The settlement lasted until the treaties of **Aigun** (1858) and **Peking** (1860) brought Russia to its present boundary with China in the Far East.

NERO (AD 37–68) Roman emperor, succeeding to the imperial title in AD 54. He murdered his mother, Agrippina, in 59; after the fire of Rome in 64 he began a systematic persecution of Christians, and in the following year executed many opponents after the discovery of a plot to depose him. He committed suicide when the governors of Gaul, Spain and Africa united in revolt.

NESTORIANS Followers of Nestorius whose Christian teachings, condemned by the councils of Ephesus (431) and Chalcedon (451), stressed the independence of the divine and human natures of Christ. They are represented in modern times by the Persian or Nestorian Church (approximately 100,000 members in Iran, Syria and Iraq) which first accepted this version of **Christianity** in 486.

NEVSKY, ALEXANDER (c.1220–63) Prince of Novgorod. He defeated the Swedes on the river Neva (hence his name) in 1240; and the Teutonic Knights on frozen Lake Peipus, 1242. He thought resistance to the Mongols hopeless and co-operated with them; in return the Khan made him Grand Prince of Vladimir (i.e. ruler of Russia) in 1252.

NEWCOMEN, THOMAS (1663–1729) English inventor of the atmospheric engine. As an ironmonger, he saw the high cost and inefficiency of using horses to drain the Cornish tin mines, and after ten years of experiment produced an effective steam machine for this purpose. The first known Newcomen engine was erected near Dudley Castle, Staffordshire, in 1712. He also invented an internal-condensing jet to produce a vacuum in the engine cylinder, and an automatic valve gear.

NEW DEAL Social and economic programme, instituted 1933–9 by President **F. D. Roosevelt** to combat the effects of world depression in the United States. He used the Federal government to promote agricultural and industrial recovery, to provide relief to the unemployed, and to institute moderate economic and social reform.

NE WIN (1911–) Military dictator of Burma. He joined the nationalistic 'We-Burmans Association' in 1936, and in 1941 went to Taiwan (Formosa) for military training with the Japanese. He was chief of staff, Burma National Army, 1943–5, commander-in-chief of the Burmese Army after independence in 1948, and Prime Minister in the 1958 'caretaker' government. He stepped down in 1960 on the restoration of parliamentary administration, but in 1962 led a *coup d'état*, establishing a Revolutionary Council of the Union of Burma and declaring the Burmese

Road to Socialism. He broke Chinese and Indian control of the economy and expelled 300,000 foreigners. He is under constant harrassment from the ethnic minorities and from Communist opposition.

NGO DINH DIEM (1901–63) President of the Republic of Vietnam. Born into one of Vietnam's royal families, he was interior minister of the emperor Bao Dai's government in the 1930s. In 1945 he was captured by **Ho Chi Minh**'s Communists, and fled after refusing Ho's invitation to join his independence movement. Returned in 1954 to head the US-backed government in South Vietnam, but took dictatorial powers, and as a Roman Catholic imprisoned and killed hundreds of Buddhists. He was abandoned by the US, and was assassinated during a military *coup d'état.*

NGUNI One of the two main Bantu-speaking groups of southern African peoples, including the Swazi, Pondo, Thembu, **Xhosa, Zulu** and **Matabele** (Ndebele) nations, occupying mainly land east of the Drakensburg mountains, from Natal to Cape Province.

NICAEA, COUNCILS OF The first council, which was also the first ecumenical gathering of the Christian Church, was called in 325 by the Emperor **Constantine**; it condemned the heresy of Arianism and promulgated the Nicene Creed, which affirms the consubstantiality of Christ the Son and God the Father. The second Nicaean (or seventh ecumenical) council took place in 787 as an attempt to resolve the controversy over **iconoclasm**; it agreed that icons deserved reverence and veneration but not adoration, which was reserved for God.

NICAEA, EMPIRE OF Founded in 1204 by the Byzantine leader Theodore I Lascaris after the Western occupation of Constantinople during the Fourth **Crusade**. Crowned emperor in 1208, Theodore gradually extended his territory to include most of western Anatolia. His successors, while fighting off the despots of Epirus and the Mongols, also attempted to retake Constantinople; success came in 1261 when the Nicaean general, Michael Palaeologus, was able to establish himself as Michael VIII and found the last dynasty of Byzantine emperors.

NICEPHORUS II PHOCAS (c.913–69) Byzantine emperor, who fought as a general under Constantine VII and Romanus II and usurped the throne in 963. He defeated Arab, Bulgarian, Italian and Western imperial enemies. He was murdered in 969 by his own general John Tzimisces, who in turn usurped the throne as John I.

NICHOLAS II (1869–1918) Last tsar of Russia, son of Alexander III. He succeeded in 1894; granted, but then largely withdrew liberal reforms after the revolution of 1905. He was forced to abdicate in March 1917, and was shot at Yekaterinburg (Sverdlovsk) by the **Bolsheviks** in July 1918.

NIEN REBELLION Insurrection led by peasant bandit confederations in Anhwei, Honan and Shantung, areas which had suffered from the disastrous flooding of the Huang Ho (Yellow River) in the 1850s.

NIMWEGEN, TREATIES OF Agreements signed 1678–9 to end the Dutch War (1672–8) between France, Spain and the Dutch Republic. France returned Maastricht to the United Provinces and suspended her anti-Dutch tariff of 1667; Spain gave up Franche-Comté, Artois and sixteen Flemish garrison towns to France, thus losing its 'corridor' from Milan to the Spanish Netherlands (the Spanish Road). In 1679 the German emperor, Leopold I, accepted the terms, slightly strengthening French rights in Alsace, Lorraine and on the Rhine.

NINE YEARS WAR Conflict between **Louis XIV** of France and his neighbours, 1689–97, led by William III of England and the Netherlands, allied in the **League of Augsburg.** Their aim was to restrain French territorial expansion, mainly at the expense of the Spanish empire, and in this they eventually succeeded.

NIMITZ, CHESTER WILLIAM (1885–1965) American naval admiral who was commander-in-chief of the Pacific Ocean Area, 1942–45.

NIVELLE, ROBERT-GEORGES (1856–1924) French general. After two brilliant victories at Verdun, he was appointed commander-in-chief of the French armies on the Western Front in 1916, but was replaced by Pétain in 1917 after the disastrous failure of the spring offensive and widespread mutiny.

NIXON, RICHARD MILHOUS (1913–) 37th President of the United States. Trained as a lawyer, he was elected to the House of Representatives in 1946 and 1948; elected Republican Senator for California, 1950. He was Vice-President to **Dwight D. Eisenhower** (1953–61); defeated for the presidency by **John F. Kennedy**, 1960, and in the contest for California governorship, 1962. He re-entered politics to defeat Humphrey in the presidential election, 1968, and was re-elected in a landslide victory, 1972. He resigned office in 1974 at the climax of the investigation into the 'Watergate scandal' arising out of an attempt to burgle the Democratic election headquarters during the 1972 campaign.

NIZAM Hereditary title of the rulers of the Indian state of Hyderabad; members of the dynasty founded by Asaf Jah, Subadhar of the Deccan, 1713–48.

NKRUMAH, KWAME (1909–72) The first Prime Minister of independent Ghana (formerly the Gold Coast colony). He graduated from Achimota College in 1930; wrote *Towards Colonial Freedom* in 1947 in opposition to British rule, and in 1949 formed the Convention People's Party, instituting a programme of non-cooperation. After independence (1957) he became first President of the Ghana republic, 1960; in 1964 he declared a one-party state, but was deposed two years later by the army while on a visit to China.

NOBEL, ALFRED BERNHARD (1833–96) Swedish industrialist, chemist and inventor of dynamite. He began the manufacture of nitroglycerine in Sweden in 1860; his first factory blew up, killing his younger brother Emil. He perfected a much safer dynamite, and patented it in 1867–8. He made an immense fortune from this and from his share of the Russian Baku oilfield. When he died he left the bulk of his money in trust to establish the Nobel prizes for peace, literature, physics, chemistry, medicine and, more recently, economics.

NOK One of the Iron Age cultures in West Africa, flourishing on the Benue Plateau of Nigeria between 500 BC and AD 200. It is characterised by its distinctive clay figurines depicting both animals and men.

NORMANS Name derived from Nordmanni, or Northmen, to describe the Viking invaders who in the late 9th century established themselves on the lower Seine, in France. In 911, under their leader Hrolfr (Rollo), they obtained from the French king, Charles the Simple, rights to territory in northern Normandy; in 924 and 933 their control was extended, particularly westward, to include the whole area now known as Normandy. In the 11th century, under Robert and Roger Guiscard, and Duke William (**William I, the Conqueror**) respectively, their descendants conquered both Sicily and England.

NORMAN CONQUEST Name given to the successful invasion of England in 1066 by Duke William of Normandy, crowned king as **William I, the Conqueror**. English resistance was broken and the whole country overrun by 1071, and the conquest stabilised by expelling **Anglo-Saxon** landowners and parcelling out the conquered territory among William's followers, as tenants-in-chief and vassals of the king.

NORTH ATLANTIC TREATY ORGANISATION (NATO) Defensive alliance, signed in 1949 between Belgium, Canada, Denmark, France, Iceland, Italy, Luxembourg, Netherlands, Norway, Portugal, United Kingdom and United States. Greece and Turkey joined in 1951; West Germany in 1954. France ceased to participate fully in 1966. NATO's headquarters are in Brussels; it deploys some 800,000 land troops in Europe.

NORTHERN RISING Attempted rebellion in northern England against **Elizabeth I** in 1569–70. Led by the Catholic earls of Northumberland and Westmorland, its object was to restore Catholicism by placing the imprisoned (Catholic) Mary Queen of Scots on the English throne; faced by royal armies, the rebels melted away, although eight hundred died in the only direct clash; the leaders fled abroad.

NORTH GERMAN CONFEDERATION Political union of north German states set up under Prussian leadership after the Seven Weeks' War in 1866. It was enlarged in 1871 after the Franco-Prussian War to become the new German Empire.

NOVATIAN (c.200–c.258) Roman theologian, author of *De Trinitate* (*On the Trinity*). He at first supported those Christians whose faith lapsed under persecution, but later strongly condemned all apostasy. After 251, when Cornelius became Pope, this led him to break with the Church and set himself up as a rigorist anti-Pope, at the head of the Novatianist Schism. He was excommunicated in 251, and probably martyred c.258 under the Emperor **Valerian**, but the sect continued to spread in east and west and lasted until the 6th century.

NU-PIEDS Peasants who rebelled in protest against high taxes in Normandy, France, in 1639; named after the salt-gatherers of Avranches, who walked barefoot on the sands. They feared that the introduction of a salt tax (*gabelle*) would reduce sales of their product, and took a leading part in the uprising, which was crushed after four months in a pitched battle with government forces outside Rouen.

NURI ES-SAID (1888–1958) Iraqi statesman. An officer in the Ottoman army, in 1916 he joined the revolt of Sherif **Hussein** against the Ottomans, and in 1921 joined Hussein's son Faysal when he became king of Iraq. He held various ministerial posts, including that of Prime Minister. In 1941 he fled Iraq with the regent, Abdullah, during the period of rule by **Rashid Ali**, returned after the British military reoccupation, and dominated Iraqi politics, with intervals, until he was killed during an army coup. He was associated with the strongly pro-Western policy which led to the formation of the Baghdad Pact (**Central Treaty Organisation**) in 1955.

NYAMWEZI A Bantu-speaking people of East Africa, occupying a large area between Lake Victoria and Lake Rukwa. In the 19th century they played a major part in the opening up of the East African interior to European trade from the coast.

NYERERE, JULIUS (1922–) President of Tanzania. Founder president of the Tanganyika African National Union in 1954, he was elected to the Tanganyika legislative council in 1958, and became Chief Minister, 1960–1, and Prime Minister, 1961–2. He was President, first of Tanganyika, 1962–4, and then of Tanzania from 1964. The author of *Freedom and Unity* (1967) and Swahili translations of Shakespeare, he developed theories of African socialism, and put these and other economic self-sufficiency policies into practice.

NYSTAD, TREATY OF Agreement in 1721 between Russia and Sweden to end the **Great Northern War**. Russia gained Sweden's Baltic provinces (Estonia and Livonia) and thus a 'window on the west', but restored Finland to Sweden.

OCTAVIAN *see* **Augustus**

OFFA (d.796) King of Mercia, central England, in the 8th century. He constructed an earthwork which still survives (Offa's Dyke) between his kingdom and Wales. He claimed the title 'King of the English' after establishing control over most of the country south of the river Humber.

OGEDEI (d.1241) Mongol ruler, third son of **Genghis Khan**. He was given chief command, in preference to his brothers, Jochi and Chagatai, during the latter part of the Khwarizian campaign, 1220–2; elected Great Khan in 1229, in 1235 he completed the conquest of the **Chin** in northern China and declared war on China's Sung dynasty, and in 1236 conquered Korea. He planned the western campaign that finally carried the Mongols from Siberia to the Adriatic.

O'HIGGINS, BERNARDO (1778-1842) Liberator of Chile, and its first head of state. The son of a Spanish officer of Irish origin; he became a member of the Chilean national congress in 1811; and then led Chilean forces in **San Martin's** Army of the Andes, triumphing over the royalists at the Battle of Chacabuco in February 1817. In 1823 he was exiled to Peru, where he died.

OJEDA, ALONSO DE (1465–1515) Spanish adventurer, who sailed under, and later quarrelled with, **Columbus**. In 1499, with **Vespucci**, he explored the coasts of Venezuela and Guiana, landing in the area later claimed by Spain (1593) under the name Surinam. He commanded the first mainland settlement in South America, on the Gulf of Urabá, 1509 – a disastrous failure.

OLDENBURGS Danish royal family, of German origin. Christian, Count of Oldenburg, was elected as king of Denmark and Norway in 1448; his direct descendants ruled until 1863, when the succession passed to the present Glücksburg branch.

OLGIERD (d.1377) Grand Duke of Lithuania, reigning 1345–77, son of **Gedymin**, father of **Wladyslaw II Jagiello.** He invaded Mongol-dominated Russia in 1362–3, seizing the principality of Kiev; he failed to take Moscow in 1368–72. He died fighting the **Tartars.**

OLOF SKÖTKONUNG (d.1022) 'The Tax King'. Christian king of the Swedes and the Gantat; son of Erik the Victorious. He joined the Danish king, **Sven Forkbeard**, to defeat Norway in 1000; though he became a Christian he failed to impose the new religion on his subjects.

OMAR IBN AL-KHATTAB (c.591–644) Second Muslim caliph, and the first to assume the title 'Commander of the Faithful'. At first he opposed Islam, but was converted c.617; his daughter Hafsa became **Mohammed**'s third wife. He aided the first caliph, **Abu Bakr**, in his campaigns, succeeding him without opposition in 634, and carried further the conquests he had begun in Palestine, Syria, Iraq, Persia and Egypt. He was assassinated by a slave of Persian origin.

OPIUM WAR Fought between Britain and China, 1839–42, over Chinese attempts to prevent the import of opium from British India in payment for British imports of Chinese tea and silk which had previously been paid in silver, the only exchange acceptable to the Chinese. After a series of defeats, under the terms of the Nanking treaty China ceded Hong Kong Island to Britain, opened five Treaty Ports to British trade, and relaxed many economic restrictions on foreign merchants.

ORIGEN (c.185–254) Scholar and theologian, deeply influential in the emergence of the early Greek Christian church. He wrote many important commentaries, treatises and polemics, culminating c.232 in his *Hexapla* reconciling six different versions of the Old Testament.

ORKHAN (1274/88–1362) Second ruler *(beg)* of the Muslim ghazi principality founded by his father, **Osman I** whom he succeeded in 1326. He captured Nicaea (Iznik) in 1331 and Nicomedia (Iznikmid) in 1337 from Byzantium; by annexing the neighbouring emirate of Karasi in 1345 he was able to involve the Ottomans in the civil wars in Byzantium, and secured a bridgehead in Europe (Rumeli). Orkhan's sons seized Tzympe in 1352, Gallipoli in 1354 and Adrianpole (Edirne) in 1361, thus opening the Balkans to Turkish conquest and Ottoman expansion.

ORMÉE REVOLT Part of the **Fronde** rebellion against **Louis XIV** of France, 1648–53. Bordeaux defied authority until reduced by a regular siege; the rebellion took its name from the *ormes* (elm trees) under which the rebels met to discuss policy.

ORTELIUS, ABRAHAM (1527–1606) Publisher of the first modern atlas *Theatrum orbis terrarum* (Antwerp, 1570). He worked as a cartographer, antiquary and book dealer. An English edition of his atlas was issued in 1606 as *Theatre of the whole World*.

OSMAN I (c.1258–c.1326) Founder of the Ottoman dynasty, a ghazi leader active among the Turks settled in the north-west Anatolian borderlands with Byzantium in the latter part of the 13th century. He emerges into history c.1301; after a constant struggle he had by his death conquered most of Bithynia from Byzantium, including Bursa (1326).

OSTROGOTHS Germanic people who occupied the Ukraine in the 4th century AD. During the reign of their great hero, king Ermanaric (d.372) they extended their empire from the Black Sea to the Baltic, but were dispossessed c.370 by the advancing Huns. The tribe then wandered and fought in eastern and central Europe until the end of Hunnish domination, c.455. Under their king, **Theodoric** (ruled 493–526), they moved into Italy and established themselves as rulers, with their capital at Verona, until finally dispersed by the armies of **Justinian I** in the mid-6th century.

OTHMAN (d.656) Third Muslim caliph after the death of **Mohammed**. Born into the rich and powerful **Umayyad** clan of Mecca, c.615 he became **Mohammed's** first influential convert, and was elected caliph in 644 after the death of **Omar.** He promulgated the first official version of the **Koran**, and continued the policy of conquest.

OTTAWA AGREEMENTS A series of arrangements, concluded at the Imperial Economics Conference in 1932, under which Great Britain, having reversed its traditional Free Trade policies and imposed tariffs on most foreign food and raw material imports, allowed free or preferential entry to goods from the British Empire. In return, the colonies and dominions agreed to use tariffs against British goods only to protect their own domestic industries. The underlying doctrine, known as Imperial Preference, was substantially modified by the General Agreement on Tariffs and Trade (GATT) in 1947, and finally evaporated on Britain's entry to the European Economic Community (EEC) in 1973.

OTTO I, THE GREAT (912–73) German emperor. As king of East Francia he crushed rebellions involving his brothers Thankmar and Henry (938–9) and his son Liudolf (953–4). He defeated the Magyars at the battle of the Lechfeld (955). He received the imperial crown in 962; by marrying his son **Otto II** to the Byzantine Princess Theophana, 972, he achieved recognition of his Western Empire in Constantinople.

OTTO II (955–83) Son of **Otto I**, and German king from 961, he held the imperial throne jointly with his father from 967 and alone from 973. He tried without success to drive the Greeks and Arabs from southern Italy, 982.

OTTO III (980–1002) German emperor, son of **Otto II**. He was German king from 983 under the regency of his mother (until 991) and grandmother (until 994), being crowned emperor in 996.

OTTO OF FREISING (c.1111–58) German bishop, historian and philosopher, half-brother to King Conrad III. He entered the Cistercian monastery at Morimond, Champagne, c.1132, and became bishop of Freising in 1138. He wrote a world history from the beginning to 1146, and also the *Gesta Friderici*, celebrating the deeds of the **Hohenstaufen** dynasty, particularly of his nephew, **Frederick I Barbarossa**.

OTTOCAR II (1230–1278) King of Bohemia, son of Wenceslaus I, reigning 1253–78. He made his kingdom briefly the strongest state in the **Holy Roman Empire**. He led crusades against the heathen Prussians and Lithuanians, and annexed lands from Styria to the Adriatic. Eclipsed after election of Rudolf of Habsburg as emperor in 1273, he was forced to renounce all territory save Bohemia and Moravia. He was killed at the Battle of Dürnkrut, attempting to reconquer Austria.

OTTOMANS Turkish Muslim emperors; *see pages 138–9, 170–1.*

OWEN THE BALD (d.1015) Last king of the Britons of Strathclyde, a state between Scotland and England, centred on Glasgow, which was annexed by Scotland after Owen's death.

OWEN, ROBERT (1771–1858) Early British socialist and social reformer. He was manager of a model cotton mill at New Lanark, 1799, and pioneered shorter working hours, employee housing, education and co-operative stores. He was partly responsible for the Factory Act of 1819; he formed the Grand National Consolidated Trades Union in 1843.

OXFORDSHIRE RISING Popular revolt in 1596 in the English Midlands against the enclosure of common land by landlords, depriving the local population of grazing rights.

PACHACUTI (d.1471) The ninth **Inca** emperor, reigning from 1438 until his death. He led his people's victorious expansion out of the Cuzco valley towards Lake Titicaca; with his son, **Topa** Inca, he conquered the **Chimú**; he founded the great fortress of Sacsahuaman. His mummified body was found by Juan Polo de Ondegardo, Spanish *corregidor* of Cuzco, in 1539.

PÁEZ, JOSÉ ANTONIO (1790–1873) First President of Venezuela. Part-Indian, he joined the revolution against Spain in 1810 and became one of the chief Venezuelan commanders to **Simon Bolívar**. He participated in the defeat of the Spaniards at Carabobo, 1821, and Puerto Cabello, 1823; in 1829 he led the movement to separate Venezuela from the larger state of Gran Colombia, and effectively controlled the new country from his election as President in 1831 until 1846, when he was forced into exile, returning as dictator in 1861. Driven out again in 1863, he retired to New York.

PAL, BIPIN CHANDRA (1858–1932) Indian schoolmaster, journalist and propagandist. After a brief visit to the United States in 1900, he became involved in the movement for Indian self-government *(swaraj)* editing newspapers and giving lectures which advocated non-cooperation with the British. In 1908 he was arrested; he lost his influence to **Tilak** and later to **Gandhi**.

PALAEOLITHIC The first part of the **Stone Age,** from the first recognisable stone tools in Africa over 2 million years ago, to the advanced reindeer-hunters who decorated their caves with wall-paintings in France and Spain around 20,000 years ago. It is divided into the Lower Palaeolithic, associated with early types of man, and the Middle and Upper Palaeolithic, associated with anatomically modern men.

PALAS Warrior dynasty of northern India, controlling most of Bengal and Bihar from the 8th to the 10th centuries. Founded by Gopala, under his son, Dharmapala, it became a dominant power in east India, with alliances from Tibet to Sumatra. It reached Benares in the 10th century but was blocked by the **Chola** king, Rajendra, and was forced back to defend Bengal, under King Mahipala, after whose death the dynasty declined, giving way to the Sena line.

PAN CH'AO Chinese general, explorer and administrator. Born into a famous scholarly family, he preferred a military life, and was despatched with a small expedition in 73 to repacify the **Hsiung-nu** tribes. He quickly established a highly effective technique for fomenting inter-tribal tensions. Appointed Protector-General of the Western Regions in 91, during the next ten years he briefly conquered virtually the whole area from the Tarim Basin and the Pamirs almost to the shores of the Caspian – the greatest westward expansion China has ever known.

PANTAENUS (died c.190) Christian teacher, convert from Stoicism. He made a missionary journey to India; the first head of the Christian Catechetical School in Alexandria, he influenced his associate and successor, **Clement of Alexandria**.

PAOLI, PASQUALE (1725–1807) Corsican patriot, elected President by the islanders during the struggle against Genoese rule. Forced to submit after Genoa sold the island to France in 1768 and in exile in Britain 1769–90, he returned in 1793 to lead the revolt against the French revolutionary government. He persuaded the British to take control of Corsica, 1794–6.

PAPACY The office or position of the Pope, as head of the Roman Catholic church. Also the papal system of government, both ecclesiastical and political, particularly during the centuries in which the papacy counted among the major states of Europe.

PAPEN, FRANZ VON (1879–1969) German politician, elected Chancellor in 1932. He played a substantial part in **Hitler's** rise to power, and helped to prepare the German annexation of Austria in 1938. He was found not guilty as a war criminal at the Nuremberg Trials in 1945, but was sentenced to eight years imprisonment; he was released in 1949.

PARAMARAS Rajput clan, prominent in northern India from the 9th to the 12th century. Mainly based in Malwa, with their capital at Dhar, near Indore, they were defeated by Turks from Afghanistan in 1192.

PARIS COMMUNE Name assumed on 26 March 1871, in emulation of the Jacobin Assembly of 1793, by a Central Committee established by rioters who had refused on 18 March to recognise the Assembly of Bordeaux which had accepted Prussian peace terms: the revolutionary socialist movement was crushed, with thousands of casualties, by government troops between 21 and 28 May.

PARIS, FIRST PEACE OF Signed on 30 May 1814, it consisted of seven separate treaties negotiated between the restored Louis XVIII of France and the principal European allies. The limits of France were fixed at approximately those of 1 January 1792; Britain restored certain colonies to France and acquired Malta. *(See also* **Congress of Vienna**.)

PARIS PEACE CONFERENCE see **Versailles, Treaty of.**

PARIS, SECOND PEACE OF Signed on 20 November 1815, following the 'Hundred Days'. It deprived **Napoleon** of Elba, reduced France to the limits of 1790, provided for an

army of occupation, and imposed an indemnity of 700 million francs. *(See also* **Congress of Vienna**.)

PARIS, TREATY OF (1763) Treaty which ended the **Seven Years War** (known in North America as the French and Indian War). France ceded to Great Britain all her territory east of the Mississippi, including Canada; Spain similarly gave up Florida to Great Britain, but received the Louisiana Territory and New Orleans from France.

PARK, MUNGO (1771–1806) Scottish explorer of Africa, who sought the true course of the river Niger; his account *Travels in the Interior of Africa* (1797) made him famous. He returned in 1805 to head a second expedition, but was drowned during a skirmish.

PARSEES Modern followers of the Iranian prophet **Zoroaster**. The majority of the sect is descended from the Persian Zoroastrians who fled to India in the 7th century to escape Muslim persecution.

PARSONS, SIR CHARLES ALGERNON (1854–1931) Inventor of the steam turbine. He entered Armstrong engineering works, Newcastle upon Tyne, in 1877 and in 1884 patented the steam turbine, at the same time thus producing the first turbo-generator. In 1897 his powered experimental ship, the *Turbinia*, attained the then record speed of $34\frac{1}{2}$ knots.

PARTHIAN EMPIRE Founded in 247 BC when Arsaces, a governor under **Diodotus**, king of the Bactrian Greeks, rebelled and fled west to found his own kingdom south of the Caspian Sea. Under **Mithridates** (171–138 BC) Parthia extended its control over the whole Iranian plateau and into the Tigris-Euphrates region. After the famous Parthian victory over the Romans at Carrhae (53 BC) Parthia was almost continuously at war with Rome, and prevented any permanent Roman expansion beyond the Euphrates. The empire was finally eclipsed in AD 224 by the rise of the **Sasanians**.

PASSAROWITZ, TREATY OF Signed on 21 July 1718, it ended the Austro-Turkish and Venetian-Turkish wars of 1716–18, and marked the end of Ottoman expansion into Europe. Under its terms, the Ottoman Empire lost substantial Balkan territories to Austria.

PATHET LAO Left-wing nationalist movement in Laos, founded in 1950. It joined with the **Viet Minh** to oppose French colonial rule in Indo-China. The first Congress of Neo Lao Hak Sat (Lao Patriotic Front) was held in 1956; throughout the 1960s and early 1970s it fought a civil war against the US-supported government in Vientiane. Its control of the north-eastern provinces of Sam Neua and Phong Saly was recognised in 1954, when Laos gained independence; it won control of the entire country in 1975.

PATRICK, ST (c.385–461) Patron saint of Ireland, to which he brought Christianity; he established the See of Armagh, c.444. He wrote *Letter to the Soldiers of Coroticus* and *Confessions*, an account of his work.

PÄTS, KONSTANTIN (1874–c.1956) Last President of independent Estonia. He founded the socialist newspaper, *Teataja (The Announcer)* in 1901, and entered politics in 1904. He was sentenced to death by the Russian authorities in 1905 after an abortive rising. Returning from exile in 1910, in 1918 he became head of the provisional government despite his arrest by German occupation forces. He was President and Prime Minister, 1921–2, 1923, and 1932–3, and became dictator after an attempted Fascist coup in 1933. He was deported to the USSR after the Soviet invasion in 1940 and was believed to have died some sixteen years later.

PAUL, ST Jewish convert to **Christianity**, who became the leading missionary and theologian of the early Church. He was born a Roman citizen in Tarsus, now in Turkey. Brought up a **Pharisee**, he persecuted the followers of **Jesus** until his conversion by a vision on the road to Damascus. He became the Apostle to the Gentiles, undertaking three great journeys to the cities of Asia Minor and Greece. His letters, maintaining contact with the communities established there, remain fundamental documents of the Christian faith. Paul was arrested in Jerusalem, c.57, taken to Rome in 60, and probably martyred during the reign of the Emperor Nero, between 62 and 68.

PAULICIANS Sect of militant Armenian Christians, founded in the mid-7th century. Influenced by earlier dualist thought, notably

Manichaeism, its members believed that there were two gods: an evil one, who created the world, and a good one responsible for the world to come. It was suppressed by Byzantine military expeditions in the late 7th and early 9th centuries; many followers then moved to Thrace as frontier soldiers, where they helped to form the ideas of the **Bogomils**.

PEASANTS' REVOLT Also known as the Peasants' War, it was a series of rural uprisings in 1524–5 in Austria and central Germany, mainly directed against heavy manorial duties and exactions. Despite the accusations of Catholics that the rebellion was provoked by Lutheran theology, there is little evidence for this: **Luther** himself condemned the peasants, and the rebels were cut down, in several bloody battles, by the combined forces of Lutheran and Catholic landlords.

PECHENEGS Turkic nomads, ruling the steppes north of the Black Sea from the 6th to the 12th century. In the 10th century they controlled the land between the rivers Don and Danube; held back with difficulty by Russians and Hungarians, they then attacked Thrace and increasingly threatened the Byzantine Empire, until they were finally annihilated, at the gates of Constantinople, by Emperor **Alexius I Comnenus** in 1091.

PEEL family The first Robert Peel introduced the calico printing industry to Lancashire, England, when he took the initiative in founding the firm of Haworth, Peel & Yates in Blackburn in 1764. His son Robert (1750–1830) greatly expanded the business and by the end of the 18th century employed some 15,000 workers in various mills. He was an enlightened employer, and when he became a Member of Parliament was responsible for introducing the first Factory Act (1802). He had been created a baronet in 1800. His son Sir Robert Peel (1788–1850) was Prime Minister from 1841 to 1846.

PEHLEVIS Dynasty in Iran, founded by **Reza Shah Pehlevi** in 1925. Overthrown 1979.

PEKING CONVENTION Series of agreements made in 1860, reaffirming and extending the Tientsin treaties of 1858. Tientsin was opened as a Treaty Port; Britain obtained control of Kowloon, the city on the mainland opposite Hong Kong island; French missionaries were given a free hand to buy and develop land; war vessels and merchant ships were allowed to navigate in the interior; and Russia obtained the Maritime Provinces east of the Ussuri river.

PELAGIUS Christian teacher and monk, whose belief in man's responsibility for his own good and evil deeds led him into bitter controversy with the 4th century Church fathers. In Rome c.380 he attacked the lax morality he attributed to doctrines of Augustine. Cleared of heresy charges at Jerusalem in 415, he responded to further attacks from **Augustine** and **Jerome** by writing *De libero arbitrio (On Free Will)*. He was excommunicated by Pope Innocent I in 417, and condemned at Carthage in 418; the date of his death is unknown.

PENINSULAR WAR Struggle, fought in the Iberian peninsula, 1808–14, between France and an alliance of Britain, Spain and Portugal, in the course of the Napoleonic Wars. Initially forced to evacuate from Corunna (1809), the British, under the future **Duke of Wellington**, returned to fight first a defensive engagement at Torres Vedras, then a successful offensive (1812–14) which drove all French troops from the region.

PEPIN THE SHORT (d.768) First **Carolingian** king, son of **Charles Martel** and father of **Charlemagne**. He became sole ruler of the Franks in 747 and was crowned king in 751.

PEQUOT WAR Massacre of the Pequot tribe of North American Indians by British colonists in 1636–8, precipitated by the murder of a Boston trader. By the early 20th century hardly any of the tribe remained in their ancestral lands in Connecticut.

PERICLES (c.495–429 BC) Athenian statesman. As a radical democrat he dominated the city-state from c.460 BC until his death. He converted the League of Delos from an equal alliance into an Athenian empire, and led Athens in the Peloponnesian War against Sparta. His famous Funeral Speech, setting out his vision of an ideal Athens, is reported by **Thucydides**.

PERKIN, SIR WILLIAM HENRY (1838–1907) Discoverer of aniline dyes. In 1853 he entered the Royal College of Chemistry, London, and while working as a laboratory assistant attempted the synthesis of quinine, but instead obtained a substance later named aniline purple, or mauve. In 1856 he produced tyrian purple, the first dyestuff to be produced from coal tar. He was knighted in 1896.

PERMIANS Finno-Ugrian speaking peoples, including the Votyaks and the **Zyrians,** living in the north-west region of Russia.

PERÓN, JUAN DOMINGO (1895–1974) Argentine head of state. He entered the army, 1911, became Minister of War and Secretary for Labour, 1944; Vice-President, 1944–5, and President, with strong backing from the trade union movement, 1946. Removed from office during the 1955 revolution and exiled to Spain, he returned and was elected to presidency, 1973.

PERRY, MATTHEW (1794–1858) US naval commander who headed the expeditions to Japan of 1853–4 which forced that country to end its 200-year isolation and open trade and diplomatic relations with the world. Perry had earlier captained the first US steamship, the *Fulton* (1837–40); his Japanese exploit, taking four warships into the fortified harbour of Uraga, made him world-famous. Later he strongly urged US expansion in the Pacific.

PERSEUS (c.212–165 BC) Last king of classical Macedonia, son of **Philip V.** He succeeded to the throne in 179 after plotting his brother's execution. He tried to dominate Greece, but by his success precipitated the Third Macedonian War (171–168) with Rome; he was finally defeated at Pydna, southern Macedonia, by the armies of Lucius Aemilius Paullus, and died after three years in captivity.

PERUZZI Important family of Florence, prominent in trade and finance in Europe in the late 13th century, and second only to the **Bardi.** During the **Hundred Years War** made large loans to **Edward III** of England; these were cancelled in 1342. The king of Naples also defaulted and the king of France exiled them and confiscated their goods; bankruptcy and collapse, both financial and political, followed.

PETER, ST (died c.AD 64) Foremost of **Jesus'** disciples and recognised by the Roman Catholic Church as its first Pope. Originally a fisherman called Simeon, or Simon, from Bethsaida, he was named by Jesus 'Cephas', meaning rock (in Greek, *petros*). After Jesus' death he emerged as the first leader of the early Church, preaching and healing. His later career is obscure, but his residence, martyrdom and burial in Rome can be taken as certain.

PETER I, THE GREAT (1672–1725) Tsar of Russia. He succeeded to the throne in 1682, and took full control in 1689. War with the Ottoman Empire, 1695–6, gave Russia access to the Sea of Azov. He made an extensive tour of western Europe, 1697–8, introduced western technology to Russia, and drastically reformed the system of government. With the **Great Northern War** (1700–21) he won through to the Baltic, and founded the city of St Petersburg on the Baltic coast which he made his capital.

PETER III (1728–62) Tsar of Russia. He succeeded his aunt, the Empress Elizabeth, in 1762, and immediately ordered Russia's withdrawal from the **Seven Years War,** thereby causing discontent among his army officers, who deposed and killed him after a reign of only six months. He was succeeded by his wife, **Catherine the Great.**

PETROBRUSIANS Followers of Peter de Bruys, leader (1104–25) of a radical opposition in France to the doctrine and organisation of the Roman church. He rejected infant baptism, transubstantiation, the sacrifice of the Mass, and the organisation of worship. He claimed scriptural authority for all his teachings, but was burned in 1125 as a heretic. His ideas were also taken up by the **Henricians.**

PHAN BOI CHAU (1867–1940) First 20th century Vietnamese resistance leader. He trained for the mandarin examinations; in 1903 he wrote *Cau huyet thu le than (Letters Written in Blood)* urging expulsion of the French colonial rulers. From Japan he directed the Duy Tan Hoi (Reformation Society) aiming to put Prince Cuong De on the throne; after exile from Japan in 1908 he reorganised in China and planned the assassination of the French governor, Albert Sarraut, in 1912. He was imprisoned until 1917; converted to Marxism; seized in 1925 and taken to Hanoi, but released after immense public protest.

PHARISEES (and Sadducees) Leading, and antagonistic, Jewish religious sects during the second temple period (to AD 70). Emphasising the interpretation of the Bible, the development of the oral law and adaptation to new conditions, the Pharisees evolved eventually into the Rabbis of the **Mishnah** and the **Talmud.** The Sadducees believed in the literal truth of the Bible and excluded all subsequent interpretations as well as beliefs in immortality, or devils and angels. The Pharisees, with their dislike of violence, survived the destruction of the temple by the Romans (AD 70); the Sadducees did not.

PHAULKON, CONSTANT (1647–88) An innkeeper's son from Cephalonia who ran away to serve as cabin boy on an English trading vessel and was later taken to Siam by a merchant of the **English East India Company.** Entering the service of King **Narai,** he was promoted to superintend foreign trade. After a quarrel with the chief of the English factory at the capital, Ayutthaya, he supported the French cause at court, but his support for **Louis XIV**'s intervention in Siam in 1687 brought about his downfall in the following year when his patron died. Narai's successor had him publicly executed.

PHIDIAS (c.490–?) Ancient Athenian sculptor. Appointed by **Pericles** to oversee all the city's artistic undertakings, he was responsible for the design and composition of the marble sculptures of the Parthenon. None of his most famous works – three monuments to Athena on the Acropolis and a colossal seated Zeus at Olympia – survive in the original. Exiled on political charges some time after 432 BC he went to Elis; his date of death is unknown.

PHILIP 'THE BOLD' (1342–1404) Duke of Burgundy, son of the French king John II. As a boy he distinguished himself at the battle of Poitiers in 1356; succeeding to the title in 1363, he was co-regent (1382–8) to Charles VI and effective ruler of France during much of the rest of his life.

PHILIP 'THE GOOD' (1396–1467) Duke of Burgundy, son of John the Fearless, he succeeded in 1419. He supported the claims of the English king, **Henry V,** to the throne but made peace with French king, Charles VII, in 1435; extended his territories into the Netherlands, and founded the Order of the Golden Fleece in 1429.

PHILIP II AUGUSTUS (1165–1223) First great Capetian king of France, son of Louis VII. He succeeded to the throne in 1179; fought a long, mainly successful campaign to win control of English possessions in France; took part in the Third **Crusade,** 1190–1; acquired major territories in the west and north of France, and began the Capetian conquest of Languedoc.

PHILIP IV (1268–1314) Known as 'the Fair'. Capetian king of France, the second son of Philip III, he became heir on the death of his brother Louis in 1276, and succeeded in 1285. He fought major wars against England, 1294–1303, and Flanders, 1302–5; continually in conflict with the papacy from 1296, he transferred the papal Curia to Avignon during the period of Pope Clement V (1305–14).

PHILIP II OF MACEDON (c.380–336 BC) Ruler of Macedon from 359 to 336 BC; father of **Alexander the Great.** He made Macedon a major power, penetrated Greece by war and diplomacy, defeated Athens and Thebes at the battle of Chaeronea, 338, bringing the warring city-states of Greece into a forced unity through a federal constitution with himself as leader. He was assassinated while planning an invasion of Persia.

PHILIP V (238–179 BC) King of Macedon, succeeding his cousin, **Antigonus Doson,** in 221. He allied with Carthage against Rome in the Second **Punic War,** and ended the resulting First Macedonian War (215–205) on favourable terms, but suffered a decisive defeat in the Second War at **Cynoscephalae** in 197. The resulting peace treaty confined him to Macedonia and imposed severe indemnities. Seven years of co-operation with Rome relaxed these conditions and his last decade was spent in trying to re-establish control in the Balkans.

PHILIP II (1527–98) King of Spain, Spanish America and the Two Sicilies (1556–98), also of the Netherlands (1555–98) and, as Philip I, of Portugal (1580–98). Son of Emperor **Charles V,** he became King of England, 1554–58, through his marriage to Mary Tudor. Sought unsuccessfully to suppress the revolt of the Netherlands from 1566 onwards; conquered Portugal in 1580; failed to invade England with his Armada in 1588.

PHRYGIANS Ancient Anatolian people, dominating central Asia Minor from the 13th to the 7th centuries BC. Traditionally of Thracian origin, they settled in north-western Anatolia in the 2nd millennium BC, and after the collapse of the **Hittites** founded a new capital, Gordium, in the central highlands. In about 730 BC the eastern territories fell to Assyria; c.700 BC the legendary king Midas was defeated by the Cimmerians, who burned Gordium and transferred the land to the Lydians.

PIAST First ruling dynasty in Poland, traditionally named after the wheelwright whose son, Ziemowit, inherited the estates of the Prince of Gniezno in the late 9th century. The dynastic territories were consolidated under **Miesko I;** his son **Boleslaw I** was the first king of Poland, and established the Polish frontiers in east and west. The last Piast, **Casimir III the Great,** died in 1370.

PICTS A group of tribes occupying Scotland north of the river Forth in early Christian times. The name, signifying 'painted people', was first mentioned in Latin texts in AD 297. Known for their fierce raiding and strongly characteristic towers, their memorial 'symbol stones' and underground shelters, they established their own kingdom in the 8th century which extended from Caithness to Fife, before amalgamating with immigrants from Ireland in 843 to form a separate Scottish nation.

PIKE, ZEBULON MONTGOMERY (1779–1813) American explorer. Commissioned in the US army in 1799, he led parties to the headwaters of the Mississippi, 1805–6, and Arkansas and Red rivers, 1806–7. He was promoted to the rank of brigadier-general in 1813, but was killed in the same year in the assault on York (now Toronto, Canada).

PILGRIMAGE OF GRACE Popular uprising in 1536 in the English counties of Yorkshire and Lincolnshire. The participants were mainly protesting against the religious policies of **Henry VIII,** especially the closure of the monasteries. Its leaders were executed in 1537.

PILGRIM FATHERS Group of English puritan refugees, mostly of the Brownist sect, who sailed in the **Mayflower** in 1620 to found Plymouth Colony, New England.

PILSUDSKI, JOSEF (1867–1935) Polish general and statesman. He struggled to liberate Poland from Russian control from 1887 (he was imprisoned in Siberia 1887–92). After the outbreak of the First World War, he commanded Polish legions under Austro-Hungarian sponsorship, 1914–16; after the Russian Revolution he assumed command of all Polish armies and proclaimed himself head of a new independent Polish state; he defeated the Soviet Union in the war of 1919–21 (see **Treaty of Riga**); he resigned in 1922, but a right-wing military *coup d'état* in 1926 brought him back to supreme power until his death.

PINEDA, ALVAREZ 16th century Spanish explorer. In 1519 he led an expedition which followed the Caribbean coast from Florida to the Pánuco river, already reached from the south by **Grijalva** in 1517. Pineda's voyage ended all hope of finding a direct sea contact between the Caribbean and the Pacific.

PINOCHET UGARTE, GENERAL AUGUSTO (1915–) Chilean head of state. He rose to prominence when appointed commander of the Santiago zone by Chile's Marxist President **Allende** in 1972. He succeeded General Carlo Prats as commander of the army, and emerged after a violent coup as head of the ruling military junta, 1973; he assumed sole leadership in 1974.

PINZÓN, MARTÍN ALONSO (c.1411–93) Part-owner of **Columbus**' two ships, the *Pinta* and the *Niña,* which took part in the discovery of the Americas. Pinzón commanded the *Pinta* under Columbus, but left the expedition after reaching the Bahamas to search independently for gold. After rejoining the main body he broke away again on the homeward voyage, hoping – but failing – to be first with the news.

PINZÓN, VICENTE YÁÑEZ (c.1460–1523) Spanish explorer, younger brother of **Martín Alonso Pinzón.** Commanded the caravel *Niña* in Columbus' fleet throughout the 1492–3 discovery voyage to the Americas. Later he probably sighted the Amazon estuary and sailed with **Juan Díaz de Solís** along the coast of central America.

PITT, WILLIAM (1759–1806) Known as 'the Younger'. English statesman, second son of the 1st Earl of Chatham (the Elder Pitt). He entered Parliament in 1781, became Chancellor of the Exchequer 1782–3, and Prime Minister 1783–1801 and again 1804–6. He played a leading part in organising coalitions against France on the outbreak of the Revolutionary Wars (1793–1802); passed the Act of Union with Ireland, 1800; resigned after George III refused to grant Catholic emancipation in 1801 but was recalled to organise new opposition to the French. He died in 1806 after **Napoleon**'s victory at Austerlitz.

PIZARRO, FRANCISCO (c.1478–1541) Conqueror of Peru, the illegitimate son of a Spanish soldier. To the Caribbean 1502; deputy to Balboa in 1513 when he discovered the Pacific Ocean. He led a small force of Spanish adventurers to conquer (and in fact to destroy) the **Inca** Empire in Peru, 1531–3, and founded the city of Lima in 1535.

PIZARRO, HERNANDO (c.1481–78) Spanish conquistador, the younger half-brother of **Francisco Pizarro.** He accompanied Francisco to Peru in 1531, and in 1534 returned to Spain with the royal share of the Inca **Atahualpa**'s ransom. He returned to Peru, and in 1537 was seized at Cuzco by the Pizarros' rival, Diego de Almagro; after his release he led an army to defeat and execute his captor, 1538. He was imprisoned in Spain, 1540–60.

PLANTAGENETS *see* **Angevins**

PLATO (c.427–347 BC) Athenian philosopher, an associate of **Socrates** and the teacher of **Aristotle.** He is best known through his twenty-five surviving Dialogues, his letters, and his *Apology,* in defence of Socrates. The ten books of *The Republic,* later modified by *The Laws,* outline a complete system for the ideal society. His Academy, outside Athens, was founded to train statesmen; it lasted nearly 900 years after his death, being closed finally by Emperor **Justinian** in 529.

PLEISTOCENE Geological era, characterised by a series of major ice advances, starting approximately 2,500,000 years ago and ending in about 8000 BC. During this period Man evolved from pre-human origins to his present appearance and bodily form.

PLINY, THE ELDER (AD 23–79) Roman encyclopaedist, accepted as the foremost Western authority on scientific matters until mediaeval times. After a short army career he settled down to accumulate knowledge and to write. His only surviving work (out of seven known titles) is the vast *Historia Naturalis;* its information, though fascinating and far-ranging, varies considerably in accuracy when checked with other sources.

POCOCK, SIR GEORGE (1706–92) British admiral. He commanded a squadron in the Indian Ocean, 1757–9, and in 1762–3 commanded the fleet which carried an expeditionary force under the Earl of Albemarle to Cuba.

POLENTA, DA Italian family dominating the city state of Ravenna from the end of the 13th to the middle of the 15th century. It first rose to power under Guido da Polenta, a leader of the **Guelph,** or pro-papal faction in the city; from 1322 it was rent by violent intra-family rivalries, and in 1441 the city fell under Venetian control.

POLO, MARCO (1254–1324) Mediaeval traveller from Venice. He went to Asia in 1271 as a merchant and jeweller with his father and uncle, who had already visited the court of the Mongol khan at Karakorum. He stayed for almost seventeen years in China and neighbouring territories in the service of **Kublai Khan.** He escorted a Chinese princess to Persia in 1292, and returned to Venice in 1295. He was captured at sea by the Genoese, and while in prison began to dictate (in French) an account of his travels – the book has been a bestseller ever since, and subsequent investigation has confirmed almost all the observations Polo made, although he was considered at the time to have made up most of what the book contained.

POLOVTSY Russian name for the Kipchak (Turkish) or Kuman (Byzantine) tribes who dominated the Eurasian steppes in the mid-11th century. They controlled a vast area between the Aral and Black Seas; fought Russians, **Pechenegs,** Byzantines and Hungarians. Dispersed in 1237, when Mongols killed

Bachman, the eastern Kipchak leader, some were absorbed into the **Golden Horde**, others (the Kumans) fled to Hungary.

POLYGNOTUS Ancient Greek painter from Thasos, at work in Athens and elsewhere 475–447 BC and famous for works such as the Fall of Troy in the Stoa Poikile at Athens and the vast murals in the Hall of the Cnidians at Delphi, now known only from contemporary descriptions. He was noted for his realism (e.g. transparent drapery) and for moralism.

POMPEY THE GREAT (106–48 BC) Roman statesman and general. He campaigned in Spain and Italy, against pirates in the Mediterranean, and against **Mithridates** of Pontus. Consul in 70 BC, in 61 he formed the First Triumvirate with **Crassus** and **Julius Caesar**. He raised an army to defend the state when civil war broke out in 49, but was defeated by Caesar at Pharsalus (Greece) in 48 and fled to Egypt, where he was murdered.

PONCE DE LEÓN, JUAN (1460–1521) Discoverer of Florida, in search of the mythical Fountain of Youth. He sailed with **Columbus** in 1493; in 1508–9, as deputy to the governor of Hispaniola, he helped to settle Puerto Rico. In 1513 he reached Florida, without realising it was part of the North American mainland; he probably sighted the north coast of Yucatán on his return passage to Puerto Rico. He was mortally wounded in 1521 by **Seminole** Indians when on a second expedition to explore his discovery.

PORTSMOUTH, TREATY OF Agreement signed in New Hampshire, USA, to end the Russo-Japanese War of 1904–5. Russia recognised Japan as the dominant power in Korea, and ceded the lease of Port Arthur, railway concessions in the south Manchurian peninsula, and the southern half of Sakhalin Island. Both powers agreed to recognise Chinese sovereignty in Manchuria.

POTASSIUM-ARGON METHOD Technique for dating the original formation of rocks of igneous origin. It involves measuring the ratio of radioactive argon to radioactive potassium in the sample, and depends for its validity on several crucial assumptions about initial purity, steadiness of decay rates, absence of other factors affecting the radioactive decay process, etc.; but in modern, improved forms it has been used to establish geological age as remote as 4500 million years and as recent as 20,000 years.

POTSDAM CONFERENCE Last inter-Allied conference of the Second World War, held from 17 July to 2 August 1945. The main participants were **Truman, Churchill** (with **Clement Attlee**, who became Prime Minister during the conference) and **Stalin**; they discussed the continuation of war with Japan and the form of the forthcoming European peace settlement.

POWELL, JOHN W. (1834–1902) United States Professor of Geology who led four expeditions to explore 900 miles of the Green and Colorado rivers, 1869–75; director of the geological survey of the Rocky Mountains, 1875–80, and of the US Geological Survey, 1880–94.

PRAIEIRA Last significant revolutionary uprising in imperial Brazil. The anti-conservative, anti-Portuguese rebellion broke out in Pernambuco in 1848 and was suppressed by 1850. 'Praieira' was the nickname given to liberals whose newspaper was printed in the Rua da Praia in Recife.

PRATIHARAS Warlike people of northern India, reputedly descended from the **Gurjaras**. By the end of the 8th century they ruled a large part of Rajasthan and Ujjain, and controlled the strategic city of Kanauj. Under King Bhoja they successfully held back the Arab advance into northern India, but were eclipsed by various enemies when a Turkish army sacked Kanauj in 1018.

PRAXITELES Ancient Athenian sculptor, working between 370 and 330 BC. Only one of his works survives in the original, the marble *Hermes carrying the infant Dionysus*, but by transforming the aloof, majestic style of his archaic and classical predecessors into more graceful and sensuous forms he changed the whole nature of Greek art. A few Roman copies of his works exist, including two of the masterpiece *The Aphrodite of Cnidus*, now in the Vatican and the Louvre.

PŘEMYSLIDS First Czech ruling family, founded by Přemysl, a ploughman, who married the Princess Libuse. They held the throne of Bohemia from c.800 to 1300. In 1198 Přemysl Ottocar I raised the country from a principality to a hereditary kingdom within the **Holy Roman Empire.**

PRESTER JOHN Legendary Christian king, variously believed to rule in central Asia and East Africa. His fabled kingdom, and its riches, captured the mediaeval imagination between the first **Crusades** and the early 16th century. His story, probably based on garbled reports of the Negus of Abyssinia, played a part in the motivation of many well-financed expeditions, including the final successful efforts of Portugal to reach Asia by sea.

PRODICUS Greek Sophist from the island of Ceos (Kea), active in the 5th century BC and renowned for his precise distinctions between words.

PROTAGORAS (c.485–c.412 BC) Most famous of the Greek Sophists, author of the constitution for the pan-Hellenic settlement of Thurii, and best known for his assertion that 'man is the measure of all things', he taught in Athens and other cities for forty years. He expressed agnosticism in his text *Concerning the Gods*, but the story of his trial for impiety may be a later invention.

PROTESTANTISM One of the three main branches of **Christianity** since the Reformation of the 16th century. It was originally characterised by belief in justification by grace through faith, the priesthood of all believers and the overriding authority of the Bible. The main early groups were **Lutherans, Calvinists**, and **Zwinglians**, with the Church of England including both Catholic and Protestant elements. Other groups from the Anabaptist and Independent traditions, as well as those emerging later such as the Society of Friends (**Quakers**) and the **Methodists**, are also included within the term.

PRUTH, TREATY OF THE A pact signed on 23 July 1711, after the Ottomans had defeated the armies of **Peter I the Great** of Russia on the River Pruth (now the frontier between Romania and the USSR). Russia agreed to relinquish the fortress of Azov, to demilitarise Taganrog and the Dnieper forts, cease interfering in Poland and the affairs of the Crimean Tartars, and allow safe conduct to **Charles XII** of Sweden. His delay in complying with these terms led to a renewed declaration of war in 1712 and the conclusion of a new, though similar, peace agreement at Adrianople (Edirne) in 1713.

PTOLEMAIC DYNASTY Line of Macedonian kings, founded by **Ptolemy I Soter**. They ruled Egypt from 323 to 30 BC, the last of the line being **Cleopatra**.

PTOLEMY Greek astronomer and geographer of the 2nd century AD. He worked in Alexandria, and wrote a *Geography*, with maps, which became the standard mediaeval work on this subject; an *Optics*, and a mathematical and astronomical treatise, popularly known as *Great Collection* or *Almagest*, which pronounced that the Earth was the centre of the Universe. He worked out a close approximation to the value of π in sexagesimal fractions; he divided the degree of angle into minutes and seconds.

PTOLEMY I SOTER (c.367–c.282 BC) Founder of the Ptolemaic dynasty, rulers of Egypt from 323 to 30 BC. He was born in Macedonia, rose to become a general with **Alexander the Great**, and after Alexander's death became satrap of Egypt, Libya and Arabia. He fought off Macedonian attacks (322–1 and 305–4) and in 304 assumed the titles of King and Soter (Saviour). An outstanding administrator, he was also author of a history of Alexander (since lost), and founder of a library and museum.

PUGACHEV, YEMELYAN IVANOVICH (1726–75) Leader of a major rebellion in 18th-century Russia. He was a **Cossack** who served in the Russian army in several wars before deserting. In 1773 he appeared at the head of a large army of discontents from the Urals. At its height the rebellion spread westwards to the Volga river and posed a threat to Moscow; Pugachev claimed to be Peter III, who had in fact been murdered to secure the succession of **Catherine II the Great** in 1762. In 1774 the revolt was put down, and Pugachev executed the following year.

PUNIC WARS Three wars in which Rome and Carthage, hitherto friendly, contested supremacy in the western Mediterranean in the 3rd and 2nd centuries BC.

First Punic War (264–241) BC: the clash came when Carthage threatened to gain control of the Straits of Messina. Carthage was a sea-power, Rome a land-power: to defeat their enemy the Romans had to build a large fleet, which gained a series of brilliant victories. The war, which was also fought by land in Sicily, resulted in the ejection of the Carthaginians from Sicily; Rome made the island its first overseas province.

The Second Punic War (218–201 BC) was caused by **Hannibal**'s advance from Spain into Italy, where after a series of great victories (especially Cannae in 216) he was gradually forced on to the defensive. In 204 Publius Scipio led an expeditionary force to Africa, thus compelling the return of Hannibal, and defeated him at Zama. Scipio had also driven the Carthaginians from Spain, which became a Roman province. Carthage survived but was no longer a great Mediterranean power.

Third Punic War (149–146 BC): Roman suspicions led to the outbreak of a final war. The Romans invaded North Africa; after a desperate siege the city of Carthage was totally destroyed and its territory made into the Roman province of Africa.

PUTTING-OUT SYSTEM Method of industrial production, widely practised in 17th-century Europe. Raw materials were supplied by manufacturers to workers in their own homes or small workshops, and the finished output was then collected and sold, after payment on a piecework or wage basis; it was gradually superseded by the development of the factory system.

PYRRHUS (319–272 BC) King of Epirus, north-west Greece. He fought Macedon, and was then called to help Greek cities in Sicily and southern Italy against the expanding power of Rome. He defeated the Romans, but with crippling losses, at Asculum in 279 BC (hence a 'Pyrrhic victory'), and was forced out of Italy in 275 BC. He died in a street fight in Argos three years later.

PYTHAGORAS (c.580–497 BC) Greek philosopher and mathematician. He emigrated from Samos to southern Italy; founded a school based on the belief that the soul could be purified by study and self-examination; taught transmigration of souls; discovered the numerical basis of the musical scale; taught that number was the basis of the Universe. Pythagoras' Theorem, which states that the square on the hypotenuse of a right-angled triangle is equal to the sum of the squares on the other two sides, is probably attributable to his school.

QADISIYA, AL- Battle, 636–7, n which the armies of Islam defeated the **Sasanian** Persians, and completed the conquest of Iraq.

QAJARS Iranian dynasty, ruling a unified Persia, 1779–1925. The reign of Fath Ali Shah (1797–1834) saw the beginning of intense European rivalry for control of the country; Naser od-Din Shah (1848–96) exploited Anglo-Russian suspicions to preserve its independence, but the Anglo-Russian division of Persia into spheres of influence in 1907, followed by Russian and British occupation of parts of the country in the First World War, led to a *coup d'état* (1921) and the emergence of the **Pehlevi**. Ahmed Shah, the last Qajar, was formally deposed in 1925.

QUAKERS (also known as the Society of Friends). Radical religious movement without clergy or creed, originating in mid-17th century England and rapidly developing in North America from the colony of Pennsylvania, founded by Quaker William Penn under royal charter in 1681. Today Quakers in the world number around 200,000.

QUEBEC ACT One of the Intolerable Acts or Coercive Acts which led up to the American War of Independence. This measure (1774) established a new administration for the North-West Territory, ceded to Great Britain by France after the French and Indian War, or **Seven Years War**, (1756–63) and extended its frontiers to the Ohio and Mississippi rivers; the trans-Appalachian claims of the other (largely Protestant) American colonies were thus jeopardised in favour of French Catholics.

QUTBUDDIN AIBAK (d.1210) Muslim ruler in India, born in Turkestan and sold as a child slave, he finally entered the service of **Muizzu-din Muhammad**. He rose from the position of stableman to that of general; led many mounted campaigns between 1193 and 1203, and was freed after Muhammad's death in 1206. He laid the foundations for the emergence of the Delhi sultanate under **Iltutmish**.

RABIH ZOBEIR (d.1900) Leader of native opposition to the French in Equatorial Africa from 1878 until his death at the battle of Lakhta.

RADCLIFFE, WILLIAM (1760–1841) An improver of cotton machinery in England. With the aid of Thomas Johnson he invented a cotton dressing machine which enabled the fabric to be starched before the warp was put onto the loom; he went bankrupt in 1807. He started another mill, but this was destroyed by **Luddite** rioters in 1812. He was the author of *Origin of the New System of Manufacture, commonly called Power Loom Weaving* (1828).

RAFFLES, SIR THOMAS STAMFORD (1781–1826) Founder of Singapore. He was appointed Assistant Secretary to the newly-formed government of Penang in 1804, and Lieutenant-Governor of Java in 1811. Recalled to England in 1816, he returned to the east as Lieutenant-Governor of Benkulen from 1818–24, and in 1819 established a British port at Singapore, henceforth the centre of British colonial activity in South-East Asia.

RAHMAN, MUJIBUR (1920–75) Usually known as Sheikh Mujib. First President of Bangladesh. He founded the East Pakistan Students' League, and during the 1950s was secretary and organiser of the Awami League, seeking autonomy for East Pakistan. He was imprisoned in 1958, and the resulting mob violence led to the breakaway of the province in 1971 as the new state of Bangladesh. Rahman was elected as its first head of state in January 1972; he was assassinated in 1975.

RAJARAJA (d.1014) King of the **Cholas** in southern India, reigning 985–1014. He attacked the alliance between Kerala, Ceylon and the Pandyas, seized the Arab trading centre of Malabar, launched a naval attack on the Arab-held Maldive Is., devastated Ceylon and its capital Anuradhapura. He was succeeded by his son Rajendra after two years of joint rule.

RAJPUTS Literally, 'Sons of Kings'; members of landowning and military castes, according to one view descendants of central Asian invaders, who dominated large parts of north and western India, especially Rajasthan, from about the 8th to the 18th century.

RAMAYANA Shorter of India's two great epic poems, composed by the poet Valmiki. Its surviving text runs to 24,000 couplets celebrating the birth, education and adventures of Rama, the ideal man and king, and his ideal wife, Sita.

RAMESSES II, THE GREAT (died c.1237 BC) Third king of Egypt's XIXth Dynasty, son of **Sethos I.** He succeeded c.1304 BC; fought the Hittites in an indecisive battle at Qadesh on the Orontes in the fifth year of his reign; sixteen years later he signed a lasting peace treaty with the Hittite king, Khattushilish. He is remembered for his military prowess and vast building activities: he constructed the famous rock-temples of Abu Simbel.

RAMESSES III The last great pharaoh of Egypt, reigning 1198–1166 BC as the second pharaoh of the XXth Dynasty. He fought two major wars against the Libyans and one against a confederation of northerners, who included Philistines, and two minor campaigns in Palestine and Syria. His greatest monument was his funerary temple at Medinet Habu (western Thebes), in which his wars are represented; he also built a small temple at Karnak, which he dedicated to Amun. Late in his reign he survived a palace conspiracy to murder him.

RAMMOHAN ROY (1774–1833) Hindu religious reformer. He published a tract against idolatry in 1790; in 1816 he founded the Spiritual Society in Calcutta, which in 1830 developed into the **Brahmo Samaj** movement. He was active in the campaign to abolish suttee, the ritual burning of Hindu widows; he was granted the title of rajah by the Delhi emperor.

RANJIT SINGH (1780–1839) Known as the Lion of the Punjab, he was the son of a **Sikh** chieftain. In 1799 he seized Lahore, capital of the Punjab, and proclaimed himself maharajah in 1801. His aim to unite all Sikh territories in India was thwarted by the British in 1809. With a modernised army, he inflicted many defeats on Afghans and Pathans in the 1820s and 1830s, and jointly with the British invaded Afghanistan in 1838.

RAPALLO, TREATY OF Agreement signed in 1922 between Germany and the USSR, which established trade relations and cancelled pre-1914 debts and war claims.

RASHID ALI AL-GAILANI (1892–1965) Iraqi Prime Minister. He supported German war aims in 1939; resigned his post, January 1941, and then seized power in April; he refused the British permission to move troops through Iraq (agreed under a 1930 treaty), but lost out in a sharp, thirty-day war when promised German help failed to arrive, and went into exile in Iran as a pro-British government was formed.

RASHTRAKUTAS South Indian dynasty, founded in the 8th century AD by Dantidurga, a feudatory of the **Chalukyas**. From their central territory in the north Deccan, they fought wars and formed alliances throughout India. The best-known king, Amoghavarsha (reigned 814–80), patronised **Jainism**. They were eclipsed in the late 10th century by the later Chalukyas.

RASULIDS Muslim dynasty, ruling in Yemen and the Hadhramaut from 1229 to 1454, named after Rasul, a Turkish officer of the **Abbasid** caliph. His grandson Umar I ibn Ali controlled Yemen and Mecca 1229–50; later Rasulid rule was confined to the Yemeni highlands.

RATANA, T.W. (1870–1939) Maori religious and political leader in New Zealand. In 1920 he founded the Ratana church, which had widespread popular appeal among Maoris and helped create for them a stronger supra-tribal identity in society and politics, notably through the Ratana-Labour Party alliance.

RATHENAU, EMIL (1838–1915) German industrialist and electrical pioneer. In 1883 he founded Deutsche Edison-Gesellschaft to exploit German rights in the patents of Thomas Edison; the company was renamed Allgemeine-Elektrizitäts-Gesellschaft (AEG) in 1887. With **Werner von Siemens** he founded the Telefunken company in 1903.

RATHENAU, WALTHER (1867–1922) German statesman. He succeeded his father, Emil, as head of the vast electrical engineering firm, AEG. In 1914 he set up the War Raw Materials Department to organise the conservation and distribution of raw materials essential to Germany's war economy; he founded the Deutsche Demokratische Partei (DDP) and advocated industrial democracy and state intervention in industry. He was Minister of Reconstruction, 1921, and as Foreign Minister in 1922 negotiated the **Treaty of Rapallo** which normalised relations with the Soviet Union. He was assassinated after accusations that he favoured 'creeping Communism'.

RAZIYYA Briefly sultan of Delhi, she succeeded to the throne during the period of anarchy following the death of her father, Iltutmish, in 1236, imposing both political stability and military leadership, but her sex and her unwillingness to share power created growing resentment, and ultimately she was murdered.

RENÉ OF ANJOU (1409–80) Duke of Lorraine, 1431–52, of Anjou, 1434–80, and Count of Provence, 1434–80. He made an unsuccessful bid to become king of Naples, 1435–42; in 1442 he retired to Anjou and later (1473) to Provence, where he patronised poets and artists. In 1481 his lands (except for Lorraine) passed to the French crown.

RESTITUTION, EDICT OF (1629) Decree of the Holy Roman Emperor Ferdinand II (1619–37) that all imperial church lands taken by secular princes since 1552 should be restored. The measure was brutally enforced by a large imperial army and provoked an alliance of German Protestant rulers against the Emperor. With Swedish aid provided by **Gustavus Adolphus**, the alliance defeated the imperial forces at the battle of Breitenfeld, 1631.

REULEAU, FRANZ (1829–1905) French engineer, best known for his geometric studies on the underlying principles of machine design, set out in his *Theoretische Kinematic*, published in Germany in 1875 and translated into English as *The Kinematics of Machinery* in 1876.

REZA SHAH PEHLEVI (1878–1944) Ruler of Iran, 1925–41. An army officer, he organised a successful revolution in 1921 and and deposed the **Qajar** dynasty to become shah in 1925. He instituted a reform and modernisation programme; he abdicated in 1941, when British and Russian armies occupied Iran.

RHODES, CECIL JOHN (1853–1902) Financier and imperialist. He emigrated from Great Britain to South Africa in 1870, and made a fortune from Kimberley diamond mines and Transvaal gold. In 1881 he entered the Cape Colony parliament; he strongly advocated British expansion in Africa: he negotiated the annexation of Bechuanaland in 1884, and having sent white settlers into Mashonaland 'founded' Rhodesia. He became Prime Minister of Cape Colony from 1890–6, but resigned after the **Jameson Raid** into the Transvaal.

RICHARD II (1367–1400) King of England, 1377–99. Son of Edward the Black Prince, he succeeded his grandfather, **Edward III**; he was in conflict with a baronial group, the Lords Appellant, to 1397, and was deposed in 1399 by a cousin, Henry of Lancaster, later crowned **Henry IV**; he died in prison, possibly murdered.

RICHELIEU, ARMAND-JEAN DU PLESSIS, DUC DE (1585–1642) French Cardinal and statesman. As Secretary of State (1616–17) and Chief Minister (1624–42) to Louis XIII, he destroyed French Protestant power (the siege of La Rochelle, 1628), undermined Spanish power in Italy (war of Mantua, 1627–31), declared war on Spain, and intervened in the Thirty Years War against the **Habsburgs** from 1635, although he died before much success had been gained (*see also* **Mazarin**).

RIENZI, COLA DI (c.1313–54) Popular leader in mediaeval Rome. In 1343 he was sent to Avignon to plead the cause of Rome's new popular party before Pope Clement VI; in 1347 he assumed dictatorial powers with popular acclaim, and reformed taxes, courts and political structure, attempting to re-establish Rome as the capital of a 'Sacred Italy'. He successfully suppressed an uprising by the nobles, but was forced to resign before the end of the year; reinstated in 1354 (but for only two months) he was seized and killed trying to quell a riot.

RIGA, TREATY OF (1920) Agreement by which the Soviet Union recognised the independence of Latvia (formerly a Russian province).

RIGA, TREATY OF (1921) Agreement between Poland and the Soviet Union following a war (1919–21) provoked largely by the claim of the new Polish state (created in 1918) that its eastern frontier of 1772 (prior to the first partition) should be restored. The treaty gave Poland large parts of Byelorussia and the Ukraine, and lasted until the **Nazi-Soviet Pact** of 1939.

RIM-SIN Last ruler of Larsa, in ancient Mesopotamia, who reigned c.1822–1763 BC. Son of Kudur-Mabuk, probably an **Amorite** chieftain from the borders of Elam, in 1794 he overthrew Isin, the old rival of Larsa, for control of southern Babylonia. He fought frequently with **Hammurabi** of Babylon, who finally defeated him in 1763.

RIPON, GEORGE FREDERICK SAMUEL ROBINSON (1827–1909) 1st Marquis and 2nd Earl of Ripon, Viceroy of India. He was appointed Viceroy in 1880, and attempted many reforms but generated much opposition, resigning in 1884 after the forced withdrawal of his proposal to give Indian judges power over European defendants. He became Secretary for the Colonies, 1892–5; Lord Privy Seal, 1905–8.

RIZAL, JOSÉ (1861–96) Filipino novelist, poet and patriot, born in Manila. At the University of Madrid he led a movement for reform of Spanish rule in the colony; he returned to the Philippines in 1892 and founded the non-violent Reform society, *Liga Filipina*. Exiled to Mindanao, he was arrested after an insurrection by a secret nationalist group, the Katipunan; although he had no connection with it, he was shot. His martyrdom and his masterly verse-farewell, *Ultimo Adiós*, inspired the fight for Filipino independence.

ROBERT I 'THE BRUCE' (1274–1329) King of Scotland, crowned in 1306 in defiance of the English king', **Edward I**. He consolidated his power during the weak reign of **Edward II**, and inflicted a heavy defeat on the English at Bannockburn in 1314. The title and Scotland's independence were recognised by the English in 1328, the year before his death.

ROBERT OF ANJOU (1278–1343) King of Naples 1309–43; he was the grandson of Charles I, conqueror of Sicily from the **Hohenstaufen** (1268). He unsuccessfully attempted to secure a dominant position in Italy, in alliance with France and the papacy. The kingdom rapidly declined after his death.

ROBESPIERRE, MAXIMILIEN FRANÇOIS MARIE-ISIDORE DE (1758–94) French revolutionary leader. He practised as a provincial lawyer; led the radical **Jacobin** faction, and played a leading part in the 1793 overthrow of the **Girondins** by the extremist Mountain group. As a member of the Committee of Public Safety, 1793–4, he became virtual dictator, establishing the Terror and eliminating his rivals Hébert and **Danton**; he introduced the cult of the Supreme Being. He was overthrown and executed after the *coup d'état* of July 1794.

RODNEY, GEORGE BRYDGES (1718–92) British admiral who commanded in the West Indies in the **Seven Years War** and again in the American War of Independence. He captured Martinique (from the French) and the neutral islands of St Lucia, Grenada and St Vincent in 1762; and defeated the Spanish fleet to relieve Gibraltar in 1780. His subsequent failures were redeemed by his victory over the French fleet at the Battle of the Saints (Dominica) in 1782, for which he was created Baron Rodney.

ROGER II (1095–1154) Founder of the Norman kingdom of Sicily. He succeeded his brother as Count of Sicily in 1105; made Palermo his capital, 1130; acquired Calabria, 1122, and Apulia, 1127; was crowned King of Sicily, 1130. He made Sicily a major meeting place for Christian and Arab scholars.

ROGGEVEEN, JACOB (1659–1729) Dutch explorer. After retirement from law practice in Batavia, he fitted out a private fleet to search for the reputed southern continent in the South Pacific, 1721–2. Though he circumnavigated the globe, his only significant discovery was Easter Island.

ROMANCE The group of languages derived from the spoken Latin of the Roman Empire. Influenced by local languages in the successor states of Rome, the Romance group comprises French, Spanish, Italian, Portuguese, Romanian, Catalan and Romansch.

ROMANOVS Ruling dynasty in Russia from 1613 until the Revolution of 1917. The family came into prominence when Anastasia Romanova became the first wife of **Ivan IV the Terrible**. In 1613 his great-grandson, Michael Romanov, was elected tsar; the succession thereafter, though remaining within the family, was frequently disorderly. In 1917 **Nicholas II** abdicated in favour of his brother Michael, who refused the throne, thus ending the royal line.

ROMANOV, MICHAEL (1596–1645) First of the Romanov tsars in Russia, reigning 1613–45. Distantly related to Fyodor I (reigned 1584–98), last tsar of the previous Rurik dynasty, he reluctantly accepted popular election to the throne at the end of Russia's fifteen-year Time of Troubles. Shared power first with relatives of his mother, who had been forced to become a nun by **Boris Godunov**, and later with his father, co-ruler from 1619 until his death in 1633.

ROOSEVELT, FRANKLIN DELANO (1882–1945) 32nd President of the United States, first elected 1933. He formulated the **New Deal** policy to combat world depression; inaugurated the Good Neighbour Policy in Latin America; in 1933 he recognised the USSR. He was re-elected in 1937 and again in 1941, when he provided lend-lease support for Great Britain. With **Churchill**, he issued the Atlantic Charter; after the Japanese attack at Pearl Harbor he led the US into the Second World War, and with **Chiang Kai-shek** at Cairo in November 1943 resolved to continue the war until Japan's unconditional surrender. Re-elected for a fourth term, he died after the 1945 Yalta conference of Allied leaders.

ROOSEVELT, THEODORE (1858–1919) 26th President of the United States. He worked as a writer, explorer and soldier before entering politics in 1881. He became Assistant Navy Secretary, then led the US **Rough Riders** in Cuba during the Spanish-American War (1898). He was Governor of New York, becoming Vice-President in 1900 and succeeding to the presidency in 1901 after the assassination of **McKinley**. He acquired the Panama Canal Zone in 1903. He left office in 1909, and failed to win back the presidency in 1912.

ROSAS, JUAN MANUEL DE (1793–1877) Dictatorial governor of Buenos Aires, 1829–52. Born into a landowning and military family, he acquired large ranches and controlled a force of *gauchos* (cowboys); in 1827 he was appointed head of the provincial militia, and distinguished himself fighting insurgents (1828–9) and Indians (1833). He accepted the governorship, 1829–32 and from 1835, and ran a ruthless police state. He was overthrown in 1852 by a coalition of Brazilians, Uruguayans and Argentine opponents at the Battle of Caseros. He fled to England and died in exile.

ROSES, WARS OF THE Civil war between rival claimants to the English throne: the dynasty of York (whose emblem was a white rose) and that of Lancaster (a red rose). The Yorkists rose against the Lancastrian king, Henry VI, in 1455, and deposed him in 1461. After a series of struggles involving Edward IV, Edward V and Richard III, the conflict was finally resolved in 1485, when Richard was defeated at Bosworth Field by the Lancastrian claimant, Henry Tudor, who was enthroned as **Henry VII** and married the Yorkist princess, Elizabeth, daughter of Edward IV, thus uniting the warring factions.

ROSKILDE, PEACE OF Treaty ending the war between Sweden and Denmark (1655–8) for control of the Baltic; it gave Sweden permanent possession of the strategically important regions of Scania, Blekinge and Bohuslän.

ROUGH RIDERS Popular name for the First Volunteer Cavalry, recruited by **Theodore Roosevelt** from cowboys, police, miners and athletes to fight in the Spanish-American War, 1898.

ROUSSEAU, JEAN-JACQUES (1712–78) French writer, born in Geneva. He quarrelled with most of the accepted conventions and established authorities of his time, and explored many of the themes later to form the basis of 19th century Romanticism and modern democracy. His main works include *Du Contrat Social* (1762), setting out a new theory of the relationship between the individual and the state; his autobiographical *Confessions* (published posthumously); and his novels *La Nouvelle Héloïse* (1761) and *Émile, ou l'éducation* (1762).

ROYAL NIGER COMPANY British trading company in West Africa. In 1886 Sir George Goldie's National African Company received a royal charter, changed its name, and was authorised to administer the delta and territories adjoining the course of the rivers Niger and Benue. It engaged in complex struggles with the French, the Germans and local rulers, conquering several emirates; in 1899, after many complaints and disputes, the charter was transferred to the British government.

RUDOLF IV (d.1365) Habsburg Duke of Austria, reigning 1358–65. He forged a charter, the *privilegium majus*, claiming vast lands, privileges and the hereditary title of archduke from his father-in-law, Emperor **Charles IV**. The document was declared fraudulent by Italian scholar-poet Petrarch; the resulting war ended with the granting of Austria's claim to the Tyrol. He founded the University of Vienna (1365).

RYSWYCK, TREATY OF Agreement, signed September-October 1697, ending the War of the Grand Alliance (1689–97). **Louis XIV** (for France) accepted William III's right to the English throne, restoration of the *status quo* in the French and British colonies, the return of Catalonia, Luxembourg and parts of the Spanish Netherlands to Spain, and a favourable trade treaty with the Dutch. The German Emperor recovered many French-fortified places along the Rhine, while Lorraine was restored to Duke Leopold.

SAAD ZAGHLUL see **Zaghlul, Saad**

SAADIS Muslim dynasty, claiming to be descendants of the Prophet ('sharifs') and ruling Morocco from the mid-16th to the mid-17th century.

SAAVEDRA, BALTAZAR DE LA CUEVA HENRÍQUEZ ÁRIAS DE (1626–86) Spanish colonial administrator. In 1674 he was appointed viceroy of Peru, Chile and Tierra Firme (a territory which included the Isthmus of Panama); his prosperous rule ended in outcry in 1678, when he tried to relax commercial monopolies. He was held captive for two years while charges were heard, and was exonerated in 1680. He returned to Spain, and held a seat on the Council of the Indies.

SABINES Ancient Apennine people of central Italy, north-east of Rome. According to legend the Sabine women were abducted by the Romans under Romulus; by the 3rd century the Sabines had become fully Romanised.

SADAT, MOHAMMED ANWAR EL- (1918–1981) Egyptian President. Commissioned in the Egyptian army in 1938, he was one of the group of officers, headed by **Nasser**, who planned the 1952 revolution. He was Vice-President, 1964–6 and 1969–70, and became President after Nasser's death in 1970. In alliance with Syria he launched war against Israel in October 1973. In 1977 he opened a new round of discussions on peace between Israel and the Arabs with his visit to Israel; assassinated in 1981 by Muslim fundamentalists.

SAFAVIDS A family of *shaykhs* (heads of a religious order – the Safaviyya) who exercised growing influence in north-western Persia and eastern Anatolia in the 14th and 15th centuries. They married into and succeeded the **Ak Koyunlu** c.1501 as rulers of these regions. Under **Ismail I** (1501–24), who took the title of shah, the **Shi'i** Safavids extended their rule over most of Persia, coming into conflict with the **Sunni** Ottomans in the west and the **Uzbeks** in Transoxania. Perhaps the most remarkable Safavid ruler was Shah **Abbas** (1587–1629), but from the mid-17th century the dynasty declined. Having capitulated to the Ghilzai Afghans (occupation of Isfahan 1722); the dynasty was finally extinguished by Nadir Shah in 1736.

SAFFARIDS Muslim dynasty ruling much of eastern Persia in the 9th century. By 873 the empire stretched from north-east India to Khurasan; after failing to annex Transoxiana in 900 its wider empire collapsed, but Saffarids retained local power in eastern Persia until the 15th century.

SAID, AL BU Muslim dynasty ruling in Oman, c.1749 to the present, and Zanzibar, c.1749–1964. It was founded by Ahmed ibn Said, who displaced the Yarubid imams of Oman to seize power there and in East Africa. In the 18th century they held Bahrein and parts of Persia; at the peak of their power under Said ibn Sultan (1806–56) they established commercial relations with the United States, France and Great Britain. The dominions were divided by Great Britain on the death of Said. The Zanzibar line was overthrown in 1964 when the island became part of Tanzania.

ST BARTHOLOMEW'S DAY MASSACRE Massacre of **Huguenots** (French Protestants) by French Catholics, which began on St Bartholomew's Day, 24 August 1572, and quickly spread from Paris to other French towns.

SALADIN (c. 1137–93) Western name of the Muslim hero, founder of the **Ayyubid** dynasty, and the Crusaders' most successful and honorable foe. He became sole ruler of Egypt and Islamic Syria, 1186; destroyed the Crusaders' army at Hattin, northern Palestine and re-entered Jerusalem, 1187. He also defeated the Third **Crusade**.

SALAZAR, ANTONIO DE OLIVEIRA (1889–1970) Dictator of Portugal. He was Finance Minister during the Depression, 1928–32, and became Prime Minister in 1932 after restoring economic order. He established authoritarian rule on Fascist lines in 1933 and maintained personal control until his death.

SALIANS One of many Frankish tribes which moved from central Europe (3rd century AD) and settled in the area north of the Rhine, near the modern Ijsselmeer. Thence, in the 5th century, they expanded south approximately to the river Loire. From them sprang the **Merovingian** dynasty, later superseded by the **Carolingians**, which conquered Aquitaine and Burgundy and reunited most of Gaul. Later a Salian Frank, Conrad of Swabia, became German king as Conrad II in 1024, and founded the Salian dynasty; the line died out with his great-grandson in 1125.

SALISBURY, ROBERT CECIL, 3rd MARQUESS OF (1830–1903) British statesman. He entered politics as a Conservative, and became Foreign Secretary 1878–80, a post which he also held through most of his three periods as Prime Minister, 1885–6, 1886–92, 1895–1902. On the whole he inclined towards co-operation with the **Triple Alliance** against Great Britain's imperial rivals, France and Russia, but was reluctant to conclude 'binding alliances' in Europe and was therefore often associated with the so-called policy of splendid isolation.

SALLE, ROBERT CAVELIER SIEUR DE LA (1643–87) French explorer. He emigrated to Montreal in 1666; traded and surveyed along the Illinois and Mississippi rivers from the Great Lakes region to the Gulf of Mexico. He founded Louisiana in 1682.

SAMANIDS Iran's first native dynasty after the Muslim conquests, ruling 819–999. It developed Samarkand and Bukhara as centres of art and culture and assumed the economic leadership of northern Persia, but weakened after the mid-10th century.

SAMNITES Ancient Italian peoples occupying the territory of Samnium, in the southern Apennines in Italy, who were subjugated by Rome in the 4th to the 3rd centuries BC.

SAMORI (c.1830–1904) Islamic hero and defender of the western Sudan against French colonial expansion in the late 19th century. Between 1865 and 1870 he built up a powerful chiefdom, and by early 1880 ruled an empire stretching from the Upper Volta and Upper Niger to Futa Jallon. In 1890 he set up his own firearms industry. He was finally defeated in 1898 on the Cavalla river, and died in exile.

SAMOYEDS People of the northern coasts of the Soviet Union, from the White Sea to the Taymyr Peninsula. Speaking a Uralic language, they are noted reindeer herders, fishermen and hunters.

SAMUDRAGUPTA (died c.375) Indian king, succeeding his father Chandragupta I, founder of the **Gupta** dynasty, c.355. From his capital, Pataliputra, in the Ganges valley, he extended control or exacted tribute throughout the greater part of the sub-continent.

SAMURAI Japanese warrior caste. Originally restricted to landed military houses, it became more open to able warriors of all kinds, especially during periods of civil war, such as that which lasted from c.1450 to 1600. After 1603, when the rule of the **Tokugawa** shoguns initiated 250 years of peace, the Samurai became a closed hereditary class, often turning from military to artistic and administrative pursuits. Its feudal privileges were quickly abolished after the **Meiji** restoration of 1868.

SAN (Bushmen) A nomadic people, speaking a distinctive click language, living in the Kalahari Desert area of Namibia and Botswana.

SAN-FAN REBELLION see **Wu San-kuei**

SAN MARTÍN, JOSÉ DE (1778–1850) Argentine liberator; with **Simon Bolívar**, he led South America's 19th-century independence struggles from Spain. After service in the Spanish army he returned to Buenos Aires in 1812 and in 1817 led an army of liberation in the epic crossing of the Andes; with **Bernardo O'Higgins** he freed Chile in 1818, and in 1821 invaded Peru from the sea and took the Spanish stronghold of Lima. After a quarrel with Bolívar, he retired to France.

SANSKRIT Classical language of ancient India, in use mainly from c.500 BC to c. AD 1000, but kept alive to the present day as the sacred language of the Hindu scriptures as well as of much secular literature. Also used in early inscriptions in south and south-eastern Asia, notably in ancient Cambodia. It is an Indo-European language, and hence ultimately related to Greek and Latin.

SAN STEFANO, TREATY OF Agreement ending the Russo-Turkish War, 1877–8. It created a large tributary state of Bulgaria, stretching from the Danube to the Aegean and covering all Macedonia except Salonika, granted independence to and enlarged Serbia, Montenegro and Romania, and gave Russia acquisitions in the Caucasus and a large indemnity. Fiercely opposed by Britain and Austria, the treaty was largely overturned at the **Congress of Berlin** in 1878.

SANTA ANNA, ANTONIO LÓPEZ DE (1794–1876) Mexican *caudillo*. He fought off the Spanish reconquest attempt in 1829, and became President of Mexico in 1834. He quelled Texan resistance at the Alamo, 1836, but was later defeated and captured; seizing power again in 1839 he ruled until 1845, but was routed by US troops in the Mexican War of 1846–8. His services were refused by both Emperor **Maximilian** and his enemies, and Santa Anna died poor and blind.

SANUSI WAR Resistance between 1912 and 1931 to Italian attempts to annex Libya, led by a brotherhood formed among the desert tribes (the 'Sanusis', founded in 1837). While the European powers were involved in the First World War, the Sanusis drove the Italians back to the coast and directed opposition to the French in Tunisia, but in the 1920s they were defeated and destroyed.

SAPPHO (born c.612 BC) Greek poetess, who lived at Mytilene in Lesbos. Her affection for a group of young women and girls associated with her in celebrating the cult of Aphrodite, is ecstatically described among the surviving fragments from her seven books of poems in the Aeolic dialect. She looks at her emotions honestly and expresses them with a rare gift of verbal music.

SARGON Semitic king of Akkad, reigning c.2371–2316 BC. One of the world's earliest empire-builders, he defeated the Sumerian ruler Lugalzagges of Uruk, seized all southern Mesopotamia, and achieved conquests as far afield as northern Syria, southern Anatolia and Elam in western Persia.

SASANIANS Iranian dynasty, named after Sasan, an ancestor of **Ardashir I**, who founded the family fortunes in AD 224. Under his leadership, Persis defeated the **Parthians** and created a major but frequently fluctuating empire extending from the Roman and Byzantine frontier in the west to central Asia where it absorbed most of the territories of the **Kushans**. They were finally eclipsed by the Islamic invasions of 637–51.

SATAVAHANAS Indian dynasty, controlling the Andhra region in the delta of the Krishna and Godavari rivers. First mentioned in the 1st century AD, when King Satakarni made many conquests, it revived under Gautamiputra and his son Vasishthiputra in the early 2nd century, under whom lands were acquired from Kathiawar on the west coast to northern Madras on the east. They were displaced by the **Vakataka** dynasty.

SATNAMIS Members of one of a group of Hindu sects in India. The oldest, founded by Birbham in the 16th century, was part of an attempt to bring together **Hinduism** and Islam. Another was launched at the end of the 17th century by the Rajput religious leader, Jagjivan Das. Modern Satnamis are found mainly among the Chamars, northern India's hereditary caste of leather-tanners; they follow the teachings of the 19th century Chamar saint, Rai Das.

SAUD, IBN (c.1880–1953) Founder of Saudi Arabia; born at Riyadh, now the Saudi Arabian capital. A member of an exiled ruling family, he recaptured Riyadh in 1902 and began the conquest of central Arabia. He accepted British Protectorate status in 1915, and established close relations with Britain in the First World War. He occupied Hejaz in 1926 and formally established the kingdom of Saudi Arabia in 1932; he signed the first oil-exploration treaty in 1933.

SAUDI (al-Saud) dynasty Founders and rulers of Saudi Arabia. Originally small rulers in central Arabia, they created their first – but short-lived – large state in the 18th century. The present state was created by **Ibn Saud**, followed after his death (1953) by four sons in succession: Saud (deposed 1964), Faisal (assassinated 1975), Khaled (d.1982) and Fahd.

SAUNDERS, SIR CHARLES (1713–75) British admiral. He commanded the fleet which carried General **James Wolfe**'s army to conquer French Canada in 1759. He was appointed First Lord of the Admiralty in 1766.

SAXONS German people originating in Schleswig-Holstein and along the Baltic. They responded to the decline of the Roman Empire with a policy of active piracy in the North Sea, developing in the 5th century AD into substantial settlements along the coasts of Britain and Gaul. The Saxon wars, initiated by **Charlemagne**, lasted 32 years and ended with the absorption of the continental Saxons into the Frankish Empire.

SAYYID MUHAMMAD BEN ABDULLAH (d.1920) Known as the 'Mad Mullah', a Somali chief who proclaimed himself **Mahdi** (religious leader) in the 1890s and began systematic raids against British and Italian positions around the Red Sea. He won territorial recognition in 1905 but resumed raids after 1908, keeping the Europeans confined to the coast until his death.

SCALA, della Italian dynastic family, also known as Scaligeri, hereditary rulers of Verona, founded by Mastino I (d.1277). Power was built up by his descendants, notably Cangrande I (1291–1329), the patron of **Dante**, but then frittered away in family quarrels. Their power was terminated by the **Visconti** of Milan, who conquered Verona in 1387.

SCANIAN WAR Fought between Sweden and Denmark, 1674–9, over the rich and strategically important province of Scania, or Skåne (at the southern tip of modern Sweden), which had been captured from the Danes in 1658.

The Danish army reconquered Scania, but **Louis XIV** vetoed the return of the territory.

SCHLEICHER, KURT VON (1882–1934) Last Chancellor of Germany's Weimar Republic, nicknamed 'the Hunger Chancellor'. He joined the German army in 1900, and in 1919 entered the newly-formed Reichswehr, becoming a major-general in the Ministry of War in 1929. He helped bring down **Brüning**, and succeeded **Papen** as Chancellor in 1932. He offered to aid **Hitler** if he could retain control of the Reichswehr, but was dismissed by **Hindenburg** in January 1933 after Hitler's refusal, and was murdered by the SS during the 'night of the long knives' the following year.

SCHLIEFFEN, ALFRED GRAF VON (1833–1913) German field-marshal, and chief of the German general staff, 1891–1906. In 1905 he devised the Schlieffen Plan, which, in the event of war, would involve the defeat of France by a vast outflanking movement through the Low Countries; in a revised form this provided the basis of German strategy at the outbreak of the First World War.

SCHOUTEN, WILLEM (1567–1625) Flemish navigator, discoverer of Le Maire Strait, between Tierra del Fuego and Staten Island, and of Cape Horn. He was the first captain to traverse the Drake Passage, linking the Atlantic and Pacific south of Tierra del Fuego (Drake himself followed the Magellan Passage, further north).

SCOTTSBORO BOYS Nine Negro youths from Alabama, USA, charged in 1931 with the rape of two white girls in a railway freight car. The death sentences pronounced by the Alabama courts provoked accusations of racial prejudice from Northern liberals and radicals, and the US Supreme Court twice reversed the Alabama court decisions. In 1937 four were finally sentenced to life imprisonment, and the others released.

SCYTHIANS Nomadic Indo-European people, settling in Scythia, north of the Black Sea, on the lower Don and Dnieper rivers, before the 7th century BC. They were famous for the skill of their mounted archers and their rich gold jewellery; they were displaced by the closely-related Sarmatians in the 3rd century BC.

SEATO see **South-East Asia Treaty Organisation**

SECOND COALITION, WAR OF THE Struggle between France and a combination of Austria, Britain and Russia in support of Turkey, 1799–1802. After initial success in Italy and Switzerland, the alliance was crippled by France's victories over Austria at Marengo and Hohenlinden in 1800. Peace was signed with Austria at Luneville (1801) and with Britain at Amiens (1802).

SECOND INTERNATIONAL Socialist organisation founded in 1889 after the collapse of the First International. One of its main objects was to reconcile the working classes of Germany and France and to prevent war, possibly by means of a general strike, but it broke up when the main socialist parties of Europe decided to support their governments on the outbreak of war in 1914.

SÉGUIN, MARC (1786–1875) Distinguished French engineer who constructed railways, locomotives and suspension bridges. In 1828 he invented a multi-tubular locomotive boiler at almost exactly the same time as – but independently of – a similar invention in England by **Robert Stephenson** and Henry Booth. In 1831 a Séguin locomotive ran on the St Etienne-Lyons line, the first railway in France.

SELEUCID Near Eastern dynasty dominating Syria and Asia Minor from 312 to 63 BC. It was founded by **Seleucus I Nicator** (reigned 312–280 BC), one of the close associates of **Alexander the Great**. Its capital established at Antioch-on-the-Orontes, the dynasty sought to Hellenise Asia through Greek settlements; it was constantly at war with the Ptolemies. Power in the east was lost in the 3rd century, in Asia Minor in 198; after 129 it became a local dynasty in northern Syria, and it was finally eclipsed during the Roman invasions of Syria and Cilicia, 65–63.

SELEUCUS I NICATOR (c.358–280 BC) Founder of the **Seleucid** dynasty, rulers of Asia Minor until the region was largely absorbed into the Roman Empire. He fought alongside **Alexander the Great** in Persia and married a Bactrian princess, 324. After Alexander's death he became governor of

Babylon, and allied with **Ptolemy I** to prevent Antigonus Monophthalmus of Macedonia from inheriting Alexander's imperial throne; he helped to defeat Antigonus at Ipsus, 301; moved his capital to Antioch-on-the-Orontes. A ruler of high integrity, he was murdered by Ptolemy Ceraunus, son of Ptolemy I.

SELIM I YAVUZ (the Inexorable) (1470–1520) Ottoman sultan, 1512-20. The youngest son of **Bayezid II,** he rebelled against his father in 1511, engineering his deposition and overcoming his own brothers Ahmed and Korkut, 1512-13. He proscribed and massacred the Anatolian Turcoman adherents of the **Safavid** shah, **Ismail,** defeating him at Chaldiran and occupying Tabriz, his capital. This radical shift in the Middle Eastern balance of power brought Selim into conflict with the **Mamelukes** of Egypt: in 1516–17 he successively conquered Syria and Egypt, abolished the Mameluke sultanate and annexed its territories to the Ottoman state. By the time of his death the Ottomans ruled in Jerusalem, in Cairo and in Mecca and Medina: a vast increase in the size, prestige and wealth of the empire.

SELJUKS Ruling family of the Oguz branch of the Turkish peoples who began settling in lands of the **Abbasid** caliphate, becoming Muslims, in the 10th century. They established a local power, quickly expanded it and occupied Baghdad, capital of the caliphate, in 1055. They ruled most of the lands of the caliphate, under Abbasid suzeraínty, with the title of sultan. The empire split after the death of Nizam al-Mulk, but a branch remained as rulers of part of Anatolia (incorporated in the Muslim world by Seljuk conquest from the Byzantines) from the early 12th century until the Mongol conquest in the 13th century.

SEMINOLE North American Indian tribe. In the early 18th century they separated from the Creek Indians ('seminole' means separate) and moved from Georgia into northern Florida. They fought two wars against the United States to avoid deportation and repel white encroachment (1817–18, while still under Spanish rule, and 1835–42); after the final surrender most of the tribe settled in Indian territory, which in 1907 became the state of Oklahoma.

SEMITES Speakers of the Semitic group of languages, of which Arabic, Hebrew and **Amharic** are the main languages still current. Akkadian, the language of Babylon and Assyria, was superseded by Aramaic during the 1st millennium BC, though still written for certain purposes down to the first Christian century; Aramaic, once widespread, survives in small enclaves and in the liturgy of the **Jews** and some Eastern churches.

SENGHOR, LEOPOLD SEDAR (1906–) President of Senegal. He studied in France (the first black African to obtain his *agrégation*), served in the French army (1939–40) and in the Resistance. He helped to draft the constitution of the Fourth French Republic in 1946 and sat in its Assembly between 1946 and 1958. He formed his own political party in Senegal in 1948, which won power in 1951, and worked in both Paris and Dakar for a federation of independent French West African states; when this failed he ran for office as President of Senegal, and was elected (1960).

SENNACHERIB King of Assyria, 704–681 BC. He gained experience as a senior commander during the reign of his father, Sargon II, and on his accession devoted himself energetically to the defence of the empire. The rising strength of **Chaldean** and Aramaean tribes in Babylonia, backed by Elam, produced a dangerous instability, which Sennacherib made repeated attempts to resolve by both political and military means, finally sacking the capital, Babylon, in 689 BC. A rebellion in the west, politically linked to the disaffection in Babylonia, led to a campaign in 701 BC which included the attack on Jerusalem mentioned in the Bible. Sennacherib had a keen interest in technological innovation; his most enduring work was the replanning of Nineveh as the Assyrian capital. He was murdered by a son or sons.

SEPHARDIM From the Hebrew word *Sepharad* for Iberia, it refers to the **Jews** of Iberia, and after the expulsion of 1492–7 their descendants down to the present day. It is used in distinction to **Ashkenazim** who have slightly different customs and rites.

SERBS Slav people. Serbia, now the largest and most populous republic of Yugoslavia, emerged as a separate principality in the 9th century and an independent kingdom in 1217. It was conquered by the Turks (1389) and incorporated into the **Ottoman** Empire (1459); it regained its independence in 1829. Blamed for the assassination of Archduke **Franz Ferdinand**, which precipitated the First World War, it became part of Yugoslavia in 1918.

SESTERCE A small silver coin, originally worth one-quarter of a Roman denarius. It was the most common unit of Roman currency.

SETHOS I (Seti I). King of Egypt's XIXth Dynasty, he reigned 1318-1304 BC. He campaigned in Syria, continued work on the Temple of Amun at Karnak, and built his own splendid temple at Abydus.

SEVEN YEARS' WAR Complex struggle, fought 1756-63, between Prussia, supported by Britain, and a coalition of Austria, Russia and France. It arose from Austrian attempts to regain Silesia, lost to Prussia in 1748 (War of the Austrian Succession) and extended by colonial rivalries between Britain and France. The untimely death of Elizabeth of Russia saved Prussia from annihilation while, overseas, Britain destroyed French power in North America, the Caribbean and India.

SÈVRES, TREATY OF Agreement between First World War Allies and the Ottoman Empire, providing for dismemberment of the Empire and Greek occupation of part of its Turkish heartland (Izmir and its surrounding region). It was signed reluctantly by the sultan's government on 10 August 1920, but was totally rejected by Turkish nationalists under Mustafa Kemal (**Atatürk);** it was replaced in 1923 by the **Treaty of Lausanne.**

SEWARD, WILLIAM (1801-72) US Secretary of State, 1861-9, best remembered for negotiating the purchase of Alaska in 1867 from Russia, called at the time 'Seward's Folly'. He was a leading anti-slavery agitator; he became governor of New York, 1839-43, and helped to found the Republican Party, 1855. A close adviser to **Lincoln**, he was stabbed by a co-conspirator of Lincoln's assassin, John Wilkes Booth, but survived.

SHAHJAHAN (1592-1658) Mughal emperor of India and builder of the Taj Mahal. Third son of the emperor Jehangir, and grandson of **Akbar,** he rebelled in 1622 in an ineffectual bid to win the succession, was reconciled with his father in 1625, and in 1628 proclaimed himself ruler after his father's death. He created the city of Shahjahanabad, and the Taj Mahal (1632-49), in memory of his favourite wife, Mumtaz Mahal. He was imprisoned in 1657 during a power struggle between his four sons, and died in captivity.

SHAILENDRA DYNASTY Rulers from c.700 to 1293 of the Srivijaya kingdom. Their ardent support of **Buddhism** is reflected in such architectural masterpieces as the great Borobudur complex in Java.

SHAKA (c.1787-1828) Zulu king. He was appointed in 1810 by the **Nguni** leader, Dingiswayo, to train and command the fighting men of north-east Natal; he pioneered the highly disciplined use of the short, stabbing assegai. He established himself as ruler on Dingiswayo's death in 1818 and crushed all rivals in Natal-Zululand before being assassinated by his half-brothers.

SHALMANESER III King of Assyria, 858–824 BC. He was the son and successor of Ashurnasirpal II, whose imperialist policies he continued, although stability and not expansion was his primary objective, as shown in Babylonia where he gave massive military aid to support the ruling dynasty without seeking personal kingship. In a long series of campaigns he broke the power of the Aramaean and Neo-Hittite states in Syria and Cilicia, consolidating control of the routes from the Mediterranean and Asia Minor. In the north he acted to defend Assyria against the growing power of Urartu (Armenia). He defended the eastern borders by sorties into the Zagros Mts to secure recognition of Assyrian suzerainty.

SHAMIL (c.1830-71) Caucasian resistance leader. In 1830 he joined the Muridis, a Sufi sect engaged in a holy war against the Russians who had seized the former Persian province of Daghestan. He succeeded as imam in 1834, establishing Daghestan as an independent state; surviving the capture of his main stronghold, Ahulgo, in 1838, he was finally defeated by massive Russian forces in 1859, and was exiled to the Moscow district. He died on a pilgrimage to Mecca.

SHAMSHI-ADAD I A major king in northern Mesopotamia, 1813–1781 BC, and older contemporary and possibly former suzerain of **Hammurabi**. The son of a minor ruler of nomad **Amorite** stock, he first gained control of Assyria, and from that base annexed the kingdom of Mari on the middle Euphrates. This gave him an empire controlling important trade routes, stretching from the Zagros Mts to the Euphrates and at times beyond, and northwards to the borders of the Anatolian plateau. Much of his correspondence, and that of his two sons appointed as sub-kings, has been found on clay tablets excavated at Mari, and shows his skill and attention to detail in diplomatic, military and administrative matters.

SHANS A Thai people now forming the Shan state of the Union of Burma. The word is a variant of 'Siam', but the Siamese came to call themselves **Thai**, 'free', and their country Thailand. The Shans infiltrated Upper Burma in the 13th century, and when Pagan fell, c.1300, strove for nearly three centuries with the Burmans for dominance; they sacked Ava, the capital, in 1527. The rulers of the Sittang state of Toungoo finally forced the Shan states in the 1550s to accept Burman overlordship. After the British annexation of Upper Burma in 1886 their *sawbwas* (chieftains) accepted British overlordship; later they were joined into the Shan States Federation. After independence in 1948 the Union government abolished the powers of the *sawbwas.*

SHANG CHIH-HSIN (1636–80) Son of Shang K'o-hsi (d.1676), governor of Kwangtung 1650–71, who succeeded his father. In 1673 his father's retirement provoked the rebellion of **Wu San-kuei**; in 1676 he joined the rebels, but the following year submitted to the **Manchus**. In 1680 he was accused of plotting a fresh rebellion, was arrested and ordered to commit suicide.

SHANKARACHARYA (c.788-820) Brahmin philosopher. He was a famous interpreter of *Vedanta* and originator of the Monist (*Advaita*) system of Hindu thought. He established influential religious centres (*mathas*) at Badrinath in the Himalayas, Puri in Orissa, Dwarka on the west Indian coast, and Sringeri in the south; he argued that the visible world is an illusion (*maya*) and that reality lies beyond the senses.

SHARIFIAN dynasty Saadi rulers of south Morocco from 1511. They secured Ottoman aid and managed to extend their control over the rest of Morocco in the 1550s and to expel the Portuguese in 1578. In 1591 they sent an expedition of Ottoman-trained troops across the Sahara and destroyed the Songhai empire. Disputed successions after 1610 weakened their authority, and the last Saadi was assassinated in 1660.

SHAYBANIDS Central Asian dynasty, controlling Transoxania in the late 15th and early 16th centuries after defeating the descendants of **Timur;** it was replaced at Bukhara by the Astrakhanids in 1599.

SHENG SHI-TS'AI (1895–1970) Warlord from Manchuria, sent to Sinkiang in 1929. He established control there, 1933–43, with strong support from the USSR, giving extensive concessions to the Soviet Union in return. In 1942 he went over to the Nationalists and demanded Soviet withdrawal, which was completed in 1943. In 1944 he tried to renew Russian links; he was removed from the province.

SHERIDAN, PHILIP HENRY (1831–88) Union general in the American Civil War. He cut off the Confederate retreat at Appomattox in 1865, forcing the surrender of the Southern commander, General **Robert E. Lee** to General **Ulysses S. Grant**. He was army commander-in-chief from 1883 until his death.

SHERMAN, WILLIAM TECUMSEH (1820-91) American Civil War general, born in Ohio. He entered the army but resigned his commission in 1853; reappointed a colonel in 1861, he was promoted to general after the first Battle of Bull Run. He destroyed the Confederate forces on his famous march through Georgia, 1864; he was appointed commanding general of the army in 1869.

SHER SHAH (c.1486-1545) Muslim emperor of northern India. A soldier under the **Mughal** king of Bihar, he became ruler of Bihar, and conquered Bengal in 1539. He defeated the Mughal emperor, Humayun, in 1539 and again in 1540, and took the royal title of Fariduddin Sher Shah. He effected notable fiscal, social and administrative reforms.

SHIH HUANG TI (c.259–210 BC) Creator of the first unified Chinese empire. He attained the throne of Ch'in, north-west China, in 246 BC; by 221 had annexed the territories of his 6 major rivals and proclaimed empire over them; he expanded Chinese control into southern China, establishing centralised administration and a network of roads, extending and consolidating the Great Wall, and unified the Chinese writing system. He entered into bitter controversy with Confucian scholars at his court, culminating in the Burning of the Books in 213.

SHI'ISM One of two main divisions of Islam, which split from the other, the **Sunni**, over the question of succession to the Prophet **Mohammed,** which Shi'is believe to have gone to his son-in-law **Ali** and then to a line of imams (hence their name, *Shi'at Ali*, party of Ali). They later split into a number of groups recognising different lines of imams: Zaidis in Yemen, **Ismailis,** and the main or Twelver group recognising a line of twelve imams, the last of whom is believed to have gone into hiding. This kind of Shi'ism is widespread today in Lebanon, Iraq, India, Pakistan and Iran, where it is the state religion.

SHIMONOSEKI Treaty of agreement ending the first Sino-Japanese war (1894-5). China recognised the independence of Korea, ceded Taiwan, the Pescadores Islands and the Liaotung Peninsula (including Port Arthur) to Japan, paid a large indemnity, and opened four new ports to foreign trade. Later in 1895 Russia, France and Germany forced Japan to return south Liaotung to China in return for a larger indemnity.

SHINTO Ancient religion of Japan. It lacks both an acknowledged founder and an organised body of teaching. It is characterised by worship of ancestors and heroes, a wide variety of local cults, and belief in the divinity of the emperor. It was largely superseded in the 6th century by **Buddhism**, but revived in the 17th century and was the official state religion from 1867 to 1946.

SHIVA Hindu god, combining within himself many apparently contradictory qualities: destruction and restoration, asceticism and sensuality, benevolence and revenge. In Sanskrit the name means 'suspicious one'; he is worshipped as the supreme deity by various Shaiva sects in India.

SHUPPILULIUMASH (died c.1346 BC) King of the **Hittites**, who won the throne c.1380 BC. He successfully invaded northern Syria, driving back Egyptians and Mitannians to add territory as far as Damascus to his empire.

SICILIAN VESPERS Revolt against the French conqueror of Sicily, **Charles I of Anjou,** during the hour of vespers on Easter Monday, 30 March, 1282. Encouraged by Peter III of Aragon, the Sicilians massacred 2000 French officials; after long wars between France and Aragon, Peter III's son, Frederick III, won recognition as king under the Peace of Caltabellotta, 1302.

SIEMENS, ERNST WERNER VON (1816-92) German engineer and inventor who discovered a process for galvanic gilding and plating, 1841. He supervised the construction of the first long telegraph line in Europe (Berlin to Frankfurt-am-Main, 1848-9). With Halske he set up a telegraph factory which constructed many telegraph lines in Russia; his brother Carl ran a subsidiary company in Russia while another brother, William, was in charge of the London branch. A new company (Siemens Brothers) manufactured and laid underwater cables. He invented the electric dynamo in 1866 and was actively concerned with the application of electric power to locomotives, trams, lifts and street lighting.

SIENAWSKI, MIKOLAJ HIERONIM (1645–83) Polish general *Voivode* (Army leader) of Volhynia (1680) and *Hetman* of the crown (1682), he fought successfully against **Tartars** and **Cossacks**. In 1683 he led the advance guard of the army led by king **John III Sobieski** to relieve Vienna.

SIGISMUND III (1566-1632) King of both Sweden and Poland, son of John III of Sweden and Catherine of Poland. Sigismund thus belonged to both the Vasa and the **Jagiello** dynasties, but his efforts to unite the two lines and the two countries ended in disaster. Elected to the throne of Poland, 1587, he also inherited the Swedish crown in 1592, and tried to restore Catholicism to Sweden. When he left Sweden for Poland the regent, his uncle (later **Charles IX**) rebelled, defeating him at Stangebro, 1598, and deposing him, 1599. The two countries remained intermittently at war until 1660.

SIHANOUK, PRINCE NORODOM (1922-) Cambodian statesman. King of Cambodia from 1941 to 1955, he then became its Prime Minister, 1955-60, and Head of State, 1960-70. In 1970 he was deposed by the National Assembly and Council of the Kingdom, and in Peking set up a Government of National Union. He returned as nominal head of state after the Communist (**Khmer Rouge**) victory in 1975, but was removed from office the following year.

SIKHS Members of an Indian religious community founded by the 16th century teacher **Nanak.** Outwardly distinguished by carrying the Five K Symbols: Kesha (uncut hair), Kanga (a small comb), Kara (an iron bangle), Kirpan (a small dagger) and Kacha (a type of underwear), in the 18th and early 19th centuries they emerged as a militant warrior brotherhood, particularly under the leadership of **Ranjit Singh.**

SIMON THE HASMONEAN (d.135 BC) Younger brother of **Judah Maccabee** who in 142 established a new Jewish state independent of the **Seleucid** rulers of the Near East; the state survived until quarrels among the descendants of Simon led to the establishment of Roman control in 63 BC.

SINCLAIR, UPTON (1875–1963) American novelist. His first major success, *The Jungle* (1906), embodied his personal, bitterly controversial investigation into working conditions in the Chicago stockyards; a series of similar works established him as a leading Socialist critic of US capitalism. He ran for governor of California as the Democratic candidate in 1934.

SINDHIAS Ruling dynasty of Gwalior, western India, founded by Ranoji, a **Maratha** official, in the 18th century. Under Sindhia Mahaduji (reigned 1761-94) the family established a virtually independent empire in northwest India, holding off the troops of the **English East India Company**, 1775–82, defeating the **Rajputs** and the **Marathas**, 1793, and taking the **Mughal** emperor, Shah Alam, under their protection. Later Sindhias, however, accepted British pre-eminence (from 1818); their kingdom survived as a native princedom under the British, and was later absorbed into the Indian union.

SIOUX (also called Dakota). North American Indian tribes once occupying vast areas of Minnesota, Montana, the Dakotas and the Western plains. From 1851 to 1876 they organised a resolute and often successful resistance to the advance of white settlers; discovery of gold in the Black Hills of Dakota brought a vast new influx of white fortune-hunters, and despite victory at the Little Big Horn (1876), the Sioux were finally crushed in the Tongue River Valley.

SIVAJI (c.1627–1680) Founder of the 17th-century **Maratha** kingdom in west India. He carved out his kingdom from **Mughal** and Bijapur territory and carried on a protracted war against the former. He was enthroned as an independent sovereign in 1674; he devoted his later life to social reform and the advancement of religious toleration.

SLOVENES South Slav people inhabiting the Yugoslav province of Slovenia; they number about two million.

SMERDIS Short-lived Persian emperor in 522 BC, son of **Cyrus II the Great** and younger brother of **Cambyses II**, on whose order he was secretly put to death by the king's officer Prexaspes. Subsequently imperial powers were usurped by Gaumata, the major-domo, who put his brother in the place of the vanished prince ('Pseudo-Smerdis') while Cambyses was campaigning in Egypt. After Cambyses' death, 'Smerdis' was recognised as king for eight months before being killed by **Darius I**.

SMETONA, ANTANAS (1874-1944) Lithuanian statesman who signed the Lithuanian declaration of independence, 1918; he became first President, 1919-20, and again after a *coup d'état* from 1926-40. After the Soviet invasion, he fled to western Europe in 1940, and then to the United States.

SMITH, ADAM (1723-90) Scottish economist and philosopher. Professor of Logic, Glasgow University, 1751, and of Moral Philosophy, 1752-64. His *Inquiry into the Nature and Causes of the Wealth of Nations*, 1776, laid the foundations for the new science of political economy.

SMITH, IAN DOUGLAS (1919–) Rhodesian political leader. In the British Royal Air Force, 1941–6; he became a member of the South Rhodesia legislative assembly, 1948–53; of the parliament of the federation of Rhodesia and Nyasaland, 1953–61, and of the right-wing Rhodesia Front Party. As Prime Minister of Rhodesia (1964–79) he declared unilateral independence (UDI) in 1965. Retired from politics 1979 after the transfer of power to a black government.

SOCIALISM Belief in communal or collective ownership of the means of economic production and distribution, and the right of all to share equally in the benefits and opportunities created by society. In Europe it reaches back to the Middle Ages ('when Adam delft and Eva span, who was then the gentilman?) and was influential in the 16th and 17th centuries (e.g. the **Levellers** in England); in the 19th century it broke up into various sub-divisions — Utopian (or Saint-Simonian) socialism, Marxian socialism, Christian socialism, democratic socialism — each differing in the emphasis placed on particular parts of the programme, and the political methods considered acceptable to achieve them.

SOCRATES (469-399 BC) Athenian thinker. None of his own work survives; he is best known through **Xenophon**'s memoirs and the early *Dialogues* of his pupil **Plato.** He was independent but critical of democracy, and was condemned to death by drinking hemlock by a popular jury. Plato's *Apology* and *Phaedo* purport to be accounts of his defence and last days.

SOLIDUS Byzantine gold coin, first issued by the Emperor **Constantine** in the 4th century AD. One of the most stable monetary tokens in economic history, it remained important in international trade for over 700 years.

SOLÍS, JUAN DÍAZ DE (c.1470-1516) Spanish explorer. He first visited central America in 1508 with **Vicente Yáñez Pinzón.** In 1515 he left Spain with three vessels and a commission to explore the lands 1700 leagues (5000 miles) south of Panama; he reached the Plate river in 1516, sailed up the Uruguay river, and was killed and eaten by Charrua Indians in sight of his crew; the survivors gave valuable information to **Sebastian Cabot.**

SOLOMONIDS Ruling dynasty in Ethiopia from 1770 to 1975. It was founded by Yekuno Amlak, prince of the inland province of Shoa, who claimed direct descent from the biblical King Solomon. Under Amda Sion (1314-44) and Zara Yaqob (1434-68) it consolidated power at home and repelled the Muslims to the north. It was finally eclipsed with the deposition of **Haile Selassie**.

SOPHIST Name applied to itinerant purveyors of higher education for fees in 5th and 4th century Greece. Their leading figures, e.g. **Protagoras**, were spoken of with much respect, but conservative opinion found their influence disturbing.

SOPHOCLES (c.496-406 BC) Athenian dramatist. Also a statesman, general and priest. He won first prize at Athenian festivals with 24 tetralogies, i.e. 96 of his 123 plays. Seven plays survive: *Ajax, The Women of Trachis, Antigone, King Oedipus, Electra, Philoctetes, Oedipus at Colonus*, and a fragment of *The Trackers.* He said that he created men as they ought to be, whereas **Euripides** wrote about men as they are.

SOTHO/TSWANA One of two main Bantu-speaking groups of southern African peoples, occupying the areas of Botswana, Lesotho, Orange Free State, and the north and east Transvaal since c.1000.

SOTO, HERNANDO DE (c.1500-42) Spanish explorer. He first sailed to Central America, c.1519, and in 1532 took part in the conquest of Peru. He was appointed governor of Cuba in 1537 by **Charles V,** and given a contract to conquer Florida: landing near Charlotte Bay in 1539, he fought his way through today's southern United States as far west as Oklahoma, discovering the Mississippi river in 1541. He died on the return journey.

SOUTH EAST ASIA TREATY ORGANISATION (SEATO) Set up in 1954 between Australia, France, New Zealand, Pakistan, the Philippines, Thailand, the United Kingdom and the United States to resist possible aggression by Communist China after the Korean War. Pakistan withdrew in 1972; at the 1975 Council meeting it was agreed that the organisation should be phased out.

SOVIETS Originally revolutionary councils elected by workers during the Russian Revolution of 1905. They were revived in 1917 to include bodies elected by workers, peasants and soldiers; it now signifies the primary units of government in the USSR.

SPARTAKISTS Members of the Spartakusbund, a German revolutionary socialist group in the First World War, led by Rosa Luxemburg and Karl Liebknecht, and named after the Roman slave-rebel, Spartacus. It later became the nucleus of the German Communist Party.

SPEER, ALBERT (1905–81) German architect and **Nazi** leader. a member from 1931 of the German Nazi party; as Minister of Armaments between 1942 and 1945 he made widespread use of slave labour from concentration camps for which, at the end of the Second World War, he was sentenced to twenty years' imprisonment. His brilliant organisation of industry contributed greatly to German strength. His memoirs, *Inside the Third Reich*, present an intimate picture of life in the entourage of **Adolf Hitler**.

SPEKE, JOHN HANNING (1827-64) British explorer who with Richard **Burton** reached Lake Tanganyika in 1858, and then journeyed alone, becoming the first European to see Lake Victoria and identify it as a source of the Nile.

SPUTNIK First artificial space satellite put into orbit, in 1957, by the USSR. Meaning 'companion', 'fellow traveller', it signalled the Soviet Union's growing technical capability and helped to precipitate the continuing US-USSR arms race.

SRIVIJAYA Maritime empire, controlling the Strait of Malacca and much of the Malay Archipelago from the 7th to the 11th century.

STALIN (1879–1953) Born Joseph Vissarionovich Dzhugashvili. Son of a Georgian shoemaker, he trained for the priesthood but was expelled in 1899 after becoming a **Marxist**. In 1917 he became Peoples' Commissar for Nationalities in the Soviet government, and General Secretary of the Communist Party of the Soviet Union from 1922 until his death. He eliminated all rivals after the death of **Lenin** in 1924; promoted an intensive industrialisation, collective agriculture and development of a police state. He signed a non-aggression pact with Nazi Germany in 1939, resulting in Russian invasion of eastern Poland and Finland, after earlier failure of attempt to form an alliance with Great Britain and France; and led ultimately successful resistance to German invasion, 1941-5. Three years after his death his regime was denounced by **Khrushchev** and a 'destalinisation' programme instituted.

STANDARD OIL US company formed in 1870 by John D. Rockefeller to refine and distribute petroleum. By 1879 it controlled almost 95 per cent of all oil refined in the United States and became the first industrial 'Trust', provoking the Sherman Anti-Trust Law of 1890. It was dissolved by the Supreme Court in 1911 and forced to operate as separate corporations chartered in different states. Its principal component, the Exxon Corporation, became the company with the highest turnover in the world in 1975, with annual sales of nearly $50,000 million.

STANISLAS II PONIATOWSKI (1732-98) Last king of independent Poland, being elected king with the support of **Catherine the Great** after the death of Augustus III in 1763. He failed to counter successive partitions of Poland by Russia, Austria and Prussia, despite the short-lived revival of 1788-94, and abdicated in 1795 as the three countries finally absorbed all Polish territory.

STANLEY, SIR HENRY MORTON (1847-1904) British explorer. As a young war-correspondent, he was sent by a New York newspaper to find the Scottish missionary traveller **David Livingstone;** he met him near Lake Tanganyika in 1871, to secure the 'scoop of the century'. He crossed Africa from Zanzibar to the mouth of the Congo, 1874-7, and founded the Congo Free State in 1879 on behalf of **Leopold II** of the Belgians, after Great Britain had turned down his offer to acquire the territory. He was a Member of Parliament, 1895-1900.

STAUFEN *see* **Hohenstaufen**

STAVISKY, SERGE ALEXANDRE (1886–1934) French financier who founded a credit organisation in Bayonne and issued bonds later found to be fraudulent. The scandal that followed his death – said by police to be suicide but widely believed to be murder – precipitated a major political crisis, culminating in the resignation of two Prime Ministers and a riot outside the Chamber of Deputies in which fifteen died.

STEFAN DUSHAN (1308-55) Most famous king of mediaeval Serbia. He deposed his father and seized the throne in 1331; annexed Macedonia, Albania and large areas of Greece from Byzantium; took the title 'Tsar of the Serbs and Greeks'; granted a major new code of laws.

STEIN, BARON HEINRICH VON (1757-1831) Prussian statesman. As Chief Minister, 1807, he instituted a programme of reform including the emancipation of serfs and municipal self-government; exiled by **Napoleon**, 1808, he became counsellor to Tsar Alexander I, 1812-13, and played a leading part in forming the anti-Napoleonic alliance between Russia and Prussia.

STEPHEN (c.1097-1154) King of England, third son of Stephen, Count of Blois and Chartres, and Adela, daughter of **William I.** Raised by Henry I and given large estates in England and Normandy, he pledged his support of Henry's daughter Matilda, but instead usurped the crown in 1135. Most of his reign was spent in civil war with Matilda (finally defeated 1148); after the death of his son, Eustace, he reluctantly designated Matilda's son, later **Henry II,** as his successor.

STEPHEN I (977-1038) First king of Hungary, a member of the **Árpád** dynasty, and son of the leading Magyar chief, Geisa (Geza). He decisively defeated a pagan uprising after the death of his father in 997, and was anointed king in 1000. He founded bishoprics, abbeys and encouraged church-building; and fought off an invasion by Emperor Conrad I in 1030. He was canonised in 1083.

STEPHEN OF PERM, ST (1335-96) Russian Orthodox bishop who led a mission to the **Zyrians**.

STEPHENSON, GEORGE (1781-1848) English railway pioneer. He built the first successful steam locomotive, 1814: constructed the Stockton and Darlington line, 1825; his *Rocket* won the first open speed contest for railway engines, 1829. With his son Robert he built many early track systems both in Great Britain and overseas.

STEPHENSON, ROBERT (1803-59) Civil engineer. He was a partner with his father, George Stephenson, and others in the firm of Robert Stephenson & Co. which built locomotives for British and many Continental railways.

STIMSON, HENRY LEWIS (1867-1950) American statesman. He was Secretary for War, 1911-13, in the Cabinet of William Howard Taft, and went on to serve in the administrations of five presidents, of both parties, up to 1945. He was Secretary for War to **F. D. Roosevelt,** 1940-45, and chief adviser to both Roosevelt and **Truman** on atomic policy: he justified the bombing of Hiroshima and Nagasaki on the grounds that it saved more lives than it cost.

STINNES, HUGO (1870-1924) German industrialist, grandson of **Matthias Stinnes.** He trained as a mining engineer, and founded the Stinnes Combine. Head of German industrial production in the First World War, he took advantage of post-war hyper-inflation to extend interests in coal, iron, power and transport into timber, insurance, paper manufacture and newspapers. At his death he was probably the most powerful financier in Europe; the company is known now as Stinneskonzern.

STINNES, MATTHIAS (1790-1845) German industrialist who built up large coal mining and river transport interests in the Ruhr; the sinking of a deep shaft in his colliery Graf Beust (near Essen) in 1839-41 began the northward expansion of mining in the Ruhr.

STOICS School of philosophers, founded by Zeno (c.334–264 BC), who taught in Athens at the Stoa. To the Stoics God is all and in all. Call him Zeus, Nature, Universe, Reason — all is in his hands. Virtue is the only good, moral weakness the only evil; to all else — health, wealth, position, pain — man should be indifferent. Notable Stoics were Zeno's successors, Cleanthes and Chrysippus; Panaetius and Posidonius, who transplanted the philosophy to Rome; and, under the Roman Empire, the statesman Seneca, the ex-slave Epictetus, and the half-agnostic Emperor Marcus Aurelius.

STOLBOVO, PEACE OF Settlement ending the Russo-Swedish war, 1610-17. The Swedes invaded northern Russia and captured Novgorod in 1611; expelled from there, they besieged Pskov. Anglo-Dutch mediation produced an agreement that Sweden would withdraw its troops, but retain Karelia and Ingria, between Finland and Estonia, thus effectively denying Russia any 'window to the Baltic' for the next century.

STOLYPIN, PIOTR ARKADEVICH (1863–1911) Russian statesman. Minister of the Interior and Prime Minister, 1906–11, he tried to save imperial Russia by agrarian reform and the forcible suppression of the revolutionary movement. He was assassinated.

STONE AGE The earliest stage in the development of human culture, characterised by the use of stone, as opposed to metal tools. It is normally sub-divided into an Old Stone Age **(Palaeolithic)**, Middle Stone Age **(Mesolithic)** and New Stone Age **(Neolithic).** The Old Stone Age covers the whole of human development during the **Pleistocene** Ice Age; the other two occupy the earlier part of the post-glacial period from 8000 BC onwards.

STROESSNER, ALFREDO (1912-) President of Paraguay. Son of a Bavarian immigrant father and Paraguayan mother; he fought in the Chaco War (1932-5); rose to be general in the Paraguayan army in 1951, associated with the Colorado party and became President in 1954 after palace revolution. He steadily accumulated dictatorial powers, and was voted President for life in 1977.

STRUTT, JEDEDIAH (1726–97) A pioneer in the development of the early English cotton industry. In 1758–9, he patented an improved stocking frame and set up a mill in Derby, England, to manufacture the 'Derby Patent Rib'. In 1768 he entered into partnership with **Arkwright** to exploit Arkwright's new spinning frame.

STUART, JOHN McDOUALL (1815-66) Explorer of South Australia. Born in Scotland, he served as draughtsman in Sturt's expeditions of 1844-6 before making six expeditions (1858-62) to the Australian interior, reaching Van Diemen Gulf.

STURT, CHARLES (1795-1869) Explorer of Australia. Born in Bengal, he was educated in England. Military Secretary to the Governor of New South Wales in 1827, in 1828-9 he traced the Macquarie, Bogan and Castlereagh rivers, then traversed the Murrumbidgee and Murray rivers, 1829-30, and in 1844-6 penetrated north from Adelaide to the Simpson Desert.

SUCRE, ANTONIO JOSÉ DE (1795-1830) Liberator of Ecuador. Born in Venezuela, at the age of twenty-six he was appointed by **Bolívar** to free the southern part of Gran Colombia, now Ecuador, from Spanish control. He defeated the royalists at Quito, May 1822; won the battle of Junín, Peru, August 1824, and routed 9,000 Spaniards at Ayacucho, forcing withdrawal; he dislodged the last Spanish survivors from Upper Peru, now Bolivia, whose legal capital carries his name.

SUEBI (SUEVES) Germanic peoples, including the Marcomanni, Quadi, Hermunduri, Semnones and Langobardi **(Lombards)**. In the 1st century AD they mostly lived along the river Elbe; apart from the Lombards, who established long-lasting control in northern Italy, their best-known group, dislodged by the Huns, entered Spain in 409 and consolidated a quasi-independent kingdom in the north-west (Galicia, Lusitania, Baetica). Their Christian king, Rechiar, was defeated by the **Visigoths** in 456, but the Visigoths finally absorbed the last Suebian territory only in 585.

SUEZ WAR Joint military intervention by Great Britain, France and Israel after Egypt nationalised the Suez Canal Company in 1956. After some early success, the action was condemned and halted by the intervention of the **United Nations**, and especially the United States. The Canal, blocked by Egypt during the fighting, was reopened in 1957.

SUI Short-lived but important Chinese dynasty, ruling from AD 581. It reunited China in 589, after three centuries of disorder following the collapse of the Han dynasty. The Sui built a great network of canals linking Lo-yang with Yangchow, Hangchow and the northern territories near Peking. It fell in 618, to be replaced by the T'ang dynasty the following year.

SUKARNO (1901–70) Indonesian statesman; he helped to found the Indonesian Nationalist party in 1928. Imprisoned by the Dutch colonial authorities, 1933–42, he was released by, and cooperated with, the Japanese, 1942–5. At the end of the Second World War he proclaimed himself President of an independent Indonesia, and spent the next four years trying to force the Dutch to relinquish their hold on the country. In 1959, after ten years of democratic rule, he assumed dictatorial powers (he declared himself President for life in 1963), and increased contacts with the Chinese Communists. Following a military coup in 1965 Sukarno was deposed (1967) and kept under house arrest until his death.

SULEIMAN I (c.1496-1566) Known as 'the Lawgiver', and to the West as 'the Magnificent'. The son of **Selim I**, he succeeded to the throne in 1520. He expanded and reinforced the Ottoman Empire and encouraged the development of art, architecture, literature and law. He conquered Belgrade (1521) and Rhodes (1522); defeated the Hungarians at Mohács (1526); seized large parts of Persia and Iraq. He developed a formidable navy to dominate the Mediterranean, and brought the **Ottoman** Empire to the practical limits of its power and expansion (unsuccessful siege of Vienna 1529, and of Malta 1565).

SULLA (138-78 BC) Roman general, led the aristocratic party in civil war with the popular leader Marius, and made himself dictator after Marius' defeat. He initiated sweeping constitutional and legal reforms, giving more power to the Senate, but was notorious for cruelty to political and military opponents.

SUMERIANS The predominant people in southern Mesopotamia from the beginning of the 3rd millennium. Immigration of Semites (*see* **Akkadians, Amorites**) changed the balance by the end of the millennium, the last Sumerian dynasty collapsing in 2006 BC. Their cultural achievements included the invention of writing and the creation of the first cities. Their language, of agglutinative type, has not been positively related to any other.

SUN CH'UAN-FANG (1884–1935) Warlord who controlled Kiangsu, Chekiang, Anhwei, Fukien and Kiangsi in 1925–7 at the time of the Northern Expedition. He lost control of his provinces in 1927, allowing the Nationalists to capture the lower Yangtze valley. With the aid of **Chang Tso-lin** he attempted to recapture Nanking in August of that year but was routed; he retired from public life. He was assassinated.

SUNNI One of the main two divisions of Islam, and the majority in most Muslim countries. It split from the other main group, the **Shi'is**, over the question of succession to the Prophet **Mohammed,** which Sunnis believe to have passed to the caliphs. The name is derived from *Sunna*, or words and deeds of the Prophet as recorded in the Hadith or Traditions; Sunnis thus claim to be following the example of the Prophet.

SUNNI ALI Emperor of Songhai in West Africa, who reigned c.1464-92. From his home territories on the Middle Niger he reduced many former Mali provinces to Songhai dependencies; he created a professional army and river-navy; seized Timbuktu, controlled the commerce of the western Sudan, and introduced many advanced administrative reforms.

SUN YAT-SEN (1866-1925) First (provisional) President of the Republic of China (1912). He studied medicine in Hong Kong and Canton; entered politics with the formation of the Revive China Society, 1884, and was exiled in 1896 after instigating an abortive uprising, but attempted to organise a series of further uprisings in south China. He returned from the United States in 1911 during the anti-**Ch'ing** (Manchu) revolution, and was elected provisional head of state but resigned after a few months. In 1923 he gained full control of the country, with Russian support; reorganised the **Kuomintang** to resemble the Soviet Communist Party. His Three Principles of the People inspired both Nationalists and Communists.

SUN YEN-LING (d.1677) Chinese general. His wife was the daughter of a commander in Kwangsi, and in 1660 she was given command of his former army. In 1666 Sun was sent to Kwangsi as its military governor; in 1673 he joined **Wu San-kuei**'s rebellion; wavering in his allegiance after 1676, he was killed on Wu San-kuei's orders.

SUTRI, SYNOD OF Council of the Roman church held in 1046, convoked at a diocesan seat north of Rome by Pope Gregory VI at the insistence of Henry III, king of Germany. The synod deposed Gregory, who had purchased his post, and two other rival pontiffs; it elected a German as Pope Clement II (1046–7), who inaugurated a thorough reform of the Church which culminated in the pontificate of **Gregory VII**.

SVEN ESTRIDSSON (c.1020-74) King of Denmark, nephew of the English and Danish king, **Cnut the Great.** He was chosen as ruler by the Danish nobles in 1047 after the death of **Magnus**; his title was vigorously disputed by Harald Hardrada, but the struggle ended early in 1066, when Harald was killed during an invasion of England (Battle of Stamford Bridge). Sven himself sponsored a serious Danish attack on England in 1069, withdrawing after an agreement with **William I** in 1070. His dynasty ruled Denmark for 300 years.

SVEN FORKBEARD (d.1014) King of Denmark, son of the Danish king, **Harald Bluetooth**. After a rebellion against his father, he seized the throne c.986. He unsuccessfully invaded Norway, and in 994 attacked England, being expensively bought off by **Æthelred II**. He was virtual ruler of Norway after 1000. He led a series of expeditions against England, and became king in 1013 after forcing Æthelred into exile.

SVYATOSLAV (d.972) Early Russian hero, Grand Prince of Kiev. He attempted to establish a Russian commercial empire over the steppes from Bulgaria to the Volga, 962-972; crushed the **Khazars**, **Volga Bulgars** and Danubian Bulgars, but was defeated by Byzantine Emperor John Tzimisces in 871. He was ambushed and killed by the **Pechenegs**.

SWAZI Bantu-speaking herdsmen and cultivators, living mainly in the independent African kingdom of Swaziland and in the adjacent South African territory of the eastern Transvaal.

SYAGRIUS Last Roman ruler of Gaul, overthrown by **Clovis** near Soissons in 486.

SYKES-PICOT AGREEMENT Secret pact between First World War Allies for the dismemberment of the Ottoman Empire. It was signed on 7 May 1916, with the assent of imperial Russia, by Sir Mark Sykes for Great Britain, and Georges Picot for France.

TACITUS, CORNELIUS (c.AD 55–c.120) Roman historian. His works include *Dialogue on Orators* (c.79–81), *Agricola* (c.98), *Germania* (c.98) and fragments of two longer works, the *Histories*, covering the period 68–70 (the original probably went down to 96), and the *Annales,* covering 14–68.

TAJIKS (Tadzhiks) Ancient Iranian people within the Soviet Union, mostly in the Tajik SSR, a mountainous region adjoining Afghanistan, Pakistan and India. They are mainly livestock keepers by occupation and Muslim by religion.

TALLEYRAND, CHARLES-MAURICE DE (1754–1838) French statesman and diplomat. Destined for the army but crippled by an accident in childhood, he entered the Church in 1775; became Bishop of Autun in 1788, but was excommunicated for his radical Church reorganisation during the French Revolution. Foreign Minister under the Directory, 1797–9, and to **Napoleon I** until resigning in 1807; he intrigued with Tsar Alexander I for Napoleon's defeat, and in 1814 became Foreign Minister to Louis XVIII. At the **Congress of Vienna** (1814–15) he secured favourable terms for France; was made Duc de Talleyrand-Périgord in 1817, and French ambassador to England, 1830–4.

TALMUD Principal repository of Jewish law and lore. It consists of the **Mishnah** and the Gemarra, an explanation of the Mishnah and a general presentation of the traditions taught and transmitted in the Rabbinical academies and preserved in two versions – the Palestinian, edited around AD 400, and the Babylonian, around 500.

TAMERLANE *see* **Timur**

TAMIL Dravidian language spoken by some 30 million southern Indians, one-third of the population of Sri Lanka (Ceylon), and scattered communities in South and East Africa, Mauritius, Malaysia and Fiji. Tamil literature dates back to the 3rd century BC; it remains the official language in the Indian state of Tamil Nadu (Madras).

TANCHELM (d.1115) Religious radical who criticised the Roman church, especially its hierarchical organisation. He preached to large congregations in the Low Countries (mainly Utrecht and Antwerp) but was eventually murdered by a priest.

T'ANG Imperial Chinese dynasty ruling AD 618 to 907; *see pages* 126–7.

T'ANG CHI-YAO (1881–1927) Chinese military leader. Appointed military governor of Kweichow, 1912, and of Yunnan Province, 1915 until his death, he gave crucial support to rebels opposing **Yüan Shih-k'ai** in his bid to re-establish the empire. After the death of **Sun Yat-sen** in 1925, he made an abortive bid to lead a new national government.

TANGUTS Tibetan-speaking peoples of north-western China, who established the 11th-century kingdom of Hsi-hsia in the area of present-day Kansu and northern Shensi. The Tangut tribes, straddling the main trade route from China to the West, remained tributaries to the Sung dynasty from 960 to 1038; from 1038 to 1044 they attempted, under their emperor, Li Yüan-hao, to conquer the whole of China, but then withdrew on payment of an annual tribute; the kingdom then survived until 1227, when it was overrun by the Mongols.

TANTRIC BUDDHISM This form of belief, evolved chiefly between the 6th and the 11th centuries AD, aimed at recreating in the individual the original spiritual experience of Gautama the **Buddha**, and emphasised sexo-yogic practices. Tantric art and sculpture made much use of male and female images to symbolise the process of spiritual growth and fulfilment; *Vajra-Yana* or the 'adamantine path' was its largest school.

TAOISM Ancient cult of China, tracing back philosophically to the legendary **Lao-tzu**, who held that there is a Way (*tao*), a sort of natural order of the universe, and that it is the duty of individuals to ensure that their life conforms to it. It developed as a mass religious movement in the 2nd century AD, with its own church and hierarchy; it emphasises salvation, aided by magical practices based on the interaction of *yin* and *yang*, the powers of darkness (female) and light (male).

TARTAR (also spelled Tatar). First found in an inscription of 731, the name came to be applied to the hosts of **Genghis Khan** and his successors, and in Europe was confused with Tartarus, the classical Hell, which seemed an appropriate place of origin for these dreadful hordes. The name was later loosely and inaccurately applied to some of the Turkic peoples of the Russian Empire – for example, Volga Tartars, Crimean Tartars; at the present time in the USSR there is a Tartar Autonomous Soviet Socialist Republic with its capital at Kazan on the Volga.

TASMAN, ABEL JANSZOON (c.1603–c.1659) Dutch explorer, discoverer of New Zealand, Tasmania, Tonga and the Fiji Islands. He served with the **Dutch East India Company,** 1633–53, carrying out two major voyages in the Indian Ocean and the South Pacific, reaching Tasmania (named after him) in 1642; he circumnavigated Australia without seeing it.

TEHERAN CONFERENCE Meeting held from 28 November 1943 to 12 January 1944 at which the Allied leaders – **Churchill, Roosevelt** and **Stalin** – concerted plans for an Anglo-American invasion of France and a Russian offensive against eastern Germany.

TE KOOTI (c.1830–93) New Zealand Maori resistance leader. While imprisoned, he founded the Ringatu cult, which is still extant. After escaping, he conducted skilful guerrilla campaigns (1868–72).

TENNANT, CHARLES (1768–1858) Scottish pioneer industrial chemist. He set up a bleachworks and in 1798 patented a new liquid for bleaching textile fabrics, which was soon widely used by Lancashire bleachers. In 1780 with three partners he set up a chemical plant near Glasgow to manufacture bleaching powder and other alkali products. When he died the firm was operating one of the largest chemical plants in the world.

TENNESSEE VALLEY AUTHORITY (TVA) United States federal agency, formed in 1933 to develop natural resources (particularly hydro-electric power) in the states drained by the Tennessee river system – Tennessee itself, Kentucky, Mississippi, Alabama, North Carolina, Georgia and Virginia.

TEN YEARS' WAR (1868–78) Cuba's first war for independence from Spain. It ended inconclusively with promises of political and economic reform, set out in the Convention of

Zanjon, 1878; the nationalist leader, Antonio Maceo, refused to accept the accompanying conditions and fled the island to prepare for renewed struggle.

TERTULLIAN (c.160–c.220) Early Christian theologian. Born in Carthage and trained as a lawyer, he was converted to **Christianity** c.195. Writing in Latin rather than Greek, he provided the Western Church with much of its basic terminology; his *De Praescriptions Haereticorum* (197–8) championed orthodoxy; in *De Testimonio Animae* he claimed that the soul is naturally Christian; in his great *Apology* he praised the martyrs: 'the blood of Christians is seed'.

TEUTONIC ORDER (also called Knights of the Cross). Organisation of German crusaders, founded in 1190 at Acre, Palestine. It moved to central Europe in 1211, and in 1226, at the invitation of Polish duke, Conrad of Masovia, began the conquest of pagan Prussia. Under its Grand Masters, with its headquarters at Marienburg, it controlled the eastern Baltic, conquering Pomerania and other areas of Poland. It absorbed the **Livonian Order** (Knights of the Sword) in 1237. It was defeated by the alliance of Poland and Lithuania at Tannenberg (Grunwald) in 1410, and broken by the Treaty of Toruń (Thorn) in 1466. It was secularised as the duchy of Prussia (1525) becoming a fief of Polish kings.

TEWFIK PASHA (1852–92) First khedive of Egypt under the British occupation. He was appointed khedive in 1879 by the Ottoman sultan in succession to **Ismail** Pasha. The growth of tension between England and France, representing the interests of foreign creditors of Egypt, and nationalist sentiment with **Arabi Pasha** as its chief spokesman, led to the weakening of Tewfik's power in favour of Arabi, but British military intervention and occupation in 1882 restored him as a figurehead under British control.

TE WHITI, ORONGOMAI (1831–1907) New Zealand Maori leader. He claimed to be a prophet and refused to take part in the Maori rebellions of the 1860s, preaching instead passive resistance and complete segregation from the Europeans. Imprisoned by the British 1881–3 and 1886, he still exercised great influence on the Maoris.

THEOCRITUS (c.300–250 BC) Pastoral poet from Syracuse, who worked in Cos and Alexandria. His *Idylls* and his lyrical descriptions of country life seem a form of escape from urban Alexandria; he strongly influenced Vergil and, through him, all pastoral poetry.

THEODORET (c.393–c.455) Christian theologian. Born in Antioch, he was appointed Bishop of Cyrrhus in Mesopotamia, and played a prominant part in the **Nestorian** controversy (for long defending Nestorians against **Cyril**), culminating with his appearance at the **Council of Chalcedon** in 451, where he finally agreed to condemn Nestorian beliefs. His works include a *Church History* and a brilliant defence of **Christianity** against paganism.

THEODORIC THE GREAT (c.454–526) Ostrogothic king of Italy, son of a chieftain. He succeeded his father in 471, led migrations of his people into Bulgaria and (in 489, on orders of the Emperor Zeno) Italy. He murdered Odoacer, the previous Italian ruler, in 493, to gain control of the country, though acknowledging imperial supremacy; he issued an edict imposing Roman law on his followers, tolerated Catholicism and sought friendship between Goths and Romans.

THEODORUS Known as Theodore the Lector, an early Greek church historian of the 6th century. Though only fragments of his work have survived, it is an essential source for events between the time of **Constantine I** (313) and Justin I (518).

THEODOSIUS I, THE GREAT (c.346–95) Roman emperor, 379–95. Appointed by Gratian to rule the Eastern Empire after the death of **Valens**, he also administered the Western Empire after the death of Maximus in 388. He established Catholicism as the official Roman religion, 380; condemned Arianism and paganism; after the massacre of Thessalonica he submitted in penance to **Ambrose.** After his death the Empire was finally divided into two halves.

THEOPHRASTUS (c.372–c.287 BC) Ancient Greek philosopher. Taught by **Aristotle** whom he succeeded as head of the Lyceum, Theophrastus was himself a great teacher, with classes attended by as many as 2000; he influenced the foundation of the Museum at Alexandria. Of his works, the *Enquiry into Plants* and the *Etiology of Plants* survive intact, and his *Doctrines of Natural Philosophers*, reconstructed by 19th century scholars, provide the main foundation for the history of early thought. His entertaining *Characters* have been much enjoyed and imitated.

THIRD COALITION, WAR OF THE Struggle between Napoleonic France and an alliance of Britain, Austria, Russia and Sweden, formed in April 1805. Britain's naval victory at Trafalgar established Allied supremacy at sea, but on land there were only defeats: Austria at Ulm (1805), Austria and Russia at Austerlitz (1805), and Prussia, joining late, at Jena (1806). Further Russian defeats, at Eylau and Friedland (1807) and the elimination of Sweden brought hostilities to an end with the Treaty of Tilsit (1807).

THIRTY TYRANTS Vituperative name given to the men who ruled Athens on behalf of Sparta for eight months after its defeat (404 BC) in the Peloponnesian War. The group included **Socrates**' former associate, Critias, who died in May 403 when a democratic army under Thrasybulus defeated the Tyrants at the Piraeus; the survivors were massacred two years later in Eleusis, where they had taken refuge.

THOMAS, ST One of the twelve Apostles. He doubted the Resurrection until he saw and touched the wounds of **Jesus**; he is traditionally believed to have gone to India as a missionary.

THOMAS, SIDNEY GILCHRIST (1850–85) English metallurgist and inventor, who discovered a new process for making steel which eliminated phosphorus from pig iron. It was applied both to the Bessemer converter (1875) and to the Siemens open-hearth process, perfected by Percy Carlyle Gilchrist.

THREE FEUDATORIES REBELLION *see* **Wu San-kuei**

THUCYDIDES (c.460–c.400 BC) Athenian historian. He served as a general in the Peloponnesian War, but was exiled after failing to defend an important strongpoint in Thrace. He had already begun his classic history of the war; he completed eight books, breaking off at 411, seven years before the end of hostilities.

THURINGIANS Germanic people, first documented c.AD 350. They were conquered by the **Huns** in the mid-5th century; by 500 their revived kingdom stretched from the Harz Mountains to the Danube, but they were defeated by the **Franks** in 531 and were subsequently ruled by them.

TIBERIUS (42 BC–AD 37) (Tiberius Claudius Nero Caesar Augustus). Second Roman emperor, stepson of the Emperor **Augustus**, he succeeded in AD 14 at the age of fifty-six. In his first years he greatly strengthened Rome's finances and institutions; after his son's death in 23 he gradually withdrew from affairs, retiring to Capri in 27 where he gained the reputation of an arbitrary, cruel and merciless tyrant. In 31 he arranged the execution of Sejanus, to whom he had delegated his authority and who plotted against him.

TIENTSIN TREATIES Agreements forced on the Chinese government in 1858 by Britain and France to allow free access, the posting of residential officials in Peking, and the opening of new trade ports. Similar agreements were then made by Russia and the United States.

TILAK, BAL GANGADHAR (1856–1920) Militant Indian nationalist. He taught mathematics, owned and edited two weekly newspapers, was twice imprisoned by the British; in 1914 he founded the Indian Home Rule League; he signed the Lucknow Pact in 1916 as the basis for a Hindu-Muslim political alliance. His books include *Secret of the Bhagavad-gita*, written in prison between 1908 and 1914.

TIMES, THE London newspaper, founded in 1785 by John Walter under the title *Daily Universal Register*; its present name was adopted in 1788. Known as 'The Thunderer' under the editorship of Delane for its incorruptibility and independence of government.

TIMUR (1336–1405) Known as Timur Lang, from his lame leg, hence Tamerlane. Born near Samarkand, later his capital, he is generally considered as bringing to an end the Mongol age of conquest, although his background was Turkish rather than Mongol, and he was no nomad but a product of the sophisticated Islamic society of Transoxiana. He conquered, with legendary barbarity, a vast Asian empire stretching from southern Russia to Mongolia and southwards into northern India, Persia and Mesopotamia. He adorned his capital with splendid buildings, many of which are standing today. He died on an expedition against **Ming** China; after his death the empire soon fell apart.

TIPU (c.1749–99) Indian sultan, known as 'the Tiger of Mysore'; son of **Haider Ali**. He fought frequently against the **Marathas**, 1767–79, despite being publicly caned by his father for cowardice in 1771. He defeated the British on the Coleroon river in 1782 and succeeded to the throne in the same year; he signed the Treaty of Mangalore with the British in 1784, though he fought several further aggressive and partially successful campaigns against them. He was killed during the final British assault on his capital, Seringapatam; he is remembered in the Mysore saying: 'Haidar was born to create an empire, Tipu to lose one'.

TITO, MARSHAL (1892–1980) (born Josip Broz). Yugoslav head of state. He led Communist resistance to German occupation of Yugoslavia, 1941–5 and in 1945 became head of the Federal People's Republic with Soviet support; he broke with the USSR in 1948 to pursue a neutralist foreign policy and an independent version of Communism. He had been President from 1953 until his death.

TITUS (AD 39–81) Roman emperor, son of **Vespasian**. He served in Britain, Germany and under his father in Judaea; on Vespasian's succession he took charge of the Jewish War, killed many (reputedly one million) Jews and sacked Jerusalem in 70; he was made commander of the Praetorian Guard in 71. He was much criticised for taking Berenice, sister of the Jewish king, Herod Agrippa II, as his mistress. He succeeded his father as emperor in 79, helped to rebuild Rome after the fire of 80, and completed the Colosseum.

TLAXCALANS Indians of the Central Mexican plateau. Relations between the Tlaxcalans and the Aztec confederation were always uneasy, and at the time of the Spanish conquest they joined **Hernan Cortés** as his principal local ally; continued loyalty to Spain brought many privileges.

TOCHARIANS Central Asian peoples, occupying the basin of the upper Oxus river in the 2nd century BC. They were joint founders, with the **Kushans**, of the Kushan Empire. They are not necessarily identical to the speakers of the 'Tocharian' language, one of the Indo-European group, whose main surviving manuscripts, found in Chinese Turkestan (Tarim Basin) date from the period AD 500–1000.

TOJO, HIDEKI (1884–1948) Japanese general and statesman, he was Prime Minister at the time of the Japanese attack on Pearl Harbor. After a military career he became Vice-Minister (1938–9), then Minister (1940–4) of War, and also Prime Minister, 1941–4. He resigned after the fall of Saipan; tried, after the war, by the Tokyo War Crimes Court, he was found guilty and hanged.

TOKUGAWA IEYASU (1542–1616) Founder of the **Tokugawa** shogunate.

TOKUGAWA Dynasty of hereditary shoguns or military dictators, effectively ruling Japan from 1603 to 1868. It was founded by Ieyasu (1542–1616), who mastered the country after the death of **Hideyoshi Toyotomi** and established his capital at the fishing village of Edo (now Tokyo). He organised a new pattern of fiefs and administration which lasted unchallenged until the 19th century. Under his son, Hidetada (1579–1632), and grandson, Iemitsu (1603–51), Japan eliminated Christianity and virtually closed itself to foreign trade and influence. These three rulers consolidated the family's control, which lasted until the 19th century when Tokugawa Keiki accepted the near-peaceful handing over of power to the emperor, **Meiji**.

TOLTECS Ruling people in Mexico from the 10th to the 12th century. The name is associated with their capital, Tula, or 'place of the reeds', located fifty miles north of Tenochtitlán, present-day Mexico City. They captured and sacked the great city of Teotihuacán c.900; under their leader Quetzalcoatl and his successors they established a wide-ranging empire, introducing to it metalwork and ambitious architectural and sculptural techniques. They were overwhelmed by nomad **Chichimec** invaders, including the Aztecs, who destroyed Tula in the mid-12th century.

TOPA (d.1493) Inca emperor, who succeeded to the title in 1471 after the abdication of his father, **Pachacuti**. After an early setback, invading the rain forests near the Tono River, he established a reputation as a great conqueror: he defeated the revolt led by the **Colla** and **Lupaca**, extended the boundaries of his empire to highland Bolivia, northern Chile and most of north-west Argentina; and finally succeeded in incorporating the previously unconquered southern coast of Peru. He devoted the rest of his reign to administration.

TORAH Hebrew name for the Law of Moses, or Pentateuch, the first five books of the Old Testament of the Bible: *Genesis, Exodus, Leviticus, Numbers and Deuteronomy;* also the scroll containing these books, used ceremonially in the synagogue.

TOTONAC Central American Indians, farming both the highlands and the hot coastal lowlands of eastern Mexico, mainly in the states of Vera Cruz, Puebla and Hidalgo. The two Totonac languages, Totonac and Tepehuan, are believed to be related to ancient **Mayan**.

TORDESILLAS, TREATY OF Treaty between Spain and Portugal, 1494, to determine ownership of lands discovered or to be discovered in the west. It granted Spain exclusive rights west of a north-south line 370 leagues west of the Cape Verde Islands – a 1493 Bull of the Spanish Pope Alexander VI had put the line 270 leagues further east – with Portugal taking lands east of the line. Portugal thus established claim to the so far undiscovered Brazil; but the treaty was never accepted by the other Atlantic powers.

TOURÉ, AHMED SEKOU (1922–84) President of the Republic of Guinea. A trade union organiser, in 1952 he started a political party, the Guinea Democratic Party; he became vice-president of the government council in 1957, and first President of Guinea on independence in 1958.

TOUSSAINT-L'OUVERTURE (1743–1803) Haitian independence leader, born into a family of African slaves in the part of Haiti which formed the French colony of St Domingue. He joined the slave rebellion and declared in favour of the French Revolutionary government; recognised by the French Directory as lieutenant-governor in 1797, he expelled British and Spanish forces and gained control of the whole island in 1801. The French government, now under Napoleon, sent invasion forces in 1802, and he was defeated and taken to France where he died in prison. The French restored slavery to Haiti.

TOWNSEND, FRANCIS (1867–1960) US doctor who helped lay the foundations for the modern American social security programme. He devised the Old Age Revolving Pension Plan, which mobilised popular support for federal action in this area.

TRAJAN (AD 53–117) (Marcus Ulpius Trajanus). First Roman emperor to be born in the provinces – in Italica, near Santiponce, Seville. He served in the army in Syria, Spain and Germany, was named Consul in 91 and chosen as Emperor in 98. He is famous as a builder, social reformer and extender of the Empire in the east and in **Dacia** modern Romania (celebrated by Trajan's Column, still standing in Rome). He died in Cilicia after invading Mesopotamia and taking Ctesiphon, the Parthian capital.

TRASTÁMARA *see* **Henry II, King of Castile**

TRIPARTITE PACT Agreement signed on 27 September 1940 between Germany, Italy and Japan, setting up a full military and political alliance (the Rome-Berlin-Tokyo Axis) to support one another in the event of a spread of the Second World War to the Far East.

TRIPLE ALLIANCE (1882–1915) Defensive treaty signed on 20 May 1882 pledging Germany and Italy to mutual support in the event of a French attack, and obliging Austria-Hungary to support Italy in such an event in return for a promise of Italian neutrality in the event of a Russian attack on Austria-Hungary. It was extended between 1887 and 1909 by supplementary agreements providing for diplomatic support in the Near East and North Africa.

TROTSKY, LEON (1879–1940) Russian revolutionary leader and theorist. Born Lev Davidovich Bronstein, he spent long periods in prison and in exile before returning to

Russia in 1917 to play a major part in bringing the **Bolsheviks** to power. He was Commissar for Foreign Affairs, 1917–18, and Commissar for War, 1918–25. The most prominent revolutionary after **Lenin**, he was effective organiser of the Red Army during the civil war; after Lenin's death in 1924 he was increasingly in conflict with **Stalin**, and was exiled in 1929. He founded the Fourth International in 1938, and published the *History of the Russian Revolution*. He was murdered by a Soviet agent in Mexico.

TRUMAN, HARRY S. (1884–1972) 33rd President of the United States, 1945–53. The son of a Missouri mule trader, he entered politics as county judge, 1922–4; US Senator, 1935 and re-elected 1940; Vice-President in 1944, succeeding as President in 1945 on the death of **F. D. Roosevelt**. He ordered the atomic bombing of Hiroshima and Nagasaki in 1945; in 1947 enunciated the Truman Doctrine on the 'containment' of the Soviet Union, and established the Central Intelligence Agency (CIA). He inaugurated the **Marshall Plan** and was re-elected, 1948, and supported in 1949 the formation of the **North Atlantic Treaty Organisation** (NATO); he ordered the US engagement in Korea in 1950.

TSHOMBE, MOISE (1919–69) Congo (Zaire) political leader. He became a member of the Katanga Provincial Council, 1951–3, and president of Conakat (Confédération des Associations Tribales du Katanga) in 1959. His plans for a federated Congo after independence were rejected in favour of a central state. He declared Katangan independence in 1960, but was defeated by UN forces in 1963. Appointed by **Kasavubu** as Premier of the Congo in 1964. Dismissed in 1965, he was sentenced to death *in absentia*, 1967; hijacked to Algeria, 1967, he died in captivity.

TUAREGS Berber nomads from the central and western Sahara; Hamitic-speaking Muslims.

TUDORS English ruling dynasty from 1485 until 1603, founded by **Henry VII** and continued through his descendants **Henry VIII**, Edward VI, Mary I and **Elizabeth I**.

TULUNIDS Muslim dynasty ruling in Egypt and Syria from 868 to 905. It was founded by Ahmed ibn Tulun, a Turk, who arrived in Egypt as vice-governor under the **Abbasids.**

TUNG-MENG-HUI Chinese political party, originally founded as a secret society by **Sun Yat-sen** in 1905.

TUNGUSY People of the sub-Arctic forest in eastern Siberia. Originally nomadic hunters, fishers and reindeer breeders, they moved from the Ob and Yenisey river basins east to the Pacific, and north from the Amur basin to the Arctic Ocean. Since the Russian Revolution (1917) most have been settled on collective farms.

TUPAMAROS Members of a Uruguayan urban guerrilla movement. It first came to prominence in 1968, preaching socialist revolution on the Cuban pattern. Its violent campaign of bombing, assassination, robbery, kidnapping – and a spectacular prison break in 1971 when 106 leading Tupamaros escaped from the Uruguayan national penitentiary – brought increasingly severe retaliation; by 1974 over 2000 members were held in a new maximum-security prison, and the movement had apparently been crushed.

TUTANKHAMUN (d.1352 BC) King of Egypt's XVIIIth Dynasty. Of uncertain parentage, as a child he succeeded his brother Smenkhkare, who had been co-regent and successor to **Akhenaten**. During his reign (1361–1352 BC) the worship of the old gods, suppressed by Akhenaten, was restored. In 1922 his long-lost tomb was discovered almost intact by the British archaeologist Howard Carter.

TUTHMOSIS I (died c.1512 BC) Third king of Egypt's XVIIIth Dynasty. He served as general in the army of Amenhotep I, and succeeded in 1525 BC when the pharaoh died without an heir. He re-established military domination in the south and conducted a brilliant campaign in Syria and across the Euphrates.

TUTHMOSIS III (d.1450 BC) Greatest of Egypt's warrior kings of the XVIIIth Dynasty. Son of Tuthmosis II (reigned 1512–1504 BC) and a minor wife named Isis, he ascended the throne as a young boy but was overshadowed for nearly twenty years by his stepmother, Queen Hatshepsut, until her death in 1482 BC. He conducted seventeen campaigns in Palestine and Syria, extending Egypt's empire to the banks of the Euphrates; his campaigns in Nubia gave Egypt control over all the gold mines and territory as far as the Fourth Cataract of the Nile.

TWENTY-ONE DEMANDS Claims pressed by Japan on China during the First World War, asking for privileges similar to, but more extensive than, those enjoyed by the Western powers, including railway and mining concessions, coastal access and power to intervene in financial, political and police affairs. An ultimatum, presented on 5 May 1915, forced capitulation on most points by the Chinese President on 25 May and greatly increased anti-Japanese feeling in China.

UIGHURS Nomadic Turkic-speaking peoples of central Asia, who ruled a substantial area north and north-west of China in the 8th and 9th centuries, and later settled in Kansu and the Tarim Basin, establishing a distinct way of life and a literary language. The modern Uighurs live mainly in Sinkiang and Soviet Central Asia.

ULFILAS (c.311–c.382) Converter of the Goths to Christianity. In 341 he was consecrated bishop of the Gothic Christians by Eusebius, the Arian patriarch of Constantinople. After initial persecution, the **Visigothic** leaders accepted the **Arianist** doctrine, while Ulfilas created a Gothic alphabet and made the first Germanic translation of the Bible, some of which still survives.

ULMANIS, KARLIS (1877–post 1942) Latvian independence leader. Trained in agronomy, he worked to free Latvia from the century-old Russian control during the 1905 revolution. He fled to the United States, was amnestied in 1913 and founded the Latvian Farmers' Union, 1917; appointed head of the provisional government by the national independence council, 1918, he held power from 1918–21, 1925–6, 1931–2 and 1934–40. He resigned in 1940 in the face of a Russian military ultimatum; was arrested in July by the Soviet authorities and deported. His fate is unknown.

UMAYYADS First Islamic dynasty, founded by Muawiya in 661, after the deposition and then murder of **Ali, Mohammed**'s son-in-law. They were deposed by the **Abbasids** in 750 although a branch continued to rule Muslim Spain from 756 to 1031

UNION, ACT OF Treaty signed in 1707 under which Scotland and England (which had shared the same rulers since 1603) became jointly the Kingdom of Great Britain. The agreement stipulated a single government, but separate churches and legal systems; Scotland recognised the Hanoverian succession.

UNITARIANS Members of a Protestant Christian denomination, characterised by belief in one God, as opposed to the more orthodox doctrine of the Trinity. It first emerged as a distinct church in Poland and Transylvania in the late 16th and 17th centuries, and was widely followed in England and North America in the 18th and 19th centuries.

UNITED FRUIT COMPANY United States-based multinational company, specialising in the shipment of tropical produce. Founded in 1899 in a merger of Central American shipping, railroad and banana-planting interests, it was merged into the United Brands Company in 1968.

UNITED NATIONS International organisation, founded in 1945 as a successor to the **League of Nations.** Its aims are to maintain world peace and security, and to promote economic, social and cultural co-operation among nations. The original membership of 50 had risen to 157 by 1982. Its main divisions are the Security Council and the General Assembly; special agencies include the World Health Organisation (WHO), Food and Agriculture Organisation (FAO), United Nations Educational, Scientific and Cultural Organisation (UNESCO), etc.

U NU (1907–) Burmese independence leader. He was expelled from Rangoon University in 1936, and in 1940 was imprisoned by the British for sedition. He became Foreign Minister in 1943 in the pro-Japanese government, and was first Prime Minister of independent Burma in 1948–58 and 1960–2, when he was ousted by General **Ne Win** in a *coup d'état*. Released from prison in 1969, he began to organise a resistance movement from abroad.

UPANISHADS Prose and verse reflections on the **Vedas** and forming with them the central corpus of Hindu sacred literature. Numbering 108 in their surviving form, the oldest were composed probably c.900 BC; teaching based on their mystical and philosophic speculations is known as the *Vedanta* – the Conclusion of the *Vedas*.

URBAN II (c.1042–99) Pope, 1088–99. He inherited many of **Gregory VII**'s ideas about the freedom of the Church from state interference, and in addition established at Rome the administrative organisation to operate it. He preached the First **Crusade** in 1099.

URNFIELD Late Bronze Age culture in central Europe, flourishing from the late 2nd to the early 1st millennium BC. It is characterised by the practice of burying the cremated ashes of the dead in ceramic urns. It was a direct predecessor of the Celtic **Hallstatt** period.

UTHMAN DAN FODIO (1754–1817) Muslim Fulani mystic and revolutionary reformer, and founder of a militant Islamic state in what later became northern Nigeria. He began teaching Sufi doctrines in 1775, and was hailed as deliverer by oppressed Hausa and fellow Fulani peoples. He launched a *jihad* (holy war) from Gabir in 1804, conquering most of northern Nigeria and beyond, establishing the Fulani-ruled Sokoto caliphate before retiring in 1815, disillusioned by the corruption of his supporters.

UTRECHT, PEACE OF Treaties concluded in 1713 which, with those of Rastadt and Baden (1714), ended the War of the Spanish Succession. **Louis XIV's** grandson Philip was recognised as king of Spain on condition that the kingdoms of France and Spain would never be united and with the cession of the Spanish Netherlands and Spain's Italian territories to Austria and Savoy. Gibraltar and Minorca were ceded to Great Britain, with a thirty-year monopoly on supplying slaves to the Spanish colonies. Portugal obtained frontier rectifications in South America at Spain's expense. Louis XIV recognised the Protestant succession in Great Britain (thus abandoning the Stuart cause) and the title of king for the ruler of Brandenburg-Prussia. He also ceded Nova Scotia, Hudson Bay, Newfoundland and St Kitts to the British, against incorporation of the principality of Orange and the Barcelonette valley into France. The Dutch Republic secured the right to garrison, at Autstrian expense, fortresses in the southern Netherlands. At the 1714 treaties between the Emperor Charles VI and Louis XIV, Landau was ceded to France and the electors of Bavaria and Cologne, Louis XIV's allies, were restored to their lands and dignities. Formal peace between Austria and Spain was not made until 1720.

UZBEKS A people of Turkish origin who arrived in the area around Samarkand and Tashkent in the 6th century AD. In the 14th century they became the core of the empire of **Timur,** and in the 16th century the basis for the conquests of the sultan, **Babur.** Later the area disintegrated into feudal city-states. Russia annexed the region in the 1860s, although incorporation was not complete until the 1920s; now mostly concentrated in the Uzbek SSR.

UZKOKS Balkan Christians who fled from the Ottoman conquest in the late 15th century and settled around the Adriatic port of Fiume, whence they attacked both Turkish and Christian (especially Venetian) shipping.

VACA, ALVARO NUÑEZ CABEZA DE (c.1490–1560) One of two Spanish survivors of a voyage of exploration from Florida to New Mexico, 1528–36, who wrote a description of the fabulous riches he claimed to have seen. Many others were thereby encouraged to go to their deaths prospecting there.

VAKATAKAS South Indian dynasty, dominating the western Deccan from the mid-3rd to the late 4th centuries AD. It achieved its greatest power under King Pravaresena I in the early 4th century; Rudrasena II married the daughter of **Chandragupta II**, and after his death c.390 the Vakataka territory was absorbed into the **Gupta** empire.

VALENS (c.328–78) Eastern Roman Emperor, who on the death of the Emperor Jovian was appointed co-emperor by his brother, Valentinian I, in 364. He twice devasted the Visigothic lands north of the Danube (in 367 and 369); fought an inconclusive war with Persia 376; was defeated and killed by the **Visigoths** at the battle of Adrianople.

VALERA, EAMON DE (1882–1975) Irish statesman. He was elected President of the Irish nationalist Party, Sinn Fein, in 1917, and President of the Irish Parliament, the Dáil, while imprisoned in England in 1918–19. He refused to accept the Irish independence treaty in 1921; in 1926 he formed a republican opposition party, Fianna Fáil. He was Prime Minister of the Irish Free State, 1937–48, and again – following full independence – in 1951-4 and 1957-9; and President of the Irish Republic 1959–73.

VALERIAN (c.190–c.260) (Publius Licinius Valerianus). Roman Emperor. He gained the throne in 253, but left government to his son Gallienus while he led campaigns against the Goths and the Persians; he was captured by the Persians in 260 and died in captivity.

VANDALS Germanic people, displaced from central Europe by the 4th-century incursion of the Huns. They reached North Africa, via Spain, and established their kingdom there in AD 429. At first federated with Rome, they seized their independence in 439 and captured Rome itself briefly in 455. Attacked in 533 by the Byzantine armies under **Belisarius,** they were obliterated in 534.

VARGAS, GETULIO DORNELLES (1883–1954) President and dicator of Brazil. He became state President of Rio Grande do Sul in 1928, and Liberal candidate for national President in 1929, seizing the presidency by force in 1930 after his defeat. Under a new constitution he was re-elected in 1934, and in 1937 he introduced the corporate-style dictatorship of Estado Nôvo (New State). He laid the foundations for the modern nation, and linked Brazil to the Western alliance in the Second World War. He was ousted in 1945, re-elected constitutional President in 1951, and committed suicide during the 1954 political crisis.

VARUS, PUBLIUS QUINTILIUS (died AD 9) Roman general. He became Consul in 13 BC. He was Governor of Syria, 6–4 BC, and was commander in Germany AD 6–9. He committed suicide after the destruction of his army by the Germans in the Teutoburg Forest.

VASVÁR, TREATY OF Agreement signed on 10 August 1664, ending an Austro-Turkish war (1663–4) after Austria had been called in to help the then independent principality of Transylvania repel a Turkish invasion. Under its terms Hungary, which had not been consulted, lost numerous fortresses to the Turks, and the resulting fury generated several later anti-Habsburg rebellions.

VAUBAN, SEBASTIEN LE PRESTRE DE (1633–1707) French engineer, military architect and town planner. He revolutionised defensive fortification, building a ring of fortresses on France's frontiers; he planned port fortifications and also towns connected with the many forts. He was made a Marshal of France in 1703.

VEDANTA Most influential among the Six Systems of Hindu philosophy. Decisive in refuting non-Brahminical schools of Hindu thought, it argues the existence of Absolute Soul in all things, and the union of the individual and his Absolute Soul as salvation. It was forcefully promoted by the Brahmin **Shankaracharya**.

VEDAS Collection of ancient Sanskrit hymns, sacred verses and devotional formulae *(mantras)*, preserved by Hindu tradition – first oral, then written – since the first appearance of Aryan-speaking peoples in north India, c.mid-2nd millennium BC. The three major compilations – *Rig*, *Yajur* and *Sama* – form the *trayividya* or 'threefold knowledge'; a fourth, the *Atharvaveda,* is made up of more homely chants, spells and incantations, of lesser religious significance.

VENDÉE UPRISING Largest and most successful royalist counter-attack against the First French Republic. In 1793 peasant troops, under their own and various aristocratic leaders, scored a number of victories, but were unable to hold the region's coastal ports and establish contact with Britain. Defeat came in October 1793, but trouble continued sporadically until finally put down by **Napoleon.**

VERONA, LEAGUE OF Alliance of Italian city states (1164), including Vicenza, Verona and Padua, formed to oppose the Emperor **Frederick I Barbarossa**; it was absorbed into the larger **Lombard League** in 1167. Verona was ruled by the da Romano and **della Scala**

families from the mid-13th century until conquered by the **Visconti** of Milan in 1387; it was then subject to Venice from 1404 until 1797.

VERRAZZANO, GIOVANNI DA (c.1485–c.1528) Florentine who in 1524 explored the North American coast from Cape Fear, North Carolina, probably as far north as Cape Breton, Nova Scotia. During his voyage he became the first European to sight New York Bay and Narragansett Bay, and he proved North America to be a continuous landmass. His name is commemorated in New York's Verrazzano-Narrows Bridge, linking Brooklyn and Staten Island.

VERSAILLES, TREATY OF (1783) (also known as the Treaty of Paris). Treaty which ended the American War of Independence. Great Britain recognised US sovereignty to the Mississippi river and ceded Florida to Spain. The agreement also called for payment of debts, US access to Newfoundland fishing-grounds and fair treatment for Americans who had stayed loyal to Great Britain.

VERSAILLES, TREATY OF (1919) Agreement signed on 28 June 1919 between Germany and the Allies after the end of the First World War. Germany was made to accept responsibility for paying heavy war reparations, to give up Alsace-Lorraine to France, yield much territory to Poland, Belgium, Denmark and Japan, and to lose all its overseas colonies. Danzig became a Free City under a **League of Nations** High Commission; the Saar was also placed under League control until 1935, when by plebiscite its citizens voted to be reunited with Germany. The Rhineland was to be permanently demilitarised and occupied by the Allies for fifteen years. The Treaty embodied the Covenant of the League of Nations; failing to secure a two-thirds majority in the United States Senate, it was not ratified by the US. The Versailles treaty with Germany was parallelled by the treaties of Trianon with Hungary, of Neuilly with Bulgaria, of St Germain with Austria and of Sèvres with the Ottoman Empire.

VESPASIAN (AD 9–79) Roman emperor. Of humble parentage, he became Proconsul in Africa, 63–6, led victorious armies in Palestine, 67–8; was proclaimed Emperor by troops during the civil wars following the death of Nero, and was recognised by the Senate in 69. He reorganised provinces in the Eastern Empire; secured the pacification of Wales and much of north Britain; and used tax reform, tolerance and a vast building programme to restore political stability.

VESPUCCI, AMERIGO (1454–1512) Explorer, cosmographer and propagandist. Born in Florence, he moved in 1492 to Seville as the **Medici** representative. He participated in several voyages of exploration, including one along the north coast of Brazil and Venezuela in 1499, and down the east coast of Brazil, possibly as far as Río de la Plata, in 1501–2. He is credited, on slender evidence, with the first suggestion that America was a continent separate from Asia; even, by some contemporaries, with being its discoverer – hence the name 'America', first used on the world map of Martin Waldseemüller in 1507. From 1508–12 Vespucci was pilot-major of the House of Trade of the Indies.

VICTOR EMMANUEL II (1820–78) First king of united Italy, son of **Charles Albert**, king of Sardinia-Piedmont, whom he succeeded on his father's abdication in 1849. He entrusted government in 1852 to Count **Cavour**, and led Italian troops in the Franco-Piedmontese victories over the Austrians at Magenta and Solferino, 1859; he encouraged **Garibaldi** to conquer Sicily and Naples. Proclaimed king of Italy in 1861, he acquired Venetia in 1866 and Rome in 1870.

VICTORIA (1819–1901) Queen of England, 1837–1901, and Empress of India, 1876–1901. She succeeded her uncle, William IV; married in 1840 Prince Albert of Saxe-Coburg-Gotha (1819–61) later styled the Prince Consort. She attached particular significance to her right to be consulted about foreign affairs and, in the latter part of her reign, identified herself with her people's imperial aspirations. She went through a period of intense unpopularity when she shut herself away from the public after the Prince Consort's death, but re-emerged as the symbol of national and imperial unity. Her diamond jubilee in 1897 was an ostentatious celebration of the apogee of Great Britain's world power.

VIENNA, CONGRESS OF Convened in fulfilment of Article XXXII of the **First Peace of Paris** and formally opened at the end of October 1814. The principal powers reconstructed Europe following the many territorial changes of the previous two decades, their decisions being embodied in the Final Act of Vienna of 9 June 1815. Legitimate dynasties were restored in Spain, Naples, Piedmont, Tuscany and Modena; the Marches, Legations and other territories were restored to the Holy See; the Swiss Confederation was restored and guaranteed; thirty-nine German states were formed into a Confederation; Belgium, Holland and part of Luxembourg were united under the kingdom of the Netherlands; the kingdom of Lombardy-Venetia was placed under the Emperor of Austria; the Congress Kingdom of Poland was created and placed under the Tsar of Russia, the rest of Poland going to Austria and Prussia; Prussia in addition acquired nearly half of Saxony, Swedish Pomerania and certain territories on both banks of the Rhine; Dalmatia, Carniola and Salzburg went to Austria.

VIET MINH League for the Independence of Vietnam, founded in 1941 by **Ho Chi Minh.** It emerged as a coalition of nationalist and Communist groups, and between 1946 and 1954 successfully fought to expel the French colonial administration. The dominant element of the party in North Vietnam, and since the military victory of 1975 throughout the country, is Lao Dong (Workers Party or Communist Party).

VIJAYANAGA Powerful Hindu kingdom of southern India, founded in 1336 by a local prince, Harihara, who in 1343 built his new capital of Vijayanagara (City of Victory) to give the state its name. In 1485 a change of dynasty brought the Saluva family to the throne. Its greatest influence was achieved under Krishna Deva Raya (1509–30); the continued struggles with the Muslim Deccan culminated in a crushing defeat at the Battle of Talikota in 1565 from which the kingdom never recovered.

VILLA, PANCHO (1877–1923) Mexican revolutionary leader, son of a farm worker. He joined **Madero** in 1909 and led a north Mexican troop in his successful revolution. Imprisoned in 1912, Villa escaped to the United States, returning in 1913 to form his famous División del Norte. He was joint leader of the successful revolt against Madero's successor, the dictator Victoriano Huerta, in 1914, but broke with his co-revolutionary **Carranza,** and fled to the mountains; he was pursued by a United States expedition in 1916 after executing sixteen Americans and attacking New Mexico, but was pardoned in 1920; he was assassinated three years later.

VILLAFRANCA, PEACE OF (1859) Preliminary peace between **Napoleon III, Victor Emmanuel II** and Francis Joseph I of Austria which brought to an end the Franco-Piedmontese hostilities against Austria. A definitive peace, which provided for the cession of Lombardy to Sardinia-Piedmont, was signed at **Zürich** on 10 November 1859.

VILLARET-JOYEUSE, LOUIS THOMAS (1750–1812) French vice-admiral. He led the French fleet during the Revolutionary Wars; ordered to protect a grain convoy by the Committee of Public Safety in 1794, he suffered severe losses at the hands of the British at the Battle of the 'Glorious' First of June, but succeeded in getting the convoy safely home to Brest; recalled by **Napoleon I** to lead the abortive expedition to recover St Domingue. In 1802 he was made Governor of Martinique, which he was forced to yield to the British in 1809; in 1811 he became Governor of Venice, where he died.

VILLENEUVE, PIERRE-CHARLES-JEAN-BAPTISTE-SILVESTRE DE (1763–1806) French vice-admiral. He commanded the French fleet at the Battle of Trafalgar in 1805; disgraced in the eyes of **Napoleon I** by his failure, he committed suicide.

VIRACOCHA (died c.1438) Inca emperor who took his name from the ancient Inca god of creation. He began in the early 15th century to substitute permanent conquest for his predecessors' pattern of intermittent raiding; he was successful in extending Inca influence into the Titicaca basin; he became embroiled in a civil war with his son, later **Pachacuti** Inca.

VISCONTI Milanese family dominating northern Italy in the 14th and 15th centuries. The family probably became hereditary viscounts of Milan in the 11th century, adopting the title as their surname; by war, diplomacy and marriage they extended their control over large territories between 1300 and 1447. The name died out with Filippo Maria (1392–1447) when he was succeeded by his son-in-law, the *condottiere* Francesco Sforza, who founded his own dynasty, ruling the Visconti domains until the 18th century. Through the female line, Visconti blood was transmitted to almost all the great European ruling houses: Valois in France, Habsburg in Austria and Spain, and Tudor in England.

VISCONTI, GIANGALEAZZO (1351–1402) Lombard ruler. He succeeded his father in 1378 as joint ruler of Pavia and Lombardy with his uncle, Bernabo, whom he put to death in 1385. Recognised as Duke of Milan in 1395, he became master of northern Italy, including Verona, Bologna and Perugia; in 1399 he bought Pisa and seized Siena; he founded Milan cathedral. He died of plague, with the conquest of Florence and his project for a great unified state in northern Italy incomplete.

VISHNU Hindu deity: God the Preserver in the Hindu trinity; the object of special or exclusive worship to Vaishnavas, a major sect of Hindu belief. Traditionally, Vishnu manifested himself in nine incarnations (most recently as the **Buddha**) to save men from evil; his tenth and final incarnation is still to come.

VISIGOTHS Germanic people, closely linked with the **Ostrogoths,** who occupied the former Roman province of Dacia (modern Romania) in the 3rd century AD. Allowed to live within the imperial frontiers, they revolted and defeated the Romans at Adrianople in 378 and began the wars and wanderings that included the Sack of Rome in 410 and the establishment of the Visigothic kingdom which, from 418 to 507, covered most of Spain and Gaul. They were defeated by the **Franks** at Vouillé in 511 and retreated to Spain, where their Christian state (first Arian, but Catholic from 589) was finally destroyed in 711 by Muslims invading from North Africa.

VLADIMIR (c.956–1015) Grand Prince of Kiev, saint and first Christian ruler in Russia. Son of **Svyatoslav** of Kiev, he became Prince of Novgorod in 970, and by 980 had linked Kiev and Novgorod, and consolidated Russia from the Ukraine to the Baltic. He signed a pact c.987 with the Byzantine emperor **Basil II** to give military aid and accept Christianity; he agreed to the appointment of a Greek Metropolitan, or archbishop, in Kiev, thus checking Roman influence on Russian religion. During his reign he expanded education, legal institutions and poor relief.

V.O.C *see* **Dutch East India Company**

VOLGA BULGARS A Turanian people, emigrating northwards from the Black Sea in the 9th century to the junction of the Volga and Kama rivers. They adopted Islam, founded an independent state, and built up a rich fur trade based on the cities of Bulgar and Suvar (early 11th century). They were conquered by the Mongols, 1237; their territory was won by Muscovy after the capture of Kazan (1552) but they themselves seem to have vanished long before.

VOLSCI Ancient Italian people, mainly known for their opposition to Roman expansion in the 5th century BC. Originally related to the Osco-Sabellian tribes of the upper Liris valley, they later moved into the fertile area of southern Latium where for two hundred years they fought against Rome and the Latins. Defeated during the Latin Revolt in 338 BC, they finally submitted in 304, and were quickly Romanised.

WAFD Egyptian nationalist party during the generation after the First World War. The name refers to the delegation, led by **Saad Zaghlul,** which asked the British High Commissioner in Cairo for permission to put the Egyptian case to the British government. Exile of leaders by the British in 1919 led to violence, martial law, and a long crisis which ended in the British declaration of limited Egyptian independence in 1922, the grant of a constitution, 1923, and the assumption of power by the Wafd, now organised as a party, in 1924. It soon lost office, but its leaders, Zaghlul and then Nahas, played an important part in later activities and negotiations which led ultimately to the Anglo-Egyptian Treaty of 1936. Subsequently Nahas was Prime Minister on several occasions, including much of the Second World War, and the Wafd continued to play the leading role as spokesmen of Egyptian aspirations for complete independence until dissolved after the military revolution of 1952.

WAHABI Member of the Muslim puritan movement founded by Mohammed ibn Abd al-Wahab in the 18th century. Originating in the Nejd district of central Arabia, it was adopted by a local dynasty, the **Saudis,** who created the first Wahabi empire, crushed by **Mohammed Ali** of Egypt acting on behalf of the Ottomans in 1818; revived in the mid-19th century, it was again destroyed, this time by the Rashidis of northern Arabia. The state was reformed, and expanded by Ibn Saud to become the modern kingdom of Saudi Arabia in 1932, with the Wahabi version of Islam as its official faith.

WALDENSIANS (Waldenses) Christian movement founded around 1170 by Peter Waldo (or Valdez) (c.1140–1217), characterised by its poverty, simplicity and evangelism. The Waldensians (also known as the Poor Men of Lyons) exalted personal conduct and the setting of a good example above priestly ordination. Waldo preached no doctrinal heterodoxy (which distinguished his movement from that of the **Cathars** with their dualistic **Manichaeism**), but he was nevertheless critical of the manners of the clerical hierarchy of his time. He was condemned at the Council of Verona (1184) for preaching without licence. As they operated in much the same areas as the Cathars, the Waldensians were also attacked in the Albigensian Crusade of 1209. Although the victim of continual persecution, the Waldensian church still survives in some districts of northern Italy.

WALLACE, SIR WILLIAM (c.1270–1305) Scottish national hero, son of Sir Matthew Wallace, a landowner near Renfrew. He organised resistance to the claims of the English king, **Edward I,** to rule Scotland, and annihilated a large English army near Stirling in 1297; he ravaged Northumberland and Durham, was badly defeated and discredited at Falkirk in the following year, and was arrested in Glasgow and executed in London in 1305.

WALLIS, SAMUEL (1728–95) Circumnavigator, discoverer of Tahiti, the Wallis Islands and some of the Tuamotu and Society Islands; in 1767 the British Admiralty sent him to survey the extent of Oceania.

WANG FU-CH'EN (d.1681) Chinese general. He was a subordinate of **Wu San-kuei** in the campaigns against the remnants of Ming forces in south-west China in the 1650s. In 1670 he became governor of Shensi. Wu San-kuei asked him to rebel in 1673 – he refused, and offered to lead his army against Wu. In 1674 he quarrelled with the Manchu commander sent against Wu and murdered him, joining the rebellion. In 1675–6 he controlled much of Shensi and Kansu, but surrendered to the Manchus in 1676 and committed suicide after the final failure of the rebellion.

WANG MANG (d.AD 23) Chinese emperor, known as 'the Usurper', founder of the short-lived Hsin dynasty, AD 9–23, which separated the two halves of the long **Han** period. He became regent to the imperial throne in 8 BC, at a time when the Han succession was confused; dismissed in 5 BC and reinstated four years later, he finally manoeuvred his way to supreme power in AD 9. By the time of his death a series of natural disasters and widespread rebellion, known as the Revolt of the Red Eyebrows, had precipitated his overthrow. This brought about the restoration of the Han line in AD 25. He instituted many reforms of administration and the economy, for which he claimed Confucian scriptural precedents. These sweeping reforms raised much discontent: for example, he attempted to nationalise land and free all slaves.

WARSAW PACT Agreement signed in 1955 which forms the basis for mutual defence co-operation within the Soviet bloc. The original participants were Albania, Bulgaria, Czechoslovakia, East Germany, Hungary, Poland, Romania and the Soviet Union, but Albania withdrew after the Soviet-led invasion of Czechoslovakia in 1968.

WASHINGTON, GEORGE (1732–99) American soldier and statesman. A farmer and country gentleman of Virginia, as a lieutenant-colonel in the Virginia militia he fought against the French, 1754–8; married 'the prettiest and richest widow in Virginia' in 1759, and became one of the largest landowners in the state. He was a member of the Virginia House of Burgesses, 1759–74, and delegate to the first Continental Congress. Appointed commander of the colonial armies in 1775 on the suggestion of **John Adams**, despite several military defeats in 1777–8 he retained the confidence of Congress, and forced the British surrender at Yorktown in 1781. After the peace of 1783 he resigned his command and returned to farming. He was elected chairman of the Constitutional Convention, 1787, and first President of the United States, 1788 (inaugurated 30 April 1789); he was re-elected in 1792. Declining to serve a third term, he gave his 'Farewell Address' in September 1796.

WATERLOO, BATTLE OF Final defeat in 1815 of **Napoleon I**, Emperor of the French, by the armies of his enemies: Dutch and British forces led by the **Duke of Wellington**, Prussians led by Marshal Blücher.

WATT, JAMES (1736–1819) Scottish inventor. At the age of seventeen he started making mathematical instruments; in 1764, while repairing a model Newcomen pump, he started a series of improvements which transformed the steam engine into the major power unit of the Industrial Revolution: separate condenser (1765), sun-and-planet gear (1781), double-acting engine (1782), centrifugal governor (1788), pressure gauge (1790). He was elected a Fellow of the Royal Society in 1785.

WEDGWOOD, JOSIAH (1730–95) Leading English potter in the 18th century. He introduced great improvements in the manufacturing process, and in 1769 he opened his new Etruria factory; in 1774 he made two dinner services for **Catherine II** of Russia. Wedgwood played an active part in securing the construction of the Trent and Mersey Canal in 1777, which greatly improved the transport facilities of the pottery industry.

WEICHSEL GLACIAL STAGE *see* **Würm**

WELLESLEY, RICHARD COLLEY (1760–1842) Marquis of Norragh. Anglo-Irish statesman and administrator, brother of the Duke of Wellington. Governor-General of Madras and of Bengal, 1797–1805, he defeated **Tipu**, Sultan of Mysore, but was recalled and threatened with impeachment over the cost and scale of his military annexations. As Lord Lieutenant of Ireland, 1821–8, and 1833–4, he tried to reconcile Protestants and Catholics.

WELLINGTON, DUKE OF (1769–1852) Victor of Waterloo and later Prime Minister of Great Britain. Born Arthur Wellesley, he gained an early military reputation in India, and was raised to the peerage after victories in the Peninsular War (1808–14). With the Prussian Marshal von Blücher he defeated **Napoleon I** in 1815 at Waterloo. A member of various Conservative Cabinets between 1818 and 1827, he became Prime Minister 1828–30, and opposition leader after the passing of the 1832 Reform Act.

WENCESLAS (1361–1419) King of Germany and Bohemia; son of Emperor Charles IV. His ineffective rule reduced Germany to anarchy between 1378 and 1389; imprisoned during a Bohemian revolt, 1394, he was deposed as king of the Romans in 1400, and of Bohemia in 1402, though later restored. He supported **Jan Hus** but failed to protect him from execution.

WESTERN RISINGS A popular English rebellion in 1549 in Cornwall and Devon against the introduction of a Protestant liturgy by Edward VI, which was defeated by government troops; also, in 1628–31, riots in south-west England against the efforts of **Charles I**'s government to enclose and cut down royal forests and thus deprive the local population of common rights.

WESTPHALIA, PEACE OF Name given to eleven separate treaties signed in 1648, after three years of negotiation, to end the Thirty Years' War. The **Habsburg** emperors lost most of their authority over the German princes, promised full toleration for Calvinist states, accepted the secularisation of all Church land (carried out 1555–1624), and formally recognised the independence of the Swiss confederation. Sweden and Brandenburg made substantial territorial gains in north Germany; France gained extensive rights and territories in Alsace and Lorraine.

WETTIN Ancient German ruling dynasty, named after the castle of Wettin on Saale below Halle, which played a major role in German eastern expansion. Conrad (died 1156) received the March of Meissen. The dynasty split into two branches in 1485: the Ernestines in Thuringia, the Albertines in Saxony, the latter was the leading territorial state in Germany from 1555 to 1763.

WHITE LOTUS REBELLION The White Lotus was a Buddhist millenarian sect founded before the 13th century. Under the Manchu (**Ch'ing**) dynasty, (1644–1911) it became an anti-dynastic movement, aiming to restore the **Ming**. In 1796–1805 White Lotus leaders led a series of large-scale risings in the mountainous regions of central China, using guerrilla tactics; however, there was no co-ordination of the rebels, who were eventually contained and put down by the organisation of local militias at vast expense.

WHITE RUSSIANS Traditional name for the people of Byelorussia (White Russia), but used during the Russian Civil War (1918–20) to describe the anti-Bolshevik forces which fought against the Communist Red Army, and since then to describe Russian emigrés.

WILFRID, ST (c.634–c.709) Born in Northumbria, he entered the monastery of Lindisfarne in 648. He fought to establish the supremacy of Rome over the Celtic church; helped convert the **Frisians**; established a monastery at Hexham and the churches of York and Ripon; and encouraged **Willibrord** and **Suidbert** to evangelise the Saxons of Germany.

WILKINSON, JOHN (1728–1808) A pioneer English ironmaster who developed a greatly improved method of boring cylinders. The new technique was first used to bore cannon, and was then adapted to the production of boilers for steam engines. In 1779 Wilkinson cast the components for the first iron bridge, over the Severn at Coalbrookedale, and in 1787 built a small iron ship on the Severn.

WILLIAM I, THE CONQUEROR (c.1028–87) First Norman King of England, son of Robert I of Normandy whose dukedom he inherited in 1035, becoming effective ruler in 1042. In 1063 he annexed Maine, and in 1066 successfully invaded England, where he introduced major legal and religious reforms. From 1072 he spent most of his time in Normandy; in 1085 he ordered the compilation of the Domesday Book, a unique survey of English landholdings.

WILLIBALD, ST (c.700–86) Anglo-Saxon missionary in Germany, a nephew and associate of **St Boniface**. He was made Bishop of Eichstätt in 741.

WILLIBRORD, ST (658–739) Anglo-Saxon bishop and missionary, disciple of St Egbert in Ireland, 678–90. He was sent to convert the **Frisians**, and became their archbishop in 695. He worked with the **Merovingian** kings, Pepin II and **Charles Martel**, to extend Christianity in northern Europe. He died at his monastery of Echternach, and was adopted as the patron saint of Holland.

WILLOUGHBY, FRANCIS (c.1613–66) Founder of the British colony of Surinam. He first supported Parliament in the English Civil War, then joined the Royalists. As Lord Willoughby of Parham he was appointed Governor of Barbados in 1650, and the following year successfully implanted settlers in Surinam.

WILSON, WOODROW (1856–1924) 28th President of the United States, an outstanding chief executive whose two terms in office (1913–21) covered the First World War and the Paris Peace Conference. A controversial figure during the first years, Wilson won temporary fame as the world's greatest leader after the war, but he fell, a tragic figure, soon after. His ardent advocacy of the **League of Nations**, which the US Senate repudiated, was the most apparent cause of his undoing.

WISCONSIN GLACIAL STAGE *see* **Würm**

WITOLD (1350–1430) Grandson of **Gedymin**, Lithuanian Grand Duke and national leader, also known in Lithuania as Vytautas the Great. He fought a long struggle with his cousin **Wladyslaw II Jagiello**, king of Poland, which ended in 1401 when Wladyslaw recognised him as Grand Duke of Lithuania, while remaining his suzerain. In alliance, the cousins broke the power of the **Teutonic Order** at the Battle of Tannenberg (Grunwald) in 1410.

WITTELSBACH Bavarian dynasty enfoeffed with the duchy of Bavaria after the fall of **Henry, Duke of Saxony** in 1180. A collateral line held the Palatinate from 1214 to 1777. The Bavarian Wittelsbachs, imperial supporters in the **Thirty Years' War**, were rewarded with the Palatinate in 1648. Raised to the rank of king by Napoleon in 1806, they continued to rule until 1918.

WLADYSLAW II JAGIELLO (1351–1434) Grandson of **Gedymin**, son of **Olgierd**, Grand Duke of Lithuania (from 1377) and (from 1386) King Wladyslaw II Jagiello of Poland. By his marriage to Queen **Jadwiga** of Poland in 1386, he united the two crowns. At the head of Polish and Lithuanian armies he defeated the knights of the **Teutonic Order** at Tannenberg (Grunwald) in 1410. He gave his name to the **Jagiellonian** dynasty.

WOLFE, JAMES (1727–59) British general. He served in the Low Countries, Scotland and Cape Breton Islands before commanding the British army at the capture of Quebec in 1759; after defeat at Beauport, he climbed the Heights of Abraham to surprise and rout the French army. He thus gained Canada for Britain, but died of wounds during the battle.

WORMS, CONCORDAT OF Agreement concluded in 1122 between Pope Calixtus II and Emperor Henry V, which ended the Investiture Contest in compromise. The Emperor conceded full freedom of election to episcopal office, surrendering the claim to bestow spiritual authority by investiture; but bishops were to be elected in his presence so that he might nevertheless influence the electors' choice. Thus neither side gained all that **Gregory VII** and **Henry IV** had demanded, but each secured valuable concessions from the other; papal headship of the Church was recognised, but the emperor retained some control over its leaders in Germany.

WRIGHT BROTHERS American aviation pioneers. Together Orville Wright (1871–1948) and his brother Wilbur (1867–1912) built the first stable, controllable, heavier-than-air flying machine, which made its first successful flights (the longest of 260m, 852 ft) at Kitty Hawk, North Carolina, in 1903.

WU P'EI-FU (1874–1939) Chinese warlord. He served with the Pei-yang armies under **Yüan Shih-k'ai**, and with the Japanese army during the Russo-Japanese war of 1904–5. After Yüan's death in 1916, Wu became the most powerful general of the Pei-yang armies, and in 1922 drove back the Manchurian armies of **Chang Tso-lin**. This made him China's most powerful military figure, and he dominated the shaky Peking government from 1922–24. His ruthless suppression of a workers' strike on the Hankow-Peking railway in 1923 cost him much of his popularity and the support of his main ally **Feng Yu-hsiang**. Decisively defeated by Chang near Tientsin in 1924, he retreated to Hupeh; in 1925–6 allied himself with Chang in a war against Feng Yu-hsiang and invaded Honan. In 1926–7 he was defeated by **Chiang Kai-shek's** Northern Expedition and took refuge in Szechwan; he took no further major part in affairs.

WÜRM GLACIAL STAGE The latest phase of major ice advance in Alpine Europe, starting c. 70,000 years ago and ending around 10,000 years ago; it is equivalent to the Wisconsin period in North America and Weichsel in Scandinavia.

WU SAN-KUEI (1612–78) Chinese general. He served in the **Ming** armies, defending the north-east frontier against the **Manchus**, but he appealed to the Manchus for aid when Peking was attacked in 1644 by the rebel **Li Tzu-ch'eng** (c.1605–45), and with their aid drove Li from Peking, where the Manchus set up the **Ch'ing** dynasty. He refused appeals to aid a restoration of the **Ming** emperors, and commanded the south-western province of Yunnan on behalf of the Manchus, growing increasingly powerful and eventually controlling much of south-west and west China. In 1673 he led the Rebellion of the Three Feudatories and attempted to set up his own Chou dynasty, invading central China in 1674. He died of dysentery three years before the rebellion was finally crushed in 1681.

WU-TI (156–87 BC) Powerful Chinese emperor of the former **Han** period, eleventh son of Emperor Ching Ti. He succeeded to the throne in 140 BC; aggressively extended China's frontiers to include much of south and south-west China, north Vietnam, northern Korea and much of central Asia, and established effective defences against the **Hsiung-nu** in the north. He finally established the supremacy of the emperor, created a tightly-knit bureaucracy, levied unprecedented taxes and made Confucianism the state religion.

WYATT'S REBELLION English uprising in 1554 against the marriage of Mary Tudor (reigned 1553–8) to Philip II of Spain. Three thousand men from Kent marched on London and reached Fleet Street before surrendering; their leader, Sir Thomas Wyatt (son of the poet of the same name), was executed, and Princess Elizabeth, later Queen **Elizabeth I** (whom Wyatt had wished to place on the throne) was imprisoned in the Tower of London.

WYCLIF, JOHN (c.1329–84) Religious reformer and translator of the Bible into English. As a vigorous anti-clerical he was patronised by John of Gaunt, who continued to support him, but not his views when he denied the miracle of transubstantiation in the Mass; he was condemned as a heretic in 1381. His followers are known as **Lollards**.

WYNFRITH *see* **Boniface, St**

WYNTER, JAN WILLEM DE (1761–1812) Dutch admiral and politician. In 1785 he led the 'patriot party' which deposed the Stadholder William V, but fled to France when William was restored in 1787. In 1795 he accompanied the French army which conquered the Netherlands, and the French placed him in charge of the Dutch navy; in 1797 he led it to its defeat by the British at the battle of Camperdown.

XENOPHON (c.430–c.355 BC) Greek soldier and author. He studied with Socrates, about whom he wrote the *Memorabilia*, *Symposium* and *Apology*. His *Anabasis* describes the epic retreat of 10,000 mercenaries from Persia after the failure of Cyrus the Younger's expedition against Artaxerxes II. In exile he wrote the *Hellenica*, a history of Greece, and other works on sport and politics.

XERXES I (c.520–465 BC) King of Persia (reigned 486–465 BC). Son of **Darius I** by his second marriage; chosen to succeed over his elder brother. He reconquered Egypt, which had rebelled at the end of Darius' reign; invaded Greece in 480 after digging a canal through the Mt Athos peninsula, forced the pass at Thermopylae and occupied Athens before meeting a crushing defeat at Salamis (480) by sea and at Plataea (479) by land. He was responsible for the finest work at the Persian capital of Persepolis. He was assassinated by conspirators headed by his chief guard, Artabanus.

XHOSA A people, and their Bantu language, in Cape Province, South Africa; now the inhabitant of the Transkei, the first independent homeland of South Africa.

YAHYA KHAN, AGHA MOHAMMED (1917–82) Pakistan soldier and politician. Commander in East Pakistan (now Bangladesh), 1962–4; commander-in-chief of the Pakistan army, 1966–9, and President of Pakistan and chief administrator of martial law, 1969–71. He was forced to resign after his failure to suppress the revolt in East Pakistan which led to the setting up of the state of Bangladesh.

YALTA CONFERENCE Meeting of Allied war leaders (led by **Roosevelt, Churchill** and **Stalin**) at Yalta in the Crimea, 4–11 February 1945. It reaffirmed the decision to demand unconditional Axis surrender, planned a four-power occupation of Germany, and agreed a further meeting to finalise plans for the **United Nations**. It was also agreed that the British and Americans would repatriate all Russians in Allied hands. Stalin, for his part, was prompted to declare war on Japan.

YAO Mountain-dwelling people of south and south-west China and of South-East Asia, related to the Miao who share a similar heritage of Sino-Tibetan languages. In Kwangtung some have turned to wet-rice cultivation, but most remain in the highlands practising primitive slash-and-burn agriculture.

YEN HSI-SHAN (1883–1960) Chinese general and military governor. A Japanese-trained army officer, he emerged as a warlord in Shansi after the overthrow of the **Ch'ing** (Manchu) dynasty in 1911, and ruled as absolute dictator of the whole region from 1917 until the end of the Second World War. In 1930 he joined **Feng Yu-hsiang** in an abortive northern alliance against **Chiang Kai-shek**, but was afterwards confirmed in command of Shansi, where he instituted a sweeping programme of provincial reforms in 1934. In 1937 he lost most of Shansi to the Japanese, and from 1939 was in constant conflict with the Chinese Communists. He was driven from the province in early 1949; he went to Taiwan and became premier until 1950.

YORKSHIRE RISING Major revolt in 1489 against the attempts of the English King **Henry**

VII to collect a parliamentary grant of £75,000. The king's lieutenant, the Earl of Northumberland, was killed before the rebels were suppressed.

YOUNG TURKS Popular name for the Committee of Union and Progress, an association of army officers and others who compelled sultan **Abdul Hamid II** to restore the 1876 constitution in 1908 and deposed him in 1909. Subsequently it became the Ottoman Empire's dominant political party, in 1914 bringing Turkey into the First World War. It was disbanded after the Central Powers' defeat in 1918.

YÜAN SHIH-K'AI (1859–1916) First President of the Republic of China. He was sent to Korea with the Anhwei army, 1882, and became Chinese commissioner in Seoul, 1885–94; he helped to create a new model army after defeat by Japan in 1895. In 1901 he became viceroy of China's metropolitan province, Chihli, and commander of China's most powerful army, the Pei-yang chün; he was removed from his post in 1907 but exercised power through his former military subordinates, and was recalled by the Ch'ing (Manchus) after the outbreak of the 1911 revolution as supreme commander. In 1912 he was recommended by the Emperor to be President, replacing the provisional President, **Sun Yat-sen**; increasingly dictatorial, he precipitated civil war in 1913 by murdering the revolutionary party chairman, and in 1916 tried to create a new imperial dynasty.

YUDENICH, NIKOLAI NIKOLAYEVICH (1862–1933) Russian general. After service in the Russo-Japanese war and the First World War, he took command of the anti-Bolshevik forces in the Baltic after the Russian Revolution. In 1919, with some British support he led an unsuccessful advance on Leningrad (then called Petrograd), and went into exile.

YÜEH-CHIH Central Asian peoples, first identified in Chinese sources in the 2nd century BC, living as nomads in Kansu, north-western China. Under attack by the **Hsiungnu**, they moved west into Sogdiana and Bactria, displacing the Greek rulers there, c.150 BC. Their descendants, with the **Tocharians**, founded the Kushan Empire, ruling northern India and central Asia until about AD 300. Yüeh-chih and Kushan missionaries helped spread **Buddhism** and Indian culture to China.

YUNG-LO (CHU TI) (1360–1424) Chinese emperor, the third of the **Ming** dynasty, and fourth son of Hung-wu. He rebelled against his nephew in 1399, and seized the throne in 1402 after two years of destructive civil war. He invaded Annam, 1406–7, and began a series of major maritime expeditions into the Indian Ocean. He personally conducted campaigns to crush the Mongols in 1410, 1414 and 1422–4, and expanded Chinese power in Manchuria and the Amur valley. He rebuilt the Grand Canal, and transferred the capital from Nanking to Peking in 1421.

ZAGHLUL, SAAD (1857–1927) Leader of Egyptian nationalism during that period when it first became a mass movement. He became prominent as a minister and politician before 1914; from 1918 he was leader of the **Wafd**, and in 1924 was appointed Prime Minister shortly after the British declaration of limited independence for Egypt; he was, however, forced to resign soon afterwards.

ZAGWE Ethiopian dynasty of Semitic origin which displaced the Axumite kings in the 12th and 13th centuries. It did much to expand and centralise the Christian empire of Ethiopia.

ZAIBATSU Large-scale Japanese business groups, normally organised around the commercial, industrial and financial interests of a single family. The biggest and best known were the Mitsui, Mitsubishi, Yasuda and Sumitomo empires, all of which grew up and flourished in the period from 1868 to 1945. In 1946, after Japan's defeat, the Zaibatsu were ordered to dissolve into their component companies, but most are now, for practical purposes, reassembled and even more formidable than before.

ZAIDI Dynasty of rulers in Yemen, southern Arabia. Founded by imam al-Hadi in northern Yemen in the 9th century, they expanded their power in the 12th century, and again after 1635 when they expelled the Ottoman Turks. Driven back to northern Yemen in the 1710s, they were forced to recognise Ottoman suzerainty in 1849. After the Ottoman collapse in 1918 they became rulers of all Yemen until a

military coup in 1962 deposed the last Zaidi imam.

ZANGI (1084–1146) Iraqi warrior who inflicted the first serious defeat on Christian crusaders, recapturing Edessa in 1144. He founded the Zangid dynasty, which ruled northern Iraq and Syria, 1127–1222.

ZANGIDS Muslim Turkish dynasty, ruling northern Iraq and part of Syria from 1127 to 1222. It was founded by Zangi (1127–46), who mounted the first Islamic counter-attack against the Christian **Crusades. Saladin**, founder of the **Ayyubid** dynasty in Egypt, was a Zangid general, and ultimately brought the family territories under his rule.

ZAPATA, EMILIANO (1879–1919) Mexican revolutionary leader. He supported **Madero** in the 1911 overthrow of **Díaz**; forbidden to redistribute land to the peasants, he issued the Plan of Ayala and renewed revolution under the slogan 'Land and Liberty'. He fought constantly, first against the dictator Huerta in 1913, and then with **Pancho Villa** against the moderate government of **Carranza**. He was ambushed and assassinated.

ZARATHUSTRA *see* Zoroaster

ZEALOTS Extremist Jewish resistance party against the Roman domination of Judaea after AD 6. It played a major part in the **Jewish uprising** of AD 66–73.

ZENO OF CITIUM (c.334–c.262 BC) Ancient Greek philosopher, founder of **Stoicism.**

ZENO OF ELEA (c.490–c.430 BC) Ancient Greek philosopher, best known for his paradoxes demonstrating the unreality of motion.

ZEUS Supreme god of Greek mythology, also identified with the Roman Jupiter; born in Crete, (Mt. Ida), son of Rhea and Cronus, whom he overthrew.

ZHUKOV, GEORGIY KONSTANTINOVICH (1896–1976) Marshal of the Soviet Union and leading Russian hero of the Second World War. He served in the Imperial Russian Army, 1915–17, joining the Red Army in 1918; he was a cavalry commander in the Civil War. In command on the Mongolian-Manchurian frontier, in 1939, he became General Officer commanding the Kiev Military District in 1940, and in 1941 Chief of the General Staff. He directed the defence of Leningrad and then Moscow after the German invasion; was appointed Marshal in 1943; and led the final assault on Berlin in 1945. He was briefly commander-in-chief of the Soviet forces in Germany, GOC of Odessa Military District 1948–52; Minister of Defence 1955, after supporting **Khrushchev** against Malenkov. He was dismissed in 1957 and retired into private life.

ZIONISM Jewish national movement. It emerged in the latter part of the 19th century, and was placed on a firm and permanent organisational basis by Theodore Herzl, author of *The Jewish State,* who convened the first Zionist Congress at Basle in 1897. It sought the creation of a revived Jewish homeland in the ancestral land of Palestine, from which most Jews had been exiled; this aim was achieved in 1948 when the **United Nations** voted to create the state of Israel.

ZIRIDS Muslim Berber dynasty ruling, under various branches, Tunisia, eastern Algeria and Granada from 972 to 1152. They were given a free hand in north-west Africa when their suzerain, the **Fatimid** caliph al-Muizz, moved his capital to Cairo. They were finally conquered by the **Almohads.**

ZOLLVEREIN German customs union established in 1834 when eighteen states, some of which had formerly belonged to the Prussian, central German and southern German customs unions, formed, under Prussian auspices, a free trade area. By 1841 most German states had joined; Hanover and Oldenburg joined in 1854; Austria remained outside; Schleswig-Holstein, Lauenburg, Lübeck and the Mecklenburgs joined after the defeat of Austria in 1866 by Prussia, whose power in Germany had been much enhanced by the Zollverein. Hamburg and Bremen joined in 1888.

ZOROASTER (Zarathustra) Prophet and religious reformer of ancient Iran, the founder of Zoroastrianism. His personal writings were the Old Iranian texts known as the *Gathas,* in which he emphasised the ethical aspects of religion against mere conformity with ritual requirements. Theologically, these ideas were expressed in the cult of Ahura Mazda, 'the Wise Lord', as the highest god, in opposition to beliefs never defined but which some have

thought included forms of Mithraism. Thus arose the 'dualistic' theology of later Zoroastrianism, which depicts creation not as the immediate rule of an omnipotent just god, but as a long contest between the divine forces of good and evil. This theology provides a simple solution for the problem of suffering, and may have influenced theories concerning the role of Satan in developing Christianity.

ZOSER (Djoser) Second king of Egypt's IIIrd Dynasty; he is traditionally said to have reigned for nineteen years during the 27th century BC. With his chief minister and architect, **Imhotep**, he built the first of the great stone pyramids at Saqqara, near his capital, Memphis.

ZULU Nguni-speaking group in Natal, southern Africa. In the early 19th century they joined with related peoples under their leader, Shaka, to form the Zulu empire; engaged in sporadic warfare with other African peoples and with the advancing European settlers, and were finally defeated at Ulundi in 1879, now capital of Kwazulu, one of South Africa's Bantu Homelands.

ZÜRICH, PEACE OF Agreement in 1859 between **Napoleon III** of France and Franz Joseph of Austria to settle the Italian problem after a general rebellion against Austrian rule. Lombardy was ceded to Piedmont, Venetia remained Austrian (to 1866); the central states of Italy voted to join Piedmont, and Nice and Savoy voted to become French (1860).

ZWINGLI, HULDREICH (1484–1531) Swiss religious reformer. He was pastor at Glarus, 1506, and rector and teacher of religion at Great Minster, Zürich, 1519, when he established the Protestant Reformation in Zurich, 1520–3; he failed to agree about doctrine with **Luther** and other German reformers, 1529; he served as chaplain in Zürich's army against the Swiss Catholics, and was killed at the Battle of Kappel.

ZYRIANS Finno-Ugrian speaking Arctic people, mostly inhabiting the Komi ASSR in the north-western USSR.

Index

1 Historical place names

Geographical names vary with time and with language, and there is some difficulty in treating them consistently in an historical atlas which covers the whole world from the beginning of human prehistory, especially for individual maps within whose time span the same place has been known by many different names. We have aimed at the simplest possible approach to the names on the maps, using the index to weld together the variations.

On the maps forms of names will be found in the following hierarchy of preference:-

a English conventional names or spellings, in the widest sense, for all principal places and features, e.g., Moscow, Vienna, Munich, Danube (including those that today might be considered obsolete when these are appropriate to the context, e.g., Leghorn).

b Names that are contemporary in terms of the maps concerned. There are here three broad categories:-

i names in the ancient world, where the forms used are classical, e.g., Latin or latinized Greek, but extending also to Persian, Sanskrit, etc.

ii names in the post-mediaeval modern world, which are given in the form (though not necessarily the spelling) current at the time of the map (e.g., St. Petersburg before 1914, not Leningrad); whose language reflects the sovereignty then existing, e.g., Usküb (Turkish) rather than Skoplje (Serbian) or Skopje (Macedonian) in maps showing Ottoman rule.

iii names in the present-day world, where the spelling generally follows that of *The Times Atlas of the World,* though in the interests of simplicity there has been a general omission of diacritics in spellings derived by transliteration from non-roman scripts, e.g., Sana rather than Şan'ā'.

Alternative names and spellings have occasionally been shown in brackets on the maps to aid in identification.

2 The Index

The index does not include every name shown on the maps. In general only those names are indexed which are of places, features, regions or countries where "something happens", i.e., which carry a date or symbol or colour explained in the key, or which are mentioned in the text.

Where a place is referred to by two or more different names in the course of the atlas, there will be a corresponding number of main entries in the index. The variant names in each case are given in brackets at the beginning of the entry, their different forms and origins being distinguished by such words as *now, later, formerly* and others included in the list of abbreviations *(right).*

"Istanbul *(form.* Constantinople, *anc.* Byzantium)" means that the page references to that city on maps dealing with periods when it was known as Istanbul follow that entry, but the page references pertaining to it when it had other names will be found under those other names.

Places are located generally by reference to the country in which they lie (exceptionally by reference to island groups or sea areas), this being narrowed down where necessary by location as E(ast), N(orth), C(entral), etc. The reference will normally be to the modern state in which the place now falls unless (a) there is a conventional or historical name which conveniently avoids the inevitably anachronistic ring of some modern names, e.g., Anatolia rather than Turkey, Mesopotamia rather than Iraq, or (b) the modern state is little known or not delineated on the map concerned, e.g., many places on the Africa plates can only be located as W.,E., Africa, etc.

Reference is generally to page number/map number (e.g., 114/2) unless the subject is dealt with over the plate as a whole, when the reference occurs as 114-5 (i.e., pages 114 and 115). All entries with two or more references have been given sub-headings where possible, e.g., Civil War 268/3. Battles are indicated by the symbol

Though page references are generally kept in numerical order, since this corresponds for the most part with chronological order, they have been rearranged occasionally where the chronological sequence would be obviously wrong, or in the interests of grouping appropriate references under a single sub-heading.

All variant names and spellings are cross-referenced in the form "Bourgogne (Burgundy)", except those which would immediately precede or follow the main entries to which they refer. The bracketed form has been chosen so that such entries may also serve as quick visual indications of equivalence. Thus Bourgogne (Burgundy) means not only "see under Burgundy" but also that Burgundy is another name for Bourgogne.

3 Abbreviations

a/c also called
Alb. Albanian
anc. ancient
Ar. Arabic
a/s also spelled
ASSR Autonomous Soviet Socialist Republic
Bibl. Biblical
Bulg. Bulgarian
C Century (when preceded by 17,18 etc.)
C Central
Cat. Catalan
Chin. Chinese
Cz. Czech
Dan. Danish
Dut. Dutch
E. East(ern)
Eng. English
Est. Estonian
f/c formerly called
Finn. Finnish
form. former(ly)
Fr. French
f/s formerly spelled
Ger. German
Gr. Greek
Heb. Hebrew
Hung. Hungarian
Indon. Indonesian
Ir. Irish
Is. Island
It. Italian
Jap. Japanese
Kor. Korean
Lat. Latin
Latv. Latvian
Lith. Lithuanian
Maced. Macedonian
Mal. Malay
med. mediaeval
mod. modern
Mong. Mongolian
N. North(ern)
n/c now called
Nor. Norwegian
n/s now spelled
NT New Testament
obs. obsolete
O.E. Old English
OT Old Testament
Pers. Persian
Pol. Polish
Port. Portuguese
Rom. Romanian
Russ. Russian
S. South(ern)
s/c sometimes called
Skr. Sanskrit
Som. Somali
Sp. Spanish
S. Cr. Serbo-Croat
SSR Soviet Socialist Republic
Sw. Swedish
Turk. Turkish
Ukr. Ukrainian
US(A) United States (of America)
var. variant
W. West(ern)
Wel. Welsh
W/G Wade-Giles
WW1 The First World War
WW2 The Second World War

Aetolian League–Antium

Aetolian League military confederation of ancient Greece 76/4
Afalou N Africa site of early man 32/2
Afars and Issas, French Territory of (form. French Somaliland now Rep. of Djibouti) NE Africa 295/1
Afghanistan under Abbasid sovereignty 135/1; under Mughal rule 173/1; independent sultanate 229/1; Anglo-Afghan war 261/1; territorial claim against Pakistan 281/3; establishment of republic 284/1; economy 218/1, 295/1; Soviet invasion 284/1
Africa early man 33/1,4; agricultural origins 39/1; early cultures 44-5; expansion of Christianity 100/1; Portuguese exploration 147/2; early trade 154; early European voyages of discovery 157/1; slave trade 166/2; early empires 167/1; 18C trade 199/1; European exploration 238/2; before partition 239/1; colonial strategy 240/3; partition 240-41; colonial empires 245/1; anti-colonial resistance 249/2; decolonisation 276/2; modern political developments 282-3
Africa (mod. Tunisia and Libya) Roman province 86/3, 89/1, 91/2; conversion to Christianity 72/1; Byzantine province 112/1
Africa Nova (mod. Tunisia) Roman province 86/3
Agadès (var. Agadez) W Africa 63/2, 136/2, 137/1, 154/2, 167/1, 241/1
Agathe (mod. Agde) SW France Ionian colony 75/1
Agathopolis Bulgaria Byzantine Empire 112/4
Agau tribe of NE Africa 137/1
Agde (Agathe)
Aggersborg N Denmark circular fortification 116/2
Aghlabids Muslim dynasty of N Africa 108/1, 135/1
Agincourt (mod. Azincourt) N France ⚔142/4
Aglar (Aquileia)
Agra N India region 173/1; centre of Mutiny 234/1
Agram (Zagreb)
Agrigentum (Gr. Acragas mod. Agrigento) Sicily Roman Empire 86/2, 3, 89/1, 91/1
Agropoli S Italy Saracen occupation 111/1
Aguascalientes state of C Mexico 227/1
Aguntum (mod. San Candido) N Italy 92/1
Ahar NW India site 64/2,3
Ahicchatra N India 64/2,3, 83/1, 131/3
Ahmadabad (Ahmedabad)
Ahmadi Kuwait oil terminal 285/3
Ahmadnagar W India sultanate 130/4; state 173/1
Ahmedabad (n/s Ahmadabad) W India industry 218/1, 235/3
Ahvenanmaa (Åland Islands)
Ahwaz (a/s Ahvaz) W Persia 82/3; oilfield 285/3
Aichi prefecture of C Japan 218/2; industry 242/1
Aigues-Mortes S France Mediterranean trade 144/1
Aigun (or Ai-hun) NE China treaty port 232/2
Ain Jalut Palestine ⚔128/1, 135/1
Ain Salah NW Africa Saharan trade 136/2, 146/1, 167/1
Ainu tribe of N Japan 35/2
Air early state of W Africa 137/1, 167/1
Aire NW France fort 193/1
Aisne river NE France WW1 252-3
Aitape New Guinea site of early man 33/4
Aix (or Aix-en-Provence anc. Aquae Sextiae) S France archbishopric 106/3; St Bartholomew Massacre 182/3; parlement 193/1
Aix-la-Chapelle (Ger. Aachen) W Germany Carolingian capital 109/6
Aizu N Japan 175/4
Ajanta C India Buddhist site 73/1
Ajayameru (mod. Ajmer) C India 83/1
Ajman United Arab Emirates 284/1
Ajmer (form. Ajayameru) N India Mughal province 173/1; British rule 234/1; industry 235/3
Ajnadain Palestine ⚔105/1
Akamagaseki (n/c Shimonoseki) W Japan 174/4
Akan W Africa early state 137/1
Akaroa S Island, New Zealand French colony 236/1
Akashi C Japan 175/4
Akhisar (Thyatira)
Akhtiar (Sevastopol)
Akita town and prefecture of N Japan 218/2; industry 243/1
Akizuki W Japan 174/4
Akjoujt W Africa stone age site 45/1
Akkadians people of Mesopotamia 54/3
Akkerman (from 1946 Belgorod-Dnestrovskiy anc. Tyras Rom. Cetatea Alba) S Russia Ottoman conquest 139/1; Ottoman control 170/1
'Akko (Acre)
Akkoyunlu Muslim dynasty of Anatolia 135/1
Ak-Mechet (Kzyl-Orda, Simferopol)
Akmolinsk (Tselinograd)
A-k'o-su (Aksu)
Akrotiri S Aegean Cretan colony 67/1
Aksai-Chin district of N India territorial dispute with China 281/4
Akşehir (Philomelium)
Aksu (a/s Aqsu Chin. A-k'o-su) Sinkiang trade 71/2; Muslim insurrection against China 175/1
Aktyubinsk Kazakhstan 230/2, 291/1
Alabama state of SE USA Civil War 233/1; 19C politics 225/2,3; Depression 267/1; income and population 289/2
Alacaluf Indian tribe of S Chile 149/1
Alagoas state of E Brazil 227/1
Alalakh (a/c Atchana) Syria 54/1, 57/1, 67/1
Alalia (or Aleria) Corsica Ionian colony 75/1
Alamannia (Alemannia)
Alamgirpur India stone age and Harappan site 64/2, 65/1
Åland Islands (Finn. Ahvenanmaa) SW Finland acquired by Russia 163/1; neutralised 265/1
Alans (Lat. Alani) E and W Europe, Africa tribal movements 89/1; 98-99
Alarcos S Spain ⚔124/3
Alaşehir (Philadelphia)
Alashiya (mod. Cyprus) early trade 54/1; under Hittite Empire 57/1; 59/2
Alaska state of USA purchase from Russia 230/2, 244/1; border dispute with Canada 246/3; income and population 289/2
Alatri (Aletrium)
Alawites people of NW Syria, uprising 261/2
Alba Fucens C Italy 87/1
Alba Iulia (anc. Apulum Hung. Gyulafehérvár Ger. Karlsburg) Romania Mithraic site 72/1
Albania Slav settlement 112/4; Black Death 143/1; Ottoman control 187/1; principality 215/2; Ottoman province 229/1; WW1 252-3; Muslim insurrection 267/2; inter-war alliances 264/2, 268/2; annexed by Italy 269/4; WW2 269/5, 272/1, 273/3; Cold War 293/1; economy 295/1
Albania ancient country of Caucasus vassal of Parthian Empire 79/3; 86/3, 89/1, 113/1
Albany (form. Fort Orange) NE USA surrenders to Dutch 161/2
Albany W Australia founded 237/5
Albazinsk SE Siberia founded 162/3
Alberta province of Canada economic development 219/3
Albertville (now Kalémié) E Belgian Congo 282/2
Alborán Island Morocco Spanish occupation 251/2
Albret region of SW France 151/4
Alcalá S Portugal site 42/2
Alcazarquivir (Al-Kasr-al-Kabir)
Aldeigjuborg (Staraya Ladoga)
Aleksandropol (Leninakan)
Alemanni tribe of C Europe 99/1
Alemannia region of C Europe 106/1, 107/3
Alençon N France fief annexed by France 151/4; provincial capital 193/1
Alep (Aleppo)
Aleppo (anc. Beroea a/c Yamkhad Fr. Alep Ar. Halab) Syria 54/1; bishopric 101/1; Byzantine Empire 113/1,5; early trade 135/1; conquest by Ottomans 139/1; Ottoman centre 170/1; economy 285/1
Aleria (Alalia)
Alesia (mod. Alise-Sainte-Reine) C France 86/3
Alessandria N Italy Lombard League 119/2; mediaeval city 123/4; Signorial domain 124/2
Aletum NW France monastery 93/3
Aletrium (mod. Alatri) C Italy 87/1
Aleutian Islands W Alaska 247/1; attacked by Japanese 271/1
Aleut tribe of Alaska 35/2
Alexander's Empire 76-77; 82/3
Alexandreschata (Alexandria Eschata)
Alexandretta (mod. Iskenderun) E Turkey Achaemenid Empire 79/1; ceded to Turkey 265/1
Alexandria (Ar. Al Iskandariyah) Egypt spread of Christianity 72/1; Alexander's route 76/1; Persian Empire 79/1; Roman Empire 86/3, 89/1, 91/1; Christian centre 92-3; patriarchate 101/2; trade 71/1, 82/4, 135/1, 144/1, 146/1, 154/2; early Jewish community 103/1; Arab conquest 105/1; conquered by Ottomans 139/1; WW2 273/3
Alexandria NW India Alexander's route 77/1
Alexandria (mod. Gulashkird) S Persia Alexander's route 77/1
Alexandria (mod. Charikar) Afghanistan 82/3
Alexandria (mod. Ghazni) Alexander's route 77/1; 82/3
Alexandria (later Merv since 1937 Mary) C Asia 77/1
Alexandria ad Caucasum Afghanistan Alexander's route 77/1
Alexandria Arachoton (mod. Qandahar Eng. Kandahar) Afghanistan Alexander's route 77/1; Achaemenid Empire 79/1; 82/3
Alexandria Areion (mod. Herat) Afghanistan Alexander's route 77/1; Achaemenid Empire 79/1; 82/3
Alexandria Eschata (a/c Alexandreschata) C Asia Alexander's route 77/1; Achaemenid Empire 79/1; 82/3
Alexandria Opiana NW India Alexander's route 77/1
Alexandria Prophthasia (mod. Farah) Afghanistan Alexander's route 77/1; Achaemenid Empire 79/1
Alexandria Troas W Anatolia Roman Empire 89/1
Al Fas (Fez)
Alger (Algiers)
Algeria under the Almohads 134/1; vassalised by Turks 186/1; Spanish conquests 186/2; economy under French rule 218/1; Ottoman province 228/1; French invasion 239/1; French colonisation 240-41, 244/1; immigration from France 209/2; overseas province of France 260/1; under Vichy control 269/5; civil war 282/3; independence 276/2; political development 283/1; economy 294-295
Algiers (Fr. Alger Sp. Argel Ar. Al Jaza'ir anc. Icosium) N Algeria Saharan trade 136/2; Mediterranean trade 144/1; Corsair city 167/1: Ottoman rule 170/1, 228/1; Spanish occupation 186/2; Allied landing WW2 273/3; 283/1
Algonkin (a/s Algonquin) Indian tribe of C Canada 35/2, 149/1
Al Hadhr (Hatra)
Al Hira Mesopotamia town of Parthian Empire 78/3
Al Hoceima (Alhucemas)
Alhucemas (n/s Al Hoceima) N Morocco Spanish occupation 251/2
Al Hudaydah (Hodeida)
Alice Springs C Australia 237/5
Aligarh N India centre of Mutiny 234/1
Ali Kosh Mesopotamia early village 40/1
Ali Murad NW India Harappan site 65/1
Alise-Sainte-Reine (Alesia)
Al Iskandariyah (Alexandria)
Al Jaza'ir (Algiers)
Al-Kasr-al-Kabir (Sp. Alcazarquivir a/c Battle of the Three Kings) Morocco ⚔167/1 (inset), 187/2
Al Khalil (Hebron)
Allahabad NE India Mughal province 173/1; industry 218/1
Allahdino NW India pre-Harappan site 65/1
Allenstein (Pol. Olsztyn) W Poland acquired by Germany after plebiscite 265/1
Allifae C Italy early town 87/1
Alma-Ata (until 1921 Vernyy) C Asia urban growth 290/3; industry 291/1
Al Madinah (Medina)
Al Mahdiya Tunisia Mediterranean trade 134/1
Al Makkah (Mecca)
Almalyk Mongolia bishopric 101/1
Almanza Spain ⚔192/3
Al Mawsil (Mosul)
Almeria S Spain Mediterranean trade 120/2, 134/1, 144/1
Almizaraque S Spain site 42/2
Almoravids Muslim dynasty of Morocco 135/1; North African empire 137/1
Almohads Muslim dynasty and empire of North Africa 134-5, 137/1
Alpes Cottiae Roman province, France/Italy, 89/1
Alpes Maritimae Roman province, France/Italy 89/1
Alpes Penninae Roman province, France/Italy 89/1
Alpirsbach SW Germany monastery 121/3
Al Qadisiya Mesopotamia ⚔78/3, 105/1
Al Qahirah (Cairo)
Al Quds (Jerusalem)
Al Raydaniyya N Egypt ⚔139/1
Alsace (anc. Alsatia Ger. Elsass) in German Empire 123/5; acquired by Habsburgs 150/2; Burgundian possession 151/3; acquired by French 192-3; customs union 217/1; WW1 252/2
Alsace-Lorraine (Ger. Elsass-Lothringen) region of E France annexed by German Empire 216/3; ceded to France 265/1
Alsatia (Alsace)
Alsium (mod. Palo) C Italy Roman colony 87/1
Altmark region of E Germany 119/1
Altona N Germany customs union 217/1
Altun Ha E Mexico Maya site 46/2
Alwa early Christian kingdom of the Sudan 137/1
Amalfi S Italy Byzantine port 120/2
Amara NW India pre-Harappan site 65/1
Amarapura C Burma early trade centre 177/1
Amasela N Turkey early archbishopric 93/1
Amasia (mod. Amasya) E Anatolia Roman Empire 89/1; Byzantine Empire 112/3
Amastris (earlier Sesamus) N Anatolia Byzantine Empire 112/3
Amasya (anc. Amasia) C Turkey Ottoman town 170/1
Amathus Cyprus ancient Greek colony 75/1
Ambianum (Amiens)
Amboina C Indonesia massacre of English 176/2; trade centre 177/1; Japanese invasion 271/1
Ambracia NW Greece 76/4
Ambriz Angola Portuguese settlement 239/1
Amchitka Aleutian Is, Alaska US air base 271/1
Amecameca Mexico on Cortés' route 159/2
America, Central (a/c Mesoamerica) early peoples 36-7; agricultural origins 38/1; early civilisations 46/2, 47/1; Aztec Empire 148/2; Indian tribes 149/1; early voyages of discovery 156/2; colonial expansion 165/1; 18C trade 199/1; exports and foreign investment 226/3; population 226/4; recent development 286-7
America, North early man 33/1, 36-7, 37/4; agricultural origins 38/1; early cultures 46/3, 47/1; Indian tribes 149/1; early voyages of discovery 156/1; colonial expansion 164-5; European colonial rivalry 194-5; 18C trade 199/1; immigration from Europe 209/2; industrialisation 219/1; range of buffalo 221/5; Peyote drug cult 221/6; Ghost dance 221/6. See also Canada, United States
America, South early peoples 36-7; agricultural origins 38/1; early civilisations 47/1, 4,5; Indian tribes 149/1; Inca Empire 149/3; early voyages of discovery 156/1; colonial expansion 165/1,2; 18C trade 199/1; revolts against Spain 202/1; industrialisation 219/1; Independence 226-7; immigration from Europe 209/2; economic development 286/2; modern politics 287/1; population 287/3
American Colonies trade 199/1
American Samoa (f/c Eastern Samoa) S Pacific 247/1, 277/2 (inset)
Amida (mod. Diyarbakir) E Anatolia 78/3; 89/1; archbishopric and monastery 93/1,3; trade 135/1
Amiens (anc. Samarobriva later Ambianum) N France bishopric 117/1; Burgundian possession 151/3; 17C revolt 185/1; provincial capital 193/1; French Revolution 203/2; industrial development 210/1; WW1 252-3
Amisus (mod. Samsun) N Anatolia Ionian colony 75/1; Roman Empire 86/3; early archbishopric 93/1; Byzantine Empire 112/3
Amiternum C Italy 87/1
Amman (Bibl. Rabbath Ammon anc. Philadelphia) Jordan 229/1, 285/1
Ammon, Sanctuary of Egypt Alexander's route 76/1
Amnisos Crete Mycenaean settlement 67/1,2
Amöneburg W Germany monastery 100/3
Amorites people of Arabia, migrations 54/3; kingdom 55/2
Amorium C Anatolia Byzantine Empire, 112-3
Amoy (W/G Hsia-men) S China early trade 147/1, 161/1; industry 218/1; treaty port 232/2; Anglo-French attacks 233/1; Japanese influence 243/2; occupied by Japanese 263/3, 268/3, 271/1
Amphipolis N Greece ⚔74/4, 78/3; Roman Empire 91/1; early church 93/1
Amri NW India Harappan site 65/1
Amritsar N India town of Punjab 235/3, 280/1, 281/3; political disturbances under British rule 261/1
Amselfeld (Kosovo)
Amsterdam Netherlands trading port 180/3; 16C urban development 180/1; 18C financial centre 181/2; imperial trade 198-9; industrial development 210/1, 212/1
Amud Palestine site of early man 33/1
Amur River (Chin. Hei-lung Chiang) Russia/China border 162/3; Russian conflict with Japan 268/2; border conflict with China 279/1
Anadyrsk E Siberia founded 162/3
Anagnia (mod. Anagni) C Italy early town 87/1
Anan N Persia early urban centre 52/1
Anantapur S India ceded to Britain 172/3
Anatolia early settlement 41/1; early trade routes 54/1; ethnic movements 54/3; Muslim conquest 135/2; Ottoman conquest 139/1; Black Death 143/1 See also Asia Minor
Anatolic Theme Anatolia district of Byzantine Empire 112/3
Anazarbus SW Anatolia early archbishopric 93/1; early Jewish community 103/1; Byzantine Empire 112/3
Ancona N Italy Roman Empire 87/1, 91/1
Ancyra (mod. Ankara obs. Eng. Angora) W Anatolia Alexander's route 76/1; Roman Empire 86/3, 89/1, 91/1; early archbishopric 93/1; Byzantine Empire 112-3
Åndalsnes C Norway WW2 269/5
Andalusia (Sp. Andalucía) region of S Spain reconquest by Castile 124/3
Andaman Islands Indian territory of Bay of Bengal 235/3, 245/1
Andegavum (earlier Juliomagus mod. Angers) W France 92/1
Anderab Afghanistan Alexander's route 82/3
Andernach (anc. Antunnacum) W Germany ⚔118/3
Andhra region of E India 65/1
Andhra Pradesh state of S India 281/3
Andover S England Industrial Revolution 201/1
Anegray E France early monastery 100/3
Anga region of NE India 65/1, 83/1,2
Angarsk S Siberia urban growth 290/3; industry 291/1
Angers (anc. Juliomagus med. Andegavum) W France 17C revolt 185/1; French Revolution 203/2
Angkor Cambodia Buddhist site 73/1
Angkor Borei S Cambodia Hindu-Buddhist remains 133/2
Angkor Wat Cambodia temple complex 133/2
Angles tribe of NW Europe, migrations 94/1, 98/1
Anglo-Egyptian Sudan Ottoman territory under British control 245/1; condominium 240/2, 260/1, 276/1
Angola SW Africa Portuguese discovery 147/2; early Portuguese trade 159/1; source of slaves 166/2; Portuguese colonisation 218/1, 240-41, 245/1; anti-Portuguese risings 249/2; independence 276/2; political development 283/1; economy 295/1
Angora (Ankara)
Angostura Venezuela 226/2
Angoulême (anc. Iculisma) C France provincial capital 193/1
Angoumois C France region annexed to France 151/4
Anguilla island of West Indies settled by English 160/3; independence 277/2 (inset)
Anhalt C Germany principality and duchy 119/1, 191/1; Reformation 182/2; 216/3
An-hsi N China trading port 71/1
An-hui (Anhwei)
Anhwei (W/G An-hui) province of E China under the Ming 169/1; Manchu expansion 175/1; T'ai-p'ing control 233/1
Ani Persia Byzantine Empire 113/1
Anjira NW India pre-Harappan site 65/1
Anjou region of NW France British possession 125/1; annexed by France 150/1, 151/4; province of France 193/1
Ankara (anc. Ancyra obs. Eng. Angora) W Turkey ⚔128/4, 139/1; revolt against Ottoman rule 170/1; Ottoman Empire 229/3
Ankole Uganda kingdom 167/1, 239/1
Annaba (Bône, Hippo Regius)
Annam N Indo-China under T'ang control 127/2; under Mongol control 129/1; expansion and early trade 177/1; anti-French resistance in 19C 248/1; French protectorate 261/1
Annapolis (until 1694 Anne Arundel Town earlier Providence) NE USA 161/2
Annesoi NW Anatolia early monastery 93/3
An-p'ing NE China Han prefecture 81/2
Ansbach S Germany Reformation 183/1; margraviate 191/1
An-shan Manchuria Russo-Japanese War 242/3; industry 263/3, 278/3
Antakya (anc. Antioch Lat. Antiochia) E Turkey Ottoman centre 170/1
Antalya (Attalia)
Antananarivo (Tananarive)
Antibes (Antipolis)
Antietam (a/c Sharpsburg) NE USA ⚔223/1
Antigua island of West Indies settlement by British 160/3; colony 227/1; independence 277/2 (inset)
An-ting NW China Han commanderie 81/2
Antioch (Lat. Antiochia mod. Antakya) E Anatolia Mediterranean trade 71/1, 82/4, 135/1; spread of Christianity 72/1; Persian Empire 79/1; Roman Empire 86/3; patriarchate 93/1; archbishopric 101/2; Jewish community 103/1; Byzantine rule 112-3, 121/2; principality 134/3
Antioch C Anatolia early archbishopric 93/1
Antiochia (anc. Antioch mod. Antakya) E Anatolia fortified Roman town 88/3, 91/1
Antiochia Margiana Persia trade 82/4
Antipolis (mod. Antibes) SE France Ionian colony 75/1
Antium (mod. Anzio) C Italy Roman colony 87/1

Antofagasta–Bad Cannstatt

Antofagasta region of N Chile dispute with Peru and Bolivia 227/5
Antrim N Ireland massacre of Catholics 184/2
An-tung *(now* Tan-tung) Manchuria treaty port 232/2; Russo-Japanese war 242/3; industry 263/3
Antunnacum (Andernach)
Antwerp *(Fr.* Anvers *Dut.* Antwerpen) Belgium Hansa city 144/1, 145/3; trade 154/2; 16C and 18C financial centre 180/1, 181/2; town of Spanish Netherlands 185/1; industrial development 212/1; WW1 252-3; WW2 273/3
Anuradhapura Ceylon Buddhist site 73/1
Anvers (Antwerp)
Anxur *(later* Tarracina *mod.* Terracina) C Italy 86/2
An-yang N China early urban settlement 53/1; Shang site 62/2
Anyer Lor W Java Iron Age site 132/1
Anzio *(anc.* Antium) C Italy WW2 273/3
Aomori N Japan town and prefecture 243/1; industry 243/1
Aornos *(mod.* Tash-Kurghan) Afghanistan Alexander's route 77/1
Ao-ts'ang C China Han prefecture 81/2
Aozou Strip N Chad occupied by Libya 283/1
Apache Indian tribe of SW USA, 35/2, 149/1
Apache Pass SW USA on trail west 220/1
Apamea Syria Peace of 77/3; Roman Empire 88/3, 91/1; early archbishopric 93/1
Apesokari Crete site 67/2
Aphrodisias SW France Ionian colony 75/1
Apodhoulou Crete site 67/2
Apollonia NE Greece Dorian colony 75/1; Roman Empire 86/3, 89/1, 91/1; early church 93/1
Apollonia *(mod.* Sozopol) Bulgaria Ionian colony 75/1
Apollonia Libya Greek colony 75/1; Roman Empire 91/1; Byzantine Empire 113/1
Apollinopolis (Edfu)
Apologos Persian Gulf port 71/1, 78/2, 79/3
Appenwihr W Germany Hallstatt site 84/1
Appenzell Switzerland Reformation 183/1
Appian Way (Via Appia)
Appomattox SE USA Confederates surrender 223/1
Apremont E France Hallstatt site 84/1
Apulia region of SE Italy unification with Naples 124/2
Apulum *(mod.* Alba Iulia) Romania Roman Empire 89/1, 91/1
Aqaba *(anc.* Aela *or* Aelana) Jordan WW1 253/4
Aqsu (Aksu)
Aquae Sextiae *(mod.* Aix) France Roman Empire 86/3
Aquileia *(med.*Aglar) N Italy Mediterranean trade 71/1; Latin colony 87/1; Roman Empire 86/3, 89/1, 91/1; early archbishopric 92/1, 107/3; monastery 93/3; invaded by Goths 99/1; Byzantine Empire 112/1
Aquincum *(mod.* Budapest) Hungary Roman Empire 89/1, 91/1
Aquino (Aquinum)
Aquinum *(mod.* Aquino) C Italy early town 87/1
Aquisgranum (Aachen)
Aquitaine *(anc.* Aquitania *mod.* Guyenne) region of SW France English possession 125/1; Black Death 143/1
Aquitania *(mod.* Aquitaine *later* Guyenne) Roman province of Gaul 89/1; invasion by Vandals 98/1; Visigothic territory conquered by Franks 106/1,3
Arabaya Arabia satrapy of Achaemenid Empire 79/1
Arabia early trade 71/1, 146/1; spread of Judaism 72/1; early Christian activity 100/1; centre of Islam 105/1; under Abbasid Caliphate 108/1; Egyptian expedition 239/1; WW1 253/4
Arabia Eudaemon S Arabia port 82/4
Arabian Gulf (Persian Gulf)
Arabia Petraea Roman province of N Arabia, 89/1
Arabissos E Anatolia Byzantine Empire 113/1
Arabs (of Mansura) NW India 131/1
Arabs (of Multan) NW India 131/1
Arachosia *(a/c* Harauvatish) Afghanistan ancient province of Persian and Alexander's Empires, 77/1, 82/3, 83/1
Aradus *(Bibl.* Arvad *later* Arwad *Fr.* Rouad) Syria Phoenician city 75/1; Alexander's route 76/1; early Jewish community 103/1
Arago S France site of early man 32/2
Aragon *(Sp.* Aragón) region of E Spain at time of Reconquista 124/3; rural uprisings 143/1; acquired by Habsburgs 150/1,2; kingdom 186/2
Arakan district of SW Burma Islamic state 133/2,3; British control 177/1; annexed by British 234/2, 235/3
Aralsk C Asia 291/1
Aramaeans people of Syria, 56/3, 60-1
Arapaho C USA Plains Indian tribe 149/1
Arash N Caucasus conquered by Ottomans 171/1
Araucanian S America Andean Indian tribe 149/1
Arausio *(mod.* Orange) S France 92/1
Arawak S America Indian tribe 149/1
Arbailu *(a/c* Arbela *mod.* Arbil) Mesopotamia 54/1
Arbe (Rab)
Arbela *(a/c* Arbailu *mod.* Arbil) Mesopotamia Alexander's route 76/1; town of Parthian Empire 78/3; under Alexander 82/3; early archbishopric 93/1, 101/1
Arcadiopolis Bulgaria Byzantine Empire 113/1
Archangel *(Russ.* Arkhangelsk) N Russia founded 157/1, 163/1; Revolution and Allied occupation 259/1; WW2 273/3; growth 290/3; industry 291/1
Arcole N Italy⚔205/1
Arcot S India ceded to British 172/3;⚔194/2
Ardabil Azerbaijan early trade 135/1
Ardea N Italy ancient town 87/1
Ardennes *forest* Belgium/France WW1 252-3; WW2 ⚔273/3
Ardmore Ireland early bishopric 92/1
Arelate *(mod.* Arles) S France Roman Empire 89/1, 90/1; archbishopric 92/1
Arène Candide SE France site 43/1
Arequipa Peru early Spanish city 158/1
Arezzo *(anc.* Arretium) C Italy mediaeval city 124/2
Argel (Algiers)
Argentina independence from Spain 226-7, 244/1; exports and foreign investment 226/3; population 226/4; industrialisation and economy 219/1, 286-7, 294-295
Argentoratum *(mod.* Strasbourg) E France Mithraic site 72/1
Arghun early kingdom of NW India 130/4
Arginusae islands of the Aegean⚔74/4
Argissa Greece site 43/1
Argonne NE France WW1 253/3 (inset)
Argos S Greece 74/3
Arguin island off NW Africa Portuguese settlement 147/2, 166/1
Århus *(a/s* Aarhus) C Denmark early bishopric 101/2, 116/2
Aria *(a/c* Haraiva) ancient region of Afghanistan 77/1, 82/3
Arica Peru trading post 158/1
Arickara E USA⚔221/4
Ariha (Jericho)
Arikamadur S India site 64/3
Ariminum *(mod.* Rimini) N Italy Latin colony 87/1; archbishopric 92/1
Arizona state of USA Depression 267/1; income and population 289/2
Arjunayanas tribe of N India 82/5
Arkansas state of C USA 19C politics 225/2,3; Depression 267/1; income and population 289/2
Arkhanes Crete settlement and palace 67/1,2
Arkhangelsk (Archangel)
Arlberg Austria tunnel 257/2
Arles *(anc.* Arelate *or* Arelas) S France early archbishopric 106/3; mediaeval kingdom 119/1; mediaeval trade 120/1
Armagh N Ireland archbishopric 92/1, 117/1; monastery 100/3
Armagnac region of SW France under English rule 125/1; annexed to France 151/4
Armenia *(anc.* Urartu) country of Caucasus spread of Christianity 72/1; Alexander's Empire 76/1, 82/3; part of Kushan Empire 78/3; Roman province 89/1, 86/3, 91/2; Muslim conquest 105/1; Ottoman Empire 229/1; Independence after WW1 265/1; Soviet Socialist Republic 290/2
Armenia, Lesser region of Asia Minor 134/3
Armeniac Theme Anatolia division of Byzantine Empire 112/3
Armenians emigration from Turkey 265/3
Armenoi Crete site 67/2
Armorica *(mod.* Brittany *and* Normandy) region of NW France, settlement by Britons 98/1
Arnhem Land N Australia Pleistocene site 48/2
Arpi C Italy early town 87/1
Arpino (Arpinum)
Arpinum *(mod.* Arpino) C Italy early town 87/1
Arrapkha Mesopotamia trading town 54/1
Arras *(anc.* Nemetocenna) N France early bishopric 117/1; fort 193/1; French Revolution 203/2; WW1 252-3
Arretium *(mod.* Arezzo) C Italy Etruscan city 75/1, 86/2; Roman Empire 91/1
Arsamosata E Anatolia city of Kushan Empire 78/3
Arsinoe *(older* Crocodilopolis) Egypt trade 82/4; Roman Empire 89/1; early Jewish community 103/1
Arsinoe Libya ancient town 89/1
Artacoana Afghanistan Alexander's route 77/1
Ártánd Hungary Thracian/Scythian site 85/1
Artashat Caucasus patriarchate 93/1
Artaxata Armenia Kushan Empire 78/3; Roman Empire 89/1
Artemision (Cape Artemisium)
Artois region of NE France Burgundian possession 151/3,4; province of France 193/1; WW1 252-3
Aruba island of Dutch West Indies 227/1, 244/1, 277/2 (inset)
Arunachal Pradesh *(form.* North East Frontier Agency) Union of NE India 281/3,4; frontier dispute with China 279/1
Arvad (Arwad)
Arvernis C France monastery 93/3
Arwad *(anc.* Aradus *Bibl.* Arvad *Fr.* Rouad) Syria Assyrian Empire 57/2; Crusader states 134/3
Asaak Persia town of Parthian Empire 79/3
Asab Abu Dhabi oilfield 285/4
Asahikawa N Japan 243/1
Asante W Africa early state 166/1, 239/1
Ascalon *(mod.* Ashqelon) S Palestine Egyptian Empire 58/2; Philistine city 75/1; early church 93/1; Venetian naval victory 121/2
Ascension Island S Atlantic British colony 244/1, 276/1,2
Ascoli Piceno (Asculum)
Ascoli Satriano (Ausculum)
Asculum *(a/c* Asculum Picenum *mod.* Ascoli Piceno) N Italy 87/1
Ashdod *(Lat.* Azotus) Palestine Philistine city 75/1
Ash Hollow C USA⚔221/4
Ashkhabad *(from 1919-27* Poltoratsk) SW Central Asia industry 291/1
Ashqelon (Ascalon)
Ash Sham (Damascus)
Ash Shariqah (Sharjah)
Ashtishat Caucasus monastery 93/3
Ashur *(mod.* Sharqat) Mesopotamia early urban centre 52/1; early trade 54/1; Assyrian Empire 56-7
Asia early man 33/1,4, 34-5, 37/1; agricultural origins 39/1; early trade routes 70-1, 146-7; tribal movements 94-5; expansion of Christianity 101/1; early empires 108-9; Chinese expansion 80/3, 127/2, 175/1; Mongol expansion 128-9; religious distribution 133/3; early voyages of discovery 157/1; Russian expansion 162/3; 18C trade 199/1; industrialisation 218/1; colonial empires 245/1; anti-colonial resistance 248/1
Asia *(Byzantine name* Asiana) Roman province of Anatolia 86/3, 89/1
Asiago N Italy WW1 253/3
Asia Minor spread of civilisation 52/1; conversion to Christianity 72/1, 101/2; Ottoman control 170/1 See also Anatolia
Asiana (Asia)
Asir SW Arabia Ottoman Empire 229/1
Asisium *(mod.* Assisi) N Italy 87/1
Asmaka ancient kingdom of S India 83/2
Asoka's Empire India 82-3
Aspanvar Mesopotamia town of Sasanian Empire 79/3
Aspendus SW Anatolia Dorian colony 75/1
Aspern/Essling Austria⚔205/1
Assam state of NE India Mongol control 129/1; conquered by Burmese 177/1; British control 232/2; 234/2, 235/3, 280/2, 281/3,4
Asselar W Africa site of early man 33/1
Assos (Lat. Assus) W Anatolia Aeolian colony 75/1; early church 93/1
Assyria empire 56-7; Roman province 89/1
Assyrians people of Middle East 60-61; risings in N Iraq 261/2
Astacus *(mod.* Izmit) NW Anatolia Dorian colony 75/1
Astarac SW France independent fief 151/4
Asti N Italy Lombard League 119/1
Astorga (Asturica Augusta)
Astoria NW USA fur station 220/1
Astrabad Ardashir Mesopotamia town of Sasanian Empire 79/3
Astrakhan S Russia occupied by Mongols 128/4; economy 162/2, 231/1; Tartar khanate 163/1; urban growth 231/1; Bolshevik seizure 259/1; WW2 273/3
Asturias region of N Spain kingdom 106/3, 108/1; part of Castile 124/3; political unrest 264/2
Asturica Augusta *(mod.* Astorga) N Spain Roman Empire 88/1; bishopric 92/1
Asunción Paraguay early Spanish settlement 158/1; 227/1
Asuristan Mesopotamia province of Achaemenid Empire 79/3
Asyut *(anc.* Lycopolis) S Egypt trade 135/1; 284/1
Atacama *(Sp.* Atacameño) S America Andean Indian tribe 47/4, 149/1
Atacama Desert Chile/Peru War of the Pacific 227/5
Atacameño (Atacama)
A-tan *(Eng.* Aden) S Arabia early trade with China 146/1
Atchana (Alalakh)
Athabaskan Indian tribe of Canada 35/2
Athenae *(Eng.* Athens *mod. Gr.* Athinai) Greece Roman Empire 86/3, 89/1, 91/1
Athenopolis SE France Ionian colony 75/1
Athens *(Lat.* Athenae *mod. Gr.* Athinai) Greece Mycenaean palace 67/1; Greek parent state 75/1; cultural centre 74/2; Persian wars 74/3; war with Sparta 74/4; 76/1,4; bishopric 93/1; invaded by Goths 99/1; early Jewish community 103/1; Byzantine Empire 112-3; WW1 253/3; WW2 269/5, 273/3
Athinai (Athens)
Athribis N Egypt early Jewish community 103/1
Athura Mesopotamia satrapy of Achaemenid Empire 79/1
Atjeh *(n/s* Aceh *var.* Acheh *a/s* Achin) N Sumatra Islamic state 133/2,3; early trade 176/2
Atlanta SE USA⚔223/1; strike 267/1; industry 289/1
Atlantic Ocean Viking voyages 111/4; U-Boat warfare WW2 273/2
Atropatene (Azerbaijan)
Attalia *(mod.* Antalya) S Anatolia early church 93/1; Byzantine Empire 112-3
Attica ancient state of SE Greece 74/3, 76/4, 91/2
Attigny NE France Frankish royal residence 106/3
Attirampakkan and Gudiyam Cave S India Stone Age site 64/2
Attleborough E England rebellion 185/1
Attu Island Aleutians, W Alaska Japanese attack 271/1
Auch *(anc.* Elimberrum *later* Augusta Auscorum) SE France *parlement* 193/1
Auckland N Island, New Zealand province and second capital 236/1
Audenarde (Oudenaarde)
Auerstädt E Germany 205/1
Aufidena C Italy early town 87/1
Augila *(n/a* Awjilah) Libya early trade 137/1
Augsburg *(anc.* Augusta Vindelicorum) S Germany town of Swabia 118/1; mediaeval trade centre 145/3; 16C financial centre 180/1; imperial city 191/1
Augusta W Australia early settlement 237/5
Augusta Auscorum (Auch)
Augusta Rauricorum *(mod.* Augst) Switzerland Roman Empire 90/1
Augusta Taurinorum *(mod.* Turin) N Italy early bishopric 92/1
Augusta Treverorum *(mod.* Trier *Eng.* Treves) W Germany Mithraic site 72/1; Roman Empire 89/1, 90/1; archbishopric 92/1; early Jewish community 103/1
Augusta Vindelicorum *(mod.* Augsburg) S Germany Roman Empire 89/1, 91/1
Augustodunum *(mod.* Autun) C France Roman Empire 89/1, 90/1; early bishopric 92/1
Augustów NE Poland WW1 253/3
Auliye-Ata (Dzhambul)
Aulon *(later* Avlona *mod.* Vlorë) Albania Dorian colony 75/1
Auranitis region of Judaea 102/2
Aurelian Way (Via Aurelia)
Aurunci early tribe of C Italy, 86/2
Auschwitz *(correctly* Auschwitz – Birkenau *Pol.* Oświęcim) concentration camp 272/1
Ausculum *(a/c* Ausculum Apulum *mod.* Ascoli Satriano) C Italy early town 87/1
Austerlitz *(mod.* Slavkov) Czechoslovakia⚔205/1
Australia *(originally called* New Holland) before the Europeans 48/1,2; early voyages of discovery and exploration 157/3, 237/2,3; early trade 237/4; settlement and development 237/5; emergence of Commonwealth 245/1; dominion status 277/1; economy and industrialisation 218/1, 266/3, 295/1
Austrasia the eastern Frankish Empire 107/1
Austria *(Ger.* Österreich) German settlement 119/1; Black Death 143/1; acquired by Habsburgs 141/1, 150/1,2; attacked by Ottomans 170/1; early industry 190/2; archduchy 191/1; Habsburg conquests 196/1, 197/3; opposition to Napoleon 204-5; Alpine tunnels and railways 257/2; inter-war alliances 264/2, 268/1; socio-political change 267/2; annexed by Germany 269/4, 272/1; Allied occupation zones 275/1; EFTA 274/2; economy 295/1
Austro-Hungarian Empire agriculture and peasant emancipation 178/1; Military Frontier with Ottoman Empire 197/3; population growth 208/3,4; industrial revolution 210/1, 213/1; customs frontier abolished 211/2; ethnic composition 214/1; in Crimean War 230/4; growth in armaments 250; European alliances 250-51; overseas trade 256-7; WW1 252-3; dismantled 265/1
Autesiodorum *(mod.* Auxerre) C France monastery 93/3, 106/3
Autum (Augustodunum)
Auvergne region of C France English possession 125/1; annexed to France 150/1, 151/4; French province 193/1
Auxerre *(anc.* Autosiodorum) C France mediaeval town 120/1, 121/4
Auximum N Italy Roman colony 87/1
Ava C Burma political centre 133/2,3; old capital 177/1
Avanti region of C India 83/1,2
Avaricum *(mod.* Bourges) C France Roman Empire 86/3
Avaris *(a/c* Tanis) Lower Egypt Hyksos capital 58/1
Avars *(Chin.* Juan-juan) ancient people of Asia and Europe 94/1, 98-9; kingdom destroyed 107/3
Avellino (Abellinum)
Avenio (Avignon)
Avesnes N France fort 193/1
Avignon *(anc.* Avenio) S France in Great Schism 143/1 (inset); Papal enclave 193/1; annexed by France 203/3
Avila C Spain expulsion of Jews 102/3
Avlona *(Gr.* Aulon *mod.* Vlorë *It.* Valona) Albania Byzantine Empire 112-3; Ottoman conquest 139/1
Avranches NW France 17C revolt 185/1
Awdaghost W Africa trans-Saharan trade 136/1,2, 167/1
Awjilah (Augila)
Axel S Netherlands town of Dutch Republic 185/1
Axim Ghana early Dutch settlement 166/1 (inset)
Axum ancient kingdom of NE Africa, 45/1, 71/1, 105/1, 137/1
Ayacucho Peru⚔226/2
Aydhab Sudan early trade 135/1
Aydin W Anatolia emirate 138/2, 139/1
Ayia Irini W Aegean ancient site 67/1
Ayia Pelagia Crete site 67/2
Ayia Triadha Crete Mycenaean village and palace 67/1,2
Aylesbury S England Industrial Revolution 201/1
Aymará Andean Indian tribe of S America, 149/1
Ayodhya *(earlier* Saketa) NC India site 64/3; town of Kosala 83/1
Ayutthaya *(a/s* Ayuthia *properly* Phra Nakhon Si Ayutthaya) S Thailand early political centre 133/2,3; early trade 177/1
Ayyubids Muslim dynasty, Egypt 135/1; Arabia 137/1
Azad Kashmir district of Pakistan 280/1
Azak *(mod.* Azov) S Russia Ottoman conquest 139/1
Azerbaijan *(anc.* Atropatene) country of the Caucasus province of Achaemenid Empire 79/3; Muslim conquest 105/1; under Abbasid sovereignty 135/1; Ottoman conquest 171/1; acquired by Russia 163/1, 229/1; independence after WW1 265/1; Soviet Socialist Republic 290/2
Azincourt (Agincourt)
Azores *(Port.* Açores) islands of N Atlantic Portuguese discovery 147/2; trade 158/1; Portuguese colony 244/1
Azotus *(mod.* Ashdod) Palestine bishopric 93/1; in Judaea 102/2
Azov *(Turk.* Azak) S Russia Ottoman town 170/1
Aztalan C USA Hopewell site 46/3
Aztec Empire Mexico growth 148/2; early economy 155/1; conquest by Spain 159/2
Baalbek (Heliopolis)
Babirush Mesopotamia satrapy of Achaemenid Empire 79/1
Babylon Mesopotamia early urban settlement 52/1; centre of Amorite kingdom 55/2; town of Parthian Empire 71/1; Achaemenid Empire 79/1; Alexander's route 77/1, 82/3; Jewish community 103/1
Babylonia ancient country of Mesopotamia fall of 56-7; under Alexander 77/1, 82/3
Baçain (Bassein)
Bactra *(a/c* Zariaspa *mod.* Balkh) Afghanistan silk route 70/2; Alexander's route 77/1, 82/3,4
Bactria *(a/c* Bactriana *Pers.* Bakhtrish *Chin.* Ta-hsia) ancient country of Afghanistan 71/1, 77/1, 82/3
Badajoz SW Spain⚔204/1
Badakhshan district of Bactria in N Afghanistan early trade 55/1; under Uzbek khans 171/1
Bad Axe N USA⚔221/4
Bad Cannstatt W Germany late Hallstatt site 85/1

California–Ch'ieh-mo

California state of SW USA ceded by Mexico 227/2; 19C politics 235/2,3; Depression 266/1; income and population 289/2; immigration from China and Japan 209/2
Callao Peru trade 158/1, 199/1
Callatis Bulgaria Ionian colony 75/1
Calleva (*mod.* Silchester) S England Roman Empire 88/1
Calliena NW India port 82/4
Callipolis (*mod.* Gallipoli) S Italy Greek colony 75/1
Calne SW England Industrial Revolution 201/1
Calusa Indian tribe of SE USA 149/1
Camarina Sicily Dorian colony 74/4, 75/1; Roman Empire 86/3
Cambaluc Mongolia early bishopric 101/1
Cambay NW India trading centre 172/2
Cambodia (*known formally as* Democratic Kampuchea *earlier* Khmer Republic) early sites 132/1; temple kingdoms 133/2; invaded by Siam and Vietman 177/1; French protectorate 261/2; independence 277/2; military growth 278/2; 279/1; Vietnamese war 292/4; economy 295/1
Cambrai N France early bishopric 117/1; centre of religious dissent 122/1; Burgundian possession 151/3; WW1 253/3 (inset)
Cambria (*mod.* Wales) expansion of Christianity 100/3
Cambridge E England Industrial Revolution 201/1
Camden SE USA ⚔164/3
Camerinum (*mod.* Camerino) N Italy Roman Empire 87/1
Cameroon (*f/s* Cameroons, Cameroun *Ger.* Kamerun) country of W Africa 218/1; German colony 240-41, 245/1; revolt 249/2; independence 276/2; political development 283/1; economy 218/1, 295/1
Cammin (*mod.* Kamień Pomorski) NW Poland founded by Germans 140/2
Campa forest Indian tribe of S America 149/1
Campania region of C Italy Roman Empire 87/1, 91/2
Campeche province of S Mexico 227/1
Camulodunum (*mod.* Colchester) S England Roman Empire 88/1, 90/1
Cana (*a/s* Cane) S Arabia early port 71/1, 82/4
Canada early trade 198/4, 199/2; immigration from Europe 209/2; economic development 219/1,3, 266/3, 295/1; Confederation 244/1; boundary dispute with USA 246/3; NATO 293/1; economy 295/1
Çanakkale (*f/s* Chanak) W Turkey Greco-Turkish War 229/3
Çanakkale Boğazi (Dardanelles)
Canal de Briare N France 193/1
Canal Royal S France 193/1
Canal Zone Panama 246/2
Canary Islands Portuguese exploration 147/2; on early trade routes 159/1; Spanish sovereignty 244/1
Canaveral, Cape (*for a short time called* Cape Kennedy) SE USA 156/2
Canberra SE Australia capital territory 237/5
Çandar (*a/c* Kastamonu) early emirate of N Anatolia 139/1
Candelaria W Cuba Soviet missile site 293/6
Candia (*mod.* Iraklion) Crete Mediterranean trade 144/1
Candida Casa S Scotland monastery 93/3, 100/3
Canea (*mod. Gr.* Khania) Crete WW2 269/5
Canhasan C Anatolia site 41/1
Çankırı (Gangra)
Cannae S Italy Roman Empire 86/3
Canterbury (*anc.* Durovernum *ecclesiastical Lat.* Cantuaria) S England monastery 100/3 and bishopric 101/2,3; archbishopric 117/1; Industrial Revolution 201/1
Canterbury S Island, New Zealand 236/1
Cantigny NE France WW1 253/3 (inset)
Canton (*Chin.* Kuang-chou) S China trade 127/2, 145/4, 147/1, 154/2, 159/1, 161/1, 168/2, 177/1, 199/1; T'ang city 109/1; treaty port 232/2; Anglo-French campaign 233/1; captured by Kuomintang 262/1; captured by Japanese 268/2, 271/1; industry 218/1, 263/3, 278/3
Canton River S China first European visit 157/1
Cantuaria (*mod.* Canterbury) archbishopric 92/1
Canusium (*mod.* Canosa di Puglia) S Italy Roman Empire 87/1
Caparcotna Palestine Roman Empire 91/1
Cape Artemisium (*mod.Gr.* Artemision) E Greece ⚔74/3
Cape Bojador NW Africa ⚔166/1
Cape Breton Island E Canada French possession 195/1
Cape Coast Castle (*a/c* Cape Coast) Ghana early British settlement 166/1 (inset), 239/1
Cape Colony S Africa captured by British from Dutch 194/2, 239/1; British colony 241/1, 244/1 (inset); immigration from Europe 209/2
Cape Finisterre NW Spain ⚔194/3
Cape Flats S Africa site of early man 32/4
Cape of Good Hope S Africa first European voyage 157/1; Dutch settlement 161/1
Cape Province S Africa established by Dutch East India Co. 167/1
Cape St. Vincent S Portugal ⚔194/3
Cape Town South Africa Dutch settlement 167/1; trade 199/1
Cape Verde Islands W Africa Portuguese exploration 147/2, 166/1; Portuguese sovereignty 244/1; independence 276/2, 283/1
Capitanata region of C Italy part of Kingdom of Naples 124/2
Capodistria (Koper)
Caporetto SW Austria-Hungary WW1 ⚔253/3
Cappadocia (*Pers.* Katpatuka) country of E Anatolia Alexander's Empire 76/1, 82/3; independent state 86/3; Roman province 89/1; Byzantine province 112/3
Capsa (*mod.* Gafsa) Tunisia Roman Empire 89/1
Capua S Italy Mithraic site 72/1; Roman Empire 87/1, 91/1; Jewish community 103/1
Carabobo Venezuela ⚔226/2
Caracas Venezuela colonised 165/1
Carajá forest Indian tribe of C Brazil, 149/1
Carales (*a/s* Caralis *mod.* Cagliari) Sardinia Roman Empire 86/2, 89/1; archbishopric 92/1
Carchemish (*Turk.* Karkamiş) E Anatolia 54/1, 57/1,2, 67/3
Cardiff S Wales Industrial Revolution 201/1
Cardigan early principality of Wales 125/1
Caria (*Per.* Karka) country of W Asia Minor Persian province 74/3, 75/1; Roman Empire 91/2
Carib Indian tribe of Caribbean 149/1
Caribbean early voyages of discovery 156/2; European settlement 158/1, 160/3; colonial expansion 165/1; imperial trade 199; US involvement 247/4
Carinthia (*Ger.* Kärnten) province of S Austria Frankish duchy 118/3; mediaeval German Empire 119/1; acquired by Habsburgs 141/1, 150/2, 197/3; Black Death 143/1; Habsburg duchy 191/1
Carlisle N England rebellion against Henry VIII 185/1; Industrial Revolution 201/1
Carmana (Kerman)
Carmania country of E Persia 77/1, 79/3, 83/1,3
Carmarthen early principality of Wales 125/1
Carmathians Muslim sect of Arabia 135/1
Carmaux S France industrial development 210/1
Carnac NW France site complex 42/2; early trade 52/1
Carnatic (*a/c* Karnata) coastal region of SE India 173/1, 194/2 (inset)
Carniola (*Ger.* Krain) region of Austria/Yugoslavia mediaeval Germany 119/1; acquired by Habsburgs 141/1, 150/2, 197/3; Habsburg duchy 191/1
Carnuntum ancient town of Austria trade 70/1; Mithraic site 72/1; Roman Empire 89/1, 99/1
Carolina N America British settlement 161/2
Caroline Islands C Pacific German sovereignty 245/1; captured by US from Japanese 271/1
Carolingian Empire (Frankish Kingdom)
Carpathos (*It.* Scarpanto) island of E Mediterranean colonisation 67/1
Carpi N Italy ⚔192/3
Carrawburgh (Procolitia)
Carrhae (*mod.* Haran) E Anatolia ⚔78/3; in Seleucia 86/3; Roman fort 88/3; Byzantine Empire 113/1
Carrier sub-arctic Indian tribe of NW Canada, 149/1
Carsioli N Italy Roman Empire 87/1
Carson City W USA mining site 220/1
Cartagena (*anc.* Carthago Nova) SE Spain naval base 195/1; Civil War 268/3
Cartagena Colombia colonial trade 158/1, 199/1
Carteia S Spain Roman Empire 89/1
Carthage (*Lat.* Carthago) Tunisia Stone Age site 45/1; Mithraic site 72/1; Phoenician colony 75/1; Roman Empire 86/3, 89/1, 91/1; early archbishopric 92/1; Byzantine reconquest 99/1; Muslim conquest 104/1
Carthago Nova (*mod.* Cartagena) SE Spain Roman Empire 86/3, 88/1, 90/1; archbishopric 92/1; Byzantine reconquest 99/1
Casablanca (*Ar.* Dar el Beida) W Morocco Ottoman Empire 228/1; French occupation 251/2
Cascades NW USA ⚔221/4
Cashel Ireland bishopric 92/1, 117/1
Caspian Gates N Persia Alexander's route 77/1
Cassano N Italy ⚔192/3
Cassian Way (Via Cassia)
Cassino C Italy WW2 273/3 See also Monte Cassino
Castellón de la Plana E Spain Civil War 268/3
Castiglione N Italy ⚔205/1
Castile region of Spain at time of Reconquista 124/3, Black Death 142/1; Kingdom 186/2; acquired by Habsburgs 150/1,2
Castillo de Teayo Mexico Aztec town 148/2
Castle Cavern S Africa Iron Age site 45/1
Castoria N Greece Byzantine Empire 113/5
Castra Regina (*mod.* Regensburg *form. Eng.* Ratisbon) C Germany Roman fort 88/2, 91/1
Castrum Novum N Italy Roman Empire 87/1
Castulo (*mod.* Cazlona) S Spain Roman Empire 88/1
Catalans people of NE Spain 214/1
Catalaunian Fields C France ⚔98/1
Çatal Hüyük C Anatolia site 41/1
Catalonia (*Sp.* Cataluña *Cat.* Catalunya) region of NE Spain reconquest by Aragon 124/3; under French rule 204/1; autonomous 265/1
Catana (*mod.* Catania) Sicily ally of Athens 74/4; Roman Empire 89/1; mediaeval German Empire 119/1
Catanzaro S Italy WW1 253/3
Catawba Indian tribe of SE USA 149/1
Cattigara S China early port 71/1
Cattaro (*mod.* Kotor) E Adriatic Venetian fort 187/3, 215/2; WW1 253/3
Caucasus early urban settlement 52/1; Muslim expansion 105/1
Caudium C Italy Roman Empire 87/1
Caulonia S Italy Roman Empire 87/1
Cawahib forest Indian tribe of W Brazil 149/1
Cawnpore (*n/s* Kanpur) N India India Mutiny 234/1
Cayapó forest Indian tribe of C Brazil 149/1
Cayenne French Guiana colonisation 165/1
Cazlona (Castulo)
Ceará NE Brazil Confederation of the Equator 227/1
Cedar Creek C USA ⚔221/4
Cedar Mountain SE USA ⚔223/1 (inset)
Cefalù (*anc.* Cephaloedium) Sicily mediaeval German Empire 119/1
Celebes (*Indon.* Sulawesi) island of East Indies Muslim expansion 104/3; occupied by Japanese 271/1
Celenderis S Anatolia Ionian colony 75/1
Celts tribe of Europe, France 60/1, 75/1; major settlements 84/3; N Italy 86/2
Cempoala Mexico Aztec town 148/2; on Cortés' route 159/1
Central African Federation (Northern Rhodesia, Southern Rhodesia, Nyasaland)
Central African Republic (*form.* Central African Empire *earlier* Ubangi-Shari) independence 276/2; political development 283/1; economy 295/1
Central Asian Gasfield USSR 291/1
Central India Agency Indian states under British control, 235/3
Central Provinces (*now* Madhya Pradesh) state of central India 235/3
Ceos (*mod.* Kea) island of the Aegean colonisation 67/1
Cephaloedium (Cefalù)
Cephalonia (*mod. Kefallinia*) *island of the Ionian* Byzantine Empire 113/5; Venetian territory 138/1, 187/3
Cerdagne (*Sp.* Cerdaña) region of France and Spain 193/1
Ceribon (Cheribon)
Cerigo (*anc.* Cythera *mod. Gr.* Kithira) *island* S Greece Venetian fort 187/1
Çerkes (Circassia)
Cernăuţi (Czernowitz)
Cerro de las Mesas C Mexico early site 46/2
Cerro de Trinidad C Andes early site 47/4
Cerveteri (Caere)
Cēsis (Wenden)
Český Těšín (Teschen)
Cetatea Alba (Akkerman)
Ceuta (*Ar.* Sebta) Spanish enclave in N Morocco early trade 147/2; transferred from Portugal to Spain 186/2; Spanish occupation 239/1, 251/2, 260/1
Ceylon (*anc.* Taprobane, Sinhala *or* Lanka *a/c* Saylan, Sarandib *Chin.* Hsi-lan) 82/4, 83/1; under Cholas 130/2; trade 145/4, 154/2; captured from Dutch 147/1, 194/2; under British rule 172/3, 235/3, 245/1, 261/1; independence 277/2; adopted title Republic of Sri Lanka 281/3,5; industry and economy 218/1, 295/1
Chad (*Fr.* Tchad) country of C Africa independence from French 276/2; political development 283/1; economy 295/1
Chad, Lake C Africa European exploration 238/2
Chaeronea C Greece 74/4
Chafarinas Islands N Morocco Spanish occupation 251/2
Chagar Bazar (*a/c* Shubat-Enlil) Mesopotamia early village 41/1
Chagatai Khanate C Asia 128/4, 129/3
Chagos Archipelago Indian Ocean British control 194/2, 245/1
Chahar former province of N China 175/1; independent of Nanking 262/2
Chaiya S Thailand Hindu-Buddhist remains 133/2
Chakipampa C Andes early site 47/5
Chalcedon (*mod.* Kadıköy) NW Anatolia centre of early Christianity 72/1; Dorian colony 75/1; Roman Empire 86/3; Council 93/1; Byzantine Empire 112/2,3
Chalcidice (*mod.* Khalkidhiki) region of N Greece Persian War 74/3
Chalcis C Greece parent state 75/1
Chaldeans people of Mesopotamia 56/3, 57/2
Chaldian Theme Byzantine province of E Anatolia, 112/3
Chaldiran (Çaldiran)
Chalon Moulineux C France mediaeval *villeneuve* 121/7
Chalon-sur-Saône S France mediaeval fair 144/1
Châlons-sur-Marne N France bishopric 117/1, seat of intendant 193/1; WW1 253/3, WW2 269/5
Chalukyas ancient dynasty of S India 130/2, 131/1
Chambéry SE France mediaeval fair 144/1
Champa Hindu-Buddhist kingdom of Indo-China 127/2; under Mongol control 129/1, 133/2,3
Champagne region of NE France mediaeval trade 120/1; French Royal domain 125/1, 151/4; 193/1; WW1 253/3
Champaubert NE France 205/1
Champion's Hill S USA ⚔223/1
Chanak (*Turk.* Çanakkale) W Turkey 1922 incident 265/1
Chancelade France site of early man 32/2
Chancellorsville SE USA ⚔223/1
Chandellas ancient dynasty of N India 130/2, 131/1
Chandernagore E India French settlement 161/1, 173/1, 194/2 (inset)
Chandigarh N India capital of Punjab 281/3
Ch'ang-an N China Han capital 82/2; T'ang city 108/2, 126/1
Chang-chia-k'ou (Kalgan)
Ch'ang-chih N China industry 218/1
Ch'ang-chou E China T'ang prefecture 126/1
Ch'ang-ch'un Manchuria treaty port 232/2; railway 242/3, 263/3; industry 278/2
Chang-i NW China Han commanderie 81/2
Changkufeng Manchuria Russo-Japanese conflict 268/2
Ch'ang-sha C China Han principality 81/2; treaty town 232/2; captured by Kuomintang 262/1; captured by Japanese 271/1; industry 218/1, 263/3, 278/3
Chang-yeh NW China conquered by Han 80/3
Chanhu-Daro N India Harappan site 65/1
Channel Islands WW2 273/6
Chansen N Thailand Iron Age site 132/1
Chao early state of N China 80/1
Chao-ming N Korea Han prefecture 81/2
Characene early kingdom of Mesopotamia 78/2; vassal state of Parthian Empire 79/1
Charax early port on Persian Gulf, 71/1, 82/4
Charcas N Mexico Spanish centre 158/1
Chard SW England Industrial Revolution 201/1
Chardzhou (*until 1940* Chardzhuy) Russ. C Asia industry 291/1
Charikar (Alexandria)
Charleroi Belgium industrial development 210/1; WW1 253/3 (inset)
Charles Town Path SE USA settlers' route 220/1
Charleville E Australia railway 237/5
Charolais region of E France Habsburg possession 151/4, 185/1
Charrúa Indian tribe of Argentina 149/1
Charsinian Theme Byzantine province of C Anatolia, 112/3
Charsianum C Anatolia Byzantine Empire 112/3
Chartres C France WW1 253/3
Château-sur-Salins E France late Hallstatt site 84/1
Château-Thierry N France ⚔205/1; WW1 252/2, 253/3 (inset)
Chatham SE England Dutch naval raid 185/1; naval base 195/1; Industrial Revolution 201/1; WW1 253/3
Chattanooga SE USA ⚔223/1
Chatti Germanic tribe of Roman Empire 89/1
Chauci Germanic tribe of Roman Empire 89/1
Chaul W India Portuguese settlement 173/1
Chavin C Andes site 47/1
Chechen-Ingush ASSR Caucasus 290/2
Che-chiang (Chekiang)
Chedi early kingdom of N India 65/1, 83/2
Chekiang (*W/G* Che-chiang) province of E China Ming economy 168/2, Manchu expansion 175/1; T'ai-p'ing control 233/1; Hsin-hai revolution 233/3
Chełm (Kholm)
Chelmno Poland concentration camp 272/1
Chelmsford (*anc.* Caesaromagus) E England Industrial Revolution 201/1
Chelyabinsk C Russia industry 231/1, 290/2, 291/1; urban growth 290/3
Chemin des Dames NE France WW1 253/3 (inset)
Chemnitz (*since 1953* Karl-Marx-Stadt) E Germany industrial development 210/1, 212/1; WW1 253/3
Chemulpo (Inchon)
Ch'en N China Chou domain 63/4
Cheng N China Late Chou domain 63/4
Cheng-chou (*a/s* Chengchow) N China Shang site 62/2; on railway 263/3
Ch'eng-tu W China on trade route 71/1; Han prefecture 81/2; T'ang prefecture 126/1; Ming provincial capital 169/1; industry 278/3
Ch'eng-tu Fu W China Sung province 127/5
Chenstokhov (*Pol.* Częstochowa) C Poland in European Russia 231/1
Chen-ting-fu N China Sung provincial capital 127/5
Ch'en-ts'ang C China Han prefecture 81/2
Chepstow W England Industrial Revolution 201/1
Chera (*mod.* Kerala) region of S India 83/1
Cherbourg N France English base in Hundred Years War 142/4; French naval base 195/1; WW1 253/3; WW2 273/3,6
Cherchell (Caesarea)
Cherchen (*Chin.* Ch'ieh-mo) Chin. C Asia silk route 71/2
Cheremkhovo S Siberia industry 291/1
Cherepovets NW Russia industry 291/1
Cheribon (*Dut.* Tjeribon *n/s* Ceribon) district of Java Dutch control 176/3
Chernigov Ukraine bishopric 101/2; principality 115/1
Chernovtsy (Czernowitz)
Cherokee Indian tribe of SE USA 149/1
Cherokees SE USA ⚔221/4
Cherso (Cres)
Chersonesus Crimea Ionian colony 75/1; bishopric 93/1
Cherusci Germanic tribe of Roman Empire 89/1
Chester (*anc.* Deva) C England county palatine 125/1; Industrial Revolution 201/1
Cheyenne plains Indian tribe of C USA 49/1
Ch'i NE China Chou domain 62/3, 63/4; state 80/1, 126/3
Chia NW China Western Chou domain 62/3
Chia-mu-ssu (Kiamusze)
Ch'iang border people of NW China 63/4
Chiang-hsi (Kiangsi)
Chiang-hsia C China Han commanderie 81/2
Chiang-hsi Nan C China Sung province 127/5
Chiang-ling C China Western Chou site 62/3; T'ang prefecture 126/1; Sung provincial capital 127/5
Chiang Mai (Chiengmai)
Chiang-nan Hsi-tao S China T'ang province 126/1
Chiang-nan Tung E China Sung province 127/5
Chiang-nan Tung-tao SE China T'ang province 126/1
Chiang-ning-fu E China Sung provincial capital 127/5
Chiang-su (Kiangsu)
Chiao N China Western Chou domain 62/3
Chiao-chih China/Vietnam Han commanderie 81/2
Chiao-ho Chin. C Asia Han expansion 80/3
Chiao-hsien (Kiaochow)
Chiao-li NE China Han prefecture 81/2
Chiapa de Corzo C Mexico early site 46/2
Chiapas province of S Mexico 227/1
Chiba C Japan city and prefecture 218/2; industry 243/1
Chibcha Andean Indian tribe 149/1
Chicago N USA industry 219/1, 289/1
Chichén Itzá Mexico Maya site 46/2; Toltec domination 148/2
Chichester S England Industrial Revolution 201/1
Ch'i-ch'i-ha-erh (Tsitsihar)
Chi-chou NE China T'ang prefecture 126/1; Ming military post 169/1
Ch'i-ch'un C China Western Chou site 62/3
Chickamauga SE USA ⚔223/1
Chickasaw Indian tribe of SE USA 149/1, 221/4
Ch'ieh-mo (*a/c* Cherchen) Chin. C Asia Han expansion 80/3